TENNESSEE TIDBITS

1778-1914

Volume II

Marjorie Hood Fischer
and Ruth Blake Burns

HERITAGE BOOKS
2008

HERITAGE BOOKS
AN IMPRINT OF HERITAGE BOOKS, INC.

Books, CDs, and more—Worldwide

For our listing of thousands of titles see our website
at
www.HeritageBooks.com

Published 2008 by
HERITAGE BOOKS, INC.
Publishing Division
100 Railroad Ave. #104
Westminster, Maryland 21157

Copyright © 1988 Ram Press
1239 Coventry Road
Vista, California 92084

Copyright © 1999 Marjorie Hood Fischer
and Ruth Blake Burns

All rights reserved. No part of this book may be reproduced or transmitted in any form or by any means, electronic or mechanical, including photocopying, recording or by any information storage and retrieval system without written permission from the author, except for the inclusion of brief quotations in a review.

International Standard Book Numbers
Paperbound: 978-0-7884-1376-6
Clothbound: 978-0-7884-4622-1

INTRODUCTION

This is the second volume in a continuing series of books with genealogical information abstracted mainly from Court Minutes. The dates, 1778-1914, are for the entire series and does not mean that records for all those dates are included in any one volume. Many court records have been lost. The earliest records found were for Washington County starting in 1778. The State of Tennessee started keeping birth and death certificates on a state-wide basis in 1914; therefore, 1914 is used as our cut-off date. Items in *Tennessee Tidbits, Volume II*, were all taken from Court Minutes but we may use other sources in other volumes.

Abstracts in this volume are from County Court Minutes, [sometimes referred to as County Court of Pleas & Quarter Sessions], Circuit Court Minutes, Chancery Court Minutes and other records included in these minutes, such as Pleas and Judgements. They are from the counties of Bedford, Claiborne, Dyer, Fentress, Jackson, Madison, McMinn, Obion, Roane, Robertson, Sevier, Stewart, Washington and Wilson.

Court Minutes contain a wealth of genealogical information and are the least used of all sources. This is probably because they are seldom indexed. It takes time and patience to read every word in these hand written documents. Sometimes the handwriting is nearly illegible. At this point we must caution the reader to check every possible way a name can be spelled, or misspelled. Be especially careful of the capital letters, "L" and "S", which are often identical.

When Court Houses have gone through fires and wars and had most of their records destroyed, then a dedicated genealogist will resort to searching anything that is left. That is how we discovered how helpful these Court Minutes can be.

Tennessee Tidbits, Volume I, contains abstracts from Blount, Davidson, Dickson, Fayette, Giles, Greene, Harden, Haywood, Hickman, Humphreys, Lincoln, Putnam, Rutherford, Washington and Williamson Counties. It was abstracted by Marjorie Hood Fischer and published by Southern Historical Press in 1986. This book, *Tennessee Tidbits, Volume II*, has been a joint effort of Marjorie Hood Fischer and Ruth Blake Burns. It follows the some format as Volume I with a few minor exceptions.

We decided to list the paupers in Volume II. It is certainly no crime to be a pauper and this is probably the only time that their names will appear in the records. We have shown more of the witnesses, securities, persons appointed to lay off dower, etc. These people often have a close relationship with the executors, administrators, widows and guardians. We have not made double entries for fathers and mothers of bastard children, or for both parties when a marriage or divorce is shown. By eliminating this duplication we were able to include more abstracts.

We have included every item of genealogical significance found in the records searched including: birth, death, marriage, divorce, guardianship, naturalization, illegitimacy, lunacy, migration, relationship, adoption, disability, military service, emancipation, apprenticeship, and tributes of respect.

The items showing certification of "good moral character and age 21" were usually because the person so certified had applied for a license to practice law. There are several entries showing the loss of part of an ear. This was because at one time, cutting off part of the ear was part of the punishment for certain crimes. Therefore, when a person lost a part of an ear by accident, they wanted this fact on record so that they would not be mistaken for a criminal.

A list of all sources used for this volume are found in the appendix.

We apologize for errors that you may find in this book. When the researcher consults the original record or the microfilm copy of these ancient documents, he or she will understand that we have made a supreme effort to determine the content as it was recorded and to present it here in its abbreviated form. We encourage the researcher to double check the original record when there is any doubt about the spelling or interpretation of the item.

You may obtain a copy of the original record from the County Court Clerk's office in the county of interest or by writing to the Tennessee State Library and Archives in Nashville for a copy from the microfilm. Send the information from the citation showing the type of record, volume, page number and date.

Marjorie Hood Fischer
Ruth Blake Burns

AARON, John Jacob
Was a pauper when he petitioned the county for maintenance for the year, 3 May 1813. (Ste TN, Co Ct Min, 4/29) Jacob Aaron was let to John Aaron on 3 May 1814. (Ibid 145)

ACUFF, Joel
6 September 1858 was released from paying poll tax as he lives in Jefferson County. (Sev TN, Co Ct Min, no#/335)

ADAIR, Robert
Died before 8 February 1804 when Whitmell Harrington was appointed administrator with Moses Winters & Shadrick Rawls as security. (Rob TN, Co Ct Min, 1/286)

ADAMS, Geo. W.
6 February 1871 made a settlement as guardian of his own children. (Dyr TN, Co Ct Min, B/190)

ADAMS, Hiram
Died before 19 February 1858 as shown in the petition of Jno. B. Boykin, executor, Robt. N. McLemore, Mary B. Adams, Josephine Adams & Wm. H. Adams, the last 3 minors by their guardian, Edward W. Matthews. (Mad TN, Ch Ct Min, 2/190)

ADAMS, J. S.
Died before 7 January l874 when Samuel Lewis was appointed administrator, with Isral Eudeley as his security. (Dyr TN, Co Ct Min, B/697)

ADAMS, James
Died before 30 August 1844 as shown in the suit of William W. Adams et al vs William H. Craig & others. Wm. Craig & Talitha Craig answered for the defendants. James Adams was the ancestor of the complainants, and had sold in his lifetime land to John Craig, who is now deceased. Talitha [Tabitha] Craig is the widow. The other defendants are the heirs of John Craig, deceased. William W. Adams is administrator of James Adams. (Bed TN, Ch Ct Min, 2/319)

ADAMS, M. C.
Died before 23 Februray 1866 when the deaths of both complainant and defendant were admitted in the suit of M. C. Adams vs Wm. H. Stone. (Mad TN, Ch Ct Min, 2/486)

ADAMS, Mich
Died before 24 August 1779 when John Clark gave bond with Andrew Greer as his security, to prosecute his suit on appeal against George Willfrong, administrator of Mich Adams, deceased. (Was TN, Co Ct Min, 1/92)

ADAMS, Nathan
Died shortly after making his will on 26 September 1850 in Weakley County, TN. Alfred Gardner qualified as executor. He left property to his wife, Nancy Adams, for life & the remainder to his 8 nephews & nieces. Nancy Adams died 16 March 1854 after making a will. Alfred Gardner was executor. The nieces & nephews are entitled to the rent from the estate since 16 March 1854. Minos C. Adams is entitled in his own right & as assignee of Elijah Adams, Nancy Ditto & Nathan Dagby, to half of the sum. (Mad TN, Ch Ct Min, 2/274)

ADAMS, William
Died before 12 November 1810 when his orphans, John Adams & Allen Adams, were bound to Jesse Skinner. (Rob TN, Co Ct Min, 2/312)

ADAMS, William
17 February l815 was appointed guardian of Sterling Adams, Harper Adams, Abner Adams, Elizabeth Ann Adams, with William Adams & Benjamin Tucker as security. (Rob TN, Co Ct Min, 3/564)

ADAMSON, William
Died before 18 June 1816 when James McAdam, the administrator, was ordered to make a report. (Wil TN, Co Ct Min, no#/16)

ADKINS
11 February 1812 William Cromwell was appointed guardian of James T. Adkins, William Adkins, Elisha Adkins, Joseph Adkins, children of Wm. Adkins. (Rob TN, Co Ct Min, 3/61)

ADKINS, Mary B.
Brought suit against Henderson W. Adkins & others, 27 June 1843, for divorce and alimony. The suit was remanded to the rules, the same being improperly set for hearing. (Bed TN, Ch Ct Min, 2/250) Mary B. Atkins was married some 12 years ago to Henderson W. Atkins in VA & lived in that state for 4 years when they removed to TN. He has become abusive. Two or three weeks before the birth of her youngest child "he whipt & beat her so that she will carry scares to her grave." He drove her out when her infant was only 8 days old & she was forced to seek shelter with a neighbor. He left when the infant was not a month old and is living, as she believes, in adultry, in VA. It will be 2 years in April since he left her. When she married she was possessed with a large estate which in settlement with her guardian, said Atkins, she received mostly in negroes, of which there are 14. He has squandered & spent all her estate. She depends on her own industry & the help of neighbors to support herself and 3 children. Several people owe notes to her husband and she wants the court to award them to her or a suitable support. [This bill is not dated but was heard at the 1844 term of Court.] (Ibid 3/173)

ADKINSON, Joshua [Atkinson]
Died before 18 March 1817 when William Babb made a settlement as guardian of the minor heirs. (Wil TN, Co Ct Min, no#/89)

AIKEN, Sarah E.
8 March 1870, W. A. Slayden was chosen & appointed guardian with J. J. Hill and G. W. Stevenson as security. (Dyr TN, Co Ct Min, B/12)

AILEY, Isaac
Died before 4 July 1859 when Cornelius Fox, guardian to Martha Ailey, John Ailey, William Ailey & Nancy Ailey, minor heirs, reported that he was guardian to above minors in Jefferson County & he desired to remove said guardianship to this county. (Sev TN, Co Ct Min, no#/455)

AILS, William
Died before 21 October 1811 when the coroner was paid for holding an inquest on his body. (Roa TN, Co Ct Min, D/329)

AIRE, Henry
21 April 1802 came into court & gave up his order for overseer of the road by reason of old age. (Rob TN, Co Ct Min, 1/215)

AIRS, Henry, Jr.
Gave bond for the maintenance of a child with which he is charged as the reputed father by Nancy Winters, 15 February 1810. (Rob TN, Co Ct. Min, 2/225)

AKEN, Aaron Johnson
"A minor son of Harrison" was bound 17 December 1816 to Obediah G. Finly for 4 years. (Wil TN, Co Ct Min, no#/56)

AKEN, Harrison
Died before 15 December 1817 when the executors were ordered to make a report. (Wil TN, Co Ct Min, no#/185) The name was also shown as Harrison Eaken. (Ibid 220)

AKIN, E. L.
Died before 6 November 1871 when C. N. Shaw and Richard F. Templeton were appointed administrators with A. G. Pierce and T. J. Frazier as security. W. H. Hendrix, C. Oakley and Jno. Milan were appointed to lay off a years allowance for the widow and family. (Dyr TN, Co Ct Min, B/314) 1 January 1872, L. J. Akin was chosen and appointed guardian of Martha Elizabeth Akin and Robert Edward Akin with W. J. Featherstone and C. K. Featherstone as her security. (Ibid 334) There were 3 children. (Ibid 351) Lucy J. Akin was the widow. Petition for dower mentioned land purchased from William Akin & land deeded by Jas. Akin. (Ibid 368-70) 3 February 1874 in a petition for division it states that Mrs. V. Shaw, Mrs. S. A. Templeton, Miss Francis Akin, Miss M. E. Akin and Robert E. Akin are the heirs of Edward L. Akin, deceased. The petition was made by C. N. Shaw. Joseph Akin was mentioned. (Ibid 708-9) Division was made. (Ibid 725-6)

ALDERSON, Alexander
Died before 4 February 1812 when Simon Alderson was appointed administrator with Silas Vinson & William Haynes as security. (Ste TN, Co Ct Min, 3/112)

ALDERSON, James C.
Died before 17 April 1811 when the will was proved by Jared Hotchkiss & H. K. Hotchkiss. (Roa TN, Co Ct Min, D/302)

ALDRIDGE, Isaac
Taxes were not collected in District 5 for 1873, "can't be found." (Dyr TN, Co Ct Min, B/759)

ALDRIDGE, Mary
Was a poor person who was let to the lowest bidder, Alfred Noel, on 11 May 1815. (Cla TN, Co Ct Min, 4/68) She was shown as Mary Oldrige when John Bullard undertook to support her. (Ibid 115) She was let to William Pruat? in 1816. (Ibid 156)

ALEXANDER, Nathaniel
Died before 1836 as shown in the suit of John P. Steele & John L. Cooper vs Amos McAdams and others. Steele, McAdams & Charles D. Cooper had purchased from the heirs of Nathaniel Alexander their share of a tract of land. McAdams purchased 1/2, or 5 shares, and Charles D. Cooper and J. P. Steele purchased the other 5 shares. Charles D. Cooper conveyed his interest in the land to John L. Cooper. Steele was then a resident of MS. In this suit over the land, John Rundleman, a citizen of NC, and John Doby, a citizen of SC and his wife Elizabeth, formerly Elizabeth Crawford, were mentioned as claiming title to part of the land by deed or devise from Martin Phifer, deceased, late of NC, land that had been granted to Caleb Phifer. Martin Phifer's land was "divided into five shares his four children." John M. Doby married Elizabeth Crawford, one of the grand daughters of said Martin Phifer who died several years ago leaving a will. He devised to his said grand daughter and her brother, William D. Crawford, jointly, 400 acres of lot 5 in said division of 5,000 acres. Rendleman purchased the part of William D. Crawford. The wife of John M. Doby has died and her children are entitled to the disputed land. This suit was filed in 1844. (Bed TN, Ch Ct Min, 3/279-290)

ALEXANDER, Nathaniel
Died before 4 February 1811 when the heirs were granted leave to return 1,000 acres for taxation for the year 1810 & be exonerated from paying double tax. (Ste TN, Co Ct Min, 3/12)

ALFORD, Hutson
Was released from paying taxes for 1804 as he and John Crudupe did not come into the county until 12 May 1804. (Wil TN, Co Ct Min, no#/112)

ALGEA, Jas. B.
Died before 6 February 1871 when James H. Hamilton was chosen and appointed guardian of the minor heirs, with F. A. McCorkle and A. J. McCorkle as security. (Dyr TN, Co Ct Min, B/183)

ALGEE, James
5 October 1870, P. E. Wilson renewed his bond as guardian of James Algee, minor heir of James Algee, with H. F. Ferguson as his security. (Dyr TN, Co Ct Min, B/118)

ALLARD, Mary
13 July 1859 dismissed her suit for divorce from James M. Allard. (Jac TN, Ch Ct Min, C/236)

ALLEN
James and Elizabeth Allen were residents of Logan County, KY, 12 August 1813 when their depositions were to be taken for the defendant in the case of George Carter against Henry Watkins. (Rob TN, Co Ct Min, 3/303)

ALLEN
Richard and Helen Allen both died before 5 October 1870 when Sam A. McKnight was chosen and appointed guardian of A. R. Allen, their minor heir, with W. C. Doyle and Jo. R. Todd as security. (Dyr TN, Co Ct Min, B/123)

ALLEN, Beverly
18 April 1798 made a deed of gift to Ann Coke Allen, John Hays Allen, Mary Allen, Beverly Allen, Jr. & Sarah Allen. (Rob TN Co Ct Min, 1/61)

ALLEN, Elizabeth
Died before 7 February 1859 when Absolem Allen was appointed administrator, with John Russell & Adam Honk as security. (Sev TN, Co Ct Min, no#/401)

ALLEN, John
Was charged by Sally Oliver of being the father of her bastard child. He gave bond for it's maintenance 20 June 1807. (Roa TN, Co Ct Min, B/329)

ALLEN, John
On 3 August 1813 John Allen [the Sheriff] was allowed a credit for taxes for 1812 on the following persons having removed out of the county or having become insolvent, Viz., Vachel Smith, Edmund Taylor, Alexander Campbell, Mark Thomason, Joseph Lockhart, John Fletcher, Joel Olive, Jordan Sandy, Thomas Wallis, William Reynolds, William Griffeth & Hyram Warnock. (Ste TN, Co Ct Min, 4/62)

ALLEN, John
Died before 17 June 1816 when Lydia Allen was appointed administratrix, with Robert Kasky & Jesse Shaw as security. (Wil TN, Co Ct Min, no#/2)

ALLEN, John
Died before 7 August 1865 when P. W. Maples, Elisha Sharp, & John H. Fraim were appointed to lay off a years support to the widow, Salina Allen, & family. Salina was also appointed guardian to the minor heirs with R. C. Low as security. (Sev TN, Co Ct Min, no#/188)

ALLEN, John B.
Was a minor orphan 4 March 1861 when A. J. Allen was appointed guardian. (Sev TN, Co Ct Min, no#/659)

ALLEN, Jonathan
Died before 1 March 1830 when Sarah E. Allen & William Maples were appointed administrators. (McM TN, Co Ct Min, 2no#/421) Robert Cowan, James Gaut & Saml. Hardy were appointed to lay off a years support to Sarah E. Allen, the widow. (Ibid 424)

ALLEN, Judith
Died before 2 August 1814 when the will was proved by James Scarborough, Nancy Blanton and Emilia Allen. Nancy Rodgers was executrix with John Allen & William M. Cooley as security. (Ste TN, Co Ct Min, 4/172)

ALLEN, Lucy A.
7 August 1865 was appointed guardian to Gideon, Matilda E., Virena H. and Barbara A. Allen, minor orphans. R. C. Low [Law] was security. (Sev. TN, Co Ct. Min, no#/188)

ALLEN, Moses
Was released from working on the public roads 4 April 1859 as he is unable to do manual labor. (Sev TN, Co Ct. Min, no#/420)

ALLEN, Neal
5 December 1870, B. C. Burgie renewed his bond as guardian of Neal Allen & others. (Dyr TN, Co Ct Min, B/137)

ALLEN, Sandford
2 May 1864, on the petition of Lemuel Bogart, a lunacy hearing was ordered as he is said to be a dangerous lunatic. (Sev TN, Co Ct Min, no#/104) John Russell was appointed his guardian. (Ibid 107) Died before 1 May 1865 when the will was proved by John Russell & R. S. Atchley, witnesses. One of the executors named is dead & the other one is in the services of the U.S., therefore John Russell was appointed administrator with the will annexed, with Thomas Maples & others as security. (Ibid 156) L. Bogart, Nelson Fox & J. Stafford were appointed to lay off a years support for Lydia Allen, widow of Sanford Allen, deceased. (Ibid 161)

ALLEN, William
Died before 25 January 1809 when William Outlaw and John Allen were appointed administrators, with William M. Cooley as security. The inventory was shown. The negroes were drawn for by lot and allotted to Mrs. Allen, John Allen for Mrs. Rodgers, Betsey Allen, William Allen, Mrs. Outlaw, John Allen & Sally Allen. (Ste TN, Co Ct Min, no#/97-104 [3 of these pages are missing]) 7 February 1810 Judith Allen was appointed guardian of William Allen, Elisabeth Allen, Milley Allen & Sarah Allen, orphan children of William Allen, deceased. (Ibid 4/no#)

ALLEN, William
Died before 1 May 1865 when a years support was ordered to be set off to the widow,

Delila Allen. (Sev TN, Co Ct Min, no#/156 &164) Delila Allen & James Smithpeter were appointed administrators. (Ibid 191) 1 October 1866 Lucy Ann Allen made a settlement as guardian to the minor heirs of William Allen, deceased. (Ibid 371)

ALLEN, William A.
Was a citizen of Giles County, TN, in 1843 as shown in the suit of Jesse M. Yorvell of Marshall County vs Alexr. Allen of Bedford County & William A. Allen of Giles County. Alexander was the father of William A. Allen. Alexander moved to TN in 1836. He had been in Montgomery County, VA. (Bed TN, Ch Ct Min, 3/92)

ALLEN, William L.
On 3 May 1814 was appointed guardian of Milley Allen & Sally Allen with John Bailey & John Allen as security. (Ste TN, Co Ct Min, 4/141)

ALLEN, Wm. M.
Died in July 1841 leaving a will. Burl Butler was the executor. Amanda Allen was his widow. They had one child, Mary Darcus, at the time of his death and another one, Amanda Milton, shortly thereafter. The mother of these children, Amanda Allen, died shortly after the birth of Amanda Milton Allen. In March 1842 Mary Darcus Allen died. In October 1842 Amanda Milton Allen died, being seven months old, the last of the family, leaving no brothers or sisters. Her grandfather, Andrew Allen, and her grandmother, Mary A. Freeman, were the next of kin. Joseph C. Smith is entitled to the share of Andrew Allen by assignment from Andrew. Burrel Butler is entitled by assignment from Edward A. Freeman & Mary his wife, to the other share. The above was shown in the suit dated 13 July 1847 of Wyatt Mooring, administrator of Joseph C. Smith, deceased vs Burrell Butler administrator of the will of Wm. M. Allen & administrator of Amanda Milton Allen, Felix R. Hardgrove administrator of Amanda Allen, deceased, Wm. M. Henry, administrator of Mary D. Allen, deceased, Edward A. Freeman & Mary his wife, & Andrew Allen. (Mad TN, Ch Ct Min, 1/22)

ALLEY, Herbert
At the August term 1810 was appointed guardian of his son, John William Alley. (Rob TN, Co Ct Min, 2/284)

ALLISON, Davidson
Died before 13 November 1812 as shown in the case of John McNairy vs John Allison, William Allison, Peggy Allison, Sally Allison & Isabell Allison, heirs of Davidson Allison, deceased. (Rob TN, Co Ct Min, 3/171)

ALLISON, Hugh
Died before 17 November 1831 as shown in the suit of James Bain vs Thomas Allison, administrator of Hugh Allison, deceased & Wm. M. Wilson, security. The suit was stricken from the docket because this court has no jurisdiction. (Obi TN, Cir Ct Min, 1/186)

ALLISON, James
Was a person who had withdrawn his allegiance. He came into Court at the February term 1789 and availed himself of the Act of Pardon and Oblivion by taking the Oaths prescribed by law. (Was TN, Co Ct Min, 1/371)

ALLISON, James
16 February 1795 made a deed of gift to his daughters, Rachael Elizabeth and Easter Allison, proven by Thomas Yourley. (Was TN, Co Ct Min, 1/527)

ALLISON, James
Died before 18 May 1795 when Nathaniel Davis qualified as executor of the will. (Was TN, Co Ct Min, 1/547) The will was proved by John Adams and Francis Allison. (Ibid 550) The widow, Jane Allison, dissented from the will. (Ibid 567)

ALLISON, John
Was a resident of Woodford County, VA, in August 1790 when he gave a power of attorney to James McCord. (Was TN, Co Ct Min, 1/454)

ALLISON, Robt.
Died before 28 December 1843 as shown in the suit of William & Thomas Allison, executors of Robt. Allison, deceased vs John & Ruthy Cook & others. Robt. Allison had been appointed by the Granville County, NC, Chancery Court in March 1837 as trustee to hold certain negroes for Ruthy Cook & her children, which had been bequeathed to them by Coleman R. White of said county of Granville. The negroes are to be delivered to John & Ruthy Cook. (Bed TN, Ch Ct Min, 2/286) 24 February 1845 the names were shown as

John & Ruthy Crook. (Ibid 322) Children of John & Ruthy Crook were Coleman R., Mary Ann, Eliza H., Elizabeth N., Colia S., & Francis C. Crook. Coleman R. White of Granvill County, NC, died leaving a will. Ruthy Crook was the daughter of Coleman R. White and was left slaves for her and her children & at her death to go to her children. James Wyche was appointed trustee for Ruthy and her children in Granville County, NC, in 1838. Wyche refused to act as trustee and Robert Allison was appointed trustee. The parties moved to TN where Robert Allison died in May 1842. The executors of Robert Allison want another trustee named for Ruthy and her children and to release the estate of Robert Allison from further liability. The trustee should reside in the county of Weakly [where the Crooks now live?] The slaves are in Bedford County. They are to be hired out until a suitable trustee can be named. John E. Vincent of Weakly County was named trustee. (Ibid 3/315)

ALSOP, John
Died before 16 September 1816 when Joshua Lester, Samuel Hill & William Alsop were appointed administrators, with Arthur Harris, Richard C. Craddock, William C. Mitchell, William Winston and Roger Qualls as security. (Wil TN, Co Ct Min, no#/27) A years support was laid off for the widow, Elizabeth Alsup, widow of John Alsup, deceased. Petition was made for dower. (Ibid 83) 2 November 1818 Joshua Lester was appointed guardian of William Alsop, Jr. & Prudence Alsop, minor heirs. (Ibid 332) Saml. Hill was appointed guardian of Sterling Alsop & Hiram Alsop, minor heirs. (Ibid 333)

ALSTON
Philip Alston, Sr. vs Sarah Alston, 14 January 1850. An estate and administrator is mentioned but not identified. (Mad TN, Ch Ct Min, 1/97) 17 January 1850 in a continuation of this suit it is stated that James Alston died intestate, leaving Sarah Alston his widow and Lydia, Mary, Jno. & Sarah Jane Alston his only children. Philip Alston Sr. was appointed administrator and agreed to make no charge for his services. Land is to be sold to satisfy debts. (Ibid 111)

ALSUP, David
Died before 1 May 1815 when Joseph Alsup was appointed administrator with John Chambers & Ephraim B. Davidson as security. (Ste TN, Co Ct Min, 4/260)

ALSUP, William
Died before 1 November 1819 when Asa Alsup was appointed administrator with Richard & Joseph Alsup as security. (Wil TN, Co Ct Min, no#/536)

AMES, John
Died before March term 1812 as shown in the case of Thomas Ames vs Daniel Cherry. (Wil TN, P&J, no#/no#)

AMES, John
Died before 18 June 1816 when Thomas Ames was appointed administrator, with Jeremiah Brown as security. (Wil TN, Co Ct Min, no#/12)

AMES, Nathan
Was a minor 24 February 1837 when Seth Bedford was allowed to stand as his next friend in the place of Wm. M. Wilson who is dead. The suit was against Loderick Farmer. (Obi TN, Cir Ct Min, 3/110)

AMONETT, William
Died intestate about March 1849, as shown in the suit of Nancy B. Ammonett, Virginia Amonett, Tennessee G. Amonett, Benjamin F. Amonett by their next friend & Martha P. Amonett, Luke T. Armstrong & Josiah H. Langford vs Thomas L. Bransford. William Amonett had been partners with the defendant & David Biggerstaff. Nancy, Virginia, Tennessee & Benjamin Amonett are the heirs and Martha Amonett is the widow. (Jac TN, Ch Ct Min, A/348) Martha P. Ammonett married James Ammonett before 13 July 1850. (Ibid 382) A suit was entered 12 February 1859 by Hall Holeman vs James J. Amonett, Martha Amonett, Virginia Amonett, Tennessee Amonett & Benjamin Amonett. The wife of Hall Holeman was Nancy B. Holeman. They sued for sale of the land for a partition, which was sold 13 December 1856, and purchased by Hall Holeman who is to have title to the land. There are infants among the defendants & James J. Amonett is their guardian. (Ibid C/212)

ANDERSON, A. C.
Died before 6 February 1871 when Jno. Hicks made a settlement as administrator. (Dyr TN, Co Ct Min, B/190)

ANDERSON, Caleb?
Died before 17 July 1858 as shown in the suit of Mary Allard vs Jose M. Allard & others. Mary is the wife of Jose M. Allard and the daughter of Calub? Anderson, deceased. The land mentioned in the proceedings was purchased with complainant's distributive share of her father's estate. [Very bad handwriting, I think Mary wants the land for her separate use & a trustee appointed.] (Jac TN, Ch Ct Min, C/165)

ANDERSON, Daniel
Died before 3 August 1819 when the heirs sold land to James McFarland. (Wil TN, Co Ct Min, no#/514)

ANDERSON, Edward
Died before 10 August 1860 as shown in the suit of F. M. Anderson & others vs Thomas Anderson & others. V. W. Anderson, one of the children of Edward Anderson, deceased, who is a grand son of Thomas Anderson, deceased, and as such is entitled to a distributive share of the estate of Thomas Anderson, deceased, had sold his share to one Thomas Anderson. [Also see Thomas Anderson] (Jac TN, Ch Ct Min, C/374)

ANDERSON, Isaac
Died before November term 1788 when his widow, Margaret Anderson, and Robert Anderson were appointed administrators of the estate, with John Stair and John Campbell as security. (Was TN, Co Ct Min, 1/344) The provisions in the inventory returned were allowed for the support of the widow and orphans. (Ibid 365)

ANDERSON, J. D.
Died before 7 November 1870 when Andrew Hart made a settlement as administrator. (Dyr TN, Co Ct Min, B/133)

ANDERSON, John
Was a resident of Davidson County 8 November 1813 when his deposition was to be taken for plaintiff [does not list case]. (Rob TN, Co Ct Min, 3/320)

ANDERSON, John H.
Died before 25 February 1845 when the suit of Elizabeth Anderson against him abated because of his death. (Bed TN, Ch Ct Min, 2/325)

ANDERSON, Joseph
3 April 1860 S. B. Henderson was paid for burying clothes for Joseph Anderson's sons. (Sev TN, Co Ct Min, no#/548)

ANDERSON, Martha Jane
On 14 July 1858 dismissed her suit against Calub Anderson for divorce. (Jac TN, Ch Ct Min, C/128)

ANDERSON, Patrick
Died before 2 August 1819 when the will was proved by H. L. Douglass & Saml. Meredeth. Francis Anderson qualified as executor. Obadiah G. Finly was also named as executor but refused to qualify. (Wil TN, Co Ct Min, no#/493)

ANDERSON, Thomas
4 March 1806 was ordered to take charge of John, Mary & Sarah Anderson until next court. (Cla TN, Co Ct Min, 2/223)

ANDERSON, Thomas
Died in Jackson County in 1858 as shown in the suit of Francis M. Anderson & others vs Ransom P. Mahony & others, 10 February 1859. It was stated that defendants Katherine Mahony and Anna Bartle? were femme coverts and Thomas H. Burton was appointed guardian ad litem for them. Land & negroes are to be sold for distribution subject to the widow's dower. (Jac TN, Ch Ct Min, C/175) Defendants Silas Anderson, James E. Reynolds, Anna K. Reynolds, John S. Reynolds, Jonas A. Reynolds, Louisa J. Clark and Isaac F. Clark are non-residents and publication has been made for them. (Ibid 194) Judith Anderson was his widow and Frances M. Anderson, Paul Anderson, Thomas Anderson, Garland Anderson, William J. Anderson, Anna wife of Andrew T. Anderson, Katherine wife of Ransom P. Mahaney, Vancil W. Anderson, Josaphine wife of Richard Waller, Adelade wife of Alfred Jones, Thomas Anderson, Jr., Elizabeth Anderson, Jane Anderson, Anna wife of Joshua Bartlett, Silas Anderson, James E. Reynolds, Anna K. Reynolds, John S. Reynolds, Jonas A. Reynolds and Louisa J. wife of Isaac F. Clark his only heirs at law. Cinderella Anderson is the regular guardian of Adelade Jones, Josephine Waller, Vancil W. Anderson, Thomas Anderson, Jr., Elizabeth Anderson and

Jane Anderson, who are minors. Anna Karr has married Andrew T. Anderson. Anna Anderson, Thomas Anderson, Jr., Vancil W. Anderson, Adelade Jones, Josephine Waller, Elizabeth Anderson and Jane Anderson are grand children of Thomas Anderson, deceased, being children of his deceased son, Edward Anderson. The Reynolds' and Louisa Clark are also grand children and the children of his deceased daughter, Fanny Reynolds. All others named as heirs-at-law are his children. Paul Anderson & F. M. Anderson are the administrators. The widow, Judith Anderson, is entitled to dower. (Ibid 200-2) Thomas Anderson had made advancements in his lifetime to his sons, Thomas, William, Paul, Silas, Edward, Garland and Francis M. Anderson, and to his daughters, Anna Bartlett, Katherine Mahaney and Fanny Reynolds. He made a bequest to the illigitimate child of his son, Silas Anderson. His widow, Judith, dissented from the will. (Ibid 373)

ANDERSON, William
Died before 18 January 1850 as shown in the suit of the administrator with will annexed [name not readable] vs Jno. A. Vincent & Sarah Adaline his wife, Wm. Anderson an infant & Mary Selasky Anderson Perkins also an infant. The will gave 1/4 part of a tract of land containing 640 acres "which came to my wife in the estate of Robt. Edmonson in the eastern part of the county.and a negro man Jerry to be sold in the way which will be most suitable to the heirs of Robt. Edmonson." The Court decided the land was the property of Sarah before her marriage to William Anderson & she should retain it. The will also stated "I give & bequeath to my grand daughter Mary Selasky Anderson Perkins 8 slaves now in the hands of Jacob Perkins my son in law living in Helms? Co. Miss... but my grand daughter shall be at liberty to give to her half brother Jacob Perkins, my son in laws sons, John & John Jacob 2 negroes when she comes of age or marries..." The will also mentioned "my son William Anderson and his children." The executor was Andrew Guthrie. Sarah Adaline Vincent was evidently the widow of William Anderson, deceased. (Mad TN, Ch Ct Min, 1/127)

ANDERSON, Wm.
Taxes were not collected in District 4 for 1873, "under age." (Dyr TN, Co Ct Min, B/759)

ANDERTON, William
Was a citizen of Franklin County, TN, as shown in the suit of William Anderton vs Thos. E. Simpson, Michael Womack & Anthony Floyd, filed 2 May 1842. Anthony Floyd was the son-in-law of Michael Womack. (Bed TN, Ch Ct Min, 1/460)

ANDREWS, Etheldred
Died before 8 November 1813 when William Andrews was appointed administrator with John Roson & Elias Fort as security. (Rob TN, Co Ct Min, 3/315)

ANTHONY, Jacob
Died before 4 November 1872 when Josiah Chitwood was appointed administrator, with Stephen Chitwood and Jo. H. Pursell his security. (Dyr TN, Co Ct Min, B/508)

ANTWINE, Martha
5 May 1873 made a settlement as guardian of A. P. Antwine, N. J. Antwine, S. E. Antwine and W. T. Antwine. (Dyr TN, Co Ct Min, B/582)

APPLE
A suit was entered 14 July 1858 by Jackson C. Apple, Mary Jane Apple, Thomas H. Butler, Sarah An Butler vs Jubal Anderson, Neadin Apple, Elizabeth Apple & George Apple. The suit was compromised. (Jac TN, Ch Ct Min, C/125)

APPLEGATE, James M.
Died before 23 October 1839 when his death was suggested in the suit of Alexr. N. Edmunds vs James M. Applegate. (Obi TN, Cir Ct Min, 4/no#)

APPLETON, James
Died before 11 May 1813 when the will was proved by Richd. Nuckols, David McMurry & Samuel McMurry. (Rob TN, Co Ct Min, 3/246) 10 May 1814 petition was made by James Appleton & Thomas Appleton for a partition of the estate of James Appleton, deceased. (Ibid 404)

APPLETON, John
Was shown to be the son of James Appleton when he was summonded for jury duty 14 November 1812. (Rob TN, Co Ct Min, 3/174)

APPLETON, John
Died before 10 May 1813 when the will was proved by Thomas Johnson, Lewis Wells & George Sprouse. James Appleton, one of the executors named, qualified. (Rob TN, Co Ct Min, 3/228) Susanna Appleton, Elijah Williams & John Hardin were granted letters of administration, with John Hutchison & Samuel McMurry as security. (Ibid 245) Susanna Appleton was appointed guardian of Henrietta Appleton & Lenore Appleton, orphans of John Appleton, deceased. (Ibid 254)

APPLEWHITE, Harry
Died before 21 February 1837 when his death was suggested in the suit of Porter & Porter vs Harry Applewhite. Thomas C. Haskins and Henry P. Westbrooks are the personal representatives of said decedant who died intestate. (Obi TN, Cir Ct Min, 3/94) 21 June 1841 petition was made to sell slaves by Henry J. P. Westbrook, administrator of Henry Applewhite, deceased, James Blankinship & Rebecca his wife, Sarah Jane Ogilsby, William H. Applewhite, Richard Applewhite, John J. Applewhite and Mary Applewhite, the later 4 who petition by their guardian, George Merreweather. (Ibid 4/no#)

ARBUCKLE, Catherine
20 September 1808 appeared in court and made choice of William Brown, Esquire as her guardian, with John Brown & Thomas Brown as security. (Roa TN, Co Ct Min, D/6)

ARCHIBALD, Richard Baxter
Died before 7 November 1870 when J. F. Dickey was appointed administrator, with J. D. Smith as security. (Dyr TN, Co Ct Min, B/127)

ARMSTEAD
21 August 1860 a suit by A. R. Reid vs James B. Carter & wife, Jno. F. Armstead, Wm. H. Armstead, Julia V. Armstead, Geo. E. & Martha A. Armstead & Thos. W. Gamwell, was dismissed. (Mad TN, Ch Ct Min, 2/353)

ARMSTRONG, John
8 July 1873 was released from paying poll tax as he is "physically unable to obtain a lively hood." (Dyr TN, Co Ct Min, B/600)

ARMSTRONG, Martin
At the June term 1806, by his attorney in fact, Thomas Armstrong, made a bill of sale to his sons, John and Joseph Armstrong and his daughter, Elizabeth Armstrong. (Wil TN, Co Ct Min, no#/236)

ARMSTRONG, Nelly?
Was a poor person who was let to the lowest bidder, Ralph Shelton, 11 May 1815. (Cla TN, Co Ct Min, 4/68) The name was shown as Polly Armstron. (Ibid 115) Polly Armstrong was let to William Bunch in 1816. (Ibid 156)

ARMSTRONG, Samuel M.
Died before 6 March 1827 when letters testamentary were issued to Benjamin D. Armstrong on his estate. (McM TN, Co Ct Min, 2no#/207)

ARMSTRONG, W. F.
Taxes were not collected in District 4 for 1873, "under age." (Dyr TN, Co Ct Min, B/759)

ARMSTRONG, William
21 January 1799 made a deed of gift to John Armstrong with Richard Clark as witness. He also made a deed of gift to Jane, Sally, & Nancy Armstrong. (Rob TN, Co Ct Min, 1/84)

ARNOLD, Euliana
19 September 1804 produced an instrument of writing to Michael Arnold, her husband, authorizing him to receive her portion or share of the estate of Jonas Rudesel, deceased, from the executors or administrators of said estate in York County, State of PA. (Roa, TN, Co Ct Min, A/261)

ARNOLD, Henry
Died before 3 February 1818 when the administrator, Wm. C. Mitchell, was ordered to sell the negro property & perishable property. (Wil TN, Co Ct Min, no#/223) Nancy Arnold petitioned for dower. (Ibid 283) Robert Bumpass was appointed guardian of John Arnold, Cooly Arnold, Booker Arnold, Richardson Arnold, Henry Arnold, Francis Arnold, Thomas Arnold, Polly Arnold & Creesey Arnold, minor heirs. (Ibid 373)

ARNOLD, Martha H.
17 January 1850, in a suit vs Martin Arnold, it is to be decided if Martha is to have custody

of her children. The separation and abandonment was mentioned. (Mad TN, Ch Ct Min, 1/109) Martha & Martin Arnold were married 19 December 1835 in Madison County, TN. They moved to Henderson County and to McNairy County and about 10 years ago came back to Madison County. They lived as husband and wife until 2 years & 10 months prior to filing this bill. At that time Martin abandonded her. Divorce was granted and Martha given custody of the children and Arnold can see his children upon prudent behavior. (Ibid 115)

ASBEL, Pierce
Died before 7 August 1804 when the heirs were shown on the delinquent tax list. (Rob TN, Co Ct Min, 1/307)

AST, Frederick
Was an orphan boy 2 February 1818 when he was bound to Abner Stewart until age 21. He is to be taught the wheelwright trade. (Wil TN, Co Ct Min, no#/218)

ATCHLEY, Albert S.
Died before 2 October 1865 when Benjamin Langston was appointed administrator with P. J. Atchly as security. (Sev TN, Co Ct Min, no#/219)

ATCHLEY, McCajah
4 October 1858 was released from paying poll tax for 1858 as he had removed out of the county before the 5th of January 1858. (Sev TN, Co Ct Min, no#/347)

ATCHLEY, Thomas
Died before 7 January 1857 when the will was proved by William Atchley and John Lindsey, witnesses. (Sev TN, Co Ct Min, no#/118)

ATCHLY, Isaac
Died before 4 August 1856 when William Atchly renewed his bond as guardian to Isaac Atchly, Mary Atchly, Malissa Atchly, John Atchly, Enoch Atchly, & Martha Ann Atchly, minor heirs. B. M. Atchly & Morgan Davis were security. (Sev TN, Co Ct Min, no#/66) John Russell was the administrator. (Ibid 85)

ATCHLY, Thos.
Died before 7 October 1856 when John C. Atchly renewed his bond as administrator with Benjamin Atchley as his security. (Sev TN, Co Ct Min, no#/84) A settlement was made by Benjamin Atchley as guardian of the minor heirs. (Ibid 89) 4 August 1862 Benjamin Atchley, Sr. resigned as guardian of Martha Atchley, McCamel Atchley, Aramicia Atchley & Patience Atchley, minor heirs of Thomas D. Atchley, deceased, and Micajah Atchley was appointed their guardian. (Ibid no#/11)

ATCHLY, William
4 August 1856 Thos. Dunn made a settlement as guardian to James H. Atchly, minor heir of William Atchly. (Sev TN, Co Ct Min, no#/65) 3 January 1859 petition to sell land was made by Benj. Langston & his wife Mary, Jas. Atchley & his guardian vs the heirs of Wm. Atchley, deceased. (Ibid 376) 4 July 1859 two interests in the land were sold & divested out of Benjamin Langston & his wife & James Atchley. (Ibid 449)

ATKINS, Anthony
Died before 4 July 1870 when J. F. Williamson was paid for making the coffin. (Dyr TN, Co Ct Min, B/73)

ATKINS, Henry
3 August 1814 gave bond with George Atkins as security, that a bastard child of Larinda Wilbourn shall not become a charge on the county. (Ste TN, Co Ct Min, 4/178) Henry Atkins was ordered to pay $25 for the expence of "Lying in of Larinda Wilbourn & the support of her child for one year." (Ibid 250)

ATKINS, Joseph
Made a deed to James Atkins which was recorded on certificate from Wythe County, VA, 7 July 1809. (Rob TN, Co Ct Min, 2/164)

ATKINS, Joshua
Died before 27 March 1806 when Benjamin Taren [Tawn] was called on to make a report as administrator. (Wil TN, Co Ct Min, no#/197)

ATKINS, William
Made a deed of gift to James T. Atkins, William Cormell Atkins & Joseph Atkins, proven by

William Cormell, Benjamin Elliott & John Yoes, 11 February 1811. (Rob TN, Co Ct Min, 2/365)

ATKINS, William
Died before 9 August 1814 when the heirs were on the tax list. (Rob TN, Co Ct Min, 3/453)

ATKINSON, Joshua
Died before 3 August 1819 when Bennett Babb was appointed guardian for Joseph Atkinson, Martha Atkinson, & Eliza Atkinson, minor heirs. (Wil TN, Co Ct Min, no#/512)

ATKINSON, Polly
17 July 1811 was fined $6 for "having a Base Born Child." (Roa TN, Co Ct Min, D/315)

ATKINSON, William
Died before 4 December 1826 when a supplemental inventory of his estate was recorded. (McM TN, Co Ct Min, 2no#/182)

ATKISON, James
Was the father of a bastard child of Nancy Bolinger and gave bond for its support 5 September 1827, with John Atkison & John Walker, Jr. as his security. (McM TN, Co Ct Min, 2no#/240)

AUST, Frederick
Died before 19 June 1816 when the administrator was ordered to make a report. (Wil TN, Co Ct Min, no#/17)

AVERETT, Joshua
Was a resident of Autanga County, AL, in 1844 when he and Adam Frelick, of the same place, filed suit against Jacob Harrison who lately resided in AL but now in Bedford County, TN, & James Burton who is from Jackson County, AL, but is also now in Bedford County. (Bed TN, Ch Ct Min, 3/162)

AVERY, Jonas
Was an orphan negro boy aged 12 years when he gave his consent, 5 September 1871, to be bound to H. B. Avery until age 21. (Dyr TN, Co Ct Min, B/286)

AYDOLETT, John
Died before 23 June 1806 when the will was proved by Isaac Mesany. (Wil TN, Co Ct Min, no#/235) Rhody Warnick was granted letters of administration with the will annexed. (Ibid 336)

AYER, Zacheus
Died before 20 April 1812 when administration was granted to Mary T. Ayer, Alpha Kingsley & John Brown, with Thos. Brown, Thos. N. Clark & James Trimble as security. Mary T. Ayer was chosen guardian by Margaret Ayer and also appointed guardian of Alexander L. Ayer, Sophia Ayer, William B. Ayer & Alpha K. Ayer. Alpha Kingsley was chosen guardian by Lewis M. Ayer and was also appointed guardian of Nancy Ayer & Thos. J. Ayer. (Roa TN, Co Ct Min, D/366)

AYERS, David B.
Died before 3 September 1827 when Susanna Ayers was appointed guardian of the orphan minor heirs: "Salina P. Thorp Joseph C. Daniel R. Susan J. and James W. Ayers." (McM TN, Co Ct Min, 2no#/229)

AYERS, Elizabeth
11 July 1844 was granted a divorce from Amos Ayers for desertion. Her maiden name of Elizabeth Fisher was restored. (Obi TN, Cir Ct Min, 4/no#)

BABB, Burwell
Was the father of a bastard child begotton on Polly Mason. He gave bond for its maintenance 11 May 1812 with John Holland & Henry Capils as security. (Rob TN, Co Ct Min, 3/79)

BABB, William
Died before 2 November 1819 when Bennet Babb was appointed administrator with Mathew Horn, Warren Moore & Benja. Wesford as security. (Wil TN, Co Ct Min, no#/542)

BACKUS, William
Was aged about 40 when he was allowed $30 for his support because of bodily infirmities, 26 June 1805. (Wil TN, Co Ct Min, no#/129)

BAILES, William
Was released from paying poll tax for 1865 & 1866 in consequence of physical disability. (Sev TN, Co Ct Min, no#/324)

BAILEY, Andrew
Died before 4 March 1829 when his will was proved by Saml. Workman & Jane McClachey, witnesses. Wesley & Lucy Bailey were named executors. (McM TN, Co Ct Min, 2no#/350)

BAILEY, Mary A.
14 October 1861 was apprenticed to John Murphy until age 21. She is now 10 years old. (Sev TN, Co Ct Min, no#/721)

BAILEY, Nancy
Died before 7 September 1829 when her will was proved by Saml. McConnell, witness. (McM TN, Co Ct Min, 2no#/383)

BAILEY, Wm.
Was a minor 2 October 1865 when George Davis was appointed guardian, with G. W. Underdown as security. (Sev TN, Co Ct Min, no#/217)

BAIN, Alexander
Died before 9 November 1830 as shown in the suit of Alexander Bain vs Joel S. Enloe. The suit was revived in the name of James Bain the administrator. Alexander Bain died in Hickman County, KY. (Obi TN, Cir Ct Min, 1/130)

BAINE, Susen M.
Divorce was granted 20 June 1838 from James Baine. (Obi TN, Cir Ct Min, 3/213)

BAIRD, W. B.
5 April 1871 N. Porter made a settlement as guardian of the heirs. (Dyr TN, Co Ct Min, B/228)

BAIRD, William
Died before 18 June 1816 when James Foster was appointed administrator with David Baird & John Baird as security. (Wil TN, Co Ct Min, no#/13) A years provision was laid off to the widow. (Ibid 15) Name also shown as Beard. (Ibid 29) 4 November 1819 Jesse Smith was appointed guardian of Ann Baird & Matilda Baird, minor daughters of William Baird, deceased. (Ibid 544)

BAITS, Isaac
Was a resident of Tryon County [NC] 23 November 1778 when his deposition was to be taken for the suit of John McNabb vs Wm. Taylor. (Was TN, Co Ct Min, 1/49)

BAKER, Francis
Was a person who had withdrawn his allegiance. He came into Court at the February term 1789 and availed himself of the Act of Pardon and Oblivion by taking the Oaths prescribed by law. (Was TN, Co Ct Min, 1/371)

BAKER, Ham
Taxes were not collected in District 5 for 1873, "Ark." (Dyr TN, Co Ct Min, B/759)

BAKER, Henry
Was released from working on public roads 1 April 1861 on account of being lame from a broken leg. (Sev TN, Co Ct Min, no#/671)

BAKER, Jas. H.
Was granted a divorce from Elizabeth Baker on 22 August 1866. They were married 27 December 1849 and lived as man & wife until 1861 when complainant discovered that defendant had been guilty of adultry and had given birth to a mulatto child. He has not lived with her after that time. (Mad TN, Ch Ct Min, 2/505)

BAKER, Joe
Taxes were not collected in District 5 for 1873, "cant be found." (Dyr TN, Co Ct Min, B/759)

BAKER, John
Died before 4 August 1856 when the administrator, Margaret Baker, filed a suggestion for insolvency of the estate. (Sev TN, Co Ct Min, no#/66)

BAKER, John
Died before 1 November 1819 when Ansel Frusly was appointed administrator with Jacob McDermit & Allen Ross as security. (Wil TN, Co Ct Min, no#/538)

BAKER, Kemp
Was the father and guardian of Sarah Ann Baker, a minor, as shown in a case 15 September 1852. (Mad TN, Ch Ct Min, 1/256)

BAKER, Martin
Died before 4 June 1866 when the will was proved by Wilson Duggan, the only living witness. (Sev TN, Co Ct Min, no#/330) Elizabeth Baker was executrix with Emanual Fox, B. F. Tipton & Calvin Fox as security. (Ibid 338)

[BAKER], Michael
Died before 19 October 1812 when the will was proved by Ja____ [page torn] & Archellas Vaughen. Fanny Baker was named executrix in the will, the other [person named] declined serving. [page torn & no last name shown for deceased but it was probably Baker.] (Roa TN, Co Ct Min, D/417)

BAKER, Morgan W.
Died before 7 August 1871 when E. A. Baker was appointed administratrix, with Jo. R. Baker, E. H. Baker and G. T. Baker as her security. J. P. Hurt, E. H. White and T. H. Johnson were appointed to lay off a years allowance for Elizabeth A. Baker and her family. (Dyr TN, Co Ct Min, B/262)

BAKER, Nathanl.
Died before 4 December 1826 when his will was proved by James Walker, one of the witnesses. (McM TN, Co Ct Min, 2no#/180)

BAKER, William
Died before 5 December 1825 when Daniel Pearce was appointed administrator, his wife, the widow of the said William Baker, having first given her consent. Daniel Pearce was appointed guardian of John Baker & Delila Baker, orphan children of William Baker, deceased, they being under 16 years of age. (McM TN, Co Ct Min, 2no#/111) 1 June 1829 Arthur Baker, minor orphan between 14 & 21, made choice of David H. Dickey as his guardian. James & Andrew Baker, under 14 and also orphans of Wm. Baker, deceased, had David H. Dickey appointed as their guardian. (Ibid 365)

BAKER, Zachariah
Died before 14 November 1814 when the heirs were on the tax list. (Rob TN, Co Ct Min, 3/488)

BALES, James
Died before 3 December 1866 when Margaret Bales was appointed guardian to Isaac Williams & James Henry, minor orphans of James Bales, deceased, with J. H. Caldwell as security. (Sev TN, Co Ct Min, no#/406)

BALES, John
Died before 8 April 1862 when Robert Bales was appointed guardian of the minor heirs. (Sev TN, Co Ct Min, no#/769)

BALES, Leroy
Died before 1 April 1867 when James M. Warren was appointed guardian to Nancy Ann Cordelia Bales, minor child, with John R. Leak as security. (Sev TN, Co Ct Min, no#/438)

BALL, Lewis
Was a resident of Franklin County, TN, 3 October 1821 when he gave power of attorney to Samuel Dixon to sell land in Wilson County. (Wil TN, Reg Bk/229)

BALLENTINE, James
Was granted a divorce from Jane Ballentine 20 February 1857 for adultry. They were married in Madison County 10 Sept 1852. (Mad TN, Ch Ct Min, 2/135)

BALZEA, J. S.
Died before 7 April 1873 when James H. Hamilton was appointed guardian of the minor heirs, with Smith Parks as security. (Dyr TN, Co Ct Min, B/556)

BANDY, Richard
Died before 1 January 1816 when the heirs made an agreement: Epeson Bandy relinquished all his right & title to the plantation for the year 1816 which he was entitled to by the will of his father, "for which cause we the heirs of said Richard Bandy agreed to make a sale on the 20th of January," signed by Jamison Bandy, Epison Bandy, Solomon Bandy, Joseph Bandy, Milcher Bandy, Peron Bandy, James Cornelious, Edward Brown & Richard Bandy. (Wil TN, Reg Bk/53)

BANDY, S.
Taxes were not collected in District 2 for 1873, "gone." (Dyr TN, Co Ct Min, B/759)

BANKS, Enock
Died before 11 September 1854 as shown in the suit of Robert Banks, executor of Enock Banks, deceased vs Jno. Finley & Geo. Snider. (Mad TN, Ch Ct Min, 2/10)

BARBER, Joel D. [Barker]
Died before 21 August 1868 as shown in the suit of Edward C. Slater vs John Hardy & Mary Hardy his wife & others. The court is to determine if the widow of Joel D. Barber is willing to take a part of the proceeds of the sale of the land in lieu of dower. (Mad TN, Ch Ct Min, 3/234)

BARCLAY, Elihu S.
10 December 1830 he has granted a certificate stating that he is of good moral character. He has been a practicing attorney in McMinn County for about 5 years and is about to remove to the State of GA. (McM TN, Co Ct Min, 2no#/498)

BARFOOT, Thomas [Barefoot]
Died before 2 May 1814 when Nathan Boon was appointed administrator with Isham Sills and Nathan Skinner as security. (Ste TN, Co Ct Min, 4/136)

BARKER, Hinchey
3 December 1827 made deeds of gift to Burt Barker, Thomas Barker and James S. Barker. (McM TN, Co Ct Min, 2no#/244 & 245) 2 June 1828 Hincha Barker made deeds of gifts to James G. Barker, Bird Barker & Thomas Barker. (Ibid 284) Hinchey Barker made a deed of gift to Alexander Barker. (Ibid 289)

BARKER, Philip
17 February 1796 was allowed forty dollars for his support as he is an object of charity. (Was TN, Co Ct Min, 1/594)

BARKER, Susan
Died before 6 November 1871 when B. C. Smith was appointed administrator, with W. B. Smith and B. F. Prichard as his security. (Dyr TN, Co Ct Min, B/315)

BARKER, Thomas
29 November 1780 it was ordered that his property be sold as he was found and taken in arms against the State. (Was TN, Co Ct Min, 1/123)

BARKSDALE, Daniel
Was a resident of Lincoln County, TN, when he filed suit against Samuel Doak of Bedford County [probably in 1837]. (Bed TN, Ch Ct Min, 1/174)

BARKSON, Aron
Died before 4 November 1782 when the will was proved by Patrick Shields. (Was TN, Co Ct Min, 1/179)

BARLEY, Walter
Died before August term 1790 when the will was proved by Thomas Reennaw and Archer Evans. Joseph Greer and Etheldred Davis were executors. (Was TN, Co Ct Min, 1/455)

BARNES, Charles
Was a resident of Hardin County, TN, in November 1820 when he gave a bond to Henry Carson of Wilson County for a military claim for 320 acres of land. (Wil TN, Reg Bk/188)

BARNET, A. M.
Died before 5 April 1870 when Edgar G. Sugg was chosen and appointed guardian of

Finis E. Barnet, minor heir, with W. P. Sugg and C. L. Nolen as security. (Dyr TN, Co Ct Min, B/43) James H. Cooper was administrator. (Ibid 48) 7 September 1874 D. S. Burgie made a settlement as guardian of Johnnie L. Barnett, minor heir of A. M. Barnett, deceased. (Ibid 783)

BARNETT, Ed
Taxes were not collected in District 4 for 1873, "insolvent." (Dyr TN, Co Ct Min, B/759)

BARNETT, John
Died before 14 January 1847 when Elizabeth Barnett petitioned for the sale of a slave. The will of the deceased was mentioned. (Mad TN, Ch Ct Min, 1/10)

BARNETT, John
Died before 5 June 1871 when David S. Burgie was chosen and appointed guardian of John L. Barnett, minor heir, with Bill C. Burgie and W. S. Bryant as security. (Dyr TN, Co Ct Min, B/242) 2 June 1873 David S. Burgie renewed his bond as guardian of Johnnie L. Barnett, minor daughter of John Barnett, deceased. (Ibid 588)

BARNETT, Martha
Died before 3 November 1818 when James Michie was appointed administrator with James Cross & Uriah Cross as security. (Wil TN, Co Ct Min, no#/341)

BARNETT, Robert
Died before 3 August 1818 when the will was proved by John M. Stoneman, Callin C. Stoneman & Jacob Thomas. Adam Young, James Michie & James Y. Barnet were executors. (Wil TN, Co Ct Min, no#/292) A years support was allotted to the widow. (Ibid 295) John Barnett qualified as executor. (Ibid 337)

BARNS, Fanny
The sheriff was ordered to bring her children into court, 3 September 1827. (McM TN, Co Ct Min, 2no#/234) Two of the children were brought into court & after mature deliberation were set at liberty. (Ibid 238)

BARNS, Nancy
25 June 1806 a warrent was issued for her to come to next court to answer a charge of bastardy. (Wil TN, Co Ct Min, no#/246)

BARRETT
Died before 6 August 1811 when land was taxed to the heirs. (Ste TN, Co Ct Min, 3/85)

BARTLETT, Isaac
Died before 16 December 1817 when the administrator, Martin Tally, was ordered to make a settlement. (Wil TN, Co Ct Min, no#/201)

BARTLETT, J. W.
7 April 1857 was released from paying poll tax for 1855 because he was not 21 years of age until the 2nd of February 1855. (Sev TN, Co Ct Min, no#/154)

BARTON, Samuel
Died before 17 September 1817 when Alexander Beard was ordered to make a report as administrator. (Wil TN, Co Ct Min, no#/171)

BARTON, Samuel
Died before June term 1824 when Stephen Barton & Gabriel Barton sold land that had belonged to Samuel Barton, deceased. (Wil TN, Reg Bk/332)

BASCOM, William
Died before 21 July 1807 when Joseph B. Neville, Esqr. returned a memorandum on the division of the estate of negroes of William Bascom, deceased. (Ste, TN, Co Ct Min, 1/46b)

BASEY, H. T.
Taxes were not collected in District 4 for 1873, "over age." (Dyr TN, Co Ct Min, B/759)

BASKINS, William
2 November 1818 gave bond to answer a charge of bastardy brought by Elizabeth Ricketts. (Wil TN, Co Ct Min, no#/337) He plead guilty and was ordered to pay support for 5 years. (Ibid 405)

BASS, Ezekiel
Made a deed of gift 15 September 1817 to Abraham Smith's children for sundry articles of property. (Wil TN, Co Ct Min, no#148)

BASS, Jno. F.
Died before 7 October 1872 when Wm. Benthal was appointed administrator, with Wilson Frost and M. P. Husley as security. (Dyr TN, Co Ct Min, B/475)

BASS, Solomon
Died before 23 March 1807 when Scion Bass was granted letters of administration, with Micajah Varett & Mosses Adam & Daniel Tilman as security. (Wil TN, Co Ct Min, no#/277)

BASS, Theophilus
17 March 1823 made a deed of gift to his son Etheldred Bass "a part of his legacy that I intend to give him at my death a Certain negro women by the name of Lucy, the sd E. Bass not to touch or tender with any part of my general stock at my death." (Wil TN, Reg Bk/297)

BATES, Richard
Died before 2 November 1863 when Philip Utinger, N. M. Baker & Carrol Martin were appointed to set off a years provisions to Elizabeth Bates, the widow, & family. (Sev TN, Co Ct Min, no#/79)

BATTE, Wm. P.
In December 1834 was a resident of McCracken? County, KY, as shown in the suit of Thomas Black. The father of William P. Batte was Henry Batte, deceased, and William Allison was one of the administrators. William P. Batte has money coming from the estate of Henry Batte, also 1/11 part of some land. Rebecca Batt was the widow of Henry Batte. William Batte owes money to Thomas Black who wants to attach the money coming to Wm. from the estate of his father. Suit filed 13 February 1837. (Bed TN, Ch Ct Min, 1/119)

BATTS, Frederick
15 May 1811 made a deed of gift to his children, namely, Rebecca Batts, Polly Batts, John Batts, Sally Batts, Rodah Batts and Nancy Batts. (Rob TN, Co Ct Min, 2/418)

BAXTER, Calvin
Taxes were not collected in District 4 for 1873, "insolvent." (Dyr TN, Co Ct Min, B/759)

BAXTER, Jeremiah
Died in 1835 as shown in the suit of William Armstrong & wife, Lucy, of Maury County, TN, vs James Baxter & Catherine Baxter, citizens of Marshall County, TN. Jeremiah Baxter died in Maury County in that part that has become Marshall County, and left a will. James & Catherine Baxter were executors. The will is shown and bequests made to "wife Catherine, my 2 children Fletcher & Mandy [unmarried], son Nathaniel Baxter, son Montgomery Baxter, daughter Eliza Hiland, my five oldest children, to wit, James Baxter, Nancy, Lucy, Sally & Eliza, to my grandson Robert Williamson a negro in the hands of William Armstrong & if said Armstrong refuse to give up the negro he is to have $400 out of the property I have left to my daughter Armstrong." His wife, Katherine, & son James Baxter, were appointed executors. The will was witnessed by Peter & James Williams. Nancy Baxter was then married to Edmund Woodman of Davidson County. Sally was then married to Edmund B. Smith & is now a resident of KY. Lucy was then married to William Armstrong & Eliza to Joseph B. Hiland of Marshall County, TN. This suit was filed 11 April 1837. (Bed TN, Ch Ct Min, 1/265)

BAYLESS, John
Was the father of a base born child by Mary Millar. 19 August 1795 he gave bond for it's maintenance with Alex Pratworth as his security. (Was TN, Co Ct Min, 1/565)

BAYLEY, Peleg
Died before 23 February 1861 as shown in the suit of Joseph W. Bayly administrator &c vs Jeremiah Bayley et als. The estate has long since been settled up leaving land subject to distribution between the heirs. The widow has had her dower. There were 3 heirs, Jos. W. Bayley, Delilah Bayley & Dicey Ann Bayly. Jos. W. & Delilah Bayley have sold their interest in the land to defendant Craig. Dicy Ann Bayly married Jeremiah Bayly & died in May 1860 leaving an infant, Eliza Jane, who died 5 November 1860. Administration was granted to complainant in said estates. (Mad TN, Ch Ct Min, 2/454)

BAYLISS, Wilie [Bayless]
Died before 22 June 1838 when his death was suggested in the suit of Wilie Bayliss vs Jubilee M. Bedford. (Obi TN, Cir Ct Min, 3/229)

BEADLES, Thomas
7 November 1814 gave power of attorney to John Fisher "to ask to demand, receive of &c from the legal Paymaster that now is or hereafter may be appointed for the paying of the Militea ordered, the Command of Major General William Carrall, I the said Thomas Beadles being one of the drafted men to go on said Tour of duty in Capt. James Blacks company, drafted out of Capt. Reazen Byrns company...the money due me for my services done on the said expedition." (Wil TN, Reg Bk/20)

BEAN, Charley
Died before 5 January 1815 when M. J. Graham was paid money from the poor fund for making his coffin. (Sev TN, Co Ct Min, no#/242)

BEAN, George
25 March 1811 gave a deposition in regards to an entry of land made by Richard Henderson, George Dougherty, Thomas Henderson & Robert Burton. George Bean answered questions about what he remembered when he was on an expedition against the "Chikamagee Indians" under the command of Col. Evan Shelby & Col. Chas. Robertson. Other names mentioned were Henry Bowen, Obediah Russell & Howell Doddy. (Roa TN, Co Ct Min, D/293) Jesse Bean gave a similar deposition. (Ibid 357)

BEAN, Jesse
Died before 24 March 1856 as shown in the suit of "David C. Travis Guardian of Emeline Pleasant D P- Sarah R Jordan Roda Jane and Jesse Bean vs James H. Beason W. F. Richardson et als." An account is to be taken of all the assets of Jesse Bean, deceased, that has come to the hands of the administrator. (Fen TN, Ch Ct Min, A/49) David C. Travis was guardian of Bean's heirs. (Ibid 107)

BEAN, William
Died before February term 1790 when Robert Bean was sworn as executor of the will. (Was TN, Co Ct Min, 1/427)

BEARDEN, Eli M. [Bearding]
Died about 1831 as shown 27 June 1843 when Nancy Beardin and the heirs petitioned for dower and sale of land. The heirs were Nancy, the widow, and Willis Bearden, Minerva now wife of William B. Hix, Nimrod Bearden, Nathan Bearden, Nancy now wife of George T. Walsh (adult children and heirs of said Eli) and Wynn Bearden, Allen Bearden and Elizabeth Bearden, minor children who sue by their next friend John T. Bearden, and no other heirs. (Bed TN, Ch Ct Min, 2/243) The land was sold 29 August 1844. (Ibid 296) There were 10 children, the 8 listed above & Charlotte wife of James E. Plannch? [Clannch?] & John T. Beardin. (Ibid 3/170)

BEASLEY, Anna B.
5 December 1870 J. T. Singleton made a settlement as guardian of Anna B. Beasley & sisters. (Dyr TN, Co Ct Min, B/141) 1 May 1871 James T. Singleton renewed his bond as guardian of Anna B. Beasley and Terriceann Beasley. (Ibid 236) One heir shown as Tracy Ann Beasley. (Ibid 381)

BEASLEY, Ephraim
11 March 1813 made a deed of gift to his son, Benney [Bunney] Barbee Beasley, for a negro woman named Dinah & a negro boy named Bob. Ephraim will keep the property as long as he & his wife shall live. Witnessed by Franklin Foster, Dillard Beasley & Polly G. Beasley. (Wil TN, Reg Bk/16) 28 January 1813 made a deed of gift of 80 acres of land to his son Dillard Beasley. (Ibid 29) On 12 September 1816 Ephraim Beasley made a deed of gift of a negro woman named Hannah & her youngest child Daniel, to the heirs of his daughter, Sally W. Cunningham. The heirs were Alexander, Sarah Ann & Prudence. This was witnessed by Jesse Warren & Bemmy Beasly. (Ibid 62) 7 September 1816, Ephraim Beasley made a deed of gift to his son, Josiah Beasley, for 6 negroes and blacksmith tools and other property. Sarah Ann was the wife of Ephrain Beasley. Another deed of gift to Josiah was made 11 March 1813. (Ibid 67) In the deed of gift to children of Sally Cunningham, the child Alexander was shown as Elender. (Ibid, Co Ct Min, no#/23)

BEASLEY, Polly
16 September 1817 it was ordered that William Willie be allowed $4 for having supported Polly Beasley ten weeks "& five dollars for the next three months if the child's father should not sooner come." (Wil TN, Co Ct Min, no#/158)

BEASON, James H.
Died before 2 August 1866 when his death was suggested in the suit of M. W. Conant? vs J. H. Beason. (Fen TN, Ch Ct Min, A/296) The suit was revived in the name of the widow, and Jane & Margaret Hudleston, his only children and heirs at law. (Ibid 320)

BEASON, Mary
Brought suit by her next friend A. Bledsoe vs Wm. Poor, administrator et al, 9 April 1860. A subpoena to answer a copy of the bill was issued to Overton County. (Fen TN, Ch Ct Min, A/226)

BEATHAL, Danl.
Died before 3 November 1818 when the executors were ordered to make a settlement. (Wil TN, Co Ct Min, no#/344)

BEATON, John
Died before 3 May 1814 when Christopher Beaton was appointed administrator with Philip Hornburger & Elijah Rushing as security. (Ste TN, Co Ct Min, 4/141)

BEATTY, Hugh
20 December 1808 Mereweather Smith was appointed commissioner to settle with the Sheriff & County Treasurer in the room of Hugh Beatty removed. (Roa TN, Co Ct Min, D/34)

BEATY, George
Died before 25 September 1855 as shown in the suit of David Beaty (Tinker), administrator of George Beaty deceased vs William C. Davidson & others. (Fen TN, Ch Ct Min, A/30)

BEATY, James
Died before 9 April 1861 as shown in the suit of A. J. Stephens vs the Heirs & Creditors of James Beaty, deceased. Defendants Cintha Beaty & Englantine Beaty are minors and W. S. Bledsoe was appointed guardian ad litem. (Fen TN, Ch Ct Min, A/264) In the suit of Geo. Smith vs the widow & heirs of James Beaty, deceased, entered 4 August 1866, it was stated that the administrator, Jackson Stephens, is deceased & has been for more than 6 months. James Beaty, Jr. was appointed administrator de bonus non for the estate of James Beaty, deceased. (Ibid 300) A defendant in the suit by George Smith was Armilda Beaty. (Ibid 314)

BEATY, John
Died in May 1854 as shown in the suit of Pleasant Taylor, administrator of D. Beaty, deceased vs William W. Wood & others, heirs at law of John Beaty, deceased, filed 12 April 1858. By his will John Beaty made a bequest to his son, David, of all the notes he held against him and in making a division he is to be made equal to the other heirs. W. W. Wood was appointed administrator with will annexed. David Beaty died intestate several years ago and before the death of John Beaty, leaving defendants William, Betsy, Melly [Milla], John, Polk, Dalles, Andrew Jackson, Anna and Pleasant Beaty, his children and heirs. In January 1856 complainant was appointed administrator of David Beaty, deceased. [It does state that David died before John & administrator was appointed for David in 1856?] On 5 March 1855 a petition was made for the sale of land and negros of the estate of John Beaty, which was sold. The court decided this sale was illegal & defective and is to be set aside. (Fen TN, Ch Ct Min, A/131-4) Under the will of John Beaty, David Beaty was entitled to 1/8th part of the personal estate. Defendants Moore, Alred & Paul were mentioned. (Ibid 161) 13 April 1859 it was reported that William Beaty and Margarett Beaty, two of the defendants and heirs of David Beaty, deceased, have died intestate pending this suit and have never been married and their heirs are their brothers & sisters. The minor heirs of David Beaty, deceased, are now residents of Fentress County. (Ibid 201) Samuel Turney, Esqr. was appointed guardian ad litem for said minors. (Ibid 221) The will of John Beaty was made 11 December 1841. (Ibid 226) In a settlement of the estate of John Beaty, deceased, it was stated that W. W. Wood, Jesse Wood, Cyntha Beaty, Pleasant Beaty, W. B. Bouden as guardian of the heirs of John Gwin, Andrew Graham & wife and Joshua Owens have all received their shares of the estate and each is to pay back a certain portion to make the heirs of David Beaty, deceased, equal with them. (Ibid 268)

BEATY, Thos. D.
Died before 20 February 1867 when Thos. H. Drake was appointed guardian ad litem for May Beaty, Posey Beaty, Elvira Beaty, Eward S. Beaty & Cicero Beaty, minors, to defend the suit of E. R. Midgett, administrator vs Mary Beaty et als. (Mad TN, Ch Ct Min, 3/17) The suit of F. A. Beaty, administrator vs May Beaty et als was also shown. (Ibid 35) In the suit

of E. R. Midgett, administrator, et als vs Mary Beaty et als, it was shown that Thos. D. Beaty died intestate in 1861 leaving complainants & defendants (except said Midgett) his only legal heirs. Midgett was appointed administrator. In the other suit of F. A. Beaty, administrator vs May Beaty et als, it was shown that Albert G. Beaty died intestate in 1861 & complainants & defendants were his only heirs. F. A. Beaty was appointed admistrator. (Ibid 114-115) 13 August 1868 the suit is shown as E. R. Midgett, administrator of Thos. D. Beaty, deceased, Francis A. Beaty, Warren G. Beaty, Martha Evelina Beaty & Ruth A. Beaty vs Mary Beaty, Posey Beaty, Elvira V. Beaty, Edward S. Beaty, Cicero Beaty and Thomas G. Carlin. The land was sold & title divested out of complainants & defendants. (Ibid 168)

BEAUMONT, Walter
Taxes were not collected in District 4 for 1873, "insolvent." (Dyr TN, Co Ct Min, B/759)

BEAVERS, Thomas
Died before 25 June 1804 when the will was duly proven and ordered to be recorded. (Wil TN, Co Ct Min, no#/42)

BECK, Elihu
5 December 1859 was a male child aged 3 years when he was bound out as an apprentice. [Does not state to whom.] (Sev TN Co Ct Min, no#/492)

BECK, Ruebin
Died bfore 13 July 1859 as shown in the suit of Sampson W. Cassitty, administrator &c vs Jesse Z. Beck & others. A report of the condition of the estate of Ruebin Beck, deceased, is to be made. (Jac TN, Ch Ct Min, C/236) Land is to be sold subject to the widow's dower. (Ibid 291) This suit was shown as Sampson W. Cassetty, administrator vs William A. Beck, Susan E. Beck, Nathaniel T. Beck, Sarah F. Beck, Mary G. Beck, Allice B. Beck & Reubin S. Beck, Jesse Z. Beck, Abner Harvey, Lucy Jane Harvey, Martha Harvey, Eliza [Elzana] Harvey, Joel W. Settle, Toliver Kirkpatrick and Robert Kirkpatrick. A negro man was sold and purchased by Ann Beck. Land was also sold and title divested out of defendants. (Ibid 321) James R. Tolbert was guardian. Land was sold & purchased by William A. Beck and Jessie Z. Beck. (Ibid 352)

BEDFORD, Jonas
Died before 19 November 1831 when a Clerk of this Court was appointed in his place, he having died since the last term of court. James L. Totten was appointed and Archibald W. O. Totten was named deputy clerk. (Obi TN, Cir Ct Min, 1/189) Lysander Adams & Seth Bedford were administrators for Jonas Bedford, deceased. Jubilee M. Bedford was security for Jonas Bedford in his lifetime. (Ibid 2/45, 84)

BEDFORD, Thos.
Died before 24 September 1806 when the heirs were in a suit vs James Crawford, ejectment. (Wil TN, Co Ct Min, no#/256)

BEDWELL, Thomas
Was a resident of Philadelphia when his land was listed for unpaid taxes, 12 February 1817. (Cla TN, Co Ct Min, 4/306)

BEEN, Wm.
Died before 27 May 1782 when the will was proved by Tho. Hardeman. (Was TN, Co Ct Min, 1/158)

BEET, Frank
Taxes were not collected in District 2 for 1873, "gone." (Dyr TN, Co Ct Min, B/759)

BEISSER, John
Taxes were not collected in District 4 for 1873, "not naturalized." (Dyr TN, Co Ct Min, B/759)

BELL
6 June 1831 Martha Bell, Wm. H. Bell, Sarah M. Bell, Polly Ann Bell, Catharine M. M. Bell, Margaret Bell & James W. Bell sold land to James Hickey. (McM TN, Co Ct Min, 2no#/533)

BELL, George
Died before 3 August 1818 when the will was proved by Charles Compton, John Barbee & Polly Barbee. Francis Bell & John Bell were named executors, John declined. (Wil TN, Co Ct Min, no#/284) An inventory was returned by Fielders [or Fielding] Bell. (Ibid 328)

BELL, John K.
Published his last will and testament on 14 April 1838 and appointed Wm. D. Ray, Leander Bell & Saml. G. Bell executors & departed this life without revoking the same. Mary M. Bell was the widow. He left a legacy to Martha Cheek. Mary M. Bell died and Adam Brown & Vincient Beal were administrators. The legacy of Mary M. Bell on her death was transmitted to & vested in complainants as her administrators. The suit dated 13 July 1847 is: Adam M. Brown and Vincent Beal, administrators of the estate of Mary M. Bell vs Wm. D. Ray [Roy], Leander Bell & Samuel G. Bell, executors of Jno. K. Bell and James Bell & E. A. Bell & others. (Mad TN, Ch Ct Min, 1/23) Other names shown in this suit were Lemuel Catham [Cotham] & Martha his wife, Elizabeth Bell & others. Also Jane Ray, wife of Wm. D. Ray. (Ibid 94)

BELL, Matthew
Died before 25 June 1806 when a deed was recorded from William Nash to William Bell, administrator of Matthew Bell. [does not say deceased] (Wil TN, Co Ct Min, no#/243)

BELL, Rebecca
Was the mother of a bastard child by George Rogers who was ordered to pay support 7 September 1874. (Dyr TN, Co Ct Min, B/783)

BELL, Thomas W.
Died before 3 October 1871 when J. D. B. Tipton was appointed administrator, with W. C. Doyle and W. H. Pate as security. (Dyr TN, Co Ct Min, B/305) W. Wynne, N. R. Prichard and John Pate were appointed to set off a years allowance for the widow and family. (Ibid 312)

BELT, Middleton
Died before 16 September 1816 when the administrator, Benjamin Bell [Belt], was ordered to give further security. (Wil TN, Co Ct Min, no#/28) 1 February 1819 Richard C. Craddock was appointed guardian of Jeremiah Belt, Dodson Belt & William Belt, minor heirs. (Ibid 385)

BENSON, Spencer
7 March 1859 made bond as guardian of J. W., S. E. & N. A. Benson, with David McMahan as his security. (Sev TN, Co Ct Min, no#/410) 1 September 1862, Spencer Benson made a settlement as guardian of the heirs of Spencer Benson & Matilda Benson. (Ibid 13) 6 August 1866 Spencer Benson made a settlement as guardian of the minor heirs of Spencer & Matilda, deceased. [sic] (Ibid 359)

BENTHAL, David [Daniel]
Died before 17 June 1816 when the will was proved by Elizabeth Johnson & Matilda Stanley. Mary Benthal, Martin Tally & [torn] Southerland were executors with Barnard Carter as security. (Wil TN, Co Ct Min, no#/1)

BENTON, Floyd
Taxes were not collected in District 2 for 1873, "gone." (Dyr TN, Co Ct Min, B/759)

BENTON, Maecenas
9 February 1870 was certified to be a resident of Dyer County from infancy, a young man of good moral character of Sober Steady habits, and that he is 21 years of age, preparatory to his application for a license to practice law. (Dyr TN, Co Ct Min, B/8)

BENTON [or Bently]
Died before 10 September 1806 when land was taxed to the heirs. (Ste TN, Co Ct Min, 1/36) 9 February 1814 land was taxed to the heirs of Jesse Benton. (Ibid 4/106)

BENTON, Prissie
6 January 1873 Ed. Barnett, colored, was paid for her care and A. B. Tigrett was paid for taking her to the poor house. (Dyr TN, Co Ct Min, B/523)

BEREN, Bazel
Died before 9 February 1813 when Augustine Cook was appointed administrator, with John Couts security. (Rob TN, Co Ct Min, 3/199) Also shown as Bazel Boren. (Ibid 201) 19 November 1813 Hosea Baren was shown as administrator for Bazel Baren, deceased. (Ibid 524)

BERRY, Mark
Died before 3 February 1819 when a committee was appointed to allot Cassandy Ashworth & Jasper R. Ashworth, her husband, her distributive share of the estate of Mark

Berry, deceased. (Wil TN, Co Ct Min, no#/407) Jasper B. Ashworth was appointed guardian of the minor heirs. (Ibid 454)

BERRYHILL, William
Died before 19 October 1838 when his death was suggested in the suit of William Berryhill for the use of the Comrs. of Common Schools &c vs William W. Watson and others. (Obi TN, Cir Ct Min, 3/282)

BERRYHILL, Wm. M.
Died before 28 September 1840 as shown in the suit of George Davidson & others vs The Bank of the State of Tenn. (Bed TN, Ch Ct Min, 1/313)

BESSENT, P. R.
Died before 8 March 1870 when Elias Parrish made a settlement as administrator. (Dyr TN, Co Ct Min, B/16) W. W. Parrish made a report as guardian of Anna and J. H. Bessent, minor heirs. (Ibid 83) J. H. was shown as James Harvey Bessent. (Ibid 88)

BETTERS, Washington
Was released from paying poll tax for 1858 as there is no such man in this county. (Sev TN, Co Ct Min, no#/408)

BETTS, Seldon
Died in the summer of 1849 having just made his last will and testament. Philander D. W. Conger was executor. He left property to his wife, Penniah, during her life or widowhood. After her death $50 was to be paid to each of his brothers & sisters being five in number, & $200 should be paid to the Baptist Union University at Murfreesboro, TN, & the balance divided between Home & Foreign Baptist Societies. (Mad TN, Ch Ct Min, 2/176) Pereniah Betts died in February 1856 having first made a will. A suit was filed by P. D. W. Conger et als vs Stokely Betts et als, 25 February 1859. (Ibid 280) 21 February 1860 in the suit of P. D. W. Conger, executor & others vs Lovel Betts & others, land was sold and title divested out of James B. Conger, John J. Betts, Lemuel Bowers [Bevers], Evelina Bowers, Stokely Betts, Lovell Betts, Eliza Colthrap, Eliza Demembrane, Isaac W. Betts, William S. Betts, Leonidas Betts, Ann Williams, Franklin Betts, Harriet Miller, John Conger, Caroline Priestly, Stephen C. Paratt [Pavatt], L. P. Wiley, Margaret Williams, Sarah Williams and Paratt Williams, John Nixen, H. E. Nixen, O. A. Nixon, Margaret Chappel, Mary Paratt & Rowena Paratt. Another listing is the same except it included Evender Betts instead of Leonidas Betts. (Ibid 298)

BEVERLY, John
Was a resident of KY in February 1790 when his deposition was to be taken for the suit of John Engle vs Henry Long. (Was TN, Co Ct Min, 1/242)

BIGEN, Matthew [Biger]
Died before 20 September 1817 as shown in an agreement made by his nephews, Thomas Drennon, James Drennon, John Drennon, David Drennon, Henry Miller & John Arnold. Matthew had given their sister, Ann Drennon, a negro girl named Nancy. (Wil TN, Reg Bk/98)

BIGGS, Francis
On 16 May 1833, in the suit of Seth Bedford vs The Commissioners of the town of Troy & others, it was stated that Francis Biggs & Didamia his wife were citizens of Spencer County, IN. In the same suit it stated that James Bain & Susan, his wife, were citizens of Hickman County, KY. Papers have been served on Jubilee M. Bedford, Lysander Adams, Jesse L. Ross, Thomas Allen & Richard B. Brown, commissioners for the town of Troy. Also on Joseph Meadows & Jane his wife. (Obi TN, Cir Ct Min, 2/84)

BIGGS, Sam
Was a nergo boy aged 9 years when he was bound 5 April 1871 to W. W. Biggs until age 21. (Dyr TN, Co Ct Min, B/226) Sam Biggs was also called Sam Jones. (Ibid 288)

BINKLEY, John
Died before 16 February 1814 when John Hutchison and Levi Hays, Esqr. were ordered to settle the estate of John Binkley, deceased, with the legatees and also with Henry Frey and Daniel Binkley, administrators of the estate of Peter Binkley, deceased. (Rob TN, Co Ct Min, 3/376)

BINKLEY, Peter
Died before 12 November 1811 when Henry Frey & Daniel Binkley were appointed

administrators. (Rob TN, Co Ct Min, 3/39) 10 May 1813 dower was ordered to be laid off to the widow. (Ibid 233)

BIRCH, George [Burch]
Was a minor orphan on 3 December 1828 when he made choice of John Neil as his guardian. (McM TN, Co Ct Min, 2no#/328)

BIRCH, Henry
Was a minor orphan 3 December 1828 when he made choice of Elijah Hurst as his guardian. Henry was of sufficient age to choose a guardian [14]. (McM TN, Co Ct Min, 2no#/328)

BIRCH, S.
Taxes were not collected in District 5 for 1873, "insolvent." (Dyr TN, Co Ct Min, B/759)

BIRD, Adam
5 June 1865 was appointed guardian to the minor heirs of A. Bird, with John Bird & Emanuel Fox as his security. (Sev TN, Co Ct Min, no#/167)

BIRD, Mark
Died before 4 September 1865 when John Bird & N. M. Baker were appointed administrators with Emanuel Fox & Calvin Fox as security. (Sev TN, Co Ct Min, no#/208) Dower is to be laid off to Mary Ann Bird, widow. (Ibid 351)

BIRD, Nancy
1 July 1861 Stephen Huff was paid for keeping Nancy Bird and child. (Sev TN, Co Ct Min, no#/697)

BIRD, Shadrack
Died before 2 May 1814 when, on the motion of Nancy Bird, she and Bryant Bird were appointed administrators, with Charles Polk & James McCulbugh as security. (Ste TN, Co Ct Min, 4/137)

BIRD, Thomas
Gave bond for the maintenance of a bastard child of Elizabeth Cohea, with Andrew Cruil & John Bird as security, 12 May 1813. (Rob TN, Co Ct Min, 3/255)

BIRD, William
Died before 11 February 1811 when an account of the sale of the estate was recorded. (Rob TN, Co Ct Min, 2/362)

BIRDSONG, Wm.
Died before 17 March 1853 as shown in the suit of James Fussell vs Jno. C. Birdsong, administrator. (Mad TN, Ch Ct Min, 1/318) In the suit of Wm. Stone & wife et als vs Jno. C. Birdsong, T. R. Birdsong et als, it was stated that Wm. Birdsong died intestate 26 October 1850. Jno. C. Birdsong was administrator & gave bond with T. R. Birdsong, B. F. Bond, Wyatt Fussell, James Fussell & J. R. Jelks as sureties. B. F. Bond has been released & G. A. Kyle & A. A. Greer substituted in his stead. The complainant & defendants Birdsong are entitled to the estate. The suit of G. M. Birdsong vs J. C. Birdsong was mentioned. (Ibid 2/226) In the suit of Geo. M. Birdsong et als vs Jno. C. Birdsong et als, Jno. C. Birdsong is to pay $1,000 to a trustee for the benefit of the wife & children of Geo. M. Birdsong. This amount is to be credited on their share of the estate when ascertained. (Ibid 360) William Fulghum was appointed trustee for Rebecca Birdsong, wife of Geo. M., and her children. (Ibid 369) William Fulghum was appointed guardian ad litem for the minor children of G. M. Birdsong. (Ibid 457) 21 February 1867 this case was heard: Geo. M. Birdsong & wife Rebecca Birdsong, Margaret Birdsong, Susan Birdsong, Ephraim Birdsong, the last 4 minors by their next friend Geo. M. Birdsong vs Jno. C. Birdsong, Wyatt Fussell, Jno. J. Anderson, administrator, Jas. Fussell, Thos. R. Richardson & Jno. R. Jelks, Wm. H. Stone & others. The entire amount of the estate of Wm. Birdsong, the ancestor of complainants, which came to the hands of the administrator, Jno. C. Birdsong, including interest to date, is $25,873.39 & the share of the complainants being 1/5 & they are entitled to a decree against Jno. C. Birdsong and his securities. A sum is to be settled upon a trustee for the use of the wife & children of said Geo. M. Birdsong. It is therefore ordered that Rebecca Birdsong, Margaret Birdsong, Susan Birdsong, Mary Birdsong and Ephrain Birdsong recover of Jno. C. Birdsong & Wyatt Fussell, Jno. R. Jelks, Thos. R. Richardson, Jno. J. Anderson, administrator, & of Aml.? Williams, administrator of B. F. Bond, the said sum. (Ibid 3/30) Wm. Birdsong had 5 children. The share of Geo. M. Birdsong is to be accounted for in another suit. Wm. Gates is entitled to one share as assignee of Wm.

Birdsong. B. F. Bond, through his administrator, A. J. Williams, is entitled to one share. (Ibid 45)

BISHOP, Joseph
Was a resident of Smith County, TN, on 17 November 1808 when he sold a slave named Peggy to Azariah Alexander of Jackson County, TN, registered in Wilson County, TN, & proved by John Cage 28 June 1817. (Wil TN, Reg Bk/85)

BLACK, Hiram
Died before 15 November 1814 when William Black was appointed administrator with William Fluellas & Abel Williams security. (Rob TN, Co Ct Min, 3/498) 13 February 1815 Moses M. Donnelson & Henry Frey were appointed administrators. (Ibid 535)

BLACK, Jonathan
Was a resident of Madison County, Mississippi Territory, 16 October 1810 when his deposition was to be taken for the defendant in the suit of John Gordon Assee. vs William Black. (Roa TN, Co Ct Min, D/257)

BLACK, William
Died before 13 February 1815 when the will was proved by Thomas Cheatam. (Rob TN, Co Ct Min, 3/537) The will was proved by Mary Black. Moses M. Donnelson & Henry Frey were executors. (Ibid 552)

BLACKBURN, Benjn.
At the May term 1789 was released from paying taxes for 1787, being over age. (Was TN, Co Ct Min, 1/381)

BLACKBURN, William H.
Died before March term 1826 as shown in a case concerning the estate of Jesse Clack, deceased. William Blackburn had married the widow of Jesse Clack. (Wil TN, Reg BK/379) [second set of page numbers]

BLAIN, James
Died before 3 June 1828 as shown in the case of William Blain vs John Armstrong, James Johnston & John Blain, Exectuors of the last will & testament of James Blain deceased. (McM TN, Co Ct Min, no#/327)

BLAIR, Hiram S.
1 June 1857 was appointed guardian to Eli M. Blair, Martha Ann Blair, & Mary Jane Blair, minor orphans. Eli Fox & Absolem Allen were his securities. (Sev TN, Co Ct Min, no#/171)

BLAIR, Jno.
Died before 18 January 1850 as shown when land he had willed to his grandchildren, Ripley B. & Hillery W. Holliday, was to be sold. Allen J. Holliday was the father and guardian of the minor children. (Mad TN, Ch Ct Min, 1/115) A suit was entered 10 July 1850; Martha L. Ross by her next friend Lewis G. Ross vs Martha Blair, James Blair, executor of Jno. Blair, deceased, in his own right & as executor, Allen Holliday & wife Nancy, Jas. Boren & wife Jane, Anderson Hays & wife Cynthia & their children James, Sally & Tennessee Hays, Jas. M. Rush & wife Tennessee, Jno. Blair, Saml. Blythe & wife Martha. Complainant's bill was dismissed. Her life estate was mentioned. (Ibid 140)

BLAIR, Joseph
6 August 1795 made over all his property, land, stock, household furniture, slave, etc. to his two daughters, Mary and Sally, recorded 17 February 1796 and proved by William Pursley and James Bean. (Was TN, Co Ct Min, 1/594)

BLAIR, Oliver H.
Died before 6 April 1858 when M. Davis was appointed administrator with J. M. Evans as security. (Sev TN, Co Ct Min, no#/288)

BLAKE, B. F.
Died before 3 January 1871 when Guy Douglass made a settlement as executor. (Dyr TN, Co Ct Min, B/154)

BLAKEMORE, Daniel
Was a resident of Lincoln County, TN, on 8 September 1825 when his deposition was to be taken for the plaintiff in the case of Joseph B. Bacon vs Ezekiel Bonner. (McM TN, Co Ct Min, no#/206)

BLAND, Nelson
Taxes were not collected in District 5 for 1873, "not found." (Dyr TN, Co Ct Min, B/759)

BLAND, Sally
Died before 3 May 1842 as shown in the suit of Samuel E. Stone and Leroy B. Settle vs Henry F. Burke and wife, Elizabeth, and Milton M. Bland. Henry F. Burke is a distributee of the estate of Sally Bland, deceased, in right of his wife, Elizabeth Burke, formerly Elizabeth Bland, who was a daughter of Sally Bland. (Jac TN, Co Ct Min, A/40) Matthew M. Bland was administrator. (Ibid 105) Henry F. Burke was not an inhabitant of this state, 7 November 1843. (Ibid 123)

BLANKENSHIP, J. H.
Died before 1 August 1870 when Rebecca Blankenship was appointed administratrix with G. W. Blankenship and J. S. Lane as security. (Dyr TN, Co Ct Min, B/87) Mrs. R. A. Blankenship made a settlement as administratrix of James H. Blankenship. (Ibid 141)

BLANKINGSHIP, C.
Taxes were not collected in District 4 for 1873, "over age." (Dyr TN, Co Ct Min, B/759)

BLANTON, William
Died before 15 August 1838 when the heirs petitioned for sale of land. The widow was Sarah Blanton and the other heirs were Wilkis Blanton, Willis Blanton, Charles Blanton, Smith Blanton, all citizens of Bedford County; Horace Blanton, Burwell Blanton and Sanford Blanton, citizens of AL; Elizabeth P. Blanton, Henderson G. Blanton, Jasper N. Blanton, minors, who petition by their guardian & mother, Sarah Blanton; daughter, Susan, wife of Leithton Cevel and daughter, Mary, wife of James Nichol, which the two latter have relinquished their rights. The last minor was also shown as Joseph N. Blanton. (Bed TN, Ch Ct Min, 1/192) The heirs were shown as Wilkins Blanton, Willis Blanton, Charles Blanton, Smith Blanton, Horace Blanton, Elizabeth P. Blanton, Henson G. Blanton, Jasper N. Blanton, Susan wife of Leighton Ewell and Mary wife of James Nichol, and Sarah Blanton, the widow. (Ibid 2/105)

BLEDSO, Anthony H.
Died before December term 1803 when the heirs were on the tax list. (Wil TN, Co Ct Min, no#/7) Anthony Bledsoe's heirs were listed on the non-resident tax list with land on Bledsoe's Pond. (Ibid 81)

BLEDSOE
A suit was entered 5 December 1867 by John Smith Admr. vs Sarah Bledsoe & others. There was an answer by the guardian ad litem. Land is to be sold to pay the debts of the estate. [does not say who's estate this is] (Fen TN, Ch Ct Min, A/352)

BLEDSOE, B. F.
Was apparently a resident of White County, TN, on 4 December 1868 when B. O. Bowden, Clerk & Master, had to send to White County for records that B. F. Bledsoe had taken with him when he left Fentress County. B. F. Bledsoe was the former Clerk & Master. (Fen TN, Ch Ct Min, A/423)

BLEDSOE, Marion B.
Died before 10 April 1860 when his death was suggested in the suit of R. T. Heldrith & M. B. Bledsoe vs Wm. C. Wood & E. B. Bledsoe & others. E. B. Bledsoe was appointed administrator. (Fen TN, Ch Ct Min, A/235) On 30 March 1868 John Smith, administrator of M. B. Bledsoe, deceased, brought suit against Sarah Bledsoe & others. The minor heirs were mentioned. Land was sold to pay debts. (Ibid 361)

BLOODWORTH, Jesse
Was bound as an apprentice to John Rhea on 27 March 1805, to learn the blacksmith trade. (Wil TN, Co Ct Min, no#/119)

BOAZ, James S.
Died before 4 March 1872 when Thomas E. Boaz was appointed administrator, with J. F. Child as security. H. R. A. McCorkle, Jo. Pope and Budd Brown were appointed to lay off a years allowance for the widow and family. (Dyr TN, Co Ct Min, B/380)

BOAZ, Josiah
Died before 1 September 1860 as shown in the bill & crossbill of Samuel P. Bell & others vs James M. Copeland et als, and vice versa. A negro was sold in 1854 by Mrs. Copeland then Mrs. Boaz. The four minors mentioned in the cross bill were Mary, James,

Thomas & William Boaz who are now in the family of James M. Copeland. Evidently Samuel P. Bell was the administrator. (Mad TN, Ch Ct Min, 2/414)

BOBBITT, Arthur
Died before 16 February 1857 as shown in the suit of Mary Jane Beard by her next friend Geo. W. Lowrance vs Jno. R. Bobbitt et als. Mary Jane is the wife of Wm. W. Beard and she is an heir of Arthur Bobbitt, deceased. Jno. R. Bobbitt was appointed administrator. Arthur Bobbitt was the grand father of Mary Jane Beard. A trustee is to be appointed for the sole & separate use of Mary Jane Beard & children and to be free from the control of her husband. Geo. W. Lourance was appointed trustee. (Mad TN, Ch Ct Min, 2/108)

BODINE, Wesly
Died before 4 April 1859 when the will was proved by H. S. Blair, one of the witnesses. The other witness, Samuel Blair, is not now present. (Sev TN, Co Ct Min, no#/424) 4 October 1859 Mary Clinton, formerly Mary Bodine, widow of Wesly Bodine, deceased, dissented from the will. (Ibid 482)

BOGLE, Jannett
Was the mother of a bastard child by Jno. Leech. He gave bond for its support 18 June 1817. (Wil TN, Co Ct Min, no#/124)

BOGLE, Joseph
Died before 16 September 1816 when the administrators, Thomas Licopk [?] & John Witherspoon, made a settlement. (Wil TN, Co Ct Min, no#/28) John Wetherspoon was appointed guardian of the minor heirs, William R. Bogle & Joseph Bogle. (Ibid 29)

BOGLE, Samuel
Died before 23 December 1806 when the will was proved by Ezekiel Alexander & Christopher Cooper. (Wil TN, Co Ct Min, no#/269)

BOHANNON, James
Died before 1 April 1867 when the will was proved. On the same date a years support was to be laid off to Sophia Bohannon [does not state widow of James] (Sev TN, Co Ct Min, no#/439)

BOLES, John
Died before 7 July 1856 when Samuel Pickens resigned as guardian to Samun Boles, William Harrison Boles and Elizabeth Jane Boles, minor heirs. He had been appointed guardian at the April term 1855. (Sev TN, Co Ct Min, no#/52)

BOND, B. F.
Died before 23 February 1860 when his death was proved in the suit of Wm. Stone & wife vs Jno. C. Birdsong et als. The suit was revived against the administrator, A. J. Williams. His death was also mentioned in the suit of Geo. W. Birdsong et als vs Jno. C. Birdsong et als. (Mad TN, Ch Ct Min, 2/316)

BOND, Geo. H.
Died before 16 February 1857 when his death was admitted in the suit of Robt. T. Chester, guardian of R. C. G. Bond vs Geo. H. Bond. (Mad TN, Ch Ct Min, 2/107) Another suit 20 February 1858, Robt C. G. Bond vs Richd. T. McKnight Exr. &c, shows the deceased to be Geo. W. Bond & his executor to be Richd. T. McKnight. A Geo. H. Bond also appeared in this suit. (Ibid 206) Geo. W. Bond was the ancestor of Robt. C. G. Bond. Evidently Geo. H. Bond was also deceased. (Ibid 219) George H. Bond died in 1856 leaving a will & Richard T. McKnight was executor. Prior to his death he had assigned a note to Francis A. Bond. (Ibid 263)

BOND, Georgie
Was an orphan boy 28 May 1782 when he was bound to John Clark, blacksmith, until the age of 21. He is now 13 years old. [on the same date John Clark was appointed guardian of Georgia Bond, an orphan boy] (Was TN, Co Ct Min, 1/160)

BOND, Henry
Was an orphan boy when he was bound to Nathl. Morrison 5 March 1827, until the age of 21. (McM TN, Co Ct Min, 2no#/200)

BOND, John
26 May 1779 was ordered to take care of Geo. & Mary Bond until there may be a proper opportunity to have said orphans properly bound to him as prescribed by law. (Was TN, Co Ct Min, 1/76)

BOND, John
Died before 29 May 1781 when Millisa Bond was granted leave to administrate on the estate of her husband. Jesse Walton, Esquire & Capt. Saml. Williams were her security. (Was TN, Co Ct Min, 1/133) Capt. Saml. Williams was appointed guardian of the orphans. (Ibid 150)

BOND, John
Died before 18 June 1816 when the will was proved by John Bond, William Palmer & Elisha Bond [all could be Baird]. Solomon Bond was executor with Thomas Beunch and John Bond, Jr. as security. (Wil TN, Co Ct Min, no#/13)

BOND, Lewis
Died before 17 March 1854 when his death was suggested and admitted in the suit of Joseph Mosely & wife vs Lewis Bond. (Mad TN, Ch Ct Min, 1/357) He made his will on 18 October1849 & afterwards departed this life. This was shown in the suit of Damon Bond et als vs William Jones et als. Slaves are to be sold for distribution to the heirs. (Ibid 2/37) All interest in some of the slaves are divested out of Dawson Bond, Eaten Bond, Lewis Bond, William Jones & Ann Jones, Lewis Jones & Helen Jones, James Turner & Susan Turner, Mary Jeffries, Mary Chapman, Perlena Newburn & Mary Walker and vested in Hance Bond. Hance Bond also had an interest in slaves purchased by Lewis Bond. (Ibid 119)

BOND, Lewis
Died before 24 August 1866 as shown in the suit of Martha E. Bond as executrix of Lewis Bond & in her own right, Lewis Bond, Jr., George Sykes & wife Martha, J. J. Hawkins & wife Eliza vs Sallie Bond, Lelia Bond, Thomas Bond, John Bond & James Bond, infants who defend by their guardian ad litem, W. L. Bond. Lewis Bond died on 18 March 1863 leaving a will which was proved in August 1865. Martha E. is the widow & a devisee under the will. The other complainants & defendants are legatees & only heirs. He left a large estate which has not been divided. In consequences of the ravages of the war, property has been taken off by violent & armed men & lost to the estate & stock & farming implements had to be bought to supply their place. The slaves have been declared free & lost to the estate. With a view to the safe keeping of the funds of the estate from robbery, such funds had to be secreted & in consequence thereof, a portion has been lost or stolen. What is left is to be divided. Land was laid off to Lewis Bond, Jr., part to the widow, the rest to the other legatees, 1/7 to each of them. Thomas Bond is to have the blacksmith tools when he comes of age. [8 children] (Mad TN, Ch Ct Min, 2/540) Division of the estate was made to Mrs. Martha E. Bond, Lewis Bond, Martha Sykes, Eliza Hawkins, Sallie Bond, Lelia Bond, Tho. Bond, Jno. Bond & Jas. Bond. (Ibid 3/21-25)

BOND, Peter
Died before 8 December 1829 when his will was proved by William H. Barnett, one of the witnesses. (McM TN, Co Ct Min, 2no#/408) John W. Barnett also proved the will. Benjamin Bond & Amon Bond were executors. (Ibid 411)

BOND, Robert C. G.
Was a minor 15 September 1855 as shown in the suit by his guardian, Robert J. Chester vs George H. Bond. (Mad TN, Ch Ct Min, 2/90)

BOND, T. B.
8 August 1871 a tract of land was divided into 4 lots, #1 to Hellen D. Johnson, #2 to J. A. Wisinger and his wife M. E. Weisinger, #3 to T. B. Bond and #4 to Joseph W. Sharber and wife Mary Jane Sharber. (Dyr TN, Co Ct Min, B/265-7)

BOND, Thomas
Died before 18 March 1817 when John Bond was appointed administrator, with James Bond as security. (Wil TN, Co Ct Min, no#/87)

BOND, William
Died before 18 June 1816 when the will was proved by Elisha Bond & John Martin. James Bond qualified as executor. (Wil TN, Co Ct Min, no#/12)

BONNER, John
21 November 1822 made a deed of gift to his daughter, Mary Wright of Limestone County, AL, a negro girl named Dilcey. (Wil TN, Reg Bk/307)

BOO, R. A.
2 July 1872 was released from paying poll tax and working on public roads. (Dyr TN, Co Ct Min, B/440)

BOON, Nathan
Died before 8 November 1814 when Nathan Skinner was appointed administrator with James H. Russell & William Campbell as security. (Ste TN, Co Ct Min, 4/202)

BOON, W. H.
Died before 6 February 1871 when B. F. Prichard renewed his bond as guardian of the minor heirs, with N. P. Tatum as security. (Dyr TN, Co Ct Min, B/187) 3 July 1872 B. F. Prichard made a settlement as guardian of Wm. A. Boone and Jeanetta Boone, minor heirs. (Ibid 442 & 737)

BOONE, E. D.
Died before 4 May 1874 when H. R. A. McCorkle was appointed administrator, with Smith Parks and D. M. Boone as his security. (Dyr TN, Co Ct Min, B/735)

BOONE, Henry
Died before 4 December 1871 when C. L. Nolan, public administrator, was appointed administrator. Geo. B. Miller, F. G. Sampson and C. J. Coker were appointed to lay off a years provision for Mrs. F. E. Boone, widow. (Dyr TN, Co Ct Min, B/323) The years provision was laid off for Mrs. Francis Brown, widow of Henry Boone. On the same page she is shown as Mrs. Francis E. Boone. (Ibid 359) 9 October 1872, application for dower was made by Frankie E. Boon vs William A. Boon, Susan J. Boon, William F. Hancock, Maggie J. Hancock, Hays W. Vaughan, Sarah F. Vaughan, and C. L. Nolan as administrator of Henry Boon, deceased. (Ibid 498)

BOONE, James H.
Was trustee for Martha Boone & children as shown in the petition of James Boone Trustee & Wm. O. Butler et als, 20 February 1857. (Mad TN, Ch Ct Min, 2/132) Petition shows Jas. H. Boone Trustee of Martha Boone, Ben F. Boone, Wm. O. Butler & Jno. L. H. Tomlin. (Ibid 145) 25 February 1861, "Ben F. Boon, husband of Martha Boon, has no means of supporting himself & family but by his own labor & his occupation is being a mechanic...he should move to Memphis where there is more demand for labor & higher wages..." The land held in trust was sold & is to be used to purchase a house in Memphis. The children were James W. Boon, Laura A. Boon, Luella Boon & Mary Boon. (Ibid 460) James H. Boon died before 21 February 1866 when his death was proved in the suit of James H. Boon et als vs J. M. Boon et als. (Ibid 474)

BOONE, Jessee
Died before 8 December 1829 when his will was proved by Asbury M. Coffey & Jonathan Allin, witnesses. (McM TN, Co Ct Min, 2no#/409) John Thompson also proved the will. Asbury M. Coffey & Israel Boone were executors. (Ibid 412)

BOREN, James
Died before 15 August 1796 when Chana [?] Bowen qualified as executor. (Was TN, Co Ct Min, 1/623) The will was proved by Horatio Foard. (Ibid 629)

BORING, Absolom
February term 1790 was ordered to give bond for the maintenance of a base born child born of Jean Oddel. Mordicae Price was his security. (Was TN, Co Ct Min, 1/433)

BORING, John Dasey
Was the reputed father of a base born child by Mary Cooper and was ordered to pay maintenance 11 May 1790. (Was TN, Co Ct Min, 1/440)

BOUNDS, Jesse
3 August 1784 made oath that his son, James Bounds, was not 21 years old when poll tax was levied against him for 1783. (Was TN, Co Ct Min, 1/243)

BOWEN, Henry
25 March 1811 gave a deposition regarding an entry of land made by Richard Henderson, George Dougherty, Thomas Henderson & Robert Burton. Henry Bowen answered questions about what he remembered when he was on an expedition against the "Chikamagee Indians" under the command of Col. Evan Shelby & Col. Chas. Robertson. Other names mentioned were George Bean, & Howell Doddy. Henry Bowen stated that he was about 43 years of age. It has been about 27 years since the campaign. (Roa TN, Co Ct Min, D/293)

BOWEN, J. B.
Died before 2 September 1872 when W. P. Rice made a final settlement as administrator. (Dyr TN, Co Ct Min, B/467)

BOWEN, John
Died before 3 December 1872 when W. H. Clarke was chosen and appointed guardian of S. C. Clarke, R. D. Bowen, J. L. Bowen, J. H. Bowen, Ebenezer Bowen and Lily Dora Bowen, minor heirs. (Dyr TN, Co Ct Min, B/518)

BOWEN, William
Died before 26 September 1806 when the heirs were on a tax list with land on Fall Creek. (Wil TN, Co Ct Min, no#/264)

BOWERS, Giles
Died before 2 November 1818 when Hezekiah Woodward & Elizabeth Bowers were appointed administrators with Jacob Caplinger & Jacob Dice as security. (Wil TN, Co Ct Min, no#/332) Elizabeth was the widow. (Ibid 336)

BOWERS, John
Died in the summer of 1836 as shown in the suit of Wm. McGrew vs Benjamin Bowers of Bedford County & William Bowers of AL. John Bowers had made a will leaving negroes to all his children, being 9 or 10 in number. Benjamin & William Bowers were executors. Wm. McGrew had purchased the interest of Green Bowers in said negroes & the executors refused to pay said legacy to him. He filed suit 3 December 1838. In the answer it was stated that John Bowers had 11 children, to wit, William, Benjamin, Jesse, John, Solomon, David, Green, Henry, Lemuel, Giles Bowers & Mary R. Hedrick. Mary Bowers, widow of John, is entitled to dower. The will was shown. His son-in-law was Wesley W. Hedricks. The will was dated 15 June 1836. (Bed TN, Ch Ct Min, 1/209) Another suit shows that William Bowers was in Blount County, AL, and Henry Bowers was in Arkansas County, AR. (Ibid 236) Jesse Bowers also lives in Blount County, AL. The widow, Mary Bowers, has now [by April 1840] died. (Ibid 286) Another suit was filed 21 January 1841 by Lemuel Bowers, a citizen of AL vs Benjamin F. Bowers of Bedford County, TN, & William Bowers of TX. Lemuel Bowers wants a settlement of his fathers estate. (Ibid 377) The widow was shown as Nancy Bowers. (Ibid 2/75)

BOWLIN, Smith
Was a resident of Rutherford County, TN, when he brought suit against William & Nehemiah Sugg, probably in 1844. (Bed TN, Ch Ct Min, 3/153)

BOWLING, Sidney
Died before 6 December 1830 when a years provision was ordered to be laid off for his widow, Denatha Bowling. (McM TN, Co Ct Min, 2no#/480) William Logan was appointed administrator. (Ibid 483)

BOYCE, Isham
Died before 24 February 1837 when land was taxed to the heirs. (Obi TN, Cir Ct Min, 3/115)

BOYD, George
Made bond 2 February 1813 to support or maintain a bastard child sworn to him by Mariah Williams. Martin Wells & Emanuel James were security. (Ste TN, Co Ct Min, 4/5) 3 November 1813 Mary Ann Williams was allowed $8 for the maintenence of a bastard child which she swore to George Boyd, Jr. until said child arrives at the age of one year. (Ibid 79)

BOYD, James M.
Died before 21 August 1866 when A. S. Savireyley? was appointed guardian ad litem for Jas. W. Boyd, Jno. Boyd, Hampton Boyd, Walter P. Boyd, Isabella Boyd & Coralin Boyd, minor defendants in the suit of Robt. J. Chester. (Mad TN, Ch Ct Min, 2/498) In the suit of Wm. E. Butler vs W. L. Sparkman & others, James M. Boyd was one of the defendants. The suit was revived in the names of his children & heirs, Jas. W. Boyd, Jr., Walter P. Boyd, Caroline A. Boyd, John M. Boyd, George H. Boyd & Isabella Boyd & Jno. L. Brown was appointed guardian ad litem for them. (Ibid 538) This suit was shown again and Jane Boyd was shown in the place of Caroline Boyd. James W. Boyd was the father of said defendants. (Ibid 3/43) Walter P. Boyd was shown as William P. Boyd. (Ibid 3/106)

BOYD, John
Died before 12 July 1850 as shown in the suit of James Boyd vs William R. Vance et al. It was stated that James Boyd is one of the heirs of John Boyd, deceased. Money was due him from the estate of the deceased on 1 October 1838. William R. Vance was the administrator & has refused to pay to James Boyd his distributive share. (Jac TN, Ch Ct Min, A/365)

BOYD, Lewis A.
Died before 27 December 1843 when his death was admitted in the suit of Lewis A. Boyd vs Joshua Hall. The suit will be revived in the name of the administrator, Richard H. Sims. (Bed TN, Ch Ct Min, 2/270) In the suit of Rosal Rollon vs Samuel & Newcom Thompson, money is to be paid to Richard H. Sims, administrator of Lewis A. Boyd assignee of Rosal Rollon. Joseph Thompson was appointed to sell negroes & pay the debt to Richard Sims & the balance to Samuel & Newcom Thompson. In the other suit against Joshua Hall it was stated that William Bullock was a resident of AL. (Ibid 303)

BOYD, M. B.
Died before 18 February 1857 when his death was suggested in the suit of M. B. Boyd vs Saml. Cromwel et als. (Mad TN, Ch Ct Min, 2/118) James A. Boyd was administrator of M. A? Boyd, deceased. (Ibid 182)

BOYD, Margaret
Died before 18 February 1858 as shown in the petition of Ro. Fenner, surviving executor and others, and F. N. W. Burton vs T. P. Jones administrator and others, tried together by consent of parties. The heirs of Margaret Boyd were Matilda F. Gibbs, Kate C. Vaulx, Mary E. Robertson & James Vaulx, Jr. This petition concerns the estate of Dr. Richard Fenner. (Mad TN, Ch Ct Min, 2/182)

BOYD, R. & J.
Died before 11 March 1844 when land was taxed to the heirs. (Obi TN, Cir Ct Min, 4/no#)

BOYER, John [Boyce]
Died before 1 August 1814 when David Collins, attorney in fact for the heirs of John Boyer, entered a plat & certificate of survey. (Ste TN, Co Ct Min, 4/168)

BOYKIN, W. A
Died before 22 August 1866 as shown in the petition of Thos. Blakemore et als. It was stated that the property bequeathed to said Martha in the will of W. A. Boykin ought to be settled to her. A trustee is to be appointed. (Mad TN, Ch Ct Min, 2/511) John W. Mathews was appointed trustee. Martha Blakemore [Blakeman] was the daughter of W. A. Boykin and the wife of Thomas Blakemore. (Ibid 522)

BOYKIN, Wm. O
Married before 15 March 1853 to Irena Lane as shown in the suit of James A. Lane et als vs Jno. Todd et als. (Mad TN, Ch Ct Min, 1/295)

BOYT, Jesse
Was a resident of Carroll County, TN, and had sold land in 1832 to Anderson Smith, a resident of Marshall County. The land was then in Maury County which is now in Marshall County, bounded by Frances Killingsworth, Joseph Duncan & Presley L. Cox. (Bed TN, Ch Ct Min, 1/78)

BRABSON, John
Died before 4 August 1856 when the executors of the will, T. C. & B. D. Brabson, gave a new bond with M. W. McCown as security. The original bond was destroyed. (Sev TN, Co Ct Min, no#/65) A certified copy of the will was entered dated 31 July 1849. (Ibid 68)

BRACKIN, Isaac
Died before 2 December 1872 when Morean S. Brackin was appointed administrator, with G. B. Miller and A. M. Stevens, Jr. as his security. (Dyr TN, Co Ct Min, B/513) F. A. Slater, T. L. Slater and M. Taylor were appointed to lay off a years allowance for the widow and her family. (Ibid 580)

BRADDY, Hezekiah [Braudy, Bruddy]
Died before 13 February 1816 when Catherine Brandy was appointed administratrix. An inventory was returned and ordered to be sold. Support is to be laid off for the widow and family. (Cla TN, Co Ct Min, 4/154) The name was shown as Brawdy when Catherine gave new security. John M. Crary and John Brawdy were security. (Ibid 250)

BRADFORD, Alexander B.
On 13 July 1848 Bradford brought suit against Mary French, George W. Hopkins, Samuel Richardson, Mary Campbell, James H. Rhodes, Thomas J. Rhodes, James M. Vaughn, Thomas J. Vaughn, John Vaughn, William Vaughn, Elizabeth Greene, Florintha Dyer, George Vaughn, Thomas H. Bradford, Campbell Vaughn, Cora Vaughn, Ann Horsley, William Hopkins, John H. Rhodes, Greene B. Rhodes, Emily J. Knight, Charles P. Rhodes,

Benjamin F. Rhodes and Cyntha McVey. No information about the suit. (Mad TN, Ch Ct Min, 1/43)

BRADFORD, David
On 10 October 1807 was excused from serving as a juror because of his bad state of health. (Ste TN, Co Ct Min, 1/49)

BRADFORD, David A., Jr.
Died before 1 December 1873 when William Jordan was appointed administrator, with Stephen J. Jordan and Thomas M. Andrews as his security. (Dyr TN, Co Ct Min, B/669)

BRADFORD, John
Died before 6 March 1837 when a slave was sold by James S. Armstrong, guardian of Amanda M. Bradford, minor heir of John Bradford, deceased. (Bed TN, Ch Ct Min, 2/14)

BRADFORD, Napolion B.
5 June 1826 he was certified to be 21 years of age & good moral character. He is an applicant for a law license. (McM TN, Co Ct Min, 2no#/154)

BRADFORD, Theodrick F.
Died between 31 January 1841 and 17 December 1841 as shown in the suit of Clemant Cannon vs John Tillman & others. (Bed TN, Ch Ct Min, 1/400) 25 December 1843 John P. Steele was appointed guardian ad litem for the minor heirs. (Ibid 2/261) In the suit of George Davidson vs Thomas C. Whiteside & others, 27 August 1845, it was stated that defendant Barkly M. Bradford was entitled to money from a trust deed made by Theoderick F. Bradford. (Ibid 368)

BRADLEY, Charles
Was a resident of Smith County, TN, 16 August 1815 when he sold to Daniel Cherry of Wilson County, TN, a negro girl named Phillis aged 13. (Wil TN, Reg Bk/39)

BRADLEY, John
On 2 December 1817 made an agreement with Hugh Bradley whereby John gives to Hugh 2 negroes, Dan & Bird, and Hugh agrees to relinquish 150 acres of land whereon he now lives and not make any claim to the land as a legatee of the said John Bradley after his death. John Bradley and his wife Martha are to have the use of the negro, Bird, so long as they live. (Wil TN, Reg Bk/97)

BRADLEY, John
Died before 18 June 1816 when the executors, Samuel Hogg, John Allcorn, & Thomas Bradley, were allowed to sell a slave to pay the debts. (Wil TN, Co Ct Min, no#/12)

BRADLY, John
Died before 19 September 1816 when William Woodward was appointed guardian for Peggy Bradly, Polly & Patsy Bradly, minor heirs of John Bradly, deceased, during the pleasure of this court and no longer. (Wil TN, Co Ct Min, no#/45)

BRADLY, John
Died before 5 August 1818 when Alexander Baird was appointed administrator, with Thomas Bradly & Edmund Crutcher as security. (Wil TN, Co Ct Min, no#/312) Thomas Bradly, one of the heirs, petitoned for division of land. (Ibid 542)

BRADSHAW
7 March 1871 in the case of J. E. Bradshaw et als vs Thos. E. Bradshaw et als, the clerk of the court reported that he had $426.00 belonging to the Bradshaw estate. (Dyr TN, Co Ct Min, B/207) 3 November 1873 a suit with the same principals as shown above lists a sale of land. It mentions a suit in Chancery Court, and a sum of $1,183.62 to be divided equally between Elizabeth S. Lack, J. E. Bradshaw, J. T. Bradshaw, Amanda & D. W. Gaulden, M. F. & Sam Walker, Sam B. Bradshaw, Clarinda A. & J. H. Hall, Thomas E. Bradshaw, Alma C. & Frank Richmond, Zenia F. Richmond, Robert and Jessee Bradshaw Smith (one share together), and one share divided between W. R. Powell, James F. Powell, C. L. F. Powell, Seymore Powell, Elizabeth Powell, minor heirs of Roberta Powell, deceased wife of R. P. Powell. There were 12 shares. (Ibid 661)

BRADSHAW, Edward
Probably died before 11 November 1844 as shown in the suit of Edward Bradshaw's heirs vs A. W. O. Totten & Benjamin C. Totten. (Obi TN, Cir Ct Min, 4/no#)

BRADSHAW, Jessee
Died before 4 May 1874 when W. T. Powell was chosen and appointed guardian of Robt. and Lena Bradshaw, minor heirs, with N. P. Tatum and R. P. Powell as his security. (Dyr TN, Co Ct Min, B/736)

BRADSHAW, Wilson
11 May 1825 made a deed of gift to Thomas Bradshaw for 5 slaves & other property. (Wil TN, Reg Bk/346) [second set of page numbers]

BRAINARD, G. W.
Was a non-resident of TN 16 March 1855 as shown in the suit of Brown & Allen vs G. W. Brainard et als. The Brainards are residents of KY. Joseph Brainard was mentioned. (Mad TN, Ch Ct Min, 2/47)

BRANCH, Joseph
Was a resident of Halifax County, NC, 12 November 1812 when his deposition was to be taken for the defendant in the case of Benjamin McCullough vs William Harwell. (Rob TN, Co Ct Min, 3/164)

BRANDON, John
Died before 7 June 1830 when his will was proved by Isaac Lane & Peter Reagan, witnesses. Philip Fry was executor. (McM TN, Co Ct Min, 2no#/449)

BRANDON, John
Died before November term 1789 when Rebekah Brandon was granted letters of administration on the estate, with William Bell as security. (Was TN, Co Ct Min, 1/411)

BRANOM, Martha Jane
4 January 1859 was bound as an apprentice to Wm. A. Baxter until age 18. She is an orphan child aged 10 years. (Sev TN, Co Ct Min, no#/380) 3 September 1866 Beverage Brannum was appointed receiver for Martha Jane Brannum to receive from Wm. A. Baxter the amount specified in his bond for the services of Martha Jane, who was bound in January 1859. (Ibid 369)

BRANTLEY
Died before 2 August 1813 as shown in the suit of Brantley's Extrs. vs Wm. Lyndsey. (Ste TN, Co Ct Min, 4/52)

BRASFIELD, George
Died before 12 November 1828 as shown in the suit of Daniel Cook, heir at law of John Cook deceased vs The heirs at Law of George Brasfield deceased. David Brasfield, Asa Brasfield, Anny Goss, Robert Flemming and Martha his wife, Edney Brasfield, Leonard Brasfield and Calvin Brasfield, who are defendants in this bill, are citizens of NC. (Obi TN, Cir Ct Min, 1/67) This suit was settled by agreement between the parties, 12 May 1830. The heirs of George Brassfield were shown as above except for Robert Fleming & wife Matilda, Cetney Brasfield instead of Edney, and the addition of Willie Brassfield, William Burton and wife Catherine and Alfred Brassfield. (Ibid 118)

BRASHEAR, Benjamin F.
Died before 7 February 1872 when C. L. Nolan was appointed administrator. (Dyr TN, Co Ct Min, B/376) O. J. P. Carter returned a report of the years allowance set off to the widow and family. (Ibid 378)

BRASHEARS, Robert S.
17 June 1805 was released from paying one white poll tax. [This usually meant he was over age or disabled.] (Roa TN, Co Ct Min, A/341)

BRAZIER, Thomas
Was an orphan white boy aged 13 years when he was bound 8 January 1874 to Elias Parrish until age 21. (Dyr TN, Co Ct Min, B/701) On the same date J. D Bradley made a petition to adopt Thomas J. Brazier who was in court and agreed to be his son. The court rejected the petition. Bradley was granted an appeal to Circuit Court. (Ibid 704)

BREDEN, John
Died before 7 November 1859 when his will was proved by Lewis Briden & Bryant Breden as witnesses. (Sev TN, Co Ct Min, no#/486)

BREEDEN, Amerel
3 January 1859 was allowed money from the poor tax for the support of his helpless children. (Sev TN, Co Ct Min, no#/374)

BREEDEN, Calvin
6 August 1860 a suit against him was dismissed on the grounds that the child sued for was not likely to become a county charge. The prosecutrix [not named] is to pay the costs. (Sev TN, Co Ct Min, no#/589)

BREEDEN, Calvin
Died before 3 July 1865 when D. B. McMahan, John Keeler & James Baker were appointed to lay off a years support to the widow, E. Breeden. (Sev TN, Co Ct Min, no#/174) The widow was Elizabeth Breeden. (Ibid 198)

BREEDEN, John
Died before 1 September 1856 when Elizabeth Breeden was appointed guardian to Harriet Breeden, Andrew Breeden, Nancy Breeden & Aaron Breeden, minor heirs. John McMahan & W. W. Casy were her securities. (Sev TN, Co Ct Min, no#/69) His children were ordered to be brought to court to be bound out 3 February 1862. (Ibid 748) Andrew Breeden was bound to Adam Bird. Harriett Breeden was bound to Nancy Breeden. John A. Breeden was bound to Anderson Thomas. Nancy Breeden was bound to John H. Frame. [The above indentures did not state children of John Breeden, deceased, but they probably were.] (Ibid 753) Elizabeth Breeden objected to the binding out of her children. (Ibid 777) 2 September 1867, John Spurgen was appointed guardian to the minor heirs of John Breeden, deceased. (Ibid no#/474)

BREEDEN, Josiah M.
5 April 1858 was released from paying poll tax for 1857, he being "a poor and decrepit person." (Sev TN, Co Ct Min, no#/281)

BREEDEN, Merrel
3 October 1859 was allowed money for keeping his four children. (Sev TN, Co Ct Min, no#/476)

BREEDEN, Nancy Jane
Was bound 6 September 1858 to Wm. Breeden until age 18. She is a girl child 11 years old. (Sev TN, Co Ct Min, no#/334)

BREEDEN, William
Died before 2 March 1863 when his will was proved by Wilson Duggan and David Hurst, witnesses. Josiah Breeden was executor with David Hurst & George Hurst as security. (Sev TN, Co Ct Min, no#/47)

BRENT, Wm.
20 April 1812 was said to have removed out of this state to some place unknown when he was to prove a deed from Robert King to John Smith. (Roa TN, Co Ct Min, D/369)

BREWER, B. A.
Taxes were not collected in District 4 for 1873, "over age." (Dyr TN, Co Ct Min, B/759)

BREWER, John J.
16 January 1850 made petition as guardian for Julia & Fanny Rodgers, Alice & Tennessee Kirksey, to sell or exchange a negro boy. (Mad TN, Ch Ct Min, 1/101)

BREWER, Sherod
7 August 1871 Amos Reed resigned as guardian of the minor heirs. (Dyr TN, Co Ct Min, B/260)

BREWTON, John
13 August 1838 his residence was unknown when he was to appear for the suit of Amelia Brewton against him. (Bed TN, Ch Ct Min, 2/86) In the suit of James M. Jones & wife vs John Brewton and others it was stated that James M. Jones had purchased the interest in the land mentioned & that complainants & defendants were owners in common. It is to be determinied if Amelia Brewton conveyed the land voluntarily & without constraint of her husband & whether the wife of James M. Jones fully consents to the sale of the land. (Ibid 110) 29 December 1840 Amelia Brewton dismissed her suit against John Brewton. (Ibid 119) On another page it was shown to be a bill for divorce. (Ibid 122)

BRICKEY, Polly
21 April 1800 was allowed $20 from the county tax for her support. (Rob TN, Co Ct Min, 1/130)

BRIDGEWATERS, John
Died before 13 July 1859 as shown in the suit of Stephen Alley vs John H. Jarritt? [Jouitt?], L. M. Grace & B. B. Washburn. A compromise was reached. Complainant agreed that the title he had in the estate of John Bridgewaters, deceased, would be divested out of him and in the defendants. (Jac TN, Ch Ct Min, C/233)

BRIGGANCE, Alfred
Died before 20 July 1853 when his death was suggested and not denied in the suit of David W. Thompson vs W. & Alfred Briggance. He left his widow, Vicy Briggance, & one daughter, an only child named C. V. Briggance. (Mad TN, Ch Ct Min, 2/16)

BRININGHAM, L. W.
Died before 3 July 1872 when Thomas E. Boaz was appointed administrator de bonis non, with J. F. Child as security. (Dyr TN, Co Ct Min, B/443)

BRINKLEY, E. W.
Died before 4 July 1870 when J. F. Williamson was paid for making the coffin. (Dyr TN, Co Ct Min, B/73)

BRINKLEY, Samuel
Died before 17 June 1816 when Cealy Brinkly was appointed administratrix with William Johnson as security. (Wil TN, Co Ct Min, no#/3)

BRINSON, Gause
Died before 10 June 1805 when Mary Brinson & Duncan Stewart were appointed administrators. (Ste TN, Co Ct Min, 1/12) Gause Brison, Jr. petitioned for his share of the real estate of Gause Brison, deceased. (Ibid 42) 25 July 1808 Gause Brison was appointed guardian of Drury Brison, an orphan of the age of 16 years. Martin Wells was security. [This is shown in the second volume on the microfilm which has no number but is page No. 74] There is an estate settlement shown in above volume. It shows payments to Mrs. Brinson, Gause Brinson, Benjamin Brinson, Drury Brinson, Arrisa Brinson, there being five legatees. (Ibid no#/77) Peter & Mary Buchanan were appointed guardians of Arisa Brinson, an orphan girl. (Ibid 83) On 24 April 1809 James Tagart was appointed guardian of Drury Brison, with Tapley Maddox & John McCarthy security. (Ibid 110)

BRINSON, Jesse
Died before 19 March 1817 when William Moss was appointed administrator, with Brittain Drake & William Steel as security. (Wil TN, Co Ct Min, no#/99)

BRISTONE, Benjamin [Bristow]
Died before 4 April 1808 when William Adams was appointed administrator with Harbet Howell & John B. Cheatam as security. (Rob TN, Co Ct Min, 2/12) The name was shown as Benjamin Brister. (Ibid 3/67)

BRISTOW, John
Died before 25 August 1807 when Darkus [Darcus] Bristow was appointed administratrix with John Owens as security. (Cla TN, Co Ct Min, 3/113)

BRITAIN, James
Died before November 1835 as shown when the administrator, William F. Long of Taledego County, AL, was mentioned in the suit of Clemant Cannon vs John Tillman & others. (Bed TN, Ch Ct Min, 1/406)

BRITTAIN, James
Had entered into a partnership with Martin C. Daniel, which was dissolved about 1 December 1831. "Martin C. Daniel is about to leave the state, has actually left his farm & residence, and will depart from Shelbyville early tomorrow morning, to go to Mississippi." Walter W. Daniel was mentioned. Brittain wants a full settlement before Martin C. Daniel leaves the state. The suit was filed 6 February 1833. The answer of Daniel was given 22 February 1834. 27 January 1837 this suit proceeded with William T. Long, executor of James Brittain, deceased vs Martin C. Daniel. (Bed TN, Ch Ct Min, 1/44) On 23 November 1839, Jason T. Brittain, a minor and only heir of James Brittain, deceased, sued by his guardian, James Wortham, against Theodrick F. Bradford, William Galbreath, John Tillman and Wilkins Blanton of Bedford County, TN, and William F. Long of Tallaselaga? County AL. James Brittian died in June or July 1833, having made a will, &

William F. Long was executor. Joseph H. Britian was former guardian. Jason T. Brittain is claiming his estate was squandered. (Ibid 307)

BRITTAIN, Joseph, Lieut.
11 May 1790 gave a power of attorney to the Honlb. John Sevier for the Pay for his Services in the Late Army of the United States. (Was TN, Co Ct Min, 1/442)

BRITTAIN, Wm.
Died before 25 February 1794 when Joseph Brittain & Hannah Brittain were appointed administrators of the estate. (Was TN, Co Ct Min, 1/470)

BRITTON, Abram
Died before 7 May 1818 when the will was proved by John Allcorn, James C. Carr & William Anderson. Edmund Crutcher was executor. (Wil TN, Co Ct Min, no#/273)

BRITTON, Mary E.
16 January 1851 sued for divorce from Adolphus Britton. They were married in 1848 in Madison County. She has been living apart from her husband and has one child. She was granted support but the divorce delayed until next term in hopes a reconciliation can be made. (Mad TN, Ch Ct Min, 1/196) 15 July 1851 divorce was granted, with alimony and custody of the child. Adolphus Britton made 2 notes payable to Henry Ba___? for his wife's alimony. [The information about the notes is written across the rest of the minutes and is hard to read.] (Ibid 205)

BROGAN, John
With his wife Betsey of Wilson County, TN, having moved to the above named state, gave power of attorney to Woodson Webb of same, "to recover from the estate of Joseph Owen, deceased, & Phebe Owen his wife of Halafax County, VA, all money, debts, negroes, land and demands whatsoever, due us from said Owens estate." Made August 1820. (Wil TN, Reg Bk/173)

BROILES, Adam
Died before 28 May 1782 when Michael Woods, Alexander More and Samuel Shervill were appointed to appraise the estate. (Was TN, Co Ct Min, 1/161) The will was proved by Jno. Waddell, Coonrod Willhite & Mathais Broils. (Ibid 165) 8 May 1783 Moses Broiles took oath as the executor. (Ibid 215) 10 August 1790 William Moore, one of the executors, was ordered to settle. (Ibid 458)

BROOKS, D. R.
Died before 6 February 1865, [this entry not clear]. "This day the Court appointed Wm. P. Brooks, Guardian ad litem to the minor heirs of David J. McMamahan, & D. R. Brooks deceased." (Sev TN, Co Ct Min, no#/135)

BROOKS, George
Died before 9 May 1815 when Mary Brooks was appointed administratrix with Jos. Clark and Ransom Day as security. A years support is to be set off for Mary Brooks. (Cla TN, Co Ct Min, 4/43) Support was set off for Mary Brooks & family; "10 barrels of corn and 100 of Bacon and two year old hoggs." (Ibid 109)

BROOKS, Mary H.
On 28 January 1848 was granted a divorce from Richard P. Brooks. They were married 27 March 1828 and have 8 children, all minors. On 4 October 1846 he abandoned her and is living in adultry with Lethe Jane Bowman beyond the limits of this state. Mary is to receive all the personal property. The title to 14 slaves is to be vested in Mary Brooks for life and at her death to the children, to wit: Albert W. W. Brooks, Cyprissa C. Brooks, Angeline A. Brooks, Mary Jane Brooks, John S. Brooks, Richard V. Brooks, Ellen W. Brooks, Elviria A. Brooks and their heirs forever. The land, part of which was purchased by Richard P. Brooks of John Brooks, the interest of Richard P. Brooks in lands of John Burke, deceased, whether of possession or reversion consisting of 3 shares, the shares of James W. Burke, William C. Burke and Esom L. Burke and the reversion of the dower of the widow of John Burke. Also the John Ramsey tract is vested in the said Mary H. during her life with reversion to her children. [There is much land described including town lots] (Ibid 297-302) There were other lands owned by Richard P. Brooks and numerous persons listed who owed him money. Everything is given to Mary H. Books and her heirs. (Ibid 325)

BROOKS, Mathew
Of Davidson County, TN, made an agreement with Charles Braden of Robertson County,

TN, about the division of some land, 16 May 1807, recorded in Wilson County in 1818. (Wil TN, Reg Bk/115)

BROOKS, Matthew
Probably died before 10 February 1855 when some land was sold that was bounded by the heirs of Matthew Brooks. (Jac TN, Ch Ct Min, B/224)

BROOKS, Stephen
Died before 27 March 1806 when the heirs were on the tax list with land on Cedar Lick Ck. (Wil TN, Co Ct Min, no#/199)

BROOKS, William
Died intestate in 1850 as shown in the suit of James H. Lee, Margaret Brooks, Adeline Lee, Prior Lee, Sidney Brooks, Marshall Brooks, Jane Brooks, Hester An Brooks, Leonidas Brooks, Peter Brooks, Jackson Brooks, Daniel Brooks, Sarah Brooks, John Brooks, Pricilla Brooks and [blank] Brooks & James W. Draper vs Mary Hobby, Letha Hollowman, Elijah Hollowman, Sarah Teel, Peter Teel, Larkin Brooks, Elijah Brooks, Tilford Brooks, Tilman Brooks, Mary King, Joshua King, Martha Mercer, Jones Mercer, Francis Rogers, Clayton Rogers, Elizabeth Rogers, William An Rogers, Joseph B. Rogers & Milton Draper. The suit was filed 15 July 1853 and James H. Lee was administrator. Previous to his death William Brooks had purchased a negro named Pheba from the defendants Jones Mercer, Joseph B. Rogers & Elijah Hollowman who are heirs of Matthew Brooks, deceased, in right of their wives, the defendants, Letha Hollowman, Martha Mercer & Elizabeth Rogers, who are daughters of said Matthew Brooks. The contract for the purchase of the negro was to be rescinded when the defendant Mary Hobby, who is the widow of said Matthew Brooks, should return home to live, which event has happened. (Jac TN, Ch Ct Min, B/98)

BROOKSHIRE, Levin
With his son Elkin, was appointed to work on a road 12 November 1810. (Rob TN, Co Ct Min, 2/316)

BROWDER, Josiah
Died before 6 February 1871 when H. H. Browder renewed his bond as guardian of the minor heirs. (Dyr TN, Co Ct Min, B/187) 5 February 1872, H. H. Browder made a settlement as guardian of John Browder and David Browder. (Ibid 364)

BROWN, Abel
Died before 13 July 1850 as shown in the petition made by Martin Thorn who had married the daughter of Abel Brown, Helena A. Brown. Helena gave birth to a child and departed this life. Thomas A. Thorn is a minor [probably the child born to Helena]. (Mad TN, Ch Ct Min, 1/152)

BROWN, C. F.
8 February 1870 L. M. Williams made a settlement as guardian. (Dyr TN, Co Ct Min, B/7)

BROWN, David [Daniel]
Died before 13 November 1834 as shown in the suit of William N. Watson, administrator of David Brown, deceased vs Merriweather, Anderson and Brown. Margaret Brown was a defendant. (Obi TN, Cir Ct Min, 2/210)

BROWN, Edward
Died before 13 August 1839 as shown in the suit of Enoch D. Rushing & William Rucker administrators of Edward Brown, deceased vs Alexander B. Moore & others. Ermine [Emin] Brown, mother of plaintiffs intestate, The Edward Brown, [sic] had advanced $100 to him in her lifetime. The mother is mentioned as the defendants intestate so she was probably also deceased. (Bed TN, Ch Ct Min, 2/71)

BROWN, Frank
3 November 1873 L. M. Williams made a final settlement as guardian. (Dyr TN, Co Ct Min, B/658)

BROWN, Jacob
Died before 8 November 1785 when Ruth Brown & Jacob Brown were qualified as administrators, with George Gillaspy & Col. Charles Robertson as security. Ruth Brown, wife of Jacob Brown, deceased, petititoned the Court: The Court decreed that the deed from Jacob Brown to Nancy Henderson was fraudulent and a writ was issued to Ruth Brown for right of Dowry, from which judgement Ann Henderson prayed an appeal which was refused. (Was TN, Co Ct Min, 1/267-8)

BROWN, Jacob, Capt.
27 February 1782 made a deed of gift to Ann Henderson. (Was TN, Co Ct Min, 1/154)

BROWN, James
Died before 17 July 1797 when his heir, William Brown, made a deed to Elizabeth Airs & Patrick Martin, heirs of Joseph Martin, deceased. (Rob TN, Co Ct Min, 1/31)

BROWN, Jeremiah
7 November 1818 was shown to have had children, Jordan Brown, the youngest surviving son, and a daughter, Hulda, who was the widow of Henry Shelby. Jeremiah Brown was probably deceased in 1818. (Wil TN, Reg Bk/121)

BROWN, Jesse
Died before 30 August 1844 as shown in the suit of Joel Whorley vs Elizabeth Brown & others. He left heirs, Elizabeth Brown, Paschal, Jesse, Thomas, Elizabeth, David [Daniel] P., John, Alvin, Henry & William Brown & Cynthia Whorley. John, Alvin & Henry were minors and William J. Whitthome was guardian ad litem. (Bed TN, Ch Ct Min, 2/308 & 318) [Also see Joel Whorley.]

BROWN, Jesse
Was reported on the delinquent tax list for 7 February 1815, "not to be found." (Ste TN, Co Ct Min, 4/247)

BROWN, Jesse
Was a base born child now 3 years & 11 months old when he was bound in August 1789 to Richard Pigg until of age. He is to be taught the trade of a Taylor. (Was TN, Co Ct Min, 1/396)

BROWN, John
Was a resident of KY 9 December 1805 when he was allowed to enter 640 acres of land by his agent, James Stewart, Esqr. (Ste TN, Co Ct Min, 1/21)

BROWN, John
Was a base born child aged 6 years and 9 months when he was bound to Richard Pigg, August term 1789. He is to be taught the weaver's trade. (Was TN, Co Ct Min, 1/396)

BROWN, John
Was a resident of Frankford County, KY, 22 April 1820, when he gave power of attorney to Edmund Crutcher of Wilson County, TN, to sell land in Wilson County. (Wil TN, Reg Bk/195)

BROWN, John, Jr.
28 August 1778 took the oath of allegiance. (Was TN, Co Ct Min, 1/47)

BROWN, John, Sr.
28 August 1778 took the oath of allegiance. (Was TN, Co Ct Min, 1/47)

BROWN, John T.
Was a minor 16 September 1852 when he petitioned by his guardian, Jno. H. Rose, to sell land. (Mad TN, Ch Ct Min, 1/262)

BROWN, Jonathan
Died before 2 June 1829 when Sarah Brown & Aron B. Brown were appointed administrators. (McM TN, Co Ct Min 2no#/365) 10 September 1829 a years provision was laid off to the widow, Sarah Brown. (Ibid 392)

BROWN, Mary
Was granted a divorce from Dison [Dixon] Brown on 16 July 1851. They were married in Jackson County and had lived here since 1827. The defendant has been guilty of adultry with one Ann Lee. The complainant was granted certain property and custody of the children. (Jac TN, Ch Ct Min, B/5)

BROWN, Matthew
Died before 18 June 1816 when the executor, Jackson Brown, sold land to Marriott Davis. (Wil TN, Co Ct Min, no#/10)

BROWN, Richard
Made a deed of gift on 3 January 1820 to his son John Brown of Cairo, Sumner County, TN. The deed was for 6 negroes. (Wil TN, Reg Bk/148)

BROWN, Robert
Was a resident of 96 District [SC] 7 August 1784 when his deposition was to be taken for the suit of Jacob Brown, Jr., plaintiff vs Jordan Roseth, defendant. (Was TN, Co Ct Min, 1/254)

BROWN, T. S.
Died before 22 August 1866 as shown in the suit of Robt. Brown, administrator of T. S. Brown vs J. M. Reavis administrator, et als. (Mad TN, Ch Ct Min, 2/511)

BROWN, Walter
Died before 1 August 1814 when John Gaston was appointed administrator with Benjamin Bradford and Charles Parvis as security. (Ste TN, Co Ct Min, 4/162)

BROWN, William
Made a quit claim deed to Abraham Dardin for 345 acres of land in Green County, NC, 20 September 1804. It was proved by James Glasgow. (Roa TN, Co Ct Min, A/261)

BROWN, William Logan
Was the son of Hiram Brown as shown in the suit 14 August 1860 of Mariah Hanner vs William Montgomery & Hiram Brown. In this suit "the Law is with the defendants and the complainants bill is to be dismissed and that the child William Logan Brown which has been attached in this cause be delivered up to its father the defendant Hiram Brown and that Mariah Hanner pay all cost." (Jac TN, Ch Ct Min, C/390)

BROWN, Wm.
Died before 3 June 1872 when T. C. Greer made a settlement as administrator. (Dyr TN, Co Ct Min, B/418)

BROWN, Zekle
25 May 1778 it was ordered that he be committed to goal immediately and kept in custody until he can be delivered to a Continental Officer. (Was TN, Co Ct Min, 1/26) Zekle Brown was discharged by the sheriff, he having enlisted in the Continental service. (Ibid 28)

BROWNING, George
16 November 1814 was appointed guardian for Spencer Browning, Malone Browning & Polly Browning with Caleb Browning, Benjamin Tucker & Austin Solomon as his security. (Rob TN, Co Ct Min, 3/507)

BROYLES, Moses
Died before August term 1789 when the executors, William Moore and Joseph Brown, were ordered to appear at the next Court to make a settlement of the estate. (Was TN, Co Ct Min, 1/402)

BRUME, Warren L. [Braum, Brum, Brame]
Died before 29 June 1841 as shown in the petition of Price C. Steel & Winfield S. Bruime. Price C. Steel was guardian of the minor heirs of Warren L. Brume, deceased, one of whom was the petitioner. The guardian has paid out to all his wards their estate except Winfield S. and Hellen P. Braime, the youngest, who is still a minor. Winfield S. has now arrived at the age of 21. The deceased's name is also shown as Samuel and as Warner L. Brume. (Bed TN, Ch Ct Min, 1/312) Slaves are to be divided. (Ibid 2/114)

BRUMON, Sarah
Was an insane girl 1 November 1813 when she was to be let out for her maintenance. (Ste TN, Co Ct Min, 4/65)

BRUNSON, Jesse
Was allowed $50 for the maintenance of Sally Brunson as a Parishioner, 8 November 1814. (Ste TN, Co Ct Min, 4/202)

BRUTEN, Thomas P.
Died before 9 July 1850 when John C. M. Garland, guardian of the minor heirs, petitioned for sale of land. Martha Bruten was the widow. (Mad TN, Ch Ct Min, 1/136) The minor heirs were: Martha, Simon, [Simpson] Addison, John, William A. & Mary Ann Bruten. Land is to be sold and another tract purchased in the neighborhood of Mount Paison near the guardian & Uncles so as to get their aid & comfort in raising said minors. The will was mentioned. Ibid 150 & 221)

BRYAN, Allen
Died before 1 June 1857 when William M. Bryan renewed his bond as guardian to Ailsay

K. D. Bryan, minor heir. Samuel Huffaker was his security. (Sev TN, Co Ct Min, no#/171) 6 May 1867 commissioners were appointed to divide his land. (Ibid 452)

BRYAN, Elizabeth
Died before 3 November 1862 when Robert Sneed was appointed adminstrator, with John Kelly & N. N. Cate as security. (Sev TN, Co Ct Min, no#/22) 7 January 1867 Robt. Sneed made a settlement as guardian to Alsey Bryan, minor heir. (Ibid 409)

BRYAN, Thomas C.
Died before 3 October 1864 when Wm. E. Bryan was appointed administrator with Samuel Mount & John H. Caldwell as security. (Sev TN, Co Ct Min, no#/122)

BRYAN, William
On 21 September 1814 sold to his son, Willis Bryan, a negro girl named Jenny about 12 or 13 years old, "for the consideration of sundry favors and kindnesses rendered me by my son and one dollar in cash." Daniel Perrett & Oring Parrett were witnesses. (Wil TN, Reg Bk/6)

BRYAN, William M.
Died before 7 May 1860 when N. J. Huffaker was appointed administrator, with Wesley Huffaker, William Thomas & W. H. Cannon as security. The widow, E. A. C. Bryan, relinquished her right to administrate. (Sev TN, Co Ct Min, no#/557) 3 November 1862 Wellington McMahan, Samuel B. Henderson & Timothy Chandles were appointed to set off the dower of Caroline Bryan, widow of William M. Bryan, deceased. (Ibid 23) The above order is null & void. L. D. Alexander, David Kelly & John A. Trotter were appointed to lay off dower to Frances Bryan widow of William M. Bryan, deceased. (Ibid 28) The last 3 appointed laid off dower to Caroline Bryan. (Ibid 33)

BRYAN, Wm.
5 November 1804 his guardian, Hardy S. Bryan, was in a suit against Philip Parchment & James H. Bryan. (Rob TN, Co Ct Min, 1/316)

BRYANT, Franklin
Was released from paying poll tax for 1860 as he is over age. (Sev TN, Co Ct Min, no#/589)

BRYANT, John
Taxes were not collected in District 2 for 1873, "gone." (Dyr TN, Co Ct Min, B/758)

BRYANT, W. J.
2 July 1872 was released from work on roads due to severe injuries. (Dyr TN, Co Ct Min, B/440)

BRYANT, William
Died in August or September 1838, intestate. William Word was administrator. He left a widow, Sophia Bryant, and children Mary Ann, Dennis, Elizabeth and Cuthbert Bryant, minors. (Bed TN, Ch Ct Min, 1/333) William D. Orr was appointed guardian of the minor heirs. (Ibid 2/48) Child Dennis was not shown when land was sold. (Ibid 187)

BUCHANAN, Elijah
Was eight years old when he was bound 25 March 1808 to Moses Archer, a Hatter. (Roa TN, Co Ct Min, C/159)

BUCHANAN, John
Was an orphan [age not given] when he was bound to William Adair on 19 December 1808. (Roa TN, Co Ct Min, D/31)

BUCHANAN, Robert
Was a resident of Washington County, VA, 2 November 1784 when his deposition was to be taken on behalf of Aron Lewis in the suit of William Griffin. (Was TN, Co Ct Min, 1/258)

BUCHANAN, William
Died before 28 July 1847 when his death was suggested in the suit of William Buchanan & wife vs Matthew C. Hogin & others. John A. Buchanan produced a power of attorney authorizing him to receive any moneys which might belong to Jane Buchanan from the estate of Sarah Hogin & Edward Hogin, deceased. [Also see Hogin] (Jac TN, Ch Ct Min, A/262)

BUCHANNAN, John
Died before 5 February 1866 when John H. Caldwell was appointed administrator with James A. Pickens as security. (Sev TN, Co Ct Min, no#/275)

BUCK, Elijah
Died before 13 October 1856 as shown in the suit of Jonathan E. C. Buck, his administrator, vs John McNamarra. Elijah Buck had sold land to John McNamarra, who is a non-reisident of this state, which has not been paid for. (Fen TN, Ch Ct Min, A/61)

BUCKHANAN, Ruth A.
14 August 1868 in the suit of Ruth A. Buckhanan by next friend vs Thos. N. Buckhanan, it was stated that the complainant is the wife of the defendant. She has a landed estate in Fayette County & some personal property that descended to her from her father. Her husband is a bad manager & is in debt therefore she wants her property to be put in trust for the sole and separate use of her and her children. Wm. M. Dunnaway was appointed trustee for this purpose. (Mad TN, Ch Ct Min, 3/181)

BUCKNER, W. E.
Died before 6 March 1871 when F. G. Sampson returned the inventory of the estate. (Dyr TN, Co Ct Min, B/201)

BULGIN, James
Was reported "not an inhabitant of this government," April term 1798, when summoned in the suit of Beverly A. Allen vs James Bulgin and Isaac Herbert. (Rob TN, Co Ct Min, 1/60)

BULLARD, John
Died before 27 November 1780 when his nuncupative will was proved by Joseph Nation, Ellenos Nation & Ann Bullen. (Was TN, Co Ct Min, 1/120)

BULLER, Isaac
27 August 1778 was ordered to be sent to Goal until he can be delivered to a Continental Officer, to serve three years or during the War. (Was TN, Co Ct Min, 1/44) Isaac Buller made bond with Joseph Buller as his security, that he would apprehend two deserters, Joshua Williams and Carter Dyer, and deliver them to the proper authority. (Ibid 45)

BULLER, Joseph
25 August 1778 moved by his counsel, Weightstel Avery, to be discharged from a commitment of Michl. Woods and Wm. Clark, Esqrs., Justices of the peace, to the Goal of said county in order to be turned over to the Continental service for three years or during the War. (Was TN, Co Ct Min, 1/39)

BUMBLEY, Smith [Rumbley]
Died before 2 May 1814 when the will was proved by Nathan Peoples & William D. Jamison. William Bumpley and Emanuel James were executors. (Ste TN, Co Ct Min, 4/138)

BUMPASS, Garrett
16 September 1816 an inventory of the property of Garrett Bumpass, a lunatic, was entered by Robert Bumpass, his guardian. (Wil TN, Co Ct Min, no#/24)

BUMPASS, Mary
Died before 1 November 1819 when Robert Bumpass was appointed administrator with T. Bradly & Bryan F. Matly as security. (Wil TN, Co Ct Min, no#/536)

BUMPASS, William
Died before 26 March 1805 when William Bumpass was granted letters of administration on the estate. (Wil TN, Co Ct Min, no#/113)

BUNCH, Martin
Died before 15 November 1815 when William Acklen and John Neal were appointed to settle with the administratrix and administrator, Anne Bunch and Wm. Bunch. (Cla TN, Co Ct Min, 4/128)

BUNDY, Sevier
Died before 29 May 1781 when his orphans, George Bundy & Reuben Bundy, were bound to William Wells. (Was TN, Co Ct Min, 1/136)

BUNDY, Simon
Died before 4 November 1782 when his orphans, Nathl. Bundy and Rueben Burdy, were

bound to James Turbott until age 21. (Was TN, Co Ct Min, 1/180) 7 August 1787 Jonathan Pugh was appointed sole administrator of the estate of Simon Bundy, deceased, with James Stuart & Robert Allison as security. (Ibid 288)

BUNN
Joel & Charity Bunn gave power of attorney to Josiah Fort on certificate of the clerk of Nash County, NC, 5 August 1806. (Rob TN, Co Ct Min, 1/402)

BUNN, Burrell
Died before 8 July 1807 when the administrator, Joel Bunn, was in a suit with Lemuel Sugg. (Rob TN, Co Ct Min, 1/454)

BURCH, Thomas
Died before 7 June 1830 when Thomas Cate was appointed administrator. (McM TN, Co Ct Min, 2no#/448) A years support is to be laid off to the widow, Sarah. (Ibid 452)

BURCH, William
Died before 2 December 1828 when Thomas Burch was appointed administrator. (McM TN, Co Ct Min, 2no#/325) A years provision is to be laid off for the widow, Elizabeth Burch. (Ibid 388) 7 December 1829 the land was divided between the widow & heirs, the widow taking a child's part; lot #1 to the widow; lot #2 to George Burch, lot #3 to Thomas Burch; lot #4 to Henry Burch. (Ibid 405) 7 June 1830 Thomas Cate was appointed administrator in the place of Thomas Burch who is deceased. (Ibid 454)

BURCHET
Jackson & Eliza Burchet were non-residents of the state in February 1855 as shown in the suit of James A. Spurlock against them. (Jac TN, Ch Ct Min, B/228)

BURDEN, Jarret
Died before 27 May 1794 when Elizabeth Burden and William Mattlock were granted leave of administration, with John Carter & Wm. Ward as security. (Was TN, Co Ct Min, 1/487) The name of the deceased was shown as Garred Burden. (Ibid 496)

BURDITT, Giles
Died before 28 September 1840 as shown in the suit of George Davidson & others vs The Bank of the State of Tenn. (Bed TN, Ch Ct Min, 1/313)

BURDITT, William
Died before 28 December 1841 when William Norton was allowed to amend his suit against Sarah Burditt et al to include all the heirs of William Burditt, deceased. (Bed TN, Ch Ct Min, 2/165) The suit was against Sarah Burditt & Giles P. Burditt, Nathan Ivy & others. (Ibid 218) Nathan Ivy was guardian of Giles P. Burditt, Samuel S. Burditt, Elizabeth G. Burditt, Wm. M. Burditt, Hampton Burditt, Hennith Burditt and Sarah Burditt, minors. Other defendants were Matilda Burditt and Mary Ann Ivy, William Caime & wife Patience, Thomas Gregory & wife Rachel. William Cairne [Caime] & wife live in MO. The original bill filed 18 December 1840, shows that William Burditt died before 3 April 1839 (Ibid 3/1)

BURDITT, Williamson R.
Died before 27 June 1843 when his death was admitted in the suit of Jacob C. Burrow & Adelade Marshall vs Williamson R. Burditt & others. (Bed TN, Ch Ct Min, 2/249)

BURFORD, David
Died before 10 October 1841 when the administrators, Edward Y. Shuck and Bennett Marshall, filed a petition to sell slaves. (Obi TN, Cir Ct Min, 4/no#)

BURGER, John
Died before 6 March 1826 when Susanah Burger was appointed administratrix, with Nathaniel Morrison security. (McM TN, Co Ct Min, 2no#/134)

BURGES, Henry A.
Died before 21 February 1839 when land was taxed to the heirs. (Obi TN, Cir Ct Min, 3/294)

BURGESS, John [Bargess]
Died before 1 May 1815 when the will was proved by James H. Russell. (Ste TN, Co Ct Min, 4/261)

BURGESS, Nathaniel
Made a deed of conveyance or gift to James Vinson 4 May 1813. (Ste TN, Co Ct Min, 4/35)

BURGESS, Wm. H.
Died in 1853 as shown in the suit of Robert Fenner, surviving executor, and others, petition to sell slaves. The widow of Wm. H. was Eugenia A. Burgess. (Mad TN, Ch Ct Min, 1/357 & 2/61)

BURGIS, Henry
Died before 24 February 1837 when land was taxed to the heirs. (Obi TN, Cir Ct Min, 3/114)

BURK, Robert
Was an orphan boy of colour 21 September 1809 when he was ordered to be put in the care of John Cooper until next court. (Roa TN, Co Ct Min, D/121) Robert was aged 14 years last June when he was bound to James Robinson on 18 April 1810. (Ibid 205)

BURKE
A suit was shown 14 July 1859 by Leonedas A. McCarver vs Milton Draper and Harvy H. Draper. Milton Draper had been guardian of America Milly J. and Matilda Burke and had money belonging to them. Said Draper was removed as guardian and complainant McCarver appointed in his place. The money is to be paid over the the new guardian. (Jac TN, Ch Ct Min, C/257)

BURKE, John
Died before 6 November 1843 as shown in the suit of Sam E. Stone & Leroy B. Settle vs Henry F. Burke et al. Henry F. Burk is not a resident of this state. His co-defendants, Wm. C. Burke and Richd. P. Brooks were administrators of John Burke, deceased. Henry F. Burk is entitled to a distributive share of the estate. (Jac TN, Ch Ct Min, A/123) Pamelia Graves, wife of Alvy Graves, is an heir of John Burke, deceased, as shown in the suit of Andrew McClellan & Beverly Graves vs Alvy Graves, Pamelia Graves et al. (Ibid 154) A suit was entered 14 July 1855 by John O. Hopkins & others vs Richard P. Brooks. It stated that the minor heirs of John Burke, deceased, were made party complainants by Richard P. Brooks, their guardian, without their knowledge or consent and that they had no day in court and no notice as required by law, of the application to sell the real estate. (Ibid B/264) Land was sold subject to the widow's dower. (Ibid C/113)

BURKE, John G.
26 July 1849 was appointed guardian ad litem for Milton E. Burk, Angelina Burke, Elizabeth Burke, John M. Burke and [blank] Burke who are minors and non-residents, to defend for them in the suit of Calaway Sizemore & William Gray, Guardians &c vs Thomas H. Butler & the Burke minors listed. John G. Burke is a resident of Jackson County. (Jac TN, Ch Ct Min, A/343)

BURKETT, Martha, Mrs.
5 April 1871 made a settlement as guardian of her children. (Dyr TN, Co Ct Min, B/228)

BURKLY, C.
Taxes were not collected in District 4 for 1873, "insolvent." (Dyr TN, Co Ct Min, B/759)

BURLASON, Aron
Died before 27 May 1782 when the will was proved by Thomas Williams. (Was TN, Co Ct Min, 1/160)

BURN, Wilson
Died before 8 July 1856 when Lewis Wayland made a settlement as guardian of William Burn, minor heir. (Sev TN, Co Ct Min, no#/63) 2 March 1857 Lewis Wayland resigned as guardian for Wm. P. Burns. L. W. Burns was appointed guardian. (Ibid 128) L. W. Burn, as guardian for William P. Burn, is to sell land grant #45l02 for 160 acres dated 4 October 1856 & issued to William P. Burn for the services of Wilson Burn as a private in the war of 1812. (Ibid 159)

BURNET, Joseph
Died before 18 June 1816 when the will was proved by John Martin & Nancy Martin. Thomas Burnet qualified as executor with Solomon Bond as security. (Wil TN, Co Ct Min, no#/13)

BURNET, Stephen
Died before 14 February 1815 when Stasha Burnet was appointed administratrix. (Rob TN, Co Ct Min, 3/541)

BURNETT, John S.
1 March 1830, with his wife, Lucinda, conveyed land in Chesterfield County, VA, to George W. Clemans. (McM TN, Co Ct Min, 2no#/420)

BURNHAM, George W.
Died before 6 January 1873 when Miles H. Davis was appointed administrator, with W. W. Davis and D. A. Chamberlain as his security. (Dyr TN, Co Ct Min, B/524) J. W. Wright, John Jones and James Rankin were appointed to lay off a years provision for the widow & family. (Ibid 525) Provisions were laid off for the widow & family. The first wife's four children were given all that was left after paying the Court fees, about $40, 1 chest & 2 beds. (Ibid 546)

BURNS, H.
Taxes were not collected in District 5 for 1873, "over age." (Dyr TN, Co Ct Min, B/759)

BURNS, James
Was a resident of Williamson County, TN, as shown in the suit of William H. Duncan & Guin [Guynn] Foster of Bedford County against James Burns, filed 25 February 1841. James mentioned Isiah Webb, his brother-in-law. (Bed TN, Ch Ct Min, 1/450)

BURNS, Jesse
Died before 29 August 1860 when his death was admitted in the suit of Ashburry Burns [Burus] et als vs Thomas Reid. (Mad TN, Ch Ct Min, 2/380) This suit was again heard on 20 February 1861, in which it was stated that one of the complainants, Jesse Burns, died in June 1860 and that he was a resident of IN. Jno. S. H. Tomlin was appointed administrator pendente lite in this state. The suit was revivived in the names of Patsy Burns, the widow, and Daniel S. Statt [Slatt] & wife Lucinda?, Beniah Moss & wife Mariah L., Leland C. Knox & wife Mary E. M. and Elihu M. Burus and Jno. S. H. Tomlin special administrator of said Jesse Burus, deceased. (Ibid 426)

BURNS, Levan W.
Died before 4 May 1863 when B. D. Brabson, Timothy Chandler and John Mullender were appointed to lay off a years support for the widow, Drucilla L. C. Burns. (Sev TN, Co Ct Min, no#/59) E. Hodges & E. Burns were appointed administrators with Wm. Catlett as security. (Ibid 81)

BURROW, Ephraim
Died after making his will dated 4 July 1833. The will was shown by which he bequeathed to his wife, [Eve Burrow], son Solomon Burrow, son Ephraim Burrow, son Jesse Burrow, son James Burrow, son Banks M. Burrow, son Dorton Alfred Burrow, son Madison Burrow, daughter Frances Black, daughter Hetty Wilhoite, daughter Nancy Black, daughter Leathy Burrow. In December 1837 a suit was brought by Jorden C. Holt vs Banks M. D. Burrow, in which Holt wants to attach the interest Banks M. D. Burrow has in his father's estate. (Bed TN, Ch Ct Min, 1/144)

BURROW, Freeman
In the suit filed 12 November 1838 by Freeman Burrow against Dudley P. T. House, Robert F. Arnold & William Burrow, it is stated that Freeman Burrow is an old man about 70 years old. William Burrow was the son of Freeman and Robert F. Arnold was his brother-in-law. Freeman Burrow claims his son & brother-in-law stole 2 of his negroes and sold them in Huntsville, AL. Dudley P. T. House is the father-in-law of both William Burrow & R. F. Arnold. (Bed TN, Ch Ct Min, 1/414) This same suit is shown again. (Ibid 3/14)

BURSHONG, Jane
Died before 6 October 1873 when J. W. Lauderdale, Coroner, was paid for holding an inquest on Jane Burshong alias McVey. He was also paid for coffin and burying Jane McVey. (Dyr TN, Co Ct Min, B/635)

BURTON, John
Died before 4 March 1805 when his widow, Margret Burton, and William Burton, were appointed administrators. (Cla TN, Co Ct Min, 2/105)

BURTON, Martin G.
Died before 2 May 1870 when F. G. Sampson was appointed administrator, with W. C. Doyle & D. E. Parker as security. (Dyr TN, Co Ct Min, B/50)

BUTLER, Bailey
Died shortly after he had made his will on 20 September 1842, as shown in the suit of Samuel B. M. Fowler & his wife Adaline Fowler vs Polly Butler, Thomas H. Butler, Franklin W. Butler Lucetta Butler, Erasmus Denton, L. L. Butler, Marium Butler, Lusanna Butler, John L. Butler, Martha Butler & Bailey Butler. Complainants & defendants were his heirs, except said Denton, who is guardian for defendant Lucetta. Thomas H. Butler is the executor. The parties wish an amicable settlement of the difficulties arising out of the ambiguous character of parts of the will. (Jac TN, Ch Ct Min, A/144) 7 February 1851 a petition was made by Samuel S. Butler & others. George M. McWhirter was guardian of Samuel S. Butler, Mary Anderson, Susan Hampton, John S. Butler, Bailey Butler & Martha Butler, minor heirs of Bailey Butler, deceased. The guardian has purchased a tract of land from Mary Anderson for said minors. (Ibid 408)

BUTLER, Burl
Died before 9 March 1852 when his death was suggested in the case of Burl Butler, administrator of A. Huntsman, deceased, vs the Heirs & Creditors of A. Huntsman, deceased. The suit was revived in the name of Jno. C. Rodgers who is administrator de bonis non. (Mad TN, Ch Ct Min, 1/233) Jas. Butler was shown as administrator. (Ibid 234)

BUTLER, Edward
Died before 18 July 1803 when Isabella Butler & Wm. P. Anderson were appointed administrators. (Rob TN, Co Ct Min, 1/254) 20 October 1803 Genl. Andrew Jackson was appointed guardian for the orphans of Captn. Edward Butler, deceased, being Caroline S. Butler, Eliza Butler, George W. Butler and Anthony Wayne Butler. (Ibid 273) Isabella Butler requested that her dower be laid off. (Ibid 308) 7 October 1809 an agreement by W. P. Anderson, administrator of Capt. Edwd. Butler, deceased, and Wm. B. Vinson, administrator in right of his wife, Robert Bell one of the legatees and Andrew Jackson, guardian for Eliza Butler, was acknowledged. (Ibid 2/190)

BUTLER, Frank N. W.
Sold a tract of land in 1855 to Jno. J. Anderson. Anderson has paid for the land but has not received a deed. Frank N. W. Burton [Butler] has left the country for parts unknown. (Mad TN, Ch Ct Min, 2/418)

BUTLER, George
Died before 2 October 1865 when Henry Butler was appointed administrator with John Butler as security. (Sev TN, Co Ct Min, no#/221)

BUTLER, Henry
Died before 5 July 1858 when his will was proved by Geo. McCown & William H. Trotter. (Sev TN, Co Ct Min, no#/311)

BUTLER, Horatio B.
Died before 1 December 1856 when the administrators, Mary Butler & Henry Butler, resigned. William H. Trotter was appointed administrator with Isaac Ogle as his security. (Sev TN, Co Ct Min, no#/91) Henry Butler was appointed guardian to George Butler & William Butler, minor heirs of H. B. Butler, deceased, with W. H. Trotter, Isaac Ogle & John Butler as his security. (Ibid 92) 2 December 1856 Mary Butler, Henry Butler and others vs Jas. D. Ernest & others, petitioned for dower & sale of land. Isaac Trotter was appointed guardian ad litem for Micajah Butler, Caleb Robison, Mary Robeson & Jemima Butler, minors, to answer said petition. (Ibid 94) 7 January 1857, Martha Butler, one of the defendants, and W. H. Trotter, administrator of H. B. Butler, deceased, failed to appear. (Ibid 118) 8 January 1857, case continued: Horatio B. Butler died several years since, leaving Mary Butler his widow & the other persons named in the petition as his heirs. Wm. H. Trotter is administrator. John Mullendore, Ashley Wynne and George W. Seaton were appointed to lay off the dower to the widow. (Ibid 120) 7 July 1857 land sale was reported. Title was divested out of Mary Butler, Isaac Ogle, Nancy Ogle, John Butler, Martha Butler, Micajah Butler, George Butler, William Butler, Marion Clabough, Anna Clabough, George Meloy, Caleb Robeson, Mary Robeson, Jemima Butler, James D. Ernest, Asa Ernest and Henry Butler. (Ibid 184-193) 2 August 1858, William H. Trotter of this county & J. M. Rambo and Martha Rambo of Knox County were made defendants to petition to sell land. (Ibid 330) 3 January 1859 some land was sold and title was to be divested out of the heirs of Horatio B. Butler, deceased, to wit: Isaac Ogle & his wife Nancy Ogle, John Butler, Henry Butler, William Butler, Marion Clabough & his wife Anna

Clabough, Martha Rambo, Micajah Butler, George Butler, George Meloy, Caleb Robeson & his wife Mary Robeson, Jemima Butler & Jas. D. Ernest & his wife Asa Ernest. William H. Trotter & Philip R. Ernest bought the land. (Ibid 370)

BUTLER, James
Died before 8 September 1857 when the court was to determine the value of the dower interest of Martha Rambo, formerly Martha Butler, and widow of James Butler, deceased. It appears that James was an heir of Horatio B. Butler, deceased. (Sev TN, Co Ct. Min, no#/203)

BUTLER, M. R.
Died before 4 December 1865 when M. A. Rawlings was appointed administrator, the widow & next of kin having relinquished the right. M. P. Thomas was security. (Sev TN, Co Ct Min, no#/250)

BUTLER, Martha A.
Married before 21 August 1867 to Charles W. Chancellor, as shown in the suit of Martha A. Butler vs R. Duckham. (Mad TN, Ch Ct Min, 3/64)

BUTLER, Mary
Died before 2 August 1858 when W. H. Trotter was appointed administrator, with Henry Butler as his security. (Sev TN, Co Ct Min, no#/323)

BUTLER, Mary E.
Was a minor 2 October 1865 when David McMahan was appointed guardian. (Sev TN, Co Ct Min, no#/217)

BUTLER, Thomas
Was not an inhabitant of this state as shown in the suit of Reuben Williams vs Thomas Butler, 22 October 1812. (Roa TN, Co Ct Min, D/431)

BUTLER, Thomas Ryan
Died before 10 August 1812 when the will was proved by James H. Bryan, John Howell & George Martin. Francis Rhoalas was executor. (Rob TN, Co Ct Min, 3/98)

BUTLER, Welcome
Died in May 1849 as shown in the suit of John Butler vs Susan Butler, William Butler, Bailey Butler, William Sarjeant & Mary his wife, William Kendall & Sarah his wife, Doctor Head & Siothy [Sinthy?] his wife, Thomas Butler & Erwin F. Langford. The parties to this suit are his widow & heirs-at-law & E. F. Langford. He had made his will 22 January 1838 leaving all his property to defendant, Susan. On 23 January 1841 he purchased the land mentioned in the pleadings. Susan sold the land to defendant Langford without title thereto, which sale is rescinded and is now to be sold for division, subject to the widows dower. Susan was the executrix. The children of Peggy Head mentioned in the answer are to be made parties to this suit and the Clerk of this Court is appointed guardian ad litem for them. (Jac TN, Ch Ct Min, A/390)

BUTLER, Welcome
He and his wife were non-residents of TN on 9 February 1856 as shown in the suit against them by Alexander Masters. (Jac TN, Ch Ct Min, B/305)

BUTTON, Mary E.
In a suit for divorce 1 August 1849 the defendant, Adolphus Button, was ordered to pay the costs. (Mad TN, Ch Ct Min, 1/92)

BYBEE, Sarah
29 May 1782 chose Isaac Mayfield as her guardian. (Was TN, Co Ct Min, 1/166)

BYRD, James [Bird]
Died before 13 November 1844 as shown in the suit of Thomas J. Byrd Admr. of John W. Byrd Deceased vs James Thomas. (Obi TN, Cir Ct Min, 4/no#)

BYRD, Thomas
Died before 6 February 1805 when the will was proved by Jas. Crabtree, Esqr. (Rob TN, Co Ct Min, 1/325)

BYRD, Wm.
Died before 3 April 1809 when letters of admistration were granted to Betsey Byrd with James Crabtree with Wm. Pate as security. (Rob TN, Co Ct Min, 2/117)

CADLE
Abraham Cadle and Polly Cadle are two of the poor of this county and are to be let to the lowest bidder for their support, 12 February 1817. (Cla TN, Co Ct Min, 4/306) Zachariah Cadle was the lowest bidder. (Ibid 309)

CAGLE
6 February 1866 B. F. Tipton was appointed guardian to C. Cagle & Jane Cagle, minor orphans, with J. A. Pickens & A. Boling as security. (Sev TN, Co Ct Min, no#/276)

CAGLE
3 June 1867 petition for dower was made by Sally Cagle vs Calloway Cagle, Jane Cagle & B. F. Tipton, guardian, (Sev TN, Co Ct Min, no#/455)

CAGLE, Shade
5 January 1857 Jourdan Honk was allowed money from the poor fund for making 2 coffins for Shade Cagle's children. (Sev TN, Co Ct Min, no#/99)

CAGLE, Wm.
Died before 2 November 1857 when a petition for dower was made, Sarah Cagle vs Isam Cagle & others, heirs of Wm. Cagle, deceased. (Sev TN, Co Ct Min, no#/223) Benjamin Tipton is one of the defendants. (Ibid 228)

CALAHAN, John
Was a resident of SC in August 1789 when he sold land in Washington County, TN. (Was TN, Co Ct Min, 1/392)

CALDWELL, _____
Died before 22 June 1836 when Steven Hanna was said to be the surviving partner of Caldwell & Hanna in their suit against William H. C. Covington. (Obi TN, Cir Ct Min, 3/66) Another suit showed Elizabeth M. Caldwell, Stephen Hanna & Edward F. Hanna vs Ferdinand C. Barber. (Ibid 77)

CALDWELL, Alexander
Died before 15 November 1834 when his death was suggested in the case of Caldwell & Hanna vs James H. Daviss. He was one of the plaintiffs. (Obi TN, Cir Ct Min, 2/223)

CALDWELL, James
On 13 November 1833 made a deed of gift to Catharin R. Davidson for certain negroes. (Obi TN, Cir Ct Min, 2/109)

CALDWELL, Mary
Died before 2 September 1872 when her will was proved by Thos. Miller and George Miller, witnesses. (Dyr TN, Co Ct Min, B/463) James P. Caldwell was executor, Wm. Caldwell waiving his rights and Robert M. being dead. (Ibid 476)

CALDWELL, Robert N.
Died before 4 March 1872 when James P. Caldwell was appointed administrator, with J. L. Webb and J. H. York as security. (Dyr TN, Co Ct Min, B/381)

CALDWELL, Wm.
Died before 6 March 1871 when J. C. Murray, John E. Bell and George Miller were appointed to lay off a years support for the widow and family. (Dyr TN, Co Ct Min, B/198) James P. Caldwell was appointed administrator. (Ibid 202)

CALVERT, Jno.
Died before 6 November 1782 as shown in the suit of Wm. Calvert vs James Ford. (Was TN, Co Ct Min, 1/184)

CAMPBELL
On the Appearance Docket included in County Court Minutes Vol. 1, is a case for slander by Richard & William Cooley vs Charles Campbell, William Campbell, James Campbell, Milley Campbell, Rachel Campbell & Nelly Campbell, filed 28 June 1806. (Ste TN, Co Ct Min, 1/63b)

CAMPBELL, Alexander
Was in the Army of the United States on 2 August 1813 when his deposition was to be taken for the defendant in the suit of George Lyndseys Admr. vs John Scarborough. (Ste TN, Co Ct Min, 4/51)

CAMPBELL, Charles
Was a resident of Christian County, KY, on 9 September 1806 when his deposition was to be taken for plaintiff in the suit of John Scott vs Aaron Fletcher. (Ste TN, Co Ct Min, 1/32)

CAMPBELL, Charles
Was a resident of Rockbridge County, VA, on 6 August 1787 when his deposition was to be taken for John Trotter respecting an article of agreement between said Trotter and John Cunningham. (Was TN, Co Ct Min, 1/288)

CAMPBELL, Elizabeth
Was the mother of a bastard child by Edward Picket, Jr. who was ordered to pay support 18 June 1817. (Wil TN, Co Ct Min, no#/123)

CAMPBELL, James
Died before 20 February 1843 when land was taxed to the heirs. (Obi TN, Cir Ct Min, 4/no#)

CAMPBELL, James H.
Died before 13 May 1817 when his death was suggested more than two terms ago in the suit of John Wallen vs James H. Campbell. The suit is abated. (Cla TN, Co Ct Min, 4/339)

CAMPBELL, Jonathan
Died before 18 June 1816 when Petter Raglin was appointed administrator. (Wil TN, Co Ct Min, no#/16)

CAMPBELL, Lysander M.
Died 23 April 1859. His widow, Annie R. Campbell, was appointed administratrix in Haywood County, TN. He had no children. B. R. Campbell, E. S. Campbell & F. D. Campbell are the only surviving brothers and Alex C. Murrell is the only son and heir of Mrs. A. E. Murrell, the sister of L. M. Campbell. Ann Elizabeth Ligon, Sue Ligon & Jno. A. Ligon are the only children of Jno. A. Ligon, who was the only son & heir of Anna? C. Ligon, also a sister of intestate L. M. Campbell. These minors are before the court. Land was mentioned that had been conveyed to L. M. Campbell by Mrs. Sarah Campbell. Alex A. Campbell was also mentioned. (Mad TN, Ch Ct Min, 3/175)

CAMPBELL, Margaret
Died before 12 February 1816 when William Graham, William Acklin and Josiah Ramsey were appointed to settle the accounts of David H. Campbell, the executor. (Cla TN, Co Ct Min, 4/149)

CAMPBELL, Thomas
Was a resident of Bedford County when a bill of sale from William Robb, Sr. was entered, 4 November 1818. (Wil TN, Co Ct Min, no#/352)

CAMPBELL, Victor Morcan
Was certified to be 21 years of age & of good reputation, 4 September 1828, preparatory to obtaining a law license. (McM TN, Co Ct Min, 2no#/311)

CAMPBELL, William
Died before 5 August 1820 when Hugh Campbell, legal heir-at-law of William Campbell, deceased, appointed [name not given] to request a military warrent to which he is entitled as the legal heir, for the service of William Campbell in the Revolutionary War as a soldier in Capt. Donohos company of the sixth regiment of the NC line. (Wil TN, Reg Bk/178)

CAMPS, T. L.
Died before 12 January 1849 as shown in the suit of Robert C. Chester vs Robert W. Crockett & William Crown [Croom], administrators. (Mad TN, Ch Ct Min, 1/67) 30 July 1849 William Croom was appointed guardian ad litem for John Camp, minor heir, in place of the former guardian, Allen S. Hoard. (Ibid 78) The name of deceased is shown as Terrell L. Camp. (Ibid 148) Camp had resided in Obion County. He died 4 May 1848, intestate, leaving his wife & only child, John Camp. His wife died prior to filing this bill. (Ibid 156)

CANADA, Anna
Died before 2 February 1874 when her will was proved by J. R. Prichard, one of the witnesses. The other witness was J. C. Hale. (Dyr TN, Co Ct Min, B/706)

CANE, James
Died before 1 August 1814 when Willis Whitford was appointed administrator, with Stephen Gardner & William Green as security. (Ste TN, Co Ct Min, 4/164)

CANE, Jesse
Died before 1 August 1814 when John Cane was appointed administrator, with Simon Fletcher & Martin Wells as security. (Ste TN, Co Ct Min, 4/165)

CANNON
On 29 July 1847 a suit was entered by Henry & Garrett Sadler vs Abisha Cannon et al. Jane Cannon, Martin V. Cannon, Henry H. Cannon and Abisha Cannon, Jr. are minor defendants and James M. Shepherd was appointed guardian pendente lite. (Jac TN, Ch Ct Min, A/274) 13 July 1850 this suit was shown as Henry Sadler and Garrett Sadler vs Abisha Cannon, Sally Cannon, James M. Shepherd Guardian ad litem of Jane Cannon, Martin V. Cannon, Henry H. Cannon, Lewis F. Cannon & Abisha Cannon minors and children of said Abisha Cannon. The suit mentioned an amount paid by complainant, Garrot, to James Williamson for accompanying him to Georgia on business of his trust. Evidently the Sadlers had been trustees of certain property for Abisha Cannon & his family. (Ibid 386) Henry H. Cannon was shown as William H. H. Cannon. (Ibid 421) The trusteeship from Abisha Cannon to Garret & Sadler was dated 12 January 1838. (Ibid C/114) When this suit was shown again on 15 August 1860 it was stated that Martin V. Cannon, Jane Cannon & Henry Cannon had arrived at full age and Jane had married Stanton Carter. (Ibid 406)

CANNON, James
Died before March term 1814 as shown in the case of Samuel Cannon, administrator of James Cannon, deceased vs William Mann & John Marshall. (Wil TN, P&J, no#/no#) Abraham W. Cannon of Rutherford County, TN, sold land that was part of the estate of James Cannon, deceased, 23 July 1821. (Ibid Reg Bk/no page # but should be 418)

CANNON, John
Died before 17 March 1807 as shown in the suit of Robert Cannon admr. vs John Jones, W. Terril Lewis & Edmond Waller. (Roa TN Co Ct Min, B/269)

CANNON, John
Died before 3 October 1864 when his death was suggested. David McCroskey is to take charge of the estate until the executor can be qualified. (Sev TN, Co Ct Min, no#/121) The will was entered 6 November 1865 and the witnesses, John Mullendore & David McCroskey, stated he was not of sound mind when he made the will. The will was set aside, the heirs contesting said will. (Ibid 237)

CANNON, Minos
Died 7 April 1823 as shown in the suit of Mary Dobson vs Robt. T. Cannon et al. The other defendants were Jastina E. Ashburn, Mary T. Ashburn, Hazzard T. Ashburn & Clemant Ashburn. Mary Dobson stated she married Minos Cannon on 14 June 1810. After his death she married Thomas F. Ashburn on 4 July 1825. Thomas F. Ashburn died 8 July 1833 and on 16 February 1834 Mary married Archibald Dobson who died 11 January 1841. By the death of Cannon, Mary obtained land as dower. By the death of Ashburn she acquired an interest in 6 negroes, conveyed to Mary by her father and at her death to go to her Ashburn children. Ashburn left a will conveying to Mary 1/5 of all his property & the balance to his children by Mary, to wit, Jastina E., Mary F., Hazzard T. & Clemant Ashburn. When Mary married Archibald Dobson he took out letters of administration with will annexed on the estate of Thomas F. Ashburn. Dobson never made a settlement & conveyed property in trust to Robert T. Cannon. Robert T. Cannon was the son of Mary Dobson. After the death of Dobson, Robert T. Cannon took out letters of administration and sold the property. The four Ashburn children are minors. The deed of trust made by Archibald Dobson to Robert T. Cannon was declared void on account of the insanity and intoxication of Archibald Dobson. Mary was given back her dower from Cannon, her interest in the negroes and dower out of the lots of Dobson. (Bed TN, Ch Ct Min, 1/540-546) The name of the child, Justina E. was also shown as Austin E. Ashburn. (Ibid 2/184)

CANNON, Newton
Died before 11 March 1845 when land was taxed to the heirs. (Obi TN, Cir Ct Min, 4/no#)

CANNON, Thomas U.
Was bound as an apprentice 16 December 1817 to Robert B. Roberts to learn the trade of a Taylor, until 1st of August 1821. (Wil TN, Co Ct Min, no#/202) 2 August 1819 the above bond was made void. (Ibid 500)

CANNON, Willis
22 August 1840 a suit was entered by Letsey Cannon vs William Pratt & others. It was stated that Samuel S., Martha, Jason T. and Letsey Cannon were minor heirs of Willis Cannon. [does not say deceased] William Pratt was appointed guardian ad litem in place of their mother who was their regular guardian, to defend the suit entered by their mother. (Bed TN, Ch Ct Min, 2/105) This suit concerns an alledged mistake in a deed from Letcy & Willis Cannon to their children. Catherine Pratt was also a child of Letcy. (Ibid 194) George Pratt was also mentioned. (Ibid 226) On 28 December 1843 the names were shown as Samuel T., Martha N., Jason H. & Letsey Cannon who sue by their guardian, Letsy Cannon, Sr., vs William & George Pratt. (Ibid 288) On 18 October 1844 a suit was entered by Samuel T., Martha M., Jason H. T. and Letsey Cannon, minors, who sue by their guardian, Letsy Cannon, Sr., vs William Pratt. They & defendant Catherine are children of Willis & Letsy Cannon who were formerly husband & wife but have since been divorced. Defendant, Catherine, is the wife of William Pratt, and they were married before 8 February 1838. George Pratt was the father of William Pratt. Letsy Cannon, Jr. is 10 years old. Minos Cannon was mentioned. Willis & Letsy Cannon had conveyed negroes to their children before the divorce, to be divided between them when the youngest came of age. When Catherine married William Pratt Letsy, Sr. loaned them 2 negroes to be returned when called for. William sold one of them and refused to give the other one back. Plaintiffs are suing to get the negroes back. (Ibid 3/61-70)

CANSLER, John
Was the reputed father of a bastard child by Susan Hogan. 9 June 1825 Susan won a judgement against him & Nath. H. Cansler & Richd. Tankersley, his securities, for support of the child. (McM TN, Co Ct Min, no#/201) 9 June 1824, same case, John Cansler pleads guilty. The child is yet unborn. (Ibid 2no#/11) Shown as John Cancillor on 7 September 1825 when he is ordered to pay support for the 2nd & 3rd year. (Ibid 2no#/101)

CANSLER, Nathaniel H.
Died before 7 June 1830 when William Cansler was appointed administrator. (McM TN, Co Ct Min, 2no#/448) A years support was laid off to the widow. (Ibid 458) Polly Cansler was the widow. (Ibid 468) 6 December 1830 the widow, Mary Canslor, petitoned for dower. (Ibid 483)

CANTER, Zechariah [Cauter]
Died before 4 May 1842 as shown in the suit of Wilson C. Carter et al vs Levi Carter et al. The widow's dower in the lands is worth a child's part, or 1/4 part. (Jac TN, Ch Ct Min, A/46) A suit was shown 6 November 1843: Wilson C. Canter, Margaret Halloman, William Wade Halloman by their next friend Dixon Brown vs Sam [or Lin, Levi?] Canter, Mary Canter, James Canter, William P. Holloman and his wife Elizabeth. Zachariah Canter, at his death, owned 80 acres of land. William P. Holloman & wife Elizabeth claim title to 40 acres of said land. (Ibid 120)

CANTERBERY, Wm.
Died before 5 August 1867 when the will was proved by George McCown & James Toomy "to be a true copy of said will as far as relates to the lands devised to Samuel Pate & his wife." (Sev TN, Co Ct Min, no#/469)

CANTRELL, Gabriel
Was the father of a bastard child by Mary Ann Lankford. He was ordered to pay support 7 September 1825. David Cantrell was his security. On the same date Gabriel petitioned the court to have the child made legitimate and change its name from Susannah Lankford to Susannah Cantrell, and made a joint heir, which was granted. (McM TN, Co Ct Min, 2no#/100)

CANTRILL, Sarah
7 November 1785 William Murphy & George Nowland were sworn to appraise a certain piece of land from Aron Lewis to the heirs of Sarah Cantrill. (Was TN, Co Ct Min, 1/266) Sarah was shown as deceased 8 November 1785 when mention was made of her executor. (Ibid 267)

CAPELL, Sam
Probably died before 4 July 1870 when W. H. Tucker was paid for services of jury of inquest. (Dyr TN, Co Ct Min, B/73)

CAPLING, Leonard [Caplinger]
Died before 6 May 1818 when Phillip Fisher was appointed administrator with James Turner & Thomas B. Reece as security. (Wil TN, Co Ct Min, no#/271)

CAPLINGER, John
Died before 2 November 1818 when Jacob Caplinger & Jacob Dees were appointed administrators with Hezekiah Woodward & James Wier, Sr. as security. (Wil TN, Co Ct Min, no#/332)

CAPSLEY, P. F. [Capley]
Died before 6 February 1871 when S. S. Hollowell was appointed administrator, with H. T. Perry and B. H. Harmon as security. W. O. Boykin, John Powell and W. P. Rice were appointed to lay off a years allowance for the widow and family. (Dyr TN, Co Ct Min, B/184)

CARDWELL, John
Died before 6 October 1862 when Joseph L. Cardwell was appointed administrator, the widow releasing her right to administrate. (Sev TN, Co Ct Min, no#/15)

CARLAND, James
Died before 16 September 1816 when the administrators, Martin Tally & Patsy Carland, were ordered to make a report. (Wil TN, Co Ct Min, no#/29)

CARLAND, Joshua
Was an orphan boy of the age of 5 years when he was bound to Joseph Willson, Esqr. on 2 February 1784. He is to be taught the Weaving trade. (Was TN, Co Ct Min, 1/235)

CARLIN, Isiah
Was a bastard child, son of Margaret Carr, of the age of four years the 15th of August last, when he was bound 3 February 1783 to Joseph Willson, Esqr. (Was TN, Co Ct Min, 1/192)

CARLIN, Jas.
Died before 18 December 1816 when William Carlin, John Phillips & Patsey Carlin for herself & the minor heirs, petitioned for a division of the property. (Wil TN, Co Ct Min, no#/65)

CARMACK, Joseph
Died before 21 January 1799 when his will was proved by Abraham Tippy. Mary Carmack & Thomas Johnson were executrix & excutor. (Rob TN, Co Ct Min, 1/83) 19 October 1802 James Bell & Thomas Johnson were executors. (Ibid 233)

CARMICHAEL, Lemuel
Died before 1 January 1866 when the hands living on the farm of Leml Carmichael were ordered to work on a road. (Sev TN, Co Ct Min, no#/255) Daniel Kelly & Louisa Carmichael were executors. The will was contested. (Ibid 306)

CARMILE, Abigale
Was the mother of a natural child begotten on her body by Charles Waddell, who gave bond for it's maintenance 17 May 1796. (Was TN, Co Ct Min, 1/606)

CARNES, Hubbard
Died before 5 February 1866 when John M. Rambo was appointed administrator with F. L. Emert as security. (Sev TN, Co Ct Min, no#/273)

CAROUTH, James
Died before 2 June 1828 when his will was proved by Nathaniel H. Cansler & Samuel McConnell, witnesses. (McM TN, Co Ct Min, 2no#/293)

CARPENTER
3 October 1871 two boys, Alexander Carpenter aged 13 years in January 1872, and John William Carpenter aged 3 years in July last, were bound to A. S. Ray until they are 21 years old. Their father was present in person and consented to indenture. (Dyr TN, Co Ct Min, B/306)

CARR, Dickison
Died before 19 July 1802 when John Carr was appointed administrator, with Laurence Carr & John Sherod as security. (Rob TN, Co Ct Min, 1/224)

CARR, William H.
Died before 26 July 1849 as shown in the suit of John W. Carr Admr. &c of the heirs of W. H. Car decd. vs Elijah Carr & Archibald M. Lindsey, who is a non-resident. (Jac TN, Ch Ct Min, A/342) On 9 February 1855 in the suit of Albert F. Car, John W. Car Admrs. &c &

Albert F. Car, John R. Car, Elijah J. Car, Riley Harris & wife Martha vs Daniel W. Car & others, petition was made to sell slaves and land. It was stated that William Car died intestate in Putnam County, in that portion formerly included in Jackson County. Hannah Car, the widow, was one of the defendants. William H. Botts was guardian ad litem. The parties named in this bill were the heirs of William Car. John W. Car & Albert F. Car were administrators. Hannah Car has not had her dower. (Ibid B/190) Plaintiffs, Riley & Martha, were shown as Harrisons. Other defendants were Wilson Stephens & wife Nancy, Joseph Stephens & wife Sally, Richard E. Mansel, William E. Mansel, Arena K. Mansel, Samuel M. Mansel, Sarah F. Mansel, John R. Mansel & Albert F. Mansel and William H. Botts guardian ad litem for the last 6 named defendants, John Alcorn & wife Elizabeth & Hannah Car, widow of said William Car, deceased. Land & negroes are to be sold for distribution subject to the widow's dower. (Ibid 195) The suit was shown as Albert F. Car, John R. Car, William H. Car, Elijah J. Car, Riley Harrison & wife Martha vs Daniel W. Car, Wilson Stephens & wife Nancy, Joseph Stephens & wife Sally, Richard E. Mansel, William E. Mansell, Sarah F. Mansell, John R. Mansell, John Allcorn & wife Elizabeth, & Hannah Car, widow of William Car, deceased, & Wm. H. Botts, guardian ad litem for the minor defendants. Dower was set off to Hannah Car of land in Putnam County by Isaac Buck, Amos Maxwell and Joseph A. Ray. Another suit the same day had the same parties except for the addition of Arena K. Mansell, Samuel M. Mansell & Albert F. Mansell. There were 6 minor defendants. Land was sold & Albert F. Car became the purchaser. Slaves were also sold & Hannah Car purchased one with A. A. Cox & Elmore Covington as security. All ot the complainants & defendants are heirs of William Car, deceased. (Ibid 253-6)

CARRIGER, Godfrey, Sr.
16 February 1795 made a deed of gift to Godfrey Carriger, Jr., proved by Pharioh Cobb. (Was TN, Co Ct Min, 1/524)

CARROL, Joseph
Was a resident of Madison County, Mississippi Territory, 16 October 1810 when his deposition was to be taken for the defendant in the suit of John Gordon Assee. vs William Black. (Roa TN, Co Ct Min, D/257)

CARROLL, M. B.
Died before 1 August 1870 when C. T. Carroll qualified as executor of the last will and testament, with J. M. Carroll and W. A. Hudson as security. (Dyr TN, Co Ct Min, B/92) The will was proved by W. A. Hudson and H. L. Fowlkes as witness. (Ibid 93)

CARROLL, M. B.
Died before 7 October 1872, intestate, when J. M. Carroll was appointed administrator cum testamento annexo. [It states intestate but the last phrase means "with will annexed."] Smith Parks and Allen Harris were his security. H. L. Fowlkes, W. A. Hudson and L. C. Wynne were appointed to lay off a years allowance for the children of M. B. Carroll, deceased. (Dyr TN, Co Ct Min, B/457)

CARSON, Charles
Died before 16 March 1853 as shown in the suit of Jas. Fussell admr. vs Margaret Carson, Jno. Calhoon? Hawkins, Charles Carson Hawkins and Ruth Matilda Hawkins, minors, who appear by their guardian, Margaret Carson. Charles Carson died intestate, living a non-resident of TN but leaving assets in Madison County, TN. Jas. Fussell was appointed administrator in January 1850. Margaret Carson was the widow. Charles Carson left one son, John Carson, & 3 grand children, viz, Jno. C. Hawkins, Charles C. Hawkins and Ruth M. Hawkins, children of his deceased daughter, Ruth Matilda. The widow is entitled to 1/3, Jno. Carson to 1/3 and the children of Ruth M. Hawkins to 1/3. Jno. Carson died intestate in 1851 since the death of his father, and his mother, Margaret, is entitled to 1/2 of his portion and his nieces & nephews named Hawkins are entitled to the other 1/2. Margaret Carson was appointed guardian of the Hawkins children by the Court of Bowie County, TX, and also appointed the administrator for Jno. Carson. (Mad TN, Ch Ct Min, 1/303, 338)

CARSON, David
12 May 1790 was shown to be the son of William Carson when he was given a road order. (Was TN, Co Ct Min, no#/100)

CARSON, Rachel
Married either John Davidson or David Billings before 19 March 1817 when a marriage contract was entered. Both names are listed and it does not state who the contracting parties were. Joseph Johnson was a witness. (Wil TN, Co Ct Min, no#/95)

CARSON, Robt.
Was shown to be the son of William Carson 12 May 1790 when he was given a road order. (Was TN, Co Ct Min, no#/100)

CARSON, William
Died before 4 September 1826 when Nancy Carson was appointed administratrix. (McM TN, Co Ct Min, 2no#/171)

CARSON, William
Was excused from paying poll tax for 1787 on account of his age. (Was TN, Co Ct Min, 1/368)

CARSON, William
Died before 17 May 1796 when Ruth Carson, John Carson and James Taylor were appointed administrators. David Carson and Robert Carson were security. (Was TN, Co Ct Min, 1/605)

CARSON, Wm.
Died before May term 1790 when the will was proved in open court by John Strain, Esquire & David Carson, who were also issued Letters Testamentry on the estate. (Was TN, Co Ct Min, 1/436)

CARTER
A suit was entered 29 January 1847 by Henry Carter vs James Carter et als, and a cross bill by James Carter vs Henry Carter. The Court decided that Henry Carter, in 1834, left a negro woman named Charlotte and her 2 children in the possession of James Carter. The woman has since had 3 more children. The deeds of gift made by said James to the other parties for said negroes are void, being executed & delivered with a knowledge of the rights of said Henry. (Jac TN, Ch Ct Min, A/257)

CARTER
In a suit filed 26 July 1849 by James A. Manear vs Richard Carter & Henry Carter, it is stated that Richard & Henry Carter are both non-residents and that Richard Carter is indebted to complainant. Land was attached that was fraudulently and wrongfully in the name of Henry Carter when it rightfully belongs to Richard Carter, and should be put to the payment of his debts. (Jac TN, Ch Ct Min, A/337)

CARTER, Betsey
Was a resident of Mecklenberg County, Va, 5 July 1809 when her deposition was to be taken for the defendant in the case of Benjn. Wells vs Wm. Roachel. (Rob TN, Co Ct Min, 2/153)

CARTER, Emanuel
Died before 8 November 1785 when an inventory of the estate was returned by Joseph Greer as administrator. (Was TN, Co Ct Min, 1/267)

CARTER, Ezekiel
Died before 21 June 1841 when his death was suggested in the suit of Walker Guthrie vs B. L. Blake & Ezekiel Carter. John B. Carter was administrator. (Obi TN, Cir Ct Min, 4/no#) 22 June 1842 Sarah Carter petitioned for dower & division of slaves. [It does not state that Sarah was the widow of Ezekiel Carter but that is the only Carter estate in these minutes] (Ibid) On 18 October 1842 the petition was heard: Sarah Carter, John B. Carter, James H. Chappell & Eliza. his wife, Benjamin L. Blake & Martha J. his wife, Tabitha Carter, and Henry Carter, guardian of Mary G. Carter, Hannah E. Carter, James L. Carter, Wesley D. Carter & Joseph D. Carter. [It still does not say these are heirs of Ezekiel Carter.] (Ibid)

CARTER, Jno., Col.
Died before 28 August 1781 when Landon Carter, Esqr. was granted leave of administration on the estate, with Valentine Sevier & Thomas Houghton & Charles Robertson as his security. (Was TN, Co Ct Min, 1/144)

CARTER, John
On the information of Andrew Crockett it is orderd that John Carter be put on the list of those poor to be supported by the county, 10 May 1815. (Cla TN, Co Ct Min, 4/60)

CARTER, John
August term 1788, was ordered to give bond for the maintenance of a Base Born Male Child of the Body of Sarah Medlock, named John. His securities were Thos. Yourley &

David Allison. (Was TN, Co Ct Min, 1/338) John Carter was the reputed father as shown when he was ordered to pay Ten pounds for the expenses and maintenance of the said child for 11 1/2 months past, May term, 1789. (Ibid 380)

CARTER, Landon
Died before 25 September 1807 when land was taxed to the heirs. (Roa TN, Co Ct Min, C/22)

CARTER, William
Died before 14 September 1837 as shown in the suit of Amos McAdams vs Robert L. Landers, administrator of Wm. Carter. McAdams had borrowed money from William Carter in 1836. He had paid part of the money back on 2 January 1837. "Your orator [McAdams] States said Carters house was burnt, and he (said Carter) together with his wife and two or three of his children, and all his furniture, papers &c were also Consumed with the house as he is informed & believes." Robert L. Landers was appointed administrator and brought suit against McAdams for the full amount of the loan from Carter. (Bed TN, Ch Ct Min, 1/294) In the suit of David Orr vs Robert L. Landers it is stated that William Carter died in January 1837 and that there are 8 heirs. Larkin Orr & Martha Orr his wife, who is one of the children of William Carter, were entitled to one share but sold it to David Orr. William Carter in his lifetime had been the security of Larkin B. Orr as the guardian of the minor children of Joseph M. Elworth. A settlement is shown. (Ibid 546-553)

CARTER, William
Was a resident of Rhea County on 5 December 1827 when his deposition was to be taken for the plaintiff in the case of William McCormick vs James Shelton. (McM TN, Co Ct Min, no#/286)

CARTER, Wm. H.
Died before 2 October 1871 when Smith Parks was chosen and appointed guardian of Nancy J. and Walker A. Carter, minor heirs, with A. L. Parks and H. Parks, Jr. as security. (Dyr TN. Co Ct Min, B/296)

CARTMEL, Nathaniel
24 March 1823 made a deed of gift to "my beloved friend Jeremiah B. McWherter and Lucinda D. McWhirter," of stock & cattle. (Wil TN, Reg Bk/290)

CARTWRIGHT, Hezekiah
Died before 7 August 1818 when Elizabeth Cartwight, John Cartwright & George Clark were appointed administrators, with John Laurence, Richard Cartwright, George Cooper, Robert W. P. Pool, William Donnell, Petis Ragland & Willam Mohollon as security. Elizabeth Cartwright was the widow. (Wil TN, Co Ct Min, no#/322) William Moholland & Elizabeth Cartwright were appointed guardian for Matthew T. Cartwright, Edward W. Cartwright, Wm. L. Cartwright, Penelope Cartwright, Peter A. Cartwright & James N. Cartwright, minor heirs. (Ibid 333) Hezekiah Cartwright, minor heir, chose Robert Pool for his guardian. (Ibid 334) Benijah Cartwright & Hannah S. Cartwright, minor heirs of Hezekiah Cartwright, deceased, chose Richard Cartwright as their guardian. Lucinda Cartwright, another minor heir, chose John Cartwright as her guardian. (Ibid, no page number, inserted between pages 334 & 335)

CARTWRIGHT, Matthew
Died before 19 November 1824 when John & Susannah Hallum of Pike County, MS, gave power of attorney to Matthew Cartwright of Pike County, MS, to receive their part of the estate of Matthew Cartwright, deceased, of Wilson County, TN. The amount when collected is to be paid to John Cartwright of Pike County, MS, who has purchased the share of John & Susannah Hallum. (Wil TN, Reg Bk/354)

CARTWRIGHT, Robert
In January 1813 sold to his brother, Jesse Cartwright of the parish of Pointcouper, State of LA, all of his claim to the estate of his father now in possession of his mother. His father is now deceased and his mother has a life estate [neither parent named]. (Wil TN, Reg Bk/94)

CARUTHERS, J. F.
Died before 4 July 1870 when S. S. Hollowell was appointed administrator, with J. Q. Craig & J. S. Moore as security. (Dyr TN, Co Ct Min, B/71) W. N. Beasly, R. C. Coffman and J. Q. Craig were appointed to lay off a years allowance for the widow and family. (Ibid 76) 4 January 1871 M. J. Caruthers petitioned for dower. J. F. Caruthers died in 1870 and Charles Caruthers is his only heir. (Ibid 175-6)

CARUTHERS, James
Probably died before 1 July 1872 when his estate and his heirs were mentioned in the suit of Stoddard Caruthers vs N. J. Sorrell et als. The estate has been charged with taxes and the land was sold to N. J. Sorrell and others in 1869. (Dyr TN, Co Ct Min, B/431)

CARUTHERS, James, Sr.
Died in March 1863 leaving a will appointing his son, William Caruthers, executor. William died before qualifing and Joseph H. Caruthers was appointed administrator with the will annexed. Joseph H., Stoddert and Susan Medora are the unmarried children and Sallie Parker Carrithers is a minor child of the deceased. His grand daughter, Fannie Freeman, is also a minor and is to be treated as one of his children. Jno. S. Brown was appointed guardian of Sallie Parker Caruthers, Wm. Caruthers, Jr., Fannie Caruthers and Fannie Freeman. James Caruthers, Jr. died in December 1864, leaving neither wife nor children. Joseph H. Caruthers was also the administrator for James, Jr. James Caruthers, Sr. owned land in Madison, Dyer, McNairy, Tipton, Lauderdale & Obion Counties. There are various entries showing this estate and heirs, Laura E. McClanahan, formerly Laura E. Caruthers, Susan Eudora Caurthers, Stoddert Carithers and Sallie Parker Caruthers as the children of James, Sr., and Fannie Freeman, William Carithers, Jr. and Fannie Carithers as the grand children. He left no wife surviving him. The land was sold 20 February 1868. (Mad TN, Ch Ct Min, 2/503, 509, 535-7, 3/152-6)

CARVER, Hiram C.
Died before 28 January 1848 as shown in the suit of Aletha Carver, et al vs Cornelius Carver. A contract between Hiram C. Carver and Cornelius Carver was mentioned. Aletha Carver was administratrix of Hiram C. Carver. (Jac TN, Ch Ct Min, A/306)

CARVER, Plesant
4 January 1859 was released from paying poll tax as he is over age. (Sev TN, Co Ct Min, no#/384)

CARY, Patsy
Died before 13 May 1817 when William Whitehead, security for William Cary, administrator on the estate of Patsy Cary, deceased, petitioned the court to have the administrator make a report. (Cla TN, Co Ct Min, 4/336)

CARY, Robert
Died before 12 November 1816 as shown when commissioners were appointed to value Nathaniel Cary's part of the lands of Robert Cary, deceased, as divised to him by the will of Robert Cary. (Cla TN, Co Ct Min, 4/262) William Cary was guardian of the minor heirs of Robert Cary, deceased. (Ibid 378)

CARY, William
Died before 14 November 1815 when Wm. Cary, Sr. was appointed administrator with George Yoakum as security. (Cla TN, Co Ct Min, 4/126)

CASH, Clark
Was a minor 10 February 1860 as shown in the suit of Clark Cash by next friend &c vs George W. Christian & others. Process is to issue against Clark Cash & Thomas Eldrige and said Eldrige to answer for himself and as regular guardian of said minor. (Jac TN, Ch Ct Min, C/313)

CASH, L. C. R.
Was a minor 15 August 1868 as shown in the suit of Jno. E. Cash vs L. C. R. Cash. The defendant is a minor and the complainant is her regular guardian. Thomas H. Drake was appointed guardian ad litem for this suit. (Mad TN, Ch Ct Min, 3/190) Shown as Lucretia E. R. Cash. (Ibid 234)

CASON
In a suit shown 14 July 1859 by Robert A. Cox and Edward M. Cason, land was sold to Thomas H. Butler and title divested out of complainants and defendants Robert A. Cox, and Edward M. Cason, Sally G. Cason, William Pully [Putty?] and his wife Adeline, William Speakman & his wife Frances, Loyd? C. Mahany & his wife Emaline, John C. Mahaney, Sarah L. Mahaney, Elizabeth Mahaney, Milan F. Mahaney, Edward P. Mahaney, Josephine D. Cason, Eliza L. Cason, Henry H. Cason, Lewis B. Cason, Tandy W. Cason and Millard F. Cason. It does not say whose estate was sold. (Jac TN, Ch Ct Min, C/256)

CASON, Edward S.
Probably died before 11 February 1859. [The writing is terrible and I can't be sure.] In a

suit entered on above date by Robert? A. Cox vs James N. Tolbert admr. &c et als, land was sold and the court is to decide "how much money is yet owing by Compt. & Edward S. Cason decd....how much said Edward S. Cason in his lifetime paid...how much is owing to compt.? Edward M. Cason by said E. S. Cason under the deed in trust set up & referred to in his answer...how much is owing to compt. by said Edward S. Cason." (Jac TN, Ch Ct Min, C/192) James R. Talbert was the administrator and Sarah G. Cason was the widow of Edward S. Cason, deceased. (Ibid 203)

CASON, James
Probably died before 30 July 1846 as shown in the suit of N. M. Cox next friend &c vs E. M. Cason & Gore. The Court found that the deed executed by James Cason to defendant Cason was executed since the making of his will by said James Cason & was not procured by fraud or undue influence, and that James Cason was of sound mind and that said deed revoked the will. (Jac TN, Ch Ct Min, A/222) Susan Cason brought suit against Edward M. Cason & Morrice [Mounce] Gore. Gore is to proceed to execute the last will and testament of James Cason, deceased, for the same is not revoked by the deed executed by testator to Edward M. Cason. (Ibid 318)

CASON, Thompson [Caison]
Died before 7 February 1855 as shown in the suit of Joel W. Settle vs Edward M. Cason & Robt. A. Cox, administrators of Thompson Cason, deceased, & others. Elizabeth Cason was the widow and Becca & James his only children, who are minors, & Elizabeth Cason is their guardian. (Jac TN, Ch Ct Min, B/186) A suit was entered 18 July 1856 by Elizabeth Cason vs Rebecca Ann Cason, James Cason, Edward M. Cason & Robert A. Cox. This was combined with the case of Allen W. DeWitt Admr. vs William H. Botts, James A. Spurlock, Edward M. Cason, Robert A. Cox, Elizabeth Cason, Becky Ann Cason and James Cason. Elizabeth has not had her dower. (Ibid C/32) Thompson Cason died about 17 October 1854. (Ibid 145)

CASTEEL, Edmond
Died before 7 March 1831 when Elizabeth Casteel & Barney Casteel were appointed administrators. (McM TN, Co Ct Min, 2no#/505) 6 June 1831 his will was entered & proved by Hesekiah Randolph, one of the witnesses. Randolph said the original will was lost & this is a copy & he has his doubts that the testator was of sound mind when he made same. Same date the security for Barney & Betsey Casteel asked to be released as they were making waste of the estate. (Ibid 538)

CATE, Charles
Died before 6 September 1824 when his will was proved by Joab Hill & Eligah Hurst. (McM TN, Co Ct Min, 2no#/22) 6 December 1824 the will was also proved by William Terry. (Ibid 33) Lucy Cate & Elijah Cate were administrators. (Ibid 155)

CATE, Elisha
4 October 1858 was released from paying poll tax as he is over 50 years of age. (Sev TN, Co Ct Min, no#/352)

CATE, Geo. W.
Was released from paying poll tax for 1859 having removed from the county before that year. (Sev TN, Co Ct Min, no#/453)

CATE, Margaret
3 July 1865 was paid her husbands per Diam for attending Courts. (Sev TN, Co Ct Min, no#/175)

CATHEY, John
Died in 1852, intestate, leaving Alexander H., John B. and Susan E. who has married William Kimbrell, his only children & heirs. Alexander H. Cathey was appointed administrator. (Mad TN, Ch Ct Min, 2/38) 19 Feb 1857 the heirs were shown to be Jno. B. Cathey, George S. Fite & Susan E. Fite, James Kimbrel & Margaret A. Kimbrell, William B. Kimbrel & Ann B. Kimbrell, in addition to Alexander H. Cathey who purchased the land. (Ibid 119)

CATHEY, Wiley
Died before 21 February 1843 when his death was suggested in the suit of Wiley Cathey vs Reuben Hammett. (Obi TN, Cir Ct Min, 4/no#) Abner Harris was the administrator as shown 19 June 1843. (Ibid)

CATLETT, A. C.
Died before 6 August 1866 when H. S. Catlett was appointed administrator with Thomas Sharp & L. H. Catlett as security. (Sev TN, Co Ct Min, no#/360)

CATLETT, J. E.
Was released from paying poll tax for 1854, he being under age 21. (Sev. TN, Co Ct Min, no#/318)

CATLETT, John
Died before 2 June 1862 when Austin Mott & William Low were appointed administrators. This entry was then crossed out. (Sev TN, Co Ct Min, no#/782) Re-entered 7 July 1862 when Joshua H. Atchley was appointed administrator. (Ibid 1) Joshua H. Atchley & wife vs George W. Catlett & others, petition to sell land. (Ibid 43) Part of the heirs are non-residents. (Ibid 50)

CATLETT, Lafayett
Was a boy of color 2 April 1867 when it was ordered that he be placed in the care of J. P. Catlett "if he is in a condition to go about if not in such condition he is to be taken to the Poor house." (Sev TN, Co Ct Min, no#/446)

CATO, Daniel
Died before 3 May 1814 when Henry Cato was appointed administrator, with David Bradford & John Allen as security. (Ste TN, Co Ct Min, 4/143)

CATO, Rufus
Was an orphan boy aged 15 years when he was bound 2 August 1814 to Alsey Bradford until age 21. (Ste TN, Co Ct Min, 4/175)

CATRIN, John, Jr.
24 February 1859 filed suit by his guardian, Joseph R. Wesly [Mosly], vs Murdock M. McKay. The complainant is owner of an undivided 1/3 of 1/2 of a tract of land originally owned by Peter R. Rooker & James Walker. A portion of the land is claimed by the defendant who lives upon the land & sets up a pretended title to complainants interest by virtue of a purchase made from O. P. Catrin, the guardian of complainant, on 15 December 1849. The sale is void and complainant to be let into possession with said McKay as tenants in common. (Mad TN, Ch Ct Min, 2/266)

CATT, Solomon P.
10 May 1830 took the oath of allegiance to become a citizen of the United States. He is from the United Kingdon of Great Brittan and has been in this country more than 5 years. He has been a citizen of this state more than 1 year, and is a man of good moral character. (Obi TN, Cir Ct Min, 1/109) On 11 May 1830 Soloman P. Catt petitioned the Court to change his name to Solomon P. Catoe, his wife's name to Jane Catoe and his daughter's name to Mary Jane Catoe. The petition was granted. (Ibid 117)

CAWTHON, Thomas, Sr.
On 15 September 1815 sold to James H. Cawthon, his heirs &c, "one negro boy Sam, one negro woman Molly, two head of horses, six head of cattle, eight head of sheep, twenty five head of hoggs, four feather Beds together with other household and kitchen furniture of all I, the said Thomas Cauthon hath on earth, the growing crop of corn and cotton, likewise, to the title of which I, the said Thomas Cauthon do give up all my right having recieved payment for the above articles." (Wil TN, Reg Bk/40)

CEARLEY, Samuel
Died before 5 June 1871 when Luke Cearley was chosen and appointed guardian of the minor heirs with E. M. Hall and Thomas Fitzhugh as security. (Dyr TN, Co Ct Min, B/242)

CERBY, Sarah, Mrs.
Made a deed of gift to her children, Nancy Cerby, William B. Cerby, John M. Cerby, Elias R. Cerby & Susan Ann Cerby, 20 March 1820. Stock & household goods are listed to each child, with Joshua Kelly & Paul P. Kelly as witness. (Wil TN, Reg Bk/168)

CHADDOCK, Alexander
3 February 1818 was bound as an apprentice to Samuel W. Sherrill until age 21. (Wil TN, Co Ct Min, no#/227)

CHAFFIN, Susan
Sued Joseph Chaffin for divorce 10 August 1860. It was stated that the two were never

legally married, that there was no license and that said marriage was never solomnized. It is therefore declared null & void. (Jac TN, Ch Ct Min, C/379)

CHALFIN, Robert
Died before 15 December 1817 when the will was proved by Richard Bryant & William Allen. (Wil TN, Co Ct Min, no#/187)

CHAMBERLAIN, Charles
Died before 29 August 1860 as shown in the suit of V. B. Woolfolk Admr. of Geo. Chamberlain vs Jesse Gray Executor of Amos Williams. Amos Williams had been appointed administrator of Charles Chamberlain, deceased, who left 7 children. One of the children of Charles Chamberlain was George Chamberlain, and V. B. Woolfolk was the administrator of George Chamberlain. George was entitled to 1/7 of the estate of Charles Chamberlain. (Mad TN, Ch Ct Min, 2/281) On 29 February 1844 Charles Chamberlain executed a deed of trust to Amos Williams as trustee for Charles' daughter, Polly Jones. The deed gave Polly all his property provided "said Charles be kept in possession of said property and decently supported during his life. At his death said Williams was to divide the whole of said estate amongst all his children." Charles died in July or August 1850 at the age of 89. He left 7 children. Polly Jones is of weak mind & easily imposed upon. Williams convinced her to sell him her interest in the estate in October 1850. He concealed from her the true value of the estate. The deceased husband of Polly Jones was Reason Burns [Burus]. A division of the estate of Charles Chamberlain had been made in 1853. The sale to Williams was declared void and Polly is entitled to an accounting from the estate of Amos Williams and her 1/7 part of the estate of Charles Chamberlain. An appeal was granted to Jesse Gray, executor of Amos Williams. (Ibid 382) On the same date as above Charles Chamberlain also executed a deed of trust to Amos Williams for his daughter, Patsy Muns, & then to her children after her death. [Amos Williams also cheated Patsy out of her share with same decision as above]. [Charles Chamberlain was another child who sold Williams his share]. (Ibid 384) Susan A. & William J. Muns are the only children of Patsy. The husband of Susan A. was Jno. A Muns [Muus]. V. B. Woolfolk is also a party to the suit as he had bought Patsy's share. William J. Muns was a minor. (Ibid 396)

CHAMBERLAIN, Mariah Susan
7 August 1871 Jno. L. Webb was chosen and appointed guardian, with Susan S. Key and W. S. Davis as security. (Dyr TN, Co Ct Min, B/263)

CHAMBERLAIN, Saml.
Was the father of a bastard child by Susannah Housman. He was ordered to pay support for the child for 5 years, 5 May 1819. (Wil TN, Co Ct Min, no#/456)

CHAMBERLAIN, Willis
6 March 1871, D. E. Parker made a settlement as administrator. [does not say deceased] (Dyr TN, Co Ct Min, B/201)

CHAMBERS, Elisabeth
20 April 1801 was bound as an apprentice to Thos. Norris, Sr. until age 18. (Rob TN, Co Ct Min, 1/170)

CHAMBERS, James
Died before 3 October 1870 when the will was proved by J. K. Strayhorn and F. M. Baker as witness. (Dyr TN, Co Ct Min, B/99) W. S. Chambers was appointed administrator with the will annexed, with J. H. Davis and W. P. Thompson as his security. (Ibid 106)

CHAMBERS, John
Was a resident of Green County 6 November 1783 when his deposition was to be taken for John Davis, defendant, at the suit of Lenox Taylor. (Was TN, Co Ct Min, 1/233)

CHAMBERS, Rachel Jane
Was the mother of a female bastard child. [Jesse Hill was probably the father.] George Russell & William J. Chambers gave bond for its maintenance 1 October 1860. (Sev TN, Co Ct Min, no#/607)

CHAMBERS, Sarah
5 October 1863 was ordered to be brought to court to be bound out. (Sev TN, Co Ct Min, no#/78)

CHAMBERS, Sarah W.
9 March 1852 dismissed her suit against Charles P. Chambers. (Mad TN, Ch Ct Min,

1/229)   17 September 1852 Sarah W. Chambers was granted a divorce from Cha. P Chambers for desertion. (Ibid 278)

CHANCY, Hesaciah
22 May 1780 was ordered to give bond for his appearance from day to day on "suggestion that sd Hesachiah Chancy having ravished and Deflourd a certain Ann Carr." Rudolph Rutherford was charged with aiding and assisting Hezekiah Chancy in committing a rape on the body of Ann Carr. (Was TN, Co Ct Min, 1/106)   Mary Carr was mentioned in the suit of Walter Carr vs Hezachiah Chaney. (Ibid 117)

CHANDLER, Anna
11 November 1811 was to be let to the lowest bidder. (Rob TN, Co Ct Min, 3/31)

CHANDLER, Joseph
Died before 4 April 1859 when Calvin Johnson was appointed administrator with J. M. Evans & Andrew Cusick as security. (Sev TN, Co Ct Min, no#/423)   B. J. Tipton, S. W. Randle & Wm. Wayland were appointed to set apart a years provision for Catherine Chandler, widow, & family. (Ibid 426)

CHANDLER, Parks
Died in 1845 leaving a will, as shown in the suit of Jno. C. Chandler et als vs Jno. W. Chandler et al. He left all his property to his wife & at her death to be equally divided between his children. Eli Chandler, deceased, was one of the sons and heirs of Parks Chandler & father of defendant, Jno. W. Chandler. Eli Chandler had purchased land as trustee for the widow & heirs of Parks Chandler. Louisa Chandler has departed this life. Complainant John Irvin is administrator de bonis non of Parks Chandler's estate. Complainants Wm. R. Chandler, Martha Chandler, Mary Young, Matilda DeJournet, John C. Chandler, Ryland J. Chandler, Carroll Chandler, Bluford Chandler & defendants Jno. W. & Joseph Chandler are the children & grand children of the said Parks Chandler & tenants in common of the land. [This is all dim and the names hard to read.] (Mad TN, Ch Ct Min, 2/324 & 428)   The land was sold 23 February 1866 and title divested out of William R. Chandler, Martha Chandler, John Young & wife Mary formerly Chandler, John DeJarnet & wife Matilda formerly Chandler, Ryland J. Chandler, Carroll Chandler, Bluford Chandler, Joseph Chandler & Jno. W. Chandler. (Ibid 490)

CHANDLER, Robert
Died before 23 September 1805 when the will was proved by William Bloodworth & Adam Tyrone. Sarah Chandler was sworn as executrix. (Wil TN, Co Ct Min, no#/162)

CHANDLER, Wm.
Died before 8 April 1856 when Timothy Chandler was appointed guardian to Rebecca E. Chandler, Narcissa Chandler, John Chandler and Joseph Chandler, minor heirs. B. M. Chandler was his security. B. M. Chandler had been the guardian and he resigned. (Sev TN, Co Ct Min, no#/32)

CHAPMAN, George
Was the reputed father of the child of Polly Pankey. 22 April 1800 he gave bond with Wm. Dorris & John Crunk as security. (Rob TN, Co Ct Min, 1/134)

CHAPMAN, Mary
Was a minor 17 March 1854 when Geo. Chapman was appointed guardian ad litem to defend in her place the suit of Dawson Bond et als vs Wm. Jones et als. (Mad TN, Ch Ct Min, 1/362)

CHAPPELL, Humphrey
6 May 1818 gave bond to come into court to answer a charge of Bastardy. (Wil TN, Co Ct Min, no#/264)   He pleaded guilty and gave bond for the support of the child of Nancy Graves. (Ibid 266)

CHAPPELL, Jno. L.
Died before 19 February 1858 as shown in the suit of Robt. A. Connally vs Archibald Rogers admr., Margaret Chappell a minor without a guardian who defends by A. Rogers guardian ad litem. Margaret is the only heir. (Mad TN, Ch Ct Min, 2/192)   Joseph [sic] Chappell died intestate in 1856 leaving Margaret Chappell his only heir. A. S. Rogers was appointed administrator at January term 1857. (Ibid 330)   In apparently the same suit the deceased is listed as J. R. Chappell. (Ibid 482)

CHARBLE, Jacob
28 August 1778 took the oath of allegiance. (Was TN, Co Ct Min, 1/47)

CHARMICHAEL, Lemuel
Died before 3 April 1865 when the will was proved by Samuel Mount and Robert R. Bryan as witness. Elizabeth Green & other heirs opposed the will & the will was not admitted until the contesting parties be notified to appear. (Sev TN, Co Ct Min, no#/152)

CHEATHAM
9 November 1813 a deed was recorded from Anderson Cheatham, William B. Cheatham, John B. Cheatham, Thomas Cheatham, Edward Cheatham, Peter Cheatham & the heirs of Giles Joyner to Joseph Washington & Archer Cheatham. (Rob TN, Co Ct Min, 3/328)

CHEATHAM, Archer
Died before 22 January 1800 when the administrators, Anderson Cheatham & Edward Cheatham, returned the inventory of the estate. (Rob TN, Co Ct Min, 1/127)

CHEATHAM, Olive
13 August 1814 Archer Cheatham was appointed administrator on the estate of Olive Cheatham, formerly Olive Deloach, with John Hutchison & Thomas Claiborne as security. [does not say Olive is deceased.] (Rob TN, Co Ct Min, 3/486)

CHEEK, Jeremiah
Died in 1823 as shown in the suit of Richard Mitchell & Cynthia H. his wife, Labitha R., Eli C., Elvina M., Susan J., Jeremiah J. and Elizabeth M. Ownly, minors, who sue by their guardian Edward Ownly, Edward Doyl & wife Labitha, Edmund R. Cheek, Eli Cheek, Arthur Alexander & wife Nancy, all citizens of Marshall County, TN, against Hugh Huston, Benjamin R. Cheek and Thomas D. Cheek also of Marshall County. These are some of the heirs of Jeremiah Cheek, deceased. Cynthia H. Mitchel and the Ownly minors listed are the heirs of Polly Ownly, deceased, who was a daughter of said Jeremiah Cheek. Labitha Doyle, Edmund R. Cheek, Eli Cheek and Nancy Alexander are children of said Jeremiah Cheek, deceased. Defendants Benjamin R. & Thomas D. Cheek and James & Jeremiah Cheek and Pattey Kaverns? are the balance of the children. Jeremiah left a will which was proved in Bedford County where he then lived. Hugh Houston & Benjamin R. Cheek were executors. The widow was Labitha [Tabitha] Cheek who died in 1834. The land was part in Bedford & part in Marshall County. The land was sold in May 1834 and at that time Edward Ownly lived in Sumner County. (Bed TN, Ch Ct Min, 1/147) The first sale was declared void and land was to be sold again. Benj. R. Cheek is to have no part of the distribution. (Ibid 2/37)

CHERRY, Cary
Died about July 1859 as shown in the suit of John W. Condran?, Sarah L. Condras?, Jackson T. Wood, Isabella Wood, J. C. Pennington, Loser M. Pennington, Sebert E. Jenkins, Mary J. Jenkins, Oliver T. Butler & Prudence L. Butler vs Wilson C. Cherry, Lemuel B. Cherry, John M. Cherry, Cary S. Cherry & Isabella Cherry. Defendant Isabella Cherry was his widow and is entitled to dower. Complainants & defendants are all over 21 and by their agreement, the rest of the land & negroes are to be sold. The Court is to take proof as to advancements made to either complainants or defendants by Cary Cherry in his lifetime. Isabella, the widow, is in a very low state of health and the other parties agree that if her life estate in said dower interest terminate before the next term of court, that it be sold also. (Jac TN, Ch Ct Min, C/324) This suit was shown as John W. Condra, Sarah T. Condra, Sebret E. Jenkins, Mary Jane Jenkins, Isaioh [or Jacob?] C. Penington, Manerva Penington, Oliver T. Butler, Lucinda Butler, Jackson T. Wood and Isabella Wood vs Lemuel B. Cherry, Cory S. Chery, John M. Chery, Wilson C. Chery and Isabella Cherry. Land and negros were sold. (Ibid 355) He had made advancements to Wilson C. Cherry, John M. Cherry, Lemuel B. Cherry, Cary C. Cherry, Jackson T. Wood & wife, Oliver H. Butler & wife, John W. Condra & wife, Sebert E. Jenkins & wife and Josiah C. Pennington & wife. (Ibid 409)

CHERRY, D. H.
4 January 1872, J. S. Spence made a settlement as guardian. (Dyr TN, Co Ct Min, B/358)

CHERRY, Daniel
Died before 14 January 1847 as shown in a suit concerning the estate of Moore Stevenson. Norman T. Cherry and Calvin W. Cherry were executors. (Mad TN, Ch Ct Min, 1/13) 14 July 1847 Matilda McIver had a suit vs the executors. (Ibid 26) Another suit on 14 July 1848: Norman T. & Calvin W. Cherry Executors of Danl Cherry deceased, John Harbert & wife Narcissa, Hiram Parte [Patee] & wife Lorania [Louania?], Henry Jones, Norman Jones, Mary Jones, Daniel Jones & Calvin H. Jones, children of Louisa J. Jones, formerly Louisa J. Cherry, by their guardian Edward K. Jones, Edward J. Read & Drusilla B. his wife, Eason Jones & Belinda his wife, Hiram Partee & Masilla [Mozella] his wife, Alvira [Almira] Cherry by her next friend Calvin W. Cherry, Sally Cherry & Norman T.

& Calvin W. Cherry heirs and distributees of Danl Cherry deceased vs Beverly Young and vs James Wright. Daniel Cherry died on the 30th day of November 1843, leaving a will. Executors & claimants are the only heirs. (Ibid 47, 63,114)

CHERRY, Daniel
Died before 11 March 1845 when land was taxed to the heirs. (Obi TN, Cir Ct Min, 4/no#)

CHERRY, Daniel
Was a resident of Haywood County, TN, 9 October 1828 when he gave power of attorney to Burchett Douglass of Wilson County to sell land in Wilson. (Wil TN, Reg Bk/396) [second set of page numbers.]

CHERRY, Darling
Was a resident of NC 4 May 1819 when his signature was proved by Daniel Cherry as witness to a title bond from Willie Cherry to James Cherry. (Wil TN, Co Ct Min, no#/446)

CHERRY, Lemuel
Died before 1 August 1870 when W. V. Redding was chosen and appointed guardian of W. M. Edwards, minor heir. (Dyr TN, Co Ct Min, B/88)

CHERRY, Wiley
Died before 26 March 1806 when the will was proved by Thomas Seawell & William Wilson. Nansey Cherry & Daniel Cherry & John Brown were sworn as executors. (Wil TN, Co Ct Min, no#/193) 24 August 1816 Darling Cherry of Marton County, NC, gave power of attorney to Daniel Cherry of Wilson County, TN, to sell lands he got by the will of Wiley Cherry, deceased. (Ibid, Reg Bk/197)

CHESTER, Archibald G.
Died before 21 October 1840 when his death was suggested in the suit of Archibald G. Chester & Robert J. Chester vs John F. Rivers. (Obi TN, Cir Ct Min, 4/no#)

CHEW, John Drury
Died before 29 May 1781 when the will was proved by Sarah Calhon & Martha Parson, which said witnesses made oath that they saw John Calhoon and Lucrecey Calhoon witness and sign their names to the will in the presence of John Drury Chew, the testator. Martha Calhoon, executor, was ordered to take into her custody the estate of John Drury Chew. (Was TN, Co Ct Min, 1/132)

CHICK, Abraham [Cheek]
Died before 14 February 1815 when Elisha Chick [Chuk] was appointed administrator with Warren Paine & George Bigbe as security. (Rob TN, Co Ct Min, 3/539)

CHILDERS, Elizabeth
Died before 11 March 1845 when land was taxed to the heirs. (Obi TN, Cir Ct Min, 4/no#)

CHILDERS, John
4 July 1870 it was ordered that a special allowance be paid to the Blind Asylum for clothing for John Childers. (Dyr TN, Co Ct Min, B/76)

CHILDERS, John
Taxes were not collected in District 5 for 1873, "can't be found." (Dyr TN, Co Ct Min, B/759)

CHILDRESS, Isaac
26 February 1807 a jury was appointed to inquire into the condition of Isaac Childress who is reported to be unable to support himself because of bodily infirmities. Jos. Powel was ordered to care for him until next court. (Cla TN, Co Ct Min, 3/63) Isaac Childress was let to Abner Childress for support until next court. (Ibid 133) Isaac Childress was let to Timothy Phillpot for John Childress until next court. (Ibid 174) He was let to John Bullard 11 May 1815. (Ibid 4/68 & 156)

CHILDRESS, Jacob
Was bound 7 February 1804 to Jacob Pinkley until age 21. (Rob TN, Co Ct Min, 1/285)

CHILDRESS, John
21 October 1803 was bound to Danl. Pinkley until age 21. (Rob TN, Co Ct Min, 1/277)

CHILDRESS, Joseph
Was an orphan 6 May 1806 when he was bound to Henry Fry until age 21. (Rob TN, Co Ct Min, 1/390)

CHILDS, Thomas
Was living in Madison County, Mississippi Territory, 23 April 1812 when his deposition was to be taken for the plaintiff in the case of Joseph Frost vs John Hawkins. (Roa TN, Co Ct Min, D/387)

CHISM, James
Died before 5 November 1840 when the heirs petitioned for sale of land. Nancy Trigg Chism and Priscilla Frances Chism by their guardian, Monna [Mounce] Gore, and Ann Frances Chism, the former minor heirs and the later the widow of James Chism who died intestate. (Jac TN, Ch Ct Min, A/5) Suit was brought 18 July 1856 by George M. McWhirter vs Reuben Beck, Ann Beck, James T. Quarles, Mourice Gore & Toliver Kirkpatrick. An account is to be made of the funds in the hands of complainant as Clerk & Master belonging to the estate of James Chism, deceased, the amount paid to the administrator James T. Quarles, the amount paid to Ann Beck as the widow of said deceased, and the amount paid to the guardian of the minor children. (Ibid C/25) 6 February 1857 Reubin Beck was shown to be guardian of Nancy T. Chism and Priscilla Chism. (Ibid 69)

CHISUM, John
Gave a power of attorney to James Chisum on certificate of two justices of Jackson County, 3 November 1806. (Rob TN, Co Ct Min, 1/412)

CHITMAN, Mary A.
21 February 1867 was granted a divorce from Fred Chitman for desertion. They were married in 1854 and he deserted her in 1856. He has refused to return & live with her. (Mad TN, Ch Ct Min, 3/38)

CHITWOOD, James
5 May 1783 John McMahone, Esqr. "petitioned the Court that James Chitwood was Indebted to him a sum of money & that said Chitwood was Inimical to the United States and was therefore executed. The petitioner prays a Jury to Try his cause according to Law." (Was TN, Co Ct Min, 1/206)

CHOATE, Mary
28 February 1782 was ordered to appear at next court to show cause if any, why her children should not be bound out. (Was TN, Co Ct Min, 1/156)

CHOATE, Thos.
Died before 24 November 1778 when Ann Choate qualified as administratrix, with Elij. Smith, James Hollis & Robert Sevier as her security. (Was TN, Co Ct Min, 1/51) 6 May 1783 a release was given from Austin Choate to Squire Smith, Sarah Smith, John Smith, Thomas Smith, of his right Title Claim and demand unto the estate of Thomas Choate, proven by Emanuel Carter, Ezekiel Smith & William Cocke, Esq. (Ibid 209)

CHOTE, Isaac
15 August 1782 it was ordered that he be executed on the 10th day of September next. (Was TN, Co Ct Min, 1/178)

CHOWNING, John
3 October 1808 made a deed of gift to his children, Jane Payne, Sarah Holman, Thos. Chowning, Elisabeth Choate, Jno. Chowning, Robert G. Chowning, Letisha Chowning & Richard Chowning, proved by Augustine Cook, Martin Walton & Chloe Walton. (Rob TN. Co Ct Min, 2/80)

CHRISMAS, Lewis
Taxes were not collected in District 4 for 1873, "insolvent." (Dyr TN, Co Ct Min, B/759)

CHRISTIANBURY, John
Died before 15 March 1802 when Elizabeth Christianbury, the widow, was granted letters of administration, with Little Page Sims, Joshua Christianbury and Gray Sims as her securities. (Roa TN, Co Ct Min, A/12)

CHRISTIE, Elizabeth
16 May 1833 her guardian, Will. M. Wilson, was in a case. (Obi TN, Cir Ct Min, 2/87 & 3/61) 21 February 1837 the death of William M. Wilson was admitted and John C. Wilson

was appointed guardian of Elizabeth Christie, as shown in their suit against Moses Parr & Charles M. Owens. The death of Moses Parr was also suggested and not denied. (Ibid 3/91) John Parr was administrator for Moses Parr. (Ibid 132)

CHRONISTER, W. E.
Died before 4 December 1871 when W. N. Beasley was appointed administrator, with F. H. Benten and J. H. Reddick as his security. E. Stevenson, H. N. Mount and Wyatt Ferguson were appointed to lay off a years allowance for the widow and family. (Dyr TN, Co Ct Min, B/323-4) Shown as W. C. Chronister. (Ibid 358)

CLACK, Jesse
Died before March term 1826 as shown in the case of James Rud vs John Cauthron. The plaintiff was one of the heirs of Jesse Clack. The defendant was administrator de bonis non. James Rud was entitled to one fourth of the estate. The widow of Jesse Clack married William H. Blackburn who is now deceased. (Wil TN, Reg Bk/379) [second set of page numbers]

CLARDY, Joseph
Died before 13 August 1838 as shown in the suit of Moffat & Marbery admrs. vs Mary Ann Clardy & others. Leonard C. Marbery and Robert Moffat were administrators of Joseph Clardy, deceased, and were authorized to sell a slave to pay debts. (Bed TN, Ch Ct Min, 2/32)

CLARDY, Richard S.
Died in 1834 as shown in the suit of Theodocia H. Clardy vs George W. Hobbs & wife Sarah, John M. James B. Allen Ann Noble L. Nancy E. Caroline P. Theodocia & Richard S. Clardy, filed 12 June 1841. Theodocia H. is the widow. Richard S. Clardy left a will. Robert H. Majors was the brother of Theodicia H. Clardy. There are now living 9 children of Richard S. Clardy, to wit, John M. Clardy, James B. Clardy, Sarah Hobbs wife of George W. Hobbs, Mary Ann Noble L. Nancy E. Caroline P. Theodocia & Richard S. Clardy, all of whom are minors without guardians except John M. Clardy ? [it appears that the minors were Mary Ann, Noble L., Nancy E., Caroline P., Theodicia and Richard S. Clardy] Dower was laid off for Theodocia H. Clardy, the widow. (Bed TN, Ch Ct Min, 1/440) George W. Hobbs was appointed guardian ad litem for the minors. (Ibid 2/144)

CLARK
On 6 September 1802 Isham Clark, Silas Clark and John Simmonds gave power of attorney to Joseph Clark to recover two negroes, Sall and Peter, supposed now to be in the possession of David Maize of Pittsylvania County, VA. Joseph Clark is also authorized to claim any legacy or property to which they have any right in Pittsylvania County, VA. (Cla TN, Co Ct Min, 1/61)

CLARK, Elizabeth
Died before 4 October 1858 when John B. Clark was appointed administrator, with Emanuel Fox as security. (Sev TN, Co Ct Min, no#/348)

CLARK, J.
Taxes were not collected in District 4 for 1873, "run away." (Dyr TN, Co Ct Min, B/759)

CLARK, J. P. H.
Died before 5 November 1856 when John B. Clark renewed his bond as executor, with Emanuel Fox as security. The original bond was destroyed by the burning of the clerks office. (Sev TN, Co Ct Min, no#/86)

CLARK, Jesse
Died before 22 November 1824 when James Rudd of Montgomery County, TN., gave power of attorney to Rutherford Rutland of Wilson County, to collect what is due him by the will of Jesse Clark, deceased. (Wil TN, Reg Bk/345) [second set of page numbers.]

CLARK, John
Was a resident of Christian County, KY, on 2 August 1813 when his deposition was to be taken for the plaintiff in the suit of Jesse Denson vs Philip Hornburger. (Ste TN, Co Ct Min, 4/50)

CLARK, John B.
Died before 7 October 1862 when Robert S. Clark was appointed administrator, the widow, Mary Clark, relinquished her right to administrate. (Sev TN, Co Ct Min, no#/18) Robert C. Hodson, Henry Butler & James C. Murphy were appointed to set off a years provision for the widow & children. (Ibid 19) There are 8 children. (Ibid 20) 7 May 1866

Mary Clark was appointed guardian to Betsy Clark, M. E. Clark, B. W. Clark, S. M. Clark, Solomon Clark, J. Clark, M. M. Clark and R. V. Clark, minor orphans, with John Williams & R. S. Clark as security. (Ibid 327)

CLARK, Mariah
Commonly called Mariah Ogle, is probably a lunatic. 8 April 1857 a jury was ordered to inquire into her lunacy. (Sev TN, Co Ct Min, no#/156) The jury found she was a lunatic. (Ibid 163)

CLARK, Nathan
Died before 14 May 1811 when Reuben Clark & John Clark were appointed administrators, with Augustin Cook & Theophilus Morgan as security. (Rob TN, Co Ct Min, 2/403)

CLARK, William
1 March 1858 a lunacy hearing was ordered to be held on him. (Sev TN, Co Ct Min, no#/261) The jury found him to be an idiot & incapable of managing his affairs. William has an undivided interest in 5,800 acres of land and about $1,000 interest in some personal property. (Ibid 276) Robert S. Clark was appointed guardian with D. B. McMahan & John Whaly as security. (Ibid 291)

CLARK, Wm.
Died before 4 January 1809 when land was taxed to the heirs. (Rob TN, Co Ct Min, 2/103)

CLAXTON, James
Died before 13 May 1817 when Sarah Claxton was appointed administratrix with Josiah Ramsey as security. (Cla TN, Co Ct Min, 4/342)

CLAXTON, John
Died before 13 August 1840 as shown in the suit of Thomas Parsons, administrator of John Claxton Decd., a citizen of Giles County, TN, vs James Claxton and Benjamin Brown of Bedford County. (Bed TN, Ch Ct Min, 3/141)

CLAY, Wm.
6 August 1783, "The Court order that Wm. Clay a trancient person gave security for his behavior and returned to his family within five months as the sd Clay is without any pass or recommendation and confesses he left his family and have taken up with another woman." (Was TN, Co Ct Min, 1/222)

CLAYTON, T. M.
Died before 22 August 1866 as shown in the suit of Martha A. Butler vs Charles Clayton et als. A. S. Swingley was appointed guardian ad litem for the minor defendants, Nancy Elizabeth Clayton, Jno. Clayton, Ivy? J. Clayton, Wm. R. Clayton, Lucy J. Clayton, Amanda P. Clayton, children of W. B. Clayton, Jno. Clayton, Jas. Clayton & Josaphin Clayton, children of T. M. Clayton, deceased, as they have no regular guardian. (Mad TN, Ch Ct Min, 2/507) 24 August 1867 this suit was shown as Charles W. Chancellor & wife Martha A. formerly Martha A. Butler vs Charles Clayton, Francis Clayton, A. C. Lett and his wife Livy, David Wilson and his wife Milley, Martha Clayton, Betsy McKaskell, [blank] Maness and wife Lucy, Haywood Hair and wife Lizzie and Nancy Elizabeth, John, Izy Jane, William Robert, Amanda Perlina Clayton, children of W. B. Clayton, deceased, and John, James and Josephine Clayton children of T. M. Clayton, deceased. (Ibid 3/105)

CLEMENS, John M.
Probably died before 12 April 1858 when some land was sold that joined the lands of John M. Clemen's heirs. (Fen TN, Ch Ct Min, A/126) A suit was entered 11 April 1859 by Owen Clemens, William A. Moffat & Permelia his wife, Samuel L. Clemens & Henry Clemens, heirs of John M. Clemens, deceased, vs George W. Keer, William A Clendenen & wife Isabella, heirs of George W. Keer, deceased. John M. Clemens, father of complainants, made an entry in April 1830 for 5,000 acres of land. The grant was issued in the name of George W. Keer, the father of the defendants, and upon his death, title was vested in his heirs. John M. Clemens paid all of the money for the land & title is to be vested in his heirs. (Ibid 175) A suit was entered 31 March 1868 by Jane Clemens, widow of John M. Clemens, deceased, Orion Clemens, Parmela A. Moffett and Samuel L. Clemens, heirs of John M. Clemens, deceased, vs Anna D. Meredith, widow of Hugh Meredith, deceased, and John D. Meridith, Henry H. Meridith, Anna R. Meridith, deceased, the heirs of Charles Meridith, deceased, and the heirs of Edward H. Meredith, deceased, heirs of Hugh Meredith, deceased. John M. Clemens had bought land from Hugh Meredith and the deed was never registered. (Ibid 364)

CLEMENT, William, Sr.
Was a resident of Gibson County, TN, 10 January 1849 when he sold land [in Gibson Co.?] to Wm. H. Stitwell, guardian of Cordelia H., Hannah R. and Mary A. Stitwell [Stilwell], witnessed by Jno. P. Thomas and Jacob Mathis. (Mad TN, Ch Ct Min, 1/58)

CLEMENTS, Henderson M.
Died before 10 February 1855 as shown in the suit of John & William Fraim vs Frame's heirs & devisees. The death of defendant Henderson M. Clements was suggested. A. W. Dewitt was administrator. (Jac TN, Ch Ct Min, B/205) Allen W. Dewitt is the administrator. (Ibid C/32)

CLEMENTS, P. G.
Died before 6 June 1870 when the administrator, J. T. Stamps, entered an account of the sale of the estate. (Dyr TN, Co Ct Min, B/64)

CLEMENTSON, C.A.
1 July 1861, "Whereas C. A. Clementson our present Clerk has left the County and joined the so called southern Confederacy we therefore declare the office vacant and will proceed to fill the office." (Sev TN, Co Ct Min, no#/70l) C. A. Clementson died before 2 June 1862 when Sarah Clementson, his mother, and Sarah Bellows relinquished their right to administratrate. Samuel B. Henderson was appointed administrator. (Ibid 777)

CLEMMONS, John [Clements]
Died before 3 May 1842 when his death was suggested in the suit of Harman Howard et al vs Christopher Clemons et al. Christopher Clemmons was executor of John Clemmons, deceased. (Jac TN, Ch Ct Min, A/41) He left a will by which he directed that the negro woman, Jin, and her child Sarah Ann, be set at liberty and the 3 yellow children, Mary, Parmer? & James, be bound out until age 21 and then be set at liberty and be taught to read the new testament. Christopher Clemons is executor of the will. Since the death of the testator the negro woman, Jin, had another child, Tim, and she is dead and all of said negroes are under the age of 21. Harman Howard and others brought suit against Christopher Clemons and others for the negroes. The Court decided camplainants were not entitled to the hire for said negroes nor distribution of them. (Ibid105) Christopher Cemmons & Harmon Howard, et als, are heirs of John Clemens. (Ibid 140) Thomas Howard & wife and Sampson Allen & wife were also defendants in this suit and are therefore heirs of John Clemens. (Ibid 199)

CLEMSTON, C. A.
Died before 3 October 1865 when W. C. Murphy was appointed administrator with J. C. Murphy as security. Name also shown as Clemenstson. (Sev TN, Co Ct Min, no#/231) W. C. Murphy administrator vs the heirs of C. A. Clemmentson, deceased, Sarah Clemmentson, Sarah J. Bellows formerly Sarah J. Clemmentson, George M. Clemmentson, Daniel Clemmentson, John Clemmentson and Mrs. Parkerson formerly Clemmentson, are non-residents. (Ibid 243)

CLENDENNON, John
Died before 22 October 1801 when his heirs were listed on the delinquent tax list. (Rob TN, Co Ct Min, 1/193)

CLIFTON, Joshua H.
Died before 2 August 1819 when Thomas Hearn was appointed administrator with George Hearn & Jno. Hearn as security. (Wil TN, Co Ct Min, no#/500)

CLINGEN, Edward
February term 1790 made a deed of gift to Mary and Margret Clingen. (Was TN, Co Ct Min, 1/424) Edward Clingen was a resident of Greene County, and the deed involved money left them by their grandfather, George Clingen. Mary and Margret were the daughters of Edward Clingen. (Ibid 425)

CLINTON, Thomas
Died before 5 February 1811 when a motion was made by Isaac Lanier to have a bill of sale registered from Thomas Clinton, deceased, to himself, for several negroes. This was opposed by counsel for the widow of said deceased. The handwriting of the witnesses, John Jennings & John Hattaway, who has moved to GA, were proved by Joshua Williams, Esqr. and Duncan McRae. Abraham Belyen was also sworn and said he lived in Anson County & acted as constable twenty odd years. He said "he was well acquainted with John Jennings and John Hattaway who was a merchant and Justice of the Peace, and Mr. Jennings was a Justice of the Peace and afterwards Sheriff, & he frequently saw him sign his name." Others also proved the handwriting. Thomas Lanier said "he saw the said

John Jennings Buried." (Ste TN, Co Ct Min, 3/31-3) Elisabeth Clinton was appointed administratrix with Henry Pugh, James H. Russel, Duncan McRae & Michael Molton as security. (Ibid 35) A years provision was allowed for Elisabeth Clinton, widow. (Ibid 55)

CLOUD, Daniel
Died before 12 August 1816 when Tabbitha Cloud, the widow, was appointed administratrix with John Bullard and Samuel Cloud as security. (Cla TN, Co Ct Min, 4/219)

CLOYD, Stephen
Died before 1 February 1819 when Molly R. Cloyd & William Thompson were appointed administrators with Andrew Wilson & John Thompson as security. (Wil TN, Co Ct Min, no#372) A years provision was allotted for Polly R. Cloyd. (Ibid 374)

CLYCE, Harriet
Died before 4 July 1870 when T. S. Robertson was paid for making the coffin. (Dyr TN, Co Ct Min, B/73)

COATS, Austin M.
Died before 23 February 1842 when land was taxed to the heirs. (Obi TN, Cir Ct Min, 4/no#)

COATS, James T.
Died before 8 September 1827 when William Hogan was appointed administrator. (McM TN, Co Ct Min 2no#/242) [this page out of order, after 254]

COBB
On 12 May 1815 the depositions of Gil Ere? and Samuel Cobb were to be taken in Knox County, KY, for the defendant in the suit of Isaac Vanbebber vs John Wright. (Cla TN, Co Ct Min, 4/80)

COBB, Christian
Died before 7 November 1870 when Thos. H. Johnson, Ed White and Willie Davis were appointed to lay off a years allowance for the widow and family. (Dyr TN, Co Ct Min, B/126) Sam J. Neely was appointed administrator with W. C. Doyle and W. M. Watkins as security. (Ibid 127) On the petition of the widow and heirs who are all adults, dower is to be laid off for Mrs. Judith Cobb, the widow. (Ibid 142)

COBB, Jesse
Died before 4 December 1867 as shown in the suit of John Cobb, Admr. of Jesse Cobb decd., & Thos. Cobb vs Mahulda Smith et als. This cause, by consent of Richard Smith, is continued. (Fen TN, Ch Ct Min, A/348)

COBB, William
Probably died before 4 March 1806 when land was taxed to Joseph Cobb & the heirs of William Cobb. (Cla TN, Co Ct Min, 2/228)

COBB, William
Taxes were not collected in District 5 for 1873, "over age." (Dyr TN, Co Ct Min, B/759)

COCHRAM, N. W.
Died before 6 June 1870 when Jno. F. Sinclair made a settlement as administrator. (Dyr TN, Co Ct Min, B/63)

COCK, Joseph L. [S.]
Died before 23 February 1866 when his death was admitted in the suit of Joseph L. Cock vs M. M. Bledsoe et als. The suit was revived in the name of John C. Cock, administrator. (Mad TN, Ch Ct Min, 2/486)

COCK, Leroy
3 September 1806 was bound to John Cock until age 21. Leroy is an orphan boy near two years old, son of Susanna Cock. The said James Cocke [sic] is to educate the said boy to read , write & cipher to the rule of three. (Cla TN, Co Ct Min, 3/14)

COE, Stephen
Was a pauper 5 June 1826 when $40 was appropriated for his maintenance. (McM TN, Co Ct Min, 2/155)

COFFEE, Asbury M.
2 June 1828 was certified to be 21 years of age and of good moral character, on the motion of R. J. Meigs. (McM TN, Co Ct Min, 2no#/292)

COFFMAN, Andrew
Died before 8 June 1802 when Mary Coffman was appointed to administer his estate. (Cla TN, Co Ct Min, 1/40)

COFFY, Marvel
With his wife, Rachael, sold land in Wayne County, KY, to Thomas Hutchinson of KY, which was proved by Asbury M. Coffy & Jessee Boone. (McM TN, Co Ct Min, 2no#/310)

COHEA, Elizabeth
Was the mother of a bastard child. Thomas Bird gave bond for it's maintenance 12 May 1813. (Rob TN, Co Ct Min, 3/255)

COLBERT, George W.
Died before 7 February 1870 when Turner Chamblin was appointed administrator, with D. C. Hibbitt & L. J. Silsby as security. (Dyr TN, Co Ct Min, B/2)

COLBERT, Mrs.
8 April 1873, $50 was allowed for Mrs. Colbert and family, to be used for clothing for said woman & children reserving enough to carry her and her children to Cape Girardeau, MO, to her friends. (Dyr TN, Co Ct Min, B/559)

COLE
21 August 1867, in the suit of Jas. B. Lovey [Long] vs Martha J. Cole et als, Peter H. Cole was appointed guardian ad litem for Ninney W. Cole, Jno. R. Cole & Susan M. Cole, to defend the above suit. Martha J. Cole is a femme covert & has no counsel. M. Bullock was appointed counsel for said Martha J. Cole & children. (Mad TN, Ch Ct Min, 3/62) Peter H. Cole is the husband of Martha J. Cole & the father of the other defendants, and was appointed trustee. (Ibid 91)

COLE, John
Died after making his will on 14 April 1859. The will was proved at April term 1860 & Thomas B. Cole & John D. Cole were executors. John Cole left land in trust to Thomas B. Cole and John D. Cole, two of his sons. The land was bounded by Doctor Thomas Ingram & Ruebin Cole & others. He also left a legacy to Mrs. Louisa Whitelaw, the rest to be divided between his four sons, said Thomas B. & John D., and Philip Cole and Stephen Cole. Thomas B. Cole has died intestate leaving Nancy D. Cole his widow and Dora T. Cole and Selia T. Cole his only children. Sugars McLemore is administrator of Thomas B. Cole and John D. Bond is guardian of the minor children. (Mad TN, Ch Ct Min, 2/516) 20 August 1868 in the suit of Jno. D. Cole et als vs Dora E. Cole et als, $3,000 is to be paid over to Jno. T. Whitelaw & wife Mariah L. or Jno. S. H. Tomlin, their attorney, being the amount of a legacy bequeathed to her by her father Jno. Cole, deceased. (Ibid 3/217)

COLE, John N.
Died before 22 February 1839 as shown in the suit of T. J. Nolen assignee &c vs Marvell Cole. Land had been willed by John N. Cole, deceased, to Marvill & Elizabeth M. Cole. (Obi TN, Cir Ct Min, 3/315)

COLEMAN, S. K.
Taxes were not collected in District 4 for 1873, "insolvent." (Dyr TN, Co Ct Min, B/759)

COLLET, Abraham
Died before 5 November 1782 when Mary Collitt & Isaac Collitt were granted leave to administrate on the estate. (Was TN, Co Ct Min, 1/181)

COLLIER, Arter [Arthur]
Died before 26 January 1809 when Feribee [Ferriby] Collier was appointed administratrix with John Tomlinson & William Tomlinson as security. (Ste TN, Co Ct Min, no#/93) The inventory was shown which included a Dictionary & Bible, Law Books & other books. (Ibid 105)

COLLIER, William
Was an orphan boy when he was bound to George Martin, Sr. on 3 August 1812. (Ste TN, Co Ct Min, 3/157) 5 August 1812 William Collier was ordered to be restored to the Mother and Stepfather of him. (Ibid 163)

COLLINS
John and Ann Collins were paupers 8 March 1831 when Obedeah Bowlin was allowed money for their support. (McM TN, Co Ct Min, 2/508)

COLLINS, Adam
Was reported to have fled from the state as shown in the suit against him by the State on 27 February 1807. (Cla TN, Co Ct Min, 3/66)

COLLINS, David
Gave power of attorney to William Skiles of Bertie County, NC, on 3 November 1813. (Ste TN, Co Ct Min, 4/77)

COLLINS, Susannah
Died before 4 March 1828 when an appropriation was made for the support of her children, Ann & John Collins. (McM TN, Co Ct Min, 2no#/271)

COLLINS, Widow
4 October 1859 it was ordered that her 3 children be brought to next court to be bound out. (Sev TN, Co Ct Min, no#/482)

COLTHORP, Clayton
Died before 16 November 1814 when Norrel Colthorp was appointed administrator. (Rob TN, Co Ct Min, 3/507)

COLTOR, John
Was a resident of Washington County, VA, 26 May 1779 when his deposition was to be taken on behalf of John Nare in a suit with James Clark. (Was TN, Co Ct Min, 1/76)

COLVILLE, Samuel
Died before 7 September 1830 when George Colville, Sr. & George Colville, Jr. were appointed administrators. (McM TN, Co Ct Min, 2no#/475)

COLVILLE, Young
Died before 5 December 1826 when a clerk pro-tem was appointed to fill his unexpired term as County Court Clerk. (McM TN, Co Ct Min, no#/255) Saml. Colvill & Nutty Colvill were his administrators. (Ibid 262) 4 June 1828 the widow, Nutty Colvill, petitioned to sell land. John Walker & John McDowell were appointed guardians pendente lite to attend the interest of the heirs. (Ibid 336) 5 September 1828, heirs were shown as Warner Elmore Colville, Bethialine Colville & Amanda Murrell Colville. (Ibid 373) 7 September 1830 Saml. H. Jordon was appointed administrator in the place of Saml. Colville who is deceased. (Ibid 475)

COLWELL, Robert
Died before 20 February 1780 when Sarah Colwell was appointed administratrix, with And. Green & Chas. Robertson as her security. (Was TN, Co Ct Min, 1/102)

COMBS, John
Died before 12 April 1859 as shown in the suit of W. E. B. Jones vs John W. Owen & others. Complainant dismissed his suit against all defendants except John W. and J. M. J. Owens, Jenny Givin & Green Combs, administrator of John Combs. (Fen TN, Ch Ct Min, A/194)

COMPTON, Edward
Died before 4 May 1818 when Charles Compton was appointed administrator, with George Clark & Wm. Lawrence as security. (Wil TN, Co Ct Min, no#/242) A years provision was allotted to the widow. (Ibid 243)

COMPTON, John B.
28 August 1860 was a non-resident of the state as stated in the suit of John B. Compton vs James H. Baker. (Mad TN, Ch Ct Min 2/370)

COMPTON, Robert
Died before 11 July 1848 as shown in the suit of Robert J. Compton, William Simmons & Caroline E. Simmons his wife, formerly Caroline E. Compton, David Compton, Mary E. Compton, Laura T. Compton & Charles Temple, administrator of Robert Compton, deceased; petition for division of slaves. Petitioner, Robert J. Compton, has arrived to the age of 21 years. Caroline E. Simmons is under the age of 21. Absolem Deberry, Solomon Freeman and William Witherspoon were appointed to divide the slaves equally among the heirs of Robert Compton. (Mad TN, Ch Ct Min, 1/33) Mary E. was shown as

Margaret E. Compton. Division of slaves was made in 5 lots. (Ibid 48) 9 March 1852, another entry stated that the wife of Robert Compton was also deceased. (Ibid 245)

COMPTON, Robert J.
Was under the age of 21 as shown in his suit for division of slaves, 14 January 1847. (Mad TN, Ch Ct Min, 1/9)

COMPTON, Vinson
Died before 23 March 1807 when John J. Soloman Harpoles, Esq. was granted letters of administration, with Just. Rullman & W. Steele as security. (Wil TN, Co Ct Min, no#/278)

CONATSER
In the suit of David Conatser Admr. vs Lavina Frogg & others, 3 December 1868, it was stated that John Conatser, Jenett Conatser, John, Phillip, Geo. Abraham Mary & Sarah Conatser are in the court by service & publication. The minors were mentioned. An account is to be taken of what is due each of the heirs & what is due Lavina Frogg. (Fen TN, Ch Ct Min, A/408)

CONATSER, Andrew
Died before 1 December 1862 when his will was proved by Absolem Allen & Nelson Fox, witnesses. Daniel Conatser was executor with Eli Fox and Nelson Fox as security. (Sev TN, Co Ct Min, no#/26)

CONATSER, Reuben
10 April 1866 was said to be a lunatic and was threatening to kill Amasa Conatser & others. A jury was ordered to determine his lunacy. (Sev TN, Co Ct Min, no#/323)

CONATSER, Sarah Jane
Was granted a divorce from James Conatser on 5 December 1867. Her maiden name of Richards was restored. (Fen TN, Ch Ct Min, A/355)

CONGO, John [Conger]
Died before 29 January 1847 as shown in the suit of Lewis R. Vance vs Alexander Dillard and Henry B. McDonald, Exr. of John Congo. (Jac TN, Ch Ct Min, A/249)

CONNALLY
Thomas D. Connally and George Anderson Connally were brothers, as shown in their suit against Calvin Thompson, et als, filed 24 December 1841. (Bed TN, Ch Ct Min, 3/41)

CONNALLY, Susan R.
Was a minor 16 January 1850 when she petitioned by her guardian, George A. Connally, for sale of land. (Mad TN, Ch Ct Min, 1/104) 12 July 1850 permission was given for her guardian to purchase a negro girl suitable for a waiting maid for Susan "as she has arrived at the age when she has need of the use of a servant of this description." (Ibid 145) 15 January 1851, "Susan R. Connally has intermarried with Edwin R. Lancaster. It is therefore ordered that he be made a party to this proceeding." (Ibid 173) Same date; Edwin R. Lancaster & his wife Susan R. Lancaster, Geo A. Connally & Samuel Lancaster, the two former minors, the said Edwin appearing by "her" next friend Saml. Lancaster & the said Susan by her regualr guardian Geo. A Connally. Susan is the owner of land & negroes which by nuptial contract was conveyed to Samuel Lancaster as trustee for her separate use. Her guardian has 4 or 5 thousand dollars in his hands which has not passed into the hands of her husband, Edwin. (Ibid 179) Edwin was shown as Edward R. Lancaster. (Ibid 2/67) G. A. Connally was deceased by 19 February 1858 as shown in the suit of Robt. A. Connally vs Archibald S. Rogers et als. (Ibid 192)

CONNALLY, Thomas D.
Died before 14 January 1847 as shown in the suit of John L. Lancaster, Samuel C. Lancaster & John L. Blue, surviving partners of the late firm of Connally, Blue & Lancaster & George A. Connally, administrator of Thomas D. Connelly, deceased, vs The President, Directors & Company of the Union Bank of the state of Tennessee and John Kerr Connally, Mary Louisa Connally, Susan Ann Connally & Fanny Sarah Connally, minors, who defend by their guardian ad litem, Joseph C. Sharp. (Mad TN, Ch Ct Min, 1/11) Geo. A. Connally was the brother of Thomas D. Connally who died in July 1846. John C., Mary & Fanny were mentioned as heirs & children who are minors. The brothers owned land in Bedford County & in Dyer County. (Ibid 209) 23 February 1861 a suit was shown by Jno. K. Connally, Mary Connally, Fanny Connally by N. S. Williams, next friend &c, vs Robert A. Connally Exr. N. S. Williams was the next friend, guardian & agent of complainants. (Ibid 2/455)

CONNELLY, Nelly
21 January 1811 was put in the care of Elizabeth Churchwell until next court and allowed $60 per annum for support. (Roa TN, Co Ct Min, D/264)

CONNER, James
Had a piece of the left ear bitten off in a fight with another man in September 1807. This was proved on the oath of Dorkus Bristow and ordered to be recorded 23 November 1807. (Cla TN, Co Ct Min, 3/128)

CONNERS, James
Died before 20 February 1843 when land was taxed to the heirs. (Obi TN, Cir Ct Min, 4/no#)

CONRAD
18 July 1797 Sampson Conrad & Peggy Conrad made choice of Martin Grider for their guardian. (Rob TN, Co Ct Min, 1/32)

CONRAD, Joseph
Died before July term 1798 when Wm. Fort, Esqr. was added to the arbitrators to decide the suit between Nichl. Conrad, Executor for ___ Conrad, deceased, against Martin Gordon & John Alston. (Rob TN, Co Ct Min, 1/69) October term 1798, Nicholas Conrad, Extecutor of Joseph Conrad vs Martin Greider. (Ibid 79)

CONRAD, Nicholas
Died before 11 November 1811 when the will was proved by Samuel Holliss, Jonathan Ferguson & James Tunstall. William C. Conrad was executor. (Rob TN, Co Ct Min, 3/31) 9 February 1813 John B. Cheatham, sheriff, made a deed to William C. Conrad, Mary Conrad, George C. Conrad, Sidney Conrad, heirs of Nicholas Conrad, deceased. (Ibid 198) 14 November 1814 Robert Whitehead petitioned to have laid off to him his part of the estate according to the will of Nicholas Conrad. (Ibid 493)

CONROD, James
Died before 11 March 1845 when land was taxed to the heirs. (Obi TN, Cir Ct Min, 4/no#)

CONROD, W. C. [Coonrod]
Died before 23 February 1842 when land was taxed to the heirs. (Obi TN, Cir Ct Min, 4/no#)

CONYERS, William
Made a deed of gift to William Young 11 February 1812, proved by Jack E. Turner. (Rob TN, Co Ct Min, 3/60)

COOK, Abraham
Sold land in Wilks County, NC, to Cornelius Sale proved by William Sale and Hannah Sale & recorded February term 1810. (Rob TN, Co Ct Min, 2/202)

COOK, Amanda
7 January 1867, John A. Trotter, D. B. McMahan & G. C. Shrader were appointed to lay off her dower. (Sev TN, Co Ct Min, no#/416)

COOK, Earl J.
Died in 1844 as shown in the suit of Eliza Cooke vs William Cooke, George Cook, Matilda C. Cook and their guardian Calvin E. Myers, William L. Stubblefield and James Young. The suit was entered 18 July 1856. Eliza Cooke is the widow and William, George & Matilda C. Cook are the minor children and only heirs. The land Earl J. Cooke lived on at his death was purchased from Leithton Myers. He had paid for same but never received title. After the death of said Earl J., James Young sold the land & William L. Stubblefield was the purchaser. The sale was set aside & the widow is to have dower. (Jac TN, Ch Ct Min, C/23)

COOK, Eli
Was released from paying poll tax for 1858 having left the county before that year. (Sev TN, Co Ct Min, no#/407)

COOK, James
Died before 14 August 1815 when Mercus Cook was appointed administrator, with Joab Hill and John Neal as security. (Cla TN, Co Ct Min, 4/89) The administrator was shown as Mercurius Cook. (Ibid 103)

COOK, John
Died before 12 November 1828 as shown in the suit of Daniel Cook, heir-at-law of John Cook, deceased, vs The heirs-at-law of George Brasfield, deceased. (Obi TN, Cir Ct Min, 1/67)

COOLEY, Cornelius
Died before 1 May 1815 when Lucinda Cooley & William Cherry were appointed administrators, with James Blanks & Henry Gibson as security. (Ste TN, Co Ct Min, 4/261)

COOLEY, Joel
Died before 3 May 1814 when William M. Cooley was appointed administrator, with John Allen, James H. Russell & Philip Hornburger as security. (Ste TN, Co Ct Min, 4/140)

COONS, Joseph
Died before 3 September 1860 when Andrew Lawson was appointed administrator with Thomas Bryan as security. (Sev TN, Co Ct Min, no#/598) [Also shown as Koons] (Ibid 621)

COOPER, James
Was a minor when he was bound to James Gorden to learn the Hatter's trade. These minutes are marked, "date is likely Feb. sessions 1794." (Was TN, Co Ct Min, 1/469)

COOPER, Jas. M.
Died before 15 August 1868 as shown in the suit of Jno. L. Couthum? vs Sallie B. Cooper et als. Complainant was the administrator. (Mad TN, Ch Ct Min, 3/185)

COOPER, John
Died before 22 December 1809 when the order binding Robert Burk [an orphan boy of color] to William Adair, was rescinded. The boy is to be returned to Mrs. Cooper, widow of John Cooper, deceased. (Roa TN, Co Ct Min, D/163)

COOPER, Martha A.
Was granted a divorce from Abram B. Cooper on 12 August 1839. They were married in 1834 in Bedford County. He left in September 1837 and went to the Republic of Texas. He had left her with her father until he returned. It was found that he had been guilty of adultry. The next friend of Martha was Joseph Thompson. (Bed TN, Ch Ct Min, 1/222)

COOPER, Mary
Was the mother of a base born child. John Dasey Boring, the reputed father, was ordered to pay maintenance 11 May 1790. (Was TN, Co Ct Min, 1/440)

COOPER, Rebecca C.
Died before 3 May 1870 when Jas. H. Cooper was appointed administrator with L. H. Benton & A. R. McKnight as security. (Dyr TN, Co Ct Min, B/60)

COOPER, Sampson
Died before 7 November 1870 when Turner Chamblin was appointed administrator, with F. S. Chamblin as his security. (Dyr TN, Co Ct Min, B/128) 5 May 1873 T. S. Chamblin was chosen and appointed guardian of A. W. Cooper, Ella Cooper, Eugene Cooper and Lula Cooper, minor heirs, with Turner Chamblin as his security. (Ibid 581)

COOPER, William
Was a minor child four years of age on the fifth day of April 1802. He was bound at the September term 1802 to Jacob Hill until age 21. (Cla TN, Co Ct Min, 1/53)

COOPER, William
In his suit against R. Cooper for words, 10 May 1811, plaintiff is allowed to take the depositions of Absalom Franklin and Whitmill Craft and John Moore of Christian County, KY. (Ste TN, Co Ct Min, 3/79)

COOPER, William
Was an orphan child about 10 years old when he was bound at the May term 1790 to Ezekiel Abell, Blacksmith, until the age 21. (Was TN, Co Ct Min, 1/438)

COPE, W. D.
4 October 1870 D. R. Hendrix was chosen and appointed guardian of Martha W. Cope a minor of W. D. Cope, with John E. McCorkle and T. H. Benton as his security. (Dyr TN, Co Ct Min, B/108) The deceased was shown as W. L. Cope. (Ibid 513)

COPELAND, Josiah
Was a resident of New Orleans, LA, on 6 November 1843 when William Gipson filed a suit against him. (Jac TN, Ch Ct Min, A/113)

COPELAND, Josiah
Died before 9 February 1855 as shown in the suit of Darcas Copeland admrx. of Josiah Copeland decd. vs Jesse Nelson, John Nelson & John Kirby. (Jac TN, Ch Ct Min, B/195)

COPELAND, Solomon
Died before 7 March 1826 when John Copeland was appointed administrator. (McM TN, Co Ct Min, 2no#/138)

COPPAGE, James
Died before 4 February 1811 when land was taxed to the heirs. (Ste TN, Co Ct Min, 3/28)

CORNWELL, Drury
Died before 8 February 1854 when his death was suggested in the suit of Logan H. McCarver Admr. &c vs Drury Cornwell et als. Benjamin Cornwell is the administrator. (Jac TN, Ch Ct Min, B/116)

COTTON, Young
13 August 1812 made a deed of gift to Nancy Wells [Miles] proved by Wyatt Wilkinson and Henry Johnson. (Rob TN, Co Ct Min, 3/123)

COVEY, John L.
Was a pauper 1 June 1829 when money was allowed for his support. (McM TN, Co Ct Min, 2/356)

COVEY, Sally
Was a pauper 8 June 1824 when Joab Hill was allowed $20 for keeping her for the ensuing year. (McM TN, Co Ct Min, 2/8) Joab Hill was released from keeping Sally Covey, 6 September 1824. (Ibid 22)

COVINGTON
1 October 1866 the following children were bound to Thomas Underwood, to wit, Elisabeth Covington aged 8 years, Wm. Covington aged 6 years & Polly Covington aged 4 years, until they arrive at age 21 for Wm. and 18 for the girls. (Sev TN, Co Ct Min, no#/372)

COVINGTON, William H. D.
Died before 20 February 1837 when his death was suggested in the suit of Stephen Hanna, surviving partner of Caldwell & Hanna vs W. H. D. Covington. Lysander Adams and A. M. Chamberlain were appointed personal representatives of said decedant, who died intestate. (Obi TN, Cir Ct Min, 3/88)

COWAN, James W.
6 December 1825 Robert Cowan was appointed guardian of Nancy Jane Cowan, minor orphan of James W. Cowan [does not say deceased.] (McM TN, Co Ct Min, 2no#/116)

COWAN, John
Was released for taxes for 1783 when his father, Robert Cowan, made oath that John was under the age of 21 at that time. (Was TN, Co Ct Min, 1/262)

COWAN, Wm. H.
Died before 5 February 1866 when James M. Evans was appointed administrator with James A. Pickens, James H. McMurry & John P. Pickens as security. (Sev TN, Co Ct Min, no#/272)

COWDEN, James
Died before 6 May 1861 when his nuncupative will was filed. Notice is to be given to Betsy Anne Gardner, John Gardner & Nancy Melvina Cowden, Sarah N. Cowden, Mariah Jane Hynds, Robt. Hynds, Mary E. Cowden & James N. Cowden to appear at next court to contest the said nuncupative will if they see proper to do so. (Sev TN, Co Ct Min, no#/689) The will was proved by Wm. Thomas & William P. Keener, witnesses. The witnesses were also appointed administrators. (Ibid 694) R. M. Creswell, Lewis Wayland & Wm. H. Cowan were appointed to lay off a years support to the minor children under 15 years old. (Ibid 698) John Cowden was appointed guardian to Mary E. Cowden & Jas. H. Cowden. (Ibid 700)

COWDEN, John
Died before 7 August 1865 when R. M. Creswell, Adam Creswell & Michael Fagala were appointed to set apart to M. J. Cowen, the widow, a years support for herself & family. (Sev TN, Co Ct Min, no#/193) 4 September 1865 Isaac Hines was appointed administrator for John B. Cowden, deceased, with R. M. Creswell & John Rose as security. Mary J. Cowden was appointed guardian to Hetty A. & Wm. T. Cowden, with Isaac Hines & R. M. Creswell as security. (Ibid 207) The widow was Mary Jane Cowden. (Ibid 230)

COWDEN, Mat
Died before 5 April 1858 when Peter H. Bryan was allowed $2.85 for "buryal clothes." (Sev TN, Co Ct Min, no#/275)

COWEN, Brison
Died before 20 March 1852 as shown in the suit of Wesley Harvey vs Thusa Cowen by her guardian Burton Ferrell. Wesley Harvey was guardian of Sophia Elizabeth Cowen, who has fits. Brison Cowen was a brother of the whole blood to said Sophia Elizabeth and a brother of the half blood to defendant Thursa. Brison died a minor and without issue. His estate belongs equally to his sisters of the half and of the whole blood. (Jac TN, Ch Ct Min, B/38)

COWEN, Hugh
Died before 4 March 1861 when the will was proved by John Chandler, witness. The hand writing of C. D. Anderson, the other witness, was proved by Thos. C. Brabson and the codicile was proved by Saml. Pickens. (Sev TN, Co Ct Min, no#/659)

COWGER, John
Was the father of a bastard child by Polly Sullivan. He gave bond 6 May 1818 with John Harpole & Thomas Bradley as security. (Wil TN, Co Ct Min, no#/265)

COX
On 29 July 1846 a suit was entered by Ann Cox, Robert Cox, Rebecca Cox, Elizabeth Cox, Sally Cox and Matilda Cox, by their next friend Nathaniel M. Cox vs Edward M. Cason and Mounce Gore. (Jac TN, Ch Ct Min, A/218) 26 July 1849 a suit was entered by Edward M. Cason vs Nathaniel M. Cox & wife. Complainant had been appointed trustee in 1842 to take charge of a negro for the use of Eliza Cox. He wishes to be relieved of said trusteeship & William H. Bates was appointed in his stead. (Ibid 341)

COX
A suit was entered 10 February 1859 by Robert A. Cox vs Edward M. Cox & others. James R. Tolbert was appointed guardian ad litem for the minor defendants. (Jac TN, Ch Ct Min, C/172)

COX, Albert F.
A suit was entered 9 February 1855 by Albert F. Cox & others vs Daniel W. Cox & others. Publication had been made for defendants Daniel W. Car, Wilson Stephens, Nancy Stephens, Joseph Stephens, Sally Stephens, John Allrorn?, Elizabeth Allcorn?, and Richard E. Monrell? who are non-residents of this state. Publication had also been made as to the defendants William E. Monsel, Arrena K. Moncil?, Samuel M. Morsel, Sarah F. Monsil, John R. Monsel and Albert F. Monsel, minor defendants, who have not appeared and have no regular guardian. William H. Batts was appointed guardian ad litem for the minor defendants. (Jac TN, Ch Ct Min, B/189)

COX, Benjamin
Died in the fall of 1824 in Dickson County, TN, as shown in the suit of Abra Parsons & wife vs Martin Walton & wife & others. A. Parson sues for himself and as administrator of Willis H. Moore, deceased. He and Eliza Ann Parsons are citizens of Rutherford County. Also in the suit are John J. Williams of Hardiman County & James Porter & [blank] Porter, administrator & administratrix of Jeremiah Baxter, deceased, citizen of Marshall County. Eliza Ann Parsons stated that she and Willis H. Moore were the children of Nancy Moore who died sometime in the year 1822 or 1823 & she & Willis were the only children. Nancy Moore was the daughter of Benjamin Cox and the wife of Thomas C. Moore. Nancy died before her father, Benjamin Cox. His widow, Winford Cox, was administratrix, with John J. Williams, Sterling Brewer & Jeremiah Baxter as security. The share of Eliza Ann & Willis Moore was paid to their father, Thomas C. Moore, who had never been appointed their guardian. Thomas C. Moore died insolvent in Bedford County in 1833. Sterling Brewer died some years since. Winford Cox has since married Martin Walton. Eliza Ann married some 3 or 4 years since to Aleia? Parsons. Willis H. Moore died intestate in Bedford County & administration granted to Aleia? [Abia] Parsons. James Baxter & Catherine Porter [Baxter was crossed out, but she is later shown as Katherine Baxter] are

administrators of Jeremiah Porter [Baxter?], deceased. Eliza Ann is suing for her share of the estate of Benjamin Cox. John J. Williams answered the complaint as Joseph J. Williams. Benjamin Cox left 10 children. The share of Nancy Moore was paid to Thomas C. Moore as administrator for Nancy Moore. (Bed TN, Ch Ct Min, 1/446) Parsons' name was shown as Abid, as shown in the suit of Willis Cannon vs Abid Parsons & wife. When Thomas C. Moore was appointed administrator of his deceased wife, Nancy Moore, Daniel McKisick & Edward Wade (who are either dead or removed from this State), became his securities. (Ibid 498)

COX, George
4 June 1827, with his wife Polly, deeded land in Wayne County, KY, to Jacob Dean. (McM Co Ct Min, 2no#/213)

COX, John
Died before 27 May 1778 when the will was proved by Col. John Carter and Emanuel Carter. (Was TN, Co Ct Min, 1/31)

COX, Stephen
Was a pauper on 5 June 1827 when James Hicks was appointed his guardian. (McM TN, Co Ct Min, 2no#/219)

COX, William
Was shown to be a County Charge 7 September 1802 when Thomas Wallen was allowed $40 for maintaining him for a year. (Cla TN, Co Ct Min, 1/64)

COX, William
Was a resident of Madison County, KY, on 31 January 1795 when he gave a power of attorney to William Willson of Green County and Western Territory [TN]. (Was TN, Co Ct Min, 1/531)

COZART, Jas. B.
Died in Penier? [Perim?] County, NC, soon after making his will in September 1846. He was the father of Winniford Howard. The 5th clause in the will states "I give & bequeath to my son in law Wm. Howard in trust & for the benefit of his wife & children, & I wish it distinctly understood that I hereby vest no title in him so that the property can be sold or disposed of in any way for the payment of any debts he may now owe, or that he may hereafter contract otherwise for the support of his family...5 slaves." Wm. Howard was removed as trustee under said will and Joseph Gill appointed in his place. (Mad TN, Ch Ct Min, 1/346) 17 March 1853 Joseph Gill declined to serve as trustee. Jno. R. Jelks, the receiver appointed, has removed to the state of AR. (Ibid 357) Wm. Hopper was appointed trustee, 16 March 1855. (Ibid 2/54)

COZEANS, John Bartley
Was an orphan child when he was bound to Abraham Earheart on 9 August 1813, to learn the trade of making guns. (Rob TN, Co Ct Min, 3/276)

CRAFT
In February 1779 Michl. Bacon was ordered to take charge of 2 orphan children, a girl named Olif Craft aged 9 years and a boy named Archillis Craft. (Was TN, Co Ct Min, 1/62)

CRAFT, Ezekiel
Had moved out of the county 29 November 1808 when William Rogers, Esqr. was elected Register in his place. (Cla TN, Co Ct Min, 3/240)

CRAIG
29 August 1844 a suit was entered by William W. Adams & others vs William H. Craig & others. Sophronia J., William, John, Polly, Ann, [or Polly Ann] James, Elisha and Elijah Craig are minors and have no regular guardian. Newcomb Thompson was appointed guardian ad litem to defend this suit for them. (Bed TN, Ch Ct Min, 2/300)

CRAIG, Amanda
Was a negro girl aged 5 years when she was bound 4 September 1871, with the consent of the child's mother, to Sarah J. Reamey until age 18. (Dyr TN, Co Ct Min, B/271)

CRAIG, James M.
Died before 7 February 1870 when John Q. Craig was appointed administrator, with Wm. H. Craig and J. H. York as security. (Dyr TN, Co Ct Min, B/3) Asa Griffin, R. C. Coffman & J. F. Caruthers were appointed to lay off a years provisions to the widow and family. (Ibid 7)

CRAIG, John
Died probably in January 1839 as shown in the suit of Wm. H. Craig and James Dillard, the later administrator of the estate of John Craig, deceased vs Flora Craig and Polly Craig, widow of William Craig, deceased, and [blank] Craig, William Craig, John Craig, James Craig, the six last of whom are minors and the only heirs of John Craig, deceased. [There are not six minors named?] William Craig died in March 1824 leaving his widow & 10 heirs at law. Wm. H. Craig has purchased the interest of some of the heirs of William Craig. James Dillard purchased the interest of one of the heirs of William Craig. John Craig, deceased, was one of the heirs of William Craig, and James Dillard was appointed administrator in February 1839. The widow of William Craig has not had her dower. "Said Flora who with widow aforsaid refused to have said land divided." Sally Craig & the minors aforesaid are to be made defendants to this bill. (Bed TN, Ch Ct Min, 1/443)

CRAIG, Moses
Died before 2 May 1814 when Polly Craig was appointed administratrix with Benjamin Bradford and Alexander Craig as security. (Ste TN, Co Ct Min, 4/136)

CRAIG, William [Crage]
Died in the early part of 1835, intestate, leaving his widow & several children, as shown in the suit of Joseph J. B. Crunk vs John Craig, son & administrator of William Craig deceased. Joseph Crunk is the attorney in fact for Benjamin F. Craig, one of the heirs of William Craig, which was acknowledged in Tipton County, TN. Joseph Crunk has purchased the interest of Benjamin F. Craig who has left the state & lives in some adjoining state or perhaps the Republic of Texas. John Craig stated that he had settled the estate & paid all the distributative shares except Benjamin F. Craig & Thomas Justice. In the settlement made by John Craig in 1837 there are 6 receipts from the heirs; Joel Bradley, Flora Craig, Robert Craig, Polly Craig, William M. Russell & Cleveland L. Harrison. (Bed TN, Ch Ct Min, 1/147) [also see John Craig] In the suit of William H. Craig & James Dillard vs Flora Craig and others, dower is to be set off to the widow of William Craig, deceased. (Ibid 2/108) Dower was laid off to Polly Craig, the widow of William Craig. (Ibid 154)

CRAIGHEAD, Stephen
Died intestate in August 1852, as shown in the suit of William Draper Admr. &c vs James M. Draper & others, and petitioner was his administrator. (Jac TN, Ch Ct Min, B/82) This suit was shown as William Draper, administrator of Stephen Craghead, deceased vs James W. Draper, James Draper, Joseph Craghead, Shelton Craghead and George Craghead. Land was sold to George W. Mosely and title was divested out of the defendants. (Ibid 113)

CRAWFORD, James
29 November 1780 it was ordered that his property be sold as he was found and taken in arms against the State. (Was TN, Co Ct Min, 1/123)

CRAWFORD, Moses
25 August 1778 it was ordered that he be imprisoned during the present War with Great Britain, and the Sheriff to take the whole of his estate into custody. Half of the estate is to be used for the state and the other half remitted to the family of the defendant. (Was TN, Co Ct Min, 1/38) Moses Crawford was ordered to appear in court and take the oath of allegiance to this state. He failed to appear but was allowed to remain in the state subject to the penalties for the crime. (Ibid 40-1) He was allowed to remain free on taking the oath of allegiance to the state of North Carolina and the United States of America. (Ibid 66)

CRAWFORD, T.
Died before 20 February 1843 when land was taxed to the heirs. (Obi TN, Cir Ct Min, 4/no#)

CRAYTON, Jane
Was a daughter of Richard Womacks as shown in the case of Jane Crayton vs Dred Bass & wife at the September term, 1815. Nancy Bass had charged Jane Crayton with having a bastard child & was not able to support said charge. It was ordered that Dredden Bass pay all costs. (Wil TN, P&J, no#/no#)

CREIGHTON, Saml. B.
Probably died before 15 July 1851 as Henry Lake was said to be the administrator. (Mad TN, Ch Ct Min, 1/207) 9 March 1852 a suit by Henry Lake, administrator of Saml. B. Creighten, deceased vs Henry & Saml. Creighten who are minors. Jno. S. H. Tomlin was appointed guardian. Saml. B. Creighton died intestate in 1840, leaving Mary Creighton

his widow and Henry & Saml. his only children. Mary Creighton died in 1851. (Mad TN, Ch Ct Min, 1/236)

CRESSLIAS, Rudolph
Died before 5 November 1787 when the will was proved. Elizabeth Cresslius and John Cathart Cusslias were executors. Wm. Nooding, Sr., John Dobbings & Abrm. Prefe were appraisers of the estate. (Was TN, Co Ct Min, 1/294) [On the same page the names are shown as Creslia & Creselia]

CRESWELL, Andrew
Died before 18 June 1816 when William Creswell & Jackson Brown were appointed administrators, with John Wilkerson & William Halbrooks security. (Wil TN, Co Ct Min, no#/15)

CRISWELL, Samuel
Died before 3 October 1859 when George Wade, E. Hodges & W. H. Cowan were appointed to lay off a years provision for Mary Criswell, the widow, & family. (Sev TN, Co Ct Min, no#/475) 6 February 1860 R. M. Criswell was appointed administrator with Henry Randels as security. (Ibid 516)

CROCKET
22 July 1800, "An article of agreement after the Nature of Indenture made between William Crocket & Jane Crocket of the one part & John Wilson of the other part was proved by Saml. Crocket." (Rob TN, Co Ct Min, 1/142)

CROCKETT, Robert H.
Died before 8 July 1844 when his death was suggested in the suit of Samuel A. Warner for the use of W. F. Hampton vs Robert H. Crockett, William H. Guy & Charles McAlister. (Obi TN, Cir Ct Min, 4/no#) William A. Brown was administrator. (Ibid, 12 March 1845)

CROMWELL
The petition of John Cromwell, Dorsey Cromwell, Rosey Lawrence, wife of Jesse Lawrence, Winnifred Cromwell, Garrard Cromwell by John Cromwell his guardian, was made to correct a mistake in a deed of conveyance, 5 November 1804. (Rob TN, Co Ct Min, 1/319)

CROMWELL, Alexr.
Died before 18 January 1802 when Ann Cromwell & Dorsey Cromwell were appointed administrators. (Rob TN, Co Ct Min, 1/196) 8 February 1805, John Cromwell & others vs Hannah Porter & others, petition to rectify an error in the deed given by John McCay Alston to Alexander Cromwell. (Ibid 331) 8 October 1807 in the suit of Wineferd Cromwell vs Dorsey Cromwell, the 1/4 share of the lands of Alexander Cromwell that Dorsey Cromwell is entitled to by heirship, was levied on to satisfy the suit. (Ibid 474)

CROMWELL, John
Died before 4 August 1806 when Winfred Cromwell was granted letters of administration, with Wm. Hart & Wm. Lundsford as her security. (Rob TN, Co Ct Min, 1/398) 7 April 1808 Jesse Lawrence was appointed administrator, with Joseph Wimberley & Assa Mason as security. (Ibid 2/23)

CROMWELL, Oliver
Died before 7 September 1829 when Patience Cromwell was appointed administratrix. (McM TN, Co Ct Min, 2no#/380) A years provision was laid off to Patience, the widow. (Ibid 384)

CROMWELL, Winefred
Died before 7 April 1808 when the administrator delivered into Court the amount of the sale of the estate. (Rob TN, Co Ct Min, 2/23)

CROOM
Valentine McMillen, next friend of Narcissa T. Croom, dismissed the suit against John W. Croom, 14 January 1850. Suit not identified. (Mad TN, Ch Ct Min, 1/98)

CROSLAND, Joshua
Died before 23 June 1807 when Jesse Holt was paid $180 for boarding & clothing the 3 orphan children, heirs of Joshua Crosland, deceased, for 3 years past. (Wil TN, Co Ct Min, no#/299)

CROSS, Ben.
Died before 4 November 1782 when his orphan, Absolom Cross, was bound to Danl. Kenedy, Esqr. until age 21. The Court adjudged Absolom to be 13 years old at this time. (Was TN, Co Ct Min, 1/179)

CROSS, Jno. B.
Died [paper is torn, it looks like 1852] intestate, & Maclin Cross was appointed administrator and filed suit vs Albert Cross et als for sale of assets, 21 September 1853. (Mad TN, Ch Ct Min, 1/342) 11 September 1854 the case was revived in the name of Richd. J. Hays, administrator of J. B. Cross, [Jr. or Sr.] deceased. (Ibid 2/10) Merideth Helm & wife Nancy have received advancements from the estate. Franklin Butler & wife, David McBride & son William & Polly McLaurin also received advancements. (Ibid 33)

CROSS, Ranson
2 July 1860 John Carmichael was paid $1.50 for making a coffin for the child of Ranson Cross. (Sev TN, Co Ct Min, no#/566)

CROSS, Robert
Was a resident of Cumberland County, KY, on 13 February 1817 when his deposition was to be taken for the defendant in the suit of Robert Nall vs William Rogers. (Cla TN, Co Ct Min, 4/319)

CROSSLAND
24 December 1805 William Davis was appointed guardian of 3 orphan children named Sally Crossland, Lucinda Crossland & Joshua Crossland. Isham Davis, Sr. was security. (Wil TN, Co Ct Min, no#/179)

CROW, J. A.
Died before 4 January 1871 when J. R. Crow and J. B. Powell made a settlement as administrators. (Dyr TN, Co Ct Min, B/165)

CROW, James
Died before 11 July 1844 when Burton L. Stovall petitioned to sell lands. George W. Bright was appointed guardian ad litem for Elizabeth Crow and Calvin Crow, minor heirs of James Crow, deceased, and Richard Nelms was appointed guardian for the two minor children of the said Richard & Jane Nelms, formerly Jane Crow. (Obi TN, Cir Ct Min, 4/no#) Narcissa Crow was the widow & dower was ordered to be set off 13 November 1844. (Ibid)

CROW, James
Was a minor 19 October 1801 when he was bound to James Hunt until age 21. (Rob TN, Co Ct Min, 1/188) 5 November 1804 this indenture was canceled because of the death of James Hunt. Mary Crow, the mother of James, was allowed to take him. (Ibid 316)

CROW, John
Died before 3 December 1827 when his will was proved by Micah Sellers & William Goldin, witnesses. (McM TN, Co Ct Min, 2no#/244)

CROW, Mary
5 February 1806 was ordered to bring her children to next court because the children "are in a likely way to suffer." (Rob TN, Co Ct Min, 1/378)

CRUDUPE, John
Was released from paying taxes for 1804 as he and Hutson Alford did not come into the county until 12 May 1804. (Wil TN, Co Ct Min, no#/112)

CRUDUPE, John
Died before 19 March 1817 when the executors, Isham David & Blake Rutland, were ordered to make a report. (Wil TN, Co Ct Min, no#/95) 4 August 1818 Thomas F. Hays was appointed guardian for Elisha Crudupe, Robert Crudupe & John Crudupe, minor heirs of John Crudupe, deceased. (Ibid 305)

CRUTCHFIELD, William
Died before 16 December 1816 when commissioners were appointed to allot to the widow her equal part of the negroes. (Wil TN, Co Ct Min, no#/53)

CULLWELL, Robert
Died before 3 February 1783 when his orphan, Wm. Cullwell, made choice of Joseph McMurty as his guardian. (Was TN, Co Ct Min, 1/193)

CULP, Daniel
Died before 16 May 1833 when his death was suggested in the suit of Thomas A. Polk vs Daniel Culp & the heirs of Rice Williams by their guardians Jesse L. Ross & Thomas Allen. It was further suggested that George W. Terril & Babrara his wife, Robert J. Gilchrist & Drucilla his wife, Susan Culp, Isabella Vanlear? Culp, Daniel Culp, Fielding Culp, Elizabeth Culp & [blank] Culp were his heirs-at-law, the last six being minors. George W. Terril was appointed guardian to defend for the minors. All of the heirs reside in Gibson County, TN. (Obi TN, Cir Ct Min, 2/85)

CULTON, Joseph
At the November term 1788 came into court and proved by the oath of Alexander Moffett that he lost a part of his left ear in a fight with a certain Charles Young and prays the same to be entered of record. (Was TN, Co Ct Min, 1/355)

CUMMINGS, B. F.
Died before 14 April 1858 as shown in the suit of James H. Beason vs John C. Flanigan et als. James H. Beason was administrator of B. F. Cummings, deceased. He had recovered a judgement against William Flanigan in 1851. William Flanigan, formerly a defendant, has been dead more than 6 months. (Fen TN, Ch Ct Min, A/148)

CUMMINGS, George
20 September 1828 made a deed of gift of some slaves to his son-in-law, William R. D. Phipps. (Wil TN, Reg Bk/366) [second set of page numbers]

CUMMINGS, Hugh
Made a deed of gift 27 May 1818 to his daughter, Sarah Rhodes of Rutherford County, TN, of a negro woman named Ester about 28 years of age. (Wil TN, Reg Bk/114)

CUMMINS, Mary A. F.
2 May 1871 was chosen and appointed guardian of her own children. (Dyr TN, Co Ct Min, B/239)

CUMMINS, W. E.
Died before 1 May 1871 when E. P. Kirk made a settlement as administrator. (Dyr TN, Co Ct Min, B/236) 1 December 1873 M. A. F. Cummings made a settlement as guardian of the heirs. (Ibid 667)

CUNNINGHAM, Christopher
28 August 1778 came to Court and took the oath of Affirmation of Alligance to this state. [The words, "oath of", were crossed out.] (Was TN, Co Ct Min, 1/45)

CUNNINGHAM, Christopher
Died before 27 August 1781 when Charles Robertson was granted leave of administration, with Wm. McNabb & Andrew Taylor as security. (Was TN, Co Ct Min, 1/141) 5 May 1783 the will of Christopher Cunningham was proved by Robert Orr. Robert Orr made oath that he saw Isaac Taylor sign the will as a witness. (Ibid 206) 3 November 1783 Mathew Talbot & Joseph Tipton, executor of the estate of Christopher Cunningham, produced an inventory of said estate. [Were there 2 Christopher Cunninghams who died?] (Ibid 225, 227)

CUNNINGHAM, George
11 February 1812, was certified to be a man of honesty, probity, good moral character, good demeanor and had attained the age of 21 years. (Rob TN, Co Ct Min, 3/62)

CUNNINGHAM, J. B.
Died before 6 June 1871 when A. S. Parks & H. Parks, Jr. were chosen and appointed guardian of the minor heirs with Smith Parks and H. Parks, Sr. as security. A years support was laid off to the widow and family. (Dyr TN, Co Ct Min, B/246) The will was proved by G. B. Tinsley and J. M. Sherrod, witnesses, and Smith Parks and J. H. Wyatt were witnesses to the codicil. (Ibid 247)

CUNNINGHAM, James
Died before 5 June 1820 when his will was proved by Robert Furgeson, one of the witnesses. Moses Cunningham & Peggy Cunningham took the oath as executors, with Robert Furgeson, Nathan M. Young & William Gardinhire as their securities. (McM TN, Co Ct Min, no#/5)

CUNNINGHAM, Jesse
Died before 1 November 1858 when the widow, Elizabeth Cunningham, vs Henry S.

Smith & other heirs, petitoned for the sale of a town lot. Ephraim Cunningham & Elizabeth Cunningham are minor heirs and Elizabeth Cunningham, Sr. was appointed their guardian ad litem. (Sev TN, Co Ct Min, no#/360) Another heir was Dorcas who has married H. S. Smith. Dorcas, Ephraim & Elizabeth Cunningham are the children and heirs of Jesse Cunningham, deceased. (Ibid 454)

CUNNINGHAM, John
28 August 1778 took the oath of allegiance. (Was TN, Co Ct Min, 1/47)

CUNNINGHAM, John, Sr.
Died intestate about 18 December 1842 in Warren County, TN. He had resided many years before his death in both Warren County and in Coffee County. His only heirs were: James Cunningham of VA; the heirs of William Cunningham who died many years ago & whose names are unknown, except that he had a son, William Cunningham, of AL; Richard Cunningham of Bedford County, TN; Austin Shepard & Richard [sic] his wife formerly Rachael Cunningham citizen of Marshall County, TN; Jesse R. Edwards & the children of said Jesse R. & Elizabeth his wife formerly Elizabeth Cunningham who is dead, that is to say Joseph Edwards of AL, William L. Binor? & Kiziah his wife formerly Kiziah Edwards of Coffee County, John Edwards of AL, David Edwards, James Edwards & Lucy C. Edwards of Warren County, the last 4 are minors; William Kinrod of Warren County & the children of he and Martha his wife, formerly Martha Cunningham who is dead, that is to say John J. Kinnrod believed to live out of the limits of TN, William Kinrod & George Kinnrod, Elizabeth Kinnrod, Martha A. Kinnrod & James A. Kinnrod of Warren County of whom being minors [this handwriting is very bad & I am not sure of some of the names. Kinnrod also looks like Rinnrod, Kinnord & Kinnard]; Joseph W. Cunningham of AL; the heirs of Langston Cunningham, deceased, that is to say, John Cunningham, Langston Cunningham, Richard Cunningham, Samuel Hancock & wife Mary formerly Mary Cummingham of Coffee County; Thomas Cunningham, a citizen of Mexico; William S. Cunningham of Warren County; Benjamin L. Douglass & wife Nancy, formerly Nancy Cunningham of KY; Joseph R. Cunningham of Coffee County who is a minor [these last 4 could have been children of Langston Cunningham deceased.]; James Cunningham of Bedford County; Nancy Cunningham widow of said Langston Cunningham, deceased, of Coffee County; Langston Martha [sic] a citizen of Coffee County [the last name entered twice]; Archibald J. Price & wife Elizabeth and Richard J. Price & Mary Price being children of Thomas Martin and Polly his wife formerly Polly Cunningham, this Price & minors being citizens of Coffee County; Nancy Shapherd widow of Anderson Shepherd, deceased, formerly Nancy Cunningham of Jackson County, AL; Linan? Cunningham whose residence is unknown but believed to be out of the state; John Odgen, Benjamin C. Ogden, Mary Ann Ogden & George W. Ogden of White County, TN, children of George Ogden & his wife Rachael formerly Rachael Cunningham being infants; Esther Ogden & S Berry Lance of White County, TN. All of the above are to be made defendants in the suit of John Williams & wife vs Jessee R. Edwards & others. John W. Williams was the husband of Kiziah Williams formerly Kiziah Cunningham. Also in the suit were William W. Cunningham of Grundy County, TN, Nancy E. Cunningham of Grundy County, Benjamin B. Cunningham of Grundy County, John M. Cunningham of Coffee County, Langston C. Cunningham, Joseph A. Cunningham, Engert Cunningham, Mary Elizabeth Cunningham, Lucy Ann Cunningham citizens of Grundy County, the said Kiziah, William H., Nancy E., Benjamin & John N., Langston C., Joseph A. George W., Mary Elizabeth and Lucy Ann Cunningham being children of Benjamin B. Cunningham, deceased, and a portion of the heirs of John Cunningham, Sr., deceased. The minors sue by their mother & next friend, Benjamin B. Cunningham [sic] [I hope somebody can make heads or tails out of this list of heirs, I can't.] John Cunningham, Sr., at the time of his death was upwards of 94 years old & was of unsound mind. This suit is a family squabble over the estate of John Cunningham, Sr. and I suggest anyone interested get a copy of it and maybe thay can sort out the names. The last entry was for February 1849. (Bed TN, Ch Ct Min, 3/340-373)

CUNNINGHAM, Margaret
Died before 5 April 1858 when the will was entered. Josias Gamble was one of the witnesses. The other witness, Thomas S. Hardin, is sick and can't attend court to prove the will. William McTeer is to take charge of the property until further order. (Sev TN, Co Ct Min, no#/284) 2 July 1866 A. B. McTeer was appointed administrator with the will annexed. (Ibid 341)

CURTIS
6 June 1870 John F. Sinclair made settlement as guardian of Sarah D. Curtis, Harriet R. C. Curtis & Lousiana Curtis. (Dyr TN, Co Ct Min, B/63)

CURTIS, Bethena
Died before 8 March 1870 when W. J. Davis was appointed administrator with Smith Parks & J. H. York as security. (Dyr TN, Co Ct Min, B/12)

CURTIS, Samuel, Jr.
Died before 5 February 1812 when Thomas Tomlinson & Hannah Tomlinson were appointed administrators, with John Tomlinson & William Tomlinson, Jr. as security. (Ste TN, Co Ct Min, 3/120)

CURTIS, William
Taxes were not collected in District 4 for 1873, "Crockett Co." (Dyr TN, Co Ct Min, B/759)

CUSICK, Samuel
Died before 1 December 1862 when his will was proved by Joseph Tipton. Andrew Cusick was appointed administrator with the will annexed with Joseph Tipton & Jas. A. Pickens as security. (Sev TN, Co Ct Min, no#/25)

DALTON, Nicholas [Daulton]
Died before 11 March 1845 when land was taxed to the heirs. (Obi TN, Cir Ct Min, 4/no#)

DARBY, J. V.
Died before 19 August 1868 as shown in the suit of J. B. Caruthers admr. of J. V. Darby decd. vs Mary A. Darby. (Mad TN, Ch Ct Min, 3/207) The suit is shown as J. B. Caruthers admr. Jas. V. Daily decd. vs Mary D. Daily et als. Jas. V. Dailey died intestate & the defendants are his children, one of whom, Ann M. Darby, has since married T. V. Burnes, who is made a defendant to these proceedings. (Ibid 214)

DARDEN, Ann
Died before 16 October 1797 when Jonathan Darden was appointed administrator with Holland Darden & Anderson Cheatham as security. (Rob TN, Co Ct Min, 1/36)

DARDEN, Betsey
7 January 1807 a jury was summoned to inquire into her lunacy. (Rob TN, Co Ct Min, 1/427) 7 April 1807 she was found to be a "Lunitick" & Jonathan Darden was appointed guardian. (Ibid 439)

DARDEN, J. H.
Taxes were not collected in District 2 for 1873, "under age." (Dyr TN, Co Ct Min, B/758)

DARDEN, James
Died before 3 December 1872 when James M. King made a settlement as guardian of James Darden's heirs. George Miller was chosen and appointed guardian of the heirs of Stephen King, deceased, "vice J. M. King removed." (Dyr TN, Co Ct Min, B/517)

DARDEN, Jonathan
Died before 9 August 1814 when Isaac Dortch & James Norfleet were ordered to settle with Hollad Darden and Anderson Cheatham, administrators of Jonathan Darden, deceased. (Rob TN, Co Ct Min, 3/452)

DARDIS, Thos.
Died before 22 September 1809 when it was ordered that $20 be paid to his representatives for his service as late Solicitor for this County for 6 months, being March & June courts. (Roa TN, Co Ct Min, D/128)

DARNAL, Nicholas
Died before 15 May 1810 when Nancy Darnal was allowed letters of administration on the estate with Jesse Martin & John Brooks as security. (Rob TN, Co Ct Min, 2/261) Name also shown as Darnell. (Ibid 3/377) 12 May 1814 Martin Duncan was appointed guardian of Nicholas Darnal & Milberry Darnal, orphans of Nicholas Darnal, deceased, with William Flewellen & Herbert Harwell as security. (Ibid 425)

DARR, Henry
Died before 10 August 1814 when Eve Darr was granted letters of administration, with Zacheriah Dunn & Jacob Grimes as security. (Rob TN, Co Ct Min, 3/462)

DARWIN, William G.
Died before 10 February 1854 as shown in the suit of George C. Darwin & Polly Darwin admrs. of William G. Darwin deceased. vs Joseph B. Rogers & Milton Draper. George C.

Darwin, Sr. has died since the start of this suit. G. C. Darwin, Jr. is his executor. (Jac TN, Ch Ct Min, B/134)

DATERIDGE, Lewis
On 10 September 1814 made a deed of gift to his sister, Milberry, for his personal property & "my draw from the United States for my Service in the Army," witnessed by Micajah Viverett, Edward Teasdale & Lanslot Viveret. (Wil TN, Reg Bk/5)

DAUGHERTY, George
Died before 21 September 1803 when land was taxed to the heirs. (Roa TN, Co Ct Min, A/144) 21 June 1804 Mary Doherty, Polly W. Burk, Francis Doherty, Hellen Doherty, Heirs & Devisees of George Doherty deceased vs Martin Armstrong: Petition for partition of Lands. Jacob Jones, George Preston, James Preston, William Campbell and Henry Breazeale were appointed to make a division. (Ibid 241) Land had been granted by NC to Dougherty & Martin Armstrong as tenants in common, formerly in Green County but now in Roane County. The heirs, [same as listed above except Polly Burch instead of Burk] petition for division. (Ibid B/259) Polly also shown as Bunch. (Ibid 265)

DAUGHERTY, Matthew
Was the father of a bastard child by Dinah Kelly. He admitted the charge & was ordered to pay support 7 September 1825. Matthew was also shown as Moses Daugherty. Charles Daugherty was his security. On the same date Matthew petitioned the court to change the name of the child from Joshua Kelly to Dennis Daugherty and have him declared legitimate and an equal heir with his other children, which was done. (McM TN, Co Ct Min, 2no#/99 & 100)

DAVENPORT, Thomas
17 June 1817 was allowed $10 for his support until next term. (Wil TN, Co Ct Min, no#/117)

DAVID, Assariah R.
Was an orphan boy aged 18 years when he was bound to Joel K. Brown on 9 March 1831, to learn the trade of a Tailor. (McM TN, Co Ct Min, 2no#/521)

DAVID, Isiah
Died before 3 August 1818 when the administrator, Thomas Patterson, was ordered to make a settlement. (Wil TN, Co Ct Min, no#/293)

DAVIDSON, Carlton
Died in 1846 as shown in the suit of Seth Thomas against Bluford Davidson in his own right and as administrator of Carlton Davidson, deceased, and against Andrew Davidson. Seth Thomas had received a judgement in 1841 against Carlton Davidson and Richard M. Davidson. Bluford Davidson was the brother of Carlton Davidson and Andrew Davidson was his father. The widow of Carlton was mentioned. Andrew Davidson sold all of his property to his son, James? S. Davidson. Bluford Davidson was administrator. (Bed TN, Ch Ct Min, 3/459)

DAVIDSON, Emanuel
Died before 4 February 1811 when land was taxed to the heirs. (Ste TN, Co Ct Min, 3/24)

DAVIDSON, Ephraim B.
Died before 12 May 1828 when Christopher C. Davidson & William Cook were ordered to appear at the next court to give evidence relative to the murder of Ephraim B. Davidson. (Obi TN, Cir Ct Min, 1/45)

DAVIDSON, Lucinda
On 8 February 1854 she dismissed her suit for divorce against Thomas Davidson. (Jac TN, Ch Ct Min, B/122)

DAVIDSON, Martha P.
Died before 2 February 1825 when her heirs, John Donnell, William B. Gill, Benjamin Davidson, William P. Davidson, Francis P. Davidson, Wilson Z. Davidson, Thomas Cartwright, & Polly Bloodworth, sold to Alfred Bloodworth a negro woman named Amy & her children. (Wil TN, Reg Bk/338) [second set of page numbers]

DAVIDSON, Richard
Died intestate in Jackson County in 1849, as shown in the petition of William Davidson Admr. of Richard Davidson & others. The other plaintiffs are the widow and heirs. Sarah Davidson was the widow. (Jac TN, Ch Ct Min, A/416) A petition was filed 17 July 1851 by

William Davidson, administrator of Richard Davidson, Sarah Davidson widow of said deceased, William Davidson son of said deceased, John Davidson, Thomas Davidson, Ansel Davidson, Jessee Chambers and wife Milly, Eli Jackson and wife Hannah, Sarah Davidson daughter of said deceased, Nathan Davidson, Martha Davidson and James C. Davidson. The land was sold and bought by the widow, Sarah Davidson, and William Davidson. Title was divested out of all of the above. (Ibid B/7)

DAVIDSON, Thomas
Was a resident of Marshall County, TN, 31 May 1838 as shown in his suit against John M. Sharp of Iredell County, NC. (Bed TN, Ch Ct Min, 1/247)

DAVIDSON, Thomas
Died before 23 February 1842 when land was taxed to the heirs. (Obi TN, Cir Ct Min, 4/no#)

DAVIE, Yarborough [Davy, David]
Died before 9 March 1852. He had been counsel for the complainant in the suit of Winiford Howard et als vs Wm. Howard et als. (Mad TN, Ch Ct Min, 1/232) Quintin Davie was administrator. (Ibid 2/11) 15 March 1855 a suit was entered by Winniford Howard, Jas. A. Howard, Beterice Howard, Robert Howard and Joseph Thomas Howard vs Quintin N. Davie, administrator of Yarboro M. David and others. Y. M. David had made advancements for the family of William Howard since 1 February 1847. (Ibid 2/28)

DAVIS, A., Mrs.
4 July 1870 several people were paid for holding a jury of inquest as to her insanity. (Dyr TN, Co Ct Min, B/75) 1 August 1870, W. G. Davis was paid $60 for carrying Adaline J. Davis to the Asylum near Nashville. (Ibid 93)

DAVIS, Benjamin
Died before 13 July 1820 when his heirs appointed a power of attorney to apply for a military land warrent for the service of Benjamin Davis in the Revolutionary War. The heirs were Joseph Gray & wife Milly, James Davis, Miles Jackson & wife Sarah, Grandy Prichard & wife Lydia, all of Pasquotank County, NC. It states that Benjamin Davis enlisted as a private soldier in NC and served until the end of the war. William Sanderlin was granted power of attorney. (Wil TN, Reg Bk/299)

DAVIS, Burgess B.
Died before 25 February 1860 as shown in the suit of Arthur Deloach et als vs Wm. J. McKinney et als. The complainants are not entitled to any part of the estate of Burgess B. Davis, deceased. An appeal was granted. (Mad TN, Ch Ct Min, 2/341)

DAVIS, David
Was a resident of Logan County, KY, on 2 August 1813 when his deposition was to be taken for the plaintiff in the suit of Jesse Denson vs Philip Hornburger. (Ste TN, Co Ct Min, 4/50)

DAVIS, Elizabeth
Made a deed of gift to her son, Nathaniel Davis, for a negro woman Isbel, 19 October 1818. (Wil TN, Reg Bk/135) On the same date she made a deed of gift to her son, John Davis, for a negro Bob, and to her son, Isham F. Davis, for all the money due from her father, John Lewis, deceased, estate. (Ibid 136-7)

DAVIS, Henry
Died before 30 August 1844 when Richard H. Sims, guardian, petitioned for division of slaves between Mary R. Stone, formerly Mary R. Davis, and Charlotte S. Davis, children & heirs of Henry Davis, deceased. (Bed TN, Ch Ct Min, 2/307) [Also see John Sims]

DAVIS, Isabella J.
Died before 2 March 1857 when the will was proved by William Wayland and Jos. M. Hodges, witnesses. Hiram Bogle, one of the executors named, qualified, with J. S. McCroskey & Jos. M. Hodges as security. (Sev TN, Co Ct Min, no#/129)

DAVIS, J. P.
Died before 6 March 1871 when G. W. Blair made a settlement as administrator. (Dyr TN, Co Ct Min, B/201)

DAVIS, James D.
4 September 1865 was appointed guardian to Andrew & John P. Davis with J. A. Pickens, Wm. B. Clark & Wm. M. Burnett as security. (Sev TN, Co Ct Min, no#/207)

DAVIS, John
Died in 1827, intestate, in Pittsylvania County VA. Winifred, now Winifred Stratton wife of Thomas Stratton, was his widow. His only child was John Davis who was a minor 27 August 1845 when he entered a suit by his next friend, Judthan Carter, vs William Robinson & others. A division of slaves was made between John, Jr. & Winifred. The boy, Ira, was allotted to Winifred. She & Thomas Stratton removed Ira to TN in 1828 without the knowledge or consent of John R. or his guardian, Judethan Carter, & thereby forfeited title to him by the laws of VA. (Bed TN, Ch Ct Min, 2/368)

DAVIS, John D.
Died before 2 December 1872 when Robert Canada made a settlement as administrator. (Dyr TN, Co Ct Min, B/514)

DAVIS, Jose M.
Died before 7 December 1840 as shown in the suit of Mansfield Whitehead vs Lydia Davis, heir-at-law & Elizabeth Davis, widow of Jose M. Davis, deceased. Some years ago William Farmer & James Russell purchased jointly a tract of land from Thomas Powell. Farmer & Pussel [sic] have since both died, but Pussel before his death, sold his interest in the land to Jose M. Davis, "and the interest of Farmer deceased to Jane Dement & Ann O. Bryant, his only heirs." Thomas Powell was at that time a resident of MS. Mansfield Whitehead has purchased the interest of Jane Dement & Ann O. Bryant and their husbands in said land and is seeking title. Lydia M. Davis was the only child of Jose M. Davis & was a minor. (Bed TN, Ch Ct Min, 1/345)

DAVIS, M. P.
Taxes were not collected in District 2 for 1873, "in Gibson Co." (Dyr TN, Co Ct Min, B/758)

DAVIS, Marriot
10 August 1824 made a deed of gift of slaves to his daughters, Sarah Davis & Elizabeth Davis. (Wil TN, Reg Bk/348)

DAVIS, Nathl., Esqr.
Died before 28 May 1781 when the will was proved by Robert Davis and Mary Davis. (Was TN, Co Ct Min, 1/132)

DAVIS, R. N.
Married before 21 August 1860 to Isabella J. McClellan and was appointed her trustee in the place of Geo. B. Hicks. Isabella was an heir of Saml. McClellan, deceased. (Mad TN, Ch Ct Min, 2/356)

DAVIS, Reps J.
Died before 4 August 1856 when the executor of the will, Thos. C. Brabson, gave a new bond with B. D. Brabson as security. The original bond was destroyed. B. D. Brabson renewed his bond as guardian of Ann Reps and John Davis, minor heirs. Personal property left to Ann Davis by the will of Reps J. Davis was ordered to be sold. (Sev TN, Co Ct Min, no#/65) William A. McNutt renewed his bond as guardian to Benj. S. Davis, minor heir of Reps J. Davis, with Jno S. McNutt & L. W. Burn as security. The original bond was destroyed by fire. (Ibid 66) Hiram Bogle renewed his bond as guardian to Joseph B. Davis & Pricilla J. Davis, minor heirs of Reps J. Davis, deceased. (Ibid 68) B. D. Brabson made a settlement as guardian to Ann E. Davis, Reps A. Davis & John E. Davis minor heirs of Reps J. Davis, deceased. (Ibid 89) 8 April 1857 Reps A. Davice chose John S. McNutt as guardian. (Ibid 156)

DAVIS, S. C.
Died before 5 August 1867 when James D. Davis made a settlement as guardian to Andrew & John P. Davis, minor heirs. (Sev TN, Co Ct Min, no#/465)

DAVIS, Samuel
Died before 7 March 1864 when James D. Davis was appointed administrator with Jas. A. Pickens as security. (Sev TN, Co Ct Min, no#/90)

DAVIS, Thomas
Died before 2 October 1871 when W. T. Agee resigned as guardian of the minor heirs. (Dyr TN, Co Ct Min, B/295)

DAVIS, Walter
Was bound 1 March 1830 to James A. Turnly to learn the potters trade. (McM TN, Co Ct Min, 2no#/422)

DAVIS, William
Died before 2 March 1830 when Nancy Davis & Anthony Davis were appointed administrators. (McM TN, Co Ct Min, 2no#/431) A years support was laid off to the widow, Nancy. (Ibid 452) 6 December 1830 John F., James A. & Francis M. Davis, minor children of William, made choice of Jackson Smith as their guardian. They are all over 14. (Ibid 488)

DAVIS, Wilson
Was released from paying poll tax for 1858 as he had left the county before that date. (Sev TN, Co Ct Min, no#/407)

DAWSON, Jane
5 April 1871 was alledged to be a pauper. (Dyr TN, Co Ct Min, B/227)

DAWSON, W. A.
Taxes were not collected in District 5 for 1873, "Ark." (Dyr TN, Co Ct Min, B/759)

DAWSON, William Johnston
Died before 22 March 1809 as shown in the suit of Penelope Lother, administratrix of William Johnston Dawson vs James Glasgow, for Debt. (Roa TN, Co Ct Min, C/287)

DAY, Jno. H.
Died before 17 February 1858 as shown in the suit of Jno. T. Andrews & wife vs Wm. Croom et als. It was stated that more than 6 months had elapsed since defendant, Robt. P. Ford, qualified as executor of Jno. H. Day, deceased. Sarah E. Moore is to be made a party complainant. (Mad TN, Ch Ct Min, 2/169) Wm. Croom was appointed guardian of Jno. T. Andrews & wife in 1843 & Jno. H. Day was his security. In 1853 there remained funds in the hands of the guardian. Jno. T. Andrews & wife Amanda & Sarah E. Moore are to recover from Croom & Robt. Ford, executor of Jno. H. Day, the funds due them. (Ibid 233) In the suit of E. H. Day & others vs Susan V. Day et als, it is stated that Jno. H. Day died 15 August 1856 leaving a will by which he gave his son, E. H. Day, an equal share of his estate. He gave Susan V. Day (after certain specified bequests) an equal share of his estate absolutely. To Wm. A. Day an equal portion for life and at his death to be equally divided among his children. To Sarah C. Lavallette an equal portion for her sole & separate use & at her death to her children. To O. T. McKee an equal portion for her sole & separate use & at her death to her children. To Malvina H. Watkins an equal portion for her sole & separate use & at her death to her children. To Martha A. Ford an equal portion for her sole & separate use & at her death to her children. Jno. R. Woolfolk, James S. Lynn, Robert B. Hunt, Martin Cartwell & Wm. H. Levy? were appointed to divide the estate. (Ibid 285) Division was made. Other names mentioned were Olivia T. McKee, Gertrude McKee, Buena Vista McKee, Martha D. McKee, Wm. Henry McKee, Haskins Ford, Mary Lavallette, Ida Watkins, Lilia Watkins, Ellen Watkins, Irvin Watkins, Martha Watkins, Susan Virginia Day, Edward H. Day. (Ibid 302-311) 21 August 1867 a suit was entered by John H. Woolfolk, administrator of Jno. H. Day, W. A. Day et als vs Eliza P. Holt. (Ibid 3/61)

DEADRICK, George M.
16 July 1799 made a deed to Mary Searcy, wife of Bennet Searcy, with Samuel Donleson as witness. The consent of Bennet Searcy to his wife's receiving the deed was also registered. (Rob TN, Co Ct Min, 1/112) 6 July 1808 Geo. M. Deadrick was shown to be of Davidson County. (Ibid 2/54)

DEAN, Alsey
Died intestate in Hardeman County in 1866 leaving Catherine Teague, wife of Joshua Teague, and Hardy J. Dean & others his only heirs. Hardy J. Dean & Jno. A. Dean are the administrators. Catherine Teague wants her part of her father's estate put in trust for the sole use of her and her children, Rebecca H. and Bedford L. Teague. Wm. G. Teague acted as the next friend of Catherine in this suit. (Mad TN, Ch Ct Min, 2/532) Jefferson C. Savage was appointed trustee for Catherine Teague & her children. (Ibid 3/73)

DEARING, William
Died before 11 March 1845 when land was taxed to the heirs. (Obi TN, Cir Ct Min, 4/no#)

DEARMAR, John
Married before 18 November 1814 to Hannah Tucker, daughter of John Tucker, deceased. (Rob Co Ct Min, 3/514)

DEASON, Shepherd
Died "some years since" as shown in a suit filed 8 July 1837 by Absolem Hally [Holly] &

wife Elvy, citizens of Ansom County, NC vs John Deason & Joseph Rushing. Shepherd Deason was the father of Elvy Hally & died when she was but a child, leaving Elvy and Joel R. Deason his only heirs. Shepherd Deason was the son of Enock Deason late of Bedford County. Enock died some 5 years since, having made a will & appointed John Deason & Joseph Rushing executors. Enock bequeathed all his property to his wife, Rebecca Deason, during her life & then to his own children then living, being 9 in number, and to his grand son, Joel Deason, he bequeathed $63. He bequeathed to his grand daughter, Elvy Hally, $25. He made other bequests to his son, John Deason, and his grandson, John Deason, son of William Deason. The widow of Enock is now deceased. Absolem Hally & Elvy [Elicy] Deason were married before the death of Enock Deason. The will of Enock Deason is shown and the name given as Enuch Dorson [I think this entire book has been recopied and there appears to be many errors in transcribing from the original.] The children named were; daughter Marth Rushing; son William Dorson; daughter Nancy Rushing; daughter Milley Rushing; son Absolem Dorson; son Absolem Dorson [named twice]; son Joel Deason; daughter Rulann? Cooper; daughter Rebecca Loyd; grand son Joel B. Deason; grand daughter Elicy Hally; grand son Joel Deason son of William Deason my son. He appointed his son John Deason and his son-in-law Joseph Rushing executors. (Bed TN, Ch Ct Min, 1/123)

DEBERRY
31 July 1849 a suit was dismissed by complainant James W. Hayley vs David Merriwether & wife Elija Jane Absalem Deberry & guar for Mathew & Allen Deberry, minors & heirs Mat Deberry Robt B. Hart & wife Susan Allen, Rebecca Merriwether Allen & Absalem Deberry Exrs of Mat Deberry & David Merriwether as admr of Jno Deberry deceased. [This suit is not clear, it is written exactly as shown.] (Mad TN, Ch Ct Min, 1/86)

DEBERRY, Absalem
Died before 17 March 1854 as shown in the petition of Caroline E. Taylor et als. 3 September 1842 Francis Merriwether conveyed slaves to Absalem Deberry in trust for the use of Caroline T. Taylor & her heirs. Absalem Deberry has departed this life & his executors desire to be divested of the trust. (Mad TN, Ch Ct Min, 1/362) David J. Merriwether was appointed trustee. (Ibid 366)

DEBERRY, Matthias
Died before 19 February 1858 as shown in the petition of Robt. B. Hunt, James W. Hayley et als. Deberry, by his will, gave a tract of land and negroes to James Hayley's children. Absolom Deberry was executor & was also appointed trustee of the estate of the Hayley children. Absolom Deberry has died leaving a will by which he appointed Robt. B. Hunt, Allen Deberry & David Merriwether executors. Wyatt Mooring was appointed trustee of the estate of the Hayley children, who have now removed to Obion County. (Mad TN, Ch Ct Min, 2/194)

DEDMAN, Edith
Was a base born child of the age of 4 years when she was bound at November term 1788 to William Carson until age 18. (Was TN, Co Ct Min, 1/343)

DEHART
Money was allowed 7 June 1830 for John Dehart for medical aid and for Mary Dehart, a pauper. (McM TN, Co Ct Min, 2/456)

DEHART, Elizabeth
Was a pauper 7 December 1829 when money was allowed for her support. (McM TN, Co Ct Min, 2/404)

DEHART, Mary
Died before 7 June 1830 when John Dehart was allowed money for her medical expense. (McM TN, Co Ct Min, 2no#/456)

DELL, John
Died before 5 April 1814 when an agreement was made by John Harpole, Asa Dell, William Dell & Thomas Dell, to release to John Dell their right & claim to a tract of land whereon Henry Johnson now lives, "the property of John Dell deceased." This was witnessed by Geo. H. Bullard, Wm. H. Peace & Adam Moser. (Wil TN, Reg Bk/7) Asa, Wm., John & Thomas Dell released to John Harpole their right to 42 acres whereon John Dell, deceased, lived. Same date & witnesses as above. (Ibid 8)

DELL, Samuel
Died before 24 September 1804 when Thomas Dell was appointed administrator. (Wil TN, Co Ct Min, no#/91)

DELOACH, Solomon
Died before 4 February 1818 when the administrator, James Whitworth, was ordered to make a settlement. (Wil TN, Co Ct Min, no#/232)

DELOCH, Samuel
Died before 9 March 1816, late of the County of Johnson and State of NC, when his widow, Jarisha Deloach & heirs, Joseph Deloach, Samuel Deloach, Shadrach Ingrum, Mary Ingrum, William Spicer & Lucretia Spicer, sold slaves to Thomas Davis. (Wil TN, Reg Bk/59)

DELOZIER, Asa
Died before 7 October 1856 when his will was proved by Andrew Kirkpatrick & David Vougtt, witnesses. Cromwell Delozier & Andrew Delozier were executors with Benjamin Tipton & B. J. Tipton as security. (Sev TN, Co Ct Min, no#/83) 7 January 1857 the widow, Caroline Delozier, dissented from the will. (Ibid 119) 7 February 1859 Caroline Delozier filed suit against the executors, exceptions to the settlement. (Ibid 403-4)

DELOZIER, Malden
5 April 1858, a lunacy hearing was ordered to be held. (Sev TN, Co Ct Min, no#/280) A jury found that he is a lunatic. (Ibid 295) 5 November 1866 Joseph H. Delozier was appointed guardian. (Ibid 390)

DELOZIER, Samuel C.
Died before 7 January 1867 when John Robeson was appointed administrator with Lankston Cunningham as security. (Sev TN, Co Ct Min, no#/413) Lewis Wayland, Calvin Chandler & John McCroskey were appointed to lay off a years support to Harriet Delozier, the widow. (Ibid 420) A bill was paid for holding an inquest over his body. (Ibid 441)

DENNIS, John
Died before 3 December 1827 when James Dennis was appointed administrator. (McM TN, Co Ct Min, 2no#/245)

DENNIS, Sarah Ann
Had apparently sued William Dennis for divorce. On 10 February 1854 in the suit of Sarah Ann vs William it was stated that since they are now living and cohabiting together the suit is dismissed. (Jac TN, Ch Ct Min, B/135) 6 February 1857 Sarah An Dennis was allowed to file an amended bill for divorce against Miles [sic] Dennis. (Ibid C/75) In the suit of Sarah An Dennis vs Miles Dennis for divorce, since the filing of this bill the defendant has died. (Ibid 89)

DENTON, Isaac
Died before 17 May 1795 when the will was proved by David Jobe and Jesse Whitson. (Was TN, Co Ct Min, 1/546)

DENTON, James
28 August 1778 took the oath of allegiance. (Was TN, Co Ct Min, 1/47)

DENTON, Joseph
28 August 1778 took the oath of allegiance to this state. (Was TN, Co Ct Min, 1/46)

DENTON, Saml.
28 August 1778 took the oath of allegiance. (Was TN, Co Ct Min, 1/47)

DERRICK, Calvin
3 February 1862 was appointed guardian of the minor heirs of Elizabeth Derrick. (Sev TN, Co Ct Min, no#/748) 1 January 1866 Calvin Derrick made a settlement as guardian of the minor heirs of Asa Derrick & wife. (Ibid 253) 5 February 1866 Calvin Derrick was granted leave to remove his guardianship to Jefferson County. (Ibid 270)

DEVERS, James
Died before 5 September 1803 when William Devers was appointed administrator with Henry Hunter as his security. (Cla TN, Co Ct Min, 1/146) Mary Dever is the widow of James Dever and a jury is to inquire into her mind as to idiocy or lunacy. (Ibid 150) William Devers was appointed guardian of William Devers & Mary Devers, orphans of James Dever, deceased. (Ibid 152) By the oath of John Overton and Jenny Devers on 4 June1804, it was proved that William Devers "is become incapacitated and void of descretion to complete his administration." Henry Hunter was appointed in his place with Thomas McLane, William Rogers, Abraham Hunter, John Miller, Jacob Dobbins & John Graves as security. (Ibid 2/29) Andrew Miller was appointed guardian of William & Mary

Dever. (Ibid 40) A settlement of the estate was made. (Ibid 51) Jane Devers was allowed $24 for services done for the estate. (Ibid 156) Andrew Miller, guardian of the widow & orphans of James Dever, deceased, petitioned the court to have all of the money from the estate turned over to him, which was refused. (Ibid 269)

DEVIN, Elizabeth
13 August 1838 in the suit of Gilbert Deer & wife, William Devin, John Devin & others vs Elizabeth Devin, defendant is given until next rule day to answer. (Bed TN, Ch Ct Min, 2/23) 14 August 1839 in above named suit it was shown that William Devin, John Devin, Susan Deer wife of Gilbert Deer & Elizabeth Nowlin wife of David Nowlin, were the legitimate children of Elizabeth Devin. A negro woman had been loaned to Elizabeth Devin, his daughter, by the will of Bryant W. Nowlin of VA, and after the death of Elizabeth Devin, to her children. Elizabeth is claiming absolute title to the negro & her increase and threatening to sell them. (Bed TN, Ch Ct Min, 2/89)

DEW, Arthur
6 May 1818 with his wife, Susanna Dew, sold to Francis P. Harris their interest in a legacy left to Susanna by the will of William Swift, deceased, late of Caswell County, NC. (Wil TN, Co Ct Min, no#/263)

DEWS, Elizabeth
Died before 2 October 1828 as shown in a bill of sale from Nathaniel Dews to William B. Dews & Sarah B. Dews. Elizabeth was the daughter of Richard Waller of Hallifax County, VA, & died prior to her father. Elizabeth was the first wife of Nathaniel Dews & William & Sarah were their children. The bill of sale concerns the inheritance of the children from the estate of Richard Waller. (Wil TN, Reg Bk/390) [second set of page numbers.]

DICE, Jacob
Was a resident of Smith County, TN, 7 November 1815 when he bought property from John Mohener [Motsener] (Wil TN, Reg Bk/43)

DICKENS, Saml.
Died before August 1840 as shown in a suit15 July 1851 by Citizen S. Woods, Saml. D. Beloate, Wm. D. Beloate, Charles R. Beloate & Reginald H. Beloate by &c vs Alex Jackson Exr. of Joseph H. Talbot decd., Francis Talbot, Almedia Talbot, Ruth Talbot, Mary Talbot, Delia Talbot and Robert F. Dickens, Jr. Saml. Dickens' will was proved in August 1840. He bequeathed to Andrew L. Martin, Jno. D. Martin & Edmund V. H. Dickens a large amount of property in trust for Elizabeth R. Beloate & her children then present & future. The trustees appointed declined to act. The Court appointed Jno. H. Talbot trustee at February term 1844 & he acted as such until February term 1849, when he was removed because of said Talbots becoming insane. Citizen S. Woods was appointed trustee. Joseph H. Talbot died leaving a will & appointed Alex. Jackson executor. Elizabeth R. Beloate died leaving Saml. D., William D., Charles R. & Reginald H. Beloate her only children and heirs-at-law. Money had been paid to V. C. Beloate who is now deceased. The Beloate heirs are entitled to land in Henderson County, Weakley County, & Gibson County. Robert F. Dickens is entitled to an undivided 3/4 of land in Lauderdale County & the Beloate heirs are jointly entitled to the remaining 1/4. Robert F. Dickens is also entitled to 1/2 of the land in Dyer County and Obion County, and the Beloate heirs are entitled to the other half. (Mad TN, Ch Ct Min, 1/211-216) The Beloates lived in Henderson [or Hardeman] County, division was made. The division between the Boyce & Dickens heirs was mentioned. (Ibid 264-273)

DICKENS, Wm.
Died in March 1845 as stated in the suit of James N. Lane et als vs Jno. Todd et als. On 30 April 1844 there was granted a tract of land to Wm. Dickins, Sr. as trustee for the children of Alfred Lane & his wife. Nancy Dickens was the widow of Wm. Dickens and Ann P. Talbot, Elizabeth Glenn, Robert Hunt, Sally Fisher Hunt, Wm. B. Dickens, Jno. R. Dickens, Saml. Dickens, Mary Hicks & Lucretia Hicks are his only heirs-at-law. On 1 May 1847, during the lifetime of said Martha Lane, wife of said Alfred Lane, the defendant, Jas. L. Talbot acting as attorney in fact for Pertius Moore, sold 400 acres of said land to Jas. & Jno. Todd. Martha Lane died in 1847 after the sale was made. The complainants Jas. A. Lane, Jno. W. Lane, Harriet Lane, Mary E. Jelks, Nancy Jelks, Emeline W. Furgerson & Irena Boyakin are the only children of Martha Lane & her husband Alfred. The complainants are entitled to said land as it was held in trust for them by said Wm. Dickens. Nancy Dickens had made a deed to defendant Todd in 1851 which is not valid. An appeal was granted. (Mad TN, Ch Ct Min, 2/56)

DICKESON, Nathaniel
4 November 1805 was exonerated from a Poll Tax for the present & all succeeding years, he being a cripple. (Rob TN, Co Ct Min, 1/361)

DICKEY, Anderson
Died before 6 June 1870 when W. C. Dickey was chosen and appointed guardian of Madison H. Dickey, Mary A. Dickey, Percilla Ann Dickey and Ann C. Dickey, the minor heirs. R. J. Dickey and Smith Parks were security. (Dyr TN, Co Ct Min, B/65) 2 September 1872 petition was made for division by R. J. Dickey et als, vs W. C. Dickey et al, heirs of Anderson Dickey, deceased. The land description mentions Robert Dickey and Matthew Dickey. (Ibid 466) The land was divided to W. C. Dickey, M. H. Dickey, A. C. Dickey, P. H. Dickey, R. J. Dickey, M. A. Dickey, 6 divisions. (Ibid 502-4) 2 June1873 W. C. Dickey made a settlement as guardian of Mary A., Asa C, & Priscilla Dickey, minor heirs. (Ibid 589)

DICKEY, Geo.
Died before 5 October 1870 when Smith Parks made a settlement as administrator. (Dyr TN, Co Ct Min, B/122)

DICKINGS, James
Died before 23 June 1807 when Samuel Dickings was granted letters of administration & also took into his possession the orphans of James Dickings. James Wilson & Nathan Clampet were his securities. (Wil TN, Co Ct Min, no#/296)

DICKINS, Saml.
Died before 20 October 1841 when his executor, John G. Martin, filed suit against Thomas Hampton et al, and another suit against Wilford Farris & Thomas Hampton. (Obi TN, Cir Ct Min, 4/no#)

DILL, Archibald, Sr.
Died before 29 July 1847 as shown in the suit of John Sommers & wife, Margaret vs Solomon Dill, Stephen Dill, Elijah Dill, Elizabeth [it looks like Dill has been erased] Lutton, Polly Rutlege, Archibald Dill, Rowland C. Dill, Stephen Dill, Jr., Solomon Dill, Jr., Dorcas Williams, Emanuel Williams, Ann Medley, Samuel Medley and Milly Loftis. Complainants & defendants are heirs of Archibald Dill, Sr., deceased. Lands are to be sold for distribution. (Jac TN, Ch Ct Min, A/265) 26 July 1849 it was stated that Solomon Dill, Stephen Dill, Elijah Dill, Elizabeth Sutton & Polly Rutledge (both widows) and Margaret Sommers, wife of John Sommers, are the only living children of Archibald Dill, Sr., deceased, and each is entitled to 1/8. Archibald Dill, Roland C. Dill, Stephen Dill, Jr., Dorcas Williams wife of Emanuel Williams, Ann Medlin wife of Samuel Medlin and Solomon Dill, Jr. are children of Arthur Dill, deceased, a son of Archibald Dill, Sr., deceased, and collectively entitled to 1/8. Milly Loftis is a widow and daughter of Archibald Dill, deceased, a son of Archibald Dill, Sr., deceased, and is entitled to 1/8. (Ibid 338)

DILL, Wm.
3 May 1819 was allowed $20 for his support for one year. (Wil TN, Co Ct Min, no#/437)

DILLARD, Edward
18 June 1817 failed to appear & answer a charge of Bastardy. William Dillard was also fined as his security. (Wil TN, Co Ct Min, no#/125) Since the mother of the child, Matilda Whershaw, has left the county, Edward was fined $3.12 1/2 & gave bond to keep the child off the county. (Ibid 131)

DILLARD, George
Died before 17 March 1817 when the will was proved by John Cartwright & Isaac Moore. Rebecca Dillard & Joshua Dillard were executors, with Edward Dillard & John Maholland as security. (Wil TN, Co Ct Min, no#/71)

DILLARD, Stacey
6 November 1787, Stacey Dillard alias Elkins made a bill of sale to Martha Dillard. Robt. Love, Esq., protested against the above bill of sale "as he Designs cancelling the Same, as guardian." (Was TN, Co Ct Min, 1/297)

DILLARD, Thos.
Died before 7 November 1785 when an inventory of the estate was returned by Robt. Love, executor. (Was TN, Co Ct Min, 1/265) The will was proved 12 May 1788 by John Webb and John Samms. Martha Dillard & Robert Love were executors. (Ibid 325)

DILLEN, Matilda
Died before 13 July 1854 as shown in the suit of James C. Webb vs Jessee Franks, administrator of Matilda Dillen, deceased, and Monterville Masters, administrator of Martin Masters, deceased. Martin Masters was one of the distributees of Matilda Dillen, deceased. His share of her estate will be used to pay a debt to James C. Webb. (Jac TN, Ch Ct Min, B/157)

DISCON, John
Died before 27 November 1778 when a suit was brought by Christopher Cunningham vs Administrator of John Discon. (Was TN, Co Ct Min, 1/54)

DITMORE, John
Died before 6 June 1831 when his will was proved by Samuel Yates, witness. (McM TN, Co Ct Min, 2no#/534)

DIXON, John M.
Was a non-resident of TN on 13 July 1854 as shown in the suit of John L. Britton vs John M. Dixon & others. (Jac TN, Ch Ct Min, B/159)

DIXON, Samuel
Was a resident of Logan or Christian County, KY, 11 February 1812 when his deposition was to be taken for the defendant in the case of Nathan Pepper vs Elijah Prichard. (Rob TN, Co Ct Min, 3/62)

DIXON, Sarah
Died before 18 October 1838. Jordan Dixon was administrator. It was stated that there was a negro woman named Juda in the possession of the administrator which belonged to the heirs of John Dixon, deceased, all of whom were of full age. The negro is to be sold and the proceeds divided among the heirs. (Obi, TN, Cir Ct Min, 3/275)

DIXON, Thomas
Died before February term 1810 when the will was proved by John Hutchison, William Adams & Assa Green. Mary Dixon, John Colemen & Geo. A. West were executors. (Rob TN, Co Ct Min, 2/202)

DIXON, William
Died before 13 February 1839 when his death was suggested in the suit of John Freeland & wife vs James Dixon & others. William Dixon was one of the defendants. His heirs were Eliza Dixon, Harriet Dixon, Emiley Dixon, Minos Dixon, Polly Dixon, Elizabeth Dixon, Amanda Dixon, Richmond Dixon and Adaline Dixon, minors. James Dixon was appointed guardian ad litem. Joel Albright & Dilly Dixon were administrators. (Bed TN, Ch Ct Min, 2/50) The final hearing on 30 June 1842 showed John Freeland & Mary his wife vs James Dixon, Nancy Dixon, Joel Albright & Delilah Dixon, administrators, & Eliza, Harriet, Emily, Polly, Minos, Elizabeth, Amanda, Richmond and Adeline Dixon children & heirs of Wm. Dixon, deceased. A cross bill was filed by Mary Freeland by her next friend &c vs John Freeland. With the assent of Mary Freeland the lands were divided among her children, the said James, William & Nancy Dixon, by deed of partition 20 March 1842. John & Mary Freeland have not lived as man & wife for upwards of 20 years & John has not provided for Mary during that time, but she has lived with her said children. The cross bill of Mary against John was for a divorce which was dismissed but he was enjoined from preventing her from living on said land. Her dower in lands in NC was mentioned. When Mary Freeland divided the lands between her 3 children it was stipulated they would support her for life & she would receive $50 per year, $25 from William & $25 from James for himself and as guardian of Nancy. (Ibid 197) [Evidently Mary Dixon was the mother of James, Nancy and William Dixon, the last of whom is deceased: More than 20 years ago she married John Freeman: Her deceased husband by the name of Dixon had owned lands in NC, out of which she had her dower. The other heirs mentioned were the children of William Dixon, deceased son of Mary Dixon Freeman. Dilly Dixon, also shown as Delilah, was probably the widow of William.]

DOAK, R. S.
Died before 4 January 1871 when Smith Parks made a settlement as administrator. (Dyr TN, Co Ct Min, B/165)

DOAK, William
Died before 26 September 1806 when John Doak, Esquire was appointed guardian of Jonathan Doak, son of William. William had left slaves to Rody Doak, Josiah Doak & Jonathan Doak. (Wil TN, Co Ct Min, no#/262)

DOBBS, Malenda
Was bound 15 August 1816 to John Cocke until age 18. She is now of the age of three years. (Cla TN, Co Ct Min, 4/247)

DOBBS, Pheby
Was the mother of a bastard child and she charged Grimes Neal with being the father. The child, Matilda Dobbs, is now three years and two months old. 16 August 1816 Grimes Neal was ordered to pay Pheby Dobbs $40 for the support of the child from her birth until the present time. Pheby appealed the award. (Cla TN, Co Ct Min, 4/251)

DOBBS, W. J. F.
3 February 1873 was chosen and appointed guardian of Amanda J. Dobbs, his daughter, with T. C. Buchanan and R. R. Watson, Sr. as his securities. (Dyr TN, Co Ct Min, B/538)

DOBSON, Archibald
Died before 26 August 1844 as shown in the suit of Benjamin Philips vs Robert T. Cannon, administrator of Archibald Dobson, deceased. The widow's dower was mentioned. (Bed TN, Ch Ct Min, 2/294) The suit also included Mary Dobson, Blackman C. Dobson, William D. Norton & wife and Joseph Dobson. (Ibid 368) Mary Dobson was the widow. A petition was mentioned that stated Dobson had no lawful issue except his brothers & sisters. John H. Kain lives in CT. Archibald Dobson died in 1840. Cannon was appointed administrator at the March term 1841. John H. Kain lived in Knox County, TN, in 1835. "16 December 1841 Mary Dobson the widow of said Archibald Dobson filed her bill against Robert T. Cannon and all her children who are named in the aforesaid deed of trust for the purpose of having said deed set aside" James Wortham was the brother-in-law of Robert T. Cannon. (Ibid 3/143)

DOBSON, B. C.
Was a non-resident of TN on 28 June 1841 when the suit of William S. Jett against B. C. Dobson showed that Dobson had absconded. (Bed TN, Ch Ct Min, 1/306)

DOBSON, Blackman C.
Was a non-resident of TN on 2 January 1839 when it was reported in the suit of John A. Furguson vs Blackman C. Dobson that Dobson had absconded. (Bed TN, Ch Ct Min, 1/286)

DODGEN, Martha Jane
7 January 1867 Albert Low was appointed guardian with Robert Cardwell as security. (Sev TN, Co Ct Min, no#/412)

DODSON, David
Died before 5 September 1826 when William Dodson & Frances Dodson were appointed administrators. (McM TN, Co Ct Min, 2no#/177)

DODSON, Jessee
2 March 1829 emancipated his slaves, Cato, Jane, Joshua, Henry, Alfred, Fanny, Milley, Letty & Harriet. (McM TN, Co Ct Min, 2no#/340)

DODSON, Lazerus
4 June 1827 made a deed of mortgage to Augustine P. Face. The land was located in Claibourne County, TN. (McM TN, Co Ct Min, 2no#/214)

DOHERTY, George
Died before 21 February 1842 when land was taxed to the heirs. (Obi TN, Cir Ct Min, 4/no#)

DONALSON, Stokely [Donaldson]
Died before 18 March 1806 as shown when some of his land was to be divided between his heirs and Zaccheus Ayer. (Roa TN, Co Ct Min, B/124)

DONELSON, Andrew
Died before 25 March 1806 when Mary Donelson, Samuel Motheral & James Grier were appointed administrators, with Ebenezer Donelson as security. (Wil TN, Co Ct Min, no#/190)

DONELSON, Rhoda
Was a free mulatto woman when her children were bound to James Trimble on 24 March 1809. The children were Betsey Donelson aged 10 years & Cresse Donelson aged 7 years. (Roa TN, Co Ct Min, D/64)

DONELSON, Samuel
Died before 26 September 1806 when the heirs were on a tax list with land on Fall Creek. (Wil TN, Co Ct Min, no#/264) Andrew Jackson, administrator, was in a case. The heirs of Samuel Donelson were John Donelson, Andrew Jackson Donelson & Daniel Donnelson, of Davidson County. (Ibid 282)

DONNEL, Callie
Was a girl of color about 6 years old when she was bound to Reuben G. Harrell 6 October 1873, until the age of 18. T. H. Bell and Robt. Hale were securities. (Dyr TN, Co Ct Min, B/628)

DONNEL, George
Was a boy of color about 10 years of age when he was bound to George Parks 6 October 1873, until age 21. Smith Parks and H. Parks, Jr. were securities. (Dyr TN, Co Ct Min, B/628)

DONNELL
Samuel & Thomas Donnell of Guilford County, NC, gave power of attorney to Samuel Donnell, Jr. of Wilson County, TN, to transfer a land warrant to William Edministon of Lincoln County, TN, 14 November 1821. (Wil TN, Reg Bk/250)

DONNELL, James, Sr.
Died before 16 September 1817 when the will was proved by Boaz Southern & Margaret Donnell. Sarah Donnell & William Donnell were executors. (Wil TN, Co Ct Min, no#/155)

DONNELL, Samuel
Died before 16 November 1818 as shown in an agreement between the heirs of William Donnell, deceased, of whom Samuel was also an heir. David Foster was executor. (Wil TN, Reg Bk/129) The will was proved 15 September 1817 by Alexander Foster & Robt. Wilson. David Foster was executor. (The executrix refused to qualify) (Ibid, Co Ct Min, no#/144)

DONNELL, William
Died before 16 November 1818 when his heirs made an agreement to divide property. The heirs were: Mary Donnell, the widow; Hugh & Mary Morrison; William Donnell; Robert Donnell; Alexander & Martha Marrs; Robert & Jane Wilson; David Foster the executor of Saml. Donnell one of said heirs, all of Wilson County, TN, and John & Sarah Gwin of Sumner County, TN. (Wil TN, Reg Bk/129)

DONNELSON, Elizabeth
20 September 1803 the Sheriff was released from the collection of taxes on 50,000 acres of land as the property of James Glasgow, in trust for Elizabeth Donnelson's heirs. (Roa TN, Co Ct Min, A/132)

DONOHO, Thomas
Was a resident of Caswell County, NC, 29 October 1805 when he gave power of attorney to his friend, James Sanders, of Warren [?] County, TN, to sell his lands in TN. (Wil TN, Reg Bk/1)

DOOLY, Thomas
Was a non-resident of TN Aug term 1819 when his signature was proved as witness to a title bond from Saml. Barton, deceased, to Isaac Moore. (Wil TN, Co Ct Min, no#/514)

DORIS, Isaac
Was shown to be the son of Samuel Doris when he was security for the suit of Joseph Dorris,18 July 1803. (Rob TN, Co Ct Min, 1/252)

DORRIS, John
Was shown to be the son of Joseph Dorris when he was appointed constable 20 January 1800, with Joseph Dorris and Wm. Dorris as security. (Rob TN, Co Ct Min, 1/122)

DORRIS, John
21 July 1802 was shown to be the son of Isaac Dorris when he was appointed road overseer. (Rob TN, Co Ct Min, 1/228)

DORRIS, John J.
5 April 1808 was allowed $40 for part of a year to support he and his family. (Rob TN, Co Ct Min, 2/13)

DORRIS, Wm.
Was shown to be the son of Isaac Dorris when he bought land, 22 April 1800. (Rob TN, Co Ct Min, 1/134)

DOSSET, Willis
Died before 14 February 1814 when Anny Dosset was granted administration, with Thornton Pryor & Jacob Young as security. (Rob TN, Co Ct Min, 3/356)

DOUGLAS, Nora
Was bound 6 June 1870 to Robt. Fuller until age 18. She is a colored orphan aged 9. (Dyr TN, Co Ct Min, B/62)

DOUGLASS, Alexr.
Died before 1 June 1857 when Rhoda Douglass gave a new bond as executrix, the original bond having been destroyed. John Douglass, J. K. Franklin & Israel Wilson were her securities. On the same date Rhoda renewed her bond as guardian of the minor heirs. (Sev TN, Co Ct Min, no#/171) The widow, Rhoda, petitioned for dower. It was stated that several years had passed since the decease of Alexr. Douglass. (Ibid 228) Dower was set off which included lands that had been bequeathed to Alexander Douglass by the will of Edward Routh, deceased. Half of this tract belongs to Rhoda apart from her dower. (Ibid 239)

DOUGLASS, William
Died before 3 August 1818 when the executor, Alfred Douglass, sold land. (Wil TN, Co Ct Min, no#/284)

DOWLER, John
Died before 22 September 1808 when the will was proved by John Purris & John McEwen. John Dowler & Thomas Dowler were executors. (Roa TN, Co Ct Min, D/15)

DOWN, John
Was bound as an apprentice to Jacob Blazer on 5 June 1865. (Sev TN, Co Ct Min, no#/167)

DOWN, Sarah Jane
Was bound as an apprentice to John B. Seaton on 3 October 1864. (Sev TN, Co Ct Min, no#/122)

DOWN, Wm. H.
Was bound as an apprentice to John Forgason, Jr. on 5 June 1865. (Sev TN, Co Ct Min, no#/167)

DOWNS, Joseph M. Filmore
Was apprenticed to John Stafford 7 August 1865. He is a minor. (Sev TN, Co Ct Min, no#/193)

DOYLE, J. H.
7 August 1871 H. P. Doyle made a settlement as guardian of the heirs of J. H. Doyle. (Dyr TN, Co Ct Min, B/260) 4 January 1872 W. C. Doyle made a settlement as administrator of James H. Doyle. (Ibid 358)

DRAKE, Francis
Was a mulatto boy about 3 months old when he and his sister, Sally, about 18 months old, were bound to Hugh Dunlap 12 Apr 1812. They were children of a free woman of colour. (Roa TN, Co Ct Min, D/378)

DRAKE, Sarah Dulaney
Was emancipated by Bird B. Drake on 30 May 1831 as shown in her suit against Martin Cartwell on 12 July 1847. (Mad TN, Ch Ct Min, 1/20)

DRAKE, Widow
3 September 1805 it was reported that Widow Drake had become so blind in her eyesight that she is incapable of getting her living without help. John Rogers, Sr. was appointed to receive her into his care until next court. (Cla TN, Co Ct Min, 2/176) A jury was appointed to review the condition of Tabitha Drake [Elizabeth had been crossed out] and report to next court. (Ibid 210) Her care was to be let to the lowest bidder. (Ibid 228) James Rogers was paid for supporting the Widow Drake. (Ibid 3/20)

DRANE, John M.
Was a negro pauper 2 January 1871 when money was allowed for his support. (Dyr TN, Co Ct Min, B/152)

DRAPER, Brice M.
Died before 12 July 1850 as shown in the suit of Edward B. Draper Exr. &c of B. M. Draper vs Reuben Rogers et al. The deposition of Mary S. Taylor is to be re-taken in the state of LA. (Jac TN, Ch Ct Min, A/364)

DRAPER, Thomas
Died before 4 May 1842 as shown in the suit of James Young and Betsy his wife vs James Draper, Obediah Evans and Sally his wife, Stephen Holliday and Henrietta his wife, John Rogers and Ann his wife, Edward B. Draper, Brice M. Draper, Milton Draper, Thomas L. Draper, Thomas Huddleston and Susana his wife and Sarah Draper, Edward P. Pate and Lucy his wife and Lawson H. Draper. James Young & Brice M. Draper were the administrators. The testator was mentioned. (Jac TN, Ch Ct Min, A/44) An accounting of settlements was made. Money had been paid to Sarah Draper starting in October 1840 and to Brice M. Draper starting in September 1840. The other legatees were paid mostly in 1841 & 1842. (Ibid 63-74)

DRENNON, John
Died before 20 September 1817 when this agreement was made: "By the will of our uncle Matthew Bigen there was given to our sister Ann Drennon a negro girl named Nancy. As our father John Drennon deceased, never had any claim to said negro we, Thomas Drennon, John Drennon, David Drennon, James Drennon, John Arnold & Henry Miller, quit claim any rights to said negro to Thomas Partlow son of said Anne Drennon & all other property said Ann Drennon died possessed of." (Wil TN, Reg Bk/98) 22 June 1816 a committee was appointed to divide the property of John Drennon, deceased. James Drennon was one of the heirs. (Ibid, Co Ct Min, no#/22)

DRENNON, Joseph
Died before 3 May 1819 when John Drennon was appointed guardian for Sally Ryal & Joseph Drennon, minor heirs, with John Arnold & Claibourn Goodman as security. (Wil TN, Co Ct Min, no#/435)

DREWRY, Nicholas
Died before 16 December 1816 when the will was entered and objected to by Ruth Drewry, the widow. Objection was sustained and Ruth appointed administrator with John Beard. Thomas Hearn & Edward Harris were security. A years provision was set off for the widow. (Wil TN, Co Ct Min, no#/47) 8 August 1818 John W. Peyton was appointed guardian of James Brantly Drury, minor heir of Nicholas Drury, deceased. (Ibid 326) 2 February 1819 Jesse Pemberton & Ruth Pemberton petitioned for dower in the land of Nicholas Drury, her late husband. (Ibid 395)

DUFFIE, John
Died before 15 July 1850 as shown in the suit of William J. G. King vs Patrick M. Duffy Executor of John Duffie deceased. (Mad TN, Ch Ct Min, 1/162) Order to produce the partnership books for the blacksmith business was to be served on defendant in Shelby or Madison County. (Ibid 167) Stephen Moore, James Moore & Lewis Duncan were security for Patrick M. Duffy, the executor of John Duffy, deceased. (Ibid 2/127)

DUFFY, Pat
Died before 14 January 1850 when the suit of Mary Duffy vs Henderson Duffy Exr. of Pat Duffy, William P. Hamilton, Mary J. Hamilton, Elijah Hamilton, William Duffy, Kitty H. & M. B. Duffy, was dismissed. (Mad TN, Ch Ct Min, 1/98)

DUKE, George M.
Was an orphan boy aged 14 years the 6th of June last. He was bound 1 December 1828 to Thomas Hoyle, a farmer, until age 21. (McM TN, Co Ct Min, 2no#/322)

DUM, Danl.
28 August 1781 "was certified to the Genl. Assembly as an infirm man & an Object of Charity and to be released from paying public or County tax." (Was TN, Co Ct Min, 1/142)

DUN, Thomas
Died before 7 January 1867 when Inman Walker was paid for burying clothes. (Sev TN, Co Ct Min, no#/415)

DUNAVIN, Michael
Removed by 6 September 1830 when a road overseer was appointed in his place. (McM TN, Co Ct Min, 2no#/469)

DUNBAR, Stephen
Was bound as an apprentice to Harbert Walker 2 August 1819 until he arrives at the age of 21. (Wil TN, Co Ct Min, no#/499)

DUNCAN, John
Died before 18 June 1816 when a sale of the estate was recorded. (Wil TN, Co Ct Min, no#/13)

DUNCAN, Martin
Was the son of John Duncan as shown on 15 July 1799 in a deed from John to Martin, proved by John Price. (Rob TN, Co Ct Min, 1/110)

DUNCAN, Stephen
Died before 4 August 1873 when the witnesses to his will were subpoenaed to appear and prove the will. The witnesses were James T. Bone and William Patten who are residents of Gibson County, TN. (Dyr TN, Co Ct Min, B/616) Smith Parks qualified as executor, William Parks the first named executor failing to qualify. (Ibid 630)

DUNEVANT, P. D.
5 October 1870 J. G. Dunevant made a settlement as guardian. (Dyr TN, Co Ct Min, B/122)

DUNEVANT, W. E.
Died before 5 February 1872 when W. T. Boatwright made a settlement as administrator. (Dyr TN, Co Ct Min, B/364)

DUNGAN, Jeremiah
27 August 1778 took the oath of allegiance. (Was TN, Co Ct Min, 1/44)

DUNLAP, Ephrim
27 August 1778 it was ordered that "the Clark certify to the Chief Justice of the state of No. Carolina that Ephrim Dunlap Is a Gentleman of honest probity and good Behavior and Well Qualified to act as an Attorney." (Was TN, Co Ct Min, 1/44)

DUNLOE, Henry
Was a resident of Davidson County, TN, on 9 October 1826 when his deposition was to be taken for the defendant in the case of William Terrell vs Daniel Dunnevant. (Obi TN, Cir Ct Min, 1/5)

DUNN, Azeriah
8 November 1813 was released from paying poll tax for 1813, it appearing that he was over the age of 50. (Rob TN, Co Ct Min, 3/317)

DUNN, John
Was a resident of Bullet County, KY, 27 August 1817 when he gave power of attorney to Ransom King of Wilson County, to sell land in Wilson County. (Wil TN, Reg Bk/93)

DUNN, John
Died before 2 November 1819 when James Cross was appointed guardian for William Dunn & Thomas Dunn, minor heirs, with William Coe & Abner Wason as security. (Wil TN, Co Ct Min, no#/539)

DUNN, Susan
Was the mother of a bastard child. Joseph Washington, who was accused of being the father, gave bond for its maintenance 11 November 1812. (Rob TN, Co Ct Min, 3/162)

DUNNEVANT, A.
Died before 8 February 1870 when G. Chitwood made a settlement as administrator. (Dyr TN, Co Ct Min, B/7)

DUNNEVANT, Ferdnand
7 February 1870 J. G. Dunnevant was chosen & appointed guardian with E. A. Dunnevant and L. M. Williams as security. (Dyr TN, Co Ct Min, B/2)

DUNNEVANT, Victoria
Was bound to E. B. Pendleton until age 18. She is now 12 years old. The indenture was with the consent of the girl's mother, her father being dead. (Dyr TN, Co Ct Min, B/649)

DUNSTAN, James
Died before 7 February 1870 when Louis M. Williams was appointed administrator with the will annexed, with Jesse F. Williamson as security. (Dyr TN, Co Ct Min, B/1)

DURDON, Jonathan
Died before 12 May 1812 when his widow, Easter Durdon, relinquished her right to administrate to Anderson Cheatam and Holland Durdon. Josiah Fort and John Bell were securities. (Rob TN, Co Ct Min, 3/88)

DURUM, James
5 December 1804 a jury was appointed to inquire into the person of James Durum who is said to be "delarious or so deranged that he cannot take care of himself or family." (Cla TN, Co Ct Min, 2/98)

DYE, Wm.
Was an orphan child adjudged to be 4 years old when he was bound 3 February 1783 to Joseph McMahon, Esqr. until age 21. (Was TN, Co Ct Min, 1/193)

DYER, James P.
Died before 2 November 1863 when Jesse Hill was appointed administrator with Jesse Stafford & Thos. Lindsey as security. (Sev TN, Co Ct Min, no#/80)

DYER, Margaret
Died in February 1860 after having made her will on 14 April 1853. Theoderick Webb was named executor. A legacy was given to Mary Webb during her life & after her death to be divided between her daughters. All the rest of the estate was to go to Theoderick Webb. Mary Webb died in the summer of 1860, about the month of August & left no living daughters, but all her daughters, to wit, Lucretia, Nancy & Mary had died intestate & without issue, before the death of the testator, that is to say, Lucretia died in 1859, Nancy in 1857 & Mary in 1855. The suit was brought by Theoderick Webb, executor of Margaret Dyer & in his own right vs Theoderick J. Webb, Stephen T. Webb & Joseph H. Webb. The legacy to Mary Webb reverts back to the estate of the deceased & therefore belongs to Theodorick Webb. (Mad TN, Ch Ct Min, 3/180)

DYKES
2 October 1866 David Keener was appointed guardian to Wm. Dykes & James Dykes, minors, with Joel Hudson as security. (Sev TN, Co Ct Min, no#/387)

EAGAN, William
Died before 17 September 1816 when the administrator, Barnaby Eagan, was ordered to make a report. (Wil TN, Co Ct Min, no#/38) Peggy Eagan was appointed guardian for Sally Siney Barnaby Samuel & William Eagan, minor heirs, with Samuel Motheral & Robert Neal security. (Ibid 59)

EAKIN
In the suit of Eakin & Brothers vs Charles Lucas & others, it was stated that John, William, Spencer and Thomas Eakin, the two former were citizens of Bedford County and the two later were citizens of Davidson County, TN. They were merchants & partners in the style of Eakin & Brothers. Charles Lucas has absconded and the process of law cannot be served upon him. It is believed he has removed to TX. (Bed TN, Ch Ct Min, 1/174)

EAKLE, Henry
Died before 11 February 1854 as shown in the suit of Samuel E. Hare & Watson M. Cooke vs Henry D. Eakle et als. Sampson W. Cassity is to be made a defendant to this suit and is to state how much funds he has in his hands belonging to the estate of Henry Eagle, deceased. (Jac TN, Ch Ct Min, B/145) Henry D. Eakle has an interest in the real estate of Henry Eakle, deceased. Christian Eakle, administrator, was mentioned. (Ibid 167) [See also William Hibbits]. In a bill & cross bill by Andrew Eakle & others, Christian Eakle & Daniel Keith & others [concerning the estate of Henry Eakle, deceased] publication was made as to non-resident defendants Curtis York, Sally York, Amos [Amon] Eakle & Henry Eakle. (Ibid 193) In the suit of Christian Eakle & others vs Daniel Keith & others process has been served on the infants Andrew Eakle, Tabitha Eakle, Jacob Eakle & William F. Eakle and publication has been made as to the infants John L. Hibit, Louisa Jane Hibit & Harland Hibit. They have no regular guardian and William H. Botts was appointed guardian ad litem of said infants. (Ibid 231) The suit was shown as

Christian Eakle & Joseph Raglin & others vs Jonathan Eakle & others. Complainants & defendants are heirs of Henry Eakle, deceased. A report is to be made. (Ibid 241) 6 February 1856 this suit was shown as Christian Eakle, Joseph A. Gaglin & John Eakle vs Jonathan Eakle, Daneil Keith, Katherine Keith, Isaac Crawford, Elizabeth Crawford, Lewis Crawford, Mary Crawford, Andrew J. Eakle, Tabitha Eakle, Jacob Eakle, Christopher Meader, Hariett Meader, Amos Ekle, Henry Eakle, Henry Hibits, John S. Hibits, Louisa J. Hibits, George Gorten, Mary Gorten, Harlin Hibits, Sally formerly Sally Hibits and her husband whose name is not known, Robert Hibits, Abraham Beely, David [Daniel] W. Bail, Henry P. Eakle, John C. Bail, Curtis W. York, Sally York, Joel Lee, Preas? B. Lee & Benjamin Hail [Hall]. [This writing is very dim] The land was divided into 14 different lots and sold. They were purchased by Leonard Jones, Daniel W. Bails, Christopher Meador [bought 4], Andrew Bowman, Parish Sims, Christian Eakle, Henry P. Eakle, James C. Cunning?, John C. Bailes, Lewis Crawford [bought 2]. Title was divested out of complainants & defendants. (Ibid 282-7) Another suit was shown as Andrew Eakle, Christopher Meadow, Harriet Meadow, Isaac Crawford, Elizabeth Crawford, Henry Hibbit, John Hibbit, Harlen Hibbit, Eliza Hibbit, Mary Cash, Richard Cash, William H. Hibbit guardian of John, Harlen, Sarah and Eliza Hibbit who are minors, Andrew Eakle by his guardian James Hibbit vs Christian Eakle, Curtis W. York, Sally York, Jacob Eakle, William T. Eakle, Talitha Eakle by William H. Botts guardian ad litem, Lewis Crawford, Mary Crawford, Daniel Keith, Catherine Keith, Henry Eakle, Amos Eakle, John Eakle & Jonathan Eakle. Aaron York & John Ferguson were in another suit vs John Eakle & Christian Eakle administrators. Jonathan Eakle claimed as an advancement the negro man David. Henry Eakle had made the following advancements to his children in his lifetime; to Christian Eakle, Henry A. Eakle, Jonathan Eakle, John Eakle, Amos Eakle, Daniel Keith & wife, Lewis Crawford & wife, Isaac Crawford & wife, Christopher Meadow & wife, William Hibbits & Rosannah Hibbits and to Curtis W. York & Sally York. $666.69 is a distributive share of the estate of Henry Eakle, deceased. $45.26 is a distributive share of Phoebe Eakle, deceased. The children of William & Rosannah Hibbits were Mary & George Garten, Harland, Sally, John S., Henry & Louisa J. Hibbit. William T. Eakle, Telitha Eakle, Andrew J. Eakle and Jacob Eakle are entitled to the full amount. The last 4 named are each entitled to receive from the estate of Phoebe Eakle $45.26. Christian Eakle was administrator for Phoebe Eakle. Other parties mentioned in these suits had made improvements in the land and recovered judgements & are entitled to money for same. (Ibid 313-8)

EAKLE, Henry, Jr.
Was not a resident of TN on 7 November 1843 as shown in the suit of Russel M. Kinnard & Thos. L. Bransford vs Henry Eakle, Jr., George Kinnard et al. (Jac TN, Ch Ct Min, A/124)

EASLY, Isaac
Died before 3 August 1818 when John L. Easly was appointed administrator with Clack Stone & Coleman Stone as security. (Wil TN, Co Ct Min, no#/283)

EASON, James K.
Was a resident of White County, TN, 7 May 1821 when he made a deed of gift to his nephews, Alfred, Monroe & Montgomery Eason & to his nieces, Eliza, Arrabilla & Frances Eason, children of Robert Eason of Wilson County,TN, for 4 slaves. (Wil TN, Reg Bk/212)

EATON, John R.
Died before 21 February 1839 when land was taxed to the heirs. (Obi TN, Cir Ct Min, 3/301)

ECHOLS, Abner
16 December 1817 was bound as an apprentice to Smith Hansbro of the Town of Lebanon until age 21. He is now 16 years the 7th of May last. (Wil TN, Co Ct Min, no#/202)

ECHOLS, Elkanah
Died before 23 September 1805 when the will was proved by James Winchester. (Wil TN, Co Ct Min, no#/164) 25 December 1817 Joel Eckols sold to his brother, Richard Eckols, his interest in the negro boy named Stephen about 6 years old," being one of the decendants of the stock of negroes willed by my father Elkanah Eckols to be divided among his 3 children at the death of my mother Elizabeth Eckols." (Ibid Reg Bk/95) 22 February 1820 Joel Echols, heir of Elkanah Echols, deceased, sold to his mother, Martha Echols, all his part of the estate of his father, Elkanah Echols. (Ibid 164) [Joel Echols made several sales in 1820 & appears to be liquidating his assets.]

ECHOLS, L.
Died before March term 1814 as shown in the case of Thomas Wilson & Co. vs Obediah

Spradlin, administrator of L. Echols, for debt. (Wil TN, P&J, no#/no#) The name was shown as Larkin Echols. (Ibid September term 1815)

ECHOLS, Larkin
Died before 19 June 1816 when an inventory of the property was recorded. (Wil TN, Co Ct Min, no#/17)

ECHOLS, W. D.
5 October 1870 Newlen Echoles made a settlement as guardian of W. D. Echols' heirs. (Dyr TN, Co Ct Min, B/122)

ECKOLS
Abigail M. Eckols, Jos. A. Eckols, Mildred Ann Eckols & Mary E. Eckols, the later of whom is a minor & files by the next friend Joseph A. Echols, petitioned for sale of land 16 January 1850. Jno. Read had been trustee but withdrew. (Mad TN, Ch Ct Min, 1/104) John L. Brown was appointed trustee. (Ibid 120)

EDLOW, John R.
Died before 21 February 1838 when land was taxed to the heirs. (Obi TN, Cir Ct Min, 3/165)

EDMONSON, Willie
Probably died before 23 February 1861 as his administrator, Jno. B. Compton, and his minor heirs were mentioned in the suit of T. W. & W. S. Bryan vs A. W. Fuller and James H. Baker. (Mad TN, Ch Ct Min, 2/448)

EDNY, C. J.
8 March 1870 N. R. Prichard made a settlement as guardian of C. J. Edny's heirs. (Dyr TN, Co Ct Min, B/16)

EDWARDS, Anderson
Was an orphan boy of the age of 19 years the 20th of May 1826. He was bound 6 March 1826 to Joel K. Brown to learn the trade of a Taylor. (McM TN, Co Ct Min, 2no#/134)

EDWARDS, Catherine
In her suit of 14 October 1856 against Arthur Edwards for divorce, the property has been attached and the defendant was ordered to pay to the court $25 so complainant could prosecute her suit. (Fen TN, Ch Ct Min, A/67)

EDWARDS, Edward
Died before 3 June 1873 when E. G. Sugg was chosen and appointed guardian of Wm. Edwards, Walter Edwards, John A. Edwards and Henry Edwards, minor heirs, with Isaac Bunnell as his security. (Dyr TN, Co Ct Min, B/591)

EDWARDS, Francis C.
31 July 1849 a suit was shown: Obadiah Gravitt & wife Sarah Francis vs David Merriwether, guardian for Frank, Henrietta, Caroline and Nathaniel Edwards, minors & heirs of Francis C. Edwards. It does not state that Francis C. Edwards was deceased. The suit was dismissed. (Mad TN, Ch Ct Min, 1/86)

EDWARDS, Labon
Died before 1 March 1802 when a deed of conveyance from Joab Hill to the heirs of Labon Edwards, deceased, was registered in Court. (Cla TN, Co Ct Min, 1/17)

ELDER, James
Died before 14 November 1844 when the administrator [not named] petitioned to sell slaves. (Obi TN, Cir Ct Min, 4/no#)

ELDRIDGE, Tyler
Was a resident of the Cherokee Nation on 5 December 1827 when his deposition was to be taken for the plaintiff in the case of William McCormicks vs James Shelton. (McM TN, Co Ct Min, no#/286)

ELGIN, John
Died before 26 March 1805 when his nuncupative will was proved by William Bumpass & William B. Elgin. Elizabeth Elgin was granted letters of administration. (Wil TN, Co Ct Min, no#/115)

ELHIERS, John
Died before 2 March 1830 when Daniel Newman was appointed administrator. (McM TN, Co Ct Min, 2no#/430)

ELISON, Alexander
Died before 6 October 1862 when Rufus M. Henderson was paid $2 for making the coffin. (Sev TN, Co Ct Min, no#/15)

ELLEDGE, James
Died before 3 April 1866 when Daniel W. Reagan was appointed guardian to William Elledge and Martha Jane Elledge, minor orphans, with R. R. Reagan & Noah Ogle as security. (Sev TN, Co Ct Min, no#/311) The above order was rescinded & James Ellege was appointed guardian. (Ibid 328)

ELLIN, William
Was charged by Patsey Galloway with being the father of her bastard child. He gave bond for the maintenance of the child 18 March 1806. (Roa TN, Co Ct Min, B/135)

ELLIOTT, John
Removed by 7 June 1824 when a road overseer was appointed in his place. (McM TN, Co Ct Min, 2no#/5)

ELLIS, Jeremiah
Was a resident of Davidson County in 1826 [or 1836] as shown in the suit of Martin Smith filed against him in 1844. (Bed TN, Ch Ct Min, 3/186)

ELLIS, John
Died before 17 June 1816 when the will was proved by John Ellis, Jr. & Velshar Bandy. Francis Ellis was executor with Peter Mosely & Saml. Meredith as security. (Wil TN, Co Ct Min, no#/3)

ELLIS, Joseph
Died before 7 August 1871 when Miles H. Davis was chosen and appointed guardian of William W. Ellis, George W. Ellis, Joseph Caroline Ellis, minor heirs, with W. W. Davis and W. C. Davis as security. (Dyr TN, Co Ct Min, B/261)

ELLIS, Michael
Died before 6 February 1871 when J. H. Hamilton made a settlement as administrator. (Dyr TN, Co Ct Min, B/190) James R. Green renewed his bond as guardian of the minor heirs. (Ibid 203) James R. Green made a settlement as guardian of S. S. Ellis, Andrew Ellis and M. L. Ellis. (Ibid 239)

ELLIS, Simeon
Died before 16 December 1816 when Jacob Ellis was appointed guardian of Simeon Ellis, 7 years old, & Sibby Ellis, minor heirs. (Wil TN, Co Ct Min, no#/53) 3 August 1818 Delila Ellis, the widow, was appointed guardian of Simeon Ellis and Sabetha Ellis, minor heirs of Simon Ellis, as Jacob Ellis, former guardian, is about to leave the state. (Ibid 287)

ELLIS, Sims
With his wife, Polly, made a deed to John L. Laughten which was ordered registered in Warren County, NC. Polly was examined separately regarding her release of her dower interest in the land, 10 May 1813. (Rob TN, Co Ct Min, 3/229)

ELLIS, Thomas
"Of Lunenburgh, VA, for $310, do loan to Polly Warren, wife of Booth M. Warren, a negro girl named Amsy during the life of said Polly Warren & at her death to be divided between James Warren, Richard L. Warren, Polly W. Warren, Rebecca Ann Warren, Ball E. Warren, Robert R. Warren & all the future increase by him the said Booth M. Warren," 19 April 1813. (Wil TN, Reg Bk/17)

ELLIS, William
Died before 10 November 1812 when Lewis [or Sims] Ellis applied for letters of administration. James Young and James Elliot were security. (Rob TN, Co Ct Min, 3/151)

ELLISON, Robert W.
Died before 3 February 1812 when the will was proved by Peter Buchanan & John Lowry. Parry W. Humphreys, George West & Robert West, three of the executors named, qualified. The executors made petition that the mulatto boy named Massina ?, according to the will of testator, be emancipated. (Ste TN, Co Ct Min, 3/108)

ELROD, James
Died before 16 January 1850 when Samuel Lancaster and Jas. L. Lyon, guardians for the minor heirs, petitioned for sale of land & negroes. (Mad TN, Ch Ct Min, 1/100) Samuel Lancaster was guardian of Samuel, James, Mary Eliza & Sarah Jane Elrod. Jas. A. Ryan was guardian of Austin Elrod. (Ibid 127) The widow was Sarah Barr, formerly Sarah Elrod. (Ibid 148) 14 July 1851 it was stated that Austin W. Elrod had come of age & is to receive his 1/5th portion. (Ibid 200) Samuel Lancaster was executor. James Elrod died in 1839 leaving Sarah K. Elrod his widow and Austin, Samuel, James, Mary Eliza & Sarah Jane his only children. The will was proved December 1839. Sarah K. afterward married Benjamin Barr. (Ibid 2/252)

ELROD, Sarah Jane
Died single & intestate in 1862. J. K. Stephens qualifed as her administrator in October 1866. Henry W. McCrorry who died about 1862 was guardian of Sarah Jane from 1857 [or 1851] to about 1860, during her minority. (Mad TN, Ch Ct Min, 3/188)

EMBREE, Moses
Died before 16 February 1795 when Thomas Embree & John Embree were appointed administrators. (Was TN, Co Ct Min, 1/524)

EMBRIE, E. Moses
3 August 1784 made affirmation that his son, Isaac Embrie, was not of the age 21 when poll tax was levied against him for 1783. (Was TN, Co Ct Min, 1/243)

EMERT, P. S.
2 April 1866 F. S. Emert was appointed guardian to James M. Emert & others, minors of P. S. Emert, with J. D. Emert & P. S. Shults as security. (Sev TN, Co Ct Min, no#/286)

EMERY
11 May 1815 the court ordered [blank] Emery to take into her possession her helpless child as one of the poor of this county until next court. (Cla TN, Co Ct Min, 4/73)

EMSON
6 August 1804 William Emson and Rebekah Emson were bound to Elijah Biggs until full age. Caleb Emson was bound to Dickeson Hall until age 21. (Rob TN, Co Ct Min, 1/303)

ENGLEMAN, Joseph
Married before 19 January 1803 to Jane Tucker as shown when Enoch Tucker was dismissed as the guardian of Jane "while she was a Lunitick." (Rob TN, Co Ct Min,1/242)

ENOCHS, Louisa
Was a negro girl aged 11 years when she was bound 5 June 1871 to Robert Hale until age 18. (Dyr TN, Co Ct Min, B/244)

EPPERSON, Samuel
Died before 28 August 1860 as shown in the suit of William H. Edwards and wife Mary Ann Edwards vs Henry A. Welch & Ruebin H. Edwards Executors of Samuel Epperson decd., Henry H. Epperson, Ben M. Hicks, Thos. N. Epperson, Elizabeth H. Epperson, Elinor S. Epperson, Samuella Newsom & Franklin E. Newsom. The complainants are to have no interest under the 9th clause of the will and are entitled to no account for the property therein bequeathed. (Mad TN, Ch Ct Min, 2/374) Samuel Epperson died in 1856 & bequeathed by his will $1,500 to Ann [Amos?] Hunt as trustee to pay out for a house for testators daughter, Mary A. Edwards, to have during her lifetime & then to her children if she should have any, otherwise to return to his estate and be divided equally between his other children. Said Hunt declined to act as trustee & G. B. Hicks was appointed. Edwards & wife are residents of Houston County, TX, & the said W. H. Edwards has been appointed by the court of said county to receive said funds as trustee. The money will be paid over to him to purchase a house in TX when he makes bond. (Ibid 378)

EPPES, Martha B.
Died before 21 February 1867 as shown in the suit of Joel S. Walker et als vs W. B. Eppes et als. (Mad TN, Ch Ct Min, 3/29) Martha died in 1863 in Buckingham, VA, having made a will. Thomas Clark of Madison County, TN, was appointed administrator. The only assets in TN belonging to the estate is a tract of land which is to be sold to pay the debts. (Mad TN, Ch Ct Min, 3/39)

ERWIN, Francis
Was charged by Sally Fletcher with being the father of her bastard child. He made bond

for the maintenance of the child, with Noah Ashley & Benjamin Moore as security. (Roa TN, Co Ct Min, D/128)

ESCUE, Samuel
Died in December 1837 having made a will, John Tillman was executor. The widow was Rachel who has married Edmond Tipton. Sarah Escue was the only child. Tipton & wife & Sarah Escue reside in Hickman County, KY. (Bed TN, Ch Ct Min, 1/466) Another suit was filed 10 July 1839 concerning the partnership of Escue & Carlos C. Steele. (Ibid 512-527) A settlement was made 30 August 1844. (Ibid 2/313-17)

ESSMAN, Thomas
Died before 10 December 1824 when John Essman was appointed administrator with Frederic Reasor his security. (McM TN, Co Ct Min, 2no#/47)

ESTIS, John
Died 23 January 1853 as shown in the suit of Penelope Estis vs Walter Keys, filed on 21 February 1857. Jno. Evans, on 23 Sept 1842 in Panola County, MS, made a deed of gift to Penelope, who was then the wife of John Estis, of some slaves for her own & separate benefit. After the death of John Estis in Madison County, TN, the administrator, Walter Keys, took possession of the slaves and Penelope is suing to get them back. (Mad TN, Ch Ct Min, 2/147)

ETHERTON, T. D. A.
Died before 4 December 1865 when Daniel Conatser, Ezekiel Conatser & Moses Cavin were appointed to lay off a years support to Louiza Etherton, widow. (Sev TN, Co Ct Min, no#/251)

EUDAILEY, J. F.
Taxes were not collected in District 4 for 1873, "insolvent." (Dyr TN, Co Ct Min, B/759)

EUDALY, Catherine
1 August 1870 Turner Chamblin was chosen and appointed guardian of Mary Jane Francis Marion and E. Bet Eudaly, minor heirs of Catherine Eudaly. W. H. Simpson and T. S. Chamblin were securities. (Dyr TN, Co Ct Min, B/92)

EVANS
On 9 April 1860 complainant B. F. Bledsoe was appointed guardian ad litem for Adam Evans, Catherine Evans & Mary Winingham, in the suit of The Bank of Tennessee vs James H. Beason et als. (Fen TN, Ch Ct Min, A/225)

EVANS
Floyd and Alexander Evans probably both died before 4 December 1867. In a suit by Margaret & Sarah Evans vs Floyd Evans & others, C. J. Sawers was appointed guardian ad litem for all of the defendants, they being minors. It was stated that Floyd Evans and Alexander Evans were joint owners of a tract of land upon which complainants now live. Floyd & Alexander Evans in their lifetime made a partition of the land and marked out a conditional line between them. The land is to be laid off for the heirs of said Floyd & Alexander and dower given to the widows of each. (Fen TN, Ch Ct Min, A/351) This suit was shown as Sary Evans & Margaret Evans vs the Heirs of Alx Evans & Stokely D. Evans. For the benefit of the widow & heirs of Alexander & Floyd Evans, deceased, dower was laid off, being the proportional part of the widow, Margaret Evans, and heirs of Floyd Evans, deceased. A partition was made for Sarah, widow of Alexander Evans, deceased, & heirs. A plot plan was shown. (Ibid 378-80)

EVANS, Andrew, Esqr.
Was a Justice of the peace for Grainger County 18 April 1799 when he proved a bond from John Stuart to Thomas Jamison, dated 2 February 1785. (Rob TN, Co Ct Min, 1/104)

EVANS, James
Was a resident of Wayne County, KY, on 8 November 1811? when his deposition was to be taken for the plaintiff in the suit of Samuel Johnson vs Abraham Price. (Ste TN, Co Ct Min, 3/6)

EVANS, L. D.
Died before 4 December 1868 as shown in the suit of George Smith Admr. &c vs John Pults. It was stated that on 25 Sept. 1866 Sampson and L. D. Evans, complainant's intestate, sold land to the defendant. (Fen TN, Ch Ct Min, A/424)

EVANS, Richard
Died before 21 February 1839 when land was taxed to the heirs. (Obi TN, Cir Ct Min, 3/294)

EVANS, Sampson
Was a non-resident of this state 14 April 1858 when he was one of the defendants in the suit of Bank vs James H. Beason & others. (Fen TN, Ch Ct Min, A/142) The death of Sampson Evans was admitted 10 April 1860 in the suit of John B. Rodgers vs F. F. Putts [Pults] et als. The complainant does not wish to revive the suit against the heirs. (Ibid 230) Sampson Evans died intestate in Fentress County. L. D. Evans, Alie Winningham & Mary his wife and Giles Clark and Thursa his wife, Adam and Catharine Evans are the only heirs. (Ibid 234)

EVANS, Samuel
Died before 4 December 1866 as shown in the suit of Deborah Evans Admrx. vs Henry W. Bow. Samuel Evans, complainant's intestate, had sold land in 1859 to the defendant, who is a non-resident of the state. The land has not been paid for. (Fen TN, Ch Ct Min, A/316)

EVINS, Evin
Was charged by Sally Miller as being the father of her bastard child. He gave bond for the maintenance of the child 18 March 1806. (Roa TN, Co Ct Min, B/135)

EWELL, Wm. [Ervell]
Died before May term 1818 when Redding B. Jones was appointed guardian of Evelina Ewing, minor heir. (Wil TN, Co Ct Min, no#/242)

EWING
12 August 1839 the suit of Rebecca Ewing by her next friend James L. Ewing vs David C. Mitchell, Tele A. Ewing & W. D. McLeary Executors &c, was transferred to the Chancery Court at Columbia. (Bed TN, Ch Ct Min, 2/64)

FAGOLA, Adam
Died before 2 June 1857 when Michael Fagola made a settlement as administrator. (Sev TN, Co Ct Min, no#/173)

FAIN
18 May 1795 Joseph Young and Adam Rader were appointed guardian to Nicholas Fain, Ruth Fain, Thomas Fain, and John Fain. (Was TN, Co Ct Min, 1/547)

FAIN, Ebenezer
Was a resident of "Ninety-six District in SC, living near the forks of Seludy," when his deposition was to be taken 8 May 1787 for John Blair McMahone in a case against John Hampton & Michael Hider. (Was TN, Co Ct Min, 1/280)

FAIN, John
Died before November term 1788 when the will was proved by Rosanna Fain, witness. Agness Fain was appointed administratrix de bonis non, with Sam Fain & William Fain as security. (Was TN, Co Ct Min, 1/347)

FAIN, Samuel
Died before 26 May 1794 when John Blair McMahon, Adam Mitchel & William Fain were appointed administrators, with Alexander Mathers & Joseph Young as security. (Was TN, Co Ct Min, 1/484)

FAN, George
Was released from paying poll tax for 1858 as he had left the county before that year. [This name could be Faw, Fair, Fau] (Sev TN, Co Ct Min, no#/406)

FANCHER, Levi
Was released from paying poll tax for 1858 as he is under 21 years of age. (Sev, TN, Co Ct Min, no#/406)

FANNING, Joe
Taxes were not collected in District 4 for 1873, "insolvent." (Dyr TN, Co Ct Min, B/759)

FARLEY, Mary Francis
Died before 4 September 1871 when LaFayette Farley was appointed administrator, with F. H. Benton as security. (Dyr TN, Co Ct Min, B/272)

FARMER, Hudson
Was a resident of Christian County, KY, 7 July 1809 when a deposition was to be taken for the case of Jesse Drake vs Benjn. Meness, Jr. (Rob TN, Co Ct Min, 2/161)

FARMER, William
Died before 29 June 1841 as shown in the suit of Mansfield Whitehead vs Elizabeth and Lydia M. Davis. Land was mentioned that was purchased from the heirs of William Farmer, deceased. (Bed TN, Ch Ct Min, 2/142)

FARR, Polly
Was an orphan child when Ephraim Farr was appointed her guardian 26 March 1805. (Wil TN, Co Ct Min, no#/118)

FARR, William
Died before June term 1804 when he was shown as deceased on the tax list. (Wil TN, Co Ct Min, no#/75)

FARRELL, William C.
Was a resident of Coweta County, GA, on 5 December 1828 when his deposition was to be taken for the defendant in the case of Daniel Carmichael vs Thomas Barclay. (McM TN, Co Ct Min, no#/399)

FAUCET, Richard
On 3 November 1812, gave bond with Philip Hall as security, for keeping a bastard child with which Lucy Davidson is now pregnant. (Ste TN, Co Ct Min, 3/unnumbered page before page 1)

FAUCETT, Richard
Made bond 7 February 1814, with Wm. Lyons, Tapley Maddox & William Dunbar as security, "that none of his Bastard Children now charged to him shall become chargeable on the county." (Ste TN, Co Ct Min, 4/86)

FAULKNER, Amos
Died before 2 May 1870 when W. P. Sugg was appointed administrator, with E. M. Hall & C. S. Nolen as security. (Dyr TN, Co Ct Min, B/55) The widow was Martha Faulkner. (Ibid 122)

FAULKNER, Jesse
Died before 20 February 1857 as shown in the suit of Wm. H. Marlow admr. vs Enos H. Faulkner et als. (Mad TN, Ch Ct Min, 2/131) 24 February 1859 land of Jesse Faulkner, deceased, was sold and title divested out of Enos H. Faulkner, Matilda E. Faulkner, Delia Ann Faulkner and Jesse C. Faulkner. (Ibid 267)

FAULKNER, LaFayette
Died before 6 June 1871 when C. L. Nolen, public administrator, was appointed administrator. (Dyr TN, Co Ct Min, B/246) 4 January 1872 the widow, Cornelia Faulkner, petitioned for dower. The heirs have been notified. (Ibid 356)

FEATHERSTON, C. R.
Died before 3 February 1873 when William J. Featherston was appointed administrator, with Z. C. Buchan as his security. (Dyr TN, Co Ct Min, B/538)

FEATHERSTON, William
Died before 7 February 1870 when A. T. Featherston and W. J. Featherston were appointed administrators, with C. R. Featherston & P. E. Wilson as security. (Dyr TN, Co Ct Min, B/3) 6 May 1872 William J. Featherstone was chosen and appointed guardian of James A. Neal, minor heir of William Featherstone, deceased. (Ibid 412)

FEEZEL, Henry
Of the county of Green, admits to being the father of an illegitimate child named Jacob, son of Polly Henegar. 4 September 1826 he petitioned the Court to change it's name from Jacob Henegar to Jacob Henegar Feezel and make it a joint heir of his estate because he "is desirous of acting towards it in such manner as to wipe from the innocent issue of his illicit amour as much of the disgrace attached to its birth as acknowledging the child will effect." Petition was granted. (McM TN, Co Ct Min, 2no#/174)

FELCKER, William
Died before 4 July 1859 when his will was proved by M. C. Murphey & C. Carey, witnesses. Shannon Felcker was named executor. (Sev TN, Co Ct Min, no#/452)

FENNER, Jno. M.
Died before 21 May 1855 as shown in the suit of Laura B. Fenner & Junius P. Fenner by their guardian, Thos. Henderson vs Julius Johnson et als. Julius Johnson & Eunice B. Jackson were administrators of the will of Jno. M. Fenner, deceased. Eunice B. intermarried with Alexander Jackson. Richd. J. Fenner & Jas. Valux were securities for J. Johnson & Eunice Jackson. An account was ordered taken of the estate. (Mad TN, Ch Ct Min, 2/61) Jno. M. Fenner was an heir of Richard Fenner, deceased. The heirs of Jno. M. are entitled to a child's part of the estate of Richard Fenner. (Ibid 182)

FENNER, Richard, Dr.
Died before 9 March 1852 as shown in the petition of Robert Fenner Surviving Executor of the Will of Dr. Richard Fenner decd & Surviving admr. of the Estate of Junius P. Fenner deceased & others. [there are 2 pages missing after this entry] (Mad TN, Ch Ct Min, 1/229) There was land claimed by E. D. Fenner in Fayette County. Mrs. Ann Fenner was mentioned. (Ibid 243) 16 March 1853, Alex Jackson et als petition to sell slaves. Alex Jackson in right of his wife Eunice B., Laura Fenner & Junius Fenner are the owners of some slaves. They are each entitled to one share. [It does not say these are heirs of Dr. Richard Fenner] (Ibid 309) The death of Mrs. Ann Fenner was mentioned. (Ibid 345) Laura B. & Junius P. Fenner were minors & Thos. Henderson is their guardian, 21 May 1855. [Also see Jno. M. Fenner] (Ibid 2/59 & 61) Larua B. Fenner intermarried with Joseph Payne before 18 Februray 1858. (Ibid 184) The heirs of Mrs. Ann W. K. Henderson were mentioned in this estate. (Ibid 244)

FENNER, Richard J.
Died before 18 February 1858 as shown in the petition of Ro. Fenner Surviving Executor and others and F. N. W. Burton vs T. P. Jones admr. and others tried together by consent of parties. The heirs of Richard J. Fenner were Mary F. Fenner, Julia Fenner & Kate E. Fenner. This petition concerns the estate of Dr. Richard Fenner. John S. Fenner was administrator. (Mad TN, Ch Ct Min, 2/182)

FENTRESS, George W.
Died before 19 October 1841 as shown in the suit of John W. Needham vs Joel S. Enloe Admr. A jury found that Joel S. Enloe had fully administered the estate of George W. Fentress, deceased. (Obi TN, Cir Ct Min, 4/no#)

FERGUSON, Douglass
Died before 4 December 1871 as shown in the suit of J. B. Powell et als vs Jo Allen Ferguson et al. The suit states that defendants, W. R. Bentley and Martha Bentley his wife, Thomas O. Jones and T. L. Jones his wife, are non-residents of TN, and that the names and residences of the decendants of James Ferguson, Eliza Chronister and Jane Whitworth (all heirs of the late Douglass Ferguson) are unknown. (Dyr TN, Co Ct Min, B/328) W. R. Ferguson is also a non-resident. (Ibid 356) 9 October 1872, when the land was sold the parties were listed; James B. Powell, Thomas Ferguson, George Ferguson, Thos. L. Ferguson, Jason H. Thompson & wife Elizabeth Thompson, K. H. Bentley & wife Paulina Bentley, Elijah Hawkins & wife Harriet Hawkins, Geo. W. Hawkins & wife Amanda Hawkins, Wm. H. Jones & wife Narcissa J. Jones, Grandison P. Ferguson vs Jo Allen Ferguson, W. R. Ferguson, Tennessee Ferguson, Orlando C. Ferguson, W. R. Bentley & wife Martha Bentley, Thomas O. Jones and wife T. L. Jones, the decendants of Jane Whitworth, James Ferguson & Eliza Chronister. The land was sold subject to the widows dower. (Ibid 499-501)

FERGUSON, J. D.
Died before 6 June 1871 when his widow, Matilda A. Terry, wife of Pleasant A. Terry, petitioned for a years provisions for her and child. (Dyr TN, Co Ct Min, B/245) Matilda and P. A. Terry were appointed administrators de bonus non, with Richard Staggs, Riley Blackwell and C. C. Moss as security. (Ibid 276)

FERGUSON, John
Died before 7 January 1867 when John Ferguson, Jr. qualified as executor of the last will & testament. (Sev TN, Co Ct Min, no#/418)

FERGUSON, Jonathan
Died before 9 November 1812 when his widow, Elizabeth Ferguson, was appointed adminstratrix, with John Hutchison and William Adams as security. (Rob TN, Co Ct Min, 3/140)

FERGUSON, Joseph G.
Died before 4 September 1871 when a tax collector was elected to fill his unexpired term. (Dyr TN, Co Ct Min, B/273) Mrs. Josephine Ferguson was appointed administrator, with L.

J. Moore and J. E. Dunlap as her securities. Geo. B. Miller, W. C. Doyle and W. B. Sampson were appointed to lay off a years provisions for the widow of Joseph G. Ferguson and her family. (Ibid 307) The family consists of the widow, Mrs. Josephine Ferguson, and an infant child. (Ibid 322)

FERGUSON, Thomas
Died before 6 February 1871 when Isaac A. Nunn renewed his bond as guardian of the minor heirs. (Dyr TN, Co Ct Min, B/187)

FERIBIE, S.
Gave a power of attorney to Enoch Douge "with the County seal of Currituch? County State of N. Carolina" which was registered 19 October 1807. (Ste TN, Co Ct Min, 1/49b)

FERRELL, Ann
Was the mother of a bastard child. She accused Colbert Arnold of being the father 8 March 1826. (McM TN, Co Ct Min, 2no#/145) [inserted between pages 158 & 159]

FERRELL, Dent
Died before 8 March 1870 as shown in the suit of C. H. Ferrell et al vs Mary E. Ferrell, Sullivan Spain et als. Answer was made by minors William B, Mary Elizabeth, Electra Hellen, and Martha Emiline Spain and Mary Alice Sullivan by their guardians ad litem. The petitioners and the defendants are entitled to an interest in the land of Dent Farrell, deceased. (Dyr TN, Co Ct Min, B/19 & 83) Dent Ferrell left five children, 1. C. H. Ferrell, 2. James S. Ferrell, 3. S. George Ferrell who has died leaving M. E. & George Ferrell as his children, 4. Thad. H. Ferrell who has died leaving 3 children, Martha, Suba & Madison Ferrell, all minors, 5. Susan Ferrell who has died, unmarried. S. G., James & Thad. had sold their interest in the land to Coleman Spain who has since died. The Sullivans and Spains mentioned in the petition are his heirs. (Ibid 145-6) 2 April 1872 the heirs of Thad. Ferrill were shown as Martha Ferrill, Lula Ferrill and Thadeus Ferrill. (Ibid 404)

FERRELL, Epperson H.
Died before 1 September 1873 when B. B. Watkins was appointed administrator, with C. C. Moss as his security. (Dyr TN, Co Ct Min, B/618)

FERRELL, James
Died before 7 September 1829 when his handwriting was proved by Napoleon B. Bradford, as witness to a deed. (McM TN, Co Ct Min, 2no#/382)

FERRELL, S. George
Died before 5 December 1870 as shown in the division of the lands of his father, Dent Ferrell. George left children, M. E. and George Ferrell as his minor heirs. (Dyr TN, Co Ct Min, B/145-6) A. Parter was administrator. (Ibid 228)

FERRELL, Thad. H.
Died before 5 December 1870 as shown in the division of the lands of his father, Dent Ferrell. Thad. left 3 children, Martha, Suba and Madison Ferrell, all minors. (Dyr TN, Co Ct Min, B/145-6) 2 April 1872 the heirs were shown as Martha, Lula, and Thadeus Ferrill. (Ibid 404)

FERRILL
7 February 1871 3 negro minors, to wit: Walie Ferrill aged 7, Alice Ferrill aged 11 and Ella Ferrill aged 4, were bound to J. S. Ferrill until age 21. (Dyr TN, Co Ct Min, B/195)

FERRILL, Thomas
8 July 1873 was released from working on the roads as he is unable to perform manual labor. (Dyr TN, Co Ct Min, B/600)

FIELDER, B. T.
Died before 6 February 1871when S. B. Fielder renewed her bond as guardian of Mary & Francis Fielder. (Dyr TN, Co Ct Min, B/182) 2 October 1871 S. B. [or L. B.] Fielder made a settlement as guardian of S. M. L. and M. A. F. Fielder. (Ibid 190) S. H. Fielder renewed her bond as guardian of the minor heirs of B. T. Fielder deceased. (Ibid 295)

FIELDER, Sarah H.
2 December 1872 resigned as guardian of her children. (Dyr TN, Co Ct Min, B/512)

FIELDS, David
Died before 13 Februray 1815 when the administratrix, Lucy Fields, returned an account which was considered to be unlawful and unjust. A sale was ordered. John Graves was

appointed guardian of the orphans of David Fields, deceased, namely, Susanna Fields, George Fields, Milly Fields, Sally Fields, Polly Fields, Dicy Fields and Betsy Fields, with John Casey & Joseph Powel as security. (Cla TN, Co Ct Min, 4/2) The heirs of David Fields objected to the administratrix being allowed $25 for her services. (Ibid 240)

FIGUERS, Thomas
16 August 1810 was said to have "removed himself out of the County," as shown in the case of James Henner vs Thomas Figuers. William Alexander stated that he owed Figuers $10.66 1/2. (Rob TN, Co Ct Min, 2/295)

FIGURES, Mathew
Probably died before 1809 when land was shown taxed to him or his heirs. (Ste TN, Co Ct Min, no#/117)

FIKES, Nathan
4 April 1808 gave bond for the maintenance of a child he had begotten on the body of Amiah Mulliz, with Frys Fikes & Jeremiah Watts as security. (Rob TN, Co Ct Min, 2/10)

FIKES, Sarah
13 August 1813 gave a deposition concerning a land boundry in which she referred to her son-in-law, Richard Perdew. (Rob TN, Co Ct Min, 3/313)

FINLEY, George
Died before 16 December 1817 when Obediah G. Finley was appointed administrator with Thos. Bradley & James Frazer as security. (Wil TN, Co Ct Min, no#/202)

FINLEY, John
Died before 5 December 1870 when B. C. Burgie was appointed administrator, with Isaac Bunnel and J. R. Todd as security. (Dyr TN, Co Ct Min, B/140) Jo. R. Todd, J. H. Heard and J. S. Singletory were appointed to lay off a years provision for the children of John Finley, deceased. (Ibid 148)

FINLEY, Lafayette
4 September 1865 John Rose was appointed guardian. (Sev TN, Co Ct Min, no#/204)

FINLEY, Thomas
Died before 4 December 1871 when Bell C. Burgie was appointed administrator, with J. W. Lauderdale and John E. Roberts as his security. (Dyr TN, Co Ct Min, B/326)

FINLEY, Thomas
Died in 1871. A suit was entered 2 April 1872 by Allen Finley et als vs Thomas Finley et als, for sale of land for partition. Thomas Finley, Susan Ann Leoata Finley, John James Finley, Martha Virginia Finley, Charles, L. Finley, Anna Finley, Ada B. Spence, Pauline Kelly and Della Wright are minor defendants without a regular guardian and J. G. Rainey, Esqr. was appointed their guardian to answer for them. (Dyr TN, Co Ct Min, B/400) This suit stated that Thomas Finley died in 1871. (Ibid 408) The land was sold and title divested out of 17 named heirs: 1. Allin Finley; 2. Mary E. Finley; 3. Wm. Finley; 4. Sarah A. Sandford & husband Joseph; 5. Susan A. Finley; 6. Nancy Tancil; 7. Thomas Finley; 8. Susan Ann Leota Finley; 9. John James Finley; 10. Martha Virginia Finley; 11. Charles L. Finley; 12. Ann Finley; 13. Ada B. Spence; 14. Perlina Kelly; 15. Mary D. Simmons & husband W. H.; 16. Martha E. Dupree and husband C. H.; 17. Della Wright. (Ibid 445-6)

FINNY, Matilda
7 July 1856 it was ordered that her oldest child be brought to next court to be bound out. Said Matilda Finny is unable to support the child. (Sev TN, Co Ct Min, no#/60) 6 April 1857 D. W. Fox was paid for a coffin for a child of Matilda Finny. (Ibid 143)

FIRESTONE, Eve
Died before 3 June 1829 when her will was proved by Sam McConnell & Gabriel Cantrell. (McM TN, Co Ct Min, 2no#/369)

FITCHPATRICK, John
Made a deed of gift to Sally Fitchpatrick on 4 June 1806. (Cla TN, Co Ct Min, 2/260)

FITE, Leonard
17 June 1816 made a deed of gift to his son, Hugh Fite. (Wil TN, Co Ct Min, no#/6)

FITTS, John
Was a resident of Winston County, MS, when he brought suit against Hiram Edy of Bedford County, TN, on 25 January 1839. John Fitts left MS in the company of his brother, Oliver Fitts, to settle in TX. (Bed TN, Ch Ct Min, 1/263)

FITZGERALD, Patrick
Died before 12 August 1817 when the coroner, Benjamin Posey, was paid $5 for holding an inquest over his dead body. (Cla TN, Co Ct Min, 4/374)

FITZHUGH, T. H.
6 February 1871 was chosen and appointed guardian of William C, John S., Thomas J, Benjamin F, Tennessee A., Margaret B. and Anzanetta H. Fitzhugh, his own children, with W. N. Beasley and W. O. Harris as security. (Dyr TN, Co Ct Min, B/184)

FLANIGAN, William
Died before 13 October 1856 when his death was suggested in the suit of James H. Benson vs John Flanigan et als. William Flanigan was a defendant. (Fen TN, Ch Ct Min, A/62) William Flanigan left the following heirs, to wit, John C., Ailsey, Martha J., Rachael, Rhoda, Sarah, George & Isabella Flanigan, some of whom are minors. John C. Flanigan was appointed administrator "pendentilite and a sciri facias is to issue to Overton County against said heirs." (Ibid 96)

FLANNERY
Isaac & Jacob Flannery were living in the Indiana Territory 6 October 1809 when their deposition was to be taken for the case of Saml. Henley & Rebekah, his wife vs Henry Mahon. (Rob TN, Co Ct Min, 2/186)

FLATT, Lucinda
On 18 March 1852 sued Pleasant Flatt for divorce. The court found she was not entitled to the relief asked for in her bill and the suit was dismissed. (Jac TN, Ch Ct Min, B/24) Lucinda was granted an appeal to the Supreme Court in Nashville. (Ibid 30) Lucinda Flatt died before 14 July 1853 when her death was admitted in the suit of Pleasant Flatt vs Lucinda Flatt & Johnson McCormack. (Ibid 75)

FLEENER, Adam
Died before 25 Jan 1799 when the land of his heirs was ordered sold for back taxes. (Rob TN, Co Ct Min, 1/94) 19 January 1803 Levi Moore, Thos. Yates, John Siglar, Wm. Sale & Joel Vaughn were appointed to lay off the dower of the widow. (Ibid 244)

FLEMING, Robert
Died before 2 April 1867 when R. J. Anderson was appointed guardian to the minor heirs, with J. H. Caldwell as security. (Sev TN, Co Ct Min, no#/447)

FLEMING, Wm.
Died before 21 February 1839 when land was taxed to the heirs. (Obi TN, Cir Ct Min, 3/299)

FLETCHER, William
Made a deed of gift at the August Term 1811 to Patsey Fletcher, Lazarus Fletcher, Betsey Fletcher, Peggy Fletcher & Peggy Fletcher [sic], proved by Charles Lockart. (Rob TN, Co Ct Min, 3/6) A deed of gift from William Fletcher to his wife and children for certain property was proved. (Ibid 60)

FLOOD, Thomas
Died before 5 May 1818 when George Michie & wife Judith Michie give other security as guardian of the minor children of Thomas Flood, deceased. Judith was Judith Flood before her marriage to George Michie. George and Judith are accused of wasting the estate of the children. (Wil TN, Co Ct Min, no#/261) The children were: Elizabeth Flood, Robert Flood, Henry Flood, Lucy Flood & John Flood. (Ibid 294)

FLOWERS, Arabel
Died before 5 April 1871 when A. Parter made a settlement as administrator. (Dyr TN, Co Ct Min, B/228)

FLOWERS, Coleman
Died before 5 October 1870 when J. W. Wright made a settlement as administrator. (Dyr TN, Co Ct Min, B/122)

FLOWERS, Nancy
Died before 2 September 1872 when Wm. Jackson was appointed administrator, with G. B. Tinsley and W. C. Dickey as security. (Dyr TN, Co Ct Min, B/464)

FLOWERS, Rowland
Died before 11 October 1858 as shown in the suit of David Wright vs William Flowers & others. The defendants were ordered to file any title papers they have for the estate of Rowland Flowers, deceased. (Fen TN, Ch Ct Min, A/159)

FLOYD, E. S.
Died before 5 December 1870 when W. S. Floyd made a settlement as administrator. (Dyr TN, Co Ct Min, B/141)

FLOYD, Thomas
Was released from paying poll tax for 1859 as he is not 21 years old. (Sev TN, Co Ct Min, no#/545)

FOGG, Francis A.
Died in May 1853 leaving Archela Ann, his widow, and his minor children named in the pleadings. 23 February 1859 Saml. Neely was the regular guardian of Thos. M., Jos. F., Jno. T. & Mary Ann Fogg. In the suit of Saml. Neely & wife vs Saml. H. Swan et als, Samel. H. Swan was appointed guardian ad litem for the said minors. (Mad TN, Ch Ct Min, 2/258 & 413) A. A. Neely was the widow & is entitled to dower. (Ibid 540)

FOGG, Joseph
Died before 24 February 1866 as shown in the suit of Wm. C. Huchison [Hutchins], administrator vs Wm. Fogg & others. (Mad TN, Ch Ct Min, 2/496 & 508)

FOGLE, Lary
Taxes were not collected in District 4 for 1873, "insolvent." (Dyr TN, Co Ct Min, B/759)

FORBES, Alexr.
Died before 2 June 1828 when his administrator returned an inventory of the estate. (McM TN, Co Ct Min, 2no#/289) James Forbes was administrator. (Ibid 424)

FORBUS, John
Died before 1 November 1819 when the will was proved by Samuel Donnell & William H. Hearn. (Wil TN, Co Ct Min, no#/534) The widow, Elizabeth Forbus, petitioned for dower and a division of land among the heirs. (Ibid 543)

FORD
11 February 1817 William Ford and Catherine Ford, two of the poor of the county, were to be let out to the lowest bidder for their support. (Cla TN, Co Ct Min, 4/294)

FORD, Charlotte dye
Made a deed of gift 6 August 1794 to her daughter, Caroline Hail, for a Negro woman named Pheebe. It was witnessed by Joseph Brittain, Nathan Shiply & George Hail, Sr. [The name is written 3 times & each time it is shown as Charlotte dye Ford] (Was TN, Co Ct Min, 1/504)

FORD, John
Died before 19 April 1803 when the land of his heirs was on the delinquent tax list of 1799. (Rob TN, Co Ct Min, 1/251)

FORD, W. S. J.
Died before 6 April 1857 when M. J. Graham was paid for making the coffin. (Sev TN, Co Ct Min, no#/143)

FORD, W. T.
Died before 5 January 1871 when J. H. Brooks made a settlement as administrator. (Dyr TN, Co Ct Min, B/179)

FORESTER, Robert
Made application for a pension 11 March 1831. He is 73 years old. He enlisted for 3 years in April or May 1778 in VA in the Company commanded by Capt. Edward Wallen & Regt. of Col. Mobile. He served until February 1779 & was discharged at Williamsburg, VA. He listed a schedule of his property. He is a farmer & has no family at all. (McM TN, Co Ct Min, 2no#/524)

FORGASON, John
Died before 5 February 1866 when the will was proved by John Templin, witness. (Sev TN, Co Ct Min, no#/275)

FORGEY, Samuel
Died before 26 September 1804 when John Studevant was granted letters of administration, with John H. Bush & Thomas Bradley as security. (Wil TN, Co Ct Min, no#/96)

FORRESTER, Alexander
Died before 14 February 1814 when William Burney was appointed administrator, with Edward Choat & William L. Armstrong as security. (Rob TN, Co Ct Min, 3/360)

FORT, Elias
At the January term 1799 made deeds to Obedience Smith, Esther Jackson, Elisabeth Lawson and Catherine Williams. (Rob TN, Co Ct Min, 1/88)

FORT, Elias, Sr.
15 February 1814 made a deed of gift to Elizabeth F. Deloach, proven by Josiah Fort & Sugg Fort. (Rob TN, Co Ct Min, 3/365)

FORT, Eliza.
Made a deed of gift to Sarah Battle 13 November 1810, proved by Whitmell Fort. (Rob TN, Co Ct Min, 2/322)

FORT, Elizabeth
Gave power of attorney to Jacob Battle 14 August 1811, which was ordered to be registered in Edgecomb County, NC. (Rob TN, Co Ct Min, 3/18)

FORT, James
Was appointed guardian of his child, Jane Vernor Hampton Fort, with Elias Fort as security, 11 February 1812. (Rob TN, Co Ct Min, 3/60)

FORT, Jeremiah
Died before 5 April 1808 when Josiah Fort was appointed administrator with Orrin D. Battle & Elias Fort, Jr. as security. (Rob TN, Co Ct Min, 2/12) 3 October 1809 an order was made to divide the property of the estate between the widow & heir according to law. (Ibid 2/174) 17 May 1810 Jethro Battle Fort, by his guardian Orrian D. Battle, filed a petition against Josiah Fort & Elias Fort, executors of the will of William Fort, for a sum of money due from them. (Ibid 266) 11 February 1813 Orrin D. Battle made a settlement as guardian of Jethro Battle Fort, orphan of Jeremiah Fort, deceased. (Ibid 3/211)

FORT, Josiah
Gave power of attorney to Jeremiah Battle 14 August 1811, which was ordered to be registered in Edgecomb County, NC. (Rob TN, Co Ct Min, 3/18)

FORT, Sugg
Removed by 23 April 1801 when a commissioner was appointed in his room. (Rob TN, Co Ct Min, 1/178)

FORT, William
Died before 14 February 1814 when William A. Fort and Jacob Fort qualified as executors of his will, with will annexed. (Rob TN, Co Ct Min, 3/361) [probably same as Wm. Fort whose will was proved in 1802]

FORT, William
Made a deed of gift to his daughter Sarah Fort, which was recorded 20 April 1802. (Rob TN, Co Ct Min, 1/214)

FORT, Wm.
Died before 18 January 1802 when the will was proved by David Smith. Josias Fort & Elias Fort were executors. (Rob TN, Co Ct Min, 1/196) 6 August 1805 the executors made a settlement with Jeremiah Fort, Sarah Fort, James Fort, Wm. A. Fort, Jacob Fort, Josiah Fort & Mary Fort, orphans of William Fort, deceased. (Ibid 351) William Anthony Fort is to receive his part of his father's estate, 11 November 1811. (Ibid 3/36) William Fort had seven children. (Ibid 64)

FORTUNE, John A.
Was a resident of Green County, AL, as shown in the suit of Preston Frazer vs John A. Fortune on 3 October 1839. Preston Frazier was a physician. He brought said Fortune's

son, a lad about 14 years of age, from Greensborough, AL, to Lincoln County, TN. [2 pages missing in this case] (Bed TN, Ch Ct Min, 1/298)

FOSTA, David [Foster]
1 February 1819 emancipated his negro man named Frederick. (Wil TN, Co Ct Min, no#/384)

FOSTER, James A.
3 January 1871 H. S. Fowlkes renewed his bond as guardian, with P. C. Ledsinger and Jo. Michell as security. (Dyr TN, Co Ct Min, B/157) 9 July 1873 a final guardian settlement was made. (Ibid 613)

FOSTER, Robert
Died before 16 December 1817 when James Foster & Alexander Foster were appointed administrators, with John Foster & Henry Moser as security. A years provisions was allotted to the widow. (Wil TN, Co Ct Min, no#/195)

FOSTER, Thomas
Died before 31 March 1821 when his heir, Joel Foster of Union District, SC, gave power of attorney to Edmund Foster, brother of the said deceased, to transact his business concerning the said estate in Wilson County, TN. Witnesses were John Norman & Edmond Simpson. (Wil TN, Reg Bk/200)

FOULING, Wm.
Died before 23 November 1778 when Betsey Fouling and John Chism, Esqr. were appointed administrators. (Was TN, Co Ct Min, 1/49) 12 May 1791 John Chisolm & Elizabeth Fauling as administrators of the estate of Wm. Fauling, were in a case against John Bean. (Ibid no#/111)

FOWLER, James S.
Was a resident of MO in November 1842 as shown in the suit of Allen Knight vs Bennett Cully & James S. Fowler. (Bed TN, Ch Ct Min, 3/71)

FOWLER, John F.
Died before 4 August 1856 when the administrator, John S. McNutt, renewed his bond with W. A. McNutt & J. Stafford as security. The original bond was destroyed by fire. (Sev TN, Co Ct Min, no#/67)

FOWLER, Robert
Died before 7 May 1787 when the will was proved and William Fowler was appointed executor, as Agness Fowler resigned her right as executrix. (Was TN, Co Ct Min, 1/278)

FOWLKES, George A.
Died before 6 February 1871 when the will was proved by Jos. Smith and Wm. P. Menzies, witnesses. Zenobia F. Fowlkes was executrix. (Dyr TN, Co Ct Min, B/188) Petition was made for dower by Zenobia Fowlkes vs George Anna Fowlkes, Jenny Fowlkes & Charles H. Fowlkes. George A. Fowlkes died in January 1871. The defendants are the only heirs. (Ibid 268) Dower was laid off. Land was mentioned that was given by H. Fowlkes to H. L. Fowlkes. (Ibid 279)

FOWLKES, Green
Taxes were not collected in District 5 for 1873, "insolvent." (Dyr TN, Co Ct Min, B/759)

FOWLKES, Henry
Taxes were not collected in District 5 for 1873, "insolvent." (Dyr Co TN, Co Ct Min, B/759)

FOWLKES, Thomas H.
Died before 3 November 1873 when Napoleon Coker was appointed administrator, with D. E. Parker and P. C. Ledsinger as his security. (Dyr Co TN, Co Ct Min, B/659)

FOX, Branson
4 June 1860 was appointed guardian of Mary Jane Fox, James M. Fox and John H. Fox, minor orphans of Branson Fox. [sic] (Sev TN, Co Ct Min, no#/562)

FOX, Emanl.
Was released from paying poll tax for 1860 as he is over age. (Sev TN, Co Ct Min, no#/589)

FOX, George
Died before 7 February 1859 when Emanuel Fox & William Fox, Jr. were appointed administrators, with M. A. Rawlings & Adam Bird as security. (Sev TN, Co Ct Min, no#/400)

FOX, John
Died before 6 October 1856 when a road order mentioned the house where John Fox, deceased, [had] lived. (Sev TN, Co Ct Min, no#/78) 7 January 1857 John Bird renewed his bond as administrator of John Fox, Jr., deceased, with C. Fox as security. The old bond was destroyed by fire. (Ibid 117) 3 August 1857 Cornelius Fox produced a certified copy of the will of John Fox, deceased, which was recorded. (Ibid 194)

FOX, Tennesse
4 January 1860 was certified to be a young man of good moral character & has attained the age of 21. He has made application for a license to practice law. (Sev TN, Co Ct Min, no#/509)

FRAIM, John
Died before 10 February 1855 as shown in the suit of William & John Fraim vs John Fraim's heirs & devisees. William H. Botts was appointed guardian ad litem for the infant defendants, to wit, Christopher Andrew, Sarah & Nancy Harling. Process has been served on defendants Preor? Fraim, Temperance Stone, Leroy & Montgomery Clemmons, and publication has been made to the non-resident defendants, Zebern Shelton & Elizabeth Shelton, Jane & Sarah Fraem. The death of defendant Henderson Clemmons was suggested. (Jac TN, Ch Ct Min, B/214) John M. Fraim is due money for supporting Sarah & Jane Fraim [apparently since 1847] The last will & testament of John M. Fraim, deceased, was mentioned. (Ibid 232) 7 February 1856 this suit was shown as John M. Fraim & William Fraim vs Sarah Fraim Jane Fraim Zeberry Sarah Clements Shelton Elizabeth Shelton Temperance? Christopher Clements Jr. Stone Leroy Clements Henderson M George C. Clements Clements Montgomery Clements Lafayette Harling Jefferson Harling Nancy Horling Sarah Horling Andrew Clements and Prior B. Fraim [witten this way with no punctuation.] Land & slaves were sold. Title was divested out of complainant John M. Fraim and the defendants & vested in William Fraim, who purchased the land. Title to the slaves was divested out of complainants & defendants. "John M. Fraim is son of one of said Lunaticks & brother to the other and that he is a responsible & trust worthy person. It is ordered and decreed by the court that upon his entering into bond with good security to account for the amount for which said land and negroes sold at the death of said Lunaticks to those intitled to the same that he be appointed their Trustee". (Ibid 290) Names above should be Sarah Fraim, Jane Fraim, Zebery Shelton, Elizabeth Shelton, Sarah Clements, Christopher Clements, Jr., George Clements, Temperence Stone, Leroy Clements, Henderson W. Clements, Montgomery Clements, Lafayette Harling, Jefferson Harling, Nancy Harling, Sarah Harling, Andrew Clements and Prior P. Fraim. "Jane & Sarah Fraim are the lunaticks, mother and sister of John W. Fraim." (Ibid C/1)

FRAIM, Ruth
Was granted support from William Fraim on 14 August 1860. (Jac TN, Ch Ct Min, C/396)

FRANKLIN
In the suit of David Beaty vs Wm. Brannon et al, 1 August 1866, it was stated that defendants Jesse Franklin, John Franklin, James Franklin and Tina Franklin are minors. B. O. Bouden was appointed guardian ad litem for them. In this same suit it showed that Edward Franklin and George W. Franklin had been dead more than six months and had no administrator. Claborn Beaty was appointed administrator. (Fen TN, Ch Ct Min, A/291)

FRANKLIN, J. K.
Died before 3 December 1866 when J. H. Caldwell was appointed guardian to the minor heirs, with W. M. Burnett as security. (Sev TN, Co Ct Min, no#/407)

FRANKLIN, Owen
Died before 14 November 1844 as shown in the suit of Bird Cannon & Lucinda his wife vs Garret Sadler, Henry Saddler, David Apple, Abisha Cannon & Sally his wife. It was stated that the complainants had failed to prove that Lucinda was a child of Owen Franklin, deceased, and distributee of his estate. (Jac TN, Ch Ct Min, A/174) An appeal was granted to Superior Court in Nashville. (Ibid 179)

FRANKLIN, William
Was released from paying poll tax for 1859 because he is under 21 years of age. (Sev TN, Co Ct Min, no#/514)

FRAZIER, Thomas J.
Died before 5 August 1872 when Thomas Frazier and John Sawyer were appointed administrators, with F. G. Sampson and R. R. Watson as securities. (Dyr TN, Co Ct Min, B/448)

FREELING, Jno. H.
Died before 17 March 1855 leaving complainant, Jno. W. Anderson & wife, and defendants, Lucy Freeling et als, his heirs-at-law. (Mad TN, Ch Ct Min, 2/41) In a suit 19 Februray 1858 by Jno. V. Anderson vs Lucy Freeling & others, land was sold and title divested out of Jno. H. Freeling, Augustus I. H. Freeling, Jas. A. Hudson & wife Nancy K., Wm. W. Freeling, Lucy Garrett, Reuben H. Freeling, Hyntin Bryant & wife Sarah E., Phillip N. Dulen & wife Susan G. (Ibid 196) 25 August 1860 in the suit of Jno. V. Anderson & wife vs Lucy Freeling & others, Thomas Clark was appointed guardian ad litem for Dansey S. Hudson, Virginia Hudson, Hamly P. Hudson, Mary L. Hudson & Nancy K. Hudson, the minor defendants. (Ibid 366)

FREEMAN, Asbury
Died before 3 August 1874 when P. C. Ledsinger made a settlement as administrator. (Dyr TN, Co Ct Min, B/766)

FREEMAN, J. D.
Taxes were not collected in district 5 for 1873, "under age." (Dyr TN, Co Ct Min, B/759)

FREEMAN, John
Was let to Alsey Bradford for one year, 3 August 1813. [He was a pauper] (Ste TN, Co Ct Min, 4/62)

FREEMAN, Solomon
Died before 18 February 1858 as shown in the suit of Radford Withers Trustee vs Joseph B. Freeman Admr. and Jas. W. Tomlin. Joseph B. Freeman was administrator for Solomon Freeman. (Mad TN, Ch Ct Min, 2/172)

FRENCH, Allen
Was an orphan boy aged 17 when he was bound to Joel K. Brown on 9 March 1831, to learn the trade of a Tailor. (McM TN, Co Ct Min, 2no#/521)

FRENCH, Thomas
Died before 2 May 1815 when Mark Rushing was appointed administrator with Thomas Brewer and Robert Lowry as security. (Ste TN, Co Ct Min, 4/269)

FRENCH, Thomas
Was a resident of Overton County, TN, on 8 June 1827 when his deposition was to be taken for the plaintiff in the case of Thomas Smith vs Booker Shockly. (McM TN, Co Ct Min, no#/265)

FRENCH, Wm.
Died before 12 April 1858 as shown in the suit of Jessee Ashburn vs C. H. Saffle & others. A compromise was made. Jesse Ashburn was administrator for Wm. French, deceased, and he agreed to deliver to said Saffle [Saffell] the widow's portion of the estate and years allowance. (Fen TN, Ch Ct Min, A/123) Jesse Ashburn filed a suit against Robert Whited, Mary French & others. (Ibid 158) An order to answer a bill was issued 10 October 1859 against the widow & heirs of Wm. French to Blount County. (Ibid 219) In the suit of Jessee Ashburn Admr. &c against the heirs of Wm. French Decd. et als, it was stated that defendants Mary French, Sarah French, J. M. French, Thomas French, John French & Josiah French were non-residents of the state and have gone to parts unknown. Publication has been made as to them and the other defendants have been served with process & have failed to answer except defendant Robert Whited. Mary French is the widow and Sarah, Melvina, James M., Thomas, John & Josiah French are the only children. Robert Whited had bought land from William French but did not yet have title. (Ibid 282) William French owned land that had been devised to him from Rebecca French. (Ibid 313) Martin French claims part of the land. (Ibid 381)

FRIM, Edward [Fum or ?]
Was granted a divorce on 17 July 1856 from Sarah Frim? for desertion. (Jac TN, Ch Ct Min, C/11)

FROGGE, Strother
Died before 26 March 1855 when his death was suggested in the suit of Lavina Frogge vs Strother Frogge. (Fen TN, Ch Ct Min, A/11) In the suit of Lavina Frogge vs Mitchel H. Frogge, 25 September 1855, they compromised the suit by Mitchel Frogge paying Lavinia Frogge for her dower interest in land where William Smith now lives. (Ibid 34)

FROST, Eli
Was a resident of GA on 8 September 1825 when his deposition was to be taken for the plaintiff in the case of Joseph B. Bacon vs Ezekiel Bonner. (McM TN, Co Ct Min, no#/206) Eli Frost was said to be a resident of Athens County, GA, on 8 December 1825. (Ibid 216)

FULLER
3 July 1872 Silas Ferrill made a settlement as guardian of Amanda Fuller (Cozart) [sic], James Fuller, Marg. Fuller and David Fuller. (Dyr TN, Co Ct Min, B/442)

FULLER, Elias
Died before 4 October 1870 when the land of his heirs was mentioned. (Dyr TN, Co Ct Min, B/104) Silas Ferrill renewed his bond as guardian of the minor heirs. (Ibid 138)

FULLER, John
Died before 1 August 1870 when L. M. Williams made a settlement as guardian of David and Stacey Fuller, minors. (Dyr TN, Co Ct Min, B/88)

FUQUA, James
4 April 1870 was allowed $20 as a pauper. (Dyr TN, Co Ct Min, B/33)

FUQUAY, Benjamin
Died before 17 July 1851 as shown in the suit of John Hughs, David G. Shepherd & Co., et als, George R. Hughes, Samuel W. Moreland, Henry Goad, B. B. Thaxton, Matthew Duke & Samuel Jones vs Dixon Brown & John M. Armstead. Property was sold at the late residence of Dixon Brown, much of it bought by Mary Brown. Also sold was a tract of land, the life estate of Gracey Fuquay in and to the lands formerly owned by Benjamin Fuquay, deceased. Land was also sold that was bounded by the land of Alsey Rogers, deceased, and by the lands of the heirs of John Hollimon, deceased. (Jac TN, Ch Ct Min, B/15-19) In the suit of Sampson McClellan Admr. vs Daniel A. Fuquay it was shown that Daniel A. Fuquay was the son of Benjamin Fuquay. (Ibid 132) The property of Daniel A. Fuquay was sold to satisfy a debt, it being 1/6 of said tract. (Ibid 149)

FUSSELL, James V.
In a suit brought by James A. W. Hess vs James V. Fussell et als, 18 February 1857, it is shown that Louisa Fussell was the wife of James V. Fussell and Ann, Susan, James, Jr., Berry & Louisa, Jr. are the children. (Mad TN, Ch Ct Min, 2/115) Another suit was filed 26 February 1859; Wyatt Fussell vs Jno. J. Anderson administrator with will annexed of Jas. Fussell. (Ibid 282)

FUSSELL, William
Died before 10 January 1849 as shown in the suit of the administrator, James Fussell, vs Jno. H. Day et als. (Mad TN, Ch Ct Min, 1/59)

FYFFE, Isaac W.
Died before 7 September 1829 when George Morgan, William Lowry & Horrace Hixkox were appointed to lay off a years provision to his widow, Peggy Fyffe. (McM TN, Co Ct Min, 2no#/384) James H. Fyffe, William Hogan & Nathaniel Smith were appointed administrators. (Ibid 386) 2 March 1830 Martin Senter was appointed guardian of Sarah Elizabeth, William C. & Isaac W. Fyffe, minor orphans of Isaac W. Fyffe, deceased. The orphans were not old enough to choose a guardian. (Ibid 431)

GAILBREATH, Isabella
Died before 6 May 1845 when her death was suggested in the suit of Nathan Montgomery vs Kinnard & Bransford et al. Isabella was one of the defendants. (Jac TN, Ch Ct Min, A/188) The suit was against Thomas L. Bransford, Russel M. Kinnard, Thomas J. Gailbreath, Isabella Gailbreath and William A. Gailbreath. Isabella had sold to complainants 2/10 of a tract of land which had been conveyed to her by William A. Gailbreath. Isabella was the widow of William Gailbreath, deceased. Thomas Gailbreath had conveyed 1/9 of the tract of land to Isabella. (Ibid 196)

GAINES, James H.
Died before 13 July 1850 as shown in the suit of Calaway Sizemore & William Gray Guardian &c vs Thomas Butler, Milton E. Burke, Angeline Burke, Elizabeth Burke, John M.

Burke, Sarah Burke & John G. Burke. Complainant Sizemore is guardian of Rufus Gaines & Margery Gaines and complainant Gray is guardian of William C. Gains, who are the only heirs of James H. Gaines, deceased. A judgement had been recovered against Henry F. Burke and the undivided interest of said Burk in the lands of his father, John Burke, deceased, was ordered to be sold which was not done. Henry F. Burk died insolvent in the state of MO & Milton E., Angelina, Elizabeth, John M. and Sarah Burke are his only heirs & are non-residents. Defendant John G. Burke is their guardian ad litem. (Jac TN, Ch Ct Min, A/378) In the suit, 15 July 1854, of Mary Ann Gaines vs William C. Gaines, Tho. H. Butler, Margery Gaines, Rufus Gaines and Robert C. Kirkpatrick, it was stated that William C. Gaines is a non-resident of TN. R. C. Kirkpatrick is guardian of Margery & Rufus Gaines. Mary Ann Gaines is the widow of James H. Gaines, deceased. Thomas Butler is evidently the administrator. Mary Ann is entitled to 1/4 of the estate. (Ibid B/173)

GAINES, William C.
Was a non-resident of Tennessee on 11 February 1854 as shown in the suit of Mary An Gaines vs William C. Gaines & others. (Jac TN, Ch Ct Min, B/144)

GALBREATH, Joseph
Died before 3 December 1827 when Thomas Galbreath was appointed guardian of Elizabeth Mary James Sarah Margaret Saml. and Joseph Galbreath, orphan minor heirs. (McM TN, Co Ct Min, 2no#/243) William Galbreath was appointed administrator. Robert W. McCleary, Joseph Cobbs & William Phillipps were appointed to lay off a years support to the widow, Elizabeth Gilbreath. (Ibid 244) 7 September 1829 Elizabeth Gilbreath asked to act as guardian for her own children, to wit: James, Sarah, Jane, Saml. L. and Joseph Gilbreath. All of said minors were not of sufficient age to choose a guardian so Elizabeth was appointed, with William Wiggins & Thomas Gilbreath her security. (Ibid 384) 5 March 1830, petition for dower states Joseph Gilbreath died 15 September 1827. Thomas Gilbreath, guardian of Mary Gilbreath, Elizabeth Gilbreath & Peggy Ann Gilbreath, were notified of the petition. (Ibid 442)

GALBREATH, Kizziah
Died in the spring of 1839 as shown in the suit of Enoch Trott & Robert Reed against Jacob Greer, administrator of Kizziah Galbreath, deceased. Levin Wood of Orange County, NC, claims to be the only living heir of Kizziah. (Bed TN, Ch Ct Min, 1/387) Keziah left no heirs of her body. Levin Wood is the lawful brother & heir of Keziah & she has no other brother or sister or the issue thereof surviving. (Ibid 2/168) 30 June 1842 the death of complainant Levin Wood was suggested by his counsel and admitted by defendants counsel. (Ibid 191) 27 December 1843 a suit was entered by William Albright & Louisa his wife, William Wood, Robert Wood & others, heirs-at-law of Levin Wood, deceased vs Enoch Trott and Clement Cannon. (Ibid 273) Kizziah was refered to as Keziah Rushing. Her will was offered for probate before 12 August 1839. Anderson & Robert Reed are brothers-in-law. [Not clear if to Kizziah or to Enoch Trott as this is stated in his answer to the bill of Levin Wood to declare the sale of Kizziah's land void.] The heirs of the late husband of Kizziah were mentioned. The heirs of Levin Wood were shown as William Albright & Louise his wife, William Wood, Ann Wood, Robert Wood, Levin Albright, Handy Wood, John Thompson & Elizabeth his wife, Silas & Sarah his wife, Vestal & Mary his wife, [No last name was given for Silas nor for Vestal] Washington Wood, Martha Wood, Layfayette Wood, Maria Wood, & Levin Wood the five last being minors with William Albright their next friend. In another place the name was written as Keziah Rushing Galbraith with Rushing crossed out. It was decided that when Keziah sold her land in 1838 to Enoch Trott that she was insane and the deed was declared void. (Ibid 3/101-7)

GALLAGY, Darcus [Gallady]
18 June 1816 was shown to be a widow and was allowed money for her support. (Wil TN, Co Ct Min, no#/16)

GALLAHAR, Lee
Died before 4 January 1871 when J. T. Montgomery was chosen and appointed guardian of John Gallahar, minor heir, with J. P. Troy and G. B. Tinsley as his securities. (Dyr TN, Co Ct Min, B/174) W. E. Troy was administrator. (Ibid 190)

GALLOWAY, Charles
Was a minor 18 December 1805 when he sued James Galloway. The suit was made with his father as his next friend. He sued Michael Baker for "Trespass on the Case for Words Spoken to the damage of the said Charles Galloway" [in other words, for slander]. On the same day, and for the same reason, he also sued John Matlock & Nelly Matlock his wife and Samuel Tummins. (Roa TN, Co Ct Min, B/97)

GALSTON, Sally G.
Petition to sell land was made 15 Feb 1858 by John Irvin, administrator of Sally G. Galston. (Mad TN, Ch Ct Min, 2/157)

GALYEAN, A. F.
Died before 2 July 1866 when Elijah Ballard was appointed administrator with James Clark as security. (Sev TN, Co Ct Min, no#/339) A years support was laid off to Eleanor Galyean. (Ibid 352)

GAMBLE, Alexander
Died before 20 September 1803 when Nancy Gamble, James Houston and Robert Gamble were granted letters of administration. John Winton, Robert Houston & George Preston were their securities. (Roa TN, Co Ct Min, A/131) An agreement between Alexander Gamble, deceased, and Robert Gamble was recorded. (Ibid 244) The petition of Agness Gamble, relict of Alexander Gamble,deceased, was made for partition. George Preston, James Rogers, Henry Breazeal, John Winton and William Ramsey were appointed to make partition. (Ibid 308) The widow was shown as Nancy Gamble when her dower was laid off. (Ibid 337) 15 January 1810 Robert Gamble deeded land to Nancy Gamble, guardian of William Gamble. (Ibid D/170)

GAMBLE, S. E. T.
Taxes were not collected in District 3 for 1873, "gone to Crockett." (Dyr TN, Co Ct Min, B/758)

GAMMELL, Thos. W.
Died before 21 February 1866 when his death was admitted in the suit of D. C. Hail vs Jas. Price et als. (Mad TN, Ch Ct Min, 2/472) The suit of M. M. Hammons vs Thos. W. Gammell, et als, is to revive against Leonella? & Frank M. Gamwell, minor children of said T. W. Gamwell. (Ibid 475) This suit was shown again as Miles M. Hammonds vs Thos W. Gammell & P. C. McConet, et al. Complainant had bought the undivided one half of some property and title is to be divested out of defendants, together with Leonilla and Melville Gammell, the heirs at law of said Thos. W. Gammell. (Ibid 520) Thos. W. Gammell died 7 October 1865. Mary Ann Gammell was the widow & sues for dower. (Ibid 3/179)

GAMMONS, Jas.
7 August 1871 M. R. Via made a settlement as administrator. (Dyr TN, Co Ct Min, B/260) Mrs. Felecia Gammons was the widow. (Ibid 287)

GANAWAY, Mary B.
In a suit by Samuel Lancaster, 10 July 1850, Mary B. is shown to have signed a mortgage jointly with her sons Samuel S. & James W. [B.] Ganaway. Mary E. R. Ganaway has since married William A. Gilliland. Mary had a life estate in a house & lot in Jackson. (Mad TN, Ch Ct Min, 1/139)

GANNON, J. P.
Died before 3 October 1870 when J. S. McCorkle was appointed administrator, with J. T. Gregory and J. C. Gregory as securities. (Dyr TN, Co Ct Min, B/98)

GANNON, James
Probably died before 4 July 1871 when the suit of M. V. Via, administrator of James Gannon vs J. R. Gannon et als was continued. (Dyr TN, Co Ct Min, B/258)

GANNON, Roda
Was a widow 5 October 1870 when A. G. Hallum, Albert Cochran and S. S. McCorkle were appointed to lay off a years allowance for her and her family. (Dyr TN, Co Ct Min, B/122)

GANT, William A.
Died intestate. He was never married and his heirs are his brothers & sisters, to wit; Absolem B. Gant of Wayne County, Jesse B. Gant & Samuel Harlson? & wife Nancy, a sister of said William A., of Hardin County, A. Gifford & wife Sarah Caroline, Benjamin Brangtin & wife Mary, S. Bryhn & wife, Elizabeth Gant, Lewis G. Roy, Martha Cotner a minor who has John Cotner for her guardian [this is bad writing & crowded together so names not certain], John Cotner, James Gant, Lewis Gant, Elizabeth, John Williams & Eliza Jane Gant, the four last being minors & have John T. Neal for their guardian, John D., Sarah and Nancy Jane Ray children of John Ray, deceased, nephew & nieces of said William A. deceased, & John R. Lewis A. Boln? P & Martha Jane Freeman children of Stephen Freeman who is their guardian being grand nephews & nieces of said William A., all citizens of Bedford County, TN, & Margret Hayzethin & William Hayzehin of Bedford

County, John Aldridge & wife Margret & Jacob Shaddy & wife Martha of MO & Aicey L. Barnt Kiziah Aldridge & Rily Aldridge minors & Robert J. B. Gant who has G. W. Redad? for his guardian & who reside in AL, said Absalam in Marshall County, said Absalim B. & Lewis Gant who are brothers of said William A. are also his administrators. George Bussey had bought land from William A. Gant before his death and he never made him a deed. He is suing for the deed to the land he bought. There is no date on the suit but the land was bought in 1840 and registered November 1844. William A. Gant was living in 1844 as he signed the document. William's name was shown as Gaunt. He died in New Orleans. The answer given by the administrators to the suit of George Bussey was dated 22 February 1847. Leave was granted to both sides to take depositions. (Bed TN, Ch Ct Min, 3/388-94)

GARDNER, John
Was an heir of Robt. Lasiter as shown 20 April 1802 when Benjn. Menes, Jr. released his claim on the land of Robt. Lasiter purchased [for taxes]. (Rob TN, Co Ct Min, 1/213)

GARNER, Jane
Was the mother of a bastard child by John Shelly who gave bond 1 October 1866 to indemnify the court. (Sev TN, Co Ct Min, no#/374)

GARNER, Sarah
Was aged 5 years when she was bound at the February term 1789 to John Hammer, Esqr. until age 18. (Was TN, Co Ct Min, 1/316)

GARRELL, Staton
Died before 23 November 1818 when Benjamin H. Garrell of Camden County, NC, the only heir of his uncle, Staton Garrell, deceased, transferred the bounty land given by NC for the service of Starton Garrell in the old Continental War, to Daniel Cherry. (Wil TN, Reg Bk/192)

GARRETT, Eliza J.
Died before 4 January 1871 when S. Seagraves was appointed administrator, with S. R. Latta & T. E. Richardson as securities. (Dyr TN, Co CT Min, B/173)

GARRISON, Baily
Died before 17 September 1816 when Benja. Garrison was appointed administrator with John Boone & Pettis Raglin as security. (Wil TN, Co Ct Min, no#/31)

GARRISON, Isaac
Was a pauper of the county and was allowed money 18 December 1816 for his support. (Wil TN, Co Ct Min, no#/65) Money was allowed for the support of he & his family. (Ibid 222) 3 May 1819 Isaac was allowed money for the support of he and his son, John. (Ibid 439)

GAUDIN, John W.
Was granted a divorce from Adelia Gaudin on 3 December 1868. He was also given custody of the children, Fanny, William, Henry and Salina Gaudin. (Fen TN, Ch Ct Min, A/410)

GAULDEN, Fletcher
Was a colored orphan boy aged 6 years when he was bound 8 January 1874 to Richard Johnson Benton, colored, until age 21. (Dyr TN, Co Ct Min, B/703)

GAULLING, John
Died before 5 September 1825 when Daniel Kelly was appointed administrator. (McM TN, Co Ct Min, 2no#/92)

GAUNT, John
Died before the end of 1837 and William A. Gaunt was administrator, as shown in the suit filed 7 December 1840 by William A. Gaunt & others vs Benjamin Broughton & wife & others. Benjamin Broughton married a daughter of John Gaunt. Alexander Bryant married another daughter of John Gaunt. Jacob Shaddy [Shadder], Jr. married another daughter of John Gaunt. John Gaunt also left a widow and children, "Elizabeth, Caroline, John William & Eliza, James who with the daughters and widow above mentioned constitute the distributees of John Gaunt deceased and who are minors and have William A. Guant for their guardian." Benjamin Broughton married Mary Gaunt in 1829. The widow was Sarah. There were 8 children. The minors were Elizabeth, Caroline, John, William & Eliza Jane. (Bed TN, Ch Ct Min, 1/328) Another suit entered 27 July 1839 shows Benjamin Braughton & wife Mary, Alexander Bryant & wife Ann, Jacob Shaddy &

wife Patsy, Elizabeth Guant, Caroline Guant, John Guant, William Guant & Eliza Jane Guant the last 5 minors who sue by next friend, Sally Guant, are the only heirs of John Guant, deceased. John Guant had purchased land from his father, Lewis Guant [Grant, Guiant], deceased. Heirs of Lewis were William Guant & Lewis Guant & James Guant of Bedford County, and Robert J. B. Grant, a minor, who has George W. Record and wife Mahulda for his guardian, and John Aldridge & wife Peggy and Caroline J. and Jessie Nathaniel Aldridge, and others, and two others whose names are not at present known and have James Aldridge, their father, for their guardian and who reside in AL, and Jessie Guant who resides in [blank] County, TN, and Samuel [blank] & wife Nancy who also reside in [blank] County and Abraham Guant who lives in Wayne County, and the children of Patsy Ray, deceased, who was a daughter of the said Louis Grant, the names of which children are unknown and are minors & have no guardian. The names of the children of Martha Ray have been learned and are Jane C. [blank], Louis G. Ray, William R. Ray, Mary D. Ray, Margaret Ray, John B. Ray, Sarah Ray & Nancy C. Ray, all of whom are minors & William A. Guant is guardian ad litem [another listing shows James G., William R., Mary D., Margaret, and John C. Freeman] (Bed TN, Ch Ct Min, 1/437)

GAUSE, G. W.
Died before 4 January 1871 when R. H. McGaughey made a settlement as administrator. (Dyr TN, Co Ct Min, B/162) The name shown was George W. Gause. (Ibid 406)

GEARHEART, Valentine
Died before 16 July 1856 as shown in the suit of An Gearheart vs William Gearheart, administrator of Valentine Gearheart, deceased. He died in Jackson County something over a year ago. He had been indebted to complainant. (Jac TN, Ch Ct Min, C/6)

GENS, David
Was a minor orphan aged 2 years when he was bound on 7 March 1825 to George Greenway until age 21. (McM TN, Co Ct Min, 2no#/52)

GENTRY, Nicholas C.
Died before 1 August 1870 when his will was proved by John H. Moss, Benj. Blackwell and J. W. Hassell, witnesses. Thos. W. Jones was executor with Thos. Miller and Henderson Clark as security. (Dyr TN, Co Ct Min, B/90)

GEORGE, Thomas
25 March 1807 was found guilty of Bastardy. He gave bond with Benjamin Clark, John Bradley & John Ward as security. (Wil TN, Co Ct Min, no#/286) Witnesses in above case were Polly Morning for defendant, Milly Ward, Peter Gressom, John Ranshaw & Hanna Renshaw. (Ibid 287)

GEORGE, William
Died before 18 June 1817 when Jesse Hunt was appointed guardian to a minor orphan named Lurena George. (Wil TN, Co Ct Min, no#/123)

GERAN, Samuel
23 March 1809 was a minor as shown when he was represented by his father, Solomon Geran, when they and Solomon Geran, Jr. were to appear in court on a peace warrant. (Roa TN, Co Ct Min, D/60) Silas Garen & Benjn. Evans were included in this suit when it came to trial. A case tried the same day had the State vs Simeon Garen & Silas Garen (Ibid 85 & 86)

GERARD, Andrew
17 June 1817 sold land in Mason County, KY, to Thos. Wells of KY. (Wil TN, Co Ct Min, no#/122)

GERARD, Charles
Probably died before 10 September 1806 when land was taxed to the estate. (Ste TN, Co Ct Min, 1/35b)

GHOLSEN, Sarah J. [Gholson, Goholson]
Died after making her will 4 March 1857 which was proved in April 1857 and James L. Talbot was named executor. Talbot refused to act and John Irvin was appointed administrator with will annexed. By the will she left all of her property in trust for her daughter Maraget J. A trustee is to be appointed for said Margaret J. Ganaway. Saml. L. Ganaway was party to the suit. (Mad TN, Ch Ct Min, 2/346) Saml. L. Gannaway was the husband of Margaret E. [J.]. Joel R. Chappell was appointed her trustee. (Ibid 357)

GIBBONS
Died before 4 December 1866 as shown in the suit of James M. Wright Admr. of A. McGinnis, deceased vs the widow & heirs and creditors of said deceased. R. F. Bryson was owed money from the estate of A. McGinnis for his own use and as administrator of Gibbons. (Fen TN, Ch Ct Min, A/305)

GIBBONS, Dennis
Was not a resident of the state on 6 March 1827 when his signature as witness to a deed from George Kees to Thomas Campbell, was proved. This entry was then crossed out. (McM TN, Co Ct Min, no#/261) Same entry, same date entered in 2no#/205

GIBBS, William
Died before 2 June 1828 when an appropriation made to him for the support of 2 orphan children was ordered to be paid to the widow of William Gibbs. (McM TN, Co Ct Min, 2no#/291)

GIBSON, David
Taxes were not collected in District 4 for 1873, "gone." (Dyr TN, Co Ct Min, B/759)

GIBSON, Hannah
Died in 1847 leaving a will, with Micajah Fly as executor. She made a bequest to Cordelia H. Stitwell [Stilwell], Harriet R. Stitwell and Mary A. Stitwell, her minor grandchildren. The father of these grandchildren was William H. Sitwell. (Mad TN, Ch Ct Min, 1/36) Some of the bequests of the will of Hannah Gibson were listed: "5th. I give to my daughter Peggy [Margaret] Williams and her children 1/7 part of my estate. 7th. I give to Thos W. Longmire & his children 1/7th part. 8th. I give to Joseph Longmire 1/7th part. 10th. I give to Rutha Byrn & her children 1/7th part." [See Benjamin Williams for names of children.] (Ibid 126)

GIBSON, Henry
Taxes were not collected in District 4 for 1873, "gone." (Dyr TN, Co Ct Min, B/759)

GIBSON, John A.
Gave a power of attorney to James Gibson to convey to Josiah Fort & the estate of William Fort, deceased, certain lands, 13 November 1810. (Rob TN, Co Ct Min, 2/322)

GIBSON, Samuel
1 July 1867 a charge of bastardy was dismissed by the defendant securing all costs. Shannon Felker was his security. (Sev TN, Co Ct Min, no#/457)

GIBSON, Samuel K.
Died before 30 August 1844 as shown in the suit of William B. Gibson, Admr. of Samuel K. Gibson Decd. vs Micajah T. Cooper. (Bed TN, Ch Ct Min, 2/306) Samuel K. Gibson was of Coffee County, TN, but died in Bedford County in February 1841. William B. Gibson was appointed administrator at the July term 1842 in Bedford County. Samuel K. Gibson had been a partner of Micajah T. Cooper in the mercantile business in Bedford County. (Ibid, 3/244)

GILBERT, John
Died before 1 May 1815 when the will was proved by Charles Hooks. Usley Gilbert was executrix. (Ste TN, Co Ct Min, 4/259)

GILCHRIST, Daniel
Was a resident of AL 6 February 1844 when he filed suit against Jessee Watson & James Hoover. (Bed TN, Ch Ct Min, 3/239)

GILCHRIST, William
Was a resident of Little Rock, AR, on 26 January 1839 as shown in the suit of Samuel Bell and James Horner of Philidelphia vs William Gilchrist. Gilchrist had been a resident of Bedford County, TN., and removed to AR near the close of 1836. (Bed TN, Ch Ct Min, 1/325) William Gilchrist died before 27 December 1843 when his death was admitted in the suit of Earps, Hooper and Wolf vs. William Gilchrist. (Ibid 2/ 271) 30 August 1844 William J. Whitthorne was appointed guardian ad litem of the minor heirs. George W. Haywood was administrator. (Ibid 317) Martha Ann Gilchrist, one of the heirs of William Gilchrist, is deceased. (Ibid 319) The minor heirs were Malcolm Gilchrist, Catharine M. Gilchrist, Adilade Gilchrist & Sarah Gilchrist. (Ibid 322) The middle name of Catherine was Mary. The widow was Martha Ann Gilchrist and she and the minor heirs did reside in AR. This estate was finally settled on 19 February 1848. (Ibid 3/298-315)

GILL, William
Was not of lawful age 8 July 1808 when James B. Reynolds, Esqr. was appointed guardian to defend the suit of Joseph Perry vs Isaac Henley & William Gill. (Rob TN, Co Ct Min, 2/67)

GILLESPIE
Jno. Gillespie & Leroy C. Gillespie were minors 14 January 1851 when they joined in a petition by their next friend, Leroy C. Gillespie. The other petitioners were: Jno. R. Alston & wife Lydia A., Jno. A. Tyson, Johnson B. Tyson, Edwin Tyson, Ambrose R. Reid & wife Fanny, Elija [Eliza] Rawlings, all of full age. They were evidently owners in common of some slaves. (Mad TN, Ch Ct Min, 1/169, & 2/15) Also mentioned were Philip Alston, Jr. & the trustee for Tempy S. Gillespie. (Ibid 2/162) Phillip Alston, Jr. was trustee for Tempy Gillespie, wife of Leroy C. Gillespie, who entered into a marriage contract on 30 Oct 1852 in view of an intended marriage. (Ibid 188)

GILLESPIE, George, Sr.
Died before 25 February 1794 when the will was proved by George Galliher & Henry Earnest. (Was TN, Co Ct Min, 1/471)

GILLESPIE, William
Died before 4 August 1818 when the executors deeded land to James McAdam, proved by Robert R. Gillespie & Barny Gillespie. (Wil TN, Co Ct Min, no#/297)

GILLILAND, William
Died before 12 February 1812 when the heirs were on the tax list. (Rob TN, Co Ct Min, 3/66)

GIRDING, George F.
Was a resident of Morgan County, TN, 14 April 1858 when he was to be made a defendant in the suit of Riley Miller vs Robert Jones. (Fen TN, Ch Ct Min, A/143)

GIST, A. F.
Died before 7 October 1856 when B. K. Mynott renewed his bond as guardian to St. Paul & Marusa Gist, minor heirs. David McCroskey was security. (Sev TN, Co Ct Min, no#/84)

GLADNEY, John
Died before 25 February 1860 as shown in the suit of Benj. F. Young et als vs Wm. H. Stone et al. The suit will be prosecuted against James Gladney, administrator of John Gladney, deceased. (Mad TN, Ch Ct Min, 2/342)

GLEAVES, Zach.
Married before 5 May 1873 to Hannah Whittington, daughter of N. A. Whittington, deceased. (Dyr TN, Co Ct Min, B/583)

GLEN, James W.
Was a resident of White County, TN, on 4 March 1824 when his deposition was to be taken for the plaintiff in the case of Daniel Newman vs Isaac Rogers. (McM TN, Co Ct Min, no#/131)

GLENN, Henry
Married before 15 March 1853 to Elizabeth Hunt as shown in the suit of James A. Lane et als vs Jno. Todd et als. (Mad TN, Ch Ct Min, 1/295)

GLENN, Thompson
Died before 6 May 1845 as shown in the suit of James T. Hughs vs Henry Cheek & wife Mary, and Mark Hollimon, Robert Sweat & Jemima Glenn. It was stated that Thompson Glenn departed this life having first made a will in which he devised all his estate to his wife, Patsy, during her life or widowhood, and then to be equally divided among his six children, the defendant, Mary, being one. The said Patsy has also departed this life. Jemima Glenn was a daughter of testator. Henry Cheek and his wife Mary have had their portion of the estate. James Hollimon was appointed trustee for Mary Cheek to receive her portion for her separate use. (Jac TN, Ch Ct Min, A/193)

GLOVER, Wm.
Died before 22 Jan 1802 when the heirs were shown on the delinquent tax list. (Rob TN, Co Ct Min, 1/206

GOBBLE, Adam
4 October 1858 was released from paying poll tax and working on public roads, he being a diseased person. (Sev TN, Co Ct Min, no#/345)

GOBBLE, Anios
2 April 1860 was released from paying poll tax as he is not 21 years old. (Sev TN, Co Ct Min, no#/544)

GODWIN, Wm. P.
Died in August 1848 having made a will. The widow, Mary M. B. Godwin, & Hardy M. Burton were appointed executors. Burton declined. The widow dissented from the will & is entitled to dower & a distributive share of the personal estate, being 1/6 part. There were 5 children, four living at the time of testators death, and 1, Thomas Hardy Godwin, was born of the marriage after his death. The other 4 were Fanny D. Godwin, William P. Godwin, Mary Susan Godwin & Frank B. Godwin, all minors. Their mother was appointed guardian. (Mad TN, Ch Ct Min, 1/87)

GOLDSTON, John
Has no permanant residence, as reported 10 October 1859 in the suit of John R. McGee vs John Goldston & others. (Fen TN, Ch Ct Min, A/215)

GOOCH, G. R.
Died before 8 January 1873 when W. C. Gooch made a settlement as executor. (Dyr TN, Co Ct Min, B/533)

GOOCH, H. A.
Died before 4 March 1872 when H. B. Fowlkes renewed his bond as guardian of W. H. E. Gooch, minor heir. (Dyr TN, Co Ct Min, B/380)

GOOCH, Sarah J.
8 March 1870 W. C. Gooch was chosen & appointed guardian, with H. B. Fowlkes & V. G. Wynne as security. (Dyr TN, Co Ct Min, B/11)

GOOCH, Wm. Henry E.
8 March 1870 H. B. Fowlkes was chosen & appointed guardian with Christian S. Cobb & R. H. McGaughey as security. (Dyr TN, Co Ct Min, B/13)

GOODALL, Charles
Was a resident of KY 17 July 1856 when his deposition was to be taken for complainant in the suit of W. W. Goodall vs James Walker & Smith. (Jac TN, Ch Ct Min, C/10)

GOODALL, John L.
Died before 4 December 1868 as shown in the suit of W. B. Armstead vs J. B. McCormack & others. John B. McCormack had conveyed land in 1842 to John L. Goodall in trust. Charles J. and Elizabeth Manning were mentioned. (Fen TN, Ch Ct Min, A/430)

GOODALL, William W.
Died before 4 February 1857 when his death was suggested in the suit of W. W. Goodall vs James Walker Secty &c & James F. Smith. Thomas Draper & Morinda Goodall were appointed administrator and administratrix. (Jac TN, Ch Ct Min, C/46) The administratrix was shown as Veronda Goodall. Said Veronda Goodall is now dead, as stated 3 February 1858. (Ibid 91) 16 July 1858 a suit was entered by Thomas J. Draper, Eliza Draper & Vorinda Goodall vs Rufus Goodall, Lucy Goodall, Martha M. Goodall, Elizabeth Goodall, Cornelia Goodall, Louisa Goodall, Zeda Goodall & James Draper, Guardian ad litem for the minor defendants. Complainant Vorinda Goodall has died since the filing of this suit & James Draper is her administrator. It will be necessary to sell the negroes to pay the debts of the estate of William W. Goodall and divide the rest of the proceeds among the children of the deceased. (Ibid 144) On 15 July 1859 the defendants in the above suit were shown as Rufus Goodall, Martha M. Goodall, Elizabeth Goodall, Lucy Goodall, Permelia Goodall & Louisa Goodall. Martha Goodall bought part of the slaves. (Ibid 283)

GOODIN, Drury
Died before 4 November 1782 when the administrator, Mary Goodin, received the inventory of the estate. (Was TN, Co Ct Min, 1/180)

GOODIN, Icam
2 November 1784 recorded a "relinquishment & instrument of Writing to Mary Dugg or other ways Mary Goodin." (Was TN, Co Ct Min, 1/259)

GOODMAN, Samuel
Was a pauper 5 June 1826 when $40 was appropriated for his maintenance. (McM TN, Co Ct Min, 2/155)

GOODPASTURE, Margaret
Had been bound to Anthony McNitt, who brought her into court and surrendered her 28 February 1794. His bond was therefore discharged. (Was TN, Co Ct Min, 1/482)

GOODRICH, Silas C.
Died before 16 March 1853 as shown in the petition of Mary M. Goodrich, Sr., Jno. Burrus & wife Elizabeth, Sarah Jane, Mary Magdalen, Jr., Benjamin Rush, Martha and James Polk Goodrich. Mary M., Sr. was the widow and the others his children. Stephen Burrus, Wyatt Mooring, William B. Watson, Wm. M. Tidwell & Cullen Lane were appointed to divide the negroes into 7 shares. (Mad TN, Ch Ct Min, 1/302, 327)

GOODWIN, Bradock
Was a resident of Dinwiddie County, VA, 5 July 1809 when a deposition was to be taken for the defendant in the case of Benjn. Wells vs Wm. Roachel. (Rob TN, Co Ct Min. 2/153)

GOODWIN, Brittain
Died before 20 January 1812 when Azariah Davis made a return of the personal estate. (Roa TN, Co Ct Min, D/345)

GOODWIN, William
Died in December 1852 as shown in the suit of Allen Goodwin and others vs James Latham. William left a will & Allen & Samuel Goodwin were named executors. He bequeathed all of his estate to the complainants. (Mad TN, Ch Ct Min, 2/88)

GORE, Mounce
Died before 12 February 1859 as shown in the suit of P. H. Lester? [Geslin?] administrator of Mounce Gore, deceased, against Joel Curtis. Joel Curtis had bought land from Mounce Gore and has not paid for it. (Jac TN, Ch Ct Min, C/217) 10 August 1860 this suit was shown as Preston H. Leslie, administrator of Mounce Gore, deceased vs Leroy Pharris, Richard Poteet & wife Elvera Poteet, William M. Picket & wife Ingolier? Picket, William Gore, Eliza J. Gore, Pauline Gore, Mounce [Mourice] L. Gore, Elender Gore & Thomas H. Butler. (Ibid 377) This suit shown again as Preston H. Leslie, administrator of Mounce Gore, deceased vs David K. Flatt, William Gore, Eliza A. Gore, Paulina Gore, Mounce L. Gore, Samuel G. Gore, Mary Ann Butler, William B. Butler, Mounce G. Butler, Elender Gore & Thomas H. Butler, Richard Poteet & wife Elvira, William M. Picket & wife Ingolier. (Ibid 386) Mounce Gore had conveyed, in his lifetime, land to his sons, William Gore & Andrew R. Gore. Andrew R. Gore died intestate & without issue never having been married. Elvira, wife of Richard Potete, Ingolier, wife of William Pickett, Eliza Jane Gore, Paulina M. Gore, Samuel Gore and Mounce L. Gore are the brothers and sisters of Andrew R. Gore. Mary Ann Butler, Bailey Butler and Mounce G. Butler are children of Polly Butler, deceased, a sister of Andrew R. and are his heirs also. Partition of the land belonging to William and Andrew R. Gore has never been made. William owns half of it and 1/8 of the other half. (Ibid 436)

GORE, Thomas
Was a resident of Augusta, GA, on 5 December 1828 when his deposition was to be taken for the defendant in the case of James Morrow vs Reuben, Elijah & Willis White. (McM TN, Co Ct Min, no#/400)

GOSSETT, West
5 October 1857 Collin Warren was paid out of the poor tax for keeping him. (Sev TN, Co Ct Min, no#/206)

GRAFFS, Frederick
Died before 10 August 1814 when Phillip Anthony, administrator, deeded land to John Young. (Rob TN, Co Ct Min, 3/460)

GRAHAM, Hannah
In the suit of Jared? H. Graham & others vs Matthew C. McKinley & others 3 February 1858, it was stated that Hannah Graham had arrived at her majority and wished to be made a party complainant instead of a party defendant in this bill. (Jac TN, Ch Ct Min, C/88) Hannah Graham married Peter Turney before 12 February 1859 as shown in the suit of Jarrett H. Graham & others vs M. C. McKinley & others. (Ibid 207)

GRAHAM, William
Died before 16 November 1815 when the widow, Susannah Graham, petitioned for dower. (Cla TN, Co Ct Min, 4/137)

GRANADE, John
Died before 2 February 1818 when the administrators, Jeremiah Stell & Deveriux Wynne, were ordered to make a report. George W. Stell was appointed guardian of John Granade & Henry Granade, minor heirs. (Wil TN, Co Ct Min, no#/219)

GRANT, H.
Taxes were not collected in District 2 for 1873, "gone." (Dyr TN, Co Ct Min, B/759)

GRANT, Jno. D.
Died before 9 March 1852 as shown in the suit of Ambrose R. Reid admr. vs the Widow & Heirs & creditors of said Grant. (Mad TN, Ch Ct Min, 1/235) 17 September 1852 the heirs of Jno. D. Grant were shown to be Robert, William, Matilda, Mary J., Geo. A., Louisa M., Eliz? H. & Asalee E. Grant, the last 6 minors by their guardian ad litem, David Merriwether. Jno. D. Grant died in February 1851, intestate. Martha was the widow. Jno. D. Grant owned a house & lots in Denmark and half of a store house & lot owned in common with the heirs of Joseph B. Love, deceased. (Ibid 283)

GRAVES, Nancy
Was the mother of a bastard child by Humphrey Chapell who gave bond for its support 6 May 1818. (Wil TN, Co Ct Min, no#/266)

GRAVES, Peter
In the suit of Peter Graves & his wife Polly vs John Bennett, 15 August 1838, land was laid off for a life estate for Peter Graves & wife Polly, "for the longest liver of the two." (Bed TN, Ch Ct Min, 2/39)

GRAVES, William
Died before 20 December 1805 when Daniel Rather, Coroner, was paid for holding an inquest on the body. (Roa TN, Co Ct Min, B/117)

GRAY, Joseph, Sr.
Made a deed of gift to Joel Cooley on 4 May 1812. (Ste TN, Co Ct Min, 3/128) He also made a deed of gift to Joseph John Gray on 2 February 1813. (Ibid 4/11) Joseph Gray, Sr. died before 7 February 1814 when his will was proved by Wm. Cooley and Anna Cooley. Robert Cooper, William Pearce & Abner Pearce were executors. (Ibid 82) According to the will of the testator, three slaves, Simon, Dinah and Chuck, were emancipated. (Ibid 85)

GREEN, Abel
Died before 20 February 1860 as shown in the suit of Samuel Wadley vs Green B. Green, Susan R. Green & others heirs at law & John McCall administrator & Catherine Green widow of Abel Green deceased. About 9 November 1852 Saml. Wadley, being embarrassed in his circumstances, applied to Abel Green, the father of the defendants named & mentioned as children & heirs of Abel Green. Abel Green became security for Wadley on a note. Abel Green died in Henderson County & Jno. McCall was appointed administrator in April 1855. (Mad TN, Ch Ct Min, 2/294)

GREEN, Alex.
5 December 1870 W. P. Rice made a settlement as guardian of the heirs of Alex Green. [does not say deceased] (Dyr TN, Co Ct Min, B/141)

GREEN, Asa
Gave a bond for the maintenance of a bastard child, which was returned into court & recorded, 11 November 1811. (Rob TN, Co Ct Min, 3/28) 14 February 1814 Asa Green made a deed of gift to his daughter, Sarah Green. (Ibid 355)

GREEN, Benjamin
Died before 1 January 1872 when B. H. Harmon was appointed administrator, with John H. York and Joseph Green as his security. (Dyr TN, Co Ct Min, B/334) W. J. Davis, Wm. Mayes and Thomas Young were appointed to set off a years allowance for the widow and family. (Ibid 347)

GREEN, David
Died before 1 January 1872 when Joseph Green was appointed administrator, with B. H.

Harmon and John H. York as his security. (Dyr TN, Co Ct Min, B/335) J. H. Davis was paid for holding an inquest over his body. (Ibid 346)

GREEN, Harriett A.
5 December 1870 W. P. Rice renewed his bond as guardian. (Dyr TN, Co Ct Min, B/138)

GREEN, Jonathan
Died before December term 1803 when the heirs were on the tax list. (Wil TN, Co Ct Min, no#/5) The heirs were listed on the 1804 non-resident tax list with land on Cumberland river. (Ibid 82)

GREEN, Letitia
Died before 1841 as shown in the suit of Thomas Davis vs John T. Shanks & David Green. David Green stated that by a marriage contract Letitia had separate property and was able to contract & trade. The heirs of said Letitia were mentioned, one of whom is a child of David Green. (Bed TN, Ch Ct Min, 3/52)

GREEN, Lucy K.
Dismissed her suit against John C. Green on 14 March 1855. (Mad TN, Ch Ct Min, 2/27)

GREEN, Richard
Was an orphan boy aged 11 on 20 March 1829. He was bound to Joel K. Brown on 2 March 1829 to learn the trade of a taylor. (McM TN, Co Ct Min, 2no#/339)

GREEN, Robert
Died before 10 August 1812 when Mansel Low, Peter Woodson, James H. Bryan, Elijah Hughes, William Adams, or any three of them, were ordered to divide the estate. (Rob TN, Co Ct Min, 3/100)

GREEN, T. C.
Died before August 1837 as shown in the suit of Lewis Shepherd vs J. N. Thomas & Co and others. Defendants Mary Green & Williamson B. Burdett are citizens of Bedford County & J. N. Thomas & Co. have residence in AL. Shepherd was security for Mary Green on a note given to William Watkins, administrator of T. C. Green, deceased. (Bed TN, Ch Ct Min, 1/156)

GREER, Francis
Died 8 April 1839, very suddenly having been well less than twenty four hours before her death. This is shown in the suit of Charles C. Talliaferro vs Nathan Eavins [Evans] admr. of Francis Greer. Taliaferro was indebted to Francis Greer (who was his sister) and executed bills of sale of negroes to secure the debt. (Bed TN, Ch Ct Min, 1/279)

GREER, Joseph
Died before 29 June 1842 as shown in the suit of John Cook & wife Margaret vs Thomas & Mary Ann Greer and John H. Moore. It was stated that "Joseph Greer deceased was a mere attorney to sell the tract of land described in complainants bill for the heirs at law of Joseph Harmon deceased, of which complainant Margaret is one." Defendants were executors of said Joseph & according to his will sold the land in 1837. Complainants are entitled to 1/10 part of the purchase money. (Bed TN, Ch Ct Min, 2/190)

GREER, Margaret
7 August 1795 her guardian, Adam Mitchel, gave as his security, Peter Millor. (Was TN, Co Ct Min, 1/560)

GREGORY, E. W.
2 December 1872 J. T. Gregory made a settlement as guardian. (Dyr, Co Ct Min, B/514)

GREGORY, Mary C.
3 October 1870 W. C. Hendrix, W. H. Franklin and J. D. Haynes were appointed to lay off a years allowance for the widow, Mary C. Gregory, and her family. [Name of her deceased husband not given.] (Dyr TN, Co Ct Min, B/101)

GREGORY, W. C.
Died before 3 October 1870 when J. C. Zaricor was appointed administrator, with J. S. McCorkle and J. T. Gregory as security. (Dyr TN, Co Ct Min, B/97) J. C. Gregory was chosen and appointed guardian of the minor heirs, with J. C. Zarecor as security. (Ibid 139) 1 January 1872 A. J. Grills was chosen and appointed guardian of Ella Grills, minor heir of W. C. Gregory, deceased, with J. T. Gregory and J. E. McCorkle as his security. (Ibid 333)

GRIER, James
17 September 1816 emancipated his negro man named Charles, about 33 years old. (Wil TN, Co Ct Min, no#/30)

GRIER, Richard
Died before August term 1789 when his orphan, Richard Grier, made choice of William Beard as his guardian, with Jeremiah Robison as security. (Was TN, Co Ct Min, 1/402)

GRIFFIN
5 March 1872 some land was sold and divided between nine persons. The first seven received an eighth part and the last two received one sixteenth each: 1. J. M. Griffin, 2. F. A. Boyd, 3. H. H. Webb, 4. L. E. Stringer, 5. E. R. McGlothlin, 6. W. D. Griffin, 7. Sarah C. Latimer, 8. Z. K. Griffin, 9. F. M. Griffin. (Dyr TN, Co Ct Min, B/384)

GRIFFIN, Margaret
Probably died before 5 July 1870 when R. C. Coffman made a settlement as administrator. (Dyr TN, Co Ct Min, B/82) 4 July 1871 R. C. Coffman made a settlement as guardian of Margaret Griffin. (Ibid 258) 9 April 1873 a settlement was made for the heirs of Margaret Griffin. (Ibid 577)

GRIFFIN, Mary
Was a resident of Shelby County, KY, on 27 October 1818 when she gave power of attorney to John Henry to sell land on Barton Creek in Wilson County, entered in the name of Mary Henry. It was witnessed by Thomas Marquess & Jesse Henry. (Wil TN, Reg Bk/109)

GRIFFITH
A suit was shown 15 August 1860, James Carnahan, W. P. Witcher & wife Polly, Sally Griffith, Sandford Ballard & wife Nancy Ballard vs John F. Griffith, Samuel T. Griffith & James G. Griffith. It is necessary to sell the land to pay the debts and said land is not susceptible of partition among the heirs. [Does not state heirs of whom.] It is also stated that the estate of David Griffith [does not say deceased] is largely indebted and there are two suits against him to sell the land as creditors, to wit, David Myers vs David Griffith & others and Leroy B. Settle vs David Griffith & others. (Jac TN, Ch Ct Min, C/416)

GRIFFITH, James P.
Died intestate before 26 July 1848 as shown in the suit of David Griffith Admr. of James P. Griffith vs Mary Josephine Griffith and Mariah Clay Griffith. The defendants are his heirs. The land is to be sold subject to the widow's dower. (Jac TN, Ch Ct Min, A/315) Both the defendants are minors and William R. Kunce was appointed guardian ad litem. (Ibid 317) Jonas Griffith was the father of James P. Griffith. Land was sold subject to the widow's dower. (Ibid B/193) Two suits were entered 15 July 1858 by Sam E. Hare vs L. B. Griffith & others and against David Griffith & others. W. P. Witcher was appointed guardian ad litem for Mary J. & Mariah C. Griffith, minors. (Ibid C/132)

GRIFFITH, John
Died before 5 March 1828 when James Hickey was appointed administrator. (McM TN, Co Ct Min, 2no#/279) 6 December 1830 the administrator made a report. He mentioned selling the land in Bledsoe County. There were receipts from Benjamin Griffith, William Baler & Jno. L. McCartey. (Ibid 487)

GRIFFITH, William C. A.
In the suit of William C. A. Griffith and others vs William J. Dixon & Emsly Willmore, 13 July 1854, complainants were given leave to take the depositions of Alexander Clark, Alexander Nevil, Solomon Wilson, Jefferson Wilson, Ephraim S. Wilson, Thomas N. Wilson, Larkin D. Sweaza, Matthias Sweaza, Sr., Matthias Sweaza, Jr., Thomas M. Wilson, Edward R. Hancock, Jonas Sweaza, Henry Lovelady, Henry Sweaza, Jefferson Price, John Sisca, Thomas Shrum, Pleasant Hendley, Joseph Roddy, John Medowel, Pharis Sweaza, Thadias C. Quarles, Alexander Keith, Valentine Vanhearer, Thompson Carson, David Myers, Burril R. Land, Jonathan Wilson, Reubin Price, Leroy Gorden, Ben C. White, Denton More, James Moss, Robert Moss, John Moss, Jonas Myers, Nathaniel M. Cox, Claiburn D. Witcher, Booker Witcher, Samuel T. Griffith, William P. Witcher & Polly Witcher. (Jac TN, Ch Ct Min, B/163) Complainants in this suit were William C. A. Griffith & Nancy Griffith and Claiburn Griffith & Polly Griffith by their next friend William C. A. Griffith. A judgement was given in favor of defendants, William J. Dixon & Ensley Wellmore. Complainants were granted an appeal to the Supreme Court in Nashville. (Ibid 265)

GRIGGS, Jane
Filed for divorce from Robert W. Griggs on 3 January 1848. They were married many

years ago in Bedford County. He is a drunkard and beats her. She left him once after a beating and went to her father's, where she stayed for 18 months. He persuaded her to return by promising to quit drinking and treat her better. She had only been back with him a few days when he started the same treatment of her. He never provided for her and their 4 children and they were forced to live in a little log hut without chimney or doors at all seasons, and very often without food or clothing. She finally left him again and took the 4 children and went to her father's. Her husband's place of residence is unknown and she believes he does not live in TN. Divorce was granted and she was given custody of the children. (Bed TN, Ch Ct Min, 3/416)

GRIMES, Emanuel
Was a base born child aged now upwards of three years, when he was bound at the February term in 1789 to John Lemmon until age 21. (Was TN, Co Ct Min, 1/371)

GRIMES, Henry
Died before 6 November 1783 when Sarah Grimes had leave to administer on the estate, with John Grimes & Saml. Tate as security. The name Isiah, written before Sarah, had been crossed out. (Was TN, Co Ct Min, 1/233)

GRIMES, M. L.
Taxes were not collected in District 2 for 1873, "Gibson Co." (Dyr TN, Co Ct Min, B/758)

GRIMM, Stephen
6 March 1873 was charged with Bastardy by Chaney Light. The court found that he was not the father of her child. (Dyr TN, Co Ct Min, B/587)

GRIMMIT, Sarah
10 March 1826 made a deed of gift to Lavinia Gillihan, proved by Asa R. Brinler. (McM TN, Co Ct Min, 2no#/150)

GRIMSLEY, J. H.
Probably died before 1 April 1868 when W. B. Grimsley brought suit against Thomas & Charles Donaldson, who are non-residents. The defendants were the surviving partners in the firm of J. H. Grimsley & Co. (Fen TN, Ch Ct Min, A/371)

GRINDSTAFF, Michael
Died before February term 1790 when it was orderd that the widow, Catrin Grindstaff, and Jacob Grindstaff be executors of the estate. Isaac Grindstaff was security. (Was TN, Co Ct Min, 1/424)

GRINDSTAFF, Nicholas
Died before May term 1789 when the widow, Catrine Grindstaff and William Moreland were appointed administrators of the estate, with Richd. White, Esqr. as security. (Was TN, Co Ct Min, 1/381)

GRISHAM, Thomas
Died before 6 September 1830 when John Grisham was appointed guardian of Meshack Grisham, John Grisham & James Grisham, minor orphans of Thomas Grisham, deceased. (McM TN, Co Ct Min, 2no#/472)

GRISHAM, William T.
Died before 6 December 1830 when his will was proved by Pleasant Chitwood & Robert W. Hamilton, witnesses. (McM TN, Co Ct Min, 2no#/484)

GRISSAM, John
Was an orphan child aged between 9 and 10 years when he was bound at February term 1789 to Isaac Lincoln until age 21. (Was TN, Co Ct Min, 1/361)

GRISUM, Wm.
Died before 13 February 1815 when Susanna Grisum was ordered to be sworn to prove the will. (Cla TN, Co Ct Min, 4/7) Thomas Grisham & Robt. Grisham presented a paper which they proposed to be the nuncupative will of Wm. Grisham, deceased. Thereupon came Samuel Davison, George Bull and George Bernard who say the paper is not the will of William Grisham. A jury is to decide. (Ibid 12) The following day in the suit of the heirs of Wm. Grisum against Susannah Grisum, the jury found there was no will. (Ibid 16) Susannah Grisum, the widow, was appointed administratrix with Robert Grisum, George Bull & Thomas Grisum as security. She also petitioned for a years support. (Ibid 21) 21 February 1815 "Jacob Shults, Ransom Day and John Evans met at the Dwelling house of William Grissam deceased in order to set apart so much of the crop and provisions on

hand as shall be sufficient for the suport of the widdo and her family for 12 months, we set apart fifteen barrels of corn and four hundred pounds of Bacon together with the vegatables now on the place such as cabage and turnips." (Ibid 68) Dower was laid off. (Ibid 168)

GROGAN, Elizabeth
Was granted a divorce from Francis Grogan on 12 July 1848. They were married 4 March 1831 in VA and moved to Madison County, TN, about 12 years before filing of this bill. They had 6 children, to wit: Jno. F., Margaret M., Elizabeth, Barzella, Robert & Patrick F. Grogan. Elizabeth was given custody of the children and all property. (Mad TN, Ch Ct Min, 1/34)

GRUBB, Allen B.
Died before 7 June 1824 when his will was proved by Samuel Love & Matthew W. McGhee & the codicil by Matthew W. McGhee & Young Colville. John L. McCahty & Joseph Rogers were the executors. (McM TN, Co Ct Min, 2no#/2)

GUANT, William A.
Died before 26 August 1845 as shown in the suit of Mary Guant vs Absolom B. & Lewis Guant. The later two were administrators of William A. Guant, deceased. A compromise was made, Mary will have certain negroes for life & at her death they will belong to the estate of William A. Guant. [Also see John Guant] (Bed TN, Ch Ct Min, 2/363)

GUFFEY, Margaret
Died before 13 February 1811 when the will was proved by George Murphey, Sr. & Robertson Murphey. (Rob TN, Co Ct Min, 2/372)

GUILLAND, William
Died before 15 February 1811 when the heirs were on a tax list. (Rob TN, Co Ct Min, 2/385)

GUTHRIE, Andrew
Died before 16 February 1857 when the death of defendant Guthrie was suggested and admitted in the suit of Wm. E. Butler vs Jane Taylor et als. R. R. Dashield was administrator. (Mad TN, Ch Ct Min, 2/107) The suit was revived against Mary Ann Guthrie, the widow, & Fanny Guthrie & William Guthrie, the only children of said Guthrie. (Ibid 115)

GUTHRIE, William Henry
Died before 19 February 1858 when his death was admitted in the suit of John Golden Guardian vs Jas. R. Stewart & others. The suit was revived in the name of Fanny Guthrie, his heir-at-law. (Mad TN, Ch Ct Min, 2/198)

GUTTNDGEWOOD, Hanna
Died before 18 May 1795 when an inventory of the estate was returned by the administrator. (Was TN, Co Ct Min, 1/553)

GUY, William R.
Was the son of William Guy as shown in the suit of James Hart vs William Guy, 14 July 1838. (Bed TN, Ch Ct Min, 1/240)

GWINN, Ahay
8 January 1861 was released from paying poll tax as "he is a poor and diseased person." He was released in the future until a better state of health is evident. (Sev TN, Co Ct Min, no#/646)

HACKETT, John
24 March 1803 made petition claiming two tracts of land. A deposition was entered by John Dearmond stating that he was present & saw John Hackett mark an Ash above the mouth of a Spring branch on the bank of Clinch River, about the first of September 1785. Dearmond was a chain carrier. (Roa TN, Co Ct Min, A/80)

HACKLER, George
Was allowed money for the support of himself & Elizabeth Hackler & Solomon Hackler, his two children, 7 March 1825 (McM TN, Co Ct Min, 2no#/51)

HACKLER, George [Hacklin]
Was a pauper 5 March 1827 when he was allowed $50 for his support. (McM TN, Co Ct Min, 2/198)

HACKNEY, Jacob
Was a resident of Hawkins County, TN, on 6 December 1828 when his deposition was to be taken for the plaintiff in the case of Daniel Carmichael vs Thomas Baily. (McM TN, Co Ct Min, no#/404)

HAGGARD
19 January 1802 Edmond and John Haggard were bound as apprentices to Jesse Jones to learn the House Carpenter trade, until they are 21 years old. (Rob TN, Co Ct Min, 1/200)

HAGGARD, Noel [Hazzard]
Died before 1 August 1814 when William Haggard, Sr. was appointed administrator with Thomas Gray & Willis Whitford as security. (Ste TN, Co Ct Min, 4/164)

HAIL, James
Died before 3 December 1827 when Thomas F. Bible was appointed guardian of William C. Hail, Jane Hail, Christopher P. Hail, Minnerva Hail, Martial C. Hail & James Hail, orphan minor heirs. (McM TN, Co Ct Min, 2no#/243) Henry Wisemore was appointed administrator. (Ibid 244) March term1828, a years provisions is to be set off to Catherine Hale, widow of James Hale, deceased. [entry very blurred] (Ibid 261) 7 December 1829 Catherine Hale was appointed guardian of her own children [as listed above.] (Ibid 403)

HAIL, William
Made an application for a pension for Revolutionary War service, 7 March 1827. He is 74 years old. He enlisted in NC [date omitted] under Capt. Alfred Moor & Col. Francis Nash for 6 months. He again enlisted for 12 months under Capt. Thomas Thompson & Col. Thos. Taylor in the line of NC & was discharged at Savannah, GA. A schedule of his property was given. He had sold land & cattle to his son Benjamin in 1823. (McM TN, Co Ct Min, 2no#/210)

HAILY, Joseph
21 June 1816 a jury was summond to enquire into his lunacy. (Wil TN, Co Ct Min, no#/21)

HAILY, Pleasant
Died before 5 May 1818 when negroes from his estate were sold for division among the heirs. Name also shown as Hayley. (Wil TN, Reg Bk/102) 20 June 1817 Thomas Harrington & Nancy Harrington petitioned for dower to be laid out of the lands of Pleasant Haily, deceased, her former husband. (Ibid, Co Ct Min, no#/138) 5 November 1819 Bennet Babb was appointed guardian of Polly Haily, minor daughter of Pleasant Haily, deceased, with William Thomas & William Tarver as security. (Ibid 544)

HAIRE, Mathew
Died before 26 February 1782 when a suit was entered by John Talley vs Robert Lucas in behalf of the orphans of Mathew Haire, deceased, for 300 acres of land on the fourth side of Holston River at Jones Falls. (Was TN, Co Ct Min, 1/150)

HALE, Frederick
Died before 7 March 1825 when his will was proved by Benjamin Isbell, William Marjors & Moses Cunningham, witnesses. George Hale & Samuel Hale were executors. (McM TN, Co Ct Min, 2no#/50)

HALE, Nicholas
Died before 27 May 1794 when Jemima Hale was appointed administratrix, with Zachariah McCubbin and Richard Hail as security. (Was TN, Co Ct Min, 1/489)

HALE, Shadrach
Died before 13 February 1815 when the administrator, John Henderson, made a report. (Cla TN, Co Ct Min, 4/3)

HALEY, Elijah G.
Died before 16 April 1810 when Polly Haley, David Haley & Daniel Alexander were appointed administrators, with James Robinson & Abraham McClellan as security. The estate was ordered to be exposed to sale. (Roa TN, Co Ct Min, D/194)

HALEY, James
Was a helpless orphan when Thomas Harrington was allowed money for his support, 18 March 1817. (Wil TN, Co Ct Min, no#/89)

HALEY, Jas.
Died before 17 March 1853 when Absolem Deberry, as trustee for Jno. W. Haley, Mary H. Haley, Henry C. Haley, Eugenia Haley & Luanna Haley, petitioned for sale of slaves. Jno. W. Haley is now of full age. Robt. B. Hunt is the guardian of the others. (Mad TN, Ch Ct Min, 1/310, 348)

HALL, Franci E.
Died before 1 September 1873 when George A. Tener made a settlement as administrator. (Dyr TN, Co CT Min, B/619)

HALL, Garrett
Was a resident of Morgan County, TN, on 10 March 1826 when his deposition was to be taken for the defendant in the case of William Brown vs Henry McKorkle. (McM TN, Co Ct Min, no#/230)

HALL, Henry
Taxes were not collected in District 2 for 1873, "gone." (Dyr TN, Co Ct Min, B/759)

HALL, Jacob
1 November 1858 was released from paying poll tax as he is under 21 years of age. (Sev TN, Co Ct Min, no#/361) He was also under 21 in 1859. (Ibid 621)

HALL, Permelia N.
Was granted a divorce from ____ Hall on 5 February 1858. [The writing is very dim & I am not sure the name is Hall. The husbands name looks like Trin, True, or ? Hall]. He had been guilty of adultry with a certain Sarah Osburn and has now left the county. (Jac TN, Ch Ct Min, C/111)

HALL, Sarah
17 July 1851 a suit was entered by Sarah Hall by her next friend James Young vs Adam Hall. On 13 October 1845 Sarah Hall & Adam Hall, being husband & wife, made a contract for the separate maintenance of Sarah where certain property was settled on her in full discharge of any claim she might have on him for alimony or maintenance. Andrew McClellan was trustee for Sarah. Said McClellan has died and James Young appointed trustee in his place & requests permission to sell part of the property. (Jac TN, Ch Ct Min, B/14)

HALL, W. C.
Died before 6 June 1870 when the will was proved by A. T. Fielder and J. Q. Craig, witnesses. S. S. Hollowell was the executor, with W. O. Boykin and A. T. Fielder as his security. (Dyr TN, Co Ct Min, B/66)

HALL, William
Died before 2 August 1819 when the will was proved by Wm. McAdow & James McAdow. James Michie was executor. (Wil TN, Co Ct Min, no#/498)

HALLIBURTON, Richard H.
Died before 6 May 1872 when E. M. Hall was appointed administrator, with G. W. Bettis and Timothy Griffin as his security. (Dyr TN, Co Ct Min, B/413) Luke Cearly, Thomas H. Fitzhugh and J. J. Follis were appointed to lay off a years allowance for the widow and family. (Ibid 416) E. M. Hall was ordered to pay cash to Mrs. R. H. Halliburton for the value of the articles allowed to her, it appearing to the court that she wishes to leave the country. (Ibid 489) 2 February 1874 Jesse B. Leggett was chosen and appointed guardian of Margaret A. Halliburton, minor child of R. H. Halliburton, deceased, with E. M. Hall & W. S. Leggett as his security. (Ibid 705)

HALLUM
There was a case at March term 1814; Jeremiah Tucker Guardian vs George & Morris Hallum for debt. (Wil TN, P&J, no#/no#)

HALLUM, David
Died before 3 June 1872 when J. N. Armstrong was appointed administrator, with N. Scoby and Jackson Pace as his security. (Dyr TN, Co Ct Min, B/417)

HALLUM, James
Died before 17 December 1816 when the widow, Elizabeth, was appointed administratrix with Robert Nichols & John Marshall security. (Wil TN, Co Ct Min, no#/58) Robt. Nichols was appointed guardian of Polly A. R. Hallum, minor heir. (Ibid 136)

HALLUM, Jno.
Died before the December term 1811 when Isham Davis was shown as the executor. (Wil TN, P&J, no#/no#) 3 August 1818 "On this Jeremiah Stephenson who became guardian to John Hallum a minor child of John Hallum deceased, in consequence of his the said Jeremiah intermarriage with the said deceased, came into court and relinquished his said guardianship." [they must mean that Jeremiah Stephenson married the widow of John Hallum.] (Ibid, Co Ct Min, no#/292) Isham Davis was appointed guardian of John Hallum, minor child of John Hallum, deceased. (Ibid 293)

HALLUM, John, Sr.
Made a deed of gift 15 September 1818 to his son, George Hallum, of a negro man named Dick about 22 years old. "But because I the said John Hallum Sr. am aged & infirm I hereby reserve to myself during my natural life and to my wife Sally Hallum during her life the entire & exclusive possession & use of the said negro man." (Wil TN, Reg Bk/118)

HAMBLIN, James
20 June 1838 sued Darcas Hamblin for divorce. Darcas is not a resident of this state. This entry was then crossed out. (Obi TN, Cir Ct Min, 3/213) The suit was re-entered and publication made for defendant. (Ibid 221) Divorce was granted 22 February 1839. (Ibid 334)

HAMBRIGHT, John
Died before 1 March 1830 when his will was proved by William Smedley & Sterling Camp, witnesses. Peter Hambright & Jessee W. Eddington were executors. (McM TN, Co Ct Min, 2no#/418)

HAMBY, William N.
5 January 1863 money was allowed for the support of his family, to be paid quarterly to John Rule. (Sev TN, Co Ct Min, no#/35) 4 July 1865 the sheriff was ordered to bring to next court the Hamby children to be bound out. (Ibid 186) 4 February 1867 it was ordered that the sheriff bring Lettitia Hamby & James M. Hamby, [children] of Wm. Hamby, to the next court to be bound out. (Ibid 430) After hearing the statements of Wm. N. Hamby he is allowed to keep his children. (Ibid 432)

HAMELTON, Hiram
Died before 10 November 1835 when his death was suggested in the suit of Partee & Partee [Porter & Porter] vs Hiram Hamelton & Charles McAlister. (Obi TN, Cir Ct Min, 3/32)

HAMELTON, Nancy
Was bound 17 May 1795 to Henry Begart until age 18. (Was TN, Co Ct Min, 1/545)

HAMILTON, James A.
Died before 6 March 1827 when Margaret Hamilton was appointed administrator. Joab Hill, Tidence Lane & John [name blurred] were appointed to set off a years provision for the widow, Margaret Hamilton. (McM TN, Co Ct Min, 2no#/207)

HAMILTON, John C.
Died before 24 February 1837 when land was taxed to the heirs. (Obi TN, Cir Ct Min, 3/113)

HAMILTON, William
Died before 13 February 1816 when commissioners were appointed to settle with Peter Hamilton, the administrator. (Cla TN, Co Ct Min, 4/160)

HAMILTON, William
"A copy of the last will & testament of William Hamilton late of Guilford county deceased, with the certificates of probate thereon was exhibited in open court and ordered to be recorded." This entry was then crossed out. (Wil TN, Co Ct Min, no#/331)

HAMM, Reuben
Died before 4 February 1812 when land was taxed to the heirs. (Ste TN, Co Ct Min, 3/117)

HAMMONTREE, Nancy
Was a minor 7 January 1861 when Morgan Davis was appointed her guardian, with Samuel Pickens as security. (Sev TN, Co Ct Min, no#/627)

HAMPSON, James
Was bound 27 February 1794 to Allexr. McKee until age 21, to learn the Shoemaking trade. Also ____ Hampson until she shall arrive at the age of 18 years. (Was TN, Co Ct Min, 1/480)

HAMPTON, Edward
Died before 28 August 1781 when Charles Robertson, Esqr. was granted leave of administration on the estate, with Jno. Newman & George Russell, Esqr. as his security. (Was TN, Co Ct Min, 1/143)

HAMPTON, John
Was a resident of SC 11 May 1790 when he bought land from Jacob Womack. (Was TN, Co Ct Min, 1/441)

HAMPTON, Robert
Died before 16 August 1796 when Mary Hampton qualified as executrix. (Was TN, Co Ct Min, 1/624) The will was proved by Saml. Wood & Reuben Bayless. (Ibid 629)

HAMPTON, William
Died before 8 December 1826 when Benjamin Hambright was appointed administrator. (McM TN, Co Ct Min, 2no#/193) James S. Bridges, Stephen Carter & Steting Camp were appointed to set off a years provision for the widow. (Ibid 207) 8 June 1827 a statement was recorded showing that William Dennis Hampton, alias William Dennis, died 8 August 1826. He had been on the pension roll for service in the Revolutionary War, Lee County, VA, dated 1819. He was a private. (Ibid 226) 2 December 1828 his widow, Nancy Hampton, petitioned for dower. (Ibid 327)

HANCOCK, Benja.
Died before 16 December 1816 when a sale of the estate was recorded. (Wil TN, Co Ct Min, no#/51)

HANCOCK, Coleman
Died before 5 April 1858 when Parrot & Coldwell was allowed $2.30 out of the poor tax for his "burying cloths." (Sev TN, Co Ct Min, no#/275)

HANCOCK, Francis M.
6 August 1866 Perry Cate was appointed guardian to the minor heirs of Francis M. Hancock. (Sev TN, Co Ct Min, no#/362)

HANCOCK, Perry
3 October 1859 was bound as an apprentice, [does not say to whom] until age 21. He is a male child aged 10. (Sev TN, Co Ct Min, no#/474)

HANCOCK, Saml.
Died before 26 January 1818 when the widow's dower was laid off. (Wil TN, Reg Bk/100) 16 September 1817 there was a suit; John Skeen, Executor of Saml. Hancock vs Virlanda Hancock, widow, Skeen Hancock, Betsy Hancock, Lee Hancock, Samuel Hancock, Sarah Hancock, Virlanda Hancock & Lesha Hancock, minor heirs of Samuel Hancock, deceased. Simon Hancock was appointed guardian of the minor heirs. John Skeen produced the will & the widow objected. A jury found it was not the last will & testament of Samuel Hancock, deceased. (Ibid, Co Ct Min, no#/163) Simon Hancock was appointed special guardian of Skeen Hancock, Elizabeth Hancock, Lee Hancock, Simon Hancock, Sally, Ruth, Samuel, Berlinda and Lythia Hancock, to defend the suit instituted by the widow for dower. (Ibid 187) Berlinda Hancock, the widow, petitioned for dower. (Ibid 203)

HANCOCK, Wm.
Died before 3 December 1866 when J. H. Caldwell was appointed guardian to the minor heirs with W. M. Burnett as security. (Sev TN, Co Ct Min, no#/406)

HAND, Samuel
Was a resident of Warren County, TN, on 3 December 1823 when his deposition was to be taken for the defendant in the case of James Capshaw vs Henry Gill. (McM TN, Co Ct Min, no#/108)

HANDCOCK, Benton B.
Was a male child aged 13 years when he was bound out as an apprentice, 3 January 1860. (Sev TN, Co Ct Min, no#/506)

HANDCOCK, Widow
Died before 4 July 1859 when J. R. Lark was paid for her coffin. (Sev TN, Co Ct Min, no#/451)

HANDLEY, Mary
28 May 1782 made motion by her attorney, Luke Bowyer, to be set free from an indenture fraudulently obtained by Wm. White. She was set at liberty. (Was TN, Co Ct Min, 1/161)

HANEY
M. L. Haney, J. R. Haney, L. A. Haney, N. E. Haney, S. A. D. Haney & M. T. Haney are minors & Thos. H. Drake was appointed guardian ad litem in the suit of Geo. W. Harris admr vs W. H. Haney et als, 18 August 1868. (Mad TN, Ch Ct Min, 3/168)

HANEY, John R.
Was granted a divorce 15 August 1860 from Nancy Haney. She has been guilty of adultry with James M. Alland [Allan]. John R. Haney was given custody of the child, William. (Jac TN, Ch Ct Min, C/413)

HANEY, Sarah
Was granted a divorce on the grounds of adultry from Caleb Haney on 14 July 1859. Her maiden name of Cantrel was restored. (Jac TN, Ch Ct Min, C/247)

HANKIN, Samuel
Died before 24 March 1807 when Richard Hankins made a settlement as administrator. (Wil TN, Co Ct Min, no#/285)

HANKINS, Nelson   [Hawkins]
Died before 2 November 1841 as shown in the suit of Russel M. Kinnarid and Thomas L. Brunsford vs Dice Hankins and John Hankins, James Alexander Hankins, Robert Hankins, Louisiana Hankins, Martha D. Hankins, Cleveland Winchester Hankins and Elizabeth Jane Hankins, minor heirs of Nelson Hankins, deceased, by their guardian, Dice Hankins. (Jac TN, Ch Ct Min, A/30)

HANKINS, William
Was probably a minor 21 September 1808 when he brought suit by James Hankins, his father & next friend. He sued William Sherral for TAP [trespass, assault & battery] (Roa TN, Co Ct Min, C/223)

HANNAH, Mrs. Julia
15 July 1853 was appointed guardian ad litem for her minor children, Virginia T. & Francis Hannah, to defend the suit of Logan H. McCarver, administrator &c vs John W. Hannah & others. (Jac TN, Ch Ct Min, B/87)

HANNAH, Samuel
Died before 8 February 1854 as shown in the suit of Logan H. McCarver admr. of Samuel Hannah Decd. and L. H. McCarver & wife Elizabeth vs Larken D. Swezea et als. The bill had been served on L. D. Swezea & wife Lucinda, William & John Hannah, Juliet Hannah & James Drennon, the executor & executrix of Samuel M. Hannah, Juliet Hannah, Dr. George W. Charlton & wife Mary Agness formerly M. A. Hannah, Virginia T. & Thomas Hannah, the two latter who are minors, & their mother Juliet Hannah their guardian ad litem. Publication has been made against the following non-resident defendants, to wit; Edward Dycus, L. Sloan and Calvin John and William James Wilson and Mary Dycus of Mo. Subpoena has also been served on Pinkney McCarver, James Young, George Darwin, Daniel Huffines, Willis Cornwell, Dr. A. Furgurson who have failed to appear and answer. (Jac TN, Ch Ct Min, B/116) The bill was taken proconfesso against all the defendants except William Young Larkin Drury & Henry Cornwell Thomas Huflines & wife Harriet Benjamin Payne Sampson McClellan & Joseph Law [no punctuation]. Those who have answered contest the right of complainants to recover as part of the estate, the money paid over to the children of Elizabeth Cornwell. Samuel Hannah died in 1840 leaving a will with no witnesses. James Young & Samuel W. Hannah qualified as executors & distributed the property to the following parties now his heirs-at-law; Melenda Dycus who married Edward Dycus, Lucinda Swezea who married Larken D. Swezea, Malinda M. McCarver who married Logan H. McCarver, Samuel W. Hannah & 2 grandsons, John & William Hannah, sons of John Hannah, the widow Elizabeth having departed this life previous to the death of said Samuel Hannah. An order was had setting aside said probate and the issue on the will was tried in 1853 and a jury found against said will. Logan H. McCarver qualified as administrator. Negroes had been delivered in 1841 to Larken D. Swezea & wife Lucinda, to Edward Dycus & wife now in MO, to Samuel W. Hannah, to Logan H. McCarver & wife Melinda, to John & William Hannah the grand

sons. Land had also been sold. Now everything will have to be undone and divided all over again. Some of the defendants were persons who had purchased land & negores. (Ibid 119-122) 12 July 1855 this suit was shown as Logan H. McCarver admr. vs Lucinda Sweezy et al. "The sums of money alledged by complainant to have been received by defts. Deny Cornwell, Larkin Cornwell, Joseph Law, Sampson McClelland, Thomas Huffhins and wife Harrit, Benjamin Payne, Alfred Cornwell and William Young from James Young and Samuel W. Hannah deceased were received during the year 1841-1842, and although said sums were paid perhaps through a mistake of the law said defts. children of Elizabeth Hannah not being devisees under the will of Samuel Hannah Dec. and the legacy of said Elizabeth being in the opinion of the court a lapsed legacy the testator Samuel Hannah surviving the devisee Elizabeth Hannah deceased...the court is of the opinion the complainant is not entitled to recovery of any thing from said defts." James Young had acted as executor of Samuel Hannah, deceased. (Ibid 236) A settlement was made. (Ibid 245)

HARBERT
13 August 1868 the following suit was entered: Rebecca C. Williamson vs Susan B. Harbert, Delestine Harbert, Corimore? Harbert, Andrw J. Smith, Francis G. Smith, Jas. Waddell, Philip Waddell, Jno. D. Cole, Andrew Cole, Philip Cole, Winnefred Henning, Lear T. Cole, Theadore E. Cole, Thos. C. Harbert, Jno. W. Harbert, Jas. A. Harbert, R. A. Hicks & wife Mary E., Lidia A. Harbert, Sarah E. Harbert, Jno. F. Hicks & wife Sarah W. Rebecca C. Williamson had bought the land belonging to all the defendants. (Mad TN, Ch Ct Min, 3/167)

HARBERT, Mrs.
Died before 19 February 1858 when her death was admitted in the suit of Thos. Reid vs Trent C. Conner et als. (Mad TN, Ch Ct Min, 2/197) In this same suit Thomas Clark was appointed guardian ad litem to answer for Celia Harbert. (Ibid 211) In another listing for this suit Sarah Harbert was mentioned. Thos. Reid & James Johnson were merchants who hired Trent C. Conner to work for them. Johnson has died. Compton was administrator of Conner? and has no assets of the estate of said Conner [has he died too?] (Ibid 283)

HARDAWAY, Edward
Made a deed of gift to James Hardaway 12 November 1813. (Rob TN, Co Ct Min, 3/341)

HARDAWAY, Manson
Died before 10 August 1812 when Elizabeth M. Hardaway, orphan of Manson, deceased, being of lawful age, made choice of Thomas Lane as her guardian. Plummer Willis and Thomas Williams were security. (Rob TN, Co Ct Min, 3/99)

HARDEN, Green A.
Died before 5 February 1866 when Wm. Headrick and Salena Headrick were appointed guardian to the minor heirs, with Wm. D. Atchley as security. (Sev TN, Co Ct Min, no#/272)

HARDEN, Nancy
6 November 1865 John A. Trotter, James N. Lawson and Wm. H. King were appointed to lay off her dower out of the lands of her deceased husband. (Sev TN, Co Ct Min, no#/237) Nancy was the widow of Thomas S. Harden. (Ibid 244)

HARDEN, William C.
Died before 5 November 1866 as shown in the partition of the lands of Thomas S. Harden, deceased. (Sev TN, Co Ct Min, no#/394-402) 4 March 1867 Richard W. Crowson, James H. Lawson & John A. Trotter were appointed to lay off dower to Sarah M. Walker out of the lands of W. C. Hardin, deceased. (Ibid 433)

HARDEN, Wm.
20 February 1780 Drurey Goodin was appointed his "Guardeen." (Was TN, Co Ct Min, 1/104)

HARDGRAVE
18 February 1858, the suit of Lavinia Hardgrave by her next friend vs Byrd Hill & Lavinia Hill, shows that Lavinia Hardgrave has married Neil M. Gardner. An agreement was reached, to wit: "Felix R. Hardgrave dismisses his suit. He is to retain possession of the negroes & pay Mrs. Lavina Hill for the hire of the same, & to keep the negroes at a reasonable hire until his daughter's right to them commences, dated Sept. 4th 1854." (Mad TN, Ch Ct Min, 2/175)

HARDGRAVE
23 August 1866 in the suit of Jas. L. McDonald vs J. R. Woolfolk et als, Jno. S. Brown was appointed guardian ad litem for America, Malvina, Cornelia Hardgrave who are minors & have no regular guardian. The names are also shown as America & Malvinia Coraline Hardgrove. (Mad TN, Ch Ct Min, 2/519)

HARDIN
4 February 1867 Wm. H. King was appointed guardian to John H. Hardin & Wm. H. Hardin with Alfred S. Hardin as security. (Sev TN, Co Ct Min, no#/429)

HARDIN, John
Died before 21 July 1802 when the will was proved by John Parks. (Rob TN, Co Ct Min, 1/228)

HARDIN, Martin R.
Was a pauper 7 June 1830 when money was allowed for his support. (McM TN, Co Ct Min, 2/445)

HARDIN, Thomas S.
Died before 2 October 1865 when Alfred S. Hardin was appointed administrator with Harvey J. Hardin, James Hedris, James W. Catter and Richard Burns as security. (Sev TN, Co Ct Min, no#/220) 2 July 1866 petition to sell land was made by Alfred S. Harden, administrator vs Harvey S. Harden & others, heirs of Thomas S. Harden, deceased. Other defendants were Nancy Ann Headrick, James Headrick, Elizabeth J. Cotter, James Cotter, Wm. Headrick, Selena Headrick, Nancy E. Hardin, Winney J. Harden, Sarah M. Harden, John H. Harden, Wm. C. Harden & Nancy Harden, R. R. Burns & Narcissa C. Burns, Wm. Headrick guardian of Nancy E. Harden & Winny J. Harden and Sarah M. Harden guardian to John H. Harden & W. C. Harden. John Harden is a non-resident. (Ibid 336) 1 October 1866 the land is to be divided in 8 equal parts between the petitioners & defendants who are heirs of Thomas S. Harden, deceased. (Ibid 373) A sale was made 2 October 1866. (Ibid 380) 5 November 1866 partition was made between the heirs of Thomas Harden, deceased, the heirs of William C. Hardin, deceased, and the heirs of Green Harden, deceased. Lot #1 to John Harden of IL, Lot#2 to the minor heirs of William C. Harden, Lot #3 to Alfred S. Harden, Lot #4 to Harvey S. Harden, Lot #5 to Nancy Ann Headrick, Lot #6 to Narcissus C. Burns, Lot #7 to the heirs of Green A. Harden, Lot #8 to Elizabeth J. Cotter, and to Nancy Ann Headrick an undivided interest in 100 acres held jointly by William E. Cotter & said Thomas S. Harden, deceased. Plat shown. (Ibid 394-402)

HARDING, Geo.
Died before 23 August 1867 as shown in the suit of Jno. J. Pack vs Jno. F. Newsom et als & John J. Mitchell vs Jno F. Newsom et als. The executor was Henry A. Welch. (Mad TN, Ch Ct Min, 3/84)

HARDISON, Alice C.
Died before 3 February 1873 when L. M. Williams was appointed administrator, with A. S. Parks and W. C. Dickey as his security. (Dyr TN, Co Ct Min, B/539)

HARGATE, Frederic
Died before 11 March 1844 when land was taxed to the heirs. (Obi TN, Cir Ct Min, 4/no#)

HARGETT, Frederick
Died before 21 February 1842 when land was taxed to the heirs. (Obi TN, Cir Ct Min, 4/no#)

HARGRAVES, Frank
Taxes were not collected in District 2 for 1873, "carried off by U.S.M." (Dyr TN, Co Ct Min, B/758)

HARIS, Jno. T.
6 August 1860 was certified to have attained the age of 21 and to be of good moral character, preparatory to obtaining a license to practice law. (Sev TN, Co Ct Min, no#/584)

HARKINS, Charles
Died before 4 May 1818 when Edward Moore was appointed administrator, with Alexander Patterson & George Moore as security. (Wil TN, Co Ct Min, no#/244)

HARKRUDER, J. W.
Died before 5 July 1870 when H. H. Phillips made a settlement as administrator. (Dyr TN, Co Ct Min, B/82)

HARLEY, Hiram
On 16 September 1853 Hiram Harley conveyed land to Hugh Swearingin and his wife Elizabeth Swearingin for the love and affection he had for them, and the further consideration that they would take care of him & his wife during their lives, which contract the Sweraingtons failed to execute. Hiram Harley later sold this land to Kinchin Pippin who brought suit 6 February 1857 for title to the land. (Jac TN, Ch Ct Min, C/72)

HARMAN, Jacob [Harmlin]
Died many years ago, having land in Bullitt County, KY, as shown in the suit of John Crook & wife Margaret vs Mary Ann Grier & others, filed 31 May 1841. John & Margaret Crook were citizens of Henderson County, TN. The defendants were Mary Ann Greer, John H. Moore & Thomas Greer, executors of Joseph Grier, deceased. The two former are citizens of Lincoln County, TN, & the latter of Bedford, Co. Jacob Harman was the father of Margaret Crook. He died intestate leaving 10 children. Joseph Grier, deceased, was the late husband of Mary Ann Greer, another of the children of Jacob Harman. Some of the heirs of Jacob Harman conveyed their interest in the land to Joseph Grier to sell and distribute the proceeds. Joseph Grier died in 1831 without having sold the land. He left a will appointing his widow, Mary Ann Grier, his son Joseph Greer and Thomas Grier & John H. Moore his executors. Son Joseph Greer removed & refused to qualify. (Bed TN, Ch Ct Min, 1/491)

HARMON, John
Died before 24 September 1855 as shown in the suit of Griffy Rigsby vs William Harmon & others. John Harmon had sold, in his lifetime, land to the plaintiff who seeks title to the land. The defendants are the only heirs of John Harmon. (Fen TN, Ch Ct Min, A/21)

HARP, Dinah
Was unable to support herself due to bodily inabilities. 23 Nov 1807 John Murphy received her into his care. (Cla TN, Co Ct Min, 3/128) She was let again to John Murphy 11 May 1815. (Ibid 4/68) She was let to Seth Botts in 1816. (Ibid 156)

HARPER, James
Died before 19 June 1839 as shown in the suit of Robert Harper & Benjamin Harper Admrs. of James Harper Decd. and others vs James F H. & William H. Harper, petition to sell land. The names of Thomas J. Harper & Mary R. Harper who intermarried with Samuel Hutchison, Martha S. Harper who intermarried with Charles McAlister, were crossed out. James F. & William H. Harper, who are heirs of James Harper, deceased, are minors & Thomas A. Polk was appointed guardian ad litem. (Obi TN, Cir Ct Min, 3/372)

HARPER, Mark
Died before 7 February 1851 as shown in the suit of John Lee Admr. of Mark Harper deceased vs Thomas Huddleston. (Jac TN, Ch Ct Min, A/407)

HARPER, Thomas M.
Died before 20 June 1836 as shown in the suit of Moses D. Harper & Robert B. Harper, administrators of Thomas M. Harper, deceased vs Terrell L. Camp. (Obi TN, Cir Ct Min, 3/56)

HARPOLE, Prior
Died before June 1805 when the heirs were on the tax list. (Wil TN, Co Ct Min, no#/157)

HARPOLE, Solomon
Died before 2 November 1818 when John Harpole resigned as guardian of William Harpole, minor heir. (Wil TN, Co Ct Min, no#/unnumbered page between 334 & 335)

HARRELL, Calvin
Died before 4 November 1872 when O. R. Robbins was appointed administrator, with W. H. Hendrix and R. Prichard as his security. W. H. Hendrix, Preston Holland and Geo. Mitchell were appointed to lay off a years provisions for the widow and family. (Dyr TN, Co Ct Min, B/509) The widow was Nancy Harrell. (Ibid 534)

HARRINGTON, Charles
Died before 7 August 1811 when the administrator was ordered to make a settlement. (Ste TN, Co Ct Min, 3/98) George Petty was administrator. (Ibid 106)

HARRINGTON, Chas.
Died before February term 1810. George Petty stated that Harrington had been a witness to a bond from Thomas Smith to John Copeland. (Rob TN, Co Ct Min, 2/201)

HARRIS
On 20 December 1840 petition was made by Sarah H. Harris and Esther J. Harris who are minors and sue by their guardian and father, Samuel S. Harris, all citizens of Mecklinburg County, NC. Samuel S. Harris has sold to Joseph R. McKinley 1/10 part of a tract of land in Bedford County, TN, belonging to said minors and they want the sale approved. (Bed TN, Ch Ct Min, 1/291)

HARRIS
1 March 1830 John M. Harris & Polly M. Harris, children of Robert M. Harris by his former wife, Deborah McEwen, came into court and asked to be allowed to choose their guardian. They are each under 21 but over 14 and chose Nathan Harris. John Lowry & Robert M. Harris were his security. (McM TN, Co Ct Min, 2no#/418)

HARRIS, D. H.
Taxes were not collected in District 4 for 1873, "run away." (Dyr TN, Co Ct Min, B/759)

HARRIS, Edmond
Taxes were not collected in District 5 for 1873, "over age." (Dyr TN, Co Ct Min, B/759)

HARRIS, Edward
Died before 24 February 1837 when land was taxed to the heirs. (Obi TN, Cir Ct Min, 3/117)

HARRIS, Edward
Died before 20 September 1815 when William Harris, Samuel Harris and Abner Harris, of Wilson County, TN, heirs of Edward Harris, Esqr., late of Craven County, NC, deceased, gave power of attorney to Eli Harris to settle any debt that may be due from the estate of Edward Harris. Witnesses were Furges S. Harris & John Adams who lives out of the state. (Wil TN, Reg Bk/68) James Harris of Franklin County & Margaret Rosenbrough of Lincoln County, TN, gave power of attorney to Eli Harris of Wilson County, to receive any property due them from the estate of Edward Harris, deceased. (Ibid 110) James McCollum & wife Mary and Thomas Stevenson & wife Lydia of Iredell County, NC, appointed Eli Harris for the same purposes. (Ibid 111) Andrew Provine & wife Rebecca and Robert McCord & wife Permelia of Madison County, KY, heirs of Edward Harris, deceased, "and Samuel P. Harris of the county and state aforesaid, heirs at law of Andrew Harris of Williamson County, TN, heirs at law of said Edward Harris," appointed Eli Harris for the same purposes. (Ibid 112)

HARRIS, Francis
Made a deed of gift to Sarah & Rhodes Harris & Joshua Harris, 6 May 1811. (Ste TN, Co Ct Min, 3/54)

HARRIS, James
Died before 22 Jan 1802 when the heirs were shown on the delinquent tax list. (Rob TN, Co Ct Min, 1/207)

HARRIS, John
Taxes were not collected in District 4 for 1873, "insol." (Dyr TN, Co Ct Min, B/759)

HARRIS, John
With his wife Elizabeth, sold land in Prince Edward County, VA, to John Stuart, 1 November 1819. (Wil TN, Co Ct Min, no#/536)

HARRIS, John
Died before 26 March 1824 when his widow, Sally Harris, made a deed of gift of a negro girl named Ester about 8 years old, to her 2 children, Eli R. Harris & Patsey S. Harris. Furgus S. Harris was guardian of the children. (Wil TN, Reg Bk/376)

HARRIS, John T.
Died before 3 October 1865 when W. C. Murphy was appointed administrator with J. C. Murphy as security. (Sev TN, Co Ct Min, no#/232) J. A. Woodside was appointed guardian to the minor heirs. (Ibid 244) John Murphy bought the house & 2 lots belonging to the estate of John T. Hauis [sic], deceased. (Ibid 268)

HARRIS, Maria
Was a minor 4 November 1805 when William Polk was appointed guardian, with James McFarlin & John Sherod as security. Maria was the daughter by a former marriage of Martha Polk, widow of John Polk, deceased. (Rob TN, Co Ct Min, 1/363 & 364) 8 February 1813 Elias Fort, Jr. made settlement as guardian. (Ibid 3/186)

HARRIS, Newton
Died before 7 November 1870 when James Copeland was chosen and appointed guardian of Nonnie [?] Harris, minor heir, with G. B. Tensley as his security. (Dyr TN, Co Ct Min, B/126) Minnie Harris was the grand daughter of James Copeland. (Ibid 539)

HARRIS, Robert
4 July 1871 J. L. Webb made a settlement as guardian of the heirs. (Dyr TN, Co Ct Min, B/258)

HARRIS, Samuel
Was a resident of Crawford County, Illinois Territory, on 1 August 1818 when he gave a power of attorney to Eli Harris of Wilson County to sell land in Wilson County. (Wil TN, Reg Bk/127)

HARRIS, W. D.
Taxes were not collected in District 5 for 1873, "run away." (Dyr TN, Co Ct Min, B/759)

HARRIS, Wiley
Died before 25 August 1860 as shown in the suit of Wiley T. Harris admr. &c of Wiley Harris decd. vs V. B. Woolfolk, Julian Woolfolk, F. R. Dailam [Dallam, Dodam] and others. (Mad TN, Ch Ct Min, 2/367)

HARRISON, J. W.
Died before 4 April 1870 when Nathaniel Porter et als reported the years provisions laid off to the widow & family. (Dyr TN, Co Ct Min, B/37) 4 July 1871 W. J. Farris made a settlement as administrator of James W. Harrison. (Ibid 258)

HARRISON, John
Died before 10 May 1815 when Elias Harrison was appointed administrator with Isaac Lane and John Neals as security (Cla TN, Co Ct Min, 4/52)

HARRISON, Robt. P.
Died before 25 December 1843 when Robert B. Davidson was appointed Clerk & Master pro tem in his place, Harrison having died since the last term of court. (Bed TN, Ch Ct Min, 2/263) Robert P. Harrison died about 1 August 1843 leaving a will, by which he appointed his widow, Eliza W. Harrison, executrix. (Ibid 3/388)

HARRISON, William
Died before 20 July 1819 when Barbary Swindle & Thomas Swindle of White County, TN, legal heirs of William Harrison, deceased, appointed John J. S. Ruffen of Raleigh, NC, to apply for a land warrent in the name of said William Harrison for his services as a soldier in the Revolutionary War of the North Carolina line of the Continental army. (Wil TN, Reg Bk/139)

HARRISON, William
Was a resident of Dinwiddie County, VA, 5 July 1809 when his deposition was to be taken for the defendant in the case of Benj. Wells vs Wm. Roachel. (Rob TN, Co Ct Min, 2/153)

HARRISON, William P.
Died before 13 November 1833 when a suit against him for riot abated because of his death. (Obi TN, Cir Ct Min, 2/106)

HART, Anthony
Died before 10 September 1806 when land was taxed to the heirs. (Ste TN, Co Ct Min, 1/36)

HART, Henry
Was the orphan of Joseph Hart when Thomas Johnson was appointed guardian, 21 April 1800. (Rob TN, Co Ct Min, 1/130) 5 April 1808, Henry Hart, being of full age to choose a guardian, made choice of Benjamin Porter, who gave bond with Martin Duncan & William Adams as his security. (Ibid 2/15)

HART, James
Died before 8 October 1872 as shown in the suit of N. R. Prichard, administrator vs D. C. Craig et al, bill to sell land to make assets. Minor defendants were mentioned. (Dyr TN, Co Ct Min, B/493) Taxes were paid on the land for 1865 by J. W. Tarkington. Taxes are due for 1867 through 1872. (Ibid 576) 1 June 1874 the land was sold. (Ibid 739-40) 8 July 1874 it was stated that James Hart was deceased as much as 10 years ago. (Ibid 762)

HART, John M.
Died before 7 October 1872 when the will was proved by R. B. Moore, one of the witnesses. Daniel E. Parker and M. J. Hart proved an addition to the will. R. L. Hart was executor with Daniel E. Parker and Milton J. Hart as his security. (Dyr TN, Co Ct Min, B/474)

HART, Joseph
Died before 16 January 1797 when Ann Hart & Noah Sugg were appointed administrators with James Norfleet & Isaac Dortch as security. (Rob TN, Co Ct Min, 1/15) 21 April 1800 James Norfleet, John Baker & Hugh Henry were appointed to divide the negroes between the widow & orphans. (Ibid 130) 3 February 1806 the estate of Joseph Hart was ordered to pay $3 to Aquilla Sugg for making the settlement between the estate of Hart and of the estate of Noah Sugg. (Ibid 371)

HART, Nathaniel
Died before 2 March 1802 when the executor, Nathaniel Hart, deeded land to Nathaniel Davis. The deed was dated 4 August 1801 and was made in Fayette County, KY. (Cla TN, Co Ct Min, 1/22)

HART, Sam
10 May 1814 was emancipated by his owner, Henry Hart. (Rob TN, Co Ct Min, 3/411)

HART, Susanna
Died before August term 1810 when the heirs were on a tax list. (Rob TN, Co Ct Min, 2/290)

HART, Thomas
Taxes were not collected in District 4 for 1873, "can't be found." (Dyr TN, Co Ct Min, B/759)

HART, William
Married before 18 December 1816 to Catharine Jones, daughter of Peter Jones, deceased. (Wil TN, Co Ct Min, no#/62)

HARTY, Pleasant
Died before September 1816 when slaves from his estate were sold for division among several heirs. (Wil TN, Reg Bk/63)

HARWELL, Frank
Died before 7 November 1870 when Turner Chamblin renewed his bond as guardian of the minor heirs. (Dyr TN, Co Ct Min, B/125)

HARWELL, R. F.
Died before 2 December 1873 when J. J. Yates was appointed guardian of R. K. Harwell, Indiana Harwell, Cleopatra Harwell, L. C. Harwell, Nancy Jane Harwell and Terry C. Scallings, minor heirs. J. H. Hardison and C. T. Nash were his security. (Dyr TN, Co Ct Min, B/670)

HASKINS
3 July 1871 two negro children, Peter and Sam Haskins, were bound to C. Haskins until age 21. They are now aged 6 and 8 years old respectively. (Dyr TN, Co Ct Min, B/255)

HASKINS, E. J.
1 May 1871 made a settlement as guardian for Rody and LaFayette Haskins, colored. (Dyr TN, Co Ct Min, B/236)

HASKINS, Edward
Died before 6 October 1873 when Harriet J. Haskins was appointed guardian of Miss Carter Haskins, minor heir of Edward Haskins, with Creed Haskins as her security. (Dyr TN, Co Ct Min, B/633) The will of Edward Haskins was proved by Smith Parks, L. M. Williams and G. B. Tinsley, proving the handwriting of J. A. C. Manley, witness who is

deceased. J. K. P. Harrell and G. B. Tinsley proved the codicil as witnesses. Mrs. Harriet J. Haskins and Creed Haskins were executors, with J. B. Ferguson and J. C. Haskins as security. (Ibid 634) The will was also proved by R. P. McCrackin, witness. (Ibid 658)

HASKINS, J. C.
1 July 1872 was released from paying poll tax and working on public roads as he is unable to do manual labor. (Dyr TN, Co Ct Min, B/430)

HASKINS, Theodoric C.
Died before 19 June 1838 when his death was suggested in the suit of Thomas Ridley vs Henry J. P. Westbrook. Theodoric C. Haskins had been administrator of Henry Applewhite, deceased. Henry J. P. Westbrook is now administrator of Henry Applewhite. (Obi TN, Cir Ct Min, 3/209)

HASTINGS, Susannah
Died before 28 December 1843 as shown in the suit of James Deery vs Samuel Pollock & John Hastings. Samuel Pollock is entitled to a share of the estate of Susannah Hastings, deceased. Samuel Pollock is a resident of AL. John Hastings is administrator of the estate of Susannah Hastings. (Bed TN, Ch Ct Min, 2/283) There are 6 distributees of the estate of Susannah Hastings of which Samuel Pollock of Benton County, AL, is one. (Ibid 3/117)

HASTINGS, Willis
Died before 12 February 1840 as shown in the suit of Dennis Bryant & wife Elizabeth, formerly Elizabeth Hastings, widow of Willis Hastings, deceased, William & Mary Jane Hastings, children of said Willis Hastings who are minors & sue by their guardian Dennis Bryant. Pearce Wilhoite, John F. Norman, William Boone, William Hurst, John C. Nix, Henry Dean & Welley F. Daniel were appointed to partition the lands & set off dower to Elizabeth. (Bed TN, Ch Ct Min, 2/102)

HATCH, Peggy
Died before 8 February 1813 when Asa Bryan, Esqr. was appointed administrator, with Marvil Lowe as security. (Rob TN, Co Ct Min, 3/185)

HATCHER, John
Died before 6 October 1856 when money was allowed for making his coffin. (Sev TN, Co Ct Min, no#/73)

HATCHER, Sally
5 January 1858 the superintendent of the poor house was allowed extra money for her while she was sick. (Sev TN, Co Ct Min, no#/242)

HAUGHTON, J. C.
Died before 13 November 1834 as shown in the suit of George W. Fentress vs Jordan Hassell, administrator of J. C. Haughton, deceased. (Obi TN, Cir Ct Min, 2/212)

HAUK, John W.
Died before 2 October 1865 when Joshua H. Atchley was appointed administrator with Robert McMahan as security. (Sev TN, Co Ct Min, no#/216)

HAVARD, George
Died before July term 1798 when his death was shown in the suit of William Barter Powel vs Danl. Lyons, Geo. Havard & Benjn. Mcintosh. Mary Havard was the wife of George Havard, deceased. (Rob TN, Co Ct Min, 1/65)

HAWKINS
22 February 1861 in the suit of Mary Haukins & others vs Jno. B. Compton & others, it is stated that Jno. B. Compton was the former guardian of Mary & Samuel Hankins, minors. H. H. Hawkins was the father of Mary & Samuel, all of whom are residents of AR, & was appointed their guardian. (Mad TN, Ch Ct Min, 2/441)

HAWKINS, James
At the May term 1789 made a deed of gift to his son, William Hawkins. (Was TN, Co Ct Min, 1/384)

HAY, David
Died before 27 May 1782 when Agness Hay was appointed administratrix with Pharoah Cobb & Wm. Ward as security. (Was TN, Co Ct Min, 1/159)

HAY, Mathew
Died before 4 February 1783 when the administratrix, Agness Hay, returned an inventory of the estate. (Was TN, Co Ct Min, 1/194)

HAY, Wm. F.
Died before 17 December 1816 when the coroner was paid for holding an inquest. (Wil TN, Co Ct Min, no#/54)

HAYDEN, Rebecca
On 1 December 1868 Rebecca Hayden, administratrix, brought suit against Peter Moody & others. Defendants David C. Travis and Lewis Glass are non-residents of TN. On 22 October 1866 Rebecca had recovered a judgement against David C. Travis in Metcalfe County, KY, which has not been paid. David C. Travis had owned land in Fentress County, TN, which he sold to Lewis Glass and he sold it to Peter Moody. The sale was made for the purpose of fraud to get out of paying the judgement to Rebecca Hayden. The sale is declared void. (Fen TN, Ch Ct Min, A/400)

HAYMES, Reuben
Died before 7 September 1824 when William Haymes was appointed administrator. (McM TN, Co Ct Min, 2no#/24) 6 December 1824 Terry Waldin, Hugh L. Lackey & James A. Templeton were appointed to lay out a years maintenance for Sarah Haymes, the widow. (Ibid 35) Provisions were laid out for Sarah & 2 children. (Ibid 36) 3 September 1827 William Haynes was appointed guardian of William & Elizabeth Haymes, the orphan minor heirs. (Ibid 229)

HAYNES, Joseph N.
Died before 14 July 1847 as shown in a suit by his widow, Margaret E. Haynes, and children, Elizabeth R. Haynes, Mary H. Haynes, Sarah J. Haynes and Matilda Haynes vs Newman Haynes. Joseph Haynes was the son of Newman [Nuoman, Nusman] Haynes. Rebecca was the wife of Newman Haynes. Joseph N. Haynes died in the spring of 1841, intestate. (Mad TN, Ch Ct Min, 1/27)

HAYNES, Stephen
Married Mary Tucker, one of the legatees of John Tucker, deceased, as shown in the case of Stephen Haynes & Mary his wife against Henry Johnson, guardian of the heirs of John Tucker, deceased, 16 May 1811. (Rob TN, Co Ct Min, 2/426) (also 3/514)

HAYS
In the suit of Sarah A. Hays et al vs Ella B. Hays et al, 19 February 1868, it was stated that the defendants were minors and Guy Lieper was appointed guardian ad litem. (Mad TN, Ch Ct Min, 3/131) This suit was shown as Sarah Ann Hays by her next friend, John L. Brown, and John L. Brown trustee vs Ella B. Hays, Angio? R. Hays, Stokley D. Hays and Charles B. Hays. On 15 April 1853 William E. Butler had deeded a lot to Sarah Ann in trust for the benefit of her and her children and not to come under the influence of her husband, Richard J. Hays, or any future husband. At her death the lot was to become the property of her children. Sarah Ann wishes to sell the unimproved lot & purchase the lot on which she & her children now live. The defendants are represented by their guardian ad litem. (Ibid 186)

HAYS, Enos [Hayes]
Died before 21 February 1839 when land was taxed to the heirs. (Obi TN, Cir Ct Min, 3/293)

HAYS, Peter
Died some time in the winter of 1834-5, intestate. He left 11 heirs, to wit, Nelly, Polly, Cooper, Mahaly, who are minors & have Samuel Jones for their guardian, Hiram Hays, Archibald Hays, Henry Hays, Elias Hays, Jane Hays, Sarah Brookshire wife of William Brookshire and Christiana wife of William Frizzel, to whom a certain tract of land descended from Peter Hays deceased, subject to the dower of Kiziah Hays, the widow. James Frizzell has purchased 6/11 of the land. (Bed TN, Ch Ct Min, 2/79) Division was made. (Ibid 96)

HAYS, Rebecca
Died before 2 August 1819 when the will was proved by Richard Drake & Thomas McGregor. (Wil TN, Co Ct Min, no#/492)

HAYS, Saml. J.
Died before 21 February 1867 when his death was proven in the suit of Saml. J. Hays vs Robt. Brown. The suit was revived in the names of A. J. Hays, Middleton Hays & R. J.

Hays, executors. (Mad TN, Ch Ct Min, 3/32) The executors names were shown as Andrew J. Hays, Richard J. Hays & Middleton Hays. (Ibid 76)

HAYWOOD, George W.
In the suit of George W. Haywood vs Dyer Pearl at August term 1830, it is shown that George W. Haywood had been a resident of Giles County in 1826; that Dyer Pearl was a resident of Nashville and had sold lottery tickets to Haywood; that Samuel Bigham was security on a note from Haywood to Pearl for the lottery tickets. (Bed TN, Ch Ct Min, 1/27)

HAYWOOD, Ruth
Was an orphan girl aged 10 years when she was bound 18 September 1809 to Barbara McClellan until age 18. (Roa TN, Co Ct Min, D/96)

HAYWOOD, Thomas
Was an orphan boy aged 7 years & 2 months when he was bound 18 September 1809 to David McClellan until age 21. (Roa TN, Co Ct Min, D/96)

HAZELWOOD, Thomas
"Moved away" by 17 September 1816 when a road overseer was appointed in his place. (Wil TN, Co Ct Min, no#/41)

HEAD, Enoch
Died intestate in January last, as shown in the suit of James W. Head and others vs Jessee P. Tucker & others. [No date, but the bill probably filed at the August term 1844] Complainant Charlotte is the widow of Enoch Head. James W. Head and Sarah Averitt who has intermarried with Littleton Averitt, John A. Head, Elizabeth Tucker wife of Jessee P. Tucker, Martha Harris wife of Israel Harris and Mary Head were the only children & heirs-at-law. Littleton & Sarah Averitt are citizens of Rutherford County, TN. John A. Head is a citzen of Giles County, TN. Mary Head has died leaving a will by which she left all her interest in the estate of said Enoch to James W. Head, Charlotte Head & Sarah Averitt. The heirs had made an agreement to divide the property among them giving Charlotte 1/7 and the other heirs each 1/7. (Bed TN, Ch Ct Min, 3/215)

HEAD, Henry
Died before 22 June 1841 when the executrix, Elizabeth Head, petitioned to sell land. (Obi TN, Cir Ct Min, 4/no#)

HEAD, Mary
Sued John Head for divorce 5 February 1858. John was ordered to pay Mary $50 for her support and attorney fees so she can prosecute this suit. (Jac TN, Ch Ct Min, C/108) Divorce was granted 15 July 1858. They have lived in the county about 10 years. Mary was given custody of the 4 children, title to personal property & land during her lifetime. At her death the land is to go the children. (Ibid 132)

HEADDEN, Moses
8 January 1873 H. H. Headden made a settlement as guardian of the heirs. (Dyr TN, Co Ct Min, B/533)

HEARD, Abraham
Died before 3 September 1822 when his death was suggested in suits of Charles McClung & John McGhee. The suits are to be revived against the executors. (McM TN, Co Ct Min, no#/58) 3 December 1822 the suits were revived against Nancy Heard & Franklin C. Heard, executors of the last will & testament of Abraham Heard, deceased. (Ibid 66)

HEARD, John D.
Died before 7 June 1830 when his will was proved by John Martin, one of the witnesses. (McM TN, Co Ct Min, 2no#/448) The will was also proved by Jesse Hannloho. Rebeccah Heard & Moses Stallcup were executors. (Ibid 472)

HEARN, Thos.
Died before 20 October 1840 when a suit against him for drunkeness was abated because of his death. (Obi TN, Cir Ct Min, 4/no#)

HEATH, William
Made a deed of gift to Elijah Heath 6 February 1804, as certified by the clerk of Garrard County, KY. (Rob TN, Co Ct Min, 1/281)

HEATWALL, John
Died before 6 July 1857 when Moses Russle was appointed administrator with William Adcock as his security. (Sev TN, Co Ct Min, no#/182)

HEDRICK, James
Died before 4 February 1867 when Manerva Hedrick was appointed guardian to the minor heirs, with Peter Hedrick as security. (Sev TN, Co Ct Min, no#/429)

HEFLIN, William
Was a resident of NC 26 March 1807 when James Heflin gave him a letter of attorney. (Wil TN, Co Ct Min, no#/288)

HEGERTY, Cynthia
9 February 1821 made a deed of gift of a feather bed to her nephew, John Evans, son of George Augustus Lyne Evans. John Evans was a minor at that time. (Wil TN, Reg Bk/214)

HELDRETH, R. T.
In his suit against W. C. Wood, Levi Harmon, John Elder and Silas Wheeler, it was stated that defendants Elder, Wheeler & Wood were non-residents of the state, 11 April 1861. (Fen TN, Ch Ct Min, A/281)

HELMS, J. W.
Taxes were not collected in District 5 for 1873, "run away." (Dyr TN, Co Ct Min, B/759)

HEMING, Abraham
24 October 1839 stated that prior to his intermarriage with his present wife that he had by her a natural child called Louisa Scott Farley. He petitioned the court to make this child legitimate and change her name to Louisa Scott Heming and that she will share alike with his other children. (Obi TN, Cir Ct Min, 4/no#)

HENDERSON, Elizabeth
Died before 6 August 1860 when her will was proved by Elizabeth Montgomery and M. W. McCowan, witnesses. James P. McMahan was executor with Robert McMahan and M. W. McCowan as security. (Sev TN, Co Ct Min, no#/587)

HENDERSON, G. B.
7 July 1856 resigned as tax assessor. His resignation was accepted in consequence of the ill health of Mr. Henderson. (Sev TN, Co Ct Min, no#/54)

HENDERSON, Hugh C.
Died before 22 August 1866 when Alex. W. Campbell was appointed guardian ad litem for Mark C. Henderson, Jas. W. Henderson, Louisa E. Henderson, Thos. J. Henderson, Nathaniel Henderson, Tennessee D. Henderson, William Henderson & Callie Henderson, minor defendants in the suit of Ro. Hicks & others. Mary S. Henderson was his widow & Hannah C. Hicks (wife of Robt. Hicks) & the minors named were his children, except that William & Callie Henderson were the only children of Elam Henderson, deceased & grand children of H. C. Henderson. Robert Hicks is the administrator. In the description of the land, the division line between Enos & Hugh Henderson was mentioned. (Mad TN, Ch Ct Min, 2/504 & 527) 21 August 1867 dower was laid off to Martha C. Henderson in the lands of Hugh C. Henderson, deceased. (Ibid 3/68)

HENDERSON, James
With his wife, Elizabeth, sold land in Champlain County, OH, to Arthur Laty, 14 May 1816. On the same day the Hendersons sold land in the same place to John Forge and to Henry Brendonburg. (Cla TN, Co Ct Min, 4/194) Elizabeth was examined separately. (Ibid 196)

HENDERSON, Jas.
Died before 7 April 1856 when Wm. Henderson renewed his bond as guardian of Amanda Henderson, Elizabeth Henderson & Robert Henderson, minor heirs. Geo. M. Henderson & Elijah Henderson were security. (Sev TN, Co Ct Min, no#/20)

HENDERSON, John
Married before 28 October 1808 to Nancy Provine, daughter of John Provine, deceased, as shown in a power of attorney to dispose of land. John Henderson was a resident of Garrard County, KY, in 1808. (Wil TN, Reg Bk/13)

HENDERSON, R. G.
Died before 4 October 1871 when the will was proved by M. Bowling and N. T. Perry, witnesses. B. H. Harman was executor, with E. H. Henderson and N. T. Perry as his security. (Dyr TN, Co Ct Min, B/309-10)

HENDERSON, Rebecca
Was granted a divorce from Kinman W. Henderson on 28 January 1847. They had married about 3 years ago and shortly thereafter he abandoned her. (Jac TN, Ch Ct Min, A/241)

HENDERSON, Richard
Died before 24 August 1807 when a deed was recorded from Robert Burton, one of the surviving executors of Richard Henderson, deceased, and Archibald Henderson, one of the other surviving executors, to George Campbell. The deed was proved by John Henderson. (Cla TN, Co Ct Min, 3/106)

HENDERSON, Richard
Died before 26 December 1807 when land was taxed to the heirs. (Roa TN, Co Ct Min, C/98)

HENDERSON, Richard
Died before 22 February 1791 when a suit was brought against "the heirs and Devisees of Richard Henderson late of Granville County Esquire deceased." The suit mentioned "Nathanial Hart of VA, deceased, William ? late of Orange County, merchant, John ? late of Chatham County & Leonard Billors ? gentlemen decd. def., John Umstead, Susanna Umstead, Leonard H. Bullock, Richard Henderson one of the heirs and devisees of Richard Henderson decd., A. Henderson, Spruce Macoy, Fanny Macoy, John Henderson by Archibald Henderson his guardian and Elizabeth Henderson by Spruce Macoy her guardian having acknowledged service of the bill and failed to appear." The rest of the heirs reside outside the limits of the territory. (Was TN, Co Ct Min, no#/2)

HENDERSON, Robert
1 April 1861 Geo. M. Henderson was appointed his guardian with M. W. McCow & Elijah Henderson as security. (Sev TN, Co Ct Min, no#/670) A final settlement was made 1 May 1865. (Ibid 155)

HENDERSON, Thomas
Was the father of William Henderson as shown in the suit of Samuel Martin vs Thomas Henderson & William Henderson, 26 July 1849. (Jac TN, Ch Ct Min, A/335)

HENDERSON, Thos.
Died before 11 March 1844 when land was taxed to the heirs. (Obi TN, Cir Ct Min, 4/no#)

HENDERSON, William
Died before 2 July 1860 when his will was proved by Basdill Scruggs & M. W. McCown witness. George M. Henderson & Elijah Henderson were executors, with M. W. McCowan, B. M. Chandler, Wellington McMahan, Jas. P. McMahan, Jas. P. Catlett & Jesse Stafford as security. (Sev TN, Co Ct Min, no#/564)

HENDERSON, William
Died before 2 June 1862 when Martha Henderson proved by the oath of Austin Mort & George W. Catlett that she was his mother. William was a single man and a private in Capt. James W. Chambers company of Volunteers in the service of the Confederate States of America. (Sev TN, Co Ct Min, no#/783)

HENDERSON, Wm. A.
Died before 5 May 1856 when Perry Cate renewed his bond as guardian of G. P. & W. A. Henderson, minor heirs. J. N. Underwood was his security. (Sev TN, Co Ct Min, no#/48) 4 August 1856 the minor heirs were shown to be William A. & Geo. P. Henderson. (Ibid 65)

HENDRICK, Drucilla
Married Peter Walker as shown when they made a marriage contract 22 June 1807, with John Williams as her trustee. (Wil TN, Co Ct Min, no#/291)

HENDRIK, Joseph
Died before 27 March 1804 when a bond from him to George Marlow, Sr. was proved by Edward Marlow. (Wil TN, Co Ct Min, no#/33) Jeremiah Hendrik was administrator. (Ibid 35) Joseph T. Williams was appointed guardian to execute a deed to Jeremiah

Hendricks, administrator of Joseph Hendricks, deceased, agreeable to the terms of a bond by said Joseph to Obediah Hendricks dated 15 October 1799, for 640 acres on Rocky Creek in Sumner County, which bond has been assigned. (Ibid 127)

HENIGAR, Jacob
Was an orphan boy 7 years old when he was bound 7 March 1826 to Henry Price, Esqr. until age 21. He is to be taught the trade of farming. (McM TN, Co Ct Min, 2no#/140)

HENLEY, Isaac
Was not of lawful age 8 July 1808 when James B. Reynolds, Esqr. was appointed guardian to defend the suit of Joseph Perry vs Isaac Henley & William Gill. (Rob TN, Co Ct Min, 2/67)

HENRY, _____
Died before 21 February 1866 when the death of complainant Henry was admitted in the suit of Rushing & Henry vs W. Witherspoon. (Mad TN, Ch Ct Min, 2/473)

HENRY
21 July 1801 receipts from Saml. Henry, John Henry, James Henry and Thomas Henry to Hugh Henry were proven by the oath of Isaac Henry. (Rob TN, Co Ct Min, 1/181)

HENRY, Albert
Died before 7 October 1856 when Thos. G. Douglass renewed his bond as guardian to Ephraim, Jane & Elizabeth Henry, minor heirs. Edward M. Douglass & Jesse Douglass were the securities. (Sev TN, Co Ct Min, no#/84)

HENRY, Benjamin
Died before 2 February 1863 when Samuel Henry was appointed administrator with J. T. Trotter & James Toomey as security. (Sev TN, Co Ct Min, no#/45) 1 August 1864, in the case of the petition of Eliza A. Henry & others, it is ordered that Samuel Henry and Oliver Henry, heirs of Benjamin Henry, deceased, be notified to appear. (Ibid 115) Samuel Mount was appointed administrator. (Ibid 121)

HENRY, Eliz [Elig?]
Died before 5 April 1858 when Thos. Henry made a settlement as guardian of Saml. Henry, minor heir. (Sev TN, Co Ct Min, no#/271)

HENRY, Hugh
28 August 1778 took the oath of allegiance. (Was TN, Co Ct Min, 1/47)

HENRY, Hugh
Died before June 1805 when the heirs were on the tax list. (Wil TN, Co Ct Min, no#/158)

HENRY, Hugh, Sr.
Died before 4 July 1808 when the will was proved by Saml. McMurry & Andrew Irwin. (Rob TN, Co Ct Min, 2/45)

HENRY, Isaac
Died before 10 May 1814 when the will was proved by Augustin Cook & Thomas Cook. (Rob TN, Co Ct Min, 3/406)

HENRY, James
Died before 1802 when the land taxed to his heirs for the years 1802 through 1808 was released from double tax on payment of the single tax. (Roa TN, Co Ct Min, D/87)

HENRY, Mary
Died before February term 1810 when the will was proved by Richd. Jones. (Rob TN, Co Ct Min, 2/200) The will was also proved by James Jones. (Ibid 224) An inventory of the estate of Polly Henry was delivered by Genl. Thomas Johnson. (Ibid 262)

HENRY, Mary, Mrs.
7 March 1871 a jury was ordered to determine if she is insane. (Dyr TN, Co Ct Min, B/205) The clerk was ordered to take the necessary steps to send Mrs. Cleek and Mrs. Mary Henry to the Insane Asylum. (Ibid 215)

HENRY, Michael
Died before 5 November 1840 when a suit was filed by George D. Allen vs Hugh P. Allen Admr. &c. It was stated that Michael Henry had received of the joint funds over and above what George Allen had received. A settlement is to be made and George D. Allen

surrender to Hugh P. Allan, administrator of M. Henry, all the notes, debts or property belonging to the said partnership. (Jac TN, Ch Ct Min, A/4) 29 January 1847 a suit was entered by Samuel E. Hare & Watson M. Cooke vs Polly Henry, James Henry, William Jordan Henry & Michael Henry and others. Polly Henry was indebted to complainants and gave them a mortgage to her dower as the widow of Michael Henry, deceased. The other defendants are the heirs of Michael Henry, deceased. (Ibid 254) Mounce Gore was appointed guardian of the minor heirs of Michael Henry in the place of Polly Henry. (Ibid 274) Dower was set off to Polly Henry. (Ibid 294)

HENRY, Samuel
4 August 1856 his guardian, Thomas Henry, renewed his bond with Ephriam Johnson and Samuel H. Ellis as security. The original bond was destroyed by fire. (Sev TN, Co Ct Min, no#/66)

HENRY, Samuel H.
Died before 3 July 1865 when Humphrey Mount was appointed administrator with Patrick Henry & David Keener as security. (Sev TN, Co Ct Min, no#/180)

HERBERT, Isaac
Was reported "not an inhabitant of this government," April term 1798, when summoned in the suit of Beverly A. Allen vs James Bulgin & Isaac Herbert. (Rob TN, Co Ct Min, 1/60)

HERRON, Andrew
Died before 15 January 1847 as shown in the suit of Samuel Roach & Mary Irvin, his wife, vs Andrew Herron, Ex. of Robert Irvin. The suit was abated because of death of the defendant. (Mad TN, Ch Ct Min, 1/15)

HESTER, James
Was released from paying poll tax for 1858 as he had left the county before that year. (Sev TN, Co Ct Min, no#/408)

HESTER, James
4 January 1860 Joel Hudson was appointed his guardian as James Hester is a lunatic. (Sev TN, Co Ct Min, no#/511)

HIBBARD, Marietta
7 January 1874 James H. Cooper made a settlement as administrator. (Dyr TN, Co Ct Min, B/698)

HIBBITS, William
Was the guardian of Harlin Hibbits, Sarah Hibbits, John Hibbits, Elizabeth Hibbits & Louisa J. Hibbits minor heirs of Henry Eakle, deceased, as shown in the suit of Peter G. Cox & Joseph Roddy vs William Hibbits, Sampson W. Cassitty & Christian Eagle, 7 February 1855. The defendant is a non-resident. (Jac TN, Ch Ct Min, B/183) 9 February 1855 the death of Elija [Eliza?] Hibbits was suggested. (Ibid 192)

HIBBITTS, Jo. R.
Died before 1 August 1870 when W. M. Watkins made a settlement as administrator. (Dyr TN, Co Ct Min, B/94)

HICKLIN, Hugh
Died shortly after making his will on 13 October 1831? A. M. Hicklin was executor. By his will he emancipated his negro Sukey. Complainants in a cross bill are Almira & Turner, the children of Sukey born after the death of testator. Sukey was emancipated in 1840 by the County Court of Jackson County. The court decreed that Almira & Turner Hicklin be free. (Jac TN, Ch Ct Min, A/34)

HICKLIN, Perry
Died several years ago as stated 8 May 1844 in the suit of Thomas Hicklin, Avery Hicklin, Benjamin Biggerstaff & Elizabeth his wife, James Parish & Polly his wife, Nelson Nunly & Letty his wife and Aaron Biggerstaff vs James Nevins & Polly his wife, George W. Atterberry & Hannah his wife, Joseph Olive and Samuel Olive, James Nevins & G. W. Atterberry, administrators of Perry Hicklin, deceased. The complainants and defendants are his heirs. A report on the estate is to be made. (Jac TN, Ch Ct Min, A/142) Samuel Olive was deceased by 30 July 1846. (Ibid 232) 29 July 1847 there was a balance in the hands of James Nivins in favor of Elizabeth Walker, Parish and wife, Nunnelly & wife, and to the heirs of Thomas Hicklin, deceased, and to Joseph Olive, Samuel Olive, Landon Armstrong & James Nevins & wife. Aaron Biggerstaff owes the estate. (Ibid 253)

HICKMAN, Edmond
Died before 14 March 1845 when a survey in the name of the heirs of Edmond Hickman was mentioned in a suit by The Bank of Tennessee vs Charles McAlister & others. (Obi TN, Cir Ct Min, 4/no#)

HICKMAN, Edmund
Died before 7 February 1806 when the heirs were shown on the delinquent tax list. (Rob TN, Co Ct Min, 1/384) He was shown as Edwin Hickman. (Ibid 393)

HICKMAN, Elizabeth
6 February 1865 James L. Haggard was appointed guardian with Joel Rudran & Daniel Kelly as security. (Sev TN, Co Ct Min, no#/135)

HICKMAN, Noah
Died before 3 August 1818 when Lemual Hickman was appointed administrator with Simon Hancock & Thos. S. Green as security. (Wil TN, Co Ct Min, no#/292)

HICKMAN, Thos.
Died before 7 November 1864 when a subpoena was issued for James Pollard and Fuqua Pollard to appear at next court to prove his will. (Sev TN, Co Ct Min, no#/127) The executor named failed to appear so David Keener was appointed administrator with the will annexed. (Ibid 145) 2 April 1866 Luticia Hickman was appointed guardian to the minor heirs, with H. Hickman & H. Mount as security. (Ibid 286) 10 April 1866 Humphrey Hickman vs Luticia Hickman and others, land was divided between Humphrey Hickman and the heirs of Thos. Hickman. (Ibid 316)

HICKS
14 February 1814 Thomas Lane made a settlement as guardian for Susan Hicks, James Hicks and Livina Hicks. (Rob TN, Co Ct Min, 3/359)

HICKS, Eliza Jane
20 February 1858 Geo. B. Hicks was appointed her trustee, as shown in the petition of Radford Withers, Geo. B. Hicks et als. (Mad TN, Ch Ct Min, 2/204) Eliza Jane was the daughter of one of the children of Saml. C. McClellan, deceased & entitled to 1/5. Geo. B. Hicks was appointed trustee in place of Radford Withers. There was also a suit of Radford Withers trustee vs Ben M. Hicks et als. (Ibid 209 & 210)

HIDE, Henry
Died before 9 February 1814 as shown in the suit of Richard Hyde Admr. of Henry Hide vs Ezekiel Cox & Nathan Skinner. (Ste TN, Co Ct Min, 4/99)

HIDER, Michael
Died before August term 1790 when the will was proved by Edmd. Williams, Robert English & Henry English. Elizabeth Hider and John Hider were executors. (Was TN, Co Ct Min, 1/456)

HIDER, Michieal
28 August 1778 took the oath of allegiance to this state. (Was TN, Co Ct Min, 1/46)

HIGGINBOTTOM, James [Higginbotham]
Died many years before 24 June 1840 when Christian Freeman & wife Eleanor, Nimrod Higginbottom & James Higginbottom who are minors and sue by their guardian Benjamin Phillips, and Jorden C. Holt & Herod F. Holt, executors of the will of Joshua Holt, deceased, and Jacob Albright and Abner Freeman, made petition. Nimrod Higginbottom was the father of complainants, Eleanor, James, Jr. & Nimrod. Joshua Holt was the guardian of the minors and sold the land to Jacob Allbright. Joshua Holt was the grand father of Eleanor Freeman & Nimrod & James Higginbottom, the last two of whom are still minors. (Bed TN, Ch Ct Min, 1/268)

HIGHSMITH, Daniel
Died before 16 February 1814 when Sukey Highsmith was appointed administratrix with William Fletcher & Isaac Morrow as security. (Rob TN, Co Ct Min, 3/374) The administratrix was shown as Susannah Highsmith. (Ibid 489)

HIGHTOWER, John
5 March 1866 Peter Headrick was appointed guardian to the minor heirs of John Hightower. (Sev TN, Co Ct Min, no#/279)

HILDRETH, P. M.
Died before 4 December 1867 as shown in the suit of R. Robinson vs the widow & heirs of P. M. Hildreth. Baily O. Bowden was appointed guardian ad litem of the minor heirs. (Fen TN, Ch Ct Min, A/349) The suit was shown as R. Roberson Admr. &c vs Lucinda Hildreth & others. A report was made of the assets of the estate of Pearce Hildreth. (Ibid 366)

HILDRETH, R. T.
Died before 31 July 1867 when his death was suggested in his suits against W. C. Wood and against James M. Wright. (Fen TN, Ch Ct Min, A/334) A suit was filed 4 December 1868 by Mary Hildreth and E. L. Gardenshire Admr. &c vs Isaac Stockton. Isaac Stockton had purchased of the intestate during his lifetime, in 1858, a "cardin machine" and has paid for same. Respondant is indebted to complainants for $50 for professional services rendered by the intestate, R. T. Hildreth, for respondant Stockton. (Ibid 422)

HILL, Chas.
Was an orphan boy aged 6 years when Michl. Bacon was ordered to take charge of him in February 1779. (Was TN, Co Ct Min, 1/62)

HILL, E. G.
Died before 5 June 1871 when B. L. Thomas made a settlement as administrator. (Dyr TN, Co Ct Min, B/243)

HILL, George
Died before 12 February 1859 as shown in the suit of John Fowler against Ruben Hill & Franklin Fowler & John W. Meadows Executors &c. The last two named were executors of George Hill, deceased. Negroes are to be sold to pay the debt of George Hill to John Fowler. (Jac TN, Ch Ct Min, C/210)

HILL, Jas. C.
Died before May term 1834 as shown in the suit of Samuel Crockett, administrator of Jas. C. Hill, deceased vs Charles McAlister. (Obi TN, Cir Ct Min, 2/163)

HILL, Jessee
1 October 1860 was charged with Bastardy. A motion was made to quash the proceedings. (Sev TN, Co Ct Min, no#/605) George Russell & William J. Chambers gave bond for the support of the female child born of Rachal Jane Chambers. (Ibid 607)

HILL, John
With his wife, Judith, sold land in Pitsylvania county, VA, 22 June 1807. (Wil TN, Co Ct Min, no#/292)

HILL, John
Died before 18 June 1816 when Edward Proctor was appointed guardian of Mary Hill, Thomas Hill, Braxton Hill, Patsy Hill, Polly Hill and John Hill, minor heirs, with Allan Ross & Thomas Proctor as security. (Wil TN, Co Ct Min, no#/16) William Walker & Amos Hill were administrators. (Ibid 162) On motion to divide the real estate among the several heirs, Edmund Proctor & Zachariah Davis, guardians, admit notice on the part of their wards. Allen Hill by letter admits notice. (Ibid 169)

HILL, M. G.
Died before 8 March 1870 when J. J. Hill was appointed administrator, with H. M. Grier & W. A. Slayden as security. (Dyr TN, Co Ct Min, B/13)

HILL, M. R.
Died before 3 January 1871 when his signature was proved as witness to the will of Thomas C. Mitchell. (Dyr TN, Co Ct Min, B/160)

HILL, Randal
Died before 3 February 1857 when a settlement was made with James Toomey, guardian of Elizabeth S. Hill, minor heir. (Sev TN, Co Ct Min, no#/124) 1 November 1858 suit was brought by W. F. Nichols & Geo. W. T. Hill, next friends of Sarah Hill, minor heir of Randal Hill, deceased. The suit is to remove James Toomey as guardian for Sarah, as Toomey has let her estate go to waste & failed to attend to her education. (Ibid 361)

HILL, Robert
Died before 1 January 1866 when Sarah A. Hill was appointed administratrix with N. B. Pate and Wm. M. Roberts as security. (Sev TN, Co Ct Min, no#/259) Sarah A. was the widow. (Ibid 278)

HILL, Robert W.
Was a resident of Maury County, TN, in 1831 as shown in the suit of James Edwards vs Robert Hill, Lydia Hill & Silas Crafton. Lydia was the mother of Robert Hill. Silas Crafton had been a resident of Maury County but now lived in the Western District. The suit of James Edwards was filed in 1837 regarding title to land. (Bed TN, Ch Ct Min, 1/127)

HILL, Sarah E.
2 January 1860 Jesse Stafford was appointed guardian with W. F. Nichols, Jesse Hill, G. M. Henderson & J. L. Trotter as security. (Sev TN, Co Ct Min, no#/499) 5 March 1860 Sarah petitioned by her next friend Eli Fox to remove Jesse Stafford as her guardian. The petition was dismissed. (Ibid 522) Sarah E. Hill was a minor heir of Randle Hill, deceased, as shown 1 May 1865. (Ibid 155)

HILL, Sarah H.
8 January 1857 her guardian, James Toomey, was ordered to renew his bond as the original one was destroyed. (Sev TN, Co Ct Min, no#/120)

HILL, Thomas
Was a minor heir of John Hill, deceased, as shown when he was bound 3 November 1818 to Obediah G. Finly for 5 years & 8 months. (Wil TN, Co Ct Min, no#/345)

HILL, William
Died before 21 February 1838 when land was taxed to the heirs. (Obi TN, Cir Ct Min, 3/161)

HIME, David
Was a minor when he was sued at a prior court and his guardian was not notified. The judgement to Jordan C. Holt against David Hime is to be set aside, 24 February 1845. (Bed TN, Ch Ct Min, 2/323)

HIME, John
Died before 24 September 1844 as shown in the suit of William Hime vs James Christian. Land had descended to the wife of James Christian from the estate of her father, John Hime. The wife of said Christian was under 21 years of age and lacks more that 2 years of reaching her majority. Christian is about to remove from the county. (Bed TN, Ch Ct Min, 3/240)

HIME, Mary Ann
Was the mother of Daniel K. Hime as shown in the suit of Moses Neely vs Daniel K. Hime filed 11 September 1841. (Bed TN, Ch Ct Min, 1/493)

HINES, Thomas   [Hynes]
Died between 15 July 1826 & 10 September 1827. He made his will 15 July 1826 and died in Chester District, SC. The will was proved 10 September 1827 in Chester District. He left a negro to his daughter, Ellener, during her life & at her death to his grand daughter, Harriet. At the time of making the will he had 2 grand daughters named Harriet, the one Harriet an illegitimate daughter of Elliner Hines. The other grand daughter, Harriet, was a legitimate daughter of Ingnatius Hines, a son of the testator. Ellener Hines removed from Chester District, SC, and settled in Madison County, TN, & brought with her the said negro, Silvy. Ellenir Hines died in 1849. While with Ellenir, Silvy had 5 children. After the death of Ellener Hines, E. F. Ferguson & Cyrus G. McCrory removed 4 of the negroes to MS & there disposed of them. Ferguson & McCrory returned from MS and sold the other child of Silvy to Ralph McKinney of Carroll County. Harriet Hines, daughter of Ignatius Hines, died intestate in SC in the lifetime of Ellener Hines. Turner J. Morgan was appointed administrator for Harriet Hines in TN in August 1855, and has a valid interest in the said negroes. (Mad TN, Ch Ct Min, 2/327 & 415)

HINTON
6 February 1871 A. T. Fielder renewed his bond as guardian of Mollie Hinton and J. A. Hinton. (Dyr TN, Co Ct Min, B/183)

HIX, Vines
Died before 11 May 1812 when Thomas Lanes made a report as guardian of the orphans. (Rob TN, Co Ct Min, 3/76)

HOARD, Stanwin   [Stanwix?]
Died before 3 December 1827 when the slaves were to be divided between the widow & heirs. (McM TN, Co Ct Min, 2no#/244) [Also see Hord]

HOBBY, Hardy
Died before 8 February 1854 when his death was suggested in the suit of Holland Denton & Hardy Hobby vs John Burrus. The suit was revived in the name of the administrator, Travis G. Hobby. (Jac TN, Ch Ct Min, B/112)

HOBBY, Mary
Was granted a divorce from Hardy Hobby on 19 March 1852. (Jac TN, Ch Ct Min, B/33)

HOBDAN, Jeannette
1 June 1874 her guardian, B. F. Prichard, resigned. She was formerly Jeannette Boon. S. M. Hobdan was chosen and appointed her guardian. (Dyr TN, Co Ct Min, B/740)

HODGE, A.
Died before 6 February 1871 when F. W. Hodge renewed his bond as guardian of the minor heirs. (Dyr TN, Co Ct Min, B/181) The name was shown as Andy Hodge. (Ibid 190)

HODGE, Wm.
3 May 1819 was bound to Wm. Hartsfield until age 21. (Wil TN, Co Ct Min, no#/436)

HODGES, E.
Died before October term 1852 when Saml Pickens was appointed administrator with the will annexed. The administrator's bond was destroyed by fire. Saml. Pickens appeared 7 July 1856 & made new bond with W. C. Pickens and Jos. M. Evos as security. (Sev TN, Co Ct Min, no#/51)

HODGES, Edmond
Died before 2 May 1864 when John Kelly, George Wade & Wm. Wayland were appointed to set off a years support to Mary Hodges, widow. (Sev TN, Co Ct Min, no#/104) David McCroskey was appointed administrator. (Ibid 107)

HODGES, Edmond
Died before 7 September 1857 when Saml. W. Randles produced a certified copy of his will. The original will had been destroyed by fire. (Sev TN, Co Ct Min, no#/199)

HODGES, H. G.
Died before January term 1855 when Saml. Pickens was appointed administrator. The administrator's bond was destroyed by fire so Saml. Pickens appeared 7 July 1856 and gave a new bond with W. C. Pickens as security. (Sev TN, Co Ct Min, no#/51)

HODGES, James
Died before 6 October 1807 when the administrator was given permission to sell negroes from the estate. (Rob TN, Co Ct Min, 1/464) Administration was granted to Hiram Hodges with Nathan Yoes & John Yoes his security. (Ibid 466) 7 July 1808 Drury Hodges was shown as the administrator. (Ibid 2/61)

HODGES, James R.
Died before 4 July 1864 when John Kelly, J. W. Ellis and J. C. Johnson were appointed to lay off a years support to the widow, Martha M. Hodges. (Sev TN, Co Ct Min, no#/113) The widow was shown as Malissa M. Hodges. Martha M. Hodges was appointed administratrix with B. C. Andes as security. (Ibid 117) 4 February 1867 Martha M. Hodges was appointed guardian to the minor heirs. (Ibid 428)

HODGES, Jas. C.
Died before 17 September 1816 when the administrator was ordered to make a report. (Wil TN, Co Ct Min, no#/34) Hannah Hodges was administratrix. (Ibid 55) 3 May 1819 James Williams was appointed special guardian for the minor heirs to attend their interest in an allotment of dower. (Ibid 440) Hannah was the widow. (Ibid 470)

HODGES, William
2 November 1818 was shown to be the father of a bastard child by Elizabeth Hubbard & he was ordered to pay $25 to her, $5 now & $5 annually until the whole is paid. (Wil TN, Co Ct Min, no#/330)

HODGES, William
Died before 7 October 1856 when Sarah Hodges renewed her bond as guardian to Martha R., Nancy S., and Mary J. Hodges, minor heirs. Wm. E. Hodges and E. Hodges were securities. (Sev TN, Co Ct Min, no#/84)

HODSDEN, Robt. H.
Died before 4 July 1864 when a Trustee of Nancy Academy was appointed to fill the vacancy occasioned by his death. (Sev TN, Co Ct Min, no#/110) His will was proved by Lemuel Bogart, one of the witnesses. (Ibid 128) 6 February 1866 Mary Hodsden was ordered to appear & give security as executrix of the last will & testament of R. H. Hodsden, deceased. (Ibid 276)

HOGAN, Humphrey
Died before 22 January 1802 when the heirs were shown on the delinquent tax list. (Rob TN, Co Ct Min, 1/206)

HOGG, Guilford
Died before 2 November 1818 when James Stewart, Esqr. was appointed administrator, with Charles Blalock & Saml. Motheral as security. (Wil TN, Co Ct Min, no#/330) The name was shown as Gifford Hogg. (Ibid 395)

HOGGE, James [Hogue]
Died before 22 February 1837 when the charge against him for Assault & Battery with intent to kill & murder was abated because of his death. (Obi TN, Cir Ct Min, 3/97) The administrator, Samuel Hutchinson, resigned and Charles McAlister? was appointed administrator. (Ibid 173)

HOGGE, John B.
Died before 11 March 1844 when land was taxed to the heirs. (Obi TN, Cir Ct Min, 4/no#)

HOGIN, Catron C.
On 12 July 1850 was granted a divorce from William C. Hogin. They were married in Jackson County in January 1847. "Before and after his marriage with complainant the defendant was afflicted with luise Veneri? in such manner as rendered it highly improper for complainant to live and cohabit with him." They have a son aged between 2 and 3 years named Anthony Wayne Hagin and complainant is allowed to keep said child until he arrive at the age of 10 years. The defendant is to have visitation rights. The name of complainant is changed from Catron C. Hogin to Catron C. Sadler. (Jac TN, Ch Ct Min, A/372)

HOGIN, Edward
Died before 14 November 1844 as shown in the suit of William Buchanan & wife vs James, Matthew, Simon Hogen & others, heirs at law of Edward Hogin Decd. & Matthew C. Hogin Admr. de bonus non. Edward Hogin died in 1838 leaving a will. Rebecca Hogin, the widow, and Anthony Hogin were executors. Both executors have died and Matthew C. Hogin was appointed administrator with will annexed and also administrator of Rebecca Hogin. James Hogin has departed this life and the complainants & defendants [are] the heirs of Rebecca and James and also of Sally [Sarah] Hogin who also departed this life. Complainant and wife are to be made equal with the balance of the legatees. (Jac TN, Ch Ct Min, A/177) The wife of William Buchanan was Jane. Advancements had been made to them from the estate of Edward Hogin. The amount given in the will of Edward Hogin to his daughter Jane Buchanan, is to go at her death to her son John. William Buchanan is an improvident man so Jane's share is to be settled on her exclusively and then to her son John. Elvis Taylor & Rawlings Hogin were security for Matthew C. Hogin, administrator. Daniel Hogin was mentioned. (Ibid 256) 28 July 1847 in the suit of John Scanland vs Isaac Hogin and Matthew C. Hogin it is stated that Isaac Hogan is indebted to John Scanland. Isaac has funds coming from the estates of Edward Hogan and Sarah Hogin. He is intitled to 1/13 part from the sale of the estate of Sarah Hogin which is to be attached for the debt. (Ibid 264) Sale was made of the estate of Rebecca & Sarah Hogin. There are 13 heirs of Rebecca & Sarah, to wit: Rawlings Hogin, Martha Shaw, Jane Buchanan, Matthew C. Hogin, Richard Hogin, Elvis Taylor & wife, Daniel Hogin, Isaac Hogin, William C. Hogin, Anthony Hogin's children, Ira Cowan's children, Simon Hogin's Estate and James Hogin's Estate. John Hughes is the administrator of the estate of James Hogin, deceased, & Rawlings is administrator of the estate of Simon Hogin, deceased. (Ibid 278-80)

HOGUE, Burrel H.
Died before 3 March 1829 when his will was proved by R. J. Meigs & Horace Hickase, witnesses. (McM TN, Co Ct Min, 2no#/346) Nathaniel Smith & James F. Bradford were executors. (Ibid 353) 8 September 1829 Mary Jane Houge, minor heir of Burrel H. Houge, chose William Hogan as her guardian, she being over 14. W. Hogan was also appointed guardian of Amanda Houge, who was not old enough to choose. (Ibid 387)

HOLDEN, Joshua
Was a non-resident of TN 2 April 1839 as shown in the suit of James G. Whitney vs John W. Gardner. Holden was believed to be in the state of AL. (Bed TN, Ch Ct Min, 1/236)

HOLDER, James
Died before 6 June 1864 when Wm. Inmans, Wm. Williams & James Williams were appointed to lay off a years support to Catherine Holder, the widow. (Sev TN, Co Ct Min, no#/105)

HOLDER, Wm.
1 October 1866 Asa Hurst was appointed guardian to Wm. Holder, a minor, with David Hurst as security. (Sev TN, Co Ct Min, no#/377)

HOLEMAN
James Holeman & David Holeman were residents of Rowan County, NC, 25 February 1808 when their depositions were to be taken for the defendant in the suit of John Rogers against James Durrum. Also the depositions of David Hickenson and his wife Sarah Hickenson were to be taken in Wilks County, NC. (Cla TN, Co Ct Min, 3/175)

HOLLADAY, Stephen
Died before 4 May 1842 when his death was admitted in the suit of James Young et ux vs Brice M. Draper et al. Stephen Holladay was one of the defendants and the suit was revived in the name of Henrietta Holladay & Brice M. Draper, his executors. (Jac TN, Ch Ct Min, A/43)

HOLLAND, Danl.
Died before 19 October 1801 when Elisabeth Holland was appointed administratrix with Wm. Stark & John Powers as security. (Rob TN, Co Ct Min, 1/188) 3 February 1806 Thomas Woodward was appointed guardian of the orphan children with Martin Duncan & Noah Woodward as security. (Ibid 375) 7 July 1808 Elisabeth Taylor was shown as administratrix. (Ibid 2/62) 11 May 1812 400 acres of land was allotted to Elizabeth Taylor, late widow of Daniel Holland, deceased. (Ibid 3/80)

HOLLAND, Edward
Died before 6 November 1871 when B. F. Prichard was appointed administrator, with B. C. Smith and W. B. Smith as his security. (Dyr TN, Co Ct Min, B/315) The name was shown as Edmond Holland. (Ibid 366)

HOLLAND, Needham
Died before 12 March 1845 as shown in the suit of Lemuel Holland Admr. of Needham Holland Decd. vs Thomas E. Page. (Obi TN, Cir Ct Min, 4/no#)

HOLLAND, Preston
Died before 6 April 1874 when W. H. Hendricks was appointed administrator, with N. P. Tatum and J. F. Dicky as his security. (Dyr TN, Co Ct Min, B/713) N. Coker, O. R. Robbins and J. F. Dickey were appointed to set off a years allowance for the widow and family. (Ibid 737)

HOLLAWAY, Chas.
Died before 5 August 1783 when John Hollaway obtained leave of administration on the estate, with James Ray & Jeremiah Terrill as his security. (Was TN, Co Ct Min, 1/220)

HOLLIS, James
Was a resident of Murry County [no state given] 15 February 1810 when his deposition was to be taken for the defendant in the case of Saml. Henly & wife vs Henry Mahon. (Rob TN, Co Ct Min, 2/232)

HOLLIS, Samuel
Died before 10 May 1813 when Isaac Hollis & Nancy Hollis were granted letters of administration. Wilson Crockett and James Strother were security. (Rob TN, Co Ct Min, 3/234) 12 May 1814 James Strother was appointed special guardian of William T. Hollis, James S. Hollis, Elizabeth Hollis, Wilson L. Hollis, orphans of Samuel Hollis, deceased. (Ibid 421)

HOLLOWELL, S. S.
Died before 1 June 1874 when Jo. Hollowell made a settlement as executor. (Dyr TN, Co Ct Min, B/737)

HOLLOWMAN, Lewis M.
Died before 14 July 1855 when his death was suggested in his suit against White Myers & others. (Jac TN, Ch Ct Min, B/273) William Q. Hughs was administrator. (Ibid 287) In the suit of White Myers & others vs Elizabeth & Susan Hollowman, it was stated the defendants are in possession of the land mentioned and are suffering the same "to delapedate." All of said land is to be rented out except the widow's dower. (Ibid C/71) A suit was entered 12 February 1859 by White Myers and wife Julia, John M. Sherly and Louisa, Benjamin D. Holliman, Samuel S. Holliman, John W. Holliman, Penelope Holliman, Robert Gilliland and wife Sarah, William H. Roberts and Jane Roberts by their guardian William Roberts, Milton Young and wife Martha, [blank] Mathis and wife Nancy vs Jefferson A. Thomas & wife [blank], Elijah B. Holliman, Oliver Richardson & wife Mary, Nancy R. Carter, Eliza Carter, Elizabeth D. Holliman, Susan Holliman, Ann Eliza Shumaker, James G. Holliman, Albert H. Ross and wife Susan Holliman and Oliver Richardson. The administrator of the estate of Lewis M. Holliman was mentioned. Lewis M. Holliman had purchased land at the sale of the estate of James A. Manian? Susan Holliman is the widow of Lewis M. Holliman and is entitled to dower. (Ibid 207)

HOLLY, John
Died before 4 November 1782 when the administratrix, Elizabeth Holly, received the inventory of the estate. (Was TN, Co Ct Min, 1/180) The administratrix is to keep the estate in her hands until the orphans of John Holly come regularly of age. (Ibid 183)

HOLMES, Benjamin D.
Died before 6 February 1856 as shown in the suit of Samuel B. Holmes, Welcome Butler & wife Sarah, Sylvanus C. Holmes, James Holmes & Adeline Holmes the last by their next friend Alexander Martins vs John N. Gates. John N. Gates had sold land to Benjamin D. Holmes in 1843. The money was paid to said Gates by Benjamin D. Holmes in his lifetime. He has since departed this life leaving Samuel B., Sarah, Sylvanus C., James & Adeline Holmes his only children. Sarah has married Welcome Butler. They sue for title to the land. (Jac TN, Ch Ct Min, B/286) In the suit of Alexander Masters vs Samuel B. M. Holmes it is stated that Benjamin D. Holmes died in Jackson County about 184_ [last digit blank]. Samuel B. M. Holmes is one of the children of Benjamin D. Holmes & entitled to 1/5 of the land. (Ibid 299)

HOLMES, Mary M.
Died after having made her last will and testament 24 May 1851. She left slaves to Julia A. McBride, wife of Archibald McBride. Jno. R. Alston is administrator with the will annexed. Archibald McBride is insolvent and if the slaves come under his control will be sold to pay his debts. Julia A. McBride sued by her next friend Wm. M. McBride to have the slaves declared her sole property for the support of herself and children. (Mad TN, Ch Ct Min, 1/360)

HOLMES, S. B. M.
Was a non-resident of TN on 13 July 1855 as shown in the suit of Alexander Martin vs S. B. M. Holmes. (Jac TN, Ch Ct Min, B/261)

HOLT
28 November 1808 a jury was appointed to inquire into the age, situation and infirmities of Francis and Martha Holt. (Cla TN, Co Ct Min, 3/235)

HOLT, Hiram
Was the brother of Herod F. Holt as shown in the suit of William S. Jett & Hillery Mosely vs Hiram Holt & Minos Cannon filed 22 January 1841. (Bed TN, Ch Ct Min, 1/457) Hiram Holt is a citizen of AL. (Ibid 490)

HOLT, Irby
Died before 2 March 1829 when Sarah Holt & James Ragan were appointed administrators. (McM TN, Co Ct Min, 2no#/333) 3 March 1829 William Hogan, John Miller & Nathl. Smith were appointed to lay off a years support to the widow, Sarah Holt. (Ibid 346) 6 March 1829, Robert Holt & Emily Holt, being over 14 but under 21, chose James Ragan as their guardian. Jane, Fanny, Serenna J., Thomas W. & Francis A. Holt are minors under the age of 14 & James H. Ragan was appointed guardian for them. (Ibid 353) 3 March 1830, the petition of Sarah Holt for dower states Irby Holt died 12 January 1829. (Ibid 441)

HOLT, Jordon C.
Died before 12 September 1854 when his widow, Julia R. Holt, and his children, Nimrod B. Holt, Adam A. Holt and Nancy E. Holt, minors, sold land and invested the proceeds in the state of MS. Julia was executrix. (Mad TN, Ch Ct Min, 2/12)

HOLT, Larkin
Died before 30 June 1842 when his death was admitted in the suit of William D. Orr vs James McKisick & others. Holt had been one of the defendants. (Bed TN, Ch Ct Min, 2/191)

HOLT, Turner J. [or C.]
23 February 1859 the following suit was entered: Alfred E. Whitworth, Eliza P. Holt, Augustus B. Alston & wife Judy Frances, Ann Eliza Holt, Jas T. Holt, Jacob H. Holt, Alfred E. Holt, Garland A. Holt & Wm. G. Holt, the last eight minors who sue by their guardian & next friend Eliza P. Holt vs Jno. T. Lovelace & Turner J. Holt. On 26 March 1846 Thos. E. Whitworth, the brother of Eliza P. Holt, executed a deed of trust in Amelia County, VA, to Alfred E. Whitworth as trustee, 2 negro slaves, Milly & Matilda, to hold said negroes & their increase for the sole benefit of Eliza P. Holt, the wife of Turner C. Holt, and her children. In 1848 Milly gave birth to a male child named Henderson & that afterward said Holt & his family emigrated to Madison County, TN. On 24 March 1853 Turner C. Holt sold said Henderson to defendant Lovelace. The sale is void and Henderson is to be returned to Eliza P. and her children. (Mad TN, Ch Ct Min, 2/261)

HOMES, Robt.
Died before 21 February 1839 when land was taxed to the heirs. (Obi TN, Cir Ct Min, 3/302)

HOOD, Brison
Was an orphan boy 12 years old on the 16th of April 1825. He was bound to Wm. R. Tucker on 6 December 1825 until age 21 to learn the trade of a blacksmith. (McM TN, Co Ct Min, 2no#/118) 4 September 1827 Bryson Hood was bound as an apprentice to Joel K. Brown to learn the Tayloring trade. (Ibid 237)

HOOD, Wm.
Died before 21 October 1803 when his heirs were on the delinquent tax list. (Rob TN, Co Ct Min, 1/278)

HOOD, Wm. H.
Died before 8 October 1872 when his widow, Martha S. Hood, was appointed administratrix, with T. L. Hamilton and Smith Parks as security. (Dyr TN, Co Ct Min, B/485) Suit to set aside the administration was brought by C. H. Hood vs Martha S. Hood. (Ibid 575) The suit stated that W. H. Hood died in 1871 and at the time of his death was a resident of Gibson County, TN. C. H. Hood was appointed administrator by the Gibson County Court in September 1871. The letters of administration issued by Dyer County to Martha S. Hood were therefore revoked. (Ibid 586)

HOOPER, Absolam, Sr.
Was a resident of Davidson County [no state given] 15 February 1810 when a deposition was to be taken for the defendant in the case of Saml. Henley & wife vs Henry Mahon. (Rob TN, Co Ct Min, 2/232)

HOOPER, James
Died sometime before April 1837 as shown in the suit of Washington Short against Judah Hooper. James Hooper left a will in which he gave negroes to his wife, Judah, and the remainder to his three sons, George, William and Joseph Hooper. Washington Short purchased the interest of William & George Hooper. Judah Hooper is about to remove to MO. The will of James Hooper was shown. The son William's wife was Elizabeth Hooper. (Bed TN, Ch Ct Min, 1/317)

HOOPER, Miles
2 January 1860 was released from paying poll tax as there is no [such] person in this county chargable with a poll tax. (Sev TN, Co Ct Min, no#/494)

HOOPER, Phillip
Was a base born child aged 12 years or thereabouts when he was bound to William Stephenson until age 21, February term 1789. (Was TN, Co Ct Min, 1/361)

HOPKINS, Charlotte
5 October 1808, on the oath of Joel Lewis, Charlotte was shown to be under 21 years of age and has sustained injury from Henry Fiser which requires a Suit at Law to redress. She applies to have Joel Lewis act for her in said suit. (Rob TN, Co Ct Min, 2/93)

HOPKINS, Thomas
Died before 21 February 1838 when land was taxed to the heirs. (Obi TN, Cir Ct Min, 3/164)

HOPSON, Joseph
Died before 4 May 1818 when Nicholas Hobson, one of the executors, qualified. (Wil TN, Co Ct Min, no#/246)

HORD, Str [Stanwix]
Died before 4 December 1826 when William Weaver was appointed administrator. (McM TN, Co Ct Min, 2no#/181) Robert W. McClary, Joseph Cobbs & Henry Bradford were appointed to lay off a years provisions to the widow, Betsy Hord, & family. (Ibid 182) 2 March 1830 a report was made which mentions money paid to Eldridge Howard, guardian of the minor heirs of Stanwix Hord, deceased. Thomas was also one of the administrators. (Ibid 437) [Also see Hoard]

HORNBACK, Anny
Made a deed of gift 10 February 1817 to John Franklin Hornback and Nancy, sister of the said John, his? [her] son and daughter. [Handwriting is very bad]. The deed was for animals and was witnessed by Reuben Harper, Jr. and Richard Harper. (Cla TN, Co Ct Min, 4/289)

HORNE, HENRY
Married before 12 October 1857 to Elizabeth Chamberlain as shown in the suit of Elizabeth Chamberlain vs Rufus M. Mason et als. The interest of Elizabeth Chamberlain in the estate of Chas. Chamberlain, deceased, was divested out of her & vested in Rufus M. Mason. (Mad TN, Ch Ct Min, 2/208)

HORTON, George
Died before 3 May 1815 when Thomas Wyatt was appointed administrator with James Wyatt & Abram Wyatt as security. (Ste TN, Co Ct Min, 4/285)

HOUGHTON, Joshua, Sr.
3 November 1783 recorded a deed of gift to Joshua Houghton, Jr. proved by Thomas Houghton, Esquire. (Was TN, Co Ct Min, 1/226)

HOUGHTON, Thomas, Esqr.
5 February 1784 Landon Carter gave other security as administrator on the estate of John Carter, as Thomas Houghton, Esqr., his present security, is about to remove out of this State. (Was TN, Co Ct Min, 1/238)

HOUK, John
Died before 1 August 1864. (Sev TN, Co Ct Min, no#/115) Joshua H. Atchley, James Maples & Wm. Ellis were appointed to lay off a years support to the widow, Nancy Houk, & family. Jordan Houk & John McMahan, Jr. were appointed administrators. (Ibid 118)

HOUSE, Duke [House, Green D.]
Died in Bedford County in 1821, as shown in the suit of John & James House vs Simms & McIntosh. The will was shown by which he made bequests to his wife, Susan House, and his two sons, Jack & James. He mentioned his mother-in-law's estate. His wife & John Sims were named executors. The two sons were minors. At the time of the suit, 2 July 1839, Jack House was a citizen of Hot Springs County, AR, and James House was a citizen of Logan County, KY, John Simms was a citizen of Bedford County, TN, & John McIntosh & wife Susan, of Robertson County, TN. The widow, Susan, married John McIntosh & moved some 16 years ago. John Simms has sold the land. Jack & James have but recently arrived at the age of 21, "one 18 months since & Junior about 1 month." Leonard P. Sims was the son of John Simms. (Bed TN, Ch Ct Min, 1/282)

HOUSE, Jacob
Died before 24 June 1805 when the will was proved by Nathan Nall & Ewel Williams. (Wil TN, Co Ct Min, no#/123)

HOUSEMAN, Nancy
Was a base born daughter of Caty Houseman and on 3 September 1804 she was bound to Thomas Cunningham until she arrives at age 18. Said Cunningham enters into bond to support said Nancy and give her 18 months of schooling when she is between the ages of 9 and 14. (Cla TN, Co Ct Min, 2/61) 2 June 1806 Nancy Houseman was given back to the custody of her mother. (Ibid 250) Nancy Houseman, daughter of Catherine Houseman, was bound on 3 September 1806 to Bluford Woodall untill she arrive to the

age of 18 years. The said Bluford Woodall will "learn or cause to be learned the said Orphan to read good english, will likewise at the expiration of eighteen years will pay to the said orphan two good commendable suits of clothes and also will keep her the said Nancy in decent good order during said Term of eighteen years." (Ibid 3/14)

HOUSER
4 July 1864 Mordica Morgan was appointed guardian of Hellen E. Houser and William Houser, minor orphans. (Sev TN, Co Ct Min, no#/109)

HOUSMAN, Susannah
Was the mother of a bastard child by Saml. Chamberlian, who was ordered to pay support for the child for 5 years, 5 May 1819. (Wil TN, Co Ct Min, no#/456)

HOUSTON, Abner
13 February 1839, in the suit of John and Jacob Forsythe vs Benjamin Williams trustee & others, it was stated that Abner Houston, one half of the defendants, had absconded & left the state. (Bed TN, Ch Ct Min, 2/49) Abner Houston & Henry B. Kelsey are said to be residents of the Republic of Texas. (Ibid 73)

HOUSTON, James
Died before 28 June 1841 as shown in the suit of James Houston vs Haynes & Ramsey Executors of Christopher Houston. The suit was revived in the name of Benjamin F. Houston, administrator of James Houston, deceased. (Bed TN, Ch Ct Min, 2/135) Defendants were James S. Haynes and John Ramsey. (Ibid 227)

HOWARD, A. J.
8 March 1870 E. M. Hall made a settlement as guardian of A. J. Howard's heirs. (Dyr TN, Co Ct Min, B/16) 2 February 1874 H. W. McGavock was chosen and appointed guardian of Joanna McGavock, formerly Johanna Howard, minor heir of A. J. Howard, deceased. (Ibid 705)

HOWARD, Henry
6 July 1857 was released from paying poll tax for 1857 because he is over the age of 50. (Sev TN, Co Ct Min, no#/176)

HOWARD, Mathew
Died before 7 March 1859 when Barbara Howard vs the heirs, petitioned for dower. Notice is to be given to Madison Howard, Lewis Howard, Saml. McMahan, Patsy McMahan & John Fraim. (Sev TN, Co Ct Min, no#/410)

HOWARD, Tilman A. [or Lilman A.]
Died before 7 August 1865 when Lewis Howard was appointed administrator with D. W. Howard as security. (Sev TN, Co Ct Min, no#/193) A years provision was set off to E. L. Howard, widow and family of L. A. Howard. (Ibid 204)

HOWELL
Power of Attorney was given by Wm. Adams, Nancy P. Howell, Susannah Howell by Wm. Adams guardian, to John Howell. It was proven by John Hutchison & Archer Cheatham, 7 July 1809. (Rob TN, Co Ct Min, 2/166)

HOWELL, A. S.
Died before 7 June 1870 when W. W. Beasley made a settlement as guardian of the minor heirs. (Dyr TN, Co Ct Min, B/69)

HOWELL, Abner
Died before 7 July 1809 when it was ordered that Jacob Binkley, Esqr., Richd. M. Howell & Joel Ragsdale divide the negroes belonging to the heirs of Abner Howell, deceased. (Rob TN, Co Ct Min, 2/167)

HOWELL, James
Made a deed of gift to William Howell 5 February 1811. (Ste TN, Co Ct Min, 3/37)

HOWELL, Paul
Died before 4 February 1813 when John Lee was appointed administrator with Benjamin Edwards and John Davidson as security. (Ste TN, Co Ct Min, 4/22)

HOWSER
3 September 1866 Green B. Nations was appointed guardian to Lemuel, Sylvester & J.

W. Howser, minors, with D. W. Reagan & R. R. Reagan as security. (Sev TN, Co Ct Min, no#/367)

HUBBARD, Elizabeth
Was the mother of a bastard child by William Hodges. 2 November 1818 he was ordered to pay her $25. (Wil TN, Co Ct Min, no#/330)

HUBBARD, Littleton G.
Died in February 1838 as shown in a statement made 21 June 1842 by Mary Hubbard, the widow of Littleton G. Hubbard. He departed this life in the Southern part of MS or AL while on a tour for the benefit of his health in the month of February 1838. His usual place of residence and the home of his family was near Lexington in Holmes County, MS. He had sold lots in Lexington to Richd. W. Gardner, and Mary Hubbard releases her right of dower in said lots. (Obi TN, Cir Ct Min, 4/no#)

HUBBARD, William
Probably died before 1 November 1813 when John Atkins, Jr. was appointed overseer of the road in the room of William Hubbard [and I think the word "deceased' was added.] (Ste TN, Co Ct Min, 4/65) The inventory of the estate of Wm. Hubbard, deceased, was returned by the executor, 7 February 1814. (Ibid 89) Dudley Williams and Sally Hubbard were executors. (Ibid 94)

HUBBART, William
Died before 2 November 1813 when the will was proved by Henry Pugh and Jesse Gilbert. (Ste TN, Co Ct Min, 4/68)

HUCCABY, Thomas
12 November 1810 was bound to Abraham Young. (Rob TN, Co Ct Min, 2/314)

HUDDLESTON, Daniel [David]
Died before 7 February 1856 as shown in the suit of John M. Clark vs Pleasant F. Huddleson, administrator of Daniel Huddleston, deceased. (Jac TN, Ch Ct Min, B/289)

HUDDLESTON, Elam
Died before 31 July 1867 as shown in the suit of Artema Huddleston vs R. Hurst et als. The minor heirs of Elam Huddleston, deceased, are to be made defendants to this suit and C. J. Sawyer was appointed guardian ad litem. (Fen TN, Ch Ct Min, A/327) Elijah Clark was the regular guardian of the minors. (Ibid 372)

HUDDLESTON, John
13 November 1815 was to be let to the lowest bidder to take care of him until next term, whereas Walter Evans undertakes the support of him for $12.00. (Cla TN, Co Ct Min, 4/120) He was let to John Huddleston, Esqr. in 1816. (Ibid 156)

HUDDLESTON, Thomas
Died before 3 December 1868 as shown in the suit of R. A. Winningham vs Thomas B. Huddleston Admr. & others. The suit came to be heard upon bills & answers of Tho. Huddleston, J. G. Huddleston and guardian ad litem of the minor heirs. Respondants Tennessee Huddleston, James Amonett [Amorett], William Amonett, Willis Amonett, Mary A. Amonett, Artema Amonett, Eliza Brown and Jackson Brown and Eliza Mungoloe have been served with process & have failed to answer. In the report there is a statement about the assets wasted by Thomas Huddleston and by Green Huddleston. There are no personal assets of the estate of Thomas Huddleston, deceased, to satisfy the debts. Thomas B. Huddleston and Joel G. Huddleston have committed waste. Land is to be sold. (Fen TN, Ch Ct Min, A/418)

HUDDLESTON, William
Died before 8 November 1813 when John Huddleston & William Huddleston were appointed administrators, with James Perry & Peter Frey as security. (Rob TN, Co Ct Min, 3/316) 16 February 1814 Elizabeth Huddleston, the widow, petitioned for dower. Notice was given to John Huddleston, William Huddleston, David Huddleston, James Huddleston, James Campbell, Elizabeth Sellers, Jonathan Huddleston, Sarah Barr & Polly Crunk. (Ibid 379)

HUDGINS, James
Died before 16 November 1814 when Edward Hudgins was appointed administrator with James Maxy & William Hudgins as security. (Rob TN, Co Ct Min, 3/502) Susanna Hudgins was appointed guardian of Rebecah Hudgins & Sally Hudgins, orphans of

James Hudgins, with Edward Hudgins and William Hudgins as security. (Ibid 506) Dower was laid off to the widow, Susanna Hudgins. (Ibid 544)

HUDSON, George
Died before 1 September 1856 when Joel Hudson, one of the executors, presented a certified copy of the will, the original will having been destroyed. (Sev TN, Co Ct Min, no#/70)

HUDSON, James
Died before 8 May 1815 when John Hodges and John Hudson were appointed administrators with Thomas Hodges and Ralph Shelton as security. (Cla TN, Co Ct Min, 4/38)

HUEY, Wm.
Died before 8 November 1813 when Elizabeth Huey, the widow and administratrix, resigned & John Hutchinson was appointed administrator, with Joseph Huey & Theophilus Morgan as security. (Rob TN, Co Ct Min, 3/318) 14 November 1814 James Gambell, Theophetus Morgan & Alexander Gordan were appointed to lay off a years support for the widow and her children. (Ibid 492)

HUFF, A. C.
Died before 4 December 1868 as shown in the suit of Martha Huff Admrx. vs the heirs of A. C. Huff, deceased. On motion of complainant an alias is awarded for defendant Eli Hatfield to Overton County. (Fen TN, Ch Ct Min, A/425)

HUFF, John
Died before 6 December 1866 as shown in the suit of Cyrus Clonch & wife vs Preston Huff Admr. et als. It was stated that publication had been made for the non-resident minor defendants, to wit, Mary and Samuel Travarse, William, Preston H., Fayette and Proctor McGee. The minor defendants who are residents have been notified, to wit, Thursey Jane, Elenor Elizabeth, Alexandre, Florida, Mary, James, Mcphillips, Ranson & Florence. [sic] Bailey O. Bowden was appointed guardian ad litem for the said several minor defendants herein before named. An order was issued to White County to be served upon Serena Huff, widow, & Florence Huff & Ransom Huff, minor children of John Huff, deceased. Publication has also been made for Claiborne Markham, a non-resident minor defendant and Martha Markham, a resident of Scott County and a minor, has been served. Charles D. McGuffey was appointed guardian ad litem for the Markham minors. (Fen TN, Ch Ct Min, A/321-2) Alvin C. Huff et als were defendants in the suit of Cyrus Clonch. (Ibid 332) In the suit of Lewis Huff vs A. C. Huff, Serelda Huff & others, A. C. & Serelda disclaim any further interest or claim in the estate of John Huff, deceased, except what they have already received. (Ibid 386) W. S. Hill is administrator de bonus non. (Ibid 400)

HUFF, Joseph
Died before 6 January 1857 when his widow, Rhoda Huff, was paid for the services of her deceased husband as a juror of inquest. (Sev TN, Co Ct Min, no#/107)

HUFFAKER, Jesse
Died before 6 July 1857 when a jury was paid for holding an inquest over his dead body. (Sev TN, Co Ct Min, no#/175)

HUFFAKER, Michael
5 March 1829 the suit of McGhee & McCarty against Michael Huffaker was deferred because he "is not a citizen of this Government." (McM TN, Co Ct Min, no#/422)

HUFFAKER, Westley
Died before 3 July 1865 when his will was proved by R. M. Creswell & Samuel Randles, witnesses. Francis G. Huffaker was executrix. (Sev TN, Co Ct Min, no#/176)

HUFFT, John
Died before 11 April 1856 when Thomas Maples renewed his bond as guardian of Benjamin Hufft, minor heir. (Sev TN, Co Ct Min, no#/45)

HUFFT, Wm.
Died before 5 May 1856 when Willis Leatherwood renewed his bond as guardian for Philip Hufft & William Hufft, minor heirs. Thomas Maples was his security. (Sev TN, Co Ct Min, no#/48)

HUGHES, John
Died before 4 November 1782 when Edward Hughes, administrator, returned an inventory of the estate. (Was TN, Co Ct Min, 1/180)

HUGHES, John
28 August 1778 took the oath of allegiance. (Was TN, Co Ct Min, 1/47)

HUGHLETT, William [Hulett]
Died before 21 February 1839 when land was taxed to the heirs. (Obi TN, Cir Ct Min, 3/300)

HUGHLETT, Wm. C.
17 September 1852 the suit of Swaney Burrus vs Heirs of Wm. C. Hughlett was transferred to the Chancery Court at Huntingdon. (Mad TN, Ch Ct Min, 1/279)

HUGHS, Daniel
Died before 23 February 1838 when his death was suggested in the suit of John Doe lessee of Owen & Cysson vs Danl. Hughs. (Obi TN, Cir Ct Min, 3/177)

HUGHS, James T.
Was a non-resident of TN on 14 July 1853 as shown in the suit of James T. Hughs vs Pinkny McCarver & others and the cross bill of Thomas L. Bransford et al vs Pinkny McCarver and others. (Jac TN, Ch Ct Min, B/84)

HUGUELY, John
Died before 4 November 1872 when his nuncupative will was proved by G. W. Blankinship and W. T. Huguely as witnesses. S. E. Huguely was executor with above witnesses as his security. (Dyr TN, Co Ct Min, B/507-8)

HUKKY, David
28 August 1778 took the oath of allegiance to this state. (Was TN, Co Ct Min, 1/46) 27 May 1779 was granted a "new Tryal in the suit of Wm. Thornton because David was in the service of the Country at the time of the Tryal." (Ibid 820

HULL, Jackson
Died before 4 February 1811 when land was taxed to the heirs. (Ste TN, Co Ct Min, 3/23)

HUMES, J. A.
Died before 7 July 1874 when he is listed as "died insol." on the delinquent tax list for 1873. (Dyr TN, Co Ct Min, B/759)

HUMPHREYS, Elisha
3 August 1784, on the oath of Suzana Humphreys, was released from paying poll tax for 1783. (Was TN, Co Ct Min, 1/243)

HUMPHREYS, John
Died before 5 February 1798 when Moses Humphreys & Jesse Humphreys were appointed administrators. Richard Humphreys and Elisha Humphreys were security. (Was TN, Co Ct Min, 1/631)

HUNDLY, Joshia
21 April 1800 made a deed of gift to Nancy Ryburn. (Rob TN, Co Ct Min, 1/131)

HUNT, A.
Taxes were not collected in District 2 for 1873, "gone" (Dyr TN, Co Ct Min, B/759)

HUNT, James
Died before 5 November 1804 when his heirs were released from the indenture of James Crow who had been bound to James Hunt. (Rob TN, Co Ct Min, 1/316)

HUNT, James
Died before 4 February 1805 when the will was proved by Miles Kirby & John Hyde. Sion Hunt & John Hunt were executors. (Rob TN, Co Ct Min, 1/322)

HUNT, Mary
Made a deed of gift to John Hunt 11 February 1811. (Rob TN, Co Ct Min, 2/356)

HUNTER, Daniel
Died before June 1805 when the heirs were on the tax list. (Wil TN, Co Ct Min, no#/154)

HUNTER, Edwin C.
Died before 12 February 1840 as shown in the suit of Melton B. Hunter, Alexander Dysart, administrators of Edwin C. Hunter, deceased, vs Thomas D. Cheek, Robert P. Harrison, Eleazer Stetwell, Wm. O. Stetwell & James Brown. (Bed TN, Ch Ct Min, 2/101)

HUNTER, Jacob
February term 1789, was ordered to deliver Jacob Hunter, a base born child, to Liddy Orseborn, mother of said child, that the same be brought before next Court for further proceedings to be had thereon. (Was TN, Co Ct Min, 1/364)

HUNTER, Martin
Died before 7 November 1870 when Turner Chamblin made a report as administrator. (Dyr TN, Co Ct Min, B/133)

HUNTER, William
7 October 1873 the sheriff was ordered to notify the woman living now at William Hunter's, to find suitable homes for her children by November court or they will be bound out. (Dyr TN, Co Ct Min, B/646)

HUNTSMAN, Adam
Died before 18 January 1850 as shown in the suit of Burl [Burwell] Butler Admr. vs Nancy Huntsman, Jno. Marring and others. (Mad TN, Ch Ct Min, 1/121) 12 July 1850 Jas. Flaherty, C. Faircloth & Peter S. Fulk were made parties defendants in above suit. (Ibid 147) Another suit 17 September 1852; Roderick McIver Trustee, America, George, Paradise, Adam and Susan Huntsman by next friend R. McIver vs George & Benjamin Hicks. On 28 January 1831 Adam Huntsman sold to Geo. Todd some negroes but was to keep them & care for them until called for by said Todd. In March 1831 said Todd executed a deed of trust to Roderick McIver as trustee for the 3 negroes settling them on the wife & children of said Huntsman. The negroes remained in the possession of the wife & children of Huntsman until the death of Mrs. Huntsman in 1843 or 1844 & in the possession of the children until 1849. [Some were sold, the suits were to get possession of some of them back.] (Ibid 286, 289)

HURLEY, G. W. [Hailey]
Married before 1 September 1860 to Mary S. W. Boyd as shown in the suit of J. W. Norwood vs Mary S. Boyd et als. (Mad TN, Ch Ct Min, 2/410)

HURST, Aaron
On 15 May 1816 a charge of bastardy against him was dismissed. (Cla TN, Co Ct Min, 4/205)

HURST, Isaac
5 February 1866 was apprenticed to John A. Thomas. (Sev TN, Co Ct Min, no#/271)

HURST, James
Was released from paying poll tax for 1858 because he was over 50 years old. (Sev TN, Co Ct Min, no#/324)

HURST, Sevier
Was released from paying poll tax for 1860 as he is over age. (Sev TN, Co Ct Min, no#/571)

HURST, Westley
5 February 1866 was apprenticed to Andrew Hurst. (Sev TN, Co Ct Min, no#/271)

HURST, Wm.
Died before 4 September 1865 when William Hurst was appointed administrator with Merrell Breeden & David Hurst as security. (Sev TN, Co Ct Min, no#/210)

HURT, Joseph [Hust]
Died before 23 August 1866 as shown in the suit of Andrew M. Hurt Surviving Partner vs Henry Nail [Noel, Noll]. (Mad TN, Ch Ct Min, 2/526)

HUSKEY, Isaac
Died before 8 April 1857 when William Huskey made a settlement as administrator. (Sev TN, Co Ct Min, no#/158)

HUSKY, William
Died before 6 May 1861 when John Husky was appointed administrator, the widow, Dolly Husky, having relinquished her right to administer. (Sev TN, Co Ct Min, no#/684)

HUTCHERSON, Daniel
Died before 3 May 1819 when Elizabeth Hutcherson was appointed guardian of Michie Hutcherson & John Hutcherson, minor heirs, with Richard Hankins & John Lay as security. (Wil TN, Co Ct Min, no#/433)

HUTCHINGS, Thomas
Died before 22 September 1806 when a deed was recorded from Andrew Jackson and John Hutchings, executor of Thomas Hutchings, deceased, to Edward Douglass. (Wil TN, Co Ct Min, no#/249)

HUTSON, Ezekiel
Died before 4 February 1811 when land was taxed to the heirs. (Ste TN, Co Ct Min, 3/24)

HUTSON, James
Died before 15 August 1815 when John Huddleston and John Hodges returned an account of sale of the estate. [Also see James Hudson] (Cla TN, Co Ct Min, 4/103)

IDLE, Adam
4 March 1806 was released from paying taxes in consequence of his infirmities. (Cla TN, Co Ct Min, 2/223)

IMPSON, Sally
3 May 1819 was allowed $40 for her support. (Wil TN, Co Ct Min, no#/441)

INGLE, John
6 September 1858 was released from paying poll tax as he is over 50 years of age. His name had been written as John England & England crossed out & Ingle written over it. (Sev TN, Co Ct Min, no#/338)

INGLE, Sarah
Was the mother of a bastard child named Mary by Henry McMott. He was ordered to pay support 2 July 1860. (Sev TN, Co Ct Min, no#/569)

INGLEMAN, Joseph
Married before 18 November 1814 to Jane, heir of John Tucker, deceased. (Rob TN, Co Ct Min, 3/514)

INGRAM, B.
Died before 10 November 1835 as shown in the suit of D. St. John & Catherine Ingram Admr. & Admrx. of B. Ingram, deceased vs Saml. Wells. (Obi TN, Cir Ct Min, 3/31)

INGRAM, Jno.
Died before 21 September 1853 as shown in the case of Thomas Ingram, administrator of Jno. Ingram, deceased vs Tho. Newbern Ex. et als. (Mad TN, Ch Ct Min, 1/337) 17 March 1854 in the suit of Thos. Ingram, administrator, vs Thos. Newbern Exr., the following persons were made defendants: Jane Taylor, Ann Deberry of full age, Jno. Ingram, Louisa Ingram, William Ingram, Adeline Ingram, under age, who sue by their guardian Thos. Ingram, the children & heirs of Jno. Ingram. [a supposed fourth heir was mentioned] (Ibid 367) Lydia Ingram is the widow of Jno. Ingram, deceased. (Ibid 2/33) In another listing of the heirs Adeline is not listed and a child, Lydia, is listed as well as the widow, Lydia. (Ibid 39) John Ingram died in February 1853. (Ibid 109) 21 August 1858 the land was sold & divested out of Lydia Ingram, Jane Taylor, Ann Deberry, Louisa Ingram, Jno. M. Ingram, Lydia Ingram [again] & Wm. Ingram. (Ibid 238)

INMAN, Willis
Died before 5 December 1864 when James Baker, Wm. Williams & John Keeler were appointed to lay off a years support to the widow, Amanda Inman. Bryant Breeden was appointed guardian to Dinah Inman & Julia Inman, minor heirs. (Sev TN, Co Ct Min, no#/128) 7 January 1867 Lewis Breeden was appointed administrator. (Ibid 417)

INMON, Mary
Was a resident of Burk County [NC] 25 May 1780 when her deposition was to be taken on behalf of Amos Bird in his suit with Saml. Sherville. (Was TN, Co Ct Min, 1/113)

IRELAND, Elizabeth
15 May 1788 John Noland "was allowed Sixty Seven pounds Ten Shillings for Supporting Elizabeth Ireland an object of Charity in this County from February 1786 till this time." (Was TN, Co Ct Min, 1/333) The name was shown as John Nolan. (Ibid no #/13, [duplicate records] November 1788)

IRVAN, James
Died before 15 February 1796 when the will was proved by Richard Jones. Benjamine Irvan and Mary Irvan were executors. (Was TN, Co Ct Min, 1/588)

IRVIN, William
Died before 1 May 1871 when Alex. Irvin made a settlement as administrator. (Dyr TN, Co Ct Min, B/236)

IRWIN, Andrew
Died before 30 July 1846 as shown in the suit of Benjamin Irwin, Andrew Wassom and wife Hester, John Garrison & wife Elizabeth, Robert Dyer & wife Cary vs Margaret Irwin, Joseph Garrison & wife Mary, Thomas Paul & wife Sally. The complainants have no right to reach the estate of Andrew Irwin, deceased, without an administrator. Andrew Wassom was the administrator. (Jac TN, Ch Ct Min, A/223) In the suit of Andrew Wassom Admr. vs Margaret Erwin, complainant is permitted to take the depositions of Henry Garrison, Elizabeth Garrison, John Garrison, George W. Clinton, Hannah Clinton, Jesse K. Clinton, John L. Clinton, Nancy Paul, Peter Anderson, Sally Anderson, Elizabeth Erwin, James Erwin, John Scarlett, Thomas Scarlett, Elizabeth Scarlett, Joshua White, Moses Scarlett, Eliza Car, Andrew Wassom, Jr., Harriet N. Wassom, Rebecca Wassom, William Stone, Nathan Judd, Dice Erwin, William H. Barns, Angeline Scarlett & Squire L. Thompson. (Ibid 242) Andrew Erwin left a will in which he left all of his property to the use of his father and mother, Benjamin Erwine & wife. Benjamin Erwine & wife have departed this life but previous to his death Benjamin Erwin had purchased a tract of land on which Margaret Erwin now lives. Margaret and her children had lived with Benjamin & his wife previous to their death. (Ibid 271) On 28 January 1848 in the suit of Andrew Wassom Admr. vs Margaret Erwin it is stated that the nuncupative will of Andrew Irvin, deceased, vested an absolute right in the property so devised to Benjamin Erwin, Sr. and said Benjamin had disposed of same to defendant as he had a right to do. (Ibid 304)

IRWIN, Enos
Was a minor 17 May 1810 when William Irwin was appointed guardian to defend the suit of Nelly Wallace by her next friend, Townly Redferren vs Enos Irwin. (Rob TN, Co Ct Min, 2/265)

IRWIN, John
Died before December term 1816 as shown in the case of John W. Payton, administrator of James Scott vs David Irwin, administrator of John Irwin. (Wil TN, P&J, no#/no#)

IRWIN, Mary
18 May 1810 William Irwin was appointed her guardian to defend the suit of Jno. Redferren against her for slander. [Also shown as Mary Erwin] (Rob TN, Co Ct Min, 2/269)

IRWIN, Robert
Was a non-resident of TN 16 October 1857 as shown in the suit of J. C. Latham vs Robert Irwin & others. (Fen TN, Ch Ct Min, A/108)

ISBELL, George
Died before 3 October 1808 when Mary Isbell relinquished her dower to the legatees. (Rob TN, Co Ct Min, 2/79) 3 April 1809 the will was admitted to record on certificate from Halafax County, VA, also the account current of said estate. (Ibid 116) James Gambell was trustee for the legatees. (Ibid 286-7)

ISBELL, John
Died before 3 October 1808 when John Hudson was appointed guardian for James, Nancy & George Isbell, minor orphans of John Isbell, deceased, with Thomas Yates & George Isbell as security. (Rob TN, Co Ct Min, 2/80)

ISBELL, Mary
Made a deed of gift 4 August 1806 to Lewis Ragsdale, proved by Joel Ragsdale & William Yates. (Rob TN, Co Ct Min, 1/397) 3 October 1808 Mary Isbell relinquished her dower left her by George Isbell, deceased, to the legatees. (Ibid 2/79) 2 October 1809 Mary Isbell made a deed of gift to John Yates, proved by Wm. Yates & John Leeper. (Ibid 171) Mary

Isbell & Wm. Ragsdale made a marriage contract which was proved by Abraham Moore & Archibald Campbell 10 February 1812. (Ibid 3/48)

ISBELL, Thomas D.
Was a minor child of Geo. Isbell, deceased, 3 October 1808, when he made choice of John Hudson as his guardian, with Thomas Yates as security. (Rob TN, Co Ct Min, 2/79)

ISRIVLE
Wm. & John Isrivle were residents of Burk County [NC] on 25 February 1779 when their depositions were to be taken in behalf of James Greenlie, Esqr., defendant, John Nare, plaintiff, on a caveat. (Was TN, Co Ct Min, 1/69)

IVY, William
6 July 1857 was stated to be an old, helpless and poor person and the commissioners of the poor house were ordered to receive him into the poor house. (Sev TN, Co Ct Min, no#/179)

JACK, Alexander
Was a pauper 7 September 1829 when money was allowed for his support. (McM TN, Co Ct Min, 2/379)

JACKSON, Henry
On 3 December 1810 a marriage contract was made between Henry Jackson and his intended wife, Mary Ramsey, widow of Zeral Ramsey, all of Dinwiddie County, VA. The agreement is four pages long and hard to understand. It involves Robert King & Berriman Jackson, also of Dinwiddie County, VA. Berriman Jackson was the son of William Jackson. Witnesses were Julius King, William T. King & Thomas B. King. It was recorded in VA in January 1811 and apparently recorded in Wilson County, TN, on 5 March 1822. (Wil TN, Reg Bk/243-8)

JACKSON, Henry D.
Died before 13 July 1850 when Caroline Jackson made petition for herself & as guardian of the minor heirs, for sale of land. (Mad TN, Ch Ct Min, 1/151)

JACKSON, James
23 September 1805 paid the fine of $3.50 as the reputed father of a bastard child which has been delivered [mother not named]. (Wil TN, Co Ct Min, no#/163)

JACKSON, James F.
Died before 7 November 1870 when Thomas M. Jackson was appointed administrator, with J. E. McCorkle and A. S. Jackson as security. (Dyr TN, Co Ct Min, B/127) W. J. Scobey, William Maxwell and E. J. Smith were appointed to lay off a years provisions for the heirs. (Ibid 233)

JACKSON, Louis E.
Died before 14 January 1847 when William Croom made petition for sale of the slaves. Heirs of Louis E. Jackson were W. A. [W. H.], Harriet M. & Martha C. Jackson. William Croom was guardian of the heirs. (Mad TN, Ch Ct Min, 1/10)

JACKSON, Mahaly
Was granted a divorce from Elias Jackson on 16 July 1851. They were married several years ago in Jackson County. In 1847 Elias Jackson was convicted of counterfeiting and was by the judgement of said Court rendered infamous. Divorce was therefore granted plus all property and custody of their 4 children. (Jac TN, Ch Ct Min, B/4)

JACKSON, Philip Whitehead
Died before 9 February 1814 when land was taxed to the heirs. (Ste TN, Co Ct Min, 4/108)

JACKSON, Robert
Was an orphan boy when he was bound 1 November 1819 to Elisha Chasten until age 21. (Wil TN, Co Ct Min, no#/535)

JACKSON, Robert
Died before 30 December 1826 when his heirs, Henry Jackson, Jesse Jackson, Bemmy B. Beasley, John M. Jackson, Dolley Jackson and Daniel Jackson, gave power of attorney to Mack Jackson, all of Wilson County, TN, to sell lands in Dinwiddie County, VA. It mentioned the widow of James Lethe, deceased, but formerly the widow of Robert Jackson, deceased. (Wil TN, Reg Bk/388) [second set of page numbers]

JACKSON, T. M.
1 July 1872 J. E. McCorkle was paid to carry him to the Insane Hospital. (Dyr TN, Co Ct Min, B/424)

JACKSON, William
Was bound 17 March 1817 to Jeremiah Horn until age 21. (Wil TN, Co Ct Min, no#/73)

JACKSON, Zebulon
Died before 16 January 1850 as shown in the suit of William B. Watson, Mathew G. Jackson, Elizabeth M. Jackson, William H. Jackson & Jno. A. Tomlinson as guardian for Virginia Jackson, minor of J. C. Jackson, deceased. The petitioners are the only persons entitled to a negro woman as the only heirs of Zebulon Jackson, deceased. (Mad TN, Ch Ct Min, 1/103)

JADWIN, Jeremiah
Was a pauper. John Williams was paid for his support 18 June 1816. (Wil TN, Co Ct Min, no#/15)

JAMES, Alfred
17 July 1866 John Roberts was ordered to renew his bond for the boy, Alfred James, who was bound to him at the last term of court. (Sev TN, Co Ct Min, no#/349)

JAMES, Frank
Died before 5 February 1872 when J. F. Sinclair was chosen and appointed guardian of Columbus James and Reese James, minor heirs. (Dyr TN, Co Ct Min, B/367)

JAMES, James
Died before 5 December 1870 when B. C. Burgie was appointed administrator, with J. W. Lauderdale as security. (Dyr TN, Co Ct Min, B/140)

JAMES, John L.
Died before 7 February 1870 when petition for dower was made by Mary J. James. Wm. L. Watkins & Andrew Hart were appointed to assign her dower out of the lands of her deceased husband. (Dyr TN, Co Ct Min, B/5) The petition for dower was made by Mary J. James vs E. A. Henderson, David C. James, E. C. James, Sarah A. James, James L. James, Giles W. James, Mary E. James & Martha James. (Ibid 17)

JAMES, Lida
Died before 8 October 1873 when Nat. P. Tatum was paid for the coffin. (Dyr TN, Co Ct Min, B/648)

JAMES, Milly
6 April 1863 John Stofle was allowed $20 annually for keeping her. (Sev TN, Co Ct Min, no#/53)

JAMES, Thomas
Died before 13 May 1816 when John Birch was appointed guardian to the orphans of Thomas James, deceased, namely, William James and John James. Thomas Shearman was his security. (Cla TN, Co Ct Min, 4/181)

JAMES, William P.
Was an orphan boy 6 April 1863 when he was bound to William Atchley until age 21. (Sev TN, Co Ct Min, no#/53)

JAMISON, William
Was an orphan boy aged 17 when he was bound to James A. Turnley on 2 December 1828, until age 21. He is to be taught the potter's trade. (McM TN, Co Ct Min, 2no#/324)

JENENS, William [Jennings]
On 7 September 1804 was refunded his poll tax as he is over age. (Cla TN, Co Ct Min, 2/81)

JENKINS, James
Died before 4 February 1811 when Larry Satterfield was appointed administrator with John Scarborough and George Martin, Sr. as security. (Ste TN, Co Ct Min, 3/13)

JENKINS, James
Was bound as an apprentice 2 October 1865 to James C. Walker. He is 15 years old. (Sev TN, Co Ct Min, no#/222)

JENKINS, Whitmell
4 October 1808 James Perry was appointed guardian with William Crocket & Jonathan Huddleston as security. (Rob TN, Co Ct Min, 2/87)

JENKINS, William
His wife died before 3 April 1860 when S. B. Henderson was paid for her burying clothes. (Sev TN, Co Ct Min, no#/548)

JENNINGS, Nancy
13 July 1850 brought suit against James Poston. The contract of 9 March 1846, so far as it obliges the defendant to keep and maintain complainant, is rescinded and instead thereof the defendant is to pay the complainant $400. (Jac TN, Ch Ct Min, A/375)

JENNINGS, Nancy
Died before 6 February 1857 as shown in the suit of Francis H. Armstrong & wife & others vs Tolaver Kirkpatrich, administrator & others. Nancy Jennings left a will giving half of her estate to Robert Stone if living & if not living to go to his heirs, and if it cannot be ascertained if Robert Stone is living or has heirs then all of the estate is to go to the support of the Gospel or the support of Christian Preachers. The court decided that the devise to Stone or heirs if any being, is effectual, but that the devise to the support of the Gospel or Christian preachers is void for uncertainty. It not appearing to the Court whether said Stone was alive or had any heirs living or whether complainants are the only heirs of Nancy Jennings, a report is to be made as to Robert Stone or any other heirs at next term. (Jac TN, Ch Ct Min, C/58) In the suit of Frances H. Armstrong & wife and Elisha Saunders & wife vs Toliver Kirkpatrick and Thomas J. Rose & others a report was made of the assets of the estate of Nancy Jennings. (Ibid 109)

JIMPSON, John [IMPSON]
Was an orphan boy who was bound 24 September 1806 to Patrick Youree to learn the trade of blacksmith. (Wil TN, Co Ct Min, no#/256)

JINENS, Ezekiah [Jenings, Hezekiah]
Died before 24 August 1807 when Sarah Jinens & Obediah Jinens were appointed administrators with John Bullard and Ryal Jinens as security. (Cla TN, Co Ct Min, 3/104) 29 November 1808 Rial Jinens was appointed guardian of Polly Jinens, Becky Jinens, Anderson Jinens, Patty Jinens, Sally Jinens & Lucy Jinens, minor orphans of Hezekiah Jinens, deceased. John Bullard & John Cocke were security. (Ibid 244)

JOHNS
9 June 1825 Andrew Johns & Hugh Johns were charged with assult. They are both under the age of 21. Samuel Johns is the father of the two boys. Ezekiel Johns paid their fine of 6 1/4 cents. (McM TN, Co Ct Min, 2no#/83)

JOHNSON
8 October 1872 a guardian settlement was made for Felix B. Johnson, Isaac C. Johnson and J. W. Johnson, heirs of [blank] Johnson, deceased. The settlement was probably made by J. A. Nunn. (Dyr TN, Co Ct Min, B/494)

JOHNSON, Alex.
Died before 17 June 1817 when Eleanor Johnson, John Johnson & Thomas Calhoon, executors of Alex. Johnson, deceased, and Robertson Johnson in his own right, deeded land to William Williams. The land was in Davidson County. (Wil TN, Co Ct Min, no#/121) George Worley was appointed guardian of Permelia Johnson, minor daughter of Alexander Johnson, deceased. (Ibid 246) The administratrix was shown as Elizabeth Johnson. (Ibid 249)

JOHNSON, Amos
Was a resident of Mulenburg County, KY, on 6 May 1813 when his deposition was to be taken for the plaintiff in the case of Jesse Denson vs James Miller. (Ste TN, Co Ct Min, 4/47)

JOHNSON, Ben
Was a pauper 4 July 1870 when $20 was allowed for his support. (Dyr TN, Co Ct Min, B/73)

JOHNSON, Clem
Died before 15 September 1817 when the widow, Absilla Johnson, was granted letters of administration, with Elijah Cross & John W. Nichols as security. (Wil TN, Co Ct Min,

no#/unnumbered page between 143 & 144) 1 February 1819 John Jones was appointed guardian of Sally Johnson & James Johnson, minor heirs of C. Johnson. (Ibid 374)

JOHNSON, Daniel
Died before 21 August 1840 as shown in the suit of Jordan C. Holt administrator of Daniel Johnson, deceased vs James M. Johnson. James M. & Daniel had been partners in the mercantile business. Daniel Johnson died in June last and Jordan C. Holt was appointed administrator in July 1839. In the answer of James M. Johnson he states that Daniel died in June 1839. Daniel was the uncle of James M. Johnson. (Bed TN, Ch Ct Min, 1/532) The deceased was also shown as Daniel John. (Ibid 2/161)

JOHNSON, David
Died before 21 February 1839 when land was taxed to the heirs. (Obi TN, Cir Ct Min, 3/293)

JOHNSON, David R.
Died before 6 February 1851 when his death was suggested in the suit of David R. Johnson vs John Burrus. The suit was revived in the name of Benjamin C. White, administrator. (Jac TN, Ch Ct Min, A/396) David R. Johnson died about September 1850. (Ibid B/35) A report was made of money due to the legatees: To Edith Johnson, Ben C. White & wife, Jacob Johnson & wife, Loyd M. Mahony & brothers & sisters the heirs of Perry Mahony, deceased, Thomas R. Mahany, William Mahany. An account was mentioned between Anderson & Ranson P. Mahany. Thomas R. Mahany has occupied the land for 4 years and is to be charged with rent. (Ibid 104)

JOHNSON, Dennis
Died before 4 July 1870 when T. S. Robertson was paid for making the coffin. (Dyr TN, Co Ct Min, B/73)

JOHNSON, Duncan
Died before 1 November 1819 when Silas Chapman was appointed administrator. (Wil TN, Co Ct Min, no#/534)

JOHNSON, Edwin
Died before 18 February 1858 as shown in the petition of Ro. Fenner Surviving Executor and others and F. N. W. Burton vs T. P. Jones admr. and others, tried together by consent of parties. The heirs of Edwin Johnson were Julius Johnson & Marianna Fenner. This petition concerns the estate of D. Richard Fenner. John S. Fenner was administrator. (Mad TN, Ch Ct Min, 2/182)

JOHNSON, Edwin
Died before 2 December 1872 when J. F. Perry was chosen and appointed guardian of Sarah R. Johnson, minor heir. (Dyr TN, Co Ct Min, B/514)

JOHNSON, Elizabeth
Died before 13 February 1815 when the will was proved by John P. Harton and William Adams. (Rob TN, Co Ct Min, 3/532) William Adams made a report of the inventory. (Ibid 564)

JOHNSON, F. B.
6 February 1871, I. A. Nunn made a settlement as guardian. (Dyr TN, Co Ct Min, B/190)

JOHNSON, F. M.
1 May 1871 J. F. Perry made a settlement as guardian. (Dyr TN, Co Ct Min, B/236)

JOHNSON, Gregory D.
Was shown to be the father of James D. Johnson when James sold land to Joseph Johnson on 12 February 1828. (Wil TN, Reg Bk/400) [second set of page numbers]

JOHNSON, Henry
Married before 10 August 1812 to Elizabeth Harper when a marriage contract was proved by John Hutchison and Matthew Day. (Rob TN, Co Ct Min, 3/97)

JOHNSON, J. C.
6 February 1871, I. A. Nunn made a settlement as guardian. (Dyr TN, Co Ct Min, B/190)

JOHNSON, J. N.
6 February 1871, I. A. Nunn made a settlement as guardian. (Dyr TN, Co Ct Min, B/190)

JOHNSON, James
Died before 14 November 1815 when the will was proved by William & Robert Whithead. William Cook was executor with Hardy Hughs as security. (Cla TN, Co Ct Min, 4/126) A suit was shown 11 February 1817, William Cook Executor of James Johnson Decd. vs Rodha Johnson. The deposition of Elizabeth Gidenns of Blount County was to be taken for the defendant. (Ibid 295)

JOHNSON, James
Died before 11 may 1812 when an inventory of the estate was recorded. (Rob TN, Co Ct Min, 3/76)

JOHNSON, James
Died before 4 August 1818 when an account of the sale of property was entered by Phillip Johnson, executor. (Wil TN, Co Ct Min, no#/298)

JOHNSON, Jas.
Died before 15 March 1853 as shown in the case of Thomas Reid vs Henry C. Beckers et als. Henry Beckers is indebted to complainant for a note executed to his deceased partner, Jas. Johnson, in 1847. (Mad TN, Ch Ct Min, 1/296)

JOHNSON, John
Died before 3 November 1812 when Henry Pugh returned an additional inventory. (Ste TN, Co Ct Min, 3/unnumbered page before page 1) Henry Pugh was appointed administrator 6 May 1812 with William King, Philip Hornberger, William M. Cooley and John Allen as security. (Ibid 139)

JOHNSON, John
Was a resident of Logan County, KY, 8 July 1808 when the deposition of he and his wife was to be taken in behalf of the defendant in the case of Joseph Dorris vs Thos. Appleton. (Rob TN, Co Ct Min, 2/67)

JOHNSON, John
14 August 1811 an indenture of apprenticeship from John Johnson to George W. West was proved by James Tunstall and ordered to be recorded. (Rob TN, Co Ct Min, 3/16)

JOHNSON, John A.
Died before 3 November 1873 when A. B. Bledsoe was appointed administrator, the widow having relinquished. Thomas H. Johnson and P. C. Ledsinger were his security. (Dyr TN, Co Ct Min, B/662)

JOHNSON, John W.
Died before 8 August 1871 when the land of the heirs was mentioned in the description of the land of George W. Folkes, deceased. (Dyr TN, Co Ct Min, B/268) 4 October 1871 Martha Johnson petitioned for dower vs Henry L. Fowlkes. Dower is to be set off from land recently occupied by J. W. Johnson. (Ibid 310) Martha Johnson was the widow of John W. Johnson. (Ibid 360)

JOHNSON, Jonathan
Died before 1 May 1865 when J. T. Johnson was appointed administrator with Jas. C. & John W. Johnson as security. (Sev TN, Co Ct Min, no#/157) Martha Johnson was the widow. (Ibid 161)

JOHNSON, Joseph
Died before 25 August 1845 as shown in the suit of Nelson Blackman vs John Johnson et als. John Johnson was the administrator. The complainants are entitled to a distributive portion of the estate of Joseph Johnson. (Bed TN, Ch Ct Min, 2/360) Joseph Johnson died in September 1842 and was at that time a citizen of Coffee County, TN. He left as his heirs; John Johnson who was the son of said Joseph; Joseph Reddin, William Reddin, John Reddin, Matilda Reddin, Elizabeth Reddin, Robt. Reddin, Susanah Blackman formerly Susan Reddin and now the wife of Nelson Blackman, Emaline Davenport formerly Emaline Reddin and now the wife of David Davenport, Martha Calhoon formerly Martha Reddin and now the wife of Wm. Calhoon, who are the grand children of said Joseph being the children of Elizabeth Reddin who was the daughter of said Joseph and who departed this life previous to the death of said Joseph; Susanah Blackman who was the daughter of said Joseph and the wife of Elisha Blackman; Catherine Chase formerly Catharine Blackman and now the wife of David Chase, James J. Blackman, J. B. Blackman, William J. Blackman, Jeremiah Blackman, John E. Blackman, Caroline Blackman, Ellenor Blackman and Mary Blackman who are grand children of said Joseph being the children of Letha Blackman who was the daughter of said Joseph and departed

this life previous to the death of said Joseph; Burrel C. Johnson who is the grand son of said Joseph being the only son of William Johnson who was the son of said Joseph and who departed this life previous to the death of said Joseph; and Susanah Johnson who is the widow of said Joseph. John Johnson was appointed administrator in Coffee County. Polly and Anna Reddin were also daughters of Elizabeth Reddin. Polly married James McLain and Ann is also married but the name of her husband is not known. A final settlement was made in February 1846. The Reddins were residents of Coffee County. The Blackmans and Elisha and Susan Blackwell were residents of Lancaster District, SC. David & Caroline Chase, James J. Blackman & Burrel J. Johnson were residents of Harris County, GA. John Johnson the administrator and Susanah Johnson the widow are residents of Coffee County, TN. (Ibid 3/262-274)

JOHNSON, Judith
Brought suit 19 March 1852 against John Johnson et als. Judith & John were married about January 1850 in Jackson County. She was granted a divorce. Andrew McClellan had bequethed to complainant a slave and it is to be her absolute property. Judith also had property which she got from her first husband, Beverly Graves, which was willed to her. Andrew McClellan was the executor of Beverly Graves' will. Judith was entitled to 1/5 of the estate of Beverly Graves there being 4 children. Sampson McClellan has now been appointed administrator. Slaves are to be sold to be divided between Judith and her 4 Graves children. (Jac TN, Ch Ct Min, B/31)

JOHNSON, Lydia J.
Was a minor 16 March 1853 when her guardian, David A. Johnson, was ordered to purchase the dower interest of Amanda Johnson for his ward. (Mad TN, Ch Ct Min, 1/297)

JOHNSON, Matthew
Died before 17 October 1797 when Mary Johnson was appointed administratrix, with Benj. Meneis & William Flinn as security. (Rob TN, Co Ct Min, 1/41) 16 January 1798 Mary Johnson was appointed guardian of James Johnson & Betsey Johnson, orphans of Matthew Johnson, deceased. (Ibid 46)

JOHNSON, Mike
1 July 1861 Jas. Walker was paid for keeping Mike Johnson when he was crippled. (Sev TN, Co Ct Min, no#/697)

JOHNSON, Nimrod
Died intestate in Jackson County about December 1856, as shown in the suit of Susannah Johnson vs Samuel Johnson & others, the heirs-at-law of Nimrod Johnson, deceased. Susannah Johnson was the widow and sued for dower. One of the tracts of land was purchased from Benjamin Johnson. (Jac TN, Ch Ct Min, C/69) In the suit of Samuel Johnson & others vs Washington Morgan & others it was stated that complainants & defendants were the heirs of Nimrod Johnson. (Ibid 90) A suit was entered by Samuel Johnson, William Johnson, David Johnson, John S. Reed & wife Louisa Reed, Paul Anderson & wife Susannah Anderson vs Washington Morgan, Polly An Morgan, Susannah Morgan, Marion Morgan, Daniel Morgan, William C. Morgan (children of A. H. Morgan), Thomas L. Mahony & wife Elizabeth Mahony, William C. Morgan & wife Polly Morgan, Vanbeuren Johnson, Benjamin T. Johnson, William Johnson, Polly An Johnson & Clay Linch Johnson (children of Jacob Johnson), Mary Johnson (child of Daniel Johnson deceased) and Susannah Johnson, widow of Nimrod Johnson, deceased, & Austin H. Morgan guardian for the minor defendants. The land & negroes were sold at the late residence of Nimrod Johnson. Some of the parties in this suit made purchases. Title was divested out of complainants & defendants. (Ibid 122-4)

JOHNSON, Rachel
1 April 1867 was appointed guardian to James Terry & Isaac Patrick Johnson, with Henry Cate & J. H. Caldwell as security. (Sev TN, Co Ct Min, no#/438)

JOHNSON, Reubin
Died before 6 December 1825 when Jacob Johnson was appointed administrator. (McM TN, Co Ct Min, 2no#/116) 4 June 1827 Andrew Cowan was appointed guardian of William Johnson, Esther Johnson & Martha Jane Johnson, infant heirs of Reubin Johnson, deceased. (Ibid 219)

JOHNSON, Robert
Was a resident of Harden County, KY, 3 October 1817 when he gave power of attorney to Elijah Truett to sell land. (Wil TN, Reg Bk/124)

JOHNSON, Robert
Died before November term 1869 when W. S. Byers, G. W. Bettis & Jas. L. Farmer were appointed to set off a years provision for the widow. Their report was made 9 February 1870. (Dyr TN, Co Ct Min, B/10) Joseph H. Brooks was administrator. (Ibid 42) M. V. Bettis was guardian of Ann Letitia Johnson and Mary A. Johnson, minor heirs. (Ibid 228 & 548)

JOHNSON, Samuel
In his suit against Abraham Price filed 6 February 1811, Samuel Johnson was given leave to take the depositions of Roger Oats, James Goodwin, James Evans of Wayne County, KY, James Montgomery & Hannah Mulka of Pulaski County, KY, & of John Sutton of Garrard County, KY. (Ste TN, Co Ct Min, 3/45)

JOHNSON, Samuel T.
Married a daughter of N. A. Whittington, deceased. Samuel Johnson's wife was deceased by 5 May 1873 leaving her husband and one son, Leroy Bruce Johnson. (Dyr TN, Co Ct Min, B/583)

JOHNSON, William
Died before 4 May 1842 as shown in the suit of William Johnson vs Enoch Carter et al. (Jac TN, Ch Ct Min, A/48)

JOHNSON, William
Died before 14 February 1814 when the will was proved by Jesse Herring & Alexander B. Porter. James Johnson, Sr. was executor. (Rob TN, Co Ct Min, 3/357)

JOHNSON, Wm.
Died before 20 February 1843 when land was taxed to the heirs. (Obi TN, Cir Ct Min, 4/no#)

JOHNSTON, Amis
Gave bond for the maintenance of two bastard children charged to him by Elisabeth Mitchel 7 March 1803. One child was a girl named Artimisse born 24 May 1793 and the other a boy named Hyram born 24 February 1796. John Rogers and Philip Williams were security for Amis Johnston. (Cla TN, Co Ct Min, 1/101)

JOHNSTON, George
Died before 2 February 1813 when land was taxed to the heirs. (Ste TN, Co Ct Min, 4/16)

JOHNSTON, Gideon
Was a resident of Buckenham County, NC, 26 February 1808 when his deposition was to be taken for the defendant in the suit of Moses Overton & wife against Francis Degraffenreed. (Cla TN, Co Ct Min, 3/177)

JOHNSTON, Saml.
Died before 5 August 1805 when Wm. Johnston was appointed administrator with James Norfleet as his security. (Rob TN, Co Ct Min, 1/349) 10 February 1812 William Johnson, Sr. was appointed guardian to Martha Johnson, orphan of Samuel Johnson, deceased. (Ibid 3/52)

JONES
Elijah Rushing was ordered to bring to next court James Jones & John Jones, orphan children in his neighborhood, 6 February 1815. (Ste TN, Co Ct Min, 4/239)

JONES
5 August 1872 Elias Johnson made a settlement as guardian of Sallie & Bettie Jones. (Dyr TN, Co Ct Min, B/447)

JONES, Abraham
Died before February term 1810 when the administratrix was given liberty to sell part of the estate. (Rob TN, Co Ct Min, 2/196) Letters of administration were granted to Elisabeth Jones, with Eli Jones & John Tylar as security. (Ibid 199) 12 February 1812, Elizabeth Jones is now Elizabeth Ragsdale. (Ibid 3/66)

JONES, Ambrose
Sold land to James Gastin & Wm. Tyrrell which was recorded on certificate from Beauford [Beaufort] County, NC, 3 July 1809. (Rob TN, Co Ct Min, 2/141)

JONES, Andrew
Taxes were not collected in District 5 for 1873, "under age." (Dyr TN, Co Ct Min, B/759)

JONES, Atlas
Died before 14 July 1848 leaving a will, as shown in the following petition: "Samuel Lancaster, Jas. D. McClellan & Montagumd? Jones, named as trustees in the will of Atlas Jones deceased - Samuel Lancaster as Executor - Octavia R. Jones, Sarah R. Jones & Catherine F. Jones, minors under 21 who petition by their regular guardian Timothy P. Jones - Doctor Robert Fenner & his wife Ann M. Fenner daughter of said Atlas Jones decd. - and of their children to wit, Rebecca Ann, Robert, John S. Richard, Walter C. Darvin P. Eliga Fanny and Rosa Matilda - minors who petition by their father Robert Fenner - and of Rebecca Jones the widow of said Atlas Jones decd." The petitioners are legatees. The 3 trustees named resigned and Timothy P. Jones, Rebecca S. Jones & Julius Johnson were appointed to act as trustees in their place. Slaves are named. The 3 children of Catherine J. Jones, deceased, were named, to wit: Octavia R., Sarah R. & Catherine F. Jones [Catherine J. Jones may have been the widow of Timothy P. Jones] (Mad TN, Ch Ct Min, 1/49) In the suit 25 February 1861 of Aniza A. Greer vs Atlas Jones, Elbert W. Massey & Lewis Jones, it is stated that Lewis Jones & Atlas Jones are brothers. (Ibid 2/459) 20 August 1868 in the suit of Alex Futrell vs Atlas Jones et als it was stated that at the time of the death of Elijah Jones, father of Atlas Jones, & at the time the will of Elijah Jones took effect that Atlas Jones was dead & left no children surviving him, & Atlas Jones had no interest in the estate of Elijah Jones. (Ibid 3/213)

JONES, Charles
Died before 30 June 1842 as shown in the suit of Michael Wommack & others vs Joseph Watson & others. All the parties of interest are before the court. The land described in the bill descended from Charles Jones to his heirs. The dower of Rebecca Jones has been heretofore alloted to her. The land cannot be divided on account of its size and the number of heirs who own same as tenants in common. The land is to be sold. (Bed TN, Ch Ct Min, 2/193) The land was sold 1 August 1842 & C. B. Jones bought the small tract of 80 acres, with D. D. Jones & Rebecca Jones his security. David Floyd bought the 100 acre tract. (Ibid 222 & 324)

JONES, Elisha
Was a minor 24 May 1808 when he was bound to Solomon Dobbins until age 21. Elisha was the son of Elijah Jones. (Cla TN, Co Ct Min, 3/187)

JONES, Elivs
Died before 6 August 1852 as shown in the suit of James Draper Admr. &c vs Parthena Jones et als. It is stated that defendants Thomas Jones, William Jones, Rebecca Jones, George Jones, Anderson Jones, Elijah Jones and Alexander Jones are minors and have no regular guardian. John P. Murray was appointed guardian ad litem. (Jac TN, Ch Ct Min, B/65) In addition to the names listed above the following were also parties to the suit: Mary Loftis, James Jones and Laborne Loftis. Elivs Jones had sold land to James Jones. Parthena is the widow and has had her dower. All of the other defendants except Laborn Loftis are children of the deceased. Laborn Loftis married Mary, a daughter of the deceased. Land is to be sold. (Ibid 103)

JONES, George W.
Died before 2 November 1818 when Russell Dance was appointed administrator with John E. Dance & Arthur Harris as security. (Wil TN, Co Ct Min, no#/332)

JONES, George W.
Died before 2 July 1872 when Jo. Michell and 7 jurors were paid for holding an inquest on his body. (Dyr TN, Co Ct Min, B/437)

JONES, J. M.
Died before 5 December 1870 when Elias Johnson was chosen and appointed guardian of the minor heirs, with J. W. Jones and F. Chamblin as security. (Dyr TN, Co Ct Min, B/139) Elias Johnson was appointed guardian of Mary Jones, minor heir. (Ibid 174)

JONES, James
Died before 15 August 1815 when Dorcus Jones was appointed administratrix with George Campbell as security. (Cla TN, Co Ct Min, 4/104)

JONES, James
Died before 6 February 1857 as shown in the suit of E. B. Jones vs C. C. Cornewell & wife Polly Cornewell. E. B. Jones stated he had purchased his freedom from James Jones, deceased, in 1828 and had fully paid the purchase price as it appeared from a receipt of

Mary Cornewell, who was the sole legatee of James Jones, deceased, who has since married C. C. Cornewell. The defendants admitted that E. B. Jones had paid all the purchase price so he was declared to be free. (Jac TN, Ch Ct Min, C/60)

JONES, James
22 July 1800 proved on the oath of John Krisel & Silas Tucker that his left ear was bit off in a fight with Richard Crunk at the house of Nathan Clark. (Rob TN, Co Ct Min, 1/143)

JONES, Jane
5 March 1827 Aaron Davis was appointed her guardian. (McM TN, Co Ct Min, 2no#/200)

JONES, John
Died before 17 September 1816 when the administratrix, Francis Jones, was ordered to make a report. (Wil TN, Co Ct Min, no#/37)

JONES, John A.
Died before 3 October 1870 when J. W. Wright, D. A. Chamberlin and M. H. Davis were appointed to lay off a years allowance for the widow and family. (Dyr TN, Co Ct Min, B/100) S. A. Jones was appointed administrator, with J. W. Wright and D. A. Chamberlin as his security. (Ibid 106) The name was shown as James Jones. (Ibid 141)

JONES, Margaret
6 June 1870 J. A. Nunn made a settlement as her guardian. (Dyr TN, Co Ct Min, B/63)

JONES, Peter
Died before 18 December 1816 when his late widow, Catharine, now the wife of Richard Watkins, petitioned for a division of the estate of Peter Jones according to his will. (Wil TN, Co Ct Min, no#/61) Peter Jones left 4 children, Alexander Jones, Amelia Jones, James Chamberlin Jones and Catharine Jones who has married William Hart. (Ibid 62) 16 December 1817 Alexander Jones petitioned for his share of his fathers estate. (Ibid 189)

JONES, Richard
Died before 6 May 1805 when the will was proved by Samuel Scott & Edward Jones. Peter Jones & Edward Ward were executors. (Rob TN, Co Ct Min, 1/337)

JONES, S. A.
Died before 6 February 1871 when the administrator, John Jones, was directed to spend $40 for sugar, flour, coffee &c for the widow and her children. (Dyr TN, Co Ct Min, B/186)

JONES, Samuel
5 June 1871 was bound as an apprentice to N. T. Perry. Samuel is a boy of color. (Dyr TN, Co Ct Min, B/240)

JONES, Sim
Taxes were not collected in District 5 for 1873, "over age." (Dyr TN, Co Ct Min, B/759)

JONES, W. D.
Died before 5 April 1870 when W. N. Beasley was chosen and appointed guardian of the minor heirs with J. H. York & T. H. Benton as security. (Dyr TN, Co Ct Min, B/46) J. A. Nunn was administrator. (Ibid 63)

JONES, Walker
On 14 November 1844 was granted a divorce from Polly Jones. They were married many years ago. Polly has deserted with one William Pankey and resides with him in adultry in the State of KY. (Obi TN, Cir Ct Min, 4/no#)

JONES, William E.
Was a resident of Davidson County, TN, on 20 March 1852 as shown in the suit of John Daws et al vs William E. Jones. (Jac TN, Ch Ct Min, B/39)

JORDAN, Elizabeth B.
Died before 4 November 1873 when her will was proved by M. J. Miller, Ella Watson and Tennie Rook, witnesses. (Dyr TN, Co Ct Min, B/663) R. Air. James was chosen and appointed guardian of Mary Truman Jordan, minor heir. (Ibid 765)

JORDAN, John
Was a citizen of VA on 9 September 1829 when Saml. Hardy & Martha Hardy, his wife, gave him a power of attorney. (McM TN, Co Ct Min, 2no#/391)

JORDAN, Robert H.
Married before 6 June 1831 to Emily Holt, daughter of Irby Holt, deceased. (McM TN, Co Ct Min, 2no#/537)

JOURDEN, Hezekiah
Was released from paying poll tax for 1805. (Cla TN, Co Ct Min, 2/163)

JUSTICE
2 April 1860 it was ordered that Polly and Louisa Justice, poor children, be sent to the poor house. (Sev TN, Co Ct Min, no#/544)

JUSTICE, Jas. B.
Died before 24 August 1867 as shown in the suit of Jas. Glidewell vs Jno. B. Justice et als. The suit is to be revived in the name of Joel T. Justice, administrator de bonis non of Jas. B. Justice, deceased. (Mad TN, Ch Ct Min, 3/112)

JUSTICE, Joseph C.
Died before 16 December 1817 when the will was proved by Isaac Easley & Peter Sullivan. (Wil TN, Co Ct Min, no#/195)

JUSTICE, Julius
7 January 1867 made a bond for the maintenance of a bastard child born of Barberry Stinnett, who named Julius Justice as the father. (Sev TN, Co Ct Min, no#/409)

JUSTICE, Mary Ann
2 October 1866 it was ordered that she be taken from R. S. Lewis to whom she had been bound because she has been "cruelly & unkindly treated." She is to be placed in the care of her brother, J. A. Justice. (Sev TN, Co Ct Min, no#/384)

KANCHLOW, George
18 May 1796, with Sarah Kenchlow, sold land to John Davis of Prince William County, VA. [Probably should be Kinchloe] (Was TN, Co Ct Min, 1/609)

KANEDY, Ann
Died before 18 July 1798 when Robert Barnet was appointed administrator, with David Henry & Isaac Henry as security. (Rob TN, Co Ct Min, 1/67)

KARR
19 April 1797 a power of attorney was given by Margaret Karr, William Karr, Henry Johnson, Willis Hix, William Brisco, Margaret Karr, Jr., Agness Karr, Robt. Karr and John Karr to James Karr. (Rob TN, Co Ct Min, 1/27) Another power of attorney was given 17 July 1798 by Margaret Karr, widow, William Karr, Henry & Mary Johnson, Willis and Eleanor Hicks, William & Sarah Briscoe to James Karr. (Ibid 66)

KARR, John
Was a resident of Ohio County, KY, 5 April 1809 when his deposition was to be taken for the defendant in the case of Wm. Parks vs Henry Johnson. (Rob TN, Co Ct Min, 2/122)

KARR, Joseph D.
Died before 3 September 1822 as shown in suit of Benjamin Harris vs William Cannon. William Cannon was summoned as a garnashee on an execution from White County. He stated he did not owe Jonathan Cannon one cent & that he holds a note on Joseph D. Car, deceased. He also mentioned debts he paid for Jonathan Cannon before he came to this county. (McM TN, Co Ct Min, no#/57) 5 March 1823 commissioners were appointed to settle with Wm. Karr, administrator of Joseph Karr, deceased. (Ibid 76) 2 December 1823 Caleb Starr was appointed guardian of Ellouer Kerr, Manerva Kerr, William Kerr, Jr. & Presha Kerr, minor heirs of the estate of Joseph Kerr, deceased. (Ibid 103) Also shown as heirs of Joseph Kerr were William Gill & wife Sena & Samuel McJenekin & wife Betsey. (Ibid 104) 5 March 1824 the heirs names are shown as Lena Gill, wife of William, and Samuel McJunkin & wife Betsey, Elonor Kerr, William Kerr, Jr., Priscilla Kerr & Minerva Kerr. (Ibid 141) Lena & Betsey were both formerly named Karr. (Ibid 150)

KARR, Margaret
Died before 5 May 1806 when the will was proved by Thomas Johnson, Mary Smith, Elisabeth Long & Jane Hardin. (Rob TN, Co Ct Min, 1/387)

KARR, Robert
Died before January 1798 when one of his heirs, James Karr, was in a suit. (Rob TN, Co Ct Min, 1/50)

KEATH, Pheribee
Died before 15 August 1860 as shown in the suit of William L. Ragland and others by next friend &c vs Allen Manear and others. Complainants produced an amended bill making E. A. Craig, administrator of Pheribee Keath, deceased, and William M. Ragland parties to this suit. Allen Maniar?, John Keath and John Brown were the defendants. It appears that there is no administrator on the estate of James H. Ragland, deceased, that is now living and it is necessary to appoint one in order for this suit to continue. James Draper was appointed administrator of James H. Ragland, deceased, and was made a defendant to this suit. (Jac TN, Ch Ct Min, C/407)

KEEFE, Thomas
8 February 1813 made a deed to Margaret Keefe, alias McKean, which was proven by Joseph McKean & Bartemaus Pack. (Rob TN, Co Ct Min, 3/177)

KEELER, John
Was released from paying poll tax for 1859 as he is over age. (Sev TN, Co Ct Min, no#/545)

KEER, Anderson
1 October 1860 was allowed money for keeping his lunatic son. (Sev TN, Co Ct Min, no#/609)

KEER, John
Died before 31 March 1868 as shown in the suit of Jane Clemens, widow of John M. Clemens, deceased, & others vs George W. Keer and William A. Clendenen and his wife Isabella Clendenen, heirs of John Kerr, deceased. John M. Clemens had bought land from John Kerr and the deed was never registered. (Fen TN, Ch Ct Min, A/365)

KEETON, John
Died before 2 June 1862 when John McMahan was appointed administrator, his widow Elizabeth Keeton, having relinquished her right to administer. (Sev TN, Co Ct Min, no#/778)

KEEWOOD, Stephen
Died before 5 March 1806 when the will was proved by the subscribing witnesses [not named]. (Cla TN, Co Ct Min, 2/231) William Rogers, Esqr., John Berry & Sarah Cawood were executors. (Ibid 238)

KEITH, Alexander
Died in 1824, as shown in a statement of Henry Bradford & Charles Carter made 6 June 1831. It is stated that Alexander Keith removed from VA & settled in TN some time in 1800 & afterwards removed to the Mississippi Country & died in 1824. His children were Kitty Keith who married James Bradford, Charles F. Keith, Isham Keith, & Maria Keith who married Wallas [Wallar, Waltar] Nash. These are the only living children of Alexander Keith. (McM TN, Co Ct Min, 2no#/528)

KELLESR, George
Was a resident of Burk County [NC] 26 May 1779 when his deposition was to be taken on behalf of John Nares, plaintiff in the suit with James Greenlee, defendant. (Was TN, Co Ct Min, 1/76)

KELLY, James
Died before August term 1820 when William Kelly & John Kelly, legal heirs at law of James Kelly, deceased, appointed [name not given] power of attorney to request a land warrent due for the service of James Kelly, deceased, in the Revolutionary War in NC. (Wil TN, Reg Bk/177)

KELLY, Michael
On 15 February 1816 John Thompson was appointed guardian of the minor heirs of Michael Kelly [does not say deceased]. Their names were, Biddy Kelly, Squire Kelly, Nancy Kelly, John Kelly, Charles Kelly, Edward Kelly & Melenda Kelly, all minors. (Cla TN, Co Ct Min, 4/167) 13 May 1817 John Thompson, guardian to the minor heirs of the estate of Michael Kelly, deceased, returned an inventory of said estate. (Ibid 348)

KENDER, George
Died before 17 February 1796 when the will was proved by Saml. Woods & Martha Snider. (Was TN, Co Ct Min, 1/596) Barbary Kender qualified as executrix. (Ibid 602)

KENNEDY, James
Died before 7 March 1826 when his will was proved by Henry Bradford & Stanwin Hord, witnesses. (McM TN, Co Ct Min, 2no#/138) Pryor Lea qualified as executor with James Kenedy & William L. Kennedy his security. (Ibid 146)

KENNEDY, James L.
Died before 13 October 1856 when his death was suggested in the suit of State for the use of A. Millers Admrs. vs E. D. Frogg & others. James L. Kennedy was one of the defendants. (Fen TN, Ch Ct Min, A/59)

KENNY, James
Died before 3 June 1806 when the will was admitted to record. (Cla TN, Co Ct Min, 2/251)

KERNEY, Henry Guston
Was a resident of Murray [Maury] County, TN, on 22 November 1816 when he sold slaves to David Marshall of Wilson County. (Wil TN, Reg Bk/90)

KERR, Joseph
Died before 18 February 1840 when land was taxed to the heirs. (Obi TN, Cir Ct Min, 4/no#)

KEY, Joseph S.
Died before 2 September 1872 when N. J. Sorrell was appointed administrator, with B. C. Burgie as his security. (Dyr TN, Co Ct Min, B/464) John H. York, A. B. Jones and Bluford Terrill were appointed to lay off a years allowance for Mrs. Carrie Key, the widow. (Ibid 465)

KEYS, Alexander D.
5 June 1829 was certified to be 21 years of age & of good moral character. (McM TN, Co Ct Min, 2no#/370)

KILBURN, Henry
Ordered that he be exempted from paying poll tax as an infirm person. [no date given but it was after February term 1788]. (Was TN, Co Ct Min, 1/320)

KIMBROUGH, Robert
1 January 1805 gave power of attorney to his friend, William G. Poindexter, of Louisa County, VA, to settle his business with Charles Yancy of said Louisa County, VA, & to receive any money due him in Louisa County, VA, concerning a partnership in Kentucky lands. (Roa TN, Co Ct Min, A/325) On 19 September 1806 Robert Kimbrough gave power of attorney to his son-in-law, Samuel Waddy, "to receive from all persons, or of & from my Attornies, Asa Thompson Capt. William Smith B. William G. Poindexter or other attornies, to transact all business in KY or VA." (Ibid B/216)

KINCHELOE
February term 1789 John and George Kincheloe were excused from paying poll taxes for 1787 &1788, having paid the same in the State of VA. (Was TN, Co Ct Min, 1/364) [Also see Kanchlow]

KING
22 September 1853 a petition was made by Worley D. King & wife Mary D., Redden A., Barbara S. S. A., & Joseph R. King, Jas W. Waldren, Kenneth R. King & William J. King. William John King executed a deed to Jas. Henry King on 9 September 1847 in Madison County, which stated: "I William John King of Fayette County, Tenn, for the love and affection which I have for my parents, brothers & sisters, and in compromise of certain suits now pending wherin I am plaintiff & my father, Worley D. King is defendant...granted certain property to Jas. Henry King of Madison Co. in trust for the benefit of my mother Mary Hopson King for life & the life of her husband Worley D. King. After the death of Mary Hopson King & her husband Worley D. King, Jas. Henry King is to convey same to my brothers & sisters, Francis Caroline King, Reddon Alonzo King, Barbara S. S. A. King & Joseph Richard King." The complainants, Worley D. King & Mary H. King, are the parents of the other petitioners. Jas. Henry King died in September 1852, intestate, without leaving a wife or issue. Francis Caroline died in 1852, intestate & without issue. Petitioners want to sell the land & buy a negro and land in AR. (Mad TN, Ch Ct Min,

1/348-351) Petition was made 18 February 1857 by Worley D. King in his own right & as administrator of Jas. Henry King, Mary Hobson King, wife of said Worley, Redden Alonzo King, Barbara S. A. King, Jos. Richard King, Kenneth Rufus King, William John King & James Waldran. Waldran bought the land. (Ibid 2/117)

KING, Edward
Died before 5 February 1811 when land was taxed to the heirs. (Ste TN, Co Ct Min, 3/39)

KING, Ellender
5 April 1859 Elijah Ogle was allowed money for the support of Ellender King. (Sev TN, Co Ct Min, no#/434)

KING, Ephraim
7 August 1787 came into court and complained that he was rendered incapable of supporting himself & family and asked to be discharged from paying public taxes, which was granted. (Was TN, Co Ct Min, 1/290)

KING, H. D.
Died before 4 September 1871 when Thomas G. Churchman was appointed administrator, with Smith Parks and G. B. Miller as security. J. F. Williamson, L. M. Williams and C. E. White were appointed to lay off a years allowance for the widow and family. (Dyr TN, Co Ct Min, B/276) The widow was Mrs. A. King. (Ibid 379) 5 May 1873 suit was brought by the administrator vs O. F. Brown et als. The names and residences of the heirs are unknown and publication is to be made. (Ibid 584) 1 September 1873 it was stated that H. D. King died without issue and that A. R. Brown was his widow. (Ibid 619)

KING, Jackson, Genl.
Died before 7 February 1871 when C. S. Nolan, the public administrator, was appointed administrator. (Dyr TN, Co Ct Min, B/193)

KING, James
Died before 5 February 1811 when land was taxed to the heirs. (Ste TN, Co Ct Min, 3/39)

KING, Joseph B.
Died before 1 January 1872 when W. A. King was appointed administrator, with William Wesson and T. M. Strange as his security. (Dyr TN, Co Ct Min, B/334)

KING, Robert
19 June 1806 the following was entered in the minutes: "I hereby certify that I raised a groundless story upon Joseph Robinson by the persuation of two men living & being on Emery river this 3rd of December 1805. (Signed) Robert King." (Roa TN, Co Ct Min, B/170)

KING, Robt.
Died before 12 February 1812 when the heirs were on a tax list. (Rob TN, Co Ct Min, 3/70)

KING, Stephen
3 December 1872 James M. King made a settlement as guardian of Stephen King's heirs. (Dyr TN, Co Ct Min, B/517)

KING, W. R.
Died before 1 August 1870 when E. M. Hall, T. D. Harwell and Thos. Fitzhugh were appointed to lay off a years allowance for the widow and family. (Dyr TN, Co Ct Min, B/86) Timothy Griffin was appointed administrator, with E. M. Hall and Willie Harris as security. (Ibid 87) The years provision was made for Mrs. E. M. King and family. (Ibid 109)

KING, William
Died before 22 March 1809 as shown in the suit of Samuel Martin & Co vs Thomas Blake. It was stated that William King, one of the plaintiffs, was dead and Hugh Martin & Samuel Martin were the surviving partners. (Roa TN, Co Ct Min, C/292)

KING, William
Died before 9 November 1814 when land was taxed to the heirs. (Ste TN, Co Ct Min, 4/233) The death of William King was suggested 23 April 1809 in the suit of Vance King & Bradley vs Abraham Davidson. (Ibid 4/no#)

KING, William
9 January 1861 was allowed money for taking care of his afflicted wife. (Sev TN, Co Ct Min, no#/648)

KING, Wyley
Died before 1 August 1859 when the nuncupetive will was entered. Notice was given to Margaret King, the widow, to appear at the September term to dissent from said will if she sees proper. (Sev TN, Co Ct Min, no#/464) 6 November 1865 Margaret King made petition for dower and John A. Trotter, R. W. Crowson & James H. Lawson were appointed to lay it off. (Ibid 236)

KIRBY
22 August 1866 Jno. L. Brown was appointed guardian of Richd. W., Mary C., Martha M. & Asa [Ara] E. King. [The name also looks like Kirby or Kieley] This is in the suit of Jas. Sowell [Lowell] vs Jno. Irvin & others. (Mad TN, Ch Ct Min, 2/506) This same suit shows that Jesse Kirby was deceased and that said Kirby had borrowed of his father to pay for land. Both the said Wiley & Jesse Kirley are dead. Jno. Irvin is administrator of Jesse Kirley, deceased, & he and Nancy M. Kirley have failed to answer this bill. The minors have answered by their guardian. Nancy M. is to have her dower. (Ibid 547)

KIRBY, Henry W.
Died before 15 July 1853 as shown in the suit of Mary Ann Stratton by next friend vs Francis M. Goolsby & Hartwell Stratton. Mary Ann is the wife of Hartwell Stratton and the daughter of Henry W. Kirby, deceased. Francis M. Goolsby is administrator of Henry W. Kirby. Mary Ann requested that her inheritance be vested in a trustee for her separate use and not in her husband. (Jac TN, Ch Ct Min, B/107) In the suit of John W. Ragland vs Jane Kirby & others it is stated that defendants Patrick & Martha Kirby are minor heirs of Henry Kirby, deceased, and Jane Kirby was appointed guardian ad litem. (Ibid 117) Mary Ann Stratton was appointed her own trustee. (Ibid 275) A suit was entered 17 July 1856 by Martha Jane Kirby, Hartwell Straton, Mary A. Straton formerly Mary A. Kirby, Patrick P. Kirby, Martha J. Kirby, Jr., the last 2 by next friend Martha Jane Kirby, Sr. vs William H. Kirby & Amon Hail. Henry W. Kirby was the ancestor of the complainants & had bought land from William H. Kirby. There was a mistake in the deed. (Ibid C/16) 6 February 1857 it was shown that Mary An Stratton was a married woman and had her property settled on her. Patrick P. Kirby was unmarried and Martha Jane Kirby was a minor. (Ibid 59) On 16 July 1858 Patrick P. Kirby was said to ba a non-resident. (Ibid 156)

KIRBY, Miles
15 May 1810 a jury found that he was an insane man and considered dangerous to his family and the rest of the community. (Rob TN, Co Ct Min, 2/261) Nicholas Conrad & Anderson Cheatham were appointed guardians. (Ibid 278)

KIRBY, Wiley
Died soon after making his will 4 July 1860. Stephen Burras was named executor but declined to serve. F. R. Dallum? was appointed administrator with will annexed. Haborn Kirby et als sued for an accounting of the estate on 20 August 1868. (Mad TN, Ch Ct Min, 3/218)

KIRK, Elijah
5 June 1871 S. R. Latta made a settlement as guardian of Elijah Kirk's heirs. (Dyr TN, Co Ct Min, B/243)

KIRKENDALL, Peter
Died before 5 May 1783 when the will was proved by Andrew Thompson and John Kirkindall. (Was TN, Co Ct Min, 1/207)

KIRKPATRICK, David
Died before 18 December 1816 when Hugh Kirkpatrick & James Stuart, Jr. were appointed administrators with Alexander Kirkpatrick as security. (Wil TN, Co Ct Min, no#/63) A years provision was set off for Rebecca Kirkpatrick, the widow, and her 6 children. (Ibid 64)

KIRKPATRICK, James
Died before 18 June 1816 when David Kirkpatrick was appointed administrator, with Allen Ross as security. (Wil TN, Co Ct Min, no#/13)

KIRKPATRICK, John
Died before 16 February 1818 when Robert & Jane Motheral sold their interest in the

estate to Samuel Motheral, witnessed by Richard Anderson, Joseph Kirkpatrick, Halem Crisswell & John Motheral. (Wil TN, Reg Bk/231)

KIRKPATRICK, Robert
Died before 23 March 1803 when Elizabeth Kirkpatrick & Soloman Geran were granted letters of administration, with Peter Crouch their security. (Roa TN, Co Ct Min, A/76)

KIRKSEY, William
Died before 6 February 1815 when Rachel Kirksey was appointed administratrix with James H. Russell & Wm. L. Allen as security. (Ste TN, Co Ct Min, 4/240)

KITTS, John
Died before 18 January 1802 when the will was proved by Nicholas Conrad. (Rob TN, Co Ct Min, 1/195) James Norfleet took oath as executor. (Ibid 198)

KNIGHT, Robert
Died before 18 March 1817 when the administrator made a report. (Wil TN, Co Ct Min, no#/86) Archibald Young was appointed guardian of Malinda Knight, Sally Knight, Sampson Knight, Thompson Knight & Polly Knight, minor heirs. (Ibid 244)

KNIGHT, Thos.
Died before 1 May 1871 when W. F. Nash made a settlement as administrator. (Dyr TN, Co Ct Min, B/236)

KNIGHT, W. P.
Died before 9 March 1870 when dower was assigned to his widow, Sarah Jane Knight, by Asa Griffin, A. B. Stalcup & Bryant White. The petition was made by Sarah J. Knight vs W. C. Fitzhugh et als. (Dyr TN, Co Ct Min, B/21) W. F. Nash was administrator. (Ibid 236)

KNIGHT, Wm.
Died before 23 February 1866 when his death was admitted in the suit of Wm. Knight vs Geo. M. Birdsong et als. The suit was revived in the name of Jno. Irvin, administrator. (Mad TN, Ch Ct Min, 2/487)

KOEN, Abraham
Died before 18 January 1802 when Benj. Koen was appointed administrator. (Rob TN, Co Ct Min, 1/196)

KOEN, Daniel
Died before 19 January 1801 when the will was proved by Benjamin Koen. (Rob TN, Co Ct Min, 1/160)

KYSER, Valentine
Died before 29 August 1844 when Demarguis D. Hix, administrator with the will annexed, petitioned to sell slaves. (Bed TN, Ch Ct Min, 2/297) The proceeds of the sale is to be divided into 8 shares and distributed to Jacob Kyser, William Kyser, Valentine Kyser, Jr., Daniel Kyser, Enoch Kyser, Jesse B. Gant and Mary Hime, each one share. He shall subdivide the remaining 1/8 into 3 parts & pay same to Mary Heasty wife of Joseph Heasty, William Seorlie? [Scorlic], and divide the remaining 1/3 of 1/8 into 2 parts & pay to Nathaniel Hubbard & Nancy Dacus wife of John Dacus. (Ibid 326)

LACAY, A. J.
Taxes were not collected in District 5 for 1873, "over age." (Dyr TN, Co Ct Min, B/759)

LACKINGS, James G.
1 April 1867 a boy calling himself James G. Lackings, supposed to be about 7 years of age, was bound to Levi S. Roberts. (Sev TN, Co Ct Min, no#/442)

LACY [Lacey]
John P. Lacy, Thos. Lacy & Martha Ann Lacy, last 2 minors who appear by their guardian Hugh R. Lacy, petition to sell land, 15 March 1855. (Mad TN, Ch Ct Min, 2/30) 30 August 1860 some land was sold & bought by James A. Hudson, Louisa Lacey, John P. Lacey, Hugh R. Lacey & Thomas P. Lacey. (Ibid 389)

LAMB, B. F.
Died before 3 October 1871 when Thomas Frazier made a settlement as administrator. (Dyr TN, Co Ct Min, B/305) 4 November 1872 a years provision was set off to the widow and family. (Ibid 505)

LAMBERT, Aaron
Died before 2 February 1819 when the heirs petitioned for a division of the real estate. (Wil TN, Co Ct Min, no#/403)

LAMBERT, Thomas
Died before 16 December 1816 when the noncupative will was proved by Daniel Dyres & Shadrach Gregg. Letters of administration with will annexed were granted to Judith Lambert, the widow, with William Draper as security. (Wil TN, Co Ct Min, no#/47)

LAMBETH, Aaron
Died before 4 May 1818 when Pleasant Irby was appointed administrator, with Carter Irby & John Irby as security. A years support was allotted to the widow. (Wil TN, Co Ct Min, no#/249)

LAMBETH, Francis
Died before 16 September 1816 when the signature was proved by James Howard as witness to a deed from John Howard to Samuel New. (Wil TN, Co Ct Min, no#/25)

LAMBETH, William
Died before 17 September 1817 when Warner Lambeth & Lawrence Sypert were appointed administrators, with William Sypert as security. (Wil TN, Co Ct Min, no#/171)

LANCASTER, Elijah
Died before 9 May 1811 as shown when the executors, Jesse Denson & William M. Cooley, were ordered to make a report. (Ste TN, Co Ct Min, 3/61)

LANCASTER, Polly
Gave consent on 9 November 1814 that her son, West Noel Haggard alias West Noel Lancaster, be bound to William Hazzard [Haggard], Sr., who agrees to give him sufficient schooling. (Ste TN, Co Ct Min, 4/218)

LANCASTER, Robert
Died before 11 March 1806 when Elijah Lancaster was appointed administrator. (Ste TN, Co Ct Min, 1/26b) 20 October 1807 the coroner, Charles B. Wilson, was allowed $10 for holding an inquest on the body of Robert Lancaster and another one on the body of a child of Nelly Cathays. (Ibid 51b)

LANCASTER, Saml.
Died before 21 February 1861 as shown in the suit of Alex Jackson vs Jno. M. Gladen, Saml C. Lancaster, John Fichwick & Jno. S. Lancaster. It is stated "that Jno. L. & Saml. C. Lancaster were the Executors & Legatees of their Father, Saml. Lancaster." (Mad TN, Ch Ct Min, 2/435)

LANCASTER, Sarah L.
Gave consent 9 November 1814 that her daughter, Crisianna Lancaster, be bound to Abram Clark until she arrive at the age of 18. She is now about 3 years old. (Ste TN, Co Ct Min, 4/224)

LANDCASTER, Eligah
Made his will 9 September 1808. He asked that his fire arms, cooper's tools & carpenter's tools be sold. He left his property to his wife, Faithey, during her widowhood and if she should marry that she shall have one child's part during her life and the balance to be sold for the benefit of his children. He mentioned sons, Aaron and Ephraim. He appointed Jessee Denson and William Cooley executors, witnessed by Nathl. Denson and Noah Sinclair. (Ste TN, Co Ct Min, no#/82)

LANE, ____
Died before 4 April 1870 when Cowles & Waits was paid for a pauper coffin. (Dyr TN, Co Ct Min, B/32)

LANE, Alec
Taxes were not collected in District 5 for 1873, "under age." (Dyr TN, Co Ct Min, B/759)

LANE, Elizabeth
8 November 1830 sued Tidence Lane for divorce. The defendant was not found. (Obi TN, Cir Ct Min, 1/126) The next friend of Elizabeth Lane was Jno. L. Doxey. (Ibid 131) Divorce was granted 11 May 1831 and they were restored to all the rights of single persons "except the right of intermarying with each other." (Ibid 171)

LANG, James
9 November 1782 was bound to Alexander Greer. (Was TN, Co Ct Min, 1/189) 3 August 1784 James Lang was said to be 14 years old when bound to Alexander Gre__. (Ibid 246)

LANGFORD, Josiah H. [Longford]
In the suit of Edwin J. Andrews vs Josiah H. Langford 14 August 1860, Josiah H. Langford was said to be a lunatic and in the Lunatic Assylum of TN. David M. Haile was appointed guardian ad litem. (Jac TN, Ch Ct Min, C/387)

LANGFORD, Stephen
Was a resident of Lincoln County, KY, 1 August 1795 when he gave a power of attorney to "my trusted friend Benjamine Shaw of Washington County in the Territory of the United States of America, South of the river Ohio." [TN], to sue Hugh Smith, acting attorney for John Smith, both of Rutherford County, NC, for 400 acres of land. Witnesses were Joseph Brittain & Ellis Bean. (Was TN, Co Ct Min, 1/552)

LANGSTON
Jerusha Langston dismissed her suit against Richard Langston on 14 January 1850. Suit not identified. (Mad TN, Ch Ct Min, 1/97)

LANGSTON, Mary H.
5 November 1856 her guardian, John Andes, resigned as guardian of Mary H. Langston formerly Mary H. Atchley. (Sev TN, Co Ct Min, no#/86) Benjamin Langston was appointed her guardian with McCajah Atchley as security. (Ibid 87)

LANHAM, Saml.
Died before 10 May 1815 when Abel Lanham was appointed administrator with Dennis Condry and John Wallen as security. (Cla TN, Co Ct Min, 4/52)

LANIER, Clement
Died before 10 February 1810 when Thomas Lanier made petition for himself & others for a division of the land of Clement Lanier, deceased. Henry Pugh, Duncan McRea and Robert Cooper were appointed to divide the property. (Ste TN, Co Ct Min, 4/no#)

LANIER, Jane
Was the mother of a bastard child by George Maggard who was ordered to pay support 2 June 1873. George was granted an appeal to Circuit Court. (Dyr TN, Co Ct Min, B/589)

LANIER, John
Was a resident of Lincoln County, TN, on 9 October 1840 as shown in the suit of Claiborne W. Black vs John Lanier. (Bed TN, Ch Ct Min, 1/320)

LANIER, William
Made a deed of gift of one ninth part of 400 acres of land to Asa Lanier. It was proved by Isaac Lanier on 7 February 1814. (Ste TN, Co Ct Min, 4/84)

LANKFORD, John L.
Died before 6 January 1863 when Andrew Cusick, John Cusick & Andrew Delozier were appointed to lay off a years support to the widow. (Sev TN, Co Ct Min, no#/42) The widow was Jane Lankford. (Ibid 46)

LANKFORD, Robert
Was the father of a bastard child on the body of Mary McMurry. He gave bond for its maintenance 7 June 1826 with Manuel Parkinson as his security. (McM TN, Co Ct Min, 2no#/163)

LANSDON, Robert
Died before 17 June 1816 when the will was proved by William Bone & Eli M. Lansdon. Susannah Lansdon, Thomas D. Lansdon & [torn] Bone were executors. The widow was allotted a years support. (Wil TN, Co Ct Min, no#/1)

LARD, Elijah
Was a minor child when he was bound at September term 1802 to George Stubblefield until age 21. Elijah will be eight years of age on 14 May 1803. (Cla TN, Co Ct Min, 1/55) George Stubblefield resigned his charge and Elijah Lard was bound to James Dodson until age 21. (Ibid 2/60)

LATHAM, James C.
Died before 13 April 1857 when his death was suggested in the suit of John R. McGee vs James C. Latham & others. (Fen TN, Ch Ct Min, A/77) C. W. Latham was appointed administrator. John W., Calvin S. & Mary E. Latham are the only heirs. (Ibid 104 &5) Gertrude Latham is a minor daughter of James C. Latham, deceased. (Ibid 116) Claborne W. Latham was appointed guardian ad litem for John W., Calvin S., and Mary E. Latham, 11 October 1858. (Ibid 158) The heirs were shown as Calvin L. Latham, Mary Latham, John W. & Laura Gertrude Latham and [blank] Latham, who are all minors. (Ibid 185) Martha Latham was the widow. (Ibid 245)

LATHAM, John
Was bound to Wm. Pauly 7 April 1809 until age 21. (Rob TN, Co Ct Min, 2/130)

LATIMER, Hugh
Died before 13 February 1815 when the will was proved by William Latimer & Nathaniel Latimer. Joseph Latimer, one of the executors named, qualified. (Rob TN, Co Ct Min, 3/533)

LATTA, James
Died before 7 November 1870 when Samuel R. Latta renewed his bond as guardian of the minor heirs. (Dyr TN, Co Ct Min, B/131)

LAUDERDALE
7 December 1824 James Cowan was appointed guardian of Robert Lauderdale, Josephus Lauderdale & Almira Lauderdale, minor heirs of [blank] Lauderdale, deceased. (McM TN, Co Ct Min, 2no#/41)

LAURENCE, Elizabeth
Died before 14 November 1814 when the will was proved by James Norfleet. Elias Lawrence was executor. (Rob TN, Co Ct Min, 3/490)

LAURENCE, Margaret
Died before March 1806 when the heirs were on the tax list with land on Spring Creek. (Wil TN, Co Ct Min, no#/233)

LAURENCE, Nathl.
Died before March term 1805 when the heirs were on the tax list with land on Spring Creek. (Wil TN, Co Ct Min, no#/117)

LAUTON [Luiton]
8 October 1873 W. W. Davis was appointed "to convey the old lady Lauton and 2 daugthers to the Poor house and the widow and her 3 children to her brothers in Gibson County, TN." (Dyr TN, Co Ct Min, B/647)

LAVELLETTE
19 February 1861 Alex. W. Campbell was appointed guardian ad litem to answer for the minor defendants in the suit of A. T. Lavellette & Sarah C. Lavellette vs Mary K., Margaret D. and Martha D. Lavellette. (Mad TN, Ch Ct Min, 2/419)

LAWSON, A.
Died before 3 August 1863 when another trustee was appointed in his place. A. Lawson had been trustee to a deed of trust from L. W. Burn to Wm. & James P. Catlett "and the trust has not been wound up satisfied." M. A. Rawlings was appointed trustee. (Sev TN, Co Ct Min, no#/64)

LAWSON, A.
Died before 3 April 1866 when W. C. Murphy was appointed administrator with J. C. Murphy as security. (Sev TN, Co Ct Min, no#/310) Evelina D. Lawson wife of A. Lawson, deceased, asked to have dower laid off for her. (Ibid 323)

LAWSON, A. P. [Alexander]
Died before 7 October 1856 when Lucinda Lawson resigned as guardian of Nancy Lawson, a minor heir. B. J. Tipton was appointed guardian with E. Hodges as security. (Sev TN, Co Ct Min, no#/82) 1 February 1858 Benj. J. Tipton made a settlement as guardian of Nancy C. Lawson, deceased. [sic] (Ibid 252) 4 September 1865 B. J. Tipton made a settlement. (Ibid 201) 1 July 1867 B. J. Tipton made a settlement as guardian to Nancy C. Lawson, minor heir of A. W. Lawson. (Ibid 461)

LAWSON, Andrew
Died before 1 December 1856 when A. Lawson made a settlement as administrator. (Sev TN, Co Ct Min, no#/92)

LAWSON, Andrew W.
Was a minor under the age of 21 when A. Lawson was appointed special guardian 2 August 1858, with permission to sell 80 acres of land. The land was warrant No. 8984 dated 26 October 1855 and was issued to Andrew W. Lawson for the services of Andrew Lawson as Captain in the War of 1812. (Sev TN, Co Ct Min, no#/323-4)

LAWSON, Ephroditus [Lossan, Lawason]
Died before 9 May 1814 when the will was proved by James Norfleet & Nicholas Nicholson. James Norfleet was the executor. (Rob TN, Co Ct Min, 3/394-5)

LAWSON, Jacob
Was charged with Bastardy 3 March 1824. The case is dismissed "because the child he is charged with being the father of, was born in Rhea County and not within the jurisdiction of this court." (McM TN, Co Ct Min, no#/130)

LAYMAN, A. M.
Died before 6 May 1867 when the will was proved by John Fargason & John Russell. John M. Layman was appointed executor. (Sev TN, Co Ct Min, no#/452)

LAYMAN, Joseph C.
17 July 1866 was released from working on the public road on account of physical disability. (Sev TN, Co Ct Min, no#/351)

LEA, William C.
Was a resident of Shelby County, AL, on 5 December 1828 when his deposition was to be taken for the defendant in the case of Daniel Carmichael vs Thomas Barclay. (McM TN, Co Ct Min, no#/399)

LEACH, Thadius
Died before 5 October 1870 when Stephen Peirce was appointed administrator, with C. H. Alston and W. C. Doyle as his security. (Dyr TN, Co Ct Min, B/122)

LEAK, Isaac
Died before 18 March 1817 when an inventory was recorded. (Wil TN, Co Ct Min, no#/80)

LEAK, Saml.
Died before 16 December 1816 as shown when a deed was entered that he had witnessed. (Wil TN, Co Ct Min, no#/51)

LEAKLEY, William
Died before 19 March 1818 when James George, one of the heirs, sold his part of the estate of William Leakley, deceased, to Eli Leakley of Warren County, TN. James George also gave power of attorney to Eli Leakley to collect a legacy, which power of attorney was recorded in 1825. (Wil TN, Reg Bk/353)

LEATH, G. W.
Taxes were not collected in District 2 for 1873, "cant be found." (Dyr TN, Co Ct Min, B/758)

LEDBETTER, David
4 January 1871 his heirs were mentioned in the petition of M. J. Caruthers for dower. (Dyr TN, Co Ct Min, B/175)

LEDBETTER, J. M.
Taxes were not collected in District 4 for 1873, "over age." (Dyr TN, Co Ct Min, B/759)

LEDBETTER, J. N.
Died before 1 September 1873 when Wilson Wynne made a settlement as administrator. (Dyr TN, Co Ct Min, B/619)

LEDBETTER, Tom
Taxes were not collected in District 2 for 1873, "gone." (Dyr TN, Co Ct Min, B/759)

LEDSINGER, Isaac
Taxes were not collected in District 5 for 1873, "over age." (Dyr TN, Co Ct Min, B/759)

LEE, Abraham
Died before 7 November 1843 as shown in the suit of Daniel Lee Admr. vs Creditors of Abraham Lee Decd. (Jac TN, Ch Ct Min, A/121) Land is to be sold subject to the widow's dower. (Ibid 181) Daniel Lee died and the suit was revived 27 January 1847 in the name of David H. Draper, administrator of said Daniel Lee, deceased. (Ibid 237)

LEE, Eliza
Was the sister of William L. Parrott as shown in the suit of William Woodfolk vs Eliza Lee, Jesse Lee & William S. Parrott. Jesse Lee was her husband. (Jac TN, Ch Ct Min, C/208)

LEE, John
Died before 14 July 1855 as shown in the suit of Agness Short vs James W. Draper Admr. The court decided that "John Lee, defendants intestate, was illigitimate and has no brothers or sisters living?, that his uncles & aunts are illigitimate and compt.? [complainant?] the grand mother of decd. or any other person cannot inherit from him." The funds in the hands of the administrator is an escheat to the common school fund of the State of TN. (Jac TN, Ch Ct Min, B/281)

LEE, John
Was a non-resident of TN 12 February 1859 as shown in the suit of A. H. Morgan & others vs John Lee and others. (Jac TN, Ch Ct Min, C/206)

LEE, Peter
Died before 26 February 1845 when his death was admitted in the suit of Elizabeth Snelling who sues &c vs Lemuel Snelling & Peter Lee Adm. of Hugh Snelling. The suit is to be revived in the name of John McGuire, administrator de bonis non of said Hugh Snelling. (Bed TN, Ch Ct Min, 2/349)

LEECH, Jno.
Was the father of a bastard child by Jannett Bogle. He gave bond for its support 18 June 1817 with Thomas Leech as security. (Wil TN, Co Ct Min, no#/124)

LEEGETT, Danl.
Was of Washington County, NC, when he sold to Daniel Cherry of said state and County of Martin, a negro man by the name of Ned, 26 March 1810, witnessed by Jesse Cherry, Hardy Aimes & Henry Cooper. (Wil TN, Reg Bk/38)

LEEK, Margaret
Died before 7 May 1866 when W. M. Burnett was appointed guardian to M. J. Leek, R. O. Leek & A. P. Leek, minor orphans, with J. M. McCroskey as security. (Sev TN, Co Ct Min, no#/327)

LEELAND, George
Was bound 5 November 1804 to Peter Brawner until age 21. (Rob TN, Co Ct Min, 1/318)

LEEPER, George
Died before 25 September 1807 when land was taxed to the heirs. (Roa TN, Co Ct Min, C/23)

LEGAN, Richard
Died before 19 June 1817 when Abraham McGehee was appointed administrator. (Wil TN, Co Ct Min, no#/130)

LEGATE, Wm.
Died before 22 June 1841 when John Legate, the administrator, petitioned to sell slaves. (Obi TN, Cir Ct Min, 4/no#) The slaves were sold 23 February 1842 and William Legate was the purchaser. (Ibid)

LEMARR, Nancy
19 July 1796 was ordered to bring her daughter, Milly Loggans, to the next court. (Rob TN, Co Ct Min, 1/5)

LEMMONS, Mary
Was stated to be an aged & infirm woman, 7 June 1824, when Reuben Lemmons was allowed money for her support. (McM TN, Co Ct Min, 2no#/5)

LENARD, John
Taxes were not collected in District 2 for 1873, "gone." (Dyr TN, Co Ct Min, B/759)

LESTER, Mary E.
Died before 2 April 1872 when J. M. Thompson was appointed administrator, with G. B. Tinsley and B. C. Burgie as his security. (Dyr TN, Co Ct Min, B/396)

LETTON, George W.
Was a resident of Davidson County, TN, on 9 October 1826 when his deposition was to be taken for the defendant in the case of William Terrell vs Daniel Dunnevant. (Obi TN, Cir Ct Min, 1/5)

LEWALLING, Jas.
14 October 1861 a charge of bastardy against him was quashed. (Sev TN, Co Ct Min, no#/722)

LEWELL, Elizabeth
Died before 7 March 1826 when William Lewell was appointed administrator. (McM TN, Co Ct Min, 2no#/138)

LEWIS, G. L.
Taxes were not collected in District 4 for 1873, "over age." (Dyr TN, Co Ct Min, B/759)

LEWIS, George
23 February 1779 was tried for Treason. Witnesses for the State were Wm. Williams and Elizabeth English. He was found to be "a spie or an officer from Feoridia (?) out of the English Army." (Was TN, Co Ct Min, 1/63)

LEWIS, Henry
Died before 16 June 1817 when the administrator was ordered to make a report. (Wil TN, Co Ct Min, no#/110) John Lewis was administrator. (Ibid 148)

LEWIS, Howel
2 May 1821 "being of that age that the laws of the State of Tennessee sanctions & authorise for the making of all legal contracts Viz, that of 21 years" sold a slave to Benjamin Wright. (Wil TN, Reg Bk/201)

LEWIS, James
Was an orphan when he was bound 8 August 1814 to George G. Brown to learn the paper making business. (Rob TN, Co Ct Min, 3/440)

LEWIS, James H.
Was a resident of Franklin County, TN, 8 May 1820 when he made a bill of sale to Matthew Figurs as trustee for Martha H. Lewis of the County of Wilson, for 7 slaves. It gives conditions should Martha H. Lewis become a widow or should be divorced from the said James W. Lewis. (Wil TN, Reg Bk/171)

LEWIS, Joel
Died before 21 February 1839 when land was taxed to the heirs. (Obi TN, Cir Ct Min, 3/297) Robert C. Nall filed a petition on 22 February 1839 stating that he was a tenant in common with others owning different quantities of a 2,500 acre grant of land issued to Robert Nall, the heirs of Joel Lewis, deceased, and James Caruthers. Robert Nall was granted 1,250 acres, James Caruthers 250 acres and the heirs of Joel Lewis, deceased 1,000 acres. Robert Nall has conveyed all his right to the land to Robert C. Nall who petitions to have the land divided. (Ibid 320) Robert's name was also shown as Naul & Nawl. (Ibid 350) On 18 October 1842 William B. Jones vs Thomas Claiborn et al petition was made for division of this same land. Jones stated he was a tenant in common with the defendants in 2,500 acres of land issued to Robert Nall, the heirs of Joel Lewis, deceased, and James Caruthers. (Ibid 4/no#)

LEWIS, John
Died before 19 October 1818 as shown when his daughter, Elizabeth Davis, made a deed of gift to her son, Isham F. Davis, for all the money due her from the estate of her father, John Lewis, deceased. (Wil TN, Reg Bk/137)

LEWIS, Katy
Was a pauper 4 April 1870 when $20 was allowed for her care. (Dyr TN, Co Ct Min, B/33)

LEWIS, William T.
Died before 6 December 1824 when Joseph Williams made a mortgage deed to William B. Lewis, attorney in fact for the executor of William T. Lewis. (McM TN, Co Ct Min, 2no#/34)

LEWIS, William T.
Died before 12 August 1813 when the executors, Thomas Crutcher, Alfred Balch & Andrew Jackson were in a suit against Oliver Edwards. (Rob TN, Co Ct Min,3/297)

LIGHT, Chaney
Was the mother of a bastard child of whom she accused Stephen Grimm with being the father. 6 May 1873 the court found that he was not the father. (Dyr TN, Co Ct Min, B/587)

LIGHT, Charlotte
Was the mother of a bastard child of whom she accused Stephen Walton of being the father. 3 June 1873 the court found that he was not the father. (Dyr TN, Co Ct Min, B/591)

LIGHT, E. P.
Died before 4 January 1871 when the heirs were released from tax on 3,360 acres of land in District No. 7 wrongfully charged to them. (Dyr TN, Co Ct Min, B/161)

LIGHT, Nancy Adaline
Was a negro girl aged 4 years and 6 months when she was bound 3 March 1873 to W. H. Walker until age 18. She was bound with the consent of her mother. (Dyr TN, Co Ct Min, B/544)

LILLARD, Wash.
Taxes were not collected in District 2 for 1873, "gone." (Dyr TN, Co Ct Min, B/759)

LINDSEY, Eli
6 May 1861 a motion was made to quash a charge of Bastardy, which was sustained. (Sev TN, Co Ct Min, no#/686)

LINDSEY, Joseph
Was a resident of Rutherford County, TN, on 9 October 1841 as shown in the suit of Jacob Morton vs D. H. Lindsey & others. Joseph was a brother of Dudley H. Lindsey. (Bed TN, Ch Ct Min, 1/393)

LINN, Andrew [Lynn]
Died before 13 November 1834 as shown in the suit of Robert B. Harper, executor of the will of Andrew Linn deceased vs Robert White. (Obi TN, Cir Ct Min, 2/207)

LINN, Jane A.
18 June 1838 her guardian was in a case: Joel S. Enloe, guardian of Jane A. Linn, for the use of George H. Long vs William Nelms & Daniel St. John. (Obi TN, Cir Ct Min, 3/192)

LIPSCUM, J. R. E.
Died before 14 July 1847 when a suit by the administrator, Samuel J. Neal, vs John T. Bryan administrator of S. G. Bryan deceased, was dismissed. (Mad TN, Ch Ct Min, 1/25)

LITTEN, Wm.
Died before 2 August 1819 when Thomas Essen [Epen] was appointed administrator with William Gray & John Ray as security. (Wil TN, Co Ct Min, no#/492)

LITTLE, Andrew
Died before 13 November 1815 when Mary Little was appointed administratrix with Wm. Howarton and John Grass as security. (Cla TN, Co Ct Min, 4/120)

LITTLE, George
28 August 1778 took the oath of allegience. (Was TN, Co Ct Min, 1/47)

LITTLE, Henry
Died before 15 December 1817 when the widow, Elizabeth Little, was appointed administratrix, with Samuel Vick & Joseph Neil as security. (Wil TN, Co Ct Min, no#/186)

LITTLE, Isabel
Was a minor 16 November 1795 when John Little was appointed her guardian. (Was TN, Co Ct Min, 1/573)

LITTLE, Thos.
28 August 1778 took the oath of allegience. (Was TN, Co Ct Min, 1/47)

LOCK, William [Locke]
Died before 2 November 1841 as shown in the suit of the administrator, William Scanland, against John Burris. (Jac TN, Ch Ct Min, A/28)

LOCKE [Lock]
A suit was entered 12 February 1859 by James Eaton & wife Polly Ann, James A. Sadler and his wife Sarah vs James W. Locke, William Locke, Augustus S. Locke & Catharine Locke. Process was served on James W. Locke & he has failed to answer. Answer was made by William Locke & Catharine Locke in proper person and of said William & Catherine and Augustus S. Locke by their guardian ad litem Sydney S. Stanton. The femmes complainants are covert & defendants William, Catherine & Augustus S. Locke are minors, the former two aged above 14 years. The Clerk & Master reports he has taken depositions of Benjamin B. Washburn, James R. Tolbert & Achilles Hare and stated that it would be to the interest of the children of James W. Lock to have title to the lands divested out of James W. Lock and James Eaton and vested in said children and to have the negroes sold to pay the debts of James W. Locke. James W. Lock had conveyed the lands to James Eaton in trust for all his children, for his own support and for the payment of his debts. Lands were mentioned that descended to James W. Locke from his father William Lock. Evidently all the children of James W. Locke were Polly Ann Eaton, Sarah Sadler, Catharine F. Locke, Augustus S. Locke & William Locke. (Jac TN, Ch Ct Min, C/219-21) A suit was entered 14 August 1860 by McCrea & Terrass & Mary Cornwell vs James Eaton, James W. Locke, Polly Ann Eaton, William Locke, Augustus S. Locke & Catherine F. Locke, James A. Sadler & wife Sally Sadler. William, Augustus & Catherine Locke are minors & David M. Haile was appointed guardian ad litem. (Ibid 387)

LOCUST, Elisabeth
15 October 1798 was certified to be a free negro girl on the testimony of Ann Barker. She had been a slave. (Rob TN, Co Ct Min, 1/74) 22 January 1799 Wm. McAdoo came into court and acknowledged that the negro woman in his possession, Elisabeth (or Betsey) Locust, was a free person. Hannah Locust, James Locust, Austin Locust & Moses Locust, children of Elisabeth are to remain in the possession of Wm. McAdoo until age 21. (Ibid 86) 21 April 1802 it was ordered that Hannah Locust, James, Austin & Moses Locust be released from Wm. McAdoo. McAdoo has treated them in an improper and unjustifiable manner. (Ibid 215) The above named children were bound to Ninian Edwards who is a resident of KY. (Ibid 216)

LOFTIN, Helen
Was a minor 15 March 1853 as shown in the petition by Jas. Holmes & Helen Loftin by her guardian. Catherine W. Loftin had sold land to Jas. Holmes and all the parties interested in said land had ratified the sale except Helen Loftin. (Mad TN, Ch Ct Min, 1/295) Her guardian was Geo. F. Jones. (Ibid 301)

LOFTIS, Sally Ann
5 February 1858 was granted a divorce from Tho. J. Loftis. (Jac TN, Ch Ct Min, C/117)

LOGG, Widow
Her heirs were listed on the 1804 non-resident tax list with land on Suggs Creek. (Wil TN, Co Ct Min, no#/83)

LOGGINS, Samuel
Was a resident of the state of KY 14 February 1811 when his deposition was to be taken for the defendant in the case of Samuel Elliott against Nathaniel Dickinson. (Rob TN, Co Ct Min, 2/382)

LOGIN, John
Died before 1805 when the heirs were on the tax list with land on Suggs Creek. (Wil TN, Co Ct Min, no#/142)

LONG
Died before 2 February 1813 when land was taxed to the heirs. (Ste TN, Co Ct Min, 4/13) Land was taxed to the heirs of Nicholas Long on 10 February 1814. (Ibid 139)

LONG, W. H.
Died before 18 February 1868 when his death was admitted in the suit of Ed Willis vs Wilhelm & others. (Mad TN, Ch Ct Min, 3/131)

LONG, William F.
Died before 28 December 1841 when his death was admitted in the suit of William F. Long & Co & Samuel Doak vs The Union Bank of Tennessee. The suit was revived in the

name of Rufus K. Flack for the firm of William F. Long & Co. (Bed TN, Ch Ct Min, 2/165) John Long was the administrator & filed suit against Mary Long & Preston Frazer. Frazer was accused of taking money from the pocket of William F. Long shortly after his death. William F. Long in his lifetime paid to James Long of AL money which was owed by said Mary Long to James Long. By a marriage contract between William F. and the said Mary she was empowered to contract as a femme sole. (Ibid 227) William F. Long was a citizen of Taladege County, AL. Rufus K. Flack was a citizen of MS. William F. Long, Rufus Flack & Joseph Long, now deceased, were partners in the firm of Wm. F. Long & Co. (Ibid 3/119)

LONGFORD, Julian
7 February 1855 sued by her next friend, Sterling Harris, for a divorce from John R. J. Longford. The plaintiff dismissed the suit. (Jac TN, Ch Ct Min, B/188)

LONGMIRE, Joseph
Martin Wiggs was guardian of the minor children of Joseph Longmire, 9 July 1850. (Mad TN, Ch Ct Min, 1/135) The minor children were: Martha J., Joseph H., Secan? E., William M. & Mary S. (Ibid 145)

LOONEY, R. A.
22 February 1861 in the suit of James Blaydes vs E. B. Mason et als, process was served on R. A. Looney while a minor & he has now attained his majority. (Mad TN, Ch Ct Min, 2/438)

LOVE, Catherine
Died before 17 October 1857 as shown in the suit of Mary Singleton vs John W. Love & others. In 1851 Mary Singleton was appointed guardian of her daughter, Catherine Singleton, & at her request purchased a tract of land. The land was a share of the dower tract of the heirs of the father of said Catherine, that is five shares out of eight. Mary Singleton took a deed to the said land in the name of Catherine. Part of this land was sold to James A. Crouch. After this sale, Catherine married John W. Love & took possession of the dower land. About seven weeks after this marriage Catherine died and John W. Love was administrator. Mary Singleton delivered to him the note from Crouch which he accepted and brought suit on Crouch. [See also Daniel Singleton] (Fen TN, Ch Ct Min, A/111) When James A. Crouch bought part of the land mentioned, he paid $50 of the price by his interest in the dower tract. (Ibid 155)

LOVE, Charles
Died before 18 February 1840 when land was taxed to the heirs. (Obi TN, Cir Ct Min, 4/no#)

LOVE, Joseph B.
Died before 13 July 1848 as shown in the suit of William T. Short vs John D. Grant surviving partner of the firm of Grant & Love & Jno. W. Love & Charles Hickox executors of Joseph B. Love the deceased partner of said firm. (Mad TN, Ch Ct Min, 1/39) 15 March 1855 John W. Love and others petitioned to sell land. It is in the interest of the legatees of Joseph B. Love, deceased, that the lot be sold. Jno. W. Love, Jr., William J. Love & Mary Love are of lawful age. All the legatees are before the court. The guardian is authorized to make a deed. (Ibid 2/31)

LOVE, Stephen
30 July 1849 suit was brought by John K. Pearce & John B. Love vs Robert Nesbit & Joseph Williams, Guardians of Stephen Love. (Mad TN, Ch Ct Min, 1/77, 105)

LOVE, Thomas
At the May term 1790 three relinquishments to Thomas Love, by Benja. Dillard, Robert Love & James Love, and Gabrial Elkens were made for the interest in a negro girl name Jude. (Was TN, Co Ct Min, 1/438)

LOVE, William K.
3 June 1829 was certified to be 21 years of age & of good moral character. (McM TN, Co Ct Min, 2no#/369)

LOVE, Wm. C.
Died before 15 September 1852 as shown in the suit of Jno. B. Love, Joseph H. & wife Mary E. Burton, Robt. B. Love, Robt. Nisbit & Joseph Williams guardians of Wm. E., Sarah E. & Stephen J. Love, heirs of Wm. C. Love, deceased vs Jas. Gadger & wife Anna, Robert Henry & wife Darcus, Jno. Patton, [blank] Johnson & wife Louisa, [blank] Miller & wife Winney, Jno. Welch & wife Mary, Jno. B. Love, Sr., Jas. R. Love, Dillard Love, Ganam

Magby & wife Sarah, Robert, Thos D., Jno. J., and E. A. S. Love, Robt. S. Deberry & wife Mary, and Robt. Love, heirs-at-law of Robert Love, deceased. Wm. C. Love, deceased, was one of the legal heirs of Robt. Love, deceased, late of the county of Haywood, NC. The complainants in this cause are the legal heirs of Wm. C. Love, deceased. Robert Love had made a distribution of lands to his children in writing in his lifetime, but died before executing a formal deed. The land was originally granted to Robt. & Thomas Love as assignees of George Gordon. Some of the land was in Gibson County. (Mad TN, Ch Ct Min, 1/259) 15 March 1855 in the suit of John B. Love et als vs Jno. B. Love et als, it is stated that Sarah E. has married Thos. C. Moore. Each petitioner was entitled to 1/6 of the land but they have sold and exchanged & now some are entitled to more than others. The proceeds in the Gibson lands now belong to Robt. B. Love, Thos. C. Moore, Sarah E. Moore, Eli W. Hale & Stephen J. Love. Jno. B. Love, Wm. E. Love & Jos. H. Bruton & wife Mary have now no interest in the Gibson lands. (Ibid 2/35)

LOVEDAY
7 January 1857 John Bird renewed his bond as guardian to Robert Loveday, Perry Loveday, Rhoton Loveday & Carroll Loveday, minor orphans, with C. Fox as security. The old bond was destroyed by fire. (Sev TN, Co Ct Min, no#/117)

LOVEDAY, Noah
2 August 1858 was released from paying poll tax because he was under 21 years of age. (Sev TN, Co Ct Min, no#/331)

LOVELACE
24 Feburary 1859 Jos. B. Freeman was appointed guardian ad litem for Fanny Lovelace & Ann Lovelace, minor defendants in the suit of Martin B. Key et als vs Jno. P. Key et als. (Mad TN, Ch Ct Min, 2/263)

LOVELADY, John
Died before 14 July 1853 as shown in the suit of Thomas A. Lovelady, administrator of Thomas Lovelady, deceased, & others vs Asa Lovelady, administrator &c of John Lovelady, deceased, & others. (Jac TN, Ch Ct Min, B/77)

LOVELADY, Thomas
Died before 9 February 1855 as shown in the suit of William H. Lovelady, Thomas A. Lovelady, Ezekiel Carnahan & wife Nancy Carnahan, Susannah G. Lovelady, Mary J. Lovelady, Elizabeth Lovelady, Samuel D. Lovelady & Darcus Lovelady in his representative character as the administrator of his father Thomas Lovelady deceased vs Asa Lovelady administrator of John Lovelady and Peter Shrum & Jesse Parker his security and Jeremiah Gammon the guardian of complainants. The three minors, Elizabeth, Samuel D. & Darcus Lovelady are entitled to more money. Thomas A. [a minor] is also entitled to money from the guardian. There was an error in the original inventory of $20 the interest on which sum for 11 years & 7 months to this time is $13.90. The widow of said John Lovelady having relinquished all further interest is said estate, the said Thomas Lovelady as administrator is entitled to recover same. (Jac TN, Ch Ct Min, B/197)

LOW
5 November 1866 Thomas Atchley was appointed guardian to A. C. & Dorah Low, minor orphans, with G. M. Maples as security. (Sev TN, Co Ct Min, no#/390)

LOW, Abner W.
Died before 5 June 1865 when John A. Trotter, Jesse Hill & W. F. Nichols were appointed to assign dower to Malissa C. Low, the widow. (Sev TN, Co Ct Min, no#/168) Gideon M. Maples was appointed admininstrator, with Thomas Maples as security. (Ibid 171) 8 August 1865 dower was set off for Malissa C. Maples, formerly Millissa C. Law. (Ibid 200)

LOWDER, Adam
Sold 112 acres of land in Montgomery County, VA, to Peter Garrent, 13 November 1815. (Cla TN, Co Ct Min, 4/120)

LOWDER, Jacob
Was ordered 23 May 1808 to pay to Rachal McFarland $8 for each month since the time she swore that he was the father of her bastard child and to pay her $33.33 for her care & trouble before the swearing said child. (Cla TN, Co Ct Min, 3/181)

LOWE, Daniel
Died in 1824 or 1825 in Bedford County, TN, as shown in the petition for division by John Lowe [Law] of Montgomery County, AL, vs Henry William Lowe. The land was bounded by a tract now owned by Isaac B. Law. Daniel Law left a will by which he left his land to

his wife, Martha Law, for life and at her death to his 3 sons, the petitioner, Henry William, George E. who is now a citizen of Tipton County, TN, and William who died in June 1833 leaving 5 children, to wit, George C., Danl. J., Seymore, Eliza Ann & Martha E., all of whom are citizens of Bedford County, and all minors. James Dillard is their guardian. Martha Low died in 1836. (Bed TN, Ch Ct Min, 1/61)

LOWE, William
Died about 1 July 1833 as shown in the suit of Martin Wisner vs Lucy Lowe & others. Martin Wisner was a citizen of Marshall County. His suit was against Lucy Lowe, the widow of William Lowe, deceased, and George C. Low, Seymore S. Lowe, Daniel Lowe, Eliza Ann Lowe and Martha Lowe, minor heirs & citizens of Bedford County. Martin Wisner is the administrator & had been the security for Daniel Barksdale & William W. Barksdale, previous administrators of the estate of said Lowe. William Lowe's share of his father's estate was mentioned. Daniel Lowe died sometime in 1825 in Bedford County, leaving land that after the death of his wife would go to his 3 sons, George E., John, and William, the last of whom is Martin Wisner's intestate. William died before his mother who died in 1836. James Dillard is guardian of the minor heirs of William Lowe. (Bed TN, Ch Ct Min, 1/137) Land was divided in February 1837 that was held in common between John Low, George E. Low and the minor heirs of William Low, deceased, to wit, George E, Jr., Seymore S., Daniel, Eliza Ann & Martha Lowe. The grave of Daniel Lowe, deceased, was mentioned. (Ibid 2/8) Another settlement made 13 February 1839. (Ibid 2/56)

LOWERY, Robert
Died before 26 February 1781 when Rebecca Lowry was granted leave to administer, with Saml. Weir & John Weir as security. (Was TN, Co Ct Min, 1/126)

LOWRY, David
Died before 3 May 1815 when Thomas Buckingham was appointed administrator with Ephraim B. Davidson and John Bailey as security. (Ste TN, Co Ct Min, 4/284)

LOWRY, John
Died before 6 December 1825 when his will was proved by Hardy L. Morris & John Newton, witnesses. (McM TN, Co Ct Min, 2no#/119)

LOYD, James
4 March 1829 he was to be tried on a charge of A. B. [assult & battery]. It was stated that "he has left this country without any probability of his returning." (McM TN, Co Ct Min, no#/416)

LOYD, Jordan
Died before 1 November 1819 when Jarratt Loyd was appointed administrator with Joshua Loyd as security. (Wil TN, Co Ct Min, no#/533)

LUCAS, Frank
Died before 4 July 1870 when F. S. Robertson was paid for making the coffin. Frank was colored. (Dyr TN, Co Ct Min, B/73)

LUCAS, I. M.
Died before 5 April 1870 when the administrator, J. A. Lucas, returned the inventory. (Dyr TN, Co Ct Min, B/44)

LUCAS, Robert
Was the brother of William Lucas as shown in a release and quit claim from Pharoah Cobb to James Barnes. It was for an entry made by Robert Lucas for his brother, William Lucas, who conveyed the land to James Barnes. (Was TN, Co Ct Min, 1/395)

LUITON, James
Is an old man in the 5th District who is very sick and suffering from want of food and fire. 4 December 1871 he was allowed $20 for food and firewood during his illness. (Dyr TN, Co Ct Min, B/326) He was put on the list of paupers. (Ibid 350)

LUNSFORD, Darling
3 January 1859 was released from paying poll taxes & working on public roads, he being a disabled person. (Sev TN, Co Ct Min, no#/376)

LYLE, Alexr.
Was a minor at February term 1788 when James Stuart, Esqr. relinquished his guardianship and Ebenezar Scroggs was appointed guardian. (Was TN, Co Ct Min, 1/303)

LYLE, Isabell
Was a minor at the February term 1788 when James Stuart, Esqr. relinquished his guardianship and Ebenezer Scroggs was appointed guardian. (Was TN, Co Ct Min, 1/303)

LYLE, John
Died before 28 August 1781 when Wm. Francis Lyle, James Stuart & James Huston have leave of administration on his estate. Danl. Kenedy, Charles Allison & John McNabb, Esqr. were security. (Was TN, Co Ct Min, 1/143) 6 November 1783 the deposition of Saml. Keyes was to be taken in Rockbridge County, VA, for the heirs of John Lyle, deceased. (Ibid 233) 2 August 1784 John Lyle, Jr., orphan of John Lyle, deceased, made choice of John Lyle for his guardian, with James Montgomery and James Scott as security. (Ibid 242) 21 February 1795 a citation was issued to James Stuart of Washington County, James Houston of Knox County, and Francis Scroggs of Mason County, KY, administrators of John Lyle, deceased, to settle the estate. (Ibid 542)

LYNDSEY, George
Died before 4 May 1813 when Sarah Lyndsey was granted letters of administration with James Miller & William Randle as security. (Ste TN, Co Ct Min, 4/33) John Lightfoot, George Berry & James Miller are to lay off provisions for Sarah Lyndsey, widow of George Lyndsey, for the support of herself and children for one year. (Ibid 43)

LYONS, Jancy
Sued for divorce from James Lyons 25 February 1837. James failed to answer and the bill will be heard at next term. (Obi TN, Cir Ct Min, 3/119) Divorce was granted 23 February 1839 for desertion. (Ibid 335)

LYONS, Thomas
Died before 16 September 1806 when his will was offered for probate by William Lyons, brother of the deceased. William Lyons was appointed administrator with will annexed. The will was quoted: "I Thomas Lyons of Greenville in Augusta & State of Virginia under apprehentions of approaching Death do make this my last will & Testament. It is my will that my Brother William Lyons of the Town County & State aforesaid shall after paying all my just Debts receive & possess all my Estate real & personal wheresoever it may be found. Given under my hand & Seal in the Chickasaw Nation this 9th day of July 1806. [signed] Thomas Lyons. Witnessed by John McKee, Samuel Mitchell & William McGhe." (Roa TN, Co Ct Min, B/197) An inventory of the estate was returned & ordered to be sold. (Ibid 237)

MacCASHTEN, Robert
Was bound 26 February 1782 to James All___. [Indenture mentioned Geroge King & Margaret, not clear.] (Was TN, Co Ct Min, 1/152)

MACK, Georgaretta [Mark, Mask]
Was granted a divorce from Jessee Mack [Mark] on 22 September 1853. Her maiden name was Tomlin. They were married in Madison County 25 February 1851 & seperated in March 1852. Jessee Mask? appealed the divorce. (Mad TN, Ch Ct Min, 1/352) 16 March 1855 Jesse was granted a divorce from Georgaretta for desertion. Georgaretta has left the state. (Ibid 2/48)

MADDOX, Notley
Died before 16 December 1816 when Notley Maddox & Fanny Maddox were appointed administrators, with Jno. W. Peyton, John Mahall & J. William Maddox as security. (Wil TN, Co Ct Min, no#/49) A years support was laid off to the widow. (Ibid 50)

MADDOX, Notley, Sr.
Was a resident of Jackson County, GA, on 14 October 1807 when he sold a slave to Notley Maddox, Jr. (Wil TN, Reg Bk/54) Notley Maddox, Sr. was a resident of Wilson County when he sold another slave to Notley W. Maddox, Jr. on 14 April 1810. (Ibid 56)

MADDOX, William
Died before 8 November 1813 when administrators, Polly Maddox and John Davis, deeded land to William C. Conrad, Mary Conrad, George C. Conrad and Sidney Conrad. (Rob TN, Co Ct Min, 3/314)

MADDUX
A suit was entered 6 February 1857 by S. H. & T. J. Maddux vs Allen Young & others. An agreement was made between S. H. Maddux, T. J. Maddux, George Maddux and C. F.

Maddux and Allen Young & John H. Young about who could have the timber on a tract of land. David Young was mentioned. (Jac TN, Ch Ct Min, C/59)

MADDUX, Silas F.
Was probably a minor on 1 November 1841 when he brought suit by his next friend against Isaac E. Ferrell et al. (Jac TN, Ch Ct Min, A/24) The next friend was Craven Maddux. (Ibid 86)

MADDUX Tapley
Died before 7 February 1815 when Elisabeth Maddux & James Tagert were appointed administrators, with Caleb Williams & Philip Hornburger as security. (Ste TN, Co Ct Min, 4/246)

MADDY, William
With his wife Elisabeth, sold 150 acres of land in VA to David Graham, 22 February 1808. (Cla TN, Co Ct Min, 3/154)

MADEN, William
6 December 1830 his guardian, James McNabb, made a report. (McM TN, Co Ct Min, 2no#/485)

MADERAS, Washington D.
Died before 16 August 1837 when his death was suggested in the suit of Gabriel Tucker and wife vs Washington D. Mademas? & others. (Bed TN, Ch Ct Min, 2/14) 15 August 1838 a suit was entered by Thomas Smith, David Yancy & wife Rachael, Benjn. W. H. Madearis & others, for sale of land. (Ibid 34) Polly was the wife of Thomas Smith. (Ibid 55) When the land was sold it was stated it was for the benefit of the heirs of John Medaris, deceased. (Ibid 64) David Yancy was administrator for Washington D. Medaris. [Evidently all persons in this suit were heirs of John Medaris deceased] (Ibid 87) Sarah Bell, daughter of Thomas Bell, deceased, was the wife of John Medaris and John & Sarah were the ancestors of the defendants Thomas Smith & wife, Benjamin W. H. Medearis, et als. Thomas Bell was the ancestor of Matilda Hicks Tucker. John & Sarah Medearis were guardians of Matilda Hicks Tucker. The court decided that if anything had ever come to the hands of the guardians of complainant, Matilda Hicks Tucker, "she has slept upon her rights and is chargable with lashees and negligance, and the court is of the opinion that by the great lapse of time, not sufficiently accounted for, has lost her right to the relief sought for by the bill." Sarah Medearis died before her husband, John. (Ibid 2/126) Land was sold & the money paid as follows: "To Thomas Smith & wife Polly 1/4 part; to John , Richard White, Haywood and Benjamin Phillips - and James Armstead & wife Martha J. 1/4 part; also 1/4 part to the heirs of Benjamin W. H. Medearis decd; and to David Yancy & wife Rachel, James Loyd & wife Sarah, Henry S. Blackmore & wife Margaret and to the guardian of Polly Catherine, George W., John T., Martha F. and William Medearis, minor orphans of Washington D. Medearis the remaining 1/4 part, subject however to the claim of Elizabeth Medearis, widow of the said Washington D. Medearis to 1/3 of the said 1/4 part for life & at her death the same shall be paid over to the heirs of said Washington D. Medearis." [These are evidently the heirs of John Mederas, deceased.] (Ibid 169) John Medearis left 4 children. Benjamin W. D. Medearis, one of the heirs, had been advanced a sum greater than his share. Mrs. Martha Phillips was a daughter of John Medearis. Washington D. Medaris was a son of John. Washington is deceased & David Yancy is his administrator. Thomas Smith, administrator for John Medaris, married a daughter of John Medaris. (Ibid 366)

MADGEHAIN, Strangman
Was a resident of Randolph County, the Illinois Territory, 18 May 1810 when a deposition was to be taken for the plaintiff in the case of Jno. Redferren vs Mary Irwin. (Rob TN, Co Ct Min, 2/269)

MADREY, Mary
Died before 8 October 1873 when Nat. P. Tatum was paid for the coffin. (Dyr TN, Co Ct Min, B/648)

MAGGARD, George
6 May 1873 was charged with Bastardy. The case was continued until next term and he gave bond with James A. Mathews as security. (Dyr TN, Co Ct Min, B/585) He was found to be the father of the child of Jane Lanier and ordered to pay support for 3 years. He was granted an appeal to Circuit Court. (Ibid 589)

MAGOFF, Jas. [or Jno.]
28 February 1782 his widow or wife was ordered to appear at the next court to show cause, if any, why her children would not be bound out. (Was TN, Co Ct Min, 1/156)

MAGUFF, Ed.
Was an orphan boy 7 years old when he was bound 28 May 1782 to Gideon Morris. (Was TN, Co Ct Min, 1/161)

MAHAN, Archibald
Died before 9 August 1813 when the inventory of the estate was reported by James Mahan, administrator. (Rob TN, Co Ct Min, 3/272) 12 November 1813 Isaac Dortch & James Norflette were appointed guardian to Martin H. W. Mahan, Nancy Mahan, Joseph H. Mahan & Prestley B. Mahan, orphans of Archibald Mahan. (Ibid 343) The widow, Nancy Mahan, petitioned for dower. Notice was given to Isaac Dortch & James Norflet as guardian shown above and to Jesse Martin as guardian of William M. Mahan, James Mahan, Henry Mahan, Sally Mahan, John Barber & Casandra Barber his wife. (Ibid 344) 18 November 1814 James Norfleet was appointed guardian for Martin H. W. Mahan, Nancy Mahan, Joseph H. Mahan, Presley B. Mahan, orphans of Archibald. (Ibid 511)

MAHAN, William H.
18 November 1814 Jesse Martin was appointed guardian, with James Mahan & Samuel Pearson security. (Rob TN, Co Ct Min, 3/510)

MAHAN, William M.
12 November 1813 chose Jesse Martin as his guardian. [probably orphan of Archibald Mahan] (Rob TN, Co Ct Min, 3/343)

MAHANY, Benjamin [Mahony, Mahoney]
Died before 20 March 1852 as shown in the suit of Benjamin C. White & wife Polly, Edith Johnson, Benjamin Mahany, John L. Mahany, Loge Mahany, Jonathan Roberts & wife Jane, Ransom Mahany, Jr., William Mahany, Jr., Marion M. Mahany, Job Mahany, Oliver P. Mahany, Thos. R. J. Mahany & William Mahany, Sr., vs Edward Anderson & wife Cinderilla, Ranson Mahany, Sr., Jacob Johnson & wife Margaret & Thomas R. Mahany. Edward Anderson was executor of Benjamin Mahany, deceased, and had purchased the land of the deceased at the sale on 8 June 1848. That sale is to be set aside and the land resold. (Jac TN, Ch Ct Min, B/51) Land was sold to Benjamin C. White and title divested out of Polly White, Edith Johnson, Benjamin Mahany, John L. Mahany, Lloyd Mahany, Jonathan Roberts & wife Jane, Ransom Mahany, Jr., William Mahany, Jr., Marion M. Mahany, Job Mahany, Oliver P. Mahany and Thomas R. J. Mahany, William Mahany, Sr., Edward Anderson & wife Cinderilla, Ransom Mahany, Sr., Jacob Johnson & wife Margaret & Thomas R. Mahany. (Ibid 62)

MAHANY, Perry
Died intestate before 27 January 1847 when his death was suggested in the suit of Perry Mahany vs Edwin F. McKinny & others. (Jac TN, Ch Ct Min, A/237)

MAHON, Henry
Was a minor 7 July 1809 when James Reynolds was appointed guardian in the suit of Saml. Henley & Rebeckah his wife vs Henry Mahon. (Rob TN, Co Ct Min, 2/164)

MAHONEY, Michl.
Died before 30 November 1780 when John Black was granted leave of administration. (Was TN, Co Ct Min, 1/125)

MALDON, Thonton
8 January 1867 was released from working on the public road on account of disability. (Sev TN, Co Ct Min, no#/425)

MALLARD, Daniel L.
Died in October 1841 & Lemuel Broadaway was appointed administrator and entered a suit against Minos Cannon on 28 December 1843. (Bed TN, Ch Ct Min, 2/284) His estate is insolvent and there are 59 creditors. The land is to be sold. (Ibid 311)

MALLORY
In the suit of William Allen vs James Mallory, 10 June 1806, defendant is allowed to take the depositions of James Mallory and Elisabeth Fox of Halifax County, NC. (Ste TN, Co Ct Min, 1/30)

MALLOY, Thomas
Died before 9 June 1806 when his executors, John Overton, Andrew Ewing & James Mulherrin, sold land to William Outlaw, proved by Nimrod Cromwill and Anderson Andrews. (Ste TN, Co Ct Min, 1/28)

MALOY, George W.
2 July 1860 his guardian, James Maloy, made application to have the guardianship transferred to Washington County, AR. The petition shows that James Maloy is the father of George W. Maloy who is about 6 years old. He is the issue of a marriage with Sarah Butler who has departed this life. George is their only child. George has coming to him about $600 from the estate of his grandfather, Oratia Butler [Horatio Butler], in Sevier County. (Sev TN, Co Ct Min, no#/574-7)

MALOY, Sarah
Died before 1 December 1856 when Henry Butler was appointed guardian to George Maloy, minor heir. J. Ogle, W. H. Trotter & Jno. Butler were securities. (Sev TN, Co Ct Min, no#/91)

MANEAR, James A.
Was granted a divorce 10 February 1860 from Sarah Manear. She had been guilty of adultry with James Crossland. (Jac TN, Ch Ct Min, C/323)

MANER, Sally
Was a resident of Wilks County, NC, 27 February 1807 when a deposition was to be taken for the suit of John Rogers vs James Darrum. (Cla TN, Co Ct Min, 3/69)

MANGRAM, W. H.
7 July 1873 was chosen and appointed guardian of Betty Mangram, his daughter. (Dyr TN, Co Ct Min, B/593)

MANIER, James A. [Marrier]
Died before 14 July 1853 when his death was suggested in the suit of Joseph Spurlock vs James A. Marrier. James A. Spurlock and Allen Marrier are the administrators. (Jac TN, Ch Ct Min, B/74)

MANIS, Fanny C.
1 February 1858 was bound to Henry Houk until age 18. She is now 9 years old. (Sev TN, Co Ct Min, no#/258)

MANIS, Polly
7 April 1857 Elizabeth Maples was paid for her support for 3 months. (Sev TN, Co Ct Min, no#/152)

MANISS, Joseph
Was a resident of Sevier County [TN] on 4 September 1820 when his deposition was to be taken for the plaintiff in the suit of William Shamblen vs Isaac Hamby. (McM TN, Co Ct Min, no#/10)

MANLEY, J. A. C.
Died before 5 February 1872 when R. G. Menzies was appointed administrator, with W. P. Menzies, W. A. Hudson and John A. King as his securities. (Dyr TN, Co Ct Min, B/368) Smith Parks, J. N. Wyatt and Louis M. Williams were appointed to lay off a years allowance for the widow and family. (Ibid 375) 6 May 1872 Mrs. M. C. Manley was appointed guardian of Mozella P., Sarah E., John A. C. and William B. Manley, minor heirs. (Ibid 413) J. A. C. Manley died in January 1872. (Ibid 421) In a bill to sell land to make assets, the names are the same except Sarah E. is shown as Ellenora. It mentioned the lot in Newbern where Dr. Manley had his drug store. (Ibid 668)

MANNING, Elizabeth
Died before 4 December 1868 as shown in the suit of W. B. Armstead vs J. B. McCormack & others. John B. McCormack had conveyed land in 1842 to John L. Goodall in trust. The deed of trust was registered in March 1842 and has been sereptitously cut out of the Registers Book. In 1848 Charles J. Manning fraudulently instituted in the Livingston Chancery Court in the name of Elizabeth Manning a dower to sell three of the tracts of land conveyed by said deed of trust and fraudulently purchased same in the name of Elizabeth Manning. Elizabeth Manning is now dead and the defendants Abram Litton, Joseph M. Litton, Charles M. Litton and Allice W. Litton claim to be her heirs. As her heirs they filed a bill in Chancery Court at Livingston on 25 Februray 1859 to sell said land. The suit is still pending. (Fen TN, Ch Ct Min, A/430)

MANSELL, Burnett
Died before 6 December 1830 when his will was proved by James D. Henly & Walter Billingsly, Sr., witnesses. Martha Mansell was named executrix. (McM TN, Co Ct Min, 2no#/483)

MANSFIELD, J. Add
4 April 1870 Thomas J. Mansfield was chosen and appointed guardian of Lee Mansfield, minor son of J. Add Mansfield, with Isaac A. Nunn and Wm. N. Beasley as security. (Dyr TN, Co Ct Min, B/34)

MANSFIELD, John
Died before 5 February 1818 when the will was proved by John Cumplon, Jr. & Walter Carr. (Wil TN, Co Ct Min, no#/238) William Walker was one of the executors. (Ibid 240)

MAP, Thomas [Mass]
Died before 28 June 1825 when the administrators, Silas Chapman & William Map [Mass], sold a slave to James Shelton. (Wil TN, Reg Bk/367)

MAPLES
7 April 1856 the constable was ordered to bring to court Redmon Maples, Samuel Maples & Sarah Maples, poor children, for the purpose of having them bound out. (Sev TN, Co Ct Min, no#/21)

MAPLES, Edward
Died before 5 May 1856 when James Maples was appointed administrator, with Thomas Maples & G. Maples as security. (Sev TN, Co Ct Min, no#/48)

MAPLES, Elijah
5 January 1857 was allowed money from the poor fund for keeping Rebecca Maples for 1857. (Sev TN, Co Ct Min, no#/99) 4 January 1858 Elijah Maples was allowed money from the poor tax for the support of his grand daughter. (Ibid 235)

MAPLES, Elizabeth
8 July 1856 John McMahan made a settlement as administrator of the estate. (Sev TN, Co Ct Min, no#/63) 5 January 1858 R. H. Hodsden was appointed guardian to Wilson Maples in place of Elizabeth Maples, removed by the court. Thos. Maples was his security. (Ibid 244) 5 December 1864 Preston Maples was appointed guardian to Wilson Maples. (Ibid 128)

MAPLES, Samuel
1 April 1867 a charge of Bastardy was dismissed. (Sev TN, Co Ct Min, no#/439)

MARGRAVE, Drury
20 October 1812 Drury Margrave was 6 years old when he was bound to John McKaney until age 21. (Roa TN, Co Ct Min, D/421)

MARGRAVE, John
Had bound his two sons to Samuel Stout. 16 July 1810, on the motion of Isaac L. McMeans, Esqr., "it was ordered to take the 2 boys out of the possession of said Stout & some couple bring Tennessee Margrave into court, the other being in court." [The writing is dim but I believe the motion was overuled] (Roa TN, Co Ct Min, D/222)

MARLOW, Edward
Died before 23 September 1805 when the will was proved by James Barrow & Josiah Thomas. William McClain & William Thomas were named executors but refused. Rebecca Marlow was appointed administratrix with will annexed. (Wil TN, Co Ct Min, no#/164)

MARLOW, Renny
Died before 19 March 1817 when William Green was allowed $8 for keeping Elizabeth Marlow, orphan of Renny Marlow, deceased. (Wil TN, Co Ct Min, no#/91)

MARLOW, Sally
On 16 May 1816 the sheriff was ordered to bring the children of Sally Marlow [name not certain, bad writing] to the court house at next term to have them bound out. The children were Edmund, Mary, Joseph, Lucy, Jane [or Lucy Jane] & Catharine [something written in between lines looks like "minors and orphans"] (Cla TN, Co Ct Min, 4/210)

MARONEY, Loyd
Was a pauper 1 December 1828 when $20 was allowed for his support. (McM TN, Co Ct Min, 2/315)

MARR, Constentine
Died before 20 February 1837 when John J. McMahan was accused of his murder. (Obi TN, Cir Ct Min, 3/85) The name was also shown as Constant P. Marr. (Ibid 99) Milton H. Marr was the prosecutor in the murder charge. (Ibid 148) John J. McMahan escaped from jail. (Ibid 166)

MARRY, John A.
Died before August term 1834 when the firm of N. & J. Dick & Co. recovered a judgement against Ezekiel W. Brown, Robert P. Harrison & Joseph C. Strong, administrators with the will annexed of John A. Marry, deceased, and against Samuel Phillips and Gordentice Waite, administrators of Robert Waite, deceased. Ezekiel W. Brown and George C. Lucas were residents of Fayette County, TN, on 25 May 1835. (Bed TN, Ch Ct Min, 1/37)

MARS, Hugh
Died before 4 May 1826 when Charles Blalock sold a slave to Polly Mars, widow of Hugh Mars, deceased. (Wil TN, Reg Bk/386)

MARS, John A.
Died before 28 September 1840 as shown in the suit of William Waite vs The Bank of Tennessee. It was stated John A. Mars died insolvent many years ago. (Bed TN, Ch Ct Min, 1/315)

MARSH
Jonathan and Nancy Marsh made a deed at the April term 1803 to Willie Cherry for land on certificate of the clerk of Beaufort County, NC. (Rob TN, Co Ct Min, 1/247)

MARSHAL, Sally
An orphan boy, son of Sally Marshall, supposed to be 6 years old in the month of March 1805, was bound 4 September 1805 to Walter Evans until age 21. The boys name is given and it looks like Chappel Car Staephen. Walter Evans is to educate the said Chappel to read, write, and cipher as far as the rule of three in arithmetic. (Cla TN, Co Ct Min, 2/181)

MARSHALL, James
Died before 29 July 1846 as shown in the suit of James Keith vs Geo. M. McWhirter Admr. &c of James Marshall Decd. (Jac TN, Ch Ct Min, A/219)

MARSHALL, Ro.
Died before 21 September 1853 as shown in the suit of William J. Smith et als vs Ro. F. Marshall and Isaac I. Roach. The defendants are the executors of Ro. Marshall, deceased. Complainants with said defendants are heirs & legatees. Two years have passed and the executors have not settled. (Mad TN, Ch Ct Min, 1/340)

MARSHALL, William B.
Died before 22 February 1866 as shown in the suit of Cyrus Simmons & Adrian Pyle Executors of W. B. Marshall vs Samuel Luskey & Geo. G. Perkins. (Mad TN, Ch Ct Min, 2/480) The executors were shown as Addison Pyles & Cyrus Simmons. (Ibid 3/76)

MARSHALL, Wm. M.
Died before 7 January 1874 when Paschal A. Fowlkes was appointed administrator, with H. L. Fowlkes and W. P. Fowlkes as his security. (Dyr TN, Co Ct Min, B/698) H. L. Fowlkes, Asa Fowlkes and P. H. Robertson were appointed to lay off a years allowance to the widow and child. (Ibid 699)

MARTIN
At the November term 1834 Adam Huntsman & Benjamin Lotten acknowledged a deed for 640 acres of land to Mary Herron, Alexander H. Martin, Jane L. Martin, Robert Martin and James L. Martin of Lincoln County, NC. The land was in Obion County, TN. (Obi TN, Cir Ct Min, 2/187)

MARTIN, David
Died before 1 January 1817 when the executor, John Martin, sold "a certain Yellow girl of said estate, called Cris," to James Johnson. (Wil TN, Co Ct Min, Reg Bk/76)

MARTIN, Francis
Died before 10 May 1813 when the will was proved by Sims Ellis, one of the witnesses. (Rob TN, Co Ct Min, 3/231) The will was also proved by William Ellis and William Sales. (Ibid 240)

MARTIN, George
Died before 3 May 1819 when Thompson Hays was appointed administrator with Richard Drake & Thomas Rhodes as security. A years provision was allotted to the widow. (Wil TN, Co Ct Min, no#/436)

MARTIN, Henry C.
Died before 14 April 1842 as shown in the suit of Baxter H. Ragsdale of Coffee County, TN, vs Matt Martin & E. Archibald Mosely, guardians of the minor heirs of Henry Martin, deceased. Theodrich F. Bradford was a brother-in-law of [Matt] Martin. Matt Martin had rented land and negroes belonging to his wards in 1838 and 1839. Bradford's death was mentioned. (Bed TN, Ch Ct Min, 1/527) Thomas B. Moseley was the administrator & brought suit against Matt Martin & Edward A. Moseley. The suit is also against William D. Martin, Andrew J. Martin & Sarah M. A. Martin, all of whom are minors, and Mat Martin being guardian of William D. Martin and Edward A. Mosely being the regular guardian. Some years ago Henry C. Martin departed this life intestate leaving a considerable estate to be divided among his four children, William D., Amanda J., Sarah N. S. & Henry Elizabeth Martin. Some time later one of the wards, Henry Elizabeth Martin, died. Many years since one Barkly Martin died in Bedford County, leaving a widow but no children, having made a will. He devised his negroes to his widow during her lifetime and at her death to his brother, Mat Martin, Sr., now deceased. A number of years after the death of said Barclay Martin, his widow, Rachael, sold her life estate in the negroes to John Tilman, who in turn sold his interest in said negroes to Mat Martin on condition Mat Martin would divide said negroes amongst his then living children and the heirs of those that were dead. There were 9 of the children of Mat Martin alive and the 10th, Henry C., being dead but leaving 4 children above mentioned, to wit, William D., Amanda J., Sarah N. A. and Henry Elizabeth Martin, his only heirs. Nine of the shares were delivered to the 9 living children and the 10th share in 1841 was placed in the hands of the said Mat Martin and Edward A. Moseley as the guardians of said children & for their benefit. The share of Henry Elizabeth should go to her mother who survives her, and her 3 surviving brother and sisters. John Tilman was evidently a son-in-law of Matt Martin, Sr. Matt Martin, Sr. died in October 1846 leaving a will by which he bequeathed negroes to the children of his deceased son, Henry C. Martin. Henry Elizabeth Martin had died before that time. William D. Martin was only a half brother to the other three. William Davenport of GA was the grandfather of William D. Martin and part of the negroes were received from his estate. The mother of William D. was a daughter of said Davenport. His mother is deceased. His half sisters are by his father's second wife. Another bill in this case is a complaint of Bark [Barkley] Martin of Mury County, TN, co-executor of the last will & testament of Matt Martin, deceased, & others. Matt Martin, Jr. was the other executor. Lucy G. Bradford was one of the children of Matt Martin, Sr. A final decree was given 27 February 1848. William D. Martin, deceased, was mentioned in this decree and Matt Martin was administrator. (Ibid 3/426-49)

MARTIN, Isaac
On 14 November 1844 dismissed his suit for divorce from Elizabeth Martin. (Obi TN, Cir Ct Min, 4/no#)

MARTIN, John J.
Died before 5 July 1870 when F. G. Sampson was appointed administrator, with F. H. Burtin and J. H. York as security. (Dyr TN, Co Ct Min, B/82)

MARTIN, Joseph
Died before 17 July 1797 when William Brown, heir of James Brown, deceased, made a deed to Elisabeth Airs & Patrick Martin, heirs of Joseph Martin, deceased. (Rob TN, Co Ct Min, 1/31)

MARTIN, Martha H.
Died before 30 July 1849 as shown in the suit of Robt. B. Mitchell & his wife Mary B. Mitchell vs George Martin, Robt. K. Martin, Margaret L. Martin, Hugh B. Martin & Martha B. Martin, minors, who defend by their guardian ad litem, Wm. P. Martin. Mary B. Mitchell and the defendants were the children of Martha H. Martin, deceased, who owned 2 tracts of land. William P. Martin, the husband of Martha B. Martin, [it should probably be husband of Martha H.] relinquished to his said wife & her children all his interest in said land on the 14th of November 1840, by deed properly registered. The children are

entitled to 1/6 part each. Report is to be made whether the land can be divided. (Mad TN, Ch Ct Min, 1/77) The regular guardian of the minors is Hugh Bradshaw. (Ibid 106)

MARTIN, Samuel J. B.
Was bound as an apprentice to John S. Wilson on 6 September 1830. (McM TN, Co Ct Min, 2no#/473)

MARTIN, Samuel J. B. [Mastin]
On 14 November 1844 was granted a divorce from Eliza Martin. (Obi TN, Cir Ct Min, 4/no#)

MARTIN, William
20 July 1801, in a suit of John Burris against Wm. Martin with Jesse Martin a garnishee, it was reported that Jesse was agent for William Martin and had in his possession notes & accounts on Robt. Boyd [Boyr] who lives in KY, Ths. Harrison of Davidson, John Cennedy who is believed to be living in Davidson, Jehu Davy of Davidson, Peter Johnson of Davidson and Mrs. Randal living in Davidson. (Rob TN, Co Ct Min, 1/180)

MARTINS, Henry C.
Probably died before 8 October 1839 as a road was laid "through the field of the heirs of Henry C. Martins." (Bed TN, Ch Ct Min, 1/297)

MASON, Henry
Evidently died before 15 September 1855 as on that date a suit is shown by James Caruthers, surviving executor of Henry Smith, deceased. James Caruthers & Henry Mason had been joint executors. (Mad TN, Ch Ct Min, 2/89)

MASON, James
Died before 14 February 1814 when Jesse Mason was appointed administrator with Willis Holland & William Mason as security. (Rob TN, Co Ct Min, 3/359)

MASON, Lucinda
Died before 5 October 1857 when Joseph Davis was paid out of the poor tax for making her coffin. (Sev TN, Co Ct Min, no#/205)

MASON, Polly
Was the mother of a bastard child by Burwell Babb who gave bond for its maintenance 11 May 1812. (Rob TN, Co Ct Min, 3/79)

MASON, R, M.
23 February 1866 a suit was entered; R. M. Mason Admr. vs S. Olliver et als. "This day Lemuel Day admr. of Z. Jane presented his petition to the Court & prayed to be made a party to this cause & file a claim due to Z. Jane his intestate & to receive his prorata distribution of the assets." (Mad TN, Ch Ct Min, 2/484)

MASON, Ralph
Died before 3 October 1808 when his will was entered. The will was objected to and case continued until Thursday next. Josiah Fort, Esqr. was ordered to attend at the house of Elisabeth Mason to take the deposition of Polly Taylor as to her signature & the signture of Ralph Mason, deceased. (Rob TN, Co Ct Min, 2/80) A jury found that it was a valid will. It was proved by McGehen ? & Jesse Lawrence. Beverly A. Allen was executor. (Ibid 94) Isaac Mason who contested the will is to pay the costs. (Ibid 95) 16 February 1815 Elizabeth Mason petitioned the court to subpoena Beverly Allen to appear & settle the estate. (Ibid 3/561)

MASON, Reuben
Died before 22 February 1808 when the will was proved by William Condry & James A. Perriman. (Cla TN, Co Ct Min, 3/150)

MASSEDA, Nathaniel
Was an orphan boy 19 October 1807 when he was bound to Archibald Cook until of age. (Ste TN, Co Ct Min, 1/49b)

MASSEY, W. B.
Died before 5 June 1871 when L. M. Williams, Green Menzies and Smith Parks were appointed to lay off a years provisions for the widow and family. (Dyr TN, Co Ct Min, B/240) J. F. Williamson was appointed administrator. (Ibid 242)

MASSEY, William
Died before 13 March 1804 when the will was proved by Phillip Hornbergar and Nathaniel Denson. Elizabeth Massey was executrix. (Ste TN, Co Ct Min, 1/1b)

MASY, J.
Taxes were not collected in District 2 for 1873. "gone." (Dyr TN, Co Ct Min, B/758)

MATHEWS, George
Died before February term 1789 when the widow, Elizabeth Mathews, was appointed administratrix, with William Woods and Alexander Mathews as securities. (Was TN, Co Ct Min, 1/366)

MATHEWS, Joshua
Was an orphan boy of the age of 6 when he was bound to William N. Slate on 17 September 1817 to learn the blacksmith trade. (Wil TN, Co Ct Min, no#/171)

MATLOCK, Moore
Died before 20 April 1812 when administration was granted to Jason Matlock, with Hugh Francis & Thomas Reyburn as security. An inventory of the estate was returned. (Roa TN, Co Ct Min, D/368)

MATTHEWS, Richard
Died before 21 October 1799 when the will was proved by James Sawyers & William Renick. Sampson Matthews & William Matthews were executors. (Rob TN, Co Ct Min, 1/117)

MATTHEWS, Wm.
Died before August 1788 when his orphan, William Matthews, aged 17 years, was bound to Ebenezer Scroggs until age 21. He is to be taught the "art & Mystry of a Tanner." (Was TN, Co Ct Min, 1/335)

MAULDEN, Leroy [Malden]
Died before 15 February 1858 when his death was admitted in the suit of Malden & Morphis vs Thos. R. Richardson. The suit was revived in the name of Samuel Maulden, administrator. (Mad TN, Ch Ct Min, 2/157)

MAXWELL, Jane
15 July 1859 a suit was entered by Jane Maxwell vs Cornelius Maxwell for divorce. It was consolidated with the suit of James Peak & others vs Cornelius Maxwell and the suit of Thomas Maxwell vs James Peak & others. (Jac TN, Ch Ct Min, C/260) In February 1860 this suit is shown again as Nancy Maxwell vs Cornelius Maxwell. Cornelius is a non-resident of this state and publication has been made for him. (Ibid 299) Nancy Maxwell dismissed her suit for divorce from Cornelius Maxwell, 10 August 1860. (Ibid 361)

MAXWELL, Jasper
Taxes were not collected in District 3 in 1873, "cant be found." (Dyr TN, Co Ct Min, B/758)

MAY, Alphonso [Mays]
Died before 16 January 1850 when James G. May made petition as guardian for the heirs, to sell land. (Mad TN, Ch Ct Min, 1/102) Alphonso left children, Amanda H., Alfred H., Almedia G., James S., Jno. W. & Joseph W. May, all minors. It will be 4 1/2 years before the oldest comes of age. (Ibid 116)

MAY, Jonathan
Was appointed guardian of Anna May and Jane May, with their consent, on 3 August 1814. Benjamin Edwards & Thomas Ross were security. (Ste TN, Co Ct Min, 4/180)

MAYFIELD, Abram [Abraham]
Was the father of John W. Mayfield as shown in the suit of John W. Mayfield vs George L. Rodgers & others, 30 August 1844. (Bed TN, Ch Ct Min, 2/313)

MAYFIELD, James S.
Was a resident of Lagrance, in the Republic of Texas, 25 February 1845 when Eliza W. Harrison of Bedford County, TN, gave him power of attorney. (Bed TN, Ch Ct Min, 2/335)

MAYO, Frederick
Died soon after making his will on 16 February 1856. John J. Boon was appointed administrator with will annexed as shown in his suit vs Redmand Mayo & others, devisees of said Frederick Mayo. R. C. Mayo was a minor defendant & Macajah Bullock was

appointed to represent his interest. There were 8 living children, Lydia Buntyn, Stephen Mayo, Redmond Mayo, Reuben Mayo, Joel Mayo, Jonas Mayo, Council Mayo & Polly Givins. The grandchildren were excluded. The children of Luce Powell are to have a share & Nance Powell is entitled to the share of his deceased daughter, Julia. The children of Hardy Mayo are to take 1/3 of the property in the 10th clause, and on the death of the Young child its share went in equal portions to its brother & mother. (Mad TN, Ch Ct Min, 2/401) 22 August 1866, a suit by Jno. J. Boon, administrator vs Joel Mayo et als. Joel Mayo has died & this cause revived in the name of J. J. Boon, administrator. Redmond Mayo has died & this cause revived in the name of Jno. D. M. Bryan, his administrator. A report was made of the distribution of the estate of Frederick Mayo & the following received a portion: Lydia Buntyn, Stephen Mayo, Redmond Mayo, Reuben Mayo, Joel Mayo, Jonas Mayo, Counsil B. Mayo, Hardy Mayo & Louisa Powell. Also mentioned was "Polly Givens & Hardy Mayo Son R. C. Mayo." (Ibid 413) Division was made 22 August 1867 to Lydia Buntin, Redmond Mayo, C. B. Mayo, Polly Givins, Hardy Mayo son of Robert. The money to be divided into 8 equal parts & paid to the 8 living children & where any of them have died to their representatives, the 8 shares being, Lydia Buntyn, Stephen Mayo, Redmond Mayo, Reuben Mayo, Joel Mayo, Jonas Mayo, Conrad B. Mayo & Polly Givins. (Ibid 3/70)

MAYO, Hardy
Died in 1855 intestate, leaving his widow, Sarah Jane & 2 children, Robert C. & Martha L. Martha L. has since that time departed this life without issue. (Mad TN, Ch Ct Min, 2/165) Sarah Jane Mayo married Jackson Smith before 19 February 1861. (Ibid 422)

MAYO, Redmond
Died before 23 August 1866 as shown in the suit of Jno. D. M. Bryan admr. et als vs Wm. Witherspoon. Redmond Mayo had sold land to the defendant in 1860 & it has not all been paid. Redmond Mayo & wife have both died intestate & Jno. D. Bryan is administrator. The other complainants [not named] are the only heirs. (Mad TN, Ch Ct Min, 2/524)

MAYO, Robert C.
Was a minor 15 February 1858 when petition was made by Sarah Jane Mayo & Robert C. Mayo to sell land. The dower right of Sarah Jane was mentioned. (Mad TN, Ch Ct Min, 2/158) Robt. Guins [Givens] was the guardian. The sale of the land was shown 22 February 1866. [There was no court from February 1861 until February 1866, Civil War] Evidently Sarah Jane had married Jackson Smith by 1866. (Ibid 480) In the suit of Jackson Smith & wife vs R. C. Mayo it is stated that Mrs. Smith is comparatively young & her life may last long, therefore she would like a portion as her dower out of the fund. (Ibid 507) She was allowed $800 as her dower. (Ibid 3/41)

MAYO, Thomas Hardy
Was a minor 21 August 1867 when Thos. H. Drake was appointed guardian ad litem to defend the suit of Geo. M. Tomlin vs Cornelia A. Tomlin & Thos. H. Mayo. Henry Brown was appointed counsel for Cornelia A. Tomlin & minor Thos. Hardy Mayo. (Mad TN, Co Ct Min, 3/62) The defendants are owners of the land in question, Cornelia A. owning dower in the land and the said Thomas H. Mayo owning the balance and the whole at the termination of the dower estate. The land belonging to the minor has no buildings on it and is thin & poor. Said minor is about 6 years old. (Ibid 115)

McALLISTER, George D.
Died before 3 February 1874 when B. C. Burgie was appointed administrator, with Charles P. Clark and B. L. Thomas as his security. (Dyr TN, Co Ct Min, B/709) N. C. White, B. L. Thomas and William E. DeBerry were appointed to lay off a years allowance for the widow and family. (Ibid 712)

McALLISTER, John
Was a resident of Cotaco [sic] County. AL, on 4 September 1820 when his deposition was to be taken for the plaintiff in the case of David Edington vs John Spears. (McM TN, Co Ct Min, no#/8)

McBEAN, William
8 April 1808 recorded a mortgage to James Morrison for 640 acres of land on certificate of the clerk of Fayette County, KY. (Rob TN, Co Ct Min, 2/38)

McCALL, Sarah Jane
Was an orphan girl aged 2, when she was bound to William Rush on 1 December 1828 until age 18. (McM TN, Co Ct Min, 2no#/322)

McCAMMELL, John
Died before 21 February 1839 when land was taxed to the heirs. (Obi TN, Cir Ct Min, 3/297)

McCAMPBELL, John
Died before 18 February 1840 when land was taxed to the heirs. (Obi TN, Cir Ct Min, 4/no#) 17 June 1840 a suit was entered by John Doe, Lessee of Stephen Cantrell and of John A. McCampbell, Mary L. McCampbell and Thomas C. McCampbell, the heirs-at-law of John McCampbell, deceased, & John C. McLemore vs Franklin Longly, Blackman H. Byrd, John B. Mithcell & William Gillam, for Ejectment. (Ibid 4/no#)

McCANEY, James
Died before 6 March 1827 when a Trustee was elected to fill his unexpired term. (McM TN, Co Ct Min, no#/260)

McCARNEY, Mary
6 March 1828 a years provision was laid off for her & her family. [name of decedant not given] (McM TN, Co Ct Min, 2no#/281)

McCARTER
4 July 1865 John McMahan was ordered to keep the McCarter children until next court when they are to be bound out. (Sev TN, Co Ct Min, no#/186)

McCARTER, John
1 January 1866 was apprenticed to Lilman Fox. (Sev TN, Co Ct Min, no#/256)

McCARTER, Mary
1 October 1860 her child was ordered to be brought to court to be bound out. (Sev TN, Co Ct Min, no#/603) 3 December 1860 it was ordered to take the child and place it in the custody of its father. (Ibid 623) 1 April 1861 George Thomas was paid for keeping Mary McCarter's child. (Ibid 665) George Thomas was also paid for keeping Mary during her confinement. (Ibid 674)

McCARTHY, Jacob
Died before 3 August 1812 when the will was proved by Henry Edwards, William Bailey & Benjamin Kelly. Joseph McCarthy & James Tagert were executors. (Ste TN, Co Ct Min, 3/158)

McCARTNEY, Lewis
Died before 23 March 1807 when the will was proved by Thomas Shannon & George Swengley. (Wil TN, Co Ct Min, no#/279)

McCARTY, James
Died before 1 February 1819 when Reuben P. Comer was appointed guardian of Jinsey McCarty, minor heir, with Jonathan Ozment & Clack Stone as security. (Wil TN, Co Ct Min, no#/390)

McCARTY, Jane
Was an orphan girl who had been bound to R. Comer, who was released from said bond 2 August 1819. (Wil TN, Co Ct Min, no#/495)

McCARVER, James
Died before 27 August 1845 as shown in the suit of American Board of Commissioners for Foreign Missions vs Saml. Doak. James McCarver had left money to the Foreign Missions by his will. Henry Blagg was the executor of the will and Samuel Doak was his security. (Bed TN, Ch Ct Min, 2/370)

McCAY, Dugal
Died before 25 January 1799 when the land of his heirs was ordered sold for back taxes. (Rob TN, Co Ct Min, 1/94)

McCLAIN, Wm.
Died before 3 August 1818 when Alfred McClain was appointed administrator with Beverly Williams & Wm. H. Doak as security. (Wil TN, Co Ct Min, no#/286)

McCLARY, Jacob
Died before 1 January 1866 when A. L. Scruggs was appointed administrator, the widow & next of kin having relinquished their right to administrate. G. M. Henderson was security. (Sev TN, Co Ct Min, no#/259)

McCLELAN, Andrew
Died in 1850. Sampson McClelan was administrator. He left his widow, Margaret McClelan, and 2 minor children, Sampson W. McClelan and Sarah Jane McClelan. (Jac TN, Ch Ct Min, B/27) 12 July 1854 Margaret McClellan petitioned by her next friend to sell land. Title was divested out of Sampson McClelan and Sarah Jane McClelan, minor heirs of Sampson McClelan, deceased. [sic] (Ibid 150)

McCLELLAN, Isabella C.
Died in October 1857. A suit was brought 21 February 1867 by Charles D. McLean vs Joseph Mosby & others. By her will she bequeathed a large portion of her estate to complainant & defendants and a portion of it to the relations of her deceased husband, James D. McClellan. In 1861 the McLean family was ordered to contribute to the McClellan family so much of their interests under the will to make the two families equal in value. The estate was valued at $76,823.20. It stated how much was bequeathed to Chas. D. McLean, the Mosbeys, the Anthonys and the McClellans. Mad TN, Ch Ct Min, 3/32)

McCLELLAN, James D.
Died in February 1852 leaving a large & valuable estate. He made his will 23 August 1841 & a codicil dated 26 January 1852. Letters testimentary were granted to his widow, Isabella C. McClellan, in 1853. In said will he gave all of his estate to his wife and in the codicil he gave $1,000 to his mother & $200 to Elizabeth Dixon. The will was made with the express understanding & agreement with his wife that at her death she bequeth half of the whole estate to the brothers & sisters of the testator & to the issue of such brothers & sisters as might be dead at that time. This agreement was the reason for leaving the whole estate to her, instead of limiting it to her for life. Isabella died in October 1857 having made her last will & testament. She had already left one negro to her nephew, James D. McLean. Radford Withers was her executor. Isabella left $1,000 to Milton Brown & Amos W. Jones for the benefit of the Methodist Church & a legacy of a horse to Henry Shelton. She left a portion of the estate to Albert G. McClellan, Jno. T. A. McClellan, Robt. Newton McClellan, Wm. B. McClellan, Bennett T. McClellan, Wm. A. Hayley, James T. Hayley, Jno. B. Hayley, Mary C. Vaden & her husband Geo. Vaden, Martha E. Plunkett & her husband Wm. Plunkett, Patrick H. Hayley, Francis M. Hayley, Newton C. Hayley, the last 2 minors by their next friend A. G. McClellan, Mary Hicks & her husband Benj M. Hicks, Jane Hicks & her husband Geo. B. Hicks, Martha Tomlin & her husband J. William Tomlin & Isabella James McClellan a minor by her next friend Benj. M. Hicks, & Radford Withers & his wife Elizabeth, who are the brothers & sisters, neices & nephews of her husband. She bequethed a much larger portion to Thos. Murrell, Milten Brown, Amos W. Jones, Henry Shelton, Charles D. McLean & wife Jane E. & their children, Charles D. McLean, Jr., Wm. L. McLean, James D. McLean, Susan Isabella McLean, the last 2 minors by their guardian ad litem Charles D. McLean, Joseph H. Mosly & wife Maria & their children Mary Isabella, Charles W., Thos. O., James D., Virginia, Marcia S. & Maria, the last 5 minors by their guardian ad litem, C. D. McLean, Archibald Wright, Harriet Somers, Sarah Somers, Eliza Brodie [Buddie] & the children of Amanda Brodie whose names are unknown. The complainants [first group listed] and Mrs. Withers are the persons to whom James McClellan intended to have half of the estate at the death of his wife, he himself having died childless. The larger share went to the kindred of Isabella in violation of the rights of the kindred of James McClellan. An appeal was granted. (Mad TN, Ch Ct Min, 2/271) The estate was valued at more than 70,000 dollars. It was to be divided according to the will of James D. McClellan. Dennis & wife were mentioned in the division. (Ibid 332-335)

McCLELLAN, Samuel
Died before 11 September 1855 as shown in the petition of George Wade, et als, to appoint a trustee. By his last will and testament Samuel McClellan appointed Valentine S. Vann and James D. McClellan trustees for the benefit of his wife and children. Valentine S. Vann and James D. McClellan have both died and another trustee should be appointed. One of the petitioners is a minor. (Mad TN, Ch Ct Min, 2/68) Radford Weathers [Withers] was appointed trustee. Samuel McClellan made his will 2 Sept 1844 and thereafter departed this life. The will is quoted..."I leave to my wife Balsorah McClellan...property to be used for the support of her & my children. If she should marry it should be divided equally between her & my children...I hereby appoint my father in law Valentine S. Vann & my brother Jas D. McClellan executors & trustees." (Ibid 85) 18 Feb 1858 it was reported that the widow had remarried and that his daughter, Martha Ann, had married James W. Tomlin in 1852 and has one or more children. (Ibid 2/172) One of the children of Samuel McClellan was Mary C. who married B. M. Hicks in 1847 & has one or more children. (Ibid 222) Another daughter of Samuel McClellan was Isabella C. McClellan. She is entitled to 1/5 of the estate. Geo. B. Hicks was appointed trustee for her in the place of Radford Withers. The widow, Balsera, married Geo. C. Wade. She is also entitled to 1/5. (Ibid 225)

McCLELLAND, Samuel
Died before 7 February 1855 as shown in the suit of Isreal McClelland, administrator of the estate of Samuel McClelland, deceased, vs Asberry York. (Jac TN, Ch Ct Min, B/184)

McCLENAN, Andrew
Died before 7 February 1851 as shown in the suit of Sarah Hall by her next friend vs Adam Hall. Sarah and Adam were married in 1829 and there was a marriage contract settling certain property on Sarah for her seperate use. Andrew McClenan had been trustee. James Young was appointed trustee in place of Andrew McClenan, deceased. (Jac TN, Ch Ct Min, A/405)

McCLENDON, George
Died before 11 February 1859 when his death was suggested in the suit of George McClendon vs Arel [Asel, Axel] Duncan. (Jac TN, Ch Ct Min, C/186) A suit was shown 12 February 1859 by James A. Spurlock vs Susannah McClendon & others. The complainant will prosecute this suit no further as to defendants Samuel W. Mortey, C. W. Jackson, William B. Campbell, Thomas Morton & wife Jane, John Rogers & wife Elizabeth Rogers, Charles Wade & wife Polly Wade & the children of George McClendon, deceased. (Ibid 215)

McCLENDON, Jacob
7 May 1818 William Algood came into court and stated that Jacob McClendon, a minor boy who had been bound to him, about October 1817 left his service and is still absent. (Wil TN, Co Ct Min, no#/277)

McCLENDON, Jessee
Died before 16 July 1858 as shown in the suit of William H. Botts vs Susannah McClendon, R. J. C. Gailbreath & Henry H. McClendon. The suit as to Henry H. McClendon was dropped. Jessee McClendon, the husband of Susannah McClendon, died in Jackson County some years ago having made a will, leaving Susannah a life estate in all his property and at her death to go to the children of said Jessee McClendon. The negroes from the estate are to be hired out to pay the debt owed by Susannah. (Jac TN, Ch Ct Min, C/157) In the suit of Susannah McClendon vs Bank of Tennessee, 10 February 1859, complainant was given leave to take the deposition of Henry H. McClendon in TX. (Ibid 172) In the suit of James A. Spurlock vs Susannah McClendon, Moriah C. Gailbreath, Robert J. E. Gailbreath & John P. Murray it was stated that Jesse McClendon died several years ago leaving a will by which he devised to his widow, Susannah McClendon, a life estate in all his lands & negroes & then to his children. Samuel W. Motley, C. W. Jackson & William B. Campbell recovered a judgement against R. J. C. Gailbreath, Susannah McClendon & John P. Murray. The land & negroes in which Susannah has a life estate are to be rented out to pay this judgement. (Ibid 215) Henry H. McClendon was a son of Jesse McClendon. His interest in the estate is one seventh part. (Ibid 311)

McCLURE, A.
Died before 11 March 1845 when land was taxed to the heirs. (Obi TN, Cir Ct Min, 4/no#)

McCLURE, Holbert
Was a resident of Blount County, TN, on 8 June 1827 when his deposition was to be taken for the defendant in the case of A. B. Baily vs William Forester. (McM TN, Co Ct Min, no#/265)

McCLURE, Mary
Was a pauper 1 March 1830 when money was allowed for her support. (McM TN, Co Ct Min, 2/417)

McCLURE, Peggy Ann
3 September 1827 John Love was appointed her guardian. (McM TN, Co Ct Min, 2no#/233)

McCOLLOUGH, John
3 May 1819 was allowed money for his support. (Wil TN, Co Ct Min, no#/442)

McCOLLUM, James J.
Died before 20 October 1840 when a suit against him for assault was abated because of his death. (Obi TN, Cir Ct Min, 4/no#) 21 October 1840 it was shown that William S. S. Harris was the administrator. (Ibid) 25 June 1842 Catherine R. McCollum petitioned for dower. (Ibid) Sidney A. McCollum & Martha A. E. McCollum were minor heirs of James J. McCollum, deceased, and William S. S. Harris was appointed guardian ad litem on 14

March 1844. (Ibid) An entry made 11 July 1844 stated that James J. McCollum died in July 1840 leaving Katharine R. McCollum his widow and the two minor children listed above. (Ibid)

McCONNELL
4 November 1818 a deed was entered from Esta Jones, James McConnell, Catherine McConnell, John M. McConnell, David McConnell & Elizabeth McConnell to John Proctor for 15 acres of land in KY. The deed was acknowledged by David McConnell & his wife, Elizabeth. (Wil TN, Co Ct Min, no#/356)

McCONNELL, Rebekah
19 July 1803 the coroner was paid $4 for holding an inquest on her child. (Rob TN, Co Ct Min, 1/259)

McCORACH, Joseph [McCovack, McCormack]
Was a pauper 4 September 1826 when he was allowed $25 for his own support. (McM TN, Co Ct Min, 2/172, 234)

McCORKLE, Anderson
Was chosen and appointed guardian of J. W. McCorkle and M. V. McCorkle, 6 March 1871 with H. R. A. McCorkle and J. E. McCorkle as his security. (Dyr TN, Co Ct Min, B/203)

McCORKLE, M. E.
6 March 1871 James Scott made a settlement as guardian of the heirs. (Dyr TN, Co Ct Min, B/200)

McCORRY, Henry W.
Died before 23 February 1866 as shown in the suit of Joseph B. Caruthers, administrator vs Henry McCorry & others. Joseph H. Carruthers was appointed guardian ad litem for the infant defendants, Henry McCorry, Mary McCorry and Corinna A. McCorry, they having no regular guardian. (Mad TN, Ch Ct Min, 2/481 & 482) Henry McCorry had left a will & Joseph B. Carruthers is administrator with will annexed. The party named as executor died before testator and the person named in the codicil declined to act as executor. Henry W. McCorry lost a large negro property due to the late war. A part of the real estate will have to be sold to pay the debts and support his children. [I believe the will also made provision for his sisters, but the handwriting is bad & I am not sure] (Ibid 495) Henry W. McCorry died in 1863. (Ibid 3/107) 19 February 1868, Mary & Corina McCorry were stated to be minors & Henry McCorry was appointed their guardian ad litem. (Ibid 137) The land was sold and title divested out of Henry McCorry, Mary McCorry, Corinna McCorry, Musadora McCorry & Ellen McCorry. (Ibid 156)

McCOWAN, James
Died before 22 January 1802 when the heirs were shown on the delinquent tax list. (Rob TN, Co Ct Min, 1/208)

McCOY, Dickson
Died before 17 March 1854 when his death was suggested and proven in the case of Nathan Haltone et als vs Thos. W. Garawell et als. The suit was revived in the name of Wm. D. Briggance. (Mad TN, Ch Ct Min, 1/357) 13 September 1854 the suit was shown as Nathan Hallom, Miles F. Roberson & Jas. Sharp vs Thos. W. Gammel, Jno. Hobbs, Louisa Hobbs, P. W. Whitworth, Rachael Whitworth, Thos. Caffrey, Margaret Caffrey, Isabella Hargis, Thos. McCoy, Jno. McCoy, Newton McCoy, Anne Eliza McCoy, Mary D. McCoy & Wm. Briggance, administrator of Dickson McCoy. (Ibid 2/21)

McCOY, Ezekiel
Died before 1850 when administration was granted to Dixon McCoy. Dixon McCoy died intestate without having settled the estate of Ezekiel McCoy. 15 March 1855 a suit was entered by Jno. G. McCoy & others vs Wm. D. Briggance, administrator of Dixon McCoy, L. C. Smith & P. D. Conger. The complainants are the distributees of deceased distributees of the estate of Ezekiel T. McCoy. (Mad TN, Ch Ct Min, 2/29) Ezekiel made his will 3 March 1838 and shortly thereafter departed this life. James H. Rogers qualified as administrator with will annexed. He had at least one minor child at that time, who has now [16 March 1855] come of age. At the March term 1841 Dickson McCoy was appointed trustee of Ezekiel T., John G., Ann E., Newton A. and Nancy D. McCoy, minor heirs of Ezekiel B. McCoy, dececeased. Dickson McCoy died about 9 February 1854, intestate, without having settled the estate of Ezekiel. (Ibid 50) 12 September 1855 a suit of Adrian B. Hargis et als vs Susan Ballard was heard. The will of Ezekiel McCoy was proved in April 1838. He devised to his daughter, Isabella Hargis, a negro girl, Rebecca, and at her

death to her children. Isabella Hargis died 24 December 1853 leaving Adrian B., Richard L., Thomas J. & Sarah L. Hargis her only children. Thos. Hargis, the husband of Isabella, delivered said negro to Benjamin P. Ballard who afterward died & Susan Ballard took possession of said negro. (Ibid 71) Dixon McCoy was a distributee of Ezekiel McCoy & entitled to 1/11 part. (Ibid 84)

McCOY, Hugh
Died before 3 May 1819 when James Williams was appointed administrator with Edward Moore & Edward B. Whellton as security. A years provision was allotted to the widow. (Wil TN, Co Ct Min, no#/435) 2 August 1819 Enoch Stiles, by his wife Catharine Stiles, petitioned for dower of the estate of Hugh McCoy, deceased. (Ibid 493) The coroner, George Clark, was paid $4 for holding an inquest on the body of Hugh McCoy. (Ibid 539)

McCOY, Jno. G.
Died before 25 February 1860 when his death was admitted in the suit of Jno. G. McCoy et al vs Wm. D. Brigance admr. &c. The suit was revived in the name of his administrator, Neuton M. McCoy. (Mad TN, Ch Ct Min, 2/341)

McCOY, John
Died before 2 March 1829 when Daniel McCoy & Susannah McCoy were appointed administrators. (McM TN, Co Ct Min, 2no#/332)

McCOY, Rachel
Was a deformed girl aged 17 years and was allowed $25 for her support. (Rob TN, Co Ct Min, 2/391)

McCOY, William
Died before 6 December 1825 when John McCoy & Daniel McCoy were appointed administrators. (McM TN, Co Ct Min, 2no#/119)

McCOY, Wm.
Died before 6 March 1871 when James McCoy renewed his bond as guardian of the minor heirs. (Dyr TN, Co Ct Min, B/203) 2 October 1871 James McCoy made guardian settlements for Sallie Vic McCoy and Eugene McCoy. (Ibid 305) James McCoy made a settlement as guadian of Sallie Vick and Eugene McCoy. (Ibid 509)

McCROSKEY, James M.
Died before 2 September 1861 when George Wade, Wm. Wayland & Wm. C. Pickens were appointed to lay off a years support for the widow, Malinda McCroskey. (Sev TN, Co Ct Min, no#/715) The widow applied for dower. Adam H. Keener was appointed administrator. (Ibid 724) 3 December 1866 S. W. Randles was appointed guardian to the minor heirs with Malinda McCroskey as security. (Ibid 406)

McCROSKEY, Robert
Died before 7 October 1856 when Mary M. McCroskey renewed her bond as guardian to William R. and Jos. M. McCroskey, minor heirs. James M. Sharp and John S. McCroskey were her securities. (Sev TN, Co Ct Min, no#/84)

McCULLOCH, Benjn.
Died before 7 August 1804 when the heirs were shown on the delinquent tax list. (Rob TN, Co Ct Min, 1/307)

McCULLOUGH, Thos.
Was a non-resident of the state on 19 March 1852 as shown in the suit of President & Directors of the Bank of Tennessee vs Edward Anderson, Joshua Bartlet, Lewis R. Vance, John H. Ammonett, Isaac Prentis & Thos McCullough. (Jac TN, Ch Ct Min, B/27)

McCUTCHEON, Medora
5 April 1871 N. Porter made a settlement as guardian. (Dyr TN, Co Ct Min, B/228)

McCUTTCHEN, John B.
3 April 1872 N. Porter made a settlement as guardian. (Dyr TN, Co Ct Min, B/406)

McDANIEL
On 11 February 1854 a suit was entered by James W. McDaniel Exr. vs John F. McDaniel, John H. Car & wife Martha A., Joseph C. Fletcher & wife Amy W., Riley W. McDaniel, Rebecca M. Hollimon, Nancy R. Whitton, Geo. W. Apple & wife Mary Ann. Two negroes were sold to Snowdon H. Maddux and title divested as to complainants and defendants and vested in said Maddux. (Jac TN, Ch Ct Min, B/145)

McDANIEL, Daniel
21 October 1801 was allowed $25 from the County Treasury for his support. (Rob TN, Co Ct Min, 1/192)

McDANIEL, Magness
Died before 2 August 1819 when James McDaniel was appointed guardian of Randal Polly Clay McDaniel [no punctuation] heirs of Magness McDaniel, deceased. (Wil TN, Co Ct Min, no#/503)

McDANIEL, Walter
Proved by the oath of George Hallum that the piece taken off of his left ear was taken off by the teeth of another man in combat in the town of Lebanon on the thirteenth of November 1804. (Wil TN, Co Ct Min, no#/105)

McDANNEL, R. Z.
Taxes were not collected in District 5 for 1873, "in Ark." (Dyr TN, Co Ct Min, B/759)

McDAVID, W. C.
Died before 4 January 1871 when W. N. McKnight made a settlement as guardian of the minor heirs. (Dyr TN, Co Ct Min, B/162) James C. McDavid was a minor heir. (Ibid 174)

McDONAL, Middleton
Was a resident of the state of TX 14 July 1853 as shown in the suit of Ridley Apple & others vs Reece C. Stewart & others. On motion of defendant, Samuel R. McDonal, the case is continued and defendants are given leave to take the depositions of Robert More, Waddy Carlisle, Isham D. Beasly, Josiah G. Beasley and Middleton McDonal of the state of TX. [Not clear if all are in TX or just McDonal.] (Jac TN, Ch Ct Min, B/78)

McDONALD, Daniel
19 January 1803 James Crabtree, Esqr. was allowed $8 for keeping him. (Rob TN, Co Ct Min, 1/243) [Same as Daniel McDaniel]

McDONALD, Henry L.
Died before 15 July 1853 as shown in the suit of James W. McDonal Exr. &c vs John F. McDonal & others. The 2 negroes mentioned in the suit are not entitled to choose their homes, that part of the will being void. All property not devised by the will is to go to the children of the testator, to wit, Martha Ann, Amy W. & Rily B McDonald. (Jac TN, Ch Ct Min, B/105)

McDONALD, Martha
Probably died before 4 December 1866 as shown in the suit of James M. Wright Admr. of A. McGinnis decd. vs the widow & heirs and creditors of said deceased. An affidavit was filed in the estate of A. McGinnis by Martha McDonald's administrators. (Fen TN, Ch Ct Min, A/305)

McDONALD, Orleana Jane
Was an orphan girl aged 3 when she was bound to Margarett Cunningham on 1 December 1828, until age 18. (McM TN, Co Ct Min, 2no#/323)

McDOWELL, John
With his wife, Elizabeth McDowell, sold land in Haywood County, NC, 2 December 1823. They hold an undivided moity of 300 acres in right of said wife. Elizabeth is infirm & unable to appear in court & commissioners were appointed to take her private examination. (McM TN, Co Ct Min, no#/106)

McDOWELL, Joseph
Died before 9 November 1812 when the will was proved by James Gambill and James McDowell. Thomas Paseley, James McDowell & Martha McDowell were executors. (Rob TN, Co Ct Min, 3/137)

McELRATH, Albert G.
Died before 11 February 1840 when his death was suggested in the suit of Albert G. McElrath and others vs Larkin B. Orr & others. The suit is to be revived in the name of the administrator, David Snoddy. (Bed TN, Ch Ct Min, 2/96)

McELRATH, Joseph
Died before August term 1833 when Larkin B. Orr was appointed administrator, with David Orr & William Carter as security. This was shown 31 December 1840 in the suit of A. G. McElrath and others vs Larkin B. Orr & others. Larkin Orr has not paid over to

complainants, who are the distributees of said Joseph McElrath, their shares. They are to recover from Larkin Orr, David Orr & Robert L. Landers, administrator of William Carter, the amount of their distributative shares. (Bed TN, Ch Ct Min, 2/130)

McELYEA, James
Made a deed of gift to the children of Mary Wit, as follows: William, Thomas, Sarah & Phebe, 7 May 1804. (Rob TN, Co Ct Min, 1/290)

McERWIN, Alexander
Died before 19 November 1795 when the jury found that the will was a good will. Margaret McCowan [McEwin] dissented from the will and also declined to be the executrix. (Was TN, Co Ct Min, 1/584) The order for recording the will was rescinded. Another jury found that it was not a good will as Alexander McErwin was not of sound mind at the time of making same. (Ibid 585) Margaret McErwin & Lewis Jordan were appointed administrators. (Ibid 586)

McEWING, John
Died before 4 June 1828 when his executor was in a case vs Wm. R. Tucker & John McAllen. (McM TN, Co Ct Min, no#/329)

McFARLAND, Alex.
Died before 5 August 1784 when Wm. Moore was granted leave to administer the estate, with George Gillaspy and Jossiah Martin as his security. (Was TN, Co Ct Min, 1/249)

McFARLAND, James
Married before 18 November 1814 to Phoebe Tucker, daughter of John Tucker, deceased. (Rob TN, Co Ct Min, 3/514)

McFARLAND, John
Died before 15 January 1847 as shown in the suit of John Umstead and Elizabeth his wife, Porter Hall & Jane his wife, John Bradberry, James M. Bradberry, Andrew Stewart, Jr. & Mary Stewart his wife, Epsey Ann Bradberry, Daniel M. Bradberry, Rebecca Bradberry, Sarah S. Bradberry, John M. Bradberry, Joel B. Bradberry, Stephen Johnson, Elizabeth M. Johnson, Martha S. Johnson, Sarah Johnson, Joseph Medlin & wife Elizabeth, John Nelson & wife Mary formerly Mary McFarlin, complainants, vs Duncan McFarlin, Quily McFarland, Richard M. Gorvan & wife Susan, Wm. P. Taylor & wife Ruthy, Wyatt Mooring, Mary J. McFarlin, James V. McFarlin & John D. McFarlin, defendants. The suit was revived in the name of John Nelson who has intermarried with Mary McFarlin, widow of John McFarlin, and Andrew Stewart who has intermarried with Mary Bradberry, complainants. Dower is to be set off for Mary Nelson, formerly Mary McFarlin. Each of the five adult complainants to wit, John Nelson, John Umstead, Stephen Johnson, John Bradberry & Porter Hall pay 1/9 of this suit & each of the adult defendants, Duncan McFarlin, Quily McFarlin, Richard M. Gorvan & William P. Taylor to pay 1/9 of the costs. (Mad TN, Ch Ct Min, 1/17)

McFARLAND, John
Died before 29 May 1794 when the administrator, William Moore, was allowed $250 for all expenditures in settling said estate. (Was TN, Co Ct Min, 1/494)

McFARLAND, Marvil
Married before 10 November 1812 to Jane Shanklin as shown when Jane was examined separately concerning a deed to land which she had received from her father, Andrew Shanklin. (Rob TN, Co Ct Min, 3/155)

McFARLIN, Jas.
Died before 15 October 1798 when the executrix, Margaret McFarlin, sold land to John Crane. (Rob TN, Co Ct Min, 1/75)

McFERSON, John
5 January 1857 the State paid the bill of cost in a case where he had been charged with Bastardy. (Sev TN, Co Ct Min, no#/96)

McGEE, Ann
12 May 1813 Robert Moses made a deed of gift to the heirs of Ann McGee proven by Elijah Hughes and Horatio Loary. Does not say that Ann was deceased. (Rob TN, Co Ct Min, 3/252)

McGHEE
4 March 1828 John & Mathew W. McGhee were deeded 640 acres of land in Monroe

County, TN, by Cheanuna or Jency Cataba, John Mink Watts, Dubetre Watts, Forked Trail Watts & Nelley, citizens & natives of the Cherokee Nation. The same date Cho Ko ha, widow of Tah Clentah, deceased, & heir of the Old Barks of Chota, deceased, deeded her dower interest in 640 acres in Monroe County to John & Mathew McGhee. (McM TN, Co Ct Min, 2no#/272) On the same date, Tah noo nah Kah tah hie, widow of the Old Barks of Chota, deeded her dower interest in 640 acres in Monroe County to John and Mathew McGhee. (Ibid 273)

McGHEE, Rachael
Was stated to be an aged & infirm woman 7 June 1824 when Reuben Lemmons was allowed money for her support. (McM TN, Co Ct Min, 2no#/5) An order for the support of Rachael McGee was rescinded from the 8th of March 1828. (Ibid 2/292)

McGINNIS, Andrew
Died before 10 October 1865 as shown in the suit of Johnathan Burnett vs the heirs-at-law & widow of Andrew McGinnis, deceased, and the heirs-at-law of Pleasant Miller, deceased, & his widow & others. The children of Pleasant Miller are minors and Sally Miller is their guardian. There is no administrator for the estate of Andrew McGinnis nor for the estate of Plesant Miller, and none can be procured and over six months has elapsed since the death of each. James M. Wright was appointed administrator of both estates. (Fen TN, Ch Ct Min, A/289) Andrew McGinnis died intestate about 1863. (Ibid 292) An accounting was made 4 December 1866. Nancy McGinnis was the widow of Andrew McGinnis. (Ibid 305) David Delk was either an heir or a creditor of Andrew McGinnis. (Ibid 368)

McGINNIS, T. J.
Died before 4 July 1870 when W. J. Farris was paid for making the coffin. (Dyr TN, Co Ct Min, B/73)

McGINNIS, W. A.
5 June 1871 L. C. White made a settlement as guardian. (Dyr TN, Co Ct Min, B/243)

McGIPSON, George
Died before 29 January 1846 when a suit was entered by William Gipson Admr. &c vs Randal McGipson et al. Lands are to be sold subject to the widow's dower. (Jac TN, Ch Ct Min, A/210) The land was sold to Tobias McGipson and title divested out of defendants, except the widow of George McGipson, deceased, who has dower therein, and the said Tobias McGipson. (Ibid 219)

McGLOHLIN, Sary
Was bound to Jane English 7 November 1785 until age 18. (Was TN, Co Ct Min, 1/265)

McGRAW, Uriah
Will be eight years of age the 4th of May next. He was bound 13 February 1815 to George G. Brown until full age. (Rob TN, Co Ct Min, 3/538)

McHANEY, Andrew
28 December 1826 made a bill of sale for several slaves to William McHaney, his son, Henry Whitlow & Lucy his wife, Thomas Pemberton & Polly his wife, and John A. Smith & Nancy his wife. The three women were daughters of Andrew McHaney. (Wil TN, Reg Bk/399)

McINTIER, J. L.
Taxes were not collected in District 4 for 1873, "over age." (Dyr TN, Co Ct Min, B/759)

McINTOSH, Alexr.
Died before 15 April 1799 when the will was proved by Bazel Boun. No executor was named so Elizabeth McIntosh was granted letters of administration with John McIntosh as security. (Rob TN, Co Ct Min, 1/95)

McINTOSH, William
Was a resident of Randolph County in Indiana Territory 5 April 1809 when his deposition was to be taken for the defendant in the case of Wm. Parks vs Henry Johnson. (Rob TN, Co Ct Min, 2/122)

McIVER, John
Died before December 1854 when the administrator, Daniel Graham, recovered a judgement against James H. Beason and Jeremiah Gwin. Lands were sold and Jane

McIver became the purchaser and she transfered the lands to John Porterfield. James H. Beason wants to redeem the lands. (Fen TN, Ch Ct Min, A/167)

McKAMY, James
Died before 4 December 1826 when William C. McKamy & Mary McKamy, the widow, who "by the articles of Partnership betwix John McEwen & James McKamy, were appointed special executors of the last will of James McKamy deceased." They were also appointed administrators of his estate. (McM TN, Co Ct Min, 2no#/181)

McKAY, Elenor
Was allowed $25 for keeping Rachel McKay for 12 months, 10 August 1813. (Rob TN, Co Ct Min, 3/283)

McKEAL, James
Was a pauper 1 December 1828 when he was sold to the lowest bidder for his support. Richard McPherson became the lowest bidder. (McM TN, Co Ct Min, 2/316)

McKEARLEY, James
11 February 1813 gave bond, with William Ledford and Azariah Jones as security, that a bastard child of Allas Thompson would not become a charge upon the county. (Rob TN, Co Ct Min, 3/214)

McKINLEY
James and Josiah McKinley had deeded to Matthew C. McKinley, on 19 March 1838, a negro slave Barbary and her increase, in trust for Elizabeth Moore and her children. A suit was brought 6 November 1843 by Matthew C. McKinley and Elizabeth Moore against Robert Becton and William Q. Hughes. The Court decided the negroes were not liable for the satisfaction of the judgement obtained by the defendants against Richard Moore. (Jac TN, Ch Ct Min, A/119) The Court decided on 8 May 1844 that the negroes were the property of Richard Moore, husband of Elizabeth Moore, by gift from Robert McKinley to said Elizabeth. (Ibid 156)

McKINLEY, James
Died before 4 May 1842. A suit was entered 8 November 1842 by Sarah McKinley, Jane McKinley, Mary McKinley, Elizabeth McKinley, Martha McKinley, minors by their guardian Elizabeth McKinley, Robert G. Hughes and wife Mariana and Elizabeth McKinley in her own right, and Simon Hogin vs Matthew C. McKinley administrator of James McKinley Decd. (Jac TN, Ch Ct Min, A/47 & 62) The heirs were listed as Eliza McKinley, Sarah McKinley, Jane McKinley, Mary McKinley, Elizabeth McKinley, James McKinley, Martha McKinley and Robert B. McKinley, the last 7 who are minor children of James McKinley, deceased. (Ibid 162)

McKINNEY, David
Died before 6 September 1821 when his administratrix, Catherine McKinney, was in a suit vs Geroge Harlin. (McM TN, Co Ct Min, no#/24)

McKINNEY, Jeremiah
Died before 19 September 1816 when Elijah Wamack was appointed administrator, with Richard Wamack & John W. Payton as security. (Wil TN, Co Ct Min, no#/45) Elijah Wamack was appointed guardian of Joel, John, Jenny, Milly, James & Fanny McKinney, minor heirs, 5 February 1819. (Ibid 431)

McKINNEY, Joel
17 March 1817 was bound as an apprentice to Nathaniel Dew until age 21. (Wil TN, Co Ct Min, no#/71)

McKINNEY, John R.
Was an orphan when he was bound 17 December 1816 to Isaac Moore until the boy comes of age. (Wil TN, Co Ct Min, no#/60)

McKINNY, Edwin F.
Was a resident of MO on 8 May 1844 as shown in the suit of Perry Mahanay vs Edwin F. McKinny, et als. (Jac TN, Ch Ct Min, A/138)

McKNIGHT
15 March 1853 a suit was entered; Marcus McKnight Next friend &c vs Hamilton McKnight et als. It mentioned a purchase made by Thos. Blair, guardian, and Margaret his ward. (Mad TN, Ch Ct Min, 1/295) In this same suit a trustee is to be appointed for Margaret

McKnight & children. (Ibid 356) David Lacy was appointed trustee for Margaret McKnight & her increase. (Ibid 364)

McKNIGHT, Elizabeth
Died before 4 May 1874 when her husband, William N. McKnight, was chosen and appointed guardian of their child, James McKnight, with W. M. Watkins and W. P. Menzies as his security. Elizabeth was formerly Elizabeth McClanahan. (Dyr TN, Co Ct Min, B/735)

McKNIGHT, John T.
Died before 4 March 1872 when Mary McKnight made a settlement as administrator. (Dyr TN, Co Ct Min, B/381)

McKNIGHT, Juliana K. M.
Died before 18 February 1858 as shown in the petition of Ro. Fenner Surviving Executor and others and F. N. W. Burton vs T. P. Jones admr. and others tried together by consent of parties. The heirs of Juliana were David McKnight, Eleanor McKnight, Mary McKnight, Matilda F. McKnight & John McKnight. John S. Fenner was administrator. This petition concerns the estate of Dr. Richard Fenner. (Mad TN, Ch Ct Min, 2/181)

McKNIGHT, Robert
Died before 11 January 1849 as shown in a suit by the administrator, James McKnight, vs John McKnight. (Mad TN, Ch Ct Min, 1/62)

McKNIGHT, Samuel A.
8 April 1874 was chosen and appointed guardian of Sammi A. McKnight, his daughter, with L. C. McClerkin and J. M. Hurt as security. (Dyr TN, Co Ct Min, B/731)

McKNIGHT, Wm.
Died before 29 August 1860 as shown in the suit of Martin Stewart & wife & others vs Caleb McKnight & others. The complainants admit that the small pecuniary legacies to them in item 6 of Wm. McKnights will have been paid. The court decided they were not entitled to more. An appeal was granted. (Mad TN, Ch Ct Min, 2/387)

McKOY, M. M. [McKay]
Died before 21 February 1860 when his death was proved in the case of John Catrin, Jr., vs M. M. McKoy. (Mad TN, Ch Ct Min, 2/296)

McLAMA, Peter
Was a resident of Tryon County [NC] 24 November 1778 when his deposition was to be taken. (Was TN, Co Ct Min, 1/51)

McLEAN, Joseph
Died before 3 September 1827 when his will was proved by Harris D. Throp & Benjamin C. Stout, witnesses. James Fyffe & John McLean were named executors. (McM TN, Co Ct Min, 2no#/229)

McLISH, Wm.
Died before 18 April 1803 when the will was proved by John Johnson & Peter Renfro. Jane McLish & George Lamb were executors. (Rob TN, Co Ct Min, 1/245)

McMACHEN, John
15 February 1786 made a deed to his son, John Blair McMachen, recorded November 1788. (Was TN, Co Ct Min, no#/14)

McMAHAN, Archabald
Died before 6 Febrauary 1865 when Rachel McMahan was appointed guardian ad litem to the minor heirs. (Sev TN, Co Ct Min, no#/135)

McMAHAN, George
Died before 1 July 1867 when M. J. Graham was paid for his coffin. George was colored. (Sev TN, Co Ct Min, no#/459)

McMAHAN, George N.
7 July 1862 made petition to be allowed to adopt two minor illegitimate children, to wit, Mary Smallwood aged near 12 years and Ned Smallwood aged 8 years, who are now at his house. They are the children of Rosanna Smallwood. He desires to make them his legitimate heirs and change their names from Smallwood to McMahan, for these reasons; he has no living children by his wife and secondly, the mother of said children some years

ago in their early infancy swore them to him and he believes they are his natural children. (Sev TN, Co Ct Min, no#/3)

McMAHAN, Iredell
Was a pauper boy of color 2 April 1867 when it was ordered that the commissioners of the poor house take charge of him. (Sev TN, Co Ct Min, no#/446)

McMAHAN, Martha B.
7 September 1857 John McMahan renewed his bond as her guardian with David McMahan as his security. (Sev TN, Co Ct Min, no#/201)

McMAHAN, Samuel
2 October 1865 was appointed guardian to David R. McMahan & Elizabeth Brooks, minors, with David McMahan & R. S. McMahan as security. (Sev TN, Co Ct Min, no#/217) 5 November 1866 Samuel McMahan made a settlement as guardian of David McMahan, minor heir of Wm. McMahan. Elizabeth Brooks was also an heir of Wm. McMahan. (Ibid 388)

McMAHAN, Wm.
Died before 7 January 1857 when Thomas McMahan renewed his bond as guardian of Jane McMahan, minor heir. Robert H. Hodsden was security. (Sev TN, Co Ct Min, no#/118) 2 March 1857 Robert H. Hodson and Redmond McMahan gave a new bond as executors, with Jesse Stafford & David McMahan as security. The original bond was destroyed. (Ibid 128) 1 February 1858 the executors vs Thomas McMahan, Sanders McMahan & others, petitioned to sell land. Land was ordered to be sold except 2 acres devised to the widow & a portion to G. N. McMahan. (Ibid 258) 6 Jan 1862 Thomas McMahan made a final settlement as guardian of Jane Rich formerly Jane McMahan. (Ibid 740)

McMAHAN, Wm.
Died before 6 February 1865 as shown in a petition to sell land made by Robert S. McMahan vs the heirs of Wm. McMahan, deceased. (Sev TN, Co Ct Min, no#/135) The land was sold to David McMahan with Robert S. McMahan & John McMahan as security. (Ibid 151) A list of the effects of Wm. McMahan, deceased, was reported. (Ibid 168)

McMAHAN, Wm.
6 May 1861 filed a plea to quash a charge of bastardy. (Sev TN, Co Ct Min, no#/687)

McMILLAN, Daniel
Died before 1 August 1814 when John McMillan was appointed administrator with James Hagert & John Chambers as security. (Ste TN, Co Ct Min, 4/162)

McMILLIN, Robert W.
Died before 6 September 1825 when administrators, Thomas Parris & Joseph W. McMillin, made a settlement. (McM TN, Co Ct Min, 2no#/96) 6 September 1830 a settlement was made by Joseph Love as guardian of David C. McMillin & Carson Caldwell as guardian of Jonathan P. McMillin, minor heirs of Robert McMillin, deceased. (Ibid 468)

McMOTT, Henry
Was the father of a bastard child, named Mary, by Sarah Ingle. He was orderd to pay support 2 July 1860. (Sev TN, Co Ct Min, no#/569) 14 October 1861 he was ordered to pay for the 2nd years support of the child. (Ibid 727)

McNABB, Baptist
Died before 3 August 1784 when an inventory of the estate was returned by John McNabb and David McNabb, executors. (Was TN, Co Ct Min, 1/245)

McNAT, Macky
Died before 4 February 1811 when David McNatt was appointed administrator with Nathan Ross & Henry Pugh as security. (Ste TN, Co Ct Min, 3/12) Provisions are to be laid off for the widow McNatt and her children for one year. (Ibid 29) A deed of gift from Macky McNat to Sarah Brandon was proved by David McNatt and John Hodges. (Ibid 37) On petition of the heirs of Macky McNatt on 5 November 1811, it was ordered that Joseph B. Neville, Dudley Williams & Nathan Ross divide the land of said deceased among his heirs. (Ibid 102)

McNEALY, Isaac
Died in 1820 or 1821 as shown in the suit filed 23 April 1838 by Rebecca McNealy and

Cynthia Ann McNealy, minor heirs who sue by their next friend, Hardin R. Cathey vs John Lane, John B. Armstrong & wife Rebecca and Amos McAdams. Rebecca & Cynthia Ann McNealy are the only heirs and distributees of their father [blank] McNealy. His widow, Margaret P. McNealy, was administrator. Margaret P. McNealy married John Lane. James B. Armstrong [or George C. Armstrong] is the guardian of the minors. (Bed TN, Ch Ct Min, 1/380)

McNEELY, Alexander
Died before 18 September 1816 when Jno. McNeely was appointed administrator with Seth McNeely & Joseph Johnson as security. (Wil TN, Co Ct Min, no#/43)

McNEELY, James
Died before 19 June 1816 when the will was proved by William Steele & Samuel Logg. John McNeely & Seth McNeely were executors with Seth McNeely, Alexander Asters & Andrew Foster as security. (Wil TN, Co Ct Min, no#/17)

McNEELY, Moses
Died before 2 November 1818 when George McNeely was appointed administrator with J. White & Saml. Bryant as security. (Wil TN, Co Ct Min, no#/331)

McNULTY, Will
Died before 17 December 1816 when the administrator was ordered to report. (Wil TN, Co Ct Min, no#/59)

McNUTT, W. A.
Died before 6 January 1862 when John Chandler, Timothy Chandler & D. B. Bradson were appointed to lay off a years support to the widow, Mary E. McNutt. (Sev TN, Co Ct Min, no#/736) John S. McNutt & W. P. Burns were appointed administrators of Wm. A. McNutt. (Ibid 738) 6 October 1862 Mary E. McNutt & Margaret J. McNutt were listed as minor heirs (Ibid 14) 3 November 1862 dower was laid off. Mary E. McNutt claimed her rights under the will of her father, Wilson Burns, it being 1/5 part of the lands belonging to her said father, which lands have never been divided. (Ibid 22) Administrator, John S. McNutt, has removed himself beyond the limits of this State. (Ibid 151) The other executor was Wm. P. Burn. (Ibid 165)

McNUTT, Wm.
Was an orphan aged 15 years when he was bound to John Dixon on 19 December 1808. (Roa TN, Co Ct Min, D/31) 18 July 1810 William McNutt was aged 16 years and 7 months when he was bound to Thomas C. Clark until age 21. (Ibid 237)

McPHAIL, David [Daniel]
Died before 12 January 1849 as shown in the suit of Daniel B. Cliff admr. vs Ranson H. Byrns [Byrus], Egbert Haywood, Stephen Burrus, Carroline C. Stafford widow of Auther Stafford deceased, James H. Stafford, Marshall C. Stafford, Jno. M. W. Stafford, Caroline Stafford, Mary A. J. Stafford & William Crown administrator of Author Stafford. McPhail died in 1846, intestate. (Mad TN Ch Ct Min, 1/70)

McPHERSON, George
Died before 17 December 1806 when Sally McPherson and Joseph McPherson were appointed administrators. (Roa TN, Co Ct Min, B/235) An inventory of the estate was returned & ordered to be sold. (Ibid 237)

McQUEAN, Saml.
Died before 25 August 1794 when Hannah McQuean was appointed administratrix, with John Vaught and Joseph Sands as her security. (Was TN, Co Ct Min, 1/495) Matthias Waggoner, Roland Jenkins and David Waggoner were appointed to appraise the estate. (Ibid 496)

McRAE, Duncan
Died before 2 May 1814 when Elisabeth McRae was appointed administratrix with James H. Russell, Wm. M. Cooley & Henry Gibson as security. (Ste TN, Co Ct Min, 4/137) Land is to be divided that is held by James. H. Russell and the heirs of Duncan McRae as tenants in common. (Ibid 151) A years support was set off for the widow. (Ibid 159)

McSHEKUS, Miles
Died before 25 January 1799 when the land of his heirs was ordered sold for back taxes. (Rob TN, Co Ct Min, 1/94)

McVEY, Thomas
Died before 14 February 1815 when the will was proved by Wm. Baker and Robert McClary. (Cla TN, Co Ct Min, 4/15) Mary McVey was appointed administratrix with the will annexed. Marcurius Cook and Daniel Rice were her security. (Ibid 43)

McWHIRTER, George M.
7 February 1825 made a deed of gift to his grand children, William Briggs, Martha Briggs, Benjamin Briggs, Elizabeth Briggs, George Briggs, Sarah Briggs & Samuel Briggs, of various household items & stock. He gave the items in trust for the grand children to "my confidential friend Samuel C. McWhirter." (Wil TN, Reg Bk/362)

McWILLIAMS, Andrew
Was a resident of Hawkins County 21 December 1804 when James McNutt, by his attorney, ordered that a subpoena issue for him and Samuel Smith to give testimony about a deed made by John Smith to William McDowell for a lot in the town of Kingston. (Roa TN, Co Ct Min, A/308)

MEADOWS, Silus
On 10 February 1860 his divorce suit against Agniss Meadows was continued until next term of Court. (Jac TN, Ch Ct Min, C/317) Silas Meaders was granted a divorce from Agness Meaders on 14 August 1860 for adultry & abandonment. They have one child, a girl about 4 years old. The father of complainant, Charles Meaders, is to have custody of the child but under the care of the father, Silas. The child will be allowed occasionally to go the the house of its grandmother, Agness Wheeler, and stay a few days at a time in order to be with its mother. (Ibid 388)

MEDDOWS, Michael
Died after making his will on 22 June 1818. He left to his wife, Jane Meddows, all his estate during her life and at her death to be divided among his children, to wit, son Riley's heirs (William & Washington), Mehaley, William, John, James, Jemima, Ann, Henderson, Rebecca, Pomphit G., Ephraim G. & Jane making in all [ten?, eleven?] legatees as well as the two heirs of Riley, (William & Washington), who are entitled to their father's part. Michael died (as well as is now recollected) in 1819. Washington has died without heirs. James has died without heirs leaving only 11 legatees. They are all of full age. Jane is a resident of Bedford County. James Meddows and Mosly Harris were named executors. [very bad writing] James died not long after "his Farther." Jane [the widow] has the property & is attempting to dispose of it. The will was entered as an exibit in this suit in 1834. This is shown in the suit of Archibald Yell of Lincoln County, & Jonathan Webster of Bedford County vs Jane Meddows. William Meddows & Henderson Meddows sold their interest to Samuel Haggard & he sold it to Yell & Webster. (Bed TN, Ch Ct Min, 1/86)

MEDGET, Massey
Was a pauper girl of this county 1 November 1819 when she was allowed $20 for her support. (Wil TN, Co Ct Min, no#/537)

MEDLIN, Grey B.
Died before 15 January 1851 as shown in the suit of Andrew Ballentine vs James H. Medlin et als. Jas. H. Medlin was appointed administrator. (Mad TN, Ch Ct Min, 1/180) 14 July 1851, heirs of Grey B. Medlin were shown as; Jas. H. Medlin, Malinda Medlin, Grey B. Medlin, Carroll Medlin, Jno. Medlin, Robertson Medlin, Thomas Medlin, Esther Medlin, Tennessee Medlin, Joseph, William & Mary Neal, Willis Evans & Elizabeth Evans his wife and Bryant Medlin. (Ibid 198)

MEDLIN, Susan
Was granted a divorce from F. B. Medlin on 22 August 1867. They were married in 1840 and he deserted her in 1845 and has not returned to her. (Mad TN, Ch Ct Min, 3/74)

MEDLOCK, Isaac
Probably died before August 1789 when his estate was released from paying poll tax for 1788. (Was TN, Co Ct Min, 1/403)

MEDLOCK, John
Probably died before August term 1789 when his estate was released from paying poll tax for 1788. (Was TN, Co Ct Min, 1/403)

MEDLOCK, Sarah
Was the mother of a base born male child named John. John Carter was ordered to make bond for it's maintenance at the August term 1788. (Was TN, Co Ct Min, 1/338)

MEDOWS, Matilda
Was granted a divorce 15 August 1860 from Meridith Medows. He has been guilty of adultry with Polly Fox. Complainant is to have the cash notes or other effects in the hands of her guardian, Milton Draper or L. A. McCarvin. She will also have custody of the child. (Jac TN, Ch Ct Min, C/413)

MEED, A.
Taxes were not collected in District 5 for 1873, "can't be found." (Dyr TN, Co Ct Min, B/759)

MEGEHEE, Norvill
Died in April or May 1836, intestate & without issue. This is shown in the suit of Henry Megehee vs John Davis. Henry Megehee was the father of Norvill McGehee and was a citizen of Wake County, NC. [There are 2 pages belonging to this suit that are missing.] In the decree Henry was shown as McGee and the suit was dismissed. (Bed TN, Ch Ct Min, 1/253)

MELTON, Garrett
Was bound as an apprentice 17 March 1817 to Elijah Cross until age 21. (Wil TN, Co Ct Min, no#/73)

MELVILLE, Levina
Was a pauper 2 March 1829 when money was allowed for her support. (McM TN, Co Ct Min, 2/331)

MELVIN, Wm.
Was an orphan boy aged 9 years on the 21st of May 1829. He was bound on 2 March 1829 to Joel K. Brown until age 21. He is to learn the trade of a taylor. (McM TN, Co Ct Min, 2no#/339)

MENEES, Benjamin
Died before 11 February 1811 when the will was proved by Nehemiah Fowler, Elisha Phelps & Levin Brookshire. Jeremiah Batts & Nimrod Browing were executors. (Rob TN, Co Ct Min, 2/365) 17 February 1814 it was ordered that Benjamin Menees be paid his bequest according to the will of Benjamin Menees, deceased. (Ibid 3/385)

MENEES, Benjamin [Menses]
9 November 1813 his deposition was to be taken for the defendant in the case of William Conrad, executor of Nicholas Coonrad deceased vs Jesse Martin, as it is believed Benjamin is about to leave the state. (Rob TN, Co Ct Min, 3/325)

MENEES, James
Was a resident of Davidson County 17 February 1814 when a deposition was to be taken for the plaintiff in the case of Benjamin Menees vs the executors of Benjamin Menees deceased. (Rob TN, Co Ct Min, 3/391)

MENEES, William D.
13 November 1811 an order was given to value the property of William D. Menees which he is to refund to the legatees of his deceased father. (Rob TN, Co Ct Min, 3/43)

MENESINGER, John
Was a pauper 4 October 1870 when $20 was allowed for his support. (Dyr TN, Co Ct Min, B/110)

MENISS, Mary
1 August 1859 it was ordered that her child be brought to court and bound out as it is in needy circumstances. (Sev TN, Co Ct Min, no#/465)

MENZIES, John C.
Died before 7 November 1870 when J. A. C. Manley was appointed administrator, with R. G. Menzies and W. P. Menzies as his securities. (Dyr TN, Co Ct Min, B/128) 6 February 1872 Smith Parks was appointed administrator de bonis non. (Ibid 374)

MERCHANT, J. P.
Died before 6 March 1871 when W. W. Davis made a settlement as administrator. (Dyr TN, Co Ct Min, B/201) W. W. Davis made a settlement as administrator of Peter Merchant, deceased. (Ibid 305)

MERCHANT, Sandford
Died before 6 June 1870 when F. G. Sampson was appointed administrator, with P. E. Wilson and J. W. Lauderdale as securities. (Dyr TN, Co Ct Min, B/67)

MEREDITH, Hugh
Died before 31 March 1868 as shown in the suit of Jane Clemens widow of John M. Clemens deceased, Orion Clemens, Parmela A. Moffett and Samuel L. Clemens, heirs of John M. Clemens deceased vs Anna D. Meredith, widow of Hugh Meredith deceased and John D. Meridith, Henry H. Meridith, Anna R. Meridith, and the heirs of Charles Meridith deceased and the heirs of Edward H. Meredith deceased, Heirs of Hugh Meredith deceased. Hugh Meredith was the husband of Anna D. Meredith and father of defendants John D. Meredith, Henry H. Meredith and Anna R. Meredith, and the grandfather of the other defendants. In 1840 or 1841 Hugh Meredith sold land to John M. Clemens but the deed was never registered and was lost or destroyed during the Civil War. (Fen TN, Ch Ct Min, A/364)

MERRITT, George Washington
Was an orphan boy 5 November 1860 when he was bound out to John Underwood. He is aged 8 1/2 years. (Sev TN, Co Ct Min, no#/619) 7 December 1863 John Underwood was released from his obligation. (Ibid 83)

MERRIWETHER, David
Died before 21 February 1861 as shown in the suit of William M. Reeves vs M. D. Merrewither et als. Defendants were Matthias D. Merriwether, William P. Merriwether and Henry A. Merriwether, administrator of David Merriwether, deceased. (Mad TN, Ch Ct Min, 2/432)

MERRIWETHER
14 August 1868 a suit was entered; E. A. Taylor & others vs Saml. Meriwither & others. James K. Stephens was appointed guardian ad litem for Samuel Merriwither, Hubbard Merriwither, Marion Merriwether, John Merriwither, Henry K. Meriwither and Sallie Merewither, the minor defendants. (Mad TN, Ch Ct Min, 3/174) In this suit R. T. McKnight was appointed surveyor to make a survey of the land embraced in the home place of the late Frank Merrwither, deceased. (Ibid 228)

MIEGS, Return J.
Died before 4 June 1823 when his administrator, Return J. Miegs, was defendant in a suit of McGlus & McCarty. (McM TN, Co Ct Min, no#/88)

MILAM, Stephen
Died before 4 December 1871 when P. A. Walker was appointed administrator, with Z. J. Milam and J. F. Child as his securities. (Dyr TN, Co Ct Min, B/324) Allen Rawles, W. L. Watkins and B. E. Burgie were appointed to lay off a years provisions for the widow and family. (Ibid 325) The widow, Eliza M. Milam, petitioned for dower. Notice has been given to defendants, Cora Walker & her husband P. A. Walker, Gladden Milam, Jack Milam, Delpha Rhodes, L. J. Rhodes and wife Eleazer Rhodes, Phelix W. Milam, John W. Milam and Louisa Milam, heirs-at-law (except D. J. Milam, a non-resident) of Stephen Milam, deceased. (Ibid 420) 8 April 1874 a suit was brought by Webb & Child vs P. A. Walker et al. Summons was served on Elija Rhodes and L. J. Rhodes his wife, Felix W. Milam, John W. Milam, Louisa E. Milam, Cora Walker, Disepha Rhodes, Jack Milam and Gladden Milam, commanding them to appear. Publication was also made for D. J. Milam. This suit concerns the estate of Stephen Milam, deceased. (Ibid 732)

MILAM, Thos. R.
Died before 2 May 1870 when R. H. McGaughey was appointed administrator, with W. C. Doyle, D. C. James, W. A. Milam and J. F. Childs as security. (Dyr TN, Co Ct Min, B/51) R. M. Tipton, W. A. Harris and Stephen Milam were appointed to lay off a years allowance for the widow and family. (Ibid 102) The widow, Martha Milam, petitioned for dower. Notice was given to Julia Milan and Dora Milan who are the only heirs. Thos. died in 1870. His land was bounded by Denten Milam. (Ibid 147)

MILEHAM, Jacob
On 3 September 1810 gave power of attorney to Archibald Simpson [both of them from Bedford County, TN] to recover money from the estate of Joseph Branch of Hallifax County, NC, witnessed by William Simpson & John Curry. (Wil TN, Reg Bk/21) On 1 March 1811 Jacob Mileham & William Simpson of Bedford County, gave power of attorney to William Scott of Wilson County to recover from Joseph Branch as above & from Nicholas Branch of Bedford County, TN, $4,000 & interest. Archibald Simpson also signed the document, witnessed by Robert Alexander & Ephraim Sherrell. (Ibid 22)

MILES, Charles
18 April 1797 John Nichols made a deed to Richard Miles & William Miles, minors, sons of Charles Miles. (Rob TN, Co Ct Min, 1/26)

MILES, James
Died before 11 November 1811 when Richard Miles was appointed guardian of the orphans. (Rob TN, Co Ct Min, 3/32) The widow, Martha Miles, was granted letters of administration. (Ibid 48)

MILES, Richard
Died before 15 May 1811 as shown in the case of Charles Miles vs Edward Lacy, executor of the last will and testament of Richard Miles, deceased. (Rob TN, Co Ct Min, 2/415)

MILES, Wm., Esqr.
"Is about to remove" 18 July 1798 when Jas. Morfleet, Esqr. was appointed to take the list of inhabitants in Captain Patterson's District in his place. (Rob TN, Co Ct Min, 1/70)

MILIGAN, Jane
Was the mother of a bastard child. James Willard was the reputed father & was ordered to pay support for 4 years, 19 March 1817. (Wil TN, Co Ct Min, no#/91)

MILLAR, Mary
Was the mother of a base born child by John Bayless who gave bond 19 August 1795 for its maintenance. (Was TN, Co Ct Min, 1/565)

MILLER
In the suit of David Delk vs Pearson Miller et als, 9 April 1861, it was stated that Joseph Miller, John Miller, Pleasant Miller and Tranguella Miller were minors and R. H. Bledsoe was appointed guardian ad litem. (Fen TN, Ch Ct Min, A/261)

MILLER, Abner
Died before 26 March 1855 as shown in the suit of Pleasant Miller & David C. Travis, administrators of Abner Miller, deceased vs Robert Montgomery, Trustee of the County of Fentress et als. (Fen TN, Ch Ct Min, A/4)

MILLER, And. [Ared.]
Died before 6 June 1820 when his executor, Joseph Crithfield, was defendant in the suit of Ephraim Walker. (McM TN, Co Ct Min, no#/6)

MILLER, Andw.
Died [no date given, but probably between February and August 1788]. Elizabeth Miller requested letters of adminstration, with Henry Miller & Adam Roder as securities. (Was TN, Co Ct Min, 1/318)

MILLER, Ann
Died before 17 May 1795 when the will was proved by William Montgomery and Abraham Campbell. (Was TN, Co Ct Min, 1/546)

MILLER, Cailar
Died before 11 November 1833 when Enoch L. Walker was charged with his murder. [The name of the deceased is in doubt as it is squeezed in between the lines.] (Obi TN, Cir Ct Min, 2/98) The charge of murder was dismissed against Enoch L. Walker. (Ibid 171)

MILLER, Cas.
Taxes were not collected in District 2 for 1873, "in MO." (Dyr TN, Co Ct Min, B/758)

MILLER, David
11 August 1790 made a deed of gift to his daughter, Margaret Hall. In the event of the death of Margaret, the negro girl named Aninece deeded to her is to go to John Hall, the youngest son of Margaret Hall, & to his heirs of his body. If John Hall have no heirs of his body, the negro is to revert back to the estate of David Miller, who lives in Greene County. (Was TN, Co Ct Min, 1/464)

MILLER, Green
Taxes were not collected in District 2 for 1873, "under age." (Dyr TN, Co Ct Min, B/759)

MILLER, James
Died before 4 December 1866 as shown in the suit of James M. Wright Admr. of A. McGinnis decd. vs the widow & heirs and creditors of said deceased. Andrew Tinch [Linch?] was owed money from the estate of A. McGinnis for the use of the estate of James Miller, deceased. (Fen TN, Ch Ct Min, A/305)

MILLER, James H.
Died before 3 February 1857 when A. G. McCallie resigned as guardian to the minor heirs. (Sev TN, Co Ct Min, no#/122)

MILLER, John
3 December 1827 sold land in Sullivan County, TN, to William Hancher. (McM TN, Co Ct Min, 2no#/245)

MILLER, Joseph
2 October 1860 it was ordered that $24 be allowed "to Joseph Miller, a feeble old man who has served his country in her past battles." (Sev TN, Co Ct Min, no#/615)

MILLER, Joseph
Died in 1860 as shown in the petition of his widow for dower made 4 December 1871. The widow was M. C. A. Miller. Cassius Miller, Thomas J. Miller and Missouri L. Miller were minor heirs. William J. Miller was also a defendant. (Dyr TN, Co Ct Min, B/327-8) Thomas Miller was administrator. (Ibid 414)

MILLER, Joseph
Died before 2 July 1861 when H. B. Baker was allowed to use a $6 claim for the support of Joseph Miller to pay for his burial clothes. (Sev TN, Co Ct Min, no#/704)

MILLER, Pleasant
Died before 10 October 1865 as shown in the suit of Johnathan Burnett vs the heirs-at-law & widow of Andrew McGinnis, deceased, and the heirs-at-law of Pleasant Miller, deceased, & his widow & others. The children of Pleasant Miller are minors and Sally Miller is their guardian. There is no administrator for the estate of Andrew McGinnis nor for the estate of Plesant Miller and none can be procured and over six months has elapsed since the death of each. James M. Wright was appointed administrator of both estates. (Fen TN, Ch Ct Min, A/289) There is money due to William Miller from the estate of Pleasant Miller being the purchase money for a tract of land deeded to said William & Pleasant Miller by Pearson Miller. Sarah Miller was the widow of Pleasant. (Ibid 302) William Miller is a non-resident of the state. (Ibid 324) William Miller was a resident of Wolf River, TN, on 3 April 1868 when he sold his interest in the estate of Pleasant Miller to John C. Wright. (Ibid 384)

MILLER, Thomas
When he was summoned as garnishee in the case of Rufus Morgan vs William McNutt, 16 September 1805, stated he owed the defendant $16.20 and he believed his son, James Miller, owed him the price of one currying comb & one yard of black ribbon. (Roa TN, Co Ct Min, B/31)

MILLER, W. B.
Taxes were not collected in District 2 for 1873. "under age." (Dyr TN, Co Ct Min, B/758)

MILLER, William
Died before 2 January 1871 when James C. Miller was chosen and appointed guardian to Sarah Ann Garland, Susan Jane Garland and Francis Garland, heirs of William Miller, deceased. (Dyr TN, Co Ct Min, B/151)

MILLS, G. G.
Died before 6 November 1871 when a Prorata settlement of the estate was made. (Dyr TN, Co Ct Min, B/318)

MILLS, John
Died before 18 June 1816 when the sale of the estate was recorded. A years provisions was laid off for the widow. (Wil TN, Co Ct Min, no#/13) Benjamin Hooker was administrator. (Ibid 208)

MILLS, John J.
Died before 5 April 1871 when J. W. Wright made a settlement as executor. (Dyr TN, Co Ct Min, B/228)

MILLSAPS, Hiram
Died before 13 April 1857 when his death was suggested in the suit of H. Millsaps & others vs N. W. Conant. (Fen TN, Ch Ct Min, A/78) Marsha Millsaps was administratrix. (Ibid 121) W. R. F. Millsaps, M. D. S. Millsaps & Jeffry H. Richardson were securities in the prosecution bond. (Ibid 198) In the suit of M. M. Brien et al vs Marsha Millsaps et als, 9 April 1860, J. D. Goodpasture was appointed guardian ad litem for all the minor heirs of Hiram Millsap, deceased. On the same day Samuel Turney was appointed guardian ad litem in the suit of James & William Nichols vs Marsha Millsaps et als and in the suit of P. M. Armstrong against same. (Ibid 224) Mitchel R. Millsaps and T. J. Millsaps were mentioned. (Ibid 250)

MILTON, Wm.
Was a resident of Warren County, KY, 5 October 1808 when a deposition was to be taken for the defendant in the case of Isom Uzzli vs Ezekiel Doyley. (Rob TN, Co Ct Min, 2/90)

MINARD, Isaac
27 February 1807 Abner Cox was allowed $4 for conveying Isaac Minard, charged with felony by Martin Beaty, Esquire of Lee County, VA, from Cumberland Gap to Sampson Davids, Esquire, Anderson County, TN. (Cla TN, Co Ct Min, 3/66)

MITCHEL, James
Died before 18 July 1811 as shown when commissioners met at his house to take depositions concerning ownership of land. (Roa TN, Co Ct Min, D/321)

MITCHEL, Josiah
Died before 22 May 1780 when the will was proved by John Colter, Richard Mitchel & Jane Colter. Mary Mitchel has leave of administration on the estate of Jacob [sic] Mitchel, with Mark Mitchel & George Russell as her securities. Wm. Been, Thomas Hardman & George Russell were appointed to appraise the estate of Jacob Mitchel, deceased. (Was TN, Co Ct Min, 1/105)

MITCHELL, B.
Died before 21 February 1861 as shown in the suit of Jno. D. Mason vs William S. Calloway Exr of B. Mitchell Decd. (Mad TN, Ch Ct Min, 2/433)

MITCHELL, Jacob [Joab]
Died before 30 May 1781 when his orphan son, Ritchard Mitchell, made choice of Chas. Robertson, Esquire as his guardian. [Joab was written in above Jacob] (Was TN, Co Ct Min, 1/137)

MITCHELL, John
Taxes were not collected in District 2 for 1873, "over age." (Dyr TN, Co Ct Min, B/759)

MITCHELL, John B.
Died before 19 October 1841 when his death was suggested and not denied in the suit of John B. Mitchell vs Robert C. Naul. (Obi TN, Cir Ct Min, 4/no#) On the same date James N. Stone was charged with the murder of John B. Mitchell. (Ibid) On 22 February 1842 the indictment against James N. Stone stated that on the 15th day of October 1841 he shot John B. Mitchell "with a rifle with 2 bulletts to the left side of the belly a little below the left pap", of which wound John B. Mitchell died instantly. (Ibid) Joseph A. Faulk [Fowlkes] & Blackman H. Byrd [Bird] were administrators, as shown 17 October 1842. (Ibid)

MITCHELL, Nelson
Died before 4 August 1856 when Cornelius Fox renewed his bond as guardian to Nancy Elizabeth Mitchell & Spencer A. Mitchell, minor heirs. Emanuel Fox & R. S. Clark were his securities. The original bond was destroyed by fire. (Sev TN, Co Ct Min, no#/67) Cornelius Fox was granted permission to sell land warrant No. 32272 for the benefit of his minor wards, Spencer A. & Nancy A. Mitchell. (Ibid 69)

MITCHELL, Robert
Died before 25 June 1804 when Drucilla Hendrick, late Drucilla Mitchell, was appointed administratrix on the part of the estate that had not been conveyed to her by deed of gift in the lifetime of Robert Mitchel, deceased. (Wil TN, Co Ct Min, no#/43) 23 December 1805 Drucilla Hendrick produced a will of Robert Mitchell. James Penkerton opposes the probate of the will. A jury is to decide. (Ibid 173)

MITCHELL, Robert
Died before 16 June 1817 when the will was proved by Drusella Walker & Peter Walker "her baron, which said Drusilla by the name of Drusilla Mitchell was named Executrix."

James Pinkerton opposed the probate of the said will. (Wil TN, Co Ct Min, no#/107) Robert McFarland acknowledged himself indebted to Peter Walker & Drucilla Walker, his wife, for a bond of $10,000 to be void if he produced the will of Robert Mitchell dated 1 July 1794 & attested by John L. Singletary & Catherine Singletary, which will was offered for probate and objected to by James Pinkerton. The deposition of Catharine Singletary is to be taken in Davidson County. (Ibid 109) 16 December 1817 trial was had. Plaintiffs, Peter & Drucilla his wife [Walker] proved that John L. Singletary & Catharine Singletary, the witnesses, were both dead; that the body of the will and attestations were in the handwriting of said John L. Singletary; that Catherine Singletary during her lifetime swore to her attestation of said will; that the signature of Robert Mitchell was in his own handwriting; and no evidence being introduced by James Pinkerton the defendant in said issue to disprove the facts, therefore, the jury finds that it is the will of Robert Mitchell, and Peter Walker & Drucilla his femme have letters testamentry. (Ibid 190)

MITCHELL, Saml.
Was a resident of Hawkins County 23 November 1793 when he sold a Mulatto Girl named Milla to Alexr. Greer. (Was TN, Co Ct Min, 1/472)

MITCHELL, Thomas
Died before 2 August 1784 when the will was proved by Robert Ivan & Mary Ivan. (Was TN, Co Ct Min, 1/241)

MITCHELL, Thomas
Died before February term 1819 when the executors, Evert & Taswell Mitchell, sold land. (Wil TN, Reg Bk/125, also 323)

MITCHELL, Thomas
21 March 1823 made a deed of gift to "my beloved cousins Levicy McWhirter and George W. McWhirter...all my goods and chattles." (Wil TN, Reg Bk/287)

MITCHELL, Thomas C.
Died before 3 January 1871 when his will was produced by Thomas W. Jones & John F. Sinclair. John Sinclair was named as an executor but refused to qualify. Ralph Sinclair, one of the executors named, is dead. John F. Sinclair nominated Thomas W. Jones as sole executor. The witnesses, M. R. Hill and John A. Wilkins, are both dead and their signatures were proved. (Dyr TN, Co Ct Min, B/160)

MITCHELL, William
Died before 16 December 1816 when the will was proved by Hardy Hunt & Bain Webb. Elizabeth Mitchell, Zadock Mitchell & Leon Mitchell were executors. (Wil TN, Co Ct Min, no#/46)

MIZER, Susannah
Her children are unprovided for and are to be brought to court for the purpose of having guardians appointed for them, 15 February 1815. (Cla TN, Co Ct Min, 4/29)

MOFFET, William
Died before 6 September 1804 as shown in the suit of John Moffet, administrator of the estate of William Moffet vs Wm. Norton. (Cla TN, Co Ct Min, 2/76)

MONDAY, James
On May 11 1815 entered a petition stating that he heretofore lived with a certain Anis Niblett [the first name of Lavinia was crossed out] who he has since married. He had by her seven children, to wit, Levinah, Levicy, Clary, James, William, Easter & Harretta who were born not in wedlock and are illegitimate and incapable of inheriting the estate of petitioner. He wants their names changed from Niblett to Monday and that they be made legitimate, which was granted. (Cla TN, Co Ct Min, 4/72)

MONGTOMERY, John
Died before 7 November 1870 when Robert Davidson was appointed guardian of the minor heirs, with J. H. York and A. G. Pierce as security. (Dyr TN, Co Ct Min, B/126)

MONTGOMERY, James A.
Died before 2 April 1866 when N. W. Emert was appointed administrator with J. B. Emert as security. John S. Troter, C. Mills & E. M. Wynn were appointed to lay off a years support to Martha E. Montgomery. (Sev TN, Co Ct Min, no#/303)

MONTGOMERY, Michael
Died before 11 October 1820 when Mary Howard, Elizabeth Montgomery & Jennett

Montgomery for herself, widow of Michael Montgomery, & also as guardian for her son, James Montgomery, of Caswell County, NC, together with Alexander Montgomery & Thomas Gunn in right of his wife Anne, being the heirs-at-law of said Michael Montgomery, gave power of attorney to Thomas Gunn & Alexander Montgomery to divide land in Wilson County, TN. (Wil TN, Reg Bk/181)

MONTGOMERY, Wm.
Died before 7 September 1857 when W. W. Montgomery was appointed special guardian for G. W. Montgomery, a minor, to sell land warrant No. 45506 for 80 acres of land. This warrent was issued to G. W. Montgomery, B. H. Montgomery and W. W. Montgomery in consideration of the service of Wm. Montgomery, deceased who served as a private in the war of 1812. (Sev TN, Co Ct Min, no#/199-200)

MOODY, John
Died before 25 September 1855 as shown in the bills & cross bills involving James C. Office, R. Bowles & others, William M. Simpson, Edley Paul, Peter Moody & W. Harmon, Edly Paul & others. The estate of John Moody, deceased, was mentioned. (Fen TN, Ch Ct Min, A/39)

MOOR, James
Was an orphan above the age of 14 years when he made choice of Wm. Cocke as his guardian, November 1789. (Was TN, Co Ct Min, 1/414)

MOORE
28 December 1841, Hugh, William N. and John Moore were the complainants in a suit against Charles D. Cooper & Ridley B. Wynn. (Bed TN, Ch Ct Min, 2/162)

MOORE, Benjamin
Was a resident of Williamson County, TN, when he made a bill of sale "for natural love & affection & $50" to Abner Moore of Wilson County, for a negro woman named Hannah about 20 years old, a sorrel mare, saddle & other property. (Wil TN, Reg Bk/176)

MOORE, D. L.
Taxes were not collected in District 2 for 1873, "gone." (Dyr TN, Co Ct Min, B/758)

MOORE, Dinkie
Was a colored orphan girl when she was bound 5 August 1872 to Geo. W. Pierce until "she shall arrive at the age of 18 years-say 13 years to come." (Dyr TN, Co Ct Min, B/449)

MOORE, Elijah
Died before 25 March 1805 when Susannah Moore was granted letters of administration with James Sanders & Peter Mosely as security. (Wil TN, Co Ct Min, no#/111)

MOORE, Evalina
3 May 1819 was bound as an apprentice to George McWhirter until she arrives at full age. (Wil TN, Co Ct Min, no#/441)

MOORE, Jackson
Was bound as an apprentice on 5 March 1830 to Wm. R. Tucker until age 21. He is to learn the trade of a blacksmith. (McM TN, Co Ct Min, 2no#/443)

MOORE, James
Died before 29 June 1842 as shown in the suit of William Yeates & wife & others vs Mary Moore Administratrix of James Moore decd. & others. Complainants & defendants are the heirs & Mary Moore is also the widow. (Bed TN, Ch Ct Min, 2/187) The suit was in the names of William Yeates & Mary Ann his wife, Edmund L. Heart & wife & others vs Mary Moore Admr., William McClure & wife & Harriett E. Moore. Complainants & defendants and one James M. Moore are the only distributees of James Moore, deceased, being 8 in number. James M. Moore has sold his interest to William Yeates. Distribution was made to William Yeates & wife, Edmond L. Hart & wife, Philip J. Thompson & wife, Elijah N. Moore, William McClure & wife, Harriett E. Moore, & to William Yeates the share of James M. Moore. [Mary Moore must have been the other distributee] (Ibid 238)

MOORE, James
Was a minor 15 February 1796 when John Blair McMahon was appointed guardian, with Adam Mitchel as his security. (Was TN, Co Ct Min, 1/589)

MOORE, John
Died before 7 February 1798 when Saml. Moore qualified as the executor. (Was TN, Co Ct Min, 1/636)

MOORE, Joseph M.
Died before 5 August 1872 when Mary J. Moore was appointed administrator, with James P. Caldwell and C. H. Lane as her security. The deceased was also shown as Joseph H. Moore. (Dyr TN, Co Ct Min, B/448) George Miller, John C. Murray and Nelson Parrish were appointed to set apart a years provisions to the widow and child of J. M. Moore, deceased. (Ibid 486)

MOORE, Kinsey
Was the father of an illegitimate child by Matilda Bennett. He petitioned the court on 9 March 1826 to change the name of the child from Polly Bennett to Polly Moore and make her his legitimate heir. He stated that he has but one child by his wife which is 5 years old & that his wife is willing & anxious to have said illegitimate child made his heir. (McM TN, Co Ct Min, 2no#/148)

MOORE, Levi
Made a deed of gift 20 May 1796 to Mary Moore & her five children, Jane, Rebecca, Elizabeth, William and James, for four negroes, Phillis, Binar, Sary & Anna [and other property and money]. On the same date Levi Moore made a deed of gift to John Moore for one stud horse named Lucellen [and other property and money], proved by Levi Roberts and Mary Moore & recorded 18 August 1796. (Was TN, Co Ct Min, 1/627)

MOORE, Levi
Died before 4 November 1805 when the will was proved by James Gambril & John Siglar. Arbraham Moore, Amos Moore & Joel Moore were excutors. (Rob TN, Co Ct Min, 1/364)

MOORE, Margaret
Died before 1 November 1819 when James Moore was appointed administrator of his late wife, with Isareal Moore, Isareal Moore, Jr. & John Hunt as security. (Wil TN, Co Ct Min, no#/536)

MOORE, Mary
Was the mother of a bastard child by W. M. Roberts. Mary gave bond 1 October 1860 with Wm. M. Roberts, L. C. Roberts, A. G. Roberts, Jesse Hill & Robert Hill as security, that she would not become a county charge. (Sev TN, Co Ct Min, no#/608) 1 May 1865 it was ordered that the sheriff take out of the possession of John Lewalling, a child named Matilda More and deliver said child to Mary More, the mother of said child. (Ibid 159)

MOORE, Nancy
Died before 30 June 1842 as shown in the suit of Willis Cannon vs Abid Parson & wife. Thomas C. Moore was the husband and the administrator for Nancy Moore. Abid Parsons claims one share of the estate of Nancy Moore in right of his wife, she being the daughter of said Nancy. Parsons also claims the other share of Nancy's estate as the administrator of Willis Moore, son of said Nancy, there being but two children of said Nancy. The court decided that Thomas C. Moore was the only distributee of Nancy Moore by virtue of his marital rights. (Bed TN, Ch Ct Min, 2/192)

MOORE, Nancy E.
Died before 4 July 1870 when J. S. Moore was appointed administrator with S. S. Hollowell and Asa Hardason as securities. (Dyr TN, Co Ct Min, B/72)

MOORE, Robert
Died before 18 June 1816 when William Woodward made a settlement as administrator. (Wil TN, Co Ct Min, no#/14) 7 August 1818, on the petition of James McDonald & Anne L. McDonnald, dower is to be allotted out of the lands of Robert Moore, deceased. John Allcorn was appointed guardian of the minor heirs, to wit: Frances, Armstead, William, Patsey & Elizabeth Moore. (Ibid 319) Dower was allotted to Anne L. McDaniel. (Ibid 375) James McDaniel was appointed guardian of Fanny B., Armstead, Polly, William & Elizabeth Moore. (Ibid 378)

MOORE, Robert A.
Died before 4 April 1870 when the will was proved by Wyatt Lunsford, one of the witnesses. (Dyr TN, Co Ct Min, B/36) J. K. Strayhorn, R. C. Coffman and W. W. Briggs were appointed to lay off a years provisions for the family. (Ibid 53) The will was also proved by A. T. Fielder, the other witness. J. S. Moore was the executor with J. Q. Craig & A. T. Fielder as his security. (Ibid 65)

MOORE, Ruthy
Died before 5 October 1857 when Wm. J. Hodges was paid out of the poor tax for coffins for Ruthy Moore & daughter. (Sev TN, Co Ct Min, no#/205)

MOORE, S. A.
Died before 5 December 1870 when S. M. Williams renewed his bond as guardian of the minor heirs. (Dyr TN, Co Ct Min, B/138)

MOORE, Sally
6 May 1806 Emanuel Skinner was allowed $30 for keeping Sally Moore one year, now on the parish. (Rob TN, Co Ct Min, 1/389)

MOORE, Wm.
24 May 1780 an inventory of his estate was made by Jacob Brown, Jonathan Tipton & Michl. Woods, assessors. (Was TN, Co Ct Min, 1/112)

MOORE, Zachariah
3 May 1819 was bound as an apprentice to Warren Moore until age 21. (Wil TN, Co Ct Min, no#/440)

MORGAN
Richard Morgan and Polly Morgan were allowed $30 each for their support for 1827, 6 March 1827. (McM TN, Co Ct Min, 2/205)

MORGAN, George
With his wife, Frances Morgan, sold land in Tuskaloosa, AL, 3 December 1827 to James Paul. (McM TN, Co Ct Min, 2no#/254)

MORGAN, Gideon
With his wife, Betsey, sold a town lot in Newhasen, Rockingham County, VA, to John Adams, 23 January 1812. (Roa TN, Co Ct Min, D/354)

MORGAN, John
Died before 12 May 1815 when commissioners were appointed to settle with Elizabeth Morgan, the administratrix. (Cla TN, Co Ct Min, 4/79)

MORGAN, John
Died before 7 March 1825 when his widow, Rebecca Morgan, was appointed administratrix. William Ballen, Moses Cunningham & John Matthews were appointed to lay off a years provisions for Rebecca. (McM TN, Co Ct Min, 2no#/49)

MORGAN, Josiah
Was placed on the poor roll of the county 10 November 1812. (Rob TN, Co Ct Min, 3/155)

MORGAN, William
Died before 16 August 1815 when John Forgerson was appointed administrator, being the highest creditor. William Morgan owes him $15. Abel Lanham and William Morgan were his securities. (Cla TN, Co Ct Min, 4/112)

MORGAN, Wm.
3 July 1865 was appointed guardian to Mary A. Morgan, a minor orphan. (Sev TN, Co Ct Min, no#/179)

MORNING, Joshua
Was a pauper of the county 17 December 1816 & money was allowed for his support. (Wil TN, Co Ct Min, no#/56)

MORRILL, J. M.
Died before 13 August 1868 as shown in the suit of W. W. Williams & wife vs Creditors of J. M. Morrill. A report is to be made as to the assets in the estate of the said deceased. (Mad TN, Ch Ct Min, 3/171)

MORRIS, Goodson
27 August 1778 took the oath of allegiance. (Was TN, Co Ct Min, 1/44)

MORRIS, Jesse
Died before 10 September 1806 when land was taxed to the heirs. (Ste TN, Co Ct Min, 1/35b)

MORRIS, Matthew
Died before 10 May 1814 when the will was proved by Laurence Clenard & Gidion Morris. Henry Frey & Jacob Binckley were executors. (Rob TN, Co Ct Min, 3/410)

MORRIS, Thomas W.
Died before 7 November 1871 when C. L. Nolan, public administrator, was appointed administrator. (Dyr TN, Co Ct Min, B/319)

MORRIS, Wm.
Died before 18 April 1803 when Joseph Woolfork was appointed administrator with Nicholas Conard as security. (Rob TN, Co Ct Min, 1/246)

MORTIMER, Sally
4 February 1819 a jury was appointed to inquire into her lunacy. They found her to be insane and has property to the value of $300. Benjamin Castleman was appointed guardian. (Wil TN, Co Ct Min, no#/420)

MORTON, Abram B.
Died before 21 December 1838 as shown in the suit of George W. Carpenter of Philadelphia, PA, vs Samuel Morton, Jessee B. Morton, Jacob Morton & Alexander B. Morton of Williamson County, TN, heirs-at-law of A. B. Morton, deceased, late of Bedford County, TN, and others. Other heirs were: Marth Tegnal Morton, Allen Morton & Solomon Morton, the last being minors, heirs of Abram B. Morton, deceased, in right of their father Elisha Morton, deceased: William Morton, Fanny G. Morton, Samuel Morton, Thomas Morton, Abraham Morton, Isaac Morton & Martha Morton, the last 5 named being minors, all residing in Williamson County, TN, and heirs of Abram B. Morton, deceased, in right of their father Abner W. Morton, deceased: Jacob J., Vina E., Abram W. and James A. Morton who are minors residing in Williamson County, TN, and who are heirs of Abram B. Morton, deceased, in right of their father, William Morton, deceased: Silas M. Morton, Bird Link and Averalla his wife, residing in Haywood County, TN, who are heirs of the said Abram B. Morton, deceased, the said Bird Link being an heir in right of his wife: Francis N. Kimbro, Solomon M. Kimbro, Dicy Kimbro, Polly H. Kimbro & Thos. H. B. Kimbro who reside in Davidson County, TN, and who are heirs of the said Abram B. Morton in right of their mother, Elizabeth Ann Kimbro, deceased: John McMurray residing in Smith County, TN, and Samuel, Sarah L., Mary, Washington, Amanda B., Lucy, America, William & Fanny McMurray, the 4 last being minors all residing in Davidson County, TN, and all of said McMurrays being heirs of Abram B. Morton in right of their mother Polly R. McMurray, deceased: John, Avrilla H., Sarah, William, Thomas, Charles, Silas & Mary McMurray, the last 6 being minors & children of Samuel & Dicy McMurray residing in Davidson County, TN, and who are hiers of Abram B. Morton in right of their mother the said Dicy, deceased: John Morton & Solomon G. Morton living in Davidson County, TN, heirs of Abram B. Morton, deceased: Absolam D. Morton residing in the state of AL who is a minor and is an heir of Abram B. Morton in right of his father, George W. Morton, deceased, together with the other children of the said George W. Morton, deceased, who also reside in AL but whose names are unknown to your orator. Clement Cannon, James McKisick & William Gilchrist were administrators of Abram B. Morton, deceased, & the plaintiff in this suit, George W. Carpenter, had obtained a judgement against them in 1834. (Bed TN, Ch Ct Min, 1/389-393)

MORTON, Nancy
Died before 10 February 1855 as shown in the suit of Wm. Morton by next friend vs Saml. E. Haire et al. The complainants were given leave to file an amended bill in their own name and in the name of James Draper, administrator of Nancy Morton, deceased. (Jac TN, Ch Ct Min, B/206) This suit was shown as William Morton Joseph Morton by next friend, James Draper administrator of Nancy Morton vs Samuel E. Haire & Rich. P. Brooks. (Ibid 230)

MORTON, Thomas
22 June 1816 a receipt was recorded from Thomas Morton to James McFarland, former guardian of said Morton. This entry was then crossed out. (Wil TN, Co Ct Min, no#/22)

MOSELEY, James M.
Married before 8 September 1874 to Ellemora Shelton, Daughter of Watson Shelton, deceased. (Dyr TN, Co Ct Min, B/785)

MOSELY [Morely]
16 September 1852 a suit was shown; Andrew J. Sharp & wife Lucinda, Thos B. Mosely, Margaret Mosely & Mary Mosely, the last two minors who appear by guardian Wm. E. Ellis vs Nancy Huntsman & Jos. Fogg. The suit was dismissed. (Mad TN, Ch Ct Min, 1/263)

MOSELY, Wm.
Was an orphan boy aged 16 years when he was bound 6 May 1783 to John Newman, Esqr., until age 21. (Was TN, Co Ct Min, 1/208)

MOSER, Adam
Died before 16 December 1817 when Henry Moser was appointed administrator, with Daniel [David] Moses & Thos. Dill as security. (Wil TN, Co Ct Min, no#/199)

MOSES, Robert
12 May 1813 made deeds of gift to the heirs of Ann McGee and to the heirs of Winifred Shepperd. It does not state that Ann or Winifred were deceased. (Rob TN, Co Ct Min, 3/252)

MOSLEY, Jesse
Made a deed of gift to Hellen Mosley, 15 February 1814. (Rob TN, Co Ct Min, 3/363)

MOSLY, Burrell [Mosely]
Died before 3 May 1819 when Thomas Rhodes was appointed administrator with Thompson Hays & Joseph Cole as security. A years provision was allotted to the widow. (Wil TN, Co Ct Min, no#/435-6)

MOSS, John T.
1 May 1871 was certified to be a young man of good moral character, a resident from infancy of Dyer County, and 21 years of age, preparatory to his application for a license to practice law. (Dyr TN, Co Ct Min, B/231)

MOSS, Robert
Died before 20 June 1816 when George Smith was appointed administrator with the will annexed, with William Glours & George Michen as security. (Wil TN, Co Ct Min, no#/19)

MOSS, Samuel
Died before 4 March 1841 as shown in the suit of Newton S. Neal Elizabeth Moss and others vs Abraham Mayfield. The bill of complaint is by Newton S Neal, John K Lovell and Elizabeth Moss. In 1819 and long before, Elizabeth was a child of Samuel Moss who is now dead. Two negroes were bequethed to Elizabeth by her father's will. On 14 August 1819 said Samuel Moss deeded to his son, James J. Moss, & to Elizabeth Moss' two sons, John K. Lovell and the said Newton F (the latter by the name of Newton Foot), the same 2 negroes & their increase. Newton F. Neal made a deed for the negroes to Abraham Mayfield, which should have been as a mortgage only. He had no legal right to dispose of more than his interest in them after the life estate of his mother, Elizabeth, and her said husband. When the deed was made Elizabeth was then a femme covert, her husband, the said Samuel was still alive, having died 14 April 1839. [Was Elizabeth the child or the widow of Samuel, both is stated?] Newton F. mentioned his brother, John K. The share of James Moss in the negroes was conveyed to Newton F. Neal. Exhibit A shows that Samuel Moss was of Mecklenburgh County, VA. The deed for the two negroes was to his son, James J. Moss, and his wife's two sons, Newton Foot and John K. Lowell. The negroes had come to Samuel by right of his wife by her father's will. He and his wife are to retain a life estate in the negroes. [This has evidently been re-copied and there are obvious errors. For instance in one place it states Elizabeth Moss was the wife of Sarah Moss.] (Bed TN, Ch Ct Min, 3/4-14)

MOTHERAL, James
Died before 23 February 1838 as shown in the suit of Joseph Motheral admr. of James Motheral Decd. vs George W. Bright. (Obi TN, Cir Ct Min, 3/179) 24 October 1839 the heirs petitioned for division of land. The heirs were: Susan Motheral the widow of James Motheral, deceased, and Martha Motheral, Jane K. Motheral, Elenor E. Motheral, Mary Motheral, William Motheral, John Motheral, Francis Susan Motheral, Robert Motheral, the children of James Motheral, deceased. James Dean was guardian of Jane K., Elenor M. & Mary Motheral. William Edmoston was guardian of William & John Motheral. Susan Motheral was guardian of Francis Susan & Robert Motheral. The land was originally granted to James H. Wilson, Samuel D. Wilson & Robert Wilson. The widow is entitled to dower. (Ibid 4/no#) On 17 June 1840 the land was divided between the widow & 8 children; Martha, William, Susan Francis, Robert, Jane, Ellen, Mary & John. Plat shown. The slaves were also divided. (Ibid 4/no#) On 22 February 1843 in the petition of Susan Motheral & others, the estate of Robert Motheral, deceased, is to be sold. (Ibid)

MOTLY, Benja. T.
With his wife Patsy Motly, sold land in Halifax County, VA. (Wil TN, Co Ct Min, no#/42)

MOTT, Wm. H.
6 February 1860 made bond with William A. McNutt as his security, to appear at April court to answer a charge of bastardy. (Sev TN, Co Ct Min, no#/515) 3 July 1860 Wm. H. Mott failed to appear to answer the charge, his security also failed to appear. (Ibid 581) Also shown as Wm. H. McMott. (Ibid 591)

MOUNT, H. N.
8 February 1870 made a settlement as guardian of his child. (Dyr TN, Co Ct Min, B/7) The child was Amanda Jane Mount. (Ibid 183)

MOYERS, Caty
15 February 1815 a jury was summoned to view the situation of Caty Moyers and her children. (Cla TN, Co Ct Min, 4/28)

MULLENDOM, W. W.
6 April 1857, it appears to the satisfaction of the court that he is a citizen of Sevier County, 21 years of age and that he sustains a good moral character. (Sev TN, Co Ct Min, no#/143)

MULLINAX, Levi
Died before 2 November 1818 when James Cross & John Fisher were appointed administrators, with Edward Moore & James Adams as security, the widow having relinquished her right to administrate. (Wil TN, Co Ct Min, no#/334)

MULLIS, James
Died before 4 August 1806 when Jeriah Mullis was granted letters of administration, with Thomas Sellars & Howel Sellars as security. (Rob TN, Co Ct Min, 1/399)

MULLIZ, Amiah
Was the mother of a child begotten by Nathan Fikes who gave bond for its maintenance 4 April 1808. (Rob TN, Co Ct Min, 2/10)

MURDOCK, Sampson
Died before 9 May 1814 when the will was proved by Greenberry Randal & Marcus Robertson. Josiah Perry & Frederick Lasiter were executors. (Rob TN, Co Ct Min, 3/403)

MURFREE, H.
Died before 21 February 1838 when land was taxed to the heirs. (Obi TN, Cir Ct Min, 3/162) The land was taxed to Hardy Murphries heirs on 21 February 1841. (Ibid 4/no#)

MURFREE, Hardy
Died before 10 May 1811 as shown when William Outlaw gave bond for his appeal of the granting to Henry Pugh leave to keep a ferry across Cumberland River, "& files his reasons &c on behalf of Robert Nelsons Heirs the heirs of Hardy Murfree and Wilie Blount." (Ste TN, Co Ct Min, 3/74) 10 February 1814 the heirs of Hardy Murphree were on the delinquent tax list. (Ibid 4/128)

MURFREE, William [Murphey]
Died before 21 February 1839 when land was taxed to the heirs. (Obi TN, Cir Ct Min, 3/297)

MURFREES, Hardy S.
Died before 13 May 1811 when the heirs were on a tax list. (Rob TN, Co Ct Min, 2/387)

MURPHEY, James
Died before 6 December 1824 when commissioners were appointed to settle with John Walker, guardian of Betsey H. Murphey, daughter & heir of James Murphey, deceased. (McM TN, Co Ct Min, 2no#/33) 6 June 1825 John Walker & Robert Murphey made a settlement as executors. (Ibid 71)

MURPHEY, Jas. H.
Was released from paying poll tax for 1858 as he had left the county before then. (Sev TN, Co Ct Min, no#/407)

MURPHEY, John
Died before 7 March 1825 when Robert Murphey was appointed administrator. (McM TN, Co Ct Min, 2no#/52)

MURPHEY, Joseph Robertson
9 November 1812 was bound out to John Mitchell. (Rob TN, Co Ct Min, 3/147)

MURPHEY, M. B.
Died before 11 March 1844 when land was taxed to the heirs. (Obi TN, Cir Ct Min, 4/no#)

MURPHEY, Patrick
Was an orphan boy 18 April 1797 when he was bound to William Crockett until age 21. (Rob TN, Co Ct Min,1/25)

MURPHEY, Patrick
Died before 15 January 1798 when it was ordered that his orphans, Peggy Murphey and Patrick Murphey, be released from their indenture to William & Jane Crockett and returned to their mother. Their property was in Montgomery County. (Rob TN, Co Ct Min, 1/44)

MURPHEY, Peggy
Was an orphan 19 April 1797 when she was bound to Jane Crocket until age 18. (Rob TN, Co Ct Min, 1/27)

MURPHEY, Richard
Died before 2 October 1871 when D. H. Jones, Esquire was paid for holding an inquest over the body. (Dyr TN, Co Ct Min, B/293)

MURPHEY, W. W.
Died before 4 January 1871 when S. Sueard, George Spence and Lee Tansil were appointed to lay off a years provisions for the widow and family. (Dyr TN, Co Ct Min, B/162) T. W. James was appointed administrator. (Ibid 173)

MURPHY, Charles
Was a resident of Christian County, KY, on 7 February 1811 when his deposition was to be taken for the defendant in the suit of Jessee Denson vs Philip Hornburger. (Ste TN, Co Ct Min, 3/53)

MURPHY, Gabril
Died before 24 May 1808 when the will was proved by Elijah Harp and Abraham Fitch. (Cla TN, Co Ct Min, 3/193)

MURPHY, Hugh S.
On 21 June 1843 was granted a divorce from Celia Murphy. Hugh Murphy had removed from NC to Obion County, TN, more than two years ago and his wife refused to come with him. (Obi TN, Cir Ct Min, 4/no#)

MURPHY, Mary
Died before 1 October 1866 when C. H. Fox was appointed administrator with John H. Murphy as security. (Sev TN, Co Ct Min, no#/374)

MURPHY, Patrick
Was the father of John Murphy as shown when the fine imposed on John for the ill treatment of his father was remitted, 26 May 1779. (Was TN, Co Ct Min, 1/77)

MURPHY, Saml.
Died before 7 February 1859 when Amos R. Trotter, one of the executors, resigned. The heirs have had legal notice. (Sev TN, Co Ct Min, no#/403) 5 April 1859 John H. Murphy resigned as one of the executors. (Ibid 433)

MURRAY, Jane C.
Was probably a minor [or a married woman] on 15 July 1858 when she brought suit by her next friend vs David J. Murray & others. She asked that S. F. Murray be made a defendant to this bill. (Jac TN, Ch Ct Min, C/132) On 11 February 1859 she dissmissed that part of her bill for divorce from David J. Murray as pertains to alimony. (Ibid 182) Divorce was granted 12 February 1859 on the grounds of adultry. Jane C. was given title to some personal property and custody of the two children, both girls and very young. The next friend of Jane C. was Richmond Darwin?. (Ibid 194) David J. Murray is a minor. (Ibid 224) On 15 August 1860 it was stated that David J. Murray had reached full age as shown in his suit against his former guardian, George C. Darwin. (Ibid 410)

MURRAY, William
Was a resident of Fayette County, KY, on 17 October 1796 when his deposition was to be taken for recording a deed from Joseph Brock to Thos. Hopkins. (Rob TN, Co Ct Min, 1/6)

MURRY, J. M.
Taxes were not collected in District 2 for 1873, "over age." (Dyr TN, Co Ct Min, B/758)

MURRY, William
Died before 3 March 1806 when Kelton Murry was appointed administrator and gave bond with James Roddy & Bernet Murry for security. (Cla TN, Co Ct Min, 2/213)

MURRY, Wm.
Died before 31 July 1867 as shown in the suit of James M. Wright Admr. of the estate of A. McGinnis decd. vs the widow, heirs & creditors of said estate. Wm. Murry was one of the defendants and T. Murry was his administrator. His only heirs were John B. Murry, Joseph C. Murry, Mary E. Taylor, W. T. Murry & Sarah B. Murry. (Fen TN, Ch Ct Min, A/324)

MURY, Thomas
Died before 8 February 1856 as shown in the suit of George C. Darwin guardian &c vs Thomas B. Murry & Thos. J. Gilbert Executors of Thomas Mury &c. (Jac TN, Ch Ct Min, B/292) A suit & cross bills were entered 6 February 1857 involving Thomas B. Murry, Thomas J. Gilbreath, George C. Darwin, guardian & David J. Murry. The court is to take an account of the legacy or distributive share of David J. Murry and James C. Darwin's ward in the estate of his father, Thomas Murry, deceased, to which he is entitled under the will of said deceased. (Ibid C/70) S. F. Murray is guardian of David J. Murray. (Ibid 159) A Suit was shown 12 February 1859 by Thomas B. Murray & Thomas J. Gailbreath vs Geroge C. Darwin guardian of David J. Murray and a cross bill by George C. Darwin guardian &c vs Thomas B. Murray, Thomas J. Gailbreath, Amon Hail, Milton Draper, James H. Carson, Thomas J. Jones & Francis M. Goolesby. The last 5 defendants were security for Thomas B. Murray & Thomas J. Gailbreath as executors of the will of Thomas Murray, deceased, who have failed to settle with David J. Murray. George C. Darwin has resigned as guardian of David J. Murray since the start of this suit and Stewart F. Murray is his now guardian. (Ibid 198)

MUTLOCK, David
Died before August term 1790 when the will was proved by Moses Humphreys. David Mutlock and Joseph Greer were the executors. (Was TN, Co Ct Min, 1/455)

MYERS, Frederick
Died before 6 August 1811 as shown in the suit of John Boyd vs Frederick Myers? admr. and administratrix. The said Frederick, deceased, had purchased land from the plaintiff in his lifetime and it has not all been paid. (Ste TN, Co Ct Min, 3/90)

MYERS, Jane
Was bound as an apprentice 7 June 1858 to Isaac Richards until age 18. She is now 2 years old. (Sev TN, Co Ct Min, no#/304)

MYLER, W. W. [Neyler, Wyler]
Probably died before 20 August 1868 as shown in the suit of H. R. Hall vs Julia Myler Ex. W. W. Myler. Since the commencement of this suit Julia Neyler has married Jas. M. Woollard & he is a necessary part of this suit. (Mad TN, Ch Ct Min, 3/214)

NAIL
15 March 1853 in the suit of George R. Scott et als vs Jacob Snipes et als, it is stated that Jane Nail, Saml. Nail, Marcus Nail, Nancy Nail & William A. Nail, defendants in this cause, are minors, & Elijah Simmons was appointed guardian ad litem. (Mad TN, Ch Ct Min, 1/292) Ro. J. Chester was appointed guardian ad litem. Mary Nail is listed instead of Marcus. (Ibid 315) [see Samuel Nail]

NAIL, Samuel
Died before 17 March 1853. He was the ancestor of Jacob Snipes & wife Jane S., Jacob Fulbright & wife Nancy P., John H. Rey & wife Mary? H. [name written over], Elijah Simmons & wife Elizabeth A., James Nauny & wife Margaret S., John Samuel & George W. Nail by the guardian James Barclay, Jane, Samuel, Mary, Nancy J. & William A. Nail. Elijah Simmons was administrator. (Mad TN, Ch Ct Min, 1/315)

NANNY, Jos. W.
Died before 21 August 1866 when his death was admitted in the suit of Jos. W. Nanny vs W. R. Haynes & suit revived in the name of Richard McKnight, administrator. (Mad TN, Ch Ct Min, 2/503)

NARIN, John
Died before 4 July 1808 when the administrator, Whitmill Harrington, was given liberty to sell the personal estate. (Rob TN, Co Ct Min, 2/44) Also shown as Narion. (Ibid 45)

NASH, James S.
Died before 4 April 1870 when Thomas Nash was appointed administrator. (Dyr TN, Co Ct Min, B/35) M. P. Warren, Jeff Love & N. C. Warren were appointed to lay off a years provision for the widow and family. (Ibid 40)

NASH, Travis C.
Died 7 April 1844, intestate. He left his widow, Johanna Nash, who is entitled to dower. He also left Levi C. Johnson & wife Elizabeth formerly Elizabeth Nash, Benjamin Garrett & wife Emily formerly Emily Nash, William M. Harwell & wife Louisa formerly Louisa Nash, James C. Nash, Travis C. Nash, Francis M. Nash, Granderson Nash, Layfayette Nash, William Nash, Thomas Nash, Augustus Nash, George W. Nash, John R. Nash who has since died leaving a son James R. Nash, Mary McGimpsey wife of John W. McGimpsey formerly Mary Nash, and none others. He left land in Bedford & Lincoln Counties. (Bed TN, Ch Ct Min, 2/339) George W. Nash was owner of one fifteenth part of the lands of Travis C. Nash. (Ibid 340) Johanna Nash was said to have an interest in the suit of Mathew Mullins vs Horatio Clagette. (Ibid 358) Fifteen Divisions were made: 1. Augustine Nash; 2. James R. Nash; 3. Thomas Nash; 4. Francis M. Nash; 5. Lafayett Nash; 6. Abner Nash; 7. Granderson Nash; 8. John McGincy & wife Mary; 9. William Nash; 10. George W. Nash; 11. T. C. Nash; 12. William N. Harvil & wife Louisa; 13. Benjamin Garret & wife Emily; 14. Levi Johnson & wife Elizabeth; 15. James Nash. Dower was also allotted to the widow. A plat map is shown. (Ibid 373-7)

NASH, W. F.
Died before 3 March 1873 when C. T. Nash was appointed administrator, with W. B. Nash and J. J. Yates as his security. John E. Bell, Geo. Miller & N. C. Warden were appointed to lay off a years allowance for the widow & family of W. S. [sic] Nash, deceased. (Dyr TN, Co Ct Min, B/545) Miranda G. Nash petitioned for dower out of the lands of William F. Nash, deceased. His heirs were James F. Nash, Nancy R. Nash, Rachel J. Nash, Rhrdam [sic] Nash, Maola Nash, F. M. Williamson & [blank] Williamson & C. F. Nash administrator. (Ibid 574)

NATIONS, Joseph
Died before 4 June 1804 when his will was proved by Luke Bowyer and William Nations. Isaac Nations was sworn as executor. (Cla TN, Co Ct Min, 2/28) Lerreata [Jerreata or Serreata] Nations & Sampson Nations were sworn to execute the will of Joseph Nations deceased. (Ibid 2/64)

NATIONS, William
Died before 24 August 1807 when the will was proved by Henry Sharp and Isaac Nations. Henry Sharp and Jane Nations were executors. (Cla TN, Co Ct Min, 3/105) Jane Nation was appointed guardian of Nancy Nations, Isaac Nations & Christopher Nations, the orphan children of Wm. Nations, deceased. (Ibid 164)

NEAL
Francis M. M. Neal and James A. Neal are minors, as shown in the suit of Wm. J. Featherston et als, 4 July 1870. A. T. Harrell was appointed guardian ad litem. (Dyr TN, Co Ct Min, B/72)

NEAL, Grimes
Gave bond 11 May 1815 as the reputed father of a bastard female child of Pheby Dobbs. Henry Baker & Christo Damson were his security. (Cla TN, Co Ct Min, 4/66)

NEAL, John
Gave power of attorney to Micajah Carter 21 February 1803. It was witnessed & proved in court by Samuel Miller. (Roa TN, Co Ct Min, A/78)

NEAL, Newton F.
15 March 1841 in the suit of Daniel G. Stephenson vs Newton F. Neal, it was shown that Neal was the owner of two thirds of a family of negroes that his mother, Mrs. Moss, has a life estate in. (Bed TN, Ch Ct Min, 1/327)

NECKINS, William B.
Died before 8 February 1854 when his death was suggested in the suit of William B. Neckins vs Sampson McClelan, administrator, and a cross bill with the same parties. (Jac TN, Ch Ct Min, B/111)

NEELY
20 February 1867 Thos. H. Drake was appointed the next friend of Elizabeth C. Neely & guardian ad litem of Wm. S., Samuel, Mary E. & Nanny P. Neely, to defend the suit of Thomas A. Simmons et als vs Caroline Neely et als. (Mad TN, Ch Ct Min, 3/11) This suit was shown again & stated that Samuel Neely, Sr. made a deed to complainants for the use and benefit of defendants on 17 February 1857. Thomas A. Simmons as trustee has sold the lot to Robert Smith. The sale is to be confirmed and divested out of Thomas Simmons as trustee and vested in Susan Smith, wife of Robert Smith, for the sole and separate use of herself and children. (Ibid 117) The death of Saml. Neely was admitted & said cause revived in the name of Saml. S. Neely, administrator. (Ibid 244)

NEELY, A. C.
Died before 4 November 1872, late a citizen of MO. H. L. W. Turney was appointed administrator of his estate in Dyer County, with Daniel E. Parker his security. (Dyr TN, Co Ct Min, B/506)

NEELY, Amanda
Was bound 1 August 1870 to C. W. Enochs until age 18. She is a negro girl aged 9. (Dyr TN, Co Ct Min, B/93)

NEELY, Jo.
Was a negro boy aged 16 years when he was bound 7 August 1871 to Robert H. Neely until age 21. (Dyr TN, Co Ct Min, B/263)

NEELY, T. G.
Taxes were not collected in District 2 for 1873, "gone." (Dyr TN, Co Ct Min, B/758)

NEIL, William
Died before 2 August 1819 when the will was exhibited in court. (Wil TN, Co Ct Min, no#/494) The will was proved by William Thweath & Thomas Hill. Moses Allen & Wm. Dale were the executors. (Ibid 496)

NELSON
Died before 11 February 1859 as shown in the suit of Tobias Gipson & Asa M. Dennon, administrators of Nelson, deceased, vs William Nelson & others. (Jac TN, Ch Ct Min, C/181)

NELSON, Henry
Died before [no date given but is probably the August term 1788] when the will was proved by William Wood & Isaac Denton, with John & Charles Nelson as executors. (Was TN, Co Ct Min, 1/316)

NELSON, James B.
Married before 18 November 1814 to Nancy Tucker, daughter of John Tucker, deceased. In another place the name looks like James B. Wilson. (Rob TN, Co Ct Min, 3/513-514)

NELSON, John
Was a non-resident of TN on 13 July 1854 as shown in the suit of Dorcas Copeland vs Jessee Nelson & others. John Nelson was a defendant. (Jac TN, Ch Ct Min, B/159)

NELSON, Robert
Died before 25 January 1809 when Hugh F. Bell made bond to keep a ferry in behalf of the heirs of Robert Nelson. (Ste TN, Co Ct Min, no#/89) Hugh F. Bell was the administrator. (Ibid 3/13) When the administrator conveyed land the name of the deceased looked like "Wilson." (Ibid 71)

NELSON, Robert
Died before 14 November 1810 as shown in the case of Hugh F. Bell, administrator of Robert Nelson, deceased, against Anderson Cheatham. (Rob TN, Co Ct Min, 2/333)

NELSON, Ruben
3 July 1865 was ordered to be sent to the poor house. (Sev TN, Co Ct Min, no#/179)

NEVILL, Sarah
Was a resident of Montgomery County, 10 August 1814, when it was ordered to take her private examination relative to a deed from John Nevill & Sarah his wife to George L. Wimberly. (Rob TN, Co Ct Min, 3/463)

NEVILL, Solomon, Sr.
Died before 12 July 1847 when the suit of George A. Connally, Surviving partner etc., vs Solomon Nevill, Sr. mentioned the death of defendant. (Mad TN, Ch Ct Min, 1/38)

NEVILLE, Thomas
Was a resident of Washington County, KY, on 16 May 1816 when his deposition was to be taken for the defendant in the suit of Stephen Lee vs John Murphy. (Cla TN, Co Ct Min, 4/214)

NEVIN, John
Died before 19 October 1838 when a petition was filed by Johnson Williamson, David Williamson, John McCoy, Elizabeth J. Williamson, a minor who petitions by her guardian D. W. McCullock, John W. Nevin, William M. Nevin, David E. Nevin, Robert P. Nevin & Marth Mary Nevin, who petition by their guardian William M. Nevin, John K. Finley and Margaret his wife, Alexander B. Brown and Elizabeth his wife and Theodore H. Nevin, heirs at law of John Nevin, deceased, William W. Morris and Mary his wife, Archibald A. Ritchie, Sally R. Ritchie, Hugh Scott and Isabella J. his wife, William L. Ritchie & also Mariah R. Ritchie, Hetta A. Ritchie and Ann Mariah Ritchie, minors who petition by their guardian Hetta Ritchie. It is ordered by the Court that Robert B. Harper, William S. S. Harris, John J. Taylor, Logan S. David and Lysander Adams be appointed commissioners to divide the tracts of land mentioned in the schedule attached to said petition into five equal shares and that they make report according to law. (Obi TN, Cir Ct Min, 3/276) On 22 February 1839 the same commissioners appointed above were given until next term to divide the lands belonging to the heirs of Hugh Williams. (Ibid 318) A deed was recorded from David Nevin & wife Mary to John McCoy, for one undivided one fifth part of 22,500 acres of land, executed on 19 December 1836 & acknowledged before a justice of the peace in Cumberland County, PA. (Ibid 373) Martha Mary Nevin & Robert P. Nevin were still minors 24 October 1839 when they petitioned by their guardian, William M. Nevin, to sell land. They each owned 1/8 of 5,367 acres. (Ibid 4/no#)

NEVIN, John
Died before 21 March 1807 as shown in the suit of James Dardis adm. vs Joseph Colvelle. (Roa TN, Co Ct Min, B/297)

NEW, William
31 March 1825 with his wife Frances New, made a deed of gift to their son, Charles Turner New, for a negro girl named Letty aged about 8. (Wil TN, Reg Bk/359)

NEWBERGER, Charles
Was a non-resident of TN on 16 March 1855 as shown in the suit of Simeon Bernhaimes, Lipman Hockstadter & Charles Hockstadter. (Mad TN, Ch Ct Min, 2/45)

NEWBERN, Perlina
Was a minor 17 March 1854 when Wm. Y. Newbern was appointed guardian ad litem to defend in her place the suit of Dawson Bond et als vs Wm. Jones et als. (Mad TN, Ch Ct Min, 1/362)

NEWMAN, Ann
26 August 1778 Saml. Tate made a motion to confirm "a Ind. of Washington Court in Virginia that Ann Newman should serve a certain time men-d in sd Order." The court ruled that the same order is illegal & that said Ann Newman be set free and discharged, she being no longer a servant. (Was TN, Co Ct Min, 1/42)

NEWMAN, Bird
Was bound as an apprentice to Tidence Lane on 4 September 1827. (McM TN, Co Ct Min, 2no#/237)

NEWMAN, James
Was bound as an apprentice to Mary Dikes 6 March 1865. He is about 4 years old. (Sev TN, Co Ct Min, no#/140)

NEWMAN, Nelson
6 September 1858 was released from paying poll tax as he is "a poor and decrepit person." (Sev TN, Co Ct Min, no#/335)

NEWMAN, William
8 January 1861 Jno. S. Trotter, P. H. Loomey & A. Lawson were appointed to see "that William Newman receive humane treatment during his unfortunate and helpless condition and that they use their own discretion as to when the county should be released from the

care and expense of said Newman." (Sev TN, Co Ct Min, no#/645) 1 April 1861 several claims were paid for Wm. Newman, one for medical treatment & one for "Berrial clothes & coffin." A claim for 2 days of hunting Newman was crossed out. (Ibid 665)

NEWSOM, Harbert
Died before 23 February 1861 as shown in the suit of Jno. F. Newsom vs H. A. Welch et als. Harbert Newsom left a will and gave his wife, Sarah E. Newsom, all his estate for life. Saml. Epperson & Eldridge M. Newsom were appointed administrators with will annexed. Sarah E. has died. John F. Newsom rendered some 6 years services for the estate, part of the time as a partner with said Sarah. Sarah died prior to 15 May 1856. Jno. F. Newsom & the other legatees entered into an agreement. (Mad TN, Ch Ct Min, 2/451)

NICHOLS
5 September 1859, 2 free negro children, Richard A. Nichols aged 8 and Alfred Nichols aged 9, were bound out as apprentices. [probably to Joab Rowland as shown in a previous entry.] (Sev TN, Co Ct Min, no#/468)

NICHOLS, Alfred
5 November 1856 was bound as an apprentice to Sanders McMahan until age 21. Alfred is a free child of color aged 7 years and in a destitute and suffering condition. (Sev TN, Co Ct Min, no#/87)

NICHOLS, Coleman
26 June 1843 his suit for divorce from Jane Nichols was dismissed. (Bed TN, Ch Ct Min, 2/236)

NICHOLS, John
Was a resident of MO in 1844, as shown in the suit of John Dean. Nichols had been a constable in Bedford County, TN, in 1840. (Bed TN, Ch Ct Min, 3/203)

NICHOLS, John, Jr.
Died before 3 April 1865 when Alexander C. B. Nichols was appointed administrator with Joshua Nichols as security. (Sev TN, Co Ct Min, no#/147) John H. Murphy was appointed guardian of the minor heirs. (Ibid 167)

NICHOLS, Joseph
Died before 3 September 1866 when A. A. Trotter was appointed guardian to Susan C. Nichols, minor heir, with M. W. McCour & E. M. Wynn as security. (Sev TN, Co Ct Min, no#/364)

NICHOLS, Margaret
Died before 2 May 1859 when her will was proved by M. W. McCown & B. M. Chandler, witnesses. The witnesses also stated that the item of the will in which the testator devised the debt owing to her by John McMahan to all her children, the name of W. F. Nichols was through mistake or oversight omitted. Margaret intended the devise to be to all her children including W. F. Nichols. W. F. Nichols was named executor. (Sev TN, Co Ct Min, no#/440-1)

NICHOLS, Neoma
Was probably a minor [or a married woman] 21 October 1840 when suit was brought by Neoma Nichols by next friend &c vs Norten Oakes & Mariah Oakes his wife, Jesse Toler & Peggy Toler his wife & Alfred Nedry & Winney Nedry his wife, for trespass. (Obi TN, Cir Ct Min, 4/no#)

NICHOLS, Richard N.
5 November 1856 was bound as an apprentice to Sanders McMahan until age 21. Richard is a free child of color aged 5 years in a destitute and suffering condition. (Sev TN, Co Ct Min, no#/87)

NICHOLS, Sally
Died before 8 January 1867 when D. P. Gap & Co. was paid for burying clothes. (Sev TN, Co Ct Min, no#/422)

NICHOLS, Tabitha
Died before 4 April 1859 when Anderson Bowers was paid for making the coffin. (Sev TN, Co Ct Min, no#/417)

NICHONS, Ellenor
"This day appeared John Crab before me Josiah Walton, one of the acting Justices of the

Peace for Sumner Co., TN, and made oath that he was acquainted with a woman by the name of Ellenor Nichons which was a White woman from appearance & generally passed for such & it was generally said that Frankey Nichons was the daughter of the said Ellenar Nichons. Sworn to and subscribed before me this 7th day of November 1826. John Crabb, attest Josiah Watson JP." (Wil TN, Reg Bk/392) [See also Frankey Scott]

NICKINS, William B.
Died before 12 July 1854 as shown in the suit of William B. Nickins vs Sampson McClelan, administrator &c and a cross bill the same. George W. McKinley, the administrator of William B. Nickins, petitioned to have the suit in his name. (Jac TN, Ch Ct Min, B/151)

NICKOLS, Henry C.
29 November 1823 made a deed of gift to Robert N. Nickols for various property. (Wil TN, Reg Bk/320)

NIGHT, Jas. [Knight]
Died before 14 September 1855 as shown in the petition of Sarah Vick et als. Another trustee is to be appointed in the place of Jas. Night, deceased. (Mad TN, Ch Ct Min, 2/82)

NIGHT, Mariah
Dismissed her suit for divorce against William Night on 9 February 1860. "They appear to have adjusted their difficulties." This suit has "Rescinded" written across it. (Jac TN, Ch Ct Min, C/304)

NIVANS, Wilson
Was a resident of the Cherokee Nation on 5 December 1827 when his deposition was to be taken for the plaintiff in the case of William McCormick vs James Shelton. (McM TN, Co Ct Min, no#/286)

NIX, Lebanan
Died before 1834 as shown in the petition of Edmond T. Doherty & others for sale of land. Edmond L. Dugherty and his wife Ann, formerly Ann Nix, Elizabeth Nix, Rebecca Nix, Francis Nix, James Nix, Lebamon Nix & Mary Nix, the last 6 who are minors & petition by their guardian, Lamuel Wilson, state that Rebecca Nix, the mother of Ann Dugherty & the above minors, after the death of her husband and in her lifetime purchased land in Marshall County, formerly Lincoln County. Rebecca Nix died during 1834 leaving Ann Nix now Ann Dugherty, James Nix, Elizabeth Nix, Rebecca Nix, Francis Nix, Mary Nix, Thomas Nix, Samuel Nix, William Nix & Lebanon Nix. Ann Dugherty, James Nix, Mary Nix, Thomas Nix & Lemuel Nix live in Marshall County. Elizabeth, Rebecca & Francis Nix live in Bedford County. The residence of William & Lebanon Nix is unknown. Samuel Nix is yet a minor but will be 21 before the next term of court. There are 10 heirs. This petition filed 24 March 1839. (Bed TN, Ch Ct Min, 1/117) John Hatchett was administrator for Rebecca Nix. (Ibid 2/104)

NOBLE, Alfred D.
Died before 18 January 1850 as shown in the suit of Simon J. Jones, guardian of the minor heirs of Alfred D. Noble - & Wm. A. Nobles, petition for sale of slave. (Mad TN, Ch Ct Min, 1/118) 14 January 1851 the slave was sold and ownership divested out of William A., Emily, Allen & Montgomery Nobles. (Ibid 166)

NOBLE, John
Died before August term 1810 when the will was proved by Robert Perry & Jacob Perry. (Rob TN, Co Ct Min, 2/281)

NOBLES, Allen J.
Died before 21 August 1860 as shown in the suit of W. A. Nables vs F. N. W. Burton et als. The court is to determine who the legal heirs are. (Mad TN, Ch Ct Min, 2/351) Allen Nobles died in 1859. William A. Nobles is his only heir. (Ibid 358)

NOBLES, H.
Taxes were not collected in District 5 for 1873, "insolvent." (Dyr TN, Co Ct Min, B/759)

NOBLES, Matt
Taxes were not collected in District 5 for 1873, "insolvent." (Dyr TN, Co Ct Min, B/759)

NODDING, Wm.
Died before 26 May 1794 when an inventory of the estate was returned by Daniel McCray & William Calvert, executors. (Was TN, Co Ct Min, 1/485)

NODING, John
Died before 3 February 1783 when the will was proved by Saml. Wood and James Scott. (Was TN, Co Ct Min, 1/192) The court appointed Priscilla Noding and Christopher Taylor as executors. (Ibid 193)

NORMAN, Willson
4 September 1827 gave power of attorney to Nelson Norman to rent certain lands in VA. (McM TN, Co Ct Min, 2no#/237)

NORMENT, Giles
Died before 7 March 1871 when the public administrator, C. L. Nolen, was appointed administrator. (Dyr TN, Co Ct Min, B/207) W. P. Menzie, E. A. Dunavant and A. G. Ferguson were appointed to lay off a years provision for the minor children. (Ibid 237) The name was shown as W. G. Norment. (Ibid 244) 3 June 1873 C. L. Nolan was ordered to pay to each of the children of W. G. Norment, deceased, an equal share of their years allowance. (Ibid 592)

NORRIS, John
Died before 4 April 1808 when Whitmill Harrington was appointed administrator with Marvill Lowe & Conrod Coon as security. (Rob TN, Co Ct Min, 2/11)

NORRIS, Thomas
Died before 6 August 1804 when the will was proved by William Norris. (Rob TN, Co Ct Min, 1/301)

NORTH, Jesse
Taxes were not collected in District 4 for 1873, "insolvent." (Dyr TN, Co Ct Min, B/759)

NORTH, John
Died before 27 May 1794 when George North & Ester North were appointed administrators, with John Tidlock as security. (Was TN, Co Ct Min, 1/489)

NORTHERN, Edward
Died before 12 November 1810 when John Sigler was appointed administrator, with John B. Cheatham & Jacob Young as security. (Rob TN, Co Ct Min, 2/314)

NORTON, Sally
Was bound 26 May 1794 to John Hunter until she arrives at the age of 18 years "to learn to Sew, Spin & Nitt." (Was TN, Co Ct Min, 1/485)

NORVILL, David
Died intestate in December [there is no date on this bill but it was probably between 1830 &1836] as shown in the petition of John W. Norvill & others vs Elizabeth W. Norvill & others. The petitioners were John W. Norvill, Sydney S. Norvill, David J. Norvill and Edward M. Norvill. David Norvill departed this life in December last. The children of David Norvill were the complainants and James D., Thomas, Felix B., Alexander S. and Mary Ann Norvill, the last 3 minors, with John Shoffner as the guardian of Felix B. and John Norvill as the guardian of Alexander & Mary Ann. There are to be 9 parts to the division. Thomas has transferred his interest in the estate to William Brown. Elizabeth W. Norvill is the widow & is entitled to dower. (Bed TN, Ch Ct Min, 1/59) A partition was made in February 1837 to the widow, Elizabeth W., and to James D., John W., Thomas, Sidney S., David J., Edward M. B., Alexander S., Felix B. & Mary Ann K. Norville, heirs-at-law. The land was bounded by the heirs of Vaughn. Plats shown. (Ibid 2/1-8)

NORVILLE, James D.
Had made a deed of trust to Samuel Phillips on 7 February 1837. Phillips resigned as trustee and Geo. W. Morris was appointed trustee and gave bond to Mary E., Robert M., David J., Geo. R., Margaret H., Heneretta F. and Sarah S. Norvell, to perform the trust. (Bed TN, Ch Ct Min, 2/37)

NUCKLES, John, Capt.
Died before 15 August 1782 when Stephen Jones was charged with killing him. The name was also shown as John Meckley. (Was TN, Co Ct Min, 1/168-9)

NUN, Frank
Died before 6 May 1872 when George W. Bettis renewed his bond as guardian of Mary Nun, minor heir. (Dyr TN, Co Ct Min, B/412)

NUNESINGER, John
Was a pauper 4 April 1870 when $35 was allowed to Nathaniel Porter for his care. (Dyr TN, Co Ct Min, B/33)

NUVELL, Dempsy [Newell, Nowell, Novell]
Died before 16 January 1850 when Harriet Nuvell made petition for herself and as guardian of the heirs of Dempsy Nuvell, deceased, for sale of land. (Mad TN, Ch Ct Min, 1/101) The heirs were James H., John A., Reuben F., Wm. C., Saml. J., Joab & Dempsy Nuvell, Jr. Harriet was given permission to sell the land and purchase another place near her brothers & relations so as to get their aid in raising the children. Harriet was the widow. (Ibid 119) 23 February 1859 it was stated that Jas. H., John A. and Reuben F. Novell are of age. (Ibid 2/257)

O'NEAL, P. P.
Died before 6 November 1871 when M. W. E. Royster made bond as guardian of Nathaniel O'Neal, minor heir, with George W. Bettis and W. H. Royster as her security. (Dyr TN, Co Ct Min, B/315) William H. Hendrix was administrator. (Ibid 418) The name was shown as A. P. O'Neal when Mrs. M. W. E. Royster renewed her bond as guardian. (Ibid 765)

O'NEAL, S. H.
Died before 6 February 1871 when O. R. Robbins made a settlement as administrator. (Dyr TN, Co Ct Min, B/190)

O'NIEL, G. W.
Died before 6 February 1871 when O. R. Robbins made a settlement as administrator. (Dyr TN, Co Ct Min, B/190)

OAKS, Susan
5 January 1858 money was allowed for taking her to the poor house. (Sev TN, Co Ct Min, no#/242) 6 January 1863 Samuel Chance was allowed to take Susan Oaks out of the poor house and off of the County. (Ibid 42)

OCONNER, Edward
20 June 1843 was granted a certificate of naturalization. He was a native of Ireland. (Obi TN, Cir Ct Min, 4/no#)

ODDEL, Jean
Was the mother of a base born child. At the February term 1790 Absolom Boring was ordered to make bond for the maintenance of the child. (Was TN, Co Ct Min, 1/433)

ODDEL, Job
Was the reputed father of a base born child of Mary Young and was ordered to pay maintenance for the child 11 May 1790. (Was TN, Co Ct Min, 1/440)

ODELL, John
28 August 1778 took the oath of allegiance. (Was TN, Co Ct Min, 1/47)

ODLE, Saml.
Died before the February term 1789 when the will was proved by Isaac Odle, witness. William Whitson and Enoch Job were named as executors but they declined. Elizabeth Odell, widow, was appointed administratrix with the will annexed. Caleb Odell and Thomas Maxwell were securities. (Was TN, Co Ct Min, 1/362)

ODONALD, Maurrice
Died before 8 September 1829 when James H. Fyffe was appointed administrator. (McM TN, Co Ct Min, 2no#/386)

ODUM, Calvin
Died about 1831 as shown in the suit of Fredrick Odum & others vs Hugh Wallace & others. The complainants were his only heirs. Defendant Jacob Cronk was the administrator and Hugh Wallace his security. Complainants want an accounting. (Jac TN, Ch Ct Min, B/89) The suit shows Fredrick Odum, Thomas Odum, Susan Thomas, Simon Odum & Nancy Bushlans vs Hugh Wallace & Jacob Cronk. (Ibid 93)

OFFICER, Robert
Died before 14 October 1856 as shown in the suit of James C. Office, his administrator vs R. Boles & Peter Moody and William Harmon executor of John Moody, deceased. (Fen TN, Ch Ct Min, A/68)

OGLE, Angeline
7 October 1856 Wm. Whaly was allowed money for keeping her child. (Sev TN, Co Ct Min, no#/80)

OGLE, Elias
7 August 1865 was shown to be the son of Thos. J. Ogle when he received a certificate for $1 for killing a wild [fox?] running wild in the woods of Sevier County. (Sev TN, Co Ct Min, no#/197)

OGLE, Elisha
Died before 2 July 1866 when J. A. Trotter, C. Mills & N. W. Emert were appointed to lay off the dower of the widow, Beda Ogle. (Sev TN, Co Ct Min, no#/344)

OGLE, Elizabeth
11 April 1856, William Whaley was allowed $15 from the poor fund to keep a child named Elizabeth Ogle, until 1 June 1857. (Sev TN, Co Ct Min, no#/42)

OGLE, Harcolas
Died before 1 September 1856 when Wm. Bohannan renewed his bond as administrator, with Stephen Husky and W. W. Ogle as his securities. The original bond was destroyed. (Sev TN, Co Ct Min, no#/69)

OGLE, Isaac
Died before 4 June 1866 when the will was proved by Isaac Trotter & J. M. Hammer, witnesses. Horatio B. Ogle and Robert Marshall were executors with Henry Butler as security. (Sev TN, Co Ct Min, no#/331)

OGLE, Perry
Died before 5 February 1866 when Wm. H. Ogle & F. L. Emert were appointed administrators, with J. M. Rambo as security. (Sev TN, Co Ct Min, no#/274)

OGLE, Thomas
Died before 3 February 1862 when his will was proved by Aron Ownley and Bradford Ogle, witnesses. (Sev TN, Co Ct Min, no#/747) Caleb Ogle & Wilson Duggan were appointed administrators with the will annexed. (Ibid 752)

OGLE, Thomas H.
5 July 1858 was released from paying poll tax as he was under 21 years of age. (Sev TN, Co Ct Min, no#/311)

OGLE, William
Died before 7 January 1857 when the executors, James Ogle and Henry Ogle, renewed their bond, with Danl. W. Reagan as security. The old bond was destroyed by fire. (Sev TN, Co Ct Min, no#/117) 3 January 1860, Thomas I. Ogle & other heirs of Wm. Ogle, deceased vs Henry Ogle & others, petition to sell land. Summons are to be issued for the residents of this state & publication to be made for the non-residents. Robert Conner was appointed guardian ad litem for the minors. (Ibid 507) Samuel Watson was one of the heirs. (Ibid 625) Milly Conner, wife of R. R. Conner & formerly Milly Ogle, and Patsy Watson, wife of S. P. Watson & formerly Patsy Ogle, were made party to a suit over the estate. (Ibid 626)

OLDHAM, Frank
Died before 4 July 1870 when F. S. Robertson was paid for making his coffin. Frank was colored. (Dyr TN, Co Ct Min, B/73)

OLDS, Arter
Died before 1 January 1872 when Martha E. Olds was chosen and appointed guardian of Lewis Olds, C. F. Olds, Mary F. Olds, James E. Olds, Sarah O. Olds, Nancy E. Olds and Laura Olds, minor heirs. (Dyr TN, Co Ct Min, B/333) Arthur C. Olds died in 1869. The widow, Martha E. Olds, petitioned for dower. (Ibid 357) Nathan King was administrator. (Ibid 358)

OLDS, Thomas, Sr.
Taxes were not collected in District 3 in 1873, "over age." (Dyr TN, Co Ct Min, B/758)

OLIVE, Samuel
Died in the state of AL in 1836 as stated in the suit of Hicklins Heirs vs Hicklins Admr., 12 July 1850. [Also see Perry Hicklin] Samuel Olive was the brother of the half blood of Perry R. Hickland, deceased. Samuel Olive left a son and daughter. The son has already

departed this life and Elizabeth Fitz, formerly Elizabeth Olive, is his only heir. The Clerk & Master is to pay to Henry B. Fitz & wife the distributive share of said Samuel Olive in the estate of Perry Hicklin. (Jac TN, Ch Ct Min, A/371)

OLIVER, Abel
In his suit of 3 February 1812 against Samuel Luton, he was granted leave to take the depositions of Robert Prince & John Shelby of Montgomery County. (Ste TN, Co Ct Min, 3/104)

OLIVER, Frank
Taxes were not collected in District 4 for 1873, "run away." (Dyr TN, Co Ct Min, B/759)

OLIVER, William
Died before 30 August 1860 as shown in the suit of Rufus M. Mason admr &c of William Oliver decd. vs Sarah Oliver and others. William Oliver left a wife & children. Sarah is entitled to dower. (Mad TN, Ch Ct Min, 2/399)

ONEAL
21 August 1858 a suit was shown by Elisha Oneal Exr. vs Matilda Oneal et als. (Mad TN, Ch Ct Min, 2/241)

ONEAL, Arthur
Died before 7 November 1814 when his nuncupative will was proved by David Carter & Elizabeth Carter. (Ste TN, Co Ct Min, 4/197)

ONEAL, Parley
At June term 1840 a paper was introduced dated November 24, 1840, whereby Parley Oneal dismissed her suit for divorce against Willie Oneal. (Bed TN, Ch Ct Min, 2/145)

ONEAL, William
Died before 21 June 1816 when John Harpole was appointed guardian of Asa L. Oneal, John H. Oneal, Wm. B. Oneal and Sally F. Oneal, minor heirs, with J. Brown & E. Centshir as security. (Wil TN, Co Ct Min, no#/21)

ONEIL, Jesse
Died before 6 September 1824 when Rebecca ONeil was appointed administratrix. (McM TN, Co Ct Min, 2no#/21)

ORR, W. E.
5 September 1871 J. H. Orr made a settlement as guardian. (Dyr TN, Co Ct Min, B/281)

ORSEBORN, Liddy
Was the mother of a base born child named Jacob Hunter, as shown when Jacob Hunter was ordered to deliver the child to the mother, February term 1789. (Was TN, Co Ct Min, 1/364)

OSBURN, Wm. R.
Died before 6 June 1870 when J. A. Nunn made a settlement as administrator. (Dyr TN, Co Ct Min, B/63)

OUTLAW, Alexander
Was a resident of Jefferson County 15 December 1806 as shown by the petition of William Terrel Lewis for a division of the land that had been granted jointly to them in 1787 by the state of NC. The land was then in the county of Green but is now in Roane County. (Roa TN, Co Ct Min, B/218)

OUTLAW, Alexander
On 3 May 1814 the court proceeded to elect a Register for said county. Alexander Outlaw & John Bailey declared themselves candidates for the office. On counting the votes Alexander Outlaw had 6 and John Bailey had 5 so Alexander Outlaw was elected. On motion of the other candidate by his attorney it appears that Alexander Outlaw is a minor & therefore incompetent to fill said office. The election was set aside. In the new election William Outlaw, William L. Allen & John Bailey declared themselves candidates. John Bailey received 6 votes and William Outlaw five. (Ste TN, Co Ct Min, 4/142)

OUTLAW, Edward
Was a resident of Sumner County 10 June 1806 when his deposition was to be taken for the defendant in the suit of John Williams vs William Outlaw. (Ste TN, Co Ct Min, 1/30b)

OUTLAW, William
Died before 9 November 1814 when on the motion of Alexander Outlaw, it was ordered that John Chambers be appointed guardian of him until he arrives at the age of 21. John Chambers was also appointed guardian of the other children of William Outlaw until a decision is had on the nuncupative will of the said Wm. Outlaw. Nathan Ross & William Hazzard were securities for John Chambers. (Ste TN, Co Ct Min, 4/218) James Tagert, Esqr. was appointed administrator with Tapley Maddux, Darrel Young, John Allen & John Chambers as security. (Ibid 219) Wilson Randle was appointed guardian of Nancy Outlaw, one of the orphans of William Outlaw, deceased. (Ibid 241) On 8 February 1815 the nuncupative will of William Outlaw was proved by Drury Bird and Jarot Bell. William Outlaw, one of the heirs of William Outlaw deceased, made choice of John Allen as his guardian. On the request of Alexander Outlaw & Harriat Outlaw, Ephraim B. Davidson was appointed guardian of Alexander & Hariat, also of George Outlaw, Drury Outlaw and Jefferson Outlaw. On the request of Mary Outlaw, widow of William Outlaw, deceased, William Allen was appointed guardian of John Outlaw, Susan Outlaw, Indiana Outlaw and Patsey Earl Outlaw. (Ibid 252) Isaac Lanier was appointed executor of the nuncupative will. (Ibid 256)

OVERTON, John
Died before 1836 as shown in the suit of Mathew Mullins against Horatio Clagett, no date on suit but an answer given in August 1846. Horatio Clagett had bought land which was part of a tract of land purchased by Mathew Mullins previous to that time, from John S. Claybrook as executor for John Overton, deceased. Richd. Rany was guardian of the minor heirs. Horatio Clagett was of Hickman County, TN, in 1835, but was a citizen of Bedford County in 1845. (Bed TN, Ch Ct Min, 3/449)

OVERTON, John
Made application for pension 7 December 1824. He served as a militia private soldier in the War of the Revolution in NC for one year & 11 months in 1779, 80 & 81, under Capt. Charles Crawford & Capt. John Honeycut, General Semington's Brigade. He was born in NC & has resided in TN 16 years. He will be 63 years of age in May 1825. He has a wife & a grandson living with him. (McM TN, Co Ct Min, 2no#/40)

OWAN, Artamissa [Owen]
13 November 1834 filed suit by her guardian William N. Watson vs Richd. L. Merriweather. The suit was dismissed. (Obi TN, Cir Ct Min, 2/203)

OWEN, Elias
Died before 31 July 1867 as shown in the suit of David Beaty vs Elias Owen. (Fen TN, Ch Ct Min, A/326) In the suit of David Beaty vs Ferby Owens et als, B. O. Bowden was appointed guardian ad litem for the minor defendants. (Ibid 335) Ferby [Pherby] Owen was administratrix. (Ibid 352) Land was sold on which Joshua Owen formerly lived. (Ibid 367)

OWENBY, John
Died before 1 October 1866 when the will was proved by Philip S. Shults, one of the witnesses. John H. Owens was executor. (Sev TN, Co Ct Min, no#/378)

OWENS, John
8 April 1862 money was paid to James Clark for the support of John Owens & family. (Sev TN, Co Ct Min, no#/771)

OWENS, Martin
Died before 3 August 1818 when William Hollingsworth was appointed guardian of the minor heirs, to wit; Johnson Owen, Francis Owen, Ann Owen & Martin Owens, with George Michie & Abner Wasson as security. (Wil TN, Co Ct Min, no#/294)

OWENS, Mary Ann
Married [blank] Webb before 14 April 1857 as shown in her suit against Jo. Matthews & others. (Fen TN, Ch Ct Min, A/91)

OZMENT, Darkus
Was the mother of a bastard child and Eli Ozment was the reputed father. He gave bond for its support 19 March 1817, with William M. Swain & Robert Shannon as security. (Wil TN, Co Ct Min, no#/91)

PACE, Asa
Died before 9 February 1813 when William Pace was appointed administraor, with

William Pace & Lenas Fox as security. (Rob TN, Co Ct Min, 3/199) Also shown as Alsy Pace. (Ibid 243)

PACE, Jackson
Died before 4 August 1873 when his will was proved by W. J. Farris and J. T. Strickton, witnesses. J. R. Herron was executor with W. J. Farris and Robert Hale as his securities. (Dyr TN, Co Ct Min, B/616)

PACE, Richd.
Was a resident of Warren County, KY, 5 October 1808 when a deposition was to be taken for the defendant in the case of Isom Uzzle vs Ezekiel Doyley. (Rob TN, Co Ct Min, 2/90)

PAGAN, Andrew Carson
Died before November term 1832 when his death was suggested in the suit of Drury Perkins vs A. C. Pagan, sued by the name of Carson Pagan. In another suit the same day the name is given as Andrew C. Pagan and he died since the last term of court. (Obi TN, Cir Ct Min, 2/8) George W. Wood & A. M. L. McBean were administrators. (Ibid 76)

PAIN, Ephriam
Died before 12 November 1813 when the widow, Catharine Pain, was granted administration, with Plummer Wellis, William S. Bradburn & George A. West as security. (Rob TN, Co Ct Min, 3/344) The name was shown as Ephraim Thompson Paine. (Ibid 345)

PAINTER, Pamilia [Pointer]
On 13 July 1854 sued John B. Painter & Thomas Painter for divorce and alimony. The defendants failed to appear. (Jac TN, Ch Ct Min, B/162) On July 12 1855 the case was continued. (Ibid 237) 14 July 1855 Permelia Painter was granted a divorce from John B. Painter. The land mentioned had been purchased by Thomas Painter with funds of Permelia and for her use and title to lands in Putnam County was divested out of Thomas Painter and vested in Permelia Painter. She was also allotted personal property and the care of the children. (Ibid 270)

PALMER, Catherine
1 February 1858 was stated to be a person of weak mind and not in condition to transact her business. R. M. Creswell was appointed her guardian. (Sev TN, Co Ct Min, no#/256)

PALMER, Catherine
Died before 2 July 1866 when A. H. Keener was appointed administrator with R. M. Cresswell as security. [The name also looks like Balmer] (Sev TN, Co Ct Min, no#/338 & 340)

PALMER, Essy
Died before 4 July 1870 when J. F. Williamson was paid for making the coffin. (Dyr TN, Co Ct Min, B/73)

PALMER, Isabella
Was bound 3 May 1870 to J. A. C. Manly "until she is 18 - say nine years." She was a colored orphan. (Dyr TN, Co Ct Min, B/57)

PALMER, W. A.
Died before 1 October 1866 when Lucinda Palmer was appointed administrator with J. A. Pickins & S. W. Randles as security. (Sev TN, Co Ct Min, no#/374)

PANKEY, Polly
Was the mother of a child of which George Chapman was the reputed father. He gave bond 22 April 1800. (Rob TN, Co Ct Min 1/134)

PARAMOUR, Amos
February term 1787 Isaac Taylor proved a bill of sale from Amos Paramour to him for the legacy of Lydia, his wife. (Was TN, Co Ct Min, 1/273)

PARISH, W. H.
Died before 5 April 1870 when John Murray made a settlement as administrator. (Dyr TN, Co Ct Min, B/42) Nelson Parrish renewed his bond as guardian of the minor heirs of W. H. Parrish, deceased. (Ibid 182)

PARKER, Henry
Died before 4 July 1870 when Chas. Love was paid for taking care of and furnishing a coffin for him. (Dyr TN, Co Ct Min, B/73)

PARKER, James
Taxes were not collected in District 4 for 1873, "run away." (Dyr TN, Co Ct Min, B/759)

PARKER, John
Made a deed of gift to Nathan Parker for a negro man Jones? and a deed of gift to David Parker and Stephen Parker for a negro boy Tom, 4 May 1813. (Ste TN, Co Ct Min, 4/36)

PARKER, John
Died before 7 February 1814 when the will was proved by William Curl & Ezikiah Rorie? (Ste TN, Co Ct Min, 4/90) Stephen Parker was one of the executors. (Ibid 196)

PARKER, Jonathan
Died before 12 February 1839, intestate, as shown in the petition of Thomas Roberts & others for sale of land. Frances was the widow and Elisha Bobo, John Stanfield, John W. Gardner, Peter R. Proby and William D. Orr were appointed to allot her dower. (Bed TN, Ch Ct Min, 2/46) Dower was laid off. Thomas Roberts & Priscilla his wife, Eps, Allen, Elijah & Martha Parker are the five heirs. (Ibid 80)

PARKER, Richard
Was a negro boy aged 12 years when he was bound 5 September 1871 to J. P. Harris until age 21. The mother of the child gave her consent. (Dyr TN, Co Ct Min, B/281)

PARKISON, Peter
Died before 11 May 1790 when Mary Parkison, the widow, and Joseph Greer, were appointed administrators of the estate. John Tipton, Andrew Greer and Joseph Tipton were security. (Was TN, Co Ct Min, 1/440)

PARKS
3 January 1871, this day was bound unto Hamilton Parks, Sr. five negro children named Blanch Parks, Margaret Parks, Anthony Parks, Fannie Parks and Sammie Parks, aged respectively 18, 15, 12, 8 & 5 years, until they reach 21 for the boys and 18 for the girls. A. A. Parks and Smith Parks were security. (Dyr TN, Co Ct Min, B/157)

PARKS, Hamilton, Jr.
8 March 1870 was chosen and appointed guardian of Faustina B. Parks, who was his wife and the daughter of Joab Hardin. Smith Parks, Hamilton Parks & J. B. Cunningham were securities. (Dyr TN, Co Ct Min, B/12)

PARR, Coleman
17 July 1810 was charged by Elizabeth Parr with being the father of her bastard child. He gave bond for the maintenence of the child with Matthias Parr as security. (Roa TN, Co Ct Min, D/227)

PARR, Moses
Died before 21 February 1843 when the petition of John Parr Admr. of Moses Parr vs LaFayette Hazlewood & Mary Parr Guardian was dismissed. (Obi TN, Cir Ct Min, 4/no#)

PARRATREE, Edward
Died before 9 February 1814 when land was taxed to the heirs. (Ste TN, Co Ct Min, 4/110)

PARRISH, W. H.
9 July 1873 Nelson Parrish made a settlement as guardian of the heirs. (Dyr TN, Co Ct Min, B/613)

PARRISH, Wm. B.
Died before 20 February 1867 when Thos. H. Drake was appointed guardian ad litem for minors, Jas. T. Parrish, Wm. S. Parrish & Alexander S. Parrish, to defend the suit of Jno. W. Parrish et als vs Jas. T. Parrish et als. Wm. B. Parrish left a will by which he directed that all his property be kept together until the death or marriage of his wife at which time the property would be divided between his children. The widow, Elizabeth Parrish, is dead. Two of his legatees, Richard Parrish & Mary T. Parrish, have died leaving complainants, Jno. W. Parrish et als and defendants, Jas T. Parrish et als, the only heirs. All of the defendants are minors. (Mad TN, Ch Ct Min, 3/12 & 52)

PARROTT, John
Died before 6 June 1864 when the widow, Emelie Parrott, petitioned for dower. Minor heirs were Diema L. Parrott, Isaac N. Parrott, Agness Mc Parrot, Mary J. Parrot, George J. R. Parrott. Benjamin M. Atchly was appointed guardian ad litem. (Sev TN, Co Ct Min, no#/105) B. M. Atchley was appointed administrator. (Ibid 124) George Parrott was the father of John Parrott, deceased. (Ibid 181)

PARTAIN, Angelina
8 April 1856 her poor child was ordered to be brought to court so it could be provided for. (Sev TN, Co Ct Min, no#/33)

PARTIN, Polly
Was the mother of a bastard child. On 26 May 1807 she paid, by Drury Lawson, six and one fourth dollars for the use of the state as her fine "for not swearing a child of which she is delivered and refuses to sware it to the Father thereof." (Cla TN, Co Ct Min, 3/80)

PARTLOW, Thomas
Was the son of Anne Drennon. Anne was the daughter of John Drennon, deceased. This was shown on 20 September 1817. [Also see John Drennon] (Wil TN, Reg Bk/98)

PARTON, Alexander
Died before 2 June 1862 when Saml. B. Henderson was appointed administrator. (Sev TN, Co Ct Min, no#/779)

PATE, Benja.
Was probably a resident of Smith County when he appeared as a witness for the plaintiff in the case of Phebe Philips by her friend vs Carter Crutcher. Benja. Pate proved 16 days attendance in the whole, 7 days from Smith County and 9 days in this county, and 54 miles. Delila Pate & John Pate were also witnesses. (Wil TN, Co Ct Min, no#/134)

PATE, Edward P.
Died before 10 February 1855 as shown in the suit of Cebert Pate vs Lawson D. Pate administrator &c of Edward P. Pate, H. H. Draper et al. Defendant Stephen C. Pate is a non-resident of the state. (Jac TN, Ch Ct Min, B/218)

PATE, John
Died before 10 May 1830 when his death was suggested in the suit of John Hubert vs John Pate & S. A. Warner. (Obi TN, Cir Ct Min, 1/106) The suit was revived in the name of Seth Bedford, administrator of John Pate. (Ibid 127)

PATE, John B.
Died before 4 March 1872 as shown when Oney C. Pate petitioned for dower. R. H. McGaughey was administrator. Defendants were William H. Pate, Ella F., Mary E., John S. and Nancy O. Pate. (Dyr TN, Co Ct Min, B/381-2) Bell C. Burgie was appointed guardian of Mary E., Ella F., John T. and Nancy O. Pate, minor heirs of John B. Pate, deceased, after Mrs. O. C. Pate had resigned. (Ibid 418)

PATE, John C.
6 March 1871 renewed his bond as guardian of Susan Pate. (Dyr TN, Co Ct Min, B/203) Susan's name is shown as Z. Susan Pate in the case of J. E. Dunlap vs John C. Pate, guardian & Z. Susan Pate. (Ibid 277)

PATE, Willeray
Died before 13 July 1850 as shown in the suit of Edward P. Pate & others vs Celert Pate & others. At the time of the death of Willeray Pate, Sabe Pate, a son of Willeray, had also died. Both of said estates are settled up and closed. Complainants & defendants are the heirs-at-law of said deceased persons except complainant Oliver Young who purchased the interest of defendant Cebert. Also said Sibert had purchased the interest of Sampson W. Pate. The lands are to be sold or partitioned. Complainant Cyrela Pate had sold her interest to Cebert. (Jac TN, Ch Ct Min, A/383) 20 March 1852 this suit is shown as Edward P. Pate, Cyrena Pate, Cyretia Pate, Leroy Pate, Stephen Pate, Anthony Pate and Oliver Young vs Cebert Pate, Alfred Cornwell & wife Zilphia A. Cornwell and Sampson Pate. (Ibid B/48)

PATEY, Charles
4 March 1861 was appointed guardian of Joseph Patey, a lunatic brother. (Sev TN, Co Ct Min, no#/663)

PATEY, Joshua
Died before 4 March 1861 when William Patey was appointed administrator with John Wear, Micajah R. Maples & Saml. Gibson as securities. (Sev TN, Co Ct Min, no#/658) Wm. Fox, John Andes & Jno. N. Trotter were appointed to lay off a years support to Nancy Patey, the widow. (Ibid 661)

PATRIC, P. H.
Taxes were not collected in District 2 for 1873, "Over age." (Dyr TN, Co Ct Min, B/758)

PATTERSON, Allen L.
Died before 17 February 1858 when his death was admitted in the suit of Allen L. Patterson vs Saml. Lucky et als. The suit is renewed in the names of Thos. Clark & wife Frances, Thos. Henderson & wife Marion, Eliza Henderson, Susan Patterson, Wm. A. Patterson & James Patterson, the only heirs of A. L. Patterson, & Thos. Clark the executor. (Mad TN, Ch Ct Min, 2/170) Same suit except the defendants were shown as Saml. Luckey, John Irvin & F. R. Hardgrave. The complainants are the heirs of A. L. Patterson. (Ibid 241) Susan Patterson married Nathan Henderson before 21 August 1860. The suit was revived in his name, also in the name of Susan P. Henderson, only child of Marion Henderson. Defendants Luckey, Irvin & Hardgrave had bought land from Allen L. Patterson and his heirs are filing suit to collect the unpaid portion. (Ibid 352) Property was sold & title divested out of Susan P. Henderson, child & heir of Marion Henderson, deceased, Frances Clark, Susan Henderson, Eliza Henderson, William A. Patterson, James Patterson, Thomas Clark executor and Felix R. Hardgraves. (Ibid 420)

PATTERSON, Austin
Was a minor 4 February 1867 when R. S. Clark was appointed guardian, with Benj. Langston as security. (Sev TN, Co Ct Min, no#/430)

PATTERSON, Charles
Died before 7 February 1859 when John Russell made a settlement as executor. (Sev TN, Co Ct Min, no#/397)

PATTERSON, Isham
Died before 2 August 1819 when Wm. McHany was appointed administrator with James Cross & Wm. Dale as security. A years provision was allotted to the widow. (Wil TN, Co Ct Min, no#/496) The widow, Peggy Patterson, petitioned for dower. (Ibid 533) Land is to be divided equally between Lucy Penneal, Patsey Gibson, Polly Patterson, Sally Short, Isham Patterson, Jr., Nancy Patterson, James Patterson, A. Patterson, Rebecca Patterson, Lewis Patterson [this last name was crossed out], Andrew Patterson & Hartwell Patterson. Geo. L. Smith was appointed special guardian of the minor heirs. William Patterson made the petition for division. Lewis Patterson was added back to the heirs. (Ibid 535)

PATTERSON, J. C. E.
Died before 5 August 1861 when the will was proved by E. M. Douglas & S. N. Douglas, witnesses. Thomas G. Douglas was executor. (Sev TN, Co Ct Min, no#/710) Shown as Joseph C. Patterson. (Ibid 716)

PATTERSON, Jacob
Died before June term 1804 when he is shown on the tax list as Jacob Patterson Deceased. (Wil TN, Co Ct Min, no#/65)

PATTERSON, Jean
Was a minor 13 May 1788 when John Rogers was appointed guardian with Jacob Brown as security. (Was TN, Co Ct Min, 1/327)

PATTERSON, John
Died before 20 January 1800 when the will was proved by Anthony Sharp. (Rob TN, Co Ct Min, 1/122) Mary Patterson & George Patterson were executors. (Ibid 130)

PATTERSON, Mary
Died before 1 June 1857 when John Russell was appointed administrator. Eli Fox & Absolum Allen were his securities. (Sev TN, Co Ct Min, no#/169)

PATTERSON, Robert
Died before 1 March 1830 when Samuel Patterson & Robert Patterson made bond as executors of his last will & testament. (McM TN, Co Ct Min, 2no#/422)

PATTERSON, Samuel
Died before 1 January 1817 when the commissioners made a division to the heirs of

Samuel Patterson, "as the annexed platt doth shew, [no plat shown]. On the petition of Elizabeth Wammock we have admitted him to draw lot No. 7" [later shown as Elijah Wammock]. Land was laid off in 7 platts (546 acres). Mention was made of the widows third, witnessed by William Patterson & Robt. Patterson. (Wil TN, Reg Bk/80-81) 19 September 1816 John W. Payton was appointed special guardian for Ann, Fulton, Rebeca, Ester, Polly & Jenny Patterson, minor heirs of Samuel Patterson, deceased, to answer the petition of Elijah Wamack for the partition of the property of the deceased. (Ibid Co Ct Min, no#/45) 16 December 1817 John Fakis? [written over] was appointed guardian of Samuel F. Patterson, Jenny Patterson, Polly Patterson, Rebecca Patterson & Hester Patterson, heirs of Samuel Patterson. (Ibid 200)

PATTERSON, Wm.
Died before 3 June 1867 when Jesse Stafford was appointed guardian to Eliza Ann Patterson, Charles Patterson, John Patterson & Martha B. Patterson, minor heirs, with W. F. Nichols as security. (Sev TN, Co Ct Min, no#/454)

PATTISON, Abijah
4 February 1867 John Kerr was appointed guardian with David Mitchell as security. (Sev TN, Co Ct Min, no#/428)

PATTON, Alexander
Died before 12 July 1847 as shown in the suit of Sarah Dulaney Drake vs Martin Cartmell [Cartwell]. Alexander left his widow, Sarah Jane, and Alexander Patton and Rachael Patton his minor children. (Mad TN, Ch Ct Min, 1/20)

PATTON, Lynne
Taxes were not collected in District 2 for 1873, "gone." (Dyr TN, Co Ct Min, B/759)

PATTON, Thomas
Died before 28 December 1841 when the administrator, Andrew Erwin, was made a defendant in the suit of Alexander Norton et al vs John Patton and others. (Bed TN, Ch Ct Min, 2/162) In the suit of Alexander Norton & wife & Thomas Patton, a minor vs Jane Patton & others, 1/4 to be laid off to complainants as the 2 shares of Archabald Patton & Daniel Patton & the said Alexander Norton in right of his wife and her ward may take immediate possession of the same. Andrew Erwin was the administrator for Thomas Patton, deceased. (Ibid 218) Another entry was made 28 June 1843 as Alexander Norton & wife & Thomas Patton vs James Patton, John Patton & others and a cross bill by John & William Patton vs A. Norton & others. John & William Patton paid money in 1814 to Patton and Erwin as part purchase of a tract of land as having been purchased by Thomas Patton from Patton & Erwin. The children and heirs of said Thomas Patton have ever since his death recognized this money as a charge against the land. Delaying and asserting the claim of said John & William has been caused by a general understanding by the heirs of Thomas Patton that Jane Patton, the widow of said Thomas, was not to be disturbed during her lifetime. Thomas sold in his lifetime several portions of the land, to wit, to Neely S. Patton, to Jones & Dobbs, to Vanoy, to Jonathan Webster. The rest of the land is to be sold and pay off the lien of John & William Patton. Jane is to have her dower out of the money left, to be refunded at her death to be divided between the heirs of Thomas Patton, being 8 in number. Thomas Patton is to have 2 shares, the share of his ancestor, Archibald Patton, and the share of Daniel Patton which was purchased by Archibald in his lifetime from said Daniel. Complainant Alexander and his wife, Jane C. W. are entitled to 1/3 of 1/9. The widow & child of Archibald were mentioned. (Ibid 256) Mrs. Jane Patton was chargeable with the rents & profits of 91 acres for the years 1831 through 1843. The widow of Archabald Patton was chargeable with rent on 18 acres for 2 years. John Patton was chargeable with rent for 1839-1843, which should have been from 1829 to 1843. Archabald Patton enjoyed the rents of the whole plantation for 1828 & 1829. William Patton purchased part of the land. Neely S. Patton was mentioned. (Ibid 265-8) A report was made 26 February 1845. It appears that Jane C. W. Patton married Alexander Norton. (Ibid 341-7)

PATTY, Nancy
Died before 4 January 1858 when John H. Murphy was paid out of the poor tax for her coffin. (Sev TN, Co Ct Min, no#/235)

PAUL, Audley, Sr.
Died before 15 July 1811 when John Walker & Peggy his wife, Coffield Taylor & Rebecca his wife, Asher Defries & Eliza his wife, John Paul & James Paul, heirs & legatees of Audley Paul, Sr., deceased, deeded land to Audley Paul, Jr. The land was in Scott County, KY. A deed from same to same for land in Fail? County, MD. (Roa TN, Co Ct Min, D/306)

PAVELY, John
Died before 27 May 1782 when the will was proved by Cha. Dodson & Lewis Pavely. (Was TN, Co Ct Min, 1/158)

PAXTON, Betsy
9 September 1830, with Eliza Barclay, gave power of attorney to Elihu Barclay to sell their interest & claim to land in Augusta County, VA. Eliza Barclay was examined apart from her husband. (McM TN, Co Ct Min, 2no#/477)

PAYN, William
Died before 5 November 1783 when the executor, Thomas Payn, was allowed thirty three pounds, one shilling & eight pence against the estate of Daniell Payn, orphan. Thomas Pain was on the jury. (Was TN, Co Ct Min, 1/230)

PAYNE, B.
6 Novmeber 1871 was chosen and appointed guardian of William H. Payne, his own son. (Dyr TN, Co Ct Min, B/313)

PAYNE, Burton P.
Married before 8 September 1874 to Burdetta Shelton, widow of Watson Shelton, deceased. (Dyr TN, Co Ct Min, B/785)

PAYNE, John, Sr.
Died before 6 April 1807 when the will was proved by Moses Beason & Edward Brewer. Josiah Payne, the surviving executor, qualified. (Rob TN, Co Ct Min, 1/436)

PAYNE, Ledford
Was a resident of KY 5 October 1808 when a deposition was to be taken for the defendant in the case of Joseph Dorris vs Thomas Appleton. (Rob TN, Co Ct Min, 2/90)

PAYNE, T. N.
Taxes were not collected in District 2 for 1873, "Gibson Co." (Dyr TN, Co Ct Min, B/758)

PAYTON, Ephraim
Was a resident of Washington County, KY, 25 August 1807 when he gave power of attorney to John Payton of Sumner County, TN, to handle all his land business in TN. Registered in Sumner County in 1808 & registered in Wilson County in 1824. (Wil TN, Reg Bk/322)

PAYTON, John Whitson
Was bound at the November term 1788 to Ezekiel Abell until age 21, he being 17 years next April, to learn the Art & Trade of a Blacksmith. (Was TN, Co Ct Min, no#/20)

PAYTON, William
Died before 24 December 1804 when Joseph Payton the administrator, reported the sale of the goods & chattles. (Wil TN, Co Ct Min, no#/99)

PEACOCK, David
Died before 4 July 1870 when E. A. Dunavant was paid for his coffin. (Dyr TN, Co Ct Min, B/73) A. R. McKnight made a settlement as administrator. (Ibid 162)

PEARCE, Burt
Taxes were not collected in District 4 for 1873, "run away." (Dyr TN, Co Ct Min, B/759)

PEARCE, J. H.
Died before 4 January 1871 when B. S. Thomas made a settlement as administrator. (Dyr TN, Co Ct Min, B/162)

PEARCE, Riley
Died before 3 April 1871 when W. N. Beasley was paid for holding an inquest over his body, furnishing coffin, &c. (Dyr TN, Co Ct Min, B/209)

PEARSON, George
Died before 6 September 1824 when his will was proved by William Weaver & Robert W. McCleary, witnesses. James Armstrong & Alla Pearson were executors. (McM TN, Co Ct Min, 2no#/18)

PEARSON, William
Died before 25 August 1845 as shown in the suit of George Simmons vs Kindred

Pearson, Jr. & Kindred Pearson, Sr. It was stated that Kindred Pearson had an interest in the estate of William Pearson, deceased, and now in the house of Kindred Pearson, Sr. (Bed TN, Ch Ct Min, 2/359)

PEEL, Joel
Died before 6 February 1871 when I. A. Nunn renewed his bond as guardian of the minor heirs. (Dyr TN, Co Ct Min, B/187) I. A. Nunn made a settlement as guardian of Robert Peel and Julia Peel. (Ibid 190)

PEERY
5 December 1871 a suit was entered by Robert Perry, et als vs Lavinia Jones, et als. It states that complainant Ann Hamilton has separated from her husband, Alex Hamilton. The proceeds from the sale of the estate of John Peery that are due to Mrs. Hamilton as the sister of John Peery, be paid to her in person. Land that had been sold in November 1869 in this cause was mentioned. (Dyr TN, Co Ct Min, B/329) Another entry shows Lavinia James. (Ibid 357)

PEERY, John [Pury]
Was reported to have removed from this state when his handwriting was proved as witness to a deed from Isaac Brunson to Nathan Ross, 2 February 1813. (Ste TN, Co Ct Min, 4/11)

PEN, Fleming [Peu]
Charged as being the father of a bastard child by Peggy Henderson. He gave bond for its maintenance 5 September 1827 with James Grigg & John Pen, Sr. his security. (McM TN, Co Ct Min, 2no#/239)

PENINGTON, Timothy
With his wife, Susanah, was an inhabitant of Barran County, KY, 19 November 1814 when their depositions were to be taken for the suit of Stephen and Mary Haynes, heirs of John Tucker, deceased, vs Joseph & Jane Ingleman, Enoch Tucker, Henry Tucker, James & Phoeba McFarland, Sarah Cagun [Eagun], John & Hannah Deamar, James B. & Nancy Nelson & Riggs Tucker by his guardian Henry Johnson. (Rob TN, Co Ct Min, 3/522)

PENNINGTON, Isaac
Died before June term 1804 when the heirs were listed on the non-resident tax list, with land on Spencers Creek. (Wil TN, Co Ct Min, no#/84)

PENNUEL, Hardy
Died before 16 September 1817 when the will was proved by Joshua Lester & Shadrach Smith. (Wil TN, Co Ct Min, no#/157)

PEPKIN, Lewis
21 July 1800 was appointed guardian to his own children, with Hugh Henry & Wm. Johnson as his security. (Rob TN, Co Ct Min, 1/141)

PERKERSON, Peter
Died before 17 May 1796 when Joseph Green made a settlement as administrator. (Was TN, Co Ct Min, 1/604) John Carter was allowed to administer the estate of Peter Perkinson on the resignation of Joseph Greer, the former administrator. (Ibid 611)

PERRY
3 July 1872 James H. Perry made a settlement as guardian of F. P. Perry and Adelade Perry. On the same date James H. Perry made a settlement as guardian of the heirs of Noah Perry. (Dyr TN, Co Ct Min, B/442) 1 December 1873 James H. Perry made a guardian settlement for Frank P. Perry (final), Adalade Perry and Noah Perry's heirs. (Ibid 667)

PERRY, Drewry
Died before 19 March 1817 when the administrator, George Smith, was ordered to make a report. (Wil TN, Co Ct Min, no#/91)

PERRY, J. S.
Taxes were not collected in District 4 for 1873, "run away." (Dyr TN, Co Ct Min, B/759)

PERRY, N. T.
3 January 1872 was released from working on public roads as he is unable to perform manual labor. (Dyr TN, Co Ct Min, B/348)

PERRY, Noah
Died before 7 November 1870 when James H. Perry renewed his bond as guardian of the minor heirs. (Dyr TN, Co Ct Min, B/125)

PERRY, Wm.
4 July 1808 Roundtree & Norfleet Perry, two of the sons of Wm. Perry, came into Court and made choice of Wm. Perry as their guardian, for receiving their legacy left them by Hardy Hunter. Wm. Benson & John Coleman were security for Wm. Perry. (Rob TN, Co Ct Min, 2/45)

PERRYMAN, J. D.
Taxes were not collected in district 4 for 1873, "run away." (Dyr TN, Co Ct Min, B/759)

PERRYMAN, James A.
Died before 15 August 1815 when William Condray returned an inventory of the estate. (Cla TN, Co Ct Min, 4/108) William Condray and Isaac Cloud were executors. (Ibid 126)

PERSIBLE, Tom
Taxes were not collected in District 2 for 1873, "gone." (Dyr TN, Co Ct Min, B/759)

PERSONS, Thomas
Died before 8 February 1813 when the heirs were released from paying double tax for 1811 & 1812. (Rob TN, Co Ct Min, 3/187)

PETERS, Richd. H.
Died before 16 July 1851 as shown in the petition of Jno. W. Peters, guardian of Jas. H. Peters & Richd. H. Peters, minor heirs. Richd. H. Peters had conveyed in his lifetime property to Theaphalus W. Pullam, in trust, for the support of Emeline W. Peters, wife of said Richd. & at her death to their children. Pullam resigned his tursteeship and in August 1845 Jas. L. Talbot was appointed trustee. Richd. H. Peters died in Lowdues? County, MS. Jno. W. Peters was appointed guardian in the state of MS. Emily W. Peters has since married Alex. J. Fergerson. (Mad TN, Ch Ct Min, 1/225)

PETERS, William   [Paters, Poters]
Died before 22 September 1807 when Samuel C. Hall & William Brown were appointed administrators, with Edward Scott & John Brown as security. (Roa TN, Co Ct Min, B/340) The administrators were ordered to expose to sale the wearing apparel of the deceased. (Ibid 202) 17 January 1810 only Wm. Brown was shown as administrator. (Ibid D/185)

PETTIT, Neamiah
Died before 6 December 1830 when his widow, Susannah Pettit, petitioned for dower. (McM TN, Co Ct Min, 2no#/483)

PETTY
1 January 1866 J. C. Douglass was appointed guardian to Martha Petty and Sarah Petty, with John Adcock as security. (Sev TN, Co Ct Min, no#/255)

PHARIS, James
Died before 10 February 1855 when his death was suggested in the suit of James Pharis vs Leroy B. Settle & W. W. Woodfolk. (Jac TN, Ch Ct Min, B/226) Various entries show that James Pharis left the following family: His widow was Mary Jane Pharis. His children were,1. Jane Pharis who married Littleton C. Collier, 2. Hannah Pharis who married Robert Wade, 3. Milly Pharis who married Hampton Wade, 4. Charlotte Pharis who married George Stout, 5. Sally Pharis who married Alexander Gettings [Gittings], 6. Mariah Pharis who married a McNabb, 7. Fanny Pharis who married James Madison Wolf, 8. Malinda Pharis who married Christopher Clark, 9. Isham Pharis, 10. Shelby Pharis, Sr, 11. Lincoln Pharis, 12. Alse Pharis, 13. Ceberry [Seabury] Pharis, 14. Rozena [Rosina] Pharis. The last four named were minors in 1859. Sally Ann Harris, widow of Wiley Harris, may have been a daughter or she may have been the same as Sally who married Alexander Gittings. The son, Isham Pharis, died before 12 February 1859 and left children, Shelby Pharis, Jr., Warren Pharis, Francis Marion Pharis, Sampson Pharis, James Pharis, William Pharis, Jane Pharis, Elizabeth Pharis and Martha Pharis, all but the first two of whom were minors. Other names mentioned in these cases were James Draper, William R. Kinnon, Dudley Brown, B. B. Washburn and Thomas H. Butler. Shelby Pharis and Christopher & Malinda Clark were non-residents. (Ibid C/39, 110, 153, 198, 255, 264, 297, 312, 331, 378) Mariah McKnabb married John Keith before 14 August 1860. (Ibid 384) In a listing 14 August 1860 it appears that the child Alse Pharis was shown as Adeline Pharis. An addition to the suit was Walker Pharis & James Pharis by their guardian Terrel Byrne. Land was sold. (Ibid 391-4, & 429)

PHARIS, Mary
9 February 1860, in the suit by Mary Pharis vs Hugh Pharis for divorce, it is stated, "It appearing to the Court that complainant and defendant since this bill was filed have had an amicable adjustment of their difficulties & are now living together & complainant desires to dismiss her bill." The word "Recinded" is written accross this item so they evidently didn't adjust their difficulties. (Jac TN, Ch Ct Min, C/304)

PHARIS, William
Died in 1836 leaving one infant child, Elizabeth, who has married James Vinson, as shown in the suit of William Lambert & wife vs James Pharis et al. James Pharis was the executor. Elizabeth Lambert is a minor and sole legatee of said estate and is entitled to an account. (Jac TN, Ch Ct Min, A/428)

PHARRIS, James
Died before 10 February 1859 as shown in the suit of Absolem Pharris & Elizabeth Pharris admr. of James Pharris decd. vs John V. Minor. (Jac TN, Ch Ct Min, C/178) 10 August 1860 Elizabeth Pharris resigned as administrator of James Pharis, deceased, and now Absolem Pharris is sole administrator. Elizabeth Pharris was appointed guardian for Amanda, Hiram, Lewis, Jane & Matilda Pharris, minor children of James Pharris, deceased. Littleton C. Hall was appointed guardian ad litem for the minors. (Ibid 377) This suit was shown as Absolum Pharis & Elizabeth Pharis vs John V. Minor, Hiram Minor, Amanda Pharis et als. The court decided the lands mentioned were the lands of Hiram Minor, Sr. The house standing upon the land is the partnership property of James Pharis, deceased, and John V. Minor and that same should be sold. (Ibid 406) Another listing showed Absolum Pharis, administrator of James Pharis, deceased, vs Joel W. Settle, Emsley Wellmore, Elizabeth Pharris, Amanda Pharris, Hyram Pharris, Lewis Pharris, Jane Pharris, Matilda Pharris, William Gore and L. C. Hall, guardian ad litem for the minor defts. On the oaths of Denton Moore & L. R. Lawson the court decided that Mrs. Elizabeth Pharris has five children and there are only four negros and they cannot be divided. The slaves are to be sold. (Ibid 409)

PHIFFS, Lambert
Taxes were not collected in District 2 for 1873, "gone." (Dyr TN, Co Ct Min, B/759)

PHILIPS, Philip
Died before July term 1798 when Michl. Campbell & Andw. Hinds, executors of Philip Philips, deceased, were in a suit against Joseph Dorris. (Rob TN, Co Ct Min, 1/72)

PHILLIPS, Abner
Died before 4 December 1867 as shown in the suit of Larson [Lonson] Bush Admr. vs the widow, heirs & creditors of A. Phillips decd. The widow was Buly Ann Phillips. Abner Phillips had land in Fentress, Morgan & Scott Counties. John I. Northrup, Anderson Tinch & David Conatser were appointed to lay off the widow's dower. (Fen TN, Ch Ct Min, A/347) Dower was laid off and plat shown. An account of the estate was made. (Ibid 373-7)

PHILLIPS, Azwell
Died before 18 June 1816 when the will was proved by John Hannah & Andrew Feaney. John P. Byrn & Stephen W. Byrn were executors. (Wil TN, Co Ct Min, no#/12)

PHILLIPS, Henry H.
Died before 5 August 1872 in the State of MO, intestate, leaving effects in Dyer County. J. A. Phillips was appointed administrator, with W. C. Doyle as his security. (Dyr TN, Co Ct Min, B/449) 8 October 1873 Mary A. Phillips was appointed guardian of William A. Phillips and Florence Phillips, minor heirs of H. H. Phillips, deceased, with P. S. Taylor and J. C. Miller as her security. (Ibid 650) T. Griffin, H. F. Ferguson and W. M. Watkins were appointed to lay off a years provisions for the widow and her 2 little children, the family of H. H. Phillips, deceased. (Ibid 652)

PHILLIPS, Payton
Was granted a divorce from Cynthia Phillips 17 July 1858 for adultry. They had lived apart for ten years. (Jac TN, Ch Ct Min, C/170)

PHILLIPS, Peter, Sr.
Died before 12 March 1805 when the will was proved by Absolom Fentriss. (Ste TN, Co Ct Min, 1/16) Peter Phillips, Jr. was executor. (Ibid 11b)

PHILLIPS, Z. B.
Died before 8 January 1873 when some land was sold that was bounded by the land of Phillips' heirs. (Dyr TN, Co Ct Min, B/536)

PICKENS, John
Died before 3 May 1814 when James H. Russell was appointed administrator with William M. Cooley & John Allen as security. (Ste TN, Co Ct Min, 4/141)

PICKENS, Mary Jane
Died before 6 March 1871. A committee was appointed to lay off a years provisions for her children. (Dyr TN, Co Ct Min, B/199) T. G. Jones was appointed administrator. (Ibid 201)

PICKENS, Samuel
Died before 3 February 1862 when Saml. W. Randles & Joseph M. Hodges were appointed administrators with the will annexed for the estate of Edmond Hodges, deceased, in place of Samuel Pickens, deceased, the former administrator. (Sev TN, Co Ct Min, no#/746) James A. Pickens and Robt. Pickins were appointed administrators with Thomas Pickins, S. W. Pickins, J. P. Pickins, Jas. D. Davis, Labon Jenkins & O. Lawson as security. (Ibid 748)

PICKENS, W. T.
Was an orphan boy about 12 years old when he was bound 4 November 1872 to H. R. A. McCorkle until age 21. (Dyr TN, Co Ct Min, B/506)

PICKERING, Jacob
Died before 13 August 1811 as shown in the case of Jacob Pickering vs John Jones & Co. (Rob TN, Co Ct Min, 3/10)

PICKET, Edward, Jr.
Was the father of a bastard child by Elizabeth Campbell. He was ordered to pay support 18 June 1817. (Wil TN, Co Ct Min, no#/123)

PICKINS, John
Died before 5 June 1828 when his administrators were in a suit vs Jackson & McConnell & William Canseller, assignee. (McM TN, Co Ct Min, no#/340) 3 December 1827 Jackson Smith, Robert McCleary & Henry Bradford were appointed to lay off a years provision for Nancy, widow of John Pickins, Sr., deceased. (Ibid 2no#/243) Nancy Pickins, Robert Pickens & Reese Pickens were appointed administrators. (Ibid 244) 1 December 1828 Nancy Pickins & George Bowman were appointed guardian for Andrew Pickins, William K. Pickins, Charles A. Pickins, Rebecka Pickins, Nancy Pickins & Martha Pickins, minor orphans [does not say of John, deceased] Each of the children are of an age to choose a guardian & they chose Nancy Pickins & George Bowman. (Ibid 322)

PICKINS, T. R.
Died before 3 March 1873 when H. R. A. McCorkle made a final settlement as administrator. (Dyr TN, Co Ct Min, B/548)

PICKLE, Amos
1 April 1861 was appointed guardian to William C. & Margaret Jane Pickle, with Andrew Henderson as security. (Sev TN, Co Ct Min, no#/670) 6 August 1866 Amos Pickle made a settlement as guardian of the minor heirs of Amos & Dicy Pickle. (Ibid 359)

PIERCE, J. S.
Died before 1 August 1870 when W. M. Watkins made a settlement as administrator. (Dyr TN, Co Ct Min, B/94) A settlement was made by the administrator of J. Sam Pierce. (Ibid 326)

PIERCE, J. W.
Died before 5 July 1870 when the administrator, W. H. Mathews, returned an inventory of the estate. (Dyr TN, Co Ct Min, B/82)

PIERCE, John M.
4 December 1871 a settlement was made by Geo. W. Pierce as guardian. (Dyr TN, Co Ct Min, B/326)

PIERCE, Joseph [Pearce]
Died befopre 22 June 1838 when his death was suggested in the suit of Joseph Pierce vs

Robert J. Rivers. The suit was revived in the names of James H. Moran & William Jones, administrators. (Obi TN, Cir Ct Min, 3/226)

PIERCE, W. F.
Died before 4 October 1871 when J. W. Hine was chosen and appointed guardian of Sallie Pierce, Albert Pierce and Marg Pierce, minor heirs. (Dyr TN, Co Ct Min, B/310)

PIERCY, Joshua
Was a resident of Pasquotank County, NC, 17 May 1828 when he gave power of attorney to Ewing Wilson of Wilson County, TN, to receive any land warrents in TN in his name or in the name of Christian Piercy, he being the heir of said Piercy. (Wil TN, Reg Bk/402) [second set of page numbers]

PILLOW, Gideon
Died before 21 February 1838 when land was taxed to the heirs. (Obi TN, Cir Ct Min, 3/163)

PINER
6 May 1783 Edmund Williams was appointed guardian of (blank) Piner, orphan of (blank) Piner. (Was TN, Co Ct Min, 1/210)

PINGLETON, G. W.
Taxes were not collected in District 4 for 1873, "run away." (Dyr TN, Co Ct Min, B/759)

PINKLEY, John
Died before 19 January 1801 when Peter Pinkley was appointed administrator with Anderson Cheatham & Matthew Day as security. (Rob TN, Co Ct Min, 1/158)

PINSON
Larkin and John Pinson were minors 5 July 1808 when they made choice of John Brooks as their guardian, with John Huddleston & Jacob Pinkley as security. (Rob TN, Co Ct Min, 2/47)

PINSON, John B.
Died before 3 May 1841 as shown in the suit of Farwick Frazer & Sarah Cooper vs James Mullins, Executor of John B. Pinson. The complainants were security, with John B. Cooper, on a note from Abraham Cooper to Sterling Goodman. Goodman sold the note to John B. Pinson who was a note shaver. Abraham Cooper has left the county. The executor of John B. Penson has brought suit against the securities of Abram Cooper for the note. (Bed TN, Ch Ct Min, 1/455)

PIPKINS, Mary E.
25 February 1861 entered a suit by her next friend vs Geo. Williamson & Hughs Pipkin. Some suitable person is to be appointed trustee for Mary. She had married Hughes Pipkin 27 Sept 1855 and her husband is an imprudent and bad manager, is largely indebted and has no means out of which to pay the same. N. W. Steadman, father of Mary E. Pipkins, died in December 1859 after making his will, by which he bequeathed Mary a negro girl named Kit, for said Mary E. & her children for their separate use and benefit. The estate has been settled up. William R. Williamson was appointed trustee for Mary E. Pipkins & children. Geo. Williamson was probably the executor for the will of N. W. Steadman. (Mad TN, Ch Ct Min, 2/461)

PIPPIN, Francis
Was a boy aged 16 years when he was bound to Nicholas Mansfield for 3 years & six months, 21 April 1812. (Roa TN, Co Ct Min, D/379)

PLUMMER, William
Died before 5 January 1809 when Plummer Willis was appointed administrator, with James Sawyers & Henry Johnson as security. (Rob TN, Co Ct Min, 2/104)

POINDEXTER
In the suit of Jno. V. McFarland et als vs Mary O. Poindexter et als, 15 August 1868, the defendants, Mary O. Poindexter, Robt. D. Poindexter & Hillary Poindexter, are minors. William McFarland was appointed guardian ad litem. (Mad TN, Ch Ct Min, 3/191)

POLK, Alexander F.
Died before 21 February 1839 when his death was admitted in the suit of Thomas P. Hoops, William B. Wolf & Abram Baker vs Thomas A. Polk, John M. Crockett, Alexander F. Polk & George Polk. (Obi TN, Cir Ct Min, 3/308)

POLK, John
On 14 May 1834 took the oath to become a citizen of the United States. He was born in the Kingdom of Ireland, a part of the dominion of the King of England. He came to this country when but a boy with his father who came to South Carolina & he believes that it was antecedent to the 29th of January, 1795. He has been a resident of America since that time and a resident of Obion County for three years. He was not of any of the orders of nobility or priviliged classes and has no titles in that respect. He was granted citizenship. (Obi TN, Cir Ct Min, 2/182)

POLK, John
Died before 22 June 1838 when his death was suggested in the suit of John Polk vs Alex Faris. (Obi TN, Cir Ct Min, 3/229) Thomas A. Porter was executor. (Ibid 291) 23 June 1843 the executor was shown as Thomas A. Polk. (Ibid 4/no#)

POLK, John
Died before 6 August 1805 when Martha Polk, William Polk & John Campbell were appointed administrators, with Thomas Polk & Joseph Wimberley as security. (Rob TN, Co Ct Min, 1/354) The court ordered the administrator to sell enough of the estate to satisfy the claim of Maria Harris, daughter of the administratrix by a former marriage. The rest is to be divided between Martha Polk, the relic of the deceased, & Olivia Polk, daughter of the deceased. (Ibid 363) 5 January 1808 the administrator of Jno. Polk "delivered into Court an Account Current of the Estate of Edmund Kearney Harris from York District in SC." (Ibid 2/4)

POLK, Thomas
Died before 14 November 1814 when Joshua Gardner was appointed administrator, with Elias Laurence & James Gardner as security. (Rob TN, Co Ct Min, 3/490) A years provision was ordered laid off for the widow, Claricy Polk, by John Gardner, Elias Laurence & Elias Ford. (Ibid 511)

POLK, Thos. A.
Was a resident of GA, Obia? County, when he was to be summoned 14 November 1844 for the suit of Porter & Neal against him. (Obi TN, Cir Ct Min, 4/no#)

POLK, William
Died before 21 February 1839 when land was taxed to the heirs. (Obi TN, Cir Ct Min, 3/300)

POOL, George
Died before 4 August 1806 when the executrix was ordered to sell the personal property. (Rob TN, Co Ct Min, 1/396) The will was proved by Martin Walton, Miller Dorris, David Jones & Nathan Frizel. Chloe Pool was executrix. (Ibid 398)

POOL, Henry P.
Was a resident of Dinwiddie County, VA, 5 July 1809 when his deposition was to be taken for the defendant in the case of Benjn. Wells vs Wm. Roachel. (Rob TN, Co Ct Min, 2/153)

POOR
4 December 1866 in the suit of William Poor Admr. &c vs J. O. Poor & others, it was stated that both complainant and defendant were dead. (Fen TN, Ch Ct Min, A/313) J. M. Frogg is administrator of J. O. Poor, deceased, and J. W. Wright is administrator of William Poor, deceased, & administrator de bonus non of Moses Poor, deceased. (Ibid 336) John W. Frogg is administrator of Jeremiah Poor, deceased. (Ibid 390)

POOR, Moses
Died before 8 October 1860 as shown in the suit of Wm. Poor Administrator of Moses Poor vs Jeremiah O. Poor et als. Complainant was appointed administrator in 1859. A report is to be made as to the advancements made to the heirs. (Fen TN, Ch Ct Min, A/240) In the suit of Mary Beason by next friend A. B. Bledsoe vs Wm. Poor & others it was stated that Moses Poor, who died some time last year, was the father of complainant. William Poor, one of the children of Moses, was administrator. James H. Beason is the husband of complainant & has no property and is in debt. Complainant has several children and she asks a settlement of the property due her from the estate of her father for the benefit of her and her children, free and clear from the claims of her husband. A. Bledsoe, Esquire, was appointed trustee for this purpose. (Ibid 255) Henry R. Poor, Sarah Mordock and Jeremiah O. Poor were allowed money from the estate for their trouble and attention to Moses Poor in his last sickness. Advancement had been made in the lifetime of Moses Poor to the following heirs: William Poor, Jeremiah O. Poor, Henry R. Poor, Sarah

Moordock, James Poor, James H. Beason & wife, R. Murphy & wife, Stokley Evans & wife, J. C. Jackson & wife and S. C. Poor. (Ibid 270)

POPE, J. W. R.
He and his wife, Mary M. Pope, were parents of an infant child, Marmian S. Pope. Thomas Clark was appointed guardian ad litem of the infant to defend with the parents the suit of D. H. C. Spence, Susan E. Spence & Sarah Ann Spence, 25 August 1860. (Mad TN, Ch Ct Min, 2/368)

POPE, Lazarus
Died before 26 June 1805 when Zebulon Baird, Jr. was granted letters of administration with Nathl. Perry as security. (Wil TN, Co Ct Min, no#/130)

PORBATE, Robert C.
Sold land in Craven County, NC, to Charles H. Pickring & John T. Pickring, 15 February 1810. (Rob TN, Co Ct Min, 2/224)

PORTER, James M.
Died before 20 February 1839 when his death was suggested in the suit of James M. Porter assignee &c vs Thomas A. Porter Executor of Jno. Polk Decd. The suit was revived in the names of Daniel St. John & Jacob Long, his administrators. (Obi TN, Cir Ct Min, 3/291)

PORTER, Scott
2 May 1859 T. C. Brobson made a settlement as guardian. (Sev TN, Co Ct Min, no#/441)

PORTER, Thomas D.
Died before 21 February 1839 when land was taxed to the heirs. (Obi TN, Cir Ct Min, 3/299)

PORTER, William M.
Died before 14 July 1855 when his death was suggested in the suit of Porter & Chaffin Admrs. &c vs Leroy B. Settle. (Jac TN, Ch Ct Min, B/267) In the suit of Rutha Porter vs John Porter & others, Rutha petitions for dower. She is the widow of William Porter, deceased. W. H. Botts was guardian of the minor defendants. (Ibid 273) Fox Chaffin was administrator. (Ibid 296)

POSTEN, W. G.
Died before 5 April 1870 when a settlement was made by William L. Poston as guardian of the minor heirs. (Dyr TN, Co Ct Min, B/42)

POSTLE
13 May 1788 "Two Indentures Between Henry Oldham and the Chairman of this Court on Behalf of John Postle and Abel Postle Was Duly perfected in open Court and the Counter parts Returned agreeable to Law." (Was TN, Co Ct Min, 1/327)

POSTON, W. F.
6 February 1871 was certified to be a young man of good moral character and steady sober habits and is 21 years of age, preparatory to obtaining a license to practice law. (Dyr TN, Co Ct Min, B/186)

POTTER, John
Died before 18 March 1807 when the will was proved on the oath of John Payne and Absolom Potter. Nicholas Nail and Thomas Gallaher were executors. (Roa TN, Co Ct Min, B/279)

POTTER, John
Died before May term 1790 when the will was proved by William Moreland and John Grindstaff. Hannah Potter, Cornelius Bowman and Thomas Whitson were executors. (Was TN, Co Ct Min, 1/437)

POTTER, John A.
Died 2 June 1843 as shown when Joshua Wallace was charged on 21 June 1843 with his murder. He was shot with a double barreled shot gun in the belly and died instantly. Lewis Potter was the prosecuter and James Mills, John C. Outlaw, Sr., Cage Hale and Bennet Marshall were witnesses. Gilbert Keesee was also charged with the same murder. (Obi TN, Cir Ct Min, 4/no#)

POTTER, William
Was the father of James Potter of Livingston, AL, as shown in the suit of Alexander Ray vs William Potter, 1844. (Bed TN, Ch Ct Min, 3/274)

POTTERS, Alexander
Died before 13 January 1847 as shown in the suit of Sarah D. Drake vs Martin Castinel & others. The defendants were minor heirs of Alexander Potters. One of the minors, also named Alexander Potters, was deceased. A guardian was to be named for the minor heirs. (Mad TN, Ch Ct Min, 1/8)

POTTS, John
Was a resident of Tryon County [NC] 23 November 1778 when his deposition was to be taken for the suit of John McNabb vs Wm. Taylor. (Was TN, Co Ct Min, 1/49)

POUEL, Robert [Pouell, Powel]
Died before 27 August 1842 as shown in the suit of Mary L. Pouel vs Thomas P. Pouel and his two sons, Robert James Pouel and Richard Henry Pouel. Mary stated that she with her husband, Robert Pouel, about 15 years ago removed to Bedford County, TN, from Sussex County, VA, where she had lived on land she had inherited from her father. Her husband convinced her to let him sell her property and that in return he would convey slaves to her as her separate property, which was done. After they had been living in Bedford County 6 or 7 years, their son Thomas P. Pouel, came out from VA and settled in the same neighborhood. He demanded that she give him the conveyance for the slaves and when she refused, he took it from her by violence. A year or two after this occurance, her husband having become intemperate in his habits and easily flattered, the said Thomas P. executed an instrument as a deed of gift by which her husband gave the slaves and all their increase to his said son, Thomas P., and his two grand sons, Robert James and Richard Henry, sons of said Thomas P. Pouel. The deed of gift was to take effect at the death of said Robert Poule, said instrument dated 25 March 1836. Mary has been told the instrument is in fact a will. A few weeks ago her husband died and Thomas P. took possession of the slaves. Robert Pouel also had a son named Seymore R. and a daughter Elizabeth H. Whitaker. In his answer Thomas P. denied that the land in VA had belonged to his mother. She did have a so called conveyance of slaves from Robert Pouel but his father claimed he had never made one and it was not in his handwriting. Thomas P. was the administrator of Robert Pouel. The will of Seymore Robinson is entered, apparently by Thomas P., to prove that his mother did not inherit land from her father for her own and separate use. Seymore Robinson was from the parish of Albermarle and County of Sussex [VA]. He made bequests to his wife, Elizabeth, of all his property during her life or widowhood. To his unborn child, if a boy land, if a girl the land is to be sold and the proceeds divided between all my daughters. Monies are to be put at interest until his youngest child arrives to age 21 or marries. The will was dated 1780. Another exhibit in the suit was a deed of gift from Mary L. Pouell to her daughter, Elizabeth H. Porter. This was dated 9 August 1842. Thomas P. must have lost the case as he filed an appeal to the Supreme Court in Nashville in December 1846. Mary is to get the slaves. (Bed TN, Ch Ct Min, 3/324-340)

POWELL, Elizabeth
Died before 6 June 1870 when W. F. Powell made a settlement as administrator. (Dyr TN, Co Ct Min, B/64)

POWELL, Exum
Died before 15 February 1815 when Willie Powell was appointed administrator, with Sampson Matthews and Daniel Gier as security. (Rob TN, Co Ct Min, 3/549)

POWELL, Levin
Died before 9 November 1812 when the heirs were exhonerated from paying double tax on 640 acres. (Rob TN, Co Ct Min, 3/135)

POWELL, Robert
Died before 30 August 1844 as shown in the suit of Thomas P. Powell vs Thomas C. Whiteside & James Mullens. It was stated that the slaves levied on were the property of the estate of Robert Powell, deceased. (Bed TN, Ch Ct Min, 2/308) Robert Powell died in the summer of 1842. Thomas P. Powell was his son and administrator. Robert had made a deed of gift to his son of some negroes & Thomas claims they are his own property and do not belong to the estate of his father. (Ibid 3/210)

POWELL, Roberta
Died before 3 November 1873 as shown in a settlement of a Bradshaw estate, from which Roberta had a share. Her share went to her children, W. R. Powell, James F. Powell, C. L.

F. Powell, Seymore Powell, Elizabeth Powell, all minors. Roberta was the wife of R. P. Powell. (Dyr TN, Co Ct Min, B/661) 4 May 1874 R. P. Powell was appointed guardian of Richard, Seymour, Bettie and Lee Powell, minor heirs of his deceased wife, Roberta Powell, formerly Bradshaw. W. T. Powell and D. M. Boone were securities. (Ibid 736)

POWERS, Ephraim, Sr.
Died before 2 December 1872 when his will was proved by Thomas D. Harwell and Timothy Griffin, witnesses. Ephraim Powers, Jr. was executor. (Dyr TN, Co Ct Min, B/513)

POWERS, James
Died before 4 August 1818 when the executors, Wm. Biggs & Jesse Cherry, sold land in Sumner County, proved by Daniel Cherry who also proved the signature of Darling Cherry. (Wil TN, Co Ct Min, no#/304)

PRESLEY, Sanders
Died before 3 May 1842 as shown in the suit of Hezekiah Crowell vs Joseph Jarod, Elizabeth Presley, Coosa M. Presley, Millenninum B. Presley, Arena H. Presley, Dyonysius B. Presley, Sarah J. Presley, Ruth E. Presley & John P. Presley. The complainant had purchased land from Sanders Presley on 24 November 1837. Sanders Presley had purchased the land from defendant, Joseph Jarod. Sanders Presley has died and defendants are his heirs except defendant Jarod. Elizabeth Presley is the widow and was appointed guardian of the minor heirs. Hezekiah Crowell is seeking title to the land. (Jac TN, Ch Ct Min, A/41)

PRESTON, George
Died before 20 June 1808 when James Preston & Jane Preston were appointed administrators, with Joseph Loony, Michael Baker & William Lumkin as security. (Roa TN, Co Ct Min, C/161) Abraham Bogart and Jane Bogart were appointed guardians of James Preston, M___ Preston, Jesse Preston, Jane Preston, Mildre? Preston, Polly Preston & George Preston. [It does not state that they were the children of George Preston] (Ibid D/348)

PREWITT, Moses H.
Died before 26 February 1859. He was the father of Robert E. Prewitt as shown in the case of Robert E. Prewitt et als vs James Prewitt et als. Apparently his other heirs were Benj. T. Harton & wife Mary Jane, Joel Rushing & wife Sarah, James Prewitt, John Wall & wife Harriet, Thomas Prewitt, Lucy Prewitt, Sally Prewitt and William Prewitt. (Mad TN, Ch Ct Min, 2/289)

PRICE
Charles N. Price & James W. Price both died before 12 July 1850 as shown in the suit of Kinnard & Bransford vs Benjamin B. Washburn & John W. Price Admrs. of Charles N. & James Price Decd. and Solomon Price. Solomon Price is the father of Charles N. & James Price, deceased, and is their legal distributee. (Jac TN, Ch Ct Min, A/374) 14 July 1853 a suit was entered by Thompson Cason vs Benjamin B. Washburn Admr. of Newton & James Price, deceased. (Ibid B/76) A suit was entered on 18 July 1856 by Joseph Cowin Guardian &c vs Benjamin B. Washburn, Lafayette Washburn, William R. Kenner, Littleton C. Hall, Holland Denton, George M. McWhirter, William Putty, Russell M. Kinnaird, Watson M. Cooke, Thomas H. Butler, Toliver Kirkpatrick, Robert C. Kirkpatrick, George White & Joel W. Settle. B. B. Washburn is administrator of the estate of Charles N. Price, deceased, and James W. Price, deceased. Kenner & Hall are his securities. He has not settled the estates. Joseph Cowin is the guardian of the children of Wm. H. & Mary A. Sallee (viz) John Sallee, Pleasant Henry Sallee, Corien Ovanda Sallee & Mary Ann Sallee, and as such guardian he had obtained a judgement against B. B. Washburn as administrator. This suit concerns debts connected with the estate and does not appear to involve any heirs. (Ibid C/28)

PRICE
19 March 1852 in the suit of William H. Dewitt & others vs Samuel T. Griffith & others, land was sold to Thomas Price and title divested out of William H. Dewitt & wife Emela, Jackson Perry & wife Sarah R., Jane T. Price, John K. Price, Thomas L. Price, Samuel T. Griffith & wife Nancy & Luke Price. Thomas Price was also appointed trustee for Nancy Griffith, wife of Samuel T. Griffith. (Jac TN, Ch Ct Min, B/26) In the suit of William H. Dewhitt & Jackson Perry et als vs Nancy Price, publication has been made to non-resident defendents Micajah Price, Elizabeth Price, William Price, Emeline Price, Sarah Price, Thomas Price & Erwin Price. Holland Denton was appointed guardian of all the minors, who have no regular guardian. (Ibid 137)

PRICE, Ann
5 November 1783 brought suit against Samuel Tate, "in Case on Marriage Contract." A jury found for the defendant and the plaintiff "has Know Cause of Action." (Was TN, Co Ct Min, 1/230) Benja. Willson & John Griner were allowed 8 days each as witnesses on behalf of Saml. Tate. (Ibid 232) Robert Tate attended 4 days as witness for Saml. Tate. (Ibid 234)

PRICE, Jas.
Died before 21 August 1866 when his death was admitted in the suit of D. C. Hall [Hail] et als vs Jas. Price et als. (Mad TN, Ch Ct Min, 2/503)

PRICE, Jno. G.
In the suit of William B. Marchall & William W. Searcy vs Jno. G. Price, Stephen Burns & Cader Sewell [Jewell], it was stated that Jno. G. Price had absconded from the county leaving personal property and an interest in 62 1/2 acres of land. (Mad TN, Ch Ct Min, 1/274) 18 February 1857 in the suit of G. M. Birdsong vs Jno. C. Birdsong et als, the death of Jno G. Price was suggested & admitted. (Ibid 2/118)

PRICE, John
Taxes were not collected in District 4 for 1873, "insolvent." (Dyr TN, Co Ct Min, B/759)

PRICE, Nathan
Died before 3 May 1842 when the suit of David Griffith Admr. &c vs William Henson was remanded to the rules to make the heirs of Nathan Price defendants. (Jac TN, Ch Ct Min, A/37) The heirs were Campbell B. Price, Susan Price, Thomas K. Price, Patrick Kernel and Elizabeth Kernal and Nancy Price. (Ibid 152)

PRICE, Thomas
Died before 10 February 1855 as shown in the suit of William H. Dewhit & Jackson Perry, admr. of Thomas Price, deceased, and Amelia H. Dewhit wife of said William H., and Sarah R. Perry wife of the said Jackson Perry, William C. Hufhens & wife Jane, Samuel T. Griffith & wife Nancy vs Nancy Price, John K. Price, Thomas L. Price, Elizabeth Price, Evalene, Elizabeth, Thomas, Irvin, Micajah, William & Sarah Price. There was a cross bill by defendant Nancy Price. Land was sold on 27 October 1851 and Thomas Price, the ancestor of complainants, became the purchaser. In October 1852, before the purchase money was paid, said Thomas Price died intestate. It appearing to the Court that said pretended marriage alledged in the amended bill of complainant between Nancy Price & Jonathan Orendine has been procured by force or fraud and without the consent of said Nancy and her subsequent marriage with the intestate, Thomas Price, on the 26 day of August 1840 was legal and valid and she was his lawful widow & entitled to dower. Nancy & Thomas Price had 2 children, to wit, Thomas L. and Elizabeth who are entitled to an equal share with the children of said intestate by his former wife & Luke Price under the will of Luke L. Price exhibited in complainants bill of review. The complainants were granted an appeal to the Supreme Court at Nashville. (Jac TN, Ch Ct Min, B/215-7) A suit was shown 6 February 1857 by Jackson Perry & wife Sarah R. Perry vs William H. Dewitt & wife Emelia H. Dewitt, Thomas L. Price, Elizabeth Price, James W. Draper, Samuel T. Griffith & wife Nancy Griffith, William S. Huffines & wife Talitha Jane Huffins. James W. Draper was guardian of the minor defendants, Thomas L. Price & Elizabeth Price: Bill to sell land. (Ibid C/63) The land in this suit was sold at the late residence of Thomas Price, deceased, and divested out of complainants & defendants. (Ibid 75-8)

PRICHARD, E. J.
Died before 2 May 1870 when F. G. Sampson was appointed administrator, with W. C. Doyle & D. E. Parker as security. (Dyr TN, Co Ct Min, B/50)

PRICHARD, H. E.
Died before 6 March 1871 when N. R. Prichard made a settlement as administrator. (Dyr TN, Co Ct Min, B/201)

PRICHARD, Harriet
Died before 3 March 1873 when B. F. Prichard was chosen and appointed guardian of Benjamin R., Fyonettie H., Frank R., and Bettie Lee Prichard, her minor heirs. N. R. Prichard had resigned as guardian. (Dyr TN, Co Ct Min, B/545)

PRICHARD, J.
Died before 7 April 1873 when Ann R. Prichard was appointed guardian of J. C. Prichard, M. M. Prichard, A. B. Prichard and C. A. Prichard, minor heirs. B. F. Prichard and W. A. Waggoner were security. (Dyr TN, Co Ct Min, B/556)

PRICHARD, Joseph
Died before 9 February 1870 when a years allowance was set apart for Mrs. Joseph Prichard & family, by Danil E. Parker & William A. Wagginer. (Dyr TN, Co Ct Min, B/10) B. F. Prichard was administator. (Ibid 48) The widow, Margaret Prichard, petitioned for dower. Notice was given to James F., Margarette, Joseph, Berryll and Jefferson Prichard, the only heirs of the deceased. (Ibid 542)

PRICHARD, N. R.
6 March 1871 made a settlement as guardian of his own children. (Dyr TN, Co Ct Min, B/200)

PRICHARD, W. T.
Died before 2 May 1870 when F. G. Sampson was appointed administrator, with W. C. Doyle & D. E. Parker as security. (Dyr TN, Co Ct Min, B/50)

PRIMMER, John
Died before 26 February 1794 when an inventory of the estate was returned by the executors. Jacob Smith, Peter Bullinger & Corneluis Bowman were appointed to appraise the estate. (Was TN, Co Ct Min, 1/477)

PROFFET, James
Died before 7 December 1863 when Jesse Stafford was appointed administrator with David Proffet & Emanuel Fox as security. (Sev TN, Co Ct Min, no#/82) Emanuel Fox was appointed guardian of Ann, Jackson, Harrison, Baxter & Margaret Proffett, minor heirs. (Ibid 83)

PROFFIT, Jackson
Died before 7 August 1865 when his will was proved by James McMahan & John Large, witnesses. The witnesses stated the will was signed "in their presents in the Armey." Wm. Benson was appointed administrator with the will annexed. (Sev TN, Co Ct Min, no#/190)

PROUT, Joshua
Was a resident of Madison County, Mississippi Territory, on 7 February 1814 when his signature was proved as witness to a deed of gift from William Lanier to Asa Lanier. (Ste TN, Co Ct Min, 4/84)

PROVINCE, John
Died before 22 November 1808 when John Province, one of the heirs, gave power of attorney to Samuel Harris & Alexander Province, who were also heirs, (there were 7 heirs) to dispose of his part of the lands of John Province. It was witnessed by Wm. Steel & Sam Hogg. (Wil TN, Reg Bk/12) John Henderson of Garrard County, KY, also gave power of attorney to Samuel Harris & Alexander Provine, which states "John Provine died having seven children, and my wife Nancy being one of the seven." Other legatees are: Frances Hall, Alexander Provine, Samuel Harris, William Provine, Polly Provine, Rebecca Provine & John Provine. (Ibid 13) Wm. Provine, Polly Provine & Rebeckah Provine gave power of attorney from Clark County, Indiana Territory, 4 October 1808. (Ibid 15)

PRUIT, Prissilla
8 September 1857 it was ordered that her children, Margaret, Catharine & William, children of colour, be brought to court to be bound out as they are suffering. (Sev TN, Co Ct Min, no#/203)

PRYOR, John
Died before September term 1804 when the heirs were on the non-resident tax list with land on Spencers Creek. (Wil TN, Co Ct Min, no#/87)

PRYOR, William [Prior]
Died about September 1854 as shown in the suit filed 10 February 1855 by Joshua Hale vs Zachareah VanHooser Admr. of William Pryor decd., Dorothy Pryor & Sarah J. Prior & Z. V. Hoozer guardian ad litem for said Sarah J. Pryor. Dorothy was his widow and Sarah J. his only child. Joshua Hale & Zachariah VanHoozer were the administrators. (Jac TN, Ch Ct Min, B/212)

PUCKET, J.
Was a resident of DeKalb County, TN, on 11 July 1850 when a deposition was to be taken for the defendant in the suit of Edward Anderson vs Lewis R. Nance [Vance]. (Jac TN, Ch Ct Min, A/352)

PUCKETT, Benjamin F.
15 January 1851 was in a suit vs William D. Briggance. It was stated that a negro boy was conveyed by Francis Puckett to complainant in trust for the support of the grand children of said Frances, to wit; Jno. R., George W., Mary E. & Joseph F. Puckett and his son Patrick R. Puckett. The conveyance was dated 9 March 1844. Another suit against William H. Jackson & Andrew Stewart for another negro was the same. (Mad TN, Ch Ct Min, 1/182)

PUGH, John
Was a resident of IN 22 September 1821 when he gave power of attorney to David Thomas of Wilson County, TN, to apply for a duplicate land warrant. (Wil TN, Reg Bk/242)

PUGH, Jonathan
Died before 12 May 1788 when the will was proved by David McNabb and Isabella McNabb. Letters testamentary were issued to Coln. Tipton and Susanna Pugh, the Relict of the said Jonathan Pugh, deceased. (Was TN, Co Ct Min, 1/325)

PUGH, Whitmell H. [Pogh]
Died before 18 February 1840 when land was taxed to the heirs. (Obi TN, Cir Ct Min, 4/no#)

PURCELL, Henry T.
3 January 1871 H. S. Fowlkes renewed his bond as guardian. (Dyr TN, Co Ct Min, B/157)

PURSELL, James J.
Was a non-resident 7 February 1851 as shown in the suit of Tandy K. Witcher vs James J. Pursell & Joseph Moss. (Jac TN, Ch Ct Min, A/409)

PUTMAN, Jesse
Died a short time after making his will which was proved in November 1833. The will was entered in the suit of Wakefield, Meeks & others vs Sarah Putman. He appointed his wife, Sarah Putman, and William Cotton as executors. He gave his estate to his wife during her life, one dollar each to his four brothers, Joseph Putman, Jaleb? Putman ___nos Putman [ink blot] and Daniel Putman, to the heirs of William Putman one dollar, to the heirs of James Putman one dollar, to the heirs of Elizabeth Ray one dollar. He listed bequests to be made after the death of his wife; to John W. Meeks; the balance of the estate to Minerva A. Cotton and to Malissa F. Meeks. The will, dated 6 August 1833, was witnessed by Joel Yowel, Thomas Gramer and W. H. Gramer. William J. W. Wakefield & his wife Malissa F. are residents of Lincoln County, TN. John W. Meeks lives in Bedford County. James Cotton & Malissa Cotton are minors who sue by their uncle & next friend John W. Meeks, said James Cotton lives in MS & Malissa Cotton in Bedford County. Defendant Samuel [probably should be Sarah] Putman lives in Bedford County. James Cotton & Malissa Cotton are the only children of Manerva A. Cotton named in said will. Manervia died since November 1833. Complainant Wakefield married Malissa F. Meeks mentioned in said will. No person ever qualified as executor of the will. John Wammock of GA was mentioned. Sarah has threatened to sell all the negroes and go the GA. John Womack was the son of Sarah Putman. [I think it states that complainants are not related to Jesse Putman but are descendants of the children of Sarah Putman by a former marriage.] (Bed TN, Ch Ct Min, 1/93)

PYLAND, J. F.
4 July 1871 Jeremiah Hay made a settlement as guardian of the heirs of J. F. Pyland. [does not say deceased] (Dyr TN, Co Ct Min, B/258)

QUARLES, James
Died before 25 March 1818 when Samuel Quarles, guardian for Sarah W. Quarles of Bedford County, VA, gave power of attorney to Doctor Manson Tregg of Wilson County, TN, to receive any property left to his ward by her father James Quarles, deceased, late of Wilson County. (Wil TN, Reg Bk/103) Maria Quarles of Bedford County, VA, also gave a power of attorney to Dr. Manson Tregg to receive property from the estate of her father, James. (Ibid 105) James Quarles' will was proved 17 December 1816 by Leonard H. Sims, S. A. Puckett & John Collings. The executors named refused to qualify. Arthur Harris was appointed administrator with the will annexed. (Ibid Co Ct Min, no#/57) 2 February 1818 Arthur Harris was appointed guardian of Saml. Quarles, Milton W. Quarles, Nancy Quarles & James M. Quarles minor heirs of James Quarles, deceased. This order is rescinded by subsequent order. (Ibid 218) 3 February 1818 Elizabeth Quarles was appointed guardian of Alexander R. Quarles, Saml. O. Quarles, Milton W. Quarles, Eliza Anne Quarles & [appears to be George with another name written over it.] (Ibid 226) Elizabeth was guardian of Milton W. Quarles, Eliza Ann Quarles [George Washington Quarles is written and crossed out] & James M. Quarles. (Ibid 443)

QUARLES, John B.
Died before 16 December 1817 when Ben Clayton was appointed guardian of [Jack was written and then crossed out] John Quarles, minor son of John B. Quarles, deceased. (Wil TN, Co Ct Min, no#/196)

QUARLES, Roger
Died before 16 December 1817 when the will was offered by Abner Johns, one of the executors, & stated the will was found among the valuable papers of the deceased. Arthur Harris, Thomas Bradley & Daniel Trigg proved the handwriting in the will, therefore it was probated. (Wil TN, Co Ct Min, no#/196)

QUESENBERRY, John
Died before 1 November 1819 when the will was proved by John Merret & Robert Edwards. (Wil TN, Co Ct Min, no#/532)

QUIGLEY, Joseph
Died before 1 September 1806 when Henry Baker, by Thomas Dardis his attorney, made a motion for the administration of the estate and was rejected. (Cla TN, Co Ct Min, 3/2) 24 February 1807 Sarah Quigley, widow of Joseph Quigley, was appointed administratrix with David Chadwell & Kar Bailey as security. (Ibid 42)

QUILLIN [Luellin]
Was a resident of Warren County, KY, 5 October 1808 when a deposition was to be taken for the defendant in the case of Isom Uzzle vs Ezekiel Doyley. (Rob TN, Co Ct Min, 2/90)

RAGSDALE, Alfred
3 February 1818 Mark Merritt was allowed $8 for keeping him from September term to this term of court. (Wil TN, Co Ct Min, no#/227)

RAGSDALE, Benjamin
Was an orphan boy of the age of 18 years the 20th of March 1826. He was bound 6 March 1826 to Joel K. Brown until age 21 to learn the trade of a tailor. (McM TN, Co Ct Min, 2no#/134)

RAGSDALE, John
Was an orphan boy aged 16 on the 11th of December 1825. He was bound 6 September 1825 to Joel K. Brown for 3 years & 6 months. He is to be taught the art of a tailor. (McM TN, Co Ct Min, 2no#/97)

RAGSDALE, Prissella
18 June 1816 was allowed money for her support. (Wil TN, Co Ct Min, no#/16)

RAGSDALE, Wm.
Made a marriage contract with Mary Isbell which was proved by Abraham Moore & Archibald Campbell, 10 February 1812. (Rob TN, Co Ct Min, 3/48)

RAINEN, Alfred [Rainey]
4 October 1870 J. W. Wright was appointed his guardian with M. H. Davis and Silas Ferrill as security. (Dyr TN, Co Ct Min, B/107)

RAINES, Susannah
On 15 July 1853 dismissed her suit against Isac E. Raines for divorce. (Jac TN, Ch Ct Min, B/106)

RAINEY, Isaac
Died in Bedford County on 18 June 1836 leaving a will. Samuel [or Lemuel, shown both ways] Rainey was appointed administrator with will annexed. Isaac had dealings with Brazilia G. Rainey & Isaac N. Rainey who reside in Marshall County. Suit was brought by Lemuel [Samuel] & Jesse G. Rainey, administrators vs Barzellie G. & Isaac Rainey for a settlement. Samuel [Lemuel] Rainey was then a resident of Giles County. Evidently Brazilla G., Isaac N. & Isaac Rainey had been partners. "The respondsnts [Brazilla G. & Isaac N.] admit that the complainants [Lemuel & Jesse G.] were appointed administrators of the estate of thir further, [their father] the said Isaac Rainey...and that he died on 17th of June, not on the 18th." Mrs. Mahala Clift had two daughters. Mahala was the widowed daughter of Isaac Rainey, deceased. (Bed TN, Ch Ct Min, 1/132) Sarah Rainey, the widow of Isaac, died in April 1842. (Ibid 2/272) Barzellia G. Rainey had taken part of the negroes to DeSoto County, MS, and has not brought them back. Commissioner Lemuel Rainey has understood & believes that some person in DeSoto County, MS, has administrated on & sold the slaves. (Ibid 363)

RAINEY, J. G.
Taxes were not collected in District 4 for 1873, "gone." (Dyr TN, Co Ct Min, B/759)

RAINS, Thos. B.
Died before 22 August 1866 as shown in the suit of David H. Parker Exr. Thos B. Rains decd. vs B. G. Hays & wife Ursula P formerly Ursula P. Rains & others. Thos. B. Rains died in October 1862 having made his will in May 1861. D. H. Parker was named executor. Ursula P. Hays & Sarah A. Hays are the sisters of testator & he was never married. Thos. Buchanan, the grandfather of the testator, & co-defendants Ursela P. Hays & Sarah A. Hays, made his will in 1855 & shortly thereafter died. Thos. Buchanan left his estate to be divided between his wife, Sarah H. Buchanan, W. M. Dunnaway the husband of his daughter Sarah E. Dunnaway & his 3 grand children, Thomas, Ursula P & Sarah Rains, the heirs of his deceased daughter, Margaret E. Rains, the three grand children drawing their mothers interest. Sarah Buchanan, widow of Thos. Buchanan, died in 1860. The suit is for a division of the land left by Thos. Buchanan. (Mad TN, Ch Ct Min, 2/509) Sarah A. Hays was formerly Sarah A. Rains. (Ibid 3/131)

RAMBO, Matt
Taxes were not collected in District 5 for 1873, "insolvent." (Dyr TN, Co Ct Min, B/759)

RAMSEY, Newet
Was of Rutherford County, TN, when he sold to Richard Ramsey of Wilson County, TN, 2 negroes named Priss & Hannah "one an old wench and the other a small Girl," 9 September 1811. The sale was proved by John Rice & William Thomas at September term 1814. (Wil TN, Reg Bk/9)

RANDAL, Jas.
Died before 6 July 1857 when Robert Lewis was allowed money from the poor tax for making his coffin. (Sev TN, Co Ct Min, no#/177)

RANDALL, Payton
Died before 7 February 1811 when commissioners were appointed to settle with Benjamin Edwards & John Lightfoot concerning the accounts of the orphan children of [blank] Randall. (Ste TN, Co Ct Min, 3/51) 9 May 1811 a settlement was to be made by John Lightfoot, guardian for the heirs of Payton Randal. (Ibid 64)

RANDLE, Osborn
Died before 7 February 1815 when Edmond Randle was appointed administrator with Benjamin Bradford & Hamblen Manly as security. (Ste TN, Co Ct Min, 4/246)

RANDLES, James
7 April 1857 was ordered to be taken to the poor house. (Sev TN, Co Ct Min, no#/151)

RASBERRY, Lot
Died before 6 January 1873 when Smith Parks was appointed administrator, with H. L. Scoby and H. R. A. McCorkle as his security. John D. Scoby, Robt. Townsend and John H. Crawford were appointed to lay off a years allowance for the widow and family. (Dyr TN, Co Ct Min, B/524) There were three children. (Ibid 578)

RATHER, Sarah G.
Apparently died 31 May 1816 as shown in the case of Read & Washington vs Baker Rather & wife, entered at the June term 1816. The signature is shown as Baker Wrather. (Wil TN, P&J, no#/no#) 21 June 1816, Baker Rather was appointed administrator for his deceased wife, Sarah G. Rather. (Ibid, Co Ct Min, no#/21)

RAWLINS, Jim
Taxes were not collected in District 5 for 1873, "can't be found." (Dyr TN, Co Ct Min, B/759)

RAWLS, Luke
Died before 21 July 1800 when the will was proved by Samuel Miles. Elizabeth Rawls was executrix. (Rob TN, Co Ct Min, 1/141) 20 October 1800 Luke Rawls, Jr. was shown as executor. (Ibid 150) Nathan Arnet was also an executor. (Ibid 153)

RAY, Amanda
Died before 5 December 1870 when Joseph Ray was appointed administrator, with W. P. Rice and J. T. Ray as security. (Dyr TN, Co Ct Min, B/139)

RAY, Delila
28 December 1843 was granted a divorce from James Ray. They were married in the early part of 1840? [written over], and at the November term following of the Circuit Court of Williamson County, he was convicted of horse stealing and sentenced to 3 years & 3 months in prison. He is now serving his time in the State Penitentiary at Nashville. (Bed TN, Ch Ct Min, 2/279) William Lamb was the next friend of Delila Ray. She & James were married 14 December 1840 in Bedford County. She is unwilling to remain the wife of an infamous man. (Ibid 3/113)

RAY, J. F.
Died before 6 November 1871 when J. H. Lasley was appointed administrator with Thomas J. Frazier as his security. W. H. Franklin, J. C. Gregory and W. H. Hendrix were appointed to set apart a years provision for the widow and family. (Dyr TN, Co Ct Min, B/312)

RAY, J. M.
Taxes were not collected in District 3 for 1873, "gone." (Dyr TN, Co Ct Min, B/758)

RAY, James
Died 5 August 1835 and Alexander Ray, John Ray, Mary Ray, James M. Ray, George M. Ray and James A. Trice, by his guardian William Trice, heirs-at-law of James Ray, deceased, petitioned to sell land. A certain tract of land descended to petitioners & to William Roberson & wife Jenny, as tenants in common. James had sold part of the land to Alexander Ray and part to John Ray in 1822, and part to Henry Moore in 1820. The widow was Jane Ray. They petitioned 18 December 1837 to sell the rest of the land. (Bed TN, Ch Ct Min, 1/202)

RAY, James, Sr.
Died in 1816 having made a will which was proved in February 1816, as shown in the suit of Mary White vs William Draper & Rolston Ray, entered 16 July 1851. Joseph Ray & James Ray were executors who have since died. On 5 March 1849 the defendants were appointed administrators with the will annexed of James Ray, deceased. Since then Raulston Ray has moved beyond the jurisdiction of this Court and William Draper is the sole administrator of said deceased. Mary White had been left certain property by the will of James Ray and she has not had her legacy. (Jac TN, Ch Ct Min, B/1)

RAY, Luke
Died before 17 September 1816 when James Gray, administrator, was ordered to make a report. (Wil TN, Co Ct Min, no#/38) William Seawell was appointed guardian of Ellison Ray & Emily Ray, minor heirs of Luke Ray, deceased. (Ibid 60)

RAY, Martha
Died before 29 June 1841 when William A. Gaunt was appointed guardian ad litem for the heirs of Martha Ray, deceased, in the suit of the heirs of John Gaunt vs the heirs of Lewis Gaunt. (Bed TN, Ch Ct Min, 2/140)

RAY, Thomas
On 9 May 1816 made a deed of gift of stock, furniture and all personal property to his 4 children, James Ray, William Ray, Sally Ray & Jane Ray. (Wil TN, Reg Bk/87)

READ, Jno.
Died 23 June 1865, intestate, as shown in the suit of Jno. L. H. Tomlin vs Polly Read et als. Polly Read is the widow & is entitled to dower. Jas. G. Read & the other heirs, who are half brothers & sisters, or the children of such & whose names are unknown & who are non-residents of the state, are his only heirs. (Mad TN, Ch Ct Min, 3/197)

READER, Franklin
Was a minor orphan over the age of 14 on 8 September 1829 when he made a choice of Michael Whitsett as his guardian. (McM TN, Co Ct Min, 2no#/385)

REAGAN, Mrs.
Died before 11 April 1856 when Philip R. Ernest was allowed $2.50 for her coffin, out of the poor fund. (Sev TN, Co Ct Min, no#/38)

REAMY, E. H.
Died before 3 June 1872 when William P. Menzies was chosen and appointed guardian of James S. Reamy, V. A. Reamy and M. O. Reamy, minor heirs, with R. G. Menzies as his security. (Dyr TN, Co Ct Min, B/417)

REASON, C. B.
Died before 4 April 1870 when W. M. Tatum was appointed administrator. (Dyr TN, Co Ct Min, B/35) E. B. Curtis, James Sinclair and J. C. Greet were appointed to lay off a years provisions for the widow and family. (Ibid 47) 2 September 1872 dower was ordered to be set off for the widow, Lavinia F. Reasons. J. R. Reasons, Moody Young, Sally Young, Polly Combs, James Lewis and wife Edna Lewis, Abitha Reasons and Dicey Reasons and Elizabeth Cherry were served with process and failed to appear. (Ibid 469) 1 December 1873 W. J. Davis was appointed administrator de bonis non. (Ibid 666)

REASONS
1 June 1874 a suit was brought by W. J. Davis administrator &c vs J. R. Reasons, bill to sell land to pay debts. Dower was laid off to Sarah F. Reasons and the rest of the land is to be sold. (Dyr TN, Co Ct Min, B/738)

REAVES, Uriah
Died before 12 March 1844 when his death was suggested in the suit of Pinkney Turnham by his next friend Uriah Reaves vs Isaac F. Crane. James McDuff was substituted in the room of said Uriah Reaves. (Obi TN, Cir Ct Min, 4/no#)

REAVIS
15 September 1855 a petition was made by Hartwell H. Reavis et als. It stated that on 24 March 1849 Horace Bledsoe conveyed to Jas Knight (now deceased) a lot in the town of Jackson, in separate trust for the separate use & maintenance of said Alice Reavis during her life, & after her death to be equally divided amongst her children. Thos C. Reavis is the husband & Hartwell, Jas., May & Robt. are the only children of said Alice. Thos. C. Reavis was appointed trustee & given permission to sell the lot. (Mad TN, Ch Ct Min, 2/94)

RECTOR, Maxemillion
9 March 1831 entered a schedule of his property. [Was this in order to get a pension for Revolutionary War service?] It states he is 73 years old. (McM TN, Co Ct Min, 2no#/520)

REDDICK
On 1 February 1813 Nathan Ross was appointed guardian of Polly Reddick, John Reddick, William Reddick, Fanny Reddick and Nancy Reddick, with John Allen and Benjamin McNatt as security. (Ste TN, Co Ct Min, 4/3)

REDDICK
5 February 1872 a suit was entered by T. T. Reddick et als vs Nancy Reddick. It concerned 80 acres of the Humphrey Reddick land that was sold 1 November 1869 by decree of this court. (Dyr TN, Co Ct Min, B/365)

REDDICK, H.
Died before 3 April 1872 when W. N. Beasley made a settlement as administrator. (Dyr TN, Co Ct Min, B/405)

REDDICK, Rice
Died before 4 February 1811 when Nathan Ross was appointed administrator with William Cherry and Thomas Ross security. (Ste TN, Co Ct Min, 3/11) Provisions are to be laid off for the widow, Nancy Reddick, & six children, for one year. (Ibid 30) Nathan Ross was guardian of the heirs. (Ibid 218)

REDMAN, Frances
Died before 4 December 1866 as shown in the suit of James M. Wright Admr. of A. McGinnis decd. vs the widow & heirs and creditors of said deceased. J. W. Simpson was owed money from the estate of A. McGinnis for the use of the heirs of Frances Redman. (Fen TN, Ch Ct Min, A/305)

REECE, Randal
Was a minor orphan 8 January 1857 when his guardian, John Reece, was ordered to make a new bond as the original one was destroyed. (Sev TN, Co Ct Min, no#/120) 8 April 1857 John Reece resigned & Eli Fox was appointed guardian. (Ibid 157)

REED, Charles
Died before April 1855 when Morgan Davis was appointed administrator. The original bond and letters were destroyed & on 4 August 1856 he renewed his bond with J. H. Atchly & Wm. Atchly as security. (Sev TN, Co Ct Min, no#/66)

REED, Charles H.
5 August 1867 was bound as an apprentice to James K. Gibson. (Sev TN, Co Ct Min, no#/468)

REED, J. A.
Died before 5 April 1870 when J. F. Williamson made a settlement as administrator. (Dyr TN, Co Ct Min, B/42)

REED, James
Died before 11 October 1858 when the death of James Reed, one of the defendants, was suggested in the suit of A. Miller vs Wm. C. Wood & others. (Fen TN, Ch Ct Min, A/160) James M. Wright is administrator. Martha, Thursa, Adam and James Reed are the only children, heirs-at-law and distributees of James Reed, deceased. (Ibid178) The heirs are all minors and B. Lee was appointed guardian ad litem. (Ibid 220)

REED, Jesse
Died before 19 April 1797 when the executors were defendants in a suit of Matthew Sellars. (Rob TN, Co Ct Min, 1/28)

REED, Joseph
Died before 3 June 1861 when James Clark, James Evans & Morgan Davis were appointed to lay off a years support for the widow, Levena Reed. (Sev TN, Co Ct Min, no#/692)

REED, S. M.
8 February 1870 T. F. Bell made a settlement as guardian. (Dyr TN, Co Ct Min, B/7)

REED, William
Died before 6 July 1874 when T. H. Atkin was chosen and appointed guardian of Robert and A. J. Akin, minor heirs of William Reed, deceased, with J. F. Dicky and M. H. Hendrix as his security. (Dyr TN, Co Ct Min, B/743)

REEVES, Gordon
28 August 1778 took his affirmation of allegiance to this state. (Was TN, Co Ct Min, 1/47)

REEVES, John George
28 August 1778 took the oath of allegience. (Was TN, Co Ct Min, 1/47)

REEVES, Tarlton J.
Died in October 1846. Joseph Thompson was appointed administrator in January 1847. Tarlton had placed property in the hands of his brother, Benjamin S. Reeves, in 1845. Alexander S. Reeves was mentioned. Tarlton J. died in AL at the residence of Benjamin S. Reeves. The widow was mentioned. Benjamin lived in Wilcox County, AL, and Tarlton J. Reeves did die there. Mrs. Neusome [Newsome] had come on a visit to AL with Tarlton J. Reeves and was with him during the whole of his sickness. She was his sister & remained with him until he died. The day after he was buried Mrs. Neusome, who lived near Tarlton J. in TN, took his clothes, papers & money back to TN. Archabald Reeves was mentioned. Moses Reeves was mentioned. Joel Rees [sic] was mentioned. The last entry in this suit was dated 28 August 1849. (Bed TN, Ch Ct Min, 3/373-88.)

REEVES, William
Was certified "to the County Court of Frederick in Commonwealth of Virginia to be a man of peaceable & honest behavior &c and that his wife, Mary Reeves, is the Daughter of Poter Wolf, Deceased, who formerly lived in the County of Frederick in Commonwealth of Virginia." (Was TN, Co Ct Min, 1/144)

REEVES, William
28 August 1778 took the oath of allegiance. (Was TN, Co Ct Min, 1/47)

REID, J. M.
Died before 19 February 1868 as shown in the suit of Archibald R. Thomas, administrator &c vs John W. Dickinson, administrator of J. M. Reid & George G. Perkins. (Mad TN, Ch Ct Min, 3/132)

REID, Richard
Died before 15 July 1811 when John Purris? was appointed administrator, with Merewether Smith & Thos. Brown as security. An inventory of the estate was returned. (Roa TN, Co Ct Min, D/305)

REID, Thomas
20 March 1805 gave power of attorney to William Cross of Botetourt County, VA, to receive any sum of money due him and his wife, Anne Reid, as a legacy or distributive share from the estate of Thomas Ramsey, deceased, formerly of York County, PA. (Roa TN, Co Ct Min, A/326)

RENFRO, Wm.
Died before 22 January 1799 when the administrator, Christopher Taylor, deeded land to Wm. Connel. (Rob TN, Co Ct Min, 1/87)

RENFROU, W. H.
Taxes were not collected in District 4 for 1873, "run away." (Dyr TN, Co Ct Min, B/759)

RENOR, Lewis
Died before 17 May 1795 when Garrett Reasoner was appointed administrator, with David Jobe as his security. (Was TN, Co Ct Min, 1/545)

RENOR, Mary
17 May 1795 came into court and made choice of Charles Renor as her guardian. (Was TN, Co Ct Min, 1/545)

RERVIES, George [Reeves ?]
Died before 17 March 1817 when the will was proved by James Michel & James Willard. Jeremiah Rervies was appointed administrator with will annexed. (Wil TN, Co Ct Min, no#/75)

RESOR, William [Rasor, Rasior, Rescor, Rasco]
Died before 9 June 1806 when Rachel Resor? was appointed administratrix with Wm. Allen & Dudley Williams security. (Ste TN, Co Ct Min, 1/27b) Dudley Williams & Rachel Rasor were appointed guardians for William Rasor, Mary Rasor and John Rasor, orphans, with Joseph B. Neville, Jesse Rasor and William Pryor as security. (Ibid 1/32) Rachel Rescor, the widow of William Rescor?, petitioned for dower. On petition of the heirs of William Rescor it is ordered that the land be divided. (Ibid 41b) The sale of the estate is shown. Buyers included Rachel Rasor, John Rasor, Laban Rasor, Jesse Rasor. [I am still not sure what the name actually is. In another record there is a Jesse Rasco and a Wm. Rasco, very plainly written, so this name may be Rasco.] (Ibid 52)

REYNOLDS, Elizabeth
Was a widow 20 June 1817 when it was ordered by the court that she be brought to court in order that provision can be made for the support of her & her children. (Wil TN, Co Ct Min, no#/133)

REYNOLDS, Henry
1 December 1828 Henry Reynolds & Ann Reynolds, minor orphans, made choice of Henry Reynolds as their guardian. (McM TN, Co Ct Min, 2no#/322)

REYNOLDS, Jane
Died before 28 December 1843 when William D. Orr was appointed guardian ad litem for the minor heirs to defend the suit of Andrew Reynolds vs Arthur Campbell and others. Alexander Campbell was the administrator of Jane Reynolds. (Bed TN, Ch Ct Min, 2/276) August 29 1844 this suit is shown as Alfred Campbell vs Andrew Reynolds & Arthur Campbell and Andrew Reynolds Admr &c vs Arthur Campbell Exr. Richard Reynolds is entitled to a share of the estate of Jane Reynolds, deceased, & Andrew Reynolds was administrator of Jane Reynolds. (Ibid 298) There are 8 distributees of the estate. They include John Reynolds, Arthur Campbell, James Reynolds, Benjamin Reynolds & David Reynolds. The former administrator, Andrew Reynolds, has failed to pay over the money to Alfred Campbell, administrator de bonis non. Arthur Campbell is his security. Henry Reynolds was a distributee & has been overpaid, also Richard Reynolds. (Ibid 372) The heirs were said to be Arthur Campbell & wife Elizabeth [Betsy] who is a daughter of Jane Reynolds & lives in Bedford County, Henry Reynolds and John Reynolds who live in Lincoln County, David Reynolds who lives in IL, Richard Reynolds who lives in MS, Moses Reynolds and the heirs of James Reynolds second? who reside in AR, and Andrew Reynolds. James Reynolds has died since the said Jane in the state of AR, leaving a widow, Sally Reynolds, and some children whose names are unknown. Moses Reynolds is a minor. Andrew Reynolds was appointed administrator of the estate of Jane Reynolds at the November term 1838. Andrew Reynolds was removed as administrator and Alford Campbell appointed in his stead. John Reynolds was one of the heirs of James Reynolds, deceased. William Reynolds died intestate many years ago, before

1816, and was the husband of Jane. John Reynolds, one of the heirs, lives in AL but did live in Lincoln County, TN. (Ibid 3/418-426)

RHEA, Richd. Joseph
Died before 7 November 1795 when a document was entered confirming that Saml. Hendley had sold land to David Hucky, and he had sold it to Richd. Joseph Rhea, who has since died. The land descended to the eldest son of Joseph Rhea, one John Rhea, and is now located in Hawkins County, TN. (Was TN, Co Ct Min, 1/613)

RHINEHEART, Betsy
2 April 1861 a female child named Rhineheart is to be brought to court to be bound out. (Sev TN, Co Ct Min, no#/680) Betsy Rinehart is to be brought from the poor house to be bound out. (Ibid 708)

RICE, Isaac
Died before 2 December 1823 when Martha Rice was appointed guardian of Henry Rice, Charles W. Rice, Eliza Rice, Miller F. Rice, Lucinda Rice and William L. Rice, minor heirs. Martha was appointed guardian of their estate. Charles Matlock was appointed their guardian in the settlement of the dower of Martha Rice. James S. Rice was appointed guardian of Tandy Rice & Isaac Rice, minor heirs of Isaac Rice, deceased, with William Matlock & John Rice as his securities. (McM TN, Co Ct Min, no#/102) On the same date Rubin Walker & Susannah his wife acknowledge that they had notice that John Rice & James S. Rice would apply for distributive shares of the estate of Isaac Rice, deceased (Ibid 103) 1 March 1824 a divison was made: Dower to Martha Rice; Lot #1 to Henry Matlock, land in Roan County, TN; Lot #2 to Henry Rice, land in Roan County, TN; Lot #3 to Miller L. Rice, land in Roan County, TN; Lot #4 to James S. Rice, land in Roan County, TN; Lot #5 to Lucinda Rice, land in Roan County, TN; Lot #6 to Isaac Rice, land in Roan County, TN; Lot #7 to Reuben Walker, land in Roan County, TN; Lot #8 to Elizabeth Rice; Lot #9 to Charles W. Rice; Lot #10 to John Rice; Lot #11 to William S. Rice; Lot #12 to Tandy Rice. (Ibid 115-120)

RICE, Isaac
Removed by 7 December 1830 when a road overseer was appointed in his place. (McM TN, Co Ct Min, 2no#/491)

RICE, James
Died before 7 March 1825 when John Rice was appointed administrator. (McM TN, Co Ct Min, 2no#/49)

RICE, John
Died before 26 September 1806 when the heirs were on a tax list with land on Sanders Fork. (Wil TN, Co Ct Min, no#/264)

RICE, Sally
Alias Sally Harpe, brought suit against Ephraim Walker & Betsy his wife, Case for Words, 20 September 1803. (Roa TN, Co Ct Min, A/128)

RICE, William
Died before 12 August 1816 when the will was proved by Adam Dale and ordered to be laid by for further probate. (Cla TN, Co Ct Min, 4/220) The will was also proved by Ann Moor. (Ibid 234)

RICHARDS
5 June 1826, James & Hannah, the two eldest servants of Gabriel Richards, were emancipated by his will. James & Hannah will assume the name of Richards. (McM TN, Co Ct Min, 2no#/160)

RICHARDS, Gabriel
Died 4 April 1826. His will was proved 5 June 1826 by John W. Barnett & James M. Barnett, witnesses. (McM TN, Co Ct Min, 2no#/160) Richard Richards was one of the executors. (Ibid 180) 1 March 1830 a report of the executor mentions a note on George Richards & an obligation on Asa Richards. The report was signed by Nancy Richards & witnessed by Asa Richards. (Ibid 423)

RICHARDS, Isaac
Died before 5 March 1866 when W. C. Murphy was appointed administrator with Wm. Catlett as security. (Sev TN, Co Ct Min, no#/282)

RICHARDS, James
Died before 5 February 1811 when land was taxed to the heirs. (Ste TN, Co Ct Min, 3/38)

RICHARDSON
18 March 1817 it was ordered that Joseph Johnson & J. Allcorn contract for schooling & boarding the children of the widow Richardson upon the best terms, which contract this Court will meet in payment. (Wil TN, Co Ct Min, no#/79)

RICHARDSON, D. M.
Died before 4 January 1871 when B. S. Thomas tendered his resignation as administrator, which was not received. (Dyr TN, Co Ct Min, B/173)

RICHARDSON, David
22 December 1807 entered a document with the following information: "David Richardson Senr. of the county of Hanover St. Martaing Parish State of Virginia, now ill with palsy, may in all probability depart this life before my intrust? may lead me to my native State. In consequence of which I David Richardson Junr. of Roane Co., TN hath this day sold unto Henry W. Richardson of Hawkins Co., TN, for $610 my interest in my Fathers estate..." (Roa TN, Co Ct Min, C/32)

RICHARDSON, Fisher
Died "in the late war" as shown 18 September 1817 when arrangements were made for the widow and minor children. The widow is to be paid to board 4 of the children. John McNeely, schoolmaster, is to be paid $100 for one year. (Wil TN, Co Ct Min, no#/172)

RICHARDSON, George
Removed by 6 September 1830 when a road overseer was appointed in his place. (McM TN, Co Ct Min, 2no#/469)

RICHARDSON, Henry H.
Died before 31 March 1868 as shown in the suit of James M. Wright Admr. & Mary Richardson vs Eli Mullinax & wife et als. It was stated that defendants, Nancy Richardson, Abigal T. Richardson and Henry O. Richardson, were minors. B. O. Bowden was appointed guardian ad litem. The suit was also shown as J. M. Wright Admr. vs Nancy F. Richardson & others. A report is to be taken of the assets of the estate of Henry Richardson, deceased. (Fen TN, Ch Ct Min, A/364 & 386) Mary Richardson was the widow and is entitled to dower. (Ibid 388)

RICHARDSON, James
Died before 7 March 1825 when James Bowers & Harritte Richardson were appointed administrators. James Cowan, Sr., George Colville & Jonathan Couch were appointed to lay off a years maintenance for Harritte Richardson, the widow. (McM TN, Co Ct Min, 2no#/49)

RICHARDSON, James
Died before 22 August 1779 when John McFarland was granted leave of administration on the estate. (Was TN, Co Ct Min, 1/87 & 89)

RICHARDSON, Stith, Doctor
Died 29 September 1872 as shown in the resolutions of respect entered in the minutes on the death of the Chairman of the Court. Condolences were extended to the aged widow and the children. (Dyr TN, Co Ct Min, B/472-3) T. E. Richardson was appointed administrator, with S. R. Latta as his security. (Ibid 502)

RICHARDSON, William
Died before 13 July 1850 as shown in the suit of Edward Vaughn vs Lawson Draper. Sarah Richardson was appointed guardian ad litem for all the minor heirs of William Richardson, deceased. (Jac TN, Ch Ct Min, A/376)

RICHMOND
In the suit of William F. Dunlap & wife vs Robert F. Richmond & others, 3 February 1858, it was stated that John M. Richmond was appointed by the Smith County Court guardian of Robert F. Richmond, Joseph H. Richmond and John R. Richmond. (Jac TN, Ch Ct Min, C/93)

RICHMOND, John
Died before 14 November 1844 as shown in the suit of Sophia and others by their next friend Joseph Eaton vs Henry & Robert Richmond. The deposition of Robert Richmond was objected to when it appeared to the court that the paper writing exhibited, purporting

to be the last will and testament of John Richmond, deceased, is not his will, he the said John Richmond at the time the same was executed, being of unsound mind and memory. (Jac TN, Ch Ct Min, A/180) In the suit of Wm. C. Burk et al vs Henry & Robert Richmond it was stated that complainants were entitled to a distribution of the estate of John Richmond, deceased. The defendants were the administrators. (Ibid 200) The others in the suit with Wm. C. Burke were Hannah D. Burke, John W. Richmond, James M. Richmond, George C. Darwin, Jr., Margaret Darwin, Dudley B. Hale [Hail], Julia Hale, Thaxton Carter & Jasie Carter vs Henry Richmond & Robert Richmond Administrators of Jno. Richmond deceased. The complainants & Henry Richmond are the heirs. (Ibid 247)

RICHMOND, John M.
14 July 1853 was appointed guardian of his minor children, Joseph Richmond, John R. Richmond & Robert F. Richmond, to defend the suit of William F. Dunlap & wife against the minors. (Jac TN, Ch Ct Min, B/84) The land in this suit was bequeathed to the complainants and defendants, except John M. Richmond, by the will of James W. Hancock, deceased. It is to be sold for distribution. (Ibid 138) Martha Dunlap, wife of William F. Dunlap, was formerly Martha Richmond. (Ibid 156)

RICKETTS, Elizabeth
Was the mother of a bastard child. 2 November 1818 William Baskins gave bond to answer the charge that he is the father. (Wil TN, Co Ct Min, no#/337)

RIDDLE, Cornelus
Died before September term 1804 when the heirs were on the non-resident tax list with land on Spring Creek. (Wil TN, Co Ct Min, no#/88)

RIDLEY, Elizabeth
Was granted a divorce from Benjamin F. Ridley on 26 July 1849. They were married in Jackson County in the Spring of 1848. Elizabeth is allowed to keep the charge of her infant daughter until it shall arrive at the age of three years and until which time the defendant is enjoined and restrained from interfering or meddling with it. (Jac TN, Ch Ct Min, A/344)

RIGGIN, Ignatius
Died before 8 April 1857 when John Mullendoor made a settlement as guardian of the minor heirs. (Sev TN, Co Ct Min, no#/158)

RIGGIN, Mary H.
Was a minor orphan 8 April 1857 when John Mullendore resigned as her guardian. Mary is living in Monroe County, and the largest part of her estate is in Monroe County. The court of Monroe County has appointed Henderson Hix as her guardian. (Sev TN, Co Ct Min, no#/158)

RIGGS, Joel
Died 13 December 1835 in Bedford County, intestate. James M. Riggs was appointed administrator. Elizabeth Riggs is the widow and James M. Zadock, & Joel D. Riggs, Mary Shepherd, Nancy Douglass, Elizabeth H. Riggs and Rebecca B. Riggs are the only children and distributees of said Joel Riggs. John H. Roberson is the guardian of Joel D., Elizabeth H. & Rebecca B. Riggs. William Shepard is the husband of Mary Shepard. Thomas L. is the husband of Nancy Douglass. The petition for division states that the widow & all the children are residents of Marshall County, TN, except William & Mary Shepherd who are citizens of Williamson County. The slaves are to be sold at the late residence of Joel Riggs, deceased, in Marshall County. (Bed TN, Ch Ct Min, 1/112)

RINEHART, E.
Died 31 March 1864 as shown when John Bird was paid for keeping her for the first quarter. [He had been paid $100 for keeping Elizabeth Rinehart for 1863] (Sev TN, Co Ct Min, no#/94)

RINEHEART, C.
Died before 2 January 1860 when B. Henderson was paid for burying clothes. On the same date John Keer was given extra pay for keeping Conrad Rineheart. (Sev TN, Co Ct Min, no#/495)

RINEHEART, Elizabeth
5 August 1861 the Superintendant of the poor house was ordered to give up a pauper child, Elizabeth Rineheart, to Elizabeth Rineheart who proposed to take and raise said child without charge to the county. (Sev TN, Co Ct Min, no#/712)

RION, John [Ryon]
Died before 11 February 1859 when his death was suggested in the suit of Horis Hatcher & wife vs David D. Rion & others. [All of these names are extremely doubtful and the handwriting is almost unreadable] Joseph H. Totem & Sarah his wife were the heirs of said John, deceased, and this suit is to be revived against them and all the other heirs of said John Rion, deceased. Clotilda Hemphill, one of the defendants, has also died leaving Caroline Hemphill her only heir. [Also see Washington Ryon] (Jac TN, Ch Ct Min, C/193) In the suit of Sarah Rion vs David D. Rion & others process had been served on all defendants except Fielding Rion. The second clause of the will of Washington Rion was quoted. John Rion was the father of Washington Rion. John Rion died in 1858, intestate. The defendants are his only heirs & Sarah is his widow. Dower is to be laid off for Sarah. (Ibid 196) The death of Sarah Ryon was suggested in this suit on 9 February 1860. (Ibid 301)

RIPLEY, John
Died before 28 November 1806 as shown in the suit of John Umstead against Samuel Lusk. Samuel Lusk stated that he was not indebted to John Ripley, deceased. (Cla TN, Co Ct Min, 3/33)

RITCHIE, James
Died before 28 April 1809 when Mary Ritchie, Thomas Clinton and William M. Cooley were appointed administrators with Bryant Oneal & Joshua Williams as security. (Ste TN, Co Ct Min, no#/111) Mary Ritchie was the widow. The will was mentioned & court to decide if it is his will. (Ibid 4/no#, 4 April 1809)

RITCHIE, John
Died before October term 1808. His will is listed. The will made bequests to Sarah Williams, all of his property, house & lot, blacksmith tools. After the death of Sarah Williams the house & lot is to be sold and divided amongst his children. Thomas Clinton was named executor. The will was dated 4 September 1808 and proved at October term by Jas. H. Russell. (Ste TN, Co Ct Min, No#/76)

RITCHTUA?, H. W.
Died before 23 February 1842 when land was taxed to the heirs. (Obi TN, Cir Ct Min, 4/no#)

ROARK, Barnabas
Died before 24 November 1806 when James Gibson was appointed administrator with Samuel Wyatt & John Owens, Jr. as security. (Cla TN, Co Ct Min, 3/20) The deceased was shown as Barnet Roark when the inventory was recorded 25 February 1807. (Ibid 50) A sale was made of the estate of Barnabas Roark. (Ibid 73) Sarah Roark petitioned to be made administratrix instead of James Gibson, which was granted. (Ibid 94) Securities for Sarah were John Bullard and John Owens. (Ibid 102)

ROBB, William, Sr.
Of Wilson County, TN, sold to Thomas Campbell of Bedford County, TN, on 25 November 1816, 2 negro children that are now in the possession of Robert Harris in Cabarris County, NC. (Wil TN, Reg Bk/113)

ROBBINS, Edward
On 23 February 1842 was granted a divorce from Polly Robbins for desertion. (Obi TN, Cir Ct Min, 4/no#)

ROBBINS, O. R.
3 July 1871 was appointed guardian of John S., Wm. E., Sallie B. and Joseph Oscar Robins, his own children, with W. H. Hendrix and R. M. Ward as security. (Dyr TN, Co Ct Min, B/256)

ROBERSON, Elizabeth J. [Robinson, Robertson]
Died 1 April 1813 in Sussex County, VA, leaving a will. William Parham was named executor but declined & Robert Powell was appointed administrator with will annexed. Elizabeth Robers made a bequest to her cousin, Ann Collier, and the rest of her estate to her sister, Mary Powell's four children, to wit, Seymore, Elizabeth, Thomas and Martha P. Powell. Elizabeth Powell, one of the four legatees, married [blank] Whidiker [Whitaker] who has since died. Semor and Marth have also died leaving Elizabeth Whitiker and Thomas Powell the sole legatees. Robert Powell took charge of the property and has probably made a settlement with Thomas Powell, but Elizabeth Whidiker has not had her portion. She brought suit in Bedford County, TN, on 29 August 1838 against Robert Powell for her share. In the answer of Robert Powell it was stated that Martha P. Powell

died without issue in 1815 and that Seymore died in 1837 leaving a wife. He claimed he made a settlement in 1823 or 1824 and paid over to Seymore his share. He said he had also given Elizabeth, who came of age in July 1820, her share. (Bed TN, Ch Ct Min, 1/214)

ROBERTS
On 18 February 1796 Sarah Roberts was bound to Wm. Patterson Chester until age 18. James Roberts was bound to the said William P. Chester until age 21. Roda Roberts was bound to Michael Harrison until age 18. They were all minors. (Was TN, Co Ct Min, 1/598)

ROBERTS
3 July 1865 Wm. & Harret Roberts were apprenticed to John Bird. (Sev TN, Co Ct Min, no#/183)

ROBERTS, Ann
Was bound to Abraham Hunter 27 May 1794, until she arrives at the age of 18. (Was TN, Co Ct Min, 1/489)

ROBERTS, Edmond
7 June 1830 made a deed of gift to Ann Wesley & Thomas Spearman. (McM TN, Co Ct Min, 2no#/452)

ROBERTS, Eli
7 April 1856 was allowed thirty dollars out of the poor fund for keeping his helpless child for one year. (Sev TN, Co Ct Min, no#/22)

ROBERTS, Eli
Died before 3 October 1859 when Mark Roberts was appointed administrator with Levi S. Roberts security. (Sev TN, Co Ct Min, no#/475)

ROBERTS, Eli
6 January 1862, J. W. Bartlett was allowed money for keeping Eli Roberts, a pauper, for 1862. (Sev TN, Co Ct Min, no#/743)

ROBERTS, Elisha
Died before 10 April 1866 when Eli H. Roberts was appointed administrator with L. C. Roberts & John S. Roberts as security. (Sev TN, Co Ct Min, no#/323)

ROBERTS, Hugh
Died the last of December 1851 as shown in the suit of Eliza Birchett & Jackson Burchitt vs William Geahart et als. The complainant, Eliza, married Hugh Roberts in June 1850 and was his lawful wife at the time of his death. She is entitled to dower out of his lands in Jackson & Overton counties. There are 5 heirs and complainant, Eliza, is entitled to 1/6 of the personal property. Eliza relinquished her rights to the defendants on 5 March 1852. Said deed was obtained from said Eliza by misrepresentation and fraud. Eliza has married complainant Jackson Burchett. William Gahert? is administrator of Hugh Roberts, deceased. Eliza is to have her dower. Her portion of the estate of Hugh Roberts is to be vested in James A. Spurlock for her sole and separate use. The defendants were granted an appeal to Supreme Court in Nashville. (Jac TN, Ch Ct Min, B/90)

ROBERTS, James
Died before 4 May 1842 as shown in the petition of Letty Roberts, executrix of Jas. Roberts, deceased, to sell slaves. (Jac TN, Ch Ct Min, A/52) Letty Roberts died before 27 January 1848 as shown in the petition of John Hughs, administrator &c. The estate of Letty Roberts, [evidently the widow of James Roberts] deceased, was mentioned. There are 8 distributees of her estate. (Ibid 283) A suit was entered 12 July 1850 by James B. Buchanan vs Ridley Roberts, Thomas J. Roberts, James M. Shepherd, administrator of Letty Roberts, deceased, & others. (Ibid 369) James Roberts executed his last will & testament in Jackson County on 14 August 1835 and departed this life on 28 August 1840. One bequest was that the rest of his estate go to his wife and after her death to be divided between his 6 children, Alitha Graham, Celina Sadler, Letty Buckannan, Patsy Sadler, Zadock B. Roberts and Buckannan W. Roberts. The testators widow died about 1844 and his daughters married as follows; Celina to John K. Sadler, Letty to James R. Buckannan, Patsy to James Sadler, Alitha to John Graham. Alitha Graham died several years prior to testator, James Roberts. About 1845 the other 5 children sold their interest to Matthew C. McKinley. Testator had 2 other children besides the 6 named in the will, to wit, Ridley Roberts & Elizabeth Holliman. A partition of land is to be made so that the children of Aletha Graham, the children of Elizabeth Holliman and the children of Ridley

Roberts have a share. The children of Elizabeth Holliman were George Holliman, William Holliman, Alexander Holliman, Granville Holliman, James Holliman and Shepherd Holliman, Gideon Mahan & wife Letty Mahan formerly Holliman, Benjamin Burton & wife Candis Burton formerly Candis Holliman. A final accounting is to be made. (Ibid 261-4)

ROBERTS, John
Freed his negro boy named Daniel, 1 March 1830. (McM TN, Co Ct Min, 2no#/419)

ROBERTS, John
Was a pauper of the county when Simon Hancock was allowed money for keeping him, 16 June 1817. (Wil TN, Co Ct Min, no#/105)

ROBERTS, Margaret
3 October 1859 was allowed money for keeping Eli C. Roberts, a helpless boy, from 1 August 1859 to 1 January 1860. (Sev TN, Co Ct Min, no#/476)

ROBERTS, Samuel
Was a minor child 7 August 1865 when he was apprenticed to Marcus Reneau. (Sev TN, Co Ct Min, no#/193)

ROBERTS, Thomas
Was a pauper, as shown when Simon Hancock was paid for keeping him, 18 June 1816. (Wil TN, Co Ct Min, no#/12)

ROBERTS, Thos. Q.
Was not a resident of this state as shown 10 February 1814 when the suit of Thomas Watson against him was stayed for six months. (Ste TN, Co Ct Min, 4/113)

ROBERTS, W. M.
1 October 1860 was charged with Bastardy. Mary Moore, the mother of the bastard child, gave bond with Wm. M. Roberts, L. C. Roberts, A. G. Roberts, Jesse Hill & Robert Hill as security, that Mary Moore would keep her from becoming a county charge. (Sev TN, Co Ct Min, no#/608)

ROBERTS, Wm., Jr.
Died before 4 April 1865 when the court ordered that all of his children be brought to next court to be bound out. County court Clerk, M. A. Rawlings, was ordered to take into his possession all the personal property of Wm. Roberts, Jr. & Sr. and hold until next court. (Sev TN, Co Ct Min, no#/154) John Bird was appointed guardian ad litem to the minor heirs. (Ibid 209)

ROBERTS, Wm. M.
2 October 1865 was appointed guardian to S. P. Roberts & J. B. Roberts, minors, with N. B. Pate & Jesse Hill as security. (Sev TN, Co Ct Min, no#/216)

ROBERTS, Wm., Sr.
Died before 3 July 1865 when M. A. Rawlings made a report of sales of the estates of Wm. Roberts, Jr. & Sr., deceased. (Sev TN, Co Ct Min, no#/173) In the suit of the administrator vs the heirs, it is stated that Samuel Roberts & Houston Roberts are non-residents of TN & publication is to be made. (Ibid 209)

ROBERTSON
In the suit of G. W. Crouch vs Nancy Robinson Admrx., on 30 March 1868, land was sold to satisfy the lien of complainant and if any money remained it was to be paid to the widow and heirs of Robertson, deceased. (Fen TN, Ch Ct Min, A/360)

ROBERTSON, Burrell
Was a blind parishioner 9 May 1814 when Marcus Robertson was paid $25 for keeping him for 12 months. (Rob TN, Co Ct Min, 3/398)

ROBERTSON, Burrell
Died before 5 April 1870 when a settlement was made by J. H. Brooks, administrator of Robt. Johnson, who was administrator of Burrell Robertson, deceased. (Dyr TN, Co Ct Min, B/42)

ROBERTSON, Charles
28 August 1778 took the oath of allegiance. (Was TN, Co Ct Min, 1/47)

ROBERTSON, Danl.
Was a pauper when he was let to the highest bidder [should be lowest bidder] 3 August 1818. (Wil TN, Co Ct Min, no#/285)

ROBERTSON, Elijah
Died before 22 January 1802 when the heirs were listed on the delinquent tax list. (Rob TN, Co Ct Min, 1/206)

ROBERTSON, F. N.
Taxes were not collected in District 4 for 1873, "can't be found." (Dyr TN, Co Ct Min, B/759)

ROBERTSON, Hugh
Died before 2 August 1819 when Zachariah T. Robertson & Andrew Robertson petitioned for division of land devised by Hugh Robertson to his heirs by his will. (Wil TN, Co Ct Min no#/502)

ROBERTSON, Joel
Died before 6 November 1865 when Nancy Robertson was appointed administrator with James Eslinger as security. (Sev TN, Co Ct Min, no#/238)

ROBERTSON, John
Was an orphan adjudged to be 10 years old when he was bound on 5 November 1782 to Elijah Robertson, until age 21. (Was TN, Co Ct Min, 1/181)

ROBERTSON, John
Died before 18 June 1816 when an account of the sale of the property was recorded. (Wil TN, Co Ct Min, no#/13) An inventory of the rent of the tanyard was recorded. (Ibid 213) 3 August 1818 John Williamson was appointed guardian of Hugh Robertson, Ann Robertson & Jane Robertson, minor heirs of Capt. John Robertson, deceased. (Ibid 284) 2 November 1818 an inventory of the halfpay pension of the minor heirs of John Robertson, deceased, was recorded. (Ibid 334)

ROBERTSON, John
Died before 8 February 1870 when W. N. Beasly made a settlement as administrator. (Dyr TN, Co Ct Min, B/7)

ROBERTSON, Julius
27 August 1778 took the oath of allegiance. (Was TN, Co Ct Min, 1/44)

ROBERTSON, Lucy
Was an orphan child one year old when she was bound to Wyatt Bettis, 18 March 1817, until age 18. (Wil TN, Co Ct Min, no#/77)

ROBERTSON, M. W.
Died before 7 November 1870 when J. F. Robertson and James H. Perry, administrators, returned an inventory of the estate. (Dyr TN, Co Ct Min, B/131)

ROBERTSON, Mark
Died before September term 1804 when the heirs were on the non-resident tax list with land on Spring Creek. (Wil TN, Co Ct Min, no#/88)

ROBERTSON, Mark
Was paid $30 on 14 May 1810 for supporting and maintaining his son Burrell, who being so infirm that he cannot support and maintain himself. (Rob TN, Co Ct Min, 2/252)

ROBERTSON, Mary E.
Died in August 1865 as shown in the suit of Charles N. Gibbs Exr. of Mary E. Robertson decd. vs Thomas Henderson, J. Carroll Terry and John S. Lancaster, partners as Henderson Terry & Co., which company was doing business in LA and owed money to Mary E. Robertson. Defendant Lancaster owns land in Madison County, TN, which was attached to pay the debt. (Mad TN, Ch Ct Min, 3/77)

ROBERTSON, Nancy
Died before 1 July 1861 when John Kear was paid for keeping her & Alexr. Mize was paid for making her coffin. Also shown as Robson. (Sev TN, Co Ct Min, no#/697)

ROBERTSON, Robert
Died before 2 August 1819 when Zachariah T. Robertson was appointed administrator

with George Smith & Alfred McLain as security. (Wil TN, Co Ct Min, no#/500) The negroes are to be sold for division among the legatees. (Ibid 501) The heirs are all of age. (Ibid 539)

ROBERTSON, William
Was a resident of Rutherford County, TN, 26 October 1819 when he bought sundry property from Delpha Drennon of Wilson County. (Wil TN, Reg Bk/142)

ROBERTSON, William Sr.
Died before 4 June1804 when his will was proved by David Chadwell and Hugh McClelland who also stated that they saw the other witness, John White, sign same. William Robertson, one of the executors named, qualified. (Cla TN, Co Ct Min, 2/36)

ROBERTSON, Wm.
Died before 5 November 1806 when on the petition of Martha Robertson, Relick of Wm. Robertson, deceased, Lewis Wells was appointed administrator with Anderson Cheatham as security. The widow's dower was ordered to be set off. A years provisons for widow and family was ordered to be set off. (Rob TN, Co Ct Min, 1/417) 6 January 1809 James Robertson & Henry Robertson, two of the orphans of Wm. Robertson, deceased, made choice of Lewis Wells as their guardian. Wells was also appointed guardian of Tabatha, Milly, Jesse & Simeon, also orphans of Wm. Robertson. (Ibid 2/108)

ROBEY, Nathan
Died before 6 November 1805 when the heirs were ordered to pay Thomas Bell $100 out of the estate for his trouble of going to NC to sell the lands of the estate. (Rob TN, Co Ct Min, 1/366)

ROBEY, Sarah
Was an orphan when Thomas Bell was appointed her guardian 21 July 1800. (Rob TN, Co Ct Min, 1/141)

ROBINS, John
Died before 7 July 1807 when Elisabeth Tucker was paid $25 for keeping the children of John Robins, deceased. (Rob TN, Co Ct Min, 1/450) 6 October 1807 Saml. Robins & John Robins, children of John Robins, deceased, were bound to Saml. Tucker until age 21, with John Johnson & John Shannon as security. (Ibid 465) Betsey & Polly Robins, daughters of John Robins deceased, were bound to Elisabeth Tucker until age 18, with same security as above. (Ibid 466)

ROBINS, John D.
Died before 10 February 1812 when his handwriting was proved as witness to a deed from William Tucker to Samuel Tucker, for land in Rutherford County. (Rob TN, Co Ct Min, 3/55)

ROBINSON, Alexander
Died before 28 December 1842 when Willis W. Wilhoit was appointed guardian ad litem for Lewis Robinson, Richard Robinson, Jesse Robinson, Henry Robinson & Houston Alexander Robinson, minor heirs of Alexander Robinson, deceased, to defend in the suit of Joseph Robinson & Jane [James] Robinson vs John Robinson & others. (Bed TN, Ch Ct Min, 2/229)

ROBINSON, Hugh
Died before 25 June 1805 when the will was proved by Andrew Wilson & Nathan Clampet. (Wil TN, Co Ct Min, no#/124)

ROBINSON, John, Sr.
Died before 28 June 1842 as shown in the suit of Joseph Robinson, administrator of John Robinson, deceased vs John Robinson and others. (Bed TN, Ch Ct Min, 2/184) In the suit of Joseph Robinson et al vs Alexander Saunders & others it was stated that complainants & defendants were the heirs of John Robinson, Sr. (Ibid 231) Rachel Robinson was the widow. Disbursments were made to David Robinson, Alexander Sanders & wife, James M. Robinson, Mary Biggirs [Beggin], William Robinson & Jane Robinson. All the other distributees of John Robinson, deceased, have been advanced in his lifetime equal to their distributive shares. (Ibid 247)

ROBISON, Abijah
6 December 1858 Preston Maples made a settlement as guardian of Abijah Robison, a lunatic. (Sev TN, Co Ct Min, no#/362)

ROBISON, Joel
7 September 1857 Nancy Robison was appointed guardian with James Eslinger as her security. (Sev TN, Co Ct Min, no#/201)

ROBISON, Mary
2 August 1858 Caleb Robeson was appointed her guardian. (Sev TN, Co Ct Min, no#/326)

RODDY, James
Died before 20 December 1805 when Daniel Rather, Coroner, was paid for holding an inquest on the body. (Roa TN, Co Ct Min, B/117)

RODDY, Joseph
Died before 15 July 1859 when his death was suggested in the suit of Adam T. Wilson & others vs Joseph Roddy & others. (Jac TN, Ch Ct Min, C/294)

RODES, B.
Taxes were not collected in District 3 in 1873, "over age." (Dyr TN, Co Ct Min, B/758)

RODGERS, Jobe
Died before 19 June 1839 as shown in the suit of Jubilee Rodgers & John W. Rodgers, Executors of Jobe Rodgers Decd. vs John W. Byrd. (Obi TN, Cir Ct Min, 3/372)

ROGERS, Aaron
Was of Wake County, NC, when he made the following on 1 March 1815: "for the natural love and affection which I hade towards my Brother Soloman Roger's children & toward his wife Rebecca Rogers & for the further consideration of fifty cents, deeded a negro woman Aney & all of her children to the children of said Sol. Rogers, Viz, William Rogers & Patsey Rogers & to any othere children Rebecca may have a share (except Elizabeth whom I have already given a girl by the name of Phepe by deed of gift.)" (Wil TN, Reg Bk/34)

ROGERS, Abraham
Died before 27 March 1804 when Sarah Rogers was appointed administratrix, with John Brady as security. (Wil TN, Co Ct Min, no#/33)

ROGERS, America
Was granted a divorce from Matthew Rogers on 4 February 1858 on the grounds of adultry with Nancy Craig. Joseph Hancock & Joseph Davenport agreed to pay $15 of the costs in this case and defendant is to pay the balance. (Jac TN, Ch Ct Min, C/96)

ROGERS, Benjn.
Died before 20 April 1801 when Jonathan Downey was appointed administrator. (Rob TN, Co Ct Min, 1/171)

ROGERS, Cornelias
Died before 6 June 1803 when Mary Rogers and Moses McSpaden were appointed administrators, with Cavanaugh Newport & James Devers as security. (Cla TN, Co Ct Min, 1/118)

ROGERS, Davis
2 March 1802 made bond for a bastard child charged to him by Mary Lewis, with Nathaniel Austin and Ezekiel Craft as his security. (Cla TN, Co Ct Min, 1/25)

ROGERS, Elisha
Died before 16 September 1816 when the administrator, Jeremiah Tucker, was ordered to make a report. (Wil TN, Co Ct Min, no#/29) Ransom King, Esqr. was appointed guardian of 5 minor heirs of Elisha Rogers, deceased, to wit, Littleton, Clabourn, Cantsriel, Emily & Jeremiah Rogers. (Ibid 43)

ROGERS, George
Was the father of a bastard child by Rebecca Bell and was ordered to pay support 7 September 1874. (Dyr TN, Co Ct Min, B/783)

ROGERS, John
Was a resident of Hall County, GA, on 8 December 1825 when his deposition was to be taken for the plaintiff in the case of Thomas C. Camp vs Gideon Morgan. (McM TN, Co Ct Min, no#/215)

ROGERS, John
19 January 1802 was bound as an apprentice to Isham Rogers to learn the trade of a Hatter, until age 21. (Rob TN, Co Ct Min, 1/200)

ROGERS, Joseph B.
Was a non-resident 13 July 1855 as shown in the suit of George C. Darwin & Polly Darwin, admrs. &c vs Joseph B. Rogers & Milton Draper. (Jac TN, Ch Ct Min, B/257)

ROGERS, Martha
Died before 5 October 1858 when A. H. Shamblin was allowed money from the poor tax for her coffin. (Sev TN, Co Ct Min, no#/353)

ROGERS, Mary Ann
18 August 1868 in the suit of H. F. Harris et als vs J. C. Rogers et als, it was stated that one undivided half of the Jno. H. Butler tract of land belongs to Mary Ann Rogers and the other half subject to the heirs herein set forth. There is now due D. B. Thomas, administrator of Battle Robinson, deceased, $4,661.08 and to said Louisa J. Harris $3,586.72 & said sums are liens on said land after cutting off the one half to Mary Ann Rogers. (Mad TN, Ch Ct Min, 3/204)

ROGERS, Nathl.
Died before 20 October 1802 when John Philips & Thomas Johnson were appointed to value the property of the estate. (Rob TN, Co Ct Min, 1/235)

ROGERS, Thomas
Died before 6 February 1860 when Saml. Pickens was appointed administrator, with W. C. Pickens as security. (Sev TN, Co Ct Min, no#/513) B. J. Tipton, C. Johnson & Saml. Davis were appointed to lay off a years provisions for Leaner Rogers & family, widow of Thos. Rogers. (Ibid 518)

ROISTER, W. H.
Taxes were not collected in District 3 for 1873, "gone." (Dyr TN, Co Ct Min, B/758)

ROLLONS, Rossel
Was a non-resident on 28 December 1843 when his attorney, Thomas C. Whiteside, was served a copy of the injunction in the suit of Rossel Rollons vs Samuel and Newsom Thompson. (Bed TN, Ch Ct Min, 2/277)

ROLSTEN, James
4 October 1870 was chosen and appointed guardian of Quintilla Rolsten, Presley Blackburn Rolsten & James Franklin Rolsten, his children, with Nathan King and J. P. Thurmond as security. (Dyr TN, Co Ct Min, B/107)

ROMINES, Abel
4 October 1859 Wm. C. Murphy was paid for trimmings for a coffin for Able Romines' child. (Sev TN, Co Ct Min, no#/483)

ROMINES, David
Died before 6 October 1857 when Mary Romines was appointed guardian of Sarah Elizabeth, Mary Jane & Samuel Romines, minor heirs. Wilson Duggan was her security. (Sev TN, Co Ct Min, no#/219) On the same date, Mary Romines petitioned for sale & partition of land. Henry Romines, John Romines, Noah Romines, Geo. Romines, Thomas Romines, Isaac Richards & his wife Jenny formerly Romines, Tabitha Abbott formerly Tabitha Romines, Elizabeth Romines and Abel Romines are to be made parties defendants to this suit. (Ibid 220)

ROMINES, Latan
Died before 2 July 1866 when D. P. Gass was paid for the burying clothes. (Sev TN, Co Ct Min, no#/347)

ROMINES, Laten
Died before 8 December 1857 when Mary Romines, guardian vs the heirs of Laten Romaine, petitioned to sell land. (Sev TN, Co Ct Min, no#/228-9)

RONK, J. S.
Died before 5 June 1871 when R. R. Watson made a settlement as administrator. (Dyr TN, Co Ct Min, B/243)

ROOT, Daniel
Gave a power of attorney 13 November 1815 to Mercellus Moss to adjust affairs in VA. (Cla TN, Co Ct Min, 4/121) Daniel Root and wife Santha sold land in VA. (Ibid 359)

ROPER, John
Taxes were not collected in District 2 for 1873, "insolvent." (Dyr TN, Co Ct Min, B/758)

ROSE, McKinsey
Died before 7 February 1859 when Adam Criswell, George Wade & Andrew Pitner were appointed to set apart one years provisions for [blank] Rose, the widow. (Sev TN, Co Ct Min, no#/397)

ROSS, James M.
Died before 13 November 1834 when his death was suggested in the suit of Louis Faust et al vs Jesse S. Ross, George McWhirter & others. James M. Ross was one of the defendants. (Obi TN, Cir Ct Min, 2/209) Jesse S. Ross is a citizen of MS. (Ibid 216)

ROSS, William
Died before 6 May 1811 when the will was proved by Charles Ross, Isaac Ross & Timothy Taylor. James Walker was executor. (Ste TN, Co Ct Min, 3/54)

ROSS, William N.
Died before 2 May 1814 when Sarah Ross was appointed administratrix with Henry Gibson & Robert Cooper as security. (Ste TN, Co Ct Min, 4/137) On the petition of Sarah Ross, John Scarborough, Ephraim B. Davidson & James H. Russell are to set aside provisions from the estate of William N. Ross, deceased, for the support of the family for one year. (Ibid 158)

ROUTH, Jeremiah
Died before 7 May 1860 when Elizabeth Routh was appointed administratrix with Jas. L. Haggard as security. (Sev TN, Co Ct Min, no#/559)

ROWHOOF, John
Died before 17 July 1866 when David Keener, A. J. Cown & J. H. Caldwell were appointed to lay off a years support to Lotty Roohoof, widow. (Sev TN, Co Ct Min, no#/352)

ROWLAND, Samuel C.
Made a deed of gift to Patsey Spencer 15 February 1815, proved by Edward Howel, a subscribing witness & Martin Beaty the other subscribing witness living in the state of VA. He also made a deed of gift to Alexander Spencer and another one to Nathan Spencer with the same witnesses. (Cla TN, Co Ct Min, 4/18)

RUCKER, John
6 December 1827 a jury found that he was the father of a male bastard child of Nancy Hill & ordered to pay support. He asked for & was granted a new trial. (McM TN, Co Ct Min, no#/287) The second jury also found that he was the father. (Ibid 301) 7 March 1828 he was granted an appeal to the Circuit court, with James Rucker as his security. (Ibid 314)

RUCKER, S. H.
Died before 4 October 1870 when Mrs. V. A. Rucker was appointed administratrix, with G. W. McDearmond, N. B. Rucker and J. H. Watson as her security. Ben Rogers, Frank Chambers and J. H. Watson were appointed to lay off a years allowance for the widow and her family. (Dyr TN, Co Ct Min, B/101 & 107) A years provision was laid off to Virginia A. Rucker, the widow. (Ibid 164)

RUDD, Herrod
Died before 7 September 1829 when his will was proved by Martin Linter & Jacob Hoss, witnesses. (McM TN, Co Ct Min, 2no#/383) William Rudd & Moses Stout were executors. (Ibid 386)

RULE, John
4 October 1858 was released from paying poll tax, as he is over 50 years of age. (Sev TN, Co Ct Min, no#/346)

RUSE, Randle
8 April 1857 John Ruse made a settlement as guardian. (Sev TN, Co Ct Min, no#/158)

RUSH, James
Was a minor 16 July 1858 when William H. Botts was appointed guardian ad litem to defend the suit of R. M. Kinnard & W. M. Cooke vs Caroline Rush & others. (Jac TN, Ch Ct Min, C/153) 17 July 1858 it was stated that since the filing of complainants bill Caroline Rush had married. Her husband, [blank] Gipson is to be made party to the bill. (Ibid 161) This suit was shown as Russell M. Kinnaird & Watson M. Cooke vs Charles C. Price, Jesse L. Case, William Case, John Rush, James M. Richmond, William M. Ragland, Caroline Gipson, Matt Gipson and James Rush. Land had passed from Richmond to Case to Ragland to Price. Charles C. Price on 18 August 1854 sold the land to John Rush and William L. Rush the last named, who has since died, leaving Caroline Rush his widow. Caroline has since married Matt Gipson. James Rush, a minor, was his only child. The purchase price for the land has not been paid so the land is to be sold. (Ibid 191)

RUSHING, Joel
Married before 21 August 1858 to Sarah Vick. Sarah Vick was one of the complainants in the suit of Robt. E. Preuett et als vs James Prewett et als. (Mad TN, Ch Ct Min, 2/235)

RUSHING, Philip
Died before 7 February 1814 when Isaac Lanier was appointed administrator on the motion of Jemima Rushing. Able Rushing and Tapley Maddux were security. John Chambers, John Brigham & Nimrod Cross were ordered to lay off a years provision for the widow. (Ste TN, Co Ct Min, 4/86) Jemima Rushing was the widow. (Ibid 199)

RUSSELL, Jas. F.
Died before 17 February 1858 when his death was admitted in the case of Croom & Russell vs Joel D. Barbour. (Mad TN, Ch Ct Min, 2/170) The heirs of James Russell were America Ann Russell, Joseph A. Russell, Edgar Russell & James F. Russell. (Ibid 314)

RUSSELL, John
Was a resident of SC 2 November 1784 when his deposition was to be taken on behalf of Leroy Taylor vs John Davis. (Was TN, Co Ct Min, 1/259)

RUSSELL, Jordan
Was a mulatto boy, who was bound 4 May 1814 to Burwell Cato until age 21. (Ste TN, Co Ct Min, 4/154)

RUSSELL, Leven [Levi]
3 August 1818 was allowed $30 for his support for one year. This order was then rescinded. (Wil TN, Co Ct Min, no#/286)

RUSSELL, Moses
7 April 1857, the order appointing him a road overseer was rescinded since Moses is over 45 years of age. Isaac Russell was appointed instead. (Sev TN, Co Ct Min, no#/154)

RUSSELL, William M.
Died before 26 August 1844 as shown in the suit of William R. Looney Executor vs Cyrus N. Allen & wife & others. Cyrus Allen was appointed guardian ad litem for William A. Russell, William E. Russell, Martha E. Russell, Samuel G. Russell, Josephus Russell and James R. Russell, who are minors and have no regular guardian. The will of William Russell was mentioned. George W. Whitsell & wife were also defendants. (Bed TN, Ch Ct Min, 2/292 & 340) Joel C. Russell shall have money for the hire of Stephen after the time he should, by the will of the testator, have been delivered to him. The saddle bequeathed to William A. Russell should be paid for out of any money not bequeathed. (Ibid 367) William M. Russell died in January 1842 having made a will. He made bequests to: my son James R. Russell; unto George W. Whitesill and his wife Mary Deltha who is my daughter; unto Cyruss N. Allen and his wife Lucy Caroline Ward who is my daughter; unto my son Joel Calaway Russell; unto my daughter Sally Matilda Freeman and the heirs of her body; unto my son William Allen Russell when he shall arrive to the age of 21; unto my daughter Margaret Ann Louisa Bathe Russell; unto my daughter Martha Freeman Russell; my three youngest children that is to say Wm. A. Russell, Martha Freeman Russell and Margaret B. Russell. He appointed William R. Loony his executor & Cyrus N. Allen guardian of Margaret Ann Bathe Russell & Martha Freeman Russell. The will was dated 7 January 1842. Sally Malvina Freeman's husband was Otheniel Freeman. James R. Russell, son of William M. Russell, is deceased. The children of James R. were William E. Russell, Martha Elizabeth Russell, Samuel S. Russell, Simpson Russell and James R. Russell. Sally's name was shown as Sally Matilda, Sally Malvina and Sally Malinda Freeman. Wm. A. Russell has died during the proceedings and William J. Barnett is his administrator. Daughter Margaret was also shown as Margaret Louisa Martha Russell.

Some slaves will have to be sold to make the legacies according to the will. (Ibid 3/255-262)

RUSSELL, Wm.
Died before 23 February 1861 when his death was admitted in the suit of William F. Steel vs Wm. Croom et als. (Mad TN, Ch Ct Min, 2/445)

RUTH, George W.
In 1839 was the jailor for Bedford County. He had in his possession a negro man called Jerry [or Drewry, Drew] & had advertised him as a runaway. He had two claims for said negro and wants the court to decide who is the rightful owner. The two claims came from Milton H. Grace for his father? Boyd M. Grace of Henry County, AL, and Samuel Williams of Martin County, NC. It was decided that Drew belonged to Samuel Williams. (Bed TN, Ch Ct Min, 1/195)

RUTHERFORD, John
Was the father of Elizabeth Rutherford as shown 16 December 1817, when he gave his consent that William Seawell be appointed guardian of Elizabeth until she arrives at full age. (Wil TN, Co Ct Min, no#/199)

RUTLAND
4 February 1812 Rhaford Rutland and Rutherford Rutland listed their land for taxes. (Ste TN, Co Ct Min, 3/111)

RUTLAND, Jno.
Died before 2 August 1819 when the widow, Clarissa Rutland, petitioned for dower. (Wil TN, Co Ct Min, no#/506)

RUTLEDGE, David
Was a citizen of Gibson County, TN, on 18 February 1842 as shown in the suit of John Wilson vs John W. Key and David Rutledge. (Bed TN, Ch Ct Min, 3/51)

RYLA, William [Rila]
Died before 25 May 1807 when John Ryla was appointed administrator with Isaac Southern & James Claxton as security. (Cla TN, Co Ct Min, 3/71) William Rogers, Luke Bowyers and William Graham were appointed to settle with John Riley as administrator of the estate of William Riley, deceased. (Ibid 232)

RYON, Sarah [Rion]
Died before 14 August 1860 as shown in the suit of Sarah Ryon vs David D. Ryon & others. Robert A. Cox was the administrator and the suit was revived in his name. It was also combined with the suit of Harris Hatcher & wife vs D. D. Rion & others. (Jac TN, Ch Ct Min, C/395)

RYON, Washington [Rion]
Died in 1847 as shown in the suit of Harris Hatcher & wife vs D. D. Ryon & others, filed 15 July 1858. D. D. Ryon was appointed administrator with the will annexed. In the second clause of said will he divised as follows, "Secondly, I give my tract of land on which I live Jointly to my father and mother and my brothers W. L. Ryon, Fielding Ryon, David D. Ryon, Joseph Ryon, to cultivate a portion of the land and have the proceeds thereof except a Suffering to Support my father and mother and sisters Courtny, & Clay Hemphill, Fielding Ryon to cultivate the portion I marked out to him being between two drains?" Whereupon the Court is of the opinion and so orders and decrees that the support of complainant Courtney and defendants, Clara Hemphill and John and Sarah Ryon, is a charge upon the real estate devised in said will. (Jac TN, Ch Ct Min, C/137) Cornelia Hemphill is a minor & R. A. Cox was appointed guardian ad litem. Cornelia was an heir at law of Matilda Hemphill, deceased. (Ibid 243)

SADLER, Henry
Died before 11 February 1859 as shown in the suit of Abisha Cannon & others vs Garret Sadler & others. (Jac TN, Ch Ct Min, C/185) Thomas H. Butler was administrator. (Ibid 235) This suit was revived against Thomas H. Butler as administrator of Henry Sadler, deceased, and Nelson Sadler, administrator de bonis non of Martha Sadler, deceased. (Ibid 317)

SADLER, Henry
Died before 16 August 1860 as shown in the suit of William P. Overstreet et als vs Thomas B. Butler, administrator of Henry Sadler & others. Henry Sadler was the original defendant to this suit and has died leaving a will by which he bequeathed some of the

slaves in controversy to certain legatees who should be made party to this suit. [It is not clear if this is the same Henry Sadler for whom Thomas B. Butler is administrator or not.] (Jac TN, Ch Ct Min, C/424)

SADLER, Ira B.
Died before 5 February 1858 as shown in the suit of Ira B. Sadler by next friend Matthew Cowen vs Nelson Sadler and Henry Sadler. Ira B. Sadler was to have land when he arrived at age 21. He died before attaining that age. He was also to have had money with interest from 1841. Oliver Sadler was mentioned. (Jac TN, Ch Ct Min, C/108)

SADLER, Lee
Died before 4 February 1858 as shown in the suit of George W. McKinley & wife Alsey McKinley vs Nancy Sadler and the heirs & distributees of Lee Sadler Decd. Complainants want an administrator appointed & William B. Botts was appointed. Defendant, Henry Sadler, was appointed guardian ad litem for the minor defendants, Charles W., Nancy & Leonidas Sadler. (Jac TN, Ch Ct Min, C/94) Dower is to be laid off for the widow. (Ibid 100) Nancy Sadler was the widow. Dower was laid off and title divested out of George W. McKenly & wife Alsey, Elmon Sadler, Henry Sadler, Charles W. Sadler, Nancy Sadler, Jr. & Leonidas Sadler, children and heirs of Lee Sadler, deceased. (Ibid 121) In the suit entered 11 February 1859 by George W. McKinley & wife vs Nancy Sadler & others and the cross bill of William F. Sadler vs Geroge M. McKinley & others, it was stated that William F. Sadler was one of the sons of Lee Sadler, deceased. (Ibid 182) A negro was sold as shown in the suit of George W. McKenly & Alsey McKeny his wife vs Nancy Sadler, Elmore Sadler, Henry Sadler, Charles W. Sadler, Mathew Anderson & his wife Nancy Anderson, Leonidas Sadler & William F. Sadler. Title was divested out of complainants & defendants. Land was also sold & purchased by Henry F. Sadler & Ellmore D. Sadler. (Ibid 346) The estate has been fully administered and divided between Nancy Sadler, Elmore D. Sadler, Charles W. Sadler, Leonidas Sadler, William F. Sadler, Henry F. Sadler, George W. McKinley and wife & Matthew Anderson & wife. In order to equalize the settlements, Mrs. Nancy Sadler must pay to each one of her children the sum of $2.41. (Ibid 438)

SADLER, Martha
Died before 3 February 1858 when her death was suggested in the suit of William P. Overstreet vs Henry Sadler & wife. The suit was revived in the name of Henry Sadler, her administrator. (Jac TN, Ch Ct Min, C/82)

SADLER, Nancy D.
Married before 10 February 1859 to Matthew J. Anderson as shown in the suit of William F. Sadler vs George W. McKinley & others. Henry F. Sadler was appointed guardian ad litem of the minor defendants in this case. (Jac TN, Ch Ct Min, C/179)

SADLER, Nelson
Brought suit for sale of land on 11 February 1860 against James K. Lunsden, Jane Lunsden, Robert O. Rogers, Mary Rogers, Travis W. Pendergrass, Nancy Pendergrass, Rachel Scanland & Benjamin Scanland. (Jac TN, Ch Ct Min, C/340)

SADLER, William
Was a resident of Jackson County, TN, 27 January 1817 when he sold a slave to Samuel Elliott of Wilson, County. (Wil TN, Reg Bk/51)

SANDERS, Joel
Died before 20 August 1858 as shown in the suit of Thos. J. Sanders admr. &c vs The Heirs & Creditors of Joel Sanders. Defendants, Clark Sanders, Jr., Elizabeth Sanders & Ann A. Tatum, are minors and are non-residents of the state. (Mad TN, Ch Ct Min, 2/232) Joel Saunders died in April 1857, intestate. Jno. P. Saunders was one of the heirs. (Ibid 317)

SANDERS, Luke
Died before 12 November 1810 when administration was granted to William D. Menees, with Elisha Fikes & Jesse Williams as security. (Rob TN, Co Ct Min, 2/312)

SANDERS, Samuel
Was a resident of Green County, GA, 18 May 1810 when his deposition was to be taken for the defendant in the case of John Redferren, Sr. vs Mary Erwin, for slander. (Rob TN, Co Ct Min, 2/268)

SANDERS, Thomas
Died after making his will on 7 April 1838. The will was proved 7 January 1839. Mary

Sanders was appointed administratrix with will annexed. Mary Sanders was his widow. A suit was filed 18 February 1858 by Wm. A. Webb & wife vs Mary Sanders et als. The will had left Mary A. Sanders a negro woman, Mariah. Mariah has had increase since the death of Thomas Sanders the following children: Edy, Tom, John, Mary, Sam, Bill & Joshua. A bill of sale for Mariah, Edy & Tom was made 20 Nov 1843 by complainants to Mary Sanders when Mary A. Webb was minor, a femme covert. The bill of sale is void and the negroes belong to Mary A. Webb at the termination of the life estate of Mary Sanders. Wm. H. Sanders & John Sanders were mentioned. (Mad TN, Ch Ct Min, 2/173) This suit was shown again 25 February 1860 and stated that Mary Saunders was dead. (Ibid 346)

SANDERS, Thos. J.
Died before 22 August 1866 as shown in the suit of Thos. J. Sanders admr. vs H. Alston et als. Land was sold & payment made to Hardaway Alston, the balance to be paid to the personal representatives of Joel Sanders. Thos. J. Sanders was administrator of Joel Sanders. The death of Thos. J. Sanders was suggested and admitted & this cause revived by consent in the names of Henry B. Wilson, administrator de bonis non, of Joel Sanders & in the name of B. F. Travsue?, administrator of Thos. J. Sanders. (Mad TN, Ch Ct Min, 2/512)

SANDERS, William
Died before 7 March 1827 when Robert Rentfroe was allowed money for holding an inquest over his body. (McM TN, Co Ct Min, 2no#/209)

SANDERS, William
Died before 25 June 1805 when the executor, James Sanders, deeded land to Walter Clopton, proved by Moses Ingram. (Wil TN, Co Ct Min, no#/124)

SANDERS, Wm.
Died before 22 February 1860 when his death was admitted in the suit of Seth Q. Waddill vs Wm. Fulgum et als. (Mad TN, Ch Ct Min, 2/316) The deceased is shown as W. S. H. Sanders. He left Butie? Sanders, Thos. D. Sanders, Jno. B. Sanders & Wm. W. Sanders, all minors, as his heirs. Benj. R. Lewis was appointed guardian ad litem. (Ibid 408)

SANDERS, Wm.
Died before 18 April 1803 when the will was proved by Benjn. Darrow. (Rob TN, Co Ct Min, 1/246)

SANDERSON, Thomas
Died before 2 August 1819 when the will was proved by Wm. Carrol & Jno. Sanderson. Wade Sanderson was executor. (Wil TN, Co Ct Min, no#/496)

SANDERSON, Wm.
Died before 2 February 1818 when a years support was set off to the widow. (Wil TN, Co Ct Min, no#/216) Thomas Sanderson was appointed administrator with Joseph T. Williams & George Smith as security. (Ibid 217) 1 February 1819 Wade Sanderson was appointed administrator with William Johnson & George Smith as security. (Ibid 383)

SANDFORD, Ezekiel
Died before 5 June 1871 when Joseph Sandford was appointed administrator, with James Sandford as security. (Dyr TN, Co Ct Min, B/242)

SANDFORD, Jo.
Taxes were not collected in District 2 for 1873, "insolvent." (Dyr TN, Co Ct Min, B/758)

SAPPINGTON, Mark
Died before 26 June 1805 when the executor, Roger B. Sappington, was on the tax list. (Wil TN, Co Ct Min, no#/130)

SAPPINGTON, Mark B.
Died before 8 May 1804 when the administrator, Roger B. Sappington, was in a case vs Jesse Martin. (Rob TN, Co Ct Min, 1/292)

SARETT, James D. [Surrett, Seratt]
Died before 1 May 1865 when Ezekiel Haggard was appointed administrator with W. F. Nichols as security. (Sev TN, Co Ct Min, no#/159) James Maples, William Atchly & Joshua Atchly, Sr. were appointed to lay off a years support to the widow & family. (Ibid 160) 2 October 1865 Francis Sarett was appointed guardian to the minor heirs, with E. L.

Haggard & W. F. Nichols as security. (Ibid 218) 1 January 1866 sale was made & Samuel H. Seratt was the purchaser. Name also shown as Saratt & Seratt. (Ibid 252)

SATTERFIELD, Larry
Was appointed guardian of Cynthia Satterfield, his infant daughter, on 5 February 1811. William Haggard & Philip Hornberger were security. (Ste TN, Co Ct Min, 3/35)

SAULSBURY, Frank
Died before 7 November 1870 when A. B. Stalcup renewed his bond as guardian of the minor heirs. (Dyr TN, Co Ct Min, B/126) A. B. Stalcup made a settlement as guardian of F. M. Saulsbury's heirs. (Ibid 243) 2 December 1872 A. B. Stallcup made a settlement as guardian of E. F. and Tennessee Saulsbury. (Ibid 513)

SAWYER, Isaac
Died before 7 November 1870 when John Sawyer made a report as administrator. (Dyr TN, Co Ct Min, B/133) John Sawyer was chosen and appointed guardian of the minor heirs. (Ibid 138) 3 July 1872 John Sawyer made a settlement as guardian of W. J. Sawyer, J. W. Sawyer, George C. Sawyer, Jame Sawyer and Daniel Sawyer. (Ibid 442) 8 January 1873 John Sawyer made a settlement as guardian of Isaac W. Sawyer, Dan T. Sawyer, Jane, Sawyer, Geo. C. Sawyer, W. J. Sawyer. (Ibid 533) These were heirs of Isaac Sawyer, deceased. (Ibid 699)

SAWYER, Jo.
7 October 1873 adopted Willie Mahon. The child and his mother, Ailsey Mahon, agree to the adoption, as Ailsey Mahon is destitute and unable to provide for the child. His name was changed from Willie Mahon to Willie Sawyer. (Dyr TN, Co Ct Min, B/645) 8 April 1874 Ailsy Mahon brought suit against Jo. Sawyer claiming that he is unable to support the child adopted by him. The charge was not allowed. Ailsy was granted an appeal to Circuit Court. (Ibid 733)

SAWYER, Joshua
Died before 8 January 1874 when his will was proved by W. C. Doyle, F. G. Sampson and W. B. Sampson, witnesses. W. H. Gooch and his wife Narcissa Gooch, contested the will. Monroe Sawyer was named executor. The case is to go to Circuit Court. (Dyr TN, Co Ct Min, B/703)

SCALES, David
Died before 14 August 1816 when his handwriting was proved by John Brock as witness to a deed from Allen Brock to John Evans. (Cla TN, Co Ct Min, 4/239)

SCALES, Joe
Taxes were not collected in District 4 for 1873, "under age." (Dyr TN, Co Ct Min, B/759)

SCANLAND, William
Died before 11 July 1850 as shown in the suit of William Scanland vs Clayton Rogers et al. Benjamin Scanland is executor. (Jac TN, Ch Ct Min, A/354) William Scanland & Clayton Rogers were partners in the tanning business. Rogers has refused to pay Scanland money due him from the partnership. One partner has died and the other removed. (Ibid B/49)

SCANLON, John
Was a non-resident of TN 30 July 1846 as shown in the suit of Nelson Sadley vs Merlin Young. (Jac TN, Ch Ct Min, A/230) John Scanland had been sheriff of Jackson County. (Ibid 269)

SCISCO, Saunders
10 Februray 1860 dismissed his suit for divorce against Mary E. Scisco. (Jac TN, Ch Ct Min, C/326)

SCITES, Abraham
Died before 6 March 1826 when Margaret Scites was appointed administratrix. Abner Lee, William L. Taylor & Isaac Carlock were appointed to lay out a years provisions for the widow, Margaret Scites. (McM TN, Co Ct Min, 2no#/133)

SCOBEY, Jonathan D.
Died before 6 July 1874 when Smith Parks was appointed administrator, with J. D. Pace and S. H. Moore as his security. R. W. Townsend, James R. Green and W. L. Meadows were appointed to lay off a years allowance for the widow and family. (Dyr TN, Co Ct Min, B/750)

SCOBY, Matilda J.
Was granted a divorce for desertion from William Scoby on 21 February 1843. (Obi TN, Cir Ct Min, 4/no#)

SCOTT
5 May 1818 a deed was entered from John Scott, William Scott, James Scott, Isabella Scott, Elizabeth Scott, Nathl. Brown, John Bell, Cornelius Anderson & Sarah Brown to Samuel Scott. (Wil TN, Co Ct Min, no#/257)

SCOTT, Allen
8 September 1874 it was stated that "one Allen Scott, a cosmopolite is insane and without friends or sustenance and in very needy circumstances." The sheriff was ordered to take him to the poor house. (Dyr TN, Co Ct Min, B/785)

SCOTT, Christian
August 1789 the presentment against him for Bastardy was ordered to be quashed. (Was TN, Co Ct Min, 1/394)

SCOTT, E. T.
Died before 16 January 1851 as shown in the suit of Elijah Turner [Tamer] vs Jas. V. Daily & others. E. T. Scott had been security for the prosecution. (Mad TN, Ch Ct Min, 1/193)

SCOTT, Frankey
Whose maiden name was Frankey Nickins, made oath that "David Manley, William Manley and Levi Manly were her children by husband Joseph Manley who was a free man of colure." Sworn 5 February 1821 [or 1826]. [Also see Eleanor Nichons.] (Wil TN, Reg Bk/393)

SCOTT, James
Died before December term 1816 as shown in the case of John W. Payton, administrator of James Scott vs David Irwin, administator of John Irwin. (Wil TN, P &J, no#/no#) 20 June 1817 Nathaniel Brown, one of the legatees, petitioned for the sale of a negro to be divided between the several heirs. (Ibid, Co Ct Min, no#/134)

SCOTT, Robert
Was a resident of Bladen County, NC, as shown in the case of William Campbell vs Philip Parchment, February term 1799. (Rob TN, Co Ct Min, 1/85)

SCOTT, Wm.
Died before 3 May 1819 when Tabetha Scott was appointed administratrix with Walter Corruth, Robt. Doak & John Y. Smith as security. George Donnel, Wm. Donnel & Ephriam Sherrill were appointed to allot a years provisions to the widow. (Wil TN, Co Ct Min, no#/441)

SCRUGGS, Archabald
Died before 3 August 1857 when Rufus M. Creswell was appointed guardian to [Rhoda is written, then crossed out] George, Nancy, Martha, Isaac, Hariet & Frederick Scruggs, minor heirs. (Sev TN, Co Ct Min, no#/197) 6 January 1858 George Wade made a settlement as executor. (Ibid 250)

SCRUGGS, Archibald
Died before 13 July 1850 when his death was admitted in the suit of Joseph C. Fletcher vs Alexander Dillard, Allen Young, John H. Young & Archibald Scruggs. (Jac TN, Ch Ct Min, A/377)

SCRUGGS, Penelope
4 May 1857 a jury was summoned to examine her as she is probably an idiot. (Sev TN, Co Ct Min, no#/163) 2 June 1857 she was found to be an idiot. She has an interest in an estate of her father. (Ibid 173) R. M. Creswell was appointed her guardian. (Ibid 198)

SCRUGGS, Rhoda
11 April 1856 G. B. Hogan was allowed money for board of Rhoda Scruggs, a lunatic, and 2 guards. (Sev TN, Co Ct Min, no#/39) 7 July 1856 R. M. Creswell was allowed money for conveying Rhoda Scruggs to the Lunatic Asylum. (Ibid 58) R. M. Creswell was appointed her guardian. (Ibid 198)

SCRUGGS, William L.
Was stated to be 21 years of age & of good moral character, 8 December 1857. (Sev TN, Co Ct Min, no#/228) 7 June 1858 he was charged with bastardy. The sheriff returned the

warrent with the note, "Search made and the defendant not found in my county." A capias was issued to the sheriff of Hamilton County. (Ibid 305)

SCURLOCK, Timothy P.
Died before 21 August 1867 when his death was proven in the suit of M. J. J. Stoddert vs Timothy P. Scurlock. The suit was revived against his widow, Ann Scurlock, and against Joseph W. Scurlock, Clarence H. Scurlock, Catherine S. Scurlock, Fanny H, Scurlock & Annie Scurlock, only heirs of Timothy P. Scurlock. (Mad TN, Ch Ct Min, 3/69) Clarence H. Scurlock & Annie F. Scurlock are minors. James K. Stephens was appointed guardian ad litem. (Ibid 130) The widow was Ann H. Scurlock and Catherine was shown as Kate. (Ibid 149) T. P. Scurlock died 20 May 1867, having made a will appointing Ann H. Scurlock, executrix, and sole devisee of his estate. Her dower has been had. He had owned land in Henderson County. His personal estate included law books. (Ibid 172)

SEARCY, Robert
Was an orphan boy 10 years of age when he was bound to Elisha Taylor, 17 June 1816. (Wil TN, Co Ct Min, no#/3)

SEARCY, William
Of the town of Centerville in Livingston County, KY, when he gave power of attorney to Robert Searcy of Nashville, TN, to dispose of lands they own jointly in TN. Given 14 December 1807 with James Tatum as witness. (Wil TN, Reg Bk/72)

SEATON, Andrew B.
10 April 1866 was released from paying poll tax on account of physical disability. (Sev TN, Co Ct Min, no#/313)

SEAWELL, John
Died before 28 March 1804 when the heirs were on the tax list. (Wil TN, Co Ct Min, no#/38) The heirs were on the 1804 non-resident tax list with land on Falling Creek. (Ibid 86)

SELLARS, Danl.
Died before 22 January 1802 when the heirs were listed on the delinquent tax list. (Rob TN, Co Ct Min, 1/206)

SENTER
John Senter & Fortena Senter were bound on 6 September 1830 to John May, as apprentices. (McM TN, Co Ct Min, 2no#/473)

SETTLE, Joel L.
Died before 5 November 1840 having bequeathed all of his property to his wife, Jane Settle, during her life or widowhood and then to be divided between his children. Jane has departed this life, leaving LaFayette, Sydney, Frederick, Sewell, Tipton and Joel their children. The property is to be sold for division. (Jac TN, Ch Ct Min, A/8) Mannie [Mounce, Maurice] Gore is administrator for Jane Settle. (Ibid 15) Peter L. Cox is guardian for Joel L. Settle & Suel Settle. (Ibid 87) There had been a partnership between J. L. Settle and L. W. Settle. (Ibid B/208) Lafayette W. Settle died previous to 6 December 1852 and on that day Peter G. Cox was appointed guardian of Tipton C. Settle, and is administrator of said L. W. Settle. (Ibid 307)

SETTLE, Lafayette W.
Probably died before 8 February 1854 as shown in the suit of Peter G. Cox et al vs Sampson W. Cassety. An account is to be made of all matters between complainants intestate and defendant and report the assets belonging to the estate of L. W. Settle, and moneys belonging to the partnership with L. W. Settle. (Jac TN, Ch Ct Min, B/115) The death of L. W. Settle was mentioned in the suit of Sidney L. Settle vs Peter G. Cox & S. W. Cassitty. (Ibid 165) A suit was entered by Peter G. Cox, administrator of L. W. Settle, deceased vs Thomas J. Jones & wife Clarissa J. Jones. Clarissa J. was the widow of L. W. Settle. She had money from the estate that had not been turned over to the administrator. (Ibid 276) A suit was shown as Peter G. Cox Admr. of L. W. Settle decd. vs Sydney L. Settle, Joel L. Settle, Tipton C. Settle & William H. Botts Guardian to T. C. Settle, Thomas J. Jones, Clarissa J. Jones & Thomas L. Bransford. It was stated Lafayette W. Settle, about 1848, purchased land from Thomas L. Bransford. This land is to be sold. (Ibid C/26) [Also see Joel L. Settle]

SEVIER, Abraham
27 August 1778 took the oath of allegiance. (Was TN, Co Ct Min, 1/44)

SEVIER, James
Was a person who had withdrawn his allegiance. He came into Court at the February term 1789 and availed himself of the Act of Pardon and Oblivion by taking the Oaths prescribed by law. (Was TN, Co Ct Min, 1/371)

SEVIER, Robert
27 August 1778 took the oath of allegiance. (Was TN, Co Ct Min, 1/44)

SEVIER, Robert
Died before 27 February 1782 when John Sevier and Charles Robertson, Esqrs. were granted leave of administration on the estate. (Was TN, Co Ct Min, 1/154) Col. Charles Robertson was appointed guardian of the orphans. (Ibid 155)

SEVIER, Val., Sr.
27 August 1778 took the oath of allegiance. (Was TN, Co Ct Min, 1/44)

SHANKLIN, Andrew
Died before 14 November 1810 when Jesse Shanklin was appointed administrator with Joseph Woolfolk and James T. Millier as security. (Rob TN, Co Ct Min, 2/326) Jane Shanklin, daughter of Andrew, married before 10 November 1812 to Marvil McFarland. (Ibid 3/155)

SHANKS, James
Made a deed of gift to his son William Shanks at May term 1789. (Was TN, Co Ct Min, no#/57)

SHANKS, John T.
Was a resident of MO in 1841 as shown in the suit of Thomas Davis vs John T. Shanks & David Green. (Bed TN, Ch Ct Min, 3/52)

SHANKS, Michl.
Was an orphan of the age of 7 years and 4 months old when he was bound 4 August 1784 to John Stram until age 21. (Was TN, Co Ct Min, 1/247)

SHANKS, William
Died before 25 June 1804 when John M. Payton returned an Inventory of the goods and chattles. (Wil TN, Co Ct Min, no#/41) The will was mentioned. (Ibid 44)

SHANNON, St. Clare
Died before 4 August 1856 when the administrator, Shannon Felker, renewed his bond with Cornelius Fox & J. M. Hammer as security. The original bond was destroyed by fire. (Sev TN, Co Ct Min, no#/66)

SHAPPARD
20 February 1857 a suit was entered by Fanny Shappard vs William Shappard & L. B. Shappard. William Shappard is indebted to the conplainant & he is a non-resident of TN. Lewis B. Shappard, as surviving partner & administrator of John Shappard, is indebted to William Shappard for more than enough to pay the debt. Complainant askes for the debt to be paid out of the money in the hands of Lewis B. Shappard. Francis E. Oliver had an indentical suit against William & Lewis B. Shappard. (Mad TN, Ch Ct Min, 2/133)

SHARKS, Jessee [Shuks]
Died before 21 February 1839 when land was taxed to the heirs. (Obi TN, Cir Ct Min, 3/301)

SHARP, Anderson
Died before 4 April 1870 when his widow, Mary Sharp, was appointed administratrix, with R. R. Watson and W. M. Watkins as security. (Dyr TN, Co Ct Min, B/35) G. W. McDearmon, Benjamine Rodgers and J. H. Watson were appointed to lay off a years provisions for the widow and family. (Ibid 40) The widow petitioned for dower. Richard Sharp, John Sharp and Mattee Sharp are the only children and heirs-at-law. (Ibid 68)

SHARP, Nicholas
Died before 14 May 1816 when the will was proved by William Lynch and William Rogers. John Sharp and Martin Sharp were apponted administrators with will annexed, with John Graves and David Wilson as security. (Cla TN, Co Ct Min, 4/189)

SHARP, William, Sr.
Was the brother-in-law of Martin Hancock and Samuel Hancock, as shown in the suit of

Ephriam Hunter against all three. The suit is not dated but is probably in 1844. John Bell is a son-in-law of William Sharp, Sr. & William Sharp, Jr. is his son. Hanoriah Hancock is the sister-in-law of William Sharp, Sr. Robert M. Sharp is a son of William Sharp, Sr. Martin & Samuel Hancock are citizens of Coffee County, TN. Jeremiah Jacob and Alfred Jacob are the father-in-law and brother-in-law of Robt. M. Sharp. James Sharp of Franklin County was mentioned. (Bed TN, Ch Ct Min, 3/291)

SHAVER, William
Was an orphan boy. 3 September 1827 the sheriff was ordered to bring him into court. (McM TN, Co Ct Min, 2no#/233) 4 September 1827 he was bound as an apprentice to Tidence Lane. (Ibid 237)

SHAW, Christopher
Was not a resident of TN on 6 November 1843 when Samuel E. Hare & Watson M. Cook filed a suit against him. (Jac TN, Ch Ct Min, A/115)

SHAW, George W. C.
Died before 4 May 1841, intestate, leaving Martha Shaw his widow, and Burchet Shaw, Matilda Shaw and Rebecca Shaw his heirs, who are minors, and the said Martha Shaw their guardian. George W. C. Shaw had been joint tenant with Ridley Roberts in some land & Roberts petitioned for division. (Jac TN, Ch Ct Min, A/17) George W. C. Shaw had been partners with Christopher Shaw and Samuel Shaw. (Ibid 18) Land was divided between the widow & heirs of G. W. C. Shaw, deceased, the heirs of Samuel Shaw, deceased, and Christopher Shaw. (Ibid 100) In a suit 30 July 1846 by James T. Hughs vs Christopher Shaw, leave was given to make Rawlings Hogin & wife Burchy of Jackson County, Thomas J. Shaw of MO, Daniel Hogan, guardian of Matilda Shaw, Jane Shaw, Buchy Shaw & Rebecca Shaw of MO, Wesley Harvey, guardian of Bryson Cowin and Sophia Cowin of Jackson County and Artie Shaw of MO parties defendant to said bill. (Ibid 224) Petition was made 27 January 1848 by Matilda Shaw, Jane Shaw, Burchy Shaw, Rebecca Shaw by their next friend Rawlings Hogin and Martha Shaw, heirs and widow of George W. C. Shaw. (Ibid 283) Martha Shaw married a Taylor before 13 July 1850. (Ibid 388) Martha's husband was George W. Taylor (Ibid 393)

SHAW, James
Was a resident of Tuskallosa County, AL, 4 July 1823 when he gave power of attorney to Simeon Hancock to collect money in Wilson County, TN. (Wil TN, Reg Bk/324)

SHAW, James G.
Died before 5 December 1870 when his heirs petitioned for a division of the land. There are shown to be 9 heirs, 1. Mary S. and J. B. McSweeny, 2. Sam B. Shaw, 3. Thos. J. Shaw, 4. Martha Shaw, 5. Craig N. Shaw, 6. David A. Shaw, 7. Margaret Giles, 8. Wiliam Shaw, 9. Sarah Jane Wagster. Sam B. Shaw has bought the interest of some of the heirs. (Dyr TN, Co Ct Min, B/143)

SHAW, Milton
Died before 8 March 1870 when S. B. Shaw was appointed administrator, with Thos. Cotten & A. G. Pierce as security. (Dyr TN, Co Ct Min, B/15) 8 August 1871 the public administrator, C. L. Nolen, was appointed administrator de bonus non. (Ibid 267)

SHAW, Sam. B.
Died before 7 August 1871 when the will was proved by H. L. W. Turney and Wm. D. Taylor, witnesses. Craig A. Shaw and David A. Shaw were executors, with A. G. Pierce and John Sawyer as security. (Dyr TN, Co Ct Min, B/261)

SHAW, Saml.
Died before 5 October 1807 when James Sawyers, Richd. Matthews, Sampson Matthews, Amos Cohia, Isaac Davis, Sr., Isaac Davis, Jr., Saml. Davis, Sr., Plummer Willis, Isaac Bridgewater, James McDonald, Robert Bates and James Shannon were appointed to lay off the dower of Mrs. Emley Shaw, relict of Saml. Shaw deceased. (Rob TN, Co Ct Min, 1/468)

SHAW, Samuel
Died before 8 November 1842 as shown in the suit of Martha Shaw & Rollins Hogin vs Christopher Shaw. David G. Shepherd, John Hughes and Henry Sadler will divide the lands in the pleadings mentioned into 3 equal parts, one part to the heirs of George W. C. Shaw, one part to Christopher Shaw and one part to the heirs of Samuel Shaw, deceased. Martha Shaw is the widow of George C. W. Shaw. James Shepherd is administrator of John Shepherd. (Jac TN, Ch Ct Min, A/77) Christopher Shaw was administrator for Samuel Shaw. (Ibid 291)

SHAW, Samuel
Died before 18 November 1794 when the will was approved by the affirmation of Margaret Spear and Samuel Breson. Francis Shaw and Samuel Shaw qualified as executors. (Was TN, Co Ct Min, 1/513)

SHAW, T. J.
Had left the State before 4 March 1872 when a new trustee was to be appointed in his place. (Dyr TN, Co Ct Min, B/382)

SHAW, W. L.
Taxes were not collected in District 4 for 1873, "run away." (Dyr TN, Co Ct Min, B/759)

SHAW, Wm. J.
Died before 8 March 1870 when a bill to sell land to pay debts was made by John H. Lasley, administrator of Wm. J. Shaw deceased vs Samuel B. Shaw, Thomas J. Shaw, Wm. C. Wagster, Jane Wagster, Martha E. Shaw, Craig N. Shaw, Milton Shaw, David A. Shaw & Mary L. Shaw. Saml. B. Shaw was the purchaser. The undivided tenth part of land in the 4th District was mentioned. (Dyr TN, Co Ct Min, B/15)

SHEARMAN, George W.
Died before 14 November 1844 as shown in the suit of Squire B. Partee Admr. of George W. Shearman vs Charles McAlister. (Obi TN, Cir Ct Min, 4/no#)

SHELBY, Evan
Died before 21 February 1843 when his death was suggested in the suit of Green B. Watson vs Evan Shelby. (Obi TN, Cir Ct Min, 4/no#) The suit was to be revived in the names of John Crockett & Thomas S. Shelby, administrators, 19 June 1843. (Ibid)

SHELBY, Henry
Died before 7 November 1818 when his widow, Hannah Shelby, confirmed a legacy he had made to Martha J. Brown for $1,000. Hannah called Martha J. Brown "my sister." (Wil TN, Reg Bk/120) The will was dated 15 August 1816 & he made a bequest to his brother-in-law, Jordon Brown, youngest son of Jeremiah Brown. He made another will in November 1817 making Hannah Shelby his residuary legatee & no provision for Jordan Brown. Hannah made provision for the education of her brother, Jordon Brown. She mentioned the slave, Isaac, that she received from her father. (Ibid 121) The will was entered 19 December 1817 by Joseph Johnson, one of the executors. Golman Donaho was the witness & stated that the will was made between the 20th and 27th of September 1817. There was a codicil which was not witnessed & the handwriting in it was proved. (Ibid, Co Ct Min, no#/210)

SHELLEY, Elijah
Died before 6 January 1862 when Boyd Clark, Andrew Delozier & Calvin Johnson were appointed to lay off a years provision for the widow, Amanda Shelly. (Sev TN, Co Ct Min, no#/744)

SHELLY, John
Was the father of a bastard child by Jane Garner and gave bond 1 October 1866 to indemify the court. (Sev TN, Co Ct Min, no#/374)

SHELTON, ____
Died before September term 1804 when the heirs were on the non-resident tax list with land on Round Lick & Cedar Creek. (Wil TN, Co Ct Min, no#/88)

SHELTON, America
Died before 7 January 1874 when J. A. Shelton was appointed guardian of Susan C., Sarah Francis and J. B. Shelton, minor heirs, with James C. Miller and C. C. Moss as his security. (Dyr TN, Co Ct Min, B/698)

SHELTON, Charles
Died before 21 February 1857 as shown in the petition of Jno. H. Williams, administrator, and others. (Mad TN, Ch Ct Min, 2/146) 24 February 1860 a suit was entered: John H. Williams, Mary Shelton, Judithen C. Shelton, Levi B. Shelton, Millard B. Shelton, Eliza J. Shelton, Eleanora Shelton, Aaron W. Haskins, Mary A. Haskins & John Sevier vs Valentine Sevier, Bethany Brown, George W. Sevier, Elizabeth Gilsen, Eldridge G. Sevier, et al. (Ibid 326)

SHELTON, David
Died before 2 January 1871 when James C. Miller was chosen and appointed guardian

of Charles H. Shelton, George N. Shelton and Solon A. Shelton, minor heirs. Burton Payne & R. W. Adams were securities. (Dyr TN, Co Ct Min, B/151) John A. Shelton was appointed administrator de bonis non. (Ibid 202)

SHELTON, Nelson P.
Died before 2 January 1871 when James C. Miller was chosen and appointed guardian of William H. Shelton, minor heir, with B. Payne and R. W. Adams as security. (Dyr TN, Co Ct Min, B/151)

SHELTON, Sandford
Died before 20 February 1858 as shown in the suit of Jno. H. Williams Admr. &c & others vs Jesse Russell & wife et als. Shelton had purchased land in 1852 from Chas. Sevier, Sr., now deceased. John M. Williams was appointed administrator for Sandford Shelton & John Sevier was appointed administrator for Charles Sevier, deceased. Mary Shelton was the widow of Sandford Shelton. (Mad TN, Ch Ct Min, 2/205) 24 February 1860 a suit was entered: John H. Williams, Mary Shelton, Judithen C. Shelton, Levi B. Shelton, Mildred B [E]. Shelton, Eliza J. Shelton, Eleanora Shelton, Aaron W. Haskins, Mary A. Haskins & John Sevier vs Valentine Sevier, Bethany Brown, George W. Sevier, Elizabeth Gilsen, Eldridge G. Sevier et al. Land was sold and divested out of all of above except John H. Williams & with the addition of Robert W. Jennings & the heirs of Catherine Langford (names not known), and the heirs of Mary R. Simentin, deceased, (names not known), the heirs of Charles Sevier, Jr., deceased, (names not known), Joseph F. S. Sevier, Jesse Russell & wife Nancy D. Russell & A. Huntsman Sevier. (Ibid 326)

SHELTON, Thomas
6 April 1874 was chosen and appointed guardian of Mahala Shelton, Susan E. Shelton, Sarah E. Shelton, John T. Shelton, William Franklin Shelton, Joseph Shelton and Robt. L. Shelton, minor heirs of Thomas and L. B. Shelton. T. H. Pain and Burton Payne were his securities. (Dyr TN, Co Ct Min, B/714)

SHELTON, W. T.
7 February 1871 resigned as administrator of the estate of David Shelton, "the said Shelton has left the country." (Dyr TN, Co Ct Min, B/195)

SHELTON, Watson
Died before 4 January 1871 when B. P. Payne made a settlement as guardian of the minor heirs. (Dyr TN, Co Ct Min, B/162) B. B. Payne was appointed guardian of Ella Nora and Mahaly Shelton, minor heirs. (Ibid 174) 8 September 1874 a suit was brought by James M. Moseley, Ellenora Moseley, Burton P. Payne & Burdetta Payne vs Mahala Shelton. It stated that Watson Shelton died some 10 years ago leaving complainant Burdetta (who has since married Burton P. Payne) as his widow, and Ellenora (now married to James M. Moseley) and Mahala Shelton (who is a minor) as his only heirs. Dower is to be laid off and land divided. (Ibid 785-6)

SHEPHERD, John
Died before 28 January 1847 as shown in the suit of James T. Hughs vs Christopher Shaw Admr. et als. James M Shepherd is administrator of John Shepherd and he and David G. Shepherd are interested in this matter and are made defendants in the suit. (Jac TN, Ch Ct Min, A/244)

SHEPHERD, Sarah Baker
Died before 5 November 1840 when David G. Shepherd and James M. Shepherd vs Augustin Shepherd et als, petitioned for sale of land. Sarah Baker Shepherd died possessed of 5 tracts of land, in which one tract the widow of John Shepherd, deceased, aged 27 years, has dower. Two of the heirs are femmes covert and there is no evidence that they have consented to sell the land. (Jac TN, Ch Ct Min, A/4 & 7) Thomas Baker was guardian of the children of Sarah Baker, formerly Sarah Shepherd. Other defendants in the suit were Jesse George Shepherd, Joseph S. Perkins and wife Nancy formerly Nancy Shepherd, Garland Farrar and wife Mary L. formerly Mary L. Shepherd, Martin B. Shepherd, Thomas Shepherd, Benjamin A. Shepherd and Joseph H. Shepherd. [This case is not clear. On page 7 it definately states that Sarah Baker Shepherd died possessed of 5 tracts of land. On page 15 it states that Thomas Baker was guardian of the children of Sarah Baker formerly Sarah Shepherd.] (Ibid 15) The estate of Sarah Baker Shepherd was mentioned in the suit of Elijah Torrey vs Augustin Shepherd and George M. McWhorter. (Ibid 30)

SHEPHERD, W. M.
13 January 1849 the sheriff of Madison County reported W. M. Shepherd was not to found in the county when attempting to serve him to appear in the suit of William J. Turner vs

Samuel S. Anderson, Jas. Fussell & W. M. Shepherd. Publication was to be made in some newspaper in the Western District. (Mad TN, Ch Ct Min, 1/74)

SHEPPERD, James
Died before 13 May 1834 when his death was suggested in the case of State of Tennessee vs James Shepperd & James M. Pound. He had died since last term of court. (Obi TN, Cir Ct Min, 2/170)

SHEROD, Henry
Died before 6 August 1805 when the administrator was given permission to sell the personal estate. (Rob TN, Co Ct Min, 1/351) Elias Lawrence was appointed administrator with Henry Gardner & John Gardner as his security. (Ibid 354)

SHERRILL, Jacob
Died before 4 June 1814 when Hulda Sherrill made an agreement with Samuel Wilson Sherrill, John Brown, Ephraim Sherrill, Able Sherrill & Ambrose Sherrill. For one cent she will convey to them, at or before her death, all her personal property except wearing clothes. In return, the above named parties agree to pay the heirs of Jacob Sherrill, deceased, $400, the purchase of a negro woman named Polly & give to the said Hulda Sherrill the negro Polly & a negro girl named Cate, during her natural life. At her death, the negroes are to revert to Samuel, John, Ephraim, Able & Ambrose and their heirs forever. (Wil TN, Reg Bk/2)

SHERRILL, Ute
Died before 2 November 1818 when the will was proved by James Jetton & James Moore. Jacob Sullivan & Ephraim Sherrill were the executors with James Wills & William Murray as security. (Wil TN, Co Ct Min, no#/334)

SHERROD, Charlotte
11 February 1812 Levi Dunn was appointed guardian with Richard Miles as security. (Rob TN, Co Ct Min, 3/60)

SHERROD, Elizabeth
14 November 1814 Holland Darden was appointed her guardian, with Elias Laurence as security. (Rob TN, Co Ct Min, 3/491)

SHIELD, Mary
Died before 4 December 1866 as shown in the suit of James M. Wright Admr. of A. McGinnis decd. vs the widow & heirs and creditors of said deceased. S. W. Shields, administrator of Mary Shield, deceased, has a lien on property in the suit. (Fen TN, Ch Ct Min, A/305)

SHIELDS, David
Died before 4 May 1857 when R. B. Brabson as guardian of the minor heir, Elizabeth Jane Shields, was given authority to sell a lot of paper & books belonging to her estate. (Sev TN, Co Ct Min, no#/161)

SHIELDS, Nancy
1 March 1858 a lunacy hearing was ordered to be held on her. (Sev TN, Co Ct Min, no#/261) She was found to be a lunatic. (Ibid 299) M. W. Shields was appointed her guardian. (Ibid 300)

SHIELDS, Richard
Died before 5 February 1866 when his will was proved by James Drennon and A. J. Kin. (Sev TN, Co Ct Min, no#/272)

SHIPLEY, Christopher
Died before 7 June 1830 when his will was proved by James H. Reagan & Philip Fry, witnesses. James Rutherford was executor. (McM TN, Co Ct Min, 2no#/449)

SHIPMAN, Daniel
Was a resident of Tryon County [NC] 24 November 1778 when his deposition was to be taken. (Was TN, Co Ct Min, 1/51)

SHIPMAN, E. P.
Died before 4 December 1871 when M. P. Shipman was appointed administratrix, with J. P. Thurmond and E. K. Manning as her security. Enoch McPherson, A. P. Mitchell and E. K. Manning were appointed to lay off a years allowance for the widow and family. (Dyr

TN, Co Ct Min, B/325) J. W. Lauderdale, coroner, was paid for holding an inquest of E. P. Shipman. (Ibid 346) Allowance was set off for the widow and her 3 children. (Ibid 495)

SHOATS, Edward
Was shown to be the son of Edward Shoats, 9 November 1812, when he was ordered to view a road. (Rob TN, Co Ct Min, 3/141) Also shown as Edward Choat. (Ibid 174)

SHOCKLEY, Caleb
Died before 14 August 1815 when Hannah Shockley was appointed administratrix with Geo. Petre and Isaac Bullard as security. (Cla TN, Co Ct Min, 4/95)

SHOOK, John, Sr.
Died before 6 March 1828 when John Shook, Jr. returned the inventory of his estate. (McM TN, Co Ct Min, 2no#/281)

SHORT, Jefferson
Was 10 years old when he was bound to Martin Eubanks on 13 February 1815. (Rob TN, Co Ct Min, 3/538)

SHORT, Martin
Was eight years old when he was bound to Joshua Spearman on 13 February 1815. (Rob TN, Co Ct Min, 3/538)

SHORT, Samuel
Died before 7 March 1829 when his administratrix, Mary Short, was in a case. (McM TN, Co Ct Min, no#/432)

SHORT, William
Died before 26 June 1843 when the suit of Elizabeth Short for divorce from William Short was abated because of the death of William. (Bed TN, Ch Ct Min, 2/236) Price C. Steele was the administrator. (Ibid 300)

SHRADER, Jacob
Died before 7 January 1857 when John Bird renewed his bond as guardian to Eliza Ann Shrader, Christopher Shrader, Saml. Shrader, Jane Shrader and William Shrader, minor orphans, with Christopher Shrader and C. Fox as security. The original bond was destroyed. (Sev TN, Co Ct Min, no#/117) 6 August 1860 Jno. Bird renewed his bond as guardian of the minor heirs of Jacob Shroder, deceased. (Ibid 590)

SHULTS, Eli H.
7 January 1861 was released from working on public roads because of disability. (Sev TN, Co Ct Min, no#/627)

SHULTS, Martin
Died before 7 January 1857 when petition was made for dower & partition of real estate: Cary Dennis & wife, heirs-at-law, of Martin Shults deceased vs William James & wife & others. Philip S. Shults was appointed guardian ad litem for Martin Shults, a minor heir of Martin Shults, deceased. (Sev TN, Co Ct Min, no#/118) John Large was administrator. (Ibid 128) 2 March 1857 "several years since Martin Shults departed this life." The widow, Sarah Shults, has married Wm. James. C. & L. M. Dennis & Martin Shults, a minor, are the heirs. (Ibid 130) 1 June 1857 dower was set off to Sarah James formerly Sarah Shults, the widow. The rest of the estate is to be divided between Cary Dennis & his wife, Amanda M. Dennis formerly Amanda Shults, & Martin M. Shults. (Ibid 165)

SILLERS, Jacob
Was a resident of Livingston County, KY, 17 February 1810 when his deposition was to be taken for the defendant in the case of William Ragsdale vs John B. Cheatham. (Rob TN, Co Ct Min, 2/247)

SILSBY, L. H.
Died before 2 May 1870 when Turner Chamblin was appointed administrator with J. E. Roberts & D. C. Hibbetts as security. (Dyr TN, Co Ct Min, B/53) The name was shown as Levi H. Silsby. (Ibid 414)

SILVESTER, F. M.
7 November 1859 was charged with bastardy and reported "not found in this county." It was suggested that he lives in Knox County and a capias was issued to that county for the defendant. (Sev TN, Co Ct Min, no#/485)

SIMMONS, Elijah
Died before 14 July 1853 as shown in the suit of Mahaly Jackson vs James Draper, administrator of Elijah Simmons. (Jac TN, Ch Ct Min, B/75)

SIMMONS, Elijah H.
12 January 1849 Elijah H. Simmons as executor [does not say for whom] settled a suit vs N. M. Price, Jas. M. McKnight, Berry Davis, Martial? Davis & Mrs. Davis, settled by agreement by the parties. (Mad TN, Ch Ct Min, 1/67)

SIMMONS, Harriet
Was granted a divorce from James Simmons 12 July 1848. They were married in the year 1826 or 1827 in Giles County, TN, and moved to Madison County some 15 years since. They had 10 children, to wit: Soloman, Martin, Peter, Martha, Mary, Wort, John C., Nancy, Lucinda & Almarine. Harriet was granted all property and custody of the children. (Mad TN, Ch Ct Min, 1/33)

SIMMONS, John
Died before 6 October 1807 when the will was proved by John McFarland & Edward Choate. John Simmons, Jr., one of the executors, qualified. (Rob TN, Co Ct Min, 1/462)

SIMMS, Bartlet
Died before 15 February 1815 when the death of the defendant was suggested in the suit of Mary Smithson vs Bartler Simms? [very poor handwriting] (Cla TN, Co Ct Min, 4/17) In the suit shown 15 August 1815 of Polly Smithson by her next friend against Bartlet Simms it was stated that death of the defendant having been suggested and no revival of this suit for more than two terms that the suit be abated. (Ibid 101)

SIMMS, Leonard H.
On 21 June 1815 gave a power of attorney to Jesse Jinnings to receive from the sheriff of Green County, GA, the monies that were collected in a suit against Roystin & Zachariah Sims. (Wil TN, Reg Bk/23)

SIMMS, Wm. E.
1 January 1866 made bond to appear at next court to answer a charge of Bastardy. (Sev TN, Co Ct Min, no#/256) The warrant was quashed & defendant "to go hence without day." (Ibid 258) 1 October 1866 he was found guilty of bastardy and ordered to pay support for the child for 3 years. He was granted an appeal to the Circuit Court. (Ibid 379)

SIMONS, Mark
Taxes were not collected in District 5 for 1873, "insolvent." (Dyr TN, Co Ct Min, B/759)

SIMPSON
D. Simpson and S. D. [or L. D.] Simpson were non-residents of the state on 9 October 1860 as shown in the suit against them by Pleasant Taylor. (Fen TN, Ch Ct Min, A/256)

SIMPSON, Adam
Was a minor, 5 years old last March, son of Marjery Simpson. He was bound 3 December 1804 to William Damron until age 21. (Cla TN, Co Ct Min, 2/83)

SIMPSON, Jeremiah
Was a resident of Hickman County, KY, on 9 October 1826 when he appeared in the Circuit Court of Obion County, TN, and made oath that he served in the Revolutionary War as a Sargent in Captain George Burrys? Co. in the 9th Regiment of the VA line and as a Corporal in Captain David Scott's Co. in the 13th Regiment of the VA line. He served 3 years and was discharged by Colonel John Gibson, Col. of the 9th & 13th Regiments, they having been consolidated. "I do solemnly swear that I was a resident citizen of the United States on the 18th day March 1818 and that I have not since that time by Gift Sale or in any manner disposed of my property..." He is applying for a pension. He had been a house joiner but is now incapable of labor. He resides with his son, Joshua Simpson. This Court is nearer and more convenient than the one in his county & state. He resides near the state line. He owns one small bay mare worth $30.00. (Obi TN, Cir Ct Min, 1/3)

SIMPSON, Jonathan
Probably died before 25 Septemner 1855 as shown in the suit of James B. Simpson et als vs Jno. W. Simpson. The complainant wants John W. Simpson to file a deed from Strother Frogge to Jonathan Simpson, the ancestor of complainants. (Fen TN, Ch Ct Min, A/36)

SIMS
In a suit filed 1 March 1840 by John A. Fergerson against William P. Sims of Davidson County, TN, and Walter B. Sims of Marshall County, TN, it is shown that Rebecca Sims is the mother of William P. Sims. (Bed TN, Ch Ct Min, 1/410)

SIMS
Walter H. and John G. Sims were citizens of Williamson County, TN, as shown in their suit against William T. McGrew, 17 May 1843. (Bed TN, Ch Ct Min, 3/139)

SIMS
6 May 1872, a suit was entered for a sale of land by W. M. Tatum, et al vs J. R. Reasons et al. It is shown that W. Sims, Albert Sims and Lula Sims are minors and J. G. Rains was appointed guardian to answer the suit for them. (Dyr TN, Co Ct Min, B/407)

SIMS, John
Died in 1841. Mary R. Davis and Charlotte Davis were his grand daughters with Richard H. Sims as their guardian. Mary and Charlotte inherited negroes from the estate of John Sims. Since Mary E. Sims will have married before the next term of court, the guardian petitioned to have the slaves divided between Mary and Charlotte S. Davis. S. Thompson, Johnathan Mosely & William Den? were appointed to divide the slaves at the December term 1843, and report made in 1844. The slaves were alloted to Mary R. Horn formerly Mary Davis and to Charlotte S. Davis, children and heirs of Henry Davis, deceased. On the same page Mary is shown as Mary R. Stone. (Bed TN, Ch Ct Min, 3/208)

SIMS, John G., Sr.
Died before 1836 as shown in the suit of Robert Cannon vs Walter H. & John G. Sims. Thomas D. Wilson was a brother-in-law of Walter H. & Thomas D. Sims, and was believed to own 1/4 part of the tract of land mentioned in the suit. In an amended bill dated 22 May 1844 it was stated that Walter H. Sims and John G. Sims were citizens of Williamson County, TN. Walter H. Sims gave an answer for himself and as administrator for John G. Sims [Jr.], deceased. The relinquishment of Boyd M. Sims to the land was mentioned. Walter & John G. Sims [Jr.] were brothers. The land had belonged to Walter, John G., and Boyd M. Sims and the wife of Thomas D. Wilson jointly. John G. Sims [Jr.] died sometime last July [1843 or 1844] in Williamson County. A power of attorney was given 4 January 1840 by Thomas D. Wilson of Caddo Parish, LA, to John A. Holland of Williamson County, TN, to convey the land he inherited as the heir of his son, Walter Sims Wilson, who inherited the same as the only heir of his mother, one of the heirs of John G. Sims, deceased, or in right of his late wife Ann H., formerly Ann H. Sims. It was stated that in October 1836 Walter H. Sims, John G. Sims, Boyd M. Sims and their sister Ann H. Sims, were heirs of their father John G. Sims, deceased. (Bed TN, Ch Ct Min, 3/229-37)

SIMS, Wm.
8 January 1861 was charged with Bastardy. (Sev TN, Co Ct Min, no#/639) 2 April 1861 $10 has been paid for the use of [blank] Chambers, the mother of the said child. (Ibid 679) 2 July 1861 the $10 was paid over to Charlottee Chambers. (Ibid 707)

SINCLAIR, Ralph
Died before 3 January 1871 as shown in proving the will of Thomas C. Mitchell. Ralph had been named as an executor for T. C. Mitchell. (Dyr TN, Co Ct Min, B/160)

SING, Isaah
Died before 3 April 1865 when the widow, Lucinda Sing, petitioned for dower vs Nancy C. Sing, Elizabeth Sing & Martha C. Sing, minor heirs. James Clark was appointed guardian ad litem to the said minors. (Sev TN, Co Ct Min, no#/149)

SING, John
Died before 5 June 1865 as shown in the description of dower lands of Lucinda Sing, widow of Isaah Sing, deceased. (Sev TN, Co Ct Min, no#/170)

SINGLETON, Daniel
Died before 12 April 1858 as shown in the suit & cross bill of Mary Singleton and John W. Love. Mary Singleton had been guardian of Catherine Singleton, heir of Daniel Singleton. A. B. Brock was administrator of Daniel Singleton, deceased. Land had been purchased for Catherine Singleton on 31 December 1853, so Daniel Singleton died prior to that date. [Also see Catherine Love] (Fen TN, Ch Ct Min, A/130)

SINGLETON, P. H.
Died before 5 December 1870 when W. P. Rice renewed his bond as guardian of the minor heirs. (Dyr TN, Co Ct Min, B/138)

SKIPPER, Jerry
8 October 1872 was released from poll tax and working on roads, it appearing to the court that he is physically unable to perform any labor. (Dyr TN, Co Ct Min, B/489)

SLATER, Perry
Died before 5 September 1871 when C. L. Nolen, public administrator, was appointed administrator. (Dyr TN, Co Ct Min, B/286)

SLAUGHTER, John P.
Was a resident of Campbell County, VA, 9 December 1816 when he gave power of attorney to his friend, Mathew Martin of same, to receive 2 slaves, to wit: Bob, Fain & Amey & their increase, in Wilson County, TN. Slaughter became entitled to the slaves by his marriage to Sarah Patrick. (Wil TN, Reg Bk/70)

SLAUGHTER, Mary
Died before 16 September 1817 when the executor, John Slaughter, sold land to Jeremiah Hendrick. (Wil TN, Co Ct Min, no#/157)

SLAYTON, Alex.
Died before 6 February 1871 when W. J. Davis renewed his bond as guardian of the minor heirs. (Dyr TN, Co Ct Min, B/182)

SLAYTON, Emily V.
8 October 1872 W. J. Davis made a settlement as guardian. (Dyr TN, Co Ct Min, B/494)

SLUDOR, Jesse
Died before 23 June 1807 when the heirs were on the tax list with land on Pond Lick Creek. (Wil TN, Co Ct Min, no#/300)

SMALLWOOD, Rosanna
Was the mother of 2 illegitimate children, Mary Smallwood & Ned Smallwood. George N. McMahan was the father and he made petition to adopt them 7 July 1862. (Sev TN, Co Ct Min, no#/3)

SMITH
March 1803 an entry was made; "The Grand Jury presented two orphant Boys named Jeremiah and Thomas commonly called Smith at the mouth of Straight Creek." William Baker was ordered to take charge of the two boys and bring them to next term of Court. (Cla TN, Co Ct Min, 1/106)

SMITH
19 December 1816 Henry & John Smith were residents of Madison County, when it was ordered to take their depositions for the plaintiff in the case of Robert Irwin vs Humphrey Chappell. (Wil TN, Co Ct Min, no#/67)

SMITH
5 December 1870 five negro minors were bound unto Allen and Mary Ann Harris, to wit: Martha Smith, Jo Smith, Spencer Smith, Rowland Smith and Hampton Smith, aged respectively 15, 13, 6, 4, & 2/12. (Dyr TN, Co Ct Min, B/141)

SMITH
Charity Smith and Dennis Smith died before 7 April 1874 when the coroner was paid for holding inquests on both of them. (Dyr TN, Co Ct Min, B/727)

SMITH, Abraham
Probably died before 23 September 1816 when Ezekiel Bass made a deed of gift to John Smith, Elizabeth Smith, Daley W. Smith & Abraham Smith, Jr., children of Abraham Smith. "Also for better maintenance of said children I give them the property I bought at their father's sale, which was sold by James Tarpley." [Named the property that he gave to each child] (Wil TN, Reg Bk/91)

SMITH, Albert
Died before 23 June 1843 as shown in the suit of John Williams vs Saml. H. Smith Extr. of Albert Smith. (Obi TN, Cir Ct Min, 4/no#)

SMITH, Allen
Was 7 years old when he was bound 3 November 1818 to James Milligan to learn the cooper's trade. (Wil TN, Co Ct Min, no#/346)

SMITH, Alonzo P.
Was a minor 17 June 1840 as shown in the suit of George W. Parker vs Alonzo P. Smith. Samuel A. Warner was his guardian. (Obi TN, Cir Ct Min, 4/no#)

SMITH, Ann C.
Was granted a divorce from Francis M. Smith on 3 December 1868. She was also given title to land and personal property. (Fen TN, Ch Ct Min, A/414)

SMITH, Caleb
Died before 6 March 1871 when E. J. Smith made a settlement as administrator. (Dyr TN, Co Ct Min, B/201)

SMITH, Charles
15 November 1832 stated that he is about 25 years of age, owes allegiance to the the King of Great Britian, left Great Britian in 1830 & landed in New York in the U. S. States of America on the 10th day of September in the same year. He renounces his allegiance to Great Britian and wishes to become a citizen of the United States. (Obi TN, Cir Ct Min, 2/36)

SMITH, Cytha A.
Died before 14 July 1855 as shown in the suit of Hardin L. Smith admr. of Cytha A. Smith vs James Medonal Admr. of H. L. Medonal & John Collins and others. Riley Medonal died intestate in Jackson County in 1840 leaving a widow and his brothers & sisters his distributees. Cytha A. Smith, a sister of said Riley Medonal, died intestate in 1840 [sic] and complainant administered on her estate in 1854. Henry L. Medonal [the name could be Mcdonel] & the widow of said Riley, the defendant Amy Collins now wife of defendant John Collins, administred on the estate of said Riley in 1840. The complainant wants an accounting of the estate of Riley Medonal. (Jac TN, Ch Ct Min, B/262)

SMITH, D. G.
Taxes were not collected in District 2 for 1873, "gone." (Dyr TN, Co Ct Min, B/758)

SMITH, David
Died before 12 August 1816 when Hannah Smith, the widow, was appointed administratrix with Absalom Hurst and John Jones as security. (Cla TN, Co Ct Min, 4/218)

SMITH, Drury
Was a resident of Hickman County, KY, 11 Nov 1835 as shown in the suit of David Thompson vs Drury Smith & Ansel Whitfield. (Obi TN, Cir Ct Min, 3/38)

SMITH, Elias
Died before 6 January 1857 when an inquest was held on his body. (Sev TN, Co Ct Min, no#/107)

SMITH, Elizabeth
8 September 1857 it was ordered that her child of colour, Sarah, be brought to court to be bound out. (Sev TN, Co Ct Min, no#/203)

SMITH, Ezekiel
Died before10 February 1859 when a suit was entered by John Smith & others vs Thomas Smith & others. It was stated that defendants, Ana Hix, Nancy Roberts, Elizabeth [blank] and Martilda Burroughs were femmes covert and Thomas H. Burton was appointed guardian ad litem for them. A report is to be made whether the sale of the land is necessary or not. In this suit it was stated that the children of Eli Swearington, defendants, are non-residents. This suit was also shown as John Smith, Labon Smith, Margaret Smith, Mary Smith, Joseph Roberts, Benjamin Howard, John Burroughs, Isaac Hix, Joseph Smith & William Smith vs Thomas H. Smith, Anna Hix, Nancy Roberts, Martula Burroughs, Elizabeth Howard and the children and heirs-at-law of Eli Swearingin. Ezekiel Smith died several years ago. Mary Smith was the widow. The widow had purchased land from Eli Swearingin who has died without making a deed to the land. The children of Ezekiel Smith were John, Labon, Margaret, Joseph & William Smith and Nancy Roberts, Elizabeth Howard, Martula Burroughs, Anne Hix & Thomas Smith. Isaac Hix is the husband of Anna. Joseph Roberts is the husband of Nancy. Benjamin Howard is husband of Elizabeth. John Burroughs is the husband of Martula. Dower was laid off to Mary Smith. There are 10 heirs & distributees. (Jac TN, Ch Ct Min, C/174 & 194-6)

SMITH, Frederick
Died before 1 May 1815 when Delilah Smith was appointed administratrix with Adam Smith and John Dunn as security. (Ste TN, Co Ct Min, 4/260)

SMITH, H. S.
Married before 4 July 1859 to Dorcas Cunningham, daughter of Jesse Cunningham, deceased. (Sev TN, Co Ct Min, no#/454)

SMITH, Henry
Died before 14 January 1847 as shown in the suit of James Caruthers & Henry D. Mason, his executors, vs Gladin Gorin & Joseph D. Mason. Henry Smith died in 1846. (Mad TN, Ch Ct Min, 1/13)

SMITH, Henry
7 June 1828 conveyed land in Knox County, TN, to Nathaniel L. Smith. (McM TN, Co Ct Min, no#/351)

SMITH, Hugh R.
2 August 1819 Wm. Smith was appointed guardian. (Wil TN, Co Ct Min, no#/503)

SMITH, Isaac
Died before 24 September 1805 when William Gray, Esquire was appointed administrator with Henry Ross security. (Wil TN, Co Ct Min, no#/167)

SMITH, Isiah
Died before 10 September 1804 when the will was proved by James Smith and Zachariah Oneal. (Ste TN, Co Ct Min, 1/3)

SMITH, James
Died before 4 May 1814 when Ephraim B. Davidson, John Allen, James H. Russell, John Scarborough & William Hazzard were ordered to divide the lands of James Smith, deceased, between the legatees. (Ste TN, Co Ct Min, 4/147)

SMITH, James
1 March 1830 was bound, by the assent of his mother, to Peter Larrisson. (McM TN, Co Ct Min, 2no#/422)

SMITH, James
Died before 7 December 1830 when William David & Jno. Smith, minor children of James Smith, made choice of Mary Smith as their guardian. They are all over 14 years old. She was also appointed guardian of Israel, Mary & Maring Smith who were also children of James Smith and not yet 14. (McM TN, Co Ct Min, 2no#/489)

SMITH, James
Died before 25 March 1806 when the will was proved by Jeremiah Brown & Andrew Harris. William Steel and Thomas B. Rees were executors. (Wil TN, Co Ct Min, no#/184)

SMITH, James
5 July 1858 was released from paying poll tax becaue he is over 50 years old. (Sev TN, Co Ct Min, no#/307)

SMITH, James
A "paritioner", was to be let to the lowest bidder 16 February 1814. (Rob TN, Co Ct Min, 3/378) James Smith died before 14 February 1815 when Thomas Helms was paid for the time he kept him and for burying said Smith. (Ibid 543)

SMITH, Jas. S.
Died before 22 February 1866 when Jno. S. Brown was appointed guardian ad litem for the infant defendants, Jas. H. Smith, Virginia E. Smith & Walter L. Harris, in the suit of E. S. Mathews Extr. et als vs James S. Smith et als. The death of Jas. S. Smith was admitted in the suit of S. V. Bell et als vs J. Copeland et als. Executors were Edward S. Mathews & Jno. M. Smith. (Mad TN, Ch Ct Min, 2/480 & 533) Martha A. Mathews was a femme covert in this case. (Ibid 546) In the suit of Samuel P. Bell et al vs James Copeland et al, since James S. Smith, the guardian of the minors has died, it is ordered that Thomas E. Boaz, one of the complainants who has come of age, be allowed to act for the minors as their next friend. (Ibid 3/170)

SMITH, Jenny
Was an orphan girl 21 January 1809 when Joseph Smith was appointed her guardian. Briant Oneal was security. (Ste TN, Co Ct Min, no#/90) Joseph Smith was the father of Jiney [Jincy] Smith. (Ibid 3/110)

SMITH, Jeremiah
Was an orphan boy 27 January 1809, aged 16, when he was bound to John Williams until age 21. (Ste TN, Co Ct Min, no#/85) On 26 January 1809 Bryant Oneal was appointed guardian of Jeremiah Smith. (Ibid 96)

SMITH, Joel
Was a pauper 7 September 1829 when William Carr was allowed money for taking care of him. (McM TN, Co Ct Min, 2/381)

SMITH, John
Taxes were not collected in District 5 for 1873, "insolvent." (Dyr TN, Co Ct Min, B/759)

SMITH, John A.
Died in 1826, intestate, in Marion County, TN, as shown in the suit of Isaac H. Roberts, Administrator of John A. Smith vs Rice T. Ross and Rachel Martin. Administration was granted to Roberts in August, 1826. Roberts stated that John A. Smith had borrowed money in 1820 from Ross, a citizen of Bedford County, and gave negroes as security. The note showing this was witnessed by Thomas A. Smith. Notes in the case were written in Franklin County, TN. (Bed TN, Ch Ct Min, 1/8)

SMITH, Joseph
Was a resident of Sullivan County, NC, [TN] May term 1790 when Robert Mason sold him land. (Was TN, Co Ct Min, 1/439)

SMITH, Joseph C.
Died before 15 January 1847 as shown in the suit of Wyatt Mooring, the administrator, vs Burrell Butler, et al. The suit was remanded to make the representatives of Amanda Allen and Mary Dorcas Allen defendants to the bill. (Mad TN, Ch Ct Min, 1/16)

SMITH, Joseph W.
Died before 6 July 1874 when Smith Parks was appointed administrator, with A. S. Parks and H. Parks, Jr. as his security. (Dyr TN, Co Ct Min, B/749) Alfred Enochs, Thomas Pace & W. L. Meadows were appointed to lay off a years allowance for the widow and family. (Ibid 750)

SMITH, Kinchen
Died before 1 November 1819 when Valuntine Vanhousen was appointed guardian of Malcom Smith, Polly Smith, Richard Smith & Susan Smith, minor heirs, with William Bloodworth & Joseph Neal as security. (Wil TN, Co Ct Min, no#/534)

SMITH, M.
Taxes were not collected in District 5 for 1873, "insolvent." (Dyr TN, Co Ct Min, B/759)

SMITH, Marion
2 October 1860 John Keer was paid for keeping him [her?] for 1 month. (Sev TN, Co Ct Min, no#/613)

SMITH, Mary
Died before 12 March 1844 when her death was suggested in the suit of the State of TN against her for Tippling, in 7 cases. (Obi TN, Cir Ct Min, 4/no#)

SMITH, Mary A.
Died before 20 February 1857 when her death was admitted in the suit of William Wetherspoon vs Mary A. Smith et als. (Mad TN, Ch Ct Min, 2/136) Thos. G. N. Smith was also a defendant in above suit. (Ibid 265)

SMITH, Mary E.
19 February 1858, Mary E. Smith brought suit by her next friend vs Elice Elstin et als. A trustee is to be appointed for Mary E. Smith. (Mad TN, Ch Ct Min, 2/191) T. W. Cooper was appointed trustee. (Ibid 354)

SMITH, Mildred
Was a resident of Overton County, TN, on 8 June 1827 when a deposition was to be taken for the plaintiff in the case of Thomas Smith vs Booker Shockly. (McM TN, Co Ct Min, no#/265)

SMITH, Mitchen
2 August 1819 petitioned for a division of land he held in common with Kinchen Smith. (Wil TN, Co Ct Min, no#/506)

SMITH, Nancy
17 July 1866 David Hurst was authorized to place her in care of the commissioners of the Poor House. (Sev TN, Co Ct Min no#/354)

SMITH, Nathan
Died before 1 July 1872 when J. H. Davis was paid for holding an inquest over him. (Dyr TN, Co Ct Min, B/424)

SMITH, Nathaniel
10 December 1830 sold land in Monroe County to John Hughes. (McM TN, Co Ct Min, 2no#/498)

SMITH, Polly
Was an orphan girl 27 January 1809, aged 17, when John Williams was appointed her guardian. James Haggard & Caleb Williams were security. (Ste TN, Co Ct Min, no#/92)

SMITH, Richard
Died before 3 February 1812 when the will was proved by James Lee. (Ste TN, Co Ct Min, 3/106) It was also proved by Charles B. Wilson. (Ibid 142) Hannah Smith was granted letters of administration with James Lee & Samuel Yarborough as security. (Ibid 156)

SMITH, Robert
7 April 1809 made a deed of gift to James Rice. (Rob TN, Co Ct Min, 2/135)

SMITH, Robert H.
Was a non-resident of TN on 27 August 1845 as shown in the suit of Wm. R. Brasee vs Robt. H. Smith & G. A. Sublett. (Bed TN, Ch Ct Min, 2/365)

SMITH, Samuel
Died before 21 February 1838 when land was taxed to the heirs. (Obi TN, Cir Ct Min, 3/163)

SMITH, Samuel
Died before 2 November 1818 when Allen Smith was appointed administrator, with Jeremiah Hendrick & William Smith as security. (Wil TN, Co Ct Min, no#/331)

SMITH, Sidney
Died before 12 February 1859 when his death was suggested in the suit of Sidney Smith vs Thomas Exr. &c. (Jac TN, Ch Ct Min, C/229)

SMITH, Silas
25 January 1799 was shown to be the son of Thomas Smith when Thos. Yates swore that Silas Smith had a part of his ear bit off in the fights. (Rob TN, Co Ct Min, 1/83)

SMITH, Solomon
Was an orphan boy 20 years of age when he was bound 27 January 1809 to James Gatlin until age 21. (Ste TN, Co Ct Min, no#/94)

SMITH, Thomas
Died before January term 1807 when the will was proved by Robert Cooper and Jesse Dawson. James Gatlin and Bryan Oneal were executors. (Ste TN, Co Ct Min, 1/39b) Thomas Clinton & James Tagart, on 28 April 1809, made a division of the lands of Thomas Smith, deceased, between his three sons, Solomon Smith, John Smith & Jeremiah Smith. (Ibid no#/114)

SMITH, William
Died before 4 September 1826 when Elizabeth Smith was appointed administratrix. (McM TN, Co Ct Min, 2no#/172) 9 March 1831 a settlement was made that states Wm. Smith had been administrator for James Smith, deceased, & guardian of the minor children of James Smith. James was the son of William Smith. A slave was purchased in SC. Evidently James Smith died before March 1824. It was later stated William was NOT guardian of James Smith's children. (Ibid 519)

SMITH, William
Died before 7 December 1829 when his will was proved by George Bowman, one of the witnesses. (McM TN, Co Ct Min, 2no#/395) John Smith, Israel C. Smith & Joseph Smith were executors. (Ibid 412)

SMITH, William
Died before 16 September 1816 when the administrator, Jeremiah Tucker, was ordered to make a report. (Wil TN, Co Ct Min, no#/29) David & William Smith, orphan children of William Smith, deceased, were ordered to be brought to court to be bound out or have guardians appointed. (Ibid 44)

SMITH, Wm.
Died before 2 August 1819 when [blank] Smith was appointed administrator with Hugh Tilford & Perry Anderson as security. (Wil TN, Co Ct Min, no#/492) A years provisions was allotted to the widow. (Ibid 494)

SMITH, Wm. G.
Married in October 1867 to Addie Morris as shown in the suit of Addie B. Smith by next friend vs Wm. G. Smith et als. Robt. Purdy had been guardian for Addie until she arrived to lawful age & has since been acting as her agent. Her property is to be put in trust for her sole and separate use & Wm. G. Smith was appointed trustee. (Mad TN, Ch Ct Min, 3/150)

SMITHER, Virginia L.
Died before 2 December 1873 when her will was proved by Dr. R. H. McGaughey and Maggie Sampson, witnesses. (Dyr TN, Co Ct Min, B/670)

SMITHPETER, John Michael
August term 1789, "On motion of John Michael Smith Peter & Mary Johnston, Ordered that George, the Son of Said Mary and John Michael Smith Peter, his reputed father, be from this time known and Called by the name of George Smith Peter." On the same date a deed of gift was recorded from Michael Smith Peter to his son, George Smith Peter. (Was TN, Co Ct Min, 1/400)

SMIZER, John, Sr.
Died before 27 December 1842 as shown in the suit of John & Alfred Smizer Executors &c vs John Crick & Alfred Balch. Balch had assigned a note to John Smizer, Sr. in his lifetime. (Bed TN, Ch Ct Min, 2/216)

SNAUFFER, Elizabeth
Died before 6 September 1802 as shown in the power of attorney given by John Snauffer, David Snauffer, George Snauffer, Nancy Snauffer & Mary Snauffer, sons and daughters of Elizabeth Snauffer, deceased, daughter of David & Margaret Jarrets, deceased. The power of attorney appointed George Snauffer, Sr. "to receive from the estate of David Jarret, deceased of the County of Barroks, State of Pensylvania, all parts of said estate unto us coming." Mary Snauffer signed as Polly Snauffer. (Cla TN, Co Ct Min, 1/59)

SNAUFFER, Jacob
At the September term 1802 made choice of George Snauffer as his guardian. On the same day the court appointed George Snauffer guardian for Margaret Snauffer & Elizabeth Snauffer. (Cla TN, Co Ct Min, 1/53)

SNELL, Elizabeth
Died before March term 1824 when the guardian of her heirs, Lawrence Sypert, sold land to pay the debts. (Wil TN, Reg Bk/337)

SNELLING, Hugh
Died before 28 June 1843 as shown in the suit of F. Peter Lee? [ink blot] Admr. of Hugh Snelling vs Lemuel Snelling & others. Complainant is the administrator & defendants are the distributees of Hugh Snelling, deceased. The defendants agreed on 23 August 1841 to make a division of the negores. Division was made to Elizabeth Snelling, R. S. McConnall & wife, Lemuel Snelling, John Snelling, Susanah Searcy and L. N. Arnold [female]. (Bed TN, Ch Ct Min, 2/259) John McGuire was administrator de bonis non, 26 February 1845, when he brought suit against Lemuel Snelling & others. John A. More was guardian of Elizabeth Snelling, an idiot, who was one of the defendants. (Ibid 349) Frances was the wife of R. S. McConnell, James H. Arnold was the husband of Louisa Arnold. (Ibid 365) Hugh Snelling died intestate in April 1841. Names mentioned in the division were his children except that Fanny McConnell, wife of Robert S. McConnell, was an illegitimate daughter of Nancy Snelling, deceased, who was a daughter of Hugh Snelling. It was mentioned that about the year 1811 Lemuel Snelling was about to move to TN from NC where his father then lived. Lemuel was at that time a single man. Hugh Snelling removed to TN some 7 or 8 years later. Thompson Gray was mentioned as a son-in-law of Hugh Snelling? In the answer of John Snelling he mentioned Granville County, NC. John lived in Bedford County in 1813 or 1814 & had to go to NC for negros

his father advanced to him. Nancy Snelling died about 20 years before her father. (Ibid 3/28-40)

SNIDER, Adam
Died before 25 February 1794 when John Venit was appointed administrator with Mathaias Waggoner as security. (Was TN, Co Ct Min, 1/470) The administrator's name was shown as John Vaught. (Ibid 484)

SNIDER, Peter
17 May 1796, with his wife Elizabeth, sold the eleventh part of 206 acres of land in Dauphin County, PA. (Was TN, Co Ct Min, 1/603)

SNODDY, Glasco
Died before 7 November 1859 when his will was proved by S. W. Randles, George Wade & James Malcom, witnesses. R. M. Creswell, one of the executors named, qualified with Andrew H. Pitner & Adam Creswell as security. (Sev TN, Co Ct Min, no#/487)

SNODGRASS, James
Died before 8 September 1824 when an inventory of his estate was filed. (McM TN, Co Ct Min, 2no#/30) 7 December 1824 William Cate, James Rucker & Elijah Gressam were appointed to lay out a years maintenance for Milly Snodgrass, widow. (Ibid 36) 7 March 1826 the 3 oldest children of the late Milly Snodgrass, present wife of Nathan Hambrick, is to be provided for until next session in court. (Ibid 140) 5 June 1826 Jeremiah Hambrick was appointed guardian of Nancy Snodgrass, Elaner Snodgrass & Thomas Snodgrass, minor orphans of James Snodgrass, deceased. They are over 14 years of age & chose Jeremiah Hambrich for their guardian. (Ibid 154) 4 June 1827 the administrator, John Miller, is entitled to money for 22 days going to & from KY on business for the estate. (Ibid 214) 5 June 1827 Jeremiah Hambrick & Robert Ellison were appointed administrators. (Ibid 219)

SOMERS, John
Died before 26 September 1806 when John Somers & Arden Somers, devisees, petitioned for division of land. (Wil TN, Co Ct Min, no#/261) James Somers & Abijah Wright, widow of Isaac Wright, deceased, were two of the heirs. (Ibid, Reg Bk/47)

SOUTHERLAND, E. G.
Sued for divorce from Janet M. Southerland on 12 November 1828. The defendant failed to appear and publication is to be made for her to appear at next term of Court. (Obi TN, Cir Ct Min, 1/67) The defendant's name was shown as Janette Moriah Sutherland. Hugh Allison was to be a witness for plaintiff and failed to appear. (Ibid 74) They were married in 1820 in LA. Elijah G. Sutherland was granted a divorce from Jannet M. Sutherland on 12 May 1828 for adultry. (Ibid 78)

SOWARD, Charles M.
Died before 9 July 1873 when George W. Soward was appointed administrator, with L. N. Stevens and T. W. Hern as security. (Dyr TN, Co Ct Min, B/613)

SPAIN
4 October 1870 P. S. Taylor was chosen and appointed guardian of John E. Spain and M. S. Spain, with J. S. Miller and M. D. Pate as his security. (Dyr TN, Co Ct Min, B/108)

SPAIN, Coleman
Died before 5 December 1870 as shown in the division of the lands of Dent Ferrell. Three of the Ferrell heirs had sold their interest in the land to Coleman Spain. Coleman left his widow, Elizabeth, and heir, Jane Francis Spain who married James Sullivan. Jane died leaving a daughter Mary Alice Sullivan. Other heirs of Coleman were Calvin [not clear if Calvin is a Spain or a Sullivan], William B. Spain, minor, Mary Elizabeth Spain, minor Electra Hellen Spain and Martha Emeline Spain. (Dyr TN, Co Ct Min, B/145-6) 2 April 1872 the heirs are shown to be James Sullivan, Mary Alice Sullivan, Elizabeth Spain, Calvin Spain, Wm. B. Spain, Mary E. Spain, Electra Hellen Spain, Martha Emiline Spain. (Ibid 403-4)

SPAIN, Wm.
5 October 1870 P. S. Taylor made a settlement as guardian of the heirs of Wm. Spain. (Dyr TN, Co Ct Min, B/122)

SPENCE, Margaret
Died before 8 January 1874 when George Spence was chosen and appointed guardian

of Elizabeth Ada Spence, minor child, with Andrew Hart and T. H. Benton as security. (Dyr TN, Co Ct Min, B/702)

SPENCER, George W.
Died before 13 February 1815 when the executor, John Dougherty, made a settlement. (Cla TN, Co Ct Min, 4/4)

SPENCER, James
Died before 4 March 1806 when George W. Spencer was appointed administrator, with William Condry & Alexander Richie as security. (Cla TN, Co Ct Min, 2/223)

SPIGHT, Mary
Was a pauper 4 April 1870 when $20 was allowed to J. P. Williamson for her care. (Dyr TN, Co Ct Min, B/33)

SPRIGS, Jno.
Was a resident of Tryon County [NC] 23 November 1778 when his deposition was to be taken for the suit of John McNabb vs Wm. Taylor. (Was TN, Co Ct Min, 1/49)

SPRING, Aaron
Died before 17 June 1816 when the administrator, Joseph Fouse, was ordered to make a report, and was appointed guardian to Elisa Spring, infant daughter of Aaron Spring deceased. (Wil TN, Co Ct Min, no#/3) An account of money received from the paymaster of the United States belonging to the estate of Aron Spring, deceased, was reported by the administrator. (Ibid 50)

SPRING, Benja.
With his wife Sally, sold land in Carretuck County, NC, to Joseph Quidly, August term 1819. (Wil TN, Co Ct Min, no#/507)

SPRINGER, Dennis
Died in July 1839 as shown in the suit of J. J. Cooper & others vs E. F. Gibbs & others, filed 16 December 1840. Jonathan J. Cooper & Edward Whitman were executors of Dennis S. Springer, who died in July last. His widow was Sarah and his children were Susan Washington Jane James Catherine Robert John Sarah and Ann. (Bed TN, Ch Ct Min, 1/462)

SQUIRE, Solomon
Died before 7 October 1808 when Martin Duncan was appointed administrator with Wm. Perry, Henry Johnson & John B. Cheatham as security. (Rob TN, Co Ct Min, 2/96)

STACY, Joseph
On 4 December 1815 made a deed of gift to his son, Joseph Stacy. (Wil TN, Reg Bk/45)

STAFFORD
John and Anna Stafford died before 11 July 1850 as shown in the suit of Nancy Nettles by her next friend W. R. Kenner vs Zebulon Nettles & others, and a cross bill of Samuel E. Hare vs Nancy Nettles & others. Nancy Nettles is entitled as one of the distributees of John Stafford and Anna Stafford, deceased, to a fund now in the hands of William Gore as administrator of John & Anna Stafford. Nancy and Zebulon Nettles are indebted to complainant Hare. (Jac TN, Ch Ct Min, A/355) Nancy Nettles is a legatee of John Stafford and a distributee of Anna Stafford. William Gore is administrator with will annexed of John Stafford and administrator of Anna Stafford. Zebulon Nettles is the husband of Nancy Nettles and is an improvident man and very much addicted to intoxication. The money coming to Nancy is to be paid to James T. Quarles, her solicitor, and he is to pay off a note given for property purchased at the administration sale with Harriett Nettles as security and the residue to William R. Kenner as trustee for Nancy. (Ibid 377) Another suit concerning parties interested in this estate was entered 20 March 1852: Zebulon M. Nettles and Nancy Nettles, Matthew & Harriet Frost vs John Stafford, Polly Anderson, Thomas H. Butler Admr. of Bailey Butler decd., William R. Kenner Guardian of James M. & Thos. J. Stafford & William Gore Admr &c. (Ibid B/50)

STAFFORD, Author
Died before 12 January 1849 as shown in the suit of Daniel B. Cliff admr. of David McPhail deceased vs Caroline C. Stafford, widow of Auther Stafford deceased, James H. Stafford, Marshall C. Stafford, Jno. M. W. Stafford, Caroline Stafford, Mary A. J. Stafford & William Crown administrator of Author Stafford, and others. The Staffords listed were his heirs. (Mad TN, Ch Ct Min, 1/70)

STAIR, William
Died before 16 January 1797 when William Harrington was appointed administrator, with Abraham Young & Thomas Howard as security. (Rob TN, Co Ct Min, 1/15)

STALLINGS, Carmah
Died before 5 February 1872 when his will was proved by B. H. Harmon and W. J. Hall, witnesses. (Dyr TN, Co Ct Min, B/370)

STALLINGS, J. H.
Died before 6 February 1871 when H. E. Stallings renewed her bond as guardian of the minor heirs. (Dyr TN, Co Ct Min, B/182)

STALLINGS, S. P.
Died before 6 February 1871 when S. F. Stallings renewed her bond as guardian of the minor heirs. (Dyr TN, Co Ct Min, B/182)

STALLINGS, Sarah Ann
Died before 5 February 1872 when her will was proved by B. H. Harmon and W. J. Hall, witnesses. (Dyr TN, Co Ct Min, B/370)

STAMPS, John
Died before 12 February 1859 when a suit was shown by Elijah C. Stamps et als vs John R. Stamps et als. It was ordered that the land mentioned be rented for the present year except the widow's dower. (Jac TN, Ch Ct Min, C/214) This suit was Elijah C. Stamps & James Stamps vs John R. Stamps, Polly Stamps, Jane Kinnaird, Montgomery Kinnaird & Mary Hale. Jane & Montgomery Kinnaird & Mary Hale are minors & Leonard J. Lovie was appointed guardian ad litem. James Gentry & Archibald M. Stafford stated they were acquainted with the children & heirs of John Stamps, deceased. There are three children of John Stamp now living. He had two more daughters who are dead, one of whom left one child & the other left two. The dower of the widow has been laid off. (Ibid 282)

STANLEY, John N.
Died before 10 July 1848 when the suit of F. W. Yancy was continued because of the death of the defendant, Stanley. (Mad TN, Ch Ct Min, 1/31)

STANLEY, Moses
Died before 15 September 1817 when the will was proved by James Michie & John Higgins. (Wil TN, Co Ct Min, no#/149)

STANSBURY, Thomas
Was a resident of Jeffeson County, KY, 26 May 1796 when Nicholas Hail of Washington County, TN, gave him power of attorney to sell land to Ezekiel Lawson of Baltimore County in KY. (Was TN, Co Ct Min, 1/601)

STARK, Thomas
Died before 19 July 1802 when the will was proved by Thomas Johnson & William Grimes. Rachel Stark & Walter Stark were executors. (Rob TN, Co Ct Min, 1/223)

STARK, Zorabable
Died before 21 April 1800 when an order was issued to take the depositions of James Edwards & James Griswitt in Southhampton County, VA, to prove the will. (Rob TN, Co Ct Min, 1/130) Shown as Zarubabul Stak when the heirs were shown on the delinquent tax list, 7 August 1804. (Ibid 308)

STARRELL, W. S.   [Starrett, Stawell]
Died before 6 February 1872 when the committee appointed to lay off a years allowance for Mrs. Sarah E. Starrell, the widow, made a report. [The committee was appointed in March 1868.] N. C. Porter was administrator of W. S. Starrett (?), deceased. (Dyr TN, Co Ct Min, B/374)

STATEN, Susan
19 February 1858 in a petition by Council B. Mays [Mayo] it was shown that he was trustee for Susan Staten who owned slaves but no land. (Mad TN, Ch Ct Min, 2/186)

STEADMAN, Benjamin   [Stedman]
Died before 11 March 1844 when land was taxed to the heirs. (Obi TN, Cir Ct Min, 4/no#)

STEADMAN, Nathan W., Sr.
Died before 23 February 1866. In the suit of Geo. W. Williams Exr. vs N. W. Steadman et

als, Jno. S. Brown was appointed guardian ad litem for the infant defendants, R. Steadman & Pleasent Steadman, and as the next friend of Sarah F. Manly. (Mad TN, Ch Ct Min, 2/491) The land mentioned in this suit was sold in October 1860 to Benj. P. Steadman with Solly? R. Steadman as his security. (Ibid 496) Nathan W. Steadman, Sr. left a will & Geo. W. Williamson was executor. (Ibid 516) Land was sold & title divested out of Nathan W. Steadman, Jno. A. Steadman, Hugh Pipkin & wife May E., Caleb Manley & wife F., Robert Steadman and Pleasant Steadman. (Ibid 3/15)

STEELE, Wilson
Died before 12 April 1836 when the administrator, C. D. Steele, sold part of the land to pay the debts. (Bed TN, Ch Ct Min, 2/14)

STEGAL, L.
Taxes were not collected in District 5 for 1873, "insolvent." (Dyr TN, Co Ct Min, B/759)

STEGALL, B. F.
Died intestate in 1864, as shown in the suit of David J. Franklin admr. vs Beverly C. Stegall et als. He left the defendants his only heirs. D. J. Franklin was his administrator. The deceased was a joint tenant in common with defendant, C. M. Alexander. Nancy W. Stegal is the widow & entitled to dower. (Mad TN, Ch Ct Min, 3/92) The suit is shown as David J. Franklin admr. of B. F. Stigall decd. & Nancy W. Stigall vs Mary L. Stigall, Harriet A. Stigall, Charles M. Alexander & wife Elizabeth L. Alexander & Beverly C. Stegal. (Ibid 209)

STEPHENS, Edwin
Died before 1 August 1814 when Thomas Gray was appointed administrator with Alsey Bradford and Peter Kindle? as security. (Ste TN, Co Ct Min, 4/164)

STEPHENS, James
7 April 1857 John Catlett was paid for making a coffin for James Stephen's child. (Sev TN, Co Ct Min, no#/152)

STEPHENS, Lorenzo
Was bound as an apprentice to Wilson McMahan 7 April 1856, until age 21. He is now 5 years of age. (Sev TN, Co Ct Min, no#/23) 1 July 1867 Wilson McMahan was released from his bond to L. D. Stevens, who had been bound to him. (Ibid 462)

STEPHENS, Noah
Was bound as an apprentice 7 April 1857 to P. M. Atchly until age 21. He is now 14 years old. (Sev TN, Co Ct Min, no#/152) 10 April 1866 P. M. Atchley was released from the apprentice bond for Noah Stevens. (Ibid 324)

STEPHENS, Solomon
Was bound as an apprentice 4 May 1857 to William Jones until he is 21. He is now 9 years old. (Sev TN, Co Ct Min, no#/162)

STEPHENS, William
Died before 12 August 1840 as shown in the suit of William Carlisle vs Harbard Smith, guardian of John Henry Stevens, Margaret Jane Stephens, William S. Stephens and Leander Stephens, minor heirs of William Stephens, and Harbard Smith in his own right. John Stephens died in 1831 and William Stephens and James Stephens, his sons, were administrators with the will annexed, and entered into bond of $16,000 with Andrew Hartsfield, Martha Stephens, Charles L. Mattox, William Carlisle, Josiah Stephens & John Stevens, Jr. as security. Some 12 or 18 months afterward, Wille Stephens, one of the administrators, also died & William Carlisle & Andrew Hartsfield were executors. Harbert Smith married Mildred, the widow of Willie Stephens, and was appointed guardian of his minor heirs. Jorden C. Holt was guardian of Tranquilla, Hiram & Lafayette Stephens, minor heirs of John Stephens, deceased. (Bed TN, Ch Ct Min, 1/359) Probably Tranquilla Stephens married Thomas Thompson before 25 August 1845, as shown in the suit of Thomas Thompson & wife vs Jordan C. Holt. It was stated that Jordon C. Holt was the regualr guardian for Tranquilla Thompson. (Ibid 2/361)

STEPHENS, William
On 24 March 1856 was appointed guardian of his minor daughter, Rebecca A. Stephens, who was one of the defendants in the suit of Mary A. Owen vs Joseph Mathews & others. (Fen TN, Ch Ct Min, A/41)

STEPHENSON, Moore
Died before 14 January 1847. He left a will making a bequest to the children of Polly

Moss. John P. Moss, husband of Polly Moss, died soon after Moore Stephenson leaving his children; Dirdimonia who married James Boles; Sarah who married Benjamin N. Perry; Elizabeth who married William Bolin; Joseph, and Moore S. Moss. Sometime after the death of John P. Moss the said Polly Moss had two illegitimate children, to wit, Almedia Moss who married Wilkin Williams. Almedia died and her husband was appointed her administrator. The other illegitimate child of Polly Moss was George W. Moss. After the birth of these two children, Polly Moss married Ruebin Dougherty and had Bamer [Bunian] Dougherty. This case evidently started before 1833. (Mad TN, Ch Ct Min, 1/12)

STEPHENSON, Moore
Died before 19 February 1825 when John Stephenson sold a slave to Isaac T. Stephenson. The slave is now in the possession of Sarah Stephenson who has title to the slave for the life of Sarah Stephenson, then agreeable to the will of Moore Stephenson deceased, the slave, Ann, will belong to John Stephenson. (Wil TN, Reg Bk/369) The will of Moore Stephenson was proved 4 May 1818 by Jeremiah Hendrick, John Comer & Thomas Rhodes. (Ibid, Co Ct Min, no#/243) The executors named, Isham F. Davis, William White & Wm. Johnson, declined. Sarah Stephenson, the widow, was appointed administratrix. (Ibid 249) Thomas Rhodes was appointed administrator with the will annexed of Moore Stephen Stephenson. (Ibid 258) 7 August 1818 Josiah Stephenson petitoned to have 100 acres of land laid off to him according to the will of Moore Stephenson. (Ibid 324)

STEPHENSON, Sarah
Made a deed of gift 20 January 1820 to her son, Isaac T. Stephenson, of a negro boy named Lewis & a roan filly. (Wil TN, Reg Bk/149)

STEVENS, Alfred
Died before 2 February 1874 when the widow, Fannie A. E. Stevens, was appointed administratrix, with E. W. Andrews, W. P. Sugg and A. M. Stevens as her security. (Dyr TN, Co Ct Min, B/705) 8 July 1874 W. P. Sugg was chosen and appointed guardian of Charley and Mollie Stevens, minor heirs. (Ibid 763)

STEVENS, James
Died before 8 April 1856 when Murphy McNutt &c was allowed money for his coffin & shroud. (Sev TN, Co Ct Min, no#/33)

STEVENS, R. G.
4 January 1871 was released from poll tax wrongfully charged to him. He is over 50 years of age. (Dyr TN, Co Ct Min, B/161)

STEVENSON, W. C.
Died before 3 January 1871 when Edward Stevenson was chosen and appointed guardian of James H., George A., Sylva Ann, John C. and Richard E. Stevenson, minor heirs, with H. N. Mount and J. H. York as security. (Dyr TN, Co Ct Min, B/158)

STEWARD, William
Was a resident of MO 27 June 1843 when his deposition was to be taken for the defendant in the suit of Lemuel Broadaway vs Minos Cannon & others. (Bed TN, Ch Ct Min, 2/250)

STEWART
A suit was shown 13 July 1854 with Ridley Apple & wife Peggy An Apple & Elizabeth Stewart vs Reece C. Stewart, John Stewart, John Lee & wife Jane Lee, Jane Williamson, Henry W. Sadler and Samuel R. McDonol. The complainants bill was dismissed. (Jac TN, Ch Ct Min, B/158)

STEWART, Charles
Was a non-resident of TN 5 May 1812 when his signature was proved as witness to a deed from Duncan Stewart to Enoch James. (Ste TN, Co Ct Min, 3/136)

STEWART, James
Died before 3 May 1819 when Cyntha Stewart & Joseph D. Young were appointed administrators with James Williams & Edward Moore as security. Saml. Stewart & John Bone were appointed to allot to Cynthia Stewart one years provisions. (Wil TN, Co Ct Min, no#/433-4)

STILLMAN, John Hants, Sr.
6 August 1794 bound his son, Thomas Hants, as apprentice to William Caldwell for the

term of 4 years. Witnessed by James Stewart & Elizabeth Stuart. (Was TN, Co Ct Min, 1/505)

STINNETT, Barberry
Was the mother of a bastard child by Julius Justice who gave bond for its maintenance 7 January 1867. James Stinnett was agent for Barberry. (Sev TN, Co Ct Min, no#/409)

STOCKTON, Isaac
Was a non-resident of TN 13 October 1856 as shown in the suit of Joseph Jones, John C. Scott & John R. Baker trading under the name & style of Jones Scott & Co. vs Isaac Stockton & others. (Fen TN, Ch Ct Min, A/63)

STODDART, William
Died before 12 January 1847 as shown in the suit of Timothy P. Jones vs The Planters Bank of Tennessee. (Mad TN, Ch Ct Min, 1/5)

STOFLE, Betsy
Died before 5 January 1858 when Yett & Brother was paid out of the poor fund for burial clothes. (Sev TN, Co Ct Min, no#/242)

STOFLE, Eliz.
Died before 5 January 1858 when Jas. McNelly was paid money from the poor fund for making her coffin. [May be the same as Betsy Stofle.] (Sev TN, Co Ct Min, no#/242)

STOFLE, John
Died before 6 April 1857 when Murphy McNutt & Co. & Jas. McNulty were paid for burying clothes & coffin. (Sev TN, Co Ct Min, no#/143)

STOFLE, John, Sr.
6 January 1857 money was allowed from the poor tax to M. W. McCowen to be applied to the support of John Stofle, Sr. & family. (Sev TN, Co Ct Min, no#/111) 7 April 1857 M. W. McCowan reported he had used $10.50 of the money allowed for the support of John Stofle & family. He is to use the balance for the support of the widow of John Stofle. (Ibid 151) 4 January 1859 Jas. McNelly was paid from the poor tax for making a coffin for John Stoffle's daughter. (Ibid 378)

STOFLE, Margaret
5 January 1858 it was ordered that she be brought to court to be bound out as she is a girl in indigent circumstances. (Sev TN, Co Ct Min, no#/247)

STOFLE, Nancy
Died before 8 April 1856 when money was allowed out of the poor fund for her burial clothes. (Sev TN, Co Ct Min, no#/36)

STOFLE, Thomas
Died before 1 July 1867 when Wm. Jones was paid for making his coffin. (Sev TN, Co Ct Min, no#/459)

STOFLE, Wm.
Died before 3 April 1865 when Jordan Houk was paid for making his coffin. (Sev TN, Co Ct Min, no#/143)

STOKES, Tennessee
Died before 2 October 1871 when D. H. Jones, Esquire was paid for holding an inquest over the body. (Dyr TN, Co Ct Min, B/293)

STONE
Mary Jane Stone & Sarah A. Stone were distributees of Wm. H. Stone, so their depositions were excluded in the suit of Hickason L. Doyle vs Thomas J. Stone & Wm. H. Stone, 13 September 1854. Mad TN, Ch Ct Min, 2/21)

STONE, H. B.
Taxes were not collected in District 4 for 1874, "can't be found." (Dyr TN, Co Ct Min, B/758)

STONE, John
Died before 15 August 1815 when Susannah Stone was appointed administratrix with William Rogers and Thomas Whithead as security. (Cla TN, Co Ct Min, 4/98)

STONE, Randolph
Died before 17 June 1840 when the widow, Lucy Stone, petitioned for dower. The heirs were James N. Stone, Richard W. Stone, Franklin Longley & Mary T. Longley his wife. (Obi TN, Cir Ct Min, 4/no#) 19 October 1841 James N. Stone was indicted for murder and for setting fire to a house. (Ibid) 21 February 1842 the sheriff of Obion County was ordered to go to Raleigh & demand from the sheriff of Shelby County the body of James N. Stone who is charged with the murder of John B. Mitchell. (Ibid) On 22 February 1842 the state entered a nole prosequi in this case. (Ibid) On the same date the charge for setting fire to a house was marked "not a true bill". The charge of murder was reinstated. (Ibid) 23 June 1842 James N. Stone was found guilty of murder in the first degree but with mitigating circumstances. (Ibid) 24 June 1842, because of the recommendation of the jury the defendant was not sentenced to death by hanging but was instead sentenced to life imprisonment at hard labor in the State Penitentiary. An appeal from the sentence was granted. (Ibid)

STONE, Sam E.
Died before 7 February 1855 as shown in the suit of Joel W. Settle vs Edward M. Cason & Robt. A. Cox Admrs. of Thompson Cason & others. Thompson Cason had executed a bill of sale for a slave to Sam E. Stone who has since departed this life. (Jac TN, Ch Ct Min, B/186) In a suit entered 6 February 1857 by Albert Kirkpatrich vs Leroy B. Settle, Willis S. Stone, William Plunket Stone, Mary Stone and Joel Haden Stone, it was shown that the defendant Stones were minor heirs of Sam E. Stone, deceased, and that Nancy P. Stone was their guardian. (Ibid C/43 & 65) Nancy P. Stone was the widow. (Ibid 78) Land was sold & Leroy B. Settle, Nancy P. Stone, Willis Stone, William P. Stone & Joel H. Stone were the purchasers. (Ibid 319)

STONE, Sarah
Died before 16 February 1858 as shown in the suit of Hickeson L. Doyle vs Thos. J. Stone et als. Wm. H. Stone was appointed administrator. Sarah Stone left 7 heirs & said Thos. J. Stone is one of them. (Mad TN, Ch Ct Min, 2/159)

STONE, Temperance
Was a non-resident of the state on 7 February 1851 as shown in the suit of James Neely vs Temperance Stone & others. Temperance Stone had a dower right in lands mentioned. (Jac TN, Ch Ct Min, A/411)

STONE, William
Was a resident of Warren County, TN, on 3 December 1823 when his deposition was to be taken for the defendant in the case of James Capshaw vs Henry Gill. (McM TN, Co Ct Min, no#/108)

STONE, William
Died in Jackson County, TN, leaving a will. In his will he asked that his black man, Thomas, be emancipated after the death of he and his wife. It states that William Stone died, or the will was dated, 24 June 1829. [This date is in error because this entry was made in 1827. It probably should be 1819 as it also states the will was proved at February session 1820 of said court.] The wife of William was also dead by 4 September 1827 when Thomas Stone (who assumed that name) asked for his freedom, which was granted. (McM TN, Co Ct Min, 2no#/236)

STORY, John
Was a resident of Augusta County, VA, 12 May 1788 when a deed was made to him from Ann Story, with John Carter & Joseph Hamilton as witnesses. (Was TN, Co Ct Min, 1/324) Anne Storey was the widow of Thomas Storey and John Storey was their son, both residents of Augusta County, VA. Ann released her dower to John. The will of Thomas Storey was mentioned. Edmd. Stevens & Wm. Hamilton were also witnesses, as shown 5 May 1788. (Ibid no#/97-98)

STOTHART, Mathew
Died before 2 February 1813 when Mary Stothart was granted letters of administration on the estate with Thomas Hardy Oneal and Philip Hornburger as security. (Ste TN, Co Ct Min, 4/6)

STOUT, Aron
Was a minor when he was bound 26 August 1794 to Nicholas Broyles until he is 21. (Was TN, Co Ct Min, 1/499)

STOUT, Benjamine C.
Died before 7 September 1829 when his will was proved by Saml. M. Gault & Alexander

D. Kays, witnesses. (McM TN, Co Ct Min, 2no#/383) Soloman Bogart and Jane C. Stout were executors. (Ibid 392) Jane C. Stout was the widow. (Ibid 424)

STOUT, Daniel
Was a minor when he was bound 18 November 1794 to Thomas Blackburn until age 21. (Was TN, Co Ct Min, 1/514)

STOUT, David
Was a minor when he was bound 18 November 1794 to Thomas Blackburn until age 21. (Was TN, Co Ct Min, 1/514)

STOUT, George
Was a minor when he was bound 18 Novmeber 1794 to Andw. Carson until age 21. (Was TN, Co Ct Min, 1/514) 20 November 1795 he was bound to John ____ to learn the shoemaking trade. (Ibid 585)

STOUT, Magdalin
Was a minor when she was bound 26 August 1794 to Nicholas Broyles until age 18. (Was TN, Co Ct Min, 1/499)

STOUT, Moses
Was a minor when he was bound 26 August 1794 to John McAllester until age 21. (Was TN, Co Ct Min, 1/499)

STRATON, Absalom
On the 15th day of July 1794 bound himself unto John Evans, as an apprentice to be taught the carpenter trade. [The bond was written in the minutes and I quote a part of it]..."to serve him from the day hereof and during the term of 3 years...he shall not commit fornification nor contract Matrimony within the said term, cards dice or any unlawful game he shall not play...he shall neither Buy nor sell during the said term without from his said Master, he shall not absent himself by night nor by day from his Master's service without leave...the said Master shall teach or cause to be taught in the trade or mistery he now occupieth and provide for him sufficient meat drink apperal & washing & lodging Suffcient for an apprentice during said term." The bond was witnessed by George Gilespie and Thos. Blackburn. (Was TN, Co Ct Min, 1/503)

STRATON, Mary Ann
Was granted a divorce on 15 July 1859 from Hartwell Straton for adultry. They were married in December [1847 is crossed out and it looks like 51 written in] Property was listed that was purchased with the money of complainant. Mary Ann was awarded the property and custody of the 3 girl children, Mary Jane, Permelia M. & Francis Maria, the eldest who is 6 years old. (Jac TN, Ch Ct Min, C/290)

STREET, David A.
On 13 July 1848 William H. Jamerson brought suit against David A. Street & wife Mary D. Street, David T. Street, Thomas D. Street, Lucy Street, Sarah Street and Henry Swan. Jamerson claimed that David A. Street conveyed land to Henry Swan in Trust for the use of Mary D. Street and the other defendants, her children. The land was under a judgement brought by Jamerson. (Mad TN, Ch Ct Min, 1/40)

STRICKLIN, John
Died before 9 May 1814 when the will was proved by Michael Finley & William Paisley. (Rob TN, Co Ct Min, 3/393) Joseph Pitts & John Barby qualified as executors. (Ibid 403)

STRODARD, William
Died before 13 March 1845 when land was taxed to the heirs. (Obi TN, Cir Ct Min, 4/no#)

STROTHER, Kemp
Was a resident of Camden Dist., SC, on 10 February 1779 when he sold a negro man named Peter, about 25 years old, to Moses Humphreys of Washington County, NC [TN]. The bill of sale was recorded 12 May 1790 and proved by Jesse Humphreys. (Was TN, Co Ct Min, 1/443)

STROTHER, Samuel K.
Died before 10 August 1813 when John Strother was appointed administrator, with Ezekiel Norman and Benjamin Gaines & Henry Frey as security. (Rob TN, Co Ct Min, 3/284)

STUARD, John
Was a resident of Lancaster District in SC 18 May 1827 when he was given power of attorney by James Harper. (Obi TN, Cir Ct Min, 1/26)

STUART, Abraham
6 October 1807 gave a power of attorney to Thos. Johnson on certificate of James Thompson & Mattw. Wilson, Esqrs. of Christian County [no state given]. Same date Abraham Stuart, Wm. Stuart, Elijah Stuart & Thomas Grayson gave power of attorney to Thomas Johnson on certificate from Christian County, KY. (Rob TN, Co Ct Min, 1/465)

STUART, John
Died before 8 November 1806 when the heirs were shown on the delinquent tax list. (Rob TN, Co Ct Min, 1/423)

STUART, Robert
Was a resident of VA 2 November 1784 when his deposition was to be taken for the defendant in the case of Shelby vs Houghton. (Was TN, Co Ct Min, 1/259)

STUART, William
Died in October 1834 leaving a will in which he appointed James Gambrill & William Stewart executors. The will is shown whereby he left to his loving wife, Peggy Steward, slaves, land & other property. Other bequests were made to his son-in-law Isaac Barnett, his grand son Burton? Barnett, his grand daughter Lucindy Barnett, his daughter Nelly Meece?, his grand son Joshua Steward, his grand son William Steward, his son John Steward, his said? [son?] Saml. Steward, Jemima Guley, Malinda Hix, Patsey Greenbruld?, William Steward, Nelly Hix, [this is not clear] slaves to be divided amongst them the Serveth?, the balance to be equally divided amongst my own children. "At the death of my wife, Peggy, the property remaining in her hands to be divided amongst my own children, that is to say Saml Steward Jemima Girly Malinda Hix Polly Gambrill Wm. Steward & Nelly Hix." He appointed his neighbor & friend James Gambrald, his son-in-law John Hix & his beloved son William Steward as executors. Peggy Stewart brought suit 16 August 1838 against James Gambrell & William Stuart, executors, for the slaves bequeathed her by said will. (Bed TN, Ch Ct Min, 1/162)

STUART, William
6 October 1807 gave a power of attorney to Thos. Johnson on certificate from Christian County, Ky. (Rob TN, Co Ct Min, 1/466)

STUBBLEFIELD, Tilman
Died about 3 May 1846 as shown in the suit of Margaret C. McCarver vs Monterville G. B. Stubblefield, William L. Stubblefield, William Procter, Thomas M. Stubblefield & Susan J. Procter. The complainant was his widow and defendants his only children. Complainant afterwards married John McCarver who is since deceased. Jane was the wife of William Procter. Slaves were divided in 1847 but title was not given. This suit brought 3 February 1858 is for title. (Jac TN, Ch Ct Min, C/91)

SUDBURG, Susannah
Died before 6 April 1871 when Ben F. Farmer was appointed administrator, with S. B. Shaw and T. A. Jordan as security. (Dyr TN, Co Ct Min, B/230)

SUGG, Aquilla
Died before September term 1804 when the heirs were on the non-resident tax list with land on Sugg Creek & Pond Lick Creek. (Wil TN, Co Ct Min, no#/88)

SUGG, Lemuel
Died before 15 March 1827 when Henry H. Sugg, an heir of Lemuel Sugg, deceased, gave a quit claim to Thomas Drennon as guardian of Nathaniel Davis, who is adjudged to be insane. Nathaniel Davis had recovered a judgement against Lemuel Sugg in 1807 & the quit claim is in settlement of that judgement. (Wil TN, Reg Bk/ no# but it should be 404, second set of page numbers.)

SUGG, Noah
Died before 20 January 1800 when the will was proved by George Sugg Allen. Aquilla Sugg was executor. (Rob TN, Co Ct Min, 1/122)

SUGG, Samuel [Lemuel]
Died before 13 August 1812 when his widow, Coily Sugg, relinquished her right to administration to John B. Blackwell. William D. Menees and Jesse Gardner were security.

(Rob TN, Co Ct Min, 3/123) 11 February 1813 Joseph Washington was paid for taking an inquest on the body of Lemuel Sugg. (Ibid 223)

SULLENS, William
Was a resident of White County on 8 March 1828 when his deposition was to be taken for the defendant in the case of Wm. W. Anderson vs Charles W. Martin. (McM TN, Co Ct Min, no#/318)

SULLIVAN, Fletcher
Died before 16 December 1817 when the will was proved by John Hancock & George Avery. (Wil TN, Co Ct Min, no#/201)

SULLIVAN, Jane Francis
Died before 5 December 1870 as shown in a division of the lands of Dent Ferrell. Jane was the daughter of Coleman Spain who had purchased part of the Ferrell land. Jane left a daughter, Mary Alice Sullivan. Jane had married James Sullivan. (Dyr TN, Co Ct Min, B/145-6)

SULLIVAN, Polly
Was the mother of a bastard child by John Cowger who gave bond for its support 6 May 1818. (Wil TN, Co Ct Min, no#/265)

SUMMERS, John
Died before 18 July 1856 as shown in the suit of Thomas E. Dennis & wife & others vs Margaret Summers, Ira F. Summers et als. Land is to be sold for distribution. There are minor heirs of John Summers, deceased. (Jac TN, Ch Ct Min, C/18) This suit was shown as Thomas E. Dennis, Catherine Dennis, Calib Simons, Elizabeth Simons, Abraham Summers, Bertie Allen & Rebecca Allen vs Margaret Summers, Rebecca Summers, Ira T. Summers, Jane Summers, Almeda Summers, Marion? Summers, Perry L. Summers and William H. Botts Guardian ad litem &c. Land was sold subject to the widow's dower. Margaret Summers was the widow. (Ibid 42)

SUMMERS, R. E.
Taxes were not collected in District 4 for 1873, "insolvent." (Dyr TN, Co Ct Min, B/759)

SUTTON, John
In the suit of Quarls T. Mayfield vs John Sutton, 3 February 1841, it was shown that Mayfield married Elizabeth F. Sutton, the daughter of John Sutton, on 27 December 1832. Mayfield is claiming that before he married Elizabeth that her father, John Sutton, had represented to him that a certain tract of land belonged to Elizabeth. In his answer John Sutton mentioned his son, John Sutton, Jr., his son, William B. Sutton and his son, C. B. Sutton. (Bed TN, Ch Ct Min, 1/274)

SUTTON [Sallie]
William H. & Mary A. Sutton died in 1850 leaving some minor children under 15 years of age, of which J. A. Spurlock is regular guardian and B. B. Washburn is the administrator. James A. Sprulock sued B. B. Washburn for an accounting of the estate. [The name of "Sutton" had been written above the name "Sallie".] (Jac TN, Ch Ct Min, B/88) 13 July 1854 the suit was heard of James A. Spurlock, guardian of the heirs of W. H. & Mary An Sallie vs Ben N. Washburn Admr. &c. Benjamin B. Washburn as administrator of William H. & Mary An Sallie is indebted to James A. Spurlock as guardian of the minor heirs. (Ibid 162)

SUTTON, William B.
Died before 23 July 1838 as shown in the suit of John Ragsdale, Sr. and William Armstrong against James L. Armstrong & Richard Warner of Marshall County, guardian of Sophia F Sutton and Elizabeth Sutton, minor heirs of William B. Sutton, deceased. William [which William?] had married the daughter of John Ragsdale, Sr. [probably William Armstrong had married the daughter of John Ragsdale, Sr., but not clear] William B. Sutton died in the later part of1833 & James L. Armstrong was executor. Sophie Sutton and Elizabeth F. Sutton were his only children. (Bed TN, Ch Ct Min, 1/168)

SWANN
29 August 1860 the court was to determine the amount due to Samuel Neely & wife for board, clothing & tuition for Saml. H. Swann & others, minors. (Mad TN, Ch Ct Min, 2/378)

SWAYNE, Amanda J.
Died before 31 August 1860 as shown in the suit of James F. Russell & Ro. Brown vs Amanda J. Suage [Swayne, or most anything else] et als. The suit was revived in the

name of W. C. McHany, administrator of J. W. Swayne with will annexed. (Mad TN, Ch Ct Min, 2/400)

SWEARINGIN
In the suit of William Night vs Pleasant C. Linville et als, entered 9 February 1860, it was reported that defendants Martha Swearingin, Elizabeth Swearingin, Adalin Swearingin, Pleasant Swearingin, Hannah Swearingin, Eliza Swearingin, Thomas Swearingin & Nancy K. Swearingin were minors and John A. Mathews is their regular guardian. Process has been served and they failed to answer. P. H. Serlis was appointed guardian ad litem. (Jac TN, Ch Ct Min, C/308) Also shown in this suit were defendants Samuel Swearingin, Thomas Swearingin, Maranda Swearingin, John Swearingin, Hariet Swearingin [in place of Hannah], Rebecca Swearingin & John Swearingin. Process has been served on all exept the last two who are non-residents. Preston H. Serlis? is guardian ad litem for Martha, Elizabeth, Adaline, Pleasant, Hannah [or Harriet], Eliza, Thomas and Nancy K. Swearingin. Land was sold and divested out of defendants and vested in William Night. (Ibid 320)

SWEET, Alexander
Died before 15 August 1815 when Elizabeth Sweet was appointed administratrix with John Casey as security. (Cla TN, Co Ct Min, 4/98)

SWIFT, Flower
12 February 1839 dismissed his suit against Thomas W. & Jacob W. Swift. (Bed TN, Ch Ct Min, 2/46)

SWIFT, Willis
Died before 3 January 1871 when William Wesson, Anthony Swift and Tom Strange were appointed to lay off a years provisions for the widow and family. (Dyr TN, Co Ct Min, B/158) Willis Swift was colored. W. A. King was appointed administrator. (Ibid 173) Milly Swift was the widow. (Ibid 192)

SWINEY, Albert A.
Died before 20 March 1852 as shown in the petition of Sarah Ann Swiney, Mary Ann Swiney, Charlotte Swiney, John Swiney, Augusta Swiney by their next friend Paul Clay and Nancy N. Swiney. Paul Clay was the administrator. Nancy N. Swiney is the widow and the other petitioners are his children. The estate has been settled and they wish to buy land with the money from the estate. (Jac TN, Ch Ct Min, B/38)

SYNDREY, William [Lyndrey]
Made a deed of gift to James Polk on 8 September 1806. (Ste TN, Co Ct Min, 1/31b)

SYPERT, Thomas
22 February 1822 made a deed of gift of a negro named Charity, to his daughter Sally Sypert. (Wil TN, Reg Bk/252) Thomas Sypert made a deed of gift to his son, William Sypert, 16 June 1817. (Ibid, Co Ct Min, no#/112)

TAILEY Wm. B. [Tasley, Tarley]
Died before 17 March 1854 as shown in the suit of Pitser Miller vs Thos. W. Harris & wife Mary, Alex Henderson & wife Mariah, Ann C. Tailey & Irene Tailey, the last a minor by her guardian ad litem, Ann C. Tailey. Ann C. was the widow and his only children were Mary Harris, Mariah Henderson & Irene Tailey. Thos. W. Harris was appointed administrator. (Mad TN, Ch Ct Min, 1/359)

TALBOT, James L.
A suit was entered 28 August 1860: James L. Talbot and wife Ann P. Talbot, petition expartee to appoint Trustee. William Dickens had deeded property in 1839 to Joseph H. Talbot in trust for Ann P. Talbot. James H. Talbot is dead and petitioners, James L. & Ann P. Talbot want another trustee. William B. Dickens was appointed. (Mad TN, Ch Ct Min, 2/370)

TALBOT, Joseph H.
Died before 12 July 1850 as shown in the suit of Planters Bank of Tennessee and others vs Alexander Jackson Exr of Jos. H. Talbot. New defendants were added to the bill; Francis Talbot, Almedia Talbot, Ruth Talbot, Mary Talbot & Delia Talbot, minor heirs of Joseph H. Talbot. Joseph B. Freeman was appointed guardian ad litem. (Mad TN, Ch Ct Min, 1/144) 15 January 1851 a suit was shown by Citizen S. Woods & others vs Alexander Jackson Extr. & others. Alex. Jackson as executor of Joseph H. Talbot, deceased, is indebted to complainants by reason of the Trusteeship of said Talbot for the said Elizabeth Beloute, now deceased, and her children. An account is to be made by

Jackson. William D., Samuel D., Charles R. & Reginald H. Beloate are entitled to a division of slaves. (Ibid 183) Alexander Jackson qualified as executor of Joseph H. Talbot in May 1849. Citizen S. Woods is of Carroll County and was appointed trustee in place of Joseph H. Talbot. There is money [from the trust] in the hands of Mr. Dunn at Mobile. (Ibid 202) The trustee sold land in Pulaski & Wayne Counties, KY. (Ibid 242, 311)

TALBOTT, Matthew, Sr.
4 August 1874 his wife, Agness Talbott, released her right to any lands belonging to her husband in VA. (Was TN, Co Ct Min, 1/247)

TALBOTT, Sarah
Died 24 December 1857 as shown in a statement made 6 February 1860 by W. A. McNutt & R. M. Criswell. Sarah left 10 children, to wit: Ephraim Talbott, James Talbott, Eliza Talbott, Catherine Talbott, Nathan Talbott, Odell Talbott, Nancy Cowan, formerly Nancy Talbott who married A. J. Cowan , Rachel Underwood, formerly Rachel Talbott who married Joel Underwood, Elizabeth Blair, formerly Elizabeth Talbott who married Harrison Blair, Emily Cowan, formerly Emily Talbot who married William H. Cowan. The said Catherine Talbott is a minor. Sarah Talbott had no other children. (Sev TN, Co Ct Min, no#/512) 5 March 1860 W. H. Cowan made a settlement as administrator. (Ibid 519)

TALBOTT, Thos.
Died before 7 June 1858 when the executor, W. H. Cowan, presented a certified copy of the will, the original will having been burned up. (Sev TN, Co Ct Min, no#/304)

TALIAFERRO
22 August 1866 in the suit of M. O. Bigelow vs J. A. McDearman admr et als, Baldwin D. Taliaferro was appointed guardian ad litem for Martha Taliaferro, Potts Taliaferro & Nerland Taliaferro, infants without a regular guardian. (Mad TN, Ch Ct Min, 2/514) In a suit concerning McDearman & Mason, John A. Taliaferro was mentioned and the death of Taliaferro. (Ibid 3/120)

TALLEY, Geo. W.
Died before 6 June 1870 when Z. G. Watkins was appointed administrator, de bonus non. W. M. Watkins had been administrator and resigned. (Dyr TN, Co Ct Min, B/66) 5 October 1870 a suit was entered by Zach. G. Watkins administrator of G. W. Talley deceased & C. C. Moss vs Sarah Talley, widow, Zachariah T. Talley, William E. Talley, Jefferson D. Talley and George A. Talley, minor heirs of G. W. Talley. George A. Talley is a non-resident. (Ibid 114) Charles C. Moss ownes a half interest in land granted to Moss and Talley. G. W. Talley died in 1868. (Ibid 115-7) 2 February 1874 it is stated that Mrs. Sarah J. Talley was 35 years of age in 1872. (Ibid 707)

TALLEY, J. N.
Taxes were not collected in District 4 for 1873, "run away." (Dyr TN, Co Ct Min, B/759)

TALLEY, John
Was bound to S. P. Latta 4 January 1871 until age 21. He is a negro boy. (Dyr TN, Co Ct Min, B/172)

TALLY, Adair
Was a non-resident of TN 1 August 1870 as shown in the suit of Z. G. Watkins administrator et als vs Sarah J. Tally et als. (Dyr TN, Co Ct Min, B/94)

TALLY, Elizabeth
Made a deed of gift to her children 6 September 1819. The children were Hannah Tally, William W. Tally, Betty Tally, Coleman Tally and Frances Tally. (Wil TN, Reg Bk/144)

TALLY, Spencer
Died before 4 May 1818 when the will was entered. Daniel Tally, one of the legatees, opposed the probate thereof. (Wil TN, Co Ct Min, no#/249) 7 May 1818, Elizabeth Tally, executrix vs Daniel Talley, contested will. A jury found that it was the will of Spencer Tally. The will was proved by Boaz Southern & Patsy Tally. Betsy Tally, executrix, returned the inventory. (Ibid 276)

TARKINGTON, W. D.
Died before 7 February 1871 when C. S. Nolan, public administrator, was appointed administrator. (Dyr TN, Co Ct Min, B/194)

TARVER, Benja.
Died before 27 March 1804 when Benja. Tarver & John Harris were appointed administrators with Blake Rutland as security. (Wil TN, Co Ct Min, no#/35)

TATOM, Absalom
Died before 5 May 1821 when Bernard Tatom sold his interest in the estate of Absalom Tatom, deceased, to Asa Tatom. Asa appointed Joseph Kirkpatrick, his attorney, to collect the proceeds of this estate. (Wil TN, Reg Bk/249)

TATUM, W. M.
Died before 1 December 1873 as shown when an administrator was appointed for the estate of C. B. Reasons in the place of W. M. Tatum, deceased. (Dyr TN, Co Ct Min, B/667)

TAYLOR
In the suit of W. S. Weaver et als vs L. J. Taylor et als, 14 February 1868, it is stated that defendants Jno. W. Taylor and Margaret Ann Taylor are minors. Stoddert Caruthers was appointed guardian ad litem to defend for them. (Mad TN, Ch Ct Min, 3/178)

TAYLOR, Absalom
Sued for divorce from Susanah Taylor 15 August 1860. It was found that Susanah Taylor was already a married woman at the time of her marriage to Absolom, having a husband then living. The marriage to Absalom Taylor was declared null and void. (Jac TN, Ch Ct Min, C/413)

TAYLOR, Andrew
Died before 5 November 1787 when the will was proved. David McNabb and Isaac Taylor were executors. (Was TN, Co Ct Min, 1/295)

TAYLOR, Caroline T.
22 February 1861 a suit was entered by Carloine T. Taylor by Thos. D. Tarver next friend &c vs James A. Taylor et als. A trustee is to be named in this case. (Mad TN, Ch Ct Min, 2/439) Caroline T. Taylor is the wife of Jas. A. Taylor. Francis Merriwether was her father & by deed & will he devised to her property held in trust by Absolem Deberry, who has died. Absolem Deberry left a will appointing D. J. Merriwether, R. B. Hast & A. Deberry executors. Francis Merriwether also died testate & appointed D. J. Merriwether, J. T. Merriwether & E. A. Taylor executors. David J. Merriwether was appointed trustee for Carloline. (Ibid 3/67)

TAYLOR, David
Died before 10 November 1830 when John Tibets was tried for his murder. On 12 November John Tibits was found not guilty of murder but guilty of manslaughter. (Obi TN, Cir Ct Min, 1/139) Wm. M. Wilson was administrator of David Taylor, deceased. (Ibid 2/23)

TAYLOR, Elizabeth
Made a deed of gift for sundry articles of property to all her children [not named] on 4 October 1816. Witnesses were Samuel Donnell, Martha Donnell, Robert Edwards & William Irvin. (Wil TN, Reg Bk/134)

TAYLOR, Elzij
Died before 4 November 1872 when W. R. G. Crow made a settlement as administrator. (Dyr TN, Co Ct Min, B/509) The name appears to be Elzy Taylor. (Ibid 540)

TAYLOR, F. C.
Died before 5 April 1870 when A. B. Stallcup made a settlement as administrator. (Dyr TN, Co Ct Min, B/42) The administrator filed a receipt from Jincy Taylor. (Ibid 61) 6 November 1871 E. M. Hall was chosen and appointed guardian of Thornton J. Taylor, Francis C. Taylor, Cora Taylor and Effie Taylor, minor heirs. (Ibid 314)

TAYLOR, Frederick
Died before 16 October 1843 when his death was suggested in the suit of Edward Y. Shuck & Bennett Marshall, administrator of David Burford, deceased. vs John T. Abington, William Hutchinson & Frederick Taylor. (Obi TN, Cir Ct Min, 4/no#)

TAYLOR, G. W.
Died before 5 July 1870 when R. C. Coffman made a settlement as administrator. (Dyr TN, Co Ct Min, B/82) 4 September 1871 Mollie E. Taylor was chosen and appointed

guardian of Edward C. Taylor and Lenard W. Taylor, minor heirs of George W. Taylor, deceased. R. C. Coffman and Thomas D. Harwell were her security. (Ibid 272)

TAYLOR, H.
Taxes were not collected in District 4 for 1873, "can't be found." (Dyr TN, Co Ct Min, B/759)

TAYLOR, Isaac
25 August 1780 was shown to be the son of Andrew Taylor when he was appointed to serve as constable in the room of Emil Carter. (Was TN, Co Ct Min, 1/119)

TAYLOR, Isaac
Died before 7 May 1787 when James Taylor was ordered to be admitted to administration "on the estate of Isaac Taylor deceased, Breeches maker." (Was TN, Co Ct Min, 1/278) 5 November 1787 James Taylor qualified as administrator of the estate of Isaac Taylor, deceased. (Ibid 295)

TAYLOR, Israel
Died before 5 April 1871 as shown in the suit of J. T. Hay and wife Francis Hay vs Elijah E. Hawkins administrator, and Fletcher Taylor and Elijah A. Taylor, children and only heirs. Israel Taylor died in Dyer County in 1862. Land is mentioned that Israel sold to Noah Taylor. Francis Hay was the widow of Israel Taylor and petitions for dower. (Dyr TN, Co Ct Min, B/221) W. P. Rice made a settlement as guardian of Fletcher Taylor and others. (Ibid 228)

TAYLOR, Leban
Died before 7 May 1819 when William Babb and his wife Ruth Babb, sold land in Sampson County, NC, to Henry Hunt. The land was part of the estate of Leban Taylor, deceased, and Ruth was one of the heirs. (Wil TN, Co Ct Min, no#/479)

TAYLOR, Mary Anne
2 February 1818 Alexander Braden was appointed her guardian with Henry Reed & Josiah Smith as security. (Wil TN, Co Ct Min, no#/217)

TAYLOR, Mary S.
Was a resident of New Orleans, LA, 26 July 1849, when her deposition was to be taken for the defendants in the suit of Edward B. Draper Exr. &c vs Reuben R. Rogers & others. (Jac TN, Ch Ct Min, A/335)

TAYLOR, Thomas
Died before 1 February 1819 when Any D. Taylor was appointed administratrix with Jno. M. Jackson, John Bonner & Benj. Jackson as security. (Wil TN, Co Ct Min, no#/378)

TAYLOR, Thomas B.
Died before 17 April 1822 when the former guardian of Thomas B. Taylor, his minor heir, turned over the notes belonging to said minor, to Allen R. Dillard, guardian. William Steel was a former guardian. (Wil TN, Reg Bk/288)

TAYLOR, Thos. H.
Died before 12 September 1855 as shown in the petition of Andrew Guthrie, administrator, and others. (Mad TN, Ch Ct Min, 2/72) He left Jane Taylor his widow & John Ingram Taylor & Fanny Thomas Taylor his only children. (Ibid 92) Land was sold in Memphis. (Ibid 320)

TAYLOR, Wm.
Married before 11 February 1812 to Elizabeth Holland, widow of Daniel Holland, deceased. (Rob TN, Co Ct Min, 3/63)

TEATER, Samuel L. [Tealer]
Died before 15 October 1838 when his death was suggested in the suit of Larkin Norrid & Samuel L. Teater vs Daniel St. John. (Obi TN, Cir Ct Min, 3/242) James Davis was administrator. (Ibid 274)

TEATIN, Sally
Died before 11 November 1835 when her death was suggested in the suit of Seth Bedford vs Lysander Adams & Lydia his wife, Jubilee M. Bedford, Samuel L. Teatin & Sally his wife & others. [The last name of Sally is very much in doubt.] She died intestate and without issue. (Obi TN, Cir Ct Min, 3/43)

TELLERS, Thomas [Sellers]
Was shown to be the son of Howell Tellers, 12 November 1810. (Rob TN, Co Ct Min, 2/316)

TELLY, Hailey [Jelly]
Died before 16 January 1816 when Thomas Harrington made a bill of sale to Joshua Bradbury, Britton Drake & Thomas Harrington [?] to indemnify his securities as guardian of two of the heirs of Hailey Telly, deceased. [Note: there had been a Hailey Tally in the county and this may be the correct name of the deceased.] (Wil TN, Reg Bk/64)

TEMPLE, Dempsey P.
Died before 7 March 1838 as shown in the suit of James L. Armstrong and Mason P. his wife, Robt. H. Temple, William P. Temple, Jane Temple and Hannah M. Temple, minor heirs of Dempsey P. Temple, deceased, who sue by their guardian Mary Temple, against Leonard C. Temple and John B. Dickson & Charlott B. His wife, the last of whom are residents of AR. They are all heirs of Elizabeth Temple, deceased, who died about January 1836. Armstrong is an heir in right of his wife, Mason P., who is one of the children of the said deceased and the said Robt. H., William P., Jane T., & Hannah N. being heirs in right of Dempsey P. Temple, deceased, who was one the children of said Elizabeth. Charlotte B. Dickson was also a child of Elizabeth. Elizabeth Temple received money from the estate of a brother, Dempsey Pouel [Powel?], of NC. Leonard C. Temple, who was administrator for Elizabeth Temple, has never made a settlement. Mary Temple was the widow of Dempsey Temple. John B. Dickson & wife Charlotte had 7 or 8 children. A settlement was made & divided into 4 shares, the heirs of Dempsey P. Temple, Leonard C. Temple, Mason P. Armstrong & Charlotte B. Dickson (Bed TN, Ch Ct Min, 1/419-431)

TEMPLE, Elizabeth
Died before February term 1836 when Leonard C. Temple was appointed administrator, as shown in the suit of John Tillman, Executor of Samuel Escue vs L. C. Temple. Samuel Escue was security for Leonard C. Temple on his administrators bond. Said Escue departed this life in December last & John Tillman was made sole executor in January 1838. Temple has removed most of the property [from the estate of Elizabeth Temple] to MS. (Bed TN, Ch Ct Min, 1/225) A settlement was made by Leonard C. Temple. [Also see Dempsey P. Temple] (Ibid 419-431) Leonard C. Temple is a resident of AR or TX. (Ibid 473) There were 4 heirs of Elizabeth Temple, Leonard C. Temple, Charlotte Dickson wife of John B., Mason P. Armstrong wife of James L. and the heirs of Dempsey P. Temple, deceased. (Ibid 2/98)

TENNIN, Alexander
Died before 5 August 1806 when Mary Tennin & Wm. Anderson were granted letters of administration, with Nathl. Simmons & Isaac Dorris security. (Rob TN, Co Ct Min, 1/402) Also shown as Alexander Tuming. (Ibid 3/26)

TENNISON, John
Died before 19 July 1802 when the will was proved by Joel Vaughn & William Sale. (Rob TN, Co Ct Min, 1/224)

TERRELL, Wm. [Lerrell, Tirrell]
Died before 24 February 1837 as shown in the suit of Geo. W. L. Marr vs William W. Jones & Moses Parr admr. of Wm. Terrell decd. Moses Parr is also now deceased. (Obi TN, Cir Ct Min, 3/109)

TERRILL, Epperson
Died before 8 April 1874 when Charles C. Moss made a settlement as administrator. [Also see Epperson Ferrill, probably same] (Dyr TN, Co Ct Min, B/732)

TERRILL, James W.
Died before 8 April 1874 when Charles C. Moss made a settlement as administrator. (Dyr TN, Co Ct Min, B/732)

TERRY, John
Died before 16 August 1860 as shown in the suit of Sarah Terry, Sr. by guardian &c vs John F. Hawkins & Sarah Hawkins, Wm. B. Webb & Rebecca Webb, Nancy Terry and Elizabeth Terry, bill for dower. E. A. Craig is guardian of Nancy Terry who is an idiot. Complainant is the widow of John Terry, deceased, & is entitled to dower. Sarah Terry, Jr. is the wife of John F. Hawkins. (Jac TN, Ch Ct Min, C/432)

TERRY, Pleasant A.
Married before 6 June 1871 to Matilda A., widow of J. D. Ferguson, deceased, as shown when Matilda applied for a years porvision. (Dyr TN, Co Ct Min, B/245)

THAXTON, Henry B.
Died intestate in 1850 as shown in the suit of Milton Draper Admr. &c vs David G. Shepherd & others. Milton Draper is his administrator. Henry B. Thaxton had purchased lands from David G. & James M. Shepherd and paid for same but did not get a title. (Jac TN, Ch Ct Min, B/56) A suit was entered by Milton Draper administrator &c, John B. Thaxton, Mary C. Thaxton and Miltilda Thaxton, the last 3 by their guardian James Draper vs David G. Shepherd, James M. Shepherd and Aletha A. Thaxton. Land was sold that was partly in Jackson and partly in Smith County. The widow's dower was mentioned. (Ibid 132)

THOMAS, Andrew
Died before 17 July 1866 when Wm. Trotter was appointed administrator. (Sev TN, Co Ct Min, no#/355)

THOMAS, Catharine
Died before 4 August 1856 when the administrator, Adam Honk, gave a new bond with Henry Honk as his security. The original bond was destroyed by fire. (Sev TN, Co Ct Min, no#/67)

THOMAS, Dicey
Was granted a divorce from D. Thomas on 10 February 1840. They were married about 14 years before filing this bill. They had been residents of Bedford County for many years. After 1 year of marriage he deserted her. She has heard that he is in KY and has remarried. (Bed TN, Ch Ct Min, 1/252)

THOMAS, Elizabeth
1 April 1861 was removed from the care of Charles Rafter to whom she had been bound. (Sev TN, Co Ct Min, no#/670)

THOMAS, James
8 March 1825 was certified to be of age when he applied for law license. (McM TN, Co Ct Min, 2no#/56)

THOMAS, Jas.
Died before 5 January 1859 when Murphy & McBath were paid for burying clothes. (Sev TN, Co Ct Min, no#/391)

THOMAS, Michael
Was a resident of Montgomery County, VA, 12 September 1781 when an agreement was made between him and Christopher Shouts for land in Washington County, recorded 17 May 1796. (Was TN, Co Ct Min, 1/606)

THOMAS, Phelimon
Gave power of attorney to Wm. Vater which was ordered to record by virtue of certificate of the clerk of Mason County, KY, 19 Jan 1803. (Rob TN, Co Ct Min, 1/242)

THOMAS, Rachel
Was bound to Charles Rafter until after age 18. She is a poor child now 11 years old. (Sev TN, Co Ct Min, no#/428) 2 September 1861 Charles Rafter was released from the apprentice indenture as Rachael Thomas was taken from him by order of this court. (Ibid 714)

THOMAS, Richard
Died before 5 August 1811 when the will was proved by John McGregor & Jesse Stone. (Ste TN, Co Ct Min, 3/81)

THOMAS, W. A.
Taxes were not collected in District 4 for 1873, "run away." (Dyr TN, Co Ct Min, B/759)

THOMAS, William
Died before 25 March 1806 when the will was proved by Joseph Thomas. William Crutchfield & William Crabtree were executors. (Wil TN, Co Ct Min, no#/185) William Crabtree & William Crutchfield were appointed guardian to 5 orphan children, sons & daughters of William Thomas, deceased. (Ibid 292) 5 August 1818 William Crabtree made a settlement as guardian of Polly, Peggy, James, Wilson & William Thomas, heirs of William Thomas, deceased. (Ibid 311)

THOMAS, Zubee
7 July 1862 Henry Newman was paid for making a coffin for the child of Zubee Thomas, a poor person. (Sev TN, Co Ct Min, no#/3)

THOMPSON, Alfred
Was appointed guardian of Anny, John, William & Sarah Thompson, minor orphans, 7 December 1830. (McM TN, Co Ct Min, 2no#/489)

THOMPSON, Allas
Was the mother of a bastard child. 11 February 1813 James McKearley gave bond that the child would not become a charge upon the county. (Rob TN, Co Ct Min, 3/214)

THOMPSON, Andrew
27 August 1778 took the oath of allegiance. (Was TN, Co Ct Min, 1/44)

THOMPSON, Andrew
Died before 6 November 1865 when James T. Trotter was appointed administrator with W. F. Nichols as security. (Sev TN, Co Ct Min, no#/238)

THOMPSON, David W.
Died before 11 September 1855 when his death was admitted in the case of David W. Thompson vs W. B. Brigance et als. (Mad TN, Ch Ct Min, 2/66) David died 16 July 1855 in Bedford County, TN. Administration was granted by Bedford County Court to James Anderson. David left the following heirs: Violet Thompson, Reuben Thompson, both of full age, Nathan W. Thompson, Thomas F. Thompson, Nancy Ann Thompson, Joseph P. Thompson, Eleaner C. Thompson, Mary Jane Thompson and David R. Thompson, all minors. (Ibid 128)

THOMPSON, Frank
Was a white orphan child when he was bound 3 November 1873 to Mrs. Polly M. Applewhite until age 21. John L. Webb was her security. (Dyr TN, Co Ct Min, B/660)

THOMPSON, Goodwin
Died before 4 February 1811 when land was taxed to the heirs. (Ste TN, Co Ct Min, 3/26)

THOMPSON, James
Died before 27 December 1842 as shown in the suit of James H. Locke administrator of James Thompson and others vs The Creditors of James Thompson deceased. Minor heirs were Martha Ann Thompson & William Thompson by their guardian, William Turrentine. (Bed TN, Ch Ct Min, 2/223) 29 August 1844 a settlement was made. Newcomb Thompson, Newcom Thompson, Sr., Mrs. Elizabeth Thompson, John F. Thompson, Calvin Thompson and the heirs of Joseph Thompson were mentioned. There was also a claim against the estate of James Thompson as administrator for John A. Thompson. (Ibid 300-3) In the suit of T. D. Connally & Brother vs Calvin Thompson et als, filed 24 December 1841, it is shown that James Thompson is dead and Calvin Thompson was the administrator. James & Calvin were brothers and Martha Thompson was their mother. James sold property to Newton C. Thompson in July 1841 and died on 26 December 1841. Newton C. was a single man and a tanner by trade. (Ibid 3/41-51)

THOMPSON, Joseph
Died before 27 June 1843 as shown in the suit of James H. Locke Admr. &c vs the Creditors of James H. Thompson decd. Some land was sold, it being the 1/5 part of an undivided 25 acre tract, being the part of the land of Joseph Thompson, deceased, which was allotted to William F. Thompson, one of the heirs of the said Joseph Thompson. Also sold was land which had descended to James Thompson from his father Joseph Thompson, deceased. Land was also sold that had been granted by the State of TN to James Thompson. Elizabeth Thompson became the purchaser. Newcom Thompson bought some of the land. (Bed TN, Ch Ct Min, 2/242) William F. Thompson was one of the heirs of Joseph Thompson. James Thompson was a son of Joseph. Newton C. Thompson was mentioned. John Thompson was mentioned. (Ibid 331)

THOMPSON, Mary J.
1 October 1866 was appointed guardian to Laura Thompson, with John Wells & Philip Cummin as security. (Sev TN, Co Ct Min, no#/372)

THOMPSON, Masten
Died before 14 August 1815 when Rachael Thompson was appointed administratrix with Joab Hill as security. (Cla TN, Co Ct Min, 4/88)

THOMPSON, Millard
Taxes were not collected in District 4 for 1873, "insolvent." (Dyr TN, Co Ct Min, B/759)

THOMPSON, Nancy M.
On 23 June 1841 dismissed her petition for divorce from Allen C. Thompson. (Obi TN, Cir Ct Min, 4/no#) The suit was evidently re-entered as a divorce was granted 18 October 1842 on the grounds of desertion. Nancy's maiden name was restored but not listed. (Ibid)

THOMPSON, Samuel
Died before March 1828 when Mary Thompson & Robert Thompson were appointed administrators. [entry very blurred] (McM TN, Co Ct Min, 2no#/261)

THOMPSON, Samuel
Was bound as an apprentice 4 May 1857 to Benjamin Atchley until age 21. He is now 14 years old. (Sev TN, Co Ct Min, no#/162)

THOMPSON, Samuel G.
Filed suit 29 December 1842 by his guardian, Joseph R. McKinley, against Samuel Mitchell & others. (Bed TN, Ch Ct Min, 2/233) The suit was against Samuel Mitchell & William R. Guy, Thomas N. McLean, John B. Cooper & Robert Dennison. William Guy was the former guardian of Samuel G. Thompson, having been appointed guardian on 16 December 1831. (Ibid 285) Money had come into the hands of the former guardian, William Guy, for his 3 wards one of whom was Samuel G. Thompson. Said Guy & Mitchell live in AR & Thomas R. McLain lives in MS & John B. Cooper lives in AL. (Ibid 3/130)

THOMPSON, Susan
Died before 6 October 1856 when money was allowed from the poor fund for her shroud. (Sev TN, Co Ct Min, no#/75)

THOMPSON, William
Was a white orphan boy when he was bound 1 December 1873 to E. C. Taylor until age 21. (Dyr TN, Co Ct Min, B/666)

THOMPSON, William H.
Died before December 1843 as shown in the suits of 20 March 1852 by L. C. Hall & wife Nancy D. Hall & R. C. Kirkpatrick & wife Elizabeth vs Garret Sadler & others. Garret Sadler had been guardian of said Nancy D, Elizabeth and Green B. Thompson and about December 1843 sold property from the estate of William H. Thompson, deceased. One Sarah Isham, and the said Nancy D., Elizabeth and Green Berry, are the only distributees of William H. Thompson. Said Sarah has collected her portion. Henry Sadler, administrator of Prudence Thompson, was mentioned in this suit. (Jac TN, Ch Ct Min, B/44) Henry Sadler was called the executor of Prudence Thompson. (Ibid 251) In a suit by Milton Draper vs James Isham & Sarah Isham, and a cross bill by Absalom Johnson vs Sarah A. Isham, James Isham, Milton Draper, Thomas H. Butler and William W. Goodall, it was stated that Sarah Fitzgerald, while a citizen of Jackson County, gave to Milton Draper a power of attorney to receive from Merlin Young or any other person, her distributive share of the estate of William H. Thompson, deceased. After giving the power of attorney said Sarah removed to the state of TX and married James Isham and issued a power of attorney to Absolum Johnson for the same purpose. Joseph Fitzgerald was the deceased husband of Sarah Isham. (Ibid 278)

THORN, David
Died before 1 August 1814 when Nathan Boon & Nathan Skinner were appointed administrators with Silas Vinson & Abel Olive as security. (Ste TN, Co Ct Min, 4/166)

THORN, Thomas A.
Was a minor 9 July 1850 when Martin Thorn petitioned for sale of land. (Mad TN, Ch Ct Min, 1/135)

THORNBURG, Anna
3 September 1866 Samuel Thornburg was appointed her guardian with J. H. Caldwell as security. Anna is a minor orphan. (Sev TN, Co Ct Min, no#/367)

THORNTON, Yancy
Died before 2 May 1814 when his death was suggested in the suit of Faulkner Elliott vs Yancy Thornton. (Ste TN, Co Ct Min, 4/140) His will was proved by William Outlaw. Amelia Thornton qualified as executrix, John Allen, the other executor named, having declined. (Ibid 144) One of the heirs came into court and questioned the validity of the

will which was dated 13 April 1814. (Ibid 219) Amelia Thornton was appointed guardian of her infant daughters, Harriet Thornton & Eliza Thornton. (Ibid 224) In the suit of William Bufford & Patsy his wife vs Amelia Thornton, 8 February 1815, a jury found that the will of Yancy Thornton was valid. (Ibid 249)

THURMAN, Joseph
Died in 1852, as shown in the petition of Richard Thurman and others. The petitioners are his only heirs. (Mad TN, Ch Ct Min, 2/76) 23 February 1859 Richd. Thurman, Van Miller & wife Nancy & Joseph Thurman sold land to Thos. T. Cardwell. (Ibid 262)

THURMOND, O. L.
Died before 5 May 1873 when James A. Thurmond was appointed administrator, with O. L. Thurmond and Davis Ford as his security. (Dyr TN, Co Ct Min, B/580)

THURMOND, Thomas
Taxes were not collected in Distric 5 for 1873, "gone." (Dyr TN, Co Ct Min, B/759)

THURSBEYS, Edward
Died before 21 February 1842 when land was taxed to the heirs. (Obi TN, Cir Ct Min, 4/no#)

TIDWELL
18 February 1861 Jno. M. Murrell was appointed guardian ad litem to answer for the minor defendants in the suit of W. M. Tidwell et als vs P. A. Tidwell et als. (Mad TN, Ch Ct Min, 2/419) Same suit shown as William M. Tidwell and F. B. Tidwell vs P. A. Tidwell & others. In October 1856 Jno. J. Brooks, William H. Watson and Sarah B. Watson his wife sold land to W. M. Tidwell for the use of P. A. Tidwell, the wife of Franklin B. Tidwell, & her children then living & to be begotten by the said F. B. Tidwell. P. A. Tidwell is the wife & the other defendants are the children of F. B. Tidwell. F. B. Tidwell has left the land & is about to move to Obion County. (Ibid 427)

TILFORD, Robert
Died before 17 September 1816 when Hugh Tilford was appointed administrator, with James Law & Rueben Woods security. (Wil TN, Co Ct Min, no#/31) A years provision was allotted for the widow. (Ibid 32) 1 November 1819 Hugh Telford was appointed guardian for Thomas C. Telford & Elizabeth Telford, minor heirs of Robert Telford, deceased. (Ibid 535)

TILLMAN, Nelly
7 July 1873 an allowance was made to A. B. Tigrett for Nelly Tillman (insane). (Dyr TN, Co Ct Min, B/598)

TIMBERLAKE, John C.
22 January 1811 entered the following statement in the records: "Whereas I have been charged with having said that I saw Joseph England and Louisa Winter Daughter of Moses Winter in the act of Fornication and Whereas, the said Moses Winter has commenced a suit against me for making said Charge which said suit is now depending in the County Court of Roane, now these are to Certify that I never made the said charge nor in any way whatever impeached or called in question the Chastity of the said Louisa Winter and that any such implication on the Character of the said Louisa would if made have been false and unfounded and I do further Certify that to the best of my Knowledge and belief the said Louisa Winter is a Chaste and Virtuous Woman. Given under my hand and seal this twenty first day of January in the year 1811. John C. Timberlake." Witnessed by Jas. Gallaher, Matthew Pryor, Joseph Nail, Wm. White & Joshua Ashmore. (Roa TN, Co Ct Min, D/271)

TIMS, Vincen
Was shown to be the ancestor of Nathaniel Tims in the suit of Nathaniel Tims et als vs Henry M. Parker. Vincen Tims had made a deed to Henry M. Parker in 1857. John Tims was also mentioned. (Mad TN, Ch Ct Min, 2/429)

TIPTON, Abraham
Died 2 September 1782 as shown in the statement of his father, Col. John Tipton. John Tipton swore that Samuel Tipton is his oldest and first born son and that Capt. Abrm. Tiption was his third son by the same marriage. His son, Abraham, was in the public Service of Col. Crocket's Regt. under the command of Genl. Clark in his Expedition against the Indians in 1782 and was killed by the Indians, the same party of Indians that killed Captain Chapman. John Tipton believes that his son Samuel, as heir of Abraham,

is entitled to all the land that would or ought to have been allowed to the said Abraham Tipton had he survived. (Was TN, Co Ct Min, 1/377)

TIPTON, Benjamin
Died before 6 November 1865 when the will was proved by Wm. M. Burnett and Andrew Rogers, witnesses. Cromwell Delozier was executor with Andrew Rogers as security. (Sev TN, Co Ct Min, no#/240)

TIPTON, Jacob
Died before 4 May 1857 when Benjamin Tipton renewed his bond as administrator, the former bond having been destroyed by fire. Jesse Hill was security. (Sev TN, Co Ct Min, no#/161) 7 May 1866 Joseph Delozier was appointed guardian to John Tipton, minor orphan of Jacob Tipton, deceased, with B. J. Tipton as security. (Ibid 327)

TIPTON, John
Was bound 10 August 1790 to Henry Jones Fuller until the age of 21. John is now 10 years and 2 months old. (Was TN, Co Ct Min, 1/459)

TIPTON, Joseph
28 August 1778 took the oath of allegiance. (Was TN, Co Ct Min, 1/47)

TIPTON, Samuel
Was bound 10 August 1790 to Joseph Hedrick, Blacksmith, until age 21. Samuel is now a boy of 13 years of age. (Was TN, Co Ct Min, 1/459)

TIPTON, W. P.
Was released from paying poll tax for 1858 as there is no such man in the county. (Sev TN, Co Ct Min, no#/407)

TISDALE, James
Died before 21 February 1842 when land was taxed to the heirs. (Obi TN, Cir Ct Min, 4/no#)

TISDELL, Edward
Died before 16 December 1816 when "a paper writing purporting to be a will or some other writing" was exhibited in Court and on motion was ordered to be deposited with the Clerk of this Court. Moore Stephenson & Ansil Whitfield were appointed administrators pendente lite on the estate. (Wil TN, Co Ct Min, no#/46) A years support was allotted to the widow & her minor children. (Ibid 60) Piety Tisdale filed her dissent to the will. (Ibid 69) Piety was the widow. (Ibid 75) 1 February 1819 Beverly Williams was appointed guardian of the minor heirs. (Ibid 377)

TOLBERT, James R.
Was a non-resident of the county on 11 February 1860 as shown in the suit of William E. Curd et als vs R. J. C. Gailbreath et als. (Jac TN, Ch Ct Min, C/345)

TOLBERT, Sarah
Died before 1 February 1858 when William H. Cowan was appointed administrator. L. W. Burns, Wm. A. McNutt, J. M. Cowan & David Keener were his security. (Sev TN, Co Ct Min, no#/255)

TOLBERT, Thomas
Died before 1 February 1858 when William H. Cowan qualified as executor with L. W. Burns, Wm. A. McNutt, J. M. Cowan & David Keener as security. (Sev TN, Co Ct Min, no#/254)

TOLIVER, Zachariah
17 September 1816 was bound as an apprentice to Saml. Sherrill as blacksmith of Lebanon, to learn the trade of a blacksmith, until the 24th day of August 1819. (Wil TN, Co Ct Min, no#/41)

TOMLIN, J. W. ?
Probably died before 20 February 1868 when a report was to be made on what advancements were made to J. W. Tomlin from the estate of his father, J. W.? Tomlin. (Mad TN, Ch Ct Min, 3/152)

TOMLIN, James W.
Married before 13 August 1868 to Penelope Estis as shown in the suit of Jas. W. Tomlin and Penelope Tomlin vs Ed. A. Clark. Penelope Estis had recovered a judgement against

Jno. F. & E. A. Clark on 23 February 1861. Penelope married Jas. W. Tomlin on 15 Dec 1862 after entering into a marriage contract by which said Jas. W. relinquished all property of Penelope, or that might descend to her, to be her sole and separate property. Jno. F. Clark is dead & his estate insolvent. The judgement granted to Penelope is to be set off against Ed A. Clark. (Mad TN, Ch Ct Min, 3/166)

TOMLINSON, Jas. M.
Died before 21 February 1866 when his death was proven in the suit of A. Vaccaro vs Simmons et als. (Mad TN, Ch Ct Min, 2/475) The suit was revived in the names of his children, Thomas, James, George & Wyatt Tomlinson, minors. (Ibid 500) The heirs were shown the same except Georgia instead of George. (Ibid 3/5)

TRAMMEL, Isabella
Noah Sinclair was appointed her guardian on 2 May 1815 with Nathan Parker & George Boyd as security. (Ste TN, Co Ct Min, 4/270)

TRAMMEL, Philip
Was a resident of Logan County, KY, 17 January 1797 when his deposition was to be taken to prove an agreement between Wm. Stair & Jethro Sumner. (Rob TN, Co Ct Min, 1/18) Said Trammel being blind, his handwriting was proved. (Ibid 23)

TRAMMEL, Sampson
Died before 5 February 1811 when Joseph Gray, Jr. was appointed guardian for all the children of Sampson Trammel, deceased, with David McNatt, James Mallory & John Hodges as security. (Ste TN, Co Ct Min, 3/34) William Pryor was administrator. (Ibid 125) William Pryor was appointed guardian of the orphan children of Sampson Trammel, deceased, in the room of Joseph Gray, Jr. (Ibid 4/63) Barney Livingston filed a petition for his distributive share (in right of his wife) of the estate of Sampson Trammel, deceased. (Ibid 221)

TRAP, Emeline [Trapt]
Was an orphan child, daughter of Mourning Trap, and on 7 March 1826 it was ordered that she be provided for until next court. (McM TN, Co Ct Min, 2no#/140) 5 June 1826 Emeline Trap was to be bound to Samuel Shelton but his application for same was rejected. (Ibid 154)

TRIMBLE, William
Listed with the court cases is, "William Trimble Abbd Marriage License for himself and Sarah Clark the 26 June 1778." (Was TN, Co Ct Min, 1/60)

TRIPLETT, John
Was a resident of Morgan County, TN, on 10 March 1826 when his deposition was to be taken for the defendant in the case of William Brown vs Henry McKorkle. (McM TN, Co Ct Min, no#/230)

TRONTHAM, Benj.
8 July 1856 M. W. Porter was allowed $3.28 out of the poor fund for clothing &c furnished to Benj. Trontham. (Sev TN, Co Ct Min, no#/61) 5 January 1858 Ben. Trentham was ordered to be received into the poor house. (Ibid 246) 4 October 1859 Benj. Trentham was discharged from being a county charge in the poor house. (Ibid 481)

TROTTER, Alexander
Died before 16 November 1795 when the will was proved by Abigale Earmile. (Was TN, Co Ct Min, 1/575)

TROTTER, James
Was admitted as a citizen of the United States and took the Oath of Fidelity, 14 November 1814. (Rob TN, Co Ct Min, 3/492)

TROTTER, Joseph
Died before 25 February 1794 when Alexr. Trotter & Jane Trotter qualified as executors of the last will and testament. An added note has, "dated January 8, 1794 Proved at February session 1794." The will was proved by John Carmichel, Isabella Trotter and Margaret Carmichel. (Was TN, Co Ct Min, 1/470)

TROTTER, Wm. J.
Died before 1 July 1867 when E. M. Wynn was appointed administrator, with John S. Trotter & N. W. Emert as security. (Sev TN, Co Ct Min, no#/461)

TRUESDALE, Jno. N.
Died before 13 September 1854 as shown in the suit of Emory Low & James Low, Jno. Henry & Edward Cunningham, Geo. W. Hardage & Jno. G. Hardage vs Jno. B. Ogden admr. of Jno. N. Truesdale, deceased. (Mad TN, Ch Ct Min, 2/20)

TRUNDLE, Ellen
Died before 5 November 1856 when Wilson L. Trundle was appointed administrator with L. W. Burns & Danl. L. Trundle as security. (Sev TN, Co Ct Min, no#/88)

TRUNDLE, James
Died before 5 November 1856 when Wilson L. Trundle renewed his bond as executor of the last will and testament, with L. W. Burns and Danl. L. Trundle as his security. (Sev TN, Co Ct Min, no#/86) Wilson L. Trundle, surviving executor of James Trundle, deceased vs David L. Trundle & others, petitioned to sell slaves for distribution. Publication was made for the non-resident heirs. Reuel Birdwell was appointed guardian ad litem of Ann Elizabeth, William, Rebecca & Winfield S. Trundle, minor heirs of John W. Trundle deceased [sic]. (Ibid 92) 2 March 1857 process was served on all defendants except David L. Trundle, Ansalam Graham & his wife Polly W. Graham. The above named & Daniel L. Trundle failed to appear. (Ibid 130) Slaves were listed. (Ibid 132)

TUBB, James
Died before 21 September 1808 when Thomas Amery, a free man of color, proved by an instrument of writing from Thomas Tubb that by the will of James Tubb, Thomas Amery had been set free. The instrument of writing was proved by James Trimble & Thomas Dardin, the witnesses thereto. (Roa TN, Co Ct Min, D/6) The instrument of writing given by Thomas Tubb was recorded. It states that Tom & his wife, Darcus, were former slaves of Col. James Tubb & by his last will & testament he liberated them. The witnesses were Thomas N. Clark, Th. Dardis, E. Pritchett & Jno. H. Norton. (Ibid 130)

TUCKER, Allen
Died before 21 July 1812 when administration was granted to John Eblin with John Freeman & Noah Ashley as security. (Roa TN, Co Ct Min, D/380) An account of the inventory was returned. (Ibid 416)

TUCKER, Enoch
Was 19 years of age when he executed a writing obligatory, as shown in the suit of Elizabeth Tucker & Chas. Simmons, administrators of Saml. Tucker, deceased. The suit was entered at November term 1805. (Rob TN, Co Ct Min, 1/400)

TUCKER, Gabriel
Died before 13 August 1839 when his death was suggested in the suit of Gabriel Tucker & wife vs John Medaris & others. The suit was revived in the name of his wife, Matilda Hicks Tucker. (Bed TN, Ch Ct Min, 2/87) [Also see Maderas]

TUCKER, Garrett
Died before 16 September 1816 when Jeremiah Tucker was ordered to make a report as guardian of the heirs. (Wil TN, Co Ct Min, no#/29) James A. Hunter was appointed guardian of Kinderick, Jeremiah, Abigale, Patsy & Rebecca, minor heirs of Garrett Tucker, deceased. (Ibid 43)

TUCKER, Henry
20 October 1802 was bound to Silas Tucker until age 21. (Rob TN, Co Ct Min, 1/236)

TUCKER, James
4 January 1871 J. F. Rays made a settlement as guardian of the heirs of James Tucker. (Dyr TN, Co Ct Min, B/162)

TUCKER, Jane
19 April 1802 a jury was appointed to enquire into her lunacy. (Rob TN, Co Ct Min, 1/209) The jury found her to be a lunatic. Enoch Tucker was appointed her guardian. (Ibid 213) Jane Tucker married Joseph Engleman before 19 January 1803. (Ibid 242)

TUCKER, Jeremiah
18 September 1816 reported that he is about to leave the State & made a report of the estate of William Smith. (Wil TN, Co Ct Min, no#/44)

TUCKER, John
Died before 18 January 1802 when the will was proved by Peter Spence. (Rob TN, Co Ct Min, 1/197) 19 April 1802 letters of administration were granted to Saml. Tucker with

Andw. Irwin, John Robins, Silas Tucker and Enoch Tucker as security. (Ibid 210) Saml. Tucker, John Robins, Charles Simmons, Enoch Tucker, Thos. Norris & Silas Tucker gave bond of $1,000 conditioned for the safe keeping & well providing for the children of John Tucker, deceased, for 6 months. (ibid 213) 20 October 1802 an order was made to pay $1 per week to Mrs. Betsy Tucker for the time she kept the child of John Tucker, deceased, the child is by the name of Samuel. Joel Lewis was allowed $20 for keeping Riggs Tucker & John Tucker, children of John Tucker, deceased. (Ibid 235) 20 October 1802 administration was granted to John Robins. (Ibid 236) Elisabeth Tucker was allowed money for keeping John Tucker. (Ibid 308) Hannah Tucker was a daughter of John Tucker, deceased. (Ibid 345) Henry Johnson was appointed guardian of Hannah, Henry, Sally & Peggy Tucker, orphans of John Tucker, deceased. John B. Cheatham was appointed guardian of Phebe, Riggs, John & Saml. Tucker, orphan children of John Tucker, deceased. (Ibid 359) Petition was made by Nancy, Phebe, Riggs, John & Saml. by their guardian, John B. Cheatham. One was also made by Hannah, Henry, Sally & Peggy Tucker by their guardian, Henry Johnson. (Ibid 360) The heirs, now of age, were mentioned. (Ibid 370) Valentine Choate was allowed $5 out of the estate for curing Riggs Tucker of the "Riptures." (Ibid 394) 12 August 1814 a suit was entered by Stephen Haynes & Mary his wife, heirs-at-law of John Tucker, deceased. (Ibid 3/481) 18 November 1814 suit to set aside the probate of a will; Stephen Haynes & Mary his wife, heirs-at-law of John Tucker deceased vs Joseph Ingleman & Jane his wife, Enoch Tucker, Henry Tucker, John Deamar & Hannah his wife, James McMartin & Pheobe his wife, Sarah Chisim, James B. Nelson & Nancy his wife & Rips Tucker, under the age of 21, by Henry Johnson, his guardian. The will was ordered recorded at the January term of this court 1802 & dated 10 October 1798. (Ibid 513) Enoch Tucker, James & Phoebe McFarland, Henry Tucker, James B. Nelson, John & Hannah Deamar & Sarah Cazun are not inhabitants of this state. (Ibid 514)

TUCKER, John
Was bound to Nehemiah Varnor until age 21, 9 May 1805. (Rob TN, Co Ct Min, 1/344)

TUCKER, Keziah
17 February 1814 made an assignment of dower rights to Patrick Darby, proved by John Howell. (Rob TN, Co Ct Min, 3/386) Above deed was for her right to the estate of John Tucker, deceased. (Ibid 443)

TUCKER, M. W.
2 July 1873 was reported to be unable to perform manual labor. He was released from work on roads until he becomes able. (Dyr TN, Co Ct Min, B/440)

TUCKER, Nancy
20 October 1802 was bound to Joseph Philips until age 18. (Rob TN, Co Ct Min, 1/235) 8 February 1805 John B. Cheatham was appointed guardian for Nancy Tucker. (Ibid 331)

TUCKER, Peggy
20 October 1802 was bound to Charles Simmons until age 18. (Rob TN, Co Ct Min, 1/235)

TUCKER, Phebe
18 January 1803 was bound to Traviss Elmon until age 18. (Rob TN, Co Ct Min, 1/239) 5 November 1804 Phebe was released from indenture and her mother, Jane Engleman, was allowed to take her. (Ibid 316)

TUCKER, Richard W.
Died before 5 April 1870 when J. G. Tucker made a settlement as administrator. (Dyr TN, Co Ct Min, B/42) John E. Webb was chosen and appointed guardian of Pattie Tucker, Etta Tucker and Richard Tucker, minor heirs, with J. G. Tucker and D. E. Parker as security. (Ibid 54)

TUCKER, Riggs
Was bound 8 May 1806 to Henry Fiser until age 21. (Rob TN, Co Ct Min, 1/395)

TUCKER, Samuel
Died before 20 October 1802 when Betty Tucker & Charles Simmons were appointed administrators, with Charles McIntosh & Joseph Philips as security. (Rob TN, Co Ct Min, 1/236) 9 May 1804, on the petition of Julius Elmore who is one of the legatees, a jury was appointed to lay off the lands amongst the legatees. (Ibid 297)

TUCKER, Sarah
20 October 1802 was bound to Silas Tucker until age 18. (Rob TN, Co Ct Min, 1/236)

TUCKER, William
Died before 10 February 1812 as shown when his deed for 100 acres in Rutherford County to Saml. Tucker was proved by Lucy Murphey & Samuel Tucker. The other witness, John D. Robins, is also deceased & his handwriting was proved. (Rob TN, Co Ct Min, 3/55)

TULLOCK, John V.
Died before 23 September 1805 when Benjamin Seawell was granted letters of administration. (Wil TN, Co Ct Min, no#/166)

TUMBLIN, William
Died before 6 December 1830 when Susannah Tumblin was appointed administrator. (McM TN, Co Ct Min, 2no#/488)

TUNIS, John
Died before 2 March 1857 when Cornelius Fox was appointed guardian to Angelina Tunis, Wesly Tunis & Ira Tunis, minor heirs. (Sev TN, Co Ct Min, no#/127) 8 April 1857 Cornelius Fox was appointed special guardian of William Tunes, Ira Tunes, Jane Tunes, Nancy Tunes & Wesley Tunes, minor children of Tunes deceased, to sell land warrant No. 55170 dated 28 January 1857 and issued to said minors for the services of John Tunes private in the war with Mexico. (Ibid 159)

TURLEY, William B.
Died before 16 July 1851 as shown in a tribute of respect entered in the minutes on that date. He was a Judge of the Common Law and Chancery Court of the city of Memphis and late one of the Judges of the Supreme Court of Tennessee. His death was sudden and unexpected. He left a family. (Mad TN, Ch Ct Min, 1/221)

TURNAGE, Solon
Died before 4 December 1871 when James S. Spence was appointed administrator, with T. H. Benton and H. M. Spence as security. (Dyr TN, Co Ct Min, B/325)

TURNER, Adam
Died before 2 December 1820 when Benjamin Turner, legal heir-at-law of Adam Turner, deceased, and attorney of John Turner & William Turner the other heirs, gave power of attorney to Josiah Hull of Smith County, TN, to ask of the land committee of NC for a military land warrant as the heir of Adam Turner who was soldier in Captain Major's company of the NC line in the Revolutionary War, a part of the 10th Regiment. (Wil TN, Reg Bk/189)

TURNER, Buford [Tanner]
Died before 14 July 1848 as shown in the suit of Philip Magavney the admr. vs Robert J. Chester, Moses Wood & Jas Hughes. (Mad TN, Ch Ct Min, 1/51)

TURNER, Daniel
Died before 25 January 1799 when the land of his heirs was ordered sold for back taxes. (Rob TN, Co Ct Min, 1/94)

TURNER, James
Gave bond 1 November 1813 to keep the county clear of all charges for the maintenance of a child with which Rachel Shaun is said to be pregnant. Christian Shaun was security. (Ste TN, Co Ct Min, 4/64)

TURNER, Jasper
Was a resident of NC 12 June 1805 when Burwell Seagraves gave him power of attorney to make a title to a certain tract of land. (Ste TN, Co Ct Min, 1/14)

TURNER, John
Died before 19 October 1819 when his legal heir, Benjamin Turner, of White County, TN, gave power of attorney to John J. S. Ruffin of the city of Raleigh, NC, to apply for a land warrant for the services of John Turner, deceased, in the Revolutionary War as a soldier in Captain Brown's company in 1st Right of the Continental line of the said state of NC. (Wil TN, Reg Bk/140)

TURNER, Robert
Died before 18 January 1827 when the administrator, Ebenezer Hearn, sold a slave to James Turner. (Wil TN, Reg Bk/387) [second set of page numbers]

TURNER, William
Died before 12 February 1822 when his son, William Turner of Smith County, TN, sold land from his father's estate to A. Beard of Wilson County. (Wil TN, Reg Bk/392) [second set of page numbers]

TURPIN, Nathan
Died before 6 January 1809 when the heirs were shown on the delinquent tax list. (Rob TN, Co Ct Min, 2/107)

TURPIN, Thomas
Died before 9 November 1812 when the heirs were exhonerated from payment of double tax on 200 acres of land. (Rob TN, Co Ct Min, 3/135)

TURRENTINE, J. F.
Died before 6 April 1874 when W. L. Hendricks was chosen and appointed guardian of Joanna, Della and Emma J. Turrentine, minor heirs, with J. R. Gammons and Jno. E. McCorkle as his security. (Dyr TN, Co Ct Min, B/714)

TURRENTINE, W. F.
Died before 3 November 1873 when W. F. Landreth was appointed administrator, with J. W. Trent and E. Jones as his security. [The name of the deceased was wirtten over. It could be J. F. Turrentine]. (Dyr TN, Co Ct Min, B/660)

TWEEDY, Jo.
Died before 4 January 1871 when J. B. Powell made a settlement as administrator. (Dyr TN, Co Ct Min, B/162)

TYSON, J. B.
Died before 19 February 1867 when Jno. L. Brown was appointed guardian ad litem for William Tysen, Edwin Tysen, Lydia Tysen & Fannie Tysen, minor defendants in the suit of Jno. R. Alston Exr. vs Margaret Tysen et als. J. B. Tyson died 5 September 1860 having made a will. He appointed Jno. R. Alston, Edwin & John Tyson his executors. He left his wife, Margaret Tyson and children, William Tyson, Edwin Tyson, Lydia Ann Tyson and Fannie Tyson. He left land that had been granted to J. B. & E. Tyson and some land deeded to J. B. & E Tyson & A. R. Reed. Edwin Tyson died having made a will in which be bequeathed all his interest in said lands to J. B. Tyson. Ambrose R. Reid is entitled to his share. The estate of J. B. Tyson is indebted to the heirs of Murphy McKay, deceased, and to Rachel Rawlings. (Mad TN, Ch Ct Min, 3/4 & 56-59)

TYSON, John A.
Died about 7 August 1865, intestate. Leroy C. Gillespie and Ambrose R. Reid were appointed administrators. He died without issue but had 4 brothers, 3 of whom, Edwin, William and Archibald, have died without issue, and the 4th, James B. Tyson, has also died leaving 4 children, William, Edwin, Fannie and Lydia surviving him. The said John A. Tyson had 4 sisters, Lydia who has married John R. Alston and died without issue, Mary Jane who married Leroy C. Gillespie and died leaving 2 children, John M. and Leroy C. Gillespie surviving her, Eliza who married [blank] Rawlings, now deceased, and Fannie who married Ambrose R. Reid. The brothers & sisters of John A. Tyson are entitled to partition and distribution of the land. Edwin, William, Lydia & Fannie are entitled to 1/4. John M. & Leroy C. Gillespie are entitled to 1/4. Eliza Rawlings is entitled to 1/4. Fannie Reid is entitled to 1/4. (Mad TN, Ch Ct Min, 3/89)

UNDERDOWN, Stephen A.
Died before 3 April 1865 when W. R. Underdown & G. W. Underdown were appointed administrators with R. M. Creswell & David Keener as security. (Sev TN, Co Ct Min, no#/146)

UNDERWOOD, George
Died before 3 April 1865 when John Underwood & I. N. Underwood proved the will. John H. Caldwell was executor. (Sev TN, Co Ct Min, no#/142)

UNDERWOOD, Jesse C.
Died before 2 July 1866 when John H. Caldwell was paid for the burial clothes. (Sev TN, Co Ct Min, no#/347)

UNDERWOOD, John
Died before 5 April 1858 when his will was entered by Joel Underwood. Payne McClary & John Kelly were witnesses. R. M. Creswell was witness to the 1st codicil. Jesse Huffaker, the other witness to the 1st codicil is dead. William H. Covington was witness to

the 2nd codicil. Payne McClary & Arnold Covington were witnesses to the 3rd codicil. Joel Underwood was appointed administrator with the will annexed with Payne McClary & George Underwood his security. (Sev TN, Co Ct Min, no#/281-2)

UNDERWOOD, Lewis
Died before 17 July 1866 when J. H. Caldwell was paid for burying clothes. (Sev TN, Co Ct Min, no#/353)

UNDERWOOD, Lewis
9 January 1861 was released from paying poll tax in the future, he being in a weak state of mind. (Sev TN, Co Ct Min, no#/652)

UNDERWOOD, Margaret
5 March 1866 John Underwood was appointed guardian. (Sev TN, Co Ct Min, no#/278)

USERY, Lucy [Urey, Ursery]
Died before 2 November 1841 as shown in the suit of Bailey Butler, Jr., et al vs Lucy Usery et al. It was stated that defendants, Lucy Usery and Joel Rich, had died since the commencement of this suit. (Jac TN, Ch Ct Min, A/29)

VADEN, Leoderick
Was a resident of Smith County, 14 November 1844, as shown in the suit of John M. Love vs Saml. T. & Leoderick Vaden. The name was also shown as Theoderic Vaden (Jac TN, Ch Ct Min, A/182 &189)

VAIL, R. H.
1 May 1871 Ben T. Porter returned the inventory as administrator of R. H. Vail. (Dyr TN, Co Ct Min, B/236) R. H. Vail was shown to be deceased. (Ibid 414) The name was shown as Roan H. Vail. (Ibid 783)

VAIL, W. C.
Died before 5 April 1870 when the administratrix, Emma Vail, returned the inventory. (Dyr TN, Co Ct Min, B/44) 7 August 1871 Mrs. E. Duffey (Mrs. E. Vail) made a settlement as administratrix. (Ibid 260) J. G. Fleming was chosen and appointed guardian of I. N. Vail, minor heir. (Ibid 272) Isaac Newton Vail is the only heir-at-law. (Ibid 280) 2 October 1871 it was stated that W. C. Vail died 10 December 1869 and Emma Duffey was his widow. (Ibid 303)

VANBEBBER, John, Jr.
Died before 9 May 1815 when John Vanbebber, Sr. was appointed administrator with Wm. Rogers as security. (Cla TN, Co Ct Min, 4/47)

VANBEBBER, Peter
Died before 11 February 1817 when Elender Vanbebber and Jacob Vanbebber were appointed administrators with John Jones & John Vanbebber as security. (Cla TN, Co Ct Min, 4/294) A years provision is to be set off for the widow and family. (Ibid 358)

VANCE, Alexr.
Died before 11 April 1856 when Henry Harris was allowed $1.08 for a shroud for him, out of the poor fund. (Sev TN, Co Ct Min, no#/38)

VANCE, William
Was a resident of IL on 3 February 1858 when his deposition was to be taken for William Jarred? in the case of William Jarred? vs Allen Young & others and a cross bill by Jas. W. McDaniel & others vs William Jarred? Jarred was also allowed to take depositions from John Simmons of MO, A. S. Rogers of White County, TN, & Joseph Jarred of Putnam County, TN. (Jac TN, Ch Ct Min, C/84)

VANDERPOOL, Abraham
24 May 1779 Teter Nave was appointed administrator of his estate. (Was TN, Co Ct Min, 1/71)

VANDERPOOL, Rebecca
Died before 24 May 1779 when her will was proved by Thos. Hoyton, Esqr. & James Grisom. (Was TN, Co Ct Min, 1/71)

VANDIKE
3 April 1865 Perry Cate was appointed guardian of Mary Vandike and Catherine Vandike, minor orphans, with J. H. Caldwell as security. (Sev TN, Co Ct Min, no#/148) 3

December 1866 Perry Cate made a settlement as guardian of Malinda C. Vandike and Mary E. Vandike. (Ibid 403)

VANHOOK, Aaron
Died before 16 January 1851 as shown in the suit of Aaron Vanhook vs Thomas R. Richardson and others. His death had been suggested at the last term of court. [July 1850] Francis Davie was appointed administrator. (Mad TN, Ch Ct Min, 1/193)

VANN, John
15 August 1782 it was ordered that he be executed on the 10th day of September next. (Was TN, Co Ct Min, 1/178)

VANNERSON, William
Died intestate in Hawkins or Sullivan County, TN, in 1802 or 1803, as shown in the suit of Francis Vannerson of Bedford County, and Sophia Person [Peaison] of Lawrance County, AL, against Elizabeth Vanuson & Catherine Vannuson of Bedford County, Thomas Vannuson of Pittsylvania County, VA, William Vannuson of Natchez, MS and Albert Vannerson of Jackson County, TN. William Vannerson left his widow, Elizabeth, now living in Bedford County and 7 children all of whom were minors. Sophia married Charles Pierson who has since died. Alford has died intestate & without issue. The other children are the ones named above except Elizabeth who is the widow. All are now of age. After the death of William Vannerson, his widow removed all of his estate to Bedford County, VA, and after several years to Bedford County, TN. Elizabeth [the widow] is now old & has a widowed daughter, who is frail, sickly and delicate, with her. This statement was given 12 February 1838. (Bed TN, Ch Ct Min, 1/228)

VANZANT, John
Was a minor 14 July 1854 as shown in the suit of James G. Cunningham vs Joshua and John Vanzant. Benjamin B. Washburn was appointed guardian ad litem. (Jac TN, Ch Ct Min, B/167)

VAUGHN, Edward
Married before 7 February 1851 to Dicy Eaton as shown in the suit of Nathan Pharis Guardian &c vs Joseph Eaton & Dicey Eaton. Edward Vaughn is of Davidson County and the suit is to be revived in his name. (Jac TN, Ch Ct Min, A/405) Victoria Eaton, who is a party to this bill, is a minor and Joseph Eaton was appointed her guardian ad litem. (Ibid B/14)

VAUGHN, John
16 October 1796 was charged with "Polygamy, he was twice married and doth at this time live in adultry with Isabella Duncan." 18 January 1797, the bill was returned "not found, Left the State." (Rob TN, Co Ct Min, 1/21)

VAUGHN, Richd.
Died before 22 January 1802 when the heirs were shown on the delinquent tax list. (Rob TN, Co Ct Min, 1/206)

VAUGHN, Thomas
Died before 23 December 1806 when the will was proved by James Stuart & Frederick Aust. Molly T. Vaughn qualified as executrix. (Wil TN, Co Ct Min, no#/271)

VENTERS, John S.
Died before 1 May 1815 when Sarah Venters qualified as executrix with Abner Pearce, Joseph Thomason, William Pearce & John Weatherford as security. (Ste TN, Co Ct Min, 4/259) The will was proved by William Pearce and Alexander Robertson. (Ibid 261)

VINCENT, Jno. A.
Married before 16 January 1850 to Sarah Anderson, as shown in the suit of Andrew Guthrie admr. vs Sarah Anderson et als. (Mad TN, Ch Ct Min, 1/102 Jno. A. Vincent died before 24 August 1866 as shown in the suit of Jno. C. M. Garland vs Sarah A. Vincent et als. (Ibid 2/538) Jno. A. Vincent died about 27 December 1865. His will was proved 3 January 1866. Sarah A. was named executrix but declined & at her request Jno. C. M. Garland was appointed administrator with will annexed. The suit to sell land also shows Thomas S. Vincent. (Ibid 3/25)

VINCENT, Thos. S.
Was a minor 22 August 1866 when A. S. Suingley? was appointed guardian ad litem to defend in the suit of Jno. C. M. Gailand vs Sarah A. Vincent & Thos S. Vincent. (Mad TN, Ch Ct Min, 2/506)

VINSON, James [Vinsen]
Probably died before 21 August 1858 as shown in the suit of Thos. Reid vs Wm. M. Vinson. The defendant had a 1/7 interest in a tract of land descended to him from James Vinson. (Mad TN, Ch Ct Min, 2/237)

VINSON, John
Died before 26 March 1806 when Jonas Vinson was granted administration, with Edward Mitchell as security. (Wil TN, Co Ct Min, no#/194)

VINSON, William
Died before 14 July 1855 as shown in the suit of James Burgess vs David G. Shepherd, Sarah Vinson & others. David G. Shepherd was the administrator. (Jac TN, Ch Ct Min, B/280) Sidney S. Stanton was appointed guardian ad litem for the minor heirs. (Ibid 302) A suit was entered by David G. Shepherd and Sally Vinson vs Jefferson A. Thomas, James Pharis, Allen Manier, Henry Vinson, Hamilton Vinson & Martha Vinson, the last 4 [sic] minors by their guardian S. S. Stanton. William Vinson had conveyed land by deed of trust to James A. Thomas on 22 July 1852. Sally Vinson is the widow. There is money owed to Allen Manier from the purchase of land. (Ibid 309) James Vinson was also a minor defendant. Land was sold subject to the widow's dower. (Ibid C/21)

VINSON, William B.
Married before 7 October 1809 to Isabella Butler, widow of Edward Butler, deceased, as shown in a case of Cornelius Conrad, Andrew Conrad & John Conrad, assignees of Duntan Robertson, against William B. Vinson & Isabella P., his wife, late Isabella Butler. (Rob TN, Co Ct Min, 2/190 & 319)

VIVRET, Micajah
Died before 19 June 1816 when an inventory of the property was recorded by the administrator and ordered to be sold. (Wil TN, Co Ct Min, no#/17) Micajah's last name looks more like Viverett. (Ibid 33) George Smith was appointed guardian of James Vivret & Thomas Vivret minor heirs of Micajah Vivret deceased. (Ibid 63)

WADDELL, Charles
17 May 1796 gave bond with George Gillaspie as security, that a natural child by him begotten on the body of Abigale Carmile would not be chargeable to the County. (Was TN, Co Ct Min, 1/606)

WADDELL, S. G.
Died before 21 August 1866 when his death was admitted in the suit of S. Q. Waddell vs W. Fulghum, and the suit revived in the name of Thos S. Freeman, administrator. (Mad TN, Ch Ct Min, 2/502)

WADDIE, W. K.
Died before 5 February 1872 when R. G. Menzies, J. F. Williamson & L. M. Williams were appointed to lay off a years allowance for the widow and family. (Dyr TN, Co Ct Min, B/366) The will was proved by Smith Parks and J. R. Westbrooks, witnesses, with Mrs. Ann Waddie as executrix of the will of William K. Waddie. Smith Parks was appointed guardian of Joseph Kimbro Waddie and John William Waddie, minor heirs, Mrs. Ann Waddie giving her consent. (Ibid 367)

WADE
4 November 1838 suit was brought by Wm. S. Wade, Martin F. Wade, Edward B. Tuck & wife Ann, Lam? Wade & Marmaduke Wade, the last 2 minors who sue by their guardian Wm. S. Wade, Mary Wade & Michael Wade, also minors who sue by Jacob Morton their guardian, all citizens of Bedford County, and Josiah C. Brassfield & wife Elizabeth who are citizens of Limestone County, AL, vs the mayor & Alderman of the town of Shelbyville, John W. Hamblin & Thomas Knott. The suit was dismissed. (Bed TN, Ch Ct Min, 1/220)

WADE
A suit was shown 14 July 1859 by Robert Wade & wife Hannah Wade, Hampton Wade & wife Milly Wade, James M. Wolf & wife Fanny Wolf vs L. C. Collier & others. An agreement was reached. (Jac TN, Ch Ct Min, C/244)

WADE, John
Died before 17 October 1803 when James Robertson was appointed administrator with Wm. Caldwell & Benjn. Mason as security. (Rob TN, Co Ct Min, 1/263)

WADE, John C.
Died in 1860 leaving a will. Mary A. Wade was appointed administratrix with will

annexed, the executor named having declined. Leonidas Utley & wife, James Wade, Miranda Wade & others were his heirs. John C. Wade had sold land to Geo. W. Day in 1859, being lot No. 1 in the division & sale of the estate of Stephen P. Wade, deceased, which had been sold in 1849 & bought by said Wade. (Mad TN, Ch Ct Min, 2/523)

WAGGONER, Stephen B.
Died before 22 August 1866 when Jno. S. Brown was appointed guardian ad litem for Geo. Waggoner & Stephen Waggoner, minors, to defend in the suit of J. W. Stewart vs Mary Waggoner et als. Stephen B. Waggoner died intestate leaving Mary Waggoner his widow & Stephen & George Waggoner his only heirs. (Mad TN, Ch Ct Min, 2/506 & 529)

WAITS, D. S.
Died before 2 December 1873 when his will was proved by John M. McGannis and F. G. Sampson, witnesses. (Dyr TN, Co Ct Min, B/671)

WAKEFIELD
25 May 1780 a Dids. was issued to Burk County [NC] to take the depositions of Charles Wakefield, John Wakefield and Henry Wakefield on behalf of Amos Bird in his suit with Saml. Sherville. (Was TN, Co Ct Min, 1/113)

WALDRAN, Jesse
19 March 1823, with his wife Sally, gave a power of attorney to Wilson Sanderlin of Camden County, NC, to dispose of lands in Pasquatant & Camden Counties which "fell to us as heirs at law by the death of Ann Chamberlin and Ann Gamberling." (Wil TN, Reg Bk/295)

WALDRON, Rebecca
Died before 24 September 1806 when the will was proved by Benjamin Gray. (Wil TN, Co Ct Min, no#/258)

WALKER, Agness
Died before 4 September 1871 when the will was proved by John M. Drane and Louisa M. Drane, witnesses. (Dyr TN, Co Ct Min, B/278) No executor was named so H. V. C. Wynne was appointed administrator of the estate cum testamento Annexeo. (Ibid 343)

WALKER, David
Died before 23 June 1806 when Elizabeth Walker & William Walker were appointed administrators, with George Mecker & Christopher Cooper as security. (Wil TN, Co Ct Min, no#/237) Elizabeth Walker requested dower. (Ibid 251)

WALKER, Elizabeth
Was living in Knox County 18 April 1810 when her deposition was to be taken for the plaintiff in the case of David McClellan vs Joseph Walker. (Roa TN, Co Ct Min, D/207)

WALKER, George
Was a resident of Fayette County, KY, on 17 October 1796 when his deposition was to be taken for recording a deed from Joseph Brock to Thos. Hopkins. (Rob TN, Co Ct Min, 1/6)

WALKER, James
Was a resident of Coffee County, TN, 22 April 1843 when he brought suit against William Brown of Bedford County. (Bed TN, Ch Ct Min, 3/110)

WALKER, James
Died before 1 May 1871 when W. B. Smith was appointed administrator with B. F. Prichard and W. H. Hendrix as his security. E. P. Kirk, T. J. Pierce and Alex Wray were appointed to lay off a years provision for the widow and family. (Dyr TN, Co Ct Min, B/236) The widow was Mrs. M. A. Walker. (Ibid 243)

WALKER, John
On 1 October 1813 made a deed of gift "of one small bay horse named Jinny" to the heirs of Robert H. Enox. (Wil TN, Reg Bk/108)

WALKER, John
Died before 6 September 1858 when Jesse Stafford was appointed administrator with R. Birchfield, Wm. Thurman, Mark Keeler, N. M. Baker, John Walker, Jos. Walker & John S. McNutt as security. (Sev TN, Co Ct Min, no#/337)

WALKER, John
Died before 18 July 1866 when Jesse Stafford was appointed trustee in the case of John

& Mark Bird to fill the vacancy occasioned by the death of John Walker. (Sev TN, Co Ct Min, no#/357)

WALKER, John, Sr.
5 December 1821 made a deed of gift to John Walker, Jr. of 3 negroes. (McM TN, Co Ct Min, no#/27)

WALKER, Kennan
Died before 3 June 1872 when C. L. Nolen, public administrator, was appointed administrator. (Dyr TN, Co Ct Min, B/420)

WALKER, Lee
Taxes were not collected in District 4 for 1873, "insolvent." (Dyr TN, Co Ct Min, B/759)

WALKER, Malissa C.
Died before 5 May 1873 when H. V. Wynne was appointed administrator, with Robert Hale and T. H. Bell as his security. (Dyr TN, Co Ct Min, B/581) 2 February 1874 her nuncupative will was proved by William Taylor and Mollie Taylor, witnesses. (Ibid 706)

WALKER, Matthew
Was a resident of Davidson County, TN, 23 February 1828 when he sold a slave to the children of Ann Dickins (to wit) Maria Enocks, Alford Enocks, Mary Ann Enocks, John G. Enocks, Joseph W. Dickins & Elijah P. Dickins. (Wil TN, Reg Bk/383) [second set of page numbers]

WALKER, P. C.
Died before 6 February 1871 when L. T. Walker made a settlement as administrator. (Dyr TN, Co Ct Min, B/190) 5 August 1872 Mrs. L. Tenne [?] Walker, administrator of Dr. P. C. Walker, was ordered to pay out the funds in her hands to the parties entitled thereto, as per settlement confirmed today. (Ibid 447)

WALKER, Peter
Married Drucilla Hendricks as shown when they entered a marriage contract 22 June 1807, with John Williams as trustee for Drucilla. (Wil TN, Co Ct Min, no#/291)

WALKER, Robert
Died shortly after making his will 1 Nov 1826 in Mecklenburg County, NC, as shown in the suit of James M. Read and others vs Robert Walker & Wm. C. Neely. He bequeathed to his daughter, Ann Reed, a negro named Barnett, and then to her children. The negro was sold several times, including to the two defendants, and the last time to a person unknown who lives outside the state. Anna Reid who had a life estate in said negro died 16 January 1850. The complainants, James M., Robert W. & Jno. Reid, Caroline Sharp & Margaret Brown, the wife of William Brown, are the only children of the said Anna Reid and they are entitled to the negro. Since Wm. Neely is unable to deliver said negro to complainants he is to pay them his value and reasonable hire from 16 January 1850. (Mad TN, Ch Ct Min, 2/95)

WALKER, Sam
Died before 5 October 1870 when the farm of his heirs was mentioned. (Dyr TN, Co Ct Min, B/120)

WALKER, Samuel
Made a petition for a pension 10 March 1826. He stated that he was about 70 years of age. He enlisted for a term of 14 months, doesn't recall the year but believes it was at the start of the American Revolution, in Chester County, SC. He was in Capt. William Brown's Regt., commanded by Col. Thomas Sumpter. He also served two periods in a volunteer Company, names battles, etc. He has 1 daughter living with him named Polly, aged 16. He has 8 other children. (McM TN, Co Ct Min, 2no#/150)

WALKER, William
Made a deed of gift of slaves & other property, 30 October 1826, to his grand children, the children of his daughter Nancy Martin, to wit: Susan Ann Martin & Dosha Martin. (Wil TN, Reg Bk/367) [second set of page numbers]

WALL, E.
Died before 3 May 1870 when W. C. Doyle was appointed administrator de bonis non, with C. C. Moss & W. M. Watkins as security. The former administrator, S. C. Pile, has left the State. (Dyr TN, Co Ct Min, B/57) Also shown as Edward Walls. (Ibid 65)

WALL, Edward
Died before 4 January 1858 when John H. Caldwell, Thomas Bryan, Jr. & Wm. E. Byran were appointed to lay off a years support to Joanna Wall, his widow. (Sev TN, Co Ct Min, no#/237) I. N. Underwood was appointed administrator with Enoch Underwood his security. (Ibid 238)

WALL, Nancy
Died before 7 April 1856 when Edward Wall was appointed administrator. John Underwood and Wm. M. Bryan were securities. (Sev TN, Co Ct Min, no#/24) 1 March 1858 Henry Randles applied for administration, which was refused as administration had been granted on the estate of Edward Wall, deceased, who was the husband & administrator of Nancy Wall, deceased. (Ibid 262) 5 April 1858 Henry Randles & Mary Underwood were appointed administrators de bonis non. Joel Underwood was security. (Ibid 283)

WALLDROPE, Richard
1 September 1828 made a deed to the United States of America for 160 acres of Military Bounty land in Arkansas Territory. (McM TN, Co Ct Min, 2no#/306)

WALLEN, Elisha
Made a deed of gift 25 May 1807 to Mary Sims, Agnes Murry and others, for his negros, goods and chattles, witnessed by John Wallen and Thomas Arnold. (Cla TN, Co Ct Min, 3/73)

WALLEN, Elisha
Died before 14 February 1815 when John Wallen was appointed administrator with John Word and James Monday as security. (Cla TN, Co Ct Min, 4/8)

WALLIS, Samuel
Was a boy nine years old when he was "deserted by his father." He was bound 3 February 1818 to John Stone until age 21. (Wil TN, Co Ct Min, no#/223)

WALTON, Steve
6 May 1873 was charged with Bastardy. The case was continued to next term of court. (Dyr TN, Co Ct Min, B/587) The court found that he was not guilty of begetting the child of Charlotte Light. (Ibid 591)

WAMOCK, Richard
Died before 1 November 1819 when the will was proved by John Green & James Crapper. John W. Payton & Elizabeth Wammack were executors. (Wil TN, Co Ct Min, no#/533)

WARD
John & Bryan Ward were residents of Smith County, TN, 25 November 1815 when they bought from John Kornegay, for $50, the following negroes; Mingo, Esther, Lovey, Jim & Dick. (Wil TN, Reg Bk/44)

WARD, Dempsy
27 August 1778 took the oath of allegiance. (Was TN, Co Ct Min, 1/44)

WARD, J. E.
Was shown to be the son of Spencer Ward when he was appointed road overseer 7 October 1873. (Dyr TN, Co Ct Min, B/641)

WARD, James
Died before 3 October 1870 when Jo. Chitwood was appointed administrator, with L. M. Williams and G. B. Tinsley as security. (Dyr TN, Co Ct Min, B/97)

WARD, John
Died before 6 June 1870 when the administrator, A. F. Fielder, returned an additional inventory of the estate. (Dyr TN, Co Ct Min, B/63)

WARD, Jonathan
Was a resident of Logan County, KY, 24 March 1823 when he sold a slave to Michael Pitner of Wilson County, TN. (Wil TN, Reg Bk/321)

WARD, Jonathan
Died before 3 November 1873 when W. D. Roberts was appointed administrator on the

written request of the widow, Mary H. Ward. J. E. Roberts and T. S. Chamblin were his securities. (Dyr TN, Co Ct Min, B/662)

WARD, Juba
2 April 1860 it was ordered that Juba Ward be sent to the poor house. (Sev TN, Co Ct Min, no#/544) 2 April 1861 Jabah Ward was dismissed from the poor house. (Ibid 680)

WARD, M.
Taxes were not collected in District 5 for 1873, "Ark." (Dyr TN, Co Ct Min, B/759)

WARD, Margarette F.
3 March 1873 R. M. Ward was appointed her guardian as she is of unsound mind and not competent to manage her affairs. J. S. Ward and N. P. Tatum were his securities. Margarette was an heir of James Ward, deceased. (Dyr TN, Co Ct Min, B/544)

WARD, Mc.
Taxes were not collected in District 2 for 1873, "gone." (Dyr TN, Co Ct Min, B/759)

WARD, Samuel
2 April 1860 Benj. Atchley, Sr. was released from his apprentice indenture. (Sev TN, Co Ct Min, no#/543)

WARD, Spions
Died before 3 October 1871 when V. M. L. Taylor was appointed administrator, with John H. York and F. C. Buchanan as his security. (Dyr TN, Co Ct Min, B/306)

WARLICK, Philip
Made his will in 1841 leaving his wife, Nancy Warlick, the whole of his estate to be held for the benefit of the children. He appointed his wife & his brother, David Warlick, executors. He afterward died leaving the same in full force. David Warlick died leaving Nancy as sole executrix to the will of Philip Warlick. Nancy sold part of the land to Thomas C. Gayle and on 11 July 1850 petitioned for confirmation of the sale: Nancy Warlick executrix of Philip Warlick, deceased, Wm. G. Smith & Synthia Jane his wife formerly Synthia Jane Warlick, Jno. N. Warlick, Laura Ann Warlick, Francis Eliza Warlick, Emeline Catherine Warlick, James P. Warlick & Thomas C. Gayle. (Mad TN, Ch Ct Min, 1/142)

WARNER, Eunice
Was the mother of William D. Warner as shown in the suit of Thomas Kimmins vs Eunice Warner filed 8 September 1837. Edward Kimmins was the father of Thomas Kimmins. Samuel J. Warner was a minor son of Eunice Warner. (Bed TN, Ch Ct Min, 1/350)

WARNER, William D.
Died before 21 October 1843 as shown in the suit of Samuel Doak vs James Smith & others. (Bed TN, Ch Ct Min, 3/57)

WARNICK, James
Died before 25 June 1804 when the will was proved by John Hannah & Peter Devault, with a codicil proved by John Rice. Robert Warnick qualified as executor. (Wil TN, Co Ct Min, no#/40)

WARREN, James
Died before 12 August 1816 when the sheriff was ordered to bring his orphans before the court to be provided for as the law directs. The orphans were Sally Warren, Alfred Warren, Milly Warren, Lucrisha Warren, Nancy Warren, James Warren, John Warren and Jesse Warren. (Cla TN, Co Ct Min, 4/219)

WARREN, James H.
Died before 5 April 1870 as shown the in suit of G. W. Bettis administrator of James H. Warren vs Martha Warren et als. (Dyr TN, Co Ct Min, B/47)

WARREN, John
Died before 16 December 1806 as shown by the suit of Jacob Warren & Alie? Warren, admrs. of John Warren deceased vs George B. Davis. [Alie was a female, maybe Alice?] (Roa TN, Co Ct Min, B/224)

WARREN, Jos.
Died before 22 February 1867 as shown in the suit of Benj. T. Horton vs Martha Warren. Jos. Warren was the ancestor of Martha Warren, his only heir. (Mad TN, Ch Ct Min, 3/44)

WARREN, Simon
Died before 6 February 1871 when Tom Griffin, J. J. Tollis and J. A. Jacox were appointed to lay off a years allowance for the widow and family. (Dyr TN, Co Ct Min, B/181) W. N. Beasley was appointed administrator. (Ibid 185) W. N. Beasley, administrator, was instructed to purchase articles for the years provision for the widow and family. (Ibid 232) 4 January 1872 petition for dower was made by Mariah Warren vs Simon E. Warren & Wm. N. Beasley. It was stated that Simon Warren died in 1870. The will was mentioned. Simon E. Warren is the only child. (Ibid 354-5) The deceased's name was shown as William Simon Warren. (Ibid 371)

WARRING, John
Died before 20 September 1803 when Elice Warring & Jacob Warren were granted letters of administration. James Blair & James Montgomery were their securities. (Roa TN, Co Ct Min, A/131)

WASHINGTON, Gray
Died before 17 March 1817 when Leonard H. Sims was appointed guardian of Nancy H. Washington, minor heir. Sims was also appointed guardian of Gray Washington, minor heir. (Wil TN, Co Ct Min, no#/75)

WASHINGTON, Joseph
11 November 1812 gave bond for the maintenance of a bastard child of Susan Dunn. Christopher Cheatham was security. (Rob TN, Co Ct Min, 3/162)

WASON, Abner [Mason]
Died before 9 August 1821 when the administrators, Geo. L. Smith, Joshua Lester & John Echols, sold a slave to Mary Quarles. (Wil TN, Reg Bk/272)

WASSON, Archibald
18 March 1817 money was allowed for his support. (Wil TN, Co Ct Min, no#/89)

WATKINS, B. B.
3 February 1874 desires to obtain a license to practice law. He is certified to be 21 years of age, has resided in Dyer County, TN, for 12 months and is a young man of good moral character. (Dyr TN, Co Ct Min, B/708)

WATKINS, John
Died before 16 November 1814 when Henry Watkins was appointed administrator with Thomas Johnson and Benjamin Tucker and Martin Duncan as security. (Rob TN, Co Ct Min, 3/505)

WATKINS, Richard
Married before 18 December 1816 to Catharine Jones, widow of Peter Jones, deceased. (Wil TN, Co Ct Min, no#/61)

WATSON
Sarah Watson and Nancy Watson were bound 3 August 1813 to James Bowen until they arrive to the age of 18 years. (Ste TN, Co Ct Min, 4/60)

WATSON, Christopher
Died before 9 October 1873 as shown in the settlement made by the administrator of John E. Watson, deceased. (Dyr TN, Co Ct Min, B/655)

WATSON, Elias
Died before 3 November 1812 when Henry Pugh was appointed to settle with the administrators. (Ste TN, Co Ct Min, 3/unnumbered page before page 1) Stephen Gilbert, one of the administrators, returned a list of the debts 4 February 1812. (Ibid 3/111) On motion of Fletcher Gilbert, 1 February 1813, he was discharged from his guardianship for the heirs of Elias Watson, deceased. (Ibid 4/2) Stephen Gilbert was allowed money for his services as guardian for the orphan children. (Ibid 8) Tapley Maddox was appointed guardian. (Ibid 10) 4 November 1813 Tapley Maddux was exonerated from serving any longer as guardian of the orphan children of Elias Watson, deceased. (Ibid 80) Reuben Elliott was appointed guardian 6 February 1815. (Ibid 240)

WATSON, I. A.
Died before 9 October 1873 as shown in the final settlement of the estate of John E. Watson, deceased. A. J. Watson was the administrator. (Dyr TN, Co Ct Min, B/654)

WATSON, John E.
Died before 7 November 1870 when F. M. Chambers was chosen and appointed guardian of the minor heirs, with A. B. Chambers and J. H. Watson as security. (Dyr TN, Co Ct Min, B/129) 9 October 1873 the administrator, J. H. Watson, presented the following receipts in full from the following named distributees, to wit: F. M. Chambers and M. J. Chambers; J. J. Young, guardian of J. E. Watson's heirs; A. J. Watson administrator of I. A. Watson, deceased; M. B. Watson; J. A. Lucky, guardian of Nancy Whitlock (formerly Watson); A. J. Watson and J. A. Lucky, guardian of T. W. Watson. Entered into the settlement book as a full and final settlement of the estate of the said Christopher Watson, deceased. [sic] (Ibid 654-5)

WATSON, Joseph
Probably died before 10 February 1817 when deeds were made by John McIver, assignee of Joseph Watson's estate. (Cla TN, Co Ct Min, 4/290)

WATSON, Mary
7 February 1806 was shown to be an heir of John Ford, on the delinquent tax list. (Rob TN, Co Ct Min, 1/384)

WATSON, Obediah
Was a resident of Jackson County, GA, on 5 June 1828 when his deposition was to be taken for the defendant in the case of Henry Glaze vs Henry Gier. (McM TN, Co Ct Min, no#/339)

WATSON, S. A.
Died before 2 September 1872 when A. J. Watson made a settlement as administrator. (Dyr TN, Co Ct Min, B/467)

WATT, James N.
Died before 17 March 1853 as shown in the petition of N. T. Nevills and others. James N. Watt [Walt] died in Madison County, having made a will in which he directed his negroes be set free but without taking any further steps towards emancipation. The petitioners, Mary Nevill, Jane Matthews, Nancy N. McClure, Permelia Hicks, Emily Cash & Nancy Ellen Jester, are his only children and grand children and claim to be each entitled to one share of said slaves. (Mad TN, Ch Ct Min, 1/320) 17 March 1854 Charlotte (alias Lotty) and her children, Frances, Martha & Ellen, persons of color, sue by their next friend Samuel Lancaster vs Wm. Boon Executor of the will of James N. Watt, deceased. James Watt died about December 1852. The slaves were declared to be free and ordered to be sent to Africa. (Ibid 369)

WAYLAND, Lewis, Sr.
Died before 1 June 1863 when Lewis Waylan presented to the court "a paper writing purporting to be a copy of the original will of Lewis Wayland, Sr. and it was ordered that the clerk spread upon the will book." (Sev TN, Co Ct Min, no#/60)

WAYLAND, Wm.
Died before 5 September 1864 when Lewis Wayland was appointed administrator with R. K. Whittle & Wm. H. Wayland as security. (Sev TN, Co Ct Min, no#/116)

WEAKLEY, D. C.
Died before 3 November 1873 when his will was proved by Hamilton Parks and R. P. McCracken, witnesses. Smith Parks was executor, with H. Parks and R. P. McCracken as his security. (Dyr TN, Co Ct Min, B/659)

WEAR, Joseph
Was a resident of Madison County, Mississippi Territory, 16 October 1810 when his deposition was to be taken for the defendant in the suit of John Gordon Assee. vs William Black. (Roa TN, Co Ct Min, D/257)

WEAR, Mary
Died before 5 April 1858 when the administrator, John Wear, brought suit against P. M. Wear, William Bradshaw, the heirs of Jno. Guthrie, David Johnson & David Cummings, to sell the land from the estate of Mary Wear, deceased. (Sev TN, Co Ct Min, no#/276) The defendants in the above suit are all non-residents of TN and publication has been made for them to answer. (Ibid 326)

WEATHERFORD, Spicy
On 1 May 1815 John Mulhaney? was appointed guardian of Spicy Weatherford with Calib Williams and Alsey Bradford as security. (Ste TN, Co Ct Min, 4/260)

WEATHERLY, Washington
Married before 23 February 1859 to Frances America Winston, as shown in the suit of J. J. Winston et als vs J. Weatherly et als. They were married since the last term of court. (Mad TN, Ch Ct Min, 2/257)

WEAVER, Saml.
22 May 1780 "came into court and voluntarily confest that he had been with the English Army some time and had been in several engagements against the American people during his stay with the enemy. He was sent to Supr. Court for further Tryale." (Was TN, Co Ct Min, 1/105)

WEBB
14 November 1814 James Gardner was appointed guardian of Mary Ann G. Webb & Tempy F. Webb, with Joshua Gardner & Elias Laurence as security. (Rob TN, Co Ct Min, 3/491)

WEBB, A. F.
Died before 6 March 1871 when J. R. Robbins made a settlement as administrator. (Dyr TN, Co Ct Min, B/201)

WEBB, Berry
6 May 1861 it was ordered that the two oldest children of Berry Webb be brought to court to be bound out, "if the said Webb don't take them into his care." (Sev TN, Co Ct Min, no#/687) 14 October 1861, it was ordered that the children & wife of Berry [or Benj] Webb be taken to the poor house unless he can procure a place for the 2 oldest children until next court, when they will be bound out. (Ibid 728)

WEBB, George
Died before 5 November 1866 when G. C. Shrader was appointed administrator with Wm. Fox as security. (Sev TN, Co Ct Min, no#/391)

WEBB, George Washington
Was bound 8 January 1867 to Marion Smith [male] until age 21. He is now 5 years old. (Sev TN, Co Ct Min, no#/425)

WEBB, Jackson
Died before 2 September 1867 when John Webb was appointed guardian to Lucinda Webb, minor heir. (Sev TN, Co Ct Min, no#/471)

WEBB, James
Was a resident of Warren County, TN, on 3 December 1823 when his deposition was to be taken for the defendant in the case of James Capshaw vs Henry Gill. (McM TN, Co Ct Min, no#/108)

WEBB, Jesse
Died before 2 November 1863 when John A. Trotter, Jesse Stafford & Joseph Snapp, Sr. were appointed to set off a years support & dower to Maranda Webb, the widow. (Sev TN, Co Ct Min, no#/79) 6 May 1867 John Webb was appointed guardian of the minor heirs, with G. C. Shrader as security. (Ibid 452)

WEBB, Mahulda J.
Died before 8 April 1874 when Charles C. Moss made a settlement as administrator. (Dyr TN, Co Ct Min, B/732)

WEBB, Matilda
8 January 1867 it was ordered that Matilda Webb, orphan child, be brought to next court to be bound out. (Sev TN, Co Ct Min, no#/426)

WEBB, Rebecca
7 October 1862 it was ordered that her female child, Matilda Webb, be brought to its mother at the residence of James Clowers. (Sev TN, Co Ct Min, no#/18) 2 April 1867 Rebecca Webb made a motion to have returned to her, her son, Geo. W. Webb, who has been bound to J. M. Smith. After hearing the testimony, the motion was dismissed. (Ibid 446)

WEBB, Ross
Died before June term 1815 as shown in the case of Ross Webb vs John B. Gofney, when his death was suggested & the case postponed. (Wil TN, P&J, no#/no#)

WEBB, William
Was a resident of Maury County, TN, 8 September 1820 when he made a deed of gift to his niece, Hannah Tally, the daughter of Spencer Tally, deceased, for a negro woman named Rachel and her child Joseph to be at her disposal. Two negroes, Charity & Elisa, are to be given to Hannah's first born child at age 18. It was witnessed by Betsey Tally & William Tally. (Wil TN, Reg Bk/183)

WELCH
27 January 1847 Levi Murphey was appointed guardian pendenti lite for Jesse Welch and Almira Welch as shown in the suit of John Barns et al vs George Welch et al. (Jac TN, Ch Ct Min, A/236)

WELCH, John
Died before 14 July 1854 as shown in the suit of Andrew Wassom, Sr. vs Andrew Wassom, Jr. Land was mentioned that was sold by decree of the Circuit Court of Jackson County in the case of James Terry & wife & others, heirs at law of John Welch, deceased, and purchased by Andrew Wassom, Jr. (Jac TN, Ch Ct Min, B/177)

WELKER, William B.
Died before 7 March 1831 when his will was proved by Thomas Crutchfield & Russell Hurst & Wm. W. Anderson, witnesses. (McM TN, Co Ct Min, 2no#/506)

WELL, Mitch.
Taxes were not collected in District 4 for 1873, "can't be found." (Dyr TN, Co Ct Min, B/759)

WELLS, Barna B.
Died before 5 March 1828 when George Wells was appointed adminsitrator. (McM TN, Co Ct Min, 2no#/279)

WELLS, Benjamin
Died before 13 August 1811 when his widow, Nancy Wells, was appointed administratrix with Amos Cohea & Garret Flippo as security. (Rob TN, Co Ct Min, 3/8) Nancy was also shown as the executrix. (Ibid 32)

WELLS, Catharine
Was a resident of Logan County, KY, 18 May 1810 when her deposition was to be taken for the plaintiff in the case of Jno. Redferren vs Mary Irwin. (Rob TN, Co Ct Min, 2/269)

WELLS, Ellison
Died before 4 December 1865 when John A. Trotter, Wm. Latham & Andrew Rogers were appointed to lay off dower for his widow, Malinda Wells. (Sev TN, Co Ct Min, no#/248 & 260)

WELLS, Jane
7 October 1857 it was ordered that the 2 children of Jane Wells be brought to court to be bound out. (Sev TN, Co Ct Min, no#/82) 2 November 1857 a female child of Jane Wells that was in the poor house is to be returned to Jane as she is now able to take care of said child. (Ibid 223)

WELLS, Jeff
Taxes were not collected in District 4 for 1873, "can't be found." (Dyr TN, Co Ct Min, B/759)

WELLS, Luticia
Died before 6 June 1870 when Green Chitwood made a settlement as administrator. (Dyr TN, Co Ct Min, B/64)

WEST, John
16 December 1817 was said to be out of the State when his signature was proved on a deed from John Hill to John Cumpton, Jr. & proved by William Walker. (Wil TN, Co Ct Min, no#/195)

WESTFALL, Abel
Was a resident of Berkley County, VA, on 18 November 1788 when he gave a power of attorney that was recorded at the February term 1790, to John Melvin of Washington County, NC [TN]. This for the purpose of recovering from George Gilespie a certain Bay horse. Witnesses were Thomas Carney & Wm. Lucas. (Was TN, Co Ct Min, 1/429)

WESTON, Jesse
Died before 1 May 1815 when Elisabeth Weston was appointed administratrix with James Tagert & William James as security. (Ste TN, Co Ct Min, 4/260)

WHALY, West. O.
Died before 3 April 1866 when Daniel W. Reagan was appointed guardian to Isham H. Whaly, minor orphan, with R. R. Reagan & Noah Ogle as security. (Sev TN, Co Ct Min, no#/311)

WHEELER, Lemuel
Died 22 September 1835, intestate, in Marshall County, TN. Sally Wheeler petitioned for dower. Sally is a resident of Marshall County, TN, & the land is in Marshall County. Elizabeth Corbitt, wife of Needham Corbitt, Lucinda, George H. & Lemuel Wheeler are the only children and heirs. The last mentioned are minors & James Ramsay is their guardian, appointed by Marshall County court. Richard Warner is the administrator. (Bed TN, Ch Ct Min, 1/111)

WHEELER, Minerva
Was granted a divorce 10 February 1860 from Hopkins Wheeler. He had been guilty of adultry with base and lewd women. She was given custody of their one child, a boy named Peyton, about 2 years old. (Jac TN, Ch Ct Min, C/318)

WHEELER, Nathan
Died before 4 May 1818 when the administrator, Edward Wheeler, was ordered to make a settlement. (Wil TN, Co Ct Min, no#/243) Edward Wheeler was appointed guardian of Polly Wheeler & Rachel Wheeler, minor heirs. William Oakley was appointed guardian of Dunnerson Wheeler & Nathan Wheeler, minor heirs. (Ibid 356)

WHEELER, Paralee E.
13 September 1854 dismissed her suit against Wm. T. Wheeler. (Mad TN, Ch Ct Min, 2/20)

WHITE, Aron
Taxes were not collected in District 5 for 1873, "insolvent." (Dyr TN, Co Ct Min, B/759)

WHITE, B. F.
Died before 3 October 1870 when A. H. White was appointed administrator, with J. H. York and J. L. Ward as security. (Dyr TN, Co Ct Min, B/97) J. H. York, A. B. Stalcup and William Royster were appointed to lay off a years allowance for the widow and family. (Ibid 101) Bryant F. White died in September 1870, as shown in the petition of Eliza White vs A. A. White et als. Eliza is the widow. (Ibid 194)

WHITE, Ben C.
Died before 10 February 1855 when his death was suggested in the suit of Ben C. White vs George M. McWhirter. The suit was revived in the names of the executors, William H. Botts & James A. Spurlock. (Jac TN, Ch Ct Min, B/225) In the suit of George White & others vs William H. Botts & James A. Spurlock Exrs &c, some negroes belonging to the estate of B. C. White were sold to pay debts. (Ibid C/89) On 16 July 1858 three suits were shown concerning this estate: Robert White, Benjamin White, William S. White, Isaac R. White, David C. White & George C. White by their next friend William White vs William H. Botts & James A. Spurlock Executors of Benjamin C. White decd., Injunction Bill: Mary White vs Robert M. White, Benjamin White, William S. White, Isaac R. White, David C. White, William H. Botts & James A. Spurlock Extrs. etc., Cross Bill: Mary White & David H. Fink vs William H. Botts & James A. Spirlock Extrs. etc., Bill for the construction? of B. C. White's will. Publication has been made to the non-resident defendants to the cross bill. Benjamin B. Washburn was guardian of the minor defendants. A final settlement has been made. Mary White was the widow. The money remaining from the estate is to be loaned out and the interest on same paid to Mary White for life and at her death the fund is to be paid to the sons of William White, deceased. (Ibid 156) Ben C. White died in August 1854. (Ibid 335)

WHITE, C. E.
Died before 7 July 1873 when his will was proved by J. N. Wyatt and R. P. McCrackin, witnesses. (Dyr TN, Co Ct Min, B/596) Smith Parks was executor with H. Parks and F. J. White as his security. (Ibid 597)

WHITE, Charles
Was charged by Matilda Hembrew? with being the father of her bastard child. He gave

bond for maintenance of the child with Daniel McPherson & John White as security. (Roa TN, Co Ct Min, D/331)

WHITE, Elisabeth
Was a minor 23 October 1799 when she was bound to Charles McIntosh until age 18. (Rob TN, Co Ct Min, 1/119)

WHITE, Gillem
Died before 6 February 1871 when W. V. White made a settlement as administrator. (Dyr TN, Co Ct Min, B/190)

WHITE, Jeremiah
Died before 4 August 1873 when E. H. White and W. A. White were appointed administrators, with James W. Baker and W. E. DeBerry as their securities. (Dyr TN, Co Ct Min, B/616)

WHITE, John
Died before 20 May 1796 when the will was proved by Joseph Brittain. (Was TN, Co Ct Min, 1/616)

WHITE, Margaret
Was an orphan girl 26 August 1778 when she was bound to Baptist McNabb until age 18. (Was TN, Co Ct Min, 1/39)

WHITE, Matthew
10 February 1854 his guardian, George M. McWhirter, filed suit against Cyntha White for interfering with his guardianship. (Jac TN, Ch Ct Min, B/131)

WHITE, P. D.
Died before 5 July 1870 when R. C. Coffman made a settlement as administrator. (Dyr TN, Co Ct Min, B/82)

WHITE, Robert
Died before 10 February 1854 as shown in the suit of Benjamin C. White vs George M. McWhirter. The defendant is permitted to proceed with the execution of the will of Robert White, deceased. (Jac TN, Ch Ct Min, B/137) This suit was heard 14 July 1854 and stated that Robert White died about October 1852 leaving a will. Complainant & defendant were appointed executors and proceeded to act as co-executors. The funds have come into the hands of George M. McWhirter who refuses to deliver any part of same to Benjamin C. White. Defendant was ordered to deliver half of the proceeds to complainant. (Ibid 172) A bill was entered by Cynthia White vs George M. McWhirter Exr. of Robert White decd., Coleman White, John Myers & wife Nancy, John Dixon & wife Jane, William White, Wm. H. Botts & James A. Spurlock Executors of Benjamin C. White decd., George White, George M. McWhirter & wife Martha, Joshua R. Stone & wife Narcissa, Hamilton Montgomery, Caroline, Penelope Robert, Earl, Thomas, Benjamin Nancy & Nathan Montgomery & John P. Cox & wife Lucinda. Cynthia White is entitled to the provisions made for her by the will of Robert White. Advancements made to Stewart White were mentioned and a special legacy made to Robert T. White, son of Stewart White, and a special legacy made to Mary Young (now Mary Settle). The executors, in making distribution to complainants & the other general legatees, are to distribute to complainant to give her an equal share with the other general legatees named in the 5th clause of said will. Cynthia was the widow. (Ibid 276) A suit was entered 11 February 1859 by Mary White vs George M. McWhirter as Surviving Executor of Robert White decd. and as of his own right and Coleman White, George White, John Myers and John M. Dixon as of their own right & Legatees of Said Robert White decd. & P. H. Leslee as agent of Deft. McWhirter et als. The estate has been settled and paid over to the distributees. By the 5th clause of said will, the slave, Booker, was to have the privelige of choosing his home amongst any of the testator's Second set of children. All defendants except P. H. Leslie are Legatees under the will and are the children of Testator or the husbands of such and are the only children of said Second Marriage living at the death of testator. Robert T. White, infant son of Stewart White, and Matthew White another grandson, and Mary Young a grand daughter of the testator, were the children of the testators second class of children to whom special legacies were bequeathed under said will, their fathers and mothers then being dead. Complainant is the widow of Ben C. White who was a child of testator by the first marriage. The slave Booker is in the possession of Mary White and is old & infirm. George M. McWhirter had told Mary if she would keep him and care for him she would be paid for same. He told her this in 1855 after the death of her husband Ben C. White, and before George M. McWhirter moved to TX where he now resides. All the other defendants also live in TX except P. H. Leslie who is the acting agent for defendants

McWhirter, Coleman White & George White. Mary is suing for compensation for keeping the slave Booker. (Ibid C/188) A settlement was made 11 February 1860. (Ibid 335)

WHITE, Robert
Died before 15 January 1851, intestate, leaving his widow, Elizabeth, and Mary Ann White, Rachael C. White & Eunice B. White his only children. Mary Ann White afterwards married Wm. L. Flowers. Rachael C. White died after having made a will in which she devised her share in the real estate of Robert White to the heirs of Wm. L. and Mary Ann Flowers. Mary Ann Flowers died leaving Joel S., Mary Eliza, William & Elizabeth Flowers her only surviving children. Jno. P. Wier was guardian of said children. Eunice B. White married Alexander Jackson. (Mad TN, Ch Ct Min, 1/185)

WHITE, Theodore
Was a non-resident of TN 5 July 1870 as shown in the suit of Arthur C. White, et als. (Dyr TN, Co Ct Min, B/84)

WHITE, Thos.
Was charged 23 March 1809 by Nancy McClenden of being the father of her bastard child. The complaint was dismissed with Thos. White paying the costs. (Roa TN, Co Ct Min, D/62)

WHITE, William
15 August 1782 was ordered to be put to death. (Was TN, Co Ct Min, 1/178) He and John White had been tried for horse stealing, William was found guilty and John found not guilty. (Ibid 176) The execution was ordered to be carried out on the 10th day of September next. (Ibid 178)

WHITE, Zacharias
27 August 1778 took the oath of allegiance. (Was TN, Co Ct Min, 1/44)

WHITEHEAD, Robert [Whited]
Died before 1 August 1866 as shown in the suit of Jessee Ashburn vs Robt. Whitehead. (Fen TN, Ch Ct Min, A/293) B. C. Bowden was guardian ad litem for the minor heirs. (Ibid 308)

WHITLOCK, William
Died before 18 September 1817 when Thomas Whitlock was appointed administrator, with George L. Smith & John Fisher as security. (Wil TN, Co Ct Min, no#/175)

WHITNEY
In the suit of McDowell vs Whitney & Organ, 31 December 1840, it was suggested that defendant Whitney had died and the suit was revived in the name of his administrator, Carlos D. Steele. (Bed TN, Ch Ct Min, 2/128)

WHITNEY, James G.
August term 1830 in the suit of James G. Whitney vs John Sutton & Levy S. Greer, it is shown that Thos. P. Whitney made a note in 1827. Thos. P. & James G. Whitney were brothers and executors of their father's estate. The father had been a merchant & kept a Tavern. It was also shown that Wm. B. Sutton was the son of John Sutton. (Bed TN, Ch Ct Min, 1/1) James G. Whitney died before 27 June 1842 as shown in the suit of Allen C. McDowell vs Carlos D. Steele Admr. of James G. Whitney decd. and John C. Organ. (Ibid 240) James G. Whitney died in August 1840. Martha was the widow. Martha gave notes belonging to the estate to William Sharp. A suit was entered by the administrator of James G. Whitney against William Sharp, George W. Fogleman, William D. Norton & Martha his wife, John Bell, William A. & Wiley Hickerson. [The widow may have married William D. Norton.] (Ibid 309) James G. Whitney had absconded from the county about 1 June 1840. He is believed to have died at Smithland, in the State of KY. Carlos D. Steel was appointed administrator at the September term 1840. A negroe belonging to said Whitney is in the possession of Peter Rowlett who is now in this county on a visit from AR, and is a single man. (Ibid 3/132)

WHITSELL, Michael
Died before 6 June 1831 when his will was proved by A. H. Napier, Lewis R. Hurst & Hilton Humphreys. Urial Johnson & Peter Kinder were executors. (McM TN, Co Ct Min, 2no#/533)

WHITSON, Wm.
Was a resident of LA 5 May 1819 when his signature was proved on a deed from Philip

Koonce to Amos Williams. [Abram Whitson was written, then Abram crossed out & Wm. written above it.] (Wil TN, Co Ct Min, no#/456)

WHITTEN, S. D.
Died before 5 June 1871 when S. R. Latta made a settlement as executor. (Dyr TN, Co Ct Min, B/243)

WHITTENTEN, M.
Died before 7 November 1870 when a settlement was made by E. M. Johnson as executrix. (Dyr TN, Co Ct Min, B/131) The deceased was shown as N. A. Whittenton. (Ibid 495)

WHITTINGTON, Jas.
Died before 21 September 1853 as shown in the suit of Kitturah Whittington vs Merritt Whittington & others. The demurrer of Solomon Whittington, Othnel Whittington and Quintithan Whittington to that part of the bill which relates to the personal estate, is disallowed. An administrator is to be appointed and made party to this suit. (Mad TN, Ch Ct Min, 1/339) James Whittinton died 20 May 1853 leaving Kitturah as his widow and distributees [not named] as his heirs. He had 50 acres of land bounded by Quintithan Whittinton, Solomon Whittinton & Ethneal Whittinton. Quintithan Whittinton & Taletha Whittinton on 17 February 1853, in consideration of lands etc. which had been conveyed to them, executed their obligation in writing to maintain & support Kiturah Whittinton (with others) with comfortable necessaries of life until her death, and they have not done so, and they are to be charged a reasonable sum from the death of James Whittinton. (Ibid 2/37) Dower was laid off for Kitturah and a yearly allowance that Quintillian & Taletha Whittington are bound to pay. (Ibid 77)

WHITTINGTON, N. A.
Died before 5 May 1873 as shown in bill to sell land for partition made by George W. Smith et al vs Zach Gleaves et al. He left as his only children and heirs at law, John & James Whittington, C. M. E. Rankin, Hannah Gleaves and [blank] Johnson. James & John Whittington and C. M. E. Rankin have sold their interest to George W. Smith. "[Blank] Johnson has departed this life leaving Leroy Bruce Johnson, his infant son & her husband, Samuel F. Johnson her husband who are entitled to her interest." (Dyr TN, Co Ct Min, B/583)

WHITTLE, John
Died before 2 January 1865 when John A. Trotter, J. S. McCroskey and S. W. Randles were appointed to lay off dower & a years support to Mary Whittle, widow, and family. O. M. Whittle was appointed administrator with R. K. Whittle as security. (Sev TN, Co Ct Min, no#/130)

WHORLEY, Joel
Married Cynthia Brown, daughter of Jesse Brown before 1843 as shown in the suit of Joel Whorley vs Elizabeth Brown & others. Joel Whorley contracted with Thomas Russell to purchase land and asked his father-in-law, Jessee Brown, Sr. to be his security. Jessee refused, but offered to purchase the land in his own name and convey it to Joel Whorley when he had paid for it. Joel has paid every dollar of the purchase money & said Brown expressed willingness to convey the land to him but became ill and died in 1843 without making the deed. The will of Jessee Brown has been presented but was made several years before the purchase of the land. The heirs were Elizabeth, the widow, and Paschall, Jessee, Thomas, Daniel P., William, John, Alvin and Henry Brown, Elizabeth Brown, Jr., Cynthia Worley wife of complainant, all citizens of Bedford County except William who is a citizen of Washington County, AR. John, Alvin & Henry Brown are minors. Title to the land was granted to Joel Whorley. (Bed TN, Ch Ct Min, 3/217-220)

WIDNER, J. H.
Died before 3 September 1866 when Jacob Widner was appointed administrator with Daniel Kelly & Joel Hudson as security. (Sev TN, Co Ct Min, no#/365) A years support was laid off to Martha Jane Widner, widow. (Ibid 366)

WILEY, John
20 April 1812 was said to have removed out of this state to some place unknown when he was to prove a deed from Robert King to John Smith. (Roa TN, Co Ct Min, D/369)

WILHOIT, Jacob
Died before 27 December 1842 as shown in the suit of William G. Cowan vs William Dwyer & wife, Jane. Process has been executed on Jane Dwyer but it appears that William Dwyer is not a resident of this state. William Dwyer owns 5/6 in his own right & 1/6

of a tract of land in right of his wife, known as Lot No. 3 in the division of the lands among the heirs of Jacob Wilhoit, deceased. He also owns land in right of his wife in Marshall County, being part of the land of Jacob Wilhoit going to his daughter, the said Jane Dwyer. (Bed TN, Ch Ct Min, 2/213) In the suit of Robert Mathews vs William Dwyer & others it was stated that Dwyer owned 5/7 of a tract of land and that Jacob Wilhoit & the wife of said Dwyer owned the other 2/7 [this Jacob evidently not the same as the deceased] Willie Wilhoit was mentioned. (Ibid 221) Land was mentioned that was devised to Jacob Wilhoit by his father. (Ibid 241)

WILHOIT, Willey
Died before 12 July 1838 as shown in the suit of James M. Jones & wife vs John Bruton & others. The wife of James M. Jones was Polly Jones, formerly Polly Wilhoit, the sister of Willey Wilhoit who died intestate without issue, but he left brothers & sisters. The suit is against Jacob Wilhoit, Jane Wilhoit, minors who have Price Wilhoit for their guardian, and Emely Brunton formerly Emily Wilhoit, all of Bedford County, and John Brunton whose residence is unknown. James M. Jones has purchased the interest of John Brunton and wife Emily. Jones has purchased 4 shares & also owns the share in right of his wife, Polly, and the other 2 shares are held by Jacob and Jane. (Bed TN, Ch Ct Min, 1/370) 28 December 1843 in the suit of Harris Austin & wife Emily vs John Brewton & Pearce Wilhoit, it is stated that Wiley Wilhoit died some 8 or 10 years ago, that he was the brother of Emily Austin, that Pearce Wilhoit was administrator. About the time of the death of Wiley Wilhoit, Emily was the wife of John Brewton and he deserted her & fled to parts unknown and that she married Harris Austin in 1841. She has since heard that John Brewton is still living and she never obtained a divorce from Brewton. The money coming to Emily from the estate of her brother is to be paid to her and neither her former husband nor her new husband is to have any part. (Ibid 2/275)

WILHOIT, William
Died before 22 June 1848 as shown in the suit of Adaline Robinson vs Jno. W. Mayfield & Richard Warner. Adaline & John W. are both from Marshall County, TN. Adaline Robinson is the widow of William Wilhoit, deceased, & she had filed a petition in Circuit Court in Bedford for sale of the lands of her husband, and preferring as she then did to receive a third part of the sale as her dower. The money she received was only hers for life and was then to go to the children of William Wilhoit. She later married James Robinson who died during the year, leaving a will. James had control of her money and he made no provision for it in his will. He appointed Richard Warner and Jno. W. Mayfield executors who refuse to pay over to her the money she had gotten as dower from her former husband. (Bed TN, Ch Ct Min, 3/458)

WILKENS, M. E.
Died before 6 March 1871 when Jo. Chitwood made a settlement as executor. (Dyr TN, Co Ct Min, B/201) Auge Chitwood was chosen and appointed guardian of the minor heirs of Mary E. Wilkins, deceased. (Ibid 245)

WILKERSON, Prudy
Died before 22 June 1807 when the will was proved by John Wilkerson. (Wil TN, Co Ct Min, no#/293)

WILKINS
Archie & Mary Wilkins both died before 5 December 1870 when W. J. Mahan, D. E. Parker and Stephen Chitwood were appointed to lay off a years provision to Lucy Bell Wilkins, Emme E. Wilkins and William Penn Wilkins, children of the late Archie and Mary Wilkins, deceased. Jo. Chitwood was the administrator. (Dyr TN, Co Ct Min, B/144) 3 July 1872 Auge Chitwood made a settlement as guardian of the heirs. (Ibid 442) 9 July 1873 Auge Chitwood made a settlement as guardian of Penn Wilkins, Emerson Wilkins & L. B. Wilkins. (Ibid 613)

WILKINS, Feribee [Feriby]
Died before 24 February 1859 when the death was admitted in the suit of Feribee Wilkins vs D. G. Helly et als. The suit was revived in the name of Catherine Wilkins, the administratrix. (Mad TN, Ch Ct Min, 2/274) 31 August 1860 the trustee, Ivy Wilkins, was mentioned. (Ibid 408)

WILKINS, John A.
Died before 3 January 1871 when his signature was proved as witness to the will of Thomas C. Mitchell. (Dyr TN, Co Ct Min, B/160)

WILKINS, Josaphine
9 July 1873 Auge Chitwood made a settlement as guardian. (Dyr TN, Co Ct Min, B/613)

WILKINSON, Mrs.
Died before 5 October 1858 when A. J. Bradley was allowed money from the poor tax for a coffin & grave. (Sev TN, Co Ct Min, no#/353)

WILKINSON, William
Died before 19 June 1843 as shown in the suit of Charles McAlister admr. of William Wilkinson for the use of Melvin H. Wilkinson vs William S. S. Harris admr. of James J. McCollum. (Obi TN, Cir Ct Min, 4/no#)

WILLARD, James
Was the reputed father of a bastard child by Jane Miligan & on 19 March 1817 was ordered to pay her $20 yearly for 4 years. (Wil TN, Co Ct Min, no#/91)

WILLARD, P.
Died before 5 April 1870 when J. L. Ward made a settlement as administrator. (Dyr TN, Co Ct Min, B/42) 6 February 1871 the name is shown as Pearson Wollord. (Ibid 190)

WILLARD, William
Was a minor boy of the age of 3 years old when he was bound 19 March 1817 to James Willard until age 21. (Wil TN, Co Ct Min, no#/94)

WILLIAMS
16 February 1858 a suit was entered, Elizabeth Williams et als vs Jesse Gray Extr. &c et als. Other defendants were Harbert W. Williams & Neuten Williams. (Mad TN, Ch Ct Min, 2/163)

WILLIAMS
22 February 1866 Jno. S. Brown was appointed guardian ad litem of defendant Geo. Williams, infant, in the suit of John H. Williams vs E. Edwards et als. On the same day Jno. S. Brown was appointed guardian ad litem of the infant defendants, Joseph H. Williams, Allen H. Williams, Sallie Williams & Frances A. Williams, in the suit of Lucy J. Williams et als vs J. H. Williams et als. (Mad TN, Ch Ct Min, 2/480)

WILLIAMS, Able
Died before 17 June 1817 when the will was proved by William Phillips & Nathaniel Williams. Jno. W. Peyton was executor with James Williams & James Turner as security. (Wil TN, Co Ct Min, no#/114)

WILLIAMS, Allen
Died in 1858 after making his will in which Jno. L. H. Tomlin was named executor & trustee for the widow & children. Tomlin resigned in May 1862. This is shown in the suit of Lucy J. Williams et al vs Joseph H. Williams et al. (Mad TN, Ch Ct Min, 2/494) Lucy was shown as Lucy Jones Williams and was the widow of Allen Williams. (Ibid 505) Land was sold and title divested out of Marthy An Williams, Fedelia E. Williams, Joseph H. Williams, Allen H. Williams, Sallie Williams & Francis A. Williams, the widow, children & heirs of said Allen Williams, deceased. (Ibid 521)

WILLIAMS, Amos
Died before 20 February 1857 as shown in several suits against him, suits by Susan A. Mans? et als, Patsy Muns?, Mary Jones & Elizabeth Chambers et als. The suits are to be revived in the name of the executor, Jesse Grey. (Mad TN, Ch Ct Min, 2/130) 23 February 1860 in the suit of Elizabeth Williams vs Jesse Gray Exr. et als it is stated that Amos Williams entered into a marriage contract with Elizabeth 3 January 1856 and they were shortly thereafter married. In 1857 Amos made his last will & testament and shortly thereafter died. [This is very dim but something is said about the survivor and 1/6 part of the personal property.] (Ibid 321) [Also see estate of Charles Chamberlain] By the marriage contract between Elizabeth & Amos Williams, she is entitled to 1/6 of his personal estate & she is not entitled to dower, house & lot or slaves given her in the will in addition to the 1/6 part. She is to decide which she will take, either the 1/6 part or house, lot & slaves under the will. (Ibid 405) Report was made 19 February 1867. The estate was divided into 7 parts, Mary Jones part was mentioned, she was a daughter of Amos Williams. Patsy Muus had a life estate, probable duration of Mrs. Muus life is said to be 22 years from 1856. She was also a daughter of Amos Williams. (Ibid 3/6-8) Wm. J. Muus was shown in this suit. (Ibid 12) In the suit of William J. Muus & Susan Muus by next friend Jno. A. Muus, it is stated thay are entitled to money at the death of their mother, Patsy Muus the tenant for life. (Ibid 19) Elizabeth Williams elected to abandon the 1/6 part and take the house, lot & slaves according to the will. (Ibid 73)

WILLIAMS, Anderson
Died before 4 February 1861 when his will was proved by Perry Large & Sanders McMahan, witnesses. D. B. McMahan and R. H. Hodsden were executors, with Saml. McMahan and Lewis Howard as security. (Sev TN, Co Ct Min, no#/654) 4 May 1863 David McMahan was appointed guardian of Samuel P. Williams & George Williams, minor heirs of Anderson Williams, deceased. (Ibid 59)

WILLIAMS, Anthony T.
Was a non-resident of TN 19 February 1858 as shown in the suit of S. S. Sykes vs Anthony T. Williams et als. (Mad TN, Ch Ct Min, 2/185)

WILLIAMS, Benjamin
In a suit by Benjamin Williams & wife vs Micajah Fly et als, 16 January 1850, a guardian is to be appointed ad litem for Jno. S., Sandford N., Nancy H.[or C.], Jennett E. & Joanah Williams, minor heirs of Ben. Williams. (Mad TN, Ch Ct Min, 1/102) 18 January 1850 this suit is shown as; Micajah Fly Executor vs Ben. Williams & wife Peggy, & the above named minors who are the children of Ben & Peggy Williams, & Robt. W. Byrn & wife Rutha C., Elija, Jas. C., Wm. T., & Robt. D. Byrns, children of Robt. & Rutha, Hugh Henderson & children Caroline, Elain & Wilson Henderson, Martha Longmire & children, William, Hannah, Mary & Malissa Longmire who appear by guardian Stephen B. Barnet, Jos. Longmire & children & James M. Meddlay and George Medley. [See the estate of Hannah Gibson.] (Ibid 125) 15 July 1851 the Williams children were mentioned again, but not Joanah Williams. (Ibid 204) 13 March 1855, Benjamin T. Williams and others, petition to exchange land in Madison County for land in Carroll County. (Ibid 2/24) The names of the Williams children were shown as Samuel N., Nancy A. H., Jemmima E. & John L. Williams. Peggy Williams was shown as Margaret. John L. Williams died intestate & without children. Margaret has had born, Smithey J. Williams & Robert Henry Williams, her children who are each entitled to 1/5 of the land. (Ibid 34)

WILLIAMS, Betsey
Was bound 25 February 1782 to Edwards Higgins until age 18. She is an orphan child the daughter of Mary Williams now Mary Newbery. (Was TN, Co Ct Min, 1/148)

WILLIAMS, Edith
Her son, an insane boy named John Williams, was to be let to the lowest bidder for a year. Edith Williams was the lowest bidder at $40.00, May 5, 1812. (Ste TN, Co Ct Min, 3/135)

WILLIAMS, Edmond
Died before 16 November 1795 when the will was proved by William Davis, Charles Whitson and William Whitson. Joshua Williams and Archibald Williams were executors. (Was TN, Co Ct Min, 1/574) 15 Febrauty 1796 a deed of gift from Edmond Williams to George Williams, was proved by Archibald Williams. (Ibid 589)

WILLIAMS, Elisha
Was a boy 12 years old when he was bound 4 August 1818 as an apprentice to John McCaffy, until age 21. (Wil TN, Co Ct Min, no#/299)

WILLIAMS, Harwin
Was a non-resident of the state on 4 December 1866 as shown when he was defendant in the suit of Edley Paul. (Fen TN, Ch Ct Min, A/311)

WILLIAMS, Henry
27 February 1872 it was ordered that the sheriff take into his custody a negro wench and two children who are in the custody of Mrs. Hannah Clark. They had been brought from GA. They were formerly the property of Henry Williams and are now confiscated. (Was TN, Co Ct Min, 1/155)

WILLIAMS, Isaac
Was a poor man on the parish 8 May 1804 when James Norfleet & John Philips were ordered to let him to the lowest bidder. (Rob TN, Co Ct Min, 1/292) Isaac Williams died before 6 May 1806 when it was ordered that John Williams be paid for keeping him until his death. (Ibid 388)

WILLIAMS, Isaac
Died before 12 November 1810 when Henry Frey was appointed administrator, with Jacob Benckley, Griffith Williams & George Massey as security. Henry Freys was chosen & appointed guardian of Rachel Williams, orphan of Isaac Williams, deceased. (Rob TN, Co Ct Min, 2/317)

WILLIAMS, Jacob
Died in 1839 as shown in the suit of Daniel Williams & others vs Simeon E. Long, Lameck W. Ezell and others. Jacob Williams died in Lauderdale County, AL, and left land in Giles County, TN. No one has administered on his estate. Rachel Carter wife of Benjamin Carter, [blank] Murrell wife of John Murrell, Daniel Williams, John Williams, Nancy Bartlett wife of William Bartlett, Cyrus A Williams, Mary Jane and Nancy Williams, and James W. Williams are the only heirs-at-law of Jacob Williams. The land in Giles County had been sold to pay a debt and complainants say the sale was not legal. (Bed TN, Ch Ct Min, 2/207)

WILLIAMS, James
Died before 6 June 1831 when Frederick S. Williams was appointed administrator. (McM TN, Co Ct Min, 2no#/533)

WILLIAMS, James
Died before 28 November 1780 when Hannah Williams was ordered to receive 40 bushels of corn that was the property of Phillip Shelby, being corn due James Williams, deceased, from said Shelby for serving as substitute in behalf of Shelby. (Was TN, Co Ct Min, 1/121) Hannah Williams was administrator with Jno. Lyer & Jno. McNabb as security. (Ibid 127)

WILLIAMS, James
Died before 28 August 1781 when John Hoskins was charged with being an accessory to his death. (Was TN, Co Ct Min, 1/143)

WILLIAMS, Jessee E.
Died some 12 or 14 years before a suit was filed by Thomas E. Williams vs William Burnett & others. The suit is not dated but was heard at August term 1844. Jessee E. Williams left as his heirs Thomas E. Williams, Martha Jane Williams who has since married Blackman C. Dobson, Julia S. Williams who has since married Israel Fonville, Airy A. Williams who has since married Thomas White, Elizabeth M. Williams who has since married Joseph A. Cunningham, Mary E. Williams who is a minor & has Gabriel B. Knight for her guardian and Elizabeth M. Williams, his widow who has since married with William Burnett, in all 7 distributees. After the widow married Thomas Burnett he was appointed guardian of the children including Thomas E., which appointment was made in May 1829 and in Novemner 1831 Burnett was appointed administrator de bonis non of said Jessee E. Williams, the former administrator having died. Thomas E. Williams is not yet 24 years old and he is the oldest child. The husband of Elizabeth M., Joseph A. Cunningham, is still a minor and George W. Cunningham is his guardian. Thomas E. Williams is suing for a final accounting and division of the estate. (Bed TN, Ch Ct Min, 3/220-8

WILLIAMS, Jno. B.
Died in 1861, intestate, leaving surviving him Martha C. who has since intermarried with Ephriam Edwards, and the minor, Geo. Williams. Jno. H. Williams was administrator. Martha C. is entitled to dower. Ben. B. Williams sold said land to Jno. B. Williams which deed has been lost. (Mad TN, Ch Ct Min, 2/548)

WILLIAMS, John
Died before 8 October 1860 when his death was suggested in the suit of Marsha Millsaps, George S. Millsaps et als vs John Williams. (Fen TN, Ch Ct Min, A/240) Jane Williams is the widow and Mary Williams, Lavina [Viny] Williams, James Williams and Sarah Ann Williams are his heirs-at-law. (Ibid 253) Samuel Turney was appointed guardian ad litem of the minors. (Ibid 261) Another entry stated that John Williams died in August 1861. The statement was made 10 April 1861 so it probably should have been August 1860. (Ibid 265) James M. Wright was administrator. Alfred Williams and Phillip Williams were mentioned. (Ibid 308)

WILLIAMS, John
Died before 8 November 1842 when his death was suggested in the suit of Williams & Clark Admrs. vs Thos. L. Clements et al. Joseph R. Williams and Peter Clarke were the administrators. (Jac TN, Ch Ct Min, A/84)

WILLIAMS, John
"Power of Attorney from John Williams of the District of Arkansas & Territory of Louisana having been acknowledged and Certified from said District was exhibited in open Court & ordered to be Registered," 3 February 1812. [It does not state to whom] (Ste TN, Co Ct Min, 3/107)

WILLIAMS, John
4 September 1865 was appointed guardian to Martha Williams, formerly Martha Clark. (Sev TN, Co Ct Min, no#/207)

WILLIAMS, Joseph
Died before 11 March 1844 when land was taxed to the heirs. (Obi TN, Cir Ct Min, 4/no#)

WILLIAMS, Margaret
4 May 1819 was appointed guardian of her daughter, Martha Williams, with John Alexander & William S. Alexander as security. (Wil TN, Co Ct Min, no#/452)

WILLIAMS, Martha E.
8 April 1857 her guardian, Sarah M. Hodges, made a settlement. (Sev TN, Co Ct Min, no#/158)

WILLIAMS, Matthew
Died before 18 July 1797 when the will was proved by Samuel Sugg. Sugg Fort & William Deloach were executors. (Rob TN, Co Ct Min, 1/34) 9 November 1813 Sugg Fort was appointed guardian of James Williams, orphan of Matthew Williams, deceased, with Thomas Appleton as security. (Ibid 3/329)

WILLIAMS, Nancy
Sold land in Green County, NC, to Abraham Dardin, 16 September 1805. This was proved on the oath of James Glasgow. (Roa TN, Co Ct Min, B/32)

WILLIAMS, Perry
3 August 1857 was bound as an apprentice to James P. McMahan until age 21. (Sev TN, Co Ct Min, no#/196)

WILLIAMS, R. C.
Died before 21 October 1839 when his death was suggested in the suit of R. C. Williams assignee vs James R. McKee et al. (Obi TN, Cir Ct Min, 4/4)

WILLIAMS, Ralph
Died before 21 February 1839 when land was taxed to the heirs. (Obi TN, Cir Ct Min, 3/299)

WILLIAMS, Rice
Died before 10 May 1831 when a special guardian was to be appointed for Elizabeth Williams, Joseph Williams, Louisa Williams and Rice Williams, minor heirs of Rice Williams, deceased, to defend the suit of George W. L. Marr vs James Dardis, Oliver Williams & the minors named. (Obi TN, Cir Ct Min, 1/161) Defendant Oliver Williams is not a resident of this state but is a resident of Hinds? County, MS. (Ibid 212) This case was heard & stated that in 1820 James Dardis placed a land warrant in the hands of Oliver Williams who agreed to locate the land & obtain a grant. The land was located in Obion County. Dardis then conveyed 1/5 of the land to Oliver Williams who in turn conveyed it to Rice Williams in 1824. Rice Williams in his lifetime, to wit, on 24 December 1829, transfered the land to George W. L. Marr. Title to the land is to be divested out of James Dardis, Oliver Williams and the heirs of Rice Williams, the 4 minors shown above by their guardians Thomas Allen & Jesse S. Ross. (Ibid 2/21)

WILLIAMS, Simon
Died before 4 February 1812 when land was taxed to the heirs. (Ste TN, Co Ct Min, 3/115)

WILLIAMS, Thomas
Died before 8 August 1814 when John Williams was appointed administrator with David Taylor as security. (Rob TN, Co Ct Min, 3/439)

WILLIAMS, Thomas
Died before 5 February 1819 when Watta Carrieth, Esquire was appointed guardian of Rachael Williams, Thomas Williams, Elizabeth Williams, Abeker Williams & Catharine Williams, minor heirs. (Wil TN, Co Ct Min, no#/431)

WILLIAMS, William
In the suit filed 27 November 1839 by William Williams & Robert McCrary of Marshall County, TN, vs Alexander E. McCord [McClure], Formerly of Marshall County & Jeremiah Holt, it is shown that McClure is about to abscond from the state & that Eli B. Dyrant [Dysart] has removed or is concealed with all of his effects. (Bed TN, Ch Ct Min, 1/324)

WILLIAMS, William
26 April 1825 made a deed of gift to his daughter, Polly Telman Mabry, of a negro girl named Penny. (Wil TN, Reg Bk/375)

WILLIAMS, William G.
Died before 18 September 1816 when Thomas Williams was appointed administrator with James Smith & Thomas Williams, Jr. as security. (Wil TN, Co Ct Min, no#/42)

WILLIAMS, Willouby
Died before 19 October 1812 as shown in the suit of Michael Montgomery Assee. for the Benefit of T. C. Clark vs Nancy Williams Exrx. of Willouby Williams. (Roa TN, Co Ct Min, D/419)

WILLIAMSON, George
Died in July 1856. His daughter, Mary Williamson, married Alvis Florence in 1836. Mary Florence is entitled to one part of her father's estate. Her brother, George Williamson, was appointed trustee & the inheritance settled on him for the benefit of Mary & her children. James O. K. Williamson was the administrator of the estate of George Williamson, deceased. (Mad TN, Ch Ct Min, 2/140)

WILLIASON, Hugh [Williams]
Died before 20 June 1839 as shown in the suit of Johnson Williamson, Heirs-at-law of Hugh Williason Decd. & John McCoy & others assignee &c vs Starkey Purvis. [Also see John Nevin.] (Obi TN, Cir Ct Min, 3/374)

WILLIS, Ed
Died before 18 February 1868 as shown in the suit of Ed Willis vs Wilhelm & others. The suit was revived in the name of Mrs. Elizabeth Burton, administratrix. (Mad TN, Ch Ct Min, 3/131) A suit was entered: "H. F. & L. J. Harris vs Jno. C. Rogers et als. Came the parties & thereupon the Death of Deft Ed Willis admr of Battle Roberson is suggested & admitted & by agreement of all the parties this cause is revived in the name of & against Davey B Thomas admr of Battle Roberson decd. and Elizabeth Burton admrx of Ed Willis decd." (Ibid 198)

WILLIS, G. W.
Died before 4 January 1872 when W. N. Beasley made a settlement as administrator. (Dyr TN, Co Ct Min, B/358)

WILLS, George
Died before 15 October 1798 when his will was proved by Robert Johnston. William Wills & Robert Wilson were executors. (Rob TN, Co Ct Min, 1/75)

WILLS, John
Was aged twelve years the 16th of June next, when he was bound to George G. Brown 13 February 1815, until full age. (Rob TN, Co Ct Min, 3/538)

WILLS, P.
Died before 6 April 1857 when A. R. Trotter & Robt. Lewis were paid for the coffin. (Sev TN, Co Ct Min, no#/143)

WILLSON, Andrew
Was a resident of SC 6 November 1787 when his deposition was to be taken for the case of Rich Woolridge vs Wm. Flanery. (Was TN, Co Ct Min, 1/298)

WILLSON, Jacob
Was a resident of Montgomery County, VA, 6 August 1783 when his deposition was to be taken on behalf of John Barlick, defendant vs George Barcley, plaintiff. (Was TN, Co Ct Min, 1/225)

WILLSON, William
Died before 3 November 1783 when the will was proved by Henry Willison, Jr., William Woods & Ruben Rider. (Was TN, Co Ct Min, 1/227)

WILMHELM & LINDSEY
There are several suits concerning this firm. In the suit 19 February 1868 by Allen Deberry vs Jno. Wilhelm, E. A. Lindsay, Geog. Metcalf, James Long and Robt. Lindsey, it is stated that Metcalf, Long & Lindsey were brothers & brothers-in-law of the members of the firm of Wilhelm & Lindsey. E. A. Lindsey had conveyed property to his father. (Mad TN, Ch Ct Min, 3/135)

WILSON, Fanny
31 August 1860 there was a suit by Richard H. Archer and Fanny Wilson by her next friend &c vs James Wilson & Richd. Mathews. James Wilson had sold some slaves to Richard Mathews without authority & the sale should be set aside. Also the slaves now in the possession of James Wilson & Fanny Wilson should be held for the support of the said Jas. and Fanny Wilson and their children during the lives of James & Fanny and then descend to their children, present & future. Ambrose R. Ried was appointed trustee for this purpose. (Mad TN, Ch Ct Min, 2/407)

WILSON, Hugh B.
Died before 18 February 1858 as shown when his death was proved in the suit of Hugh B. Wilson vs Thos. Ingram et als. The suit was revived in the names of James R. Wilson, Amanda M. Farris & her husband, William Farris, Nancy C. Wilson, Mary E. Wilson, Martha J. Wilson, Wm. N. Wilson, Geo. W. Wilson, Hugh J. Wilson, the only children & heirs of Hugh B. Wilson, deceased, & James R. Wilson the administrator. Jno. M. Merrill was appointed guardian ad litem for defendants, Lydia Ingram & Wm. Ingram, minors. Thos. Ingram was administrator of John Ingram, deceased. Lydia Ingram, Jane Taylor, Ann Deberry, Louisa Ingram & John M. Ingram have been served with process & failed to answer. (Mad TN, Ch Ct Min, 2/178) Hugh Wilson was living in Haywood County at the time of his death. (Ibid 279)

WILSON, Israil
4 October 1858 was released from paying poll tax for 1858 because he had removed from Sevier County for two years. (Sev TN, Co Ct Min, no#/352)

WILSON, Jacob R.
Was released from paying tax on a pleasure carriage & one poll tax for 1859 as he had left the county. (Sev TN, Co Ct Min, no#/545)

WILSON, James
7 June 1825 was appointed guardian to Sarah Wilson, Betsey Wilson, John Wilson, Polly Wilson & Washington Wilson, being chosen by the two former and appointed by the court to the three latter, they being minors under the age of 14. (McM TN, Co Ct Min, 2no#/71)

WILSON, Jason C.
Died before 18 February 1840 when land was taxed to the heirs. (Obi TN, Cir Ct Min, 4/no#)

WILSON, Jno. Read
Was a minor 22 August 1866 when Alex W. Campbell was appointed guardian ad litem to defend in the suit of Mary C. Wilson Ex. vs Jas. M. Wilson et als. (Mad TN, Ch Ct Min, 2/505)

WILSON, Joab
Died before 19 January 1850 as shown in the suit of John Ingram and Andrew J. Turner vs Thos. Newbern Extr. of Joab Wilson decd. This suit also mentions the supposed fourth heir of Jno. Reaves [Reeves], deceased. (Mad TN, Ch Ct Min, 1/130, 284) 17 March 1854 in the suit of Thos. Ingram Admr. vs Thos. Newbern Exr., the following persons were made defendants: Thos. H. Newbern & Emeline his wife, Alsey Bradford & Mary Ellen his wife, Jno. Clack [Clark] & Martha his wife, Parmelia F. Wilson & Jas T. Wilson, the children & heirs of Joab Wilson, deceased. (Ibid 367)

WILSON, Joseph
25 September 1805 his wife, Martha Wilson, was appointed joint guardian with James Wilson for the purpose of securing the personal property of Joseph Wilson who is reputed to be "in a State of Lunacy." William Steel & Perry Taylor were security. (Wil TN, Co Ct Min, no#/171)

WILSON, Joseph
Died before 17 February 1820 when his son, Joseph L. Wilson, sold to his mother, Martha Wilson, the interest he had in certain negroes of the estate of his father, Joseph Wilson, deceased. (Wil TN, Reg Bk/159) Joseph L. Wilson was guardian of Mary Wilson, one of the minor heirs of Joseph Wilson, deceased. Ewing Wilson was another heir. (Ibid 381) Joseph Wilson died before 16 September 1816 when administrators, Martha Wilson & Joseph Love, made a settlement. (Ibid, Co Ct Min, no#/28) Joseph Johnson, Esqr. was appointed guardian for James Wilson, a minor heir. (Ibid 29) Martha Wilson was appointed guardian of Ewin Wilson & Mary Wilson, minor heirs. (Ibid 30)

WILSON, Lucinda
Died before 14 January 1847 as shown in the suit of William Croom, guardian, vs J. F. Edwards, administrator. The defendant, James F. Edwards, released any claim for his wife's portion of the estate of Lucinda Wilson which was in his hands. (Mad TN, Ch Ct Min, 1/9)

WILSON, Permelia F.
Was a minor 15 January 1851 when Thomas H. Newbern was appointed guardian ad litem to answer for her in the suit of Thomas L. Sullivan vs Jno. Ingram, T. H. Newbern et als. (Mad TN, Ch Ct Min, 1/178)

WILSON, R. W.
Died before 23 August 1866 as shown in the suit of Mary C. Wilson Ex. vs Jas. M. Wilson & others. It is necessary to sell the real estate to pay the debts. (Mad TN, Ch Ct Min, 2/527)

WILSON, Robert
Was a minor child aged aged 6 years when he was bound to Leeroy Taylor at November term 1789, until of age. He is to be taught the "art and mistry of Silversmith." (Was TN, Co Ct Min, 1/411)

WILSON, Robert W. [L.]
Died before 12 January 1849 as shown in the suit of Willis B. Dickerson, Admr., vs Robert Livingston & Jas. P. Collins and others. The estate was insolvent. (Mad TN, Ch Ct Min, 1/68)

WILSON, Samuel
Died before 28 November 1827 when William McGready of Sumner County, TN, sold land to Isreal Moore & Jonathan Wilson, executors of Samuel Wilson, deceased. (Wil TN, Reg Bk/319)

WILSON, Samuel A.
Died before 1831. On 2 November 1841 a suit was filed by John N. Gates, William H. Wilson, James T. Wilson, George Martin & wife Mary T., Robert K. Chism & wife Nancy H., Samuel T. Wilson, Elizabeth B. Wilson, Narcissa J. Wilson and John A. Wilson by their guardian, William H. Wilson, and James T. Galder & wife Sarah vs Wilson McCalgin. Land is to be divided giving Wilson McCalgin his share which is one tenth. (Jac TN, Ch Ct Min, A/26) Wilson McCalgin was allotted his 1/10 part of the land and the rest was sold to be distributed between the rest of the parties. (Ibid 81) James T. Galder exhibited a record of the County Court of Monroe County, KY, appointing Samuel T. Wilson guardian of Narcissa J., Elizabeth B. & John A. Wilson and also a power of attorney from Samuel T. Wilson for himself & as guardian. (Ibid 211) On 10 February 1855 a suit was entered by Jno. A. Wilson, Samuel Garvin & wife Elizabeth, John W. Rhineheart & wife Nancy & others vs John N. Gates & Ervin H. Langford. It was stated that Samuel Wilson, father of complainants Jno. A., Elizabeth and Narcissa, about 1831 died intestate possesed of 800 acres of land. Part of the land was granted to Samuel Wilson by the states of TN & KY. At his death Samuel A. Wilson left the said John A., Narcissa J. & Elizabeth, William H. Wilson, James T. Wilson, Mary T., Nancy H., Sameul T. Wilson, Sarah C. & George Wilson his only children & heirs-at-law. Sarah C. married James T. Golden. Nancy H. married Robert K. Chism. Mary T. married George Martin. Narcissa J. married John W. Rhineheart. Elizabeth B. married Samuel Graven. All the above heirs held the land as tenants in common. In August 1836 James T. Wilson sold his interest, it being one tenth, to James McColegin. Defendant Gates has purchased the interest of William H. Wilson, George Martin & wife, Robert K. Chism & wife and James T. Goldin & wife. On 28 September 1841 John N. Gates & William H. Wilson, who represented himself to be guardian of John A., Narcissa & Elizabeth B., and Samuel T. Wilson, filed a bill against Willson T. McColgin as heir-at-law of James McColgin then deceased, praying for a sale of said land. George Wilson has died without issue leaving his brothers & sisters his only heirs. James T. Wilson died without issue leaving his brothers & sisters his only heirs. Defendant Gates & Langford took possession of said lands and have occupied the same until the present time. Complainants John A., Narcissa J. & Elizabeth B. were all minors and femme coverts. This suit was commenced in this court within one year after the said John A. Wilson arrived at full age. William H. Wilson who had represented himself as guardian to complainants was not their guardian so all proceedings is declared null & void and is set aside. The defendants were granted an appeal to the Supreme Court of the State of Tennessee. (Ibid B/202-5)

WILSON, Thomas
Died before 19 November 1831 as shown in the suit of Lucy Wilson & others vs William M.

Wilson & others. The court will decide if the paper presented be the last will and testament of Thomas Wilson, deceased, or not. The property in the County of Williamson was restrained from being removed until the decision of the Court. (Obi TN, Cir Ct Min, 1/195) At the May term 1832 a jury found it was not the will of Thomas Wilson, deceased. (Ibid 204)

WILSON, William M.
Died before 22 February 1837 when William C. Edwards was charged with his murder. (Obi TN, Cir Ct Min, 3/96) Samuel C. Wilson was prosecutor in the murder charge. (Ibid 143) In a motion for continuance of the trial it was stated that William Hutchinson is a material witness whose testimony is vital and that said Hutchinson is in a lingering state of health and may not survive until next term. His deposition is to be taken to be read at the trial in case he cannot attend. (Ibid 170) The defendant, William C. Edwards, was found not guilty. (Ibid 224) John C. Wilson & Rebecca Wilson were administrators. (Ibid 280) On 23 June 1841 Rebecca Willson, the widow, petitioned for dower. The other heirs were Thomas D., Robert B., James P., William M., Ruth C., Rebecca H., Mary M., Saml. D. and Katharine C. Wilson. (Ibid 4/no#)

WIMBERLY, Joseph
Died before 11 May 1812 when his widow, Sarah Wimberly, relinquished her right to administrate to Josiah Fort, who gave bond with Orrin D. Battle & Thomas Appleton as security. (Rob TN, Co Ct Min, 3/80) 10 November 1812 Sugg Fort was appointed guardian to the orphans with Josiah Fort and Thomas Appleton as security. (Ibid 148) Dower was ordered to be laid off to the widow. (Ibid 150)

WINCHESTER, David
Died before 1 August 1849 as shown in the suit of Charles B. Winchester admr. and others vs Merlin Marsh and others, suit dismissed. (Mad TN, Ch Ct Min, 1/94)

WINGWOOD, Elias
Died before 2 April 1866 when the nuncupative will was entered. It was made during his last illness at the home of Jadah Maples in the presence of Louisa Etherton & Judah Maples and reduced to writing on the 20th day of February 1866. Judah Maples is to have his mare & colt & George Maples is to have the balance of the personal property. (Sev, TN, Co Ct Min, no#/299)

WINKLER, Ch. Ph.
Was a non-resident of TN on 16 March 1855 as shown in the suit of H. C. Caruth & William Terry. (Mad TN, Ch Ct Min, 2/44)

WINN, Edmund
Was a resident of Lunenburg County, VA, 27 September 1824 when his agent, Edmund Hardy, gave power of attorney to Charles Blaylock of Wilson County, TN, "give him full authority to use in any way that he may think proper for the special benefit and use of my daughter Francis Bacon all the property I have placed in his hands as Trustee for the above purpose." Slaves & household equipment were listed. (Wil TN, Reg Bk/356)

WINSET, John
Died before 15 September 1817 when the administrator, Jesse Rhodes, was ordered to make a settlement. (Wil TN, Co Ct Min, no#/149)

WINSTON, Fountain
Died before 21 February 1838 when land was taxed to the heirs. (Obi TN, Cir Ct Min, 3/159)

WINSTON, Joseph
Died before 24 February 1837 when land was taxed to the heirs. (Obi TN, Cir Ct Min, 3/114)

WINSTON, Lewis
Died before 24 February 1837 when land was taxed to the heirs. (Obi TN, Cir Ct Min, 3/115)

WINSTON, Samuel
Died before 21 February 1838 when land was taxed to the heirs. (Obi TN, Cir Ct Min, 3/160)

WINSTON, Wm. L.
Died before 21 February 1860 when his death was admitted in the suit of Isaac J. Winston

et al vs James Weatherly et als. Wm. L. Winston had been a complainant in this suit. Stephen Carter was appointed administrator. (Mad TN, Ch Ct Min, 2/296) Isaac J. & Wm. L. Winston had come of age before filing their bill in this cause. Jno. J. Winston was the father of complainants. (Ibid 355) James Weatherly was guardian of Isaac J. Winston & of Wm. S. [L] Winston who has died. (Ibid 450)

WINSTON, Wm. N.
Died in 1854 leaving a will. He left his widow, Winny Ann, & one child, Wm. Robt. Winston, to whom he left land when he came of age. In the event his son did not live to age 21 the land was to go to the children of his brothers. Wm. Robert Winston died a short time after his father. John Winston is the only child of Joseph Winston & William, Candis & James Winston are the only children of Henry Winston. Joseph & Henry were the only brothers of Wm. N. Winston. Winney Ann, the widow, is insisting that the land descended to her. In the suit, Jno. Winston by his guardian Arnold Winston vs Joel R. Chappell & others, the court decided the land should be sold and the proceeds go the the children of Wm. N. Winston's brothers. (Mad TN, Ch Ct Min, 2/171) Joel R. Chappell & Nathan H. Whitlow were executors. (Ibid 318)

WINTERS, Elisha
Died before 2 November 1818 when the nuncupative will was proved by Archibald Campbell, Patsy Campbell & Rebecca Campbell. It was ordered that Rhoda Winters, widow, be appointed administratrix with will annexed. It was also proved that the next of kin lived in KY and that the estate did not exceed $100. (Wil TN, Co Ct Min, no#/336)

WINTERS, Moses
Died before 15 October 1798 when his will was proved by William Flewellen. Elisabeth Winters was executrix. (Rob TN, Co Ct Min, 1/74)

WINTERS, Nancy
Was the mother of a child of which Henry Airs, Jr. was charged as the reputed father. Henry gave bond for its manitenance 15 February 1810. (Rob TN, Co Ct Min, 2/225)

WISEMAN, Thomas
Died before 13 May 1817 as shown in the suit of Benjamin White & John Wiseman, administrator of Thomas Wiseman Decd. vs Henry Dobbs. (Cla TN, Co Ct Min, 4/339)

WITCHER
A suit was heard 14 August 1860 of Joseph Eaton vs William P. Witcher, George M. McWhirter admr. & Danl. K. Witcher, James H. Witcher, Tandy W. Witcher, Junison Brown & wife Jane Brown, Samuel Ballard & wife Nancy Ballard, Jessie Witcher, Martha Witcher, Hogin W. Witcher & Martha G. Witcher. The defendants [except George M. McWhirter & Danl. K. Witcher] are indebted to complainant for $100, that is, William P. Witcher in the sum of $37.50, $25 as guardian of Martha Witcher & Jessie Witcher and the other parties in the sum of $12.50 each. (Jac TN, Ch Ct Min, C/395) Jessie Witcher is now of full age as stated 16 August 1860. (Ibid 423)

WITCHER, Daniel K.
Died before 7 February 1851 as shown in the suit of Garrett Sadler vs Merlin Young et al. McWhirter was a defendant in this case and Daniel K. Witcher, deceased, had been his security. (Jac TN, Ch Ct Min, A/417)

WITCHER, Jane
On 9 February 1860 dismissed her suit for divorce from William Witcher. They are now living together. (Jac TN, Ch Ct Min, C/304)

WITCHER, Tandy K.
Died before 15 July 1859 as shown in the suit of Joseph Eaton vs Wm. P. Witcher et als. A report is to be made as to what has come into the hands of George M. McWhirter, administrator of the estate of Tandy K. Witcher, deceased. (Jac TN, Ch Ct Min, C/286)

WITHERINGTON, Robert
Died before 10 January 1849 as shown by the suit of R. W. Witherington next friend of Lovey Ann Wright vs Thomas W. P. Wright. Lovey Ann was the wife of Thomas W. P. Wright and was entitled to 3 negroes derived from her father, Robert Witherington, deceased. Thomas Wright had sold the negroes and the suit was to recover the money for them and a trustee was to be named to hold same for her benefit. (Mad TN, Ch Ct Min, 1/61) Lovey Ann had received the negroes from her father's estate while she was single. She will retain two of them for herself and her children and they will not be subject to the debts of her husband. Jno. R. Jelks was appointed to act as trustee. (Ibid 65) 16 January

1850, Thomas W. P. Wright & wife, Lucy Gideon Witherington Amos Jonier & wife Martha vs David Outlaw & wife Lovey, Halliday H. Fife & wife Mary & Robt. H. Witherington [punctuation as shown]. Plaintiffs dismissed their bill. Defentant Outlaw & wife withdrew Ex. No. 1 filed in their answer & filed another: "Recd. of Lovey Witherington guardian to my wife all of her part of her fathers Estate, This 10th Feby 1837. EX. No. 1. [signed] H. H. Fife." (Ibid 103)

WITHERS, John
Was bound as an apprentice to Samuel Workman on 5 June 1827, to learn the tanning and currying trade. (McM TN, Co Ct Min, 2no#/219)

WITT
7 September 1829 Sally Witt, John Witt, Nathaniel Witt, Silas Witt, James Witt, Mourning Witt, Patsey Witt & Edward G. Sellers, sold land in Jefferson County, to Charles Cate. The handwriting of James Ferrell, deceased, was proved as the witness by Napoleon B. Bradford. On the same date Edward G. Sellers, Sarly Sellers, Sarah Witt, guardian for "an ediot named Martha Witt" & Joseph Witt, sold land in Jefferson County to the heirs of Charles Cate, deceased. (McM TN, Co Ct Min, 2no#/382)

WITT, Nathaniel
Died before 5 June 1826 when William Cate was appointed administrator, the widow being present and consenting. (McM TN, Co Ct Min, 2no#/155)

WOFFORD, Jesse
Died before 2 May 1814 when John Wofford was appointed administrator with George Boyd & John Gardner as security. (Ste TN, Co Ct Min, 4/137)

WOLF, Elizabeth
Sued George Wolf for divorce. On 14 July 1853 she dismissed her suit. (Jac TN, Ch Ct Min, B/74) On 10 February 1859 the suit for divorce of Elizabeth Wolf against George W. Wolf was continued until next term of Court. (Ibid C/172)

WOLF, Jacob
Died before 25 February 1807 when Robert Depreast was ordered to receive into his care Michael Wolf and Elijah Wolf, sons of Jacob Wolf, deceased, and support them until next term of court. (Cla TN, Co Ct Min, 3/50) Robert Depreast was paid for supporting the widow Wolf's children. (Ibid 79)

WOLF, Polly
Was an orphan girl between 10 and 11 years of age, a daughter of Jacob Wolf, deceased, when she was bound 25 August 1807 to John Word, Esqr. until age 18. (Cla TN, Co Ct Min, 3/108)

WOLLIN, Joshua
On 12 September 1815 gave power of attorney to Jesse Rhodes to take care of any of his business in the State of NC, witnessed by Fras. Palmer & Edward Wollin. (Wil TN, Reg Bk/41)

WOLLOS, Jesse
7 November 1785 Col. Charles Robertson gave a deposition relating to something said by Jesse Wollos "when he was about to Remove out of this County." (Was TN, Co Ct Min, 1/267)

WOOD, Archer S.
Made a deed to his son Larkin Wood for a negro boy Robin, 10 February 1820. (Wil TN, Reg Bk/162)

WOOD, Hanna Gallege
Died before 19 February 1795 when Jesse Patrick was appointed administrator, with Ethelred Cobb and Joseph Sevier as his security. (Was TN, Co Ct Min, 1/535)

WOOD, Jackson
Was not a resident of this state 4 May 1842 as shown in the suit of John M. Richmond vs Pinckney McCarver. (Jac TN, Ch Ct Min, A/53)

WOOD, Jenny
Was a free woman of color when she brought suit against John McDowell on 3 February 1858. She is to be allowed to visit and see her children, Rhoda & Daniel, on proper occasions under the supervision & direction of James Draper. (Jac TN, Ch Ct Min, C/86)

WOOD, John
Was a resident by Burk County, GA, on 11 September 1794 when he sold a negro boy named Isaac about 19 years old, to John Tedlock, witnessed by Moses Humphreys & Lewis Tombleson. (Was TN, Co Ct Min, 1/543)

WOOD, John
Was a mulatto boy 3 years old when he was bound 3 May 1819 to Hezekiah Rhodes until age 21. (Wil TN, Co Ct Min, no#/441)

WOOD, Jonathan
Died before 28 December 1843 as shown in the suit of Elisha G. Forrest vs John P. Wood and Green L. Poplin. John B. Wood is not an inhabitant of this state. He is a distributee of Jonathan Wood, deceased, and entitled to a share of his estate in the hands of Green L. Poplin, administrator. (Bed TN, Ch Ct Min, 2/275) There were 7 legatees, one of whom was John P. Wood. (Ibid 292) John P. Wood is a citizen of AL. Elisha G. Forest is a citizen of Marshall County, TN. In May 1843 it was stated that Jonathan Wood died a few months ago. (Ibid 3/136)

WOOD, S. D.
Died before 3 January 1871 when H. S. Fowlkes renewed his bond as guardian of the minor heirs of S. D. Wood. (Dyr TN, Co Ct Min, B/157) 3 July 1872 Mary A. Wood made a settlement as administratrix of S. D. Wood, deceased. (Ibid 442)

WOODFORK, William
Died before 15 July 1859 when his death was suggested in the suit of Willis Cornwell vs William Woodfork. (Jac TN, Ch Ct Min, C/279)

WOODRUM, Jacob
Died before 13 July 1850 as shown in the suit of Matthew C. McKindly vs William Woodrum & James Drennum Exrs. &c of Jacob Woodrum decd. (Jac TN, Ch Ct Min, A/376)

WOODS, David
Died before 11 March 1844 when land was taxed to the heirs. (Obi TN, Cir Ct Min, 4/no#)

WOODS, Feryl
Was a resident of Jackson County, GA, on 5 June 1828 when his deposition was to be taken for the defendant in the case of Henry Glaze vs Henry Gier. (McM TN, Co Ct Min, no#/339)

WOODS, John
Died before 22 May 1780 when Laneas Wood was granted "leave of aportempore of Administration on the estate." (Was TN, Co Ct Min, 1/106) The name of the administratrix looks like Haneas Woods. She gave bond with David Hughes & Peter McName as security. In another place the name looks like Agness Woods. (Ibid 107)

WOODS, Minor
Died before 7 July 1874 when he was listed on the tax list for 1873 as "dead." (Dyr TN, Co Ct Min, B/759)

WOODS, Wm. H.
Died before 13 January 1851 as shown by the petition of Cary H. Woods, admr. of Wm. H. Woods decd., Levi S. Wood, Henry Woods, Dezart? Woods, Jas. W. Drake & wife Margaret, David H. Woods, & Hester Ann, Levi B., John, Emily & Margaret Herron, last five of whom are minors & petition by their Father, Jno. Herron, & of Martha D. Woods a minor by her guardian Levi S. Woods & of Jno. P. Clark a minor by his father, James M. Clark. These are the distributees of the intestate, Wm. H. Woods. (Mad TN, Ch Ct Min, 1/164)

WOODSIDES, M. M.
Died before 5 February 1872 when J. J. McLemore was appointed administrator, with J. M. Cochrane and S. F. Waggoman as his security. (Dyr TN, Co Ct Min, B/368)

WOODWARD, Thomas
Died before 1836 as shown in the suit of J. M. Yowell vs Thomas Brunts [Bunts] & Solomon Meadows, all of Marshall County. Yowell was administrator for Thomas Meadows. [All other statements say administrator for Thomas Woodward.] The widow of Thomas Woodward was mentioned. Egbert Campbell, administrator of P. Campbell, deceased, was also mentioned. (Bed TN, Ch Ct Min, 1/159) 30 December 1840, in the suit of Elizabeth Harwell and others vs Thomas Reeves and others, it was shown that

Thomas Woodward had executed a deed of trust to defendant Chitwood for Elizabeth Harwell and not liable for the debts of Bowling Harwell. Chitwood has not performed the duties of trustee and Jesse M. Yowell was appointed in his stead. (Ibid 2/124)

WOOLDRIDGE, William
On 6 December 1816 sold to his daughter, Sally Cox, for good will & affection & one dollar, a negro girl named Fortune. Thomas Wooldridge was witness. (Wil TN, Reg Bk/77) William made a deed of gift 29 January 1816 to his daughter Polly Edwards. (Ibid 107)

WOOLDRIDGE, William
Died before 3 August 1818 when Martha Wooldridge was appointed administratrix with William Edward & William Coe as security. (Wil TN, Co Ct Min, no#/293) Martha was the widow. (Ibid 362)

WOOLFOLK, Jno.
Died before 22 August 1867 as shown in the suit of James S. McDonald vs Jno. R. Woolfolk et als. The defendants were the only heirs of Jno. Woolfolk. America Hardgraves & Malvina C. Hardgraves are minors & have answered by their guardian, Jno. L. Brown. Some defendants are non-residents. Also mentioned were Milly & Jno. R. Woolfolk. (Mad TN, Ch Ct Min, 3/78)

WOOLFOLK, Jno. R.
Died before 17 February 1868 as shown in the suits of Stephens & Stephens vs Jno. R. Woolfolk et al and Nock Wicks &c vs Jno R. Woolfolk et als. It was stated that Mildred Ann, Julietta, Lee Cornelia, Almira, Gilbreth, Jas. Graves, Lizzie Love, Gilbreth Niell & Florence Preston Woolfolk are minors having no regular guardian and R. H. Fenner was appointed guardian ad litem to defend these suits for them. (Mad TN, Ch Ct Min, 3/122) Julia R. Woolfolk was the widow of Jno. R. Woolfolk and the minors listed were his children, all of whom were minors on 20 February 1868, except Mildred Ann. (Ibid 148)

WOOLRIDGE, Thomas
Died before 4 November 1818 when the administrator entered the inventory of the estate. (Wil TN, Co Ct Min, no#/353)

WOOTON, John
Died before 19 March 1817 when Dorothy Wooton was appointed administratrix, with William Wooton as security. (Wil TN, Co Ct Min, no#/96)

WORD, Cuthbert
Died before 25 February 1845 as shown in the petition of William Word, executor, to sell slaves. Jane Word was the widow and she has lately departed this life. There are 7 children. (Bed TN, Ch Ct Min, 2/327) Slaves were sold to Thomas S. Word. (Ibid 359)

WORDLOW, Michael
6 September 1830 came into Court and asked that his son, James Wordlow, aged 16 years the 16th day of July last, be set at liberty to trade for himself as though he were 21. This entry is then marked "Error." (McM TN, Co Ct Min, 2no#/465)

WORMACK, Dave
Taxes were not collected in District 2 for 1873, "gone." (Dyr TN, Co Ct Min, B/759)

WORMACK, Jim
Taxes were not collected in District 2 for 1873, "gone." (Dyr TN, Co Ct Min, B/759)

WORRELL, Daniel
Was bound 5 December 1870 to J. F. Perry. He is a white boy aged 11 years. (Dyr TN, Co Ct Min, B/141)

WORRELL, James H.
Was bound 5 December 1870 to Wilson Frost. He is a white boy aged 9 years. (Dyr TN, Co Ct Min, B/141)

WRAY, George
Died before 4 March 1872 when a settlement was made by Elizabeth Wray as administrator. (Dyr TN, Co Ct Min, B/381)

WRENSHAW, Matilda
Was the mother of a bastard child by Edward Dillard. 20 June 1817 it was reported that Matilda had left the county of Wilson. (Wil TN, Co Ct Min, no#/131)

WRIGHT
In the suit of Polly Brannum et als vs B. Findly et als, 9 April 1861, it was stated that defendants Richard, Polly, Joshua, James & Elizabeth Wright are minors and R. H. Bledsoe was appointed guardian ad litem. (Fen TN, Ch Ct Min, A/261)

WRIGHT, Bird
Died before 16 September 1816 when Benj. Wright was appointed administrator, with John Deny & Thomas Sypert as security. (Wil TN, Co Ct Min, no#/26)

WRIGHT, Henry
17 June 1817 came into court and by the oath of Capt. Rich. A. Robertson proved that he lost nearly the whole of his right ear in a fight with a certain Asaph Alsup on the 15th day of April 1817. The proof being satisfactory to the court it is ordered that the same be certified. (Wil TN, Co Ct Min, no#/122)

WRIGHT, Isaac
Died before 19 December 1815 when his widow, Abijah Wright, one of the heirs of John Somers, deceased, late of Caswell County, NC, appointed her brother, James Somers, of Wilson County, TN, her attorney to recover her part of the estate of her deceased father. (Wil TN, Reg Bk/47)

WRIGHT, J___
[Name written over, could be James, Jennie, Joshua, etc.] Died before 3 August 1818 when Phillip Smart was appointed guardian for Abraham Wright, Martha Wright, Rebecca Wright & Isaac Wright, minor heirs. [the name of the deceased could be Isaac] (Wil TN, Co Ct Min, no#/287)

WRIGHT, James
Died before 14 July 1854 as shown in the suit of George W. Wolfe & Elizabeth Wolfe vs Patsy Wright and James A. Spurlock & Allen Manear. James Wright left a will by which he left to his wife, Patsy Wright, certain negroes during her life and afterwards to his daughters, Jenny, Betsy the complainant, Sally and Patty. At the time of the bequest Betsy or Elizabeth was married to George W. Wolfe & said marriage still subsists. On 8 March 1852 Elizabeth Wolfe deeded to James A. Manear her interest in the estates of James Wright & Martha Wright & her husband did not join her in said conveyance. The deed was declared void and Martha Wright was ordered not to sell or remove the negroes beyond this state. (Jac TN, Ch Ct Min, B/175) On 10 February 1855 a suit was entered by Jane Haile vs James A. Spurlock, Alen Manear, Mariah Manear et al. The transfer procured by James A. Marear, of whose estate the said James A. Spurlock and Alen Manear were administrators, was procured by fraud and the same is to be cancelled. Anyone claiming under James A. Manear is enjoined from interfering with the negroes devised to Jane Haile by her father James Wright. James A. Manear, deceased, in his lifetime, and Denton Hale the husband of Jane Hale, had procured a transfer or bill of sale to their interest in one of the negroes devised as aforesaid. A judgement had been recovered from Garritt H. Graham, administrator of John Graham, deceased, and Ridly Roberts in March 1850. This is void since Jane Hale was never examined separately from her husband. (Ibid 207)

WRIGHT, John J.
17 March 1817 was bound as an apprentice to John McMinn until age 21. (Wil TN, Co Ct Min, no#/76)

WRIGHT, Lemuel
Died before 13 October 1856 as shown in the suit of John R. McGee & others vs Jessee Woods et als. Lemuel Wright was a defendant. (Fen TN, Ch Ct Min, A/62) Mitchel Wright was his only heir. (Ibid 91)

WRIGHT, Martha
Died before 3 February 1858 when her death was suggested in the suit of James A. Spurlock vs John P. Murray et als. Martha Wright had been a defendant in this suit. Her administrator, Syrus W. Russell, resided in the county of Hickman. (Jac TN, Ch Ct Min, C/89)

WRIGHT, Stephen
Was a deserter. February term 1779 it was ordered that he be sent to the district Goal of Salisbury or delivered to some Contl. Officer. (Was TN, Co Ct Min, 1/62)

WROE, Original
Died before 20 March 1809 when Sarah Wroe & George Wroe were appointed administrators, with Milton Center & Gilbreath Barton as security. This entry was crossed out & under it an order for Sarah & George Wroe to expose the perishable part of the estate to sale. (Roa TN, Co Ct Min, D/45)

WYATT
2 November 1813 John Wyatt, Daniel Wyatt, Abraham Wyatt, Thomas Wyatt, Zachariah Wyatt and Solomon Wyatt were among the crew ordered to work on a road. [Also in the county were James Wyatt, Robert Wyatt, Martin Wyatt & William Wyatt.] (Ste TN, Co Ct Min, 4/66)

WYATT, Edward
Was a resident of Dinwiddie County, VA, 5 July 1809 when his deposition was to be taken for the defendant in the case of Benjn. Wells vs Wm. Roachel. (Rob TN, Co Ct Min, 2/153)

WYATT, Samuel
Died before 16 August 1815 when his widow, Catharine Wyatt, petitioned for dower. (Cla TN, Co Ct Min, 4/115) An entry was made and crossed out that stated that Samuel Wyatt was living on the 11th day of June 1815, on the evidence of David Lantern. (Ibid 125) 14 November 1815, "On motion it is ordered by the Court that the report of the Jury heretofore appointed to lay off the dower or one third part of the real estate of Samuel Wyatt for the benefit of his widow be set aside it appearing to the satisfaction of the Court that said Samuel Wyatt is still living." (Ibid 127)

WYLIS, Darlin A.
Was bound on 6 September 1825 to Joel K. Brown until age 21. He is now 18 years of age on the 11th of November 1825. He is to be taught the trade of a tailor. (McM TN, Co Ct Min, 2no#/97)

WYN, William
November term 1788 made a bill of sale to David Allison for a negro woman named Lucy, "Which Wyn, the grandfather of the said William Wyn, gave unto him also her children Viz: Chloe, Clayburn, Ginney, Will, Nede & Joe and the issue of the said Negroes from the first Day of August 1785." On the same day William Wynne of Burke County sold to David Allison of Washington County the negro boy, Clayburn. (Was TN, Co Ct Min, no#/21)

WYNN, Ashley
Died before 4 June 1866 when the will was proved by Curtis Mills & Baschil Scruggs, witnesses. E. M. Wynn was executor with Basdill Scruggs as security. (Sev TN, Co Ct Min, no#/331)

WYNN, Isham
Died before 16 December 1816 when John Wynn, Sr. made a deed of gift to his grandchildren, Robert Wynn, Betsy Wynn, John Wynn, Jr., Joel Wynn, William Wynn & Polly Wynn, children of Isham Wynn, deceased. John Wynn, Sr. gave them 5 negroes, Betsy, Harry, Cynthia & 2 children Ned & Carlisle, stock of every [kind], household & kitchen furniture, except that he retained the use of the property during the life of he & his wife. (Wil TN, Reg Bk/75) Deveraux Wynn was guardian of the heirs of Isham Wynn. (Ibid 191)

WYNN, Quaker [Quarker]
On 27 June 1835 Wm. E. Butler sold to Quaker Wynn & Jane Carson a lot of ground as tenants in common. Both Quaker Wynn & Jane Carson were free persons of color. On 24 August 1866 it was stated that Quaker Wynn & Jane Carson had both died several years since, without issue, children or relatives capable of inheriting so the land escheated to the state. (Mad TN, Ch Ct Min, 2/543)

WYNNE, Robert
Died before 22 December 1806 when the executor, John K. Wynne, returned an additional inventory. (Wil TN, Co Ct Min, no#/267) John K. Wynne was appointed guardian of 2 orphans of Robert Wynne deceased, viz, Alford Wynne & Sinthia Wynne. (Ibid 276)

WYNNE, Thomas
Was a negro boy 5 years old when he was bound 5 January 1872, with his mother's consent, to W. P. Fowlkes until age 21. (Dyr TN, Co Ct Min, B/363)

WYNNE, V. G.
Taxes were not collected in District 4 for 1873, "insolvent." (Dyr TN, Co Ct Min, B/759)

WYNNE, William
Died before 17 June 1816 when John K. Wynne was appointed administrator, with John Harpole & Harry L. Douglass as security. (Wil TN, Co Ct Min, no#/3)

WYNNE, William R.
Died 26 December 1814 in Brunswick County, VA, after making his will, as shown in the suit of Abner Vincent and others vs George R. Scott & Wife. The complainants, Abner Vincent and his wife Susan Parthena W., Harriett J. Wynne and William R. Wynne, the latter a minor who sues by by his next friend Abner Vincent, are all of Weakley County, TN. The defendants, George R. Scott and Polly his wife are of Bedford County, TN. The complainants are the only children of William R. Wynne, deceased, except Abner Vincent who is here in right of his wife, she being a child of William R. Wynne. By his will he bequeathed all of his estate to his wife Polly Wynne and at her death to his children. The widow married 3 or 4 years later (about 1821 or 1822) to George R. Scott. They resided in VA for some years and then removed to TN. George R. Scott has treated his wife with great cruelty and has driven her from his home & refused to support her and is claiming as his own the negroes that had come to Polly as a life estate by the will of William Wynne. The will named his 2 children, Susan Parthena William Wynne & Stanott [Harriett?] James Wynne & mentioned the child his wife was then pregnant with. Polly was the daughter of Peter Wynne whose will is entered in this suit. [not shown] Peter Wynne died in 1815. Peter & Polly Scott moved from VA to TN in 1825. The children of Peter Scott were mentioned. An agreement was reached 1 November 1837 between Abram Vincent for himself & wife, William R. Wynne for himself and attorney in fact for Harriett J. Wynne and George R. Scott for himself & wife Polly. (Bed TN, Ch Ct Min, 1/99)

WYNNE, William R.
Died before 9 October 1872 when the land of his heirs was mentioned in the division of the land of Anderson Dickey. (Dyr TN, Co Ct Min, B/503)

YANCY, Kavenaugh
Married Elizabeth Watts in Virginia about 35 years ago. Elizabeth was the daughter of Fredrick Watts, deceased, who bequeathed by his will certain property and a negro woman named Violet, to Elizabeth during her life and after her death to her children. The children are Henry, James, William, Elizabeth, Francis, Louisa, Rebecca & Jane, minors, who sue by their next friend and brother, Henry Yancy, and Alexander Yancy of Virginia. [Probably Henry & James were not minors as they had purchased the interest of Kavenaugh Yancy in the negro.] They are suing to prevent the negro from being sold to pay the debts of Kavenaugh Yancy. Louisa Yancy was also shown as Hanna. Elizabeth Yancy, the mother, was also a complainant in this suit, filed 9 March 1843. (Bed TN, Ch Ct Min, 3/96)

YANDELL, Henry
Died before 13 August 1839 as shown by the suit of John M. Schorn & wife Martha vs George Davidson. A judgement in favor of defendant was rendered in Rutherford County against Frederick E. Becton as administrator of Henry Yandell, deceased, who was appointed administrator in MS & has never been appointed by TN. (Bed TN, Ch Ct Min, 2/84)

YARBROUGH, Henry
Was a resident of Franklin County, NC, 10 April 1819 when he sold a slave to John Brown of Wilson, County, TN. (Wil TN, Reg Bk/133)

YARBROUGH, John
Died before 2 October 1871 when J. A. Nunn, JP, was paid for holding an inquest over the body. (Dyr TN, Co Ct Min, B/293)

YATES, John B.
10 September 1820 made a deed of gift of a slave to his son, Lemuel Yates. (Wil TN, Reg Bk/213)

YATES, William
17 November 1795 was allowed money to maintain his daughter, Louisa Yates, one of the poor of the county. (Was TN, Co Ct Min, 1/578)

YEARLY, Isam
22 May 1780, "came into Court and Volentary Confest that he had been Incrimical to the Common Cause of Liberty. He was sent to supr Court for further Tryal." (Was TN, Co Ct Min, 1/106)

YEARWOOD, J. G.
Died before 5 October 1870 when F. G. Sampson was appointed administrator, with P. E. Wilson as his security. (Dyr TN, Co Ct Min, B/118)

YEARWOOD, Wm.
Died before 6 September 1871 as shown in the suit of the administrator, E. M. Hall vs John Jones & others. The residences of the heirs are unknown and publication has been made requiring said unknown heirs to appear and they have failed to appear. William Yearwood died in January 1867 without issue, leaving the defendant, Kate Jones his widow. (Dyr TN, Co Ct Min, B/288-90) The sale of the land mentioned land sold by Wm. Yearwood to John Yearwood. (Ibid 353-4)

YORK, G. W., Dr.
2 May 1871 was released from working on public roads as he is physically unable to do manual labor. (Dyr TN, Co Ct Min, B/239)

YOUNG, America
By consent of the parties, her bill for divorce against Merlin Young was continued until next term, 13 July 1854. (Jac TN, Ch Ct Min, B/166) Divorce was granted 10 February 1855. They were married in October 1842. She was given title to all the property mentioned in the bill and custody of the children. (Ibid 213) The minor children of this marriage, Milton Bertram Young & Napoleon B. Young, were left in the care of the mother together with the two other youngest children subject to further order. A proposition was made by William Young of Smith County who is their paternal uncle to take them and send them to school & to clothe and board them gratuitously. William Young was appointed guardian of the two eldest, that is Milton Bertrund and Napolion B. Young. (Ibid C/21) America Young was guilty of contempt of court by refusing to give up the children to the guardianship of William Young. Joseph Eaton & Elizabeth Eaton have been guilty of a like contempt in aiding America Young in defeating the execution of said order. (Ibid 72) In the suit of Merlin Young vs America Young it was decreed that J. C. G. Young, one of the minor children of Merlin and America Young, be taken from the guardianship of Joseph Eaton and placed under the guardianship of Wm. Young of Smith County, who is known by the Court to be a man of fortune and of good moral character. On the same day another suit ordered the sheriff to take into custody Napoleon B. Young & Milton B. Young and deliver them to Wm. Young, brother of said Merlin Young. (Ibid 116) Mary Young brought her two children, Bertram Young and Josephus, alias James Young into court. The sheriff had already delivered her oldest child, Napoleon B. Young to Wm. Young in Smith County. It was agreed that Mary could have custody of Josephus, alias James Young and Wilson Clements Young until they arrive at the age of 21. (Ibid 134)

YOUNG, Banister
Died before 2 November 1818 when the will was proved by Wm. Crabtree & Joseph Crabtree. Stephen Young was executor with Joseph Crabtree & Brinkly Rogers as security. (Wil TN, Co Ct Min, no#/333)

YOUNG, Charles
Died before 18 May 1796 when a jury found that his will was not a sufficient will in law. Rebecca Young & George Gillaspie were appointed administrators, with Francis Allison and Nathaniel Davis as security. (Was TN, Co Ct Min, 1/608)

YOUNG, David
Died before 10 February 1855 as shown in the suit of William Jared? vs Allen Young et als. An amended bill is to be filed making the administrator of David Young a defendant. (Jac TN, Ch Ct Min, B/210)

YOUNG, Henry
Was a minor 16 July 1858 as shown in the suit of Abner Chaffin & others vs Henry Young & others. Robert Hail is also a minor defendant and L. J. Lane was appointed guardian ad litem for both. The suit concerns sale of land for distribution. (Jac TN, Ch Ct Min, C/155)

YOUNG, Isaac
6 September 1830 emancipated his woman slave named Malinda. (McM TN, Co Ct Min, 2no#/471)

YOUNG, James G.
In the suit 6 August 1852 by Littleberry Young et als vs Thomas Young and others it was stated that John Stafford, James Stafford, Merlin Young, Henderson Young, Harrison Young, Zebulon Young & Sally Young are minors and have no regular guardian. Thomas D. Cassitty was appointed guardian ad litem. (Jac TN, Ch Ct Min, B/66) This case probably concerns the estate of James Young, deceased. (Ibid 76) When the suit was heard it listed Littleberry Young & Joseph Stafford vs Thomas Young, John M. Young, Rada Dudney, Partick N. Dudny, Elizabeth Stafford, Lorinsa J. Stafford, Duke Young, Sally Young, Zebulon Young, Harrison Young, H. Young, Merlin Young, James Stafford & John Stafford. It was stated that the administrator had paid from the estate of his intestate, L. Young [J. Young had been written and the J. crossed out]. On the testimony of L. B. Young the land should be sold. James L. Young died intestate in Jackson County in 1848 & complainant Littlebry Young is his administrator. The deceased had owned lands jointly with Joseph Stafford. The deceased is also shown as James G. Young. (Ibid 80) Names listed again as Littleberry Young, Joseph Stafford, Thomas Young, John Young, Rhoda Dudney, Patrick N. Dudny, Elizabeth Stafford, Lorenza J. Stafford, Duke Young, Sally Young, Zebulon Young, Harrison Young, Henderson Young, Merlin Young, James Stafford and John Stafford. (Ibid 109 & 292) The land was sold to LeRoy B. Settle & divested out of defendants as shown above except Joseph Stafford was not listed. It was bounded by the land where Robert Young lived on the 6 day of July 1846. (Ibid 343)

YOUNG, Mary
Was the mother of a base born child. Job Odell, the reputed father, was ordered to pay for its maintenance 11 May 1790. (Was TN, Co Ct Min, 1/440)

YOUNG, Parker
Died before 10 April 1861 when Benjamin Buch, administrator of Parker Young, was to be made a defendant to the suit of E. R. Taylor et als vs James Young & others. (Fen TN, Ch Ct Min, A/279)

YOUNG, Robert
Probably died before 12 February 1859 as shown in the suit of Abner Chaffin, Elizabeth Chaffin, Joshua Young, William Chaffin, Barberry Chaffin, Elijah Stamps, Sally Stamps, William Young, James Stamps, John Young, Bailey McClendon & Temperance McClendon vs Henry Young, Robert Hale & their guardian ad litem L. J. Lowe. Land was sold, including the house farm &c where Robert Young lived on the 8th day of February 1841, and title divested out of complainants and defendants. (Jac TN, Ch Ct Min, C/224)

YOUNG, Thomas
Died before 16 February 1795 when Mary Young and Joseph Young were appointed adminstrators, with John Tipton and David Jobe as security. (Was TN, Co Ct Min, 1/524)

YOUNG, Worley
Died before 14 July 1859 as shown in the suit of William H. Botts, administrator with the will annexed of Worly Young, deceased, and James Y. Putty vs Rebecca Young, Thomas Young, William [or Wallis] W. Davis & wife Elizabeth Davis, Marion Young, Nancy Young, Josiah Young, Martha Young, Polly J. Young, Matilda Putty, John S. Putty & wife Rhoda Putty & William Young. All the defendants have been served except William Young and publication has been made for him. Defendants Elizabeth Davis, Rhoda Putty, Matilda Putty, Marion Young, Nancy Young, the femme coverts & the minors who are over the age of 14, have filed their answers. All the rest have failed to enter their defense. Rebecca Young was the widow and she is to have dower. Benjamin B. Washburn was appointed guardian ad litem for Rhoda Putty & Matilda Putty, femme coverts, and Marion Young, Nancy Young, Josiah Young, Polly Jane Young, Martha Young, the minor defendants. (Jac TN, Ch Ct Min, C/246) There were nine children & heirs-at-law of Worley Young. (Ibid 280) Dower was laid off. (Ibid 305) This suit was shown as James Y. Putty, Matilda Putty, Thomas Young, Wallace W. Davis, Elizabeth Davis, John L. Putty, Rhoda M. Putty, William Young vs Marion Young, Nancy Young, Josiah Young, Martha Young & Polly J. Young. The defendants are all minors & Benjamin B. Washburn is guardian ad litem. Land was sold. (Ibid 359 & 431)

YOUNGTON, ___
Died before 4 April 1870 when Cowles & Waits was paid for a pauper coffin. (Dyr TN, Co Ct Min, B/32)

YOWELL
6 November 1783 an order was issued to the Justices of Culpeper County, VA, to take the depositions of "Saml. Yowell & Jas. Yowell, Son to Chris & James Yowell Son to David on behalf of Saml. Leathers plaintiff vs Moses Broils defendant." (Was TN, Co Ct Min, 1/233)

ZELLERS, Thos.
Was a resident of Montgomery County, TN, on 9 October 1826 when his deposition was to be taken for the plaintiff in the case of William Terrell vs Daniel Dunnevant. (Obi TN, Cir Ct Min, 1/6)

ZIMMERMAN, J. J.
Died before 5 April 1870 when J. G. Tucker made a settlement as administrator. (Dyr TN, Co Ct Min, B/42)

APPENDIX

SOURCES

BEDFORD COUNTY Microfilm Roll No. 27
Clerk & Masters Minutes [Chancery Court Minutes] - 1830-1848

[Vol. 1], 1830-1842. There is no volume number on the microfilm. These are Bills, Answers, Decrees, etc. in Chancery Court. They are very long, very detailed and very difficult to read. It appears that this entire book has been recopied from the original. There are many obvious mistakes in names and spelling. 553 pages.

[Vol. 2], 1837-1845. There is no volume number on the microfilm. These appear to be the minutes of the Chancery Court. 379 pages.

[Vol. 3], 1840-1848. There is no volume number on the microfilm. These are not minutes but are Bills, Answers, etc., very long, apparently recopied from the original with some very bad handwriting with many obvious mistakes. 462 pages.

CLAIBORNE COUNTY Microfilm Roll No. 8
County Minutes - 1801-1817

[Vol 1], Dec. 1801-June 1802. There is no volume number on the microfilm. These are County Court Minutes ending with December 1803. Some pages are illegible. 189 pages.

Vol. 2, Mar. 1804-Sept. 1804. The dates shown on the microfilm label are incorrect. They go through June 1806. 279 pages.

[Vol. 3], Sept. 1806-Dec. 1808. There is no volume number on the microfilm. There are no minutes from December 1808 to August 1815. 251 pages

[Vol. 4], Aug. 1815-Aug. 1817. There is no volume number on the microfilm. 383 pages.

FENTRESS COUNTY Microfilm Roll No. 2
Chancery Court Minutes, 1854-1881. These Chancery Court minutes include the counties of Morgan and Scott. Only Vol. A was abstracted for this book.

Vol. A, Sept. 1854-Dec. 1868. There are no minutes from June, 1861 to October, 1865, Civil War. 433 pages.

DYER COUNTY Microfilm Roll No. 67
County Court Minutes

[Vol. B], Feb. 1865-Jan. 1870. [Actually February 1870 through September 1874]. There is no Vol. A. Vol. C was not abstracted. 786 pages

JACKSON COUNTY Microfilm Roll No. 1
Chancery Court Minutes - 1840-1860.

Vol. A, Nov. 1840-July 1851. 430 pages.

Vol. B, July 1851-Apr. 1856. 320 pages.

Vol. C, July 1856-Aug. 1860. Parts of this book are very dim and the handwriting very small. Some of it is illegible. 442 pages.

MADISON COUNTY   Microfilm Roll No. 366
Chancery Court Minutes - 1846-1869. The handwriting in these minutes varies, sometimes very good and sometimes very bad. There are some dim pages. Deciphering the vowels and the letters, "w", "n" and "m" was a challenge.

Vol. 1, 1846-1853. 371 pages.

Vol. 2, 1854-1866. The first 9 pages were used for a partial index. The minutes start on page 10. There were no minutes between February 1861 and February 1866 because of the Civil War. 550 pages.

Vol. 3, 1867-1869. This volume has very bad handwriting. 246 pages.

McMINN COUNTY   Microfilm Roll No. 82
County Court Minutes - 1819-1831.

[Vol. no#], Nov. 1819-June 1829. There is no volume number on the microfilm. 445 pages.

[Vol. 2no#], June 1824-June 1831. There is no volume number on the microfilm. Both of these volumes are called Court of Pleas & Quarter Sessions. Some of the dates overlap. The first book is mostly Court cases and the second book appears to be the other County business. Since the dates overlap, we have referred to the second volume as [2no#/--]. There are many irregularities: Pages 143-146 for March 1826 are inserted between pages 158 and 159; pages 253 & 254 are inserted between 240 & 241 and pages 252 through 267, Dec. 1827 & Mar. 1828, are mostly illegible because they are out of focus. There are a total of 540 pages in the volume.

OBION COUNTY   Microfilm Roll No. 6
Circuit Court Minutes

[Vol. 1], Oct. 1826-May 1832. There is no volume number on the microfilm. 249 pages.

[Vol. 2], May 1829-Nov. 1834. There is no volume number on the microfilm. The first 14 pages are a State Docket. Circuit Court Minutes start on page 15 with Nov. 1832. 234 pages.

[Vol. 3], May 1835-June 1839. There is no volume number on the microfilm. 381 pages.

[Vol. 4], Oct. 1839-Mar. 1845. There is no volume number on the microfilm. There are no page numbers.

ROANE COUNTY   Microfilm Roll No. 92
Court Minutes - 1801-1812

Vol. A, County Court Minutes   Dec. 1801-June 1805.   This book is mostly law suits.   353 pages.

Vol. B, June 1805-Sept. 1807.   352 pages.

Vol. C, Sept. 1807-Mar. 1809.   294 pages.

[Vol. D], Sept. 1808-Oct. 1812.   There is no volume number on the microfilm. 432 pages.

ROBERTSON COUNTY   Microfilm Roll No. 121
There is no heading on the microfilm box but the film shows the records to be County Court Minutes. There are volume numbers on the film. There are several indexes on the first part of the reel.

Vol. 1, July 1796-Oct. 1807.   477 pages.

Vol. 2, Jan. 1808-May 1811.   430 pages.

Vol 3, Aug. 1811-Feb. 1815.   571 pages.

SEVIER COUNTY   Microfilm Roll No. 15
County Court Minutes

[Vol. no#], Apr. 1856-June 1862.   There is no volume number on the microfilm. The court house burned 24 March 1856 and prior records were destroyed.   784 pages.

[Vol. no#], July 1862-Sept. 1867.   475 pages.

STEWART COUNTY   Microfilm Roll number 38
County Court Minutes, 1804-1825.

[Vol. 1], March 1804-Jan. 1807.   The microfilm is marked "Vol. 1804." Pages are numbered every other page through page no. 48. There are no page numbers following page no. 48. The writing is very dim and the handwriting is very bad.

[Vol. 2], 1808. The microfilm is marked "Vol. 1808." Contains various items. The first 17 pages are a partial tax list for 1808. Some pages are missing. There are bonds, wills, inventories, sales, guardian & apprentice bonds. Pages 115-121 are tax lists for 1809.   121 pages.

[Vol. 3], County Court Minutes - 1811 & 1812. The microfilm is marked "Vol 1812." Pages are mixed up, some are not numbered, some too dim to read and some are missing.   167 pages.

[Vol. 4], County Court Minutes - 1813-1815. The microfilm is marked "Vol. 1813-1815." This volume is marked "This Book is in poor condition." There are some torn pages and no page numbers after page 286. There are 47 unnumbered pages. The records then revert to some Minutes for 1809 and 1810.

WASHINGTON COUNTY Microfilm Roll No. 129
Minutes - 1778-1809

Vol. 1, County Court Minutes - Jan. 1778-May 1798. [Should be Feb. 1778-May 1798]. There is a typed index. The first 20 pages are blank. This book was recopied from the original in 1887. The minutes skip from Aug. 1790 to Feb. 1794 and again from Aug. 1796 to Feb. 1798. 640 pages.

[Vol. no#], Starts in Nov. 1788 and is duplicated in Vol. 1 up to page 103. Starting on page 103, Nov. 1790, until May 1793, all the records in this volume are trials. There are two page numbers on each page and we have used the one at the bottom of the page. 134 pages.

WILSON COUNTY Microfilm Roll No. 150
Court Min. - 1803-1819. [County Court Minute Books]

[Vol. no#], Dec. 1803-June 1807. There is no volume number on the microfilm. Some tax lists are included. 331 pages.

[Vol. P&J], Jan. 1812-Nov. 1819. There is no volume number on the microfilm. This is a book of Pleas & Judgements and referred to as "P&J" in these abstracts. There are some items as early as 1808. There are no page numbers and some dates are out of order.

[Vol. Reg. Bk.], June 1814-May 1829. These are not minutes but are records from a Registers Book and are cited as "Reg. Bk." in these abstracts. Pages are numbered from 1 through 420. Page numbers 319 through 403 are repeated. These repeated page numbers are shown as "(Second set of page numbers)" following the citation and the abstracts contain different items from those on the original numbered pages 319-403. There are 4 unnumbered pages at the end of the book and a page number 208 appears as the last page. This book contains bills of sale, powers of attorney and articles of agreement. There is a partial index but the pages are mixed up.

[Vol. no#], June 1816-Nov. 1819. These are County Court Minutes. The first part of the book is very badly damaged and some pages are out of order. There is an index in the back. Apparently the Court Minutes from Nov. 1807 to June 1816 are missing. 547 pages.

INDEX

Aaron, Jacob 1
Aaron, John 1
Aaron, John Jacob 1
Abbott, Tabitha 264
Abell, Ezekiel 69, 236
Abington, John T. 299
Acklen, William 39
Acklin, William 46
Acthley, B. M. 233
Acuff, Joel 1
Adair, Robert 1
Adair, William 38, 69
Adams, Abner 1
Adams, Allen 1
Adams, Elijah 1
Adams, Elizabeth Ann 1
Adams, Geo. W. 1
Adams, Harper 1
Adams, Hiram 1
Adams, J. S. 1
Adams, James 1, 218
Adams, John 1, 5, 132, 215
Adams, Josephine 1
Adams, Lydia 300
Adams, Lysander 19, 21, 70, 223, 300
Adams, M. C. 1
Adams, Mary B. 1
Adams, Mich 1
Adams, Minos C. 1
Adams, Mosses 16
Adams, Nancy 1
Adams, Nathan 1
Adams, R. W. 276
Adams, Sterling 1
Adams, William 1, 33, 72, 87, 101, 120, 133, 151, 161
Adamson, William 1
Adcock, John 238
Adcock, William 138
Adkins, Elisha 1
Adkins, Henderson W. 2
Adkins, James T. 1
Adkins, Joseph 1
Adkins, Mary B. 2
Adkins, William 1
Adkinson, Joshua 2
Adlridge, Margaret 113
Agee, W. T. 81
Aiken, Sarah E. 2
Ailey, Isaac 2
Ailey, John 2
Ailey, Martha 2
Ailey, Nancy 2
Ailey, William 2
Ails, William 2
Aimes, Hardy 177
Aire, Henry 2
Airs, Elizabeth 36, 190
Airs, Henry 336
Aken, Aaron Johnson 2
Aken, Harrison 2
Akin, A. J. 253
Akin, E. L. 2
Akin, Edward L. 2
Akin, Francis 2
Akin, Jas. 2

Akin, Joseph 2
Akin, L. J. 2
Akin, Lucy J. 2
Akin, M. E. 2
Akin, Martha El. 2
Akin, Robert 2, 253
Akin, William 2
Albright, Jacob 142
Albright, Joel 87
Albright, Levin 111
Albright, Louisa 111
Albright, William 111
Alcorn, Elizabeth 50
Alcorn, John 50
Alderson, Alexander 2
Alderson, James C. 3
Alderson, Simon 2
Aldridge, Caroline J. 114
Aldridge, Isaac 3
Aldridge, James 114
Aldridge, Jessie N. 114
Aldridge, John 113, 114
Aldridge, Kizah 113
Aldridge, Mary 3
Aldridge, Peggy 114
Aldridge, Rily 113
Alexander, Arthur 58
Alexander, Azariah 23
Alexander, C. M. 290
Alexander, Daniel 124
Alexander, Elizabeth L. 290
Alexander, Ezekiel 25
Alexander, John 331
Alexander, L. D. 38
Alexander, Nancy 58
Alexander, Nathaniel 3
Alexander, Robert 208
Alexander, Wm. 103, 331
Alford, Hutson 3, 75
Alfred [a slave] 88
Algee, James 3
Algood, William 196
Allan, Hugh P. 141
Allan, James M. 128
Allard, James M. 3
Allard, Jose M. 7
Allard, Mary 3, 7
Allcorn, Elizabeth 71
Allcorn, J. 256
Allcorn, John 30, 34, 214
Allen, A. J. 4
Allen, A. R. 3
Allen, Absolem 3, 23, 67, 234
Allen, Alexr. 5
Allen, Amanda 5, 284
Allen, Andrew 5
Allen, Ann Coke 3
Allen, Barbara A. 4
Allen, Bertie 296
Allen, Betsey 4
Allen, Beverly 3, 39, 141, 191
Allen, Cyrus N. 266
Allen, Delila 5
Allen, Elizabeth 3, 4
Allen, Emilia 4

Allen, George D. 140
Allen, George S. 295
Allen, Gideon 4
Allen, Helen 3
Allen, Hugh P. 140
Allen, James 3
Allen, John 3, 4, 5, 55, 69, 162, 230, 240, 252, 283, 304
Allen, Jonathan 4
Allen, Judith 4
Allen, Lucy A. 4, 5
Allen, Lydia 4
Allen, Mary 3
Allen, Mary Darcus 5, 284
Allen, Matilda E. 4
Allen, Milley 4, 5
Allen, Moses 4, 222
Allen, Neal 4
Allen, Rebecca 83, 296
Allen, Richard 3
Allen, Salina 4
Allen, Sally 4, 5
Allen, Sampson 63
Allen, Sandford 4
Allen, Sarah 3, 4
Allen, Susan 83
Allen, Thomas 21, 76, 331
Allen, Virena H. 4
Allen, William 4, 5, 56, 172, 186, 229-230, 254
Alley, Herbert 5
Alley, John William 5
Alley, Stephen 33
Allin, Jonathan 27
Allison, Charles 184
Allison, David 52, 341
Allison, Davidson 5
Allison, Esther 5
Allison, Francis 5, 342
Allison, Hugh 5, 287
Allison, Isabell 5
Allison, Jame 5
Allison, Jane 5
Allison, John 5
Allison, Peggy 5
Allison, Rachael E. 5
Allison, Robert 5, 6, 40
Allison, Sally 5
Allison, Thomas 5
Allison, William 5, 16
Allrorn, John 71
Almira [a slave] 141
Alsop, Hiram 6
Alsop, John 6
Alsop, Prudence 6
Alsop, Sterling 6
Alsop, William 6
Alston, Augustus B. 149
Alston, C. H. 176
Alston, Hardaway 269
Alston, James 6
Alston, Jno. 6, 68, 74, 116, 148, 311
Alston, Judy Frances 149
Alston, Lydia 6, 116
Alston, Mary 6

Alston, Phillip 6, 116
Alston, Sarah 6
Alsup, Asa   6
Alsup, Asaph 240
Alsup, David 6
Alsup, Elizabeth 6
Alsup, Joseph 6
Alsup, Richard 6
Alsup, William 6
Amery, Thomas 308
Ames, John 6
Ames, Nathan 6
Ames, Thomas 6
Amey [a slave] 281
Ammonett, James 6
Ammonett, John H. 198
Ammonett, Nancy B. 6
Amonett, Artema 152
Amonett, Benjamin F. 6
Amonett, James 6, 152
Amonett, Martha P. 6
Amonett, Mary A. 152
Amonett, Tennessee G. 6
Amonett, Virginia 6
Amonett, William 6, 152
Amonett, Willis 152
Amorett, James 152
Amsy [a slave] 96
Amy [a slave] 79
Anderson, A. C. 6
Anderson, Andrew T. 8
Anderson, Anna 7, 8
Anderson, C. D. 71
Anderson, Caleb 7
Anderson, Cinderella 7, 186
Anderson, Cornelius 271
Anderson, Daniel 7
Anderson, Edward 7, 8, 186, 198, 247
Anderson, Elizabeth 7, 8
Anderson, F. M. 7 8
Anderson, Francis 7-8
Anderson, Garland 7, 8
Anderson, Isaac 7
Anderson, J. D. 7
Anderson, James 303
Anderson, Jane 8
Anderson, John 7, 22, 43, 109-110
Anderson, Joseph 7
Anderson, Jubal 8
Anderson, Judith 7, 8
Anderson, Margaret 7
Anderson, Martha Jane 7
Anderson, Mary 7, 43
Anderson, Mathew 268
Anderson, Nancy 268
Anderson, Patrick 7
Anderson, Paul   7, 8,163
Anderson, Perry 286
Anderson, Peter 157
Anderson, Polly   288
Anderson, R. J. 104
Anderson, Richard 172
Anderson, Robert 7
Anderson, Sally 157
Anderson, Samuel S. 277

Anderson, Sarah 7, 313
Anderson, Silas   7, 8
Anderson, Susannah 163
Anderson, Thomas 7, 8
Anderson, Vancil W. 7, 8
Anderson, W. P. 43
Anderson, William 7, 8, 34, 43, 296, 301, 322
Anderton, William 8
Andes, John 174, 234
Andres, B. C. 145
Andrew, Andrew T. 7
Andrews, Amanda 82
Andrews, Anderson 187
Andrews, E. W. 291
Andrews, Edwin J. 174
Andrews, Etheldred 8
Andrews, Jno. T.82
Andrews, Thomas M. 30
Andrews, William 8
Aney [a slave] 263
Aninece [a slave] 209
Ann [a slave] 291
Anna [a salve] 214
Anthony, Jacob 8
Anthony, Phillip 118
Antwine, A. P. 8
Antwine, Martha 8
Antwine, N. J. 8
Antwine, S. E. 8
Antwine, W. T. 8
Apple, David 108
Apple, Elizabeth 8
Apple, George 8, 198
Apple, Jackson C. 8
Apple, Mary 8, 198
Apple, Neadin 8
Apple, Peggy An 291
Apple, Ridley 199, 291
Applegate, James M. 8
Appleton, Henrietta 9
Appleton, James 8, 9
Appleton, John 8, 9
Appleton, Lenore 9
Appleton, Susanna 9
Appleton, Thomas 8, 162, 236, 331, 335
Applewhite, Harry 9
Applewhite, Henry 9, 135
Applewhite, John J. 9
Applewhite, Mary 9
Applewhite, Polly M. 303
Applewhite, Richard 9
Applewhite, William H. 9
Arbuckle, Catherine 9
Archer, Moses 38
Archer, Richard H. 333
Archibald, Richard B. 9
Armestead, W. B. 117
Armstead, Geo. E. 9
Armstead, James 185
Armstead, John 9, 110
Armstead, Julia V. 9
Armstead, Martha 9, 185
Armstead, W. B. 187
Armstead, Wm. H. 9
Armstrong, Benjamin D. 9

Armstrong, Elizabeth 9
Armstrong, Francis H. 160
Armstrong, George C. 205
Armstrong, J. N. 125
Armstrong, James 30, 205, 236, 296, 301
Armstrong, Jane 9
Armstrong, John 9, 23, 205
Armstrong, Joseph 9
Armstrong, Landon 141
Armstrong, Lucy 16
Armstrong, Luke T. 6
Armstrong, Martin 9, 79
Armstrong, Mason P. 301
Armstrong, Nancy 9
Armstrong, Nelly 9
Armstrong, P. M. 211
Armstrong, Polly 9
Armstrong, Rebecca 205
Armstrong, Sally 9
Armstrong, Samuel M.9
Armstrong, Thomas 9
Armstrong, W. F. 9
Armstrong, William 9, 16, 106, 296
Arnet, Nathan 250
Arnold, Booker 9
Arnold, Colbert 102
Arnold, Cooly 9
Arnold, Creesey 9
Arnold, Euliana 9
Arnold, Francis 9
Arnold, Henry 9
Arnold, James H. 286
Arnold, John 9, 21, 91
Arnold, L. N. 286
Arnold, Louisa 286
Arnold, Martha 9-10
Arnold, Martin 9-10
Arnold, Michael 9
Arnold, Nancy 9
Arnold, Polly 9
Arnold, Richardson 9
Arnold, Robert F. 42
Arnold, Thomas 9, 317
Asbel, Pierce 10
Ashburn, Austin E. 47
Ashburn, Clemant 47
Ashburn, Hazzard T. 47
Ashburn, Jastina E. 47
Ashburn, Jessee 109, 325
Ashburn, Mary 47
Ashburn, Thomas F. 47
Ashley, Noah 98, 308
Ashmore, Joshua 305
Ashworth, Cassandy 20
Ashworth, Jasper 20, 21
Assee, John G. 23, 50, 320
Assee, Michael M. 332
Ast, Frederick 10
Asters, Alexander 205
Atchely, Micajah   10
Atchley, Albert S. 10
Atchley, Aramicia 10
Atchley, Benjamin 10, 304, 318

Atchley, Joshua H. 55, 135, 150
Atchley, Martha 10
Atchley, Mary H. 174
Atchley, McCajah 10, 174
Atchley, McCamel 10
Atchley, Patience 10
Atchley, R. S. 4
Atchley, Thomas 10, 182
Atchley, William 10, 129, 159
Atchly, B. M. 10
Atchly, Enoch 10
Atchly, Isaac 10
Atchly, J. H. 252
Atchly, James H. 10
Atchly, John 10
Atchly, Joshua 269
Atchly, Malissa 10
Atchly, Martha A. 10
Atchly, Mary 10
Atchly, P. J. 10, 290
Atchly, Thos. 10
Atchly, William 10, 252, 269
Atkin, T. H. 253
Atkins, Anthony 10
Atkins, George 10
Atkins, Henry 10
Atkins, James 10
Atkins, John 152
Atkins, Joseph 10
Atkins, Joshua 10
Atkins, William 10, 11
Atkinson, Eliza 11
Atkinson, Joseph 11
Atkinson, Joshua 2, 11
Atkinson, Martha 11
Atkinson, Polly 11
Atkinson, William 11
Atkison, James 11
Atkison, John 11
Atterberry, George W. 141
Atterberry, Hannah 141
Aust, Frederick 11, 313
Austin, Harris 327
Austin, Nathaniel 263
Averett, Joshua 11
Averitt, Littleton 137
Averitt, Sarah 137
Avery, George 296
Avery, H. B. 11
Avery, Jonas 11
Avery, Weightstel 39
Aydolett, John 11
Ayer, Alexander L. 11
Ayer, Alpha K. 11
Ayer, Lewis M. 11
Ayer, Margaret 11
Ayer, Mary T. 11
Ayer, Nancy 11
Ayer, Sophia 11
Ayer, Thos. J. 11
Ayer, William B. 11
Ayer, Zaccheus 11, 88
Ayers, Amos 11
Ayers, Daniel R. 11
Ayers, David B. 11

Ayers, Elizabeth 11
Ayers, James W. 11
Ayers, Joseph C. 11
Ayers, Salina P. 11
Ayers, Susan J. 11
Ayers, Susanna 11
Ayers, Thorp 11
Babb, Bennett 11, 124
Babb, Burwell 11, 191
Babb, Ruth 300
Babb, William 2, 11, 300
Backus, William 12
Bacon, Francis 335
Bacon, Joseph B. 23, 110
Bacon, Michl. 72, 143
Bail, Daniel W. 94
Bail, David W. 94
Bailes, John C. 94
Bailes, William 12
Bailey, Andrew 12
Bailey, John 5, 183, 229
Bailey, Kar 249
Bailey, Lucy 12
Bailey, Mary A. 12
Bailey, Nancy 12
Bailey, Wesley 12
Bailey, William 12, 194
Baily, A. B. 196
Baily, Thomas 124
Bain, Alexander 12
Bain, James 5, 12, 21
Bain, Susan 21
Baine, James 12
Baine, Susen M. 12
Baird, Alexander 30
Baird, Ann 12
Baird, David 12
Baird, Elisha 26
Baird, John 12
Baird, Matilda 12
Baird, W. B. 12
Baird, William 12
Baird, Zebulon 243
Baits, Isaac 12
Baker, Abram 241
Baker, Andrew 13
Baker, Arthur 13
Baker, Delila 13
Baker, E. A. 13
Baker, E. H. 13
Baker, Elizabeth 12, 13
Baker, F. M. 56
Baker, Fanny 13
Baker, Francis 12
Baker, G. T. 13
Baker, H. B. 210
Baker, Ham 12
Baker, Henry 12, 221, 249
Baker, James 12-13, 32, 66, 95, 156, 324
Baker, Jo. R. 13
Baker, Joe 12
Baker, John 13, 134, 292
Baker, Kemp 13
Baker, Margaret 13
Baker, Martin 13
Baker, Michael 13, 111, 245

Baker, Morgan W. 13
Baker, N. M. 16, 22, 315
Baker, Nathanl. 13
Baker, Sarah Ann 13
Baker, Thomas 14, 276
Baker, William 13, 206, 281
Baker, Zachariah 13
Balch, Alfred 179, 286
Baler, William 121
Bales, Isaac Wm. 13
Bales, James 13
Bales, John 13
Bales, Leroy 13
Bales, Margaret 13
Bales, Nancy A. C. 13
Bales, Robert 13
Ball, Lewis 13
Ballard, Benjamin P. 198
Ballard, Elijah 112
Ballard, Nancy 121, 336
Ballard, Samuel 336
Ballard, Sandford 121
Ballard, Susan 197, 198
Ballen, William 215
Ballentine, Andrew 206
Ballentine, James 13
Ballentine, Jane 13
Balmer, Catherine 231
Balzea, J. S. 14
Bandy, Epison 14
Bandy, Jamison 14
Bandy, Joseph 14
Bandy, Milcher 14
Bandy, Peron 14
Bandy, Richard 14
Bandy, Solomon 14
Bandy, Velshar 96
Banks, Enock 14
Banks, Robert 14
Barbary [a slave] 202
Barbee, John 19
Barbee, Polly 19
Barber, Casandra 186
Barber, Ferdinand C. 45
Barber, Joel D. 14
Barber, John 186
Barbour, Joel D. 266
Barby, John 294
Barclay, Elihu 14, 236
Barclay, Eliza 236
Barclay, James 220
Barclay, Thomas 100, 176
Barcley, George 332
Barefoot, Thomas 14
Baren, Hosea 20
Bargess, John 40
Barker, Alexander 14
Barker, Ann 180
Barker, Bird 14
Barker, Burt 14
Barker, Hincha 14
Barker, James 14
Barker, Joel D. 14
Barker, Philip 14
Barker, Susan 14
Barker, Thomas 14
Barksdale, Daniel 14, 183

Barksdale, Wm. W.183
Barkson, Aron 14
Barley, Walter 14
Barlick, John 332
Barnes, Charles 14
Barnes, James 183
Barnet, A. M. 14
Barnet, Finis E. 15
Barnet, James Y. 15
Barnet, Robert 167
Barnet, Stephen B. 329
Barnett, A. M. 15
Barnett [a slave] 316
Barnett, Burton 295
Barnett, Ed 15, 20
Barnett, Elizabeth 15
Barnett, Isaac 295
Barnett, James M. 255
Barnett, John 15, 26, 255
Barnett, Lucindy 295
Barnett, Martha 15
Barnett, Robert 15
Barnett, William 26, 266
Barns, Fanny 15
Barns, John 322
Barns, Nancy 15
Barns, William H. 157
Barnt, Aicey L. 113
Barr, Benjamin 97
Barr, Sarah 97, 152
Barrett, [no name] 15
Barrow, James 188
Bartle, Anna 7
Bartlet, Joshua 198
Bartlett, Anna 8
Bartlett, Isaac 15
Bartlett, J. W. 15, 259
Bartlett, Joshua 7
Bartlett, Nancy 330
Bartlett, William 330
Barton, Gabriel 15
Barton, Gilbreath 341
Barton, Samuel 15, 89
Barton, Stephen 15
Bascom, William 15
Basey, H. T. 15
Baskins, William 15, 257
Bass, Dred 73
Bass, Dredden 73
Bass, Etheldred 16
Bass, Ezekiel 16, 281
Bass, Jno. F. 16
Bass, Lucy 16
Bass, Scion 16
Bass, Solomon 16
Bass, Theophilus 16
Bates, Elizabeth 16
Bates, Richard 16
Bates, Robert 274
Bates, William H. 71
Batt, Rebecca 16
Batte, Henry 16
Batte, Wm. P. 16
Battle, Jacob 106
Battle, Jeremiah 106
Battle, Orrin D. 106, 335
Battle, Sarah 106

Batts, Frederick 16
Batts, Jeremiah 207
Batts, John 16
Batts, Nancy 16
Batts, Polly 16
Batts, Rebecca 16
Batts, Rodah 16
Batts, Sally 16
Batts, William H. 71
Baxter, Calvin 16
Baxter, Catherine 16
Baxter, Eliza 16
Baxter, Fletcher 16
Baxter, James 16, 71
Baxter, Jeremiah 16, 71, 72
Baxter, Katherine 16,
Baxter, Mandy 16
Baxter, Montgomery 16
Baxter, Nancy 16
Baxter, Nathaniel 16
Baxter, Sally 16
Baxter, Wm. A. 31
Bayless, John 16, 209
Bayless, Reuben 127
Bayless, Wilie 17
Bayley, Delilah 16
Bayley, Eliza Jane 16
Bayley, Jeremiah 16
Bayley, Peleg 16
Bayliss, Wilie 17
Bayly, Dicey Ann 16
Bayly, Joseph W. 16
Beadles, Thomas 17
Beal, Vincent 20
Bean, Charley 17
Bean, D. P. 17
Bean, Ellis 174
Bean, Emeline 17
Bean, George 17, 27
Bean, James 23
Bean, Jesse 17
Bean, John 107
Bean, Jordan 17
Bean, Pleasant 17
Bean, Robert 17
Bean, Roda Jane 17
Bean, Sarah R. 17
Bean, William 17
Beard, A. 311
Beard, Alexander 15
Beard, John 91
Beard, Mary Jane 25
Beard, William 12, 25, 121
Bearden, Allen 17
Bearden, Charlotte 17
Bearden, Eli M. 17
Bearden, Elizabeth 17
Bearden, John T.17
Bearden, Minerva 17
Bearden, Nathan 17
Bearden, Nimrod 17
Bearden, Willis 17
Bearden, Wynn 17
Beardin, Nancy 17
Bearding, Eli M. 17
Beasley, Anna B. 17

Beasley, Bemmy B. 158
Beasley, Benney B. 17
Beasley, Dillard 17
Beasley, Ephraim 17
Beasley, Isham D. 199
Beasley, Josiah 17, 199
Beasley, Polly 17
Beasley, Sarah Ann 17
Beasley, Terriceann 17
Beasley, Tracy Ann 17
Beasley, W. N. 52, 61, 104, 166, 188, 236, 252, 261, 319, 332
Beasley, W. W. 151
Beasly, Bemmy 17
Beason, J. H. 18
Beason, James H.17, 18, 76, 98-99, 201-202, 242-243
Beason, Mary 18, 242
Beason, Moses 236
Beathal, Danl. 18
Beaton, Christopher 18
Beaton, John 18
Beatty, Hugh 18
Beaty, Alfred G. 19
Beaty, Andrew Jackson 18
Beaty, Anna 18
Beaty, Armilda 18
Beaty, Betsy 18
Beaty, Cicero 18-19
Beaty, Claborn 108
Beaty, Cyntha 18
Beaty, Dalles 18
Beaty, David 18, 108, 230
Beaty, Edward S.18, 19
Beaty, Elvira 18-19
Beaty, Englantine 18
Beaty, F. A. 18, 19
Beaty, George 18
Beaty, James 18
Beaty, John 18
Beaty, Margarett 18
Beaty, Martha E. 19
Beaty, Martin 211, 265
Beaty, Mary 18, 19
Beaty, May 18,19
Beaty, Melly 18
Beaty, Milla 18
Beaty, Pleasant 18
Beaty, Polk 18
Beaty, Posey 18, 19
Beaty, Ruth A. 19
Beaty, Thos. D. 18, 19
Beaty, Warren G. 19
Beaty, William 18
Beaumont, Walter 19
Beavers, Thomas 19
Beck, Allice B. 19
Beck, Ann 19, 60
Beck, Elihu 19
Beck, Jesse Z. 19
Beck, Mary G. 19
Beck, Nathaniel T. 19
Beck, Reubin 19, 60
Beck, Sarah F. 19
Beck, Susan E. 19

Beck, William A. 19
Beckers, Henry C, 162
Becton, Frederick 342
Becton, Robert 202
Bedford, Jonas 19
Bedford, Jubilee 17, 19, 21 300
Bedford, Seth 6, 19, 21, 233, 300
Bedford, Thos. 19
Bedwell, Thomas 19
Beely, Abraham 94
Been, Wm. 9, 211
Beet, Frank 19
Begart, Henry 126
Beggin, Mary 262
Beisser, John 19
Bell, Benjamin 20
Bell, Catharine M. M. 19
Bell, E. A. 20
Bell, Elizabeth 20
Bell, Fielders 19
Bell, Fielding 19
Bell, Francis 19
Bell, George 19
Bell, Hugh F. 222
Bell, James 20, 49
Bell, James W. 19
Bell, Jarot 230
Bell, John 19-20, 45, 93, 221, 271, 274, 325
Bell, Leander 20
Bell, Margaret 19
Bell, Martha 19
Bell, Mary M. 20
Bell, Matthew 20
Bell, Polly Ann 19
Bell, Rebecca 20, 263
Bell, Robert 43
Bell, S. V. 283
Bell, Samuel 20, 24-25, 115, 283
Bell, Sarah 185
Bell, Sarah M. 19
Bell, T. F. 253
Bell, T. H. 89, 316
Bell, Thomas 20, 185, 262
Bell, William 19-20, 31
Bellows, Sarah 63
Beloate, Charles R. 85, 298
Beloate, Elizabeth R. 85
Beloate, Reginald H. 85, 298
Beloate, Saml. D. 85, 298
Beloate, V. C. 85
Beloate, Wm. D. 85, 298
Beloute, Elizabeth 297
Belt, Benjamin 20
Belt, Dodson 20
Belt, Jeremiah 20
Belt, Middleton 20
Belt, William 20
Belyen, Abraham 63
Benckley, Jacob 329
Bennett, John 119
Bennett, Matilda 214
Bennett, Polly 214

Benson, J. W. 20
Benson, James H. 104
Benson, Matilda 214
Benson, N. A. 20
Benson, S. E. 20
Benson, Spencer 20
Benson, Wm. 238, 247
Benten, F. H. 61
Benthal, Daniel 20
Benthal, David 20
Benthal, Mary 20
Benthal, Wm. 16
Bentley, K. H. 101
Bentley, Martha 101
Bentley, Paulina 101
Bentley, W. R. 101
Benton, F. H. 99
Benton, Floyd 20
Benton, Jesse 20
Benton, L. H. 69
Benton, Maecenas 20
Benton, Prissie 20
Benton, Richard J. 113
Benton, T. H. 69, 166, 288, 310
Beren, Bazel 20
Bernard, George 122
Bernhaimes, Simeon 223
Berry, George 184
Berry, John 168
Berry, Mark 20
Berryhill, William 21
Bessent, Anna 21
Bessent, James Harvey 21
Bessent, P. R. 21
Betsy [a slave] 341
Betters, Washington 21
Bettis, G. W. 125, 164, 318
Bettis, George W. 226, 227
Bettis, M. V. 164
Bettis, Wyatt 261
Betts, Evender 21
Betts, Franklin 21
Betts, Isaac W. 21
Betts, John J. 21
Betts, Leonidias 21
Betts, Lovel 21
Betts, Pereniah 21
Betts, Seldon 21
Betts, Stokley 21
Betts, William S. 21
Beunch, Thomas 26
Beverly, John 21
Bevers, Lemuel 21
Bible, Thomas F. 124
Bigbe, George 59
Bigelow, M. O. 298
Bigen, Matthew 21, 91
Biger, Matthew 21
Biggerstaff, Aaron 141
Biggerstaff, Benjamin 141
Biggerstaff, David 6
Biggerstaff, Elizabeth 141
Biggirs, Mary 262
Biggs, Didamia 21
Biggs, Elijah 97
Biggs, Francis 21

Biggs, Sam 21
Biggs, W. W. 21
Biggs, Wm. 245
Bigham, Samuel 137
Bill [a slave] 269
Billings, David 50
Billingsly, Walter 188
Billors, Leonard 139
Binar [a slave] 214
Binckley, Jacob 216
Binkley, Daniel 21
Binkley, Jacob 151
Binkley, John 21
Binkley, Peter 21
Binor, Kiziah 77
Binor, William L. 77
Birch, George 22
Birch, Henry 22
Birch, John 159
Birch, S. 22
Birchett, Eliza 259
Birchfield, R. 315
Bird, A. 22
Bird [a slave] 30
Bird, Adam 22, 32, 108
Bird, Amos 156, 315
Bird, Blackman H. 211
Bird, Bryant 22
Bird, Drury 230
Bird, James 44
Bird, John 22, 108, 182, 257, 259-260, 278, 315
Bird, Lucinda 108
Bird, Mark 22, 316
Bird, Mary Ann 22
Bird, Nancy 22
Bird, Shadrack 22
Bird, Thomas 22, 65
Bird, William 22
Birdsong, Ephraim 22
Birdsong, G. M. 22, 246
Birdsong, Geo. 25, 172
Birdsong, Jno. C. 22, 25, 246
Birdsong, Margaret 22
Birdsong, Mary 22
Birdsong, Rebecca 22
Birdsong, Susan 22
Birdsong, T. R. 22
Birdsong, Wm. 22
Birdwell, Reuel 308
Bishop, Josoph 23
Black, Claiborne W. 174
Black, Frances 42
Black, Hiram 23
Black, Jamas 17
Black, John 186
Black, Jonathan 23
Black, Mary 23
Black, Nancy 42
Black, Thomas 16
Black, William 23, 50, 320
Blackburn, Benjn. 23
Blackburn, Thomas 294
Blackburn, William 23, 61
Blackman, Caroline 162
Blackman, Catharine 162

Blackman, Elisha 162
Blackman, Ellenor 162
Blackman, J. B. 162
Blackman, James J. 162, 163
Blackman, Jeremiah 162
Blackman, John E. 162
Blackman, Letha 162
Blackman, Mary 162
Blackman, Nelson 162
Blackman, Susanah 162
Blackman, William J. 162
Blackmore, Henry S. 185
Blackmore, Margaret 185
Blackwell, Benj. 114
Blackwell, Elisha 163
Blackwell, John B. 295
Blackwell, Riley 101
Blackwell, Susan 163
Blagg, Henry 194
Blain, James 23
Blain, John 23
Blain, William 23
Blair, Eli M. 23
Blair, Elizabeth 298
Blair, G. W. 80
Blair, H. S. 25
Blair, Harrison 298
Blair, Hiram S. 23
Blair, James 23, 319
Blair, Jno. 23
Blair, Joseph 23
Blair, Martha 23
Blair, Mary 23
Blair, Oliver H. 23
Blair, Sally 23
Blair, Samuel 25
Blair, Thos. 202
Blake, B. F. 23
Blake, B. L. 51
Blake, Benjamin L. 51
Blake, Martha J. 51
Blake, Thomas 170
Blakeman, Martha 29
Blakemore, Daniel 23
Blakemore, Martha 29
Blakemore, Thomas 29
Blalock, Charles 146, 189
Bland, Elizabeth 24
Bland, Matthew M. 24
Bland, Milton M. 24
Bland, Nelson 24
Bland, Sally 24
Blankenship, G. W. 24
Blankenship, J. H. 24
Blankenship, R. A. 24
Blankenship, Rebecca 24
Blankingship, C. 24
Blankinship, G. W. 154
Blankinship, James 9
Blankinship, Rebecca 9
Blanks, James 69
Blanton, Burwell 24
Blanton, Charles 24
Blanton, Elizabeth P. 24
Blanton, Henderson G. 24
Blanton, Henson G. 24
Blanton, Horace 24

Blanton, Jasper N. 24
Blanton, Joseph N. 24
Blanton, Nancy 4
Blanton, Sanford 24
Blanton, Sarah 24
Blanton, Smith 24
Blanton, Wilkins 24, 33
Blanton, Wilkis 24
Blanton, William 24
Blanton, Willis 24
Blaydes, James 181
Blaylock, Charles 335
Blazer, Jacob 90
Bledso, Anthony H. 24
Bledsoe, A. 18, 242
Bledsoe, A. B. 162, 242
Bledsoe, B. F. 24, 98
Bledsoe, E. B. 24
Bledsoe, Horace 252
Bledsoe, M. B. 24
Bledsoe, M. M. 64
Bledsoe, R. H. 209, 340
Bledsoe, Sarah 24
Bledsoe, W. S. 18
Bloodworth, Alfred 79
Bloodworth, Jesse 24
Bloodworth, Polly 79
Bloodworth, William 57, 284
Blount, Wilie 218
Blue, John L. 67
Blythe, Martha 23
Blythe, Saml. 23
Boatwright, W. T. 92
Boaz, James 24
Boaz, Josiah 24
Boaz, Mary 24
Boaz, Thomas E. 24, 25, 33, 283
Boaz, William 25
Bob [a slave] 17, 80, 281
Bobbitt, Arthur 25
Bobbitt, Jno. R. 25
Bobo, Elisha 232
Bodine, Mary 25
Bodine, Wesley 25
Bogart, Abraham 245
Bogart, Jane 245
Bogart, Lemuel 4, 146
Bogart, Soloman 294
Bogle, Hiram 80-81
Bogle, Jannett 25, 177
Bogle, Joseph 25
Bogle, Samuel 25
Bogle, William R. 25
Bohannan, Wm. 228
Bohannon, James 25
Bohannon, Sophia 25
Boles, Elizabeth J. 25
Boles, James 291
Boles, John 25
Boles, R. 227
Boles, Samuel 25
Boles, William H. 25
Bolin, Elizabeth 291
Bolin, William 291
Boling, A. 45
Bolinger, Nancy 11

Bond, Amon 26
Bond, B. F. 22-23, 25
Bond, Benjamin 26
Bond, Damon 26
Bond, Dawson 26, 57, 223
Bond, Eaten 26
Bond, Elisha 26
Bond, Francis A. 25
Bond, Geo. W. 25
Bond, George H. 25-26
Bond, Georgia 25
Bond, Hance 26
Bond, Henry 25
Bond, James 26
Bond, John 25-26, 65
Bond, Lelia 26
Bond, Lewis 26
Bond, Martha E. 26
Bond, Mary 25
Bond, Millisa 26
Bond, Peter 26
Bond, R. C. G. 25
Bond, Robert C. G. 26
Bond, Sallie 26
Bond, Solomon 26, 41
Bond, T. B. 26
Bond, Thomas 26
Bond, W. L. 26
Bond, William 26
Bone, James T. 92
Bone, John 291
Bone, no name 174
Bone, William 174
Bonner, Ezekiel 23, 110
Bonner, John 26, 300
Boo, R. A. 26
Booker [a slave] 324-325
Boon, Ben F. 27
Boon, Frankie E. 27
Boon, Henry 27
Boon, J. J. 193
Boon, J. M. 27
Boon, James W. 27
Boon, Jeannette 145
Boon, John J. 192-193
Boon, Laura A. 27
Boon, Luella 27
Boon, Martha 27
Boon, Mary 27
Boon, Nathan 14, 27, 304
Boon, Susan J. 27
Boon, W. H. 27,
Boon, William 27, 320
Boone, Ben F. 27
Boone, D. M. 27, 245
Boone, E. D. 27
Boone, Francis E. 27
Boone, Henry 27
Boone, Israel 27
Boone, James H. 27
Boone, Jeanetta 27
Boone, Jesse 27, 65
Boone, John 113
Boone, Martha 27
Boone, William 27, 135
Boren, Bazel 20
Boren, James 23, 27

Boren, Jane 23
Boring, Absolom 27, 227
Boring, John Dasey 27, 69
Borrow, Ephraim 42
Botts, Seth 131
Botts, W. H. 243
Botts, William 50, 54, 93-94
108, 196, 266, 268, 272,
296, 323-324 344
Bouden, B. O. 108
Bouden, W. B. 18
Boun, Bazel 201
Bounds, James 27
Bounds, Jesse 27
Bow, Henry W. 99
Bowden, B. C. 325
Bowden, B. O. 24, 230, 256
Bowden, Baily O.143, 153
Bowen, Chana 27
Bowen, Ebenezer 28
Bowen, Henry 17, 27
Bowen, J. B. 27
Bowen, J. H. 28
Bowen, J. L. 28
Bowen, James 319
Bowen, John 28
Bowen, Lily Dora 28
Bowen, R. D. 28
Bowen, William 28
Bowers, Anderson 224
Bowers, Benjamin 28
Bowers, David 28
Bowers, Elizabeth 28
Bowers, Evelina 21
Bowers, Giles 28
Bowers, Green 28
Bowers, Henry 28
Bowers, James 256
Bowers, Jesse 28
Bowers, John 28
Bowers, Lemuel 21, 28
Bowers, Mary 28
Bowers, Nancy 28
Bowers, Solomom 28
Bowers, William 28
Bowles, R. 213
Bowlin, Obedeah 66
Bowlin, Smith 28
Bowling, Denatha 28
Bowling, M. 139
Bowling, Sidney 28
Bowman, Andrew 94
Bowman, Cornelius 243, 247
Bowman, George 240, 285
Bowman, Lethe Jane 34
Bowyer, Luke 128, 221,
Boyakin, Irena 85
Boyce, Isham 28
Boyce, John 29
Boyd, Caroline A. 28
Boyd, Coralin 28
Boyd, F. A. 121
Boyd, George 28, 307, 337
Boyd, Hampton 28
Boyd, Isabella 28
Boyd, J. 29

Boyd, James 28-29
Boyd, Jane 28
Boyd, John 28, 220
Boyd, Lewis A. 29
Boyd, M. A. 29
Boyd, M. B. 29
Boyd, Margaret 29
Boyd, Mary S. 155
Boyd, R. 29
Boyd, Robt. 191
Boyd, Walter P. 28
Boyd, William P. 28
Boyer, John 29
Boykin, Jno. B. 1
Boykin, W. A. 29
Boykin, W. O. 29, 49, 129
Boyr, Robt. 191
Boyt, Jesse 29
Brabson, B. D. 29, 42, 81
Brabson, John 29
Brabson, R. B. 277
Brabson, T. C. 29
Brabson, Thos. C. 71, 81
Brackin, Isaac 29
Brackin, Morean S. 29
Bradberry, Daniel M. 200
Bradberry, Epsey Ann 200
Bradberry, James M. 200
Bradberry, Joel B. 200
Bradberry, John 200
Bradberry, Rebecca 200
Bradberry, Sarah S. 200
Bradburn, William S. 231
Bradbury, Joshua 301
Braddy, Hezekiah 29
Braden, Alexander 300
Braden, Charles 34
Bradford, Alexander 29
Bradford, Alsey 55, 109, 290, 320, 333
Bradford, Amanda M. 30
Bradford, Barkly M. 30
Bradford, Benjamin 37, 73, 250
Bradford, David 30, 55
Bradford, Henry 50, 168-169, 240
Bradford, James 146, 168
Bradford, John 30
Bradford, Lucy G.190
Bradford, Mary Ellen 333
Bradford, Napoleon B. 30, 102, 337
Bradford, Theodrick F. 30, 33, 190
Bradford, Thomas H. 29
Bradley, A. J. 328
Bradley, Charles 30
Bradley, Hugh 30
Bradley, J. D. 31
Bradley, Joel 73
Bradley, John 30, 114
Bradley, Martha 30
Bradley, Thomas 30, 71, 103, 106, 249
Bradly, John 30
Bradly, Patsy 30

Bradly, Polly 30
Bradly, T. 39
Bradly, Thomas 30
Bradshaw, Edward 30
Bradshaw, Hugh 191
Bradshaw, J. E. 30
Bradshaw, J. T. 30
Bradshaw, Jesse 31
Bradshaw, Lena 31
Bradshaw, Roberta 245
Bradshaw, Robt. 31
Bradshaw, Sam B. 30
Bradshaw, Thomas 30-31
Bradshaw, William 20
Bradshaw, Wilson 31
Bradson, D. B. 205
Brady, John 263
Braime, Hellen P. 37
Braime, Winfield S. 37
Brainard, G. W. 31
Brainard, Joseph 31
Brame, Warren L. 37
Branch, Joseph 31, 208
Branch, Nicholas 208
Brandon, John 31
Brandon, Rebekah 31
Brandon, Sarah 204
Brandy, Catherine 29
Brangtin, Benjamin 112
Brangtin, Mary 112
Brannon, Wm.108
Brannum, Beverage 31
Brannum, Martha Jane 31
Brannum, Polly 340
Branom, Martha Jane 31
Bransford, Thomas L. 6, 94, 110, 154, 272
Brasee, Wm. R. 285
Brasfield, Asa 31
Brasfield, Calvin 31
Brasfield, Cetney 31
Brasfield, David 31
Brasfield, Edney 31
Brasfield, George 31, 69
Brasfield, Leonard 31
Brashear, Benjamin F. 31
Brassfield, Alfred 31
Brassfield, Elizabeth 314
Brassfield, Josiah C. 314
Brassfield, Willie 31
Braudy, Hezekiah 29
Braum, Warren L. 37
Brawdy, Catherine 29
Brawdy, John 29
Brawner, Peter 77
Brazier, Thomas 31
Breashears, Robert S. 31
Breazeale, Henry 79, 112
Breden, Bryant 31
Breden, John 31
Breeden, Aaron 32
Breeden, Amerel 32
Breeden, Andrew 32
Breeden, Bryant 156
Breeden, Calvin 32
Breeden, Elizabeth 32
Breeden, Harriet 32

Breeden, John 32
Breeden, Josiah 32
Breeden, Lewis 156
Breeden, Merrel 32, 155
Breeden, Nancy 32
Breeden, William 32
Brendonburg, Henry 138
Brent, Wm. 32
Breson, Samuel 275
Brewer, B. A. 32
Brewer, Edward 236
Brewer, John J. 32
Brewer, Sherod 32
Brewer, Sterling 71
Brewer, Thomas 109
Brewton, Amelia 32
Brewton, John 32, 327
Brian, M. M. 211
Brickey, Polly 33
Briden, Lewis 31
Bridges, James S. 127
Bridgewater, Isaac 274
Bridgewaters, John 33
Brigance, W. B. 303
Briggance, Alfred 33
Briggance, C. V. 33
Briggance, Vicy 33
Briggance, W. 33
Briggance, Wm. 197-198, 248
Briggs, Benjamin 206
Briggs, Elizabeth 206
Briggs, George 206
Briggs, Martha 206
Briggs, Samuel 206
Briggs, Sarah 206
Briggs, W. W. 214
Briggs, William 206
Brigham, John 266
Bright, George W. 75, 217
Briningham, L. W. 33
Brinkley, E. W. 33
Brinkley, Samuel 33
Brinkly, Cealy 33
Brinler, Asa R. 122
Brinson, Arrisa 33
Brinson, Benjamin 33
Brinson, Drury 33
Brinson, Gause 33
Brinson, Jesse 33
Brinson, Mary 33
Brisco, William 167
Briscoe, Sarah 167
Brison, Drury 33
Brison, Gause 33
Brister, Benjamin 33
Bristow, Benjamin 33
Bristow, Darcus 33
Bristow, Dorkus 68
Bristow, John 33
Britain, James 33
Britian, John H. 34
Brittain, Hannah 34
Brittain, James 33
Brittain, Jason T. 33-34
Brittain, Joseph 34, 105, 174, 324

Brittain, Wm. 34
Britton, Abram 34
Britton, Adolphus 34
Britton, John L. 87
Britton, Mary E. 34
Broadaway, Lemuel 186, 291
Brobson, T. C. 243
Brock, A. B. 280
Brock, Allen 270
Brock, John 270
Brock, Joseph 219, 315
Brodie, Amanda 195
Brodie, Eliza 195
Brogan, Betsy 34
Brogan, John 34
Broiles, Adam 34, 345
Broiles, Moses 34
Broils, Mathais 34
Brooks, Albert W. W. 34
Brooks, Angeline A. 34
Brooks, Cyprissa C. 34
Brooks, D. R. 34
Brooks, Daniel 35
Brooks, Elijah 35
Brooks, Elizabeth 204
Brooks, Ellen W. 34
Brooks, Elvira A. 34
Brooks, George 34
Brooks, Hester An 35
Brooks, J. H. 105, 260
Brooks, Jackson 35
Brooks, Jane 35
Brooks, John 34-35, 78, 241, 305
Brooks, Joseph H. 164
Brooks, Larkin 35
Brooks, Leonidas 35
Brooks, Margaret 35
Brooks, Marshall 35
Brooks, Mary 34
Brooks, Mathew 34-35
Brooks, Peter 35
Brooks, Pricilla 35
Brooks, Richard 34, 41, 216
Brooks, Sarah 35
Brooks, Sidney 35
Brooks, Stephen 35
Brooks, Tilford 35
Brooks, Tilman 35
Brooks, William 35
Brooks, Wm. P. 34
Brookshire, Elkin 35
Brookshire, Levin 35, 207
Brookshire, Sarah 136
Brookshire, William 136
Broughton, Benjamin 113
Browder, David 35
Browder, H. H. 35
Browder, John 35
Browder, Josiah 35
Browing, Nimrod 207
Brown, A. R. 170
Brown, Abel 35
Brown, Adam 20
Brown, Alexander B. 223
Brown, Alvin 36, 326

Brown, Aron B. 36
Brown, Benjamin 62
Brown, Bethany 275-276
Brown, Budd 24
Brown, C. F. 35
Brown, Cynthia 326
Brown, Daniel 35-36, 326
Brown, David 35-36
Brown, Dixon 36, 48, 110
Brown, Dudly 238
Brown, Edward 14, 35
Brown, Eliza 152
Brown, Elizabeth 36, 223, 326
Brown, Ermine 35
Brown, Ezekiel W. 189
Brown, Francis 27
Brown, Frank 35
Brown, George G. 178, 201, 332
Brown, Helena A. 35
Brown, Henry 36, 193, 326
Brown, Hiram 37
Brown, Hulda 36
Brown, J. 229
Brown, Jackson 36, 74, 152
Brown, Jacob 35-37, 215, 234
Brown, James 36, 155, 190
Brown, Jane 336
Brown, Jeremiah 6, 36, 275, 283
Brown, Jesse 36, 326
Brown, Jno. L. 28, 95, 136, 171, 311, 339
Brown, Jno. S. 53, 130, 283, 290, 315, 328
Brown, Joel K. 79, 95, 109, 120, 149, 207, 249, 341
Brown, John 9, 11, 36, 59, 168, 238, 277, 326, 342
Brown, Jonathan 36
Brown, Jordan 36, 275
Brown, Joseph 37
Brown, Junison 336
Brown, Margaret 35, 316
Brown, Martha J. 275
Brown, Mary 36, 110
Brown, Matthew 36
Brown, Milton 195
Brown, Nathaniel 271
Brown, O. F. 170
Brown, Paschall 36, 326
Brown, Richard 36
Brown, Richard B. 21
Brown, Ro. 296
Brown, Robert 37, 136
Brown, Ruth 35
Brown, Sarah 36, 271
Brown, T. S. 37
Brown, Thomas 9, 11, 36, 253, 326
Brown, Walter 37
Brown, William 9, 36-37, 74, 125, 190, 226, 238, 307, 315-316, 326
Brown, Zekle 37

Browning, Caleb 37
Browning, George 37
Browning, Malone 37
Browning, Polly 37
Browning, Spencer 37
Broyles, Moses 37
Broyles, Nicholas 293-294
Bruddy, Hezekiah 29
Bruime, Winfield S. 37
Brume, Samuel 37
Brume, Warren L. 37
Brumon, Sarah 37
Brunsford, Thomas L. 128
Brunson, Isaac 237
Brunson, Jesse 37
Brunson, Sally 37
Brunton, Emely 327
Brunts, Thomas 338
Bruten, Addison 37
Bruten, John 37
Bruten, Martha 37
Bruten, Mary Ann 37
Bruten, Simon 37
Bruten, Simpson 37
Bruten, Thomas P. 37
Bruten, William A. 37
Bruton, John 327
Bruton, Jos. H. 182
Bruton, Mary 182
Bryan, Ailsey K. D. 37-38
Bryan, Allen 37
Bryan, Asa 135
Bryan, Asley 38
Bryan, Caroline 38
Bryan, E. A. C. 38
Bryan, Elizabeth 38
Bryan, Frances 38
Bryan, Hardy S. 38
Bryan, James H. 38, 44, 120
Bryan, John 179, 193
Bryan, Peter H. 71
Bryan, Robert R. 58
Bryan, S. G. 179
Bryan, T. W. 95
Bryan, Thomas 38, 69, 317
Bryan, W. S. 95
Bryan, William 37-38, 317
Bryan, Willis 38
Bryant, Alexander 113
Bryant, Ann 81, 113
Bryant, Cuthbert 38
Bryant, Dennis 38, 135
Bryant, Elizabeth 38
Bryant, Franklin 38
Bryant, Hyntin 109
Bryant, John 38
Bryant, Mary Ann 38
Bryant, Richard 56
Bryant, Saml. 205
Bryant, Sarah E. 109
Bryant, Sophia 38
Bryant, W. J. 38
Bryant, W. S. 15
Bryant, William 38
Bryhn, S. 112
Bryson, R. F. 115
Buch, Benjamin 344

Buchan, Z. C. 100
Buchanan, Elijah 38
Buchanan, F. C. 318
Buchanan, James B. 259
Buchanan, Jane 38, 146
Buchanan, John 38, 146
Buchanan, Mary 33
Buchanan, Peter 33, 96
Buchanan, Robert 38
Buchanan, Sarah H. 250
Buchanan, T. C. 88
Buchanan, Thos. 250
Buchanan, William 38, 146
Buchannan, John 39
Buck, Elijah 39
Buck, Isaac 50
Buck, Jonathan E. C. 39
Buckannan, James R. 259
Buckannan, Letty 259
Buckhanan, Ruth A. 39
Buckhanan, Thos. N. 39
Buckingham, Thomas 183
Buckner, W. E. 39
Buddie, Eliza 195
Bufford, Patsy 305
Bufford, William 305
Bulgin, James 39, 141
Bull, George122
Bullard, Geo. H. 83
Bullard, Isaac 278
Bullard, John 3, 39, 59, 64, 160, 258
Bullen, Ann 39
Buller, Isaac 39
Buller, Joseph 39
Bullinger, Peter 247
Bullock, Leonard H. 139
Bullock, M. 65
Bullock, Macajah 192
Bullock, William 29
Bumbley, Smith 39
Bumpass, Garrett 39
Bumpass, Mary 39
Bumpass, Robert 9, 39
Bumpass, William 39, 95
Bumpley, William 39
Bunch, Anne 39
Bunch, Martin 39
Bunch, Polly 79
Bunch, Wm. 39
Bundy, George 39
Bundy, Nathl. 39
Bundy, Reuben 39
Bundy, Sevier 39
Bundy, Simon 39, 40
Bunn, Burrell 40
Bunn, Charity 40
Bunn, Joel 40
Bunnell, Isaac 95, 103
Buntin, Lydia 193
Bunts, Thomas 338
Buntyn, Lydia 193
Burch, Elizabeth 40
Burch, George 22, 40
Burch, Henry 40
Burch, Polly 79
Burch, Sarah 40

Burch, Thomas 40
Burch, William 9, 40
Burchet, Eliza 40
Burchet, Jackson 40
Burchitt, Jackson 259
Burden, Elizabeth 40
Burden, Garred 40
Burden, Jarret 40
Burdett, Williamson B. 120
Burditt, Elizabeth G. 40
Burditt, Giles 40
Burditt, Hampton 40
Burditt, Hennith 40
Burditt, Matilda 40
Burditt, Samuel S. 40
Burditt, Sarah 40
Burditt, William 40
Burditt, Williamson R. 40
Burford, David 40, 299
Burger, John 40
Burger, Susanah 40
Burges, Henry A. 40
Burgess, Eugenia A. 41
Burgess, James 314
Burgess, John 40
Burgess, Nathaniel 41
Burgess, Wm. H. 41
Burgie, B. C. 4, 103, 159, 169, 178, 193
Burgie, B. E. 208
Burgie, Bell C. 15, 103, 233
Burgie, D. S. 15
Burgis, Henry 41
Burk, Milton E. 41
Burk, Polly W. 79
Burk, Robert 41, 69
Burk, Wm. C. 257
Burke, America Milly J. 41
Burke, Angelina 41, 110-111
Burke, Elizabeth 24, 41, 110-111
Burke, Esom L. 34
Burke, Hannah D. 257
Burke,Henry F. 24, 41, 111
Burke, James W. 34
Burke, John 34, 41, 110-111
Burke, Matilda 41
Burke, Milton E. 110-111
Burke, Sarah 111
Burke, William C. 34, 41
Burkett, Martha 41
Burkly, C. 41
Burlason, Aron 41
Burn, L. W. 41, 81, 175
Burn, William 41
Burn, Wilson 41
Burn, Wm. P. 41, 205
Burnes, T. V. 78
Burnet, Joseph 41
Burnet, Stasha 42
Burnet, Stephen 42
Burnet, Thomas 41
Burnett, John S. 42
Burnett, Jonathan 201, 210
Burnett, Lucinda 42

Burnett, Thomas 330
Burnett, W. M. 108, 127, 177
Burnett, William 80, 306, 330
Burney, William 106
Burnham, George W. 42
Burns, Ashburry 42
Burns, Drucilla L. C. 42
Burns, E. 42
Burns, H. 42
Burns, James 42
Burns, Jesse 42
Burns, L. W. 306, 308
Burns, Levan W. 42
Burns, Narcissa C. 130
Burns, Patsy 42
Burns, R. R. 130
Burns, Reason 56
Burns, Richard 130
Burns, Stephens 246
Burns, W. P. 205
Burns, Wilson 205
Burras, Stephen 171
Burris, John 180, 191
Burroughs, John 282
Burroughs, Martilda 282
Burroughs, Martula 282
Burrow, Banks M. 42
Burrow, Dorton Alfred 42
Burrow, Eve 42
Burrow, Freeman 42
Burrow, Jacob C. 40
Burrow, James 42
Burrow, Jesse 42
Burrow, Leathy 42
Burrow, Madison 42
Burrow, Solomon 42
Burrow, William 42
Burrus, John 118,145, 161
Burrus, Stephen 118, 205
Burrus, Swaney 154
Burry, George 279
Burshong, Jane 42
Burtin, F. H. 190
Burton, Benjamin 260
Burton, Candis 260
Burton, Catherine 31
Burton, Elizabeth 332
Burton, F. N. W. 29, 101, 161, 203, 225
Burton, Frank N. W. 43
Burton, Hardy M. 117
Burton, James 11
Burton, John 42
Burton, Joseph H. 181
Burton, Margret 42
Burton, Martin G. 43
Burton, Mary E. 181
Burton, Robert 17, 27, 139
Burton, Thomas H. 7, 282
Burton, William 31, 42
Burus, Ashburry 42
Burus, Elihu M. 42
Burus, Jesse 42
Burus, Reason 56
Bush, John H. 106

Bush, Larson 239
Bush, Lonson 239
Bushlans, Nancy 227
Bussey, George 113
Butler, Anthony Wayne 43
Butler, Bailey 43-44, 118, 288, 312
Butler, Burl 5, 43, 155
Butler, Burrell 284
Butler, Burwell 155
Butler, Caroline S. 43
Butler, Edward 43, 314
Butler, Eliza 43
Butler, Frank N. W. 43
Butler, Franklin 75
Butler, Franklin W. 43
Butler, George 43-44
Butler, Henry 43-44, 61, 187, 228
Butler, Horatio 43-44, 187
Butler, Isabella 43, 314
Butler, James 43-44
Butler, Jemima 43-44
Butler, John 43-44, 187, 264
Butler, L. L. 43
Butler, Lucetta 43
Butler, Lucinda 58
Butler, Lusanna 43
Butler, M. R. 44
Butler, Marium 43
Butler, Martha 43-44, 62
Butler, Mary 43-44
Butler, Mary Ann 118
Butler, Mary E. 44
Butler, Micajah 43-44
Butler, Mounce G. 118
Butler, Oliver 58
Butler, Oratia, 187
Butler, Polly 43, 118
Butler, Prudence L. 58
Butler, Samuel S. 43
Butler, Sarah 148, 187
Butler, Sarah An 8
Butler, Susan 44
Butler, Thomas 8, 41, 43-44, 53, 110-111, 118, 238, 245, 267-268, 288, 304
Butler, Welcome 44, 148
Butler, William 27-28, 43-44, 118, 123, 136, 341
Button, Adolphus 44
Button, Mary E. 44
Bybee, Sarah 44
Byers, W. S. 164
Byrd, Betsey 44
Byrd, Blackman H. 194, 211
Byrd, James 44
Byrd, John W. 44, 263
Byrd, Thomas 44
Byrd, Wm. 44
Byrn, John P. 239
Byrn, Robt. W. 329
Byrn, Ruth 115
Byrn, Stephen W. 239
Byrne, Terrel 238
Byrns, Elija 329

Byrns, Jas. 329
Byrns, Ranson H. 205
Byrns, Reazen 17
Byrns, Robt. D. 329
Byrns, Rutha C. 329
Byrns, Wm. T. 329
Byrus, Ranson H. 205
Cadle, Abraham 45
Cadle, Polly 45
Cadle, Zachariah 45
Caffrey, Margaret 197
Caffrey, Thos. 197
Cage, John 23
Cagle, C. 45
Cagle, Calloway 45
Cagle, Isam 45
Cagle, Jane 45
Cagle, Sally 45
Cagle, Sarah 45
Cagle, Shade 45
Cagle, Wm. 45
Cagun, Sarah 237
Caime, Patience 40
Caime, William 40
Caison, Thompson 54
Calahan, John 45
Caldwell, Alexander 45
Caldwell, Carson 204
Caldwell, Elizabeth M. 45
Caldwell, J. H. 13, 104, 108, 127, 163, 265, 304, 312
Caldwell, James 45, 214
Caldwell, John H. 38-39, 311, 317
Caldwell, Mary 45
Caldwell, Robert 45
Caldwell, William 45, 291, 314
Calhon Sarah 59
Calhoon, John 59
Calhoon, Lucrecey 59
Calhoon, Martha 59, 162
Calhoon, Thomas 160
Calhoon, Wm. 162
Calloway, William S. 211
Calvert, Jno. 45
Calvert, William 45, 225
Camp, John 46
Camp, Sterling 126-127
Camp, Terrell L. 46, 131
Camp, Thomas C. 263
Campbell, Abraham 209
Campbell, Alexander 4, 45-46, 138, 175, 254, 333
Campbell, Alfred 254
Campbell, Annie R. 46
Campbell, Archibald 158, 249, 336
Campbell, Arthur 254
Campbell, B. R. 46
Campbell, Betsy 254
Campbell, Charles 45-46
Campbell, David H. 46
Campbell, E. S. 46
Campbell, Egbert 338
Campbell, Elizabeth 46, 240, 254

Campbell, F. D. 46
Campbell, George 139, 165
Campbell, Hugh 46
Campbell, James 45-46, 152
Campbell, John 7, 242
Campbell, Jonathan 46
Campbell, L. M. 46
Campbell, Lysander M. 46
Campbell, Margaret 46
Campbell, Mary 29
Campbell, Michl. 239
Campbell, Milley 45
Campbell, Nelly 45
Campbell, P. 338
Campbell, Patsy 336
Campbell, Rachel 45
Campbell, Rebecca 336
Campbell, Sarah 46
Campbell, Thomas 46, 115, 258
Campbell, Victor Morcan 46
Campbell, William 27, 45-46, 79, 196, 271
Camps, T. L. 46
Canada, Anna 46
Canada, Robert 81
Cancillor, John 48
Cane, James 47
Cane, Jesse 47
Cane, John 47
Cannon, Abisha 47, 108, 267
Cannon, Abraham W. 47
Cannon, Bird 108
Cannon, Clemant 30, 33, 111, 216
Cannon, Henry H. 47
Cannon, James 47
Cannon, Jane 47
Cannon, Jason 48
Cannon, John 47
Cannon, Jonathan 167
Cannon, Letsey 48
Cannon, Lewis F. 47
Cannon, Martha 48
Cannon, Martin V. 47
Cannon, Minos 47-48, 148, 186, 291
Cannon, Newton 47
Cannon, Robert 47, 88, 280
Cannon, Sally 47, 108
Cannon, Samuel 47-48
Cannon, Thomas U. 47
Cannon, W. H. 38
Cannon, William 47, 167
Cannon, Willis 48, 72, 214
Canseller, William 240
Cansler, John 48
Cansler, Nathaniel H. 48-49
Cansler, Polly 48
Cansler, William 48
Canslor, Mary 48
Canter, James 48
Canter, Levi 48
Canter, Lin 48
Canter, Mary 48
Canter, Sam 48
Canter, Wilson C. 48
Canter, Zechariah 48
Canterberry, Wm. 48
Cantrel, Sarah 128
Cantrell, David 48
Cantrell, Gabriel 48, 103
Cantrell, Stephen 194
Cantrell, Susannah 48
Cantrill, Sarah 48
Capell, Sam 48
Capley, P. F. 49
Capling, Lenord 48
Caplinger, Jacob 28, 49
Caplinger, John 49
Caplinger, Leonard 48
Caplis, Henry 11
Capshaw, James 127, 293, 321
Capsley, P. F. 49
Car, Albert F. 49-50
Car, Daniel W. 50, 71
Car, Elijah J. 50
Car, Eliza 157
Car, Hannah 50
Car, John 50, 198
Car, Joseph D. 167
Car, Martha A. 198
Car, William 50
Cardwell, John 49
Cardwell, Joseph L. 49
Cardwell, Robert 88
Cardwell, Thos. T. 305
Carey, C. 100
Carithers, Fannie 53
Carithers, Stoddert 53
Carithers, William 53
Carland, James 49
Carland, Joshua 49
Carland, Patsy 49
Carlin, Isiah 49
Carlin, Jas. 49
Carlin, Patsy 49
Carlin, Thomas G. 19
Carlin, William 49
Carlisle [a slave] 341
Carlisle, Waddy 199
Carlisle, William 290
Carlock, Isaac 270
Carlson, Jane 341
Carmack, Joseph 49
Carmack, Mary 49
Carmichael, Daniel 100, 124, 176
Carmichael, John 75
Carmichael, Lemuel 49
Carmichael, Louisa 49
Carmichel, John 307
Carmichel, Margaret 307
Carmile, Abigale 49, 314
Carnahan, Ezekiel 182
Carnahan, James 121
Carnahan, Nancy 182
Carnes, Hubbard 49
Carney, Thomas 322
Carouth, James 49
Carpenter, Alexander 49
Carpenter, George W. 216
Carpenter, John William 49
Carr, Ann 57
Carr, Dickison 49
Carr, Elijah 49
Carr, James C. 34
Carr, John 49
Carr, Laurence 49
Carr, Margaret 49
Carr, Mary 57
Carr, W. H. 49
Carr, Walter 57, 188
Carr, William 49, 284
Carrall, William 17
Carrieth, Watta 331
Carriger, Godfrey 50
Carrithers, Sallie P. 53
Carrol, Wm. 269
Carroll, C. T. 50
Carroll, J. M. 50
Carroll, Joseph 50
Carroll, M. B. 50
Carson, Andw. 294
Carson, Charles 50
Carson, David 50-51
Carson, Henry 14
Carson, James H. 220
Carson, John 50-51
Carson, Margaret 50
Carson, Nancy 51
Carson, Rachel 50
Carson, Robert 51
Carson, Ruth 51
Carson, Thompson 121
Carson, William 50, 51, 83
Carter, Barnard 20
Carter, Benjamin 330
Carter, Betsey 51
Carter, Charles 168
Carter, David 229
Carter, Eliza 148
Carter, Elizabeth 229
Carter, Emanuel 51, 60, 72
Carter, Emil 300
Carter, Enoch 164
Carter, Ezekiel 51
Carter, George 3
Carter, Hannah E. 51
Carter, Henry 51
Carter, James 9, 51
Carter, Jasie 257
Carter, John 40, 51-52, 72, 150, 206, 237, 293
Carter, Joseph D. 51
Carter, Judthan 81
Carter, Landon 51-52, 150
Carter, Levi 48
Carter, Mary G. 51
Carter, Micajah 221
Carter, Nancy J. 52, 148
Carter, O. J. P. 31
Carter, Rachel 330
Carter, Richard 51
Carter, Sarah 51
Carter, Stanton 47
Carter, Stephen 127, 336
Carter, Tabitha 51
Carter, Thaxton 257

Carter, Walker A. 52
Carter, Wesley D. 51
Carter, William 52, 199, 200
Carter, Wilson C. 48
Cartmel, Nathaniel 52
Cartmell, Martin 235
Cartwell, Martin 82, 90, 235
Cartwright, Benijah 52
Cartwright, Edward W. 52
Cartwright, Elizabeth 52
Cartwright, Hannah S. 52
Cartwright, Hezekiah 52
Cartwright, James N. 52
Cartwright, Jesse 52
Cartwright, John 52, 86
Cartwright, Lucinda 52
Cartwright, Matthew 52
Cartwright, Penelope 52
Cartwright, Peter A. 52
Cartwright, Richard 52
Cartwright, Robert 52
Cartwright, Thomas 79
Cartwright, Wm. L. 52
Caruth, H. C. 335
Caruthers, Charles 52
Caruthers, Fannie 53
Caruthers, J. B. 78
Caruthers, J. F. 52, 72
Caruthers, James 53, 178, 191, 283
Caruthers, Joseph 53, 197
Caruthers, Laura E. 53
Caruthers, M. J. 52, 176
Caruthers, Stoddard 53,
Caruthers, Susan Eudora 53
Caruthers, Susan Medora 53

Caruthers, William 53
Carver, Althea 53
Carver, Cornelius 53
Carver, Hiram C. 53
Carver, Plesant 53
Cary, Nathaniel 53
Cary, Patsy 53
Cary, Robert 53
Cary, William 53
Case, Jesse L. 266
Case, William 266
Casey, John 103, 297
Cash, Clark 53
Cash, Emily 320
Cash, Jno. E. 53
Cash, L. C. R. 53
Cash, Lucretia E. R. 53
Cash, Mary 94
Cash, Richard 94
Cason, Becca 54
Cason, Becky Ann 54
Cason, Edward 53-54, 71, 293
Cason, Eliza L. 53
Cason, Elizabeth 54
Cason, Henry H. 53
Cason, James 54
Cason, Josephine D. 53
Cason, Lewis B. 53
Cason, Millard F. 53

Cason, Rebecca Ann 54
Cason, Sally G. 53
Cason, Sarah G. 54
Cason, Susan 54
Cason, Tandy W. 53
Cason, Thompson 54, 245, 293
Cassitty, Sampson W. 19, 93, 141, 272
Cassitty, Thomas D. 344
Casteel, Barney 54
Casteel, Betsey 54
Casteel, Edmond 54
Casteel, Elizabeth 54
Castinel, Martin 244
Castleman, Benjamin 216
Casy, W. W. 32
Cataba, Cheanuna 201
Cataba, Jency 201
Cate [a slave] 277
Cate, Charles 54, 337
Cate, Elijah 54
Cate, Elisha 54
Cate, Geo. W. 54
Cate, Henry 163
Cate, Lucy 54
Cate, Margaret 54
Cate, N. N. 38
Cate, Perry 127, 139, 312-313
Cate, Susan E. 54
Cate, Thomas 40
Cate, William 287, 337
Catham, Martha 20
Cathays, Nelly 173
Cathey, Alexander H. 54
Cathey, Hardin R. 205
Cathey, John 54
Cathey, Wiley 54
Catlett, A. C. 55
Catlett, George W. 55, 139
Catlett, H. S. 55
Catlett, J. E. 55
Catlett, J. P. 55
Catlett, James P.139, 175
Catlett, John 55, 290
Catlett, L. H. 55
Catlett, Lafayett 55
Catlett, Wm. 42, 175, 255
Cato [a slave] 88
Cato, Burwell 266
Cato, Daniel 55
Cato, Henry 55
Cato, Rufus 55
Catoe, Jane 55
Catoe, Mary Jane 55
Catoe, Solomon P. 55
Catrin, John 55, 203
Catrin, O. P. 55
Catt, Solomon P. 55
Catter, James W. 130
Cauter, Zechariah 48
Cauthon, Thomas 55
Cauthron, John 61
Cavin, Moses 98
Cawood, Sarah 168

Cawthon, James H. 55
Cawthon, Thomas 55
Cazun, Sarah 309
Cearley, Luke 55, 125
Cearley, Samuel 55
Cennedy, John 191
Center, Milton 341
Centshir, E. 229
Cerby, Elias R. 55
Cerby, John M. 55
Cerby, Nancy 55
Cerby, Sarah 55
Cerby, Susan Ann 55
Cerby, William B. 55
Cevel, Leithton 24
Cevel, Susan 24
Chaddock, Alexander 55
Chadwell, David 249, 262
Chaffin, Abner 343-344
Chaffin, Barberry 344
Chaffin, Elizabeth 344
Chaffin, Fox 243
Chaffin, Joseph 55
Chaffin, Susan 55
Chaffin, William 344
Chalfin, Robert 56
Chamberlain, A. M. 70
Chamberlain, Charles 56, 150, 328
Chamberlain, D. A. 42
Chamberlain, Elizabeth 150
Chamberlain, M.Susan 56
Chamberlain, Saml. 56, 151
Chamberlain, Willis 56
Chamberlin, Ann 315
Chamberlin, D. A. 166
Chamberlin, Geoorge 56
Chambers, A. B. 320
Chambers, Charles P. 56-57
Chambers, Charlottee 280
Chambers, Elizabeth 56, 328
Chambers, F. M. 320
Chambers, Frank 265
Chambers, James 56, 139
Chambers, Jessee 80
Chambers, John 6, 56, 204, 230, 266
Chambers. M. J. 320
Chambers, Milly 80
Chambers, Rachel Jane 56, 143
Chambers, Sarah 56-57
Chambers, W. S. 56
Chambers, William J. 56, 143

Chamblin, F. 69, 165
Chamblin, T. S. 69, 98, 318
Chamblin, Turner 65, 69, 98, 134, 155, 278
Chance, Samuel 227
Chancellor, Charles W. 44, 62
Chancellor, Martha A. 62
Chancy, Hezekiah 57
Chandler, Anna 57

Chandler, B. M. 57, 139, 224
Chandler, Bluford 57
Chandler, Calvin 84
Chandler, Carroll 57
Chandler, Catherine 57
Chandler, Eli 57
Chandler, John 57, 71, 205
Chandler, Joseph 57
Chandler, Louisa 57
Chandler, Martha 57
Chandler, Mary 57
Chandler, Matilda 57
Chandler, Narcissa 57
Chandler, Parks 57
Chandler, Rebecca E. 57
Chandler, Robert 57
Chandler, Ryland J. 57
Chandler, Sarah 57
Chandler, Timothy 42, 57, 205
Chandler, William 57
Chandles, Timothy 38
Chaney, Hezechiah 57
Chapell, Humphrey 119
Chapman, George 57, 231
Chapman, Mary 26, 57
Chapman, Silas 161, 188
Chappel, Margaret 21
Chappell, Eliza 51
Chappell, Humphrey 57, 281
Chappell, J. R. 57
Chappell, James H. 51
Chappell, Jno. L. 57
Chappell, Joel R. 114, 336
Chappell, Joseph 57
Chappell, Margaret 57
Charble, Jacob 57
Charity [a slave] 297, 322
Charles [a slave] 121
Charlotte [a slave] 51, 320
Charlton, George W. 128
Charmichael, Lemuel 58
Chase, Caroline 163
Chase, Catherine 162
Chase, David 162-163
Chasten, Elisha 158
Cheatam, John B. 33
Cheatam, Thomas 23
Cheatham, Anderson 58, 78, 93, 171, 222, 241, 262,
Cheatham, Archer 58, 151
Cheatham, Christopher 319
Cheatham, Edward 58
Cheatham, John B. 58, 68, 226, 278, 288, 309
Cheatham, Olive 58
Cheatham, Peter 58
Cheatham, Thomas 58
Cheatham, William B. 58
Cheek, Abraham 59
Cheek, Benjamin R. 58
Cheek, Edmund R. 58
Cheek, Eli 58
Cheek, Henry 116

Cheek, James 58
Cheek, Jeremiah 58
Cheek, Labitha 58
Cheek, Martha 20
Cheek, Mary 116
Cheek, Tabitha 58
Cheek, Thomas D. 58, 155
Cherry, Almira 58
Cherry, Alvira 58
Cherry, Calvin W. 58-59
Cherry, Cary S. 58
Cherry, D. H. 58
Cherry, Daniel 6,30, 58-59, 113, 177, 245
Cherry, Darling 59, 245
Cherry, Elizabeth 252
Cherry, Isabella 58
Cherry, James 59
Cherry, Jesse 177, 245
Cherry, John M. 58
Cherry, Lemuel 58-59
Cherry, Louisa J.58
Cherry, Nansey 59
Cherry, Norman T. 58
Cherry, Sally 58
Cherry, Wiley 59
Cherry, William 69, 252
Cherry, Willie 59, 189
Cherry, Wilson C. 58
Chery, Cory S. 58
Chery, John M. 58
Chery, Wilson C. 58
Chester, Archibald G. 59
Chester, Robert J. 25-26, 28, 46, 59, 220, 310
Chester, William P. 259
Chew, John Drury 59
Chick, Abraham 59
Chick, Elisha 59
Child, J. F. 24, 33, 208
Childers, Elizabeth 59
Childers, John 59
Childress, Abner 59
Childress, Isaac 59
Childress, Jacob 59
Childress, John 59
Childress, Joseph 60
Childs, J. F. 208
Childs, Thomas 60
Chisim, Sarah 309
Chism, Ann Frances 60
Chism, James 60
Chism, John 60, 107
Chism, Nancy H. 334
Chism, Nancy Trigg 60
Chism, Priscilla Frances 60
Chism, Robert K. 334
Chisolm, John 107
Chitman, Fred 60
Chitman, Mary A. 60
Chitwood, Auge 327
Chitwood, G. 92
Chitwood, Green 322
Chitwood, James 60
Chitwood, Jo. 317, 327
Chitwood, Josiah 8
Chitwood, [no name] 339

Chitwood, Pleasant 122
Chitwood, Stephen 8, 327
Chloe [a slave] 341
Cho Ko ha [an Indian] 201
Choat, Edward 106, 278
Choate, Ann 60
Choate, Austin 60
Choate, Edward 279
Choate, Elisabeth 60
Choate, Mary 60
Choate, Thomas 60
Choate, Valentine 309
Chote, Isaac 60
Chowning, John 60
Chowning, Letisha 60
Chowning, Richard 60
Chowning, Robert G. 60
Chowning, Thos. 60
Chrismas, Lewis 60
Christian, George W. 53
Christian, James 144
Christianbury, Elizabeth 60
Christianbury, John 60
Christianbury, Joshua 60
Christie, Elizabeth 60-61
Chriswell, R. M. 298
Chronister, Eliza 101
Chronister, W. C. 61
Chronister, W. E. 61
Chuck [a slave] 119
Chuck, Elisha 59
Churchman, Thomas G. 170
Churchwell, Elizabeth 68
Clabough, Anna 43-44
Clabough, Marion 43
Clack, Jesse 23, 61
Clack, Jno. 333
Clack, Martha 333
Clagette, Horatio 221, 230
Claiborne, Thomas 58, 178
Clampet, Nathan 86, 262
Clannch, James E. 17
Clardy, Allen 61
Clardy, Ann 61
Clardy, Caroline P. 61
Clardy, James B. 61
Clardy, John M. 61
Clardy, Joseph 61
Clardy, Mary Ann 61
Clardy, Nancy E. 61
Clardy, Nobel L. 61
Clardy, Richard S. 61
Clardy, Theodocia H. 61
Clark, Abram 173
Clark, Alexander 121
Clark, B. W. 62
Clark, Benjamin 114
Clark, Betsy 62
Clark, Boyd 275
Clark, Charles P. 193
Clark, Christopher 238
Clark, Ed. A. 306-307
Clark, Elijah 152
Clark, Elizabeth 61
Clark, Frances 234
Clark, George 52, 66, 198
Clark, Giles 99

363

Clark, Hannah 329
Clark, Henderson 114
Clark, Isaac F. 7
Clark, Isham 61
Clark, J. 61-62
Clark, J. P. H. 61
Clark, James 66, 112, 230, 253, 280, 333
Clark, Jesse 61
Clark, John 1, 25, 61-62, 152, 307, 333, 338
Clark, Joseph 34, 61
Clark, Louisa 7, 8
Clark, M. E. 62
Clark, M. M. 62
Clark, Mariah 62
Clark, Martha 331
Clark, Mary 61-62
Clark, Nathan 62, 166
Clark, R. S. 62, 211, 234
Clark, R. V. 62
Clark, Reuben 62
Clark, Richard 9
Clark, Robert S. 61-62
Clark, S. M. 62
Clark, Sarah 307
Clark, Silas 61
Clark, Solomon 62
Clark, T. C. 332
Clark, Thomas 11, 97, 109, 129, 205, 234, 243, 308
Clark, Thursa 99
Clark, William 39, 62, 80
Clarke, Peter 330
Clarke, S. C. 28
Clarke, W. H. 28
Claxon, James 267
Claxton, James 62
Claxton, John 62
Claxton, Sarah 62
Clay, Paul 297
Clay, Wm. 62
Claybrook, John S. 230
Clayburn [a slave] 341
Clayton, Amanda P. 62
Clayton, Ben 249
Clayton, Charles 62
Clayton, Francis 62
Clayton, Ivy J. 62
Clayton, Izy Jane 62
Clayton, James 62
Clayton, John 62
Clayton, Josaphine 62
Clayton, Lucy J. 62
Clayton, Martha 62
Clayton, Nancy E. 62
Clayton, T. M. 62
Clayton, W. B. 62
Clayton, William R. 62
Cleek, no name 140
Clemans, George W. 42
Clemens, Henry 62
Clemens, Jane 62, 168, 208
Clemens, John 62-63,168, 208
Clemens, Orion 62, 208
Clemens, Owens 62

Clemens, Samuel L. 62, 208
Clemenstson, C. A. 63
Clement, William 63
Clements, Christopher 108
Clements, George 108
Clements, Henderson M. 63
Clements, H. W. 108
Clements, John 63
Clements, Leroy 108
Clements, Montgomery 108
Clements, P. G. 63
Clements, Sarah 108
Clements, Thos. L. 330
Clementson, C. A. 63
Clementson, Sarah 63
Clemments, Andrew 108
Clemmentson, C. A. 63
Clemmentson, Daniel 63
Clemmentson, Geo. M. 63
Clemmentson, John 63
Clemmentson, Sarah 63
Clemmons, John 63
Clemons, Christopher 63
Clemston, C. A. 63
Clenard, Laurence 216
Clendenen, Isabella 62, 168
Clendenen, Wim. A. 62, 168
Clendennon, John 63
Cliff, Daniel B. 205, 288
Clift, Mahala 249
Clifton, Joshua H. 63
Clingen, Edward 63
Clingen, George 63
Clingen, Margaret 63
Clingen, Mary 63
Clinton, Elisabeth 64
Clinton, George W. 157
Clinton, Hannah 157
Clinton, Jesse K. 157
Clinton, John L. 157
Clinton, Mary 25
Clinton, Thomas 63,258, 285
Clonch, Cyrus 153
Clopton, Walter 269
Cloud, Daniel 64
Cloud, Isaac 238
Cloud, Samuel 64
Cloud, Tabbitha 64
Clowers, James 321
Cloyd, Molly R. 64
Cloyd, Polly R. 64
Cloyd, Stephen 64
Clyce, Harriet 64
Coats, Austin M. 64
Coats, James T. 64
Cobb, Christian 64, 117
Cobb, Ethelred 337
Cobb, Jesse 64
Cobb, John 64
Cobb, Joseph 64
Cobb, Judith 64
Cobb, Pharoah 50, 135, 183

Cobb, Samuel 64
Cobb, Thos. 64
Cobb, William 64

Cobbs, Joseph 111, 150
Cochram, N. W. 64
Cochran, Albert 112
Cochrane, J. M. 338
Cock, John 64
Cock, Joseph 64
Cock, Leroy 64
Cock, Susanna 64
Cocke, James 64
Cocke, John 88, 160
Cocke, William 60, 213
Coe, Stephen 64
Coe, William 92, 339
Coffee, Asbury M. 27, 65
Coffman, Andrew 65
Coffman, Mary 65
Coffman, R. C. 52, 72, 121, 214, 299, 300, 324
Coffy, Asbury M. 65
Coffy, Marvel 65
Coffy, Rachael 65
Cohea, Amos 322
Cohea, Elizabeth 22, 65
Cohia, Amos 274
Coker, C. J. 27
Coker, N. 147
Coker, Napoleon 107
Colbert, George W. 65
Cole, Andrew 129
Cole, Dora E. 65
Cole, Dora T. 65
Cole, Elizabeth M. 65
Cole, John 65, 129
Cole, Joseph 217
Cole, Lear T. 129
Cole, Martha J. 65
Cole, Marvell 65
Cole, Nancy D. 65
Cole, Ninney W. 65
Cole, Peter H. 65
Cole, Phillip 65, 129
Cole, Reubin 65
Cole, Selia T. 65
Cole, Stephen 65
Cole, Susan M. 65
Cole, Theadore E.129
Cole, Thomas B. 65
Coleman, John 87, 238
Coleman, S. K. 65
Collet, Abraham 65
Collier, Ann 258
Collier, Arthur 65
Collier, Feribee 65
Collier, L. C. 314
Collier, Littleton C. 238
Collier, William 65
Collings, John 248
Collins, Adam 66
Collins, Amy 282
Collins, Ann 66
Collins, David 29, 66
Collins, Jas. P. 334
Collins, John 66, 282
Collins, Susannah 66
Collins, Widow 66
Collitt, Isaac 65
Collitt, Mary 65

Collville, Young 66
Colter, Jane 211
Colter, John 211
Colthorp, Clayton 66
Colthorp, Norrel 66
Colthrap, Eliza 21
Coltor, John 66
Colvelle, Joseph 223
Colvill, Nutty 66
Colvill, Saml. 66
Colville, Amanda M. 66
Colville, Bethialine 66
Colville, George 66, 256
Colville, Samuel 66
Colville, Warner 66
Colville, Young 123
Colwell, Robert 66
Colwell, Sarah 66
Combs, Green 66
Combs, John 66
Combs, Polly 252
Comer, John 291
Comer, Reuben P. 194
Compton, Caroline E. 66
Compton, Charles 19, 66
Compton, David 66
Compton, Edward 66
Compton, John B. 66, 95, 135
Compton, Laura T. 66
Compton, Margaret E. 67
Compton, Mary E. 66
Compton, Robert 66-67
Compton, Vinson 67
Conant, N. W. 18, 211
Conard, Nicholas 216
Conaster, David 239
Conatser, Abraham 67
Conatser, Amasa 67
Conatser, Andrew 67
Conatser, Daniel 67, 98
Conatser, David 67
Conatser, Ezekiel 98
Conatser, Geo. A.67
Conatser, James 67
Conatser, Jenett 67
Conatser, John 67
Conatser, Mary 67
Conatser, Phillip 67
Conatser, Reuben 67
Conatser, Sarah 67
Condra, John W. 58
Condra, Sarah T. 58
Condran, John W. 58
Condras, Sarah L. 58
Condray, William 238
Condry, Dennis 174
Condry, William 191, 288
Conger, James B. 21
Conger, John 21, 67
Conger, P. D. 197
Conger, Philander D. W.21
Congo, John 67
Connally, Fanny 67
Connally, George A. 67, 223
Connally, John 67
Connally, Mary 67

Connally, Robert A. 57, 67
Connally, Susan 67
Connally, T. D. 303
Connally, Thomas D. 67
Connel, Wm. 254
Connelly, Nelly 68
Conner, James 68
Conner, Milly 228
Conner, R. R. 228
Conner, Robert 228
Conner, Trent C. 129
Conrad, Andrew 314
Conrad, Cornelius 314
Conrad, George C. 68, 184
Conrad, John 314
Conrad, Joseph 68
Conrad, Mary 68, 184
Conrad, Nicholas 68, 171-172
Conrad, Peggy 68
Conrad, Sampson 68
Conrad, Sidney 68, 184
Conrad, William 68, 184, 207

Conrod, James 68
Conrod, W. C. 68
Conyers, William 68
Cook, Abraham 68
Cook, Amanda 68
Cook, Archibald 191
Cook, Augustin 62, 140
Cook, Augustine 20, 60
Cook, Daniel 31, 69
Cook, Earl J. 68
Cook, Eli 68
Cook, George 68
Cook, James 68
Cook, John 5, 31, 69, 120
Cook, Marcurius 206
Cook, Margaret 120
Cook, Matilda C. 68
Cook, Mercurius 68
Cook, Ruthy 5
Cook, Thomas 140
Cook, Watson M. 141, 274
Cook, William 79, 162
Cooke, Eliza 68
Cooke, W. M. 266
Cooke, Watson M. 93, 245, 266
Cooke, William 68
Cooley, Anna 119
Cooley, Cornelius 69
Cooley, Joel 69, 119
Cooley, Lucinda 69
Cooley, Richard 45
Cooley, William 4, 45, 69, 119, 162, 173, 205, 240, 258
Coon, Conrod 226
Coonrad, Nicholas 207
Coonrod, W. C. 68
Coons, Joseph 69
Cooper, A. W. 69
Cooper, Abraham 241
Cooper, Abram 69, 241
Cooper, Charles D. 3, 213

Cooper, Christopher 25, 315
Cooper, Ella 69
Cooper, Eugene 69
Cooper, George 52
Cooper, Henry 177
Cooper, J. J. 288
Cooper, James 15, 69, 141
Cooper, John 3, 41, 69, 241, 304
Cooper, Jonathan J. 288
Cooper, Lula 69
Cooper, Martha A. 69
Cooper, Mary 27, 69
Cooper, Micajah T. 115
Cooper, R. 69
Cooper, Rebecca C. 69
Cooper, Robert 119, 174, 265, 285
Cooper, Rulann 83
Cooper, Sallie B. 69
Cooper, Sampson 69
Cooper, Sarah 241
Cooper, T. W. 284
Cooper, William 69
Cope, Martha W. 69
Cope, W. D 69
Cope, W. L. 69
Copeland, Darcas 70, 222
Copeland, J. 283
Copeland, James 243-25, 133, 283
Copeland, John 70, 132
Copeland, Josiah 70
Copeland, Solomon 70
Coppage, James 70
Corbitt, Elizabeth 323
Corbitt, Needham 323
Cormell, William 11
Cornelious, James 14
Cornewell, C. C. 165-166
Cornewell, Mary 166
Cornewell, Polly 165
Cornwell, Alfred 129, 233
Cornwell, Benjamin 70
Cornwell, Deny 129
Cornwell, Drury 70
Cornwell, Elizabeth 128
Cornwell, Henry128
Cornwell, Larkin129
Cornwell, Mary180
Cornwell, Willis128, 338
Cornwell, Zilphia 233
Cornwill, Nimrod 187
Corruth, Walter 271
Cotham, Lemuel 20
Cotner, John 112
Cotner, Martha 112
Cotten, Thos. 274
Cotter, Elizabeth J. 130
Cotter, James 130
Cotter, William E. 130
Cotton, James 248
Cotton, Malissa 248
Cotton, Minerva A. 248
Cotton, William 248
Cotton, Young 70

Couch, Jonathan 256
Couthum, Jno. L. 69
Couts, John 20
Covey, John L. 70
Covey, Sally 70
Covington, Arnold 312
Covington, Elisabeth 70
Covington, Elmore 50
Covington, Polly 70
Covington, William 45, 70, 311
Cowan, A. J. 298
Cowan, Andrew 163
Cowan, Emily 298
Cowan, Ira 146
Cowan, J. M. 306
Cowan, James 70, 175, 256
Cowan, John 70
Cowan, Nancy 70, 298
Cowan, Robert 4, 70
Cowan, W. H. 74, 298
Cowan, William 70, 298, 306, 326
Cowden, Hetty A. 71
Cowden, James 70
Cowden, John 70-71
Cowden, Mary 70-71
Cowden, Mat 71
Cowden, Nancy Melvina 70
Cowden, Sarah N. 70
Cowden, Wm. T. 71
Cowen, Brison 71
Cowen, Hugh 71
Cowen, M. J. 71
Cowen, Mathew 268
Cowen, Sophia Elizabeth 71
Cowen, Thusa 71
Cowger, John 71, 296
Cowin, Bryson 274
Cowin, Joseph 245
Cowin, Sophia 274
Cown, A. J. 265
Cox, A. A. 50
Cox, Abner 211
Cox, Albert F. 71
Cox, Ann 71
Cox, Benjamin 71-72
Cox, Daniel W. 71
Cox, Edward M. 71
Cox, Eliza 71
Cox, Elizabeth 71
Cox, Ezekiel 142
Cox, George 72
Cox, John 72, 324
Cox, Lucinda 324
Cox, Matilda 71
Cox, N. M. 54, 71, 121
Cox, Peter 141, 272
Cox, Polly 72
Cox, Presley L. 29
Cox, R. A. 267
Cox, Rebecca 71
Cox, Robert 53-54, 71, 267, 293
Cox, Sally 71, 339
Cox, Stephen 72
Cox, William 72

Cox, Winford 71
Cozart, Amanda 110
Cozart, Jas. B. 72
Cozeans, John Bartley 72
Crab, John 224-225
Crabtree, James 44, 199
Crabtree, Joseph 343
Crabtree, William 302, 343
Craddock, Richard C. 6, 20
Craft, Archillis 72
Craft, Ezekiel 72, 263
Craft, Olif 72
Craft, Whitmill 69
Crafton, Silas 144
Crage, William 73
Craghead, George 73
Craghead, Joseph 73
Craghead, Shelton 73
Craghead, Stephen 73
Craig, Alexander 73
Craig, Amanda 72
Craig, Ann 72
Craig, Benjamin F. 73
Craig, D. C. 134
Craig, E. A. 168, 301
Craig, Elijah 72
Craig, Elisha 72
Craig, Flora 73
Craig, J. Q. 52, 125, 214
Craig, James 72-73
Craig, John 1, 72-73
Craig, Moses 73
Craig, Nancy 263
Craig, Polly 72-73
Craig, Robert 73
Craig, Sally 73
Craig, Sophronia J. 72
Craig, Tabitha 1
Craig, William 1, 72-73
Craighead, Stephen 73
Crane, Isaac F. 252
Crane, Jane 200
Crapper, James 317
Crary, John M. 29
Crawford, Charles 230
Crawford, Elizabeth 3, 94
Crawford, Isaac 94
Crawford, James 19, 73
Crawford, John H. 250
Crawford, Lewis 94
Crawford, Mary 94
Crawford, Moses 73
Crawford, T. 73
Crawford, William D. 3
Crayton, Jane 73
Creighten, Henry 73
Creighten, Mary 73
Creighten, Saml. 73
Creighton, Henry 74
Creighton, Mary 74
Creighton, Saml. 73-74
Creselia, Rudolph 74
Creslia, Rudolph 74
Cresslias, Rudolph 74
Cresslius, Elizabeth 74
Creswell, R. M. 231
Creswell, Adam 71, 287

Creswell, Andrew 74
Creswell, R. M. 70-71, 153, 231, 271, 287, 311
Creswell, William 74
Crick, John 286
Cris [a slave] 189
Crisswell, Halem 172
Criswell, Adam 265
Criswell, Mary 74
Criswell, R. M. 74
Criswell, Samuel 74
Crithfield, Joseph 209
Crocket, Jane 74
Crocket, Saml. 74
Crocket, William 74, 160
Crockett, Andrew 51
Crockett, Jane 219
Crockett, John 241, 275
Crockett, Robert 46, 74
Crockett, Samuel 143
Crockett, William 219
Crockett, Wilson 147
Cromwel, Saml. 29
Cromwell, Alexander 74
Cromwell, Ann 74
Cromwell, Dorsey 74
Cromwell, Garrard 74
Cromwell, John 74
Cromwell, Oliver 74
Cromwell, Patience 74
Cromwell, William 1
Cromwell, Winnifred 74
Cronk, Jacob 227
Crook, Coleman R. 6
Crook, Colia S. 6
Crook, Eliza H. 6
Crook, Elizabeth N. 6
Crook, Francis C. 6
Crook, John 6, 131
Crook, Margaret 131
Crook, Mary Ann 6
Crook, Ruthy 6
Croom, John W. 74
Croom, Narcissa T. 74
Croom, William 46, 82, 158, 267, 334
Crosland, Joshua 74
Cross, Absolom 75
Cross, Albert 75
Cross, Ben 75
Cross, Elijah 160, 207
Cross, J. B. 75
Cross, James 15, 92, 218, 234
Cross, Jno. B. 75
Cross, Maclin 75
Cross, Nimrod 266
Cross, Ranson 75
Cross, Robert 75
Cross, Uriah 15
Cross, William 254
Crossland, James 187
Crossland, Joshua 75
Crossland, Lucinda 75
Crossland, Sally 75
Crouch, G. W. 260
Crouch, James A. 181

Crouch, Peter 172
Crow, Calvin 75
Crow, Elizabeth 75
Crow, J. A. 75
Crow, J. R. 75
Crow, James 75, 154
Crow, Jane 75
Crow, John 75
Crow, Mary 75
Crow, Narcissa 75
Crow, W. R. G. 299
Crowell, Hezekiah 245
Crown, William 46, 205, 288
Crowson, R. W. 171
Crowson, Richard W. 129
Crudupe, Elisha 75
Crudupe, John 3, 75
Crudupe, Robert 75
Cruil, Andrew 22
Crunk, John 57
Crunk, Joseph J. B. 73
Crunk, Polly 152
Crunk, Richard 166
Crutcher, Carter 233
Crutcher, Edmund 30, 34, 36
Crutcher, Thomas 179
Crutchfield, Thomas 322
Crutchfield, William 75, 302
Cullwell, Robert 75
Cullwell, Wm. 75
Cully, Bennett 107
Culp, Daniel 76
Culp, Elizabeth 76
Culp, Fielding 76
Culp, Isabella Vanlear 76
Culp, Susan 76
Culton, Joseph 76
Cummin, Philip 303
Cummings, B. F. 76
Cummings, David 320
Cummings, George 76
Cummings, Hugh 76
Cummins, Mary A. F. 76
Cummins, W. E. 76
Cumpton, John 188, 322
Cunning, James C. 94
Cunningham, Alexander 17
Cunningham, Benjamin B. 77
Cunningham, Christopher 76, 87
Cunningham, Dorcas 77, 283
Cunningham, Edward 308
Cunningham, Elender 17
Cunningham, Elizabeth 76-77
Cunningham, Engert 77
Cunningham, Ephraim 77
Cunningham, George 76, 330
Cunningham, J. B. 76, 232
Cunningham, James 76-77, 313
Cunningham, Jesse 76-77, 283
Cunningham, John 46, 77
Cunningham, Joseph 77, 330
Cunningham, Kiziah 77
Cunningham, Langston 77, 84
Cunningham, Linan 77
Cunningham, Lucy Ann 77
Cunningham, Margaret 77, 199
Cunningham, Martha 77
Cunningham, Mary 77
Cunningham, Moses 76, 124, 215
Cunningham, Nancy 77
Cunningham, Peggy 76
Cunningham, Polly 77
Cunningham, Prudence 17
Cunningham, Rachael 77
Cunningham, Richard 77
Cunningham, Sally W. 17
Cunningham, Sarah Ann 17
Cunningham, Thomas 77, 150
Cunningham, William 777
Curd, William E. 306
Curl, William 232
Curry, John 208
Curtis, Bethena 78
Curtis, E. B. 252
Curtis, Harriet R. C. 77
Curtis, Joel 118
Curtis, Louisana 77
Curtis, Samuel 78
Curtis, Sarah D. 77
Curtis, William 78
Cusick, Andrew 57, 78, 174
Cusick, John 174
Cusick, Samuel 78
Cusslias, John Cathart 74
Cynthia [a slave] 341
Dacus, John 172
Dacus, Nancy 172
Dagby, Nathan 1
Dailam, F. R. 133
Daily, Jas. V. 78, 271
Daily, Mary D. 78
Dale, Adam 255
Dale, Wm. 222, 234
Dallam F. R. 133, 171
Dalton, Nicholas 78
Damron, William 279
Damson, Christo 221
Dan [a slave] 30
Dance, John E. 165
Dance, Russell 165
Daniel [a slave] 17, 260
Daniel, Martin C. 33
Daniel, Walter W. 33
Daniel, Welley F. 135
Darby, Ann M. 78
Darby, J. V. 78
Darby, Mary A. 78
Darby, Patrick 309
Darden, Ann 78
Darden, Betsey 78
Darden, Holland 78, 277
Darden, J. H. 78
Darden, James 78
Darden, Jonathan 78
Dardin, Abraham 37
Dardin, Thomas 308
Dardis, James 223, 331
Dardis, Thomas 78, 249, 308
Darnal, Milberry 78
Darnal, Nancy 78
Darnal, Nicholas 78
Darr, Eve 78
Darr, Henry 78
Darrow, Benjn. 269
Darrum, James 187
Darwin, G. C. 79
Darwin, George 78, 128, 219-220, 257, 264,
Darwin, James C. 220
Darwin, Margaret 257
Darwin, Polly 78, 264
Darwin, Richmond 219
Darwin, William G. 78
Dashield, R. R. 123
Dateridge, Lewis 79
Dateridge, Milberry 79
Daugherty, Charles 79
Daugherty, Dennis 79
Daugherty, George 79
Daugherty, Matthew 79
Daugherty, Moses 79
Daulton, Nicholas 78
Davenport, David 162
Davenport, Emaline 162
Davenport, Joseph 263
Davenport, Thomas 79
Davenport, William 190
Davice, Reps A. 81
David [a slave] 94
David, Assariah R. 79
David, Isham 75
David, Isiah 79
David, Logan S. 223
David, William 283
David, Y. M. 80
David, Yarborough 80
Davids, Sampson 211
Davidson, Abraham 170
Davidson, Andrew 79
Davidson, Ansel 80
Davidson, Benjamin 79
Davidson, Bluford 79
Davidson, Carlton 79
Davidson, Catharin R. 45
Davidson, Christopher C. 79
Davidson, Emanuel 79
Davidson, Ephraim B. 6, 79, 183, 230, 265, 283
Davidson, Francis P. 79
Davidson, George 21, 30, 40, 342
Davidson, James 79-80
Davidson, John 50, 80, 151
Davidson, Lucinda 79
Davidson, Lucy 100
Davidson, Martha 79-80
Davidson, Nathan 80

Davidson, Richard 79-80
Davidson, Robert 133, 212
Davidson, Sarah 79-80
Davidson, Thomas 79-80
Davidson, William 18, 79-80
Davidson, Wilson Z. 79
Davie, Francis 313
Davie, Quintin 80
Davie, Yarborough 80
Davis, A. 80
Davis, Aaron 166
Davis, Adaline J. 80
Davis, Andrew 80-81
Davis, Ann 81
Davis, Anthony 82
Davis, Azariah 118
Davis, Benjamin 80-81
Davis, Berry 279
Davis, Burgess B. 80
Davis, Charlotte 80, 280
Davis, David 80
Davis, Elizabeth 80, 81, 100, 178, 344
Davis, Etheldred 14
Davis, Francis M. 82
Davis, George 12, 318
Davis, Henry 80, 280
Davis, Isaac 274
Davis, Isabella J. 80
Davis, Isham 75, 80, 126, 178, 291
Davis, J. H. 56, 120, 285
Davis, J. P. 80
Davis, James 80-82, 240, 300
Davis, John 56, 80-82, 167, 187, 207, 266
Davis, Joseph 81, 191
Davis, Lydia 81, 100
Davis, M. 23
Davis, M. H. 166, 249
Davis, M. P. 81
Davis, Marriott 36, 81
Davis, Martial 279
Davis, Mary R. 80-81, 280
Davis, Miles H. 42, 96
Davis, Morgan 10, 126, 252-253
Davis, Nancy 82
Davis, Nathaniel 5, 80-81, 134, 295, 343,
Davis, Pricilla J. 81
Davis, R. N. 81
Davis, Reps 81
Davis, Robert 81
Davis, S. C. 81
Davis, Saml. 81, 264, 274
Davis, Sarah 81
Davis, Thomas 81, 84, 120, 273
Davis, W. C. 96
Davis, W. G. 80
Davis, W. J. 78, 119, 252, 281,
Davis, W. S. 56
Davis, W. W. 42, 96, 175, 207

Davis, Wallace W. 344
Davis, Walter 81
Davis, William 75, 82, 329, 344
Davis, Willie 64
Davis, Wilson 82
Davis, Zachariah143
Davison, Samuel122
Daviss, James H. 45
Davy, Jehu 191
Davy, Yarborough 80
Daws, John 166
Dawson, Jane 82
Dawson, Jesse 285
Dawson, W. A. 82
Dawson, William J. 82
Day, E. H. 82
Day, Geo. W. 315
Day, Jno. H. 82, 110
Day, Lemuel 191
Day, Matthew 161, 241
Day, Ransom 34, 122
Day, Susan V. 82
Day, Wm. A. 82
Deadrick, George M. 82
Deamar, Hannah 237, 309
Deamer, John 237, 309
Dean, Alsey 82
Dean, Hardy J. 82
Dean, Henry 135
Dean, Jacob 72
Dean, James 217
Dean, John 82, 224
Dearing, William 82
Dearmar, John 82
Dearmond, John123
Deason, Elicy 83
Deason, Elvy 83
Deason, Enock 83
Deason, Joel 83
Deason, John 83
Deason, Rebecca 83
Deason, Shepherd 82-83
Deason, William 83
Deberry, A. 299
Deberry, Absolem 66, 83, 125, 299
Deberry, Allen 83, 332
Deberry, Ann 156, 333
Deberry, Elija J. A. 83
Deberry, Jno. 83
Deberry, Mary 182
Deberry, Mathew 83
Deberry, Matthias 83
Deberry, Robt. S. 182
Deberry, W. E. 193, 324
Dedman, Edith 83
Deer, Gilbert 85
Deer, Susan 85
Deery, James 135
Dees, Jacob 49
Defries, Asher 235
Defries, Eliza 235
Degraffenreed, Francis 164
Dehart, Elizabeth 83
Dehart, John 83
Dehart, Mary 83

DeJarnet, John 57
DeJarnet, Matilda 57
DeJournet, Matilda 57
Delk, David 201, 209
Dell, Asa 83
Dell, John 83
Dell, Samuel 83
Dell, Thomas 83
Dell, William 83
Deloach, Arthur 80
Deloach, Elizabeth F. 106
Deloach, Jarisha 84
Deloach, Joseph 84
Deloach, Olive 58
Deloach, Samuel 84
Deloach, Solomon 84
Deloach, William 331
Deloch, Samuel 84
Delozier, Andrew 84, 174, 275
Delozier, Asa 84
Delozier, Caroline 84
Delozier, Cromwell 84, 306
Delozier, Harriet 84
Delozier, Joseph 84, 306
Delozier, Malden 84
Delozier, Samuel C. 84
Demembrane, Eliza 21
Dement, Jane 81
Den, William 280
Dennis, Amanda M. 278
Dennis, Cary 278
Dennis, Catherine 296
Dennis, James 84
Dennis, John 84
Dennis, L. M. 278
Dennis, Miles 84
Dennis, Sarah Ann 84
Dennis, Thomas E. 296
Dennis, William 84, 127
Dennison, Robert 304
Dennon, Asa M. 222
Denson, Jesse 61, 80, 160, 173, 219
Denson, Nathaniel 173, 192
Denton, Erasmus 43
Denton, Holland 145, 245
Denton, Isaac 84, 222
Denton, James 84
Denton, Joseph 84
Denton, Saml. 84
Deny, John 340
Depreast, Robert 337
Derrick, Asa 84
Derrick, Calvin 84
Derrick, Elizabeth 84
Devault, Peter 318
Dever, James 85
Dever, Mary 84
Devers, James 84, 263
Devers, Jane 85
Devers, Jenny 84
Devers, William 84
Devin, Elizabeth 85
Devin, John 85
Devin, William 85
Dew, Arthur 85

Dew, Nathaniel 202
Dew, Susanna 85
Dewhit, Amelia H. 246
Dewhit, William H. 246
DeWitt, Allen W. 54, 63
Dewitt, Emelia H. 245-246
Dewitt,William H. 245-246
Dews, Elizabeth 85
Dews, Nathaniel 85
Dews, Sarah B. 85
Dews, William B. 85
Dice, Jacob 28, 85
Dick [a slave] 126, 317
Dickens, E. V. H. 85
Dickens, Jno. R. 85
Dickens, Nancy 85
Dickens, Robert F. 85
Dickens, Saml. 85
Dickens, William 85, 297
Dickerson, Willis B. 334
Dickeson, Nathaniel 86
Dickey, A. C. 86
Dickey, Anderson 86, 342
Dickey, Ann C. 86
Dickey, Asa C. 86
Dickey, David H.13
Dickey, Geo. 86
Dickey, J. F. 9
Dickey, M. A. 86
Dickey, Madison H. 86
Dickey, Mary A. 86
Dickey, Matthew 86
Dickey, P. H. 86
Dickey, Percilla Ann 86
Dickey, Priscilla 86
Dickey, R. J. 86
Dickey, Robert 86
Dickey, W. C. 86, 105, 130
Dickings, James 86
Dickings, Samuel 86
Dickins, Ann 316
Dickins, Elijah P. 316
Dickins, Joseph W. 316
Dickins, Saml. 86
Dickinson, John W. 253
Dickinson, Nathaniel 180
Dickson, Charlott B. 301
Dickson, John B. 301
Dicky, J. F. 147, 253
Dikes, Mary 223
Dilcey [a slave] 26
Dill, Archibald 86
Dill, Arthur 86
Dill, Elijah 86
Dill, Rowland C. 86
Dill, Solomon 86
Dill, Stephen 86
Dill, Thos. 217
Dill, William 86
Dillard, Alexander 67, 271
Dillard, Allen R. 300
Dillard, Benja. 181
Dillard, Edward 86, 340
Dillard, George 86
Dillard, James 73, 183
Dillard, Joshua 86
Dillard Martha 86

Dillard, Rebecca 86
Dillard, Stacey 86
Dillard, Thos. 86
Dillard, William 86
Dillen, Matilda 87
Dinah [a slave] 17, 119
Discon, John 87
Ditmore, John 87
Ditto, Nancy 1
Dixon, Adaline 87
Dixon, Amanda 87
Dixon, Delilah 87
Dixon, Dilly 87
Dixon, Eliza 87
Dixon, Elizabeth 87, 195
Dixon, Emiley 87
Dixon, Harriet 87
Dixon, James 87
Dixon, Jane 324
Dixon, John 87, 205, 324
Dixon, Jordan 87
Dixon, Mary 87
Dixon, Minos 87
Dixon, Nancy 87
Dixon, Polly 87
Dixon, Richard 87
Dixon, Samuel 13, 87
Dixon, Sarah 87
Dixon, Thomas 87
Dixon, William 87, 121
Doak, John 87
Doak, Jonathan 87
Doak, Josiah 87
Doak, R. S. 87
Doak, Robt. 271
Doak, Rody 87
Doak, Samuel 14, 180, 194, 318
Doak, William 87, 194
Dobbings, John 74
Dobbins, Jacob 84
Dobbins, Solomon 165
Dobbs, Amanda J. 88
Dobbs, Henry 336
Dobbs, Malenda 88
Dobbs, Matilda 88
Dobbs, Pheby 88, 221
Dobbs, W. J. F. 88
Dobson, Archibald 47, 88
Dobson, B. C. 88, 330
Dobson, Joseph 88
Dobson, Mary 47, 88
Doby, Elizabeth 3
Doby, John 3
Dodam, F. R. 133
Doddy, Howell 17, 27
Dodgen Mary Jane 88
Dodson, Cha. 236
Dodson, David 88
Dodson, Frances 88
Dodson, James 174
Dodson, Jessee 88
Dodson, Lazerus 88
Dodson, William 88
Doe, John 154, 194
Doherty, Edmond T. 225
Doherty, Francis 79

Doherty, George 79, 88
Doherty, Hellen 79
Doherty, Mary 79
Donaho, Golman 275
Donaldson, Charles 122
Donaldson, Thomas 122
Donalson, Stokely 88
Donelson, Andrew 88-89
Donelson, Betsey 88
Donelson, Cresse 88
Donelson, Daniel 89
Donelson, Ebenezer 88
Donelson, John 89
Donelson, Mary 88
Donelson, Rhoda 88
Donelson, Samuel 82, 89
Donnel, Callie 89
Donnel, George 89, 271
Donnel, Wm. 271
Donnell, James 89
Donnell, John 79
Donnell, Margaret 89
Donnell, Martha 299
Donnell, Mary 89
Donnell, Robert 89
Donnell, Samuel 89, 105, 299
Donnell, Sarah 89
Donnell, Thomas 89
Donnell, William 52, 89
Donnelson, Elizabeth 89
Donnelson, Moses M. 23
Donoho [no name] 46
Donoho, Thomas 89
Dooly, Thomas 89
Doris, Samuel 89
Dorris, Isaac 89, 90, 301
Dorris, John 89
Dorris, Joseph 89, 162, 236, 239
Dorris, Miller 242
Dorris, Wm. 57, 89-90
Dorson, Absolem 83
Dorson, Enuck 83
Dorson, William 83
Dortch, Isaac 78, 134, 186
Dosset, Anny 90
Dosset, Willis 90
Dougalss, Harry L. 342
Douge, Enoch102
Dougherty, Bamer 291
Dougherty, Bunian 291
Dougherty, George 17, 27
Dougherty, John 288
Dougherty, Ruebin 291
Douglas, E. M. 234
Douglas, Nora 90
Douglas, S. N. 234
Douglas, Thomas G. 234
Douglass, Alexr. 90
Douglass, Alfred 90
Douglass, Benjamin L. 77
Douglass, Burchett 59
Douglass, Edward 140, 156
Douglass, Guy 23
Douglass, H. L. 7
Douglass, J. C. 238

Douglass, Jesse 140
Douglass, John 90
Douglass, Nancy 77, 257
Douglass, Rhoda 90
Douglass, Thomas140, 257
Douglass, William 90
Dowler, John 90
Dowler, Thomas 90
Down, John 90
Down, Sarah Jane 90
Down, Wm. H. 90
Downey, Jonathan 263
Downs, Joseph M. F. 90
Doxey, Jno. L. 173
Doyl, Edward 58
Doyl, Labitha 58
Doyle, H. P. 90
Doyle, Hickason L. 292-293
Doyle, J. H. 90
Doyle, James H. 90
Doyle, Labitha 58
Doyle, W. C. 3, 20, 43, 64, 90, 102, 176, 208, 239, 246-247, 270, 316
Doyley, Ezekiel 211, 231, 249
Drake, Bird B. 90
Drake, Brittain 33, 301
Drake, Francis 90
Drake, Jas. W. 338
Drake, Jesse 100
Drake, Margaret 338
Drake, Richard 136, 190
Drake, Sally 90
Drake, Sarah D. 90, 235, 244
Drake, Tabitha 90
Drake, Thos. H.18, 53, 128, 193, 222-232
Drake, Widow 90
Drane, John M. 91, 315
Drane, Louisa M. 315
Draper, B. M. 91
Draper, Brice M. 91, 147
Draper, David H. 177
Draper, Edward B. 91, 300
Draper, Eliza 117
Draper, H. H. 41, 2331
Draper, James 35, 73, 91, 117, 165, 168, 177, 216, 238, 246, 279, 302, 337,
Draper, Lawson 91, 256
Draper, Milton 35, 41, 78, 91, 207, 220, 264, 302, 304
Draper, Sarah 91
Draper, Thomas 91, 1171
Draper, William 73, 173, 251
Drennon, Ann 21, 91, 233
Drennon, David 21, 91
Drennon, Delpha 262
Drennon, James 21, 91, 128, 277
Drennon, John 21, 91, 233
Drennon, Joseph 91
Drennon, Thomas 21, 91, 295
Drennum, James 338

Drew [a slave] 267
Drewry, Nicholas 91
Drewry, Ruth 91
Drury, James Brantly 91
Drury, Larkin 128
Duckham, R. 44
Dudney, Rhoda 344
Dudny, Patrick N. 344
Duffey, E. 312
Duffey, Emma 312
Duffie, John 91
Duffy, Henderson 91
Duffy, John 91
Duffy, Kitty H. 91
Duffy, M. B. 91
Duffy, Mary 91
Duffy, Patrick M. 91
Duffy, William 91
Dugg, Mary117
Duggan, Wilson 13, 32, 228, 264
Dugherty, Ann 225
Dugherty, Edmond L. 225
Duke, George M. 91
Duke, Matthew 110
Dulen, Phillip N.109
Dulen, Susan G.109
Dum, Danl.91
Dun, Thomas 91
Dunavant, E. A. 226, 236
Dunavin, Michael 92
Dunbar, Stephen 92
Dunbar, William100
Duncan, Arel 196
Duncan, Asel 196
Duncan, Axel 196
Duncan, Isabella 313
Duncan, John 92
Duncan, Joseph 29
Duncan, Lewis 91
Duncan, Martin 78, 92, 133, 147, 288, 319
Duncan, Stephen 92
Duncan, William H. 42
Dunevant, J. G. 92
Dunevant, P. D. 92
Dunevant, W. E. 92
Dungan, Jerimiah 92
Dunlap, Ephrim 92
Dunlap, Hugh 90
Dunlap, J. E. 102, 233
Dunlap, Martha 257
Dunlap, William F. 256-257
Dunloe, Henry 92
Dunn, Azeriah 92
Dunn, John 92, 282
Dunn, Levi 277
Dunn, Susan 92, 319
Dunn, Thomas 10, 92
Dunn, William 92
Dunn, Zacheriah 78
Dunnaway, Sarah E. 250
Dunnaway, W. M. 39, 250
Dunnevant, A. 92
Dunnevant, Daniel 92, 178, 345
Dunnevant, E. A. 92

Dunnevant, Ferdnand 92
Dunnevant, J. G. 92
Dunnevant, Victoria 93
Dunstan, James 93
Dupree, C. H. 103
Dupree, Martha E. 103
Durdon, Easter 93
Durdon, Holland 93
Durdon, Jonathan 93
Durrum, James 93, 147
Dwyer, Jane 326-327
Dwyer, William 326-327
Dycus, Edward 128
Dycus, Mary 128
Dycus, Melenda 128
Dye, Wm. 93
Dyer, Carter 39
Dyer, Cary 157
Dyer, Florintha 29
Dyer, James P. 93
Dyer, Margaret 93
Dyer, Robert 157
Dykes, James 93
Dykes, Wm. 93
Dyrant, Eli B. 331
Dyres, Daniel 173
Dysart, Alexander 155
Dysart, Eli B. 331
Eagan, Barnaby 93
Eagan, Peggy 93
Eagan, Sally 93
Eagan, Siney 93
Eagan, William 93
Eagen, Samuel 93
Eagle, Christian 141
Eagle, Henry 93
Eagun, Sarah 237
Eaken, Harrison 2
Eakin, John 93
Eakin, Spencer 93
Eakin, Thomas 93
Eakin, William 93
Eakle, Amon 93
Eakle, Amos 93-94
Eakle, Andrew 93-94
Eakle, Christian 93-94
Eakle, Henry 93-94, 141
Eakle, Jacob 93-94
Eakle, John 94
Eakle, Jonathan 94
Eakle, Phoebe 94
Eakle, Tabitha 93-94
Eakle, William 93-94
Earheart, Abraham 72
Earmile, Abigale 307
Earnest, Henry 116
Easley, Isaac 94, 167
Easly, John L.94
Eason, Alfred 94
Eason, Arrabilla 94
Eason, Eliza 94
Eason, Frances 94
Eason, James K. 94
Eason, Monroe 94
Eason, Montgomery 94
Eason, Robert 94
Eaton, Dicy 313

Eaton, Elizabeth 343
Eaton, James 180
Eaton, John R. 94
Eaton, Joseph 256, 313, 336, 343
Eaton, Polly Ann 180
Eaton, Victoria 313
Eavins, Nathan 120
Eblin, John 308
Echoles, Newlen 95
Echols, Abner 94
Echols, Elkanah 94
Echols, John 319
Echols, L. 94
Echols, Larkin 95
Echols, Martha 94
Echols, W. D. 95
Eckols, Abigal 95
Eckols, Elizabeth 94
Eckols, Joel 94
Eckols, Jos. A. 95
Eckols, Mary E. 95
Eckols, Mildred A. 95
Eckols, Richard 94
Eddington, Jessee W. 126
Edington, David 193
Edlow, John R. 95
Edminston, William 89
Edmonson, Robt. 8
Edmonson, Willie 95
Edmoston, William 217
Edmunds, Alexr. N. 8
Edny, C. J. 95
Edward, William 339
Edwards, Anderson 95
Edwards, Arthur 95
Edwards, Benjamin 151, 192, 250
Edwards, Caroline 95
Edwards, Catherine 95
Edwards, David 77
Edwards, E. 328
Edwards, Edward 95
Edwards, Elizabeth 77
Edwards, Ephraim 330
Edwards, Francis C. 95
Edwards, Frank 95
Edwards, Henrietta 95
Edwards, Henry 95, 194
Edwards, J. F. 334
Edwards, James 77, 144, 289, 334
Edwards, Jesse R. 77
Edwards, John 77, 95
Edwards, Joseph 77
Edwards, Kiziah 77
Edwards, Labon 95
Edwards, Lucy C. 77
Edwards, Mary A. 97
Edwards, Nathaniel 95
Edwards, Ninian 180
Edwards, Oliver 179
Edwards, Polly 339
Edwards, Robert 249, 299
Edwards, Ruebin H. 97
Edwards, W. M. 59
Edwards, Walter 95

Edwards, William 95, 97, 335
Edy [a slave] 269
Edy, Hiram 104
Ekle, Amos 94
Elder, James 95
Elder, John 138
Eldridge, Tyler 95
Eldrige, Thomas 53
Elgin, Elizabeth 95
Elgin, John 95
Elgin, William B. 95
Elhiers, John 96
Elisa [a slave] 322
Elison, Alexander 96
Elkens, Gabrial 181
Elkins, Stacey 86
Elledge, James 96
Elledge, Martha J. 96
Elledge, William 96
Ellen [a slave] 320
Ellin, William 96
Elliot, James 96
Elliott, Benjamin 11
Elliott, Faulkner 304
Elliott, John 96
Elliott, Reuben 319
Elliott, Samuel 180, 268
Ellis, Andrew 96
Ellis, Delila 96
Ellis, Francis 96
Ellis, George W. 96
Ellis, J. W. 145
Ellis, Jacob 96
Ellis, Jeremiah 96
Ellis, John 96
Ellis, Joseph 96
Ellis, Lewis 96
Ellis, M. L. 96
Ellis, Michael 96
Ellis, Polly 96
Ellis, S. S. 96
Ellis, Sabetha 96
Ellis, Samuel H. 141
Ellis, Sibby 96
Ellis, Simeon 96
Ellis, Sims 96, 190
Ellis, Thomas 96
Ellis, William 96, 150, 190, 216
Ellison, Robert 96, 287
Elmon, Traviss 309
Elmore, Julius 309
Elrod, Austin 97
Elrod, James 97
Elrod, Mary Eliza 97
Elrod, Samuel 97
Elrod, Sarah 97
Elstin, Elice 284
Elworth, Joseph M. 52
Embree, John 97
Embree, Moses 97
Embree, Thomas 97
Embrie, E. Moses 97
Embrie, Isaac 97
Emert, F. L. 49, 228
Emert, F. S. 97
Emert, J. B. 212

Emert, J. D. 97
Emert, James M. 97
Emert, N. W. 212, 228, 307
Emert, P. S. 97
Emery, [no name] 97
Emson, Caleb 97
Emson, Rebekah 97
Emson, William 97
Encoks, Mary Ann 316
England, John 156
England, Joseph 305
Engle, John 21
Engleman, Jane 309
Engleman, Joseph 97, 308
English, Elizabeth 178
English, Henry 142
English, Robert 142
Enloe, Joel S. 12, 101, 179
Enochs, Alfred 284
Enochs, C. W. 222
Enochs, Louisa 97
Enocks, Alford 316
Enocks, John G. 316
Enocks, Maria 316
Enox, Robert H. 315
Epen, Thomas 179
Epperson, Elinor S. 97
Epperson, Elizabeth H. 97
Epperson, Henry H. 97
Epperson, Saml. 97, 224
Epperson, Thos. N. 97
Eppes, Martha B. 97
Eppes, W. B. 97
Ere, Gil 64
Ernest, Asa 43-44
Ernest, Jas. D. 43-44
Ernest, Phillip R. 44, 251
Ervell, Wm. 99
Erwin, Andrew 157, 235
Erwin, Dice 157
Erwin, Elizabeth 157
Erwin, Francis 97
Erwin, James 157
Erwin, Margaret 157
Erwin, Mary 157, 268
Erwine, Benjamin 157
Escue, Rachel 98
Escue, Samuel 98, 301
Escue, Sarah 98
Eslinger, James 261, 263
Essen, Thomas 179
Essman, John 98
Essman, Thomas 98
Ester [a slave] 76, 132
Esther [a slave] 317
Estis, John 9
Estis, Penelope 98, 306
Etherton, Louisa 98, 335
Etherton, T. D. A. 98
Eubanks, Martin 278
Eudailey, J. F. 98
Eudaly, Catherine 98
Eudaly, E. Bet 98
Eudaly, Francis Marion 98
Eudaly, Mary Jane 98
Eudeley, Isral 1
Evans, Adam 98-99

Evans, Alexander 98
Evans, Andrew 98
Evans, Archer 14
Evans, Benjn. 114
Evans, Catharine 98, 99
Evans, Deborah 99
Evans, Elizabeth 206
Evans, Floyd 98
Evans, George A. L. 138
Evans, J. M. 23, 57
Evans, James 70, 98, 164, 253
Evans, John 98, 122, 138, 270, 294
Evans, L. D. 98-99
Evans, Margaret 98
Evans, Nathan 120
Evans, Obediah 91
Evans, Richard 99
Evans, Sally 91
Evans, Sampson 99
Evans, Samuel 99
Evans, Sarah 98
Evans, Sary 98
Evans, Stokely 243
Evans, Stokely D. 98
Evans, Walter 152, 189
Evans, Willis 206
Evins, Evin 99
Evos, Jos. M. 145
Ewell, Leighton 24
Ewell, Wm. 99
Ewing, Andrew 187
Ewing, Evelina 99
Ewing, James L. 99
Ewing, Rebecca 99
Ewing, Tele A. 99
Ezell, Lameck W. 330
Face, Ausustine P. 88
Fagola, Adam 99
Fagola, Michael 71, 99
Fain [a slave] 281
Fain, Agness 99
Fain, Ebenezer 99
Fain, John 99
Fain, Nicholas 99
Fain, Rosanna 99
Fain, Ruth 99
Fain, Samuel 99
Fain, Thomas 99
Fain, William 99
Faircloth, C.155
Fakis, John 235
Fan, George 99
Fancher, Levi 99
Fanning, Joe 99
Fanny [a slave] 88
Fargason, John 176
Faris, Alex 242
Farley, LaFayette 99
Farley, Louisa Scott 138
Farley, Mary Francis 99
Farmer, Ben F. 295
Farmer, Hudson 100
Farmer, Jas. L. 164
Farmer, Loderick 6
Farmer, William 81, 100

Farr, Ephraim 100
Farr, Polly 100
Farr, William 100
Farrar, Garland 276
Farrar, Mary L. 276
Farrell, Epperson H. 102
Farrell, William C. 100
Farris, Amanda M. 333
Farris, W. J. 133, 201, 231
Farris, Wilford 86
Farris, William 333
Faucet, Richard 100
Fauling, Elizabeth 107
Fauling, Wm. 107
Faulk, Joseph A. 211
Faulkner, Amos 100
Faulkner, Cornelia 100
Faulkner, Delia Ann 100
Faulkner, Enos H. 100
Faulkner, Jesse 100
Faulkner, LaFayette 100
Faulkner, Martha 100
Faulkner, Matilda 100
Faust, Louis 265
Feaney, Andrew 239
Featherston, A. T. 100
Featherston, C. R. 100
Featherston, Wm.100, 221
Featherstone, C. K. 2
Featherstone, W. J. 2
Feezel, Henry 100
Feezel, Jacob Henegar 100
Felcker, Shannon 100
Felcker, William 100
Felker, Shannon 115, 273
Fenner, Ann 101, 165
Fenner, D. Richard 161
Fenner, Darvin P. 165
Fenner, E. D. 101
Fenner, Eliga Fanny 165
Fenner, John101, 161, 165, 203
Fenner, Julia 101
Fenner, Junius 101
Fenner, Kate E. 101
Fenner, Laura 101
Fenner, Marianna 161
Fenner, Mary F.101
Fenner, R. H. 339
Fenner, Rebecca Ann165
Fenner, Richard 29, 100-101, 165, 203,
Fenner, Ro. 29, 101, 161, 203
Fenner, Robert 41, 101, 165
Fenner, Rosa Matilda 165
Fenner, Walter C. 165
Fentress, George W. 101, 135
Fentriss, Absolom 239
Fergerson, Alex. J. 238
Fergerson, John A. 280
Ferguson, A. G. 226
Ferguson, Douglass 101
Ferguson, E. F. 144
Ferguson, Elizabeth 101

Ferguson, George 101
Ferguson, Grandison 101
Ferguson, H. F. 3, 239
Ferguson, J. B. 135
Ferguson, J. D. 101, 301
Ferguson, James 101
Ferguson, Jo Allen 101
Ferguson, John 94, 100
Ferguson, Jonathan 68, 101
Ferguson, Joseph G. 101-102
Ferguson, Josephine 101-102
Ferguson, Orlando C. 101
Ferguson, Tennessee 101
Ferguson, Thomas 101-102
Ferguson, W. R. 101
Ferguson, Wyatt 61
Feribie, S. 102
Ferrell, Ann 102
Ferrell, Burton 71
Ferrell, C. H. 102
Ferrell, Dent 102, 287, 296
Ferrell, Isaac E.185
Ferrell, James 102, 337
Ferrell, Madison 102
Ferrell, Martha 102
Ferrell, Mary E. 102
Ferrell, S. George 102
Ferrell, Suba 102
Ferrell, Susan 102
Ferrell, Thad. H. 102
Ferrill, Alice 102
Ferrill, Ella 102
Ferrill, Epperson 301
Ferrill, J. S. 102
Ferrill, Lula 102
Ferrill, Martha 102
Ferrill, Silas 110, 249
Ferrill, Thadeus 102
Ferrill, Thomas 102
Ferrill, Walie 102
Fichwick, John173
Fielder, A. F. 317
Fielder, A. T. 125, 144, 214
Fielder, B. T. 102
Fielder, Francis 102
Fielder, L. B. 102
Fielder, M. A. F.102
Fielder, Mary 102
Fielder, S. B. 102
Fielder, S. H. 102
Fielder, S. M. L. 102
Fielder, Sarah H. 102
Fields, Betsy 103
Fields, David 102-103
Fields, Dicy 103
Fields, George 103
Fields, Lucy 102
Fields, Milly 103
Fields, Polly 103
Fields, Sally 103
Fields, Susanna 103
Fife, H. H. 337
Fife, Halliday H. 337
Fife, Mary 337

Figuers, Thomas 103
Figures, Mathew 103, 178
Fikes, Elisha 268
Fikes, Frys 103
Fikes, Nathan 103, 218
Fikes, Sarah 103
Findly, B. 340
Fink, David H. 323
Finley, Allen 103
Finley, Anna 103
Finley, Charles L.103
Finley, George 103
Finley, John 14, 103, 223
Finley, Lafayette 103
Finley, Margaret 223
Finley, Martha Virginia103
Finley, Mary E. 103
Finley, Michael 294
Finley, Susan A. L.103
Finley, Thomas 103
Finley, Wm. 103
Finly, Obediah G. 2, 7, 103, 144
Finny, Matilda 103
Firestone, Eve 103
Fiser, Henry 149, 309
Fisher, Elizabeth 11
Fisher, John 17, 218, 325
Fisher, Phillip 48
Fitch, Abraham 219
Fitchpatrick, John 103
Fitchpatrick, Sally 103
Fite, George S. 54
Fite, Hugh 103
Fite, Leonard 103
Fite, Susan E. 54
Fitts, John 104
Fitts, Oliver 104
Fitz, Henry B. 229
Fitzgerald, Joseph 304
Fitzgerald, Patrick 104
Fitzgerald, Sarah 304
Fitzhugh, Anzanetta H. 104
Fitzhugh, Benjamin F. 104
Fitzhugh, John S. 104
Fitzhugh, Margaret B.104
Fitzhugh, T. H.104
Fitzhugh, Tennessee A. 104
Fitzhugh, Thomas 55, 104, 125, 170
Fitzhugh, W. C.104, 172
Flack, Rufus K.181
Flaherty, Jas.155
Flanery, Wm. 332
Flanigan, Ailsey 104
Flanigan, George 104
Flanigan, Isabella 104
Flanigan, John 76,104
Flanigan, Martha J. 104
Flanigan, Rachael 104
Flanigan, Rhoda104
Flanigan, Sarah 104
Flanigan, William 76, 104
Flannery, Isaac104
Flannery, Jacob104
Flatt, David K.118

Flatt, Lucinda 104
Flatt, Pleasant 104
Fleener, Adam 104
Fleming, J. G. 312
Fleming, Matilda 31
Fleming, Robert 104
Fleming, Wm. 104
Flemming, Martha 31
Flemming, Robert 31
Fletcher, Aaron 46
Fletcher, Amy W.198
Fletcher, Betsey104
Fletcher, John 4
Fletcher, Joseph C.198, 271
Fletcher, Lazarus104
Fletcher, Patsey104
Fletcher, Peggy104
Fletcher, Sally 97
Fletcher, Simon 47
Fletcher, William104, 142
Flewellen, William 78, 336
Flinn, William 163
Flippo, Garret 322
Flood, Elizabeth104
Flood, Henry 104
Flood, John 104
Flood, Judith 104
Flood, Lucy104
Flood, Robert 104
Flood, Thomas 104
Florence, Alvis 332
Florence, Mary 332
Flowers, Arabel 104
Flowers, Coleman 104
Flowers, Elizabeth 325
Flowers, Joel S. 325
Flowers, Mary 325
Flowers, Nancy105
Flowers, Rowland105
Flowers, William105, 325
Floyd, Anthony 8
Floyd, David165
Floyd, E. S.105
Floyd, Thomas105
Floyd, W. S. 105
Fluellas, William 23
Fly, Micajah 115, 329
Foard, Horatio 27
Fogg, Archela Ann 105
Fogg, Francis A. 105
Fogg, Jno. T. 105
Fogg, Joseph 105, 216
Fogg, Mary Ann 105
Fogg, Thos. M.105
Fogg, Wm. 105
Fogle, Lary 105
Fogleman, G. W.162, 325
Follis, J. J.125
Fonville, Israel 330
Forbes, Alexr. 105
Forbes, James 105
Forbus, Elizabeth 105
Forbus, John 105
Ford, Catherine 105
Ford, Charlotte dye 105
Ford, Davis 305

Ford, Elias 242
Ford, Haskins 82
Ford, James 45
Ford, John 105, 320
Ford, Martha A. 82
Ford, Robt. P. 82
Ford, W. S. J.105
Ford, W. T. 105
Ford, William 105
Forester, Robert 105
Forester, William 196
Forge, John 138
Forgerson, John 90, 106, 215
Forgey, Samuel 106
Forrest, Elisha G. 338
Forrester, Alexander 106
Forsythe, Jacob 151
Forsythe, John 151
Fort, Elias 8, 106, 133
Fort, Eliza 106
Fort, Elizabeth 106
Fort, Jacob 106
Fort, James 106
Fort, Jane V. H.106
Fort, Jeremiah 106
Fort, Jethro Battle 106
Fort, Joshia 93
Fort, Josiah 40, 106, 115, 191, 335,
Fort, Josias 106
Fort, Mary106
Fort, Sarah106
Fort, Sugg106, 331, 335
Fort, Whitmell 106
Fort, William 68, 106, 115
Fortune [a slave] 339
Fortune, John A. 106
Fosta, David 107
Foster, Alexander 89, 107
Foster, Andrew 205
Foster, David 89, 107
Foster, Edmund 107
Foster, Franklin 17
Foster, Guin 42
Foster, Guynn 42
Foster, James 12, 107
Foster, Joel 107
Foster, John 107
Foster, Robert 107
Foster, Thomas 107
Fouling, Betsey 107
Fouling, Wm. 107
Fouse, Joseph 288
Fowler, Adaline 43
Fowler, Agness 107
Fowler, Franklin 143
Fowler, James S. 107
Fowler, John 107, 143
Fowler, Nehemiah 207
Fowler, Robert 107
Fowler, Samuel B. M. 43
Fowler, William 107
Fowlkes, Asa 189
Fowlkes, Charles H. 107
Fowlkes, George A. 107
Fowlkes, Green 107

Fowlkes, H. 107
Fowlkes, H. B. 117
Fowlkes, H. L. 50, 107, 189
Fowlkes, H. S. 107, 248, 338
Fowlkes, Henry 107, 162
Fowlkes, Jenny 107
Fowlkes, Joseph A. 211
Fowlkes, Paschal A. 189
Fowlkes, Thomas H. 107
Fowlkes, W. P. 189, 342
Fowlkes, Zenobia F. 107
Fox, Branson 107
Fox, C. 108, 182, 278
Fox, C. H. 219
Fox, Calvin 13, 22
Fox, Cornelius 2, 108, 211, 273, 310
Fox, D. W. 103
Fox, Eli 23, 67, 144, 234, 252
Fox, Elizabeth 186
Fox, Emanuel 13, 22, 61, 107-108, 211, 247
Fox, George 108
Fox, James M. 107
Fox, John 107-108
Fox, Lenas 231
Fox, Lilman 194
Fox, Mary Jane 107
Fox, Nelson 4, 67
Fox, Polly 207
Fox, Tennessee 108
Fox, William 108, 234, 321
Fraim, Jane 108
Fraim, John 4, 63, 108, 151
Fraim, Prior P. 108
Fraim, Ruth 108
Fraim, Sarah 108
Fraim, William 63, 108
Frame, John H. 32
Frances [a slave] 320
Francis, Hugh 192
Franklin, Absalom 69
Franklin, David J. 290
Franklin, Edward 108
Franklin, George W. 108
Franklin, J. K. 90, 108
Franklin, James 108
Franklin, Jesse 108
Franklin, John 108
Franklin, Owen 108
Franklin, Tina 108
Franklin, W. H. 120, 251
Franklin, William 109
Franks, Jessee 87
Frazer, Farwick 241
Frazer, James 103
Frazer, Preston 106, 181
Frazier, T. J. 2
Frazier, Thomas 109, 172, 251
Frederick [a slave] 107
Freeland, John 87
Freeling, Augustus I. H. 109
Freeling, Jno. H. 109
Freeling, Lucy 109

Freeling, Reuben H. 109
Freeling, Wm. W. 109
Freeman, Abner 142
Freeman, Asbury 109
Freeman, Boln P. 112
Freeman, Christian 142
Freeman, Edward A. 5
Freeman, Eleanor 142
Freeman, Fannie 53
Freeman, J. D. 109
Freeman, James G. 114
Freeman, John 109, 112, 114, 308
Freeman, Joseph B. 109, 182, 297
Freeman, Lewis A. 112
Freeman, Margaret 114
Freeman, Martha Jane 112
Freeman, Mary 5, 87, 114
Freeman, Otheniel 266
Freeman, Sally M. 266
Freeman, Solomon 66, 109
Freeman, Stephen 112
Freeman, Thos. S. 314
Freeman, William R. 114
Frelick, Adam 11
French, Allen 109
French, James M. 109
French, John 109
French, Josiah 109
French, Martin 109
French, Mary 29, 109
French, Melvina 109
French, Rebecca 109
French, Sarah 109
French, Thomas 109
French, Wm. 109
Frey, Henry 21, 23, 216, 294, 329
Frey, Peter 152
Frim, Edward 109
Frim, Sarah 109
Fritz, Elizabeth 229
Frizel, Nathan 242
Frizzel, Christiana 136
Frizzel, William 136
Frizzell, James 136
Frogg, E. D. 169
Frogg, J. M. 242
Frogg, John W. 242
Frogg, Lavina 67, 110
Frogge, Mitchel H. 110
Frogge, Strother 110, 279
Frost, Eli 110
Frost, Harriet 288
Frost, Joseph 60
Frost, Matthew 288
Frost, Wilson 16, 339
Frusly, Ansel 13
Fry, Henry 60,
Fry, Philip 31, 277
Fulbright, Jacob 220
Fulbright, Nancy P. 220
Fulghum, W. 314
Fulghum, William 22, 269
Fulk, Peter S. 155
Fuller, A. W. 95

Fuller, Amanda 110
Fuller, David 110
Fuller, Elias 110
Fuller, Henry J. 306
Fuller, James 110
Fuller, John 110
Fuller, Marg. 110
Fuller, Robt. 90
Fuller, Stacey 110
Fum, Edward 109
Fuqua, James 110
Fuquay, Benjamin 110
Fuquay, Daniel A. 110
Fuquay, Gracey 110
Furgerson, Emeline W. 85
Furgeson, Robert 76
Furguson, A. 128
Furguson, John A. 88
Fussell, Ann 110
Fussell, Berry 110
Fussell, James 22, 50, 110, 277
Fussell, Louisa 110
Fussell, Susan 110
Fussell, William 110
Fussell, Wyatt 22, 110
Futrell, Alex 165
Fyffe, Isaac W. 110
Fyffe, James 110, 203, 227
Fyffe, Peggy 110
Fyffe, Sarah Elizabeth 110
Fyffe, William C. 110
Gadger, Anna 181
Gadger, Jas. 181
Gaglin, Joseph A. 94
Gailbreath, Isabella 110
Gailbreath, Moriah C. 196
Gailbreath, R. J. C. 196, 306
Gailbreath, Robert J. E. 196
Gailbreath, Thomas J. 110
Gailbreath, William A. 110
Gaines, Benjamin 294
Gaines, James H. 110-111
Gaines, Margery 111
Gaines, Mary Ann 111
Gaines, Rufus 111
Gains, William C. 111
Galbraith, Keziah R. 111
Galbreath, Joseph 111
Galbreath, Kizziah 111
Galbreath, Thomas 111
Galbreath, William 33, 111
Galder, James T. 334
Galder, Sarah 334
Gallagy, Darcus 111
Gallahar, John 111
Gallahar, Lee 111
Gallaher, Jas. 305
Gallaher, Thomas 243
Galliher, George 116
Galloway, Charles 111
Galloway, James 111
Galloway, Patsey 96
Galston, Sally G. 112
Galyean, A. F. 112
Galyean, Eleanor 112
Gambell, James 153, 157

Gamberling, Ann 315
Gambill, James 199
Gamble, Agness 112
Gamble, Alexander 112
Gamble, Josias 77
Gamble, Nancy 112
Gamble, Robert 112
Gamble, S. E. T. 112
Gamble, William 112
Gambrald, James 295
Gambril, James 214, 295
Gambrill, Polly 295
Gammel, Thos. W. 197
Gammell, Mary Ann 112
Gammell, Melville 112
Gammell, Thos. W. 112
Gammon, Jeremiah 182
Gammons, Felecia 112
Gammons, J. R. 311
Gammons, Jas. 112
Gamwell, Frank M 112
Gamwell, Leonella 112
Gamwell, T. W. 9, 112
Ganaway, James W. [B] 112
Ganaway, Margaret J. 114
Ganaway, Mary 112
Ganaway, Samuel 112, 114
Gannon, J. P. 112
Gannon, J. R. 112
Gannon, James 112
Gannon, Roda 112
Gant, Absolem B. 112-113
Gant, Eliza Jane 112
Gant, Elizabeth 112
Gant, James 112
Gant, Jesse B. 112, 172
Gant, John William 112
Gant, Lewis 112-113
Gant, Robert J. B. 113
Gant, William A. 112-113
Gap, D. P. 224
Garawell, Thos. W. 197
Gardenshire, E. L. 143
Gardinhire, William 76
Gardner, Alfred 1
Gardner, Betsy A. 70
Gardner, Henry 277
Gardner, James 242, 321
Gardner, Jesse 295
Gardner, John 70, 113, 147, 232, 242, 277, 337
Gardner, Joshua 242, 321
Gardner, Neil M. 129
Gardner, Richd. W. 152
Gardner, Stephen 47
Garen, Silas 114
Garen, Simeon 114
Garland, Francis 210
Garland, John C. M. 37, 313
Garland, Sarah Ann 210
Garland, Susan Jane 210
Garner, Jane 113, 275
Garner, Sarah 113
Garrell, Benjamin H. 113
Garrell, Staton 113
Garrent, Peter 182
Garrett, Benjamin 221

Garrett, Eliza J. 113
Garrett, Emily 221
Garrett, Lucy 109
Garrison, Baily 113
Garrison, Benja. 113
Garrison, Elizabeth 157
Garrison, Henry 157
Garrison, Isaac 113
Garrison, John 113, 157
Garrison, Joseph 157
Garrison, Mary 157
Garten, George 94
Garten, Mary 94
Garvin, Elizabeth 334
Garvin, Samuel 334
Gass, D. P. 264
Gastin, James 164
Gaston, John 37
Gates, John N. 148, 344
Gates, Wm. 22
Gatlin, James 285
Gaudin, Adelia 113
Gaudin, Fanny, 113
Gaudin, Henry 113
Gaudin, John W. 113
Gaudin, Salina 113
Gaudin, William 113
Gaulden, Amanda 30
Gaulden, D. W. 30
Gaulden, Fletcher 113
Gaulling, John 113
Gault, Saml. M. 293
Gaunt, Caroline 113
Gaunt, Eliza 113
Gaunt, Elizabeth 113
Gaunt, James 113
Gaunt, John 113, 251
Gaunt, Lewis 251
Gaunt, Mary 113
Gaunt, Sarah 113
Gaunt, William A. 113, 251
Gause, G. W. 114
Gaut, James 4
Gayle, Thomas C. 318
Geahart, William 259
Gearheart, An 114
Gearheart, Valentine 114
Gearheart, William 114
Gens, David 114
Gentry, James 289
Gentry, Nicholas C. 114
George, James 176
George, Lurena 114
George, Thomas 114
George, William 114
Geran, Samuel 114
Geran, Solomon 114, 172
Gerard, Andrew 114
Gerard, Charles 114
Geslin, P. H. 118
Gettings, Alexander 238
Gholsen, Sarah J. 114
Gibbons, Dennis 115
Gibbs, Charles N. 261
Gibbs, E. F. 288
Gibbs, Matilda F. 29
Gibbs, William 115

Gibson, David 115
Gibson, Hannah 115, 329
Gibson, Henry 69, 115, 205, 265
Gibson, James 115, 253, 258
Gibson, John 115, 279
Gibson, Patsey 234
Gibson, Samuel 115, 234
Gibson, William B. 115
Gidenns, Elizabeth 162
Gier, Daniel 244
Gier, Henry 320, 338
Gifford, A. 112
Gifford, Sarah Caroline 112
Gilbert, Fletcher 319
Gilbert, Jesse 152
Gilbert, John 115
Gilbert, Stephen 319
Gilbert, Thos. J. 220
Gilbert, Usley 115
Gilbreath, Elizabeth 111
Gilbreath, James 111
Gilbreath, Jane 111
Gilbreath, Joseph 111
Gilbreath, Mary 111
Gilbreath, Peggy Ann 111
Gilbreath, Saml. L. 111
Gilbreath, Sarah 111
Gilbreath, Thomas J. 220
Gilchrist, Adilade 115
Gilchrist, Catharine M. 115
Gilchrist, Daniel 115
Gilchrist, Drucilla 76
Gilchrist, Malcolm 115
Gilchrist, Martha Ann 115
Gilchrist, Robert J. 76
Gilchrist Sarah 115
Gilchrist, William 115, 216
Giles, Margaret 274
Gilespie, Eliza 311
Gilespie, George 294
Gilespie, John M. 311
Gilispie, George 322
Gill, Henry 127, 293, 321
Gill, Joseph 72
Gill, Lena 167
Gill, Sena 167
Gill, William 79,116, 140, 167, 194
Gillaspie, George 314, 343
Gillaspy, George 35, 200
Gillespie, Barny 116
Gillespie, George 116
Gillespie, Jno. 116
Gillespie, Leroy C. 116, 311
Gillespie, Robert R. 116
Gillespie, Tempy S. 116
Gillespie, William 116
Gillihan, Lavinia 122
Gilliland, Robert 148
Gilliland, Sarah 148
Gilliland, William 112, 116
Gilsen, Elizabeth 275-276
Ginney [a slave] 341
Gipson, Caroline 266
Gipson, Matt 266

Gipson, Tobias 222
Gipson, William 70, 201
Girding, George F. 116
Girly, Jemima 295
Gist, A. F. 116
Gist, Marusa 116
Gist, St. Paul 116
Gittings, Alexander 238
Givin, Jenny 66
Givins, Polly 193
Givins, Robt. 193
Gladen, Jno. M. 173
Gladney, James 116
Gladney, John 116
Glasgow, James 37, 82, 89, 331
Glass, Lewis 136
Glaze, Henry 320, 338
Gleaves, Hannah 326
Gleaves, Zach 116, 326
Glen, James W. 116
Glenn, Elizabeth 85
Glenn, Henry 116
Glenn, Jemima 116
Glenn, Patsy 116
Glenn, Thompson 116
Glidewell, Jas. 167
Glours, William 217
Glover, Wm. 116
Goad, Henry 110
Gobble, Adam 117
Gobble, Anios 117
Godwin, Fanny D. 117
Godwin, Frank B. 17
Godwin, Mary M. B. 17
Godwin, Mary S. 117
Godwin, Thomas H. 117
Godwin, William P. 117
Gofney, John B. 321
Golden, James T. 334
Golden, John 123
Goldin, William 75
Goldston, John 117
Gooch, G. R. 117
Gooch, H. A. 117
Gooch, Narcissa 270
Gooch, Sarah J. 117
Gooch, W. C. 117
Gooch, W. H. 270
Gooch, W. H. E. 117
Goodall, Charles 117
Goodall, Cornelia 117
Goodall, Elizabeth 117
Goodall, John L. 117, 187
Goodall, Louisa 117
Goodall, Lucy 117
Goodall, Martha M. 117
Goodall, Morinda 117
Goodall, Permelia 117
Goodall, Rufus 117
Goodall, Veronda 117
Goodall, Vorinda 117
Goodall, W. W. 117
Goodall, Wm. W. 117, 304
Goodall, Zeda 117
Goodin, Drurey 117, 129
Goodin, Icam 117

Goodin, Mary 117
Goodman, Claibourn 91
Goodman, Samuel 118
Goodman, Sterling 241
Goodpasture, J. D. 211
Goodpasture, Margaret 118
Goodrich, Benjamin 118
Goodrich, Elizabeth 118
Goodrich, James Polk 118
Goodrich, Martha 118
Goodrich, Mary M. 118
Goodrich, Sarah Jane 118
Goodrich, Silas C. 118
Goodwin, Allen 118
Goodwin, Bradock 118
Goodwin, Brittain 118
Goodwin, James 164
Goodwin, Samuel 118
Goodwin, William 118
Goolsby, F. M. 171, 220
Gordan, Alexander 153
Gorden, James 69
Gorden, Leroy 121
Gordon, George 182
Gordon, Martin 68
Gore, Andrew R. 118
Gore, Elender 118
Gore, Eliza A. 118
Gore, Eliza Jane 118
Gore, Mannie 272
Gore, Maurice 272
Gore, Monna 60
Gore, Morrice 54
Gore, Mounce 54, 60, 71, 118, 141, 272
Gore, Mourice 60
Gore, Pauina M. 118
Gore, Samuel G. 118
Gore, Thomas 118
Gore, William 118, 239, 288
Gorin, Gladin 283
Gorten, George 94
Gorten, Mary 94
Gorvan, Richard M. 200
Gorvan, Susan 200
Goss, Anny 31
Gossett, West 118
Grace, Boyd M. 267
Grace, L. M. 33
Grace, Milton H. 267
Graffs, Frederick 118
Graham, Alitha 259
Graham, Andrew 18
Graham, Ansalam 308
Graham, Daniel 201
Graham, David 185
Graham, Garritt H. 340
Graham, Hannah 118
Graham, Jarrett H. 118
Graham, John 259, 340
Graham, M. J. 17, 105, 203
Graham, Polly W. 308
Graham, Susannah 119
Graham, Wim. 46, 119, 267
Gramer, Thomas 248
Gramer, W. H. 248
Granade, Henry 119

Granade, John 119
Grant, Asalee E. 119
Grant, Eliz. H. 119
Grant, Geo. A. 119
Grant, H. 119
Grant, John D. 119, 181
Grant, Lewis 114
Grant, Louisa M. 119
Grant, Martha 119
Grant, Mary J. 119
Grant, Matilda 119
Grant, Robert 1 114, 19
Grant, William 119
Grass, John 179
Graven, Samuel 334
Graves, Alvy 41
Graves, Beverly 41, 163
Graves, John 84, 102, 273
Graves, Nancy 57, 119
Graves, Pamelia 41
Graves, Peter 119
Graves, Polly 119
Graves, William 119
Gravitt, Obadiah 95
Gravitt, Sarah Francis 95
Gray, Benjamin 315
Gray, James 251
Gray, Jesse 56, 328
Gray, Joseph 80, 119, 307
Gray, Joseph John 119
Gray, Milly 80
Gray, Thomas 124, 290
Gray, Thompson 286
Gray, Wim. 41, 110, 179, 283
Grayson, Thomas 295
Green, Abel 119
Green, Alex. 119
Green, And. 66
Green, Asa 87, 119
Green, Benjamin 119
Green, Catherine 119
Green, David 119-120, 273
Green, Elizabeth 58
Green, Green B. 119
Green, Harriet A. 120
Green, James R. 96, 270
Green, John 120, 317
Green, Jonathan 120
Green, Joseph 119, 237
Green, Letitia 120
Green, Lucy K. 120
Green, Mary 120
Green, Richard 120
Green, Robert 120
Green, Sarah 119
Green, Susan R. 119
Green, T. C. 120
Green, Thos. S. 142
Green, William 47, 188
Greenbruld, Patsey 295
Greene, Elizabeth 29
Greenlee, James 158, 168
Greenway, George 114
Greer, A. A. 22
Greer, Alexander 174, 212
Greer, Andrew 1, 232

Greer, Aniza A. 165
Greer, Francis 120
Greer, Jacob 111
Greer, Joseph 14, 51, 120, 131, 220, 232, 237
Greer, Levy S. 325
Greer, Margaret 120
Greer, Mary Ann 120, 131
Greer, T. C. 37
Greer, Thomas 120, 131
Greet, J. C. 252
Gregg, Shadrach 173
Gregory, E. W. 120
Gregory, J. C. 112, 120, 251
Gregory, J. T. 112, 120
Gregory, Mary C. 120
Gregory, Rachel 40
Gregory, Thomas 40
Gregory, W. C. 120
Greider, Martin 68
Gressman, Elijah 287
Gressom, Peter 114
Grey, Jesse 328
Grider, Martin 68
Grier, H. M. 143
Grier, James 88, 121
Grier, Joseph 131
Grier, Mary Ann 131
Grier, Richard 121
Grier, Thomas 131
Griffeth, William 4
Griffin, Asa 72, 172
Griffin, F. M. 121
Griffin, J. M. 121
Griffin, Margaret 121
Griffin, Mary 121
Griffin, T. 239
Griffin, Timothy 125, 170, 245
Griffin, Tom 319
Griffin, W. D. 121
Griffin, William 38
Griffin, Z.. K. 121
Griffith, Benjamin 121
Griffith, Claiburn 121
Griffith, David 121, 246
Griffith, James 121
Griffith, John 121
Griffith, Jonas 121
Griffith, L. B. 121
Griffith, Mariah Clay 121
Griffith, Mary Josephine 121
Griffith, Nancy 121, 245-246
Griffith, Polly 121
Griffith, Sally 121
Griffith, Samuel T. 121, 245-246
Griffith, William C. A. 121
Grigg, James 237
Griggs, Jane 121
Griggs, Robert W. 121
Grills, A. J. 120
Grills, Ella 120
Grimes, Emanuel 122
Grimes, Henry 122
Grimes, Jacob 78
Grimes, John 122

Grimes, M. L. 122
Grimes, Sarah 122
Grimes, William 289
Grimm, Stephen 122, 179
Grimmit, Sarah 122
Grimsley, J. H. 122
Grimsley, W. B. 122
Grindstaff, Catrin 122
Grindstaff, Isaac 122
Grindstaff, Jacob 122
Grindstaff, John 243
Grindstaff, Michael 122
Grindstaff, Nicholas 122
Griner, John 246
Grisham, James 122
Grisham, John 122
Grisham, Meshack 122
Grisham, Thomas 122
Grisham, William 122
Grisom, James 312
Grissam, John 122
Grissam, William 122
Grisum, Robert 122
Grisum, Susanna 122
Grisum, Wm. 122
Griswitt, James 289
Grogan, Barzella 123
Grogan, Elizabeth 123
Grogan, Francis 123
Grogan, Jno. F. 123
Grogan, Margaret M. 123
Grogan, Patrick F. 123
Grogan, Robert 123
Grubb, Allen B. 123
Guant, Abraham 114
Guant, Absolom B. 123
Guant, Caroline 114
Guant, Eliza Jane 114
Guant, Elizabeth 114
Guant, James 114
Guant, Jesse 114
Guant, John 114, 123
Guant, Lewis 114, 123
Guant, Mary 123
Guant, Sally 114
Guant, William 113-114, 123
Guffey, Margaret 123
Guiant, Lewis 114
Guilland, William 123
Guins, Robt. 193
Guley, Jemima 295
Gunn, Anne 213
Gunn, Thomas 213
Guthrie, Andrew 8, 123, 300, 313
Guthrie, Fanny 123
Guthrie, Jno. 320
Guthrie, Mary Ann 123
Guthrie, Walker 51
Guthrie, William 123
Guttndgewood, Hanna 123
Guy, William 74, 123, 304
Gwin, Jeremiah 201
Gwin, John 18, 89
Gwin, Sarah 89
Gwinn, Ahay 123
Hackett, John 123

Hackler, Elizabeth 123
Hackler, George 123
Hackler, Solomon 123
Hacklin, George 123
Hackney, Jacob 124
Hagert, James 204
Haggard, E. L. 269-270
Haggard, Edmond 124
Haggard, Ezekiel 269
Haggard, James 142, 265, 285
Haggard, Noel 124
Haggard, Samuel 206
Haggard, West Noel 173
Haggard, Wm. 124, 173, 270
Hagin, Anthony Wayne 146
Hail, Amon 171, 220
Hail, Benjamin 94, 124
Hail, Caroline 105
Hail, Christopher P. 124
Hail, D. C. 112, 246
Hail, Dudley B. 257
Hail, George 105
Hail, James 124
Hail, Jane 124
Hail, Martial C. 124
Hail, Minnerva 124
Hail, Nicholas 289
Hail, Richard 124
Hail, Robert 343
Hail, William 124
Haile, David M. 174, 180
Haile, Jane 340
Hailey, G. W. 155
Haily, Joseph 124
Haily, Pleasant 124
Haily, Polly 124
Hair, Haywood 62
Hair, Lizzie 62
Haire, Mathew 124
Haire, Saml. 216
Halbrooks, William 74
Hale, Cage 243
Hale, Catherine 124
Hale, Denton 340
Hale, Dudley B. 257
Hale, Eli W. 182
Hale, Frederick 124
Hale, George 124
Hale, J. C. 46
Hale, Jane 340
Hale, Jemima 124
Hale, Joshua 247
Hale, Julia 257
Hale, Mary 289
Hale, Nicholas 124
Hale, Robert 89, 97, 231, 316, 344
Hale, Samuel 124
Hale, Shadrach 124
Haley, David 124
Haley, Elijah G. 124
Haley, Eugenia 125
Haley, Henry C. 125
Haley, James 124-125
Haley, Jno. W. 125

Haley, Luanna 125
Haley, Mary H. 125
Haley, Polly 124
Hall, Adam 125, 196
Hall, Benjamin 94
Hall, Clarinda A. 30
Hall, D. C. 246
Hall, Dickeson 97
Hall, E. M. 55, 100, 125, 151, 170, 299, 343
Hall, Frances 247
Hall, Franci E. 125
Hall, Garrett 125
Hall, H. R. 220
Hall, Henry 125
Hall, J. H. 30
Hall, Jacob 125
Hall, Jane 200
Hall, John 209
Hall, Joshua 29
Hall, L. C. 239, 304
Hall, Littleton C. 239, 245
Hall, Margaret 209
Hall, Nancy D. 304
Hall, Permelia N. 125
Hall, Phillip 100
Hall, Porter 200
Hall, Samuel C. 238
Hall, Sarah 125, 196
Hall, True 125
Hall, W. C. 125
Hall, W. J. 289
Hall, William 125
Halliburton, Margaret A. 125
Halliburton, Richard H. 125
Hallom, Nathan 197
Halloman, Margaret 48
Halloman, William Wade 48
Hallum, A. G. 112
Hallum, David 125
Hallum, Elizabeth 125
Hallum, George 125-126, 199
Hallum, James 125
Hallum, John 52, 126
Hallum, Morris 125
Hallum, Polly A. R. 125
Hallum, Sally 126
Hallum, Susannah 52
Hally, Absolem 82-83
Hally, Elicy 83
Hally, Elvy 83
Haltone, Nathan 197
Hamblin, Darcus 126
Hamblin, James 126
Hamblin, John W. 314
Hambrick, Jeremiah 287
Hambrick, Nathan 287
Hambright, Benjamin 127
Hambright, John 126
Hambright, Peter 126
Hamby, Isaac 187
Hamby, James M. 126
Hamby, Lettitia 126
Hamby, William N. 126
Hamelton, Hiram 126
Hamelton, Nancy 126

Hamilton, Alex 237
Hamilton, Ann 237
Hamilton, Elijah 91
Hamilton, J. H. 96
Hamilton, James 3, 14, 126
Hamilton, John C. 126
Hamilton, Joseph 293
Hamilton, Margaret 126
Hamilton, Mary J. 91
Hamilton, Peter 126
Hamilton, Robert W. 122
Hamilton, T. L.149
Hamilton, Wm. 91, 126, 293
Hamm, Reuben 126
Hammer, J. M. 228, 273
Hammer, John 113
Hammett, Reuben 54
Hammons, M. M. 112
Hammontree, Nancy 126
Hampson, James 127
Hampton, Edward 127
Hampton, John 99, 127
Hampton, Mary 127
Hampton, Nancy 127
Hampton, Robert 127
Hampton, Susan 43
Hampton, Thomas 86
Hampton, W. F. 74
Hampton, William 127
Hancher, William 210
Hancock, Benja. 127
Hancock, Benton B. 127
Hancock, Berlinda 127
Hancock, Betsy 127
Hancock, Coleman 127
Hancock, Edward R. 121
Hancock, Elizabeth 127
Hancock, Francis M. 127
Hancock, Hanoriah 274
Hancock, James W. 257
Hancock, John 296
Hancock, Joseph 263
Hancock, Lee 127
Hancock, Lesha 127
Hancock, Lythia 127
Hancock, Maggie J. 27
Hancock, Martin 273-274
Hancock, Mary 77
Hancock, Perry 127
Hancock, Ruth 127
Hancock, Sally 127
Hancock, Samuel 77, 127, 273-274
Hancock, Sarah 127
Hancock, Simeon 274
Hancock, Simon 127, 142, 260
Hancock, Skeen 127
Hancock, Virlanda 127
Hancock, Widow 128
Hancock, Wm. 127
Hand, Samuel 127
Handley, Mary 128
Haney, Caleb 128
Haney, John R. 128
Haney, L. A. 128
Haney, M. L. 128

Haney, M. T. 128
Haney, N. E. 128
Haney, Nancy 128
Haney, S. A. D. 128
Haney, Sarah 128
Haney, W. H. 128
Haney, William 128
Hankin, Samuel 128
Hankins, Cleveland W. 128
Hankins, Dice 128
Hankins, Elizabeth Jane 128
Hankins, James 128
Hankins, John 128
Hankins, Louisiana 128
Hankins, Martha D. 128
Hankins, Mary 135
Hankins, Nelson 128
Hankins, Richard 128, 156
Hankins, Robert 128
Hankins, Samuel 135
Hankins, William 128
Hanna, Edward F. 45
Hanna, Stephen 70
Hanna, Steven 45
Hannah [a slave] 17, 213, 250, 255
Hannah, Elizabeth 128-129
Hannah, Francis 128
Hannah, John 128, 239, 318
Hannah, Julia 128
Hannah, Juliet 128
Hannah, Lucinda 128
Hannah, Mary Agness 128
Hannah, Samuel 128-129
Hannah, Thomas 128
Hannah, Virginia T. 128
Hannah, William 128
Hanner, Mariah 37
Hannloho, Jesse 137
Hansbro, Smith 94
Hants, Thomas 291
Harbert, Celia 129
Harbert, Corimore 129
Harbert, Delestine 129
Harbert, Jas. A. 129
Harbert, John 58, 129
Harbert, Lidia A.129
Harbert, Narcissa 58
Harbert, Sarah 129
Harbert, Susan B. 129
Harbert, Thos. C. 129
Hardage, Geo. W. 308
Hardage, Jno. G. 308
Hardason, Asa 214
Hardaway, Edward 129
Hardaway, Elizabeth M. 129
Hardaway, James 129
Hardaway, Manson 129
Hardeman, Tho. 19
Harden, Green 129-130
Harden, Harvey S. 130
Harden, John 130
Harden, Nancy 129-130
Harden, Sarah M. 130
Harden, Thomas S. 129-130
Harden, William C. 129-130

Harden, Winney J. 130
Harden, Wm. 129
Hardgrave, America 130, 339
Hardgrave, Cornelia 130
Hardgrave, Felix R. 129, 234
Hardgrave, Lavinia 129
Hardgrave, Malvina 130, 339
Hardgrove, Coraline 130
Hardin, Alfred S. 130
Hardin, Harvey J. 130
Hardin, Jane 167
Hardin, Joab 232
Hardin, John 9, 130
Hardin, Martin R. 130
Hardin, Nancy E. 130
Hardin, Thomas S. 77, 130
Hardin, W. C. 129
Hardin, Wm. H. 130
Harding, Geo. 130
Hardison, Alice C. 130
Hardison, J. H. 134
Hardman, Thomas 211
Hardy, Edmund 335
Hardy, John 14
Hardy, Martha 166
Hardy, Mary 14
Hardy, Saml. 4, 166
Hare, Achilles 180
Hare, Samuel 93, 121, 141, 274, 288
Hargate, Frederic 130
Hargett, Frederick 130
Hargis, Adrain B. 197-198
Hargis, Isabella 197-198
Hargis, Richard L. 198
Hargis, Sarah L. 198
Hargis, Thomas 198
Hargraves, Frank 130
Hargrove, Felix R. 5
Haris, Jno. T. 130
Harkins, Charles 130
Harkruder, J. W. 131
Harley, Hiram 131
Harlin, George 202
Harling, Christopher A. 108
Harling, Jefferson 108
Harling, Lafayette 108
Harling, Nancy 108
Harling, Sarah 108
Harlson, Nancy 112
Harlson, Samuel 112
Harman, Jacob 131
Harmon, B. H. 49, 119, 120, 139, 289
Harmon, John 131
Harmon, Joseph 120
Harmon, Levi 138
Harmon, W. 213
Harmon, William 131, 227
Harp, Dinah 131
Harp, Elijah 219
Harpe, Alias S. 255
Harper, Benjamin 131
Harper, Elizabeth 161
Harper, James 131, 295
Harper, Mark 131
Harper, Mary R. 131
Harper, Moses D. 131
Harper, Reuben 150
Harper, Richard 150
Harper, Robert 131, 179, 223
Harper, Thomas 131
Harper, William H. 131
Harpole, John 71, 83, 131, 229, 342
Harpole, Prior 131
Harpole, Solomon 131
Harpole, William 131
Harpoles, J. J. S. 67
Harrell, A. T. 221
Harrell, Calvin 131
Harrell. J. K. P. 135
Harrell, Nancy 131
Harrell, Reuben G. 89
Harriet [a slave] 88
Harrington, Charles 131-132
Harrington, Nancy 124
Harrington, Thos. 124, 301
Harrington, Whitmill 1, 221, 289
Harrington, William 289
Harris, Abner 54, 132
Harris, Allen 50, 281
Harris, Andrew 132, 283
Harris, Arthur 6, 165, 248-249
Harris, Benjamin 167
Harris, D. H. 132
Harris, Edmond 132, 242
Harris, Edward 91, 132
Harris, Eli 132-133
Harris, Elizabeth 132
Harris, Emily 327
Harris, Esther J. 132
Harris, Francis 85, 132
Harris, Furges S. 132
Harris, Geo. W. 128
Harris, H. F. 264, 332
Harris, Henry 312
Harris, Israel 137
Harris, J. P. 232
Harris, James 132
Harris, John 132, 299
Harris, Joshua 132
Harris, L. J. 332
Harris, Louisa J. 264
Harris, Maria 133
Harris, Martha 50, 137, 242
Harris, Mary 281, 297
Harris, Minnie 133
Harris, Mosly 206
Harris, Nathan 132
Harris, Newton 133
Harris, Nonnie 133
Harris, Patsey S. 132
Harris, Polly M. 132
Harris, Rhodes 132
Harris, Riley 50
Harris, Robert 132, 133, 258
Harris, Sally 132, 238
Harris, Samuel 132-133,
Harris, Sarah 132
Harris, Sterling 181
Harris, Thos. W. 297
Harris, W. A. 208
Harris, W. D. 133
Harris, W. O. 104
Harris, Walter L. 283
Harris, Wiley 133, 238
Harris, Wm. 132, 196, 233, 328
Harris, Willie 170
Harrison, Cleveland L. 73
Harrison, Elias 133
Harrison, Eliza W. 133, 192
Harrison, J. W. 133
Harrison, Jacob 11
Harrison, James W. 133
Harrison, John 133
Harrison, Martha 50
Harrison, Michael 259
Harrison, Riley 50
Harrison, R. P. 133, 155, 189
Harrison, Ths. 191
Harrison, William 133
Harry [a slave] 341
Hart, Andrew 7, 159, 288
Hart, Ann 134
Hart, Anthony 133
Hart, Edmond L. 213
Hart, Henry 133-134
Hart, James 123, 134
Hart, John M. 134
Hart, Joseph 133-134
Hart, M. J. 134
Hart, Milton J. 134
Hart, Nathanial 134, 139
Hart, R. L. 134
Hart, Robt. B. 83
Hart, Sam 134
Hart, Susanna 134
Hart, Thomas 134
Hart, William 74, 134, 166
Hartman, Jacob 131
Harton, Benj. T. 245
Harton, John P. 161
Harton, Mary Jane 245
Hartsfield, Andrew 290
Hartsfield, Wm. 145
Harty, Pleasant 134
Harvard, George 135
Harvard, Mary 135
Harvey, Abner 19
Harvey, Eliza 19
Harvey, Elzana 19
Harvey, Lucy Jane 19
Harvey, Martha 19
Harvey, Wesley 71, 274
Harvil, Louisa 221
Harvil, William N. 221
Harwell, Bowling 339
Harwell, Cleopatra 134
Harwell, Elizabeth 338-339
Harwell, Frank 134
Harwell, Herbert 78
Harwell, Indiana 134
Harwell, L. C. 134
Harwell, Louisa 221

Harwell, Nancy Jane 134
Harwell, R. F. 134
Harwell, R. K. 134
Harwell, T. D. 170
Harwell, Thomas D. 245, 300

Harwell, William 31, 221
Haskins, Aaron W. 275-276
Haskins, C. 134
Haskins, Carter 134
Haskins, Creed 134-135
Haskins, E. J. 134
Haskins, Edward 134
Haskins, Harriet J. 134-135
Haskins, J. C. 135
Haskins, LaFayette 134
Haskins, Mary A. 275-276
Haskins, Peter 134
Haskins, Rody 134
Haskins, Sam 134
Haskins, Theodoric C. 135
Haskins, Thomas C. 9
Hassell, J. W. 114
Hassell, Jordan 135
Hast, R. B. 299
Hastings, Elizabeth 135
Hastings, John 135
Hastings, Mary Jane 135
Hastings, Susannah 135
Hastings, William 135
Hastings, Willis 135
Hatch, Peggy 135
Hatcher, Harris, 267
Hatcher, Horis 258
Hatcher, John 135
Hatcher, Sally 135
Hatchett, John 225
Hatfield, Eli 153
Hattaway, John 63
Haughton, J. C. 135
Hauis, John 132, 135
Hauk, John W. 135
Haukins, Mary 135
Hawkins, Amanda 101
Hawkins, Charles Carson 50
Hawkins, Elijah 101, 300
Hawkins, Eliza 26
Hawkins, Geo. W. 101
Hawkins, H. H. 135
Hawkins, Harriet 101
Hawkins, J. J. 26
Hawkins, James 135
Hawkins, John 50, 60, 301
Hawkins, Nelson 128
Hawkins, Ruth Matilda 50
Hawkins, Sarah 301
Hawkins, William 135
Hay, Agnes 135-136
Hay, David 135
Hay, Francis 300
Hay, J. T. 300
Hay, Jeremiah 248
Hay, Mathew 136
Hay, Wm. F. 136
Hayden, Rebecca 136
Hayes, Enos 136
Hayley, Francis M. 195

Hayley, James 83, 195
Hayley, John B. 195
Hayley, Newton C. 195
Hayley, Patrick H. 195
Hayley, Pleasant 124
Hayley, Wm. A. 195
Haymes, Elizabeth 136
Haymes, Reuben 136
Haymes, Sarah 136
Haymes, William 136
Haynes, Elizabeth R. 136
Haynes, J. D. 120
Haynes, James S. 151
Haynes, Joseph N. 136
Haynes, Margaret E. 136
Haynes, Mary 136, 237, 309
Haynes, Matilda 136
Haynes, Newman 136
Haynes, Nusman 136
Haynes, Rebecca 136
Haynes, Sarah J. 136
Haynes, Stephen 136, 237, 309
Haynes, W. R. 220
Haynes, William 2
Hays, A. J. 136
Hays, Anderson 23
Hays, Andrew J. 137
Hays, Angio R. 136
Hays, Archibald 136
Hays, B. G. 250
Hays, Charles B. 136
Hays, Cooper 136
Hays, Cynthia 23
Hays, Elias 136
Hays, Ella B. 136
Hays, Enos 136
Hays, Henry 136
Hays, Hiram 136
Hays, James 23
Hays, Jane 136
Hays, Kiziah 136
Hays, Levi 21
Hays, Mahaly 136
Hays, Middleton 136-137
Hays, Nelly 136
Hays, Peter 136
Hays, Polly 136
Hays, R. J. 136-137
Hays, Rebecca 136
Hays, Richard J. 75, 136-137
Hays, Sally 23
Hays, Saml. J. 136
Hays, Sarah A. 136, 250
Hays, Stokley D. 136
Hays, Tennessee 23
Hays, Thomas F. 75
Hays, Thompson 190, 217
Hays, Ursula P. 250
Haywood, Egbert 205
Haywood, George W. 115, 137
Haywood, Ruth 137
Haywood, Thomas 137
Hayzehin, William 112
Hayzethin, Margaret 112

Hazelwood, LaFayette 232
Hazelwood, Thomas 137
Hazzard, Noel 124
Hazzard, William173, 230, 283
Head, Charlotte 137
Head, Doctor 44
Head, Elizabeth 137
Head, Enoch 137
Head, Henry 137
Head, James W. 137
Head, John 137
Head, Mary 137
Head, Peggy 44
Head, Sinthy 44
Head, Siothy 44
Headden, H. H. 137
Headden, Moses 137
Headrick, James 130
Headrick, Nancy Ann 130
Headrick, Peter 142
Headrick, Selena 129-30
Headrick, Wm. 129-130
Heard, Abraham 137
Heard, Franklin C. 137
Heard, J. H. 103
Heard, John D. 137
Heard, Nancy 137
Heard, Rebeccah 137
Hearn, Ebenezer 310
Hearn, George 63
Hearn, Jno. 63
Hearn, Thomas 63, 91, 137
Hearn, William H. 105
Heart, Edmund L. 213
Heasty, Joseph 172
Heasty, Mary 172
Heath, Elijah 137
Heath, William 137
Heatwall, John 138
Hedrick, James 138
Hedrick, Joseph 306
Hedrick, Manerva 138
Hedrick, Mary R. 28
Hedrick, Peter 138
Hedricks, Wesley W. 28
Hedris, James 130
Heflin, James 138
Heflin, William 138
Hegerty, Cynthia 138
Heldreth, R. T. 24, 138
Helly, D. G. 327
Helm, Meredith 75
Helm, Nancy 75
Helms, J. W. 138
Helms, Thomas 283
Hembrew, Matilada 323
Heming, Abraham 138
Heming, Louisa Scott 138
Hemphill, Caroline 258
Hemphill, Clara 267
Hemphill, Clay 267
Hemphill, Clotilda 258
Hemphill, Cornelia 267
Hemphill, Matilda 267
Henderson, A. 139
Henderson [a slave] 149

Henderson, Alex 297
Henderson, Amanda 138
Henderson, Andrew 240
Henderson, Ann 35-36, 101
Henderson, Archibald 139
Henderson, B. 257
Henderson, Callie 138
Henderson, Caroline 329
Henderson, E. A. 159
Henderson, E. H. 139
Henderson, Elain 329
Henderson, Elam 138
Henderson, Elijah 138-139
Henderson, Eliza 234
Henderson, Elizabeth 138-139
Henderson, Enos 138
Henderson, G. B. 138
Henderson, G. M. 139, 144, 194
Henderson, G. P. 139
Henderson, George M. 138-139
Henderson, Hugh 138, 329
Henderson, James 138
Henderson, John 124, 138-139, 247
Henderson, Kinman W. 139
Henderson, Louisa E. 138
Henderson, Mariah 297
Henderson, Marion 234
Henderson, Mark C. 138
Henderson, Martha 138-139
Henderson, Mary S. 138
Henderson, Nancy 35
Henderson, Nathan 234
Henderson, Nathaniel 138
Henderson, Peggy 237
Henderson, R. G. 139
Henderson, Rebecca 139
Henderson, Richard 17, 27, 139
Henderson, Robert 138-
Henderson, Rufus M. 96
Henderson, S. B. 7, 160
Henderson, Samuel B. 38, 63, 233
Henderson, Susan P. 234
Henderson, Tennessee D. 138
Henderson, Thomas 17, 27, 101, 138-139, 234, 261,
Henderson, W. A. 139
Henderson, William 138-139
Henderson, Wilson 329
Hendley, Pleasant 121
Hendley, Saml. 255
Hendrick, Drucilla 139, 211, 316
Hendrick Jeremiah 140, 281, 285, 291
Hendricks, Joseph 140
Hendricks, Obediah 140
Hendricks, W. H. 147
Hendricks, W. L. 311
Hendrik, Jeremiah 139
Hendrik, Joseph 139
Hendrix, D. R. 69
Hendrix, M. H. 253
Hendrix, W. C. 120
Hendrix, W. H. 2, 131, 251, 258, 315
Hendrix, William H. 227
Henegar, Jacob 100, 140
Henegar, Polly 100
Henley, Isaac 116, 140
Henley Rebekah 104, 186
Henley Saml. 104, 147, 149, 186
Henly, James D. 188
Henner, James 103
Henning, Winnefred 129
Henry [a slave] 88
Henry, Albert 140
Henry, Benjamin 140
Henry, Darcus 181
Henry, David 167
Henry, Elig 140
Henry, Eliz 140
Henry, Eliza A. 140
Henry, Elizabeth 140
Henry, Ephraim 140
Henry, Hugh 134, 140, 237
Henry, Isaac 140, 167
Henry, James 140-141
Henry, Jane 140
Henry, Jesse 121
Henry, John 121, 140, 308
Henry, M. 141
Henry, Mary 121, 140
Henry, Michael 140-141
Henry, Oliver 140
Henry, Patrick 141
Henry, Polly 140-141
Henry, Robert 181
Henry, Samuel 140-141
Henry, Thomas 140-141
Henry, William 5, 141
Henson, William 246
Herbert, Isaac 39, 141
Hern, T. W. 287
Herring, Jesse 164
Herron, Andrew 141
Herron, Emily 338
Herron, Hester Ann 338
Herron, J. R. 231
Herron, John 338
Herron, Levi B. 338
Herron, Margaret 338
Herron, Mary 189
Hess, James A. W. 110
Hester, James 141
Hibbard, Marietta 141
Hibbetts, D. C. 278
Hibbit, Eliza 94
Hibbit, Harlan 94
Hibbit, Henry 94
Hibbit, James 94
Hibbit, John 94
Hibbit, William H. 94
Hibbits, Elijah 141
Hibbits, Eliza 141
Hibbits, Elizabeth 141
Hibbits, Harlin 141
Hibbits, Jo. R. 141
Hibbits, John 141
Hibbits, Louisa J. 141
Hibbits, Rosannah 94
Hibbits, Sarah 141
Hibbits, William 93-94, 141
Hibbitt, D. C. 65
Hibit, Harland 93
Hibit, John L. 93
Hibit, Louisa Jane 93
Hibits, Harlin 94
Hibits, Henry 94
Hibits, John S. 94
Hibits, Louisa J. 94
Hibits, Robert 94
Hibits, Sally 94
Hickase, Horace 146
Hickenson, David 147
Hickenson, Sarah 147
Hickereson, Wiley 325
Hickerson, William A. 325
HicMcMahan, R. S. 204
Hickland, Perry R. 228
Hicklin, A. M. 141
Hicklin, Almira 141
Hicklin, Avery 141
Hicklin, Hugh 141
Hicklin, Perry 141, 228-229
Hicklin, Thomas 141
Hicklin, Turner 141
Hickman, Edmond 142
Hickman, Edwin 142
Hickman, Elizabeth 142
Hickman, Humphrey 142
Hickman, Lemuel 142
Hickman, Luticia 142
Hickman, Noahn 142
Hickman, Thos. 142
Hickox, Charles 181
Hicks, Ben M. 97, 142, 195
Hicks, Benjamin 155
Hicks, Eleanor 167
Hicks, Eliza Jane 142
Hicks, G. B. 97
Hicks, George 81, 142, 155, 195
Hicks, Hannah C. 138
Hicks, James 72, 142
Hicks, Jane 195
Hicks, Jno. 6, 129
Hicks, Livinia 142
Hicks, Lucretia 85
Hicks, Mary 85, 129, 195
Hicks, Permilia 320
Hicks, R. A. 129
Hicks, Robt. 138
Hicks, Sarah W. 129
Hicks, Susan 142
Hicks, Willis 167
Hide, Henry 142
Hyde, Elizabeth 142
Hider, John 142
Hider, Michael 99, 142
Higginbottom, James 142
Higginbottom, Nimrod 142
Higgins, Edward 329
Higgins, John 289

Highsmith, Daniel 142
Highsmith, Sukey 142
Highsmith, Susannah 142
Hightower, John 142
Hiland, Eliza 16
Hiland, Joseph B. 16
Hildreth, Lucinda 143
Hildreth, Mary 143
Hildreth, P. M. 143
Hildreth, Pearce 143
Hildreth, R. T. 143
Hill, Allen 143
Hill, Amos 143
Hill, Braxton, 143
Hill, Byrd 129
Hill, Chas. 143
Hill, E. G. 143
Hill, Elizabeth S.143
Hill, George 143
Hill, J. J. 2, 143
Hill, Jacob 69
Hill, Jas. C. 143
Hill, Jesse 56, 93, 143-144, 182, 214, 260, 306,
Hill, Joab 54, 68, 70, 95, 126, 303
Hill, John 143-144, 322
Hill, Judith 143
Hill, Lavinia 129
Hill, Lydia 144
Hill, M. G.143
Hill, M. R. 143, 212
Hill, Mary 143
Hill, Nancy   265
Hill, Patsy 143
Hill, Polly 143
Hill, Randal 143,144
Hill, Robert 143-144, 214, 260
Hill, Ruben   143
Hill, Samuel 6
Hill, Sarah 143-144
Hill, Thomas 143-144, 222
Hill, W. S. 153
Hill, William 144
Hime, Daniel K. 144
Hime, David 144
Hime, John   144
Hime, Mary 144, 172
Hime, William 144
Hinds, Andw. 239
Hine, J. W. 241
Hines, Ellener 144
Hines, Harriet 144
Hines, Ingnatius 144
Hines, Isaac 71
Hines, Thomas 144
Hinton, J. A. 144
Hinton, Mollie 144
Hix, Anna 282
Hix, Demarguis D. 172
Hix, Henderson 257
Hix, Isaac 282
Hix, John 295
Hix, Malinda 295
Hix, Nelly 295
Hix, Vines 144

Hix, William B. 17
Hix, Willis167
Hixkox, Horrace   110
Hoard, Allen S. 46
Hoard, Stanwix 144
Hobbs, George W. 61
Hobbs, Jno. 197
Hobbs, Louisa 197
Hobbs, Sarah 61
Hobby, Hardy 145
Hobby, Mary 35, 145
Hobby, Travis G.145
Hobdan, Jeannette 145
Hobdan, S. M. 145
Hobson, Nicholas 150
Hobson, Robert C. 61
Hockstadter, Charles 223
Hockstadter, Lipman 223
Hodge, Andy 145
Hodge, F. W. 145
Hodge, Wm. 145
Hodges, Drury 145
Hodges, E. 42, 74, 145, 175
Hodges, Edmond 145, 240
Hodges, H. G. 145
Hodges, Hannah 145
Hodges, Hiram 145
Hodges, James 145
Hodges, John 153, 156, 204, 307
Hodges, Joseph M. 80, 240
Hodges, Malissa M. 145
Hodges, Martha 145
Hodges, Mary 145
Hodges, Nancy S. 145
Hodges, Sarah 145, 331
Hodges, Thomas 153
Hodges, William 145, 152, 215
Hodsden, Mary 146
Hodsden, R. H. 188, 329
Hodsden, Robert H. 146, 204
Hogan, Daniel 274
Hogan, G. B. 271
Hogan, Humphrey 146
Hogan, Susan 48
Hogan, William 64, 110, 146, 148
Hogen, James 146
Hogen, Matthew 146
Hogen, Simon 146
Hogg, Guilford146
Hogg, Samuel 30, 247
Hogge, James 146
Hogge, John B. 146
Hogin, Anthony 146
Hogin, Burchy 274
Hogin, Catron C. 146
Hogin, Daniel 146
Hogin, Edward 38, 146
Hogin, Isaac 146
Hogin, Matthew C. 38, 146
Hogin, Rawlings 146, 274
Hogin, Rebecca 146
Hogin, Richard 146
Hogin, Rollins 274

Hogin, Sally 146
Hogin, Sarah 38, 146
Hogin, Simon 202
Hogin, William C. 146
Hogue, Burrel H. 146
Hogue, James 146
Holden, Joshua 147
Holder, Catherine 147
Holder, James 147
Holder, Wm. 147
Holeman, David 147
Holeman, Hall 6
Holeman, James 147
Holeman, Nancy B. 6
Holladay, Henrietta 147
Holladay, Stephen 147
Holland, Daniel 147, 300
Holland, Edmond147
Holland, Edward 147
Holland, Elisabeth 147, 300
Holland, John 11, 280
Holland, Lemuel 147
Holland, Needham 147
Holland, Preston 131, 147
Holland, Willis 191
Hollaway, Chas. 147
Hollaway, John 147
Holliday, Allen 23
Holliday, Henrietta 91
Holliday, Hillery W. 23
Holliday, Nancy 23
Holliday, Ripley B. 23
Holliday, Stephen 91
Holliman, Alexander 260
Holliman, Benjamin D. 148
Holliman, Candis 260
Holliman, Elijah B. 148
Holliman, Elizabeth 148, 259-260
Holliman, George 260
Holliman, Granville 260
Holliman, James 148, 260
Holliman, John W. 148
Holliman Letty 260
Holliman, Penelope 148
Holliman, Samuel S. 148
Holliman, Shepherd 260
Holliman, Susan 148
Holliman, William 260
Hollimon, James 116
Hollimon, John 110
Hollimon, Mark 116
Hollimon, Rebecca M. 198
Hollingsworth, William 230
Hollis, Elizabeth 147
Hollis, Isaac 147
Hollis, James 60, 147
Hollis, Nancy 147
Hollis, Samuel 147
Hollis, William T. 147
Hollis, Wilson L. 147
Holliss, Samuel 68
Holloman, Elizabeth 48
Holloman, William P. 48
Hollowell, Jo. 147
Hollowell, S. S. 49, 52, 125, 147, 214

Hollowman, Elijah 35
Hollowman, Elizabeth 148
Hollowman, Letha 35
Hollowman, Lewis M. 148
Hollowman, Susan 148
Holly, Absolem 82
Holly, Elizabeth 148
Holly, John 148
Holman, Sarah 60
Holmes, Adeline 148
Holmes, Benjamin D. 148
Holmes, James 148, 180
Holmes, Mary M. 148
Holmes, S. B. M. 148
Holmes, Sylvanus C. 148
Holt, Adam A. 148
Holt, Alfred E. 149
Holt, Ann Eliza 149
Holt, Eliza P. 82, 149
Holt, Emily 148, 167
Holt, Fanny 148
Holt, Francis 148
Holt, Garland A. 149
Holt, Herod F. 142, 148
Holt, Hiram 148
Holt, Irby 148, 167
Holt, Jacob H. 149
Holt, Jane 148
Holt, Jas. T. 149
Holt, Jeremiah 331
Holt, Jesse 74
Holt, Jordan C. 42, 142, 144, 148, 161, 290
Holt, Joshua 142
Holt, Julia R. 148
Holt, Larkin 149
Holt, Martha 148
Holt, Nancy E. 148
Holt, Nimrod B. 148
Holt, Robert 148
Holt, Sarah 148
Holt, Serenna J. 148
Holt, Thomas W. 148
Holt, Turner 149
Holt, Wm. G. 149
Homes, Robt. 149
Honeycut, John 230
Honk, Adam 3, 302
Honk, Henry 302
Honk, Jourdan 45
Hood, Bryson 149
Hood, C. H. 149
Hood, Martha S. 149
Hood, W. H. 149
Hood, Wm. 149
Hooker, Benjamin 210
Hooks, Charles 115
Hooper, Absolam 149
Hooper, Elizabeth 149
Hooper, George 149
Hooper, James 149
Hooper, Joseph 149
Hooper, Judah 149
Hooper, Miles 149
Hooper, Phillip 149
Hooper, William 149
Hoops, Thomas P. 241

Hoover, James 115
Hoozer, Z. V. 247
Hopkins, Charlotte 149
Hopkins, George W. 29
Hopkins, John O. 41
Hopkins, Thomas 150, 219, 315,
Hopkins, William 29, 72
Hopson, Joseph 150
Hord, Betsy 150
Hord, Stanwin 169
Hord, Stanwix 144, 150
Hord, Str 150
Horn, Jeremiah 159
Horn, Mary R. 280
Horn, Mathew 11
Hornback, Anny 150
Hornback, John Franklin 150

Hornback, Nancy 150
Hornbergar, Phillip 162, 192, 270
Hornburger, Philip 18, 61, 69, 80, 185, 219, 293
Horne, Henry 150
Horner, James 115
Horsley, Ann 29
Horton, Benj. T. 318
Horton, George 150
Hoskins, John 330
Hoss, Jacob 265
Hotchkiss, H. K. 3
Hotchkiss, Jared 3
Houge, Amanda 146
Houge, Mary Jane 146
Houghton, Joshua 150
Houghton, Thomas 51, 150
Houk, Henry 187
Houk, John 150
Houk, Jordan 150, 292
Houk, Nancy 150
House, Dudley P. T. 42
House, Duke 150
House, Green D. 150
House, Jack 150
House, Jacob 150
House, James 150
House, John 150
House, Susan 150
Houseman, Catherine 150
Houseman, Caty 150
Houseman, Nancy 150-151
Houser, Hellen E. 151
Houser, William 151
Housman, Susannah 56, 151
Houston, Abner 151
Houston, Benjamin F. 151
Houston, Christopher 151
Houston, James 112, 151, 184
Houston, Robert 112
Howard, A. J. 151
Howard, Barbara 151
Howard, Benjamin 282
Howard, Beterice 80
Howard, D. W. 151

Howard, E. L. 151
Howard, Eldridge 150
Howard, Elizabeth 282
Howard, Harman 63
Howard, Henry 151
Howard, James 80, 173
Howard, Johanna 151
Howard, John 173
Howard, Joseph Thomas 80
Howard, L. A. 151
Howard, Lewis 151, 329
Howard, Lilman A. 151
Howard, Madison 151
Howard, Mary 212
Howard, Mathew 151
Howard, Robert 80
Howard, Thomas 63, 289
Howard, Tilman A. 151
Howard, William 72, 80, 179
Howard, Winniford 72, 80
Howel, Edward 265
Howell, A. S. 151
Howell, Abner 151
Howell, Harbet 33
Howell, James 151
Howell, John 44, 151, 309
Howell, Nancy P. 151
Howell, Paul 151
Howell, Richd. M. 151
Howell, Susannah 151
Howell, William 151
Howser, J. W. 151-152
Howser, Lemuel 151
Howser, Sylvester 151
Hoyle, Thomas 91
Hoyton, Thos. 312
Hubbard, Elizabeth 145, 152
Hubbard, Littleton G. 152
Hubbard, Mary 152
Hubbard, Nathaniel 172
Hubbard, Sally 152
Hubbart, William 152
Hubert, John 233
Huccaby, Thomas 152
Huchison, Wm. C. 105
Hucky, David 255
Huddleston, Artema 152
Huddleston, Daniel 152
Huddleston, David 152
Huddleston, Elam 152
Huddleston, Elizabeth 152
Huddleston, Green 152
Huddleston, J. G. 152
Huddleston, James 152
Huddleston, Joel G. 152
Huddleston, John 152, 156, 241
Huddleston, Jonathan 152, 160
Huddleston, Pleasant F. 152
Huddleston, Susana 91
Huddleston, Tennessee 152
Huddleston, Thomas 91, 131, 152
Huddleston, William 152

Hudgins, Edward 152-153
Hudgins, James 152-153
Hudgins, Rebecah 152
Hudgins, Sally 152
Hudgins, Susanna 152-153
Hudgins, William 152-153
Hudleston, Jane 18
Hudleston, Margaret 18
Hudson, Dansey S. 109
Hudson, George 153
Hudson, Hamly P. 109
Hudson, James A. 109, 153, 172
Hudson, Joel 93, 141, 153, 326
Hudson, John 153, 156-
Hudson, Mary L. 109
Hudson, Nancy K. 109
Hudson, Virginia 109
Hudson, W. A. 50, 187
Huey, Elizabeth 153
Huey, Joseph 153
Huey, Wm. 153
Huff, A. C. 153
Huff, Alexandre 153
Huff, Alvin C. 153
Huff, Elenor Elizabeth 153
Huff, Florence 153
Huff, Florida 153
Huff, James 153
Huff, John 153
Huff, Joseph 153
Huff, Lewis 153
Huff, Martha 153
Huff, Mary 153
Huff, McPhillips 153
Huff, Preston 153
Huff, Ranson 153
Huff, Rhoda 153
Huff, Serelda 153
Huff, Serena 153
Huff, Stephen 22
Huff, Thursey Jane 153
Huffaker, Francis G. 153
Huffaker, Jesse 153, 311
Huffaker, Michael 153
Huffaker, N. J. 38
Huffaker, Samuel 38
Huffaker, Wesley 38, 153
Huffhins, Harrit 129
Huffhins, Thomas 129
Huffines, Daniel 128
Huffines, William S. 246
Huffins, Talitha Jane 246
Hufft, Benjamin 153
Hufft, John 153
Hufft, Phillip 153
Hufft, William 153
Hufhens, Jane 246
Hufhens, William C. 246
Huflines, Harriet 128
Huflines, Thomas 128
Hughes, David 338
Hughes, Edward 154
Hughes, Elijah 120, 200
Hughes, George R.110
Hughes, Jas. 310

Hughes, John 146, 154, 274, 285
Hughes, Mariana 202
Hughes, Robert G. 202
Hughes, William Q. 202
Hughlett, William 154
Hughs, Daniel 154
Hughs, Hardy 162
Hughs, James T. 116, 154, 274, 276
Hughs, John 110, 259
Hughs, William Q. 148
Huguely, John 154
Huguely, S. E. 154
Huguely, W. T. 154
Hukky, David 154
Hulett, William 154
Hull, Jackson154
Hull, Josiah 310
Humes, J. A. 154
Humphreys, Elisha 154
Humphreys, Hilton 325
Humphreys, Jesse 154, 294
Humphreys, John 154
Humphreys, Moses 154, 220, 294, 338
Humphreys, Parry W. 96
Humphreys, Richard 154
Humphreys, Suzana 154
Hundly, Joshia 154
Hunt, A. 154
Hunt, Amos 97
Hunt, Ann 97
Hunt, Elizabeth 116
Hunt, Hardy 212
Hunt, Henry 300
Hunt, James 75, 154
Hunt, Jesse 114
Hunt, John 154, 214
Hunt, Mary 154
Hunt, Robert 82-83, 85, 125
Hunt, Sally Fisher 85
Hunt, Sion 154
Hunter, Abraham 84, 259
Hunter, Daniel 154
Hunter, Edwin C. 155
Hunter, Ephraim 274
Hunter, Hardy 238
Hunter, Henry 84
Hunter, Jacob 155, 229
Hunter, James A. 308
Hunter, John 226
Hunter, Martin 155
Hunter, Melton B.155
Hunter, William155
Huntsman, A.43
Huntsman, Adam155, 189
Huntsman, America155
Huntsman, George155
Huntsman, Nancy155, 216
Huntsman, Paradise155
Huntsman, Susan155
Hurley, G. W.155
Hurst, Aaron 155
Hurst, Absalom 282
Hurst, Andrew 155

Hurst, Asa 147
Hurst, David 32, 147, 155, 285
Hurst, Eligah 54
Hurst, Elijah 22
Hurst, George 32
Hurst, Isaac 155
Hurst, James 155
Hurst, Lewis R. 325
Hurst, R. 152
Hurst, Russell 322
Hurst, Sevier 155
Hurst, Westley 155
Hurst, William 135, 155
Hurt, Andrew M. 155
Hurt, J. M. 203
Hurt, J. P. 13
Hurt, Joseph 155
Huskey, Isaac 155
Huskey, William 155
Husky, Dolly 156
Husky, John 156
Husky, Stephen 228
Husky William 156
Husley, M. P. 16
Hust, Joseph 155
Huston, Hugh 58
Hutcherson, Daniel 156
Hutcherson, Elizabeth 156
Hutcherson, John 156
Hutcherson, Michie 156
Hutchings, John 156
Hutchings, Thomas 156
Hutchins, Wm. C. 105
Hutchinson, J. 153
Hutchinson, Samuel 146
Hutchinson, Thomas 65
Hutchinson, William 299, 335
Hutchison, John 9, 21, 58, 87, 101, 151, 161
Hutchison, Samuel 131
Hutson, Ezekiel 156
Hutson, James 156, 184
Hyde, John 154
Hyde, Richard 142
Hynds, Mariah Jane 70
Hynds, Robt. 70
Hynes, Thomas 144
Idle, Adam 156
Impson, John 160
Impson, Sally 156
Ingle, John 156
Ingle, Mary 156, 204
Ingle, Sarah 156, 204
Ingleman, Jane 156, 237, 309
Ingleman, Joseph 156, 237, 309
Ingram, Adeline 156
Ingram, B. 156
Ingram, Catherine 156
Ingram, John 333, 334
Ingram, Louisa 156, 333
Ingram, Lydia 156, 333
Ingram, Moses 269

Ingram, Thomas 65, 156, 333
IIngram, William 156, 333
Ingrum, Mary 84
Ingrum, Shadrach 84
Inman, Amanda 156
Inman, Dinah 156
Inman, Julia 156
Inman, Willis 156
Inmans, Wm. 147
Inmon, Mary 156
Ira [a slave] 81
Irby, Carter 173
Irby, John 173
Ireland, Elizabeth 157
Irvan, Benjamin 157
Irvan, James 157
Irvan, Mary 157
Irvin, Alex. 157
Irvin, John 57, 112, 114, 171-172, 234
Irvin, Mary 141
Irvin, Robert 141
Irvin, William 157, 299
Irwin, Andrew 140, 157, 309
Irwin, Benjamin 157
Irwin, David 157, 271
Irwin, Enos 157
Irwin, John 157, 271
Irwin Margaret 157
Irwin, Mary 157, 185, 322
Irwin, Robert 157, 281
Irwin, William 157
Isaac [a slave] 338
Isbel [a slave] 80
Isbell, Benjamin 124
Isbell, George 157-158
Isbell, James 157
Isbell, John 157
Isbell, Mary 157-158, 249
Isbell, Nancy 157
Isbell, Thomas D. 158
Isham, James 304
Isham, Sarah 304
Isrivle, John 158
Isrivle, Wm. 158
Ivan, Mary 212
Ivan, Robert 212
Ivy, Mary Ann 40
Ivy, Nathan 40
Ivy, William 158
Jack, Alexander158
Jackson, A. S. 158
Jackson, Alexander 85, 101, 173, 297-298, 325
Jackson, Andrew 43, 89, 156, 179
Jackson, Benj. 300
Jackson, Berriman 158
Jackson, C. W. 196
Jackson, Caroline 158
Jackson, Daniel 158
Jackson, Dolley 158
Jackson, Eli 80
Jackson, Elias 158
Jackson, Elizabeth M. 159
Jackson, Esther 106

Jackson, Eunice B. 101
Jackson, Hannah 80
Jackson, Harriet M. 158
Jackson, Henry 158
Jackson, J. C. 159, 243
Jackson, James 158
Jackson, Jesse 158
Jackson, John M. 158, 300
Jackson, Louis E. 158
Jackson, Mack 158
Jackson, Mahaly 158, 279
Jackson, Martha C. 158
Jackson, Mathew G. 159
Jackson, Miles 80
Jackson, Phillip W. 158
Jackson, Robert 158
Jackson, Sarah 80
Jackson, T. M. 159
Jackson, Thomas M.158
Jackson, Virginia 159
Jackson, W. A. 158
Jackson, W. H. 158
Jackson, William105,158-159, 248
Jackson, Zebulon 159
Jacob, Alfred 274
Jacob, Jeremiah 274
Jacox, J. A. 319
Jadwin, Jeremiah 159
Jamerson, William H. 294
James [a slave] 63, 255
James, Alfred 159
James, Columbus 159
James, D. C. 208
James, David C. 159
James, E. C. 159
James, Emanuel 28, 39
James, Enoch 291
James, Frank 159
James, Giles W. 159
James, James 159
James, John 159
James, Lavinia 237
James, Lida 159
James, Martha 159
James, Mary 159
James, Milly 159
James, R. Air. 166
James, Reece 159
James, Sarah 159, 278
James, T. W. 219
James, Thomas 159
James, William 159, 278, 323, 278
Jamison, Thomas 98
Jamison, William 39, 159
Jane [a slave] 88
Jane, Z. 191
Jared, William 343
Jarod, Joseph 245
Jarred, Joseph 312
Jarred, William 312
Jarret, David 286
Jarrets, Margaret 286
Jarritt, John H. 33
Jeffries, Mary 26
Jelks, J. R. 22

Jelks, Jno. R. 22, 72, 336
Jelks, Mary E. 85
Jelks, Nancy 85
Jelly, Hailey 301
Jenens, William 159
Jenings, Hezekiah 160
Jenkins, James 159
Jenkins, Labon 240
Jenkins, Mary Jane 58
Jenkins, Roland 205
Jenkins, Sebert E. 58
Jenkins, Whitmell 160
Jenkins, William 160
Jennings, John 63-64
Jennings, Nancy160
Jennings, Robert W. 276
Jennings, William 159
Jenny [a slave] 38
Jerry [a slave] 8, 267
Jester, Nancy E. 320
Jett, William S. 88, 148
Jetton, James 277
Jewell, Cader 246
Jim [a slave] 317
Jimpson, John 160
Jin [a slave] 63
Jinens, Anderson160
Jinens, Becky 160
Jinens, Ezekiah 160
Jinens, Lucy 160
Jinens, Obediah 160
Jinens, Patty 160
Jinens, Polly 160
Jinens, Ryal 160
Jinens, Sally 160
Jinens, Sarah 160
Jinnings, Jesse 279
Job, Enoch 227
Jobe, David 84, 254, 344
Joe [a slave] 341
John [a slave] 269
John, Daniel 161
Johns, Abner 249
Johns, Andrew 160
Johns, Ezekiel 160
Johns, Hugh 160
Johns, Samuel 160
Johnson, Absalom 304
Johnson, Absilla 160
Johnson, Alex, 160
Johnson, Amanda 163
Johnson, Amos 160
Johnson, Ann Letitia 164
Johnson, Ben 160
Johnson, Benjamin 163
Johnson, Betsey 163
Johnson, Burrel163
Johnson, C. 161, 264
Johnson, Calvin 57, 275
Johnson, Clay Linch 163
Johnson, Clem 160
Johnson, Daniel 161, 163
Johnson, David 161, 163, 320
Johnson, Dennis 161
Johnson, Duncan 161
Johnson, E. M. 326

Johnson, Edith 161, 186
Johnson, Edwin 161
Johnson, Eleanor 160
Johnson, Elias 164-165
Johnson, Elizabeth 20, 160-161, 220, 221
Johnson, Ephraim 141
Johnson, Esther 163
Johnson, F. B. 161
Johnson, F. M. 161
Johnson, Felix B. 160
Johnson, Gregory D. 161
Johnson, Hellen D. 26
Johnson, Henry 70, 83, 136, 161, 167, 201, 237, 241, 288, 309
Johnson, Isaac 160, 163
Johnson, J. C. 145, 161
Johnson, J. N. 161
Johnson, J. T. 162
Johnson, J. W. 160-162
Johnson, Jacob 161, 163, 186
Johnson, James 129, 161-164
Johnson, John 160, 162-163, 203, 263
Johnson, Jonathan 162
Johnson, Joseph 50, 161-163, 205, 256, 275, 333
Johnson, Judith 163
Johnson, Julius 101, 161, 165
Johnson, Leroy B. 164, 326
Johnson, Levi C. 221
Johnson, Louisa 181
Johnson, Lydia J. 163
Johnson, Margaret 186
Johnson, Martha 162-163, 164, 200
Johnson, Mary 163-164, 167
Johnson, Matthew 163
Johnson, Mike 163
Johnson, Nimrod 163
Johnson, Permelia 160
Johnson, Peter 191
Johnson, Phillip 162
Johnson, Polly An 163
Johnson, Rachel 163
Johnson, Reuben 163
Johnson, Rhoda 162
Johnson, Robert 163-164, 260
Johnson, Robertson 160
Johnson, Sally 161
Johnson, Samuel 98, 163-164, 326
Johnson, Sarah 161, 200
Johnson, Stephen 200
Johnson, Susannah 163
Johnson, T. H. 13
Johnson, Thomas 9, 49, 133, 140, 167, 264, 289, 319, 295
Johnson, Thomas H. 162, 295
Johnson, Urial 325
Johnson, Vanbeuren 163
Johnson, William 33, 163-164, 269, 237, 291
Johnston, Amis 164
Johnston, George 164
Johnston, Gideon 164
Johnston, James 23, 189
Johnston, Mary 286
Johnston, Robert 332
Johnston, Samuel 164
Johnston, William 164
Jones, A. B. 169
Jones [a slave] 232
Jones, Abraham 164
Jones, Adelade 7-8
Jones, Alexander 165-166
Jones, Alfred 7
Jones, Ambrose 164
Jones, Amelia 166
Jones, Amos W. 195
Jones, Anderson 165
Jones, Andrew 165
Jones, Ann 26
Jones, Atlas 165
Jones, Azariah 202
Jones, Belinda 58
Jones, Bettie 164
Jones, C. B. 165
Jones, Calvin H. 58
Jones, Catharine 134, 165-166, 319
Jones, Charles 165
Jones, Clarissa J. 272
Jones, D. D. 165
Jones, D. H. 219, 292
Jones, Daniel 58
Jones, David 242
Jones, Dorcus 165
Jones, E. 311
Jones, E. B. 165-166
Jones, Eason 58
Jones, Edward 58, 166
Jones, Eli 164
Jones, Elijah 165
Jones, Elisabeth 164
Jones, Elisha 165
Jones, Elivs 165
Jones, Esta 197
Jones, Francis 166
Jones, George 165, 180
Jones, Helen 26
Jones, Henry 58
Jones, J. M. 165
Jones, J. W. 165
Jones, Jacob 79
Jones, James 32, 140, 164-166, 327
Jones, Jane 166
Jones, John 42, 47, 161, 164, 166, 240, 282, 312, 343
Jones, Joseph 292
Jones, Kate 343
Jones, Lavinia 237
Jones, Leonard 94
Jones, Lewis 26, 165
Jones, Louisa J. 58
Jones, Margaret 166
Jones, Mary 58, 165, 328
Jones, Montagumd 165
Jones, Narcissa J. 101
Jones, Norman 58
Jones, Octavia R. 165
Jones, Parthena 165
Jones, Peter 134, 166, 319
Jones, Polly 56, 166, 327
Jones, Rebecca 165
Jones, Redding B. 99
Jones, Richard 140, 157, 166
Jones, Robert 16
Jones, S. A. 166
Jones, Sallie 164
Jones, Samuel 21, 110, 136, 166
Jones, Sarah R. 165
Jones, Sim 166
Jones, Simon J. 225
Jones, Stephen 226
Jones, T. G. 240
Jones, T. L. 101
Jones, T. P. 29, 101, 161, 203
Jones, Thomas 101, 114, 165, 212, 220, 272
Jones, Timothy P. 165, 292
Jones, W. D. 166
Jones, W. E. B. 66
Jones, Walker 166
Jones, William 26, 57, 101, 165-166, 178, 223, 241, 290, 292, 301
Jonier, Amos 337
Jonier, Martha 337
Jordan, Elizabeth B. 166
Jordan, John 166
Jordan, Lewis 200
Jordan, Mary Truman 166
Jordan, Robert H. 167
Jordan, T. A. 295
Jordon, Saml. H. 66
Jordon, Stephen J. 30
Jordon, William 30
Joseph [a slave] 322
Joshua [a slave] 88, 269
Jouitt, John H. 33
Jourden, Hezekiah 167
Joyner, Giles 58
Juda [a slave] 87
Judd, Nathan 157
Jude [a slave] 181
Justice, J. A. 167
Justice, Jas. B. 167
Justice, Jno. B. 167
Justice, Joel T. 167
Justice, Joseph C. 167
Justice, Julius 167, 292
Justice, Louisa 167
Justice, Mary Ann 167
Justice, Polly 167
Justice, Thomas 73
Kain, John H. 88
Kanchlow, George 167

Kanchlow, John 169
Kanedy, Ann 167
Karr, Agness 167
Karr, Anna 8
Karr, James 167-168
Karr, John 167
Karr, Joseph 167
Karr, Margaret 167
Karr, Robert 167-168
Karr, William 167
Kasky, Robert 4
Kaverns, Pattey 58
Kays, Alexander D. 293-294
Kear, John 261
Keath, John 168
Keath, Pheribee 168
Keefe, Margaret 168
Keefe, Thomas 168
Keeler, John 32, 156, 168
Keeler, Mark 315
Keener, A. H. 231
Keener, Adam H. 198
Keener, David 93, 141-142, 265, 306, 311
Keener, William P. 70
Keer, Anderson 168
Keer, George W. 62, 168
Keer, John 168, 257, 284
Kees, George 115
Keesee, Gilbert 243
Keeton, Elizabeth 168
Keeton, John 168
Keewood, Stephen 168
Keith, Alexander 121, 168
Keith, Charles F. 168
Keith, Daniel 93-94
Keith, Isham 168
Keith, James 189
Keith, John 238
Keith, Katherine 94
Keith, Kitty 168
Keith, Maria 168
Kellesr, George 168
Kelly, Benjamin 194
Kelly, Biddy 168
Kelly, Charles 168
Kelly, Daniel 49, 113, 142, 326,
Kelly, David 38
Kelly, Dinah 79
Kelly, Edward 168
Kelly, James 168
Kelly, John 38, 145, 168, 311
Kelly, Joshua 55, 79
Kelly, Melenda 168
Kelly, Michael 168
Kelly, Nancy 168
Kelly, Paul P. 55
Kelly, Pauline 103
Kelly, Perina 103
Kelly, Squire 168
Kelly, William 168
Kelsey, Henry B. 151
Kenchlow, Sarah 167
Kendall, Sarah 44
Kendall, William 44

Kender, Barbary 169
Kender, George 169
Kenedy, Danl. 75, 184
Kennedy, James 169
Kennedy, William L. 169
Kenner, William R. 245, 288
Kenny, James 169
Kernal, Elizabeth 246
Kernel, Patrick 246
Kerney, Henry Guston 169
Kerr, Elonor 167
Kerr, John 235
Kerr, Joseph 167, 169
Kerr, Minerva 167
Kerr, Presha 167
Kerr, Priscilla 167
Kerr, William 167
Key, Carrie 169
Key, Jno. P. 182
Key, John W. 267
Key, Joseph S. 169
Key, Martin B. 182
Key, Susan S. 56
Keyes, Saml. 184
Keys, Alexander D. 169
Keys, Walter 98
Kilburn, Henry 169
Killingsworth, Frances 29
Kimbrel, James 54
Kimbrel, William B. 54
Kimbrell, Ann B. 54
Kimbrell, Margaret A. 54
Kimbrell, William 54
Kimbro, Dicy 216
Kimbro, Elizabeth Ann 216
Kimbro, Francis N. 216
Kimbro, Polly H. 216
Kimbro, Solomon M. 216
Kimbro, Thomas H. B. 216
Kimbrough, Robert 169
Kimmins, Edward 318
Kimmins, Thomas 318
Kin, A. J. 277
Kincheloe, George 167, 169
Kincheloe, John 169
Kinder, Peter 325
Kindle, Peter 290
King, A. 170
King, Ara 171
King, Asa E. 171
King, Barbara S. A. 169, 170
King, Edward 170
King, Ellender 170
King, Ephraim 170
King, Francis C. 169
King, George 184
King, H. D. 170
King, J. M. 78
King, Jackson 170
King, James 78, 169-170
King, John A. 187
King, Joseph B. 170
King, Joseph R. 169, 170
King, Joshua 35
King, Julius 158
King, Kenneth R. 169, 170
King, Margaret 171

King, Martha M. 171
King, Mary 35, 169-171
King, Nathan 264
King, Ransom 92, 263
King, Redden A. 169, 170
King, Richd. W. 171
King, Robert 32, 158, 170, 326
King, Stephen 78, 170
King, Thomas B. 158
King, Vance 170
King, W. A. 170, 297
King, W. R. 170
King, William 91, 129-130, 158, 162, 170-171
King, Worley D. 169-170
King, Wyley 171
Kingsley, Alpha 11
Kinnaird, Jane 289
Kinnaird, Montgomery 289
Kinnard, George 94
Kinnard, Russel M. 94, 110, 128, 245, 266
Kinnon, William R. 238
Kinnord, John J. 77
Kinnrod, Elizabeth 77
Kinnrod, George 77
Kinnrod, James A. 77
Kinnrod, Martha A. 77
Kinrod, William 77
Kirby, Haborn 171
Kirby, Henry W. 171
Kirby, Jane 171
Kirby, Jesse 171
Kirby, John 70
Kirby, Martha 171
Kirby, Mary A. 171
Kirby, Miles 154, 171
Kirby, Patrick 171
Kirby, Wiley 171
Kirby, William H. 171
Kirk, E. P. 76, 315
Kirk, Elijah, 171
Kirkendall, Peter 171
Kirkindall, John 171
Kirkpatrick, Albert 293
Kirkpatrick, Alexander 171
Kirkpatrick, Andrew 84
Kirkpatrick, David 171
Kirkpatrick, Elizabeth 172, 304
Kirkpatrick, Hugh 171
Kirkpatrick, James 171
Kirkpatrick, John 171
Kirkpatrick, Joseph 172, 299
Kirkpatrick, R. C. 304
Kirkpatrick, Rebecca 171
Kirkpatrick, Robert 19, 111, 172, 245
Kirkpatrick, Toliver 19, 60, 160, 245
Kirksey, Alice 32
Kirksey, Rachel 172
Kirksey, Tennessee 32
Kirksey, William 172
Kirley, Jesse 171
Kirley, Nancy M. 171

Kirley, Wiley 171
Kit [a slave] 241
Kitts, John 172
Knight, Allen 107
Knight, Emily J. 29
Knight, Gabriel B. 330
Knight, Jas. 225, 252
Knight, Malinda 172
Knight, Polly 172
Knight, Robert 172
Knight, Sally 172
Knight, Sampson 172
Knight, Sarah Jane 172
Knight, Thompson 172
Knight, Thos. 172
Knight, W. P. 172
Knight, Wm. 172
Knott, Thomas 314
Knox, Leland C. 42
Knox, Mary E. M. 42
Koen, Abraham 172
Koen, Benjamin 172
Koen, Daniel 172
Koonce, Philip 325-326
Koons, Joseph 69
Kornegay, John 317
Krisel John 166
Kunce, William R. 121
Kyle, G. A. 22
Kyser, Daniel 172
Kyser, Enoch 172
Kyser, Jacob 172
Kyser, Valentine 172
Kyser, William 172
Lacay, A. J. 172
Lacey, John P. 172
Lacey, Louisa 172
Lacey, Thomas P. 172
Lack, Elizabeth S. 30
Lackey, Hugh L. 136
Lackings, James G. 172
Lacy, David 203
Lacy, Edward 209
Lacy, Hugh R. 172
Lacy, John P. 172
Lacy, Martha Ann 172
Lacy, Thos. 172
Lake, Henry 73
Lamb, B. F. 172
Lamb, George 203
Lamb, William 251
Lambert, Aaron 173
Lambert, Elizabeth 239
Lambert, Judith 173
Lambert, Thomas 173
Lambert, William 239
Lambeth, Aaron 173
Lambeth, Francis 173
Lambeth, Warner 173
Lambeth, William 173
Lancaster, Crisianna 173
Lancaster, Edwin R. 67
Lancaster, Elijah 173
Lancaster, John 67, 173, 261
Lancaster, Polly 173
Lancaster, Robert 173

Lancaster, Samuel 67, 97, 112, 165, 173, 320,
Lancaster, Sarah L. 173
Lancaster, Susan R. 67
Lancaster, West Noel 173
Lance, S. Berry 77
Land, Burril R. 121
Landcaster, Aaron 173
Landcaster, Eligah 173
Landcaster, Ephraim 173
Landcaster, Faithey 173
Landers, Robert L. 52, 200
Landreth, W. F. 311
Lane, Alec 173
Lane, Alfred 85
Lane, C. H. 214
Lane, Cullen 118
Lane, Elizabeth 173
Lane, Harriet 85
Lane, Irena 29
Lane, Isaac 31, 133
Lane, J. S. 24
Lane, James 29, 85, 116
Lane, John 85, 205
Lane, L. J. 343
Lane, Martha 85
Lane, Thomas 129, 142, 144
Lane, Tidence 126, 173, 223, 274
Lang, James 174
Langford, Catherine 276
Langford, Ervin H. 334
Langford, Erwin F. 44
Langford, Josiah H. 6, 174
Langford, Stephen 174
Langston, Benjamin 10, 174, 234
Langston, Jerusha 174
Langston, Mary 10, 174
Langston, Richard 174
Lanham, Abel 174, 215
Lanham, Saml. 174
Lanier, Asa 174, 247
Lanier, Clement 174
Lanier, Isaac 63, 174, 230, 266
Lanier, Jane 174, 185
Lanier, John 174
Lanier, Thomas 63, 174
Lanier, William 174, 247
Lankford, Jane 174
Lankford, John L. 174
Lankford, Mary Ann 48
Lankford, Robert 174
Lankford, Susannah 48
Lansdon, Eli M. 174
Lansdon, Robert 174
Lansdon, Susannah 174
Lansdon, Thomas D. 174
Lantern, David 341
Lard, Elijah 174
Large, John 247, 278
Large, Perry 329
Lark, J. R. 128
Larrisson, Peter 283
Lasiter, Frederick 218

Lasiter, Robt. 113
Lasley, J. H. 251
Lasley, John H. 275
Latham, C. W. 175
Latham, Calvin S. 175
Latham, Claborne W. 175
Latham, Gertrude 175
Latham, J. C. 157
Latham, James 118, 175
Latham, John 175
Latham, Laura G. 175
Latham, Martha 175
Latham, Mary E. 175
Latham, Wm. 322
Latimer, Hugh 175
Latimer, Joseph 175
Latimer, Nathaniel 175
Latimer, Sarah C. 121
Latimer, William 175
Latta, James 175
Latta, S. P. 298
Latta, S. R. 113, 171, 256, 326
Latta, Samuel R. 175
Laty, Arthur 138
Lauderdale, Almira 175
Lauderdale, J. W. 42, 103, 159, 208, 278
Lauderdale, Josephus 175
Lauderdale, Robert 175
Laughten, John L. 96
Laurence, Elias 242, 277, 321
Laurence, Elizabeth 175
Laurence, John 52
Laurence, Margaret 175
Laurence, Nathl. 175
Lauton, no name 175
Lavalette, Mary 82
Lavallette, Sarah C. 82
Lavellette, A. T. 175
Lavellette, Margaret D. 175
Lavellette, Martha D. 175
Lavellette, Mary K. 175
Lavellette, Sarah C. 175
Law, Danl. J. 183
Law, Eliza Ann 183
Law, George 183
Law, Isaac B. 182
Law, James 305
Law, John 182
Law, Joseph 128-129
Law, Martha 183
Law, Millissa C.182
Law, R. C. 4
Law, Seymour 183
Law, William 183
Lawrence, Elias 175, 277
Lawrence, Jesse 74, 191
Lawrence, Rosey 74
Lawrence, Wm. 66
Lawson, A. 175-176, 223
Lawson, A. P. 175
Lawson, A. W. 175
Lawson, Alexander 175
Lawson, Andrew 69, 176
Lawson, Drury 233

Lawson, Elizabeth 106
Lawson, Ephroditus 176
Lawson, Evelina D. 175
Lawson, Ezekiel 289
Lawson, Jacob 176
Lawson, James 129, 171
Lawson, L. R. 239
Lawson, Lucinda 175
Lawson, Nancy 175
Lawson, O. 240
Lay, John 156
Layman, A. M. 176
Layman, John M. 176
Layman, Joseph C. 176
Lea, Pryor 169
Lea, William C. 176
Leach, Thadius 176
Leak, Isaac 176
Leak, John R. 13
Leak, Saml. 176
Leakley, Eli 176
Leakley, William 176
Leath, G. W. 176
Leathers, Saml. 345
Leatherwood, Willis 153
Ledbetter, David 176
Ledbetter, J. M. 176
Ledbetter, J. N. 176
Ledbetter, Tom 176
Ledford, William 202
Ledsinger, Isaac 176
Ledsinger, P. C. 107, 109, 162
Lee, Abner 270
Lee, Abraham 177
Lee, Adeline 35
Lee, Anna 36
Lee, B. 253
Lee, Daniel 177
Lee, Eliza 177
Lee, F. Peter 286
Lee, James 35, 285
Lee, Jane 291
Lee, Jesse 177
Lee, Joel 94
Lee, John 131, 151, 177, 291
Lee, Peter 177
Lee, Preas B. 94
Lee, Prior 35
Lee, Stephen 223
Leech, Jno. 25, 177
Leech, Thomas 177
Leegett, Danl. 177
Leek, A. P. 177
Leek, M. J. 177
Leek, Margaret 177
Leek, R. O. 177
Leeland, George 177
Leeper, George 177
Leeper, John 157
Legan, Richard 177
Legate, John 177
Legate, Wm. 177
Leggett, Jesse B. 125
Leggett, W. S. 125
Lemarr, Nancy 177

Lemmon, John 122
Lemmons, Mary 177
Lemmons, Reuben 177, 201
Lenard, John 177
Lerrell, Wm. 301
Leslee, P. H. 324
Leslie, Preston H. 118
Lester, Joshua 6, 237, 319
Lester, Mary E. 178
Lester, P. H. 118
Lethe, James 158
Lett, A. C. 62
Lett, Livy 62
Letton, George W. 178
Letty [a slave] 88, 223
Levy, Wm. H. 82
Lewalling, Jas. 178
Lewalling, John 214
Lewell, Elizabeth 178
Lewell, William 178
Lewis [a slave] 291
Lewis, Aron 38, 48
Lewis, Benj. R. 269
Lewis, Edna 252
Lewis, G. L. 178
Lewis, George 178
Lewis, Henry 178
Lewis, Howel 178
Lewis, James 178, 252
Lewis, Joel 149, 178, 309
Lewis, John 80, 178
Lewis, Katy 178
Lewis, Martha H. 178
Lewis, Mary 263
Lewis, R. S. 167
Lewis, Robert 250, 332
Lewis, Samuel 1
Lewis, W. Terril 47
Lewis, William 178-179, 229
Licopk, Thomas 25
Lieper, Guy 136
Light, Chaney 122, 179
Light, Charlotte 179, 317
Light, E. P. 179
Light, Nancy Adaline 179
Lightfoot, John 184, 250
Ligon, Ann Elizabeth 46
Ligon, Anna C. 46
Ligon, Jno. A. 46
Ligon, Sue 46
Lillard, Wash. 179
Linch, Andrew 210
Lincoln, Isaac 122
Lindsay, E. A. 332
Lindsey, Archibald M. 49
Lindsey, Dudley H. 179
Lindsey, Eli 179
Lindsey, John 10
Lindsey, Joseph 179
Lindsey, Robt. 332
Lindsey, Thos. 93
Link, Averalla 216
Link, Bird 216
Linn, Andrew 179
Linn, Jane A. 179
Linter, Martin 265

Linville, Pleasant C. 297
Lipscum, J. R. E. 179
Litten, Wm. 179
Little, Andrew 179
Little, Elizabeth 179
Little, George 179
Little, Henry 179
Little, Isabel 179
Little, John 179
Little, Mary 179
Little, Thos. 179
Litton, Abram 197
Litton, Allice W. 187
Litton, Charles M. 187
Litton, Joseph M. 187
Livingston, Barney 307
Livingston, Robert 334
Loary, Horatio 200
Lock, William 180
Locke, Augustus S. 180
Locke, Catharine F. 180
Locke, James 180, 303
Locke, William 180
Lockhart, Charles 104
Lockhart, Joseph 4
Locust, Austin 180
Locust, Betsey 180
Locust, Elisabeth 180
Locust, Hannah 180
Locust, James 180
Locust, Moses 180
Loftin, Catherine W. 180
Loftin, Helen 180
Loftis, Laborne 165
Loftis, Mary 165
Loftis, Milly 86
Loftis, Sally Ann 180
Loftis, Tho. J. 180
Logan, William 28
Logg, Samuel 205
Logg, Widow 180
Loggans, Milly 177
Loggins, Samuel 180
Login, John 180
Long, Elisabeth 167
Long, George H. 179
Long, Henry 21
Long, Jacob 243
Long, James 65, 181, 332
Long, John 181
Long, Joseph 181
Long, Mary 181
Long, Nicholas 180
Long, Simeon E. 330
Long, W. H. 180
Long, William 33-34, 180-181
Longford, John R. J. 181
Longford, Josiah H. 174
Longford, Julian 181
Longley, Franklin 293
Longley, Mary T. 293
Longly, Franklin 194
Longmire, Hannah 329
Longmire, Joseph 115, 181, 329
Longmire, Malissa 329

Longmire, Martha 181, 329
Longmire, Mary 181, 329
Longmire, Secan E. 181
Longmire, Thos. W. 115
Longmire, William 181, 329
Loomey, P. H. 223
Looney, R. A. 181
Looney, William R. 266
Loony, Joseph 245
Lossan, Ephroditus 176
Lother, Penelope 82
Lotten, Benjamin 189
Lotty [a slave] 320
Lourance, Geo. W. 25
Love, Catherine 181, 280
Love, Charles 181, 232
Love, Dillard 181
Love, E. A. S. 182
Love, James 181
Love, Jeff 221
Love, John 181-182, 196, 280, 312
Love, Joseph 119, 181, 204, 333
Love, Mary 181
Love, Robert 86, 181-182
Love, Samuel 123
Love, Sarah E. 181
Love, Stephen 181-182
Love, Thomas 181-182
Love, William 181-182
Loveday, Carroll 182
Loveday, Noah 182
Loveday, Perry 182
Loveday, Rhoton 182
Loveday, Robert 182
Lovelace, Ann 182
Lovelace, Fanny 182
Lovelace, Jno. T. 149
Lovelady, Asa 182
Lovelady, Darcus 182
Lovelady, Elizabeth 182
Lovelady, Henry 121
Lovelady, John 182
Lovelady, Mary J. 182
Lovelady, Samuel D. 182
Lovelady, Susannah G. 182
Lovelady, Thomas 182
Lovelady, William H. 182
Lovell, John K. 217
Lovell, Newton Foot 217
Lovey [a slave] 317
Lovey, Jas. B. 65
Lovie, Leonard J. 289
Low, A. C. 182
Low, Abner W. 182
Low, Albert 88
Low, Dorah 182
Low, Emory 308
Low, George 183
Low, James 308
Low, John 183
Low, Malissa C. 182
Low, Mansel 120
Low, Martha 183
Low, R. C. 4
Low, William 55, 183

Lowder, Adam 182
Lowder, Jacob 182
Lowe, Daniel 182-183
Lowe, Eliza Ann 183
Lowe, George E. 183
Lowe, Henry William 182
Lowe, John 182-183
Lowe, L. J. 344
Lowe, Lucy 183
Lowe, Martha 183
Lowe, Marvil 135, 226
Lowe, Seymore S. 183
Lowe, William 183
Lowell, Jas. 171
Lowell, John K. 217
Lowery, Robert 183
Lowrance, Geo. W. 25
Lowry, David 183
Lowry, John 96, 132, 183
Lowry, Rebecca 183
Lowry, Robert 109
Lowry, William 110
Loyd, James 183, 185
Loyd, Jarratt 183
Loyd, Jordan 183
Loyd, Joshua 183
Loyd, Rebecca 83
Loyd, Sarah 185
Lucas, Charles 93
Lucas, Frank 183
Lucas, George C. 189
Lucas, I. M. 183
Lucas, J. A. 183
Lucas, Robert 124, 183
Lucas, William 183, 322
Lucky, J. A. 320
Lucky, Saml. 234
Lucy [a slave] 341
Luiton, James 183
Lumkin, William 245
Lundsford, Wm. 74
Lunsden, James K. 268
Lunsden, Jane 268
Lunsford, Darling 183
Lunsford Wyatt 214
Lusk, Samuel 258
Luskey, Samuel 189
Luton, Samuel 229
Lutton, Elizabeth 86
Lyer, Jno. 330
Lyle, Alexr. 183
Lyle, Isabell 184
Lyle, John 184
Lyle, Wm. Francis 184
Lynch, William 273
Lyndrey, William 297
Lyndsey, George 45, 184
Lyndsey, Sarah 184
Lyndsey, Wm. 31
Lynn, Andrew 179
Lynn, James S. 82
Lyons, Danl. 135
Lyons, James 97, 184
Lyons, Jancy 184
Lyons, Thomas 184
Lyons, William 100, 184
MacCashten, Robert 184

Mack, Georgaretta 184
Mack, Jessee 184
Macoy, Fanny 139
Macoy, Spruce 139
Maddox, Fanny 184
Maddox, J. William 184
Maddox, Notley 184
Maddox, Polly 184
Maddox, Tapley 33, 100, 319
Maddox, William 184
Maddux, C. F. 184-185
Maddux, Craven 185
Maddux, Elisabeth 185
Maddux, George 184
Maddux, S. H. 184
Maddux, Silas F. 185
Maddux, Snowdon H. 198
Maddux, T. J. 184
Maddux, Tapley 185, 230, 266
Maddy, Elisabeth 185
Maddy, William 185
Madearis, Benjn. W. H. 185
Mademas, W. D. 185
Maden, William 185
Maderas, W. D. 185
Madgehain, Strangman 185
Madrey, Mary 185
Magavney, Philip 310
Magby, Ganam 181-182
Magby, Sarah 182
Maggard, George 174, 185
Magoff, Jas. 186
Magoff, Jno. 186
Maguff, Ed. 186
Mahall, John 184
Mahan, Archibald 186
Mahan, Gideon 260
Mahan, Henry 186
Mahan, James 186
Mahan, Joseph H. 186
Mahan, Letty 260
Mahan, Martin H. W. 186
Mahan, Nancy 186
Mahan, Prestley B. 186
Mahan, Sally 186
Mahan, W. J. 327
Mahan, William 186
Mahanay, Perry 202
Mahaney, Edward P. 53
Mahaney, Elizabeth 53
Mahaney, John C. 53
Mahaney, Katherine 7-8
Mahaney, Milan F. 53
Mahaney, Ransom P. 7
Mahaney, Sarah L. 53
Mahany, Benjamin 186
Mahany, Emaline 53
Mahany, Job 186
Mahany, John L. 186
Mahany, Lloyd 186
Mahany, Loge 186
Mahany, Loyd C. 53
Mahany, Marion M. 186
Mahany, Oliver P. 186
Mahany, Perry 186

Mahany, Ranson 161, 186
Mahany, Thomas R. 161, 186
Mahany, William 161, 186
Maholland, John 86
Mahon, Ailsey 270
Mahon, Henry 104, 147, 149, 186
Mahon, Willie 270
Mahoney, Katherine 7
Mahoney, Michl. 186
Mahony, Benjamin 186
Mahony, Elizabeth 163
Mahony, Loyd M. 161
Mahony, Perry 161
Mahony, Ransom P. 7
Mahony, Thomas L. 163
Maize, David 61
Majors, Robert H. 61
Malcom, James 287
Malden, Leroy 192
Maldon, Thonton 186
Malinda [a slave] 344
Mallard, Daniel L. 186
Mallory, James 307
Malloy, James 186
Malloy, Thomas 187
Maloy, George 187
Maloy, James 187
Maloy, Sarah 187
Manear, Alen 340
Manear, Allen 168, 340
Manear, James A. 51, 187, 340
Manear, Mariah 340
Manear, Sarah 187
Maner, Sally 187
Maness, Lucy 62
Mangram, Betty 187
Mangram, W. H. 187
Manian, James A. 148
Maniar, Allen 168, 314
Manier, James A. 187
Manis, Fanny C. 187
Manis, Polly 187
Maniss, Joseph 187
Manley, Caleb 290
Manley, David 271
Manley, Ellenora 187
Manley, F. 290
Manley, J. A. C. 134, 187, 207
Manley, Joseph 271
Manley, M. C. 187
Manley, Mozella P. 187
Manley, Sarah E. 187
Manley, William 187, 271
Manly, Hamblen 250
Manly, J. A. C. 231
Manly, Levi 271
Manly, Sarah F. 290
Mann, William 47
Manning, Charles J. 117, 187
Manning, E. K. 277
Manning, Elizabeth 117, 187

Mans, Susan A. 328
Mansel, Albert F. 50
Mansel, Arena K. 50
Mansel, John R. 50
Mansel, Richard E. 50
Mansel, Samuel M. 50
Mansel, Sarah F. 50
Mansel, William E. 50
Mansell, Burnett 188
Mansell, Martha 188
Mansfield, J. Add 188
Mansfield, John 188
Mansfield, Lee 188
Mansfield, Nicholas 241
Mansfield, Thomas J. 188
Map, Thomas 188
Map, William 188
Maples, Edward 188
Maples, Elijah 188
Maples, Elizabeth 187-188
Maples, G. 188
Maples, G. M. 182
Maples, George 335
Maples, Gideon M. 182
Maples, Jadah 335
Maples, James 150, 188, 269
Maples, Judah 335
Maples, Malissa C. 182
Maples, Micajah R. 234
Maples, P. W. 4
Maples, Preston 188, 262
Maples, Rebecca 188
Maples, Redmon 188
Maples, Samuel 188
Maples, Sarah 188
Maples, Thomas 4, 153, 182, 188
Maples, William 4
Maples, Wilson 188
Marbery, Leonard 61
Marby, Polly T. 332
Marchall, William B. 246
Marear, James 340
Margrave, Drury 188
Margrave, John 188
Margrave, Tennessee 188
Mariah [a salve] 269
Marjors, William 124
Mark, Georgaretta 184
Mark, Jessee 184
Markham, Claiborne 153
Markham, Martha 153
Marlow, Catharine 188
Marlow, Edmund 188
Marlow, Edward 139, 188
Marlow, Elizabeth 188
Marlow, George 139
Marlow, Jane 188
Marlow, Joseph 188
Marlow, Lucy Jane 188
Marlow, Mary 188
Marlow, Rebecca 188
Marlow, Renny 188
Marlow, Sally 188
Marlow, Wm. H. 100
Maroney, Loyd 189

Marquess, Thomas 121
Marr, Constant P. 189
Marr, Constentine 189
Marr, George W. L. 331
Marr, Milton H. 189
Marrier, Allen 187
Marrier, James A. 187
Marring, Jno. 155
Marrs, Alexander 89
Marrs, Geo. W. L. 301
Marrs, Martha 89
Marry, John A. 189
Mars, Hugh 189
Mars, John A. 189
Mars, Polly 189
Marsh, Jonathan 189
Marsh, Merlin 335
Marsh, Nancy 189
Marshal, Sally 189
Marshall, Adelade 40
Marshall, Bennett 40, 299, 243
Marshall, Chappel 189
Marshall, David 169
Marshall, James 189
Marshall, John 47, 125
Marshall, Robert 189, 228
Marshall, W. B. 189
Marshall, Wm. M. 189
Martha [a slave] 320
Martin, Alexander 148, 189
Martin, Amanda J. 190
Martin, Andrew 85, 190
Martin, Barclay 190
Martin, Carrol 16
Martin, Charles W. 296
Martin, David 189
Martin, Dosha 316
Martin, Eliza 191
Martin, Elizabeth 190
Martin, Francis 190
Martin, George 44, 65, 159, 190, 344
Martin, Henry 190
Martin, Hugh 170, 190
Martin, Isaac 190
Martin, James L. 189
Martin, Jane L. 189
Martin, Jesse 78, 186, 191, 207, 269
Martin, John 26, 41, 85-86, 137, 189-190
Martin, Joseph 36, 190, 200
Martin, Margaret L. 190
Martin, Martha 190
Martin, Mary T. 334
Martin, Mathew 281
Martin, Matt 190
Martin, Nancy 41, 316
Martin, Patrick 36, 190
Martin, Polly 77
Martin, Rachael 190, 284
Martin, Robert 189, 190
Martin, Samuel 139, 170, 191
Martin, Sarah 190
Martin, Susan Ann 316

Martin, Thomas 77
Martin, William 190-191
Martins, Alexander 148
Martins, Henry C. 191
Mary [a slave] 63, 269
Mask, Georgaretta 184
Mask, Jessee 184
Mason, Abner 319
Mason, Assa 74
Mason, Benjn. 314
Mason, E. B. 181
Mason, Elizabeth 191
Mason Henry 191, 283
Mason, Isaac 191
Mason, James 191
Mason, Jesse 191
Mason, Jno. D. 211
Mason, Joseph D. 283
Mason, Lucinda 191
Mason, Polly 11, 191
Mason, R. M. 191
Mason, Ralph 191
Mason, Reuben 191
Mason, Robert 284
Mason, Rufus M. 150, 229
Mason, William 191
Mass, Thomas 188
Masseda, Nathaniel 191
Massey, Elbert W. 165
Massey, Elizabeth 192
Massey, George 329
Massey, W. B. 191
Massey, William 192
Massina [a slave] 96
Masters, Alexander 44, 148
Masters, Martin 87
Masters, Monterville 87
Mastin, Samuel J. B. 191
Masy, J. 192
Mathers, Alexander 99
Mathews, Alexander 192
Mathews, E. S. 283
Mathews, Elizabeth 192
Mathews, George 192
Mathews, James A. 185
Mathews, John 29, 297
Mathews, Joseph 290
Mathews, Joshua 192
Mathews, Martha A. 283
Mathews, Richd. 333
Mathews, Robert 327
Mathews, W. H. 240
Mathis, Jacob 63
Mathis, Nancy 148
Mathis, no name 148
Matilda [a slave] 149
Matlock, Charles 255
Matlock, Henry 255
Matlock, Jason 192
Matlock, John 111
Matlock, Moore 192
Matlock, Nelly 111
Matlock, William 255
Matly, Bryan F. 39
Matthews, Edward W. 1
Matthews, Jane 320
Matthews, Jo. 230

Matthews, John 215
Matthews, Richard 192, 274
Matthews, Sampson 192, 244, 274
Matthews, William 192
Mattlock, William 40
Mattox, Charles L. 290
Maulden, Leroy 192
Maulden, Samuel 192
Maxwell, Amos 50
Maxwell, Cornelius 192
Maxwell, Jane 192
Maxwell, Jasper 192
Maxwell, Nancy 192
Maxwell, Thomas 192, 227
Maxwell, William 158
Maxy, James 152
May, Alfred H. 192
May, Almedia G. 192
May, Alphonso 192
May, Amanda H. 192
May, Anna 192
May, James 192
May, Jane 192
May, John 192, 272
May, Jonathan 192
May, Joseph W. 192
Mayes, Wm. 119
Mayfield, Abraham 217
Mayfield, Abram 192
Mayfield, Isaac 44
Mayfield, James S. 192
Mayfield, John W. 192, 327
Mayfield, Quarls T. 296
Mayo, C. B. 193
Mayo, Council 193, 289
Mayo, Frederick 192-193
Mayo, Hardy 193
Mayo, Joel 193
Mayo, Jonas 193
Mayo, Martha L. 193
Mayo, R. C. 192-193
Mayo, Redmond 192-193
Mayo, Reuben 193
Mayo, Robert 193
Mayo, Sarah Jane 193
Mayo, Stephen 193
Mayo, Thomas H. 193
Mays, Alphonso 192
Mays, Council B. 289
McAdams, Amos 3, 52, 205
McAdams, James 1, 116
McAdoo, Wm. 180
McAdow, James 125
McAdow, Wm. 125
McAlister, Charles 74, 126, 131, 142-143, 146, 275, 328
McAllen, John 200
McAllester, John 294
McAllister, George D. 193
McAllister, John 193
McBean, A. M. L. 231
McBean, William 193
McBride, Archibald 148
McBride, David 75
McBride, Julia A. 148

McBride, William 75
McBride, Wm. M. 148
McCaffy, John 329
McCahty, John L. 123
McCalgin, Wilson 334
McCall, John 119
McCall, Sarah Jane 193
McCallie, A. G. 210
McCammell, John 194
McCampbell, John 194
McCampbell, Mary L. 194
McCampbell, Thos. C. 194
McCaney, James 194
McCarney, Mary194
McCarter, John 194
McCarter, Mary 194
McCartey, Jno. L. 121
McCarthy, Jacob 194
McCarthy, John 33
McCartney, Lewis 194
McCarty, James 194
McCarty, Jane 194
McCarty, Jinsey 194
McCarver, James 194
McCarver, John 295
McCarver, L. H. 128
McCarver, Leonedas A. 41
McCarver, Logan H. 70, 128-129
McCarver, Malinda M. 128
McCarver, Margaret C. 295
McCarver, Pinkney 128, 154, 337
McCarvin, L. A. 207
McCay, Dugal 194
McClachey, Jane 12
McClain, Alfred 194
McClain, William 188, 194
McClanahan, Elizabeth 203
McClanahan, Laura E. 53
McClary, Jacob194
McClary, Payne 311-312
McClary, Robert 150206
McCleary, Robert 111, 236, 240
McClelan, Andrew 195
McClelan, Margaret 195
McClelan, Sampson 195, 221, 225
McClelan, Sarah Jane 195
McClellan, A. G. 195
McClellan, Abraham 124
McClellan, Albert G. 195
McClellan, Andrew 41, 125, 163
McClellan, Balsorah 195
McClellan, Barbara 137
McClellan, Bennett T. 195
McClellan, David 137, 315
McClellan, Hugh 262
McClellan, Isabella 81, 195
McClellan, James D. 165, 195
McClellan, Jno. T. A. 195
McClellan, Martha Ann 195
McClellan, Mary C. 195

McClellan, Robt. Newton 195
McClellan, Saml. 81, 142
McClellan, Sampson 110, 128, 163, 195
McClellan, Wm. B. 195
McClelland, Isreal 196
McClelland, Sampson 129
McClelland, Samuel 196
McClenan, Andrew 196
McClenden, Nancy 325
McClendon, Bailey 344
McClendon, George 196
McClendon, Henry H. 196
McClendon, Jacob 196
McClendon, Jessee 196
McClendon, Susannah 196
McClendon, Temperance 344
McClerkin, L. C. 203
McClung, Charles 137
McClure, A. 196
McClure, Alexander E. 331
McClure, Holbert 196
McClure, Mary 196
McClure, Nancy N. 320
McClure, Peggy Ann 196
McClure, William 213
McColegin, James 334
McCollough, John 196
McCollum, Catherine R. 196
McCollum, James 132, 196-197, 328
McCollum, Katherine R. 197
McCollum, Martha A. E. 196
McCollum, Mary 132
McCollum, Sidney A. 196
McConet, P. C. 112
McConnall, R. S. 286
McConnell, Catherine 197
McConnell, David 197
McConnell, Elizabeth 197
McConnell, Fanny 286
McConnell, Frances 286
McConnell, James 197
McConnell, John M. 197
McConnell, R. S. 286
McConnell, Rebelah 197
McConnell, Robert S. 286
McConnell, Samuel 12, 49, 103
McCorach, Joseph 197
McCord, Alexander E. 331
McCord, James 5
McCord, Permelia 132
McCord, Robert 132
McCorkle, A. J. 3
McCorkle, Anderson 197
McCorkle, F. A. 3
McCorkle, H. R. A. 24, 27, 197, 240, 250
McCorkle, J. E. 120, 158-159, 197
McCorkle, J. S. 112, 120
McCorkle, J. W. 197
McCorkle, John E. 69, 311
McCorkle, M. E. 197

McCorkle, M. V. 197
McCorkle, S. S. 112
McCormack, J. B. 117, 187
McCormack, Johnson 104
McCormack, Joseph 197
McCormick, William 52, 95, 225
McCorry, Corinna A. 197
McCorry, Ellen 197
McCorry, Henry W. 197
McCorry, Mary 197
McCorry, Musadora 197
McCoullough, Benjamin 31
McCour, M. W. 224
McCovack, Joseph 197
McCow, M. W. 139
McCowan, James 197
McCowan, M. W. 29, 138-139, 224, 292
McCowan, Margaret 200
McCown, George 43, 48
McCoy, Ann E. 197
McCoy, Daniel 198
McCoy, Dickson 197
McCoy, Dixon 197-198
McCoy, Eugene 198
McCoy, Ezekiel 197-198
McCoy, Hugh 198
McCoy, James 198
McCoy, John 197-198, 223, 332
McCoy, Mary D. 197
McCoy, Nancy D. 197
McCoy, Neuton M. 198
McCoy, Newton A. 197
McCoy, Rachel 198
McCoy, Sallie Vic 198
McCoy, Susannah 198
McCoy, Thos. 197
McCoy, William 198
McCrackin, R. P. 135, 320, 323
McCrary, Robert 331
McCray, Daniel 225
McCrorry, Henry W. 97
McCrory, Cyrus G. 144
McCroskey, David 47, 116, 145
McCroskey, J. M. 177
McCroskey, J. S. 80, 326
McCroskey, James M. 198
McCroskey, John 84, 198
McCroskey, Jos. M. 198
McCroskey, Malinda 198
McCroskey, Mary M. 198
McCroskey, Robert 198
McCroskey, William R. 198
McCubbin, Zachariah 124
McCulbugh, James 22
McCulloch, Benjn. 198
McCullock, D. W. 223
McCullough, Thos. 198
McCutcheon, Medora 198
McCuttchen, John B. 198
McDaniel, Anne L. 214
McDaniel, Clay 199
McDaniel, Daniel 199

McDaniel, James 198-199, 214, 312
McDaniel, John F. 198
McDaniel, Magness 199
McDaniel, Polly 199
McDaniel, Randal 199
McDaniel, Riley W. 198
McDaniel, Walter 199
McDannel, R. Z. 199
McDavid, James C. 199
McDavid, W. C. 199
McDearman, J. A. 298
McDearmon, G. W. 265, 273
McDermit, Jacob 13
McDonal, James W. 199
McDonal, John F. 199
McDonal, Middleton 199
McDonal, Samuel R. 199
McDonald, Amy W. 199
McDonald, Daniel 199
McDonald, Henry 67, 199
McDonald, James 130, 214, 274, 339
McDonald, Martha 199
McDonald, Orlena Jane 199
McDonald, Rily B. 199
Mcdonel, Henry L. 282
McDonnald, Anne L. 214
McDonol, Samuel R. 291
McDowell, Allen C. 325
McDowell, Elizabeth 199
McDowell, James 199
McDowell, John 66, 199, 337
McDowell, Joseph 199
McDowell, Martha 199
McDowell, William 206
McDuff, James 252
McElrath, Albert G. 199
McElrath, Joseph 199, 200
McElyea, James 200
McErwin, Alexander 200
McErwin, Margaret 200
McEwen, Deborah 132
McEwen, John 90, 202
McEwin, Margaret 200
McEwing, John 200
McFarland, Alex. 200
McFarland, James 7, 200, 216, 237, 309
McFarland, John 200, 241, 256, 279
McFarland, Marvil 200, 273
McFarland, Phoeba 237, 309
McFarland, Quily 200
McFarland, Rachal 182
McFarland, Robert 212
McFarland, William 241
McFarlin, Duncan 200
McFarlin, James 133, 200
McFarlin, John D. 200
McFarlin, Margaret 200
McFarlin, Mary J. 200
McFerson, John 200
McGannis, John M. 315

McGaughey, R. H. 114, 117, 208, 233, 286
McGavock, H. W. 151
McGavock, Joanna 151
McGee, Ann 200, 217
McGee, Fayette 153
McGee, Henry 207
McGee, John R. 117, 175, 340
McGee, Preston H. 153
McGee, Proctor 153
McGee, William 153
McGehee, Abraham 177
McGhe, William 184
McGhee, John 137, 200-201
McGhee, Matthew 123, 200, 201
McGhee, Rachael 201
McGimpsey, John W. 221
McGimpsey, Mary 221
McGincy, John 221
McGincy, Mary 221
McGinnis, A. 115, 199, 210, 220, 252, 277
McGinnis, Andrew 201, 210
McGinnis, Nancy 201
McGinnis, T. J. 201
McGinnis, W. A. 201
McGipson, George 201
McGipson, Randal 201
McGipson, Tobias 201
McGlohlin, Sary 201
McGlothlin, E. R.121
McGraw, Uriah 201
McGready, William 334
McGregor, John 302
McGregor, Thomas 136
McGrew, William 28, 280
McGuffey, Charles D. 153
McGuire, John 177, 286
McHaney, Andrew 201
McHaney, William 201, 234
McHany, W. C. 297
McIntier, J. L. 201
McIntosh, Alexr. 201
Mcintosh, Benjamin 135
McIntosh, Charles 309, 324
McIntosh, Elizabeth 201
McIntosh, John 150, 201
McIntosh, Susan 150
McIntosh, William 201
McIver, Jane 201-202
McIver, John 201, 320
McIver, Matilda 58
McIver, Roderick 155
McJenekin, Betsey 167
McJenekin, Samuel 167
McJunkin, Betsey 167
McJunkin, Samuel 167
McKamy, James 202
McKamy, Mary 202
McKamy, William C. 202
McKaney, John 188
McKaskell, Betsy 62
McKay, Elenor 202
McKay, M. M. 203

McKay, Murdock M. 55
McKay, Murphy 311
McKay, Rachael 202
McKeal, James 202
McKean, Jospeh 168
McKean, Margaret 168
McKearley, James 202, 303
McKee, Allexr. 127
McKee, Buena Vista 82
McKee, Gertrude 82
McKee, James R. 331
McKee, John 184
McKee, Martha D. 82
McKee, Olivia T. 82
McKee, Wm. Henry 82
McKenly, George W. 268
McKeny, Alsy 268
McKindly, Matthew C. 338
McKinley, Alsey 268
McKinley, Eliza 202
McKinley, Elizabeth 202
McKinley, George W. 225, 268
McKinley, James 202
McKinley, Jane 202
McKinley, Joseph R. 132, 304
McKinley, Josiah 202
McKinley, Martha 202
McKinley, Mary 202
McKinley, Matthew C. 118, 202, 259
McKinley, Robert B. 202
McKinley, Sarah 202
McKinney, Catherine 202
McKinney, David 202
McKinney, Fanny 202
McKinney, James 202
McKinney, Jenny 202
McKinney, Jeremiah 202
McKinney, Joel 202
McKinney, John 202
McKinney, Milly 202
McKinney, Ralph 144
McKinney, Wm. J. 80
McKinny, Edwin F. 186, 202
McKisick, Daniel 72
McKisick, James 149, 216
McKnight, A. R. 69, 236
McKnight, Caleb 203
McKnight, David 203
McKnight, Eleanor 203
McKnight, Elizabeth 203
McKnight, Hamilton 202
McKnight, James 203, 279
McKnight, John 203
McKnight, Juliana K. M. 203
McKnight, Marcus 202
McKnight, Margaret 202-
McKnight, Mary 203
McKnight, Matilda F. 203
McKnight, R. T. 208
McKnight, Richard 25, 220
McKnight, Robert 203
McKnight, Sam A. 3
McKnight, Sammi A. 203
McKnight, W. N. 199

McKnight, William N. 203
McKorkle, Henry 125, 307
McKoy, M. M. 203
McLain, Alfred 262
McLain, James 163
McLain, Thomas R. 304
McLama, Peter 203
McLane, Thomas 84
McLaurin, Polly 75
McLean, Charles D.195
McLean, James D. 195
McLean, Jane E. 195
McLean, John 203
McLean, Joseph 203
McLean, Susan Isabella 195
McLean, Thomas N. 304
McLean, Wm. L.195
McLeary, W. D. 99
McLemore, J. J. 338
McLemore, John C. 194
McLemore, Robt. N. 1
McLemore, Sugars 65
McLish, Jane 203
McLish, Wm. 203
McMachen, John 203
McMahan, Archabald 203
McMahan, D. B. 32, 62, 68, 329
McMahan, David 20, 44, 204, 329
McMahan, G. N. 204
McMahan, George 203, 281
McMahan, Iredell 204
McMahan, James 138-139, 247 331
McMahan, Jane 204
McMahan, John 32, 150, 168, 188-189, 194, 204, 213, 224
McMahan, Martha B. 204
McMahan, Patsy 151
McMahan, R. S. 204
McMahan, Rachael 203
McMahan, Redmond 204
McMahan, Robert 135, 138, 204
McMahan, Saml. 151, 204, 329
McMahan, Sanders 204, 224, 329
McMahan, Thomas 204
McMahan, Wellington 38, 139
McMahan, Wilson 290
McMahan, Wm. 204
McMahon, Joseph 93
McMahone John 60, 99
McMamahan, David J. 34
McMartin, James 309
McMartin, Pheobe 309
McMeans, Isaac L.188
McMillan, Daniel 204
McMillan, John 204
McMillen, Valentine 74
McMillin, David C. 204
McMillin, Jonathan P. 204
McMillin, Joseph W. 204

McMillin, Robert W. 204
McMinn, John 340
McMott, Henry 156, 204
McMott, Wm. H. 218
McMurray, Amanda B. 216
McMurray, America 216
McMurray, Arvilla H. 216
McMurray, Charles 216
McMurray, Dicy 216
McMurray, Fanny 216
McMurray, John 216
McMurray, Lucy 216
McMurray, Mary 216
McMurray, Polly R. 216
McMurray, Samuel 216
McMurray, Sarah 216
McMurray, Silas   216
McMurray, Thomas 216
McMurray, Washington 216
McMurray, William 216
McMurry, David 8
McMurry, James H. 70
McMurry, Mary 174
McMurry, Samuel 8-9, 140
McMurty, Joseph 75
McNabb, Baptist 204, 324
McNabb, David 204, 248, 299
McNabb, Isabella 248
McNabb, James 185
McNabb, John 12, 184, 204, 244, 288, 330
McNabb, Mariah 238
McNabb, Wm. 76
McNairy, John 5
McNamarra, John 39
McName, Peter 338
McNat, Macky 204
McNatt, Benjamin 252
McNatt, David 204, 307
McNealy, Cynthia Ann 205
McNealy, Isaac 204
McNealy, Margaret P. 205
McNealy, Rebecca 204-205
McNeely, Alexander 205
McNeely, George 205
McNeely, James 205
McNeely, John 205, 256
McNeely, Moses 205
McNeely, Seth 205
McNelly, Jas. 292
McNitt, Anthony 118
McNulty, Jas. 292
McNulty, Will 205
McNutt, James 206
McNutt, John S. 81, 107, 205, 315
McNutt, Margaret J. 205
McNutt, Mary E. 205
McNutt, Murphy   291-292
McNutt, W. A. 107, 205, 298
McNutt,William 81, 205, 210, 218, 306
McPhail, Daniel 205
McPhail, David, 205, 288
McPherson, Daniel 324
McPherson, Enoch 277

McPherson, George 205
McPherson, Joseph 205
McPherson, Richard 202
McPherson, Sally 205
McQuean, Hannah 205
McQuean, Saml. 205
McRae, Duncan 63-64, 174, 205
McRae, Elisabeth 205
McShekus, Miles 205
McSpaden, Moses 263
McSweeny, J. B. 274
McSweeny, Mary S. 274
Mcteer, A. B. 77
McTeer, William 77
McVey, Cynthia 30
McVey, Jane 42
McVey, Mary 206
McVey, Thomas 206
McWherter, Jeremiah 52
McWhirter, George 43, 60, 189, 206, 212-213, 245, 265, 323-324, 336,
McWhirter, Levicy 212
McWhirter, Lucinda D. 52
McWhirter, Martha 324
McWhirter, Samuel C. 206
McWhorter, George M. 276
McWilliams Andrew 206
Meader, Christopher 94
Meader, Hariett 94
Meaders, Agness 206
Meaders, Charles 206
Meadow, Christopher 94
Meadow, Harriet 94
Meadows, Agniss 206
Meadows, Jane 21
Meadows, John W. 143
Meadows, Joseph 21
Meadows, Silus 206
Meadows, Solomon 338
Meadows, Thomas 338
Meadows, W. L. 270, 284
Meaks, John W. 248
Mecker, George 315
Meckley, John 226
Medaris, John 185, 308
Meddlay, James M. 329
Meddows, Ann 206
Meddows, Ephraim G. 206
Meddows, Henderson 206
Meddows, James 206
Meddows, Jane 206
Meddows, Jemima 206
Meddows, John 206
Meddows, Mehaley 206
Meddows, Michael 206
Meddows, Pomphit G. 206
Meddows, Rebecca 206
Meddows, Riley 206
Meddows, Washington 206
Meddows, William 206
Medearis, B. W. H. 185
Medearis, Elizabeth 185
Medearis, George W. 185
Medearis, John T. 185
Medearis, Martha F. 185

Medearis, Polly C. 185
Medearis, Sarah 185
Medearis, William 185
Medget, Massey 206
Medley, Ann 86
Medley, George 329
Medley, Samuel 86
Medlin, Ann 86
Medlin, Bryant 206
Medlin, Carroll 206
Medlin, Elizabeth 200
Medlin, Esther 206
Medlin, F. B. 206
Medlin, Grey B. 206
Medlin, James H. 206
Medlin, Jno. 206
Medlin, Joseph 200
Medlin, Malinda 206
Medlin, Robertson 206
Medlin, Samuel 86
Medlin, Susan 206
Medlin, Tennessee 206
Medlin, Thomas 206
Medlock, Isaac 206
Medlock, John 206
Medlock, Sarah 51, 206
Medonal, Henry L. 282
Medonal, James 282
Medonal, Riley 282
Medowel, John 121
Medows, Matilda 207
Medows, Meridith 207
Meece, Nelly 295
Meed, A. 207
Meeks, John W. 248
Meeks, Malissa F. 248
Megehee, Henry 207
Megehee, Norvill 207
Meigs, R. J. 65, 146
Meloy, George 43-44
Melton, Garrett 207
Melville, Levina 207
Melvin, John 322
Melvin, Wm. 207
Menees, Benjamin 207
Menees, James 207
Menees, William D. 207, 268, 295
Meneis, Benj.113, 163
Menesinger, John 207
Meness, Benjn. 100
Meniss, Mary 207
Menses, Benjamin 207
Menzies, Green 191
Menzies, John C. 207
Menzies, R. G. 187, 207, 251, 314
Menzies, W. P. 107,187, 203, 207, 226
Menzies, William P. 251
Mercer, Jones 35
Mercer, Martha 35
Merchant, J. P. 207
Merchant, Peter 207
Merchant, Sandford 208
Meredith, Anna 62, 208
Meredith, Charles 62

Meredith, Ed. H. 62, 208
Meredith, Henry H. 62
Meredith, Hugh 62, 208
Meredith, John D. 62
Meredith, Saml. 7, 96
Merewither, Sallie 208
Meridith, Anna R. 208
Meridith, Charles 208
Meridith, Henry H. 208
Meridith, John D. 208
Meriwither, Henry K. 208
Meriwither, Saml. 208
Merret, John 249
Merreweather, George 9
Merrewither, M. D. 208
Merrill, Jno. M. 333
Merritt, George W. 208
Merritt, Mark 249
Merriweather, Richd. L. 230
Merriwether, D. J. 83, 299
Merriwether, David 83, 95, 119, 208, 299
Merriwether, Francis 83, 299
Merriwether, Henry A. 208
Merriwether, J. T. 299
Merriwether, Marion 208
Merriwether, Matthias D. 208
Merriwither, Hubbard 208
Merriwither, John 208
Merriwither, William P. 208
Merrwither, Frank 208
Mesany, Isaac 11
Metcalf, Georg. 332
Michel, James 254
Michell, Jo. 107, 165
Michen, George 217
Michie, Adam 15
Michie, George 104, 230
Michie, James 15, 125, 289
Michie, Judith 104
Midgett, E. R. 18-19
Miegs, Return J. 208
Milam, D. J. 208
Milam, Denten 208
Milam, Eliza M. 208
Milam, Felix W. 208
Milam, Gladden 208
Milam, Jack 208
Milam, John W. 208
Milam, Louisa E. 208
Milam, Martha 341
Milam, Phelix W. 208
Milam, Stephen 208
Milam, Thos. R. 208
Milam, W. A. 208
Milam, Z. J. 208
Milan, Dora 208
Milan, Jno. 2
Milan, Julia 208
Mileham, Jacob 208
Miles, Charles 209
Miles, James 209
Miles. Martha 209
Miles, Nancy 70
Miles, Richard 209, 277
Miles, Samuel 250
Miles, William 209

Miligan, Jane 209, 328
Milla [a slave] 212
Millar, Mary 16, 209
Miller, A. 253
Miller, Abner 209
Miller, Andrew 84-85, 209,
Miller, Ann 209
Miller, Ared. 209
Miller, Cailar 209
Miller, Cas. 209
Miller, Cassius 210
Miller, David 209
Miller, Elizabeth 209
Miller, G. B. 29, 170
Miller, George 27, 45, 78, 102, 214, 221
Miller, Green 209
Miller, Harriet 21
Miller, Henry 21, 91, 209
Miller, J. C. 239
Miller, J. S. 287
Miller, James 160, 184, 210, 273, 275-276
Miller, John 84, 148, 209-210, 287
Miller, Joseph 209-210
Miller, M. C. A. 210
Miller, M. J. 166
Miller, Missouri L. 210
Miller, Nancy 305
Miller, [no name 181
Miller, Pearson 209-210
Miller, Pitser 297
Miller, Pleasant 201, 209-210
Miller, Riley 116
Miller, Sally 99, 201, 210
Miller, Samuel 221
Miller, Sarah 210
Miller, Thomas 45, 114, 210
Miller, Tranquella 209
Miller, Van 305
Miller, W. B. 210
Miller, William 210
Miller, Winney 181
Millers, A. 169
Milley [a slave] 88
Milligan, James 281
Millor, Peter 120
Mills, C. 212, 228
Mills, Curtis 341
Mills, G. G. 210
Mills, James 243
Mills, John J. 210
Millsaps, Hiram 211
Millsaps, M. D. S. 211
Millsaps, Marsha 211, 330
Millsaps, Mitchel R. 211
Millsaps, T. J. 211
Millsaps, W. R. F. 211
Milly [a slave] 149
Milsaps, George S. 330
Milton, Wm. 211
Minard, Isaac 211
Mingo [a slave] 317
Minor, Hiram 239
Minor, John V. 239

Mitchel, Adam 99, 120, 213
Mitchel, Artimisse 164
Mitchel, Elizabeth 164
Mitchel, Hyram 164
Mitchel, Jacob 211
Mitchel, James 211
Mitchel, Josiah 211
Mitchel, Mark 211
Mitchel, Mary 211
Mitchel, Richard 211
Mitchell, A. P. 277
Mitchell, B. 211
Mitchell, Cynthia H. 58
Mitchell, David 99, 235
Mitchell, Drucilla 211
Mitchell, Edward 314
Mitchell, Elizabeth 212
Mitchell, Evert 212
Mitchell, Geo. 131
Mitchell, Jacob 211
Mitchell, Joab 211
Mitchell, John 130, 194, 211, 219, 293
Mitchell, Leon 212
Mitchell, Mary B. 190
Mitchell, Nancy A. 211
Mitchell, Nancy E. 211
Mitchell, Nelson 211
Mitchell, Richard 58, 211
Mitchell, Robert 190, 211-212
Mitchell, Samuel 184, 212, 304
Mitchell, Spencer A. 211
Mitchell, T. C. 280
Mitchell, Taswell 212
Mitchell, Thomas C. 143, 212, 280, 327
Mitchell, William 6, 9, 212
Mitchell, Zadock 212
Mize, Alexr. 261
Mizer, Susannah 212
Mobile, Col. 105
Moffat, Robert 61
Moffat, William A. 62
Moffet, John 212
Moffet, William 212
Moffett, Alexander 76
Moffett, Parmela A. 62, 208
Mohener, John 85
Mohollon, William 52
Molly [a slave] 55
Molton, Michael 64
Moncil, Arrena K. 71
Monday, Clary 212
Monday, Easter 212
Monday, Harretta 212
Monday, James 212, 317
Monday, Levicy 212
Monday, Levinah 212
Monday, William 212
Monrell, Richard E. 71
Monsel, Albert F. 71
Monsel, John R. 71
Monsel, William E. 71
Monsil, Sarah F. 71
Montgomery, Alexander 213

Montgomery, B. H. 213
Montgomery, Benjamin 324
Montgomery, Caroline 324
Montgomery, Earl 324
Montgomery, Elizabeth 138, 212
Montgomery, G. W. 213
Montgomery, Hamilton 324
Montgomery, J. T. 111
Montgomery, James 164, 184, 212-213, 319,
Montgomery, Jennet 212-213
Montgomery, John 212
Montgomery, Martha E. 212
Montgomery, Michael 212-213
Montgomery, Nancy 324
Montgomery, Nathan 110, 324
Montgomery, Penelope 324
Montgomery, Robert 209, 324
Montgomery, Thomas 324
Montgomery, W. W. 213
Montgomery, William 37, 209, 213
Moody, John 213, 227
Moody, Peter 136, 213, 227
Moor, Alfred 124
Moor, Ann 255
Moor, James 213
Moordock. Sarah 242
Moore, Abner 213
Moore, Abraham 158, 214, 249
Moore, Alexander B. 35
Moore, Amos 214
Moore, Armstead 214
Moore, Benjamin 98, 213
Moore, D. L. 213
Moore, Denton 239
Moore, Dinkie 213
Moore, Edward 130, 198, 218
Moore, Elijah 213
Moore, Elizabeth 202, 214
Moore, Evalina 213
Moore, Fanny B. 214
Moore, Frances 214
Moore, George 130
Moore, Harriet E. 213
Moore, Henry 251
Moore, Hugh 213
Moore, Isaac 86, 89, 202
Moore, Isareal 214, 334
Moore, J. M. 214
Moore, J. S. 52, 214
Moore, Jackson 213
Moore, James 91, 213, 214, 277
Moore, Jane 214
Moore, Joel 214
Moore, John 69, 120, 131, 213-214
Moore, Joseph 214
Moore, Kinsey 214

Moore, L. J. 102
Moore, Levi 104, 214
Moore, Margaret 214
Moore, Mary 213-214, 260
Moore, Nancy 71-72, 214
Moore, Patsy 214
Moore, Pertius 85
Moore, Polly 214
Moore, R. B. 134
Moore, Rebecca 214
Moore, Richard 202
Moore, Robert 214
Moore, Ruthy 215
Moore, S. A. 215
Moore, S. H. 270
Moore, Sally 215
Moore, Saml. 214
Moore, Sarah E. 82, 182
Moore, Stephen 91
Moore, Susannah 213
Moore, Thomas C. 71-72, 182, 214
Moore, Warren 11, 215
Moore, William 34, 37, 200, 213-215
Moore, Willis 71, 214
Moore, Zachariah 215
Mooring, Wyatt 5, 83, 118, 200, 284
Moran, James H. 241
Mordock, Sarah 242
More, Alexander 34
More, Denton 121
More, John A. 286
More, Mary 214
More, Matilda 214
More, Robert 199
Moreland, Samuel W. 110
Moreland, William 122, 243
Morfleet, Jas. 209
Morgan, A. H. 163, 177
Morgan, Austin H. 163
Morgan, Betsy 215
Morgan, Daniel 163
Morgan, Elizabeth 215
Morgan, Frances 215
Morgan, George 110, 215
Morgan, Gideon 215, 263
Morgan, John 215
Morgan, Josiah 215
Morgan, Marion 163
Morgan, Mary A. 215
Morgan, Mordica 151
Morgan, Polly 163, 215
Morgan, Rebecca 215
Morgan, Richard 215
Morgan, Rufus 210
Morgan, Susannah 163
Morgan, Theophilus 62, 153
Morgan, Turner J. 144
Morgan, Washington 163
Morgan, William 215, 163
Morning, Joshua 215
Morning, Polly 114
Morrill, J. M. 215
Morris, Addie 286
Morris, Geo. W. 226

Morris, Gideon 186, 216
Morris, Goodson 215
Morris, Hardy L. 183
Morris, Jesse 215
Morris, Mary 223
Morris, Matthew 216
Morris, Thomas W. 216
Morris, Wm. 216, 223
Morrison, Hugh 89
Morrison, James 193
Morrison, Mary 89
Morrison, Nathl. 25, 40
Morrow, Isaac 142
Morrow, James 118
Morsel, Samuel M. 71
Mort, Austin, 139
Mortey, Samuel W. 196
Mortimer, Sally 216
Morton, A. B. 216
Morton, Abner W. 216
Morton, Abraham 216
Morton, Abram 216
Morton, Absolam D. 216
Morton, Alexander B. 216
Morton, Allen 216
Morton, Elisha 216
Morton, Fanny G. 216
Morton, George W. 216
Morton, Isaac 216
Morton, Jacob 179, 216, 314
Morton, James A. 216
Morton, Jane 196
Morton, Jessee B. 216
Morton, John 216
Morton, Joseph 216
Morton, Martha 216
Morton, Nancy 216
Morton, Samuel 216
Morton, Silas M. 216
Morton, Solomon 216
Morton, Thomas 196, 216
Morton, Vina E. 216
Morton, William 216
Mosby, Joseph 195
Moseley, Edward A. 190
Moseley, Jas. M. 216, 276
Moseley, Thomas B. 190
Mosely, Burrell 217
Mosely, Ellenora 276
Mosely, George W. 73
Mosely, Hillery 148
Mosely, James D. 195
Mosely, Johnathan 280
Mosely, Joseph 26
Mosely, Margaret 216
Mosely, Maria 195
Mosely, Mary 195, 216
Mosely, Peter 96, 213
Mosely, Thos. 195, 216
Mosely, Virginia 195
Mosely, Wm. 217
Moser, Adam 83, 217
Moser, Henry 107, 217
Moses, Daniel 217
Moses, David 217
Moses, Robert 200, 217

Mosley, Charles W. 195
Mosley, E. Archibald 190
Mosley, Hellen 217
Mosley, Jesse 217
Mosley, Joseph H. 195
Mosley, Marcia S. 195
Mosly, Burrell 217
Mosly, Joseph R. 55
Moss, Almedia 291
Moss, Beniah 42
Moss, C. C. 101-102, 275, 298, 316
Moss, Charles C. 298, 301, 321
Moss, Dirdimonia 291
Moss, Elizabeth 217
Moss, George W. 291
Moss, James 121, 217
Moss, John 114, 121, 217, 291
Moss, Joseph 248, 291
Moss, Mariah L. 42
Moss, Mercellus 265
Moss, Moore S. 291
Moss, Polly 290, 291
Moss, Robert 121, 217
Moss, Samuel 217
Moss, Sarah 217
Moss, William 33
Motheral, Elenor E. 217
Motheral, Francis S. 217
Motheral, James 217
Motheral, Jane 171, 217
Motheral, John 172, 217
Motheral, Joseph 217
Motheral, Martha 217
Motheral, Mary 217
Motheral, Robert 171, 217
Motheral, Samuel 88, 93, 146, 172,
Motheral, William 217
Motley, Samuel W. 196
Motly, Benja. T. 217
Motly, Patsy 217
Motsener, John 85
Mott, Austin 55
Mott, Wm. H. 218
Mount, Amanda Jane 218
Mount, H. 142
Mount, H. N. 61, 218, 291
Mount, Humphrey 141
Mount, Samuel 38, 58, 140
Moyer, Caty 218
Mulhaney, John 320
Mulherrin, James 187
Mulka, Hannah 164
Mullender, John 42
Mullendom, W. W. 218
Mullendore, John 43, 47, 257,
Mullens, James 244
Mullinax, Eli 256
Mullinax, Levi 218
Mullins, James 241
Mullins, Mathew 221, 230
Mullis, James 218
Mullis, Jeriah 218

Mulliz, Amiah 103, 218
Mungoloe, Eliza 152
Muns, Jno. A. 56
Muns, Patsy 56, 328
Muns, Susan A. 56
Muns, William J. 56
Murdock, Sampson 218
Murfree, H. 218
Murfree, Hardy 218
Murfree, William 218
Murphey, Betsey H. 218
Murphey, George 123
Murphey, James 218
Murphey, John 218
Murphey, Joseph R. 219
Murphey, Levi 322
Murphey, Lucy 310
Murphey, M. B. 219
Murphey, M. C. 100
Murphey, Patrick 219
Murphey, Peggy 219
Murphey, Richard 219
Murphey, Robert 218
Murphey, Robertson 123
Murphey, W. W. 219
Murphey, William 218
Murphrie, Hardy 218
Murphy, Celia 219
Murphy, Charles 219
Murphy, Gabril 219
Murphy, Hugh 219
Murphy, J. C. 61, 63, 132, 175
Murphy, John 12, 131-132, 219, 223-224, 235
Murphy, Mary 219
Murphy, Patrick 219
Murphy, R. 243
Murphy, Saml. 219
Murphy, W. C. 63, 132, 175, 255, 264
Murphy, William 48
Murray, David J. 219
Murray, J. C. 45
Murray, Jane C. 219
Murray, John 165, 196, 214, 231, 340
Murray, S. F. 219-220
Murray, Stewart F. 220
Murray, William 219, 277
Murrell, A. E. 46
Murrell, Alex C. 46
Murrell, John 305, 330
Murrell, Thos. 195
Murry, Agnes 317
Murry, Bernet 220
Murry, David J. 220
Murry, J. M. 220
Murry, John B. 220
Murry, Joseph C. 220
Murry, Kelton 220
Murry, Sarah B. 220
Murry, T. 220
Murry, Thomas B. 220
Murry, W. T. 220
Murry, William 220
Mury, Thomas 220

Muss, Patsy 328
Mutlock, David 220
Muus, Jno. A. 56, 328
Muus, Susan 328
Muus, Wm. J. 328
Myers, Calvin E. 68
Myers, David 121
Myers, Frederick 220
Myers, Jane 220
Myers, Jonas 121
Myers, Julia 148
Myers, Leithton 68
Myers, Nancy 324
Myers, White 148
Myler, Julia 220
Myler, W. W. 220
Mynott, B. K. 116
Myres, John 324
Nables, W. A. 225
Nail, George W. 220
Nail, Henry 155
Nail, Jane 220
Nail, John Samuel 220
Nail, Joseph 305
Nail, Marcus 220
Nail, Mary 220
Nail, Nancy 220
Nail, Nicholas 243
Nail, Saml. 220
Nail, William A. 220
Nall, Nathan 150
Nall, Robert 75, 178
Nance, Lewis R. 247
Nancy [a slave] 21, 91
Nanny, Jos. W. 220
Napier, A. H. 325
Nare, John 66, 158, 168
Narion, John 221
Nash, Abner 221
Nash, Augustine 221
Nash, Augustus 221
Nash, C. F. 221
Nash, C. T. 134, 221
Nash, Elizabeth 221
Nash, Emily 221
Nash, Francis 124, 221
Nash, George W. 221
Nash, Granderson 221
Nash, James 221
Nash, Johanna 221
Nash, John R. 221
Nash, Lafayette 221
Nash, Louisa 221
Nash, Maola 221
Nash, Mary 221
Nash, Miranda G. 221
Nash, Nancy R. 221
Nash, Rachel J. 221
Nash, Rhrdam 221
Nash, T. C. 221
Nash, Thomas 221
Nash, Travis C. 221
Nash, W. B. 221
Nash, W. F. 172, 221
Nash, W. S. 221
Nash, Wallas 168
Nash, William 20, 221

Nation, Ellenos 39
Nation, Joseph 39
Nations, Christopher 221
Nations, Green B. 151
Nations, Isaac 221
Nations, Jane 221
Nations, Jerreata 221
Nations, Joseph 221
Nations, Lerreata 221
Nations, Nancy 221
Nations, Sampson 221
Nations, Serreata 221
Nations, William 221
Naul, Robert 178, 211
Nauny, James 220
Nauny, Margaret S. 220
Nave, Teter 312
Nawl, Robert 178
Neal, Francis M. M. 221
Neal, Grimes 88, 221
Neal, James A. 100, 221
Neal, John 39, 68, 112, 133, 221
Neal, Joseph 206, 284
Neal, Mary 206
Neal, Newton 217, 221
Neal, Robert 93
Neal, Samuel J. 179
Neal, William 206
Neckins, William B. 221
Ned [a slave] 177, 341
Nede [a slave] 341
Nedry, Alfred 224
Nedry, Winney 224
Needham, John W. 101
Neely, A. A. 105
Neely, A. C. 222
Neely, Amanda 222
Neely, Caroline 222
Neely, Elizabeth C. 222
Neely, James 293
Neely, Jo. 222
Neely, Mary E. 222
Neely, Moses 144
Neely, Nanny P. 222
Neely, Robert H. 222
Neely, Saml. 64, 105, 222, 296
Neely, T. G. 222
Neely, Wm. 222, 316
Neil, John 22
Neil, Joseph 179
Neil, William 222
Nelms, Jane 75
Nelms, Richard 75
Nelms, William 179
Nelson, Charles 222
Nelson, Henry 222
Nelson, James B. 222, 237, 309
Nelson, Jesse 70, 222
Nelson, John 70, 200, 222
Nelson, Mary 200
Nelson, Nancy 237, 309
Nelson, Robert 218, 222
Nelson, Ruben 222
Nelson, William 222

Nesbit, Robert 181
Nettles, Harriett 288
Nettles, Nancy 288
Nettles, Zebulon 288
Neusome, [no name] 253
Nevil, Alexander 121
Nevill, John 222
Nevill, Mary 320
Nevill, Sarah 222
Nevill, Solomon, 223
Neville, Joseph B. 15, 204, 254
Neville, Thomas 223
Nevills, N. T. 320
Nevin, David E. 223
Nevin, John 223, 332
Nevin, Martha Mary 223
Nevin, Robert P. 223
Nevin, Theodore H. 223
Nevin, William M. 223
Nevins, David 223
Nevins, James 141
Nevins, Mary 223
Nevins, Polly 141
New, Charles T. 223
New, Frances 223
New, Samuel 173
New, William 223
Newberger, Charles 223
Newbern, Emeline 333
Newbern, Perlina 223
Newbern, T. H. 334
Newbern, Thomas 156, 333-334
Newbern, Wm. Y. 223
Newbery, Mary 329
Newburn, Perlena 26
Newell, Dempsy 227
Newman, Ann 223
Newman, Bird 223
Newman, Daniel 96, 116
Newman, Henry 303
Newman, James 223
Newman, John 127, 217
Newman, Nelson 223
Newman, William 223-224
Newport, Cavanaugh 263
Newsom, Eldridge M. 224
Newsom, Franklin E. 97
Newsom, Harbert 224
Newsom, Jno. F. 130, 224
Newsom, Samuella 97
Newsom, Sarah E. 224
Newsome, [no name] 253
Newton, John 183
Neyler, Julia 220
Neyler, W. W. 220
Niblett, Anis 212
Niblett, Lavinia 212
Nichols, Alexander C. B. 224

Nichols, Alfred 224
Nichols, Coleman 224
Nichols, James 24, 211
Nichols, Jane 224
Nichols, John 160, 209, 224
Nichols, Joseph 224

Nichols, Joshua 224
Nichols, Margaret 224
Nichols, Mary 24
Nichols, Neoma 224
Nichols, Richard 224
Nichols, Robert 125
Nichols, Sally 224
Nichols, Susan C. 224
Nichols, Tabitha 224
Nichols, W. F. 143-144, 182, 224, 235, 269-270, 303
Nichols, William 211
Nicholson, Nicholas 176
Nichons, Eleanor 271, 224-225
Nichons, Frankey 225, 271
Nickins, William B. 225
Nickols, Henry C. 225
Nickols, Robert N. 225
Night, Jas. 225
Night, Mariah 225
Night, William 225, 297
Nisbit, Robt. 181
Nivans, Wilson 225
Nix, Ann 225
Nix, Elizabeth 225
Nix, Francis 225
Nix, James 225
Nix, John C. 135
Nix, Lebanon 225
Nix, Mary 225
Nix, Rebecca 225
Nix, Samuel 225
Nix, Thomas 225
Nix, William 225
Nixen, H. E. 21
Nixen, John 21
Nixon, O. A. 21
Noble, Alfred D. 225
Noble, John 225
Nobles, Allen J. 225
Nobles, Emily 225
Nobles, H. 225
Nobles, Matt 225
Nobles, Montgomery 225
Nobles, William A. 225
Nodding, Wm. 225
Noding, John 226
Noding, Priscilla 226
Noel, Alfred 3
Noel, Henry 155
Nolan, C. L. 15, 27, 31, 100, 216, 226, 274, 280, 316
Nolan, C. S. 100, 170, 298
Nolan, John 157
Nolen, T. J. 65
Nooding, Wm. 74
Norfleet, James 78, 134, 164, 172, 175-176, 186, 329, 186
Norman, Ezekiel 294
Norman, John 107, 135
Norman, Nelson 226
Norman, Willson 226
Norment, Giles 226
Norment, W. G. 226

Norrid, Larkin 300
Norris, John 226
Norris, Thomas 56, 226, 309
Norris, William 226
North, Ester 226
North, George 226
North, Jesse 226
North, John 226
Northern, Edward 226
Northrop, John I. 239
Norton, Alexander 235
Norton, Jno. H. 308
Norton, Martha 325
Norton, Sally 226
Norton, William 40, 88, 212, 325
Norvell, Jas. H. 227
Norvell, John A. 227
Norvell, Reuben 227
Norvill, Alexander S. 226
Norvill, David 226
Norvill, Edward M. 226
Norvill, Elizabeth W. 226
Norvill, Felix B. 226
Norvill, Geo. R. 226
Norvill, Heneretta F. 226
Norvill, James D. 226
Norvill, John W. 226
Norvill, Margaret H. 226
Norvill, Mary 226
Norvill, Robert M. 226
Norvill, Sarah S. 226
Norvill, Sydney S. 226
Norvill, Thomas 226
Norville, Edward M. B. 226
Norville, James D. 226
Norville, Mary Ann K. 226
Norwood, J. W. 155
Novell, Dempsy 227
Nowell, Dempsy 227
Nowland, George 48
Nowlin, Bryant W. 85
Nowlin, David 85
Nowlin, Elizabeth 85
Nuckles, John 226
Nuckols, Richd. 8
Nun, Frank 226
Nun, Mary 226
Nunesinger, John 227
Nunly, Letty 141
Nunly, Nelson 141
Nunn, I. A. 161, 237
Nunn, Isaac A. 102, 188
Nunn, J. A. 160, 166, 229, 342
Nuvell, Dempsy 227
Nuvell, Harriet 227
Nuvell, James H. 227
Nuvell, Joab 227
Nuvell, John A. 227
Nuvell, Reuben F. 227
Nuvell, Saml. J. 227
Nuvell, Wm. C. 227
O'Neal, A. P. 227
O'Neal, Nathaniel 227
O'Neal, P. P. 227
O'Neal, S. H. 227

O'Neil, G. W. 227
Oakes, Mariah 224
Oakes, Norten 224
Oakley, C. 2
Oakley, William 323
Oaks, Susan 227
Oats, Roger 164
OConner, Edward 227
Oddel, Jean 27, 227
Oddel, Job 227
Odell, Caleb 227
Odell, Elizabeth 227
Odell, Job 344
Odell, John 227
Odle, Isaac 227
Odle, Saml. 227
ODonald, Maurrice 227
Odum, Calvin 227
Odum, Fredrick 227
Odum, Simon 227
Odum, Thomas 227
Office, James C. 213, 227
Officer, Robert 227
Ogden, Benjamin C. 77
Ogden, Esther 77
Ogden, George 77
Ogden, Jno. B. 308
Ogden, John 77
Ogden, Mary Ann 77
Ogden, Rachael 77
Ogilsby, Sarah Jane 9
Ogle, Angeline 228
Ogle, Beda 228
Ogle, Bradford 228
Ogle, Caleb 228
Ogle, Elias 228
Ogle, Elijah 170
Ogle, Elisha 228
Ogle, Elizabeth 228
Ogle, Harcolas 228
Ogle, Henry 228
Ogle, Horatio B. 228
Ogle, Isaac 43, 228
Ogle, J. 187
Ogle, James 228
Ogle, Mariah 62
Ogle, Milly 228
Ogle, Nancy 43
Ogle, Noah 96, 323
Ogle, Patsy 228
Ogle, Perry 228
Ogle, Thomas 228
Ogle, W. W. 228
Ogle, William 228
Old Barks [an Indian] 201
Oldham, Frank 228
Oldham, Henry 243
Oldrige, Mary 3
Olds, Arter 228
Olds, Arthur C. 228
Olds, C. F. 228
Olds, James E. 228
Olds, Laura 228
Olds, Lewis 228
Olds, Martha E. 228
Olds, Mary F. 228
Olds, Nancy E. 228

Olds, Sarah O. 228
Olds, Thomas 228
Olive, Abel 304
Olive, Elizabeth 229
Olive, Joel 4
Olive, Joseph 141
Olive, Samuel 141, 228-229
Oliver, Abel 229
Oliver, Francis E. 273
Oliver, Frank 229
Oliver, S. 191
Oliver, Sally 4
Oliver, Sarah 229
Oliver, William 229
Oneal, Arthur 229
Oneal, Asa L. 229
Oneal, Bryant 258, 283-285
Oneal, Elisha 229
Oneal, John H. 229
Oneal, Matilda 229
Oneal, Parley 229
ONeal, Rebecca 229
Oneal, Sally F. 229
Oneal, Thomas H. 293
Oneal, William 229
Oneal, Willie 229
Oneal, Zachariah 283
Oneil, Jesse 229
Orendine, Jonathan 246
Organ, John C. 325
Orr, David 52, 199-200
Orr, J. H. 229
Orr, Larkin 52, 199-200
Orr, Martha 52
Orr, Robert 76
Orr, W. E. 229
Orr, W. D. 38, 149, 232, 254
Orseborn, Liddy 155, 229
Osburn, Sarah 125
Osburn, Wm. R. 229
Outlaw, Alexander 229-230
Outlaw, David 337
Outlaw, Drury 230
Outlaw, Edward 229
Outlaw, George 230
Outlaw, Harriat 230
Outlaw, Indiana 230
Outlaw, Jefferson 230
Outlaw, John 230, 243
Outlaw, Lovey 337
Outlaw, Mary 230
Outlaw, Nancy 230
Outlaw, Patsey Earl 230
Outlaw, Susan 230
Outlaw, William 4, 187, 218, 229-230, 304
Overstreet, Wim. P. 267-268
Overton, John 84, 187, 230
Overton, Moses 164
Owen, Ann 230
Owen, Artamissa 230
Owen, Elias 230
Owen, Francis 230
Owen, Johnson 230
Owen, Joseph 34
Owen, Joshua 230
Owen, Mary A. 290

Owen, Phebe 34
Owen, Pherby 230
Owenby, John 230
Owens, Charles M. 61
Owens, Ferby 230
Owens, J. M. J. 66
Owens, John 33, 66, 230, 258
Owens, Joshua 18
Owens, Martin 230
Owens, Mary Ann 230
Ownly, Aron 228
Ownly, Edward 58
Ownly, Eli C. 58
Ownly, Elizabeth M. 58
Ownly, Elvina M. 58
Ownly, Jeremiah J. 58
Ownly, Labitha R. 58
Ownly, Polly 58
Ownly, Susan J. 58
Ozment, Darkus 230
Ozment, Eli 230
Ozment, Jonathan 194
Pace, Alsy 231
Pace, Asa 230
Pace, J. D. 270
Pace, Jackson 125, 231
Pace, Richd. 231
Pace, Thomas 284
Pace, William 230-231
Pack, Bartemaus 168
Pack, Jno. J. 130
Pagan, A. C. 231
Pagan, Andrew C. 231
Pagan, Carson 231
Page, Thomas E. 147
Pain, Catharine 231
Pain, Ephraim 231
Pain, T. H. 276
Paine, Ephraim T. 231
Paine, Warren 59
Painter, John B. 231
Painter, Pamilia 231
Painter, Thomas 231
Paisley, William 294
Palmer, Catherine 231
Palmer, Essy 231
Palmer, Fras. 337
Palmer, Isabella 231
Palmer, Lucinda 231
Palmer, W. A. 231
Palmer, William 26
Pankey, Polly 57, 231
Pankey, William 166
Paramour, Amos 231
Paramour, Lydia 231
Paratt, Mary 21
Paratt, Rowena 21
Paratt, Stephen C. 21
Parchment, Philip 38, 271
Parham, William 258
Parish, James 141
Parish, Polly 141
Parish, W. H. 231
Parker, Allen 232
Parker, D. E. 43, 56, 107, 246-247, 309, 327

Parker, Daniel E. 134, 222, 247
Parker, David 232, 250
Parker, Elijah 232
Parker, Eps 232
Parker, Frances 232
Parker, George W. 282
Parker, Henry 232, 305
Parker, James 232
Parker, Jesse 182
Parker, John 232
Parker, Jonathan 232
Parker, Martha 232
Parker, Nathan 232, 307
Parker, Richard 232
Parker, Stephen 232
Parkerson, [no name] 63
Parkinson, Manuel 174
Parkison, Mary 232
Parkison, Peter 232
Parks, A. 232
Parks, A. L. 52
Parks, A. S. 76, 130, 284
Parks, Anthony 232
Parks, Blanch 232
Parks, Fannie 232
Parks, Faustina B. 232
Parks, George 89
Parks, H. 52, 76, 89, 284, 320, 323
Parks, Hamilton 232, 320
Parks, John 130
Parks, Margaret 232
Parks, Sammie 232
Parks, Smith 14, 27, 50, 52, 76, 78, 86-87, 89, 92, 134, 149, 170, 187, 191, 207, 232, 250, 270, 284, 314, 320, 323
Parks, William 92, 167, 201
Parmer [a slave] 63
Parr, Cunningham 232
Parr, Elizabeth 232
Parr, John 61, 232
Parr, Mary 232
Parr, Matthias 232
Parr, Moses 61, 232, 301
Parratree, Edward 232
Parrett, Oring 38
Parris, Thomas 204
Parrish, Alexander S. 232
Parrish, Elias 21, 31
Parrish, Elizabeth 232
Parrish, Jas. T. 232
Parrish, Jno. W. 232
Parrish, Mary T. 232
Parrish, Nelson 214, 231-232
Parrish, Richard 232
Parrish, W. H. 232
Parrish, W. W. 21
Parrish, William 232
Parrott, Agness Mc 233
Parrott, Diema L. 233
Parrott, Emelie 233
Parrott, George 233
Parrott, Isaac N. 233

Parrott, John 233
Parrott, Mary J. 233
Parrott, William 177
Parson, Martha 59
Parsons, Abid 72, 214
Parsons, Eliza Ann 71-72
Parsons, Thomas 62
Partain, Angelina 233
Parte, Hiram 58
Parte, Lorania 58
Partee, Hiram 58
Partee, Masilla 58
Partee, Mozella 58
Partee, Squire B. 275
Parter, A. 104
Partin, Polly 233
Partlow, Thomas 91, 233
Parton, Alexander 233
Parvis, Charles 37
Paseley, Thomas 199
Pate, Anthony 233
Pate, Benja. 233
Pate, Cebert 233
Pate, Cyrela 233
Pate, Cyrena 233
Pate, Cyretia 233
Pate, Delila 233
Pate, Edward P. 91, 233
Pate, Ella F. 233
Pate, John 20, 233
Pate, Lawson D. 233
Pate, Leroy 233
Pate, Lucy 91
Pate, M. D. 287
Pate, Mary E. 233
Pate, N. B. 143, 260
Pate, Nancy O. 233
Pate, Oney C. 233
Pate, Sabe 233
Pate, Sampson W. 233
Pate, Samuel 48
Pate, Stephen C. 233
Pate, Susan 233
Pate, W. H. 20
Pate, Willeray 233
Pate, William 44, 233
Pate, Z. Susan 233
Patee, Hiram 58
Paters, William 238
Patey, Charles 233
Patey, Joseph 233
Patey, Joshua 234
Patey, Nancy 234
Patey, William 234
Patric, P. H. 234
Patrick, Jesse 337
Patrick, Sarah 281
Patten, William 92
Patterson, A. 234
Patterson, A. L. 234
Patterson, Alexander 130
Patterson, Allen L. 234
Patterson, Andrew 234
Patterson, Ann 235
Patterson, Austin 234
Patterson, Charles 234-235
Patterson, Eliza Ann 235

Patterson, Ester 235
Patterson, Fulton 235
Patterson, George 234
Patterson, Hartwell 234
Patterson, Hester 235
Patterson, Isham 234
Patterson, J. C. E. 234
Patterson, Jacob 234
Patterson, James 234
Patterson, Jean 234
Patterson, Jenny 235
Patterson, John 234-235
Patterson, Joseph C. 234
Patterson, Lewis 234
Patterson, Martha B. 235
Patterson, Mary 234
Patterson, Nancy 234
Patterson, Peggy 234
Patterson, Polly 234-235
Patterson, Rebecca 234-235
Patterson, Robert 234-235
Patterson, Samuel 234-235
Patterson, Susan 234
Patterson, Thomas 79
Patterson, William 234-235
Pattison, Abijah 235
Patton, Alexander 235
Patton, Archibald 235
Patton, Daniel 235
Patton, James 235
Patton, Jane 235
Patton, John 181, 235
Patton, Lynne 235
Patton, Neely S. 235
Patton, Rachael 235
Patton, Sarah Jane 235
Patton, Thomas 235
Patton, William 235
Patty [a slave] 340
Patty, Nancy 235
Paul, Audley 235
Paul, Edley 213, 329
Paul, James 215, 235
Paul, John   235
Paul, Nancy 157
Paul, Sally 157
Paul, Thomas 157
Pauly, Wm. 175
Pavatt, Stephen C. 21
Pavely, John 236
Pavely, Lewis 236
Paxton, Betsy 236
Payn, Daniell 236
Payn, Thomas 236
Payn, William 236
Payne, B. B. 236, 276
Payne, Benjamin 128-129
Payne, Burdetta 276
Payne, Burton 236, 276
Payne, Jane 60
Payne, John 236, 243
Payne, Joseph 101
Payne, Josiah 236
Payne, Ledford 236
Payne, T. N. 236
Payne, William H. 236

Payton, Ephraim 236
Payton, John 157, 202, 235-236, 271, 273, 317
Payton, Joseph 236
Payton, William 83, 236
Peace, Wm. H. 83
Peacock, David 236
Peaison, Sophia 313
Peak, James 192
Pearce, Abner 119, 313
Pearce, Burt 236
Pearce, Daniel 13
Pearce, J. H. 236
Pearce, John K. 181
Pearce, Joseph 240
Pearce, Riley 236
Pearce William 119, 313
Pearl, Dyer 137
Pearson, Alla 236
Pearson, George 236
Pearson, Kindred 236-237
Pearson, Samuel 186
Pearson, William 236-237
Peel, Joel 237
Peel, Julia 237
Peel, Robert 237
Peery, John 237
Peggy [a slave] 23
Peirce, Stephen 176
Pemberton, Jesse 91
Pemberton, Polly 201
Pemberton, Ruth 91
Pemberton, Thomas 201
Pen, Fleming 237
Pen, John 237
Pendergrass, Nancy 268
Pendergrass, Travis W. 268
Pendleton, E. B. 93
Penington, Isaioh C. 58
Penington, Jacob C. 58
Penington, Manerva 58
Penington, Susanah 237
Penington, Timothy 237
Penkerton, James 211
Penneal, Lucy 234
Pennington, Isaac 237
Pennington, J. C. 58
Pennington, Loser M. 58
Pennuel, Hardy 237
Penny [a slave] 332
Penson, John B. 241
Peoples, Nathan 39
Pepkin, Lewis 237
Pepper, Nathan 87
Perdew, Richard 103
Perkerson, Peter 237
Perkins, Drury 231
Perkins, Geo. G. 189, 253
Perkins, Jacob 8
Perkins, John 8
Perkins, Joseph S. 276
Perkins, Mary S. P. 8
Perkins, Nancy 276
Perkinson, Peter 237
Perrett, Daniel 38
Perriman, James A. 191
Perry, Adelade 237

Perry, Benjamin N. 291
Perry, Drewry 237
Perry, F. P. 237
Perry, H. T. 49
Perry, J. F. 161, 339
Perry, J. S. 237
Perry, Jackson 245-246
Perry, Jacob 225
Perry, James 152, 160 237-238, 261
Perry, Joseph 116, 140
Perry, Josiah 218
Perry, N. T.139, 166, 237
Perry, Nathl. 243
Perry, Noah 237-238
Perry, Norfleet 238
Perry, Robert 225, 237
Perry, Rountree 238
Perry, Sarah 245-246, 291
Perry,Wm. 238, 246, 288
Perryman, J. D. 238
Perryman, James A. 238
Persible, Tom 238
Person, Sophia 313
Persons, Thomas 238
Peter [a slave] 61, 294
Peters, Emeline W. 238
Peters, Emily W. 238
Peters, Jas. H. 238
Peters, Jno. W. 238
Peters, Richd. H. 238
Peters, William 238
Petre, Geo. 278
Pettit, Neamiah 238
Pettit, Susannah 238
Petty, George 131-132
Petty, Martha 238
Petty, Sarah 238
Peu, Fleming 237
Peyton, Jno. W. 91, 184, 328
Pharis, Adeline 238
Pharis, Alse 238
Pharis, Ceberry 238
Pharis, Charlotte 238
Pharis, Elizabeth 238-239
Pharis Fanny 238
Pharis, Francis M. 238
Pharis, Hannah 238
Pharis, Hugh 239
Pharis, Isham 238
Pharis, James 238-239, 314
Pharis, Jane 238
Pharis, Lincoln 238
Pharis, Malinda 238
Pharis, Mariah 238
Pharis, Martha 238
Pharis, Mary 238-239
Pharis, Milly 238
Pharis, Nathan 313
Pharis, Rosina 238
Pharis, Rozena 238
Pharis, Sally 238
Pharis, Sampson 238
Pharis, Seabury 238
Pharis, Shelby 238
Pharis, Walker 238

Pharis, Warren 238
Pharis, William 238-239
Pharris, Absolem 239
Pharris, Amanda 239
Pharris, Elizabeth 239
Pharris, Hiram 239
Pharris, James 239
Pharris, Jane 239
Pharris, Leroy 118
Pharris, Lewis 239
Pharris, Matilda 239
Pheba [a slave] 35
Pheebe [a slave] 105
Phelps, Elisha 207
Phepe [a slave] 263
Phifer, Caleb 3
Phifer, Martin 3
Phiffs, Lambert 239
Philips, Benjamin 88
Philips, John 264, 329
Philips, Joseph 309
Philips, Phebe 233
Philips, Philip 239
Phillipps, William 111
Phillips, Abner 239
Phillips, Azwell 239
Phillips, Benjamin 142, 185
Phillips, Buly Ann 239
Phillips, Cynthia 239
Phillips, Florence 239
Phillips, H. H. 131, 239
Phillips, Haywood, 185
Phillips, Henry H. 239
Phillips, J. A. 239
Phillips, John 49
Phillips, Martha 185
Phillips, Mary A. 239
Phillips, Payton 239
Phillips, Peter 239
Phillips, Samuel 189, 226
Phillips, William 328-239
Phillips, Z. B. 240
Phillis [a slave] 30, 214
Phillpot, Timothy 59
Phipps, William R. D. 76
Pickens, J. A. 45, 80
Pickens, James A. 39, 70, 78, 81, 240
Pickens, John 70, 240
Pickens, Mary Jane 240
Pickens, Reese 240
Pickens, Robert 240
Pickens, Samuel 25, 71, 126, 145, 240, 264
Pickens, W. C. 145, 264
Pickens, Wm. C. 198
Pickering, Jacob 240
Picket, Edward 46, 240
Picket, Ingolier 118
Picket, William M. 118
Pickins, Andrew 240
Pickins, Charles A. 240
Pickins, J. A. 231
Pickins, J. P. 240
Pickins, John 240
Pickins, Martha 240
Pickins, Nancy 240

Pickins, Rebecka 240
Pickins, Robt. 240
Pickins, S. W. 240
Pickins, T. R. 240
Pickins, Thomas 240
Pickins, William K. 240
Pickle, Amos 240
Pickle, Dicy 240
Pickle, Margaret J. 240
Pickle, William C. 240
Pickring, Charles H. 243
Pickring, John T. 243
Pierce, A. G. 2, 212, 274
Pierce, Albert 241
Pierce, Geo. W. 213, 240
Pierce, J. S. 240
Pierce, J. W. 240
Pierce, John M. 240
Pierce, Joseph 240
Pierce, Marg 241
Pierce, Sallie 241
Pierce, T. J. 315
Pierce, W. F. 241
Piercy, Christian 241
Piercy, Joshua 241
Pierson, Charles 313
Pigg, Richard 36
Pile, S. C. 316
Pillow, Gideon 241
Piner, [no name] 241
Pingleton, G. W. 241
Pinkerton, James 212
Pinkley, Danl. 59
Pinkley, Jacob 59, 241
Pinkley, John 241
Pinkley, Peter 241
Pinson, John 241
Pinson, Larkin 241
Pipkin, Hugh 241, 290
Pipkin, Mary E. 241, 290
Pippin, Francis 241
Pippin, Kinchin 131
Pitner, Andrew 265, 287
Pitner, Michael 317
Pitts, Joseph 294
Plannch James E.17
Plummer, William 241
Plunkett, Martha E. 195
Plunkett, Wm. 195
Pogh, Whitmell H. 248
Poindexter, Hilary 241
Poindexter, Mary O. 241
Poindexter, Robt. D. 241
Poindexter, William G.169
Pointer, Pamilia 231
Polk, Alexander F. 241
Polk, Charles 22
Polk, George 241
Polk, James 297
Polk, John 133, 242-243
Polk, Martha 133, 242
Polk, Olivia 242
Polk, Thos.76, 131, 241-242
Polk, William 133, 242
Pollard, Fuqua 142
Pollard, James 142

Pollock, Samuel 135
Polly [a slave] 277
Pool, Ch loe 242
Pool, George 242
Pool, Henry P. 242
Pool, Robert 52
Poor, Henry R. 242
Poor, J. O. 242
Poor, James 243
Poor, Jeremiah 242
Poor, Moses 242
Poor, S. C. 243
Poor, William 18, 242
Pope, J. W. R. 243
Pope, Jo. 24
Pope, Lazarus 243
Pope, Marmian 243
Pope, Mary M. 243
Poplin, Green L. 338
Porbate, Robert C. 243
Porter, Alexander B. 164
Porter, Benjamin 312, 133
Porter, Catherine 71
Porter, Elizabeth H. 244
Porter, Hannah 74
Porter, James 71, 243
Porter, Jeremiah 72
Porter, John 243
Porter, N. 12, 198
Porter, N. C. 289
Porter, Nathaniel 133, 227
Porter, Rutha 243
Porter, Scott 243
Porter, Thomas A. 242-243
Porter, William M. 243
Porterfield, John 202
Posey, Benjamin104
Posten, W. G. 243
Postle, Abel 243
Postle, John 243
Poston. James 160
Poston, W. F. 243
Poston, William L. 243
Poteet, Elvira 118
Poteet, Richard 118
Poters, William 238
Potter, Absolom 243
Potter, Hannah 243
Potter, James 244
Potter, John 243
Potter, Lewis 243
Potter, William 244
Potters, Alexander 244
Potts, John 244
Pouel, Dempsey 301
Pouel, Mary L. 244
Pouel, Richard H. 244
Pouel, Robert 244
Pouel, Seymore R. 244
Pouel, Thomas P. 244
Pouell, Robert 244
Pound, James M. 277
Powel, Dempsey 301
Powel, Joseph 103
Powel, Robert 244
Powel, William Barter 135
Powell, Bettie 245

Powell, C. L. F. 30, 244-245
Powell, Elizabeth 30, 244-245, 258-259
Powell, Exum 244
Powell, J. B. 75, 101, 311
Powell, James 30, 101, 244
Powell, John 49
Powell, Jos. 59
Powell, Julia 193
Powell, Lee 245
Powell, Levin 244
Powell, Louisa 193
Powell, Luce 193
Powell, Martha P. 258
Powell, Mary 258
Powell, Nance 193
Powell, R. P. 30-31, 245
Powell, Richard 245
Powell, Robert 244, 258
Powell, Roberta 30, 244-245
Powell, Seymore 30, 145, 258-259
Powell, Thomas 81, 244, 258
Powell, W. F. 244
Powell, W. R. 30, 244
Powell, W. T. 31, 245
Powell, Willie 244
Powers, Ephraim 245
Powers, James 245
Powers, John 147
Pratt, Catherine 48
Pratt, George 48
Pratt, William 48
Pratworth, Alex 16
Prefe, Abrm. 74
Prentis, Isaac 198
Presely, Elizabeth 245
Presely, John P. 245
Presley, Arena H. 245
Presley, Coosa M. 245
Presley, Dyonysius B. 245
Presley, Millenninum B. 245
Presley, Ruth E. 245
Presley, Sanders 245
Presley, Sarah J. 245
Preston, George 79, 112, 245
Preston, James 79, 245
Preston, Jane 245
Preston, Jesse 245
Preston, M. 245
Preston, Mildre 245
Preston, Polly 245
Preuett, Robt. E. 266
Prewitt, James 245, 266
Prewitt, Lucy 245
Prewitt, Moses H. 245
Prewitt, Robert E. 245
Prewitt, Sally 245
Prewitt, Thomas 245
Prewitt, William 245
Price, Abraham 98, 164
Price, Ann 246
Price, Archibald J. 77
Price, Campbell B. 246

Price, Charles 245, 266
Price, Elizabeth 77, 245-246
Price, Emeline 245
Price, Erwin 245
Price, Evalene 246
Price, Henry 140
Price, Irvin 246
Price, James 112, 245-246
Price, Jane T. 245
Price, Jefferson 121
Price, John 92, 245-246
Price, Luke 245-246
Price, Mary 77
Price, Micajah 245-246
Price, Mordicae 27
Price, N. M. 279
Price, Nancy 245-246
Price, Nathan 246
Price, Newton 245
Price, Reubin 121
Price, Richard J. 77
Price, Sarah 245-246
Price, Solomon 245
Price, Susan 246
Price, Thomas 245-246
Price, William 245-246
Prichard, A. B. 246
Prichard, Ann R. 246
Prichard, B. F. 14, 27, 145, 147, 246-247, 315
Prichard, Benjamin R. 246
Prichard, Berryll 247
Prichard, Bettie Lee 246
Prichard, C. A. 246
Prichard, E. J. 246
Prichard, Elijah 87
Prichard, Frank R. 246
Prichard, Fyonettie H. 246
Prichard, Grandy 80
Prichard, H. E. 246
Prichard, Harriet 246
Prichard, J. 246
Prichard, J. C. 246
Prichard, J. R. 46
Prichard, James F. 247
Prichard, Jefferson 247
Prichard, Joseph 247
Prichard, Lydia 80
Prichard, M. M. 246
Prichard, Margaret 247
Prichard, N. R. 20, 95, 134, 246-247
Prichard, R. 131
Prichard, W. T. 247
Prichett, E. 308
Priestly, Caroline 21
Primmer, John 247
Prince, Robert 229
Prior, Sarah J. 247
Prior, William 247
Priss [a slave] 250
Proby, Peter R. 232
Procter, Jane 295
Procter, Susan J. 295
Procter, William 295
Proctor, Edmund 143
Proctor, Edward 143

Proctor, John 197
Proctor, Thomas 143
Proffet, James 247
Proffett, Ann 247
Proffett, Baxter 247
Proffett, David 247
Proffett, Harrison 247
Proffett, Jackson 247
Proffett, Margaret 247
Prout, Joshua 247
Province, Alexander 247
Province, John 247
Provine, Andrew 132
Provine, John 138, 247
Provine, Nancy 138, 247
Provine, Polly 247
Provine, Rebecca 132, 247
Provine, William 247
Pruat, William 3
Prudy, Robt. 286
Pruit, Catharine 247
Pruit, Margaret 247
Pruit, Prissilla 247
Pruit, William 247
Pryor, Dorothy 247
Pryor, John 247
Pryor, Matthew 305
Pryor, Thornton 90
Pryor, William 247, 254, 307
Pucket, J. 247
Puckett, Benjamin F. 248
Puckett, Francis 248
Puckett, George W. 248
Puckett, Jno. R. 248
Puckett, Joseph F. 248
Puckett, Mary E. 248
Puckett, Patrick R. 248
Puckett, S. A. 248
Pugh, Henry 64, 152, 162, 174, 204, 218, 319
Pugh, John 248
Pugh, Jonathan 40, 248
Pugh, Susanna 248
Pugh, Whitmell H. 248
Pullman, Theaphalus W. 238

Pully, Adeline 53
Pully, William 53
Pults, F. F. 99
Pults, John 98
Purcell, Henry T. 248
Purris, John 90, 253
Pursell, James J. 248
Pursell, Jo H. 8
Pursley, William 23
Purvis, Starkey 332
Pury, John 237
Putman, Daniel 248
Putman, Jaleb 248
Putman, James 248
Putman, Jesse 248
Putman, Joseph 248
Putman, Samuel 248
Putman, Sarah 248
Putman, William 248
Putts, F. F. 99

Putty, James Y. 344
Putty, John 344
Putty, Matilda 344
Putty, Rhoda 344
Putty, William 53, 245
Pyland, J. F. 248
Pyle, Adrian 189
Pyles, Addison 189
Qualls, Roger 6
Quarles, Alexander R. 248
Quarles, Eliza Ann 248
Quarles, Elizabeth 248
Quarles, George 248
Quarles, Jack 249
Quarles, James 60, 248, 288
Quarles, John 249
Quarles, Maria 248
Quarles, Mary 319
Quarles, Milton W. 248
Quarles, Nancy 248
Quarles, Roger 249
Quarles, Samuel 248
Quarles, Sarah W. 248
Quarles, Thadias C. 121
Quesenberry, John 249
Quidly, Joseph 288
Quigley, Joseph 249
Quigley, Sarah 249
Quillin, [no name] 249
Rachel [a slave] 322
Rader, Adam 99
Rafter, Charles 302
Ragan, James 148, 168
Ragland, John W. 171
Ragland, Petis 52
Ragland, William 168, 266
Raglin, Joseph 94
Raglin, Petter 46
Raglin, Pettis 113
Ragsdale, Alfred 249
Ragsdale, Baxter H. 190
Ragsdale, Benjamin 249
Ragsdale, Elizabeth 164
Ragsdale, Joel 151, 157
Ragsdale, John 249, 296
Ragsdale, Lewis 157
Ragsdale, Prissella 249
Ragsdale, William 158, 249, 278
Rainen, Alfred 249
Raines, Isac E. 249
Raines, Susannah 249
Rainey, Alfred 249
Rainey, Brazillia G. 249
Rainey, Isaac 249
Rainey, J. G. 103, 250
Rainey, Jesse G. 249
Rainey, Lemuel 249
Rainey, Samuel 249
Rainey, Sarah 249
Rains, J. G. 280
Rains, Margaret E. 250
Rains, Sarah A. 250
Rains, Thos. B. 250
Rains, Ursula P. 250
Rambo, J. M. 43, 49, 228

Rambo, Martha 43-44
Rambo, Matt 250
Ramsey, James 323
Ramsey, John 34, 151
Ramsey, Josiah 46, 62
Ramsey, Mary 158
Ramsey, Newet 250
Ramsey, Richard 250
Ramsey, Thomas 254
Ramsey, William 112
Ramsey, Zeral 158
Randal, Greenberry 218
Randal, Jas. 250
Randal, [no name] 191
Randall, Payton 250
Randels, Henry 74
Randle, Edmond 250
Randle, Osborn 250
Randle, S. W. 57
Randle, William 184
Randle, Wilson 230
Randles, Henry 317
Randles, James 250
Randles, S. W. 145, 198, 231, 153, 240, 287, 326
Randolph, Hesekiah 54
Rankin, C. M. E. 326
Rankin, James 42
Ranshaw, John 114
Rany, Richd. 230
Rasberry, Lot 250
Rasco, William 254
Rasior, William 254
Rasor, Jesse 254
Rasor, John 254
Rasor, Laban 254
Rasor, Mary 254
Rasor, Rachel 254
Rasor, William 254
Rather, Baker 250
Rather, Daniel 119, 263
Rather, Sarah G. 250
Rawles, Allen 208
Rawlings, Elija 116
Rawlings, Eliza 311
Rawlings, M. A. 44, 108, 175, 260
Rawlings Rachel 311
Rawlins, Jim 250
Rawls, Elizabeth 250
Rawls, Luke 250
Rawls, Shadrick 1
Ray, A. S. 49
Ray, Alexander 244, 251
Ray Amanda 250
Ray, Delila 251
Ray, Elizabeth 248
Ray, Ellison 251
Ray, Emily 251
Ray, George M. 251
Ray, J. F. 251
Ray, J. M. 251
Ray, J. T. 250
Ray, James 147, 251
Ray, Jane 20, 114, 251
Ray, John 112, 114, 179, 251

Ray, Joseph 50, 250-251
Ray, Louis G. 114
Ray, Luke 251
Ray, Margaret 114
Ray, Martha 114, 251
Ray, Mary 114, 251
Ray, Nancy C. 112, 114
Ray, Patsy 114
Ray, Raulston 251
Ray, Rolston 251
Ray, Sally 251
Ray, Sarah 112, 114
Ray, Thomas 251
Ray, William 20, 114, 251
Rays, J. F. 308
Read, Drusilla B. 58
Read, Edward J. 58
Read, James 251, 316
Read, Jno. 95, 251
Read, Polly 251
Reader, Franklin 251
Reagan, D. W. 152
Reagan, Daniel W. 96, 228, 323
Reagan, James H. 277
Reagan, [no name] 251
Reagan, Peter 31
Reagan, R. R. 96, 152, 323
Reamey, Sarah J. 72
Reamy, E. H. 251
Reamy, James S. 251
Reamy, M. O. 251
Reamy, V. A. 251
Reason, C. B. 252
Reasoner, Garrett 254
Reasons, Abitha 252
Reasons, C. B. 299
Reasons, Dicy 252
Reasons, J. R. 252, 280
Reasons, Lavinia F. 252
Reasons, Sarah F. 252
Reasor, Frederic 98
Reaves, Jno. 333
Reaves, Uriah 252
Reavis, Alice 252
Reavis, Hartwell 252
Reavis, J. M. 37
Reavis, James 252
Reavis, May 252
Reavis, Robt. 252
Reavis, Thos. C. 252
Rebecca [a slave] 197
Record, George W. 114
Record, Mehulda 114
Rector, Maxemillion 252
Redad, G. W. 113
Reddick, Fanny 252
Reddick, Humphrey 252
Reddick, J. H. 61
Reddick, John 252
Reddick, Nancy 252
Reddick, Polly 252
Reddick, Rice 252
Reddick, T. T. 252
Reddick, William 252
Reddin, Anna 163
Reddin, Elizabeth 162-163

Reddin, Emaline 162
Reddin, John 162
Reddin, Joseph 162
Reddin, Martha 162
Reddin, Matilda 162
Reddin, Polly 163
Reddin, Robt. 162
Reddin, Susan 162
Reddin, William 162
Redding, W. V. 59
Redferren, Jno. 157, 185, 268, 322
Redman, Frances 252
Reece, John 252
Reece, Randal 252
Reece, Thomas B. 48
Reed, A. R. 311
Reed, Adam 253
Reed, Amos 32
Reed, Anderson 111
Reed, Ann 316
Reed, Charles 252-253
Reed, Henry 300
Reed, J. A. 253
Reed, James 253
Reed, Jesse 253
Reed, John S. 163
Reed, Joseph 253
Reed, Lavena 253
Reed, Louisa 163
Reed, Martha 253
Reed, Robert 111
Reed, S. M. 253
Reed, Thursa 253
Reed, William 253
Reennaw, Thomas 14
Rees, Joel 253
Rees, Thomas B. 283
Reeves, Alexander S. 253
Reeves, Archabald 253
Reeves, Benjamin S. 253
Reeves, George 254
Reeves, Gordon 253
Reeves, Jno. 333
Reeves, John George 253
Reeves, Mary 253
Reeves, Moses 253
Reeves, Tarlton J. 253
Reeves, Thomas 338
Reeves, William 208, 253
Reid, A. R. 9
Reid, Ambrose R. 116, 119, 311, 333
Reid, Anna 316
Reid, Anne 254
Reid, Fanny 116, 311
Reid, J. M. 253
Reid, Jno. 316
Reid, Richard 253
Reid, Robert W. 316
Reid, Thomas 42, 129, 162, 254, 314
Reneau Marcus 260
Renfro, Peter 203
Renfro, Wm. 254
Renfrou, W. H. 254
Renick, William 192

Renor, Charles 254
Renor, Lewis 254
Renor, Mary 254
Renshaw, Hannah 114
Rentfroe, Robert 269
Reps, Ann 81
Rervies, George 254
Rervies, Jeremiah 254
Rescor, William 254
Resor, Rachel 254
Resor, William 254
Rey, John H. 220
Rey, Mary H. 220
Reyburn, Thomas 192
Reynolds, Andrew 254
Reynolds, Ann 254
Reynolds, Anna K. 7
Reynolds, Benjamin 254
Reynolds, David 254
Reynolds, Elizabeth 254
Reynolds, Fanny 8
Reynolds, Henry 254
Reynolds, James 7, 116, 140, 186, 254
Reynolds, Jane 254-255
Reynolds, John 7, 254-255
Reynolds, Jonas A. 7
Reynolds, Moses 254
Reynolds, Richard 254
Reynolds, Sally 254
Reynolds, William 4, 254
Rhea, John 24, 255
Rhea, Joseph 255
Rhea, Richd. J. 255
Rhineheart, Betsy 255
Rhineheart, John W. 334
Rhineheart, Nancy 334
Rhoalas, Francis 44
Rhodes, Benjamin F. 30
Rhodes, Charles P. 29
Rhodes, Delpha 208
Rhodes, Disepha 208
Rhodes, Eleazer 208
Rhodes, Elija 208
Rhodes, Greene B. 29
Rhodes, Hezekiah 338
Rhodes, James H. 29
Rhodes, Jesse 335, 337
Rhodes, John H. 29
Rhodes, L. J. 208
Rhodes, Sarah 76
Rhodes, Thomas 29, 190, 217, 291
Rice, Charles W. 255
Rice, Daniel 206
Rice, Eliza 255
Rice, Elizabeth 255
Rice, Henry 255
Rice, Isaac 255
Rice, James 255, 285
Rice, John 250, 255, 318
Rice, Lucinda 255
Rice, Martha 255
Rice, Miller 255
Rice, Sally 255
Rice, Tandy 255

Rice, W. P. 27, 49, 119-120, 250, 280, 300
Rice, William 255
Rich, Jane 204
Rich, Joel 312
Richards, Asa 255
Richards, Gabriel 255
Richards, George 255
Richards, Hannah 255
Richards, Isaac 220, 255, 264
Richards, James 255-256
Richards, Jenny 264
Richards, Nancy 255
Richards, Richard 255
Richards, Sarah Jane 67
Richardson, Abigal T. 256
Richardson, D. M. 256
Richardson, David 256
Richardson, Fisher 256
Richardson, George 256
Richardson, Harritte 256
Richardson, Henry 256
Richardson, James 256
Richardson, Jeffry H. 211
Richardson, Mary 148, 256
Richardson, Nancy 256
Richardson, Oliver 148
Richardson, Samuel 29
Richardson, Sarah 256
Richardson, Stith 256
Richardson, T. E. 113, 256
Richardson, Thomas R. 22, 192, 313
Richardson, W. F. 17
Richardson, William 256
Richie, Alexander 288
Richie, Ann Mariah 223
Richie, Archibald A. 223
Richie, Sally R. 223
Richie, William L. 223
Richmond, Alma C. 30
Richmond, Frank 30
Richmond, Henry 256-257
Richmond, James M. 257, 266
Richmond, John 237, 256-257
Richmond, Joseph 256-257
Richmond, Martha 257
Richmond, Robert 256-257
Richmond, Sophia 256
Richmond, Zenia F. 30
Ricketts, Elizabeth 15, 257
Riddle, Cornelus 257
Rider, Ruben 332
Ridley, Benjamin F. 257
Ridley, Elizabeth 257
Ridley, Thomas 135
Riggin, Ignatius 257
Riggin, Mary H. 257
Riggs, Elizabeth 257
Riggs, James M. 257
Riggs, Joel 257
Riggs, Rebecca B. 257
Rigsby, Griffy 131
Rila, William 267

Riley, John 267
Riley, William 267
Rineheart, Conrad 257
Rineheart, Elizabeth 257
Rion, D. D. 258, 267
Rion, Fielding 258
Rion, John 258
Rion, Sarah 258, 267
Rion, Washington 258, 267
Ripley, John 258
Ritchie, Hetta A. 223
Ritchie, James 258
Ritchie, John 258
Ritchie, Mariah R. 223
Ritchie, Mary 258
Ritchua, H. W. 258
Rivers, John F. 59
Rivers, Robert J. 241
Roach, Isaac I. 189
Roach, Samuel 141
Roachel, Wm. 51, 118, 133, 242, 341
Roark, Barnabus 258
Roark, Barnet 258
Roark, Sarah 258
Robb, William 46, 258
Robbins, Edward 258
Robbins, J. R. 321
Robbins, John S. 258
Robbins, Joseph O. 258
Robbins, O. R. 131, 147, 227, 258
Robbins, Polly 258
Robbins, Sallie B. 258
Robbins, Wm. E. 258
Robers, Elizabeth 258
Roberson, Battle 332
Roberson, Elizabeth J. 258
Roberson, Jenny 251
Roberson, John H. 257
Roberson, Miles F. 197
Roberson, William 251
Roberts, A. G. 214, 260
Roberts, Ann 259
Roberts, Buckannan W. 259
Roberts, Edmond 259
Roberts, Eli 259-260
Roberts, Elisha 259
Roberts, Harret 259
Roberts, Houston 260
Roberts, Hugh 259
Roberts, Isaac H. 284
Roberts, J. B. 260
Roberts, J. E. 278, 318
Roberts, James 259
Roberts, Jane 148, 186
Roberts, John 103, 159, 259-260
Roberts, Jonathan 186
Roberts, Joseph 282
Roberts, L. C. 214, 259-260
Roberts, Letty 259
Roberts, Levi 172, 214,
Roberts, Margaret 260
Roberts, Mark 259
Roberts, Nancy 282
Roberts, Priscilla 232

Roberts, Ridley 259, 274, 340
Roberts, Robert B. 47
Roberts, Roda 259
Roberts, S. P. 260
Roberts, Samuel 260
Roberts, Sarah 259
Roberts, Thomas 232, 259-260
Roberts, W. D. 317
Roberts, W. M. 214, 260
Roberts, William 143, 148, 214, 259-260
Roberts, Zadack B. 259
Robertson, Alexander 313
Robertson, Andrew 261
Robertson, Ann 261
Robertson, Burrell 260-261
Robertson, Chas. 17, 27, 35, 51, 66, 76, 127, 211, 260-261, 273, 337
Robertson, Danl. 261
Robertson, Duntan 314
Robertson, Elijah 261
Robertson, Elizabeth J. 258
Robertson, F. N. 261
Robertson, F. S. 183, 228
Robertson, Henry 262
Robertson, Hugh 261
Robertson, J. F. 261
Robertson, James 262, 314
Robertson, Jane 261
Robertson, Jesse 262
Robertson, Joel 261
Robertson, John 261
Robertson, Julius 261
Robertson, Lucy 261
Robertson, M. W. 261
Robertson, Marcus 218, 260
Robertson, Mark 261
Robertson, Martha 262
Robertson, Mary E. 29, 261
Robertson, Milly 262
Robertson, Nancy 261
Robertson, P. H. 189
Robertson, Rich. A. 340
Robertson, Robert 261
Robertson, Simeon 262
Robertson, T. S. 64, 161
Robertson, Tabatha 262
Robertson, William 262
Robertson, Zachariah T. 261
Robeson, Caleb 43-44, 263
Robeson, John 84
Robeson, Mary 43-44
Robey, Nathan 262
Robey, Sarah 262
Robin [a slave] 337
Robins, Betsey 262
Robins, John 262, 309-310
Robins, Polly 262
Robins, Saml. 262
Robinson, Adaline 327
Robinson, Alexander 262
Robinson, Battle 264
Robinson, David 262

Robinson, Elizabeth 244, 258
Robinson, Henry 262
Robinson, Houston A. 262
Robinson, Hugh 262
Robinson, James 41, 124, 262, 327
Robinson, Jane 262
Robinson, Jesse 262
Robinson, John 262
Robinson, Joseph 170, 262
Robinson, Lewis 262
Robinson, Nancy 260
Robinson, R. 143
Robinson, Rachel 262
Robinson, Richard 262
Robinson, Seymore 244
Robinson, William 81, 262
Robison, Abijah 262
Robison, Caleb 43
Robison, Jeremiah 121
Robison, Joel 263
Robison, Mary 263
Robison, Nancy 263
Robson, Nancy 261
Roddy, James 220, 263
Roddy, Joseph 121, 141, 263
Roder, Adam 209
Rodes, B. 263
Rodgers, Benjamine 273
Rodgers, Fanny 32
Rodgers, George L. 192
Rodgers, Jobe 263
Rodgers, John 43, 99, 263
Rodgers, Jubilee 263
Rodgers, Julia 32
Rodgers, Nancy 4
Rogers, A. S. 57, 312
Rogers, Aaron 263
Rogers, Abraham 263
Rogers, Alsey 110
Rogers, America 263
Rogers, Andrew 306, 322
Rogers, Ann 91
Rogers, Archibald 57, 67
Rogers, Benjn. 263, 265
Rogers, Brinkly 343
Rogers, Cantsriel 263
Rogers, Clabourn 263
Rogers, Clayton 35, 270
Rogers, Cornelias 263
Rogers, Davis 263
Rogers, Elisha 263
Rogers, Elizabeth 35, 196, 263
Rogers, Emily 263
Rogers, Francis 35
Rogers, George 20, 263
Rogers, Isaac 116
Rogers, Isham 264
Rogers, J. C. 264
Rogers, James 90, 112, 197,
Rogers, Jeremiah 263

Rogers, John 90-91, 147, 164, 187, 196, 234, 263-264, 332
Rogers, Joseph 35, 78, 123, 264
Rogers, Leaner 264
Rogers, Littleton 263
Rogers, Martha 264
Rogers, Mary 263-264, 268
Rogers, Matthew 263
Rogers, Nathl. 264
Rogers, Patsey 263
Rogers, Rebecca 262
Rogers, Reuben 91, 300
Rogers, Robert O. 268
Rogers, Sarah 263
Rogers, Soloman 263
Rogers, Thomas 264
Rogers, William 72, 75, 84, 168, 263, 267, 273, 292, 312
Rogers, William An 35
Roister, W. H. 264
Rollons, Rossel 29, 264
Rolsten, James 264
Rolsten, Presley B. 264
Rolsten, Quintilla 264
Romines, Abel 264
Romines, David 264
Romines, Elizabeth 264
Romines, Geo. 264
Romines, Henry 264
Romines, Jenny 264
Romines, John 264
Romines, Laten 264
Romines, Mary 264
Romines, Noah 264
Romines, Samuel 264
Romines, Sarah E. 264
Romines, Tabitha 264
Romines, Thomas 264
Ronk, J. S. 264
Roohoof, Lotty 265
Rook, Tennie 166
Rooker, Peter R. 55
Root, Daniel 265
Root, Santha 265
Roper, John 265
Rorie Ezikiah 232
Rose, Jno. H. 36
Rose, John 71, 103
Rose, McKinsey 265
Rose, Thomas J. 160
Rosenbrough, Margaret 132
Roseth, Jordan 37
Roson, John 8
Ross, Albert H. 148
Ross, Allen 13, 143, 171
Ross, Charles 265
Ross, Henry 283
Ross, Isaac 265
Ross, James M. 265
Ross, Jesse 21, 76, 265, 331
Ross, Lewis G. 23
Ross, Martha L. 23

Ross, Nathan 204, 230, 237, 252
Ross, Rice T. 284
Ross, Sarah 265
Ross, Thomas 192, 252
Ross, William 265
Routh, Edward 90
Routh, Elizabeth 265
Routh, Jeremiah 265
Rowhoof, John 265
Rowland, Joab 224
Rowland, Samuel C. 265
Rowlett, Peter 325
Roy, Lewis G. 112
Roy, Wm. D. 20
Royster, M. W. E. 227
Royster, W. H. 227
Royster, William 323
Rucker, James 265, 287
Rucker, John 265
Rucker, N. B. 265
Rucker, S. H. 265
Rucker, Virginia A. 265
Rucker, William 35
Rud, James 61
Rudd, Herrod 265
Rudd, James 61
Rudd, William 265
Rudesel, Jonas 9
Rudran, Joel 142
Ruffen, John J. S. 133, 310
Rule, John 126, 265
Rullman, Just. 67
Rumbley, Smith 39
Rundleman, John 3
Ruse, John 265
Ruse, Randle 265
Rush, Caroline 266
Rush, James 23, 266
Rush, John 266
Rush, Tennessee 23
Rush, William 193, 266
Rushing, Able 266
Rushing, Elijah 18, 164
Rushing, Enoch D. 35
Rushing, Jemima 266
Rushing, Joel 245, 266
Rushing, Joseph 83
Rushing, Keziah 111
Rushing, Mark 109
Rushing, Martha 83
Rushing, Milley 83
Rushing, Nancy 83
Rushing, Philip 266
Rushing, Sarah 245
Russell, America Ann 266
Russell, Edgar 266
Russell, George 56, 127, 143, 211
Russell, Isaac 266
Russell, James 27, 40, 64, 69, 81, 172, 205, 240, 258, 265-266, 283, 296
Russell, Jesse 276
Russell, Joel C. 266
Russell, John 3-4, 10, 176, 234, 266

Russell, Jordan 266
Russell, Joseph A. 266
Russell, Josephus 266
Russell, Leven 266
Russell, Levi 266
Russell, Margaret 266
Russell, Martha 266
Russell, Moses 266
Russell, Nancy D. 276
Russell, Obediah 17
Russell, Samuel 266
Russell, Simpson 266
Russell, Syrus W. 340
Russell, Thomas 326
Russell, William 73, 266-267
Russle, Moses 138
Ruth, George W. 267
Rutherford, Elizabeth 267
Rutherford, James 277
Rutherford, John 267
Rutherford, Rudolph 57
Rutland, Blake 75, 299
Rutland, Clarissa 267
Rutland, Jno. 267
Rutland, Rhaford 267
Rutland, Rutherford 61, 267
Rutledge, David 267
Rutledge, Polly 86
Ryal, Sally 91
Ryan, Jas. A. 97
Ryburn, Nancy 154
Ryla, John 267
Ryla, William 267
Ryon, Courtney 267
Ryon, David D. 267
Ryon, Fielding 267
Ryon, John 258, 267
Ryon, Joseph 267
Ryon, Sarah 258, 267
Ryon, W. L. 267
Ryon, Washington 258, 267
Saddler, Henry 108
Sadler, Catron C. 146
Sadler, Celina 259
Sadler, Charles W. 268
Sadler, Elmore 268
Sadler, Garrett 47, 108, 267, 304, 336
Sadler, Henry 47, 267-268, 274, 291, 304
Sadler, Ira B. 268
Sadler, James 180, 259
Sadler, John K. 259
Sadler, Lee 268
Sadler, Leonidas 268
Sadler, Martha 267-268
Sadler, Nancy 268
Sadler, Nelson 267-268
Sadler, Oliver 268
Sadler, Patsy 259
Sadler, Sarah 180
Sadler, William 268
Sadley, Nelson 270
Saffle, C. H. 109
Sale, Cornelius 68
Sale, Hannah 68

Sale, William 68, 104, 190, 301
Sall [a slave] 61
Sallee, Corien O. 245
Sallee, John 245, 296
Sallee, Mary Ann 245
Sallee, Pleasent H. 245
Sallee, Wm. H. 245, 296
Sally [a slave] 340
Sam [a slave] 55, 269
Samms, John 86
Sampson, F. G. 27, 39, 43, 109, 190, 208, 246-247, 270, 315, 343
Sampson, Maggie 286
Sampson, W. B. 102, 270
Sanderlin, William 80
Sanderlin, Wilson 315
Sanders, Alexander 262
Sanders, Butie 269
Sanders, Clark 268
Sanders, Elisha 160
Sanders, Elizabeth 268
Sanders, James 89, 213, 269
Sanders, Jno B. 269
Sanders, Joel 268-269
Sanders, John 269
Sanders, Luke 268
Sanders, Mary 268-269
Sanders, Samuel 268
Sanders, Thomas 268-269
Sanders, W. S. H. 269
Sanders, William 269
Sanderson, Jno. 269
Sanderson, Thomas 269
Sanderson, Wade 269
Sanderson, Wm. 269
Sandford, Ezekiel 269
Sandford, James 269
Sandford, Joseph 103, 269
Sandford, Sarah A. 103
Sands, Joseph 205
Sandy, Jordan 4
Sanland, William 270
Sappington, Mark 269
Sappington, Roger B. 269
Sarah Ann [a slave] 63
Sarett, Francis 269
Sarett, James D. 269
Sarjeant, Mary 44
Sarjeant, William 44
Sary [a slave] 214
Satterfield, Cynthia 270
Satterfield, Larry 159, 270
Saulsbury, E. F. 270
Saulsbury, F. M. 270
Saulsbury, Frank 270
Saulsbury, Tennessee 270
Saunders, Alexander 262
Saunders, Jno. P. 268
Saunders, Mary 269
Savage, Jefferson C. 82
Savireyly, A. S. 28
Sawers, C. J. 98, 152
Sawyer, Daniel 270
Sawyer, George C. 270

Sawyer, Isaac 270
Sawyer, J. W. 270
Sawyer, Jane 270
Sawyer, Jo. 270
Sawyer, John 109, 270, 274
Sawyer, Joshua 270
Sawyer, Monroe 270
Sawyer, W. J. 270
Sawyer, Willie 270
Sawyers, James 192, 241, 274
Scales, David 270
Scales, Joe 270
Scallings, Terry C. 134
Scanland, Benjamin 268, 270
Scanland, John 146
Scanland, Rachel 268
Scanland, William 180
Scanlon, John 270
Scarborough, James 4, 45, 159, 265, 283
Scarlett, Angeline 157
Scarlett, Elizabeth 157
Scarlett, John 157
Scarlett, Moses 157
Scarlett, Thomas 157
Schorn, John M. 342
Scisco, Mary E. 270
Scisco, Saunders 270
Scites, Abraham 270
Scites, Margaret 270
Scobey, Jonathan D. 270
Scobey, W. J. 158
Scoby, H. L. 250
Scoby, John D. 250
Scoby, Matilda J. 271
Scoby, N. 125
Scoby, William 271
Scorlic, William 172
Scott, Allen 271
Scott, Christian 271
Scott, David 279
Scott, E. T. 271
Scott, Edward 238
Scott, Elizabeth 271
Scott, Frankey 271
Scott, George R. 220, 342
Scott, Hugh 223
Scott, Isabella 223, 271
Scott, James 157, 184, 197, 226, 271
Scott, John 46, 271, 292
Scott, Jones 292
Scott, Peter 342
Scott, Polly 342
Scott, Robert 271
Scott, Samuel 166, 271
Scott, Tabetha 271
Scott, William 208, 271
Scroggs, Ebenezer 183-184, 192
Scroggs, Francis 184
Scruggs, A. L. 194
Scruggs, Archibald 271
Scruggs, Basdill 139, 341
Scruggs, Frederick 271

Scruggs, George 271
Scruggs, Hariet 271
Scruggs, Isaac 271
Scruggs, Martha 271
Scruggs, Nancy 271
Scruggs, Penelope 271
Scruggs, Rohoda 271
Scruggs, William L. 271
Scurlock, Annie 272
Scurlock, Catherine S. 272
Scurlock, Clarence H. 272
Scurlock, Fanny H. 272
Scurlock, Joseph W. 272
Scurlock, Kate 272
Scurlock, Timothy P. 272
Seagraves, Burwell 310
Seagraves, S. 113
Searcy, Bennet 82
Searcy, Mary 82
Searcy, Robert 272
Searcy, Susanah 286
Searcy, William 246, 272
Seaton, Andrew B. 272
Seaton, George W. 43
Seaton, John B. 90
Seawell, Benjamin 310
Seawell, John 272
Seawell, Thomas 59
Seawell, William 251, 267
Secty, James Walker 117
Sellars, Danl. 272
Sellars, Howell 218
Sellars, Matthew 253
Sellars, Thomas 218
Sellers, Edward G. 337
Sellers, Elizabeth 152
Sellers, Micah 75
Sellers, Sarly 337
Sellers, Thomas 301
Senter, Fortena 272
Senter, John 272
Senter, Martin 110
Seorlie, William 172
Seratt, James D. 269
Seratt, Samuel H. 270
Serlis, P. H. 297
Serlis, Preston H. 297
Settle, Frederick 272
Settle, J. L. 272
Settle, Jane 272
Settle, Joel 19, 54, 239, 245, 293
Settle, L. W. 272
Settle, LaFayette 272
Settle, Leroy B. 24, 41, 121, 238, 243, 293, 344
Settle, Mary 324
Settle, Sewell 272
Settle, Sidney L. 272
Settle, Suel 272
Settle, T. C. 272
Settle, Tipton 272
Sevier, A. Huntsman 276
Sevier, Abraham 272
Sevier, Chas. 276
Sevier, Eldridge G. 275-276
Sevier, George W. 275-276

Sevier, James 273
Sevier, John 34, 273, 275-276
Sevier, Joseph 276, 337
Sevier, Robert 60, 273
Sevier, Valentine 51, 273, 275-276
Sewell, Cader 246
Shadder, Jacob 113
Shaddy, Jacob 113
Shaddy, Martha 113
Shaddy, Patsy 114
Shamblen, William 187
Shamblin, A. H. 264
Shanklin, Andrew 200, 273
Shanklin, Jane 200, 273
Shanklin, Jesse 273
Shanks, James 273
Shanks, John T. 120, 273
Shanks, Michl. 273
Shanks, William 273
Shannon, James 274
Shannon, John 262
Shannon, Robert 230
Shannon, St. Clare 273
Shannon, Thomas 194
Shapherd, Nancy 77
Shappard, Fanny 273
Shappard, John 273
Shappard, L. B. 273
Shappard, Lewis B. 273
Shappard, William 273
Sharber, Joseph W. 26
Sharber, Mary Jane 26
Sharks, Jesse 273
Sharp, Anderson 273
Sharp, Andrew J. 216
Sharp, Anthony 234
Sharp, Caroline 316
Sharp, Elisha 4
Sharp, Henry 221
Sharp, James 197-198, 274
Sharp, John 80, 273
Sharp, Joseph C. 67
Sharp, Lucinda 216
Sharp, Martin 273
Sharp, Mary 273
Sharp, Mattee 273
Sharp, Nicholas 273
Sharp, Richard 273
Sharp, Robert M. 274
Sharp, Thomas 55
Sharp, William 273-274, 325
Shaun, Christian 310
Shaun, Rachel 310
Shaver, William 274
Shaw, Artie 274
Shaw, Benjamine 174
Shaw, Burchet 274
Shaw, C. N. 2
Shaw, Christopher 274, 276
Shaw, Craig 274-275
Shaw, David A. 274-275
Shaw, Emley 274
Shaw, Francis 275
Shaw, George W. C. 274
Shaw, James 274

Shaw, Jane 274
Shaw, Jesse 4
Shaw, Martha 146, 274
Shaw, Martha E. 275
Shaw, Mary L. 275
Shaw, Matilda 274
Shaw, Milton 274-275
Shaw, Rebecca 274
Shaw, S. B. 274, 295
Shaw, Samuel 274-275
Shaw, Thomas J. 274-275
Shaw, V. 2
Shaw, W. L. 275
Shaw, William 274-275
Shearman, Thomas 159
Sheild, Mary 277
Sheilds, Elizabeth J. 277
Sheilds, M. W. 277
Sheilds, Nancy 277
Sheilds, Richard 277
Sheilds, S. W. 277
Shelby Evan 17, 27, 275
Shelby, Hannah 275
Shelby, Henry 36, 275
Shelby, Hulda 36
Shelby, John 229
Shelby, Phillip 330
Shelby, Thomas S. 275
Shelly, Amanda 275
Shelly, Elijah 275
Shelly, John 113, 275
Shelton, America 275
Shelton, Burdetta 236
Shelton, Charles 275-276
Shelton, David 275-276
Shelton, Eleanora 275-276
Shelton, Eliza J. 275-276
Shelton, Elizabeth 108
Shelton, Ella Nora 276
Shelton, Ellemora 216
Shelton, George N. 276
Shelton, Henry 195
Shelton, J. A. 275
Shelton, J. B. 275
Shelton, James 52, 95, 188, 225
Shelton, John 276
Shelton, Joseph 276
Shelton, Judithen C. 275-276
Shelton, L. B. 276
Shelton, Levi B. 275-276
Shelton, Mahala 276
Shelton, Mary 275-276
Shelton, Millard B. 275-276
Shelton, Nelson P. 276
Shelton, Ralph 9, 153
Shelton, Robt. L. 276
Shelton, Samuel 307
Shelton, Sandford 276
Shelton, Sarah 275-276
Shelton, Solon A. 276
Shelton, Susan 275-276
Shelton, Thomas 276
Shelton, W. T. 276
Shelton, Watson 216, 236, 276

Shelton, William 276
Shelton, Zebery 108
Shepard, Austin 77
Shepard, Richard 77
Shepherd, Anderson 77
Shepherd, Augustin 276
Shepherd, Benjamin A. 276
Shepherd, David G. 110, 274, 276, 302, 314
Shepherd, James M. 47, 259, 274, 276, 302
Shepherd, Jesse G. 276
Shepherd, John 274, 276
Shepherd, Joseph H. 276
Shepherd, Lewis 120
Shepherd, Martin B. 276
Shepherd, Mary 257, 276
Shepherd, Nancy 276
Shepherd, Sarah B. 276
Shepherd, Thomas 276
Shepherd, W. M. 276-277
Shepherd, William 257
Shepperd, James 277
Shepperd, Winifred 217
Sherly, John M. 148
Sherly, Louisa 148
Sherman, George W. 275
Sherod, Henry 277
Sherod, John 49, 133
Sherral, William 128
Sherrill, Able 277
Sherrill, Ambrose 277
Sherrill, Ephraim 208, 271, 277
Sherrill, Hulda 277
Sherrill, Jacob 277
Sherrill, Samuel 55, 277, 306
Sherrill, Ute 277
Sherrod, Charlotte 277
Sherrod, Elizabeth 277
Sherrod, J. M. 76
Sherville, Samuel 34, 156, 315
Shields, David 277
Shields, Patrick 14
Shipley, Christopher 277
Shiply, Nathan 105
Shipman, Daniel 277
Shipman, E. P. 277-278
Shipman, M. P. 277
Shoats, Edward 278
Shockley, Caleb 278
Shockley, Hannah 278
Shockly, Booker 109, 284
Shoffner, John 226
Shook, John 278
Shorn, Martha 342
Short, Agness 177
Short, Elizabeth 278
Short, Jefferson 278
Short, Martin 278
Short, Mary 278
Short, Sally 234
Short, Samuel 278
Short, Washington 149
Short, William 181, 278

Shouts, Christopher 302
Shrader, Christopher 278
Shrader, Eliza Ann 278
Shrader, G. C. 68, 321
Shrader, Jacob 278
Shrader, Jane 278
Shrader, Saml. 278
Shrader, William 278
Shroder, Jacob 278
Shrum, Peter 182
Shrum, Thomas 121
Shuck, Edward Y. 40, 299
Shuks, Jesse 273
Shults, Amanda 278
Shults, Eli H. 278
Shults, Jacob 122
Shults, Martin 278
Shults, P. S. 97
Shults, Philip S. 230, 278
Shults, Sarah 278
Shumaker, Ann Eliza 148
Siglar, John 104, 214, 226
Sillers, Jacob 278
Sills, Isham 14
Silsby, L. H. 278
Silsby, L. J. 65
Silsby, Levi H. 278
Silvester, F. M. 278
Silvy [a slave] 144
Simentin, Mary R. 276
Simmonds, John 61
Simmons, Almarine 279
Simmons, Caroline E. 66
Simmons, Charles 308, 309
Simmons, Cyrus 189
Simmons, Elijah 220, 279
Simmons, Elizabeth A. 220
Simmons, George 236
Simmons, Harriet 279
Simmons, James 279
Simmons, John 279, 312
Simmons, Lucinda 279
Simmons, Martha 279
Simmons, Martin 279
Simmons, Mary 103, 279
Simmons, Nancy 279
Simmons, Natl. 301
Simmons, Peter 279
Simmons, Solomon 279
Simmons, Thomas A. 222
Simmons, W. H. 103
Simmons, William 66
Simmons, Wort 279
Simms, Bartlet 279
Simms, John 150
Simms, Leonard H. 279
Simms, Roystin 279
Simms, Wm. E. 279
Simms, Zachariah 279
Simon [a slave] 119
Simons, Calib 296
Simons, Elizabeth 296
Simons, Mark 279
Simpson, Adam 279
Simpson, Archibald 208
Simpson, D. 279
Simpson, Edmond 107

Simpson, J. W. 252
Simpson, James B. 279
Simpson, Jeremiah 279
Simpson, Jno. W. 279
Simpson, Jonathan 279
Simpson, Joshua 279
Simpson, L. D. 279
Simpson, Majery 279
Simpson, S. D. 279
Simpson, Thos. E. 8
Simpson, W. H. 98
Simpson, William 208, 213
Sims, Albert 280
Sims, Ann H. 280
Sims, Boyd M. 280
Sims, Gray 60
Sims, John 80, 150, 280
Sims, Leonard 150, 248, 319
Sims, Little Page 60
Sims, Lula 280
Sims, Mary 280, 317
Sims, Parish 94
Sims, Rebecca 280
Sims, Richard H. 29, 80, 280
Sims, Thomas D. 280
Sims, W. 280
Sims, Walter 280
Sims, William 280
Sinclair, J. F. 159
Sinclair, James 252
Sinclair, John F. 64, 77, 212
Sinclair, Noah 173, 307
Sinclair, Ralph 212, 280
Sing, Elizabeth 280
Sing, Isaah 280
Sing, John 280
Sing, Lucinda 280
Sing, Martha C. 280
Sing, Nancy C. 280
Singletary, Catherine 212
Singletary, John L. 212
Singleton, Catherine 181, 280
Singleton, Daniel 181, 280
Singleton, J. T. 17
Singleton, Mary 181, 280
Singleton, P. H. 280
Singletory, J. S. 103
Sisca, John 121
Sizemore, Calaway 41, 110
Skeen, John 127
Skiles, William 66
Skinner, Emanuel 215
Skinner, Jesse 1
Skinner, Nathan 14, 27, 142, 304
Skipper, Jerry 281
Slate, William N. 192
Slater, Edward C. 14
Slater, F. A. 29
Slater, Perry 281
Slater, T. L. 29
Slatt, Daniel S. 42
Slaughter, John 281
Slaughter, Mary 281
Slaughterm, John P. 281

Slayden, W. A. 2, 143
Slayton, Alex. 281
Slayton, Emily V. 281
Sludor, Jesse 281
Smallwood, Mary 203, 281
Smallwood, Ned 203, 281
Smallwood, Rosanna 203, 281
Smart, Phillip 340
Smedley, William 126
Smith, Abraham 16, 281
Smith, Adam 282
Smith, Addie B. 286
Smith, Albert 281
Smith, Allen 281, 285
Smith, Alonzo P. 282
Smith, Anderson 29
Smith, Andrw J. 129
Smith, Ann C. 282
Smith, B. C. 14, 147
Smith, Caleb 282
Smith, Charity 281
Smith, Charles 282
Smith, Cytha A. 282
Smith, D. G. 282
Smith, Daley W. 281
Smith, David 106, 282, 286
Smith, Delilah 282
Smith, Dennis 281
Smith, Dorcas 77
Smith, Drury 282
Smith, E. J. 158, 282
Smith, Edmund B. 16
Smith, Elias 282
Smith, Elij. 60
Smith, Elizabeth 281-282, 285
Smith, Ezekiel 60, 282
Smith, Francis 129, 282
Smith, Frederick 282
Smith, Geo. L. 234, 319, 325
Smith, George 18, 98, 217, 237, 262, 269, 314,
Smith, George W. 326
Smith, H. S. 77, 283,
Smith, Hampton 281
Smith, Hannah 282, 285
Smith, Harbard 290
Smith, Harbet 290
Smith, Hardin L. 282
Smith, Henry 76-77, 191, 281, 283
Smith, Hugh 174, 283
Smith, Isaac 283
Smith, Isiah 283
Smith, Israel 283, 285
Smith, J. D. 9
Smith, J. M. 321
Smith, Jackson 82, 193, 240
Smith, Jacob 247
Smith, James 117, 283, 285, 318, 332,
Smith, Jenny 283
Smith, Jeremiah 281, 284, 285
Smith, Jesse 12, 30

Smith, Jincy 283
Smith, Jiney 283
Smith, Jo 281
Smith, Joel 284
Smith, John 24, 32, 60, 174, 201, 206, 271, 281-
Smith, Joseph 5, 107, 282-285
Smith, Josiah 300
Smith, Kinchen 284
Smith, L. C. 197
Smith, Labon 282
Smith, M. 284
Smith, Mahulda 64
Smith, Malcom 284
Smith, Margaret 282
Smith, Maring 283
Smith, Marion 284, 321
Smith, Martha 281
Smith, Martin 96
Smith, Mary 167, 282-284
Smith, Mereweather 18, 253
Smith, Mildred 284, 290
Smith, Mitchen 284
Smith, Nancy 201, 285
Smith, Nathan 285
Smith, Nathaniel 110, 146, 148, 283, 285
Smith, Obedience 106
Smith, Polly 185, 284-285
Smith, Richard 64, 284-285
Smith, Robert 30, 222, 285
Smith, Rowland 281
Smith, Samuel 206, 281, 285
Smith, Sarah 60, 282
Smith, Shadrack 237
Smith, Sidney 285
Smith, Silas 285
Smith, Solomon 285
Smith, Spencer 281
Smith, Squire 60
Smith, Susan 222, 284
Smith, Synthia Jane 318
Smith, Thomas 60, 109, 132, 185, 281-282, 284-285
Smith, Vachel 4
Smith, Virginia E. 283
Smith, W. B. 14, 147, 315
Smith, William 110, 169, 189, 282-283, 285-286, 308, 318
Smither, Virginia L. 286
Smithpeter, George 286
Smithpeter, James 5
Smithpeter, John Michael 286
Smithson, Mary 279
Smithson, Polly 279
Smizer, Alfred 286
Smizer, John 286
Snapp, Joseph 321
Snauffer, David 286
Snauffer, Elizabeth 286
Snauffer, George 286
Snauffer, Jacob 286

Snauffer, John 286
Snauffer, Margaret 286
Snauffer, Mary 286
Snauffer, Nancy 286
Snauffer, Polly 286
Sneed, Robert 38
Snell, Elizabeth 286
Snelling, Elizabeth 177, 286
Snelling, Hugh 177, 286
Snelling, John 286
Snelling, Lemuel 177, 286
Snelling, Nancy 286-287
Snider, Adam 287
Snider, Elizabeth 287
Snider, Geo. 14
Snider, Martha 169
Snider, Peter 287
Snipes, Jacob 220
Snipes, Jane S. 220
Snoddy, David 199
Snoddy, Glasco 287
Snodgrass, Elaner 287
Snodgrass, James 287
Snodgrass, Milly 287
Snodgrass, Nancy 287
Snodgrass, Thomas 287
Solomom, Austin 37
Somers, Arden 287
Somers, Harriet 195
Somers, James 287, 340
Somers, John 287, 340
Somers, Sarah 195
Sommers, John 86
Sommers, Margaret 86
Sorrell, N. J. 53, 269
Southerland, E. G. 287
Southerland, Janet M. 287
Southerland, [name torn] 20
Southern, Boaz 89, 298
Southern, Isaac 267
Soward, Charles M. 287
Soward, George W. 287
Sowell, Jas. 171
Spain, Calvin 287
Spain, Coleman 102, 287, 296
Spain, Electra H. 102, 287
Spain, Elizabeth 287
Spain, Jane F. 287
Spain, John E. 287
Spain, M. S. 287
Spain, Martha E. 102, 287
Spain, Mary E. 102, 287
Spain, Sullivan 102
Spain, William 102, 287
Sparkman, W. L. 28
Speakman, Frances 53
Speakman, William 53
Spear, Margaret 275
Spearman, Joshua 278
Spearman, Thomas 259
Spears, John 193
Spence, Ada B. 103
Spence, D. H. C. 243
Spence, Elizabeth A. 288
Spence, George 219, 287
Spence, H. M. 310

Spence, J. S. 58
Spence, James S. 310
Spence, Margaret 287
Spence, Peter 308
Spence, Sarah Ann 243
Spence, Susan E. 243
Spencer, Alexander 265
Spencer, George W. 288
Spencer, James 288
Spencer, Nathan 265
Spencer, Patsey 265
Spicer, Lucretia 84
Spicer, William 84
Spight, Mary 288
Spirlock, James A. 323
Spradlin, Obediah 94-95
Sprigs, Jno. 288
Spring, Aaron 288
Spring, Benja. 288
Spring, Elisa 288
Spring, Sally 288
Springer, Ann 288
Springer, Catherine 288
Springer, Dennis 288
Springer, James 288
Springer, Jane 288
Springer, John 288
Springer, Robert 288
Springer, Sarah 288
Springer, Susan 288
Springer, Washington 288
Sprouse, George 9
Spurgen, John 32
Spurlock, J. A. 296
Spurlock, James A. 40, 54, 187, 196, 259, 296, 323-324, 340
Spurlock, Joseph 187
Squire, Solomon 288
St. John, D. 156
St. John, Daniel 179, 243, 300
Staark, Thomas 289
Stacy, Joseph 288
Staephen, Chappel Car 189
Stafford, Anna 288
Stafford, Archibald M. 289
Stafford, Author 205, 288
Stafford, Caroline 205, 288
Stafford, Elizabeth 344
Stafford, J. 4, 107
Stafford, James 205, 288, 344
Stafford, Jesse 93, 139, 144, 204, 235, 247, 315, 321
Stafford, John 90, 205, 288, 344
Stafford, Joseph 344
Stafford, Lorenza J. 344
Stafford, Lorinsa 344
Stafford, Marshall C. 205, 288
Stafford, Mary A. J. 205, 288
Stafford, Thos. J. 288
Staggs, Richard 101
Stair, John 7

Stair, William 289, 307
Stak, Zarubabul 289
Stalcup, A. B. 172, 270, 323, 299
Stallcup, Moses 137
Stallings, Carmah 289
Stallings, H. E. 289
Stallings, J. H. 289
Stallings, S. F. 289
Stallings, S. P. 289
Stallings, Sarah Ann 289
Stamps, Elijah 289, 344
Stamps, J. T. 63
Stamps, James 289, 344
Stamps, John 289
Stamps, Polly 289
Stamps, Sally 344
Stanfield, John 232
Stanley, John N. 289
Stanley, Matilda 20
Stanley, Moses 289
Stansbury, Thomas 289
Stanton, S. S. 180, 314
Stark, Rachel 289
Stark, Walter 289
Stark, Wm. 147
Stark, Zorabable 289
Starr, Caleb 167
Starrell, Sarah E. 289
Starrell, W. S. 289
Staten, Susan 289
Statt, Daniel S. 42
Statt, Lucinda 42
Stawell, W. S. 289
Steadman, Benjamin 289-290
Steadman, N. W. 241, 289
Steadman, Nathan W. 289-290
Steadman, Pleasent 290
Steadman, Robert 290
Steadman, Solly R. 290
Stedman, Benjamin 289
Steel, Price C. 37
Steel, William 33, 247, 267, 283, 300, 333,
Steele, C. D. 290
Steele, Carlos C. 98, 325
Steele, John P. 3, 30
Steele, Price C. 278
Steele, W. 67
Steele, William 205
Steele, Wilson 290
Stegal, L. 290
Stegal, Nancy W. 290
Stegall, B. F. 290
Stegall, Beverly C. 290
Stell, George W. 119
Stell, Jeremiah 119
Stephen [a slave] 94
Stephens, A. J. 18
Stephens, Edwin 290
Stephens, Hiram 290
Stephens, J. K. 97
Stephens, Jackson 18
Stephens, James K. 208, 272, 290

Stephens, John 290
Stephens Joseph 50, 71
Stephens, Josiah 290
Stephens, Lafayette 290
Stephens, Leander 290
Stephens, Lorenzo 290
Stephens, Margaret J. 290
Stephens, Martha 290
Stephens, Nancy 50, 71
Stephens, Noah 290
Stephens, Rebecca A. 290
Stephens, Sally 50, 71
Stephens, Solomon 290
Stephens, Tranquilla 290
Stephens, William 290
Stephens, Willie 290
Stephens, Wilson 50, 71
Stephenson, Daniel G. 221
Stephenson, Isaac T. 291
Stephenson, Jeremiah 126
Stephenson, John 291
Stephenson, Josiah 291
Stephenson, Moore 290-291, 306,
Stephenson, Sarah 291
Stephenson, William 149
Stetwell, Eleazer 155
Stetwell, Wm. O. 155
Stevens, A. M. 29, 291
Stevens, Alfred 291
Stevens, Charly 291
Stevens, Edmd. 293
Stevens, Fannie A. E. 291
Stevens, James 291
Stevens, John 290
Stevens, L. D. 290
Stevens, L. M. 287
Stevens, Mollie 291
Stevens, R. G. 291
Stevenson, E. 61
Stevenson, Edward 291
Stevenson, G. W. 2
Stevenson, George A. 291
Stevenson, James H. 291
Stevenson, John C. 291
Stevenson, Lydia 132
Stevenson, Moore 58
Stevenson, Richard E. 291
Stevenson, Sylva Ann 291
Stevenson, Thomas 132
Stevenson, W. C. 291
Steward, John 295
Steward, Joshua 295
Steward, Peggy 295
Steward, Saml. 295
Steward, William 291, 295
Stewart, Abner 10
Stewart, Andrew 200, 248
Stewart, Charles 291
Stewart, Cyntha 291
Stewart, Duncan 33, 291
Stewart, Elizabeth 291
Stewart, J. W. 315
Stewart, James 36, 123, 146, 291-292,
Stewart, John 291
Stewart, Martin 203

Stewart, Mary 200
Stewart, Reece C. 199, 291
Stewart, Saml. 291
Stigall, B. F. 290
Stigall, Harriet A. 290
Stigall, Mary L. 290
Stiles, Catharine 198
Stiles, Enoch 198
Stillman, John H. 291
Stilwell, Cordelia H. 115
Stilwell, Mary A. 63
Stinnett, Barberry 167, 292
Stinnett, James 292
Stitwell, Cordelia H. 63,115
Stitwell, Hannah R. 63
Stitwell, Harriet R. 115
Stitwell, Mary A. 63, 115
Stitwell, William H. 63, 115
Stockton, Isaac 143, 292
Stoddart, William 292
Stoddert, M. J. J. 272
Stofle, Betsy 292
Stofle, Eliz. 292
Stofle, John 159, 292
Stofle, Margaret 292
Stofle, Nancy 292
Stofle, Thomas 292
Stofle, Wm. 292
Stokes, Tennessee 292
Stone, Clack 94, 194
Stone, Coleman 94
Stone, H. B. 292
Stone, James N. 211, 293
Stone, Jesse 302
Stone, Joel H. 293
Stone, John 292, 317
Stone, Joshua R. 324
Stone, Lucy 293
Stone, Mary 80, 280, 292, 293
Stone, Nancy P. 293
Stone, Narcissa 324
Stone, Randolph 293
Stone, Richard W. 293
Stone, Robert 160
Stone, Samuel E. 24, 41, 293
Stone, Sarah 292, 293
Stone, Susannah 292
Stone, Temperence 108, 293
Stone, Thomas 292-293
Stone, William 1, 22, 25, 116, 157, 292-293
Stone, Willis S. 293
Stoneman, Callin C. 15
Stoneman, John M. 15
Storey, Anne 293
Storey, John 293
Storey, Thomas 293
Story, Ann 293
Story, John 293
Stothart, Mary 293
Stothart, Mathew 293
Stout, Aron 293
Stout, Benjamin C. 203. 293
Stout, Daniel 294

Stout, David 294
Stout, George 238, 294
Stout, Jane C. 294
Stout, Magdalin 294
Stout, Moses 265, 294
Stout, Samuel 188
Stovall, Burton L. 75
Strain, John 51
Stram, John 273
Strange, T. M. 170
Strange, Tom 297
Straton, Absalom 294
Straton, Francis M. 294
Straton, Hartwell 294
Straton, Mary 294
Straton, Permelia M. 294
Stratton, Hartwell 171
Stratton, Mary Ann 171
Stratton, Thomas 81
Stratton, Winifred 81
Strayhorn, J. K. 56, 214
Street, David 294
Street, Lucy 294
Street, Mary D. 294
Street, Sarah 294
Street, Thomas D. 294
Stricklin, John 294
Strickton, J. T. 231
Stringer, L. E. 121
Strodard, William 294
Strong, Joseph C. 189
Strother, James 147
Strother, John 294
Strother, Kemp 294
Strother, Samuel K. 294
Stuard, John 295
Stuart, Abraham 295
Stuart, Elijah 295
Stuart, Elizabeth 292
Stuart, James 40, 171, 183-184, 313
Stuart, John 98, 132, 295
Stuart, Robert 295
Stuart, William 295
Stubblefield, William L. 295
Stubblefield, George 174
Stubblefield, M. G. B. 295
Stubblefield, Thomas M. 295
Stubblefield, Tilman 295
Stubblefield, William L. 68
Studevant, John 106
Suage, Amanda J. 296
Sublett, G. A. 285
Sudburg, Susannah 295
Sueard, S. 219
Sugg, Aquilla 134, 295
Sugg, Coily 295
Sugg, E. G. 14, 95
Sugg, Henry H. 295
Sugg, Lemuel 40, 295
Sugg, Nehemiah 28
Sugg, Noah 134, 295
Sugg, Samuel 295, 331
Sugg, W. P. 15, 100, 291
Sugg, William 28
Suingley, A. S. 313

Sukey [a slave] 141
Sullens, William 296
Sullivan, Calvin 287
Sullivan, Fletcher 296
Sullivan, Jacob 277
Sullivan, James 287, 296
Sullivan, Jane F. 296
Sullivan, Mary A. 102, 296, 287
Sullivan, Peter 167
Sullivan, Polly 71, 296
Sullivan, Thomas L. 334
Summers, Abraham 296
Summers, Almeda 296
Summers, Ira 296
Summers, Jane 296
Summers, John 296
Summers, Margaret 296
Summers, Marion 296
Summers, Perry L. 296
Summers, R. E. 296
Summers, Rebecca 296
Sumner, Jethro 307
Sumpter, Thomas 316
Surrett, James D. 269
Sutherland, Elijah G. 287
Sutton, C. B. 296
Sutton, Elizabeth 86, 296
Sutton, John 164, 296, 325
Sutton, Mary A. 296
Sutton, Sophia F. 296
Sutton, William 296, 325
Swain, William M. 230
Swan, Henry 294
Swan, Saml. H. 105, 296
Swayne, Amanda J. 296
Swayne, J. W. 297
Swearingin, Adalin 297
Swearingin, Eliza 297
Swearingin Elizabeth 131, 297
Swearingin, Hannah 297
Swearingin, Hariet 297
Swearingin Hugh 131
Swearingin, John 297
Swearingin, Maranda 297
Swearingin, Martha 297
Swearingin, Nancy K. 297
Swearingin, Pleasant 297
Swearingin, Rebecca 297
Swearingin, Samuel 297
Swearingin, Thomas 297
Swearington, Eli 282
Sweat, Robert 116
Sweaza, Henry 121
Sweaza, Jonas 121
Sweaza, Larkin D. 121
Sweaza, Matthias 121
Sweaza, Pharis 121
Sweet, Alexander 297
Sweet, Elizabeth 297
Sweezy, Lucinda 129
Swengley, George 194
Swezea, Elizabeth 128
Swezea, Larken D. 128
Swift, Anthony 297
Swift, Flower 297

Swift, Jacob W. 297
Swift, Milly 297
Swift, Thomas W. 297
Swift, William 85
Swift, Willis 297
Swindle, Barbara 133
Swindle, Thomas 133
Swiney, Albert A. 297
Swiney, Augusta 297
Swiney, Charlotte 297
Swiney, John 297
Swiney, Mary Ann 297
Swiney, Nancy N. 297
Swiney, Sarah Ann 297
Swingley, A. S. 62
Sykes, George 26
Sykes, Martha 26
Sykes, S. S. 329
Syndrey, William 297
Sypert, Lawrence 173, 286
Sypert, Sally 297
Sypert, Thomas 297, 340
Sypert, William 173, 297
Tagert, James 33, 185, 194, 230, 285, 323
Tah Clentah [an Indian] 201
Tah noo nah Kah [an Indian] 201
Tailey, Ann C. 297
Tailey, Irene 297
Tailey, Wm. B. 297
Talbert, James R. 54
Talbot, Almedia 85, 297
Talbot, Ann P. 85, 295
Talbot, Delia 85, 297
Talbot, Francis 85, 297
Talbot, James 85, 114, 238, 297
Talbot, Jno. H. 85
Talbot, Joseph H. 85, 297-298
Talbot, Mary 85, 297
Talbot, Mathew 76
Talbot, Ruth 85, 297
Talbott, Agness 298
Talbott, Catherine 298
Talbott, Eliza 298
Talbott, Elizabeth 298
Talbott, Emily 298
Talbott, Ephraim 298
Talbott, James 298
Talbott, Matthew 298
Talbott, Nancy 298
Talbott, Nathan 298
Talbott, Odell 298
Talbott, Rachel 298
Talbott, Sarah 298
Talbott, Thos. 298
Taliaferro, Baldwin D. 298
Taliaferro, John A. 298
Taliaferro, Martha 298
Taliaferro, Nerland 298
Taliaferro, Potts 298
Talley, George A. 298
Talley, J. N. 298
Talley, Jefferson D. 298
Talley, John 124, 298

Talley, Sarah 298
Talley, William E. 298
Talley, Zachariah T. 298
Talliaferro, Charles C. 120
Tally, Adair 298
Tally, Betsey 298, 322
Tally, Betty 298
Tally, Coleman 298
Tally, Daniel 298
Tally, Elizabeth 298
Tally, Frances 298
Tally, Hannah 298, 322
Tally, Martin 15, 20, 49
Tally, Patsy 298
Tally, Spencer 298, 322
Tally, William 298, 322
Tamer, Elijah 271
Tancil, Nancy 103
Tankersley, Richd. 48
Tanner, Buford 310
Tansil, Lee 219
Taren, Benjamin 10
Tarkington, J. W. 134
Tarkington, W. D. 298
Tarley, Wm. B. 297
Tarpley, James 281
Tarver, Benja. 299
Tarver, Thos. D. 299
Tarver, William 124
Tasley, Wm. B. 297
Tate, Robert 246
Tate, Samuel 122, 223, 246
Tatom, Absalom 299
Tatom, Asa 299
Tatom, Bernard 299
Tatum, Ann A. 268
Tatum, James 272
Tatum, N. P. 27, 31, 147, 318
Tatum, Nat. P. 159, 185
Tatum, W. M. 252, 280, 299
Tawn, Benjamin 10
Taylor, Absalom 299
Taylor, Andrew 76, 299-300
Taylor, Any D. 300
Taylor, Caroline 83, 299
Taylor, Christopher 226, 254
Taylor, Coffield 235
Taylor, Cora 299
Taylor, David 299, 331
Taylor, E. A. 208, 299
Taylor, E. C. 304
Taylor, E. R. 344
Taylor, Edmund 4
Taylor, Edward C. 300
Taylor, Effie 299
Taylor, Elijah A. 300
Taylor, Elisha 272
Taylor, Elizabeth 147, 299
Taylor, Elvis 146
Taylor, Elzij. 299
Taylor, Elzy 299
Taylor, F. C. 299
Taylor, Fanny T. 300
Taylor, Fletcher 300
Taylor, Francis C. 299
Taylor, Frederick 299

Taylor, G. W. 274, 299-300
Taylor, H. 300
Taylor, Isaac 76, 231, 299-300
Taylor, Israel 300
Taylor, James 51, 299-300
Taylor, Jane 123, 156, 300, 333
Taylor, Jincy 299
Taylor, Jno. W. 223, 299-300
Taylor, L. J. 299
Taylor, Leban 300
Taylor, Leeroy 334
Taylor, Lenox 56
Taylor, Leonard W. 300
Taylor, Leroy 266
Taylor, Lydia 231
Taylor, M. 29
Taylor, Margaret A. 299
Taylor, Mary 91, 220, 300
Taylor, Mollie 299, 316
Taylor, Noah 300
Taylor, P. S. 239, 287
Taylor, Perry 333
Taylor, Pleasant 18, 279
Taylor, Polly 191
Taylor, Rebecca 235
Taylor, Ruthy 200
Taylor, Susanah 299
Taylor, Thomas 124, 300
Taylor, Thornton J. 299
Taylor, Timothy 265
Taylor, V. M. L. 318
Taylor, William 12, 200, 244, 270, 274, 288, 300, 316
Teague, Bedford L. 82
Teague, Catherine 82
Teague, Joshua 82
Teague, Rebecca H. 82
Teague, Wm. G. 82
Tealer, Samuel L. 300
Teasdale, Edward 79
Teater, Samuel L. 300
Teatin, Sally 300
Teatin, Samuel L. 300
Tedlock, John 338
Teel, Peter, 35
Teel, Sarah 35
Telford, Elizabeth 305
Telford, Hugh 305
Telford, Thomas C. 305
Tellers, Howell 301
Tellers, Thomas 301
Telly, Hailey 301
Temple, Charles 66
Temple, Dempsey P. 301
Temple, Elizabeth 301
Temple, Hannah 301
Temple, Jane 301
Temple, L. C. 301
Temple, Leonard C. 301
Temple, Mary 301
Temple, Robt. H. 301
Temple, William P. 301
Templeton, James A. 136
Templeton, Richard F. 2

Templeton, S. A. 2
Templin, John 106
Tener, George A. 125
Tennin, Alexander 301
Tennin, Mary 301
Tennison, John 301
Terrell, William 92, 178, 301, 345,
Terril, Barbara 76
Terril, George W. 76
Terrill, Bluford 169
Terrill, Epperson 301
Terrill, James W. 301
Terrill, Jeremiah 147
Terry, Elizabeth 301
Terry, J. Carroll 261
Terry, James 322
Terry, Jerry 163
Terry, John 301
Terry, Matilda A. 101, 301
Terry, Nancy 301
Terry, Pleasant A. 101, 301
Terry, Sarah 301
Terry, William 54, 335
Thaxton, Aletha A. 302
Thaxton, B. B. 110
Thaxton, Henry B. 302
Thaxton, John B. 302
Thaxton, Mary C. 302
Thaxton, Matilda 302
Thomas [a slave] 293
Thomas, Anderson 32
Thomas, Andrew 302
Thomas, Archibald R. 253
Thomas, B. L. 143, 193
Thomas, B. S. 236, 256
Thomas, Catharine 302
Thomas, D. 302
Thomas, D. B. 264
Thomas, Davey B. 332
Thomas, David 248
Thomas, Dicey 302
Thomas, Elizabeth 302
Thomas, George 194
Thomas, J. N. 120
Thomas, Jacob 15
Thomas, James 44, 302, 314
Thomas, Jefferson A. 148, 314
Thomas, John 63, 155
Thomas, Joseph 302
Thomas, Josiah 188
Thomas, M. P. 44
Thomas, Michael 302
Thomas, Peggy 302
Thomas, Phelimon 302
Thomas, Polly 302
Thomas, Rachel 302
Thomas, Richard 302
Thomas, Seth 79
Thomas, Susan 227
Thomas, W. A. 302
Thomas, William 38, 70, 124, 188, 250, 302
Thomas, Wilson 302
Thomas, Zubee 303

Thomason, Joseph 313
Thomason, Mark 4
Thompson, Alfred 303
Thompson, Allas 202, 303
Thompson, Allen C. 304
Thompson, Andrew 171, 303
Thompson, Anny 303
Thompson, Asa 169
Thompson, Calvin 67, 303
Thompson, David 33, 282, 303
Thompson, Eleaner C. 303
Thompson, Elizabeth 101, 111, 303-304
Thompson, Frank 303
Thompson, Goodwin 303
Thompson, Green B. 304
Thompson, J. M. 178
Thompson, James 295, 303,
Thompson, Jason H. 101
Thompson, John 27, 64, 111, 168, 303
Thompson, Joseph 29, 69, 253, 303
Thompson, Laura 303
Thompson, Martha A. 303
Thompson, Mary 303-304
Thompson, Masten 303
Thompson, Millard 304
Thompson, Nancy Ann 303
Thompson, Nancy M. 304
Thompson, Nathan W. 303
Thompson, Newcomb 29, 72, 303
Thompson, Newsom 264
Thompson, Newton C. 303
Thompson, Philip J. 213
Thompson, Prudence 304
Thompson, Rachel 303
Thompson, Reuben 303
Thompson, Robert 304
Thompson, S. 280
Thompson, Samuel 29, 264, 304
Thompson, Sarah 303
Thompson, Squire L.157
Thompson, Susan 304
Thompson, Thomas 124, 290, 304
Thompson, Violet 303
Thompson, W. P. 56
Thompson, William 64, 303-304,
Thorn, David 304
Thorn, Martin 35, 304
Thorn, Thomas A. 35, 304
Thornburg, Anna 304
Thornburg, Samuel 304
Thornton, Amelia 304-305
Thornton, Eliza 305
Thornton, Harriet 305
Thornton, Wm. 154
Thornton, Yancy 304-305
Throp, Harris D. 203
Thurman, J. P. 277

Thurman, Joseph 305
Thurman, Richard 305
Thurman, Wm. 315
Thurmond, J. P. 264
Thurmond, James A. 305
Thurmond, O. L. 305
Thurmond, Thomas 305
Thursbeys, Edward 305
Thweath, William 222
Tibets, John 299
Tidlock, John 226
Tidwell, Franklin B. 305
Tidwell, P. A. 305
Tidwell, W. M. 305
Tidwell, Wm. M. 118
Tigrett, A. B. 20, 305
Tilford, Hugh 286, 305
Tilford, Robert 305
Tillman, John 30, 33, 98, 301
Tillman, Nelly 305
Tilman, Daniel 16
Tilman, John 190
Tim [a slave] 63
Timberlake, John C. 305
Tims, John 305
Tims, Nathaniel 305
Tims, Vincen 305
Tinch, Anderson 239
Tinch, Andrew 210
Tinsley, G. B. 76, 105, 111, 134-135, 178, 317
Tippy, Abraham 49,
Tipton, Abraham 305-306
Tipton, B. F. 13, 45
Tipton, B. J. 57, 175, 264, 306
Tipton, B. T. 84
Tipton, Benjamin 45, 84, 175, 306
Tipton, Coln. 248
Tipton, Edmond 98
Tipton, J. D. B. 20
Tipton, Jacob 306
Tipton, John 232, 305-306, 344
Tipton, Jonathan 215
Tipton, Joseph 76, 78, 232, 306
Tipton, R. M. 208
Tipton, Samuel 305-306
Tipton, W. P. 306
Tirrell, Wm. 301
Tisdale, James 306
Tisdell, Edward 306
Tisdell, Piety 306
Todd, Geo. 155
Todd, J. R. 103
Todd, Jas. 85
Todd, Jno. 29, 85, 116
Todd, Jo. R. 3
Tolbert, James N. 54
Tolbert, James R. 19, 71, 180, 306
Tolbert, Sarah 306
Tolbert, Thomas 306
Toler, Jesse 224

Toler, Peggy 224
Toliver, Zachariah 306
Tollis, J. J. 319
Tom [a slave] 232, 269
Tombleson, Lewis 338
Tomlin, Cornelia A.193
Tomlin, Geo. M. 193
Tomlin, Georgaretta 184
Tomlin, J. W. 195, 306
Tomlin, James W. 109, 195, 306, 307
Tomlin, Jno. L. H. 27, 42, 65, 73, 251, 328
Tomlin, Martha 195
Tomlin, Penelope 306-307
Tomlinson, George 307
Tomlinson, Georgia 307
Tomlinson, Hannah 78
Tomlinson, James 307
Tomlinson, John 65, 78, 159
Tomlinson, Thomas 78, 307
Tomlinson, William 65, 78
Tomlinson, Wyatt, 307
Toomey, James 48, 140, 143-144
Torrey, Elijah 276
Totem, Joseph H. 258
Totem, Sarah 258
Totten, A. W. O. 30
Totten, Archibald W. O. 19
Totten, Benjamin C. 30
Totten, James L. 19
Townly, Redferren 157
Townsend, R. W. 270
Townsend, Robt. 250
Trammel, Isabella 307
Trammel, Philip 307
Trammel, Sampson 307
Trap, Emeline 307
Trap, Mourning 307
Trapt, Emeline 307
Travarse, Mary 153
Travarse, Samuel 153
Travis, David C. 17, 136,
Travsue, B. F. 269
Tregg, Manson 248
Trent, J. W. 311
Trice, James A. 251
Trice, William 251
Trigg, Daniel 249
Trimble, James 11, 88
Trimble, William 307
Triplett, John 307
Trontham, Benj. 307
Troter, John S. 212
Trott, Enoch 111
Trotter, A. A. 224
Trotter, A. R. 332
Trotter, Alexander 307
Trotter, Amos R. 219
Trotter, Isaac 43, 228
Trotter, Isabella 307
Trotter, J. A. 228
Trotter, J. L. 144
Trotter, J. T. 140
Trotter, James 303, 307

Trotter, Jane 307
Trotter, John 38, 46, 68, 129, 171, 182, 223, 234, 307, 321-322, 326,
Trotter, Joseph 307
Trotter, W. H. 43-44, 187
Trotter, William H. 43-44, 302, 307
Troy, J. P. 111
Troy, W. E. 111
Truesdale, Jno. N 308
Truett, Elijah 163
Trundle, Ann E. 308
Trundle, Danl. L. 308
Trundle, David L. 308
Trundle, Ellen 308
Trundle, James 308
Trundle, John W. 308
Trundle, Rebecca 308
Trundle, William 308
Trundle, Wilson L. 308
Trundle, Winfield S. 308
Tubb, Darcus 308
Tubb, James 308
Tubb, Thomas 308
Tuck, Ann 314
Tuck, Edward B. 314
Tucker, Abigale 308
Tucker, Allen 308
Tucker, Benjamin 1, 37, 319
Tucker, Betsy 309
Tucker, Betty 309
Tucker, Elisabeth 137, 262, 308-309,
Tucker, Enoch 97, 237, 308-309
Tucker, Etta 309
Tucker, Gabriel 185, 308
Tucker, Garrett 308
Tucker, Hannah 82, 309
Tucker, Henry 237, 308-309
Tucker, J. G. 309, 345
Tucker, James 308
Tucker, Jane 97, 308
Tucker, Jeremiah 125, 263, 286, 308
Tucker, Jessee P. 137
Tucker, John 82, 136, 156, 200, 222, 237, 308-309
Tucker, Kendrick 308
Tucker, Keziah 309
Tucker, M. W. 309
Tucker, Mary 136
Tucker, Matilda H. 185, 308
Tucker, Nancy 222, 309
Tucker, Patsy 308
Tucker, Pattie 309
Tucker, Peggy 309
Tucker, Phoebe 200, 309
Tucker, Rebecca 308
Tucker, Richard W. 309
Tucker, Riggs 237, 309
Tucker, Rips 309
Tucker, Sally 309
Tucker, Saml. 262, 308-310
Tucker, Sarah 309
Tucker, Silas 166, 308-309

Tucker, W. H. 48
Tucker, William 149, 200, 213, 262, 310
Tullock, John V. 310
Tumblin, Susannah 310
Tumblin, William 310
Tuming, Alexander 301
Tummins, Samuel 111
Tunes, Ira 310
Tunes, Jane 310
Tunes, John 310
Tunes, Nancy 310
Tunes, Wesley 310
Tunes, William 310
Tunis, Angelina 310
Tunis, Ira 310
Tunis, John 310
Tunis, Wesley 310
Tunstall, James 68, 162
Turbott, James 40
Turley, William B. 310
Turnage, Solon 310
Turner [a slave] 141
Turner, Adam 310
Turner, Andrew J. 333
Turner, Benjamin 310
Turner, Buford 310
Turner, Daniel 310
Turner, Elijah 271
Turner, Jack E. 68
Turner, James 26, 48, 310, 328
Turner, Jasper 310
Turner, John 310
Turner, Robert 310
Turner, Susan 26
Turner, William 276, 310-311
Turney, H. L. W. 222, 274
Turney, Peter 118
Turney, Samuel 18, 211, 330
Turnham, Pinkney 252
Turnley, James A. 81, 159
Turpin, Nathan 311
Turpin, Thomas 311
Turrentine, Della 311
Turrentine, Emma J. 311
Turrentine, J. F. 311
Turrentine, Joanna 311
Turrentine, W. F. 311
Turrentine, William 303
Tweedy, Jo. 311
Tylar, John 164
Tyrone, Adam 57
Tyrrell, Wm. 164
Tysen, Edwin 311
Tysen, Fannie 311
Tysen, Lydia 311
Tysen, Margaret 311
Tysen, William 311
Tyson, Archibald 311
Tyson, E. 311
Tyson, Edwin 116
Tyson, Fannie 311
Tyson, J. B. 311
Tyson, John 116, 311

Tyson, Johnson B. 116
Tyson, Lydian Ann 311
Tyson, Mary Jane 311
Umstead, Elizabeth 200
Umstead, John 139, 200, 258
Umstead, Susanna 139
Underdown, G. W. 12, 311
Underdown, Stephen A. 311
Underdown, W. R. 311
Underwood, Enoch 317
Underwood, George 311
Underwood, I. N. 317
Underwood, J. N. 139
Underwood, Jesse C. 311
Underwood, Joel 298, 311-312, 317
Underwood, John 208, 311-312, 317
Underwood, Lewis 312
Underwood, Margaret 312
Underwood, Mary 317
Underwood, Rachel 298
Underwood, Thomas 70
Underwoood, I. N. 311
Ursery, Lucy 312
Utinger, Philip 16
Utley, Leonidas 315
Uzzle, Isom 211, 231, 249
Vaccaro, A. 307
Vaden, Geo. 195
Vaden, Leoderick 312
Vaden, Mary C. 195
Vaden, Saml. T. 312
Vaden, Theoderic 312
Vail, E. 312
Vail, Emma 312
Vail, I. N. 312
Vail, Isaac N. 312
Vail, R. H. 312
Vail, Roan H. 312
Vail, W. C. 312
Valux, Jas. 101
Vanbebber, Elender 312
Vanbebber, Isaac 64
Vanbebber, Jacob 312
Vanbebber, John 312
Vanbebber, Peter 312
Vance, Alexr. 312
Vance, Lewis R. 67, 198, 247
Vance, William 28, 312
Vanderpool, Abraham 312
Vanderpool, Rebecca 312
Vandike, Catherine 312
Vandike, Malina C. 313
Vandike, Mary 312-313
Vanhearer, Valentine 121
Vanhook, Aaron 313
VanHooser, Zacharean 247
Vanhousen, Valuntine 284
Vann, John 313
Vann, Valentine S. 195
Vannerson, Albert 313
Vannerson, Alford 313
Vannerson, Elizabeth 313

Vannerson, Francis 313
Vannerson, William 313
Vannuson, Catherine 313
Vannuson, Thomas 313
Vannuson, William 313
Vanuson, Elizabeth 313
Vanzant, John 313
Vanzant, Josuha 313
Varett, Micajah 16
Varnor, Nehemiah 309
Vater, Wm. 302
Vaughen, Archellas 13
Vaughn, Campbell 29
Vaughn, Cora 29
Vaughn, Edward 256, 313
Vaughn, George 29
Vaughn, Hays W. 27
Vaughn, James M. 29
Vaughn, Joel 104, 301
Vaughn, John 29, 313
Vaughn, Molly T. 313
Vaughn, Richd. 313
Vaughn, Sarah F. 27
Vaughn, Thomas 29, 313
Vaughn, William 29
Vaught, John 205, 287
Vaulx, James 29
Vaulx, Kate C. 29
Venit, John 287
Venters, John S. 313
Venters, Sarah 313
Via, M. R. 112
Via, M. V. 112
Vick, Samuel 179
Vick, Sarah 225, 266
Vincent, Abner 342
Vincent, John 6, 8, 313
Vincent, Sarah A. 8, 313
Vincent, Susan P. W. 342
Vincent, Thomas S. 313
Vinsen, James 314
Vinson, Hamilton 314
Vinson, Henry 314
Vinson, Isabella P. 314
Vinson, James 41, 239, 314
Vinson, John 314
Vinson, Jonas 314
Vinson, Martha 314
Vinson, Sally 314
Vinson, Sarah 314
Vinson, Silas 2, 304
Vinson, William 43, 314
Vinson, Wm. M. 314
Violet [a slave] 342
Viverett, Lanslot 79
Viverett, Micajah 79, 314
Vivret, James 314
Vivret, Micajah 314
Vivret, Thomas 314
Vougtt, David 84
Waddell, Charles 49, 314
Waddell, Jas. 129
Waddell, Jno. 34
Waddell, Phillip 129
Waddell, S. G. 314
Waddell, S. Q. 314
Waddie, Ann 314
Waddie, John William 314
Waddie, Joseph K. 314
Waddie, William K. 314
Waddill, Seth Q. 269
Waddy, Samuel 169
Wade, Charles 196
Wade, Edward 72
Wade, George 74, 145, 195, 198, 265, 271, 287,
Wade, Hampton 238, 314
Wade, Hannah 314
Wade, James 315
Wade, John 314, 315
Wade, Lam 314
Wade, Marmaduke 314
Wade, Martin F. 314
Wade, Mary 314
Wade, Michael 314
Wade, Milly 314
Wade, Miranda 315
Wade, Polly 196
Wade, Robert 238, 314
Wade, Stephen P. 315
Wade, Wm. S.314
Wadley, Samuel 119
Wagginer, William A. 247
Waggoman, S. F. 338
Waggoner, David 205
Waggoner, Geo. 315
Waggoner, Mary 315
Waggoner, Matthias 205, 287
Waggoner, Stephen 315
Wagster, Jane 275
Wagster, Sarah Jane 274
Wagster, Wm. C. 275
Waite, Gordentice 189
Waite, Robert 189
Waite, William 189
Waits, D. S. 315
Wakefield, Charles 315
Wakefield, Henry 315
Wakefield, John 315
Wakefield, Malissa F. 248
Wakefield, William J. W. 248
Waldin, Terry 136
Waldran, James 170
Waldran, Jesse 315
Waldran, Sally 315
Waldren, Jas. W. 169
Waldron, Rebecca 315
Walker, Agness 315
Walker, Betsy 255
Walker, Cora 208
Walker, David 315
Walker, Drucilla 211, 212
Walker, Elizabeth 141, 315
Walker, Enoch L. 209
Walker, Ephraim 209, 255
Walker, George 315
Walker, Harbert 92
Walker, Inman 91
Walker, James 13, 55, 117, 159, 163, 265, 315
Walker, Joel S. 97
Walker, John 11, 66, 218, 235, 315-316,
Walker, Joseph 315
Walker, Kennan 316
Walker, L. T. 316
Walker, Lee 316
Walker, M. A. 315
Walker, M. F. 30
Walker, Malissa C. 316
Walker, Mary 26
Walker, Matthew 316
Walker, P. A. 208
Walker, P. C. 316
Walker, Peggy 235
Walker, Peter 139, 211-212, 316
Walker, Polly 316
Walker, Reuben 255
Walker, Robert 316
Walker, Samuel 30, 316
Walker, Sarah M. 129
Walker, Susannah 255
Walker, W. H. 179
Walker, William 143, 188, 315-316, 322
Wall, E. 316
Wall, Edward 317
Wall, Harriet 245
Wall, Joanna 317
Wall, John 245
Wall, Nancy 317
Wall, W. J. 289
Wallace, Hugh 227
Wallace, Joshua 243
Wallace, Nelly 157
Walldrope, Richard 317
Wallen, Edward 105
Wallen, Elisha 317
Wallen, John 46, 174, 317
Wallen, Thomas 72
Waller, Edmond 47
Waller, Josephine 7-8
Waller, Richard 7, 85
Wallis, Samuel 317
Wallis, Thomas 4
Walls, Edward 316
Walsh, George T. 17
Walton, Chloe 60
Walton, Jesse 26
Walton, Josiah 224
Walton, Martin 60, 71, 242
Walton, Stephen 179
Walton, Steve 317
Wamack, Elijah 202, 235
Wamack, Richard 202
Wammack, Elizabeth 235, 317
Wammock, John 248
Wamock, Richard 317
Ward, Bryan 317
Ward, Dempsey 317
Ward, Edward 166
Ward, J. E. 317
Ward, J. L. 323, 238
Ward, J. S. 318
Ward, Jabah 318
Ward, James 317-318
Ward, John 114, 317
Ward, Jonathan 317

Ward, Juba 318
Ward, Lucy C. 266
Ward, M. 318
Ward, Margarette F. 318
Ward, Mary H. 318
Ward, Mc. 318
Ward, Milly 114
Ward, R. M. 258, 318
Ward, Samuel 318
Ward, Spencer 317
Ward, Spions 318
Ward, Wm. 40, 135
Warden, N. C. 221
Warlick, David 318
Warlick, Emeline C. 318
Warlick, Francis E. 318
Warlick, James P. 318
Warlick, Jno. N. 318
Warlick, Laura Ann 318
Warlick, Nancy 318
Warlick, Philip 318
Warlick, Synthia J. 318
Warner, Eunice 318
Warner, Richard 296, 323, 327
Warner, S. A. 233
Warner, Samuel A. 74, 282, 318
Warner, William D. 318
Warnick, James 318
Warnick, Rhody 11
Warnick, Robert 318
Warnock, Hyram 4
Warren, Alfred 318
Warren, Alice 318
Warren, Ball E. 96
Warren, Booth M. 96
Warren, Collin 118
Warren, Jacob 318-319
Warren, James 13, 96, 318
Warren, Jesse 17, 318
Warren, John 318
Warren, Jos. 318
Warren, Lucrisha 318
Warren, M. P. 221
Warren, Mariah 319
Warren, Martha 318
Warren, Milly 318
Warren, N. C. 221
Warren, Nancy 318
Warren, Polly 96
Warren, Rebecca Ann 96
Warren, Richard L. 96
Warren, Robert R. 96
Warren, Sally 318
Warren, Simon 319
Warren, William S. 319
Warring, Elice 319
Warring, John 319
Washburn, B. B. 33, 238, 296
Washburn, Ben N. 296
Washburn, Benjamin B. 180, 245, 296, 313, 323, 344
Washburn, Lafayette 245
Washington, Gray 319

Washington, Joseph 58, 92, 296, 319
Washington, Nancy H. 319
Wason, Abner 92, 319
Wassom, Andrew 157, 322
Wassom, Harriet N. 157
Wassom, Hester 157
Wassom, Rebecca 157
Wasson, Abner 230
Wasson, Archibald 319
Watkins, B. B. 102, 319
Watkins, Catherine 166
Watkins, Ellen 82
Watkins, Henry 3, 319
Watkins, Ida 82
Watkins, Irvin 82
Watkins, John 319
Watkins, Lilia 82
Watkins, Malvina H. 82
Watkins, Martha 82
Watkins, Richard 166, 319
Watkins, W. L. 159, 208
Watkins, W. M. 64, 141, 203, 239-240, 273, 298, 316
Watkins, William 120
Watkins, Zach G. 298
Watson, A. J. 319-320
Watson, Christopher 319-320
Watson, Elias 319
Watson, Ella 166
Watson, Green B. 275
Watson, I. A. 319-320
Watson, J. E. 320
Watson, J. H. 265, 273, 320
Watson, Jessee 115
Watson, John E. 319-320
Watson, Joseph 165, 320
Watson, Josiah 225
Watson M. B. 320
Watson, Mary 320
Watson, Nancy 319
Watson, Obediah 320
Watson, Patsy 228
Watson, R. R. 88, 109, 264, 273
Watson, S. A. 320
Watson, S. P. 228
Watson, Samuel 228
Watson, Sarah 319
Watson, Sarah B. 305
Watson, T. W. 320
Watson, Thomas 260
Watson, William 21, 35, 118, 159, 230, 305
Watt, James N. 320
Watts, Dubetre 201
Watts, Elizabeth 342
Watts, Forked Tail 201
Watts, Frederick 342
Watts, Jeremiah 103
Watts, John Mink 201
Watts, Nelley 201
Wayland, Lewis 41, 70, 84, 320
Wayland, Wm. 57, 80, 145, 198, 320

Weakley, D. C. 320
Wear, John 234, 320
Wear, Joseph 320
Wear, Mary 320
Wear, P. M. 320
Weatherford, John 313
Weatherford, Spicy 320
Weatherly, J. 321
Weatherly, James 336
Weatherly, Washington 321
Weathers, Radford 195
Weaver, Saml. 321
Weaver, W. S. 299
Weaver, William 150, 236
Webb, A. F. 321
Webb, Bain 212
Webb, Berry 321
Webb, George 321
Webb, H. H. 121
Webb, Isiah 42
Webb, J. L. 45, 133
Webb, Jackson 321
Webb, James 87, 321
Webb, Jesse 321
Webb, John 56, 86, 309, 321
Webb, Joseph H. 93
Webb, Lucinda 321
Webb, Lucretia 93
Webb, Mahulda J. 321
Webb, Maranda 321
Webb, Mary 93, 269, 321
Webb, Matilda 321
Webb, Nancy 93
Webb, [no name] 230
Webb, Rebecca 301, 321
Webb, Ross 321
Webb, Stephen T. 93
Webb, Tempy F. 321
Webb, Theoderick 93
Webb, Wm. 269, 301, 322
Webb, Woodson 34
Webster, Jonathan 206,
Weir, John 183
Weir, Saml. 183
Weisinger, M. E. 26
Welch, Almira 322
Welch, George 322
Welch, H. A. 224
Welch, Henry A. 97, 130
Welch, Jesse 322
Welch, Jno. 181, 322
Welch, Mary 181
Welker, William B. 322
Well, Mitch. 322
Wellis, Plummer 231
Wellmore, Emsley 239
Wellmore, Ensley 121
Wells, Barna B. 322
Wells, Benjamin 51, 118, 133, 242, 322, 341
Wells, Catharine 322
Wells, Ellison 322
Wells, George 322
Wells, Jane 322
Wells, Jeff 322
Wells, John 303

Wells, Lewis 9, 262
Wells, Luticia 322
Wells, Malinda 322
Wells, Martin 28, 33, 47
Wells, Nancy 70, 322
Wells, Saml. 156
Wells, Thos. 114
Wells, William 39
Wesford, Benja 11
Wesley, Ann 259
Wesley, Joseph R. 55
Wesson, William 170, 297
West, George 87, 96, 162, 231
West, John 322
West, Robert 96
Westbrook, Henry J. P. 9, 135
Westbrooks, J. R. 314
Westfall, Abel 322
Weston, Elisabeth 323
Weston, Jesse 323
Wetherspoon, John 25
Wetherspoon, William 284
Whaley, William 228
Whaly, Isham H. 323
Whaly, John 62
Whaly, West O. 323
Wheeler, Agness 206
Wheeler, Dunnerson 323
Wheeler, Edward 323
Wheeler, George H. 323
Wheeler, Hopkins 323
Wheeler, Lemuel 323
Wheeler, Lucinda 323
Wheeler, Minerva 323
Wheeler, Nathan 323
Wheeler, Paralee E. 323
Wheeler, Peyton 323
Wheeler, Polly 323
Wheeler, Rachel 323
Wheeler, Sally 323
Wheeler, Silas 138
Wheeler, Wm. T. 323
Whellton, Edward B. 198
Whershaw, Matilda 86
Whidiker, Elizabeth 258
Whirter, George M. 324
Whitaker, Elizabeth 244, 258
White, A. A. 323
White, A. H. 323
White, Aron 323
White, Arthur C. 325
White, B. F. 323
White, Ben C. 121, 161,
White, Benjamin 161, 186, 323-324, 336
White, Bryant 172, 323
White, C. E. 170, 323
White, Charles 323
White, Coleman 5-6, 324-325,
White, Cynthia 324
White, David C. 323
White, E. H. 13, 324
White, Ed 64

White, Elijah 118
White, Eliza 323
White, Elizabeth 324-325
White, Eunice B. 325
White, F. J. 323
White, George 245, 323-325
White, Gillem 324
White, Isaac R. 323
White, J. 205
White, Jeremiah 324
White, John 185, 262, 324-325
White, Joshua 157
White, L. C. 201
White, Margaret 324
White, Mary 251, 323-325
White, Matthew 324
White, N. C. 193
White, P. D. 324
White, Polly 186
White, Rachael C. 325
White, Reuben 118
White, Richard 122, 185
White, Robert 179, 323-325
White, Stewart 324
White, Theodore 325
White, Thomas 325, 330
White, W. A. 324
White, W. V. 324
White, William 128, 291, 305, 324-325
White, Willis 118
White, Zacharias 325
Whited, Robert 109, 325
Whitehead, Mansfield 81, 100
Whitehead, Robert 68, 325
Whitehead, William 53
Whitelaw, Jno. T. 65
Whitelaw, Louisa 65
Whitelaw, Mariah L. 65
Whiteside, Thomas C. 30, 244, 264
Whitfield, Ansel 282, 306
Whitford, Willis 47, 124
Whithead, Robert 162
Whithead, Thomas 292
Whithead, William 162
Whitlock, Nancy 320
Whitlock, Thomas 325
Whitlock, William 325
Whitlow, Henry 201
Whitlow, Lucy 201
Whitlow, Nathan H. 336
Whitman, Edward 288
Whitney, James G. 147, 325
Whitney, Martha 325
Whitney, Thos. P. 325
Whitsell, George W. 266
Whitsell, Mary Deltha 266
Whitsell, Michael 325
Whitsett, Michael 251
Whitson, Abram 326
Whitson, Charles 329
Whitson, Jesse 84
Whitson, Thomas 243

Whitson, William 227, 325-326, 329
Whitten, S. D. 326
Whittenten, M. 326
Whittenton, N. A. 326
Whitthome, William J. 36, 115
Whittington, Hannah 116
Whittington, James 326
Whittington, John 326
Whittington, Kitturah 326
Whittington, Merritt 326
Whittington, N. A. 116, 164, 326
Whittington, Othnel 326
Whittington, Quintithan 326
Whittington, Solomon 326
Whittinton, Ethneal 326
Whittinton, James 326
Whittinton, Kiturah 326
Whittinton, Taletha 326
Whittle, John 326
Whittle, Mary 326
Whittle, O. M. 326
Whittle, R. K. 320, 326
Whitton, Nancy R. 198
Whitworth, Alfred E. 149
Whitworth, James 84
Whitworth, Jane 101
Whitworth, P. W. 197
Whitworth, Rachael 197
Whitworth, Thos. E. 149
Whorley, Cynthia 36, 326
Whorley, Joel 36, 326
Wicks, Nock 339
Widner, J. H. 326
Widner, Jacob 326
Widner, Martha Jane 326
Wier, James 49
Wier, Jno. P. 325
Wiggins, William 111
Wiggs, Martin 181
Wilbourn, Larinda 10
Wiley, John 326
Wiley, L. P. 21
Wilhelm, Jno. 332
Wilhoit, Emily 327
Wilhoit, Jacob. 326-327
Wilhoit, Jane 327
Wilhoit, Pearce 327
Wilhoit, Polly 327
Wilhoit, Price 327
Wilhoit, Willey 327
Wilhoit, William 327
Wilhoit, Willis W. 262
Wilhoite, Hetty 42
Wilhoite, Pearce 135
Wilkens, M. E. 327
Wilkerson, John 74, 327
Wilkerson, Purdy 327
Wilkins, Archie 327
Wilkins, Catherine 327
Wilkins, Emerson 327
Wilkins, Emme E. 327
Wilkins, Feriby 327
Wilkins, Ivy 327
Wilkins, John A. 212, 327

Wilkins, Josephine 327
Wilkins, Lucy Bell 327
Wilkins, Mary 327
Wilkins, Penn 327
Wilkins, William P. 327
Wilkinson, Melvin H. 328
Wilkinson, William 328
Wilkinson, Wyatt 70
Will [a slave] 341
Willard, James 209, 254, 328
Willard, P. 328
Willard, William 328
Willfrong, George 1
Willhite, Coonrod 34
Williams, A. J. 23, 25
Williams, Abeker 331
Williams, Abel 23, 328
Williams, Airy A. 330
Williams, Alfred 330
Williams, Allen 328
Williams, Aml.? 22
Williams, Amos 56, 326, 328
Williams, Anderson 329
Williams, Ann 21
Williams, Anthony T. 329
Williams, Archibald 329
Williams, Ben B. 330
Williams, Benjamin 115, 151, 329
Williams, Betsey 329
Williams, Beverly 194, 306
Williams, Caleb 185, 285, 320
Williams, Catharine 106, 331
Williams, Cyrus A. 330
Williams, Daniel 330
Williams, Dorcas 86
Williams, Dudley 152, 204, 254
Williams, Edith 329
Williams, Edmd. 142, 241, 329
Williams, Elijah 9
Williams, Elisha 329
Williams, Elizabeth 328, 330-331
Williams, Emanuel 86
Williams, Ewel 150
Williams, Fedelia E. 328
Williams, Frances A. 328
Williams, Frederick S. 330
Williams, Geo. 328-330, 289
Williams, Griffith 329
Williams, Hannah 330
Williams, Harbert W. 328
Williams, Harwin 329
Williams, Henry 329
Williams, Hugh 223, 332
Williams, Isaac 329
Williams, J. H. 328
Williams, Jacob 330
Williams, James 16, 145, 147, 198, 291, 328, 330-331
Williams, Jane 330
Williams, Jannett E. 329

Williams, Jemmima E. 329
Williams, Jesse 268
Williams, Jessee E. 330
Williams, Joanah 329
Williams, John 62, 71-72, 77, 139, 159, 229, 275-276, 281, 284-285, 316, 328-331
Williams, Joseph 72, 139, 178, 181, 269, 330-331
Williams, Joshua 39, 63, 258, 329
Williams, Julia S. 330
Williams, Kiziah 77
Williams, L. M. 35, 92,110, 130, 134, 170, 191, 317
Williams, Lavina 330
Williams, Louis M. 93, 187
Williams, Louisa 331
Williams, Lucy J. 328
Williams, Margaret 21, 329, 331
Williams, Martha 330-331
Williams, Marthy An 328
Williams, Mary 28, 329-330
Williams, Matthew 331
Williams, Miriah 28
Williams, N. S. 67
Williams, Nancy 330-332, 329
Williams, Nathaniel 328
Williams, Neuten 328
Williams, Oliver 331
Williams, Paratt 21
Williams, Peggy 115, 329
Williams, Perry 331
Williams, Peter 16
Williams, Phillip 164, 330
Williams, R. C. 331
Williams, Rachael 329, 331
Williams, Ralph 331
Williams, Reuben 44
Williams, Rice 76, 331
Williams, Robert H. 329
Williams, S. M. 215
Williams, Sallie 328
Williams, Samuel 26, 267, 329
Williams Sandford N. 329
Williams, Sarah 21, 258, 330
Williams, Simon 331
Williams, Smithey J. 329
Williams, Thomas 41, 129-332
Williams, Viny 330
Williams, W. W. 215
Williams, Wilkins 291
Williams, William 147, 156, 178, 160, 331-332
Williams, Willouby 332
Williamson, David 223
Williamson, Elizabeth J. 223
Williamson, F. M. 221
Williamson, Geo. 241, 290, 332
Williamson, J. F. 10, 33, 170, 191, 231, 253, 314

Williamson, J. P. 288
Williamson, James 47, 332
Williamson, Jane 291
Williamson, Jesse F. 93
Williamson, John 261
Williamson, Johnson 223, 332
Williamson, L. M. 314
Williamson, Mary 332
Williamson, Rebecca C. 129
Williamson, Robert 16
Williamson, William R. 241
Williason, Hugh 332
Willie, William 17
Willis, Ed 180, 332
Willis, G. W. 332
Willis, Plummer 129, 241, 274
Willmore, Emsly 121
Wills, George 332
Wills, James 277
Wills, John 332
Wills, P. 332
Wills, William 332
Willson, Andrew 332
Willson, Henry 332
Willson, Jacob 332
Willson, Joseph 49
Willson, William 72, 332
Wilson, Adam T. 263
Wilson, Andrew 64, 262
Wilson, Benja. 246
Wilson, Betsey 333
Wilson, Calvin John 128
Wilson, Charles B. 173, 285
Wilson, David 62, 273
Wilson, Elizabeth B. 334
Wilson, Ephraim S. 121
Wilson, Ewing 241, 333
Wilson, Fanny 333
Wilson, George 333, 334
Wilson, Henry B. 269
Wilson, Hugh 333
Wilson, Israel 90
Wilson. Israil 333
Wilson, Jacob R. 333
Wilson, James 86, 217, 222, 333-335
Wilson, Jane 89
Wilson, Jaob 333
Wilson, Jason C. 333
Wilson, Jefferson 121
Wilson, John 60, 74, 191, 267, 333-335
Wilson, Jonathan 121, 334
Wilson, Joseph 333
Wilson, Katharine C. 335
Wilson, L. Sloan 128
Wilson, Lamuel 225
Wilson, Lucinda 334
Wilson, Lucy 334
Wilson, Martha 333
Wilson, Mary 333-335
Wilson, Mattw. 295
Wilson, Milley 62
Wilson, Nancy C. 333
Wilson, Narcissa J. 334

Wilson, P. E. 3, 100, 208, 343
Wilson, Parmelia F. 333-334
Wilson, Polly 333
Wilson, R. W. 334
Wilson, Rebecca 335
Wilson, Robert 89, 217, 332, 334-335
Wilson, Ruth C. 335
Wilson, Samuel 217, 334-335
Wilson, Sarah 333-334
Wilson, Solomon 121
Wilson, Thomas 94, 121, 280, 334-335
Wilson, Walter Sims 280
Wilson, Washington 333
Wilson, William 5-6, 59-60, 128, 299, 333-335
Wimberley, Joseph 74, 242
Wimberly, George L. 222
Wimberly, Joseph 335
Wimberly, Sarah 335
Winchester, Charles B. 335
Winchester, David 335
Winchester, James 94
Wingwood, Elias 335
Winingham, Mary 98
Winkler, Ch. Ph. 335
Winn, Edmund 335
Winningham, Alie 99
Winningham, Mary 99
Winningham, R. A. 152
Winset, John 335
Winston, Arnold 336
Winston, Candis 336
Winston, Fountain 335
Winston, Frances A. 321
Winston, Henry 336
Winston, Isaac J. 335-336
Winston, J. J. 321
Winston, James 336
Winston, John 336
Winston, Joseph 335-336
Winston, Lewis 335
Winston, Samuel 335
Winston, William 6, 336
Winston, Winny Ann 336
Winston, Wm. 335-336
Winter, Elisha 336
Winter, Louisa 305
Winters, Elizabeth 336
Winters, Moses 1, 305, 336
Winters, Nancy 2, 336
Winters, Rhoda 336
Winton, John 112,
Wiseman, John 336
Wiseman, Thomas 336
Wisemore, Henry 124
Wisinger, J. A. 26
Wisner, Martin 183
Witcher, Booker 121
Witcher, Claiburn D. 121
Witcher, Danl. K. 336
Witcher, Hogin W. 336
Witcher, James H. 336
Witcher, Jane 336
Witcher, Jessie 336
Witcher, Martha 336
Witcher, Martha G. 336
Witcher, Polly 121
Witcher, Tandy 248, 336
Witcher, W. P. 121
Witcher, William 121, 336
Witherington, Lovey 337
Witherington, Lacy G. 337
Witherington, R. W. 336
Witherington, Robert 336-337
Withers, Elizabeth 195
Withers, John 337
Withers, Radford 109, 142, 195
Witherspoon, John 25
Witherspoon, W. 140
Witherspoon, William 66, 193
Witt, James 337
Witt, John 337
Witt, Joseph 337
Witt, Martha 337
Witt, Mary 200
Witt, Mourning 337
Witt, Nathaniel 337
Witt, Patsy 337
Witt, Phebe 200
Witt, Sally 337
Witt, Sarah 200, 337
Witt, Silas 337
Witt, Thomas 200
Witt, William 200
Wofford, Jesse 337
Wofford, John 337
Wolf, Elijah 337
Wolf, Elizabeth 337
Wolf, Fanny 314
Wolf, George 337
Wolf, Jacob 337
Wolf, James M. 238, 314
Wolf, Michael 337
Wolf, Polly 337
Wolf, Poter 253
Wolf, William B. 241
Wolfe, Betsy 340
Wolfe, Elizabeth 340
Wolfe, George W. 340
Wollard, Jas. M. 220
Wollin, Edward 337
Wollin, Joshua 337
Wollord, Peason 328
Wollos, Jesse 337
Womack, Jacob 127
Womack, John 248
Womack, Michael 8, 165
Womacks, Richard 73
Wood, Ann 111
Wood, Archer S. 337
Wood, Daniel 337
Wood, George W. 231
Wood, Handy 111
Wood, Hanna G. 337
Wood, Isabella 58
Wood, Jackson 58, 337
Wood, Jenny 337
Wood, Jesse 18
Wood, John 338
Wood, Jonathan 338
Wood, Laneas 338
Wood, Larkin 337
Wood, Layfayette 111
Wood, Levi S. 338
Wood, Levin 111
Wood, Maria 111
Wood, Martha 111
Wood, Mary A. 338
Wood, Moses 310
Wood, Rhoda 337
Wood, Robert 111
Wood, S. D. 338
Wood, Saml. 127, 226
Wood, W. C. 138, 143
Wood, W. W. 18
Wood, Washington 111
Wood, William 18, 24, 111, 222, 253
Woodall, Bluford 150-151
Woodfolk, W. W. 238
Woodfolk, William 17
Woodfork, William 338
Woodman, Edmund 16
Woodrum, Jacob 338
Woodrum, William 338
Woods, Agness 338
Woods, Cary H. 338
Woods, Citizen S. 85, 297-298
Woods, David 338
Woods, Desart 338
Woods, Feryl 338
Woods, Haneas 338
Woods, Henry 338
Woods, Jessee 340
Woods, John 338
Woods, Martha D. 338
Woods, Michael 34, 39, 215
Woods, Minor 338
Woods, Reuben 305
Woods, Saml. 169
Woods, William 192, 332, 338
Woodside, J. A. 132
Woodsides, M. M. 338
Woodson, Peter 120
Woodward, Hezekiah 28, 49
Woodward, Noah 147
Woodward, Thomas 147, 338-339
Woodward, William 30, 214
Wooldridge, Martha 339
Wooldridge, Thomas 339
Wooldridge, William 339
Woolfolk, Almira 339
Woolfolk, Florence P. 339
Woolfolk, Gilbreth N. 339
Woolfolk, J. R. 130
Woolfolk, Jas. Graves 339
Woolfolk, Jno. 82, 339
Woolfolk, Joseph 216, 273
Woolfolk, Julia R. 339
Woolfolk, Julian 133
Woolfolk, Julietta 339

Woolfolk, Lee C. 339
Woolfolk, Lizzy Love 339
Woolfolk, Mildred Ann 339
Woolfolk, Milly 339
Woolfolk, V. B. 56, 133
Woolfork, Gilbreth 339
Woolridge, Rich 332
Woolridge, Thomas 339
Wooton, Dorothy 339
Wooton, John 339
Wooton, William 339
Word, Cuthbert 339
Word, Jane 339
Word, John 317, 337
Word, Thomas S. 339
Word, William 38, 339
Wordlow, James 339
Wordlow, Michael 339
Workman, Samuel 12, 337
Worley, George 160
Worley, Mary D. 169
Wormack, Dave 339
Wormack, Jim 339
Worrell, Daniel 339
Worrell, James H. 339
Wortham, James 33, 88
Wrather, Baker 250
Wray, Alex 315
Wray, Elizabeth 339
Wray, George 339
Wrenshaw, Matilda 340
Wright, Abijah 287, 340
Wright, Abraham 340
Wright, Archibald 195
Wright, Benjamin 178, 340
Wright, Betsy 340
Wright, Bird 340
Wright, David 105
Wright, Della 103
Wright, Elizabeth 340
Wright, Henry 340
Wright, Isaac 287, 340
Wright, J. 340
Wright, J. R. 249
Wright, J. W. 42, 104, 166, 210, 242
Wright, James 59, 115, 143, 199, 201, 210, 220, 252-253, 256, 277, 330, 340
Wright, Jenny 340
Wright, John 64, 210, 340
Wright, Joshua 340
Wright, Lemuel 340
Wright, Lovey Ann 336
Wright, Martha 340
Wright, Mary 26
Wright, Michael 340
Wright, Patsy 340
Wright, Polly 340
Wright, Rebecca 340
Wright, Richard 340
Wright, Stephen 341
Wright, Thomas W. P. 336-377
Wroe, George 341
Wroe, Original 341
Wroe, Sarah 341

Wyatt, Abraham 341
Wyatt, Abram 150
Wyatt, Catharine 341
Wyatt, Daniel 341
Wyatt, Edward 341
Wyatt, J. H. 76
Wyatt, J. N. 187, 323
Wyatt, James 150, 341
Wyatt, John 341
Wyatt, Martin 341
Wyatt, Robert 341
Wyatt, Samuel 258, 341
Wyatt, Solomon 341
Wyatt, Thomas 150, 341
Wyatt, William 341
Wyatt, Zachariah 341
Wyche, James 6
Wyler, W. W. 220
Wylis, Darlin A. 341
Wyn, William 341
Wynn, Ashley 341
Wynn, Betsy 341
Wynn, Deveraux 341
Wynn, E. M. 212, 224, 307, 341
Wynn, Isham 341
Wynn, Joel 341
Wynn, John 341
Wynn, Polly 341
Wynn, Quaker 341
Wynn, Ridley B. 213
Wynn, Robert 341
Wynn, William 341
Wynne, Alford 341
Wynne, Ashley 43
Wynne, Deveriux 119
Wynne, H. V. 315-316
Wynne, Harriett J. 342
Wynne, John K. 341-342
Wynne, L. C. 50
Wynne, Peter 342
Wynne, Polly 342
Wynne, Robert 341
Wynne, Sintha 341
Wynne, Stanott H. J. 342
Wynne, Thomas 342
Wynne, V. G. 117, 342
Wynne, W. 20
Wynne, William 341-342
Wynne, Wilson 176
Yancy, Alexander 342
Yancy, Charles 169
Yancy, David 185
Yancy, Elizabeth 342
Yancy, F. W. 289
Yancy, Francis 342
Yancy, Hanna 342
Yancy, Henry 342
Yancy, James 342
Yancy, Jane 342
Yancy, Kavenaugh 342
Yancy, Louisa 342
Yancy, Rachael 185
Yancy, Rebecca 342
Yancy, William 342
Yandell, Henry 342
Yarborough, Samuel 285

Yarbrough, Henry 342
Yarbrough, John 342
Yates, J. J. 134, 221
Yates, John 157, 342
Yates, Lemuel 342
Yates, Louisa 343
Yates, Samuel 87
Yates, Thomas 104, 157-158, 285
Yates, William 157, 343
Yearly, Isam 343
Yearwood, J. G. 343
Yearwood, John 343
Yearwood, Wm. 343
Yeates, Mary Ann 213
Yeates, William 213
Yell, Archibald 206
Yoakum, George 53
Yoes, John 11,145
Yoes, Nathan 145
York, Aaron 94
York, Asberry 196
York, Curtis 93-94
York, G. W. 343
York, J. H. 45, 72, 78, 166, 190, 212, 291, 323
York, John H. 119-120, 169, 318
York, Sally 93-94
Yorvell, Jesse M. 5
Young, Abraham 152, 289
Young, Adam 15
Young, Allen 184-185, 271, 312, 343
Young, America 343
Young, Archibald 172
Young, Banister 343
Young, Benj. F. 116
Young, Bertram 343
Young, Betsy 91
Young, Beverly 59
Young, Charles 76, 343
Young, Darrel 230
Young, David185, 343
Young, Duke 344
Young, H. 344
Young, Harrison 344
Young, Henderson 344
Young, Henry 343-344
Young, Isaac 344
Young, J. C. G. 343
Young, J. J. 320
Young, Jacob 90, 226
Young, James 68, 91, 96, 125, 128-129, 147, 196, 343-344
Young, John 57, 118, 185, 271, 344
Young, Joseph 99, 244, 291
Young, Josephus 343
Young, Joshua 344
Young, Josiah 344
Young, L. 344
Young, L. B. 344
Young, Littleberry 344
Young, Marion 344

Young, Martha 148, 344
Young, Mary 57, 227, 324, 343-344
Young, Merlin 270, 304, 336, 343-344
Young, Milton 148, 343
Young, Moody 252
Young, Nancy 344
Young, Napolean B. 343
Young, Nathan M. 76
Young, Oliver 233
Young, Parker 344
Young, Polly J. 344
Young, Rebecca 343-344
Young, Robert 344
Young, Sally 252, 344
Young, Stephen 343
Young, Thomas 119, 344
Young, William 68, 128-129, 343-344
Young, Wilson C. 343
Young, Worley 344
Young, Zebulon 344
Youree, Patrick 160
Yourley, Thomas 5, 51
Yowel, Joel 248
Yowell, Chris 345
Yowell, David 345
Yowell, J. M. 338
Yowell, James 345
Yowell, Jesse M. 339
Yowell, Samuel 345
Zadock, James M. 257
Zaricor, J. C. 120
Zellers, Thos. 345
Zimmerman, J. J. 345

Other Heritage Books by Marjorie Hood Fischer:

*Dickson County, Tennessee Cemetery Records
Part I and II: Revised Edition*

*Haywood County, Tennessee Marriage Records:
Books 1, 2, 3, 4, 5, 6, 7, & 8; 1859-1878*

Tennesseans Before 1800: Davidson County

Tennesseans Before 1800: Washington County

Tennessee Tidbits: Volume IV, 1778-1914

Other Heritage Books by Marjorie Hood Fischer and Ruth Blake Burns:

*Bakerville Review Abstracts (Humphreys Co., Tennessee)
Volume II, 1897-1898*

*Bakerville Review Abstracts (Humphreys Co., Tennessee)
Volume III, 1898-1899*

Humphreys County, Tennessee Marriage Records, 1861-1888

*Humphreys County, Tennessee Records: Tax Lists, 1837-1843
and Marriages, 1888-1900*

Tennessee Tidbits: Volume I

Tennessee Tidbits: Volume II, 1778-1914

Tennessee Tidbits: Volume III, 1778-1914

www.ingramcontent.com/pod-product-compliance
Lightning Source LLC
Chambersburg PA
CBHW050327230426
43663CB00010B/1765